# CALIFORNIA CAMPING

TOM STIENSTRA

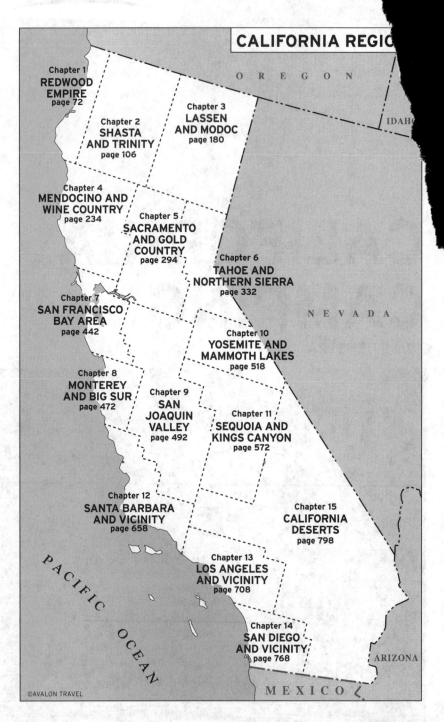

**CALIFORNIA REGIO**

OREGON

IDAHO

Chapter 1
**REDWOOD EMPIRE**
page 72

Chapter 2
**SHASTA AND TRINITY**
page 106

Chapter 3
**LASSEN AND MODOC**
page 180

Chapter 4
**MENDOCINO AND WINE COUNTRY**
page 234

Chapter 5
**SACRAMENTO AND GOLD COUNTRY**
page 294

Chapter 6
**TAHOE AND NORTHERN SIERRA**
page 332

Chapter 7
**SAN FRANCISCO BAY AREA**
page 442

NEVADA

Chapter 10
**YOSEMITE AND MAMMOTH LAKES**
page 518

Chapter 8
**MONTEREY AND BIG SUR**
page 472

Chapter 9
**SAN JOAQUIN VALLEY**
page 492

Chapter 11
**SEQUOIA AND KINGS CANYON**
page 572

Chapter 12
**SANTA BARBARA AND VICINITY**
page 658

Chapter 15
**CALIFORNIA DESERTS**
page 798

PACIFIC

Chapter 13
**LOS ANGELES AND VICINITY**
page 708

OCEAN

Chapter 14
**SAN DIEGO AND VICINITY**
page 768

ARIZONA

©AVALON TRAVEL

MEXICO

# Contents

# How to Use This Book
## ABOUT THE CAMPGROUND PROFILES

The campgrounds are listed in a consistent, easy-to-read format to help you choose the ideal camping spot. If you already know the name of the specific campground you want to visit, or the name of the surrounding geological area or nearby feature (town, national or state park, forest, mountain, lake, river, etc.), look it up in the index and turn to the corresponding page. Here is a sample profile:

Campground name and number →

**1 SOMEWHERE USA CAMPGROUND**

Icons noting activities and facilities at or nearby the campground

General location of the campground in relation to the nearest major town or landmark →

**Scenic rating: 10**

south of Somewhere USA Lake

Rating of scenic beauty on a scale of 1-10 with 10 the highest rating

Map the campground can be found on and page number the map can be found on →

**Map 1.2, page 4**   **BEST (**

Symbol indicating that the campground is listed among the author's top picks

Each campground in this book begins with a brief overview of its setting. The description typically covers ambience, information about the attractions, and activities popular at the campground.

**Campsites, facilities:** This section notes the number of campsites for tents and RVs and indicates whether hookups are available. Facilities such as restrooms, picnic areas, recreation areas, laundry, and dump stations will be addressed, as well as the availability of piped water, showers, playgrounds, stores, and other amenities. The campground's pet policy and wheelchair accessibility is also mentioned here.

**Reservations, fees:** This section notes whether reservations are accepted, and provides rates for tent sites and RV sites. If there are additional fees for parking or pets, or discounted weekly or seasonal rates, they will also be noted here.

**Directions:** This section provides mile-by-mile driving directions to the campground from the nearest major town or highway.

**Contact:** This section provides an address, phone number, and website, if available, for the campground.

## ABOUT THE ICONS

The icons in this book are designed to provide at-a-glance information on activities, facilities, and services available on-site or within walking distance of each campground.

- 🗻 Hiking trails
- 🚲 Biking trails
- 🏊 Swimming
- 🎣 Fishing
- 🚤 Boating
- 🛶 Canoeing and/or kayaking
- ❄ Winter sports

- ♨ Hot springs
- 🐾 Pets permitted
- 🎠 Playground
- ♿ Wheelchair accessible
- 5️⃣ 5 Percent Club
- 🚐 RV sites
- ⛺ Tent sites

## ABOUT THE SCENIC RATING

Each campground profile employs a scenic rating on a scale of 1 to 10, with 1 being the least scenic and 10 being the most scenic. A scenic rating measures only the overall beauty of the campground and environs; it does not take into account noise level, facilities, maintenance, recreation options, or campground management. The setting of a campground with a lower scenic rating may simply not be as picturesque that of as a higher rated campground, however other factors that can influence a trip, such as noise or recreation access, can still affect or enhance your camping trip. Consider both the scenic rating and the profile description before deciding which campground is perfect for you.

## MAP SYMBOLS

| Symbol | Description | Symbol | Description | Symbol | Description |
|---|---|---|---|---|---|
| ▭ | Expressway | (80) | Interstate Freeway | ✕ | Airfield |
| ▭ | Primary Road | (101) | U.S. Highway | ✈ | Airport |
| ▭ | Secondary Road | (21) | State Highway | ○ | City/Town |
| ▭ | Unpaved Road | (66) | County Highway | ▲ | Mountain |
| ▭ | Ferry | | Lake | ⚑ | Park |
| ▭ | National Border | | Dry Lake | ⟩( | Pass |
| ▭ | State Border | | Seasonal Lake | ◉ | State Capital |

## ABOUT THE MAPS

This book is divided into chapters based on major regions in the state; an overview map of these regions precedes the table of contents. Each chapter begins with a map of the region, which is further broken down into detail maps. Campgrounds are noted on the detail maps by number.

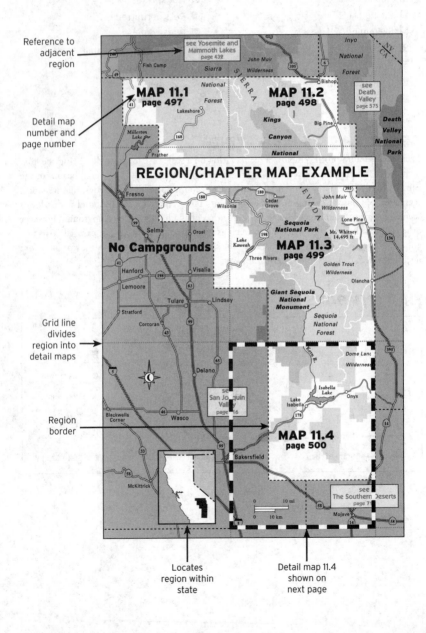

Reference to adjacent region

Detail map number and page number

**REGION/CHAPTER MAP EXAMPLE**

**No Campgrounds**

Grid line divides region into detail maps

Region border

Locates region within state

Detail map 11.4 shown on next page

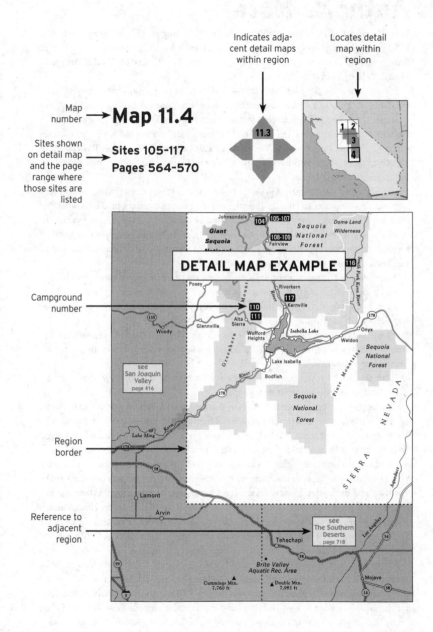

Indicates adjacent detail maps within region

Locates detail map within region

Map number → **Map 11.4**

Sites shown on detail map and the page range where those sites are listed → **Sites 105-117
Pages 564-570**

DETAIL MAP EXAMPLE

Campground number

Region border

Reference to adjacent region

# Author's Note

When I wrote the first edition of this book, I began: "Going on a camping trip can be like trying to put hiking boots on an octopus. You've tried it too, eh? Instead of a relaxing and fun trip full of adventure, it turns into a scenario called 'You Against the World.' You might as well try to fight a volcano."

It's still much the same for many folks—and with the reservation crush at many marquee sites, it can take a winter of planning to book sites for peak summer weekends. For example, the cabins at Steep Ravine on the Marin coast and the campsites with views at Doheny State Beach near Dana Point can be booked six months out within 10 minutes of the reservation lines opening. The sites at state beaches near Monterey Bay can fill in a day. But there are many other options. That's why I wrote this book: to never get stuck for the night without a spot.

I can always find a spot—often a great spot—all summer long. But you have to know every spot out there in order to take the pressure off and put the fun back in. That's what this book is all about. Put the mystery, excitement, and fun back into your camping vacations.

*Mystery?* The mystery awaits you out there on the road as you camp your way amid a series of adventures. There are hundreds of hidden campgrounds listed and mapped in this book that most people have never dreamed of.

*Excitement?* At many campgrounds, there's a great payoff to crown your trip: a hike to a great lookout or the big fish at the end of a line.

*Fun?* The Camping Tips section of this book will help you put the fun back in your trips, especially for families.

Camping is like religion: many paths, one truth. This book is designed for campers from all paths—from fully outfitted RVers to backpackers headed to trail camps on a month-long expedition.

With this book in your hands, the real question is this: *"What sets you free?"* Answer that question and you can transform your life.

California has roughly 400 lakes that you can drive to, 1,000 lakes that you can hike to, 185 major streams, 20 million acres of national forest, 1,200 miles of coast, and more than 100 major wilderness areas. The best campsites at these lakes, streams, coastal bluffs, and trailheads can offer a portal to a new life and a launch point for daily adventures.

Once you answer the question "What sets you free?" your mission becomes "This is the year I start doing it." I once almost moved to the Northwest Territories to become a guide, outfitter, and bush pilot. I was offered a great job and at the time thought there was nowhere else to go in California. Hah! In the process of taking flight lessons, I looked down from the pilot's seat and saw places that I never dreamed existed. That set *me* free. Since then, I've flown 1,700 hours and driven more than one million miles in California and have found more hidden gems than can be explored in my lifetime.

I've learned that 95 percent of people go to about 5 percent of these destinations. With this book, you can leave the herd, wander, and be free. Join the 5 Percent Club—the 5 Percenters who find the great hidden spots used by so few. Look at the maps in this book for the areas you want to visit and find the corresponding campground listings. As you study the camps, a sense of excitement builds—a feeling that you are about to unlock a door and venture into a world that is rarely viewed. When you feel that excitement, act. Parlay that energy into a great trip.

The campground maps and campsite listings can serve you in two ways: 1) If you're on the road late in the day and stuck for a spot for the night, you can find one nearby; or 2) if you are planning a trip, you can tailor a vacation to fit your plans rather than heading off and hoping—maybe praying—that it turns out all right.

You may wish to obtain additional maps, particularly if you are venturing into areas governed by the U.S. Forest Service or Bureau of Land Management. Both are federal agencies that offer low-cost maps detailing all hiking trails, lakes, streams, and backcountry camps reached via logging roads. The Resources section at the back of this book details how to obtain these and other maps.

This book lists roughly 1,500 campgrounds. For the 20th edition, each campground was reviewed and checked by two research editors, Donna Sager and Ronda Elliot, with the help of hundreds of recreation specialists. Within these pages is the full spectrum of what's out there. At one end of the spectrum are developed RV parks. These offer a home away from home, with everything from full hookups to a grocery store and laundry room. An RV park provides a place to shower, to buy food, and to clean clothes. For RV cruisers, it's a place to stay within a small community of like-minded souls.

At the opposite end of that spectrum are remote and primitive sites that provide a sense of isolation. These are good jumping-off points for backpacking trips like the John Muir Trail, my favorite trek. For this edition, I've added a new section on hiking what is widely considered America's No. 1 hike.

Somewhere in between the two extremes are roughly 800 campgrounds with beautiful settings and some facilities. Most have piped drinking water, flush or chemical toilets, and picnic tables for each site. Reservations are advised for summer weekends, but even when full, the sites at state parks won't make campers feel as if they've been squeezed in with a shoehorn. Even better, these same state parks are often uncrowded during the off season and on weekdays.

Before your trip, you'll want to get organized, and that's when you must start putting boots on that giant octopus. The trick to organization for any task is breaking it down to its key components and then solving each element independent of the others. Remember the octopus. Grab a moving leg, jam on a boot, and make sure it's on tight before reaching for another leg. Do one thing at a time, in order, and all will get done quickly and efficiently.

In the Camping Tips section, I have divided the different elements of planning a trip: 1) Food and cooking gear; 2) Clothing and weather protection; 3) Hiking and foot care and how to choose the right boots and socks; 4) Sleeping gear; 5) Combating bugs and some commonsense first-aid; 6) Catching fish, avoiding bears, and camp fun; 7) Outdoors with kids; and 8) Weather prediction. I've also included sections on boat-in and desert camping and ethics in the outdoors, as well as a camping gear checklist.

Getting organized is an unnatural act for many. By splitting up these tasks, you can take the pressure out of planning and put the fun back in. Once you nail these elements down, you won't need to break down your gear after every trip. In fact, I keep my gear intact so that when I decide to go, I just buy the food and bail for yonder. Some years I've spent 150-200 days outdoors, writing through the early afternoon then heading out for adventure in the evening.

Don't put your life on hold for anything. Make this the year where you start having the fun you deserve—and let this book be the portal to a new life.

—Tom Stienstra, March 2017

# Best Campgrounds

The most common emails I get are those from readers asking me to plan their adventures and to rate campgrounds as launch points for specific activities. While I can't respond to all emails, I do often rate the top 10 campgrounds in California for scenery, hiking, fishing, boating, water sports, rafting, and family activities.

I've organized the following selections by activity, then rated them 1 through 10, starting with my pick for the best. These are among America's preeminent campgrounds, so if you plan a trip to any of them, be sure to plan your stay far in advance.

## BEST( Scenic Campgrounds

1. **Emerald Bay State Park and Boat-In,** Tahoe and the Northern Sierra, page 435.
2. **Steep Ravine Environmental Campsites,** San Francisco Bay Area, page 451.
3. **Doheny State Beach,** San Diego and Vicinity, page 771.
4. **Seacliff State Beach,** Monterey and Big Sur, page 474.
5. **Lower Pines and Upper Pines,** Yosemite and Mammoth Lakes, pages 529 and 530.
6. **Wildcat Camp Hike-In,** San Francisco Bay Area, page 449.
7. **Camino Cove,** Tahoe and the Northern Sierra, page 390.
8. **Mary Smith,** Shasta and Trinity, page 170.
9. **Angel Island State Park Walk-In/Boat-In,** San Francisco Bay Area, page 455.
10. **Santa Rosa Island,** Santa Barbara and Vicinity, page 703.

## BEST( Boat-In Campgrounds

1. **Emerald Bay State Park and Boat-In,** Tahoe and the Northern Sierra, page 435.
2. **Santa Rosa Island,** Santa Barbara and Vicinity, page 703.
3. **Pleasant Hike-In/Boat-In,** Tahoe and the Northern Sierra, page 388.
4. **Greens Creek Boat-In,** Shasta and Trinity, page 164.
5. **Bullards Bar Reservoir,** Sacramento and Gold Country, pages 309, 310, and 311.
6. **Azalea Cove Hike-In/Boat-In,** Tahoe and the Northern Sierra, page 391.
7. **Stone Lagoon Boat-In,** Redwood Empire, page 87.
8. **Tomales Bay Boat-In,** San Francisco Bay Area, page 447.
9. **Lake Sonoma Recreation Area,** Mendocino and Wine Country, page 275.
10. **Englebright Lake Boat-In,** Sacramento and Gold Country, page 313.

## BEST( for Families

1. **Lake Siskiyou Resort & Camp,** Shasta and Trinity, page 127.
2. **Historic Camp Richardson Resort,** Tahoe and the Northern Sierra, page 438.
3. **Pine Cliff Resort,** Yosemite and Mammoth Lakes, page 548.
4. **Lake Alpine Campground,** Tahoe and the Northern Sierra, page 419.
5. **Serrano,** Los Angeles and Vicinity, page 750.
6. **Silver Lake West,** Tahoe and the Northern Sierra, page 399.
7. **El Capitan Canyon,** Santa Barbara and Vicinity, page 680.
8. **Rancho Seco Recreation Area,** Sacramento and Gold Country, page 319.
9. **Dorst Creek,** Sequoia and Kings Canyon, page 623.
10. **Elk Prairie,** Redwood Empire, page 86.

## BEST◖ for Fishing

1. **Arbuckle Flat Boat-In,** Shasta and Trinity, page 165.
2. **Convict Lake,** Yosemite and Mammoth Lakes, page 562.
3. **Lake Pardee Marina,** Sacramento and Gold Country, page 326.
4. **Camanche Lake North,** Sacramento and Gold Country, page 327.
5. **Upper Soda Springs,** Yosemite and Mammoth Lakes, page 553.
6. **Snug Harbor Resort,** Sacramento and Gold Country, page 321.
7. **Almanor North, South, and Legacy,** Lassen and Modoc, page 219.
8. **Campland on the Bay,** San Diego and Vicinity, page 776.
9. **Hirz Bay,** Shasta and Trinity, page 162.
10. **Panther Flat,** Redwood Empire, page 79.

## BEST◖ for Hikes with Views

1. **Yosemite Creek (hike to Yosemite Point in Yosemite National Park),** Yosemite and Mammoth Lakes, page 526.
2. **Canyon View Group Camp (hike to Lookout Peak in Kings Canyon National Park),** Sequoia and Kings Canyon, page 620.
3. **Wilderness Walk-In Camps (climb San Jacinto Peak),** Los Angeles and Vicinity, page 759.
4. **Whitney Trailhead Walk-In (climb Mount Whitney),** Sequoia and Kings Canyon, page 636.
5. **Angel Island State Park Walk-In/Boat-In (hike to Mount Livermore),** San Francisco Bay Area, page 455.
6. **Manker Flats (climb Mount Baldy in Angeles National Forest),** Los Angeles and Vicinity, page 732.
7. **D. L. Bliss State Park (hike Rubicon Trail),** Tahoe and the Northern Sierra, page 434.
8. **Panther Meadows Walk-In (climb Mount Shasta),** Shasta and Trinity, page 129.
9. **Tuolumne Meadows (hike the Pacific Crest Trail north to Grand Canyon of the Tuolumne),** Yosemite and Mammoth Lakes, page 527.
10. **Summit Lake: North, South, and Stock Corral (climb Lassen Peak),** Lassen and Modoc, page 209.

## BEST◖ Island Retreats

1. **Catalina Island Boat-In,** Los Angeles and Vicinity, page 724.
2. **Santa Cruz Island,** Santa Barbara and Vicinity, page 704.
3. **Two Harbors,** Los Angeles and Vicinity, page 722.
4. **Santa Rosa Island,** Santa Barbara and Vicinity, page 703.
5. **Angel Island State Park Walk-In/Boat-In,** San Francisco Bay Area, page 455.
6. **Anacapa Island,** Santa Barbara and Vicinity, page 705.
7. **San Miguel Island,** Santa Barbara and Vicinity, page 703.
8. **Little Harbor Hike-In,** Los Angeles and Vicinity, page 723.
9. **Parsons Landing Hike-In,** Los Angeles and Vicinity, page 721.
10. **Brannan Island State Recreation Area,** Sacramento and Gold Country, page 320.

## BEST( Trailhead Camps

1. **Tuolumne Meadows,** Yosemite and Mammoth Lakes, page 527.
2. **Yosemite Creek,** Yosemite and Mammoth Lakes, page 526.
3. **Saddlebag Lake and Trailhead Group,** Yosemite and Mammoth Lakes, page 545.
4. **Onion Valley,** Sequoia and Kings Canyon, page 634.
5. **Buckhorn,** Los Angeles and Vicinity, page 259.
6. **Panther Meadows Walk-In,** Shasta and Trinity, page 129.
7. **Upper Soda Springs,** Yosemite and Mammoth Lakes, page 553.
8. **Pantoll Walk-In,** San Francisco Bay Area, page 452.
9. **Woods Lake,** Tahoe and the Northern Sierra, page 399.
10. **Goldfield,** Shasta and Trinity, page 134.

## BEST( for Waterskiing

1. **Havasu Landing Resort and Casino,** California Deserts, page 818.
2. **Rainbo Beach Resort,** California Deserts, page 812.
3. **Eddos Harbor and RV Park,** Sacramento and Gold Country, page 323.
4. **Historic Camp Richardson Resort,** Tahoe and the Northern Sierra, page 438.
5. **Holiday Harbor Resort,** Shasta and Trinity, page 163.
6. **Lake Perris State Recreation Area,** Los Angeles and Vicinity, page 742.
7. **Lake Piru Recreation Area,** Los Angeles and Vicinity, page 712.
8. **La Laguna Resort,** Los Angeles and Vicinity, page 747.
9. **Los Alamos,** California Deserts, page 814.
10. **Snug Harbor Resort,** Sacramento and Gold Country, page 321.

## BEST( for White-Water Rafting

1. **Lumsden,** San Joaquin Valley, page 505.
2. **Camp Lotus,** Sacramento and Gold Country, page 324.
3. **Auburn State Recreation Area,** Sacramento and Gold Country, pages 315 and 316.
4. **Kirch Flat,** Sequoia and Kings Canyon, page 612.
5. **Merced River Recreation Area,** Yosemite and Mammoth Lakes, page 531.
6. **Tree of Heaven,** Shasta and Trinity, page 122.
7. **Hobo,** Sequoia and Kings Canyon, page 653.
8. **Fairview,** Sequoia and Kings Canyon, page 643.
9. **Dillon Creek,** Shasta and Trinity, page 116.
10. **Matthews Creek,** Shasta and Trinity, page 120.

# Camping Tips

## SLEEPING GEAR

The most important part of every camping trip is this: Get a good night's sleep. While camping, some people might sleep 7-8 hours . . . but in about a half dozen installments. They wake up with their body half paralyzed, sore in spots, with headaches and general discomfort that makes it impossible to rest deeply. If you get it right, not only will you feel great, but a good night's sleep will transform your outlook for the great things possible in the coming day.

When I was a little boy, one eve long ago I was in the mountain pines with my dad and my brother. We had rolled out our sleeping bags and were bedded down for the night. After the pre-trip excitement, a long drive, an evening of trout fishing, and a barbecue, we were like three tired puppies who had played too much.

But as I looked up at the stars, I was suddenly wide awake. I was still wired. A half hour later? No change. Wide awake.

And as little kids can do, I had to wake up ol' Dad to tell him about it. "Hey, Dad, I can't sleep."

After the initial grimace, he said: "This is what you do. Watch the sky for a shooting star and tell yourself that you cannot go to sleep until you see at least one shooting star. As you wait and watch, you will start getting tired, then sleepy; your breathing will become rhythmic and it will be difficult to keep your eyes open. But tell yourself, you must keep watching. Then you'll start to really feel tired. When you finally see a shooting star, you'll go to sleep so fast you won't know what hit you."

Well, I tried it that night and I don't even remember seeing a shooting star, I went to sleep so fast.

It's a good trick, and along with having a good sleeping bag, ground insulation, maybe a tent, or a few tricks for bedding down in a pickup truck or RV, you can get a great night's sleep on every camping trip.

More than 20 years after that camping episode with my dad and brother, we made a trip to the planetarium at the Academy of Sciences in San Francisco to see a show. The lights dimmed, and the ceiling turned into a night sky, filled with stars and a setting moon. A scientist began explaining the phenomena of the heavens.

After a few minutes, I began to feel drowsy. Just then, a shooting star zipped across the planetarium ceiling. I went into such a deep sleep, well, it was like I was in a coma. I didn't wake up until the show was over, the lights were turned back on, and the people were leaving.

Feeling drowsy, I turned to see if Dad had liked the show. Oh yeah? Not only had he gone to sleep too, but he apparently had no intention of waking up, no matter what. Just like a camping trip.

## Sleeping Bags

The first rule of a good night's sleep is that you must be dry, warm, and safe. A good sleeping bag can help plenty. A sleeping bag is a shell filled with heat-retaining insulation. By itself, it is not warm. Your body provides the heat, and the sleeping bag's ability to retain that heat is what makes it warm or cold.

The cheap cotton bags are heavy, bulky, cold, and, when wet, useless. With other options available, their function is limited. Anybody who sleeps outdoors or backpacks should choose otherwise. Use a sleeping bag filled with down or one of the quality poly-fills. Down is light, warm, and aesthetically pleasing to those who don't think camping and technology mix. Down bags are also light, which makes them desirable for backpacking. If you choose a down bag, be sure to keep it double wrapped in plastic garbage bags on your trips to keep it dry. Once it's wet, you'll spend your nights howling at the moon.

The polyfiber-filled bags are not necessarily better than those filled with down, but they can be. Their one key advantage is that even when wet, some poly-fills can retain up to 85 percent of your body heat. This allows you to sleep and

## KEEP IT WILD TIP 1: CAMP WITH CARE

1. Choose an existing, legal site. Restrict activities to areas where vegetation is compacted or absent.
2. Camp at least 75 steps (200 feet) from lakes, streams, and trails.
3. Always choose sites that won't be damaged by your stay.
4. Preserve the feeling of solitude by selecting camps that are out of view when possible.
5. Don't dig trenches or build structures or furniture.

get valuable rest even in miserable conditions. In my camping experience, no matter how lucky you may be, there will come a time when you will get caught in an unexpected, violent storm and everything you've got will get wet, including your sleeping bag. That's when a poly-fill bag becomes priceless. You have one and can sleep. Or you don't have one and suffer. It is that simple.

Another key factor is a bag's temperature rating and weight. The temperature rating of a sleeping bag refers to how cold it can get outside before you start actually feeling cold. Many campers make the mistake of thinking, "I only camp in the summer, so a bag rated at 30 or 40°F should be fine." Later, they find out it isn't so fine, and all it takes is one cold night to convince them of that. When selecting the right temperature rating, visualize the coldest weather you might ever confront, and then get a bag rated for even colder weather.

For instance, if you are a summer camper, you may rarely experience a night in the low 30s or high 20s. A sleeping bag rated at 20°F would be appropriate, keeping you snug, warm, and asleep. For most campers, I advise bags rated at 0 or 10°F.

But guess how the companies come up with their temperature ratings? Usually it's a guy like me field-testing a bag before it is commercially released, and then saying, "Well, it got down to 40°F and I was pretty warm." So they rate it at 30 degrees. Obviously, testers can have different threshold levels for cold, while others base their ratings on how much fill is used.

If you buy a poly-filled sleeping bag, try not to leave it squished in your stuff sack between camping trips. Instead, keep it on a hanger in a closet or use it as a blanket. One thing that can reduce a poly-filled bag's heat-retaining qualities is if the tiny hollow fibers that make up the fill lose their loft. You can avoid this with proper storage.

The weight of a sleeping bag can also be a key factor, especially for backpackers. When you have to carry your gear on your back, every ounce becomes important. Sleeping bags that weigh just 2-3 pounds are available, although they are expensive. But if you hike much, it's worth the price to keep your weight to a minimum. For an overnighter, you can get away with a 4- or 4.5-pound bag without much stress. However, bags that weigh six pounds or more may be comfy at car camps but add too much weight for backpacking.

I have several sleeping bags; they range from a seven-pounder that feels like a giant sponge to a feather-light three-pounder. The heavy-duty model is for pickup truck camping in cold weather and doubles as a blanket at home. The lightweight bag is for expeditions.

## Insulation Pads

Even with the warmest sleeping bag in the world, if you just lay it down on the ground and try to sleep, you will likely get as cold as a winter cucumber. That is because the cold ground will suck the warmth right out of your body. The solution is to have a layer of insulation between you and the ground. For this, you can use a thin Insulite pad, a lightweight Therm-a-Rest inflatable pad, a foam pad or mattress, an airbed, or a cot. Here is a capsule summary of each:

- **Insulite pads:** They are light, inexpensive, roll up quickly for transport, and can double as a seat pad at your camp. The negative side is that in one night, they will compress, making you feel like you are sleeping on granite. But they are light and they help keep you warm in the wilderness.
- **Therm-a-Rest pads:** These are a real luxury for wilderness travel because they do everything an Insulite pad does, but they also provide a cushion. The negative side is that they are expensive by comparison, and if they get a hole in them, they become worthless without a patch kit. Most wilderness campers carry one "bonus item"—and a full-length Therm-A-Rest is often what they choose.
- **Foam mattresses, airbeds, and cots:** These are excellent for car campers. The new air beds, especially the thicker ones, are outstanding and inflate quickly with an electric motor inflator that plugs into a power plug or cigarette lighter in your vehicle. Foam mattresses are also excellent; I think they are the most comfortable of all, but their size makes it impossible for many to bring them along. I've found that cots work great, too. I've always had one and they're great for drive-in tent sites. For camping in the back of a pickup truck with a camper shell, the cots with three-inch legs can work great. Here's the trick: On the canvas cot, put a blanket over it, then add a Therm-A-Rest pad; that will provide insulation to keep the cold air beneath you from sucking out the warmth.

## A Few Tricks

When surveying a camp area, the most important consideration should be to select a good spot for sleeping. You want a flat area that is wind-sheltered and on ground soft enough to drive stakes into. Yeah, and I want to win the lottery, too.

Sometimes, the ground will have a slight slope to it. In that case, always sleep with your head on the uphill side. If you sleep parallel to the slope, every time you roll over, you'll find yourself rolling down the hill. If you sleep with your head on the downhill side, you might get a headache that feels as if an ax is embedded in your brain.

When you've found a good spot, clear it of all branches, twigs, and rocks, of course. Do not clear the ground with your foot as a broom, but instead pick up each rock with your hands and toss them aside. A good tip is to dig a slight indentation, almost imperceptible, in the ground where your hip will fit. Since your body is not flat, but has curves and edges, it often will not feel comfortable on flat ground. Some people even get severely bruised on the sides of their hips when sleeping on flat, hard ground. For that reason alone, they learn to hate camping.

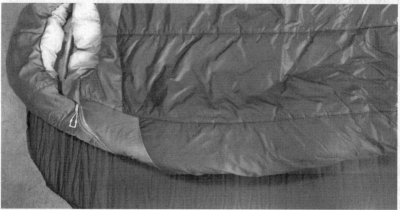

For maximum comfort, be sure to use an insulation pad beneath your sleeping bag.

The problem is solved with a Therm-a-Rest pad, foam insulation, an airbed, or a cot.

After the ground is prepared, throw a ground cloth over the spot, which will keep much of the morning dew off you. In some areas, particularly where fog is a problem, morning dew can be heavy and get the outside of your sleeping bag quite wet. In that case, you need overhead protection, such as a tent or some kind of roof, like a poncho or tarp with its ends tied to trees.

## A Great Night's Sleep

Some people sleep seven, eight hours at camp, but it comes in 10 installments. They keep waking up. They wake up and half their body is paralyzed. They can't get comfortable. To solve this, practice camp-style sleeping at home until you get it perfect. At home, you have flexibility and complete control over your sleeping surface. Get it right. Get it just how you like it.

For wilderness travel, my bonus item is an extra inflatable pillow; that's right, I carry two air pillows, not one. I inflate them about half full. It puts my head at a perfect comfort zone for deep sleep. Whatever it takes, know how to get a great night's sleep and your entire trip has the chance to feel epic, no matter what you do.

Got it? Get it right. There is no replacement for this.

## Tents and Weather Protection

All it takes is to get caught in the rain once without a tent and you will never go anywhere without one again. A tent provides protection from rain, wind, and mosquito attacks. In exchange, you can lose a starry night's view, though some tents now provide moon roofs.

A tent can be as complex as a four-season, tubular-jointed dome with a rain fly or as simple as a tarp roped up to a tree. They can be as cheap as a $10 tube tent, which is nothing more than a hollow piece of plastic, or as expensive as a $500 five-person deluxe expedition, multi-room dome. They vary greatly in size, price, and assembly time. For those who camp

infrequently and want to buy a tent without paying much, off-brand models are available at considerable price discounts. My experience in field-testing outdoor gear, though, is that cheap tents often rip at the seams if subjected to regular use. If you plan on getting a good one, plan on doing plenty of shopping and asking lots of questions. With a little bit of homework, you can get the right answers to these questions:

### WILL IT KEEP ME DRY?

On many one-person and two-person tents, the rain fly does not extend far enough to keep water off the bottom sidewalls of the tent. In a driving rain, water can also drip from the rain fly and onto those sections of the tent. Eventually, the water can leak through to the inside, particularly through the seams.

You must be able to stake out your rain fly so it covers the entire surface of the tent inside it. If you are tent shopping and this does not appear possible, then don't buy the tent. To prevent potential leaks, use a waterproof gel for seams, such as Seam Lock, a glue-like substance that can close potential leak areas on tent seams. For large umbrella tents, keep a patch kit handy. Coleman tents, by the way, are guaranteed to keep campers dry.

Another way to keep water out of your tent is to store all wet garments outside the tent, under a poncho. Moisture from wet clothes stashed in the tent will condense on the interior tent walls. If you bring enough wet clothes into the tent, by the next morning you'll feel as if you're camping in a duck blind.

### HOW HARD IS IT TO PUT UP?

Some tents can go up in just a few minutes, without requiring help from another camper. This might be the kind of tent you want. If a tent is difficult to erect in full sunlight, you can just about forget it at night, especially the first night out if you arrive late to camp.

The way to compare put-up times when shopping for tents is to count the number of connecting points from the tent poles to the tent and the number of stakes required; the

© SABRINA YOUNG

Tents vary in complexity, size, and price. Be sure to buy the one that's right for you.

fewer, the better. Think simple. My two-person-plus-a-dog tent has seven connecting points and, minus the rain fly, requires no stakes. It goes up in a few minutes.

My bigger family tent, which has three rooms with walls (so we can keep two kids isolated on each side if necessary), takes 20 minutes to put up. That's without anybody's help. With their help, add about 15 minutes. Heh, heh.

Another factor is the tent poles themselves. Always make sure the poles are connected by an interior bungee cord. It takes only an instant to convert them to a complete pole.

Some outdoor shops have tents on display on their showroom floors. Before buying the tent, have the salesperson show you how to take the tent down and put it back up. If they say they don't have time, then keep looking.

### IS IT ROOMY ENOUGH?

Don't judge the size of a tent on floor space alone. Some tents that are small on floor space can give the illusion of roominess with a high ceiling. You can be quite comfortable and snug in them.

But remember that a one-person or two-person tent is just that. A two-person tent has room for two people plus some gear. That's it. Don't buy a tent expecting it to hold more than it is intended to.

### HOW MUCH DOES IT WEIGH?

If you're a hiker, this becomes the preeminent question. When my son hiked the Pacific Crest Trail, his tent weighed about two pounds. The first time I hiked the John Muir Trail, I brought a five-pound tent. The next time, I brought a bivy bag that weighed 31 ounces. A typical 12-pound tent is a nightmare to hike with. If it gets wet, it's like carrying a piano on your back. On the other hand, if you only car camp then weight is scarcely a factor. My dad used to have this giant canvas umbrella tent that folded down to a neat little pack that weighed about 500 pounds.

## Family Tents

It is always worth spending the time and money to buy a tent you and your family will be happy with.

Many excellent family tents are available for

$125-200, particularly from Cabela's, Coleman, Eureka!, North Face, Remington, and Sierra Designs. Guide-approved expedition tents for groups cost more, generally $350-600. Here is a synopsis of some of best tents available:

## REI
800/423-2320
www.rei.com
REI has 94 backpacking tents and 27 tents available for car camping, including their own designs as well as those from other manufacturers. A great backpacking tent for two is the REI Half Dome 2 Plus. The Eureka! Copper Canyon 6 is one of the better family values.

## CABELA'S TWO- OR THREE-ROOM CABIN
800/237-4444
www.cabelas.com
This beautiful tent features two to three rooms, a 10- by 16-foot floor available in different configurations with removable interior walls. Three doors mean everybody doesn't tromp through the center room for access to the side rooms. It will stand up to wind, rain, and frequent use.

## COLEMAN MODIFIED DOME
800/835-3278
www.coleman.com
Coleman Modified Dome tents are available in six different single- and multi-room designs. The pole structure is unique, with all four upright poles and one ridgepole shock-corded together for an integrated system that makes setup extremely fast and easy. Yet, because of the ridgepole's engineering, the tent has passed tests in high winds. Mesh panels in the ceiling are a tremendous plus for ventilation.

## COLEMAN WEATHERMASTER
800/835-3278
www.coleman.com
The Weathermaster series features tents with multiple rooms, walls, and ample headroom, and they are guaranteed to keep rain out. The 17- by 9-foot model sleeps six to eight, has a 76-inch ceiling, and has zippered dividers. Since the dividers are removable, you can configure the tent in multiple layouts. The frame is designed with poles adjustable to three different heights to accommodate uneven ground.

## KELTY
800/423-2320
www.kelty.com
Kelty offers top-of-the-line tents based on a sleek dome profile. This is a great package, with mesh sides, tops, and doors, along with a full awning fly and coverage for weather protection. Clip sleeves and rubber-tipped poles for easy sliding during setup are nice bonuses.

# Bivouac Bags
If you like going light or solo, you may choose not to own a tent at all. A bivy bag or tarp can be the way to go. Bivy is short for bivouac bag and pronounced "bivvy" as in dizzy, not "bivy" as in ivy, and can provide extremely lightweight weather protection. A bivy bag is a water-repellent shell in which your sleeping bag fits. It is light and tough, and for some is the perfect alternative to a heavy tent. My own bivy weighs 31 ounces and cost around $250; it's made by OR (Outdoor Research), and I just plain love the thing on expeditions. Some say it can be a bit difficult getting settled just right in it, and others say they feel claustrophobic in such close quarters. Once you get used to a bivy, spend a night in a tent; the tent will feel like a room at the Mirage. For me, not a problem.

The idea of riding out a storm in a bivy can be quite worrisome for some. You can hear the rain hitting you, and sometimes even feel the pounding of the drops through the bivy bag. For some, it can be unsettling to try to sleep under such circumstances. On the other hand, I've always looked forward to it. In cold weather, a bivy also helps keep you warm. I've had just one miserable night in mine. That was when my sleeping bag was a bit wet when I started the night. By the middle of the night, the water was condensing from the sleeping bag on the interior walls of the bivy, and then

---

## KEEP IT WILD TIP 2:
## KEEP THE WILDERNESS WILD

1. Let nature's sound prevail. Avoid loud voices and noises. Don't shout or talk too much. Listen instead.
2. Leave radios and music players at home. At drive-in camping sites, never open car doors with music playing.
3. Careful guidance is necessary when choosing any games to bring for children. Most toys, especially any kind of gun toys with which children simulate shooting at each other, shouldn't be allowed on a camping trip.
4. Control pets at all times or leave them with a sitter at home.
5. Treat natural heritage with respect. Leave plants, rocks, and historical artifacts where you find them.

---

soaking the bag, like a storm cycle. The night hit only about 45°F, not too cold—but since I was wet I just about turned into an ice cube. Otherwise, I've used it on more than 100 expeditions with great results: warm, dry quarters and deep, restful sleeps by night, and a pack lightened without carrying a tent by day.

Many long-distance hikers are switching to light tarps in the continuing mission to minimize weight. They work great in rain and the spacious feel beneath them is fantastic. You just need a tree to tie to and soft enough ground for stakes, so they don't work in the alpine (above tree line). Tarps aren't so great when there are bug problems; then you will need some kind of mosquito netting. A bivy or tent solves that, of course.

## Pickup Truck Campers

If you own a pickup truck with a camper shell, you can turn it into a self-contained campground with a little work. This can be an ideal way to go: It's fast and portable, and you are guaranteed a dry environment.

But that does not necessarily mean it is a warm environment. In fact, without insulation from the metal truck bed, it can be like trying to sleep on an iceberg. The metal truck bed will get as cold as the air temperature, which is often much colder than the ground temperature. Without insulation, it can be much colder in your camper shell than it would be on the open ground.

When I camp in my rig, I use a large piece of foam for a mattress and insulation. The foam measures four inches thick, 48 inches wide, and 76 inches long. It makes for a bed as comfortable as anything one might ask for. In fact, during the winter, if I don't go camping for a few weeks because of writing obligations, I sometimes will throw the foam on the floor, lay down the old sleeping bag, light a fire, and camp right in my living room. It's in my blood, I tell you. Airbeds and cots are also extremely comfortable and I've used both many times. Whatever you choose, just make sure you have a comfortable sleeping unit. Good sleep makes for great camping trips.

## RVs

The problems RVers encounter come from two primary sources: lack of privacy and light intrusion.

The lack of privacy stems from the natural restrictions of where you can go. Without careful use of the guide section of this book, owners of RVs can find themselves in parking-lot settings, jammed in with plenty of neighbors. Because RVs often have large picture windows, you lose your privacy, causing some late nights; then, come daybreak, light intrusion forces an early wake-up. As a result, you get shorted on your sleep.

The answer is to carry inserts to fit over the inside of your windows. These close off the outside and retain your privacy. And if you don't want to wake up with the sun at daybreak, you don't have to. It will still be dark.

Many campgrounds and RV parks enforce a quiet time. If that is important to you, make sure you don't end up somewhere where a quiet time is optional.

If you go the RV route, the key to any purchase is determining the length of the trailer or motor home (not the amenities that are packed into them). Length is key: A 21-foot trailer can fit into virtually any Forest Service campsite. Once you get over 25 feet, you become excluded from hundreds of RV sites. If you go over 30 feet, you will need a pull-through site at a private RV park in order to find a spot. For each campsite in this book where there is space for RVs, we detail the length limit.

There is a real movement toward buying smaller and lighter campers. Smaller vehicles fit into more campsites, plus they are easier to back in and park. A light vehicle means you don't need to buy a big pickup truck in order to tow it, something that could be quite an additional expense for a larger, heavy camper trailer.

If cost is not an issue, some fifth wheels come with amazing luxury packages, multiple pullouts for added space, great kitchens and bedrooms, and living rooms with flat-screen TVs.

## HIKING AND FOOT CARE

I really loved the days with my old pal, Foonsky. We went everywhere—hiking, camping, and fishing and usually with my dog, Rebel, creating problems. Around the campfire, we'd talk all about the new country we wanted to see: lakes, streams, and mountain rims. We were always getting into all kinds of trouble.

On one trip, we had set up a nice little camp in the woods. Foonsky, sitting against a big Douglas fir, was strapping on his hiking boots.

"New boots," he said with a grin. "But they seem pretty stiff."

We decided to hoof it down the trail for a few hours, exploring the mountain wildlands that are said to hide Bigfoot and other strange creatures. After just a short while on the trail, a sense of peace and calm seemed to settle in. The forest provides the chance to be purified with clean air and the smell of trees, freeing you from all troubles.

But it wasn't long before a look of trouble was on Foonsky's face. And no, it wasn't from seeing Bigfoot.

"Got a hot spot on my toe," he said.

Immediately, we stopped. He pulled off his right boot, then his sock, and inspected the left side of his big toe. Sure enough, a blister had bubbled up, filled with fluid, but hadn't popped. From his medical kit, Foonsky cut a small piece of moleskin to fit over the blister and taped it to hold it in place. In a few minutes we were back on the trail.

A half hour later, there was still no sign of Bigfoot. But Foonsky stopped again and pulled off his other boot. "Another hot spot." On the little toe of his left foot was another small blister, over which he taped a Band-Aid to keep it from further chafing against the inside of his new boot.

In just a few days, ol' Foonsky, a strong, 6-foot-5, 220-pound guy, was walking around like a sore-hoofed horse that had been loaded with a month's worth of supplies and ridden over sharp rocks. Well, it wasn't the distance that had done Foonsky in; it was those blisters. He had them on eight of his 10 toes and was going through Band-Aids, moleskin, and tape like a walking emergency ward. If he'd used any more tape, he would've looked like a mummy from an Egyptian tomb.

If you've ever been in a similar predicament, you know the frustration of wanting to have a good time, wanting to hike and explore the area where you have set up a secluded camp, only to be held up by several blisters. No one is immune—all are created equal before the blister god. You can be forced to bow to it unless you get your act together.

## Blisters

What causes blisters? In almost all cases, it is the simple rubbing of a foot against the interior of a boot. That can be worsened by several factors:

1. A very stiff boot or one in which your foot moves inside as you walk, instead of a boot that flexes as if it were another layer of skin.

2. Thin, ragged, or dirty socks. Thin socks will allow your feet to move inside your boots, ragged socks will allow your skin to chafe directly against the boot's interior, and dirty socks will wrinkle and fold, also rubbing against your feet instead of cushioning them.

3. Soft feet. By themselves, soft feet will not cause blisters, but in combination with a stiff boot or thin socks, they can cause problems. The best way to toughen up your feet is to go barefoot. In fact, some of the biggest, toughest-looking guys you'll ever see, from Hells Angels to pro football players, have feet that are as soft as a baby's butt. Why? Because they never go barefoot and don't hike much. Another trick is to wear Tevas, which can help build a tough layer on the bottom of your feet.

## The Perfect Boot

Every hiker eventually conducts a search for the perfect boot in the mission for ideal foot comfort and freedom from blisters. While there are many entries in this search—in fact, so many that it can be confusing—there is a way to find that perfect boot for you.

I've tried every combination of sock and insole in every style of boot. After 25,000 trail miles, I have found the perfect boot setup for me. What works for me is this: I wear thick SmartWool socks (not the thin ones), Dr. Scholl's Double Air-Pillo insoles, and Merrill Reflex Gore-Tex Mid Hikers. I've had no blisters in the past 1,500 miles. But the same setup will not work for you. Like my pal, the great hiker Francis Tapon, says, "Hike your own hike." Figure out what works for you and do not compromise based on what works for anybody else.

Gel insoles may be great for people who stand for long hours at their jobs, but they're not good for hiking. Your foot can shift and rub against the gel insole, causing a blister, rather than conforming to a fitted shape. A cushion-type insert is best.

To stay blister-free, the most important

© SABRINA YOUNG

Hiking shoes are perfect for short treks or day-long trips.

factors are socks and boot flexibility. If there is any foot slippage from a thin sock or a stiff boot, you can rub up a blister in minutes. For instance, I never wear stiff boots and I sometimes wear two fresh sets of SmartWools.

My search for the perfect boot included discussions with the nation's preeminent long-distance hikers, Brian Robinson of Mountain View (7,200 miles in one year) and Ray Jardine of Oregon (2,700 miles of Pacific Crest Trail in three months). Both believe that the weight of a shoe is the defining factor when selecting hiking footwear. They both go as light as possible, believing that heavy boots will eventually wear you out by forcing you to pick up several pounds on your feet over and over again.

It is absolutely critical to stay away from very stiff, heavy, leather boots and thin socks. Always wear the right style boots for what you have in mind and then protect your feet with carefully selected socks. If you are still so unfortunate as to get a blister or two, you must know how to treat them fast so they don't turn your walk into a sore-footed endurance test.

## Selecting the Right Boots

The first time we did the John Muir Trail, I hiked 400 miles in three months; that is, 150 miles in a two-month general-training program, then 250 miles in three weeks from Mount Whitney to Yosemite Valley. In that span, I got just one blister, suffered on the fourth day of the 250-miler. I treated it immediately and suffered no more. One key is wearing the right boot, and for me, that means a boot that acts as a thick layer of skin that is flexible and pliable to my foot. I want my feet to fit snugly in them, with no interior movement.

For many years, people have had four choices of footwear for hiking: hiking boots, hunting boots, mountaineering boots, and athletic shoes. I've tried them all, each for hundreds of miles. My opinion is to stay away from hunting boots, mountaineering boots, or athletic shoes. (The only exception is while rock climbing, when mountaineering boots work best.)

### HIKING BOOTS

The era of lightweight hiking boots is dominated by what are best described as Gore-Tex walking shoes. These shoes are designed for day walks or short backpacking trips. At first look, they can appear to be a rugged version of athletic shoes, designed with a Gore-Tex top for lightness and a Vibram sole for traction. There is no reason to get anything else because: 1) They are flexible, 2) They are easy to break in, and 3) With fresh socks, they rarely cause blisters. Since they are light, general hiking fatigue is greatly reduced. The models I like have some extra muscle built into them so that they can work for backpacking (and weight bearing).

On the negative side, because hiking boots are light, traction can be far from great on steep, gravelly surfaces. In addition, some provide less than ideal ankle support, which can be a problem in rocky areas, such as along a stream where you might want to go trout fishing. (I prefer midlevel for ankle support.)

Regardless of the distance you anticipate, they are the footwear of choice. My personal preference is Merrell's, but New Balance, Salomon, Asolo, Zamberlan, Vasque, and others make great hiking boots.

### MOUNTAINEERING BOOTS

You can identify mountaineering boots by their midrange tops, laces that extend almost as far as the toe area, and stiff ankle areas. This lack of "give" is what makes them great for rock climbing. Their stiffness is preferred when walking off-trail on craggy surfaces or hiking along the edge of streambeds, where walking across small rocks could cause you to turn your ankle. Because these boots don't give on rugged, craggy terrain, they reduce ankle injuries and provide better traction. Vasque makes my favorite mountaineering boots for rock climbing.

But for long hikes, they don't work. The drawback is that if you don't have the proper socks and your foot starts slipping around in the boot, blisters will inevitably follow.

## KEEP IT WILD TIP 3: TRAVEL LIGHTLY

1. Visit the backcountry in small groups.
2. Below tree line, always stay on designated trails.
3. Don't cut across switchbacks.
4. When traveling cross-country where no trails are available, follow animal trails or spread out with your group so no new routes are created.
5. Read your map and orient yourself with landmarks, a compass, and an altimeter. Avoid marking trails with rock cairns, tree scars, or ribbons.

### AT THE STORE

There are many styles, brands, and price ranges to choose from. A store like REI can have hundreds of hiking shoes available—Merrill alone offers a dozen different choices. If you wander around the aisles trying to look at all of them, you'll get as confused as my wife in a chocolate factory—you'll want to try everything.

Instead, go into the store with your mind clear about what you want, find it, and buy it. If you want the best, expect to spend $100-175 for hiking boots. If you go much cheaper, well, then you are getting cheap footwear.

Walk into the store believing you deserve the best and that's exactly what you'll pay for. However, you don't always *get* what you pay for. Once out of necessity for an unexpected hike, I spent $175-plus on some boots that turned out to be miserable blister-makers. I had to throw them out. *Adios.* Then move on to what works.

If you plan to use the advice of a shoe salesperson, first look at what kind of boots he or she is wearing. If the salesperson isn't even wearing boots, then their advice may not be worth much. Most people I know who own quality boots, including salespeople, often wear them almost daily if their jobs allow, since boots are the best footwear available. However, even these well-meaning folks can offer sketchy advice. Every hiker I know claims that they have chosen the world's greatest boot! Instead of asking how great the boot is, ask, "How many blisters did you get when you hiked 12 miles a day every day for a week?"

Enter the store with a precise use and style in mind. Rather than fish for suggestions, tell the salesperson exactly what you want, try two or three brands of the same style, and always try on both boots in a pair simultaneously so you know exactly how they'll feel. If possible, walk up and down stairs with them. Are they too stiff? Are your feet snug yet comfortable, or do they slip? Do they have that "right" kind of feel when you walk?

If you get the appropriate answers to those questions, then you're on your way to blister-free, pleasure-filled days of walking.

### Socks

People can spend so much energy selecting the right kind of boots that they virtually overlook wearing the right kind of socks. One goes with the other.

Your socks should be thick enough to cushion your feet as well as fit snugly. Without good socks, you might tie your bootlaces too tight—and that's like putting a tourniquet on your feet. You should have plenty of clean socks on hand, or plan on washing what you have on your trip. As socks are worn, they become compressed, dirty, and damp. If they fold over, you'll rub up a blister in minutes.

My companions believe I go overboard when it comes to socks—I bring too many and wear too many. But it works, so that's where the complaints stop. So how many do I wear? Well, it varies. On day hikes, SmartWool socks make my size 13s feel as if they're walking on pillows. I often wear two of them; that is, two on each foot (one medium-heavyweight sock and one medium-weight sock). Several manufacturers now produce socks that are the equivalent of SmartWools but are a lot less expensive. SmartWool socks and other similar socks are a synthetic composite that can partially wick moisture away from the skin.

It is critical to keep the interior sock clean. If you wear a sock over and over again, it will compact, lose its cushion, and start wrinkling or folding over while you hike and a blister will be born.

Do not wear thin cotton socks. Your foot can get damp and mix with dirt, which can cause a hot spot to start on your foot. Eventually, you get blisters, lots of them.

## Inner Sole

If you are like most folks, the bottoms of your feet are rarely exposed and can be quite soft. Take additional steps in their care by keeping a fresh inner sole footpad in your boot. I prefer Dr. Scholl's Double Air-Pillo insoles (or the equivalent). Just like new boots and new socks, insoles need to be broken in before an expedition. Some new inner soles can be slippery for a few days; if your foot slides around while you're hiking, this can cause blisters.

Another cure for soft feet is to walk or jog regularly before your camping trip. On one trip on the Pacific Coast Trail, I ran into the long-distance master Jardine. He swore that regularly going barefoot was the best way to build up foot strength and arch support, while also toughening up the bottoms of your feet.

If you plan to use insoles and to wear two socks, bring them with you when sizing boots. Put on the socks you plan to wear when hiking, insert the inner sole, and then see how the boots feel. That's the only right way to size a hiking boot.

## Treating Blisters

The key to treating blisters is fast work at the first sign of a hot spot. If you feel a hot spot, never keep walking, figuring that the problem will go away or that you will work through it. Wrong! Stop immediately and go to work.

Before you remove your socks, check to see if the sock has a wrinkle in it, a likely cause of

the problem. If so, either change socks or pull them tight, removing the tiny folds, after taking care of the blister.

To take care of the blister use Second Skin, which adheres over the top of the blister and does not dislodge. For small blisters, Band-Aids can do the job, but these have to be replaced daily (sometimes more than that). At night, clean your feet and sleep without socks, which will allow your feet to dry and heal.

For the big round blisters that occasionally form on your heel, the great Brian Robinson told me that in an emergency he used duct tape around the back of his heel to create a second skin. He then put Vaseline on top of the second skin to stop the abrasion at the hot spot.

Moleskin, once a great blister treatment, is no longer the must-have in your first-aid kit. Over the years, they've changed the manufacturing and I've found it slides off the blister while hiking.

## Tips in the Field

Three other items that can help your walking are an Ace bandage, a pair of gaiters, and hiking poles.

For sprained ankles and twisted knees, an Ace bandage can be like an insurance policy to get you back on the trail and out of trouble. In many cases, a hiker with a twisted ankle or sprained knee has relied on a good wrap with a four-inch bandage for the added support to get home. Always buy the Ace bandages that come with the clips permanently attached, so you don't have to worry about losing them.

Gaiters are leggings made of Gore-Tex that fit from just below your knees, over your calves, and attach under your boots. They are of particular help when walking in damp areas or in places where rain is common. As your legs brush against ferns or low-lying plants, gaiters deflect the moisture. Without them, pants can get soaking wet in short order.

Many hikers would never hit the trail without hiking poles. Personally, they are not for me; I like to hike in rhythm and keep my arms swinging effortlessly. I don't like to have to watch where I'm putting my poles all the time. But for those who have trouble with footing, a cranky knee or ankle, or want the upper body workout, poles can be a good fit. If it floats your boat, bring 'em.

Another tip: Should your boots become wet, never try to force-dry them. Some well-meaning folks will try to dry them quickly at the edge of a campfire or, at home, actually put the boots in an oven. While this may dry the boots, it can also loosen the glue that holds them together, ultimately weakening them until one day they fall apart in a heap. A better bet is to treat the leather so the boots become water-repellent. Silicone-based liquids are the easiest to use and least greasy of the treatments available.

A final tip is to have another pair of light-weight shoes or moccasins that you can wear around camp and, in the process, give your feet the rest they deserve.

## Clothing and Weather Protection
### A HELL OF A MESS

It was what we called "A Hell of a Mess." For Foonsky and me, what started as an innocent pursuit of the perfect campground evolved into an impossible predicament.

We had parked at the end of a logging road and then bushwhacked our way off trail down a canyon to a pristine trout stream. On my first cast—a little flip into the plunge pool of a waterfall—I caught a 16-inch rainbow trout, a real beauty that jumped three times. Magic stuff.

Then, just across the stream, we saw it: the Perfect Camping Spot. On a sandbar on the edge of the forest, there lay a flat spot, high and dry above the river. Nearby was plenty of downed wood collected by past winter storms that we could use for firewood. And, of course, this beautiful trout stream was bubbling along just 40 yards from the site.

But nothing is perfect, right? To reach it, we had to wade across the river, although it didn't appear to be too difficult. The cold water tingled a bit, and the river came up surprisingly

high, just above the belt. But it would be worth it to camp at the Perfect Spot.

Once across the river, we put on some dry clothes, set up camp, explored the woods, and fished the stream, catching several nice trout for dinner. But late that afternoon, it started raining. What? Rain in the summertime? Nature makes its own rules. By the next morning, it was still raining from a solid gray sky, pouring like a Yosemite waterfall.

That's when we noticed the Perfect Spot wasn't so perfect. The rain had raised the river level too high for us to wade back across. We were marooned, wet, and hungry.

"Now we're in a hell of a mess," said Foonsky, the water streaming off him.

Both of us were soaking wet on that sandbar. With no other choice, we tried holing up in the tent for the night. A sleeping bag with polyester fiberfill can retain warmth even when wet, because the fill is hollow and retains its loft. So as miserable as it was, the night passed without incident.

The rain stopped the next day and the river dropped a bit, but it was still rolling big and angry. Using a stick as a wading staff, 6-foot 5-inch Foonsky crossed about 80 percent of the stream before he was dumped, but he made a jump for it and managed to scramble to the riverbank. He waved for me to follow. "No problem," I thought.

It took me 20 minutes to reach nearly the same spot where Foonsky had been dumped. The heavy river current was above my belt and pushing hard. Then, in the flash of an instant, my wading staff slipped on a rock. I teetered in the river current and was knocked over like a bowling pin. I became completely submerged. I went tumbling down the river, heading right toward the waterfall. While underwater, I looked up at the surface, and I can remember how close it seemed yet how out of control I was. Right then, this giant hand appeared, and I grabbed it. It was Foonsky. If it weren't for that hand, I would have sailed right over the waterfall.

My momentum drew Foonsky right into the river, and we scrambled in the current, but

I suddenly sensed the river bottom under my knees. On all fours, the two of us clambered ashore. We were safe.

"Thanks, ol' buddy," I said.

"Man, we're wet," he responded. "Let's get to the rig and get some dry clothes on."

My best friend had saved my life.

Getting cold and wet on a camping trip with no way to warm up is unnecessary and uncomfortable. Worse, it can be a ticket to hypothermia, the number one killer of campers in the woods. By definition, hypothermia is a condition in which body temperature is lowered to the point that it causes illness. It is particularly dangerous because the afflicted are usually unaware it is setting in. The first sign is a sense of apathy, then a state of confusion, which can lead eventually to collapse (or what appears to be sleep), then death.

You must always have a way to get warm and dry in short order, regardless of any conditions you may face. If you have no way of getting dry, then you must take emergency steps to prevent hypothermia. (See the steps detailed in First Aid and Insect Protection in this chapter.)

But you should never reach that point. For starters, always have spare sets of clothing tucked away so no matter how cold and wet you might get, you have something dry to put on. On hiking trips, I always carry a second set of clothes, sealed to stay dry, in a plastic garbage bag. I keep a third set waiting back at the truck. It's a great insurance policy—when you get wet, you'll know you have dry clothes waiting.

If you are car camping, your vehicle can cause an illusory sense of security. But with an extra set of dry clothes stashed safely away, there is no illusion. The security is real. And remember, no matter how hot the weather is when you start your trip, always be prepared for the worst. Or just like Foonsky and me, you'll learn the hard way.

## The Art of Layering

The most important element for enjoying the outdoor experience in any condition is to stay dry and warm. There is no substitute. You must stay dry and you must stay warm. If you are a parent and have children, remember to make sure your youngsters are always dry and warm.

Thus comes the theory behind layering, which suggests that as your body temperature fluctuates or the weather shifts, you simply peel off or add available layers as needed—and have a waterproof shell available in case of rain. What you need to do is create a system that effectively combines elements of breathability, durability, insulation, rapid drying, water repellence, wicking, and wind resistance, while still being lightweight and offering the necessary freedom of movement, all with just a few garments.

The introduction of a new era of outdoor clothing has made it possible for campers to turn choosing clothes into an art form.

### What Works For Me

When facing severe conditions, this is what works for me. Start with a base layer, a bi-component knit underwear, such as Polartec (there are many others). I prefer medium to heavyweight because a thin layer can feel clingy and can creep up on you. For the next layer, I wear a long-sleeve Dynafit thermal on top and quick-dry, water-repellent Kuhl pants on the bottom. The Kuhl pants are good in all conditions; in cold weather, just add a bi-component knit underwear layer next to your skin or, in rain, a waterproof shell.

In extreme cold, the next strategy is my own invention. Over these first two layers, I wear a tight-fitting Under Armour long-sleeve shirt. This creates a tight shell to retain core warmth and it works great for me. Then I wear a fleece vest on top.

For rain, snow, or wind, I add a super-lightweight shell that is waterproof and wind-proof. Berghaus hydroshells have worked for me. In a blizzard, I also have an insulated Gore-Tex snow bib that goes over the top of everything and a mountaineering jacket, like a Spyfire. I wear Black Diamond gloves and both a skullcap and a ski cap.

Of course, we haven't had weather like in

1937, when it was minus 45 degrees at Boca near Truckee. It was so cold that winter that, according to a campfire story, the cats licked themselves to stay warm. Then in the spring when their litters came, all the kittens were born with sweaters.

## Hats

Always pack a wide-brimmed hat. You lose a large percentage of heat through your head. When it gets cold, a hat will help seal in warmth. At night in cold weather, I also wear a skullcap; when it's freezing cold, I wear a ski hat on top of that. During the day, I almost always wear a wide-brimmed hat. My favorite hat is made of waterproof canvas and is rigged with a lariat that can be cinched down when windy. The wide brim keeps the tops of my ears from getting sunburned. If you're outside a lot, do not wear baseball hats—the tops of your ears will burn to a red crisp. Years ago, that's how an old friend of mine lost his ears to skin cancer. Good ol' Dave.

### Head Light

I've tried many head lights and the Trail Torch Hat Light is the best for the money (www.halibut.net). It comes with five LED lights in a horizontal row that clips under the bill of your hat. For the best option, order the set with three green lights (for night vision) and two white lights. At night, walking around camp, you'll look like a jet coming in for a landing. I have several lightweight headlamps as well, which work better than the Trail Torch when caving. Their brightness can hurt your night vision, making it difficult to see the night sky and the stars.

## Vests and Parkas

In cold weather, take the layer system one step further with a warm vest and a parka jacket. Vests are especially useful as they provide warmth without the bulk. I often wear a Cabela's medium-weight fleece vest and I prefer that to the park-type vests. For many, the answer can be to combine a fleece vest with a lightweight parka.

## Rain Gear

One of the most miserable nights of my life was on a camping trip for which I hadn't brought my rain gear or a tent. Hey, it was early August, the temperature had been in the 90s for weeks, and if anybody had said it was going to rain, I would have told them to consult a brain doctor. But rain it did. And as I got wetter and wetter, I kept saying to myself, "Hey, it's summer, it's not supposed to rain." Then I remembered one of the commandments of camping: Forget your rain gear and you can guarantee it will rain.

To stay dry, you need some form of water-repellent shell. It can be as simple as a $5 poncho made out of plastic or as elaborate as a Gore-Tex jacket-and-pants set that costs hundreds of dollars. What counts is not how much you spend, but how dry you stay.

Waterproof and water-resistant are completely different things. In addition, there is no such thing as rain gear that is both waterproof and breathable. The more waterproof a jacket is, the less it breathes. Conversely, the more breathable a jacket is, the less waterproof it becomes.

If you wear water-resistant rain gear in a sustained downpour, you'll get soaked. Water-resistant rain gear is appealing because it breathes and will keep you dry in the light stuff, such as mist, fog, or even a little splash from a canoe paddle. But in rain? Forget it.

So what is the solution?

I've decided that the best approach is a set of fairly light but 100 percent-waterproof rain gear. I bought a hooded jacket and pants from Coleman, and my assessment is that it is the most cost-efficient rain gear I've ever had. Many duck hunters use Gore-Tex based rain gear and it keeps them dry no matter what.

The best foul-weather gear made is by Simms, both jacket and bib. While it is expensive, you will stay dry and warm in any condition but that in which you need a survival suit.

Their motto is: There is no such thing as bad weather, only bad gear.

You can also stay dry with any of the waterproof plastics and even heavy-duty rubber-coated outfits made for commercial fishers. But these are uncomfortable during anything but a heavy rain. Because they are heavy and don't breathe, you'll likely get soaked anyway (that is, from your own sweat), even if it isn't raining hard.

On backpacking trips, I still stash a super-lightweight, water-repellent slicker for day hikes and a poncho, which I throw over my pack at night to keep it dry.

Some do just fine with a cheap poncho, and note that ponchos can serve other uses in addition to a raincoat. Ponchos can be used as a ground tarp, as a rain cover for supplies or a backpack, or can be snapped together and roped up to trees in a pinch to provide a quick storm ceiling if you don't have a tent. The problem with ponchos is that in a hard rain, you just don't stay dry. First your legs get wet. Then they get soaked. Then your arms follow the same pattern. If you're wearing cotton, you'll find that once part of the garment gets wet, the water spreads until, alas, you are dripping wet, poncho and all. Before long, you start to feel like a walking refrigerator.

If cost is no factor, buy a Gore-Tex rain jacket and pants. Gore-Tex is actually not a fabric, but a laminated film that coats a breathable fabric. The result is lightweight, water-repellent, breathable jackets and pants. They are perfect for campers, but they cost a fortune.

If you don't want to spend the big bucks for Gore-Tex rain gear but want more rain protection than a poncho affords, a coated nylon jacket is the compromise that many choose. They are cheap, have the highest water-repellency of any rain gear, and are warm, providing a good outer shell for your layers of clothing.

But they are not without fault. These jackets don't breathe at all, and if you zip them up tight, you can sweat a river.

My brother Rambob gave me a nylon jacket before we climbed 14,179-foot Mount Shasta the first time. I wore that cheap special all the way to the top with no complaints; it's warm and 100 percent waterproof. The one problem with nylon comes when temperatures drop below freezing. It gets so stiff that it feels as if you are wearing a straitjacket.

## Other Gear

Question: Can you guess the three most commonly forgotten items on a camping trip? Answer: A hat, sunglasses, and lip balm.

A hat is crucial, especially when you are visiting high elevations. Without one you are constantly exposed to everything nature can give you. The sun will dehydrate you, sap your energy, sunburn your head, and in worst cases, cause sunstroke. Start with a comfortable hat. Then finish with sunglasses, lip balm, and sunscreen for additional protection. They will help protect you from extreme heat.

To guard against extreme cold, it's a good idea to keep a pair of thin ski gloves stashed away with your emergency clothes, along with a wool ski cap, or a skull cap. Any glove should be thick enough to keep your fingers from stiffening up, but pliable enough to allow full movement so you don't have to take them off to complete simple tasks, like lighting a stove. While expensive, Black Diamond gloves are irreplaceable in extreme cold, snow, or ice.

An alternative is glovelets, which look like gloves with no fingers. A lot of fishing guides wear glovelets in winter, when it gets cold but they still need to tie knots. In any case, just because the weather turns cold doesn't mean that your hands have to.

# FOOD AND COOKING GEAR

On a clear, warm day, Foonsky decided to go skydiving. He jumped out of the plane and pulled on the ripcord: His parachute didn't open. In total free fall, Foonsky watched the earth below getting closer and closer. Not one to panic, he calmly pulled the ripcord on the emergency parachute. Again, nothing happened. No parachute, no nothing. The ground was getting ever closer and as he tried to search for a soft place to land, Foonsky detected a small object shooting up toward him, growing larger as it approached. It looked like a camper. Figuring this was his last chance, Foonsky shouted as they passed in midair, "Hey, do you know anything about parachutes?"

The other fellow just yelled back as he headed off into space, "Do you know anything about lighting camping stoves?"

Well, Foonsky got lucky and his parachute opened. As for the other guy, well, he's probably in orbit like a NASA weather satellite. If you've ever had a mishap while lighting a camping stove, you know exactly what I'm talking about.

If your stove does not work right, your trip can turn into a disaster, regardless of how well you have planned the other elements. In addition, a bad stove will add an underlying sense of foreboding to your day. You will constantly have the inner suspicion that your darn stove is going to foul up again. It is important to be able to light your stove easily and to have it reach full heat without feeling as though you're playing with a short fuse to a big bomb.

I once almost burned my beard completely off in a mini-explosion while lighting one of the larger car camping stoves. I was in the middle of cooking dinner when the flame suddenly shut down. Sure enough, the fuel tank was empty. After refilling it, I pumped the tank 50 or 60 times to regain pressure. When I lit the match, the sucker ignited from three feet away. The resulting explosion was like a stick of dynamite and immediately the smell of burning beard was in the air. In a flash, my once thick, dark beard had been reduced to a mass of little, yellow, burned curlicues.

My error? After filling the tank, I forgot to shut the fuel cock off while pumping up the pressure in the tank. As a result, the stove burners were slowly emitting the gas/air mixture as I pumped the tank, filling the air above the stove. Then, strike a match from even a few feet away and ka-boom!

## Camping Stoves

If you are buying a camping stove, remember this one critical rule: Do not leave the store with a new stove unless you have been shown exactly how to use it.

Know what you are getting. Many stores that specialize in outdoor recreation equipment now staff experienced campers/employees who will demonstrate the use of every stove they sell. While they're at it, they'll also describe the stoves' respective strengths and weaknesses.

The best backpacking stove is the MSR Reactor 1.7L Stove System. I used this baby when I climbed the Lyell Glacier, camping at 12,800 feet, and I've never seen water boil so fast—in less than two minutes. It uses a butane fuel canister that will last 80 minutes.

The MSR Whisperlite is an icon among backpackers. I've gone through several of them. It uses white gas in a separate fuel container so you can easily monitor fuel consumption. The one flaw is the connector links from the fuel line. After a few years of heavy use, they can develop leaks; ignite and you've got a meltdown.

For heavy, long-term use, the ease with which you can clean the burner is most important. If you camp often, especially with a smaller stove, the burner holes will eventually become clogged. Some stoves have a built-in cleaning needle: a quick twist of the knob and you're in business. Others require disassembly and a protracted cleaning session using special tools. If a stove is difficult to clean, you will tend to put off the tiresome chore. Your stove will sputter and pant while you watch that pot of water sitting there, staying cold.

The standard Coleman car camping stove

© SABRINA YOUNG

Stoves are available in many sizes and burn a variety of fuels.

(the green one with the two burners) is a legend around the world. Electronic ignition has solved all the old lighting problems. In addition, you can get the version with free-standing legs so that you don't need to place the stove on a picnic table or a folded-out tailgate to use as a platform.

A little stove with a cult-like following is the Sierra, which burns small twigs and pinecones, then uses a tiny battery-driven fan to develop increased heat and cooking ability. It's an alternative for long-distance backpacking trips, as it solves the problem of carrying a fuel bottle, especially on expeditions for which large quantities of fuel would otherwise be needed. Some tinkering with the flame (a very hot one) is required, and they are legal and functional only in the alpine zone where dry wood is available. Also note that in years with high fire danger, the U.S. Forest Service enacts rules prohibiting open flames, and fires are also often prohibited above an elevation of 10,000 feet.

## Building Fires

One summer expedition took me to the Canadian wilderness in British Columbia for a 75-mile canoe trip on the Bowron Lake Circuit, a chain of 13 lakes, six rivers, and seven portages. It is one of the greatest canoe trips in the world, a loop that ends just a few hundred feet from its starting point. But at the first camp at Kibbee Lake, my stove developed a fuel leak at the base of the burner, and the fire that followed looked like a Roman candle.

As a result, we had to complete the final 70 miles of the trip without a stove, cooking instead on open fires each night. The problem was compounded by the weather. It rained eight of the 10 days. In Canada, raindrops the size of silver dollars fall so hard they actually bounce on the lake surface. We had to stop paddling a few times to empty the rainwater out of the canoe. At the end of the day, we'd make camp and then face the critical decision: either make a fire or go to bed cold and hungry.

Equipped with an ax, at least we had a chance for success. Although the downed wood was soaked, I was able to make my own fire-starting tinder from the chips of split logs. That's because no matter how hard it rains, the inside of a log is always dry.

In heavy rain, matches don't stay lit long

# KEEP IT WILD TIP 4: CAMPFIRES

1. Fire use can scar the backcountry. If a fire ring is not available, use a lightweight stove for cooking.
2. Where fires are permitted, use existing fire rings away from large rocks or overhangs.
3. Don't char rocks by building new rings.
4. Gather sticks from the ground that are no larger than the diameter of your wrist.
5. Don't snap branches of live, dead, or downed trees, which can cause personal injury and also scar the natural setting.
6. Put the fire "dead out" and make sure it's cold before departing. Remove all trash from the fire ring and sprinkle dirt over the site.
7. A campfire that appears to be out can still start a forest fire. Hot embers burning deep in the pit can cause tree roots to catch fire and burn underground. If you ever see smoke rising from the ground, seemingly from nowhere, dig down and put the fire out.

enough to get tinder started. Instead, we used either a candle or the little waxlike fire-starter cubes that remain lit for several minutes. From those, we could get the tinder going. Then we added small, slender strips of wood that had been axed from the interior of the logs. When the flame reached a foot high, we added the logs, their dry interior facing in. By the time the inside of the logs had caught fire, the outside was drying from the heat. It wasn't long before a royal blaze was brightening the rainy night.

Being able to build a good fire and cook on it can be one of the more satisfying elements of a camping trip. At times, just looking into the flames can provide a special satisfaction at the end of a good day.

However, never expect to build a fire for every meal or, in some cases, even to build one at all. During fire season, the danger of forest fires often prohibits fires altogether or may restrict these to existing fire rings in designated campgrounds. Many state and federal campgrounds have also been picked clean of downed wood, though you may be able to buy wood bundles from a camp store or a camp host.

When you can build a fire and the resources for doing so are available, it will enhance the quality of your camping experience. Of the campgrounds listed in this book, those where you are permitted to build fires will usually have fire rings. In primitive areas where you can make your own fire, you should dig a ring

eight inches deep and clear all the needles and twigs in a five-foot radius. The next day, when the fire is dead, you can fill over the black charcoal with dirt, and then spread pine needles and twigs over it. Nobody will even know you camped there. That's the best way I know to keep a secret spot a real secret.

When you start to build a campfire, the first thing you will notice is that your fellow campers will not be able to resist moving the wood around. Watch. You'll be getting ready to add a key piece of wood at just the right spot, and your companion will stick his mitts in, believing he has a better idea. He'll shift the fire around and undermine your best-thought-out plans.

We enforce a rule on camping trips: One person makes the fire while everybody else stands clear or is involved with other camp tasks, such as gathering wood, getting water, putting up tents, or planning dinner. Once the fire is going strong, then it's fair game; anyone adds logs at his or her discretion. But in the early, delicate stages of the campfire, it's best to leave the work to one person. Then you can rotate who gets to make the campfire each evening.

Before a match is ever struck, you should gather a complete pile of firewood. Then, start small, with the tiniest twigs you can find, and slowly add larger twigs as you go, crisscrossing them like a miniature tepee. Eventually, you will get to the big chunks that produce high heat. The key is to get one piece of wood burning into another, which then burns into another, setting off what I call the chain of flame. Conversely, single pieces of wood set apart from each other will not burn, of course.

On a dry summer evening at a campsite where plenty of wood is available, about the only way you can blow the deal is to get impatient and try to add the big pieces too quickly. Do that and you'll get smoke, not flames, and it won't be long before every one of your fellow campers is poking at your fire. It will drive you crazy, but they just can't help it.

## Cooking Gear

I like traveling light, and I've found that all I need for cooking is a pot, small frying pan, metal pot grabber, fork, knife, cup, and a lighter. If you want to keep the price of food low and also cook customized dinners each night, a small pressure cooker can be just the ticket. (See Keeping the Price Down in this chapter.) I store all my gear in one small bag that fits into my pack. If I'm camping out of my four-wheel-drive rig, I can easily keep track of the little bag of cooking gear. Going simple, not complicated, is the key to keeping a camping trip on the right track.

You can get more elaborate by buying complete kits with plates, a coffeepot, large pots, and other cookware, but what really counts is having a single pot that makes you happy. It needs to be just the right size, not too big or small, and stable enough so it won't tip over, even if it is at a slight angle on a fire, filled with water at a full boil. Mine is just six inches wide and 4.5 inches deep. It holds better than a quart of water and has served me well for thousands of camp dinners.

The rest of your cook kit is easy to complete. The frying pan should be small, light-gauge aluminum, and Teflon-coated, with a fold-in handle so it's no hassle to store. A pot grabber is a great addition. This little aluminum gadget clamps to the edge of pots and allows you to lift them and pour water with total control and without burning your fingers. For cleanup, take

along a plastic scrubber and a small bottle filled with dish soap, and you're in business.

A Sierra Cup, a wide aluminum cup with a wire handle, can be an ideal item to carry because you can eat out of it as well as use it for drinking. This means no plates to scrub after dinner, so washing up is quick and easy. In addition, if you go for a hike, you can clip its handle to your belt. Some people bring a giant cup called a "Fair Share." These look like Sierra Cups, but are twice as big. In expeditions where food has to be rationed, people with "Fair Share" cups manage to get a lot more than their "fair share" because a cup of food looks so small in these giant vessels. If you see these giant cups on an expedition, serve the owner last and use a separate measuring device.

If you opt for a more formal setup for car camping, complete with plates, glasses, silverware, and the like, you can end up spending more time preparing and cleaning up after meals than enjoying the country you are exploring. In addition, the more equipment you bring, the more loose ends you will have to deal with, and loose ends can cause plenty of frustration. If you have a choice, go simple.

## Food and Cooking Tricks

On a trip to the Bob Marshall Wilderness in western Montana, I woke up one morning, yawned, and said, "What've we got for breakfast?"

The silence was ominous. "Well," finally came the response, "we don't have any food left."

"What!?"

"Well, I figured we'd catch trout for meals every other night."

On the return trip, we ended up eating wild berries, buds, and, yes, even roots (not too tasty). When we finally landed the next day at a suburban pizza parlor, we nearly ate the wooden tables.

Running out of food on a camping trip can do more to turn reasonable people into violent grumps than any other event. There's no excuse for it, not when figuring meals can be

# HOW TO MAKE BEEF JERKY IN YOUR OWN KITCHEN

Start with a couple of pieces of meat: lean top round, sirloin, or tri-tip. Cut them into 3/16-inch strips across the grain, trimming out the membrane, gristle, and fat. Marinate the strips for 24 hours in a glass dish. The fun begins in picking a marinade. Try two-thirds teriyaki sauce, one-third Worcestershire sauce. You can customize the recipe by adding pepper, ground mustard, bay leaf, red wine vinegar, garlic, and, for the brave, Tabasco sauce.

After a day or so, squeeze out each strip of meat with a rolling pin, lay them in rows on a cooling rack over a cookie sheet, and dry them in the oven at 125°F for 12 hours. Thicker pieces can take as long as 18-24 hours.

That's it. The hardest part is cleaning the cookie sheet when you're done. The easiest part is eating your own homemade jerky while sitting at a lookout on a mountain ridge. The do-it-yourself method for jerky may take a day or so, but it is cheaper and can taste better than any store-bought jerky.

−My thanks to Jeff Patty for this recipe

done precisely and with little effort. You should not go out and buy a bunch of food, throw it in your rig, and head off for yonder. That leaves too much to chance. And if you've ever been really hungry in the woods, you know it's worth a little effort to guard against a day or two of starvation. Here's a three-step solution:

1. Draw up a general meal-by-meal plan and make sure your companions like what's on it.

2. Tell your companions to buy any specialty items (such as a special brand of coffee) on their own and not to expect you to take care of everything.

3. Put all the food on your living room floor and literally plan out every day of your trip, meal by meal, putting the food in plastic bags as you go. That way, you will know exact food quotas and you won't go hungry.

Fish for your dinner? There's one guarantee as far as that goes: If you expect to catch fish for meals, you will most certainly get skunked. If you don't expect to catch fish for meals, you will probably catch so many they'll be coming out of your ears. I've seen it a hundred times.

## Keeping the Price Down

"There must be some mistake," I said with a laugh. "Whoever paid $750 for camp food?"

But the amount was as clear as the digital numbers on the cash register: $753.27.

"How is this possible?" I asked the clerk.

"Just add it up," she responded, irritated.

Then I started figuring. The freeze-dried backpack dinners cost $8-10 apiece. A pack of turkey jerky went for $6, a box of Clif bars for $20. Multiply it all by four hungry men, including Foonsky.

The dinners alone cost close to $500. Add in the usual goodies—candy, coffee, dried fruit, granola bars, jerky, oatmeal, soup, and Tang—and I felt as if an earthquake had struck when I saw the tab.

A lot of campers have received similar shocks. In preparation for their trips, campers shop with enthusiasm. Then they pay the bill in horror.

Well, there are solutions, lots of them. You can eat gourmet-style in the outback without having your wallet cleaned out. But it requires do-it-yourself cooking, more planning, and careful shopping. It also means transcending the push-button, I-want-it-now attitude that so many people can't leave behind when they go to the mountains.

Now when Foonsky, Mr. Furnai, Rambob, and I sit down to eat such a meal, we don't call it "eating." We call it "hodge packing" or "time to pack your hodge." After a particularly long day on the trail, you can do some serious hodge packing.

If your trip is a shorter one, say for a weekend, consider bringing more fresh food to add some sizzle to the hodge. You can design a hot soup/stew mix that is good enough to eat at home.

Start by bringing a pot of water to a full boil, and then add pasta, ramen noodles, or macaroni. While it simmers, cut in a potato, carrot, onion, and garlic clove, and cook for about 10 minutes. When the vegetables have softened, add in a soup mix or two, maybe some cheese, and you are just about in business. But you can still ruin it and turn your hodge into slodge. Make sure you read the directions on the soup mix to determine cooking time. It can vary widely. In addition, make sure you stir the whole thing up; otherwise, you will get those hidden dry clumps of soup mix that taste like garlic sawdust.

How do I know? Well, it was up near Kearsage Pass in the Sierra Nevada, where, feeling half-starved, I dug into our nightly hodge. I will never forget that first bite—I damn near gagged to death. Foonsky laughed at me, until he took his first bite (a nice big one) and then turned green.

Another way to trim food costs is to make your own beef jerky, the trademark staple of campers for more than 200 years. We make our own and get big strips of jerky that taste better than anything you can buy.

For a crew of four, you can get by with two freeze-dried dinners that you cook right in the container pouch. Liam Furniss discovered that by adding a separate bonus pack of garlic-seasoned mashed potatoes, which cook in 90 seconds; everybody has plenty of food. That goes even for his dad Mo, with his gigantic, crater-of-the-moon Fair Share cup.

You can supplement your eats with sweets, nuts, freeze-dried fruits, and drink mixes. In any case, make sure you keep the dinner menu varied. If you and your buddies look into your dinner cups and groan, "Ugh, not this again," you will soon start dreaming of cheeseburgers and French fries instead of hiking, fishing, and finding beautiful campsites.

If you are car camping and have a big ice chest, you can bring virtually anything to eat and drink. If you are on the trail and don't mind paying the price, the newest freeze-dried dinners provide another option.

Some of the biggest advances in the outdoors industry have come in the form of freeze-dried dinners. Some of them are almost good enough to serve in restaurants. Sweet-and-sour pork over rice, tostadas, Burgundy chicken—it sure beats the poopy goop we used to eat, like the old soupy chili-mac dinners that tasted bad and looked so unlike food that consumption was nearly impossible, even for my dog, Rebel. Foonsky usually managed to get it down, but just barely.

To provide an idea of how to plan a menu, consider what we ate while hiking 250 miles over the course of 21 days and 20 nights on the John Muir Trail:

- Breakfast: instant soup, oatmeal (never get plain), jerky, coffee or hot chocolate.
- Lunch: one beef stick, two jerky sticks, dried fruit, half cup of trail mix, Tang, one small bag of M&Ms with nuts.
- Trail snack: one Clif bar, trail mix.
- Dinner: instant soup, one freeze-dried dinner (split between two people), one milk bar, rainbow trout.

What was that last item? Rainbow trout? Right! Unless you plan on it, you can catch them every night.

## Trout Dinner

If all this still doesn't sound like your idea of a gourmet but low-cost camping meal, well, you are forgetting the main course: rainbow trout. Remember: If you don't plan on catching them for dinner, you'll probably land more than you can finish in one night's hodge packing.

Some campers go to great difficulties to cook their trout, bringing along frying pans, butter, grills, tinfoil, and more, but all you need is some seasoned salt and a campfire.

Rinse the gutted trout, and while it's still wet, sprinkle on a good dose of Lawry's seasoned salt, both inside and out. Clear any burning logs to the side of the campfire, then lay the trout right on the coals, turning it once so both sides are cooked. Sound ridiculous? Sound like you are throwing the fish away? Sound like the fish will burn up? Sound like you will have to eat the campfire ash? Wrong on all counts. The fish cooks perfectly, the ash doesn't stick, and after cooking trout this way, you may never fry trout again.

If you can't convince your buddies that insist that trout should be fried, then make sure you have butter to fry it in, not oil. Also make sure you cook them all the way through, so the meat strips off the backbone in two nice, clean fillets. The fish should end up looking like one that Sylvester the Cat just drew out of his mouth—only the head, tail, and a perfect skeleton.

## FIRST AID AND INSECT PROTECTION

One summer night, as I lay in my sleeping bag gazing up at the night sky full of stars, I thought, "It doesn't get any better than this." The sky looked like a mass of jewels and the air tasted sweet and smelled of pines. A shooting star fireballed across the sky.

Just then, as I was drifting into sleep, a mysterious buzz appeared from nowhere and deposited itself inside my left ear. Suddenly awake, I whacked my ear with the palm of my hand, hard enough to cause a near concussion. The buzz disappeared. I pulled out my flashlight and shined it on my palm, and there, lit in the blackness of night, lay the squished intruder: a mosquito, dead amid a stain of blood.

Satisfied, I turned off the light, closed my eyes, and thought of the fishing trip planned for the next day. Then I heard them. It was a squadron of mosquitoes flying in landing patterns around my head. I tried to grab them with an open hand, but they dodged the assault and flew off. Just 30 seconds later, another landed in my left ear. I promptly dispatched the invader with a rip of the palm.

Now I was completely awake, so I got out of my sleeping bag to retrieve some mosquito repellent. But en route, several of the buggers

swarmed and nailed me in the back and arms. After I applied the repellent and settled snugly again in my sleeping bag, the mosquitoes would buzz a few inches from my ear. After getting a whiff of the poison, they would fly off. It was like sleeping in a sawmill.

The next day, drowsy from little sleep, I set out to fish. I'd walked but 15 minutes when I brushed against a bush and felt a stinging sensation on the inside of my arm, just above the wrist. I looked down: A tick had his clamps in me. I ripped it out before he could embed his head into my skin.

After catching a few fish, I sat down against a tree to eat lunch and just watch the water go by. My dog, Rebel, sat down next to me and stared at the beef jerky I was munching as if it were a T-bone steak. I finished eating, gave him a small piece, patted him on the head, and said, "Good dog." Right then, I noticed an itch on my arm where a mosquito had drilled me. I unconsciously scratched it. Two days later, in that exact spot, some nasty red splotches started popping up. Poison oak. By petting my dog and then scratching my arm, I had transferred the oil residue of the poison oak leaves from Rebel's fur to my arm.

When I returned home, Foonsky asked me about the trip.

"Great," I said. "Mosquitoes, ticks, poison oak. Can hardly wait to go back."

"Sorry I missed out," he answered.

## Mosquitoes, No-See-Ums, Horseflies

On a trip to Canada, Foonsky and I were fishing a small lake from the shore when suddenly a black horde of mosquitoes could be seen moving across the lake toward us. It was like when the French army looked across the Rhine and saw the Wehrmacht coming. There was a buzz in the air. We fought them off for a few minutes, then made a fast retreat to the truck and jumped in, content the buggers had been foiled. But in some way still unknown to us, the mosquitoes gained entry to the truck. In 10 minutes, we squished 15 of them as they attempted to plant their oil drills into our skins. Just outside the truck, the black horde waited for us to make a tactical error, such as rolling down a window. It finally took a miraculous hailstorm with lightning to squelch the attack.

When it comes to mosquitoes, no-see-ums, gnats, and horseflies, there are times when there is nothing you can do. However, in most situations, you can muster a defense to repel the attack.

When under heavy attack by mosquitoes, the first key is to wear clothing too heavy for them to drill through. Expose a minimum of skin, wear a hat, and tie a bandanna around your neck, preferably one that has been sprayed with repellent. If you try to get by with just a thin cotton T-shirt and nylon shorts, you will be declared a federal mosquito sanctuary.

When under bombardment, your skin must be well covered with only your hands and face exposed. Second, you should have your companion spray your clothes with repellent. I prefer Deep Woods Off! Then dab liquid repellent directly on what little skin is exposed.

At night, the easiest way to get a good sleep without mosquitoes buzzing in your ear is to sleep in a bug-proof tent. If the nights are warm and you want to see the stars, new tent models are available that have a skylight covered with mosquito netting. If you don't like tents on summer evenings, mosquito netting rigged with an air space at your head can solve the problem.

If your problems are with no-see-ums or biting horseflies, then you need a slightly different approach. No-see-ums are tiny black insects that look like nothing more than a sliver of dirt on your skin. Then you notice something stinging, and when you rub the area, you scratch up a little no-see-um. The results are similar to mosquito bites, making your skin itch, splotch, and, when you get them bad, swell. In addition to using the techniques described to repel mosquitoes, you should go one step further.

The problem is that no-see-ums are tricky little devils. Somehow, they can actually get under your socks and around your ankles. If you wear your socks in your sleeping bag, they will bite to their hearts' content all night long while you sleep, itch, sleep, and itch some more. The best solution is to apply a liquid repellent to your ankles, then wear clean socks.

Horseflies are another story. They are rarely a problem, but when they get their dander up, they can cause trouble you'll never forget. Always wear sunglasses when you hike. If you enter an area with flies, the moisture from your eyes will attract them. The sunglasses will keep them from getting in your eyes.

On one trip, Foonsky and I were paddling a canoe along the shoreline of a Lake Quesnel in British Columbia. This giant horsefly, about the size of a fingertip, started dive-bombing the canoe. After 20 minutes, it landed on Foonsky's thigh. He immediately slammed it with an open hand, then let out a blood-curdling "Yeeeee-ow!" that practically sent ripples across the lake. When Foonsky whacked it, the horsefly had somehow turned around and bit him on the hand, leaving a huge red welt.

In the next 10 minutes, that big fly strafed the canoe on more dive-bomb runs. I finally got my canoe paddle, swung it as if it were a baseball bat, and nailed that horsefly as if I'd hit a home run. It landed about 15 feet from the boat, still alive and buzzing in the water. While I was trying to figure what it would take to kill this bugger, a large rainbow trout surfaced and snatched it out of the water, finally avenging the assault.

When I climbed Mount Katahdin in Maine at the northern end of the Appalachian Trail, horseflies bit so deep that they took craters of meat out of my arms. I still have the scars.

If you have yellow jackets at the campsite, avoid bringing mango-style drinks and don't leave meat (even jerky) out in the open. That's what brings them in. A few sheets of Bounce can help repel them. If you are facing a relentless swarm, go somewhere else. One, two, or a few can be dealt with. More than that and your fun camping trip will be about as fun as being roped to a tree and stung by an electric shock rod.

On most trips, you will spend time doing everything possible to keep from getting bitten by mosquitoes or no-see-ums. When your attempts fail, you must know what to do next, and fast, especially if you are among those ill-fated campers who get big, red lumps from a bite inflicted from even a microscopic mosquito.

A fluid called After Bite or a dab of ammonia should be applied immediately to the bite. To start the healing process, apply a first-aid gel (not a liquid), such as the one made by Campho-Phenique. For yellow jacket stings, use SSsstingStop, a mudpack, Ancient Healing Salve, witch hazel, and later, anti-itch cream and Medicaine swabs or vinegar for wasps.

## DEET

What is DEET? You're not likely to find the word DEET on any repellent label. That's because DEET stands for N,N diethyl-m-toluamide. If the label contains this scientific name, the repellent contains DEET. Despite fears of DEET-associated health risks and the increased attention given natural alternatives, DEET-based repellents are long acknowledged as the best option when serious insect protection is required.

On one trip, I had a small bottle of mosquito repellent in the same pocket as a Swiss army knife. Guess what happened? The mosquito repellent leaked a bit and literally melted the insignia right off the knife. DEET will also melt synthetic clothes. That is why, in bad mosquito country, I'll expose a minimum of skin, just hands and face (with full beard), apply the repellent only to my cheeks and the back of my hands, and perhaps wear a bandanna sprinkled with a few drops as well. That does the trick, with a minimum of exposure to the repellent.

### Natural Repellents

Are natural alternatives a safer choice than DEET? Some are potentially hazardous if ingested, and most are downright painful if they find their way into the eyes or onto mucus membranes. For example, pennyroyal is perhaps the most toxic of the essential oils used to repel insects and can be deadly if taken internally. Other oils used include cedarwood, citronella, and perhaps the most common, eucalyptus and peppermint.

How effective are natural repellents? The average effective repelling time of a citronella product appears to range from 1.5-2 hours, so it must be reapplied to be effective.

### Other Options

What other chemical alternatives are there? Another line of defense against insects is the chemical permethrin, used on clothing, not on skin. Permethrin-based products are designed to repel and kill arthropods or crawling insects, making them a preferred repellent for ticks. The currently available products remain effective—repelling and killing chiggers, mosquitoes, and ticks—for two weeks and through two launderings.

## Ticks

Ticks are nasty little vermin that will wait in ambush, jump on unsuspecting prey, and then crawl to a prime location before filling their bodies with their victim's blood.

I call them Dracula bugs, but by any name they can be a terrible camp pest. Ticks rest on grass and low plants and attach themselves to those who brush against the vegetation (dogs are particularly vulnerable). Typically, they can be found no more than 18 inches above ground, and if you stay on the trails, you can usually avoid them.

There are two common species of ticks. The common coastal tick is larger, brownish in color, and prefers to crawl around before putting its clamps on you. The feel of any bug crawling on your skin can be creepy, but consider it a forewarning of assault; you can just pick the tick off and dispatch it. The coastal tick's preferred destination is usually the back of your neck, just where the hairline starts. The other species, the wood tick, is small and black, and when it puts its clamps in, it's immediately painful. When a wood tick gets into a dog for a few days, it can cause a large red welt. In either case, ticks should be removed as soon as possible.

If you have hiked in areas infested with ticks, it is advisable to shower as soon as possible, washing your clothes immediately. If you just leave your clothes in a heap, a tick can crawl out and invade your home. They like warmth, and one way or another, they can end up in your bed. Waking up in the middle of the night with a tick crawling across your chest can be unsettling, to put it mildly.

Once a tick has its clampers in your skin, you must determine how long it has been there. If it has been a short time, the most painless and effective method for removal is to take a pair of sharp tweezers and grasp the little devil, making certain to isolate the mouth area, then pull it out. Reader Johvin Perry sent in the suggestion to coat the tick with Vaseline, which will cut off its oxygen supply, after which it may voluntarily give up the hunt.

If the tick has been in longer, you may wish to have a doctor extract it. Some people will burn a tick with a cigarette or poison it with lighter fluid, but neither is advisable. No matter how you do it, you must take care to remove all of the tick, especially its clawlike mouth.

The wound, however small, should then be cleansed and dressed. First, apply liquid peroxide, which cleans and sterilizes, and then apply a dressing coated with a first-aid gel, such as First Aid Cream, Campho-Phenique, or Neosporin.

Lyme disease, which can be transmitted by the bite of a deer tick, is rare but common enough to warrant some attention. To prevent tick bites, some people tuck their pant legs into their hiking socks and spray tick repellent, called Permamone, on their pants.

The first symptom of Lyme disease is a bright red, splotchy rash that develops around the bite area. Other possible early symptoms include headache, nausea, fever, and/or a stiff neck. If any of these happen, or if you have any doubts, you should see your doctor immediately. If you do get Lyme disease, don't panic. Doctors say it is easily treated in the early

stages with simple antibiotics. If you are nervous about getting Lyme disease, carry a small plastic bag with you when you hike. If a tick manages to get his clampers into you, put the tick in the plastic bag after you pull it out. Then give it to your doctor for analysis to see if the tick is a carrier of the disease. Lyme disease becomes a problem when it goes undetected and untreated for a long period of time, resulting in long-term health issues.

During the course of my hiking and camping career, I have removed ticks from my skin thousands of times without any problems. However, if you are worried about ticks, you can buy a tick removal kit from any outdoors store. These kits allow you to remove ticks in such a way that their toxins are guaranteed not to enter your bloodstream.

If you are particularly wary of ticks or perhaps even have nightmares of them, wear long pants that are tucked into your socks, as well as a long-sleeved shirt tucked securely into your pants and held with a belt. Clothing should be light in color, making it easier to see ticks, and tightly woven so ticks have trouble hanging on. On one hike with my mom, Eleanor, I brushed more than 100 ticks off my blue jeans in less than an hour, while she did not pick up a single one on her polyester pants.

Perform tick checks regularly, especially on the back of the neck. Often you can see or feel the ticks and just brush them off. The combination of DEET insect repellents applied to the skin and permethrin repellents applied directly to clothing is considered to be the most effective line of defense against ticks.

## Poison Oak

After a nice afternoon hike, about a five-miler, I was concerned about possible exposure to poison oak, so I immediately showered and put on clean clothes. Then I settled into a chair with my favorite foamy elixir to watch the end of a baseball game. But the game went on for hours, 18 innings; meanwhile, my dog, tired from the hike, went to sleep on my bare ankles.

A few days later, I had a case of poison oak.

My feet looked as though they had been on fire and put out with an ice pick. The lesson? Don't always trust your dog, give him a bath as well, and beware of extra-inning ball games.

You can get poison oak only from direct contact with the oil residue from the plant's leaves. It can be passed in a variety of ways, as direct as skin-to-leaf contact or as indirect as leaf to dog, dog to sofa, sofa to skin. Once you have it, there is little you can do but feel horribly itchy. Applying Caladryl lotion or its equivalent can help because it contains antihistamines, which attack and dry the itch.

My pal Furniss offers a tip that may sound crazy but seems to work. You should expose the afflicted area to the hottest water you can stand, then suddenly immerse it in cold water. The hot water opens the skin pores and gets the "itch" out, and the cold water then quickly seals the pores.

In any case, you're a lot better off if you don't get poison oak to begin with. Remember that poison oak can disguise itself. In the spring, it is green; then it gradually turns reddish in the summer. By fall, it becomes a bloody, ugly-looking red. In the winter, it loses its leaves altogether and appears to be nothing more than the barren, brown sticks of a small plant. However, at any time and in any form, its contact with skin can quickly lead to infection.

Some people are more easily afflicted than others, but if you are one of the lucky few who aren't, don't cheer too loudly. While some people can be exposed to the oil residue of poison oak with little or no effect, the body's resistance can gradually be worn down with repeated exposure. At one time, I could practically play in the stuff and the only symptom would be a few little bumps on the inside of my wrist. Now, more than 15 years later, my resistance has broken down. If I merely brush against poison oak now, in a few days the exposed area can look as if it were used for a track meet.

So regardless of whether you consider yourself vulnerable or not, you should take heed to reduce your exposure. Stay on trails when you hike and make sure your dog does the same. Remember, the worst stands of poison oak are usually brush-infested areas just off the trail. Also protect yourself by dressing so your skin is completely covered, wearing long-sleeved shirts, long pants, and boots. If you suspect you've been exposed, immediately wash your clothes and then wash yourself with aloe vera, rinsing with a cool shower.

And don't forget to give your dog a bath as well.

## Sunburn

The most common injury suffered on camping trips is sunburn, yet some people wear it as a badge of honor, believing that it somehow enhances their virility. Well, it doesn't. Neither do suntans. Too much sun can lead to serious burns or sunstroke.

Both are easy enough to avoid. Use a high-level sunscreen on your skin, apply lip balm, and wear sunglasses and a hat. If any area gets burned, apply First Aid Cream, which will soothe and provide moisture to the parched skin.

## Giardia and Cryptosporidium

You have just hiked in to your backwoods spot, you're thirsty and a bit tired, but you smile as you consider the prospects. Everything seems perfect—there's not a stranger in sight, and you have nothing to do but relax with your pals.

You toss down your gear, grab your cup, dip it into the stream, and take a long drink of that ice-cold mountain water. It seems crystal pure and sweeter than anything you've ever tasted. It's not till later that you find out it can be just like drinking a cup of poison.

Whether you camp in the wilderness or not, if you hike, you're going to get thirsty. And if your canteen runs dry, you'll start eyeing any water source. Stop! Do not pass Go. Do not drink.

By drinking what appears to be pure mountain water without first treating it, you can ingest a microscopic protozoan called

© PUTT SAKDHNAGOOL/123RF.COM

**Always filter water before drinking.**

*Giardia lamblia*. The ensuing abdominal cramps can make you feel like your stomach and intestinal tract are in a knot, ready to explode. With that comes long-term diarrhea that is worse than even a bear could imagine.

Doctors call the disease giardiasis, or giardia for short, but it is difficult to diagnose. One friend of mine who contracted giardia was told he might have stomach cancer before the proper diagnosis was made.

Drinking directly from a stream or lake does not mean you will get giardia, but you are taking a giant chance. There is no reason to assume such a risk, potentially ruining your trip and enduring weeks of misery.

A lot of people are taking that risk. I made a personal survey of campers in the Yosemite National Park wilderness, and found that roughly only one in 10 was equipped with some kind of water-purification system. The result, according to the Public Health Service, is that an average of 4 percent of all backpackers and campers suffer giardiasis. According to the Parasitic Diseases Division of the Center for Infectious Diseases, the rates range from 1 percent to 20 percent across the country. But if you get giardia, you are not going to care about the statistics.

The stream might be running free, gurgling over boulders in the high country, tumbling into deep, oxygenated pools. It looks pure. Then in a few days, the problems suddenly start. Drinking untreated water from mountain streams is a lot like playing Russian roulette. Sooner or later the gun goes off.

## SteriPEN

We would never do another wilderness trip without one and I keep mine with me all the time. By using UV light, the SteriPEN destroys viruses, bacteria, and protozoa (like *Giardia*) that can make you sick. Dip your water bottle in a cold stream, purify the water with the UV light in less than two minutes, and drink all the cold, clean mountain water you can. It's like having a cooler full of ice-cold water with you all the time. On expeditions of more than four days, make sure you bring extra batteries. There are several sizes of SteriPENs, based on the level of need.

# KEEP IT WILD TIP 5: SANITATION

If no refuse facility is available:
1. Deposit human waste in "cat holes" dug 6-8 inches deep. Cover and disguise the cat hole when finished.
2. Deposit human waste at least 75 paces (200 feet) from any water source or camp.
3. Use toilet paper sparingly. When finished, carefully burn it in the cat hole, then bury it.
4. If no appropriate burial locations are available, such as in popular wilderness camps above tree line in granite settings, then all human refuse should be double-bagged and packed out.
5. At boat-in campsites, chemical toilets are required. Chemical toilets can also solve the problem of larger groups camping for long stays at one location where no facilities are available.
6. To wash dishes or your body, carry water away from the source and use small amounts of biodegradable soap. Scatter dishwater after all food particles have been removed.
7. Scour your campsites for even the tiniest piece of trash and any other evidence of your stay. Pack out all the trash you can, even if it's not yours. Finding cigarette butts, for instance, provides special irritation for most campers. Pick them up and discard them properly.
8. Never litter. Never. Or you become the enemy of all others.

## FILTERS

Handheld filters are getting more compact, lighter, easier to use, and often less expensive. Having to boil water or endure chemicals that leave a bad taste in the mouth has been all but eliminated.

With a filter, you just pump and drink. Filtering strains out microscopic contaminants, rendering the water clear and somewhat pure. How pure? That depends on the size of the filter's pores—what manufacturers call pore-size efficiency. A filter with a pore-size efficiency of one micron or smaller will remove protozoa, such as *Giardia lamblia* and cryptosporidium, as well as parasitic eggs and larva, but it takes a pore-size efficiency of less than 0.4 micron to remove bacteria. All but one of the filters recommended here do that.

A good backcountry water filter weighs less than 20 ounces, is easy to grasp, simple to use, and a snap to clean and maintain. At the very least, buy one that will remove protozoa and bacteria. (A number of cheap, pocket-sized filters remove only *Giardia lamblia* and cryptosporidium. That, in my book, is risking your health to save money.) Consider the flow rate, too: A liter per minute is good.

All filters will eventually clog—it's a sign that they've been doing their job. If you force water through a filter that's becoming difficult to pump, you risk injecting a load of microbial nasties into your bottle. Some models can be back-washed, brushed, or, as with ceramic elements, scrubbed to extend their useful lives. And if the filter has a pre-filter to screen out the big stuff, use it: It will give your filter a boost in mileage, which can then top out at about 100 gallons per disposable element. Any of the filters reviewed here will serve well on an outing into the wilds, providing you always play by the manufacturer's rules.

- **First Need Deluxe:** The filter pumps smoothly and puts out more than a liter per minute. The 15-ounce First Need Deluxe from General Ecology does something no other handheld filter will do: It removes protozoa, bacteria, and viruses without using chemicals. Such effectiveness is the result of a fancy three-stage matrix system. The First Need has been around since 1982. Additional cartridges mean you just replace the cartridge, not the entire unit. If you drop the filter and unknowingly crack the cartridge, all the little nasties can get through—a small point worth noting.
- **Katadyn Hiker Pro:** The Katadyn effectively removes protozoa and bacteria. I found it challenging to put any kind of

power behind the pump's tiny handle, and the filtered water comes through at a paltry half-liter per minute. It also requires more cleaning than most filters—though the good news is that the element is made of long-lasting ceramic.

- **MSR MiniWorks:** The 14-ounce MiniWorks looks similar to the more expensive WaterWorks and, like the WaterWorks, is fully field-maintainable, while guarding against protozoa, bacteria, and chemicals. It attaches directly to a standard one-quart Nalgene water bottle. Takes about 90 seconds to filter that quart.
- **SweetWater WalkAbout:** The WalkAbout is perfect for the day hiker or backpacker who obsesses on lightening the load. The filter weighs just 8.5 ounces, is easily cleaned in the field, and removes both protozoa and bacteria: a genuine bargain. There are some trade-offs, however, for its diminutiveness. Water delivery is a tad slow at just under a liter per minute, but filter cartridges are now good for up to 100 gallons.

The big drawback with filters is that if you pump water from a mucky lake, the filter can clog in a few days. Therein lies the weakness. Once plugged up, it is useless, and you have to replace it or take your chances. One trick to extend the filter life is to fill your cook pot with water, let the sediment settle, then pump from there. As an insurance policy, always have a spare filter canister on hand.

## BOILING WATER

Except for water filtration, this is the only treatment that you can use with complete confidence. According to the federal Parasitic Diseases Division, it takes a few minutes at a rolling boil to be certain you've killed *Giardia lamblia*. At high elevations, boil for 3-5 minutes. A side benefit is that you'll also kill other dangerous bacteria that live undetected in natural waters. Boiling drinking water is a thorn for most people on backcountry trips. For one thing, if you boil water on an open fire, what

should taste like crystal-pure mountain water tastes instead like a mouthful of warm ashes. If you don't have a campfire, it wastes stove fuel. And if you are thirsty *now*, forget it. The water takes hours to cool. The only time boiling always makes sense, however, is when you are preparing dinner. The ash taste will disappear in whatever freeze-dried dinner, soup, or hot drink you make.

## WATER-PURIFICATION PILLS

I bring water-purification pills for backup use only. They are cheap and, in addition, they kill most of the bacteria, regardless of whether you use iodine crystals or potable aqua iodine tablets. The problem is they just don't always kill *Giardia lamblia*, and that is the one critter worth worrying about on your trip. That makes water-treatment pills unreliable and dangerous.

Another key element is the time factor. Depending on the water's temperature, organic content, and pH level, these pills can take a long time to do the job. A minimum wait of 20 minutes is advised. Most people don't like waiting that long, especially when they're hot and thirsty after a hike and thinking, "What the heck, the water looks fine."

And then there is the taste. On one trip, my water filter clogged and we had to use the iodine pills instead. It doesn't take long to get tired of iodine-tinged water. Mountain water should be one of the greatest tasting beverages of the world, but the iodine kills that.

## NO TREATMENT

This is your last resort and, using extreme care, can be executed with success. Michael Furniss, the renowned hydrologist, has shown me the difference between safe and dangerous water sources.

When I was in the Boy Scouts, I remember a scoutmaster actually telling me if you could find water running over a rock for at least five feet, it was a guarantee of its purity. Imagine that. What we've learned is that the safe water sources are almost always small springs in high, craggy mountain areas. The key is making sure no one has been upstream from where you drink. We drink untreated water only when we can see the source, such as a spring.

Furniss mentioned that another potential problem in bypassing water treatment is that even in settings free of *Giardia lamblia*, you can still ingest other bacteria that cause stomach problems.

## Hypothermia

No matter how well planned your trip might be, a sudden change in weather can turn it into a puzzle for which there are few answers. Bad weather or an accident can set in motion a dangerous chain of events.

Such a chain of episodes occurred for my brother Rambob and me on a fishing trip one fall day just below the snow line. The weather had suddenly turned very cold, and ice was forming along the shore of the lake. Suddenly, the canoe became terribly imbalanced, and, just that quickly, it flipped. The little life vest seat cushions were useless, and using the canoe as a paddleboard, we tried to kick our way back to shore where my dad was going crazy at the thought of his two sons drowning before his eyes.

It took 17 minutes in that 38-degree water, but we finally made it to shore. When they pulled me out of the water, my legs were dead, not strong enough even to hold up my weight. In fact, I didn't feel so much cold as tired, and I just wanted to lie down and go to sleep.

My brother-in-law, Lloyd Angal, slapped me in the face several times, then got me on my feet and pushed and pulled me about. My brother-in-law had saved my life, but at the time, I didn't even realize it.

Amid the celebration over our making it to shore, Lloyd had realized that hypothermia was setting in. Hypothermia is the condition in which the temperature of the body is lowered to the point that it causes poor reasoning, apathy, and collapse. It can look like the afflicted person is just tired and needs to sleep, but that sleep can be the first step toward a coma.

Ultimately, my brother and I shared what little dry clothing remained. Then we began walking around to get muscle movement, creating internal warmth. We ate whatever munchies were available because the body produces heat by digestion. But most important, we got our heads as dry as possible. More body heat is lost through wet hair than any other single factor.

A few hours later, we were in a pizza parlor replaying the incident, talking about how only a life vest can do the job of a life vest. We decided never again to rely on those little flotation seat cushions that disappear when the boat flips. Now I have about a dozen different life vests for any situation.

Because I was with people who understood hypothermia, we had done everything right to prevent it: Don't go to sleep, start a physical activity, induce shivering, put dry clothes on, dry your head, and eat something. That's how you fight hypothermia. In a dangerous situation, whether you fall in a lake or a stream or get caught unprepared in a storm, that's how you can stay alive.

After being in that ice-bordered lake for almost 20 minutes and then finally pulling ourselves to the shoreline, we discovered a strange thing. My canoe was flipped right side up and almost all of its contents were lost: tackle box, flotation cushions, and cooler. But remaining were one paddle and one fishing rod, the trout rod my grandfather had given me for my 12th birthday.

Lloyd gave me a smile. "This means that you are meant to paddle and fish again," he said with a laugh.

## Getting Unlost

I could not have been more lost. There I was, a guy who is supposed to know about these things, transfixed by confusion, snow, and hoofprints from a big deer.

I discovered that it is actually quite easy to get lost. If you don't get your bearings, getting found is the difficult part. This occurred on a wilderness trip where I'd hiked in to a remote

Rock cairns (small piles of rocks) can act as directional signs to keep you from getting lost.

lake and then set up a base camp for a deer hunt.

"There are some giant bucks up on that rim," confided Mr. Furnai, who lives near the area. "But it takes a mountain man to even get close to them."

That was a challenge I answered. After four-wheeling it to the trailhead, I tromped off with pack and rifle, gut-thumped it up 100 switchbacks over the rim, then followed a creek drainage up to a small but beautiful lake. The area was stark and nearly treeless, with bald granite broken only by large boulders. To keep from getting lost, I marked my route with piles of small rocks to act as directional signs for the return trip.

But at daybreak the next day, I stuck my head out of my tent and found eight inches of snow on the ground. I looked up into a gray sky filled by huge, cascading snowflakes. Visibility was about 50 yards, with a low ceiling that concealed the mountain rim and all landmarks. "I better get out of here and get back to my truck,"

I said to myself. "If my truck gets buried at the trailhead, I'll never get out."

After packing quickly, I started down the mountain. But after 20 minutes, I began to get disoriented. You see, all the little piles of rocks I'd stacked to mark the way were now buried in snow, and I had only a smooth white blanket of snow to guide me. Everything looked the same, and it was snowing even harder now.

Five minutes later, I started chewing on some jerky to keep warm, then suddenly stopped. Where was I? Where was the creek drainage? Isn't this where I was supposed to cross over a creek and start the switchbacks down the mountain?

Right then, I looked down and saw the tracks of a huge deer, the kind Mr. Furnai had talked about. What a predicament: I was lost and snowed in and seeing big hoofprints in the snow. Part of me wanted to abandon all safety and go after that deer, but a little voice in the back of my head won out. "Treat this as an emergency," it said.

The first step in any predicament is to secure your present situation, that is, to make sure it does not get any worse. I unloaded my rifle (too easy to slip, fall, and have a misfire), took stock of my food (three days' worth), camp fuel (plenty), and clothes (rain gear keeping me dry). Then I wondered, "Where the hell am I?"

I took out my map, compass, and altimeter, then opened the map and laid it on the snow. It immediately began collecting snowflakes. I set the compass atop the map and oriented it to north. Because of the fog, there was no way to spot landmarks, such as prominent mountaintops, to verify my position. Then I checked the altimeter, which read 4,900 feet. Well, the elevation at my lake was 5,320 feet. That was critical information.

I scanned the elevation lines on the map and was able to trace the approximate area of my position, somewhere downstream from the lake, yet close to a 4,900-foot elevation. "Right here," I said, pointing to a spot on the map with my finger. "I should pick up the switchback trail down the mountain somewhere off to the left, maybe just 40 or 50 yards away."

Slowly and deliberately, I pushed through the light, powdered snow. In five minutes, I suddenly stopped. To the left, across a 10-foot depression in the snow, appeared a flat spot that veered off to the right. "That's it! That's the crossing."

In minutes, I was working down the switchbacks, on my way, no longer lost. I thought of the hoofprints I had seen, and now that I knew my position, I wanted to head back and spend the day hunting. Then I looked up at the sky, saw it filled with falling snowflakes, and envisioned my truck buried deep in snow. Alas, this time logic won out over dreams.

In a few hours, now trudging through more than a foot of snow, I was at my truck at a spot called Doe Flat, and next to it was a giant, all-terrain U.S. Forest Service vehicle and two rangers.

"Need any help?" I asked them.

They just laughed. "We're here to help you,"

one answered. "It's a good thing you filed a trip plan with our district office in Gasquet. We wouldn't have known you were out here."

"Winter has arrived," said the other. "If we don't get your truck out now, it will be stuck here until next spring. If we hadn't found you, you might have been here until the end of time."

They connected a chain from the rear axle of their giant rig to the front axle of my truck and started towing me out, back to civilization. On the way to pavement, I figured I had gotten some of the more important lessons of my life. Always file a trip plan and have plenty of food, fuel, and a camp stove you can rely on. Make sure your clothes, weather gear, sleeping bag, and tent will keep you dry and warm. Always carry a compass, altimeter, and map with elevation lines, and know how to use them, practicing in good weather to get the feel of it.

And if you get lost and see the hoofprints of a giant deer, well, there are times when it is best to pass them by.

And one other thing: Never give up hope.

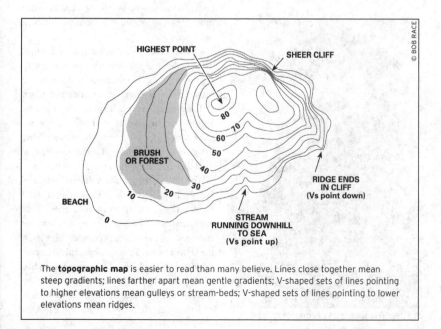

The **topographic map** is easier to read than many believe. Lines close together mean steep gradients; lines farther apart mean gentle gradients; V-shaped sets of lines pointing to higher elevations mean gulleys or stream-beds; V-shaped sets of lines pointing to lower elevations mean ridges.

## CATCHING FISH, AVOIDING BEARS, AND HAVING FUN

Feet tired and hot, stomachs growling, we stopped our hike for lunch beside a beautiful little river pool that was catching the flows from a long but gentle waterfall. My brother Rambob passed me a piece of jerky. I took my boots off, then slowly dunked my feet into the cool, foaming water.

I was gazing at a towering peak across a canyon when suddenly, Wham! There was a quick jolt at the heel of my right foot. I pulled my foot out of the water to find that, incredibly, a trout had bitten it.

My brother looked at me as if I had antlers growing out of my head. "Wow!" he exclaimed. "That trout almost caught himself an outdoors writer!"

It's true that in remote areas trout sometimes bite on almost anything, even feet. On one high-country trip, I caught limits of trout using nothing but a bare hook. The only problem is that the fish will often hit the splitshot sinker instead of the hook. Of course, fishing isn't usually that easy. But it gives you an idea of what is possible.

America's wildlands are home to a remarkable abundance of fish and wildlife. Deer browse with little fear of man, bears keep an eye out for your food, and little critters, such as squirrels and chipmunks, are daily companions. Add in the fishing, and you've got yourself a camping trip.

Your camping adventures will evolve into premium outdoor experiences if you can work in a few good fishing trips, avoid bear problems, and occasionally add a little offbeat fun with some camp games.

### Trout and Bass

I remember watching my brother stalk trout in a mountain stream when I was a little boy. By the time he was a man, there was nobody better at it.

He creeps up on the stream as quietly as an Indian scout, keeping his shadow off the water. With his little spinning rod he'll zip his lure within an inch or two of its desired mark, probing along rocks, the edges of riffles, pocket water, or wherever he can find a change in river habitat. Rambob is trout fishing, and he's a master at it.

In most cases, he'll catch a trout on his first or second cast. After that, it's time to move up the river, giving no spot much more than five minutes' due. Stick and move, stick and move, stalking the stream like a bobcat zeroing in on an unsuspecting rabbit. He might keep a few trout for dinner, but mostly he releases what he catches. Rambob doesn't necessarily fish for food. It's the feeling that comes with it.

You don't need a million dollars' worth of fancy gear to catch fish. What you need is the right outlook, and that can be learned. That goes regardless of whether you are fishing for trout or bass, the two most popular fisheries in the United States. Your fishing tackle selection should be as simple and clutter-free as possible.

At home, I've got every piece of fishing tackle you might imagine, more than 30 rods and many tackle boxes, racks and cabinets

brother Rambob's big Almanor trout

filled with all kinds of stuff. I've got one lure that looks like a chipmunk and another that resembles a miniature can of beer with hooks. If I hear of something new, I want to try it and usually do. It's a result of my lifelong fascination with the sport.

But if you just want to catch fish, there's an easier way to go. And when I go fishing, I take that path. I don't try to bring everything. It would be impossible. Instead, I bring a relatively small amount of gear. At home, I scan my tackle boxes for equipment and lures, make my selections, and bring just the essentials. Rod, reel, and tackle will fit into a side pocket of my backpack or a small carrying bag.

So what kind of rod should be used on an outdoor trip? For most camper/anglers, I suggest the use of a light, multi-piece spinning rod that will break down to a small size. The lowest-priced, quality six-piece rod on the market is the Daiwa 6.5-foot pack rod, which is made of a graphite/glass composite that gives it the quality of a much more expensive model. And it comes in a hard plastic carrying tube for protection. Other major rod manufacturers, such as Fenwick, offer similar premium rods. It's tough to miss with any of them.

If you haven't bought a fishing reel in some time, you will be surprised at the quality and price of micro spinning reels on the market. The reels come tiny and strong, with rear-control drag systems. Daiwa, Shimano, and many other companies all make premium micro reels.

The one downside to spinning reels is that after long-term use, the bail spring will sometimes weaken. As a result, after casting and beginning to reel, the bail will sometimes not flip over and allow the reel to retrieve the line. Then you have to do it by hand. This can be incredibly frustrating, particularly when stream fishing, where instant line pickup is essential. The solution is to have a new bail spring installed every few years. This is a cheap, quick operation for a tackle expert.

You might own a giant tackle box filled with lures, but on your fishing trip you are better off to fit just the essentials into a small container. One of the best ways to do that is to use the Plano Micro-Magnum, a tiny two-sided tackle box for trout anglers that fits into a shirt pocket. In mine, I can fit 20 lures in one side of the box and 20 flies, split-shot weights, and snap swivels in the other. For bass lures, which are bigger, you need a slightly larger box, but the same principle applies.

There are more fishing lures on the market than you can imagine. For bass alone, I have more than 30 boxes that are packed with all kinds of stuff, but a few special ones do the job. I make sure these are in my box on every trip. For trout, I carry a small black Panther Martin spinner with yellow spots, a small gold Kastmaster, a yellow Roostertail, a gold Z-Ray with red spots, a Super Duper, and a Mepps Lightning spinner.

You can take it a step farther using insider's wisdom. My old mentor Ed "the Dunk" Dunckel showed me his trick of taking a tiny Dardevle spoon, spray painting it flat black, and dabbing five tiny red dots on it. It's a real killer, particularly in tiny streams where the trout are spooky. We call it the Mr. Dunckel Special.

The best trout catcher I've ever used on rivers is a small metal lure made in the 1960s called a Met-L Fly. On days when nothing else works, it can be like going to a shooting gallery. The problem is that the lure is nearly impossible to find. When I was on Mr. Dunckel's Little League team, he gave my brother Rambob and me two of them. Since then, I've received a half dozen others from readers who have found them in their garages and sent them to me. Rambob and I consider the few we have so valuable that if the lure is snagged on a rock, you're going for a cold swim to get it back.

For bass, you can also fit all you need into a small plastic tackle box. I have fished with many bass pros, and all of them actually use just a few lures: twist-tail grubs, Senkos, Brush Hog, a white spinner bait, a surface plug called a Zara Spook, and AC plug. At times, like when the bass move into shoreline areas during the spring, shad minnow imitations like those made by Rebel or Rapala can be dynamite. My favorite is the one-inch, black-gold Rapala. Every spring as the lakes begin to warm and the fish snap out of their winter doldrums, I like to float and paddle around in my small raft. I'll cast that little Rapala along the shoreline and catch and release hundreds of bass, bluegill, and sunfish. The fish are usually sitting close to the shoreline, awaiting my offering.

## Fishing Tips

There's an old angler's joke about how you need to think like a fish. But if you're the one getting zilched, you may not think it's so funny.

The irony is that it is your mental approach, what you see and what you miss, that often determines your fishing luck. Some people will spend a lot of money on tackle, lures, and fishing clothes, and that done, just saunter up to a stream or lake, cast out, and wonder why they are not catching fish. The answer is their mental outlook. They are not attuning themselves to their surroundings.

You must live on nature's level, not your own. Try this and you will become aware of things you never believed even existed. Soon you will see things that will allow you to catch fish. You can get a head start by reading about fishing, but to get your degree in fishing, you must attend the University of Nature.

On every fishing trip, regardless of what you fish for, try to follow three hard-and-fast rules:
1. Always approach the fishing spot so you will be undetected.
2. Present your lure, fly, or bait in a manner so it appears completely natural, as if no line was attached.
3. Stick and move, hitting one spot, working it the best you can, then moving to the next. You'll find that 5 percent of the water has 95 percent of the fish.

### Approach

No one can just walk up to a stream or lake, cast out, and start catching fish as if someone had waved a magic wand. Instead, give the fish credit for being smart. After all, they live there.

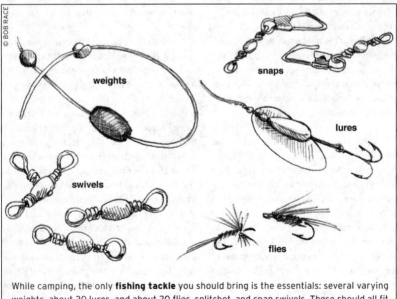

© BOB RACE

weights

snaps

lures

swivels

flies

While camping, the only **fishing tackle** you should bring is the essentials: several varying weights, about 20 lures, and about 20 flies, splitshot, and snap swivels. These should all fit into a container just bigger than a deck of cards.

Your approach must be completely unde-tected by the fish. Fish can sense your presence through sight and sound, though most people often misinterpret these factors. By sight, fish rarely actually see you; more often, they see your shadow on the water or the movement of your arm or rod while casting. By sound, they don't necessarily hear you talking, but they do detect the vibrations of your footsteps along the shore, a rock being kicked, or the unnatu-ral plunking sound of a heavy cast hitting the water. Any of these elements can spook them off the bite. In order to fish undetected, you must walk softly, keep your shadow off the water, and keep your casting motion low. All of these key elements become easier at sunrise or sunset, when shadows are on the water. At midday, the sun is at its peak, causing a high level of light penetration in the water. This can make the fish skittish to any foreign presence.

Like a hunter, you must stalk the spots. When my brother Rambob sneaks up on a fish-ing spot, he is like a burglar sneaking through an unlocked window.

## Presentation

Your lure, fly, or bait must appear in the water as if no line were attached, so it looks as natural as possible. My pal Mo Furniss has snorkeled in rivers to watch what the fish see when some-body is fishing.

"You wouldn't believe it," he said. "When the lure hits the water, every trout within 40 feet, like 15, 20 trout, will do a little zigzag. They all see the lure and are aware something is going on. Meanwhile, onshore the guy casting doesn't get a bite and thinks there aren't any fish in the river."

If your offering is aimed at fooling a fish into striking, it must appear as part of the natural habitat, like an insect just hatching or a small fish looking for a spot to hide. That's where you come in.

After you have sneaked up on a fishing spot, you should zip your cast upstream and start your retrieval as soon as it hits the water. If you let the lure sink to the bottom and then start the retrieval, you have no chance. A minnow, for instance, does not sink to the bottom, then start swimming. On rivers, the retrieval should be more of a drift, as if the "minnow" is in trou-ble and the current is sweeping it downstream.

When fishing on trout streams, always hike and cast upriver and retrieve as the offering drifts downstream in the current. This is ef-fective because trout will sit almost motionless, pointed upstream, finning against the current. This way, they can see anything coming their direction, and if a potential food morsel arrives, all they need to do is move over a few inches, open their mouths, and they've got an easy lunch. Thus, you must cast upstream.

Conversely, if you cast downstream, your retrieval will bring the lure from behind the fish, where it cannot see it approaching. And I've never seen a trout that had eyes in its tail. In addition, when retrieving a downstream lure, the river current will tend to sweep your lure inshore to the rocks.

## Finding Spots

A lot of anglers don't catch fish, and a lot of hikers never see any wildlife. The key is where they are looking.

My cousin Andy Eldridge taught me the rule of the wild: Fish and wildlife will congre-gate wherever there is a distinct change in the habitat. This is where you should begin your search. To find deer, for instance, forget prob-ing a thick forest, but look for where it breaks into a meadow or a clear-cut has splayed a stand of trees. That's where the deer will be.

In a river, it can be where a riffle pours into a small pool, a rapid plunges into a deep hole and flattens, a big boulder in the middle of a long riffle, a shoreline point, a rock pile, a sub-merged tree. Look for the changes. Conversely, long, straight stretches of shoreline will not hold fish—the habitat is lousy.

On rivers, the most productive areas are often where short riffles tumble into small, oxygenated pools. After sneaking up from the downstream side and staying low, you should zip your cast so the lure plops gently into the

© BOB RACE

The rule of the wild is that wildlife will congregate wherever there is a distinct change in habitat. To find where fish are hiding, look where a riffle pours into a small pond, where a rapid plunges into a deep hole and flattens, and around submerged trees, rock piles, and boulders in the middle of a long riffle.

white water just above the pool. Start your retrieval instantly; the lure will drift downstream and plunk into the pool. Bang! That's where the trout will hit. Take a few more casts and then head upstream to the next spot.

With a careful approach and lure presentation and by fishing in the right spots, you have the ticket to many exciting days on the water.

## Of Bears and Food

The first time you come nose-to-nose with a bear can make your skin quiver.

Even the sight of mild-mannered black bears, the most common bear in America, can send shock waves through your body. They weigh 250-400 pounds and have large claws and teeth that are made to scare campers. When they bound, the muscles on their shoulders roll like ocean breakers. But in California, you don't have to be scared of them. They aren't interested in you, just your food.

Bears in camping areas are accustomed to sharing the mountains with hikers and campers. They have become specialists in the food-raiding business. As a result, you must be able to bear-proof your camp or be able to scare the fellow off. Many campgrounds provide bear- and raccoon-proof food lockers. In most wilderness areas, bear-proof food canisters are required. Never leave your food or trash in your car!

Bear-proof food canisters are so effective in wilderness areas at Yosemite, Kings Canyon-Sequoia, and Mount Whitney that I never see bears on trips there anymore—they've given up on backpackers. Instead, they head to the drive-in campgrounds where they can walk right in and often find food sitting out on top of picnic tables.

Never leave food outside of your reach at a campsite and never leave food or garbage in your vehicle. Use the bear-proof food lockers. Then the bear will just move on to the next site on his daily mooching round.

## Food Hangs

If you are staying at one of the backpack sites listed in this book, it is unlikely that there will be food lockers available. Your car will not be there, either. The solution is to make a

© CESLO DINIZ/123RF.COM

Use bear-proof containers to protect your campsite.

## HIKING IN BEAR TERRITORY

If you are hiking in a wilderness area that may have grizzlies (Canada or Alaska; there are no grizzlies in California) or black bears, it is necessary to wear bells on your pack. That way the bear will hear you coming and likely get out of your way. Keep talking, singing, or maybe even debating the country's foreign policy, but do not fall into a silent hiking vigil. And if a breeze is blowing in your face, you must make even more noise (a good excuse to rant and rave about the government's domestic affairs). Noise is important because your smell will not be carried in the direction you are hiking. As a result, the bear will not smell you coming.

If a bear can hear you and smell you, it will tend to get out of the way and let you pass without your knowing it was even close by. The exceptions are if you are carrying fish or lots of sweets in your pack or if you are wearing heavy, sweet deodorants or makeup. All of these are bear attractants.

bear-proof food hang, suspending all of your food wrapped in a plastic garbage bag from a rope in midair, 10 feet from the trunk of a tree and 20 feet off the ground. (Counterbalancing two bags with a rope thrown over a tree limb is very effective, but finding an appropriate limb can be difficult.)

The food hang is accomplished by tying a rock to a rope, then throwing it over a high but sturdy tree limb. Next, tie your food bag to the rope and hoist it in the air. When you are satisfied with the position of the food bag, tie off the end of the rope to another tree. In an area frequented by bears, a good food bag is a necessity—nothing else will do.

I've been there. On one trip, my pal Foonsky and my brother Rambob left to fish. I was stoking up an evening campfire when I felt the eyes of an intruder on my back. I turned around and saw a big bear heading straight for our camp. In the next half hour, I scared the bear off twice, but then he got a whiff of something sweet in my brother's pack.

The bear rolled into camp like a truck, grabbed the pack, ripped it open, and plucked out the Tang and the Swiss Miss. The 350-pounder then sat astride a nearby log and lapped at the goodies like a thirsty dog drinking water.

Once a bear gets his mitts on your gear, he considers it his. I took two steps toward the pack, and that bear jumped off the log and galloped across the camp right at me. Scientists say a man can't outrun a bear, but they've never seen how fast I can go up a granite block with a bear on my tail.

Shortly thereafter, Foonsky returned to find me perched on top of the rock and demanded to know how I could let a bear get our Tang. It took all three of us, Foonsky, Rambob, and me, charging at once and shouting like madmen, to clear the bear out of camp and send him off over the ridge. We learned never to let food sit unattended.

## The Grizzly

When it comes to grizzlies, well, my friends, you need what Hank Williams, Jr. described as an "attitude adjustment." Or that big ol' bear, that is, may just decide to adjust your attitude for you.

Grizzlies are nothing like black bears. They are bigger, stronger, have little fear, and take what they want. Some people believe there are many different species of this critter, such as Alaskan brown, silvertip, cinnamon, and Kodiak, but the truth is are all grizzlies. Any difference in appearance has to do with diet, habitat, and life habits, not speciation. By any name, they all come big.

The first thing is to determine if there are grizzlies in the area where you are camping. If you're hiking in California, then no problem—no grizzlies. If you are unsure, ask the local rangers. If you are heading into Yellowstone or Glacier National Park, or the Bob Marshall Wilderness of Montana, well, you don't have to ask. They're out there, and they're the biggest and potentially most dangerous critters you could run into. Unlike the bears in Alaska, they don't have salmon to eat and that makes them smaller, meaner, hungrier, and territorial. Beware.

One general way to figure the size of a bear is from its footprint. Take the width of the footprint in inches, add one to it, and you'll have an estimated length of the bear in feet. For instance, a nine-inch footprint equals a 10-foot bear. Any bear that big is a grizzly. In fact, most grizzly footprints average about 9-10 inches across, and black bears (though they may be brown in color) tend to have footprints only 4.5-6 inches across (though I've seen bigger).

Most encounters with grizzlies occur when hikers fall into a silent march in the wilderness with the wind in their faces, and they walk around a corner and right into a big, unsuspecting grizzly. If you do this and see a big hump just behind its neck, don't think twice. It's a grizzly.

And then what should you do? Get up a tree, that's what. Grizzlies are so big that their claws cannot support their immense weight, and thus they cannot climb trees. And although young grizzlies can climb, they rarely want to get their mitts on you.

If you do get grabbed, every instinct in your body will tell you to fight back. Don't believe it. Play dead. Go limp. Let the bear throw you around a little. After a while, you'll become unexciting play material and the bear will get bored. My grandmother was grabbed by a grizzly in Glacier National Park and, after a few tosses and hugs, was finally left alone to escape.

Some say it's a good idea to tuck your head under its chin, since that way the bear will be unable to bite your head. I'll take a pass on that one. If you are taking action, any action, it's a signal that you are a force to be reckoned with,

and it'll likely respond with more aggression. And bears don't lose many wrestling matches.

What grizzlies really like to do, believe it or not, is to pile a lot of sticks and leaves on you. Just let them, and keep perfectly still. Don't fight them; don't run. And when you have a 100 percent chance (not 98 or 99) to dash up a nearby tree, that's when you let fly. Once safely in a tree, you can hurl down insults and let your aggression out.

In a wilderness camp, there are special precautions you should take. Always hang your food at least 100 yards downwind of camp and get it high; 30 feet is reasonable. In addition, circle your camp with rope and hang the bells from your pack on it. Thus, if a bear walks into your camp, it'll run into the rope, the bells will ring, and everybody will have a chance to get up a tree before ol' griz figures out what's going on. Often, the unexpected ringing of bells is enough to send it off in search of a quieter environment.

You see, more often than not, grizzlies tend to clear the way for campers and hikers. So be smart, don't act like bear bait, and always have a plan if one confronts you.

My pal Foonsky had such a plan during a wilderness expedition in Montana's northern Rockies. On our second day of hiking, we started seeing scratch marks on the trees 13-14 feet off the ground.

"Mr. Griz made those," Foonsky said. "With spring here, the grizzlies are coming out of hibernation and using the trees like a cat uses a scratch board to stretch the muscles."

The next day, I noticed Foonsky had a pair of track shoes tied to the back of his pack. I just laughed.

"You're not going to outrun a griz," I said. "In fact, there's hardly any animal out here in the wilderness that man can outrun."

Foonsky just smiled.

"I don't have to outrun a griz," he said. "I just have to outrun you!"

## Fun and Games

"Now what are we supposed to do?" the young boy asked his dad.

"Yeah, Dad, think of something," said another son.

Well, Dad thought hard. This was one of the first camping trips he'd taken with his sons and one of the first lessons he received was that kids don't appreciate the philosophic release of mountain quiet. They want action and lots of it. With a glint in his eye, Dad searched around the camp and picked up 15 twigs, breaking them so each was four inches long. He laid them in three separate rows, three twigs in one row, five twigs in another, and seven in the other.

"OK, this game is called 3-5-7," said Dad. "You each take turns picking up sticks. You are allowed to remove all or as few as one twig from a row, but here's the catch: You can pick only from one row per turn. Whoever picks up the last stick left is the loser."

I remember this episode well because those two little boys were my brother Bobby, as in Rambobby, and me. And to this day, we still play 3-5-7 on campouts, with the winner getting to watch the loser clean the dishes. What I have learned in the span of time since that original episode is that it does not matter what your age is: Campers need options for camp fun.

Some evenings, after a long hike or ride, you feel too worn out to take on a serious romp downstream to fish or a climb up to a ridge for a view. That is especially true if you have been in the outback for a week or more. At that point, a lot of campers will spend their time resting and gazing at a map of the area, dreaming of the next day's adventure, or just take a seat against a rock, watching the colors of the sky and mountain panorama change minute by minute. But kids in the push-button video era, and a lot of adults too, want more. After all, "I'm on vacation. I want some fun."

There are several options, such as the 3-5-7 twig game, and they should be just as much a part of your trip planning as arranging your gear.

For kids, plan on games, the more physically challenging the competition, the better. One of the best games is to throw a chunk of wood into a lake and challenge the kids to hit it by throwing rocks. It wreaks havoc on the fishing, but it can keep kids totally absorbed for some time. Target practice with a wrist-rocket slingshot—firing rocks at small targets, like pinecones set on a log—is also all-consuming for kids.

You can also set kids off on little missions near camp, such as looking for the footprints of wildlife, searching out good places to have a "snipe hunt," picking up twigs to get the evening fire started, or having them take the water purifier to a stream to pump some drinking water into a canteen. The latter is an easy, fun, yet important task that will allow kids to feel a sense of equality they often don't get at home.

For adults, the appeal should be more to the intellect. A good example is star and planet identification, and while you are staring into space, you're bound to spot a few asteroids or shooting stars. A star chart can make it easy to find and identify many distinctive stars and constellations, such as Pleiades (the Seven Sisters), Orion, and others from the zodiac, depending on the time of year. With a little research, this can add a unique perspective to your trip. You could point to Polaris, one of the most easily identified of all stars, and note that navigators in the 1400s used it to find their way. Polaris, of course, is the North Star and is at the end of the handle of the Little Dipper. Pinpointing Polaris is quite easy. First find the Big Dipper and then find the outside stars of the ladle of the Big Dipper. They are called the "pointer stars" because they point right at Polaris.

A tree identification book can teach you a few things about your surroundings. It is also a good idea for one member of the party to research the history of the area you have chosen and another to research the geology. With shared knowledge, you end up with a deeper love of wild places.

Another way to add some recreation into your trip is to bring a board game, a number of which have been miniaturized for campers. The most popular are chess, checkers, and cribbage. The latter comes with an equally miniature set of playing cards. And if you bring those little cards, that opens a vast set of other possibilities. With kids along, for instance, you can play Crazy Eights.

But there are more serious card games, and they come with high stakes. Such occurred on one high-country trip where Foonsky, Rambob, and I sat down for a late-afternoon game of poker. In a game of seven-card stud, I caught a straight on the sixth card and felt like a dog licking on a T-bone. Already, I had bet several Skittles and peanut M&Ms on this promising hand.

Then I examined the cards Foonsky had face up. He was showing three sevens, and acting as happy as a grizzly with a pork chop—or a full house. He matched my bet of two peanut M&Ms, then raised me three SweetTarts, one Starburst, and one sour apple Jolly Rancher. Rambob folded, but I matched Foonsky's bet and hoped for the best as the seventh and final card was dealt.

Just after Foonsky glanced at that last card, I saw him sneak a look at my grape stick and beef jerky stash.

"I raise you a grape stick," he said.

Rambob and I both gasped. It was the highest bet ever made, equivalent to a million dollars laid down in Las Vegas. Cannons were going off in my chest. I looked hard at my cards. They looked good, but were they good enough?

Even with a great hand like I had, a grape stick was too much to gamble, my last one with 10 days of trail ahead of us. I shook my head and folded my cards. Foonsky smiled at his victory.

But I still had my grape stick.

## Old Tricks Don't Always Work

Most people are born honest, but after a few camping trips, they usually get over it.

I remember some advice I got from Rambob, normally an honest soul, on one camping trip. A giant mosquito had landed on my arm and he alerted me to an expert bit of wisdom.

"Flex your arm muscles," he commanded, watching the mosquito fill with my blood. "He'll get stuck in your arm, then he'll explode."

For some reason, I believed him. We both proceeded to watch the mosquito drill countless holes in my arm.

Alas, the unknowing face sabotage from their most trusted companions on camping trips. It can arise at any time, usually in the form of advice from a friendly, honest-looking face, as if to say, "What? How can you doubt me?" After that mosquito episode, I was a little more skeptical of my dear old brother. Then the next day, when another mosquito was nailing me in the back of the neck, out came this gem:

"Hold your breath," he commanded. I instinctively obeyed. "That will freeze the mosquito," he said, "then you can squish him."

But in the time I wasted holding my breath, the little bugger was able to fly off without my having the satisfaction of squishing him. When he got home, he probably told his family, "What a dummy I got to drill today!"

Over the years, I have been duped numerous times with dubious advice:

On a grizzly bear attack: "If he grabs you, tuck your head under the grizzly's chin; then he won't be able to bite you in the head." This made sense to me until the first time I saw a nine-foot grizzly 40 yards away. In seconds, I was at the top of a tree, which suddenly seemed to make the most sense.

On coping with animal bites: "If a bear bites you in the arm, don't try to jerk it away. That will just rip up your arm. Instead, force your arm deeper into his mouth. He'll lose his grip and will have to open it to get a firmer hold, and right then you can get away." I was told this in the Boy Scouts. When I was 14, I had a chance to try it out when a friend's dog bit me as I tried to pet it. What happened? When I shoved my arm deeper into his mouth, he bit me three more times.

On cooking breakfast: "The bacon will curl up every time in a camp frying pan. So make sure you have a bacon stretcher to keep it flat." As a 12-year-old Tenderfoot, I spent two hours looking for the bacon stretcher until I figured out the camp leader had forgotten it. It wasn't for several years that I learned that there is no such thing.

On preventing sore muscles: "If you haven't hiked for a long time and you are facing a rough climb, you can keep from getting sore muscles in your legs, back, and shoulders by practicing the Dead Man's Walk.' Simply let your entire body go slack, and then take slow, wobbling steps. This will clear your muscles of lactic acid, which causes them to be so sore after a rough hike." Foonsky pulled this one on me. Rambob and I both bought it and tried it while we were hiking up Mount Whitney, which requires a 6,000-foot elevation gain in six miles. In one 45-minute period, about 30 other hikers passed us and looked at us as if we were suffering from some rare form of mental aberration.

Fish won't bite? No problem: "If the fish are not feeding or will not bite, persistent anglers can still catch dinner with little problem. Keep casting across the current, and eventually, as they hover in the stream, the line will feed across their open mouths. Keep reeling and you will hook the fish right in the side of the mouth. This technique is called 'lining.' Never worry if the fish will not bite, because you can always line 'em." Of course, heh, heh, heh, that explains why so many fish get hooked in the side of the mouth.

On keeping bears away: "To keep bears away, urinate around the borders of your campground. If there are a lot of bears in the area, it is advisable to go right on your sleeping bag." Yeah, surrrrrre.

On disposing of trash: "Don't worry about packing out trash. Just bury it. It will regenerate into the earth and add valuable minerals." Bears, raccoons, skunks, and other critters will dig up your trash as soon as you depart, leaving one huge mess for the next camper. Always pack out everything.

Often the advice comes without warning. That was the case after a fishing trip with a female companion, when she out-caught me two to one, the third such trip in a row. I explained this to a shopkeeper, and he nodded, then explained why.

"The male fish are able to detect the female scent on the lure, and thus become aroused into striking."

Of course! That explains everything!

## Getting Revenge

I was just a lad when Foonsky pulled the old snipe-hunt trick on me. It took nearly 30 years to get revenge.

You probably know about snipe hunting. The victim is led out at night in the woods by a group, and then is left holding a bag.

"Stay perfectly still and quiet," Foonsky explained. "You don't want to scare the snipe. The rest of us will go back to camp and let the woods settle down. Then when the snipe are least expecting it, we'll form a line and charge through the forest with sticks, beating bushes and trees, and we'll flush the snipe out right to you. Be ready with the bag. When we flush the snipe out, bag it. But until we start our charge, make sure you don't move or make a sound or you will spook the snipe and ruin everything."

I sat out there in the woods with my bag for hours, waiting for the charge. I waited, waited, and waited. Nothing happened. No charge, no snipe. It wasn't until well past midnight that I figured something was wrong. When I finally returned to camp, everybody was sleeping.

Well, I tell ya, don't get mad at your pals for the tricks they pull on you. As my old pal Waylon Jennings told me, "Get revenge." About 25 years later, on the last day of a camping trip, the time finally came.

"Let's break camp early," Foonsky suggested to Mr. Furnai and me. "Get up before dawn, eat breakfast, pack up, and be on the ridge to watch the sun come up. It will be a fantastic way to end the trip."

"Sounds great to me," I replied. But when Foonsky wasn't looking, I turned his alarm clock ahead three hours. So when the alarm sounded at the appointed 4:30am wake-up time, Mr. Furnai and I knew it was actually only 1:30am.

Foonsky clambered out of his sleeping bag and whistled with a grin. "Time to break camp."

"You go ahead," I answered. "I'll skip breakfast so I can get a little more sleep. At the first sign of dawn, wake me up, and I'll break camp."

"Me, too," said Mr. Furnai.

Foonsky then proceeded to make some coffee, cook a breakfast, and eat it, sitting on a log in the black darkness of the forest, waiting for the sun to come up. An hour later, with still no sign of dawn, he checked his clock. It now read 5:30am. "Any minute now we should start seeing some light," he said.

He made another cup of coffee, packed his gear, and sat there in the middle of the night, looking up at the stars, waiting for dawn. "Anytime now," he said. He ended up sitting there all night long.

Revenge is sweet. Before a fishing trip at a lake, I took Foonsky aside and explained that the third member of the party, Jimbobo, was hard of hearing and very sensitive about it. "Don't mention it to him," I advised. "Just talk real loud."

Meanwhile, I had already told Jimbobo the same thing. "Foonsky just can't hear very good."

We had fished less than 20 minutes when Foonsky got a nibble.

"GET A BITE?" shouted Jimbobo.

"YEAH!" yelled back Foonsky, smiling. "BUT I DIDN'T HOOK HIM!"

"MAYBE NEXT TIME!" shouted Jimbobo with a friendly grin.

Well, they spent the entire day yelling at each other from the distance of a few feet. They never did figure it out. Heh, heh, heh.

That is, I thought so, until we made a trip salmon fishing. I got a strike that almost knocked my fishing rod out of the boat. When I grabbed the rod, it felt as if Moby Dick was on the other end. "At least a 25-pounder," I said. "Maybe bigger."

The fish dove, ripped off line, and then bulldogged. "It's acting like a 40-pounder," I announced, "Huge, just huge. It's going deep. That's how the big ones fight."

Some 15 minutes later, I finally got the "salmon" to the surface. It turned out to be a coffee can that Foonsky had clipped on the line with a snap swivel. By maneuvering the boat, he made the coffee can fight like a big fish.

This all started with a little old snipe hunt years ago. You never know what your pals will try next. Don't get mad. Get revenge.

# CAMPING OPTIONS
## Boat-In Seclusion

Most campers would never think of trading in their cars, pickup trucks, or RVs for a boat, but people who go by boat on a camping trip enjoy virtually guaranteed seclusion and top-quality outdoor experiences.

Camping with a boat is a do-it-yourself venture in living under primitive circumstances. Yet at the same time, you can bring along any luxury item you wish, from giant coolers, stoves, and lanterns to portable gasoline generators. Weight is almost never an issue.

Many outstanding boat-in campgrounds in beautiful surroundings are available. The best are on the shores of lakes accessible by canoe or skiff, and at offshore islands reached by saltwater cruisers. Several boat-in camps are detailed in this book.

If you want to take the adventure a step further and create your own boat-in camp, perhaps near a special fishing spot, this is a go-for-it deal that provides the best way possible to establish your own secret campsite. But most people who set out freelance style forget three critical items for boat-in camping: a shovel, a sunshade, and an ax. Here is why these items can make a key difference in your trip:

- **Shovel:** Many lakes and virtually all reservoirs have steep, sloping banks. At reservoirs subject to drawdowns, what was lake bottom in the spring can be a campsite in late summer.
- **Sunshade:** The flattest spots to camp along lakes often have a tendency to support only sparse tree growth. As a result, a natural shield from sun and rain is rarely available. What? Rain in the summer? Oh

Claim your own boat-in island.

yeah, don't get me started. A light tarp, set up with poles and staked ropes, solves the problem.

- **Ax:** Unless you bring your own firewood, which is necessary at some sparsely wooded reservoirs, there is no substitute for a good, sharp ax. With an ax, you can almost always find dry firewood, since the interior of an otherwise wet log will be dry. When the weather turns bad is precisely when you will most want a fire. You may need an ax to get one going.

In the search to create your own personal boat-in campsite, you will find that the flattest areas are usually the tips of peninsulas and points, while the protected back ends of coves are often steeply sloped. At reservoirs, the flattest areas are usually near the mouths of the feeder streams and the points are quite steep. On rivers, there are usually sandbars on the inside of tight bends that make for ideal campsites.

Almost all boat-in campsites developed by government agencies are free of charge, but you are on your own. Only in extremely rare cases is piped water available.

Any way you go, by canoe, skiff, or power cruiser, you end up with a one-in-a-million campsite you can call your own.

## Desert Outings

It was a cold, snowy day in Missouri when 10-year-old Rusty Ballinger started dreaming about the vast deserts of the West.

"My dad was reading aloud from a Zane Grey book called *Riders of the Purple Sage*," Ballinger said. "He would get animated when he got to the passages about the desert. It wasn't long before I started to have the same feelings."

That was in 1947. Since then Ballinger has spent a good part of his life exploring the West, camping along the way. "The deserts are the best part. There's something about the uniqueness of each little area you see," Ballinger said. "You're constantly surprised. Just the time of day and the way the sun casts a different color. It's like the lady you care about. One time she smiles, the next time she's pensive. The desert is like that. If you love nature, you can love the desert. After a while, you can't help but love it."

A desert adventure is not just an antidote for a case of cabin fever in the winter. Whether you go by RV, pickup truck, car, or on foot, it provides its own special qualities.

If you go camping in the desert, your approach has to be as unique as the setting. For starters, don't plan on any campfires, but bring a camp stove instead. And unlike in the mountains, do not camp near a water hole. That's because an animal, such as a badger, coyote, or desert bighorn, might be desperate for water, and if you set up camp in the animal's way, you may be forcing a confrontation.

In some areas, there is a danger of flash floods. An intense rain can fall in one area, collect in a pool, then suddenly burst through a narrow canyon. If you are in its path, you could be injured or drowned. The lesson? Never camp in a gully.

"Some people might wonder, 'What good is this place?'" Ballinger said. "The answer is that it is good for looking at. It is one of the world's unique places."

## CAMP ETHICS AND POLITICS

The perfect place to set up a base camp turned out to be not so perfect. Field scout Doug Williams and his son, James, had driven deep into Angeles National Forest, prepared to set up camp and then explore the surrounding area on foot. But when they reached their destination, no campground existed.

"I wanted a primitive camp in a national forest where I could teach my son some basics," said the senior Williams. "But when we got there, there wasn't much left of the camp, and it had been closed. It was obvious that the area had been vandalized."

It turned out not to be an isolated incident. A lack of outdoor ethics practiced by a few people using the unsupervised campgrounds available on national forestland has caused the U.S. Forest Service to close a few of them and make extensive repairs to others.

There have been sites closed, especially in Angeles and San Bernardino National Forests in Southern California. It's an urban type of thing, affecting forests near urban areas, and not just Los Angeles. They get a lot of urban users and they bring with them a lot of the same ethics they have in the city. They get drinking and they're not afraid to do things. They vandalize and run. Of course, it is a public facility, so they think nobody is getting hurt.

But somebody is getting hurt, starting with the next person who wants to use the campground. And if the ranger district budget doesn't have enough money to pay for repairs, the campground can be closed for the next arrivals. Posting camp hosts at campgrounds has helped solve many problem sites.

The National Park Service had similar problems some years back, especially with rampant littering. Park Director Bill Mott responded by creating an interpretive program that attempts to teach visitors the wise use of natural areas, and to have all park workers set examples by picking up litter and reminding others to do the same. At the entrance station, rangers ask each visitor to pick up at least one piece of litter per day.

The U.S. Forest Service has responded with a similar program. They made brochures available at district offices that detail the ethical use of national forests. These include: "Rules for Visitors to the National Forest," "Recreation in the National Forests," "Is the Water Safe?" and "Backcountry Safety Tips." Brochures include details on campfires, drinking water from lakes or streams, hypothermia, safety, and outdoor ethics.

Even experienced campers sometimes unintentionally cross the ethics line. A common example is when campers toss garbage into the chemical toilets rather than packing it out in a plastic garbage bag. The result is some poor guy has to pick that stuff out piece by piece before it can be pumped.

At most backcountry sites the U.S. Forest Service has implemented a program called "Pack it in, pack it out." Posted signs remind all visitors to do just that. But a lot of people don't, and we've seen evidence where others may even uproot the signs and burn them for firewood.

# THE JOHN MUIR TRAIL AND THE PACIFIC CREST TRAIL

You can have a foothold in the sky with every step on the John Muir Trail (JMT). The trail starts at practically the tip-top of North America—Mount Whitney—and takes you northward across a land of 12,000-foot passes and Ansel Adams-style vistas, then eventually pours you into nature's showpiece of the world, Yosemite Valley.

How could you top that? There is only one way: to hike the Pacific Crest Trail (PCT), which the JMT partially overlaps. The PCT extends from the Mexico border for 1,700 miles north to Oregon, and then beyond all the way to its end, at the Canadian border—a total distance of 2,650 miles.

The JMT and the PCT are the two premier expeditions in North America. The JMT usually takes about three weeks to complete, covering about 250 miles, including side trips for food drops and other forays. Some swear that the trip should be hiked from north to south, but most prefer south to north, starting with the awesome climb from Whitney Portal to the Whitney Summit, a climb of more than 5,000 feet. Three weeks later, the trip ends with a spectacular descent into Yosemite Valley, past hundreds of gawking tourists on the final three miles on the Mist Trail. Some cheat by starting at Tuolumne Meadows, thus avoiding a 4,000-foot climb out of Yosemite Valley, then heading south, but that is a hollow victory, having technically not completed the trip.

John Muir called the Sierra Nevada the "Range of Light." The trail that traverses it has become America's greatest hike—officially 211 miles from the Whitney Summit to Happy Isles in Yosemite Valley. It is a land spiked by 13,000-foot granite spires, untouched sapphire lakes loaded with trout, and canyons that drop as if they were the edge of the earth. There are many highlights, including the Mount Whitney Wilderness, John Muir Wilderness, Kings Canyon National Park, crossing the ice cut at Forester Pass, topping Muir Pass at Muir Hut, the incredible pyramidlike ridgeline near Selden Pass, catching golden trout where a cast can be like tossing

## Getting Along with Fellow Campers

The most important thing about a camping, fishing, or hunting trip is not where you go, how many fish you catch, or how many shots you fire. It often has little to do with how beautiful the view is, how easily the campfire lights, or how sunny the days are.

Oh yeah? Then what is the most important factor? The answer: the people you are with. It is that simple.

Who would you rather camp with? Your enemy at work or your dream mate in a good mood? You get the idea. A camping trip is a fairly close-knit experience, and you can make lifetime friends or lifelong enemies in the process. That is why your choice of companions is so important. Your own behavior is equally consequential.

Yet most people spend more time putting together their camping gear than considering why they enjoy or hate the company of their chosen companions. Here are 10 rules of behavior for good camping mates:

1. **No whining:** Nothing is more irritating than being around a whiner. It goes right to the heart of adventure, since often the only difference between a hardship and an escapade is simply whether or not an individual has the spirit for it. The people who do can turn a rugged day in the outdoors into a cherished memory. Those who don't can ruin it with their incessant sniveling.

2. **Activities must be agreed upon:**

a dog a bone, crossing the headwaters of Rush Creek, and finally dropping over Donohue Pass down to Lyell Fork and Tuolumne Meadows.

Yet the PCT goes far beyond this scope. It crosses through 37 wilderness areas, 20 national forests, and seven national parks, topping out at 13,180 feet at Forester Pass in the south Sierra. It also features the worst parts of the entire 2,700-mile route, the Hat Creek Rim (30 miles without water) and across the Mojave, where a siege of hot weather can have you praying for a sip of water out of a cow's hoof print.

Many hikers choose not to hike the entire JMT or PCT in one shot. Rather, they camp near a JMT or PCT trailhead then head up to the crest, taking off on side trips as they choose. The following campsites provide trailhead access to the JMT and the PCT:

- Tuolumne Meadows (page 527)
- Agnew Meadows Equestrian Camp (page 551)
- Pumice Flat (page 552)
- Upper Soda Springs (page 553)
- Minaret Falls (page 554)
- Devils Postpile National Monument (page 555)
- Vermillion (page 584)
- Jackass Meadow (page 597)
- Onion Valley (page 634)
- Lone Pine and Lone Pine Group (page 635)
- Whitney Trailhead Walk-In (page 636)
- Whitney Portal and Group (page 637)

Always have a meeting of the minds with your companions over the general game plan. Then everybody will possess an equal stake in the outcome of the trip. This is absolutely critical. Otherwise they will feel like merely an addendum to your trip, not an equal participant, and a whiner will be born (see number one).

3. **Nobody's in charge:** It is impossible to be genuine friends if one person is always telling another what to do, especially if the orders involve simple camp tasks. You need to share the space on the same emotional plane, and the only way to do that is to have a semblance of equality, regardless of differences in experience. Just try ordering your mate around at home for a few days. You'll quickly see the results, and they aren't pretty.

4. **Equal chances at the fun stuff:** It's fun to build the fire, fun to get the first cast at the best fishing spot, and fun to hoist the bagged food for a bear-proof food hang. It is not fun to clean the dishes, collect firewood, or cook every night. So obviously, there must be an equal distribution of the fun stuff and the not-fun stuff, and everybody on the trip must get a shot at the good and the bad.

5. **No heroes:** No awards are bestowed for achievement in the outdoors, yet some guys treat mountain peaks, big fish, and big game as if they are prizes in a trophy competition. Actually, nobody cares how wonderful you are, which is always a surprise to trophy chasers. What people care about is the heart of the adventure, the gut-level stuff.

---

# KEEP IT WILD TIP 6: PLAN AHEAD AND PREPARE

1. Learn about the regulations and issues that apply to the area you're visiting.
2. Avoid heavy-use areas.
3. Obtain all maps and permits.
4. Bring extra garbage bags to pack out any refuse you come across.

---

6. **Agree on a wake-up time:** It is a good idea to agree on a general wake-up time before closing your eyes for the night, and that goes regardless of whether you want to sleep in late or get up at dawn. Then you can proceed on course regardless of what time you crawl out of your sleeping bag in the morning, without the risk of whining (see number one).

7. **Think of the other guy:** Be self-aware instead of self-absorbed. A good test is to count the number of times you say, "What do you think?" A lot of potential problems can be solved quickly by actually listening to the answer.

8. **Solo responsibilities:** There are a number of essential camp duties on all trips, and while they should be shared equally, most should be completed solo. That means that when it is time for you to cook, you don't have to worry about me changing the recipe on you. It means that when it is my turn to make the fire, you keep your mitts out of it.

9. **Don't let money get in the way:** Of course everybody should share equally in trip expenses, such as the cost of food, and it should be split up before you head out yonder. Don't let somebody pay extra, because that person will likely try to control the trip. Conversely, don't let somebody weasel out of paying a fair share.

10. **Accordance on the food plan:** Always have complete agreement on what you plan to eat each day. Don't figure that just because you like Steamboat's Sludge, everybody else will, too, especially youngsters. Always, always, always check for food allergies, such as nuts, onions, or cheese, and make sure each person brings his or her own personal coffee brand. Some people drink only decaffeinated; others might gag on anything but Burma monkey beans.

Obviously, it is difficult to find companions who will agree on all of these elements. This is why many campers say that the best camping buddies they'll ever have are their mates, who know all about them and like them anyway.

## OUTDOORS WITH KIDS

How do you get a youngster excited about the outdoors? How do you compete with the television and remote control? How do you prove to a kid that success comes from persistence, spirit, and logic, which the outdoors teaches, and not from pushing buttons?

The answer is in the Ten Camping Commandments for Kids. These are lessons that will get youngsters excited about the outdoors and that will make sure adults help the process along, not kill it. I've put this list together with the help of my own kids, Jeremy and Kris, and their mother, Stephani. Some of the commandments are obvious, some are not, but all are important:

1. Take children to places where there is a guarantee of action. A good example is camping in a park where large numbers of wildlife can be viewed, such as squirrels, chipmunks, deer, and even bears. Other good choices include fishing at a small pond loaded with bluegill or hunting in a spot where a kid can shoot a .22 at pinecones all day. Boys and girls want action, not solitude.

2. Enthusiasm is contagious. If you aren't excited about an adventure, you can't expect a child to be. Show a genuine zest for life in the outdoors, and point out everything as if it is the first time you have ever seen it.

3. Always, always, always be seated when talking to someone small. This allows the adult and child to be on the same level. That is why fishing in a small boat is perfect for adults and kids. Nothing is worse for youngsters than having a big person look down at them and give them orders. What fun is that?

4. Always *show* how to do something, whether it is gathering sticks for a campfire, cleaning a trout, or tying a knot. Never tell— always show. A button usually clicks to "off" when a kid is lectured. But kids can learn behavior patterns and outdoor skills by watching adults, even when the adults are not aware they are being watched.

5. Let kids be kids. Let the adventure happen, rather than trying to force it within some preconceived plan. If they get sidetracked watching pollywogs, chasing butterflies, or sneaking up on chipmunks, let them be. A youngster can have more fun turning over rocks and looking at different kinds of bugs than sitting in one spot, waiting for a fish to bite.

6. Expect short attention spans. Instead of getting frustrated about it, use it to your advantage. How? By bringing along a bag of candy and snacks. Where there is a lull in the camp activity, out comes the bag. Don't let them know what goodies await, so each one becomes a surprise.

7. Make absolutely certain the child's sleeping bag is clean, dry, and warm. Nothing is worse than discomfort when trying to sleep, but a refreshing sleep makes for a positive attitude the next day. In addition, kids can become quite scared of animals at night. A parent should not wait for any signs of this, but always play the part of the outdoor guardian, the one who will take care of everything.

8. Kids quickly relate to outdoor ethics. They will enjoy eating everything they kill, building a safe campfire, and picking up all their litter, and they will develop a sense of pride that goes with it. A good idea is to bring extra plastic garbage bags to pick up any trash you come across. Kids long remember when they do something right that somebody else has done wrong.

9. If you want youngsters hooked on the outdoors for life, take a close-up photograph of them holding up fish they have caught, blowing on the campfire, or completing other camp tasks. Young children can forget how much fun they had, but they never forget if they have a picture of it.

10. The least important word you can ever say to a kid is "I." Keep track of how often you

## KEEP IT WILD TIP 7: RESPECT OTHER USERS

1. Horseback riders have priority over hikers. Step to the downhill side of the trail and talk softly when encountering horseback riders.

2. Hikers and horseback riders have priority over mountain bikers. When mountain bikers encounter other users even on wide trails, they should pass at an extremely slow speed. On very narrow trails, they should dismount and get off to the side so hikers or horseback riders can pass without having their trip disrupted.

3. Mountain bikes aren't permitted on most single-track trails and are expressly prohibited in designated wilderness areas and all sections of the Pacific Crest Trail. Mountain bikers breaking these rules should be confronted and told to dismount and walk their bikes until they reach a legal area.

4. It's illegal for horseback riders to break off branches that may be in the path of wilderness trails.

5. Horseback riders on overnight trips are prohibited from camping in many areas and are usually required to keep stock animals in specific areas where they can do no damage to the landscape.

© TOM STIENSTRA

are saying "Thank you" and "What do you think?" If you don't say them very often, you'll lose out. Finally, the most important words of all are: "I am proud of you."

## PREDICTING WEATHER

Foonsky climbed out of his sleeping bag, glanced at the nearby meadow, and scowled hard.

"It doesn't look good," he said. "Doesn't look good at all."

I looked at my adventure companion of 25 years and noted his discontent. Then I looked at the meadow and immediately understood why. "We better get ready for it."

This is why: *"When the grass is dry at morning light, look for rain before the night."*

"How bad you figure?" I asked him.

"We'll know soon enough, I reckon," Foonsky answered.

This is why: *"Short notice, soon to pass. Long notice, long it will last."*

When you are out in the wild, spending your days fishing and your nights camping, you learn to rely on yourself to predict the weather. If a storm hits the unprepared, it can quash the

trip and possibly endanger the participants. But if you are ready, a potential hardship can be an adventure.

You can't rely on TV weather forecasters, people who don't even know that when all the cows on a hill are facing north, it will rain that night for sure. God forbid if the cows are all sitting. But what do you expect from TV?

Foonsky made a campfire, started boiling some water for coffee and soup, and we started to plan the day. In the process, I noticed the smoke of the campfire: It was sluggish, drifting and hovering.

"You notice the smoke?" I asked, chewing on a piece of homemade jerky.

"Not good," Foonsky said. "Not good."

This is why: Sluggish, hovering smoke indicates rain.

"You'd think we'd have been smart enough to know last night that this was coming," Foonsky said. "Did you take a look at the moon or the clouds?"

"I didn't look at either," I answered. "Too busy eating the trout we caught."

This why: If the moon is clear and white, the weather will be good the next day. But if there is a ring around the moon, the number of stars you can count inside the ring equals the number of days until the next rain. As for clouds, the high, thin ones—called cirrus—indicate a change in the weather.

We were quiet for a while, planning our strategy, but as we did so, some terrible things happened: A chipmunk scampered past with his tail high, a small flock of geese flew by very low, and a little sparrow perched on a tree limb quite close to the trunk.

"We're in for trouble," I told Foonsky.

"I know, I know," he answered. "I saw 'em, too. And come to think of it, no crickets were chirping last night either."

"Damn, that's right!"

These are all signs of an approaching storm. Foonsky pointed at the smoke of the campfire and shook his head as if he had just been condemned. Sure enough, now the smoke was blowing toward the north, a sign of a south wind.

This is why: *"When the wind is from the south, the rain is in its mouth."*

"We'd best stay hunkered down until it passes," Foonsky said.

I nodded. "Let's gather as much firewood now as we can, get our gear covered up, then plan our meals."

"Then we'll get a poker game going."

As we accomplished these camp tasks, the sky clouded up, then darkened. Within an hour, we had gathered enough firewood to make a large pile, enough wood to keep a fire going no matter how hard it rained. The day's meals had been separated out of the food bag so it wouldn't have to be retrieved during the storm. We buttoned two ponchos together, staked two of the corners with ropes to the ground, and tied the other two with ropes to different tree limbs to create a slanted roof/shelter.

As the first raindrop fell with that magic sound on our poncho roof, Foonsky was just starting to shuffle the cards.

"Cut for deal," he said.

Just as I did so, it started to rain a bit harder. I pulled out another piece of jerky and started

chewing on it. It was just another day in paradise.

Weather lore can be valuable. Here is the list I have compiled:

*When the grass is dry at morning light,*
*Look for rain before the night.*

*Short notice, soon to pass.*
*Long notice, long it will last.*

*When the wind is from the east,*
*'Tis fit for neither man nor beast.*

*When the wind is from the south,*
*The rain is in its mouth.*

*When the wind is from the west,*
*Then it is the very best.*

*Red sky at night, sailors' delight.*
*Red sky in the morning, sailors take warning.*

*When all the cows are pointed north,*
*Within a day rain will come forth.*

*Onion skins very thin, mild winter coming in.*
*Onion skins very tough, winter's going to be very rough.*
*When your boots make the squeak of snow,*
*Then very cold temperatures will surely show.*

*If a goose flies high, fair weather ahead*
*If a goose flies low, foul weather will come instead.*

Small signs provided by nature and wildlife can also be translated to provide a variety of weather information:

- A thick coat on a woolly caterpillar means a big, early snow is coming.
- Chipmunks will run with their tails up before a rain.
- Bees always stay near their hives before a rainstorm.
- When the birds are perched on large limbs near tree trunks, an intense but short storm will arrive.

# CAMPING GEAR CHECKLIST

## Cooking Gear
- Camp stove and fuel
- Dish soap and scrubber
- Fire-starter cubes
- Heavy-duty paper plates
- Ice chest and drinks
- Itemized food, separated by groups
- Knife, fork, cup
- Large, heavy-duty garbage bags
- Matches stored in ziplock bags
- One lighter for each camper
- Paper towels
- Plastic spatula and stir spoon
- Pot grabber or pot holder
- Salt, pepper, spices
- Two pots and no-stick pan
- Water jug or lightweight plastic "cube"

## Optional Cooking Gear
- Aluminum foil
- Ax or hatchet
- Barbecue tongs
- Can opener
- Candles
- Dustpan
- Grill or hibachi
- Plastic clothespins
- Tablecloth
- Whisk broom
- Wood or charcoal for barbecue

## Clothing
- Cotton/canvas pants
- Gore-Tex parka or jacket
- Gore-Tex rain pants
- Lightweight, breathable shirt
- Lightweight fleece jacket
- Medium-weight fleece vest
- Polypropylene underwear
- Rain jacket and pants, or poncho
- Sunglasses
- Waterproofed, oilskin wide-brimmed hat

## Optional Clothing
- Gloves
- Shorts
- Ski cap
- Swimsuit

## Hiking Gear
- Backpack or daypack
- Hiking boots
- Fresh bootlaces
- Innersole or foot cushion (for expeditions)
- Moleskin and medical tape
- SmartWool (or equivalent) socks
- Water-purification system

## Optional Hiking Gear
- Backup lightweight shoes or moccasins
- Gaiters
- Water-repellent boot treatment

## Sleeping Gear
- Ground tarp
- Sleeping bag
- Tent or bivy bag
- Therm-a-Rest pad

## Optional Sleeping Gear
- Air bed
- Cot
- Catalytic heater
- Foam pad for truck bed

- Mosquito netting
- Mr. Heater and propane tank (for use in pickup truck camper shell)
- Pillow (even in wilderness)
- RV windshield light screen
- Seam Lock for tent stitching

## First Aid

- Ace bandage
- After-Bite for mosquito bites (before you scratch them)
- Aspirin
- Biodegradable soap
- Caladryl for poison oak
- Campho-Phenique gel for bites (after you scratch them)
- Mosquito repellent
- Lip balm
- Medical tape to affix pads
- Neosporin for cuts
- Roller gauze
- Sterile gauze pads
- Sunscreen
- Tweezers

## Optional First Aid

- Athletic tape for sprained ankle
- Cell phone or coins for phone calls
- Extra set of matches
- Mirror for signaling
- Thermometer

## Recreation Gear

- All required permits and licenses
- Fishing reel with fresh line
- Fishing rod
- Knife
- Leatherman tool or needle-nose pliers

- Small tackle box with flies, floats, hooks, lures, snap swivels, and splitshot

## Optional Recreation Gear

- Backpacking cribbage board
- Deck of cards
- Folding chairs
- Guidebooks
- Hammock
- Mountain bike
- Reading material

## Other Necessities

- Bear-proof food canister (if required)
- Duct tape
- Extra plastic garbage bags
- Flashlight and batteries
- Lantern and fuel
- Maps
- Nylon rope for food hang
- Spade for cat hole
- Toilet paper
- Toothbrush and toothpaste
- Towelettes
- Wristwatch

## Other Optional Items

- Altimeter
- Assorted bungee cords
- Binoculars
- Camera with fresh battery and digital card or film
- Compass
- Feminine hygiene products
- GPS unit
- Handkerchief
- Notebook and pen

- On the coast, if groups of seabirds are flying a mile inland, look for major winds.
- If crickets are chirping very loudly during the evening, the next day will be clear and warm.
- If the smoke of a campfire at night rises in a thin spiral, good weather is assured for the next day.
- If the smoke of a campfire at night is sluggish, drifting and hovering, it will rain the next day.
- If there is a ring around the moon, count the number of stars inside the ring, and that is how many days until the next rain.
- If the moon is clear and white, the weather will be good the next day.
- High, thin clouds, or cirrus, indicate a change in the weather.
- Oval-shaped lenticular clouds indicate high winds at the crest or mountaintops.
- Two levels of clouds moving in different directions indicate changing weather soon.
- Huge, dark, billowing clouds, called cumulonimbus, suddenly forming on warm afternoons in the mountains mean that a short but intense thunderstorm with lightning can be expected.
- When squirrels are busy gathering food for extended periods, it means good weather is ahead in the short term, but a hard winter is ahead in the long term.

And God forbid if all the cows are sitting down. . . .

# REDWOOD EMPIRE

© DREAMSTIME.COM

## Visitors come to the Redwood Empire for one

reason: to see groves of giant redwoods, the tallest trees in the world. But the redwoods are only one of the attractions in this area. The Smith River canyon, Del Norte and Humboldt Coasts, and the remote edge of the Siskiyou Wilderness in Six Rivers National Forest all make this region like none other in the world. Three stellar areas should be on your must-see list for outstanding days of adventure: the redwood parks from Trinidad to Klamath River, the Smith River Recreation Area, and the Lost Coast. Redwood campgrounds are in high demand, and reservations are necessary in the peak vacation season. On the opposite end of the spectrum are primitive and remote settings in Six Rivers National Forest, the Lost Coast, and even a few surprise nuggets in Redwood National Park.

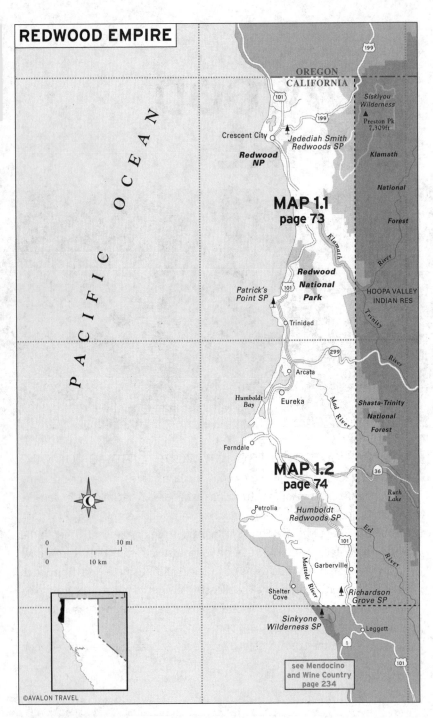

# Map 1.1

## Sites 1-31
## Pages 75-90

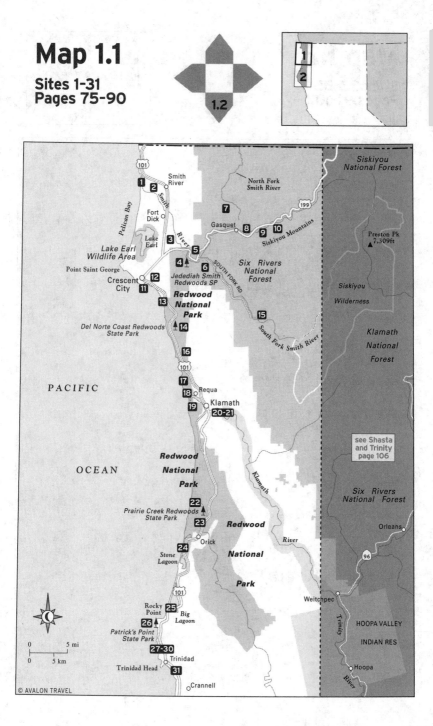

# Map 1.2

## Sites 32-55
## Pages 91-102

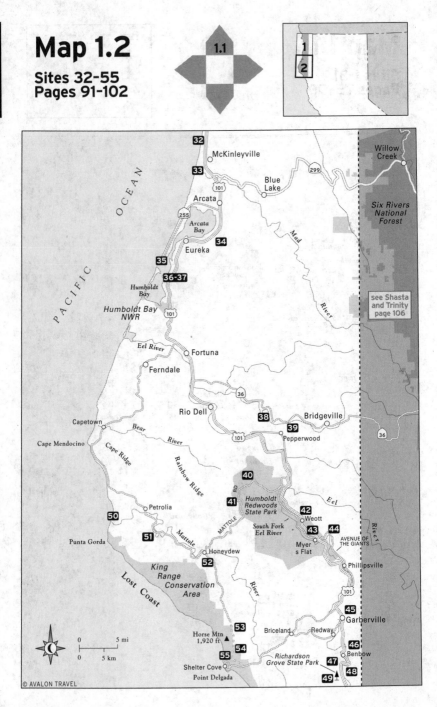

1.1

1
2

McKinleyville

Willow Creek

299

Blue Lake

Arcata

101

Arcata Bay

255

Six Rivers National Forest

34

Eureka

35

Mad River

36-37

Humboldt Bay

Humboldt Bay NWR

101

see Shasta and Trinity page 106

Eel River

Fortuna

Ferndale

36

Rio Dell

38

Bridgeville

Capetown

Bear River

39

Pepperwood

36

Cape Mendocino

Cape Ridge

Rainbow Ridge

40

Humboldt Redwoods State Park

Eel River

41

42

Weott

50

Petrolia

Mattole RD

South Fork Eel River

43

44

AVENUE OF THE GIANTS

Punta Gorda

51

Mattole

Myers Flat

Honeydew

52

King Range Conservation Area

Lost Coast

River

Phillipsville

101

45

Garberville

Briceland

Redway

0    5 mi
0    5 km

Horse Mtn 1,920 ft

53

54

46

Benbow

55

Shelter Cove
Point Delgada

Richardson Grove State Park

47

48

49

© AVALON TRAVEL

# 1 SALMON HARBOR RV RESORT

Scenic rating: 6

on the Smith River

**Map 1.1, page 73**

If location is everything, this privately operated campground rates high for salmon and steelhead anglers in the fall. It is near the mouth of the Smith River, where salmon enter and school in the deep river holes in October. The fish are big, often in the 20-pound range, occasionally surpassing even 40 pounds. Year-round this is a good layover for RV cruisers looking for a spot near the Oregon border. It is actually an RV parking area with hookups, set within a mobile home park. Salmon Harbor RV Resort overlooks the ocean, with good beachcombing and driftwood and agate hunting nearby. Note that most sites are filled for the entire summer, but several sites are kept open for overnight campers. Restaurants are within walking distance and golfing only 20 minutes away.

**Campsites, facilities:** There are 93 sites for tents or RVs up to 40 feet; most sites have full hookups (30 and 50 amps) and some are pull-through. Picnic tables and fire grills are provided. Drinking water, restrooms with flush toilets and showers, cable TV, coin laundry, storage sheds, Wi-Fi (some sites), and a recreation room are available. A grocery store, ice, gas, propane, a restaurant, boat ramp, fish-cleaning station, RV storage, snack bar, and a bar are available within three miles. Leashed pets are permitted with a pet walk on the beach.

**Reservations, fees:** Reservations are accepted at 800/332-6139. Sites are $38 per night, plus $3 per person for more than two people. Monthly rates are available. Open year-round.

**Directions:** From Crescent City, drive north on U.S. 101 for 13 miles to the town of Smith River. Continue three miles north on U.S. 101 to the Salmon Harbor Road exit. Turn left on Salmon Harbor Road, drive a short distance, and look for Salmon Harbor Resort at the end of the road.

**Contact:** Salmon Harbor RV Resort, 707/487-3341, www.salmonharborrvresort.com.

# 2 SHIP ASHORE RESORT

Scenic rating: 7

on the Smith River

**Map 1.1, page 73**

This is a famous spot for Smith River anglers in late fall and all through winter, when the tales get taller as the evening gets late. In the summer, the resort has become quite popular with people cruising the coast on U.S. 101. The park is set on five acres of land adjacent to the lower Smith River. Note that in addition to the 120 RV sites, another 80 sites have mobile homes. The salmon and steelhead seem to come in one size here—big—but they can be as elusive as Bigfoot. If you want to hear how big these fish can be, just check into the Captain's Galley restaurant any fall or winter evening. Salmon average 15-25 pounds, occasionally bigger, with 50-pounders caught each year, and steelhead average 10-14 pounds, with bigger fish occasionally hooked as well.

**Campsites, facilities:** There are 200 sites for RVs and a separate area for 10-15 tents. Most RV sites have full hookups (30 amps); some sites are pull-through. Two houses and motel rooms are also available. Picnic tables are provided. Restrooms with flush toilets and showers, boat dock, boat ramp, coin laundry, propane, and a restaurant are available. A grocery store is two miles away. Leashed pets are permitted, with a maximum of two pets.

**Reservations, fees:** Reservations are not accepted. Tent sites are $16 per night, RV sites are $28 per night, plus $2.50 per person per night for more than two people and an additional fee for cable TV. Weekly rates are available. Some credit cards are accepted. Open year-round.

**Directions:** From Crescent City, drive north on U.S. 101 for 16 miles, three miles past the town of Smith River, to the Ship Ashore sign at Chinook Street. At Chinook Street, turn left and drive a short distance (less than half a block) to the motel lobby to register.

**Contact:** Ship Ashore Resort, 707/487-3141, www.ship-ashore.com.

# 3 CRESCENT CITY REDWOODS KOA

**Scenic rating: 6**

five miles north of Crescent City

**Map 1.1, page 73**

This KOA camp is on the edge of a recreation wonderland, a perfect jumping-off spot for a vacation. The park covers 17 acres, with 10 acres of redwood forest. A few farm animals live here, and guests are allowed to feed them. In addition, there are three golf courses nearby. The camp is only two miles from Redwood National Park, Jedediah Smith Redwoods State Park, and the Smith River National Recreation Area. It is also only a 10-minute drive to the beach and Tolowa Dunes Wildlife Area to the east, and to Crescent City Harbor to the south.

**Campsites, facilities:** There are 12 sites for tents and small RVs with partial hookups, 28 sites with full hookups (30 and 50 amps), including some pull-through sites for RVs of any length, and 35 sites with no hookups. Seventeen cabins and one lodge are also available. Picnic tables and fire grills are provided. A dump station, restrooms with flush toilets and showers, a coin laundry, free Wi-Fi, cable TV, playground, propane, convenience store, ice, firewood, recreation room, pool table, tetherball, table tennis, horseshoes, go-carts, and volleyball are available. Some facilities are wheelchair-accessible. Leashed pets are permitted.

**Reservations, fees:** Reservations for RV sites are accepted at 800/562-5754 or online at www.crescentcitykoa.com. RV sites are $42-65 per night, tent sites are $32-38, plus $3-4 per person per night for more than two people. Some credit cards are accepted. Open mid-March to mid-November.

**Directions:** From Crescent City, take U.S. 101

north for five miles to the campground entrance on the right (east) side of the road.

**Contact:** Crescent City Redwoods KOA, 707/464-5744, www.crescentcitykoa.com.

# 4 JEDEDIAH SMITH REDWOODS STATE PARK

**Scenic rating: 10**

on the Smith River

**Map 1.1, page 73**

This is a beautiful park set along the Smith River, where the campsites are sprinkled amid a grove of old-growth redwoods. Reservations are usually a necessity during the summer. This park covers 10,000 acres on both sides of the Smith River, a jewel and California's last major free-flowing river. There are 20 miles of hiking and nature trails. The park has hiking trails that lead right out of the campground; one is routed along the beautiful Smith River, and another heads through forest, across U.S. 199, and hooks up with Simpson-Reed Interpretive Trail. In the summer, interpretive programs are available. There is also a good put-in spot at the park for river access in a drift boat, canoe, or raft. The fishing is best for steelhead from mid-January through March. In the summer, a seasonal footbridge connects the campground with more extensive trails. The best hikes are on the south side of the Smith River, accessible via Howland Hill Road, including the Boy Scout Tree Trail and Stout Grove. Note that in winter, 100 inches of cumulative rainfall is common.

South Fork Road provides an extended tour into Six Rivers National Forest along the South Fork Smith River, with the option of visiting many of the largest trees in Jedediah Smith Redwoods State Park. The turnoff is on U.S. 199 just northeast of the town of Hiouchi. Turn right, cross two bridges, and you will arrive at a fork in the road. Turning left at the fork will take you along the South Fork Smith River and deep into Six Rivers National Forest.

Turning right at the fork will take you to a series of trailheads for hikes into redwoods. Of these, the best is the Boy Scout Tree Trail.

**Campsites, facilities:** There are 89 sites for tents or RVs up to 36 feet (no hookups) and trailers up to 31 feet, five hike-in/bike-in sites, and one group site for up to 15 vehicles and 50 people. Picnic tables, fire grills, and food lockers are provided. Drinking water, showers, flush toilets, and a dump station are available. There is a visitors center with exhibits and a nature store. Propane gas and groceries are available within one mile. Some facilities are wheelchair-accessible. Leashed pets are permitted only in the campground and on roads.

**Reservations, fees:** Reservations are accepted May through early September at 800/444-7275 or www.reserveamerica.com ($8 reservation fee). Sites are first-come, first-served September through May. Sites are $35 per night, plus $8 per night for each additional vehicle; the group site is $300 per night; and it's $5 per person per night for hike-in/bike-in sites. Cabins are $100 per night. Open year-round.

**Directions:** From Crescent City, drive north on U.S. 101 for four miles to the junction with U.S. 199. Turn east at U.S. 199 and drive five miles. Turn right at the well-signed entrance station.

**Contact:** Jedediah Smith Visitors Center, 707/458-3496; Jedediah Smith Redwoods State Park, 707/465-7335, www.parks.ca.gov.

## 5 REDWOOD MEADOWS RV RESORT

🚶 🏊 🎣 🐕 ♿ 🚐 ⛺

### Scenic rating: 7

near the Smith River

**Map 1.1, page 73**

This camp is out of the wind and fog you get on the coast and set instead in the heart of the forest country. It makes a good base camp for a steelhead trip in winter. Insiders know that right next door, the fried chicken at the Hamlet's market can be good for a quick hit. An excellent side trip is to drive just east of Hiouchi on U.S. 199, turn right, and cross over two bridges, where you will reach a fork in the road. Turn left for a great scenic drive along the South Fork Smith River or turn right to get backdoor access to Jedediah Smith Redwoods State Park and three great trailheads for hiking in the redwoods. My favorite of the latter is the Boy Scout Tree Trail. Note that about one-fourth of the RV sites are filled with long-term renters, and many other sites fill up quickly with summer vacationers.

**Campsites, facilities:** There are 120 sites with full hookups (30 and 50 amps) for RVs of any length, six tent sites, and one yurt. Some sites are pull-through. Two park-model cabins and six furnished apartments are also available. Restrooms with flush toilets and showers, a dump station, coin laundry, Wi-Fi, cable TV, recreation room, fish-cleaning station, horseshoe pits, basketball court, grocery store, propane, and deli are available. A motel and café are nearby. A golf course is within four miles. Some facilities are wheelchair-accessible. Leashed pets are permitted.

**Reservations, fees:** Reservations are accepted at 800/722-9468. RV sites are $43-51 per night, plus $3.50 per person per night for more than two people; tent sites are $27-30 per night; cabins, apartments, and a yurt are available. Some credit cards are accepted. Open year-round.

**Directions:** From Crescent City, drive five miles north on U.S. 101 to U.S. 199. Turn east (right) on U.S. 199 and drive about five miles (just past the entrance to Jedediah Smith Redwoods State Park) to the town of Hiouchi. In Hiouchi, turn left at the well-signed campground entrance.

**Contact:** Redwood Meadows RV Resort, 707/458-3321, www.redwoodmeadowsrv.com.

# 6 LITTLE BALD HILLS

🚶 🚵 5% ⛺

## Scenic rating: 8

in Jedediah Smith Redwoods State Park

**Map 1.1, page 73**

Little Bald Hills is a little-known campground in the backcountry at Jedediah Smith. The camp, set in a deep forest, is very quiet and is often overlooked because of its location off Howland Hill Road on the far side of the Smith River (not at the main entrance along U.S. 199). Reaching the camp requires a 3.3-mile trip, accessible for hikers, mountain bikers, and horseback riders. For newcomers, the drive to the trailhead can seem circuitous and remote compared to other state and national parks. Nearby Stout Grove and the Boy Scout Tree Trail provide excellent side trips. Bears are occasional visitors at night, so be sure to use the food lockers provided.

**Campsites, facilities:** There are four tent sites and one group site for up to 20 people. Picnic tables and fire rings are provided. Pit toilets, bear-proof lockers, a horse corral, and a water trough are available. Drinking water is not available, but there is a spigot for stock water. Garbage must be packed out.

**Reservations, fees:** Reservations are not accepted. A free backcountry permit is required (available at the visitors centers in Crescent City and Hiouchi). There is no fee for camping. Open year-round.

**Directions:** From Crescent City, drive north on U.S. 101 for four miles to the junction with U.S. 199. Turn east at U.S. 199 and drive just past Hiouchi to the turnoff on the right for South Fork Road. Turn right and drive over two bridges to the junction with South Fork Road (on the left) and Howland Hill Road (on the right). Turn right and drive a short distance to the Little Bald Hills Trailhead on the left (just before Stout Grove).

**Contact:** Redwood National and State Parks, 707/465-7335, www.nps.gov/redw.

# 7 NORTH FORK

🚶 🛶 🚐 ⛺

## Scenic rating: 7

on the North Fork of the Smith River in Six Rivers National Forest

**Map 1.1, page 73**

This remote and primitive camp is a put-in for rafting and kayaking the North Fork Smith River in winter. Since there is no dam it can only be run in the rainy season, but this is a sensational Class III rafting trip in a rainstorm, including a spot at an overhanging rock along the northern shore where you can raft right through a waterfall. In the summer, the flows on the North Fork turn into a trickle and you can virtually walk down the stream. The campsites are primitive, open, and located within view of the river—not in the forest. Though there is space for RVs at the camp, the road in can be impassable for RVs during wet weather.

**Campsites, facilities:** There are five sites for tents or RVs up to 18 feet (no hookups). Large RVs are not advised. Picnic tables and fire rings are provided. Vault toilets are available, but there is no drinking water. Garbage must be packed out.

**Reservations, fees:** Reservations are not accepted. Sites are $8 per night, plus $5 per night per additional vehicle. Open year-round.

**Directions:** From Crescent City, drive north on U.S. 101 (straight ahead past the U.S. 199 turnoff) to Rowdy Creek Road. Turn right on Rowdy Creek Road (it becomes Forest Road 308) and drive about 4.5 miles on Rowdy Creek Road/FR 308 to Forest Road 305. Turn left on Forest Road 305 (a dirt road) and drive 11 miles to the campground.

**Contact:** Smith River Recreation Area, Six Rivers National Forest, 707/457-3131, www.fs.usda.gov/srnf.

# 8 PANTHER FLAT

🥾 🏊 🛶 ⛵ 🐕 ♿ 🚐 ⛺

### Scenic rating: 8

on the Smith River in Six Rivers National Forest

**Map 1.1, page 73**　　　　　**BEST (**

This is an ideal alternative to the often-crowded Jedediah Smith Redwoods State Park. The park provides easy road access since it is right along U.S. 199, the two-laner that runs beside the Smith River. This is one of the featured campgrounds in the Smith River Recreation Area, with excellent prospects for salmon and steelhead fishing in the fall and winter respectively, and outstanding hiking and backpacking in the summer. A 0.25-mile interpretive trail and viewing area is one mile north of the campground, off U.S. 199. A great nearby hike is Stony Creek Trail, an easy walk along the North Fork Smith River; the trailhead is in nearby Gasquet on Stoney Creek Road. Redwood National Park is a short drive to the west. The Siskiyou Wilderness is a short drive to the southeast via forest roads detailed on Forest Service maps. The wild and scenic Smith River system provides fishing, swimming, sunbathing, kayaking for experts, and beautiful scenery.

**Campsites, facilities:** There are 38 sites for tents or RVs up to 40 feet (no hookups). Picnic tables and fire grills are provided. Drinking water, restrooms with flush toilets and coin showers, a visitors center, and horseshoe pits are available. Propane gas, groceries, and coin laundry are nearby. Some facilities are wheelchair-accessible. Leashed pets are permitted.

**Reservations, fees:** Reservations are accepted at 877/444-6777 ($10 reservation fee) or www. recreation.gov ($9 reservation fee). Sites are $15-30 per night, plus $5 per night for each additional vehicle. Open year-round.

**Directions:** From Crescent City, drive north on U.S. 101 for three miles to the junction with U.S. 199. At U.S. 199, turn east and drive 14.5 miles to Gasquet. From Gasquet, continue for 2.3 miles east on U.S. 199 and look for the entrance to the campground on the left side of the highway.

**Contact:** Smith River Recreation Area, Six Rivers National Forest, 707/457-3131, www. fs.usda.gov/srnf.

# 9 GRASSY FLAT

🛶 🏊 🐕 ♿ 🚐 ⛺

### Scenic rating: 4

on the Smith River in Six Rivers National Forest

**Map 1.1, page 73**

This is one in a series of three easy-to-reach Forest Service camps near U.S. 199 along the beautiful Middle Fork of the Smith River. It's a classic wild river, popular in the summer with kayakers, and the steelhead come huge in the winter for the crafty few. The camp itself is directly across from a CalTrans waste area, and if you hit it when the crews are working, it can be noisy here. Most of the time, however, it is peaceful and quiet.

**Campsites, facilities:** There are 15 sites for tents or RVs up to 30 feet (no hookups) and four walk-in tent sites. Picnic tables and fire grills are provided. Drinking water and vault toilets are available. Propane gas and groceries are available nearby. Some facilities are wheelchair-accessible. Leashed pets are permitted.

**Reservations, fees:** Reservations are accepted at 877/444-6777 ($10 reservation fee) or www. recreation.gov ($9 reservation fee). Sites are $10 per night, plus $5 per night for each additional vehicle. Open June through September.

**Directions:** From Crescent City, drive north on U.S. 101 for three miles to the junction with U.S. 199. Turn east on U.S. 199 and drive 14.5 miles to Gasquet. From Gasquet, continue east on U.S. 199 for 4.4 miles and look for the campground entrance on the right side of the road.

**Contact:** Smith River Recreation Area, Six Rivers National Forest, 707/457-3131, www. fs.usda.gov/srnf.

## 10 PATRICK CREEK

### Scenic rating: 8

in Six Rivers National Forest

**Map 1.1, page 73**

This is one of the prettiest spots along U.S. 199, where Patrick Creek enters the upper Smith River. It is also a historic California Conservation Corps site that was built in the 1930s. This section of the Smith looks something like a large trout stream, rolling green past a boulder-lined shore, complete with forest canopy. There are small cutthroat trout in summer and salmon and steelhead in fall and winter. A big plus for this camp is its nearby access to excellent hiking in the Siskiyou Wilderness, especially the great day hike to Buck Lake. It is essential to have a map of Six Rivers National Forest, both for driving directions to the trailhead and for the hiking route. You can buy maps at the information center for the Smith River National Recreation Area on the north side of U.S. 199 in Gasquet. Patrick Creek Lodge, on the opposite side of the highway from the campground, has a restaurant and bar. A paved trail connects the campground to Patrick Creek Lodge.

**Campsites, facilities:** There are 13 sites for tents or RVs up to 35 feet (no hookups). Picnic tables and fire grills are provided. Drinking water and flush toilets are available. Some facilities are wheelchair-accessible, including a fishing area. Leashed pets are permitted.

**Reservations, fees:** Reservations are accepted for individual sites and are required for group sites at 877/444-6777 or www.recreation.gov ($9 reservation fee). Sites are $14 per night, plus $5 per night for each additional vehicle. Open May through September.

**Directions:** From Crescent City, drive north on U.S. 101 for three miles to the junction with U.S. 199. Turn east on U.S. 199 and drive 14.5 miles to Gasquet. From Gasquet, continue east on U.S. 199 for 7.5 miles and look for the campground entrance on the right side of the road.

**Contact:** Smith River Recreation Area, Six Rivers National Forest, 707/457-3131, www.fs.usda.gov/srnf.

## 11 BAYSIDE RV PARK

### Scenic rating: 6

in Crescent City

**Map 1.1, page 73**

If you are towing a boat, you just found your personal heaven: This RV park is directly adjacent to the boat docking area in Crescent City Harbor. There are several walks in the immediate area, including exploring the harbor and ocean frontage. The Crescent City Harbor provides views of seals and sea lions lounging on floating docks. For a quick change of scenery, it is only a 15-minute drive to Redwood National Park and Jedediah Smith Redwoods State Park along U.S. 199 to the north. Note that about 20 sites are filled with long-term renters, and most of the spaces book up for the entire season.

**Campsites, facilities:** There are 110 sites for RVs up to 34 feet. Most sites have full hookups (30 amps) and/or are pull-through. No tents. Picnic tables are provided. Restrooms with flush toilets and showers, cable TV, Wi-Fi, and a coin laundry are available. A restaurant is adjacent to the park. Leashed pets are permitted.

**Reservations, fees:** Reservations are accepted at 800/446-9482 or at www.baysidervcc.com/reservations. Sites are $35-40 per night, plus $5 per person per night for more than two people. Open year-round.

**Directions:** From U.S. 101 at the southern end of Crescent City, drive to Citizen Dock Road and continue one-half block south to the park office.

**Contact:** Bayside RV Park, 750 U.S. 101, Crescent City, 707/464-9482, www.baysidervcc.com.

## 12 VILLAGE CAMPER INN RV PARK

### Scenic rating: 7

in Crescent City

**Map 1.1, page 73**

Woods and water attract visitors to California's north coast. Village Camper Inn provides nearby access to big woods and big water. This RV park is on 20 acres of wooded land, about a 10-minute drive away from the giant redwoods along U.S. 199. In addition, you'll find some premium beachcombing for driftwood and agates a mile away on the spectacular rocky beaches just west of town. Note that about half of the sites fill up for the entire summer season.

**Campsites, facilities:** There are 135 sites for RVs of any length and a separate area for tents. Most RV sites have full hookups (30 and 50 amps); some sites are pull-through. A one-bedroom vacation cottage is also available. Picnic tables are provided. Drinking water, a dump station, restrooms with flush toilets and showers, coin laundry, pickleball court, Wi-Fi, and cable TV are available. Leashed pets are permitted, with certain restrictions.

**Reservations, fees:** Reservations are accepted at 800/470-3544. Sites are $37.50-40.50 per night, plus $2 per person per night for more than two people and $5 per day for extra vehicles; Wi-Fi costs $3 daily. Monthly rates are available. Some credit cards are accepted. Open year-round.

**Directions:** From Crescent City, drive north on U.S. 101 to the Parkway Drive exit. Take that exit and drive 0.5 mile to the campground on the right.

On U.S. 101, driving south in Crescent City: Drive south on U.S. 101 to the Washington Boulevard exit. Turn left on Washington Boulevard and drive one block to Parkway Drive. Turn left on Parkway and drive one block to the campground on the right.

**Contact:** Village Camper Inn RV Park, 707/464-3544, www.villagecamperinn.com.

## 13 NICKEL CREEK

### Scenic rating: 8

in Redwood National Park

**Map 1.1, page 73**

This camp is 100 yards from the beach on a bluff, right near the mouth of Nickel Creek. One of the least-known national park campgrounds in the whole state, Nickel Creek Walk-In provides a backpacking-type experience, yet it requires only a short, moderate walk (some steep grades and switchbacks). In return for the effort, you get seclusion and beach frontage, with seashore walks and tidepool exploration available. Enjoy ocean vistas from the high bluff.

**Campsites, facilities:** There are five hike-in tent sites. There is no drinking water. Picnic tables, food lockers, and fire pits are provided. Composting toilets are available. Garbage must be packed out. No pets are allowed.

**Reservations, fees:** Reservations are not accepted, but a free backcountry permit is required (available at the visitors center or online at www.nps.gov/redw). There is no fee for camping. Open year-round.

**Directions:** From Crescent City, drive south on U.S. 101 for two miles to Enderts Beach Road. Turn right on Enderts Beach Road and drive about a mile to the trailhead at the end of the road. From the trailhead, hike in 0.5 mile to the campground.

**Contact:** Crescent City Information Center, 707/465-7335, www.crescentcity.org; Redwood National and State Parks, 707/465-7335, www.nps.gov/redw.

## 14 DEL NORTE COAST REDWOODS STATE PARK

### Scenic rating: 8

near Crescent City

**Map 1.1, page 73**

The campsites are set in a series of loops in the

forest, so while there are a lot of camps, you still feel a sense of privacy. In addition to redwoods, there are good stands of alders, along with a rambling stream fed by several creeks. It makes for a very pretty setting, with four loop trails available right out of the camp. This park covers 6,400 acres, featuring 50 percent old-growth coastal redwoods and eight miles of wild coastline. Topography is fairly steep, with elevations ranging from sea level to 1,277 feet. This range is oriented in a north-south direction, with steep cliffs adjacent to the ocean. That makes most of the rocky seacoast generally inaccessible except by Damnation Trail and Footsteps Rock Trail. The best coastal access is at Wilson Beach or False Klamath Cove, where there is a half mile of sandy beach bordered by excellent tidepools.

The forest interior is dense, with redwoods and tanoaks, madrones, red alders, bigleaf maples, and California bays. One reason for the lush growth is what rangers call the "nurturing" coastal climate. Nurturing, in this case, means rain like you wouldn't believe in the winter—often more than 100 inches in a season—and lots of fog in the summer. Interpretive programs are conducted here. Insider's note: Hike-in and bike-in campers beware. There is a 900-foot elevation change over the course of two miles between the U.S. 101 access road and the campground.

**Campsites, facilities:** There are 145 sites for tents or RVs up to 31 feet (no hookups). Hike-in/bike-in sites are also available. Picnic tables, fire pits, and food lockers are provided. Drinking water, a dump station, and restrooms with flush toilets and coin showers are available. Some facilities are wheelchair-accessible. Leashed pets are permitted only in the campground.

**Reservations, fees:** Reservations are accepted at 800/444-7275 or www.reserveamerica.com ($8 reservation fee); search for Del Norte Coast Redwoods. Sites are $35 per night, plus $8 per night for each additional vehicle; it's $5 per person per night for hike-in/bike-in sites. Open May through September.

**Directions:** From Crescent City, drive seven miles south on U.S. 101 to a signed access road for Mill Creek Campground/Del Norte Coast Redwoods State Park. Turn east at the park entrance and continue 1.5 miles to the campground entrance.

**Contact:** Del Norte Coast Redwoods State Park, 707/465-7335, www.parks.ca.gov; Redwood National and State Parks, 707/465-7335, www.nps.gov/redw.

## 15 BIG FLAT

**Scenic rating: 7**

on Hurdygurdy Creek in Six Rivers National Forest

**Map 1.1, page 73**

This camp provides an ideal setting for those who know of it, which is why it gets quite a bit of use for a relatively remote camp. Set along Hurdygurdy Creek, near where the creek enters the South Fork of the Smith River, it provides nearby access to South Kelsey Trail, an outstanding hiking route whether you are walking for a few hours or backpacking for days. In the summer, it is a good layover for rafters or kayakers paddling the South Fork of the Smith River.

**Campsites, facilities:** There are 23 sites for tents or RVs up to 22 feet (no hookups). Picnic tables and fire grills are provided. Vault toilets and food lockers are available. There is no drinking water and garbage must be packed out. Some facilities are wheelchair-accessible. Leashed pets are permitted.

**Reservations, fees:** Reservations are not accepted. Sites are $8 per night, plus $5 per night for each additional vehicle. Open May through mid-September.

**Directions:** From Crescent City, drive north on U.S. 101 for three miles to the junction with U.S. 199. Turn east on U.S. 199 and drive five miles to Hiouchi. Continue just past Hiouchi to South Fork Road. Turn right and cross two bridges. At the Y, turn left on South Fork Road and drive about 14 miles to Big Flat Road/ County Road 405. Turn left and drive 0.25 mile to the campground entrance road (Forest Road 15N59) on the left. Turn left and drive a short distance to the camp on the left.

**Contact:** Smith River Recreation Area, Six Rivers National Forest, 707/457-3131, www. fs.usda.gov/srnf.

# 16 DEMARTIN

## Scenic rating: 9

in Redwood National Park

**Map 1.1, page 73**

For hikers on the California Coastal Trail, this camp is ideal for an overnight spot. It is set in a grassy prairie area on a bluff overlooking the ocean along the DeMartin section of the trail beside Wilson Creek. Sound good? You can chase the waves, hike the Coastal Trail, or just hunker down and let the joy of a peaceful spot renew your spirit.

**Campsites, facilities:** There are 10 tent sites. Picnic tables, fire pits, and food storage lockers are provided. Composting toilets are available. There is no drinking water. Garbage must be packed out. No pets are allowed.

**Reservations, fees:** Reservations are not accepted. A free backcountry permit is required (available from the visitors center or online). There is no fee for camping. Open year-round.

**Directions:** From Crescent City, drive south for approximately 18 miles on U.S. 101 to Wilson Creek Road. At Wilson Creek Road, turn left and drive 0.25 mile to the trailhead at the end of the road. From the trailhead, marked Coastal Trail, hike in about 3.5 miles to the campground.

**Contact:** Redwood National and State Parks, 707/465-7335, www.nps.gov/redw.

# 17 MYSTIC FOREST RV PARK

## Scenic rating: 6

near the Klamath River

**Map 1.1, page 73**

The park features gravel roads, redwood trees, and grassy sites amid a 50-acre park designed primarily for RVs with a separate area for tents. Set in a unique natural environment, campsites are nestled among the redwoods, and RV sites are on open grass (no blacktop). A bonus is the 18-hole miniature golf course. The Trees of Mystery attraction is less than a mile away and features a nearly 50-foot-tall Paul Bunyan and his blue ox, Babe. (You may recall the tale of Babe's head falling off in a storm in the winter of 2008. Have no fear—Babe again has a head.) The park is about 1.5 miles away from the ocean and 3.5 miles from the Klamath River. Jet-boat tours are available on the Klamath River.

**Campsites, facilities:** There are 30 sites with full hookups (30 amps) for RVs of any length and 14 tent sites. Some of the RV sites are pull-through. Picnic tables and fire rings are provided. Drinking water, restrooms with flush toilets and showers, Wi-Fi, cable TV, playground, recreation room, horseshoes, miniature golf, a coin laundry, convenience store and gift shop, group facilities, and firewood are available. Some facilities are wheelchair-accessible. Leashed pets are permitted.

**Reservations, fees:** Reservations are accepted. RV sites are $36 per night, tent sites are $20 per night, plus $4 per person per night for more than two people. Group rates are available. Some credit cards are accepted. Open year-round.

**Directions:** From Eureka, drive north on U.S. 101 to Klamath and continue north for five miles. Look for the entrance sign on the left side of the road. If you reach the Trees of Mystery, you have gone a mile too far north.

**Contact:** Mystic Forest RV Park, 707/482-4901, www.mysticforestrv.com.

## 18 CHINOOK RV RESORT

**Scenic rating: 7**

on the Klamath River

**Map 1.1, page 73**

The camping area at this park consists of grassy RV sites that overlook the Klamath River. Chinook RV Resort is one of the more well-known parks on the lower Klamath. A boat ramp and fishing supplies are available.

**Campsites, facilities:** There are 70 sites with full hookups (30 and 50 amps) for RVs of any length and a grassy area for tents. Some RV sites are pull-through. An apartment is also available. Picnic tables and fire grills are provided. Restrooms with flush toilets and showers, free cable television, Wi-Fi, coin laundry, fish-cleaning station, recreation room, horseshoes, propane, convenience store, RV supplies and storage, boat ramp, boat rentals, and a tackle shop are available. Leashed pets are permitted.

**Reservations, fees:** Reservations are accepted at 866/482-3511. RV sites are $30-35 per night, tent sites are $20 per night, plus $3 per person per night for more than two people and $3 per night for each additional vehicle. Some credit cards are accepted. Open year-round.

**Directions:** From Eureka, drive north on U.S. 101 to Klamath. After crossing the bridge at the Klamath River, continue north on U.S. 101 for a mile to the campground on the left.

**Contact:** Chinook RV Resort, 707/482-3511, www.chinookrvresort.com.

## 19 FLINT RIDGE HIKE-IN

**Scenic rating: 7**

in Redwood National Park

**Map 1.1, page 73**

This little-known camp is on a grassy bluff overlooking the ocean along the Flint Ridge section of the California Coastal Trail. From the parking area at the trailhead, it's only a five-minute walk to reach a meadow surrounded by a thicket of wild blackberries, alders, and redwoods, with the ocean looming huge to the west, but there is no trail to the beach from here. The parking area, by the way, is an excellent perch to watch for the "puff-of-smoke" spouts from passing whales. A hike out of camp is routed into the forest; it's a two-mile climb to reach a hill filled solid with redwoods. The only problem is that there is no real destination—just in and out with your friend. It's the "Trail to Nowhere."

**Campsites, facilities:** There are eight tent sites. Picnic tables, fire pits, and food lockers are provided. Composting toilets are available. There is no drinking water. Garbage must be packed out. No pets are allowed.

**Reservations, fees:** Reservations are not accepted. A free backcountry permit is required (available from the visitors center or online). There is no fee for camping. Open year-round.

**Directions:** From Eureka, drive north on U.S. 101 to the Klamath River. Just before reaching the bridge at the Klamath River, take the Coastal Drive exit and head west up the hill for four miles to a dirt parking area on the right side of the road. Park here. The campground trailhead is adjacent to the parking area on the east side of the road. Hike 0.25 mile to the camp.

**Contact:** Crescent City Information Center, 707/465-7335, www.crescentcity.org; Redwood National and State Parks, 707/465-7335, www.nps.gov/redw.

## 20 KLAMATH'S CAMPER CORRAL RV PARK AND CAMPGROUND

**Scenic rating: 6**

on the Klamath River

**Map 1.1, page 73**

This 50-acre resort offers 3,000 feet of Klamath River frontage, grassy tent sites, berry picking, access to the ocean, and hiking trails nearby.

And, of course, in the fall it has salmon and steelhead, the main attraction on the lower Klamath. A boat launch is about 1.5 miles from the resort. Nature trails are on the property, and there is room for bike riding. River swimming is popular in summer. A nightly campfire is usually available. Organized recreation is available in summer. A free pancake breakfast is offered to campers on Sundays.

**Campsites, facilities:** There are 134 sites for RVs of any length and 50 tent sites. Many RV sites have full or partial hookups (30 amps) and are pull-through. Picnic tables and fire rings are provided at the tent sites. Drinking water, restrooms with flush toilets and showers, seasonal heated swimming pool, recreation hall, general store, playground, dump station, coin laundry, cable TV, ice, firewood, bait and tackle, fish-cleaning station, fishing guide service, group facilities, arcade, basketball, volleyball, badminton, shuffleboard, horseshoes, table tennis, croquet, and tetherball are available. Leashed pets are permitted.

**Reservations, fees:** Reservations are accepted at 800/701-7275. RV sites are $45-50 per night, tent sites are $35 per night, plus $6 per night for each additional vehicle and $6 per person per night for more than two people. Weekly and monthly rates are available. Some credit cards are accepted. Open April through October.

**Directions:** From Eureka, drive north on U.S. 101 to Klamath. Just after crossing the Klamath River/Golden Bear Bridge, take the Terwer Valley/Highway 169 exit. At the stop sign, turn left, drive under the highway, and continue a short distance west to the campground.

**Contact:** Klamath's Camper Corral, 707/482-5741, www.campercorral.net.

## 21 TERWER PARK

**Scenic rating: 7**

on the Klamath River

**Map 1.1, page 73**

This RV park is situated near the Terwer Riffle, one of the better shore-fishing spots for steelhead and salmon on the lower Klamath River. You'll find grassy sites, river access, and some fair trails along the Klamath. When the salmon arrive in late August and September, Terwer Riffle can be loaded with fish, as well as boaters and shore anglers—a wild scene. Note that at this park, tent campers are separated from the RV park, with tent camping at a grassy area near the river. Some sites are taken by monthly renters.

**Campsites, facilities:** There are 35 sites with full hookups (30 amps) for RVs up to 34 feet, plus a separate tent area. Several sites are pull-through. Five cabins are also available. Picnic tables are provided. Restrooms with flush toilets and showers are available. A pulley boat launch is nearby. Leashed pets are permitted.

**Reservations, fees:** Reservations are accepted. RV sites are $30 per night, tent sites are $25 per night, plus $5 per night for each additional vehicle. Weekly and monthly rates are available. Open April through October.

**Directions:** From Eureka, drive north on U.S. 101 to Klamath and the junction with Highway 169. Turn east on Highway 169 and drive 3.5 miles to Terwer Riffle Road. Turn right on Terwer Riffle Road and drive two blocks, then bear right on Terwer Riffle Road and continue five blocks (about 0.5 mile) to the park at the end of the road.

**Contact:** Terwer Park, 641 Terwer Riffle Rd., Klamath, 707/482-3855 or 866/662-1219.

## 22 GOLD BLUFFS BEACH

### Scenic rating: 8

in Prairie Creek Redwoods State Park

**Map 1.1, page 73**

The campsites are in a sandy, exposed area with windbreaks and with a huge, expansive beach on one side and a backdrop of 100- to 200-foot cliffs on the other side. You can walk for miles at this beach, often without seeing another soul, and there is a great trail routed north through forest, with many hidden little waterfalls. In addition, Fern Canyon Trail, one of the best 30-minute hikes in California, is at the end of Davison Road. Hikers walk along a stream in a narrow canyon, its vertical walls covered with magnificent ferns. Sturdy hikers can continue heading north on the Coastal Trail through its pristine woodlands and fantastic expanses of untouched beaches.

There are some herds of elk in the area, often right along the access road. These camps are rarely used in the winter because of the region's heavy rain and winds. The expanse of beach here is awesome, covering 10 miles of huge, pristine ocean frontage. (See listing for Elk Prairie in this chapter for more information about Prairie Creek Redwoods.)

**Campsites, facilities:** There are 26 sites for tents or RVs up to 24 feet (no hookups). There is one backcountry site (#25). No trailers or vehicles wider than 8 feet are permitted. Fire grills, food lockers, and picnic tables are provided. Drinking water and restrooms with flush toilets and showers are available. Leashed pets are permitted.

**Reservations, fees:** Reservations are not accepted. Sites are $35 per night, plus $8 per night for each additional vehicle. The backcountry site is $10 per night; a free permit is required. Open year-round, weather permitting.

**Directions:** From Eureka, drive north on U.S. 101 for 45 miles to Orick. At Orick, continue north on U.S. 101 for three miles to Davison Road. Turn left (west) on Davison Road and drive six miles to the campground on the left. Note: No vehicles more than 24 feet long or 8 feet wide are permitted on gravel Davison Road, which is narrow and very bumpy.

**Contact:** Redwood National and State Parks, 707/465-7335 or 707/464-6101, www.nps.gov/redw; Prairie Creek Redwoods State Park, 707/465-7335, Visitors Center, 707/465-7354, www.parks.ca.gov.

## 23 ELK PRAIRIE

### Scenic rating: 9

in Prairie Creek Redwoods State Park

**Map 1.1, page 73**     **BEST (**

A small herd of Roosevelt elk wander free in this remarkable 14,000-acre park. Great opportunities for photographs abound, including a group of about five elk often found right along the highway and access roads. Where there are meadows, there are elk; it's about that simple. An elky here, an elky there, making this one of the best places to see wildlife in California. Remember that these are wild animals, they are huge, and they can be unpredictable; in other words, enjoy them, but don't harass them or get too close.

This park consists of old-growth coastal redwoods, prairie lands, and 10 miles of scenic, open beach (Gold Bluff Beach). The interior of the park can be reached by 70 miles of hiking, biking, and nature trails, including a trailhead for a great bike ride at the visitors center. There are many additional trailheads and a beautiful tour of giant redwoods along the Drury Scenic Parkway. Summer interpretive programs with guided walks and junior ranger programs are available through the visitors center. On the James Irvine Trail (trailhead near the visitors center), you can see world-class redwoods, Sitka spruce, western hemlock, and Douglas fir in the span of a few miles. The forest understory is very dense due to moisture from coastal fog. Western azalea and rhododendron blooms, peaking in May and June, are best seen from the Rhododendron Trail. November through May, always bring your rain gear. Summer temperatures range 40-75°F; winter temperatures range 35-55°F.

**Campsites, facilities:** There are 75 sites for tents or RVs up to 27 feet (no hookups), plus one hike-in/bike-in site. Picnic tables, fire rings, and bear-proof food lockers are provided. Drinking water and restrooms with flush toilets and coin showers are available. Some facilities are wheelchair-accessible. Leashed pets are permitted.

**Reservations, fees:** Reservations are accepted January through September at 800/444-7275 or www.reserveamerica.com ($8 reservation fee). Sites are first-come, first-served October through December. Sites are $35 per night, plus $8 per night for each additional vehicle and $5 per person per night for the hike-in/bike-in site. Open year-round.

**Directions:** From Eureka, drive 45 miles north on U.S. 101 to Orick. At Orick, continue north on U.S. 101 for five miles to the Newton B. Drury Scenic Parkway. Take the exit for the Newton B. Drury Scenic Parkway and drive north for a mile to the park. Turn left at the park entrance.

**Contact:** Redwood National and State Parks, 707/465-7335 or 707/464-6101, www.nps.gov/redw; Prairie Creek Redwoods State Park, 707/488-2039 or Visitors Center, 707/465-7335, www.parks.ca.gov.

## 24 STONE LAGOON BOAT-IN

### Scenic rating: 10
in Humboldt Lagoons State Park

**Map 1.1, page 73**     **BEST (**

Virtually nobody knows about this ideal spot for canoeists. While Stone Lagoon is directly adjacent to U.S. 101, the camp is set in a cove that is out of sight of the highway. That makes it a secret spot for a lucky few. It is a great place to explore by canoe or kayak, especially paddling upstream to the lagoon's inlet creek.

After setting up camp, it is possible to hike to a secluded sand spit and stretch of beachfront. You may see elk in this area on the rare occasion. The water is usually calm in the morning but often gets choppy from afternoon winds. Translation: Get your paddling done early on Stone Lagoon. There is also good fishing for cutthroat trout here. The early 1900s saw several dairy ranches established along Stone Lagoon's shore; however, today's regenerated marshland habitat is home to a wide range of marsh flora, as well as birdlife and other creatures.

**Campsites, facilities:** There are six primitive tent sites accessible by boat only. There is no drinking water. Picnic tables, food lockers, and fire rings are provided. Pit toilets are available. Garbage must be packed out. No pets are allowed.

**Reservations, fees:** Reservations are not accepted. Sites are $20 per night; fee includes one vehicle, with a second vehicle costing $8 per night (two-vehicle limit). All campers must register at the Patrick's Point State Park entrance station. Open year-round.

**Directions:** From Eureka, drive 41 miles north on U.S. 101 (15 miles north of Trinidad) to Stone Lagoon. At Stone Lagoon, turn left at the visitors information center. The boat-in campground is in a cove directly across the lagoon from the visitors center. The campsites are dispersed in an area covering about 300 yards in the landing area.

**Contact:** Patrick's Point State Park, 4150 Patrick's Point Dr., 707/677-3570, www.parks.ca.gov.

## 25 BIG LAGOON COUNTY PARK

### Scenic rating: 7
north of Trinidad overlooking the Pacific Ocean

**Map 1.1, page 73**

This is a remarkable, huge lagoon that borders the Pacific Ocean. It provides good boating, excellent exploring, fair fishing, and good duck hunting in the winter. It's a good spot to paddle a canoe around on a calm day. A lot of out-of-towners cruise by, note the lagoon's proximity to the ocean, and figure it must be saltwater. Wrong! Not only is it freshwater, but it provides a long shot for anglers trying for rainbow trout. One reason not many RV drivers stop here is that most of them are drawn farther north (another eight miles) to Freshwater Lagoon.

**Campsites, facilities:** There are 25 sites for tents or small RVs (no hookups). Picnic tables and fire grills are provided. Drinking water and restrooms with flush toilets and showers are available. A boat ramp is also available. Some facilities are wheelchair-accessible. Leashed pets are permitted.

**Reservations, fees:** Reservations are not accepted. Sites are $20 per night per vehicle (maximum 10 people per site), bike-in/walk-in sites are $8 per person per night, there's no charge for children 12 and under with adult, each additional vehicle is $5 per night, and it's $2 per pet per night. Maximum stay is 10 days. Open year-round.

**Directions:** From Eureka, drive 22 miles north on U.S. 101 to Trinidad. At Trinidad, continue north on U.S. 101 for eight miles to Big Lagoon Park Road. Turn left (west) at Big Lagoon Park Road and drive two miles to the park.

**Contact:** Humboldt County Public Works/County Parks, 707/445-7651, www.co.humboldt.ca.us or http://humboldtgov.org; Humboldt Lagoons State Park Visitor Center, 707/488-2041.

## 26 PATRICK'S POINT STATE PARK

### Scenic rating: 10

near Trinidad

**Map 1.1, page 73**

This pretty park covers 640 acres of coastal headlands and is filled with Sitka spruce, dramatic ocean lookouts, and several beautiful beaches, including one with agates, one with tidepools, and another with an expansive stretch of beachfront leading to a lagoon. You can see it best on the Rim Trail, which has many little cutoff routes to the lookouts and down to the beaches. The campground is sheltered in the forest, and while it is often foggy and damp in the summer, it is always beautiful. A Native American village, constructed by the Yurok tribe, is also here. At the north end of the park, a short hike to see the bizarre "Octopus Trees" is a good side trip, with trees that are growing atop downed logs, their root systems exposed like octopus tentacles; the trail here loops through a grove of old-growth Sitka spruce. In addition, there are several miles of pristine beach to the north that extends to the lagoons. Interpretive programs are available. The forest is dense, with spruce, hemlock, pine, fir, and red alder covering an ocean headland. Night and morning fog are common almost year-round, and there are periods when it doesn't lift for days. This area gets 60 inches of rain per year on average. For camping, plan on making reservations.

**Campsites, facilities:** There are 85 sites for tents or RVs (no hookups), 39 sites for RVs up to 31 feet, and two group sites for up to 100 people. Fire grills, storage lockers, and picnic tables are provided. Drinking water and restrooms with flush toilets and coin showers are available. Some facilities are wheelchair-accessible. Leashed pets are permitted at campsites, but not on trails or beaches.

**Reservations, fees:** Site-specific reservations are accepted at 800/444-7275 or www.reserveamerica.com ($8 reservation fee). Abalone and Penn Creek sites are $35 per night, Agate Campground sites are $35-45 per night, plus $8 per night for each additional vehicle. It's $300 per night for the group sites. Open year-round.

**Directions:** From Eureka, drive north on U.S. 101 for 22 miles to Trinidad. At Trinidad, continue north on U.S. 101 for 5.5 miles to Patrick's Point Drive. Take that exit, and at the stop sign turn left and drive 0.5 mile to the park entrance.

**Contact:** Patrick's Point State Park, 707/677-3570, www.parks.ca.gov.

## 27 SOUNDS OF THE SEA RV PARK

🏃 🏊 🏠 🚐 ⛺

### Scenic rating: 6

in Trinidad

**Map 1.1, page 73**

The Trinidad area, about 20 miles north of Eureka, is one of the great places on this planet. Nearby Patrick's Point State Park is one of the highlights, with a Sitka spruce forest, beautiful coastal lookouts, a great easy hike on the Rim Trail, and access to several secluded beaches. To the nearby south at Trinidad Head is a small harbor and dock, with deep-sea and salmon fishing trips available. A breezy beach is to the immediate north of the Seascape Restaurant. A bonus at this privately operated RV park is good berry picking in season.

**Campsites, facilities:** There are 52 sites with full hookups (30 and 50 amps) for tents or RVs of any length; some sites are pull-through. RV rentals and four park-model cabins are also available. Picnic tables and fire rings are provided at most sites. Restrooms with showers, cable TV, Wi-Fi, exercise room and indoor spa (fee), dump station, coin laundry, convenience store, gift shop, propane, firewood, and ice are available. Leashed pets are permitted with certain restrictions.

**Reservations, fees:** Reservations are accepted at 877/489-6360. RV sites are $37-50 per night, tent sites are $35-38 per night, plus $3-5 per person per night for more than two people. Some credit cards are accepted. Open year-round.

**Directions:** From Eureka, drive north on U.S. 101 for 28 miles to Trinidad. In Trinidad, continue north on U.S. 101 for five miles to the Patrick's Point exit. Take the Patrick's Point exit, turn left, and drive 0.5 mile to the park.

**Contact:** Sounds of the Sea RV Park, 707/677-3271, www.soundsofthesea.us.

## 28 SYLVAN HARBOR RV PARK AND CABINS

🏃 🏊 🏠 🦌 🚐

### Scenic rating: 8

in Trinidad

**Map 1.1, page 73**

This park is designed as an RV park and fish camp, with cleaning tables and canning facilities available on-site. It is a short distance from the boat hoist at the Trinidad pier. Beauty surrounds Sylvan Harbor on all sides for miles. Visitors come to enjoy the various beaches, go agate hunting, or look for driftwood on the beach. Nearby Patrick's Point State Park is an excellent side-trip getaway. This is one of several privately operated parks in the Trinidad area, offering a choice of shaded or open sites. (For more information about recreation options nearby, see Sounds of the Sea RV Park listing.)

**Campsites, facilities:** There are 73 sites with full hookups (30 amps) for RVs up to 35 feet. No tents. A storage shed and cable TV are provided. Three cabins are available. Restrooms with showers, fish-cleaning stations, fish smokers, canning facilities, coin laundry, and propane are available. Leashed pets are permitted.

**Reservations, fees:** Reservations are accepted for cabins only. Sites are $34.95 per night, plus $3 per person per night for more than two people. Weekly and monthly rates are available during the summer. Cash or checks only; no credit cards. Open year-round, weather permitting.

**Directions:** From Eureka, drive north on U.S. 101 for 28 miles to the Trinidad exit. Take that exit to Main Street. Turn left on Main Street and drive 0.1 mile under the freeway to Patrick's Point Drive. Turn right on Patrick's Point Drive and drive one mile to the campground on the right at 875 Patrick's Point Drive.

**Contact:** Sylvan Harbor RV Park and Cabins, 707/677-9988, www.sylvanharbor.com.

## 29 VIEW CREST LODGE

### Scenic rating: 8

in Trinidad

**Map 1.1, page 73**

View Crest Lodge is one of the premium spots in Trinidad, with pretty cottages available as well as campsites for RVs and tents. A bonus is the remarkable flights of swallows, many of which have nests at the cottages. Recreation options include deep-sea and salmon fishing at Trinidad Harbor to the nearby south, and outstanding easy hiking at Patrick's Point State Park to the nearby north.

**Campsites, facilities:** There are 36 sites with full hookups (20 and 30 amps) for RVs of any length and a separate area for 12 tent sites. Some sites are pull-through. Twelve cottages are also available. Picnic tables and fire rings are provided. Restrooms with showers, cable TV, Wi-Fi, a coin laundry, fish-cleaning station, and firewood are available. Leashed pets are permitted only in the campground.

**Reservations, fees:** Reservations are accepted. RV sites are $29-40 per night, tent sites are $27, plus $3 per person per night for more than two people over age 12. Monthly rates are available. Some credit cards are accepted. Open year-round.

**Directions:** From Eureka, drive north on U.S. 101 for 28 miles to Trinidad. Take the Patrick's Point State Park exit. Continue north for five miles to Patrick's Point Drive. Turn left and drive 0.9 mile to the lodge on the left.

**Contact:** View Crest Lodge, 707/677-3393, www.viewcrestlodge.com.

## 30 EMERALD FOREST

### Scenic rating: 5

in Trinidad

**Map 1.1, page 73**

This campground is set on 12 acres of redwoods, often dark and wet, with the ocean at Trinidad Head only about a five-minute drive away. The campground owners emphasize that they are a vacation and overnight park only, and not a mobile home or long-term park.

**Campsites, facilities:** There are 46 sites with full or partial hookups (30 amps) for RVs up to 45 feet, along with 30 tent sites. Some sites are pull-through. There are also 19 cabins. Picnic tables, fire rings, and barbecues are provided. Restrooms, showers, free cable TV in RV sites, playground, convenience store, ice, firewood, coin laundry, group facilities, fish-cleaning station, dump station, propane, telephone hookups, Wi-Fi, volleyball, horseshoes, badminton, bicycle rentals, and video arcade are available. Leashed pets are permitted, except in the tent sites or cabins.

**Reservations, fees:** Reservations are recommended in the summer. RV sites are $38-48 per night, plus $3 per person per night for more than two people; tent sites are $35 per night. Winter rates are available. Some credit cards are accepted. Pets are permitted in RV sites only. Open year-round.

**Directions:** From Eureka, drive north on U.S. 101 for 28 miles to the Trinidad exit. Take that exit to Main Street. Turn left on Main Street and drive 0.1 mile under the freeway to Patrick's Point Drive. Turn right on Patrick's Point Drive and drive 0.9 mile north to the campground.

**Contact:** Emerald Forest, 753 Patrick's Point Dr., 707/677-3554, www.rvintheredwoods.com.

## 31 HIDDEN CREEK

### Scenic rating: 5

in Trinidad

**Map 1.1, page 73**

To tell you the truth, there really isn't much hidden about this RV park, but you might be hard-pressed to find year-round Parker Creek. Regardless, it is in a pretty location in Trinidad, with the Trinidad pier, adjacent harbor, restaurants, and beach all within a drive of just a minute or two. Deep-sea fishing for salmon, lingcod, and rockfish is available on boats out of Trinidad Harbor. Crab and albacore tuna are also caught here, and there's beachcombing for agates and driftwood on the beach to the immediate north. Note that half of the sites are filled with long-term renters.

**Campsites, facilities:** There are 56 sites with full or partial hookups (30 and 50 amps) for RVs up to 40 feet, and a grassy area for tents. Six park-model cabins are also available. Picnic tables are provided. Cable TV, restrooms with showers, fish-cleaning station, ice, picnic area, and a dump station are available. Leashed pets are permitted.

**Reservations, fees:** Reservations are recommended in the summer. RV sites are $30 per night, tent sites are $20 per night, plus $2 per person per night for more than two people. Villas and cabins are available. Long-term rates are available. Open year-round.

**Directions:** From Eureka, drive north on U.S. 101 for 28 miles to Trinidad. Take the Trinidad exit to the stop sign. Turn right at Westhaven Drive and drive a short distance to the RV park on the left.

**Contact:** Hidden Creek RV Park, 199 N. Westhaven, 707/677-3775, www.hidden-creekrvpark.com.

## 32 CLAM BEACH COUNTY PARK

### Scenic rating: 7

near McKinleyville

**Map 1.2, page 74**

Here awaits a beach that seems to stretch on forever, one of the great places to bring a lover, dog, children, or, hey, all three. While the campsites are a bit exposed, making winds out of the north a problem in the spring, the direct beach access largely makes up for it. The park gets its name from the fair clamming that is available, but you must come equipped with a clam gun or special clam shovel, and then be out when minus low tides arrive at daybreak. Most people just enjoy playing tag with the waves, taking long romantic walks, or throwing sticks for the dog.

**Campsites, facilities:** There are nine tent sites and a parking lot for nine RVs of any length (no hookups). Picnic tables and fire rings are provided. Drinking water and vault toilets are available. Propane gas, grocery store, and a coin laundry are available in McKinleyville. Some facilities are wheelchair-accessible. Leashed pets are permitted.

**Reservations, fees:** Reservations are not accepted. Sites are $15 per night per vehicle, plus $5 per night for one additional vehicle and $2 per pet per night; it's $8 per person per night for hike-in/bike-in. Maximum stay is three days. Open year-round.

**Directions:** From Eureka, drive north on U.S. 101 to McKinleyville. Continue past McKinleyville to the Clam Beach Park exit. Take that exit and turn west at the sign for Clam Beach. Drive two blocks to the campground, which is adjacent to Little River State Beach.

**Contact:** Humboldt County Public Works, 707/445-7651, www.co.humboldt.ca.us.

## 33 MAD RIVER RAPIDS RV PARK

### Scenic rating: 7

in Arcata

**Map 1.2, page 74**

This park is near the farmlands on the outskirts of town, in a pastoral, quiet setting. There is a great bike ride nearby on a trail routed along the Mad River, and it is also excellent for taking a dog for a walk. Nearby Arcata is a unique town, a bit of the old and a bit of the new, and the Arcata Marsh at the north end of Humboldt Bay provides a scenic and easy bicycle trip, as well as an excellent destination for hiking, sightseeing, and bird-watching. About half of the sites are filled with long-term renters.

**Campsites, facilities:** There are 92 sites with full hookups (30 and 50 amps) for RVs of any length; some sites are pull-through. Picnic tables are provided. Fire grills are provided at two sites. Cable TV, Wi-Fi, a dump station, restrooms with showers, a recreation room, tennis courts, fitness room, playground, basketball courts, jogging trail, arcade, billiards, table tennis, horseshoe pits, heated seasonal swimming pool, spa, group facilities, restaurant and bar, convenience store, RV supplies, and coin laundry are available. A motel is adjacent to the park. Some facilities are wheelchair-accessible. Leashed pets are permitted.

**Reservations, fees:** Reservations are accepted at 800/822-7776. Sites are $39-49 per night, plus $3 per night per additional vehicle and $3 per person per night for more than two people. Some credit cards are accepted. Weekly and monthly rates are available. Open year-round.

**Directions:** From the junction of U.S. 101 and Highway 299 in Arcata, drive 0.25 mile north on U.S. 101 to the Giuntoli Lane/Janes Road exit. Take that exit and turn left (west) on Janes Road, then drive two blocks to the park on the left.

**Contact:** Mad River Rapids RV Park, 707/822-7275, www.madriverrv.com.

## 34 REDWOOD COAST CABIN AND RV RESORT

🚶 🚴 🏊 🛶 🎣 🐕 ♿ 🚐 ⛺

**Scenic rating: 2**

in Eureka

**Map 1.2, page 74**

This is a year-round camp for U.S. 101 cruisers looking for a layover spot in Eureka. A bonus is that there are a few cabins, log-style jobs that win on cuteness alone, as well as a giant playground for kids. The closest significant recreation option is the Arcata Marsh on Humboldt Bay, a richly diverse spot with good trails for biking and hiking or just parking and looking at the water. Another option is excellent salmon fishing in June, July, and August.

**Campsites, facilities:** There are 140 sites with full or partial hookups (30 and 50 amps) for RVs of any length, 30 tent sites, and eight hike-in/bike-in sites. Most RV sites are pull-through. Ten camping cabins and two cottages are also available. Picnic tables and fire pits are provided. Drinking water, restrooms with flush toilets and showers, cable TV, playground, recreation room, seasonal heated swimming pool, two spas, convenience store, coin laundry, horseshoe pits, volleyball and basketball court, mini golf, dog run/park, dump station, propane, ice, firewood, fax machine, and Wi-Fi are available. Some facilities are wheelchair-accessible. Leashed pets are permitted.

**Reservations, fees:** Reservations are accepted for cabins and tents at 707/822-4243 and for RVs at 707/798-6444. RV sites are $40-65 per night, tent sites are $39-45 per night, plus $3 per person per night for more than two people, $3 per pet per night, and $2 per night for each additional vehicle; it's $17 per person per night for hike-in/bike-in sites. Some credit cards are accepted. Open year-round.

**Directions:** From Eureka, drive north on U.S. 101 for four miles to KOA Drive (well signed on east side of highway). Turn right on KOA Drive and drive a short distance to the end of the road.

**Contact:** Redwood Coast Cabin and RV Resort, 707/822-4243, www.redwoodcoastrv.com.

## 35 SAMOA BOAT RAMP COUNTY PARK

🏊 🛶 🎣 🐕 🚐 ⛺

**Scenic rating: 7**

on Humboldt Bay near Eureka

**Map 1.2, page 74**

The nearby vicinity of the boat ramp, with access to Humboldt Bay and the Pacific Ocean, makes this a star attraction for campers towing their fishing boats. Near the campground you'll find good beachcombing and clamming at low tides, and a chance to see a huge variety of seabirds, highlighted by egrets and herons. There's a reason: Directly across the bay is the Humboldt Bay National Wildlife Refuge. Adjacent to the park is the Samoa Dunes Recreation Area, which is popular with ATV enthusiasts who are allowed to ride on the beach. This park is set near the famed all-you-can-eat, logger-style Samoa Cookhouse. The park is on the bay, not on the ocean.

**Campsites, facilities:** There are 25 sites for tents or RVs of any length (no hookups). Overflow camping for tents or RVs of any length is also available in a parking lot. Picnic tables and fire grills are provided. Drinking water and restrooms with flush toilets and coin showers are available. A boat ramp, grocery store, propane, and a coin laundry are available in Eureka (about five miles away). Leashed pets are permitted.

**Reservations, fees:** Reservations are not accepted. Sites are $20 per night with one vehicle, plus $5 per night for each additional vehicle and $2 per pet per night; hike-in/bike-in sites are $8 per person per night. Maximum stay is seven days. Open year-round.

**Directions:** From U.S. 101 in Eureka, turn west on Highway 255 and drive two miles until it dead-ends at New Navy Base Road. At New Navy Base Road, turn left and drive five miles to the end of the Samoa Peninsula and the campground entrance.

**Contact:** Humboldt County Public Works, 707/445-7651, www.co.humboldt.ca.us.

## 36 E-Z LANDING RV PARK AND MARINA

**Scenic rating: 6**

on Humboldt Bay

**Map 1.2, page 74**

In July and August, big schools of king salmon often teem just west of the entrance of Humboldt Bay. E-Z Landing provides a good base camp for salmon fishing, with a nearby boat ramp with access to Humboldt Bay. It's not the prettiest camp in the world, with quite a bit of asphalt, but most people use this camp as a simple parking spot for sleeping and getting down to the business of the day: fishing. This spot is ideal for ocean fishing, clamming, beachcombing, and boating. There are a few long-term and seasonal renters here.

**Campsites, facilities:** There are 45 RV sites with full hookups (30 amps); some sites are pull-through. Restrooms with flush toilets and showers, marine gas, ice, coin laundry, bait, and boat slips are available. Some facilities are wheelchair-accessible. Leashed pets are permitted.

**Reservations, fees:** Reservations are accepted. RV sites are $20.40 per night. Some credit cards are accepted. Open year-round.

**Directions:** From Eureka, drive 3.5 miles south on U.S. 101 to King Salmon Avenue. Turn west (right) on King Salmon Avenue (it becomes Buhne Drive) and drive for 0.5 mile to where the road turns. Turn left (south) on Buhne Drive and go 0.5 mile to the park on the left.

**Contact:** E-Z Landing RV Park and Marina, 1875 Buhne Dr., 707/442-1118.

## 37 JOHNNY'S MARINA AND RV PARK

**Scenic rating: 5**

on Humboldt Bay near Eureka

**Map 1.2, page 74**

This is a good base camp for salmon fishing during the peak season—always call, since the season changes each year as set by the Department of Fish and Game. Mooring for private boats is available, a nice plus for campers trailering boats. Other recreation activities include beachcombing, clamming, and perch fishing from shore. The owners have run this place since 1948. Note that a number of sites are filled with long-term renters, usually anglers who come for the season. So when the fishing is good, more space is tied up.

**Campsites, facilities:** There are 53 sites with

full hookups (30 and 50 amps) for self-contained RVs up to 38 feet. There are no toilets or showers. Coin laundry and a boat dock are available. Leashed pets are permitted.

**Reservations, fees:** Reservations are accepted. Sites are $30 per night, plus $1 per person per night for more than two people. Open year-round.

**Directions:** From Eureka, drive 3.5 miles south on U.S. 101 to King Salmon Avenue. Turn west (right) on King Salmon Avenue (it becomes Buhne Drive). Continue about 0.5 mile to the park on the left.

**Contact:** Johnny's Marina and RV Park, 1821 Buhne Dr., 707/442-2284.

## 38 VAN DUZEN COUNTY PARK: SWIMMER'S DELIGHT

🏃 ≈ 🛶 🏊 🐕 🏕 ♿ 🚐 ⛺

### Scenic rating: 6

on the Van Duzen River

**Map 1.2, page 74**

This campground is near the headwaters of the Van Duzen River, one of the Eel River's major tributaries. The river is subject to tremendous fluctuations in flows and height, so low in the fall that it is often temporarily closed to fishing by the Department of Fish and Game, so high in the winter that only fools would stick their toes in. For a short period in late spring, it provides a benign run for rafting and canoeing, putting in at Grizzly Creek and taking out at Van Duzen. In October, you'll find an excellent salmon fishing spot where the Van Duzen enters the Eel.

**Campsites, facilities:** There are 30 sites for tents or small RVs; some sites have partial hookups (30 amps). Picnic tables and fire grills are provided. Drinking water and restrooms with flush toilets and coin showers are available. A grocery store and coin laundry are nearby. Some facilities are wheelchair-accessible. Leashed pets are permitted in the campground but not on the beach.

**Reservations, fees:** Reservations are not accepted. Sites are $20 per night, hike-in/bike-in sites are $8 per person per night, plus $5 per night for each additional vehicle and $2 per pet per night. Maximum stay is 10 days. Open year-round.

**Directions:** From Eureka, drive south on U.S. 101 to the junction of Highway 36 at Alton. Turn east on Highway 36 and drive 12 miles to the campground.

**Contact:** Humboldt County Public Works, 707/445-7651, www.co.humboldt.ca.us.

## 39 GRIZZLY CREEK REDWOODS STATE PARK

🏃 ≈ 🛶 🐕 ♿ 🚐 ⛺

### Scenic rating: 8

near Bridgeville

**Map 1.2, page 74**

Most summer vacationers hit the campgrounds on the Redwood Highway; that is, U.S. 101. However, this camp is just far enough off the beaten path to provide some semblance of seclusion. It is set in redwoods, quite beautiful, with fair hiking and good access to the adjacent Van Duzen River. The park encompasses only a few acres, yet it is very intimate. There are 4.5 miles of hiking trails, a visitors center with exhibits, and a bookstore. The Cheatham Grove in this park is an exceptional stand of coast redwoods. Fishing is catch-and-release only with barbless hooks. Nearby attractions include the Victorian village of Ferndale and Fort Humboldt to the north, Humboldt Redwoods State Park to the south, and Ruth Lake to the more distant east. Insider's tip: Half of the park borders Highway 36, and you can hear highway noise from some campsites.

**Campsites, facilities:** There are 10 tent sites, nine sites for tents or small RVs, 11 sites for RVs up to 30 feet or trailers up to 24 feet, one hike-in/bike-in site, and one group site (no hookups). Picnic tables, food lockers, and fire grills are provided. Drinking water and restrooms with flush toilets and showers are available. A grocery store is available within 3.5 miles. Some facilities are wheelchair-accessible. Leashed pets are permitted in the campground but not on trails or the beach area.

**Reservations, fees:** Reservations are accepted at 800/444-7275 or www.reserveamerica.com ($8 reservation fee); the group site may be reserved by calling 707/777-3683. Sites are $35 per night, plus $8 per night for each additional vehicle; it's $5 per person per night for the hike-in/bike-in site and $90 per night for the group site. Open year-round.

**Directions:** From Eureka, drive south on U.S. 101 to the junction of Highway 36 at Alton. Turn east on Highway 36 and drive about 17 miles to the campground on the right.

**Contact:** Humboldt County Parks and Recreation, 707/445-7651, http://co.humboldt.ca.us; Grizzly Creek Redwoods State Park, 707/777-3683, www.parks.ca.gov.

## 40 ALBEE CREEK

### Scenic rating: 8
in Humboldt Redwoods State Park

**Map 1.2, page 74**

Humboldt Redwoods State Park is a massive sprawl of forest that is known for some unusual giant trees in the Federation Grove and Big Tree Area. The park covers nearly 53,000 acres, including more than 17,000 acres of old-growth coast redwoods. It has 100 miles of hiking trails, many excellent, both short and long. The camp is set in a redwood grove, and the smell of these trees has a special magic. Nearby Albee Creek, a benign trickle most of the year, can flood in the winter after heavy rains. Seasonal interpretive programs, campfire talks, nature walks, and junior ranger programs are available.

**Campsites, facilities:** There are 40 sites for tents or RVs up to 33 feet and trailers up to 24 feet (no hookups); five environmental sites; and a hike-in/bike-in site. Picnic tables, fire grills, and food lockers are provided. Drinking water, restrooms with flush toilets and showers, and firewood are available. Some facilities are wheelchair-accessible. Leashed pets are permitted.

**Reservations, fees:** Reservations are accepted at 800/444-7275 or www.reserveamerica.com ($8 reservation fee). Sites are $45-55 per night. Open Memorial Day weekend through mid-October.

**Directions:** From Eureka, drive south on U.S. 101 about 43 miles to the Honeydew exit (if you reach Weott, you have gone two miles too far). At Mattole Road, turn west and drive five miles to the campground on the right.

**Contact:** Humboldt Redwoods State Park, 707/946-2472 or 707/946-2409; Visitor Center, 707/946-2263, www.parks.ca.gov.

## 41 CUNEO CREEK HORSE CAMP

### Scenic rating: 7
in Humboldt Redwoods State Park

**Map 1.2, page 74**

This is a horse camp within Humboldt Redwoods State Park near the South Fork Eel River. The site is woodsy and far enough away from other camps in the park to often make it feel all your own. Though it is primarily a camp set up for equestrians, you can also use it as a base camp for kayak trips on the nearby South Fork Eel, or for hiking and biking trips nearby.

**Campsites, facilities:** There are five individual (environmental sites) and two group sites for tents and RVs for up to 25 and 65 people, with parking space for horse trailers. Picnic tables and fire rings are provided. Drinking water, coin showers, and flush toilets are available. There are water troughs and corrals for horses. Some facilities are wheelchair-accessible. Leashed pets are permitted.

**Reservations, fees:** Reservations are accepted May through September at 800/444-7275 or www.reserveamerica.com ($8 reservation fee). Individual sites are $35 per night, plus $8 per night for each additional vehicle. Group sites are $135-200. Open mid-April to mid-October.

**Directions:** From Eureka, drive south on U.S. 101 about 43 miles to the Honeydew exit (if you reach Weott, you have gone two miles too far). At Mattole Road, turn west and drive eight miles to the Cuneo Creek Horse Campground sign. Turn right onto the entrance road and continue to the campground.

**Contact:** Humboldt Redwoods State Park, 707/946-2409; Visitor Center, 707/946-2263, www.parks.ca.gov.

## 42 BURLINGTON

### Scenic rating: 7
in Humboldt Redwoods State Park

**Map 1.2, page 74**

This camp is one of the centerpieces of Humboldt Redwoods State Park. Humboldt is California's largest redwood state park and also includes the largest remaining contiguous old-growth coastal redwood forest in the world: the Rockefeller Forest. The trees here are thousands of years old and have never been logged; they are as pristine now as 200 years ago. The park has hundreds of miles of trails, but it is little 0.5-mile Founders Grove Nature Trail that has the quickest payoff and requires the least effort. The average rainfall here is 65 inches per year, with most occurring between October and May. Morning and evening fog in the summer keeps the temperature cool in the river basin.

At Burlington, you get shady sites with big redwood stumps that kids can play on. There's good hiking on trails routed through the redwoods, and in winter, steelhead fishing is often good on the nearby Eel River. However, this camp is often at capacity during the tourist months, and sites tend to be packed close together with plenty of RVs. There's road noise from Avenue of the Giants a few feet away.

**Campsites, facilities:** There are 57 sites for tents or RVs up to 33 feet (no hookups) and trailers up to 24 feet, plus three hike-in/bike-in

sites. Picnic tables, fire grills, and food lockers are provided. Drinking water, restrooms with flush toilets and showers, and firewood are available. Some facilities are wheelchair-accessible. Leashed pets are permitted.

**Reservations, fees:** Reservations are accepted at 800/444-7275 or www.reserveamerica.com ($8 reservation fee). Sites are $35 per night, plus $8 per night for each additional vehicle, and it's $5 per person per night for hike-in/bike-in sites. Open year-round.

**Directions:** From Eureka, drive south on U.S. 101 for 45 miles to the Weott/Newton Road exit. Turn right on Newton Road and continue to the T junction where Newton Road meets the Avenue of the Giants. Turn left on the Avenue of the Giants and drive two miles to the campground entrance on the left.

**Contact:** Humboldt Redwoods State Park, 707/946-1811 or 707/946-2409; Visitor Center, 707/946-2263, www.parks.ca.gov.

## 43 HIDDEN SPRINGS

### Scenic rating: 7
in Humboldt Redwoods State Park

**Map 1.2, page 74**

This camp gets heavy use from May through September, but the campsites have been situated in a way that offers relative seclusion. Side trips include good hiking on trails routed through redwoods and a touring drive on Avenue of the Giants. The park has more than 100 miles of hiking trails, many of them amid spectacular giant redwoods, including Bull Creek Flats Trail and Founders Grove Nature Trail. Bears are occasionally spotted by mountain bikers on rides out to the park's outskirts. In winter, nearby High Rock on the Eel River is one of the better shoreline fishing spots for steelhead. (For more information on Humboldt Redwoods, see Albee Creek and Burlington listings.)

**Campsites, facilities:** There are 155 sites for tents or RVs up to 33 feet (no hookups) and trailers up to 24 feet. Picnic tables, fire grills, and food lockers are provided. Drinking water, restrooms with flush toilets and showers, and firewood are available. A grocery store and coin laundry are available within one mile in Myers Flat. Leashed pets are permitted.

**Reservations, fees:** Reservations are accepted at 800/444-7275 or www.reserveamerica.com ($8 reservation fee). Sites are $35 per night, plus $8 per night for each additional vehicle. Open mid-April through Labor Day weekend.

**Directions:** From Eureka, drive south 50 miles on U.S. 101 to the Myers Flat/Avenue of the Giants exit. Continue south and drive less than a mile to the campground entrance on the left.

**Contact:** Humboldt Redwoods State Park, 707/943-3177 or 707/946-2409; Visitor Center, 707/946-2263, www.parks.ca.gov.

## 44 GIANT REDWOODS RV AND CAMP

### Scenic rating: 8
on the Eel River near Myers Flat

**Map 1.2, page 74**

This privately operated park is in a grove of redwoods and covers 23 acres, much of it fronting the Eel River. Trip options include the scenic drive on Avenue of the Giants.

**Campsites, facilities:** There are 26 tent sites and 55 sites for RVs of any length. RV sites have full or partial hookups (50 amps), and some are pull-through. Picnic tables and fire rings are provided. Restrooms with showers, free Wi-Fi, cable TV, a convenience store, ice, coin laundry, playground, volleyball court, tetherball, horseshoe pits, boat launch, dog "freedom area," and a recreation room are available. A camp host is on-site. Leashed pets are permitted.

**Reservations, fees:** Reservations are recommended in the summer. RV sites are $40-49 per night, tent sites are $40-43 per night, primitive sites are $35 per night, plus $3 per person per night for more than two people and $5 per night per additional vehicle. Discounted winter

rates and weekly rates are available. Some credit cards are accepted. Open year-round.

**Directions:** From Eureka, drive south 50 miles on U.S. 101 to the Myers Flat/Avenue of the Giants exit. Turn right on Avenue of the Giants and make a quick left onto Myers Avenue. Drive 0.25 mile on Myers Avenue to the campground entrance at 351 Myers Avenue.

**Contact:** Giant Redwoods RV and Camp, 707/943-9999, http://giantredwoodsrv.com.

## 45 DEAN CREEK RESORT

### Scenic rating: 7
on the South Fork Eel River

**Map 1.2, page 74**

This very family-oriented year-round RV park is on the South Fork Eel River. In the summer, it makes a good base camp for a redwood park adventure, with Humboldt Redwoods State Park (well north of here) providing 100 miles of hiking trails, many routed through awesome stands of giant trees. In the winter heavy rains feed the South Fork Eel, inspiring steelhead upstream on their annual winter journey. Fishing is good in this area, best by shore at nearby High Rock. Bank access is good at several other spots. Note that there is catch-and-release fishing only; check fishing regulations. Contact information for fishing guides is available at the resort, and they offer winter steelhead fishing specials. An excellent side trip is to drive three miles south to the Avenue of the Giants, a tour through giant redwood trees. The campground also offers volleyball, shuffleboard, badminton, and horseshoes. You get the idea.

**Campsites, facilities:** There are 64 sites for tents or RVs of any length with full or partial hookups (30 and 50 amps); some sites are pull-through. Picnic tables and fire grills are provided. Restrooms with showers, a recreation room, a coin laundry, a motel, a convenience store, and Wi-Fi access, RV supplies, firewood, ice, a giant spa, a sauna, a seasonal heated swimming pool, a dump station, an amphitheater, group facilities, an arcade, basketball, tetherball, shuffleboard, volleyball, mini golf, and a playground are available. Some facilities are wheelchair-accessible. Leashed pets are permitted.

**Reservations, fees:** Reservations are recommended in the summer at 877/923-2555. RV sites are $33-49 per night, tent sites are $25-40 per night, plus $5 per person per night for more than two people and $1.50 per night for each additional vehicle. Some credit cards are accepted. Open year-round.

**Directions:** From Eureka, drive 60 miles south on U.S. 101 to the Redwood Drive exit. Exit onto Redwood Drive and continue about one-half block to the motel/campground entrance on the right; check in at the motel.

**Contact:** Dean Creek Resort, 707/923-2555, www.deancreekresort.com.

## 46 BENBOW KOA

**Scenic rating: 7**

on the South Fork Eel River

**Map 1.2, page 74**

This is an RV park with a pretty nine-hole regulation golf course set along U.S. 101 and the South Fork Eel River. It takes on a dramatically different character in the winter, when the highway is largely abandoned, the river comes up, and steelhead migrate upstream to the stretch of water here. Cooks Valley and Benbow provide good shore fishing access. Note that fishing restrictions for steelhead are extremely severe and subject to constant change; always check with the DFG before fishing for steelhead.

**Campsites, facilities:** There are 112 sites for RVs or tents with full hookups (30 and 50 amps), including six "VIP" sites for RVs of any length. Many sites are pull-through. Cottages and park-model cabin rentals are also available. Picnic tables and cable TV are provided. Restrooms with showers, a coin laundry, convenience store, snack bar, playground, recreation room, seasonal heated swimming pool, seasonal spa, Wi-Fi, fax and copy services, group facilities, organized activities, shuffleboard, table tennis, horseshoes, game room, RV supplies, and a nine-hole golf course are available. Some facilities are wheelchair-accessible. Leashed pets are permitted. A doggy playground and pet wash are available.

**Reservations, fees:** Reservations are accepted at 800/562-7518. Sites are $46-73 per night, plus $5 per person per night for more than two people and $3 per pet per night. Discounted rates are offered fall through spring. Some credit cards are accepted. Open year-round.

**Directions:** From the junction of U.S. 101 and Highway 1 in Leggett, drive north on U.S. 101 past Richardson Grove State Park to the Benbow Drive exit (two miles south of Garberville). Take that exit and turn right at the stop sign. Drive a short distance to the end of the road and Benbow Drive. Bear left on Benbow Drive and continue a short distance to the resort on the left.

**Contact:** Benbow KOA, 7000 Benbow Dr., 707/923-2777, www.benbowrv.com.

## 47 MADRONE, HUCKLEBERRY, AND DAWN REDWOOD

**Scenic rating: 8**

in Richardson Grove State Park

**Map 1.2, page 74**

The highway cuts a swath right through Richardson Grove State Park, and everyone slows to gawk at the tallest trees in the world, one of the most impressive groves of redwoods you can drive through in California. To explore further, there are several campgrounds available at the park, as well as a network of outstanding hiking trails. The best of these are the short Exhibit Trail, Settler's Trail, and Toumey Trail. The Eel River runs through the park, providing swimming holes in summer. Richardson Grove is one of the prettiest and most popular state parks, making reservations a necessity from Memorial Day through Labor Day weekend. When arriving from points south on U.S. 101, this is the first park in the Redwood Empire where you will encounter significant old-growth redwoods. There are nine miles of hiking trails, fishing in the winter for steelhead, and several trees of significant note.

**Campsites, facilities:** At Madrone Camp, there are 40 sites for tents or RVs up to 30 feet. At Huckleberry, there are 36 sites for tents or RVs up to 30 feet (no hookups). Dawn Redwood is a group camp (9-40 people) open in summer only. Picnic tables, food lockers, and fire grills are provided. Drinking water and restrooms with flush toilets and coin showers are available. Wi-Fi is available near the ranger station. A dump station is three miles away. Some facilities are wheelchair-accessible. Leashed pets are permitted at campsites only.

**Reservations, fees:** Reservations are accepted January through September at 800/444-7275 or www.reserveamerica.com ($8 reservation fee). October through December sites are first-come, first-served. Sites are $35 per night, plus $8 per night for each additional vehicle. The group camp is $150 per night and a special-use permit is required. Open year-round but subject to occasional winter closures.

**Directions:** From the junction of U.S. 101 and Highway 1 in Leggett, drive north on U.S. 101 for 16 miles (past Piercy) to the park entrance along the west (left) side of the road (eight miles south of Garberville).

**Contact:** Richardson Grove State Park, 707/247-3318, www.parks.ca.gov.

## 48 OAK FLAT

🏃 🏊 🛶 🐾 🚙 🚐 ⛺

### Scenic rating: 8
in Richardson Grove State Park

Map 1.2, page 74

Oak Flat is on the eastern side of the Eel River in the shade of forest and provides easy access to the river. The campground is open only in the summer. (For side-trip information, see the listing for Madrone, Huckleberry, and Dawn Redwood in this chapter.)

**Campsites, facilities:** There are 94 sites for tents or RVs up to 24 feet (no hookups) and trailers up to 18 feet. Picnic tables, food lockers, and fire grills are provided. Drinking water, restrooms with flush toilets and coin showers, and Wi-Fi are available. A grocery store and propane gas are available nearby. Leashed pets are permitted.

**Reservations, fees:** Reservations are accepted at 800/444-7275 or www.reserveamerica.com ($8 reservation fee). Sites are $45 per night, plus $8 per night for each additional vehicle. Open mid-June through mid-September, weather permitting.

**Directions:** From the junction of U.S. 101 and Highway 1 in Leggett, drive north on U.S. 101 for 16 miles (past Piercy) to the park entrance on the west (left) side of the road (eight miles south of Garberville).

**Contact:** Richardson Grove State Park, 707/247-3318, www.parks.ca.gov.

## 49 RICHARDSON GROVE CAMPGROUND AND RV PARK

🏃 🏊 🛶 🐾 🏕 🚐 ⛺

### Scenic rating: 7
on the South Fork Eel River

Map 1.2, page 74

This private camp provides a nearby alternative to Richardson Grove State Park, complete with cabin rentals. The state park, with its grove of giant redwoods and excellent hiking, is the primary attraction. The RV park is family-oriented, with volleyball and basketball courts and horseshoe pits. The adjacent South Fork Eel River may look like a trickle in the summer, but there are some good swimming holes. It also provides good steelhead fishing in January and February, with especially good shore fishing access here as well as to the south in Cooks Valley (check DFG regulations before fishing). This campground is owned and operated by the Northern California/Nevada District Assemblies of God.

**Campsites, facilities:** There are 98 sites for tents or RVs; some sites are pull-through, and many have full or partial hookups (30 amps). Two log cabins are also available. Picnic tables and fire rings are provided. Restrooms with showers, dump station, Wi-Fi, playground, coin laundry, convenience store, group facilities, propane, and ice are available. Leashed pets are permitted.

**Reservations, fees:** Reservations are recommended in the summer. RV sites are $35-45 per night; tent sites are $30 per night. Weekly, winter, and group rates are available. Some credit cards are accepted. Open year-round.

**Directions:** From the junction of U.S. 101 and Highway 1 in Leggett, drive north on U.S. 101 for 15 miles (1 mile before reaching Richardson Grove State Park) to the camp entrance on the west (left) side of the road.

**Contact:** Richardson Grove Campground and RV Park, 707/247-3380, www.redwoodfamily-camp.com.

## 50 MATTOLE

**Scenic rating: 8**

in King Range National Conservation Area

**Map 1.2, page 74**

The Lost Coast is often overlooked by visitors because of the difficulty in reaching it; your only access is via a slow, curvy road through the Mattole River Valley, past Petrolia, and out to a piece of coast. The experience is like being in suspended animation—your surroundings peaceful and pristine, with a striking lack of people. One of the best ways to capture the sensation is to drive out near the mouth of the Mattole, then hike south on the Coastal Trail long enough to get a feel for the area.

This is a little-known camp set at the mouth of the Mattole River, right where it pours into the Pacific Ocean. It is beautiful and isolated.

An outstanding hike leads to the Punta Gorda Lighthouse. Hike from the campground to the ocean and head south. It's a level walk, and at low tide, there's a chance to observe tidepool life. Perch fishing is good where the Mattole flows into the ocean, best during low tides. In the winter, the Mattole often provides excellent steelhead fishing. Check the Department of Fish and Game regulations for closed areas. Be sure to have a full tank on the way out—the nearest gas station is quite distant.

**Campsites, facilities:** There are 14 sites for tents or RVs up to 16 feet (no hookups). Picnic tables and fire rings are provided. Drinking water and vault toilets are available. Some facilities are wheelchair-accessible. Leashed pets are permitted.

**Reservations, fees:** Reservations are not accepted. Sites are $8 per night. Open year-round.

**Directions:** From U.S. 101 north of Garberville, take the South Fork-Honeydew exit and drive west to Honeydew. At Honeydew and Mattole Road, turn right on Mattole Road and drive toward Petrolia. At the second bridge over the Mattole River, one mile before Petrolia, turn west on Lighthouse Road and drive five miles to the campground at the end of the road.

**Contact:** King Range National Conservation Area, 707/986-5400; Bureau of Land Management, Arcata Field Office, 707/825-2300, www.blm.gov/ca; Department of Fish & Game, Low-Flow Fishing Information, 707/442-4502.

## 51 A. W. WAY COUNTY PARK

**Scenic rating: 8**

on the Mattole River

**Map 1.2, page 74**

This secluded camp provides a home for visitors to the Lost Coast, the beautiful coastal stretch of California far from any semblance of urban life. The highlight is the Mattole River, a great steelhead stream when flows are suitable between January and mid-March. Nearby is excellent hiking in the King Range National Conservation Area. For the great hike out to the abandoned Punta Gorda Lighthouse, drive to the trailhead on the left side of Lighthouse Road (see the Mattole listing in this chapter). This area is typically bombarded with monsoon-level rains in winter.

**Campsites, facilities:** There are 30 sites for tents or small RVs (no hookups). Overflow camping is also available. Picnic tables and fire grills are provided. Drinking water, restrooms with flush toilets, and coin showers are available. A grocery store, coin laundry, and propane gas are available nearby. Leashed pets are permitted.

**Reservations, fees:** Reservations are not accepted. Sites are $20 per night, hike-in/bike-in sites are $8 per person per night, plus $5 per night for each additional vehicle and $2 per pet per night. Maximum stay is 10 days. Open year-round.

**Directions:** From Garberville, drive 22 miles north on U.S. 101 to the South Fork-Honeydew exit. Turn west on South Fork-Honeydew Road and drive 31 miles (the road changes between pavement, gravel, and dirt, and is steep and curvy) to the park entrance on the left side of the road. The park is 7.5 miles east of the town of Petrolia. (South Fork-Honeydew Road can be difficult for larger vehicles.)

**Contact:** Humboldt County Public Works, 707/445-7651, www.co.humboldt.ca.us.

## 52 HONEYDEW CREEK

### Scenic rating: 6
in the King Range National Conservation Area

**Map 1.2, page 74**

This little known and little used camp is located on Honeydew Creek, a tributary to the Mattole River in California's Lost Coast. In summer, it's a hideaway that you can use as base camp to explore the Lost Coast and the King Range. In late winter, steelhead fishing can be good on the Mattole River between Honeydew and Petrolia, providing for good access and stream flows. One problem is rain. It can pound here and the river can get too high to fish; winters with 100 inches of rain are typical in average-to-wet years.

**Campsites, facilities:** There are five sites for tents or RVs (no hookups). Picnic tables and fire rings are provided. Vault toilets are available, but there is no drinking water; creek water is available but must be purified before drinking. Some facilities are wheelchair-accessible.

**Reservations, fees:** Reservations are not accepted. Sites are $8 per night.

**Directions:** From Garberville, drive north on U.S. 101 to the South Fork-Honeydew exit. Turn west on South Fork-Honeydew Road and drive to Wilder Ridge Road in Honeydew. Turn left (south) on Wilder Ridge Road and drive one mile to the campground.

**Contact:** King Range National Conservation Area, 707/986-5400; Bureau of Land Management, Arcata Field Office, 707/825-2300, www.blm.gov/ca.

## 53 HORSE MOUNTAIN

### Scenic rating: 6
in the King Range

**Map 1.2, page 74**

Few people know of this spot. The campground is along the northwest flank of Horse Mountain. A primitive road (Saddle Mountain Road) leads west from the camp and then goes left at the Y, up to Horse Mountain (1,920 feet), which offers spectacular ocean and coastal views on clear days. If you turn right at the Y, the road leads to the trailhead for the King Crest Trail near Saddle Mountain (3,290 feet). This hike is an ambitious climb to King Peak (4,087 feet), rewarding hikers with a fantastic panorama, including Mount Lassen poking above the Yolla Bolly Wilderness to the east.

**Campsites, facilities:** There are nine sites for tents only. Picnic tables and fire rings are provided. Vault toilets are available. No drinking water is available. Leashed pets are permitted.

**Reservations, fees:** Reservations are not accepted. Sites are $5 per night. Open year-round.

**Directions:** From Eureka, drive 60 miles south on U.S. 101 to the Redway/Shelter Cove exit. Take that exit and drive 2.5 miles north on Redwood Road to Briceland-Thorne Road. Turn right on Briceland-Thorne Road (which will become Shelter Cove Road) and drive 17 miles to King Peak Road (Horse Mountain). Turn right and continue six miles to the campground on the right.

**Contact:** King Range National Conservation Area, 707/986-5400, Bureau of Land Management, Arcata Field Office, 707/825-2300, www.blm.gov/ca.

## 54 TOLKAN

### Scenic rating: 6

in the King Range

**Map 1.2, page 74**

This remote camp is set at 1,840 feet, a short drive south of Horse Mountain. (For nearby side-trip options, see the listing for Horse Mountain in this chapter.)

**Campsites, facilities:** There are nine sites for tents or RVs up to 20 feet (no hookups). Picnic tables and fire rings are provided. Drinking water and vault toilets are available. Some facilities are wheelchair-accessible. Leashed pets are permitted.

**Reservations, fees:** Reservations are not accepted. Sites are $8 per night. Open year-round.

**Directions:** From Eureka, drive 60 miles south on U.S. 101 to the Redway exit. Take the Redway/Shelter Cove exit onto Redwood Drive into the town of Redway. Drive 2.5 miles (look on the right for the King Range Conservation Area sign) to Briceland-Thorne Road. Turn right on Briceland-Thorne Road (which will become Shelter Cove Road) and drive 17 miles to King Peak (Horse Mountain) Road. Turn right

on King Peak Road and continue 3.5 miles to the campground on the right.

**Contact:** King Range National Conservation Area, 707/986-5400; Bureau of Land Management, Arcata Field Office, 707/825-2300, www.blm.gov/ca.

## 55 SHELTER COVE RV AND CAMPGROUND

### Scenic rating: 8

in Shelter Cove

**Map 1.2, page 74**

This is a prime recreation area and a great ocean-side spot to set up a base camp for deep-sea fishing, whale-watching, tidepool gazing, beachcombing, and hiking. Long-term renters occupy some of the campsites. A wide boat ramp makes it perfect for campers who have trailered boats and don't mind the long drive. Reservations are strongly advised. The park's backdrop is the King Range National Conservation Area, offering spectacular views. The deli is well known for its fish-and-chips. The salmon, halibut, and rockfish fishing is quite good in the summer; always call first for current regulations and seasons, which change every year. Clamming is best during winter's low tides; hiking is best in the King Mountain Range during the summer. Seasonal abalone diving and shore fishing for redtail perch are also options. There is heavy rain in winter. Insider's tip: Two miles north is one of the few black-sand beaches in the continental United States.

**Campsites, facilities:** There are 103 sites for tents or RVs; many have full hookups (30 amps); some sites are pull-through. Picnic tables and fire rings are provided. Restrooms with showers, a dump station, coin laundry, grocery store, deli, propane, ice, and RV supplies are available. A boat ramp and marina are across the street. Leashed pets are permitted.

**Reservations, fees:** Reservations are recommended. Sites are $36-46 per night, plus $10 per person per night for more than two people, $1 per pet per night, and $1 per night per additional vehicle. Some credit cards are accepted. Open year-round.

**Directions:** From Eureka, drive 60 miles south on U.S. 101 to the Redway/Shelter Cove exit. Take that exit and drive 2.5 miles north on Redwood Road to Briceland-Thorne Road (which will become Shelter Cove Road). Turn right (west) and drive 18 miles (following the truck/RV route signs) to Upper Pacific Drive. Turn left (south) on Upper Pacific Drive and proceed (it becomes Machi Road) 0.5 mile to the park on the right.

**Contact:** Shelter Cove RV and Campground, 492 Machi Rd., 707/986-7474, http://sheltercov-erv.com.

# SHASTA AND TRINITY

© SABRINA YOUNG

At 14,179 feet, Mount Shasta rises like a diamond in a field of coal. Its sphere of influence spans a radius of 125 miles, and its shadow is felt everywhere in the region. This area has much to offer, with giant Shasta Lake, the Sacramento River above and below the lake, the McCloud River, and the wonderful Trinity Divide with its dozens of pretty backcountry lakes and several wilderness areas. This is one of the best regions anywhere for outdoor adventures, with remote campgrounds set near quiet wilderness. The most popular destinations are Shasta Lake, the Trinity Alps and their surrounding lakes and streams, and the Klamath Mountains.

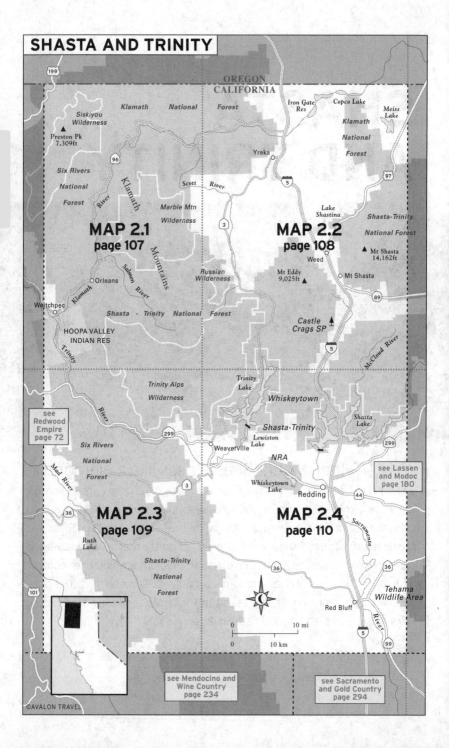

# SHASTA AND TRINITY

OREGON
CALIFORNIA

Klamath    National    Forest

Siskiyou
Wilderness

▲
Preston Pk
7,309ft

Six Rivers

National

Forest

Iron Gate
Res

Copco Lake

Meiss
Lake

Klamath

National

Forest

Yreka

Scott    River

Marble Mtn
Wilderness

Lake
Shastina

Shasta-Trinity

National Forest

**MAP 2.1
page 107**

**MAP 2.2
page 108**

Weed

▲ Mt Shasta
14,162ft

Orleans

Russian
Wilderness

Mt Eddy
9,025ft ▲

▲ Mt Shasta

Weitchpec

Shasta - Trinity National Forest

Castle
Crags SP

McCloud River

HOOPA VALLEY
INDIAN RES

see
Redwood
Empire
page 72

Trinity Alps
Wilderness

Trinity
Lake

Whiskeytown

Shasta
Lake

Six Rivers

National

Forest

Shasta-Trinity

Lewiston
Lake

Weaverville

NRA

see Lassen
and Modoc
page 180

Mad River

Whiskeytown
Lake

Redding

**MAP 2.3
page 109**

**MAP 2.4
page 110**

Sacramento

Ruth
Lake

Shasta-Trinity

National

Forest

Tehama
Wildlife Area

0        10 mi

0      10 km

Red Bluff

see Mendocino and
Wine Country
page 234

see Sacramento
and Gold Country
page 294

©AVALON TRAVEL

# Map 2.1

## Sites 1–21
## Pages 112–121

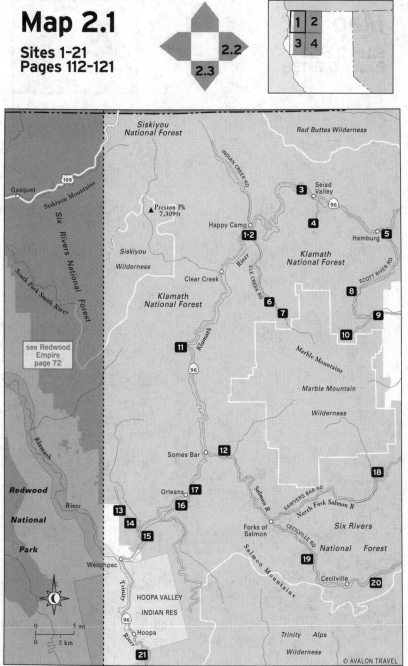

2.2

2.3

| 1 | 2 |
| 3 | 4 |

Siskiyou
National Forest

Red Buttes Wilderness

199

Gasquet

**3** Seiad Valley

96

**4**

Happy Camp

**1·2**

Hamburg **5**

Preston Pk
7,309ft

INDIAN CREEK RD

Klamath
National Forest

Siskiyou
Wilderness

Clear Creek

River

ELK CREEK RD

SCOTT RIVER RD

**8**

Klamath
National Forest

**6**

**7**

**9**

**10**

**11**

Klamath

96

Marble Mountains

Marble Mountain

Wilderness

see Redwood
Empire
page 72

South Fork Smith River

Six Rivers National Forest

Siskiyou Mountains

Klamath

River

Somes Bar

**12**

**18**

Orleans **17**

**16**

Redwood

**13**

**14**

Salmon R

SAWYERS BAR RD

North Fork Salmon R

National

**15**

Forks of
Salmon

CECILVILLE RD

Six Rivers

Park

Weitchpec

Trinity

HOOPA VALLEY

INDIAN RES

96

River

Hoopa

**21**

**19**

National Forest

Salmon Mountains

Cecilville **20**

Trinity  Alps

Wilderness

0        5 mi
0        5 km

© AVALON TRAVEL

# Map 2.2

## Sites 22-53
## Pages 122-138

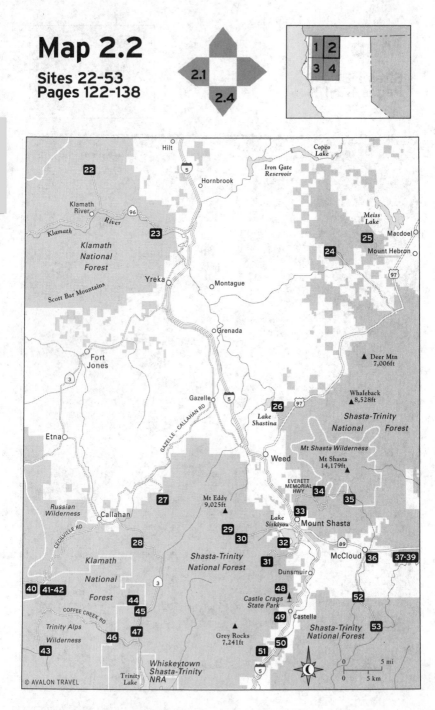

# Map 2.3

Sites 54-73
Pages 139-147

2.1 2.4

1 2
3 4

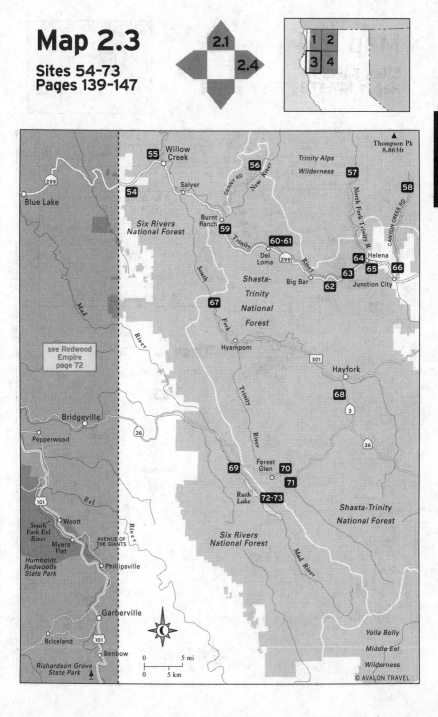

© AVALON TRAVEL

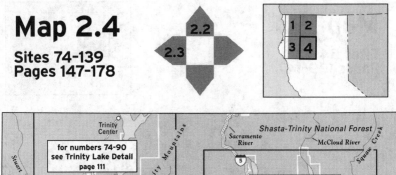

# Map 2.4
## Sites 74–139
## Pages 147–178

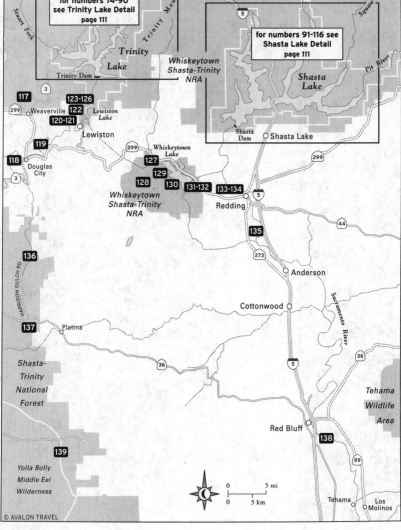

for numbers 74-90
see Trinity Lake Detail
page 111

for numbers 91-116 see
Shasta Lake Detail
page 111

© AVALON TRAVEL

# TRINITY LAKE DETAIL

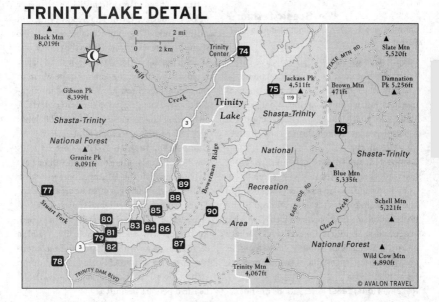

# SHASTA LAKE DETAIL

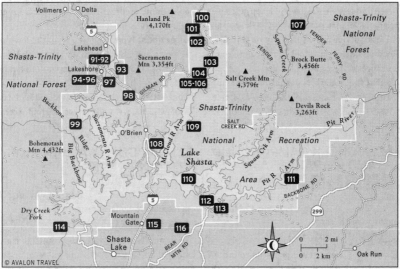

# 1 CURLY JACK

**Scenic rating: 7**

on the Klamath River in Klamath National Forest

**Map 2.1, page 107**

This campground at 1,000 feet elevation on the Klamath River provides opportunities for fishing, light rafting, and kayaking. What's special about Curly Jack, though, is that the water is generally warm enough through the summer for swimming.

**Campsites, facilities:** There are 12 sites for tents or RVs up to 42 feet, with two specially designed sites for RVs up to 60 feet (no hookups) and three group sites for up to 30 people. Fire grills and picnic tables are provided. Drinking water and vault toilets are available. Garbage pickup is available in summer. Some facilities are wheelchair-accessible. Leashed pets are permitted.

**Reservations, fees:** Reservations are not accepted for individual sites but are required for group sites at 877/444-6777 ($10 reservation fee) or www.recreation.gov ($9 reservation fee). Sites are $15 per night; group sites are $50 per night. Open May through October.

**Directions:** From the town of Happy Camp on Highway 96, turn south on Elk Creek Road and drive about one mile. Turn right on Curly Jack Road and drive one block to the campground entrance on the right.

**Contact:** Klamath National Forest, Happy Camp and Oak Knoll Ranger Districts, 530/493-2243, www.fs.usda.gov/klamath.

# 2 ELK CREEK CAMPGROUND AND RV PARK

**Scenic rating: 8**

on the Klamath River

**Map 2.1, page 107**

Elk Creek Campground is a year-round RV park set where Elk Creek pours into the Klamath River. It is a beautiful campground, with sites right on the water in a pretty, wooded setting. The section of the Klamath River nearby is perfect for inflatable kayaking and rafting. Guided trips are available, with a wide scope of white water, rated from the easy Class I stuff all the way to the Class V to-hell-and-back rapids. In addition, the water is quite warm in the summer and flows are maintained throughout the year, making it ideal for water sports. A swimming hole gets use in summer. The park is popular with anglers and hunters.

**Campsites, facilities:** There are 34 sites for RVs of any length, some with full or partial hookups (30 and 50 amps); some sites are pull-through. There is a separate area for tents. Three cabins and three rental trailers are available. Picnic tables and fire grills are provided. Restrooms with showers, cable TV, Wi-Fi, a recreation room with billiards and table tennis, horseshoes, a beach, coin laundry, dump station, propane, and firewood are available. Leashed pets are permitted.

**Reservations, fees:** Reservations are recommended. RV sites are $20-30 per night, tent sites are $20 per night, plus $7 per night for each additional person for more than four people. Weekly, monthly, and group rates are available. Some credit cards are accepted. Open year-round.

**Directions:** From Highway 96 in the town of Happy Camp, turn south on Elk Creek Road and drive 0.75 mile to the campground on the right.

**Contact:** Elk Creek Campground and RV Park, 530/493-2208, www.elkcreekcampground.com.

# 3 FORT GOFF WALK-IN

**Scenic rating: 7**

in Klamath National Forest

**Map 2.1, page 107**

This small, primitive campground is right along the Klamath River, an ideal location for both fishing and rafting. Many productive shoreline fishing spots on the Klamath River are in this area, with fair trout fishing in summer, good steelhead fishing in the fall and early winter, and a wild card for salmon in late September. There are pullouts along Highway 96 for parking, with short trails/scrambles down to the river. This is also a good spot for rafting, especially in inflatable kayaks, and commercial rafting operations have trips (Class II+ and III) available on this stretch of river. On the opposite side of Highway 96 (within walking distance, to the west) is a trailhead for a hike that is routed along Little Fort Goff Creek, an uphill tromp for five miles to Big Camp and Boundary National Recreation Trail. The creek also runs near the camp, and the elevation is 1,300 feet.

**Campsites, facilities:** There are five walk-in tent sites. Picnic tables and fire grills are provided. Vault toilets are available. There is no drinking water and garbage must be packed out. Supplies are available in Seiad Valley. Leashed pets are permitted.

**Reservations, fees:** Reservations are not accepted. There is no fee for camping. Open May through October.

**Directions:** From Yreka, drive north on I-5 to the junction with Highway 96. At Highway 96, turn west and drive to Seiad Valley. At Seiad Valley, continue west on Highway 96 for five miles to the campground on the left side of the road. Walk a very short distance (20-75 feet) to the campsites.

**Contact:** Klamath National Forest, Happy Camp and Oak Knoll Ranger Districts, 530/493-2243, www.fs.usda.gov/klamath.

## 4 GRIDER CREEK

### Scenic rating: 6

in Klamath National Forest

**Map 2.1, page 107**

This obscure little camp is used primarily by hikers, since a trailhead for the Pacific Crest Trail is available, and by deer hunters in the fall.

It is also popular with equestrians. The camp is at 1,400 feet along Grider Creek. Access to the Pacific Crest Trail is provided from a bridge across the creek. From here, the PCT is routed uphill along Grider Creek into the Marble Mountain Wilderness, about an 11-mile ripper to Huckleberry Mountain at 6,303 feet. There are no lakes along the route, only small streams and feeder creeks.

**Campsites, facilities:** There are 10 sites for tents or RVs up to 16 feet (no hookups). Picnic tables and fire grills are provided. Vault toilets, horse corrals, and a loading ramp are available. No drinking water is provided, but there is water for stock horses. Garbage must be packed out. Leashed pets are permitted.

**Reservations, fees:** Reservations are not accepted. There is no fee for camping. Two vehicles maximum per site. Open May through October.

**Directions:** From Yreka, drive north on I-5 to the junction with Highway 96. At Highway 96, turn west and drive to Walker Creek Road/Forest Road 46N64, one mile before Seiad Valley. Turn left to enter Walker Creek Road and stay to the right as it runs adjacent to the Klamath River to Grider Creek Road. At Grider Creek Road, turn left and drive south for three miles to the camp entrance.

**Contact:** Klamath National Forest, Happy Camp and Oak Knoll Ranger Districts, 530/493-2243, www.fs.usda.gov/klamath.

## 5 SARAH TOTTEN

### Scenic rating: 7

on the Klamath River in Klamath National Forest

**Map 2.1, page 107**

This is one of the more popular Forest Service camps on the Klamath River, and it's no mystery why. In the summer, its placement is perfect for rafters (Class II+ and III), who camp here and use it as a put-in spot. In fall and winter, anglers arrive for the steelhead run. It's in the "banana belt," or good-weather area of the Klamath, in a pretty grove of oak trees. Fishing is often good for salmon in early October and for steelhead from November through spring, providing there are fishable water flows.

**Campsites, facilities:** There are eight sites for tents or RVs up to 28 feet, and two group sites for tents or RVs up to 22 feet that can accommodate up to 30 people each (no hookups). Picnic tables and fire grills are provided. Drinking water and vault toilets are available. A small grocery store is nearby. Some facilities are wheelchair-accessible. Leashed pets are permitted.

**Reservations, fees:** Reservations are not accepted for individual sites but are required for the group sites at 877/444-6777 ($10 reservation fee) or www.recreation.gov ($9 reservation fee). Sites are $10 per night; group sites are $50 per night. Open May through October.

**Directions:** From Yreka, drive north on I-5 to the junction with Highway 96. At Highway 96, turn west and drive to Horse Creek, continuing west for five miles to the campground on the right side of the road. If you reach the town of Hamburg, you have gone one mile too far.

**Contact:** Klamath National Forest, Happy Camp and Oak Knoll Ranger Districts, 530/493-2243, www.fs.usda.gov/klamath.

# 6 SULPHUR SPRINGS
🏃🏊🎿🐕 5% ⛺

### Scenic rating: 8
on Elk Creek in Klamath National Forest

**Map 2.1, page 107**

This hidden spot is along Elk Creek on the border of the Marble Mountain Wilderness. The camp is at a trailhead that provides access to miles and miles of trails that follow streams into the backcountry of the wilderness area. It is a 12-mile backpack trip one-way and largely uphill to Spirit Lake, one of the prettiest lakes in the entire wilderness. The nearby hot springs (which are usually around 75 degrees) provide a side attraction. There are also some swimming

holes nearby in Elk Creek, but these aren't hot springs, so expect the water to be cold. Sulphur Springs Camp is at 2,300 feet.

**Campsites, facilities:** There are six walk-in tent sites. Picnic tables and fire grills are provided. Vault toilets are available. No drinking water is available. Garbage must be packed out. Leashed pets are permitted.

**Reservations, fees:** Reservations are not accepted. There is no fee for camping. Open late May through early October.

**Directions:** From Yreka, drive north on I-5 to the junction with Highway 96. At Highway 96, turn west and drive to Happy Camp. In Happy Camp, turn south on Elk Creek Road and drive 12 miles to the campground.

**Contact:** Klamath National Forest, Happy Camp and Oak Knoll Ranger Districts, 530/493-2243, www.fs.usda.gov/klamath.

# 7 NORCROSS
🏃🏊🎿🐕👤♿🚐⛺

### Scenic rating: 7
near Happy Camp in Klamath National Forest

**Map 2.1, page 107**

This camp at 2,400 feet in elevation serves as a staging area for various trails that provide access into the Marble Mountain Wilderness. The Elk Creek Trail offers four different loops that access various destinations and mountain lakes. There is also access to the popular Kelsey National Recreation Trail and to swimming and fishing activities.

**Campsites, facilities:** There are six sites for tents or RVs up to 25 feet (no hookups). Picnic tables and fire pits are provided. Vault toilets, a horse corral, stock water, and a loading ramp are available. No drinking water is available. Garbage must be packed out. Some facilities are wheelchair-accessible. Leashed pets are permitted.

**Reservations, fees:** Reservations are not accepted. There is no fee for camping. Open May through October.

**Directions:** From Yreka on I-5, drive north on

I-5 to the junction with Highway 96. Drive west on Highway 96 to the town of Happy Camp. In Happy Camp, turn south onto Elk Creek Road and drive 16 miles to the campground.

**Contact:** Klamath National Forest, Happy Camp and Oak Knoll Ranger Districts, 530/493-2243, www.fs.usda.gov/klamath.

## 8 BRIDGE FLAT

### Scenic rating: 7
in Klamath National Forest

**Map 2.1, page 107**

This camp is at 2,000 feet along the Scott River. Though commercial rafting trips are only rarely available, the river is accessible during the early spring for skilled rafters and kayakers, with a good put-in and take-out spot four miles downriver; others begin their trip at the Buker Bridge or the Kelsey Creek Bridge (a popular swimming hole). For backpackers, a trailhead for the Kelsey Trail is nearby, leading into the Marble Mountain Wilderness. A fish-spawning area is on Kelsey Creek, upriver from camp.

**Campsites, facilities:** There are four sites for tents or RVs up to 22 feet (no hookups). Picnic tables and fire grills are provided. Vault toilets are available. There is no drinking water and garbage must be packed out. Some facilities are wheelchair-accessible. Leashed pets are permitted.

**Reservations, fees:** Reservations are not accepted. There is no fee for camping. Open May through September.

**Directions:** From Redding, drive north on I-5 to Yreka. In Yreka, turn southwest on Highway 3 and drive 16.5 miles to Fort Jones. In Fort Jones, turn right on Scott River Road and drive 17 miles to the campground on the right side of the road, just after crossing a bridge.

**Contact:** Klamath National Forest, Scott River and Salmon River Ranger Districts, 530/468-5351, www.fs.usda.gov/klamath.

## 9 INDIAN SCOTTY

### Scenic rating: 7
on the Scott River in Klamath National Forest

**Map 2.1, page 107**

This popular camp provides direct access to the adjacent Scott River. Because it is easy to reach (no gravel roads) and shaded, it gets a lot of use. The camp is at 2,400 feet. The levels, forces, and temperatures on the Scott River fluctuate greatly from spring to fall. In the spring, it can be a raging cauldron, but cold from snowmelt. Come summer it quiets, with some deep pools providing swimming holes. By fall, it can be reduced to a trickle. Keep your expectations flexible according to the season.

**Campsites, facilities:** There are 28 sites and a group site (parking lot) for tents or RVs up to 30 feet (no hookups). Picnic tables and fire grills are provided. Drinking water and vault toilets are available. There is a playground in the group-use area. Some facilities are wheelchair-accessible. Leashed pets are permitted.

**Reservations, fees:** Reservations are not accepted for individual sites but are required for the group site at 877/444-6777 ($10 reservation fee) or www.recreation.gov ($9 reservation fee). Individual sites are $10 per night, and the group site is $50 per night. Open May through October.

**Directions:** From Redding, drive north on I-5 to Yreka. In Yreka, turn southwest on Highway 3 and drive 16.5 miles to Fort Jones. In Fort Jones, turn right on Scott River Road and drive 14 miles to a concrete bridge and the adjacent signed campground entrance on the left.

**Contact:** Klamath National Forest, Scott River and Salmon River Ranger Districts, 530/468-5351, www.fs.usda.gov/klamath.

## 10 LOVERS CAMP

### Scenic rating: 5

in Klamath National Forest

**Map 2.1, page 107**

Lovers Camp isn't set up for lovers at all, but for horses and backpackers. This is a trailhead camp at 4,300 feet at the edge of the Marble Mountain Wilderness, one of the best in the entire wilderness for packers with horses. The trail is routed up along Canyon Creek to the beautiful Marble Valley at the foot of Black Marble Mountain. The most common destination is Sky High Lakes, a good one-day huff-and-puff away. Now *there's* a place for lovers.

**Campsites, facilities:** There are eight walk-in tent sites. Picnic tables and fire grills are provided. Vault toilets are available. There are also facilities for stock unloading and a corral. There is no drinking water, but water is available for stock. Garbage must be packed out. Leashed pets are permitted.

**Reservations, fees:** Reservations are not accepted. There is no fee for camping. Open May through October.

**Directions:** From Redding, drive north on I-5 to Yreka. In Yreka, turn southwest on Highway 3 and drive to Fort Jones and Scott River Road. Turn right on Scott River Road and drive 14 miles to Forest Road 44N45. Turn left (south) on Forest Road 44N45 and drive eight miles to the campground at the end of the road.

**Contact:** Klamath National Forest, Scott River and Salmon River Ranger Districts, 530/468-5351, www.fs.usda.gov/klamath.

## 11 DILLON CREEK

### Scenic rating: 7

on the Klamath River in Six Rivers National Forest

**Map 2.1, page 107**          **BEST (**

This is a prime base camp for rafting or a steelhead fishing trip. A put-in spot for rafting is adjacent to the camp, with an excellent river run available from here on down past Presidio Bar to the take-out at Ti-Bar. If you choose to go on, make absolutely certain to take out at Green Riffle river access, or risk death at Ishi Pishi Falls. The water is warm in the summer, and there are many excellent swimming holes in the area. In addition, this is a good stretch of water for steelhead fishing from September to February, best in early winter from Dillon Creek to Ti-Bar, with shoreline access available at Dillon Beach. The elevation is 1,780 feet.

**Campsites, facilities:** There are 21 sites for tents or RVs up to 25 feet (no hookups). Picnic tables, food lockers, and fire grills are provided. Drinking water and vault toilets are available. There are dump stations in Happy Camp (25 miles north of the campground) and at Aikens Creek (nine miles west of the town of Orleans). Some facilities are wheelchair-accessible. Leashed pets are permitted.

**Reservations, fees:** Reservations are accepted for some sites three days in advance at 877/444-6777 ($10 reservation fee) or www.recreation.gov ($9 reservation fee). Sites are $10 per night, plus $5 per night for each additional vehicle. Open mid-May through early November.

**Directions:** From Yreka, drive north on I-5 to the junction with Highway 96. At Highway 96, turn west and drive to Happy Camp. Continue south from Happy Camp for 35 miles and look for the campground on the right side of the road.

Coming from the west, from Somes Bar, drive 15 miles north on Highway 96.

**Contact:** Six Rivers National Forest, Orleans Ranger District, 530/627-3291, www.fs.usda.gov/srnf.

## 12 OAK BOTTOM

### Scenic rating: 7

on the Salmon River in Six Rivers National Forest

**Map 2.1, page 107**

This camp is just far enough off Highway 96 that it gets missed by zillions of out-of-towners every year. It is across the road from the lower Salmon River, a pretty, clean, and cold stream that pours out of the surrounding wilderness high country. Swimming is very good in river holes, though the water is cold, especially when nearby Wooley Creek is full of snowmelt pouring out of the Marble Mountains to the north. In the fall, there is good shoreline fishing for steelhead, though the canyon bottom is shaded almost all day and gets very cold.

**Campsites, facilities:** There are 26 sites for tents or RVs up to 25 feet (no hookups). Picnic tables and fire grills are provided. Drinking water and vault toilets are available. There is a dump station at the Elk Creek Campground in Happy Camp and another at Aikens Creek, 13 miles southwest of the town of Orleans. Supplies are available in Somes Bar. Some facilities are wheelchair-accessible. Leashed pets are permitted.

**Reservations, fees:** Reservations are accepted at 877/444-6777 ($10 reservation fee) or www. recreation.gov ($9 reservation fee). Sites are $10 per night, plus $5 per night for each additional vehicle. Open April through mid-October, weather permitting.

**Directions:** From the junction of U.S. 101 and Highway 299 near Arcata, turn east on Highway 299 and drive to Willow Creek. In Willow Creek, turn north (left) on Highway 96 east and drive to Salmon River Road (0.25 mile before Somes Bar). Turn right on Salmon River Road and drive 2.3 miles to the campground on the left side of the road.

**Contact:** Six Rivers National Forest, Orleans Ranger District, 530/627-3291, www.fs.usda. gov/srnf.

## 13 FISH LAKE

### Scenic rating: 8

in Six Rivers National Forest

**Map 2.1, page 107**

This is a pretty little lake that provides good fishing for stocked rainbow trout from the season opener on Memorial Day weekend through July. The camp gets little pressure in other months. It's in the heart of Bigfoot Country, with numerous Bigfoot sightings reported near Bluff Creek. No powerboats are permitted on the lake, but it's too small for that anyway, being better suited for a canoe, float tube, raft, or pram. The elevation is 1,780 feet. The presence here of Port-Orford-cedar root disease, spread by spores in the mud, forces closure from October through May in some years; call for current status.

**Campsites, facilities:** There are 24 sites for tents or RVs up to 20 feet (no hookups). Picnic tables and fire grills are provided. Drinking water, vault toilets, and a boat ramp are available. Some facilities are wheelchair-accessible. Leashed pets are permitted.

**Reservations, fees:** Reservations are required three days in advance at 877/444-6777 ($10 reservation fee) or www.recreation.gov ($9 reservation fee). Sites are $10 per night, plus $5 per night for each additional vehicle. Open late May through September, weather permitting.

**Directions:** From I-5 in Redding, turn west on Highway 299 and drive to Willow Creek. In Willow Creek, turn north (left) on Highway 96 east and drive to Weitchpec, continuing seven miles north on Highway 96 to Fish Lake Road/ Bluff Creek Road. Turn left on Fish Lake Road/ Bluff Creek Road and drive five miles (stay to the right at the Y) to Fish Lake.

**Contact:** Six Rivers National Forest, Orleans Ranger District, 530/627-3291, www.fs.usda. gov/srnf.

# KLAMATH MOUNTAINS

The neighboring Klamath Mountains are well known as Bigfoot Country. If you drive up the Forest Service road at Bluff Creek, just off Highway 96 upstream of Weitchpec, you can even find the spot where the famous Bigfoot movie was shot in the 1960s. Well, I haven't seen Bigfoot, but I have discovered tons of outdoor recreation. This remote region features miles of the Klamath and Salmon Rivers, as well as the Marble Mountain Wilderness. Options include canoeing, rafting, and fishing for steelhead on the Klamath River, or hiking to your choice of more than 100 wilderness lakes.

## 14 E-NE-NUCK

### Scenic rating: 7

in Six Rivers National Forest

**Map 2.1, page 107**

The campground gets its name from a Karuk chief who lived in the area in the late 1800s. It's a popular spot for anglers; Bluff Creek and the Klamath are within walking distance, and Fish Lake is eight miles to the west. Bluff Creek is the legendary site where the Bigfoot film of the 1960s was shot. While it was finally admitted that the film was a phony, it still put Bluff Creek on the map. A unique feature at this campground is a smokehouse for lucky anglers along with a knowledgeable campground host who can show you how to use it.

**Campsites, facilities:** There are 10 sites for tents or RVs up to 30 feet (no hookups). Picnic tables, fire rings, and cast-iron firebox stoves are provided. Drinking water, vault toilets, and a smokehouse are available. Some facilities are wheelchair-accessible. Leashed pets are permitted.

**Reservations, fees:** Reservations are not accepted. Sites are $10 per night, plus $5 for each additional vehicle. Open late June through October.

**Directions:** From the junction of U.S. 101 and Highway 299 near Arcata, turn east on Highway 299 and drive to Willow Creek. In Willow Creek, turn north (left) on Highway 96 east and drive to Weitchpec, continuing on Highway 96 for about five miles to the campground. E-Ne-Nuck is just beyond Aikens Creek West campground.

**Contact:** Six Rivers National Forest, Orleans Ranger District, 530/627-3291, www.fs.usda.gov/srnf.

## 15 AIKENS CREEK WEST

### Scenic rating: 7

on the Klamath River in Six Rivers National Forest

**Map 2.1, page 107**

The Klamath River is warm and green here in summer, and this camp provides an ideal put-in spot for a day of easy rafting, especially for newcomers in inflatable kayaks. The camp is at 340 feet in elevation along the Klamath. From here to Weitchpec is an easy paddle, with the take-out on the right side of the river just below the confluence with the Trinity River. The river flows through a beautiful canyon with lots of birds and enters the Yurok Indian Reservation. The steelhead fishing can be good in this area from August through mid-November. Highway 96 is a scenic but slow cruise.

**Campsites, facilities:** There are dispersed sites for tents or RVs up to 35 feet (no hookups). Picnic tables and fire grills are provided. Vault toilets and a dump station are available, but there is no drinking water. There are reduced services in winter, and all garbage must be packed out. Leashed pets are permitted.

**Reservations, fees:** Reservations are not

accepted. Sites are $8 per night, plus $5 per night for each additional vehicle; no fees during winter. Open year-round, weather permitting.

**Directions:** From the junction of U.S. 101 and Highway 299 near Arcata, turn east on Highway 299 and drive to Willow Creek. In Willow Creek, turn north (left) on Highway 96 east and drive to Weitchpec, continuing on Highway 96 for five miles to the campground on the right side of the road.

**Contact:** Six Rivers National Forest, Orleans Ranger District, 530/627-3291, www.fs.usda. gov/srnf.

## 16 KLAMATH RIVERSIDE RV PARK

### Scenic rating: 8
on the Klamath River

**Map 2.1, page 107**

Klamath Riverside RV Park and Campground is an option for RV cruisers touring Highway 96—designated the Bigfoot Scenic Byway—and looking for a place in Orleans. The camp has large grassy sites among pine trees, right on the river. There are spectacular views of Mount Orleans and the surrounding hills. A 12-foot Bigfoot statue is on the property. Through the years, I've seen many changes at this park. It has been transformed from a dusty fishing spot to a park more resembling a rural resort that attracts hikers, cyclists, gold panners, river enthusiasts, anglers, and hunters. One big plus is that the park offers guided fishing trips during the season.

**Campsites, facilities:** There are 45 sites with full hookups (30 and 50 amps) for RVs of any length. Picnic tables and fire rings are provided. Restrooms with showers, a seasonal swimming pool, group pavilion, fish-cleaning station, coin laundry, horseshoes, Wi-Fi, pay phone, and RV storage are available. Restrooms are super clean. Guided drift-boat fishing in season is available. Leashed pets are permitted.

**Reservations, fees:** Reservations are

accepted. RV sites are $35 per night, tent sites with hookups are $10 per person per night, plus $6 per person per night for more than four people. Group, weekly, and monthly rates are available. Open year-round.

**Directions:** From the junction of U.S. 101 and Highway 299 near Arcata, drive east on Highway 299 to Willow Creek, turn north (left) on Highway 96 east and drive past Weitchpec to Orleans. This campground is at the west end of the town of Orleans on Highway 96 on the right.

**Contact:** Klamath Riverside RV Park and Campground, 530/627-3239, www.krrvp.com.

## 17 PEARCH CREEK

### Scenic rating: 7
on the Klamath River in Six Rivers National Forest

**Map 2.1, page 107**

This is one of the premium Forest Service camps on the Klamath River because of its easy access from the highway and easy access to the river. The camp is on Pearch Creek, about a quarter mile from the Klamath at a deep bend in the river. Indeed, the fishing is often excellent for one- to five-pound steelhead from August through November. The elevation is 400 feet.

**Campsites, facilities:** There are 10 sites for tents or RVs up to 30 feet (no hookups). Picnic tables and fire grills are provided. Drinking water and vault toilets are available. A grocery store, coin laundry, and propane gas are available within one mile. Some facilities are wheelchair-accessible. Leashed pets are permitted.

**Reservations, fees:** Reservations are accepted at 877/444-6777 ($10 reservation fee) or www. recreation.gov ($9 reservation fee). Sites are $10 per night, plus $5 per night for each additional vehicle. Open late May through October.

**Directions:** From I-5 in Redding, turn west on Highway 299 and drive to Willow Creek. In Willow Creek, turn north (right) on Highway

96 east, drive past Weitchpec, and continue to Orleans. In Orleans, continue for one mile and look for the campground entrance on the right side of the road.

**Contact:** Six Rivers National Forest, Orleans Ranger District, 530/627-3291, www.fs.usda.gov/srnf.

## 18 IDLEWILD

### Scenic rating: 8

on the North Fork of the Salmon River in Klamath National Forest

**Map 2.1, page 107**

This is one of the prettiest drive-to camps in the region, set on the North Fork of the Salmon River, a beautiful, cold, clear stream and a major tributary to the Klamath River. Most campers use the camp for its nearby trailhead (two miles north on a dirt Forest Service road out of camp). The hike is routed to the north, climbing alongside the Salmon River for miles into the Marble Mountain Wilderness (wilderness permits are required). It's a rugged 10-mile, all-day climb to Lake of the Island, with several other lakes (highlighted by Hancock Lake) to the nearby west, accessible on weeklong trips. The elevation is 2,560 feet.

**Campsites, facilities:** There are 11 sites for tents or RVs up to 24 feet (no hookups). Picnic tables and fire grills are provided. Vault toilets are available. Drinking water is unreliable, especially in the off-season. Some facilities are wheelchair-accessible. Leashed pets are permitted.

**Reservations, fees:** Reservations are not accepted. Sites are $10 per night, with no fee during the winter. Open May through October.

**Directions:** From Yreka, turn southwest on Highway 3 and drive to Etna. In Etna, turn west on Etna-Somes Bar Road (Main Street in town) and drive about 16 miles to the campground on the right side of the road. Note: A shorter, more scenic, and more complex route is available from Gazelle (north of Weed on Old

Highway 99). Take Gazelle-Callahan Road west over the summit and continue north to Etna.

**Contact:** Klamath National Forest, Salmon River and Scott River Ranger Districts, 530/468-5351, www.fs.usda.gov/klamath.

## 19 MATTHEWS CREEK

### Scenic rating: 8

on the Salmon River in Klamath National Forest

**Map 2.1, page 107**   **BEST (**

This camp is set in a dramatic river canyon, with the beautiful South Fork of the Salmon River nearby. Rafters call it the "Cal Salmon," and good put-in and take-out spots are found every few miles all the way to the confluence with the Klamath. In early summer the water is quite cold from snowmelt, but by midsummer it warms up significantly. The best fishing for steelhead on the Salmon is in December and January in the stretch of river downstream from the town of Forks of Salmon or upstream in the South Fork (check regulations for closed areas). In winter the mountain rims shield the canyon floor from sunlight and it gets so cold you'll feel like a human glacier. The elevation is 1,760 feet.

**Campsites, facilities:** There are 12 sites for tents or RVs up to 24 feet (no hookups). Picnic tables and fire grills are provided. Drinking water and vault toilets are available, with limited winter facilities. Five sites are wheelchair-accessible. Leashed or controlled pets are permitted.

**Reservations, fees:** Reservations are not accepted. Sites are $10 per night. Open May through October.

**Directions:** From the junction of U.S. 101 and Highway 299 near Arcata, head east on Highway 299 and drive to Willow Creek. In Willow Creek, turn north on Highway 96 and drive past Orleans to Somes Bar. At Somes Bar, turn east on Salmon River Road/Forest Road 2B01 and drive to the town of Forks of Salmon.

Turn right on Cecilville Road/Forest Road 1002 and drive about nine miles to the campground. Cecilville Road is very narrow.

**Contact:** Klamath National Forest, Salmon River and Scott River Ranger Districts, 530/468-5351, www.fs.usda.gov/klamath.

## 20 EAST FORK

**Scenic rating: 6**

on the Salmon River in Klamath National Forest

**Map 2.1, page 107**

This is one of the more spectacular areas in the fall when the leaves turn different shades of gold. It's at 2,600 feet along the Salmon River, just outside the town of Cecilville. There are some great pools for swimming and fishing. Directly adjacent to the camp is Forest Road 37N02, which leads to a Forest Service station four miles away, and to a trailhead for the Trinity Alps Wilderness three miles beyond that. Note to steelhead anglers: Check the Department of Fish and Game regulations for closed areas on the Salmon River.

**Campsites, facilities:** There are six sites for tents or RVs up to 16 feet (no hookups). Picnic tables and fire grills are provided. Vault toilets are available. No drinking water is available. Garbage must be packed out. Some facilities are wheelchair-accessible. Leashed pets are permitted.

**Reservations, fees:** Reservations are not accepted. There is no fee for camping. Open May through October.

**Directions:** From Weed, drive north on I-5 to the Edgewood exit. Take the Edgewood exit, turn left at the stop sign, and drive a short distance under the freeway to another stop sign at Old Highway 99. Turn right (north) and drive six miles to Gazelle and Gazelle-Callahan Road. Turn left (west) on Gazelle-Callahan Road, and drive to Callahan and Cecilville Road. Turn left (southwest) on Cecilville Road and drive about 30 miles to the campground on

the right side of the road. If you reach the town of Cecilville, you have gone two miles too far.

**Contact:** Klamath National Forest, Salmon River and Scott River Ranger Districts, 530/468-5351, www.fs.usda.gov/klamath.

## 21 TISH TANG

**Scenic rating: 8**

in Six Rivers National Forest

**Map 2.1, page 107**

This campground is adjacent to one of the best swimming holes in all of Northern California. By late July the adjacent Trinity River is warm and slow, perfect for tubing, a quick dunk, and paddling a canoe. There is a large gravel beach, and some people will bring along their short lawn chairs and just take a seat on the edge of the river in a few inches of water. Though Tish Tang is a good put-in spot for rafting in the late spring and early summer, the flows are too slow and quiet for most rafters to even ruffle a feather during the summer. The elevation is 300 feet.

**Campsites, facilities:** There are 40 sites for tents or RVs up to 22 feet (no hookups). Picnic tables and fire grills are provided. Drinking water and vault toilets are available, and there is a camp host. Some facilities are wheelchair-accessible. Leashed pets are permitted.

**Reservations, fees:** Reservations are accepted at 530/625-4284. Single sites are $15 per night, plus $5 per night for each additional vehicle, and it's $20 per night for double sites. Open late May through September.

**Directions:** From the junction of U.S. 101 and Highway 299 near Arcata, turn east on Highway 299 and drive to Willow Creek. In Willow Creek, turn north (left) on Highway 96 east and drive eight miles north to the campground entrance on the right side of the road.

**Contact:** Hoopa Valley Tribal Council, Forestry Department, 530/625-4284, www. hoopa-nsn.gov.

## 22 BEAVER CREEK

**Scenic rating: 8**

in Klamath National Forest

**Map 2.2, page 108**

This camp is along Beaver Creek, a feeder stream to the nearby Klamath River, with two small creeks entering Beaver Creek on the far side of the river near the campground. It is quiet and pretty. There are several historic mining sites in the area; you'll need a map of Klamath National Forest (available for a fee at the district office) to find them. In the fall, this campground is usually taken over by deer hunters. The elevation is 2,400 feet.

**Campsites, facilities:** There are eight sites for tents or RVs up to 28 feet (no hookups). Picnic tables and fire grills are provided. Vault toilets are available. There is no drinking water. Garbage must be packed out. Leashed pets are permitted.

**Reservations, fees:** Reservations are not accepted. There is no fee for camping. Open June through October.

**Directions:** From Yreka, drive north on I-5 to Highway 96. Turn west on Highway 96 and drive approximately 15 miles to Beaver Creek Road (if you reach the town of Klamath River, you have gone 0.5 mile too far). Turn right on Beaver Creek Road/Forest Road 11 and drive five miles to the campground on the right.

**Contact:** Klamath National Forest, Happy Camp and Oak Knoll Ranger Districts, 530/493-2243, www.fs.usda.gov/klamath.

## 23 TREE OF HEAVEN

**Scenic rating: 7**

in Klamath National Forest

**Map 2.2, page 108**   **BEST (**

This outstanding riverside campground provides excellent access to the Klamath River for fishing, rafting, and hiking. The best deal is to put in your raft, canoe, or drift boat upstream

at the ramp below Iron Gate Reservoir, then make the all-day run down to the take-out at Tree of Heaven. This section of river is an easy paddle (Class II, II+, and III) and also provides excellent steelhead fishing in the winter. A 0.25-mile paved interpretive trail is near the camp. On the drive in from the highway, you can watch the landscape turn from high chaparral to forest.

**Campsites, facilities:** There are 20 sites for tents or RVs up to 35 feet (no hookups). Picnic tables and fire grills are provided. Drinking water and vault toilets are available. A river access spot for put-in and take-out for rafts and drift boats is available. Some facilities are wheelchair-accessible. Leashed pets are permitted.

**Reservations, fees:** Reservations are accepted for some sites at 877/444-6777 ($10 reservation fee) or www.recreation.gov ($9 reservation fee). Sites are $15 per night. Open May through October.

**Directions:** From Yreka, drive north on I-5 to Highway 96. Turn west on Highway 96 and drive seven miles to the campground entrance on the left side of the road.

**Contact:** Klamath National Forest, Happy Camp and Oak Knoll Ranger Districts, 530/493-2243, www.fs.usda.gov/klamath.

## 24 MARTINS DAIRY

**Scenic rating: 8**

on the Little Shasta River in Klamath National Forest

**Map 2.2, page 108**

This camp is set at 6,000 feet, where the deer get big and the country seems wide open. A large meadow is nearby, directly across the road from this remote camp, with fantastic wildflower displays in late spring. This is one of the prettiest camps around in the fall, with dramatic color from aspens, elderberries, and willows. It also makes a good base camp for hunters in the fall. Before heading into the surrounding backcountry, obtain a map (fee) of Klamath National Forest at the Goosenest Ranger Station on Highway 97, on your way in to camp.

**Campsites, facilities:** There are six sites for tents or RVs up to 30 feet (no hookups). There are also four equestrian sites with four small corrals and a shared water tank to the north about 0.25 mile up the road. Picnic tables and fire grills are provided. Drinking water and vault toilets are available. Leashed pets are permitted.

**Reservations, fees:** Reservations are not accepted. Sites are $10 per night. Open June through October, weather permitting.

**Directions:** From I-5 in Weed, turn north on U.S. 97 (Klamath Falls exit) and drive to Grass Lake. Continue about seven miles to Forest Road 70/46N10 (if you reach Hebron Summit, you have driven about a mile too far). Turn left, drive about 10 miles to a Y, take the left fork, and drive three miles (including a very sharp right turn) to the campground on the right side of the road. A map of Klamath National Forest is advised.

**Contact:** Klamath National Forest, Goosenest Ranger District, 530/398-4391, www.fs.usda.gov/klamath.

# 25 JUANITA LAKE

**Scenic rating: 7**

in Klamath National Forest

Map 2.2, page 108

Small and relatively unknown, this camp is along the shore of Juanita Lake at 5,100 feet. Swimming is not recommended because the water is cold and mucky, and mosquitoes can be abundant as well. It is stocked with rainbow trout, brown trout, bass, and catfish, but a problem with golden shiners has cut into the lake's fishing productivity. It's a small lake and forested, set near the Butte Valley Wildlife Area in the plateau country just five miles to the northeast. The latter provides an opportunity

to see waterfowl and, in the winter, bald eagles. Campers will discover a network of Forest Service roads in the area, providing an opportunity for mountain biking. There are designated fishing areas and a paved trail around the lake that is wheelchair-accessible and spans approximately 1.25 miles.

**Campsites, facilities:** There are 22 sites for tents or RVs up to 42 feet (no hookups) and a group tent site that can accommodate up to 50 people. Picnic tables and fire grills are provided. Drinking water and vault toilets are available. Boating is allowed, but no motors are permitted on the lake. Many facilities are wheelchair-accessible. Leashed pets are permitted.

**Reservations, fees:** Reservations are not accepted for individual sites but are required for the group site at 877/444-6777 ($10 reservation fee) or www.recreation.gov ($9 reservation fee). Individual sites are $15 per night, the double site is $20 per night, and the group site is $50 per night. Open late May through mid-October, weather permitting.

**Directions:** From Weed and I-5, turn north on U.S. 97 (Klamath Falls exit) and drive approximately 37 miles to Ball Mountain Road. Turn left on Ball Mountain Road and drive 2.5 miles, veer right at the fork, and continue to the campground entrance at the lake.

**Contact:** Klamath National Forest, Goosenest Ranger District, 530/398-4391, www.fs.usda.gov/klamath.

# 26 LAKE SHASTINA

**Scenic rating: 5**

near Klamath National Forest and Weed

Map 2.2, page 108

Lake Shastina is at the northern foot of Mount Shasta at an elevation of 3,000 feet. The campground is on the access road to the boat ramp, about 0.25 mile from the lake. It offers sweeping views, good swimming on hot summer days, waterskiing, and all water sports. There is fishing for catfish and bass in the spring and summer, an occasional opportunity for crappie, and a chance for trout in late winter and spring. The lake level is often low, with the water drained for hay farmers to the north. One reason the views of Mount Shasta are so good is that this is largely high sagebrush country with few trees. As such, it can get very dusty, windy, and, in the winter, nasty cold. Since this campground is remote (yet not far from I-5), provides free access, and there is no campground host, the nearby lakeshore can be the site of late-night parties with bonfires, drinking, and worse—amplified music from open car doors. This is one of the few lakes in Northern California that has property with lakeside housing (not near the campground). Locals often run their dogs off-leash. Lake Shastina Golf Course is nearby.

**Campsites, facilities:** There is a small primitive area for tents or RVs of any length (no hookups). There is one faucet, but you should bring your own water in case it is not turned on. A vault toilet is available and a boat launch is nearby; the boat ramp is nonfunctional when the lake level drops below the concrete ramp. Garbage service is available May to September only. There is a 14-day limit for camping. Supplies can be obtained five miles away in Weed. Some facilities are wheelchair-accessible. Pets are permitted.

**Reservations, fees:** Reservations are not accepted. There is no fee for camping. Open May through September.

**Directions:** From Redding, take I-5 north to the central Weed exit and U.S. 97. Take the exit to the stop sign, turn right, drive through Weed, exiting for U.S. 97/Klamath Falls. Merge right (north) on U.S. 97 and drive about five miles to Big Springs Road. Turn left (west) on Big Springs Road and drive about two miles to Jackson Ranch Road. Turn left (west) on Jackson Ranch Road and drive about one mile to Emerald Isle Road (watch for the signed turnoff). Turn right and drive one mile to the campground.

**Contact:** Siskiyou County Flood Control and

Water Conservation District, 530/842-8250, www.co.siskiyou.ca.us.

## 27 KANGAROO LAKE

**Scenic rating: 9**

in Klamath National Forest

**Map 2.2, page 108**

A remote paved road leads to the parking area for Kangaroo Lake, set at 6,500 feet. This provides a genuine rarity: a beautiful and pristine mountain lake with a campground, good fishing for brook and rainbow trout, and an excellent trailhead for hikers. The walk to the walk-in campsites is very short, 1-3 minutes, with many sites very close. Campsites are in a forested setting with no lake view. Reaching the lake requires another five minutes, but a paved wheelchair-accessible trail leads right to the lake's edge. In addition, a switchback ramp for wheelchairs makes it one of the best wheelchair-accessible fishing areas in California. The lake is small, 25 acres, but deep at 100 feet. No boat motors are allowed. A hiking trail rises steeply out of the campground and connects to the Pacific Crest Trail, from which you turn left to gain a dramatic lookout of Northern California peaks as well as the lake below.

**Campsites, facilities:** There are 13 sites for tents or RVs up to 30 feet (no hookups), plus five walk-in sites that require a short walk. Picnic tables and fire grills are provided. Drinking water and vault toilets are available. Some facilities are wheelchair-accessible, including a nearby fishing pier. Leashed pets are permitted.

**Reservations, fees:** Reservations are not accepted. Sites are $15 per night. Open June through October, weather permitting.

**Directions:** From Weed, drive north on I-5 and take the Edgewood exit. At the stop sign, turn left and drive a short distance under the freeway to the stop sign at Old Highway 99. Turn right (north) on Old Highway 99 and drive six miles to Gazelle and Gazelle-Callahan Road. Turn left at Gazelle-Callahan Road and drive over the summit. From the summit, continue about five miles to Rail Creek Road. Turn left at Rail Creek Road and drive approximately eight miles to where the road dead-ends near the campground. Walk approximately 30-150 yards to reach the campsites.

**Contact:** Klamath National Forest, Scott River and Salmon River Ranger Districts, 530/468-5351, www.fs.usda.gov/klamath.

# 28 SCOTT MOUNTAIN
🏃 🐕 🚐 ⛺

### Scenic rating: 7
in Shasta-Trinity National Forest

**Map 2.2, page 108**

This camp is a jumping-off point for hikers, with the Pacific Crest Trail passing right by. If you hike southwest, it leads into the Scott Mountains and skirts the northern edge of the Trinity Alps Wilderness. Another option is driving on Forest Road 40N08, which begins directly across from camp and Highway 3. On this road, it's only two miles to Big Carmen Lake, a small, largely unknown and pretty little spot. Campground elevation is 5,400 feet. A Forest Service map is advisable.

**Campsites, facilities:** There are seven sites for tents or RVs up to 15 feet. Picnic tables and fire grills are provided. Vault toilets are available. No drinking water is available. Garbage must be packed out. Leashed pets are permitted.

**Reservations, fees:** Reservations are not accepted. There is no fee for camping. Open year-round, weather permitting.

**Directions:** From Weed, drive north on I-5 and take the Edgewood exit. At the stop sign, turn left and drive a short distance under the freeway to the stop sign at Old Highway 99. Turn right (north) and drive six miles to Gazelle and Gazelle-Callahan Road. Turn left at Gazelle-Callahan Road and drive to Callahan and Highway 3. Turn south on Highway 3 and drive to Scott Mountain Summit and look for the campground on the right side of the road.

**Contact:** Shasta-Trinity National Forest,

Weaverville Ranger District, 530/623-2121, www.fs.usda.gov/stnf.

# 29 TOAD LAKE WALK-IN
🏃 🏊 🛶 🐕 5% ⛺

### Scenic rating: 9
in Shasta-Trinity National Forest

**Map 2.2, page 108**

Some people think this site is closed, since the Forest Service no longer lists it as an active campground. Nope. There are six primitive campsites at Toad Lake, including two with picnic tables. Because it is a free site with no maintenance provided, it is off the mainstream grid. So if you want the remote beauty and splendor of an alpine lake on the Pacific Crest Trail, yet you don't want to walk far to get there, this is the place. Toad Lake is no easy trick to get to, with a bone-jarring ride for the last half hour followed by a 15-minute walk, but it's worth the effort. It's a beautiful little lake, just 23.5 acres, set at 6,900 feet in the Mount Eddy Range, with lakeside sites, excellent swimming, fair fishing for small trout, and great hiking. The best hike is a 45-minute trail out of the Toad Lake Basin to pristine Porcupine Lake. To get there, follow the trail to the head of the lake. There it rises up the slope and to the top of the ridge, intersecting with the Pacific Crest Trail. Turn left and walk a short distance to a spur trail junction on the right, which leads to Porcupine Lake.

**Campsites, facilities:** There are six walk-in tent sites. A vault toilet is available but is rather dilapidated. No drinking water is available. Garbage must be packed out. A campfire permit is required. Leashed pets are permitted.

**Reservations, fees:** Reservations are not accepted. There is no fee for camping. Open May through October, weather permitting.

**Directions:** From the town of Mount Shasta on I-5, take the Central Mount Shasta exit and drive to the stop sign. Turn west and drive less than a mile to Old Stage Road. Turn left and drive 0.25 mile to a Y intersection at W. A. Barr Road. Bear right and drive past Box Canyon

Dam and the entrance to Lake Siskiyou, and continue up the mountain (the road becomes Forest Road 26). Just past a concrete bridge, turn right on Forest Road 41N53 and drive 0.2 mile to a fork and Toad Lake Road. Turn left onto Toad Lake Road (a dirt road) and continue for 11 miles to the parking area. The road is bumpy and twisty, and the final half mile to the trailhead is rocky and rough. High-clearance or four-wheel-drive vehicles are recommended. Walk in about 0.5 mile to the lake and campsites. Note: Access roads may be closed because of flooding; call ahead for status.

**Contact:** Shasta-Trinity National Forest, Mount Shasta Ranger District, 530/926-4511, www.fs.usda.gov/stnf.

## 30 GUMBOOT

**Scenic rating: 9**

in Shasta-Trinity National Forest

**Map 2.2, page 108**

This pretty spot at 6,080 feet elevation provides a few small campsites beside a small yet beautiful high mountain lake—the kind of place many think can only be reached only after a long hike. The fishing has been good here, suited for a pram, raft, or float tube, but Fish and Game stopped stocking trout. No motors of any kind are permitted, including electric motors. Floating in a pram or inflatable to the far end of the lake and fly-fishing with black leeches and a sink-tip line is one of the best possibilities. Another option is hiking 10 minutes through forest to Upper Gumboot Lake, which is more of a pond with small trout. Another excellent hike is available here, tromping off-trail beyond Upper Gumboot Lake and up the back slope of the lake to the Pacific Crest Trail, then turning left and scrambling to a great lookout of Mount Shasta in the distance and Gumboot in the foreground.

**Campsites, facilities:** There are four sites for tents or RVs up to 16 feet (no hookups), and across the creek there are four walk-in tent sites. One unmaintained vault toilet is available. There is no drinking water. Garbage must be packed out. Some facilities are wheelchair-accessible. Leashed pets are permitted.

**Reservations, fees:** Reservations are not accepted. There is no fee for camping. Open June through October, weather permitting.

**Directions:** From the town of Mount Shasta on I-5, take the Central Mount Shasta exit and drive to the stop sign. Turn west and continue less than a mile to Old Stage Road. Turn left and drive 0.25 mile to a Y intersection at W. A. Barr Road. Bear right on W. A. Barr Road and drive two miles past Box Canyon Dam and the Lake Siskiyou Campground entrance. Continue 10 miles to a fork, signed for Gumboot Lake. Bear left and drive 0.5 mile to the lake and campsites. Note: Access roads may be closed because of flooding; call for current status.

**Contact:** Shasta-Trinity National Forest, Mount Shasta Ranger District, 530/926-4511, www.fs.usda.gov/stnf.

## 31 CASTLE LAKE

**Scenic rating: 10**

in Shasta-Trinity National Forest

**Map 2.2, page 108**

Castle Lake is a beautiful spot, a deep blue lake set in a granite bowl with a spectacular wall on the far side. The views of Mount Shasta are great, fishing is decent (especially ice fishing in winter), canoeing or floating around on a raft is a lot of fun, and a terrific hike loops around the left side of the lake, rising to the ridge overlooking the lake for dramatic views. Locals use this lake for ice-skating in winter. The campground is not right beside the lake, to ensure the pristine clear waters remain untouched, but is rather just a short distance downstream along Castle Lake Creek. There is no dispersed camping allowed within 0.5 mile of the lake. The lake is only 47 acres, but 120 feet deep. The elevation is 5,280 at the camp and 5,450 feet at the lake.

**Campsites, facilities:** There are six sites for tents or RVs up to 10 feet (no hookups). Picnic tables and fire grills are provided. Vault toilets are available. No drinking water is available. Garbage must be packed out. Leashed pets are permitted.

**Reservations, fees:** Reservations are not accepted. There is no fee for camping. Open May through October, weather permitting.

**Directions:** From the town of Mount Shasta on I-5, take the Central Mount Shasta exit and drive to the stop sign. Turn west and drive less than a mile to Old Stage Road. Turn left and drive 0.25 mile to a Y intersection at W. A. Barr Road. Bear right on W. A. Barr Road and drive two miles past Box Canyon Dam. Turn left at Castle Lake Road and drive seven miles to the campground access road on the left. Turn left and drive a short distance to the campground. Note: Castle Lake is another 0.25 mile up the road; there are no legal campsites along the lake's shoreline.

**Contact:** Shasta-Trinity National Forest, Mount Shasta Ranger District, 530/926-4511, www.fs.usda.gov/stnf.

## 32 LAKE SISKIYOU RESORT & CAMP

**Scenic rating: 9**

near Mount Shasta

**Map 2.2, page 108**    **BEST (**

This is a true gem of a lake, a jewel set at the foot of Mount Shasta at 3,181 feet, the prettiest lake on the I-5 corridor in California. The lake level is almost always full (because it was built for recreation, not water storage) and offers a variety of quality recreation options, with great swimming, low-speed boating, and fishing. The campground complexes are huge, yet they are tucked into the forest so visitors don't get their styles cramped. The water in this 435-acre lake is clean and fresh. There is an excellent beach and swimming area, the latter protected by a buoy line. In spring, the fishing

is good for trout, and then as the water warms, for smallmouth bass. A good boat ramp and boat rentals are available, and a 10-mph speed limit is strictly enforced, keeping the lake pristine and quiet. The City of Mount Shasta holds its Fourth of July fireworks display above the lake. The campgrounds are huge and often fill on weekends and summer holidays.

**Campsites, facilities:** There are 150 sites with full or partial hookups (30 and 50 amps) for RVs of any length, including some pull-through sites, and 225 additional sites for tents, seven of which are group areas. There are also 30 cabins and five park-model cabins. Picnic tables and fire pits are provided. Drinking water, restrooms with flush toilets and showers, a playground, propane, a convenience store, gift shop, coin laundry, and a dump station are available. Other amenities include a marina, boat rentals (canoes, kayaks, pedal boats, motorized boats), free boat launching, a fishing dock, a fish-cleaning station, boat slips, a swimming beach, horseshoes, volleyball, group facilities, and a recreation room. A free movie plays every night in the summer. Some facilities are wheelchair-accessible. Leashed pets are permitted at the campground only.

**Reservations, fees:** Reservations are accepted. RV sites are $26-29 per night, plus $3 per person per night for more than two people, $5 per night for each additional vehicle, and $2 per pet per night; tent sites are $20 per night. Some credit cards are accepted. Open April through October, weather permitting.

**Directions:** From the town of Mount Shasta on I-5, take the Central Mount Shasta exit and drive to the stop sign. Turn west and drive less than a mile to Old Stage Road. Turn left and drive 0.25 mile to a Y intersection at W. A. Barr Road. Bear right on W. A. Barr Road and drive past Box Canyon Dam. Two miles farther, turn right at the entrance road for Lake Siskiyou Campground and Marina and drive a short distance to the entrance station.

**Contact:** Lake Siskiyou Resort & Camp, 530/926-2610 or 888/926-2618, www.siskiyou-lakeresort.com.

## 33 KOA MOUNT SHASTA

### Scenic rating: 7

in Mount Shasta City

Map 2.2, page 108

Despite this KOA camp's relative proximity to the town of Mount Shasta, the extended driveway, wooded grounds, and view of Mount Shasta offer some feeling of seclusion. There are many excellent side trips. The best is driving up Everitt Memorial Highway, which rises up the slopes of Mount Shasta to the tree line at Bunny Flat, where you can take outstanding, short day hikes with great views to the south of the Sacramento River Canyon and Castle Crags. In the winter, you can play in the snow, including heading up to Bunny Flat for snowplay or to the Mount Shasta Board and Ski Park for developed downhill and cross-country skiing. An ice skating rink is in Mount Shasta. One of the biggest events of the year in Mount Shasta is the Fourth of July Run for Fun (billed as the largest small-town foot race anywhere) and associated parade and fireworks display at nearby Lake Siskiyou.

**Campsites, facilities:** There are 35 sites with full hookups (20, 30, and 50 amps) for RVs of any length, 42 additional sites with partial hookups (water only) for tents or RVs, and seven camping cabins. All sites are pull-through. Picnic tables are provided, and fire grills are provided at tent sites only. Restrooms with showers, a playground, propane gas, a convenience store, recreation room with arcade, horseshoe pit, shuffleboard, a seasonal swimming pool, Wi-Fi, and coin laundry are available. Some facilities are wheelchair-accessible. Leashed pets are permitted.

**Reservations, fees:** Reservations are accepted at 800/562-3617. RV sites are $34-42 per night, tent sites are $25 per night, plus $3-4 per person per night for more than two people, $3.50 per night for each additional vehicle, and a $5 site guarantee fee. Some credit cards are accepted. Open year-round.

**Directions:** From Redding, drive north on I-5 to the town of Mount Shasta. Continue past the first Mount Shasta exit and take the Central Mount Shasta exit. At the stop sign, turn right (east) on Lake Street and drive 0.6 mile to Mount Shasta Boulevard. Turn left and drive 0.5 mile to East Hinckley Boulevard. Turn right (signed KOA) on East Hinckley, drive a very short distance, then turn left at the entrance to the extended driveway for KOA Mount Shasta.

**Contact:** KOA Mount Shasta, 530/926-4029, http://koa.com/campgrounds/mount-shasta.

## 34 MCBRIDE SPRINGS

### Scenic rating: 8

on Mount Shasta in Shasta-Trinity National Forest

Map 2.2, page 108

This camp sits at 4,880 feet on the slopes of the awesome Mount Shasta (14,179 feet), California's most majestic mountain. Stargazing is fantastic, and during full moons, an eerie glow is cast on the adjoining high mountain slopes. A good side trip is to drive to the end of Everitt Memorial Highway to Bunny Flat Trailhead at 6,950 feet. Or continue beyond to the Old Ski Bowl at 7,800 feet (below towering Green Butte). You'll find great lookouts to the west and a jumping-off point for a Shasta expedition or day hike to Panther Meadows.

In 2009, a root disease decimated the white fir trees in this campground. Infected trees were removed in 2011 and the campground has since reopened. The Forest Service has replanted disease-free native species and eventually nature will do the rest.

**Campsites, facilities:** There are 12 sites for tents or RVs up to 16 feet (no hookups). Picnic tables and fire grills are provided. Drinking water (from a single well with a hand pump at the north end of the campground) and vault toilets are available. Supplies and a coin laundry are available in the town of Mount Shasta. Some facilities are wheelchair-accessible. Leashed pets are permitted.

**Reservations, fees:** Reservations are not accepted. Sites are $10 per night; pay at the self-registration fee station at the entrance. Open Memorial Day weekend through October, weather permitting.

**Directions:** From Redding, drive north on I-5 to the town of Mount Shasta and the Central Mount Shasta exit. Take that exit and drive to the stop sign and Lake Street. Turn right and continue on Lake Street through town; once out of town, the road becomes Everitt Memorial Highway. Continue on Everitt Memorial Highway for four miles to the campground entrance on the left side of the road.

**Contact:** Shasta-Trinity National Forest, Mount Shasta Ranger District, 530/926-4511, www.fs.usda.gov/stnf.

## 35 PANTHER MEADOWS WALK-IN

🚶 🐕 ⛺

**Scenic rating: 9**

on Mount Shasta in Shasta-Trinity National Forest

**Map 2.2, page 108**          **BEST (**

This quiet site, on the slopes of Mount Shasta at 7,500 feet, features access to the pristine Panther Meadows, a high mountain meadow set just below tree line. It's a sacred place, regardless of your religious orientation. The hiking is excellent; the short hike out to Gray Butte (elevation 8,119 feet) offers a panoramic view to the south of Castle Crags, Lassen Peak, and the Sacramento River Canyon. A three-night maximum stay is enforced to minimize long-term impacts.

**Campsites, facilities:** There are 10 walk-in tent sites (trailers not allowed). Picnic tables and fire grills are provided. Vault toilets are available. No drinking water is available. Garbage must be packed out. Supplies are available in the town of Mount Shasta. Leashed pets are permitted.

**Reservations, fees:** Reservations are not accepted. There is no fee for camping. Open mid-June through mid-October, weather permitting.

**Directions:** From Redding, drive north on I-5 to the town of Mount Shasta and the Central Mount Shasta exit. Take that exit and drive to the stop sign and Lake Street. Turn right and continue on Lake Street through town; once out of town, Lake Street becomes Everitt Memorial Highway. Continue on Everitt Memorial Highway for about 12 miles (passing the Bunny Flat parking area) to the campground parking area on the right. Park and walk a short distance to the campsites. Note: When the gate is closed just past Bunny Flat, the walk in is 1.5 miles from the gate to the campground.

**Contact:** Shasta-Trinity National Forest, Mount Shasta Ranger District, 530/926-4511, www.fs.usda.gov/stnf.

## 36 MCCLOUD DANCE COUNTRY RV PARK

🚶 🏊 ❄ 🎣 🐕 ♿ 🚐 ⛺

**Scenic rating: 6**

in McCloud

**Map 2.2, page 108**

McCloud Dance Country RV Park has became a draw for RV travelers. The park is sprinkled with old-growth pine trees and bordered by Squaw Valley Creek, a pretty stream. The RV sites are grassy and manicured; many are shaded. (Note that some RV campers have complained about early morning highway noise from logging trucks.) The town of McCloud is the home of McCloud Dance Country Hall, a large dance hall dedicated to square and round dancing, and tango. McCloud River's three waterfalls are accessible from the McCloud River Loop, five miles south of the park on Highway 89. McCloud Lake is just up the road (south of Squaw Valley Road); when leaving the park, make a left and continue 12 miles for boating, fishing, hiking, and day use. Mount Shasta Board and Ski Park also offers summer activities such as biking, a rock-climbing structure, and chairlift rides to great views of the surrounding forests. The ski park access road is six miles west of McCloud off Highway 89 at Snowman's Hill Summit. (For more information, see the listing for Fowlers Camp in this chapter.)

**Campsites, facilities:** There are 136 sites with full or partial hookups (30 and 50 amps) for RVs of any length, a grassy area for dispersed tent camping, and seven cabins. There are a few long-term rentals. Large groups are welcome. Picnic tables are provided. Drinking water, restrooms with hot showers and a heated bathhouse, a central barbecue and campfire area, cable TV, pay telephone, coin laundry, dump station, propane, horseshoes, two trout ponds, fish-cleaning station, and two pet walks are available. Some facilities are wheelchair-accessible. Leashed pets are permitted, except in cabins.

**Reservations, fees:** Reservations are recommended. RV sites are $38-45 per night, tent sites are $28 per night, plus $2 per person per night for more than two people. Weekly and monthly rates are available. Some credit cards are accepted. Open May through October.

**Directions:** From Redding, drive north on I-5 and continue just past Dunsmuir to the junction with Highway 89. Turn east on Highway 89 and drive nine miles to McCloud and Squaw Valley Road. Turn right on Squaw Valley Road and then turn immediately left into the park entrance.

**Contact:** McCloud Dance Country RV Park, 530/964-2252, www.mccloudrvpark.com.

## 37 FOWLERS CAMP

### Scenic rating: 10

on the McCloud River in Shasta-Trinity National Forest

**Map 2.2, page 108**

This campground sits beside the beautiful McCloud River at 3,400 feet. Nearby are three distinct waterfalls, including Middle Falls, one of the stellar sights in Northern California.

From the camp, the trail is routed upstream through forest, a near-level walk of only 15 minutes; it then arrives at awesome Middle Falls, a wide-sweeping curtainlike cascade. By summer, the flows subside and warm to the point that some people will swim in the pool at the base of the falls. The trail is also routed from camp downstream to Lower Falls, a chutelike fall and an outstanding swimming hole in midsummer. Above Middle Falls is Upper Falls, a stair-step falls with a trail that runs nearby. Fishing the McCloud River here is fair, with trout stocks made from Lakin Dam on downstream to the camp. If this camp is full, Cattle Camp and Algoma (see listings in this chapter) offer overflow areas.

**Campsites, facilities:** There are 38 sites and one double site for tents or RVs up to 30 feet (no hookups). Picnic tables and fire grills are provided. Drinking water and vault toilets are available. Some facilities are wheelchair-accessible. Leashed pets are permitted.

**Reservations, fees:** Reservations are not accepted. Sites are $15 per night. Open year-round, weather permitting.

**Directions:** From Redding, drive north on I-5 and continue just past Dunsmuir to the junction with Highway 89. Turn east on Highway 89 and drive 12 miles to McCloud. From McCloud, continue driving on Highway 89 for five miles to the campground entrance road on the right. Turn right and drive a short distance to a Y intersection, then turn left into the campground.

**Contact:** Shasta-Trinity National Forest, McCloud Ranger District, 530/964-2184, www.fs.usda.gov/stnf.

## 38 ALGOMA

### Scenic rating: 7

on the McCloud River in Shasta-Trinity National Forest

**Map 2.2, page 108**

This little-known, undeveloped spot is an alternative to Fowlers Camp and Cattle Camp (see listings in this chapter). Algoma sits along the McCloud River at 3,800 feet elevation; note that it can get quite dusty in August. A dirt road out of Algoma (turn right at the junction) follows the headwaters of the McCloud River past Cattle Camp to Upper Falls. There is a parking area for a short walk to view Middle Falls, and then on to Fowlers Camp and Lower Falls.

**Campsites, facilities:** There are eight sites for tents or RVs up to 24 feet (no hookups). Picnic tables and fire grills are provided. There are no toilet facilities. A campfire permit is required. Leashed pets are permitted.

**Reservations, fees:** Reservations are not accepted. There is no fee for camping. Open year-round, weather permitting.

**Directions:** From Redding, drive north on I-5 and continue just past Dunsmuir to the junction with Highway 89. Turn east on Highway 89 and drive to McCloud. From McCloud, continue driving on Highway 89 for 13 miles to the campground entrance road on the right (signed). Turn right and drive one mile to the campground by the bridge.

**Contact:** Shasta-Trinity National Forest, McCloud Ranger District, 530/964-2184, www.fs.usda.gov/stnf.

## 39 CATTLE CAMP

### Scenic rating: 5
on the McCloud River in Shasta-Trinity National Forest

Map 2.2, page 108

This campground at 3,700 feet is best suited for RV campers who want a rustic setting, or as an overflow area when the more attractive and popular Fowlers Camp (see listing in this chapter) is filled. A small swimming hole in the McCloud River is near the camp, although the water is typically cold. There are several good side trips in the area, including fishing on the nearby McCloud River, visiting the three waterfalls near Fowlers Camp, and exploring the north slopes of Mount Shasta (a

map of Shasta-Trinity National Forest details the back roads).

**Campsites, facilities:** There are 19 individual sites and four double sites for tents or RVs up to 32 feet (no hookups). Picnic tables and fire grills are provided. Drinking water and vault toilets are available. Some facilities are wheelchair-accessible. Leashed pets are permitted.

**Reservations, fees:** Reservations are not accepted. Sites are $15 per night. Open year-round, weather permitting.

**Directions:** From Redding, drive north on I-5 and continue just past Dunsmuir to the junction with Highway 89. Turn east on Highway 89 and drive to McCloud. From McCloud, continue driving on Highway 89 for 11 miles to the campground entrance road on the right. Turn right and drive 0.5 mile to the campground on the left side of the road.

**Contact:** Shasta-Trinity National Forest, McCloud Ranger District, 530/964-2184, www.fs.usda.gov/stnf.

## 40 TRAIL CREEK

### Scenic rating: 7
in Klamath National Forest

Map 2.2, page 108

This simple and quiet camp is set beside Trail Creek, a small tributary to the upper Salmon River, at an elevation of 4,700 feet. A trailhead is about a mile to the south, accessible via a Forest Service road, that provides access to a two-mile trail routed along Fish Creek and leads to little Fish Lake. From Fish Lake the trail climbs steeply, with switchbacks at times, for another two miles to larger Trail Gull Lake, a very pretty spot set below Deadman Peak (7,741 feet).

**Campsites, facilities:** There are 13 sites for tents or RVs up to 20 feet (no hookups). Picnic tables and fire grills are provided. Drinking water and vault toilets are available. Garbage must be packed out. Some facilities are wheelchair-accessible. Leashed pets are permitted.

# TRINITY ALPS

At the charmed center of this beautiful region are the Trinity Alps, where lakes are sprinkled everywhere. It's also home to the headwaters for feeder streams to the Trinity River, Klamath River, New River, Wooley Creek, and others. Trinity Lake provides outstanding boating and fishing, and just downstream, smaller Lewiston Lake offers a quiet alternative. One advantage to Lewiston Lake is that it is always full of water, even all summer long, making for a very pretty scene. Downstream of Lewiston, the Trinity River provides low-cost rafting and outstanding shoreline access along Highway 299 for fishing for salmon and steelhead.

**Reservations, fees:** Reservations are not accepted. Sites are $10 per night. Open May through October.

**Directions:** From Weed, drive north on I-5 to the Edgewood exit. Take the Edgewood exit, turn left at the stop sign, and drive a short distance under the freeway to another stop sign at Old Highway 99. Turn right (north) and drive six miles to Gazelle and Gazelle-Callahan Road. Turn left (west) on Gazelle-Callahan Road and continue to Callahan and Cecilville Road. Turn left (southwest) on Cecilville Road (becomes narrow) and drive 17 miles to the campground. Those with RVs should bear right upon entering the campground to align properly with aprons.

**Contact:** Klamath National Forest, Scott River Ranger District, 530/468-5351, www.fs.usda.gov/klamath.

## 41 HIDDEN HORSE

🏕️ ♿ 🚐 ⛺

**Scenic rating: 7**

in Klamath National Forest

**Map 2.2, page 108**

Hidden Horse provides an alternative horse camp to nearby Carter Meadows (see listing in this chapter). The horse camps are in close proximity to the Pacific Crest Trail, which passes through the area and serves as access to the Russian Wilderness to the north and the Trinity Alps Wilderness to the south. Trail Creek and East Fork campgrounds are nearby. The elevation is 6,000 feet.

**Campsites, facilities:** There are six sites for tents or RVs up to 35 feet (no hookups). Picnic tables and fire grills are provided. Drinking water and vault toilets are available. A horse-mounting ramp and corrals are also available. There is no designated water for stock available, so bring a bucket. Some facilities are wheelchair-accessible. Leashed pets are permitted.

**Reservations, fees:** Reservations are not accepted. Sites are $10 per night. Open June through October, weather permitting.

**Directions:** From Weed, drive north on I-5 to the Edgewood exit. Take the Edgewood exit, turn left at the stop sign, and drive a short distance under the freeway to Old Highway 99. Turn right (north) and drive six miles to Gazelle and Gazelle-Callahan Road. Turn left (west) on Gazelle-Callahan Road, and continue to Callahan and Cecilville Road. Turn left (southwest) on Cecilville Road (becomes narrow) and drive 11 miles to Carter Meadows Horse Camp. Continue 0.25 mile to the campground on the left.

**Contact:** Klamath National Forest, Scott River and Salmon River Ranger Districts, 530/468-5351, www.fs.usda.gov/klamath.

## 42 CARTER MEADOWS GROUP HORSE CAMP

**Scenic rating: 7**

in Klamath National Forest

**Map 2.2, page 108**

Carter Meadows offers an extensive trail network for riding and hiking. The Pacific Crest Trail passes through the area and serves as access to the Russian Wilderness to the north and the Trinity Alps Wilderness to the south. Stream fishing is another option. Trail Creek and East Fork campgrounds are nearby.

**Campsites, facilities:** There is one dispersed group equestrian site for tents or RVs up to 35 feet (no hookups) that can accommodate up to 25 people and 25 horses. Group barbecues and picnic tables are provided. Drinking water, vault toilets, and three horse corrals are available. Leashed pets are permitted.

**Reservations, fees:** Reservations are required at 877/444-6777 ($10 reservation fee) or www.recreation.gov ($9 reservation fee). The camp is $50 per night. Open June through October, weather permitting.

**Directions:** From Weed, drive north on I-5 to the Edgewood exit. Take the Edgewood exit, turn left at the stop sign, and drive a short distance under the freeway to Old Highway 99. Turn right (north) and drive six miles to Gazelle and Gazelle-Callahan Road. Turn left (west) on Gazelle-Callahan Road, and continue to Callahan and Cecilville Road. Turn left (southwest) on Cecilville Road and drive 11 miles to the campground on the left.

**Contact:** Klamath National Forest, Scott River and Salmon River Ranger Districts, 530/468-5351, www.fs.usda.gov/klamath.

## 43 BIG FLAT

**Scenic rating: 8**

on Coffee Creek in Klamath National Forest

**Map 2.2, page 108**

This is a great jumping-off spot for a wilderness backpacking trip into the adjacent Trinity Alps. An 11-mile hike will take you into the beautiful Caribou Lakes Basin for lakeside campsites, excellent swimming, dramatic sunsets, and fair trout fishing. The trail is routed out of camp, crosses the stream, then climbs a series of switchbacks to the ridge. From here it gets easier, rounding a mountain and depositing you in the basin. Bypass Little Caribou, Lower Caribou, and Snowslide Lakes, and instead head all the way to Caribou, the biggest and best of the lot. Big Flat is set at 5,800 feet elevation along Coffee Creek, and on the drive in, you'll see big piles of boulders along the stream, evidence of past gold mining activity.

**Campsites, facilities:** There are nine sites for tents or RVs up to 24 feet (no hookups). Picnic tables and fire grills are provided. Vault toilets and a small corral are available. No drinking water is available, but there is stock water for horses. Garbage must be packed out. Leashed pets are permitted.

**Reservations, fees:** Reservations are not accepted. There is no fee for camping. Open June through October, weather permitting.

**Directions:** From Redding, turn east on Highway 299 and drive to Weaverville. In Weaverville, turn right (north) on Highway 3 and drive just past the north end of Trinity Lake to Coffee Creek Road/Forest Road 104, adjacent to a Forest Service ranger station. Turn left on Coffee Creek Road and drive 21 miles to the campground at the end of the road.

**Contact:** Klamath National Forest, Salmon River Ranger District, 530/468-5351, www.fs.usda.gov.

## 44 HORSE FLAT

### Scenic rating: 6

on Eagle Creek in Shasta-Trinity National Forest

**Map 2.2, page 108**

This camp is used by commercial pack operations as well as horse owners preparing for trips into the Trinity Alps. A trail leads out of camp and is routed deep into the Trinity Alps Wilderness. The trail starts at 3,200 feet in elevation, then climbs all the way along Eagle Creek to Eagle Peak, where it intersects with the Pacific Crest Trail, then drops over the ridge to little Telephone Lake, a nine-mile hike. Note: Horse owners should call for the conditions of the corral and trail before making the trip.

**Campsites, facilities:** There are 10 sites for tents or RVs up to 16 feet (no hookups). Picnic tables and fire grills are provided. Vault toilets are available. No drinking water is available. Horse corrals are available. Garbage must be packed out. Leashed pets are permitted.

**Reservations, fees:** Reservations are not accepted. There is no fee for camping. Open mid-May through October.

**Directions:** From Redding, drive west on Highway 299 to Weaverville and Highway 3. Turn right (north) on Highway 3 and drive to Trinity Center at the north end of Trinity Lake. From Trinity Center, continue north on Highway 3 for 16.5 miles to Eagle Creek Campground (on the left) and Forest Road 38N27. Turn left on Forest Road 38N27 and drive two miles to the campground.

**Contact:** Shasta-Trinity National Forest, Weaverville Ranger Station, 530/623-2121, www.fs.usda.gov/stnf.

## 45 EAGLE CREEK

### Scenic rating: 7

in Shasta-Trinity National Forest

**Map 2.2, page 108**

This campground is where little Eagle Creek enters the north Trinity River. Some campers use it as a base camp for a fishing trip, with the rainbow trout often abundant but predictably small in this stretch of water. The elevation is 2,800 feet.

**Campsites, facilities:** There are 10 sites for tents and seven sites that can accommodate RVs up to 35 feet (no hookups). Picnic tables and fire grills are provided. Drinking water and vault toilets are available. Leashed pets are permitted.

**Reservations, fees:** Reservations are not accepted. Sites are $15 per night, plus $6 per night for an additional vehicle. Open mid-May through October.

**Directions:** From Redding, drive west on Highway 299 to Weaverville and Highway 3. Turn right (north) on Highway 3 and drive to Trinity Center at the north end of Trinity Lake. From Trinity Center, continue north on Highway 3 for 16.5 miles to the campground on the left side of the road.

**Contact:** Shasta-Trinity National Forest, Weaverville Ranger Station, 530/623-2121, www.fs.usda.gov/stnf.

## 46 GOLDFIELD

### Scenic rating: 6

in Shasta-Trinity National Forest

**Map 2.2, page 108**    BEST (

For hikers, this camp makes a perfect first stop after a long drive. You wake up, get your gear organized, and then take the trailhead to the south. The trail is routed along Boulder Creek, and a left turn at the junction (about four miles in) will take you to Boulder Lake (another two miles), inside the edge of the Trinity Alps

Wilderness. Back in the day, former 49ers coach George Seifert told me about the beauty of this place and how perfectly this campground is situated for the hike. The elevation is 3,000 feet.

**Campsites, facilities:** There are six sites for tents or RVs up to 16 feet (no hookups). Picnic tables and fire grills are provided. Vault toilets and hitching posts for horses are available. No drinking water is available. Garbage must be packed out. Leashed pets are permitted.

**Reservations, fees:** Reservations are not accepted. There is no fee for camping. Open year-round.

**Directions:** From Redding, head west on Highway 299 and drive to Weaverville. Turn right (north) on Highway 3 and drive about 36 miles, just past the north end of Trinity Lake to Coffee Creek Road/Forest Road 104 (a Forest Service ranger station is nearby). Turn left on Coffee Creek Road/Forest Road 104 and drive 4.7 miles to the campground on the left side of the road.

**Contact:** Shasta-Trinity National Forest, Weaverville Ranger Station, 530/623-2121, www.fs.usda.gov/stnf.

## 47 TRINITY RIVER

### Scenic rating: 7
in Shasta-Trinity National Forest

Map 2.2, page 108

This camp offers easy access off Highway 3, yet it is fairly secluded and provides streamside access to the upper Trinity River. It's a good base camp for a fishing trip when the upper Trinity is loaded with small trout. The elevation is 2,500 feet.

**Campsites, facilities:** There are seven sites for tents or RVs up to 35 feet (no hookups). Picnic tables and fire grills are provided. Drinking water and vault toilets are available. Leashed pets are permitted.

**Reservations, fees:** Reservations are not accepted. Sites are $10 per night, plus $6 for an additional vehicle. Open May through October.

**Directions:** From Redding, drive west on Highway 299 to Weaverville and Highway 3. Turn right (north) on Highway 3 and drive to Trinity Center at the north end of Trinity Lake. From Trinity Center, continue north on Highway 3 for 9.5 miles to the campground on the left side of the road.

**Contact:** Shasta-Trinity National Forest, Weaverville Ranger Station, 530/623-2121, www.fs.usda.gov/stnf.

## 48 CASTLE CRAGS STATE PARK

### Scenic rating: 9
on the Sacramento River

Map 2.2, page 108

This park is named for the awesome granite spires that tower 6,000 feet above the park. Beyond to the north is giant Mount Shasta (14,179 feet), which encompasses a spectacular natural setting. The campsites are within the forest, shaded, very pretty, and sprinkled along a paved access road. But not a year goes by when people don't write in complaining of the highway noise from I-5 echoing in the Sacramento River Canyon, as well as of the occasional passing freight trains in the night. The Pacific Crest Trail passes through the park. Pristine and quiet, this campground is not. At the end of the access road is a parking area for the two-minute walk to the Crags Lookout, a beautiful view. Nearby is the trailhead (at 2,500 feet elevation) for hikes up the Crags, featuring a 5.4-mile round-trip that rises to the base of Castle Dome at 4,800 feet, the leading spire on the crag's ridge. Again, road noise echoing up the canyon provides a background once you clear the tree line. Trout fishing is good in the nearby Sacramento River and requires driving, walking, and exploring to find the best spots. There are also some good swimming holes, but the water is cold. Severe weather may cause closures; contact the Cascade Sector Office for current conditions.

**Campsites, facilities:** There are 62 sites for tents only and three sites for RVs up to 27 feet (no hookups). There are also six walk-in environmental sites (100-yard walk required) with limited facilities, and a hike-in/bike-in site. The Riverside Campground is an overflow area with 12 sites and limited facilities (first-come, first-served). Picnic tables, food lockers, and fire grills or fire rings are provided. Drinking water, restrooms with flush toilets and showers, and firewood are available. Some facilities are wheelchair-accessible. Leashed pets are permitted at campsites only.

**Reservations, fees:** Reservations are accepted seasonally at 800/444-7275 or www.reserveamerica.com ($8 reservation fee). Tent and RV sites are $25-30 per night, plus $8 per night for each additional vehicle; primitive drive-in tent sites are $15 per night; hike-in/bike-in sites are $5 per person per night. Open year-round.

**Directions:** From Redding, drive north on I-5 for 45 miles to the Castle Crags State Park exit. Take that exit, turn west, and drive a short distance to the well-signed park entrance on the right side of the road.

**Contact:** Castle Crags State Park, 530/235-2684, Cascade Sector Office, 530/225-2065, www.parks.ca.gov.

## 49 RAILROAD PARK RV AND CAMPGROUND

🏊 🛶 🐕 ♿ 🚐 ⛺

**Scenic rating: 7**

south of Dunsmuir

**Map 2.2, page 108**

The resort adjacent to the RV park and campground was designed in the spirit of the railroad, when steam trains ruled the rails. The property features old stage cars (available for overnight lodging) and a steam locomotive. The railroad theme does not extend to the campground, however. What you'll find at the park is a classic campground amid tall trees. There is a swimming hole in Little Castle Creek alongside the park. Many good side trips are available in the area, including excellent hiking and sightseeing at Castle Crags State Park (where there is a series of awesome granite spires) and outstanding trout fishing on the upper Sacramento River. At night, the sound of occasional passing trains soothes some, wakes others.

**Campsites, facilities:** There are 25 sites with full or partial hookups (30 amps) for RVs of any length, 31 sites with no hookups for tents or RVs. Some sites are pull-through. Cabins and a motel are next door at the resort. Picnic tables and fire rings are provided. Restrooms with showers, ice, coin laundry, group barbecue pit, game room, and horseshoes are available. A restaurant and lounge are within walking distance. Some facilities are wheelchair-accessible. Leashed pets are permitted.

**Reservations, fees:** Reservations are accepted. RV sites are $37 per night, tent sites are $23 per night, plus $3 per person per night for more than two people and $3 per night for each additional vehicle. Some credit cards are accepted. Open April through November, weather permitting.

**Directions:** From Redding, drive north on I-5 for 45 miles to Exit 728 for Cragview Drive/Railroad Park Road. Take that exit and drive to the stop sign and Railroad Park Road. Turn left and drive under the freeway and continue to the campground on the left.

**Contact:** Railroad Park RV and Campground, 530/235-4440, www.rrpark.com.

## 50 SIMS FLAT

🚶 🏊 🛶 🐕 ♿ 🚐 ⛺

**Scenic rating: 7**

on the Sacramento River

**Map 2.2, page 108**

The upper Sacramento River is one of the best trout streams in the West, with easy and direct access off an interstate highway, and this camp is a good example. Sitting beside the upper Sacramento River at an elevation of 1,600 feet, it provides access to some of the better spots for trout fishing, particularly from late April through July. In the spring, this is a good put-in for rafting down through Pollard Flat. There is also a wheelchair-accessible interpretive trail. If you want to literally get away from it all, there is a trailhead about three miles east on Sims Flat Road that climbs along South Fork, including a terrible, steep, one-mile section near the top, eventually popping out at Tombstone Mountain. The noise from passing trains can be a shock, even when you know it's coming.

**Campsites, facilities:** There are 19 sites for tents or RVs up to 16 feet (no hookups). Picnic tables and fire grills are provided. Drinking water and flush and vault toilets are available. A nearby seasonal grocery store is open intermittently. Supplies are available to the north in Castella and Dunsmuir. Some facilities are wheelchair-accessible. Leashed pets are permitted.

**Reservations, fees:** Reservations are not accepted. Sites are $15 per night. Open late April through October.

**Directions:** From Redding, drive north on I-5 for about 40 miles to the Sims Road exit. Take the Sims Road exit (on the east side of the highway) and drive south for a mile (crossing the railroad tracks and a bridge) to the campground on the right.

**Contact:** Shasta-Trinity National Forest, Mount Shasta Ranger District, 530/926-4511, www.fs.usda.gov/stnf.

## 51 BEST IN THE WEST RESORT

### Scenic rating: 5

near Dunsmuir

**Map 2.2, page 108**

This is a good layover spot for RV cruisers looking to take a break. The proximity to Castle Crags State Park, the Sacramento River, and Mount Shasta makes the location a winner. Meers Creek runs through the property, and the local area has outstanding swimming holes

on the Sacramento River. Trains make regular runs every night in the Sacramento River Canyon and the noise is a problem for some visitors.

**Campsites, facilities:** There are 15 sites with full hookups (30 and 50 amps) for RVs, a separate grassy area for dispersed tent camping, eight cabins, and a lodge. Picnic tables are provided. Coin laundry, cable TV, and restrooms with showers are available. Leashed pets are permitted.

**Reservations, fees:** Reservations are recommended. Sites are $30 per night. Cabins are $60-110 per night (two-night minimum). Weekly and monthly rates are available. Open year-round.

**Directions:** From Redding, drive north on I-5 for about 40 miles to the Sims Road exit. Take the Sims Road exit and drive one block west on Sims Road to the resort on the left.

**Contact:** Best in the West Resort, 530/235-2603, www.eggerbestwest.com.

## 52 FRIDAY'S RV RETREAT & MCCLOUD FLY FISHING RANCH

### Scenic rating: 7

near McCloud

**Map 2.2, page 108**

Friday's RV Retreat and McCloud Fly Fishing Ranch offers great recreation opportunities across 400 wooded and grassy acres. The property features a small private fishing lake, two casting ponds, 1.5 miles of Squaw Valley Creek frontage, and five miles of hiking trails. The ranch specializes in fly-fishing packages, with both lodging and fly-fishing for one price. In addition, the McCloud River's wild trout section is a 45-minute drive to the south, the beautiful McCloud Golf Course (nine holes, play it twice at different tee boxes) is within a five-minute drive, and a trailhead for the Pacific Crest Trail is also only five minutes away.

Owner Bob Friday is quite a character, and

he figured out that if he planted giant rainbow trout in the ponds for catch-and-release fishing, fly fishers would stop to catch a monster, take a photograph, and then tell people they caught the fish on the McCloud River, where they are smaller and elusive. (Weeds are occasionally a problem at the ponds; call ahead if that is a concern.) The park also has an area for miniature radio-controlled airplanes, a subject of fascination for Bob.

**Campsites, facilities:** There are 30 sites with full hookups (30 and 50 amps) for RVs of any length (7 back-in spaces, 23 pull-through), a large, grassy area for dispersed tent camping, and two cabins. Picnic tables and fire pits are provided. Drinking water, restrooms with showers and flush toilets, coin laundry, pay phone, propane gas, a recreation room, and a large community deck with table and chairs are available. A fly-fishing school is available by arrangement. Some facilities are wheelchair-accessible. Leashed pets are permitted.

**Reservations, fees:** Reservations are recommended. RV sites are $35 per night, tent sites are $23 per night, plus $5 per person per night for more than two people. Monthly rates are available for RVs. Open early May through September.

**Directions:** From Redding, drive north on I-5 and continue just past Dunsmuir to the junction with Highway 89. Bear right on Highway 89 and drive nine miles to McCloud and Squaw Valley Road. Turn right at Squaw Valley Road and drive six miles to the park entrance on the right.

**Contact:** Friday's RV Retreat & McCloud Fly Fishing Ranch, 530/964-2878, www.fridaysrvretreat.com.

## 53 AH-DI-NA

**Scenic rating: 9**

on the McCloud River in Shasta-Trinity National Forest

**Map 2.2, page 108**

This is the base camp for trout fishing on the lower McCloud River, with campsites just a cast away from one of the prettiest streams in California. You get access to the McCloud, which includes a special two-mile stretch of river governed by The Nature Conservancy, where all fish must be released, no bait is permitted, single, barbless hooks are mandated, and only 10 rods are allowed on the river at any one time. Wildlife is abundant in the area, the Pacific Crest Trail passes adjacent to the camp, and an excellent nature trail is also available along the river in the McCloud Nature Conservancy.

**Campsites, facilities:** There are 17 sites for tents. Picnic tables and fire grills are provided. Drinking water, flush toilets, and garbage bins are available. Leashed pets are permitted.

**Reservations, fees:** Reservations are not accepted. Sites are $10 per night. Open late April through October, weather permitting.

**Directions:** From Redding, drive north on I-5 past Dunsmuir to the junction with Highway 89. Turn right and drive nine miles to McCloud and Squaw Valley Road. Turn right on Squaw Valley Road and drive to Lake McCloud. Turn right at Lake McCloud and continue along the lake to a signed turnoff on the right side of the road (at a deep cove in the lake). Turn right (the road turns to dirt) and drive four miles to the campground entrance on the left side of the road. Turn left and drive a short distance to the campground. The road in is dusty and winding—RVs and trailers are not advised.

**Contact:** Shasta-Trinity National Forest, McCloud Ranger District, 530/964-2184, www.fs.usda.gov/stnf.

## 54 EAST FORK

### Scenic rating: 8

on Willow Creek

Map 2.3, page 109

This is a beautiful spot along Willow Creek at a 2,000-foot elevation. It's one of the prettiest campgrounds in the area. While you can dunk into the cold creek, it's not really a good swimming area. Fishing is prohibited.

**Campsites, facilities:** There are 10 sites for tents or RVs up to 20 feet (no hookups). Picnic tables and fire rings are provided. Vault toilets are available. No drinking water is available. Some facilities are wheelchair-accessible. Leashed pets are permitted.

**Reservations, fees:** Reservations are not accepted. Sites are $8 per night, plus $5 per night for each additional vehicle. Open late May through September, weather permitting.

**Directions:** From the junction of U.S. 101 and Highway 299 near Arcata, turn east on Highway 299 and drive 32 miles (six miles west of Willow Creek); look for the camp's entrance road (well signed) on the right (south) side of the road.

**Contact:** Six Rivers National Forest, Lower Trinity Ranger District, 530/629-2118, www. fs.usda.gov/stnf.

## 55 BOISE CREEK

### Scenic rating: 7

in Six Rivers National Forest

Map 2.3, page 109

This camp features a 0.25-mile trail down to Willow Creek and nearby access to the Trinity River. If you have ever wanted to see Bigfoot, you can do it while camping here—there's a giant wooden Bigfoot on display in nearby Willow Creek. After your Bigfoot experience, your best bet during summer is to head north on nearby Highway 96 (turn north in Willow Creek) to the campground at Tish Tang, where there is excellent river access, swimming, and rafting in the late summer's warm flows. The Trinity River also provides good salmon and steelhead fishing during fall and winter, respectively. Note that fishing is prohibited in nearby Willow Creek.

**Campsites, facilities:** There are 17 sites for tents or RVs up to 35 feet (no hookups). Picnic tables and fire grills are provided. Drinking water and vault toilets are available. A camp host is on-site. A grocery store, gas station, restaurant, and propane gas are nearby. Some facilities are wheelchair-accessible. Leashed pets are permitted.

**Reservations, fees:** Reservations are accepted at 877/444-6777 ($10 reservation fee) or www. recreation.gov ($9 reservation fee). Sites are $10 per night, plus $5 per night for each additional vehicle. Open year-round.

**Directions:** From the intersection of U.S. 101 and Highway 299 near Arcata, drive 38 miles east on Highway 299 and look for the campground entrance on the left side of the road. If you reach the town of Willow Creek, you have gone 1.5 miles too far.

**Contact:** Six Rivers National Forest, Lower Trinity Ranger District, 530/629-2118, www. fs.usda.gov/stnf.

## 56 DENNY

### Scenic rating: 6

on the New River in Shasta-Trinity National Forest

Map 2.3, page 109

This is a secluded and quiet campground along the New River, a tributary to the Trinity River and a designated Wild and Scenic River. The stream is OK for swimming but too cold to even dip a toe in until late summer. If you drive north from the camp on Denny Road, you will find several trailheads for trips into the Trinity Alps Wilderness. The best of them is at the end of the road, where there is a good parking area, with a trail that is routed along the East Fork

New River up toward Limestone Ridge. Note that the stretch of river near the camp is closed to fishing year-round. The campground is at 1,400 feet.

**Campsites, facilities:** There are five sites for tents or RVs up to 22 feet (no hookups). Picnic tables and fire grills are provided. Vault toilets are available. No drinking water is available. Garbage must be packed out. Supplies are available about one hour away in Salyers Bar. Leashed pets are permitted.

**Reservations, fees:** Reservations are not accepted. There is no fee for camping. Open year-round.

**Directions:** From the junction of U.S. 101 and Highway 299 near Arcata, turn east on Highway 299 and drive to Willow Creek. In Willow Creek, continue east on Highway 299 and, after reaching Salyer, continue for four miles to Denny Road/County Road 402. Turn north (left) on Denny Road and drive about 14 miles on a paved but very windy road to the campground.

**Contact:** Shasta-Trinity National Forest, Weaverville Ranger Station, 530/623-2121, www.fs.usda.gov/stnf.

## 57 HOBO GULCH

### Scenic rating: 7

on the North Fork of the Trinity River in Shasta-Trinity National Forest

**Map 2.3, page 109**

Only the ambitious need apply. This is a trailhead camp on the edge of the Trinity Alps Wilderness, and the reason only the ambitious show up is that it is a 20-mile uphill haul all the way to Grizzly Lake, at the foot of the awesome Thompson Peak (8,663 feet), with no other lakes available en route. The camp is at 2,200 feet along the North Fork of the Trinity River. The adjacent slopes of the wilderness are known for little creeks, woods, and a few pristine meadows, but are largely devoid of lakes.

**Campsites, facilities:** There are 10 sites for tents only. Picnic tables and fire grills are provided. Vault toilets are available. No drinking water is available. Garbage must be packed out. Supplies can be obtained in Junction City, about one hour away. Leashed pets are permitted.

**Reservations, fees:** Reservations are not accepted. There is no fee for camping. Open year-round.

**Directions:** From Redding, turn on Highway 299 west and drive west past Weaverville, then continue 13 miles to Helena and County East Fork Road. Turn right on County East Fork Road and drive four miles to Hobo Gulch Road. At Hobo Gulch Road, turn left (north) and drive 16 miles (very rough road) to the end of the road at the campground.

**Contact:** Shasta-Trinity National Forest, Weaverville Ranger Station, 530/623-2121, www.fs.usda.gov/stnf.

## 58 RIPSTEIN

### Scenic rating: 8

on Canyon Creek in Shasta-Trinity National Forest

**Map 2.3, page 109**

This is one of the great trailhead camps for the neighboring Trinity Alps. It is at 3,000 feet on the southern edge of the wilderness and is a popular spot for a late-night arrival followed by a backpacking trip the next morning. The Canyon Creek Lakes await you via a six-mile uphill hike along Canyon Creek. The destination is extremely beautiful—two alpine lakes set in high granite mountains. The route passes Canyon Creek Falls, a set of two different waterfalls, about 3.5 miles out. This is one of the most popular backpacking destinations in Northern California. Seasonal guided rafting trips on Canyon Creek are also available.

**Campsites, facilities:** There are 10 sites for tents only. Picnic tables and fire grills are provided. Vault toilets are available. No drinking water is available. Garbage must be packed out.

Supplies can be obtained 25 minutes away in Junction City. Leashed pets are permitted.

**Reservations, fees:** Reservations are not accepted. There is no fee for camping. Open year-round.

**Directions:** From Redding, turn on Highway 299 west and drive west to Junction City and Canyon Creek Road. Turn right on Canyon Creek Road and drive 10 miles to the campground on the left side of the road.

**Contact:** Shasta-Trinity National Forest, Weaverville Ranger Station, 530/623-2121, www.fs.usda.gov/stnf; Trinity River Rafting Company, 530/623-3033 or 800/307-4837, www. trinityriverrafting.com.

## 59 BURNT RANCH

### Scenic rating: 7
on the Trinity River in Shasta-Trinity National Forest

**Map 2.3, page 109**

This campground is on a bluff above the Trinity River and is one of its most compelling spots. This section of river is very pretty, with deep, dramatic canyons nearby. The elevation is 1,000 feet. Note that the trail to Burnt Ranch Falls is not maintained and is partially on private land—the landowners will not take kindly to anyone trespassing.

**Campsites, facilities:** There are 16 sites for tents or RVs up to 25 feet (no hookups). Picnic tables and fire grills are provided. Drinking water and vault toilets are available. Garbage must be packed out. Supplies can be obtained in Hawkins Bar about one hour away. Leashed pets are permitted.

**Reservations, fees:** Reservations are not accepted. Sites are $6 per night. Open year-round, weather permitting.

**Directions:** From Redding, take Highway 299 west and drive past Weaverville to Burnt Ranch. In Burnt Ranch, continue 0.5 mile and look for the campground entrance on the right side of the road.

**Contact:** Shasta-Trinity National Forest, Weaverville Ranger Station, 530/623-2121, www.fs.usda.gov/stnf; Trinity River Rafting Company, 530/623-3033 or 800/307-4837, www. trinityriverrafting.com.

## 60 DEL LOMA RV PARK AND CAMPGROUND

### Scenic rating: 7
on the Trinity River

**Map 2.3, page 109**

RV cruisers looking for a layover spot near the Trinity River will find just that at Del Loma. Shady sites and sandy beaches are available along the Trinity. Rafting and tubing trips are popular in this area during the summer. Salmon fishing is best in the fall, steelhead fishing in the winter. This camp is popular for family reunions and groups. Salmon fishing can be sensational on the Trinity in the fall, and some anglers will book a year in advance to make certain they get a spot. About two-thirds of the sites are rented for extended periods.

**Campsites, facilities:** There are 41 sites, including two pull-through, with full hookups (50 amps) for RVs and tents, as well as five park-model cabins. Picnic tables and fire grills are provided. Restrooms with flush toilets and showers, dump station, convenience store, clubhouse, heated pool, deli, Wi-Fi, RV supplies, firewood, coin laundry, recreation room, volleyball, tetherball, 18-hole mini golf, laser tag, and horseshoe pits are available. Some facilities are wheelchair-accessible. Leashed pets are permitted.

**Reservations, fees:** Reservations are accepted at 800/839-0194. Sites are $30 per night, plus $2 per person per night for more than two people. Group and monthly rates are available. Some credit cards are accepted. Open year-round.

**Directions:** From the junction of U.S. 101 and Highway 299 in Arcata, turn east on Highway 299 and drive to Burnt Ranch. From Burnt Ranch, continue 10 miles east on Highway 299 to the town of Del Loma and look for the campground entrance on the right.

**Contact:** Del Loma RV Park and Campground, 530/623-2834 or 800/839-0194, www.dellomarv.com.

## 61 HAYDEN FLAT CAMPGROUND

### Scenic rating: 7

on the Trinity River in Shasta-Trinity National Forest

**Map 2.3, page 109**

This campground is split into two pieces, with most of the sites grouped in a large, shaded area across the road from the river and a few on the river side. A beach is available along the river; it is a good spot for swimming as well as a popular put-in and take-out spot for rafters. The elevation is 1,200 feet.

**Campsites, facilities:** There are 35 sites for tents or RVs up to 25 feet (no hookups); it can also be used as a group camp with a three-site minimum. Picnic tables and fire grills are provided. Drinking water and vault toilets are available. Some facilities are wheelchair-accessible. Leashed pets are permitted.

**Reservations, fees:** Reservations are required for groups (minimum of three sites) at 530/623-2121. Single sites are $12 per night, and group sites are $40 per night. Open year-round.

**Directions:** From the junction of U.S. 101 and Highway 299 in Arcata, head east on Highway 299 and drive to Burnt Ranch. From Burnt Ranch, continue 10 miles east on Highway 299 and look for the campground entrance. If you reach the town of Del Loma, you have gone 0.5 mile too far.

**Contact:** Shasta-Trinity National Forest, Weaverville Ranger Station, 530/623-2121, www.fs.usda.gov/stnf.

## 62 SKUNK POINT GROUP CAMP

### Scenic rating: 7

on the Trinity River in Shasta-Trinity National Forest

**Map 2.3, page 109**

This is an ideal site for groups on rafting trips. You get easy access to the nearby Trinity River with a streamside setting and privacy for the group. A beach on the river is nearby. In the spring, this section of river offers primarily Class II rapids (only more difficult during high water), but most of it is rated Class I. By late summer, the water is warm and benign, ideal for families. Guided rafting trips and inflatables are available for hire and rent in nearby Big Flat. The camp elevation is 1,200 feet.

**Campsites, facilities:** Two group sites can accommodate up to 50 people each. Picnic tables and fire grills are provided. Vault toilets are available. No drinking water is available. Some facilities are wheelchair-accessible. Leashed pets are permitted.

**Reservations, fees:** Reservations are accepted at 530/623-2121. The camp is $40 per night per site. Open seasonally (closed to camping in winter).

**Directions:** From Redding, turn on Highway 299 west, drive west past Weaverville, Junction City, and Helena, and continue for about seven miles. Look for the campground entrance on the left side of the road. If you reach the town of Big Bar, you have gone two miles too far.

**Contact:** Shasta-Trinity National Forest, Weaverville Ranger Station, 530/623-2121, www.fs.usda.gov/stnf; Trinity River Rafting Company, 530/623-3033 or 800/307-4837, www.trinityriverrafting.com.

## 63 BIG FLAT

**Scenic rating: 6**

on the Trinity River in Shasta-Trinity National Forest

**Map 2.3, page 109**

This level campground is off Highway 299, just across the road from the Trinity River. The sites are close together, and it can be hot and dusty in midsummer. No problem. That is when you will be on the Trinity River, taking a rafting or kayaking trip—as low as $40 to rent an inflatable kayak from Trinity River Rafting in nearby Big Bar. It's fun, exciting, and easy (newcomers are welcome).

**Campsites, facilities:** There are 10 sites for tents or RVs up to 22 feet (no hookups). Picnic tables and fire grills are provided. Vault toilets are available. There is no drinking water. Some facilities are wheelchair-accessible. Leashed pets are permitted.

**Reservations, fees:** Reservations are not accepted. Sites are $6 per night. Open year-round.

**Directions:** From Redding, turn on Highway 299 west, drive west past Weaverville, Junction City, and Helena, and continue for about seven miles. Look for the campground entrance on the right side of the road. If you reach the town of Big Bar, you have gone three miles too far.

**Contact:** Shasta-Trinity National Forest, Weaverville Ranger Station, 530/623-2121, www.fs.usda.gov/stnf; Trinity River Rafting Company, 530/623-3033 or 800/307-4837, www. trinityriverrafting.com.

## 64 PIGEON POINT AND GROUP

**Scenic rating: 7**

on the Trinity River in Shasta-Trinity National Forest

**Map 2.3, page 109**

In the good old days, huge flocks of bandtail pigeons flew the Trinity River Canyon, swooping and diving in dramatic shows. Nowadays you don't see too many pigeons, but this camp still keeps its namesake. It is better known for its access to the Trinity River, with a large beach for swimming. The elevation is 1,100 feet.

**Campsites, facilities:** There are six sites for tents or RVs up to 22 feet, two multi-family sites, and one group site that can accommodate up to 50 people with tents or RVs up to 16 feet (no hookups). Picnic tables and fire grills are provided. Vault toilets are available. No drinking water is available. Supplies can be obtained within 10 miles in Big Bar or Junction City. Some facilities are wheelchair-accessible. Leashed pets are permitted.

**Reservations, fees:** Reservations are not accepted for individual sites but are required for the group site at 530/623-2121. Rates are $12 per night for singles sites, $15 for multi-family sites, and $75 per night for the group site. Open year-round.

**Directions:** From Redding, turn on Highway 299 west and drive west to Weaverville. Continue west on Highway 299 to Helena and continue 0.5 mile to the campground on the left (south) side of the road.

**Contact:** Shasta-Trinity National Forest, Weaverville Ranger Station, 530/623-2121, www.fs.usda.gov/stnf.

## 65 BIGFOOT CAMPGROUND AND RV PARK

**Scenic rating: 8**

on the Trinity River

**Map 2.3, page 109**

This private RV park has become one of the most popular spots along the Trinity River. Rafting and fishing trips are featured, along with cabin rentals. It is also a popular layover for Highway 299 cruisers, but it provides an option for longer stays with rafting, gold panning, and, in the fall and winter, fishing for salmon and steelhead, respectively. RV sites are exceptionally large, and a bonus is that a storage area is available. A three-acre site for tent camping is along the river.

**Campsites, facilities:** There are 46 sites with full or partial hookups (30 and 50 amps) for RVs of any length, a separate area for tent camping, and four cabins. Tent camping is not allowed during the winter. Picnic tables and barbecues are provided. Restrooms with flush toilets and coin showers, coin laundry, convenience store, dump station, propane gas, solar-heated swimming pool (summer only), and horseshoe pits are available. TV hookups and a tackle shop are also available. Some facilities are wheelchair-accessible. Leashed pets are permitted.

**Reservations, fees:** Reservations are recommended from June through October. RV sites are $26-35 per night, tent sites are $26 per night, plus $2.50 per night per person for more than two people at RV sites. Some credit cards are accepted. Open year-round.

**Directions:** From Redding, turn on Highway 299 west and drive west to Junction City. Continue west on Highway 299 for three miles to the camp on the left.

**Contact:** Bigfoot Campground and RV Park, 530/623-6088 or 800/422-5219, www.bigfoot-rvcabins.com.

## 66 JUNCTION CITY

**Scenic rating: 7**

on the Trinity River

Map 2.3, page 109

Some of the Trinity River's best fall salmon fishing is in this area in September and early October, with steelhead following from mid-October into the winter. That makes it an ideal base camp for a fishing or camping trip.

**Campsites, facilities:** There are 22 sites for tents or RVs up to 40 feet (no hookups). Picnic tables, fire grills, and bear-proof food lockers are provided. Drinking water and vault toilets are available. Groceries and propane gas are available within two miles in Junction City. Some facilities are wheelchair-accessible. Leashed pets are permitted.

**Reservations, fees:** Reservations are not accepted. Sites are $10 per night per vehicle, plus $5 per additional vehicle. Open May through November.

**Directions:** From Redding, turn on Highway 299 west and drive west to Junction City. At Junction City, continue west on Highway 299 for 1.5 miles to the camp on the right.

**Contact:** Bureau of Land Management, Redding Field Office, 530/224-2100, www.blm.gov/ca.

## 67 BIG SLIDE

**Scenic rating: 7**

on the South Fork of the Trinity River in Shasta-Trinity National Forest

Map 2.3, page 109

This camp is literally out in the middle of nowhere, a tiny, secluded, little-visited spot along the South Fork of the Trinity River. Free? Of course it's free. Otherwise, someone would actually have to show up now and then to collect. The elevation is 1,250 feet.

**Campsites, facilities:** There are eight sites for tents only. Picnic tables and fire grills are provided. Vault toilets are available. No drinking water is available. Leashed pets are permitted.

**Reservations, fees:** Reservations are not accepted. There is no fee for camping. Open late May to early October, weather permitting.

**Directions:** From Redding, turn on Highway 299 west and drive west over the Buckhorn Summit to the junction with Highway 3 near Douglas City. Turn south on Highway 3 and drive to Hayfork. From Hayfork, turn right on County Road 301 and drive about 20 miles to the town of Hyampom. In Hyampom, turn right on Lower South Fork Road/County Road 311 and drive five miles on County Road 311 to the campground on the right.

**Contact:** Shasta-Trinity National Forest,

Hayfork Ranger Station, 530/628-5227, www. fs.usda.gov/stnf.

# 68 PHILPOT

### Scenic rating: 7

on the North Fork of Salt Creek in Shasta-Trinity National Forest

**Map 2.3, page 109**

It's time to join the 5 Percent Club; that is, the 5 percent of the people who know the little-used, beautiful spots in California. This is one of those places, set on the North Fork of Salt Creek on national forest land at an elevation of 2,600 feet. Remember: 95 percent of the people use just 5 percent of the available open space. Why would anyone come here? To join the 5 Percent Club, that's why. Note: The road is too rough for many vehicles, and the sites are too small for most RVs. Trailers and RVs are not recommended.

**Campsites, facilities:** There are 13 sites for tents only. Picnic tables and fire grills are provided. Vault toilets are available. No drinking water is available. Garbage must be packed out. Leashed pets are permitted.

**Reservations, fees:** Reservations are not accepted. There is no fee for camping. Open late May to early November, weather permitting.

**Directions:** From Redding, turn on Highway 299 west and drive west over the Buckhorn Summit, then continue to the junction with Highway 3 near Douglas City. Turn left (south) on Highway 3 and drive to Hayfork. From Hayfork, continue southwest on Highway 3 for eight miles to County Road 353 (Rattlesnake Creek Road). Turn right and drive one mile to Forest Road 30N31. Turn right and drive 0.5 mile to the campground on the left. Trailers and RVs are not recommended.

**Contact:** Shasta-Trinity National Forest, Hayfork Ranger Station, 530/628-5227, www. fs.usda.gov/stnf.

# 69 MAD RIVER

### Scenic rating: 7

in Six Rivers National Forest

**Map 2.3, page 109**

This Forest Service campground sits along an alluvial flood terrace, a unique landscape for this region, featuring a forest of manzanita and Douglas fir. It is often hot, always remote, in a relatively unknown section of Six Rivers National Forest at an elevation of 2,600 feet. The headwaters of the Mad River pour right past the campground, about two miles downstream from the Ruth Lake Dam. People making weekend trips to Ruth Lake sometimes end up at this little-used camp. Ruth Lake is a designated Watchable Wildlife Site and is the only major recreation lake within decent driving range of Eureka, offering a small marina with boat rentals and a good boat ramp for access to trout and bass fishing and waterskiing. Swimming and all water sports are allowed at Ruth Lake. Note: All boats must be certified mussel-free before launching.

**Campsites, facilities:** There are 40 sites for tents or RVs up to 22 feet (no hookups). Picnic tables and fire grills are provided. Drinking water and vault toilets are available. Some facilities are wheelchair-accessible. Leashed pets are permitted.

**Reservations, fees:** Reservations are accepted at 877/444-6777 ($10 reservation fee) or www.recreation.gov ($9 reservation fee). Sites are $12 per night, plus $5 per night for each additional vehicle. Open late May through mid-September.

**Directions:** From Eureka, drive south on U.S. 101 to Alton. Turn east on Highway 36 and drive about 50 miles to the town of Mad River. Turn southeast on Lower Mad River Road and drive four miles to the camp on the right side of the road.

**Contact:** Six Rivers National Forest, Mad River Ranger District, 707/574-6233, www.fs.usda. gov/srnf.

## 70 FOREST GLEN

### Scenic rating: 7

on the South Fork of the Trinity River in Shasta-Trinity National Forest

**Map 2.3, page 109**

If you get stuck for a spot in this region, this camp almost always has sites open, even during three-day weekends. It is on the edge of a forest near the South Fork of the Trinity River. If you hit it during a surprise storm, a primitive shelter is available at the nearby Forest Glen Guard Station, a historic cabin that sleeps eight and rents out from the Forest Service.

**Campsites, facilities:** There are 15 sites for tents or RVs up to 16 feet (no hookups). Picnic tables and fire grills are provided. Drinking water and vault toilets are available. Some facilities are wheelchair-accessible. Leashed pets are permitted.

**Reservations, fees:** Reservations are accepted for the cabin at 877/444-6777 ($10 reservation fee) or www.recreation.gov ($9 reservation fee). The cabin is $35-75 per night. Reservations are not accepted for campsites. Sites are $12 per night. Open late May through early November, weather permitting.

**Directions:** From Red Bluff, turn west on Highway 36 (very twisty) and drive past Platina to the junction with Highway 3. Continue west on Highway 36 for 12 miles to Forest Glen. The campground is at the west end of town on the right side of the road.

**Contact:** Shasta-Trinity National Forest, Hayfork Ranger Station, 530/628-5227, www.fs.usda.gov/stnf.

## 71 HELLS GATE

### Scenic rating: 7

on the South Fork of the Trinity River in Shasta-Trinity National Forest

**Map 2.3, page 109**

This is a pretty spot bordering the South Fork of the Trinity River. The prime feature is for hikers. The South Fork National Recreation Trail begins at the campground and follows the river for many miles. Additional trails branch off and up into the South Fork Mountains. This area is extremely hot in summer. The elevation is 2,300 feet. It gets moderate use and may even fill on three-day weekends. Insider's note: If Hells Gate is full, there are seven primitive campsites at Scott's Flat Campground, 0.5 mile beyond Hells Gate, that can accommodate RVs up to 20 feet.

**Campsites, facilities:** There are 17 sites for tents or RVs up to 16 feet (no hookups). Picnic tables and fire grills are provided. Vault toilets are available. There is no potable water. Some facilities are wheelchair-accessible. Leashed pets are permitted.

**Reservations, fees:** Reservations are not accepted. Sites are $6 per night. Open late May through early November, weather permitting.

**Directions:** From Red Bluff, turn west on Highway 36 (very twisty) and drive past Platina to the junction with Highway 3. Continue west on Highway 36 for 10 miles to the campground entrance on the left side of the road. If you reach Forest Glen, you have gone a mile too far.

**Contact:** Shasta-Trinity National Forest, Hayfork Ranger Station, 530/628-5227, www.fs.usda.gov/stnf.

## 72 FIR COVE

### Scenic rating: 7

on Ruth Lake in Six Rivers National Forest

**Map 2.3, page 109**

This spot is situated along Ruth Lake adjacent to Bailey Cove. The elevation is 2,600 feet, and the lake covers 1,200 acres. Swimming and all water sports are allowed on Ruth Lake, and there are three boat ramps. In the summer the warm water makes this an ideal place for families to spend some time swimming. Fishing is decent for rainbow trout in the spring and for bass in the summer. Note: All boats must be certified mussel-free before launching.

**Campsites, facilities:** There 19 sites for tents or RVs up to 22 feet (no hookups). Picnic tables and fire grills are provided. Drinking water and vault toilets are available. Some facilities are wheelchair-accessible. Leashed pets are permitted.

**Reservations, fees:** Reservations are accepted at 877/444-6777 ($10 reservation fee) or www.recreation.gov ($9 reservation fee). Sites are $12 per night, plus $5 per night for each additional vehicle. Open late May through mid-September.

**Directions:** From Eureka, drive south on U.S. 101 to Alton and the junction with Highway 36. Turn east on Highway 36 and drive about 50 miles to the town of Mad River. Turn right at the sign for Ruth Lake/Lower Mad River Road and drive 12 miles to the campground on the right side of the road.

**Contact:** Six Rivers National Forest, Mad River Ranger District, 707/574-6233, www.fs.usda.gov/stnf.

## 73 BAILEY CANYON

### Scenic rating: 7
on Ruth Lake in Six Rivers National Forest

**Map 2.3, page 109**

Ruth Lake is the only major lake within a reasonable driving distance of U.S. 101, although some people might argue with you over how "reasonable" this twisty drive is. Regardless, you end up at a camp along the east shore of Ruth Lake, where fishing for trout or bass and waterskiing are popular. What really wins out is that it is hot and sunny all summer, the exact opposite of the fogged-in Humboldt coast. The elevation is 2,600 feet. Note: All boats must be certified mussel-free before launching.

**Campsites, facilities:** There are 25 sites for tents or RVs up to 22 feet (no hookups). Picnic tables and fire grills are provided. Drinking water and vault toilets are available. A boat

ramp and small marina are available nearby. Some facilities are wheelchair-accessible. Leashed pets are permitted.

**Reservations, fees:** Reservations are not accepted. Sites are $12 per night, plus $5 per night for each additional vehicle. Open late May through mid-September.

**Directions:** From Eureka, drive south on U.S. 101 to Alton and the junction with Highway 36. Turn east on Highway 36 and drive about 50 miles to the town of Mad River. Turn right at the sign for Ruth Lake/Lower Mad River Road and drive 13 miles to the campground on the right side of the road.

**Contact:** Six Rivers National Forest, Mad River Ranger District, 707/574-6233, www.fs.usda.gov/stnf.

## 74 TRINITY LAKE KOA

### Scenic rating: 8
on Trinity Lake

**Map 2.4 Trinity Lake, page 111**

This huge resort (some may remember this as the former Wyntoon Resort) is an ideal family vacation destination. Set in a wooded area covering 90 acres on the north shore of Trinity Lake, it provides opportunities for fishing, boating, swimming, and waterskiing, with access within walking distance. The lake boasts a wide variety of fish, including smallmouth bass and rainbow trout. The tent sites are spread out on 20 forested acres. The lake sits at the base of the dramatic Trinity Alps, one of the most beautiful regions in the state.

**Campsites, facilities:** There are 97 tent sites, 136 sites with full hookups (30 and 50 amps) for RVs of any length, two group sites for 12-48 people, and 19 cottages. Some RV sites are pull-through. Picnic tables and fire rings are provided. Drinking water, restrooms with showers, coin laundry, two playgrounds, miniature golf, summer recreation program for kids, seasonal heated pool, dump station, gasoline, convenience store, ice, snack bar, fish-cleaning area, boat rentals, and slips are available. Some facilities are wheelchair-accessible. Leashed pets are permitted, with certain restrictions.

**Reservations, fees:** Reservations are accepted. RV sites are $45-60 per night, tent sites are $38-50 per night, plus $3-6 per person per night for more than two people. Some credit cards are accepted. Open year-round.

**Directions:** From Redding, drive west 40 miles on Highway 299 to Weaverville and Highway 3. Turn right (north) on Highway 3 and drive approximately 30 miles to Trinity Lake. At Trinity Center, continue 0.5 mile north on Highway 3 to the resort on the right.

**Contact:** Trinity Lake KOA, 530/266-3337 or 800/562-7706, www.trinitylakekoa.com or www.koa.com.

## 75 JACKASS SPRINGS
🏃 🚣 ⛵ 🚤 🐕 🚐 ⛺

### Scenic rating: 6
near Trinity Lake in Shasta-Trinity National Forest

**Map 2.4 Trinity Lake, page 111**

If you're poking around for a more secluded campsite on this end of the lake, halt your search and pick the best spot you can find at this campground, since it's the only one in this area of Trinity Lake. The campground is 0.5 mile from Trinity Lake, but you can't see the lake from the camp. It is most popular in the fall as a base camp for deer hunters. The elevation is 2,500 feet.

**Campsites, facilities:** There are 10 sites for tents or RVs up to 32 feet (no hookups). Picnic tables and fire grills are provided. Vault toilets are available. No drinking water is available. Garbage must be packed out. Leashed pets are permitted.

**Reservations, fees:** Reservations are not accepted. There is no fee for camping. Open year-round, weather permitting.

**Directions:** From Redding, drive west on Highway 299 to Weaverville and the junction with Highway 3. Turn right (north) on Highway 3 and drive 29 miles to Trinity Center. Continue five miles past Trinity Center to County Road 106. Turn right on County Road 106 and drive 12 miles to the Jackass Springs/County Road 119 turnoff. Turn right on County Road 119 and drive five miles to the campground near the end of the road.

**Contact:** Shasta-Trinity National Forest, Weaverville Ranger Station, 530/623-2121, www.fs.usda.gov/stnf.

## 76 CLEAR CREEK
🏃 🐕 5% 🚐 ⛺

### Scenic rating: 6
in Shasta-Trinity National Forest

**Map 2.4 Trinity Lake, page 111**

This is a primitive, little-known camp that gets little use. It is near Clear Creek at 3,400 feet elevation. In fall hunters will occasionally turn it into a deer camp, with the adjacent slopes of Blue Mountain and Damnation Peak in the Trinity Divide country providing fair numbers of large bucks three points or better. Trinity Lake is only seven miles to the west, but it seems as if it's in a different world.

**Campsites, facilities:** There are six sites for tents or RVs up to 22 feet (no hookups). Picnic tables and fire grills are provided. Vault toilets are available. No drinking water is available. Garbage must be packed out. Leashed pets are permitted.

**Reservations, fees:** Reservations are not accepted. There is no fee for camping. Open year-round.

**Directions:** From Redding, drive west on Highway 299 for 17 miles to Trinity Mountain Road. Turn right (north) on Trinity Mountain Road and continue past the town of French Gulch for about 12 miles to East Side Road/County Road 106. Turn right on the gravel road and drive north for about 11 miles to the campground access road (dirt) on the right. Turn right on the access road and drive two miles to the campground.

**Contact:** Shasta-Trinity National Forest,

Weaverville Ranger District, 530/623-2121, www.fs.usda.gov/stnf.

## 77 BRIDGE CAMP

### Scenic rating: 8

on Stuarts Fork in Shasta-Trinity National Forest

**Map 2.4 Trinity Lake, page 111**

This remote spot is an ideal jumping-off point for backpackers. It's at the head of Stuarts Fork Trail, about 2.5 miles from the western shore of Trinity Lake. The trail leads into the Trinity Alps Wilderness, along Stuarts Fork, past Oak Flat and Morris Meadows, and up to Emerald Lake and the Sawtooth Ridge. It is a long and grueling climb, but fishing is excellent at Emerald Lake as well as at neighboring Sapphire Lake. There's a great view of the Alps from this camp. It is set at 2,700 feet and remains open year-round, but there's no piped water in the winter and it gets mighty cold up here.

**Campsites, facilities:** There are 10 sites for tents or RVs up to 20 feet (no hookups). Picnic tables and fire grills are provided. Drinking water (summer season), vault toilets, and horse corrals are available. Leashed pets are permitted.

**Reservations, fees:** Reservations are not accepted. Sites are $10 per night in the summer, $5 per night in the winter. Open year-round.

**Directions:** From Redding, drive west on Highway 299 to Weaverville. In Weaverville, turn right (north) on Highway 3 and drive 17 miles to Trinity Alps Road (at Stuarts Fork of Trinity Lake). Turn left at Trinity Alps Road and drive about two miles to the campground on the right side of the road.

**Contact:** Shasta-Trinity National Forest, Weaverville Ranger Station, 530/623-2121, www.fs.usda.gov/stnf; Shasta Recreation Company, 530/275-8113.

## 78 RUSH CREEK

### Scenic rating: 4

in Shasta-Trinity National Forest, north of Weaverville

**Map 2.4 Trinity Lake, page 111**

This small, primitive camp provides overflow space during busy holiday weekends when the camps at Lewiston and Trinity Lakes are near capacity. It may not be much, but hey, at least if you know about Rush Creek, you'll never get stuck for a spot. The camp borders Rush Creek and is secluded, but again, it's nearly five miles to the nearest access point to Trinity Lake.

**Campsites, facilities:** There are eight sites for tents or RVs up to 20 feet (no hookups). Picnic tables and fire pits are provided. Vault toilets are available. No drinking water is available. Leashed pets are permitted.

**Reservations, fees:** Reservations are not accepted. Sites are $10 per night. Open mid-May through mid-September.

**Directions:** From Redding, drive west on Highway 299 to Weaverville. In Weaverville, turn right (north) on Highway 3 and drive about eight miles to the signed turnoff on the left side of the road. Turn left and drive 0.25 mile on the short spur road to the campground on the left side of the road. If you get to Forest Road 113, you've gone too far.

**Contact:** Shasta-Trinity National Forest, Weaverville Ranger Station, 530/623-2121, www.fs.usda.gov/stnf; Shasta Recreation Company, 530/275-8113.

## 79 PINEWOOD COVE

### Scenic rating: 7

on Trinity Lake

**Map 2.4 Trinity Lake, page 111**

This is a privately operated camp with full boating facilities at Trinity Lake. If you don't have a boat but want to get on Trinity Lake, this can be a good starting point. A reservation is advised during the peak summer season. The elevation is 2,300 feet.

**Campsites, facilities:** There are 45 sites with full or partial hookups (30 and 50 amps) for RVs up to 40 feet, including 10 RV sites rented for the entire season and wait-listed. There are also 28 tent sites and 15 park-model cabins. Picnic tables and fire grills are provided. Restrooms with showers, a coin laundry, dump station, RV supplies, seasonal heated swimming pool, playground, children's treehouse, volleyball, badminton, free movies three nights a week in summer, video rentals, recreation room with billiards and video arcade, convenience store, ice, fishing tackle, library, boat dock with 32 slips, beach, and canoe and kayak rentals are available. Some facilities are wheelchair-accessible. Leashed pets are permitted.

**Reservations, fees:** Reservations are recommended in the summer. RV sites are $36-46 per night, tent sites are $19.50-28.50 per night, plus $4 per person per night for more than six people and $4 per pet per night. Some credit cards are accepted. Open mid-May through September.

**Directions:** From Redding, drive west on Highway 299 to Weaverville. In Weaverville, turn north (right) on Highway 3 and drive 14 miles to the campground entrance on the right.

**Contact:** Pinewood Cove Resort, 45110 Highway 3, Trinity Center, 530/286-2201, www. pinewoodcove.com.

## 80 STONEY CREEK GROUP CAMPGROUND

### Scenic rating: 7

on Trinity Lake in Shasta-Trinity National Forest

Map 2.4 Trinity Lake, page 111

A couple of camps sit on the northern shore of the Stuarts Fork arm of Trinity Lake. This is one of two designed for groups (the other is Fawn), and it is clearly the better. It is along the Stoney Creek arm, a cove with a feeder creek, with the camp large but relatively private. A swimming beach nearby is a bonus. The elevation is 2,400 feet.

**Campsites, facilities:** This group tent site can accommodate up to 50 people. Picnic tables and fire grills are provided. Drinking water and flush toilets are available. Leashed pets are permitted.

**Reservations, fees:** Reservations are required (find Stoney Group) at 877/444-6777 ($10 reservation fee) or www.recreation.gov ($9 reservation fee). The camp is $100 per night. Open early May through late September.

**Directions:** From Redding, drive west on Highway 299 to Weaverville. In Weaverville, turn right (north) on Highway 3 and drive 14.5 miles (about a mile past the Stuarts Fork Bridge) to the campground on the left.

**Contact:** Shasta-Trinity National Forest, Weaverville Ranger Station, 530/623-2121, www.fs.usda.gov/stnf; Shasta Recreation Company, 530/275-8113.

## 81 TANNERY GULCH

### Scenic rating: 8

on Trinity Lake in Shasta-Trinity National Forest

Map 2.4 Trinity Lake, page 111

This is one of the more popular Forest Service camps on the southwest shore of huge Trinity Lake. There's a nice beach near the campground, provided the infamous Bureau of Reclamation hasn't drawn the lake level down too far. It can be quite low in the fall. The elevation is 2,400 feet. Side note: This campground was named by the tannery that once operated in the area; bark from local trees was used in the tanning process.

**Campsites, facilities:** There are 82 sites for tents or RVs up to 40 feet (no hookups). Picnic tables and fire grills are provided. Drinking water, flush and vault toilets, and a boat ramp are available. In summer, programs are held in the amphitheater. Leashed pets are permitted.

**Reservations, fees:** Reservations are accepted at 877/444-6777 ($10 reservation fee) or www. recreation.gov ($9 reservation fee). Single sites are $20 per night, double sites are $35 per night, plus $6 per night for each additional vehicle. Open early May through late September.

**Directions:** From Redding, drive west on Highway 299 to Weaverville. In Weaverville, turn right (north) on Highway 3 and drive 13.5 miles north to County Road 172. Turn right on County Road 172 and drive 1.5 miles to the campground entrance.

**Contact:** Shasta-Trinity National Forest, Weaverville Ranger Station, 530/623-2121, www.fs.usda.gov/stnf; Shasta Recreation Company, 530/275-8113.

## 82 FAWN GROUP CAMP

### Scenic rating: 7
on Trinity Lake in Shasta-Trinity National Forest

**Map 2.4 Trinity Lake, page 111**

If you want Trinity Lake all to yourself, one way to do it is to get a group together and then reserve this camp near the shore of Trinity Lake. The elevation is 2,500 feet.

**Campsites, facilities:** There are two group sites for tents or RVs up to 37 feet (no hook-ups) that can accommodate up to 100 people each. Picnic tables and fire grills are provided. Drinking water and flush toilets are available. A marina is nearby. Leashed pets are permitted.

**Reservations, fees:** Reservations are required at 877/444-6777 ($10 reservation fee) or www. recreation.gov ($9 reservation fee). Sites are $120 per night. Open early May through late September.

**Directions:** From Redding, drive west on Highway 299 to Weaverville. In Weaverville, turn right (north) on Highway 3 and drive

about 15 miles to Fawn Road. Turn right and drive 0.25 mile to the campground.

**Contact:** Shasta-Trinity National Forest, Weaverville Ranger Station, 530/623-2121, www.fs.usda.gov/stnf; Shasta Recreation Company, 530/275-8113.

## 83 MINERSVILLE

### Scenic rating: 7
on Trinity Lake in Shasta-Trinity National Forest

**Map 2.4 Trinity Lake, page 111**

The setting is near lakeside, quite beautiful when Trinity Lake is fullest in the spring and early summer. This is a good camp for boaters, with a boat ramp in the cove a short distance to the north. But note that the boat ramp is not always functional. When the lake level drops to 65 feet below full, the ramp is not usable. The elevation is 2,400 feet.

**Campsites, facilities:** There are 14 sites for tents or RVs up to 36 feet, some with electricity. Picnic tables and fire grills are provided. Flush toilets and a low-water boat ramp are available. Drinking water was not available at time of publication. Leashed pets are permitted.

**Reservations, fees:** Reservations are not accepted. Single sites with electricity are $16-24 per night, single sites are $12, and walk-in sites are $8 per night. Open year-round, with limited winter services.

**Directions:** From Redding, drive west on Highway 299 to Weaverville. Turn right (north) on Highway 3 and drive about 18 miles (if you reach the Mule Creek Ranger Station, you have gone 0.5 mile too far). Turn right at the signed campground access road and drive 0.5 mile to the camp.

**Contact:** Shasta-Trinity National Forest, Weaverville Ranger Station, 530/623-2121, www.fs.usda.gov/stnf; Shasta Recreation Company, 530/275-8113.

## 84 RIDGEVILLE BOAT-IN CAMP

### Scenic rating: 9

on Trinity Lake in Shasta-Trinity National Forest

**Map 2.4 Trinity Lake, page 111**

This is one of the ways to get a camping spot to call your own—go by boat. The camp is exposed on a peninsula, providing beautiful views. Prospects for waterskiing and trout or bass fishing are often outstanding. The early part of the season is the prime time for boaters, before the furnace heat of full summer. A great view of the Trinity Alps is a bonus. The only downer is the typical lake drawdown at the end of summer and beginning of fall, when this boat-in camp becomes a long traipse from water's edge.

**Campsites, facilities:** There are seven tent sites. Picnic tables and fire grills are provided. Vault toilets are available. No drinking water is available. Garbage must be packed out. Boat ramps can be found near Clark Springs, Alpine View, or farther north at Trinity Center. Leashed pets are permitted.

**Reservations, fees:** Reservations are not accepted. There is no fee for camping. Open year-round.

**Directions:** From Redding, drive west on Highway 299 to Weaverville. In Weaverville, turn right (north) on Highway 3 and drive seven miles to the Stuarts Fork arm of Trinity Lake. You'll find boat launches at Stuarts Fork. After launching, drive your boat to the mouth of Stuarts Fork. The campground is on the western shore at the end of a peninsula at the entrance to that part of the lake.

**Contact:** Shasta-Trinity National Forest, Weaverville Ranger Station, 530/623-2121, www.fs.usda.gov/stnf.

## 85 CLARK SPRINGS

### Scenic rating: 7

on Trinity Lake in Shasta-Trinity National Forest

**Map 2.4 Trinity Lake, page 111**

At time of publication, this site was closed due to water system repairs. Please check with the ranger station before planning a trip.

This former day-use-only picnic area is now a Forest Service campground with a nearby boat ramp and a beach at Trinity Lake. The primitive campground is best suited to tent campers but can accommodate some trailers. The elevation is 2,400 feet.

**Campsites, facilities:** There are 19 sites for tents or RVs up to 25 feet (no hookups). Picnic tables and fire grills are provided. Drinking water and flush toilets may be available, with limited facilities in the winter; call ahead to confirm. Supplies are available in Weaverville. Leashed pets are permitted.

**Reservations, fees:** Reservations are not accepted. Sites are $14 per night. Open early April through October.

**Directions:** From Redding, drive west on Highway 299 to Weaverville. In Weaverville, turn right (north) on Highway 3 and drive 16.5 miles (about four miles past the Stuarts Fork Bridge) to the campground entrance road on the right.

**Contact:** Shasta-Trinity National Forest, Weaverville Ranger Station, 530/623-2121, www.fs.usda.gov/stnf.

## 86 RIDGEVILLE ISLAND BOAT-IN CAMP

### Scenic rating: 9

on Trinity Lake in Shasta-Trinity National Forest

**Map 2.4 Trinity Lake, page 111**

How would you like to be on a deserted island? You'll learn the answer at this tiny, little-known island with a great view of the Trinity Alps. Located at 2,400 feet, it is one of several boat-in camps in the Trinity Lake region. Note that the lake level at Trinity Lake typically drops significantly from September through October.

**Campsites, facilities:** There are three tent sites. Picnic tables and fire grills are provided. Vault toilets are available. No drinking water is available. Garbage must be packed out. Several boat ramps are available at campgrounds and private resorts at Trinity Lake. Leashed pets are permitted.

**Reservations, fees:** Reservations are not accepted. There is no fee for camping. Open year-round.

**Directions:** From Redding, drive west on Highway 299 to Weaverville. In Weaverville, turn right (north) on Highway 3 and drive seven miles to the Stuarts Fork arm of Trinity Lake. You'll find boat launches at Stuarts Fork. After launching, drive your boat to the campground on a small island near Estrellita Marina, between Minersville and Mariners Roost.

**Contact:** Shasta-Trinity National Forest, Weaverville Ranger Station, 530/623-2121, www.fs.usda.gov/stnf.

## 87 MARINERS ROOST BOAT-IN CAMP

### Scenic rating: 8
on Trinity Lake in Shasta-Trinity National Forest

**Map 2.4 Trinity Lake, page 111**

A perfect boat camp? This comes close at Trinity because it's positioned perfectly for boaters, with spectacular views of the Trinity Alps to the west, and it is an ideal spot for water-skiers. That is because it is on the western side of the lake's major peninsula, topped by Bowerman Ridge. Secluded and wooded, this area is at 2,400 feet elevation.

**Campsites, facilities:** There are seven tent sites. Picnic tables and fire grills are provided. Vault toilets are available. No drinking water is

available. Garbage must be packed out. Several boat ramps are available at campgrounds and private resorts at Trinity Lake. Leashed pets are permitted.

**Reservations, fees:** Reservations are not accepted. There is no fee for camping. Open year-round.

**Directions:** From Redding, drive west on Highway 299 to Weaverville. In Weaverville, turn right (north) on Highway 3 and drive seven miles to the Stuarts Fork arm of Trinity Lake. You'll find boat launches at Stuarts Fork. After launching, drive your boat to West Bowerman Ridge (near the point of the main arm of the lake) and look for the camp on the peninsula, just east of and on the shore opposite Ridgeville Island Boat-In Camp.

**Contact:** Shasta-Trinity National Forest, Weaverville Ranger Station, 530/623-2121, www.fs.usda.gov/stnf.

## 88 HAYWARD FLAT

### Scenic rating: 7
on Trinity Lake in Shasta-Trinity National Forest

**Map 2.4 Trinity Lake, page 111**

When giant Trinity Lake is full of water, Hayward Flat is one of the prettiest places you could ask for. The camp has become one of the most popular Forest Service campgrounds on Trinity Lake because it sits right along the shore and offers a beach. The elevation is 2,400 feet.

**Campsites, facilities:** There are 98 sites for tents or RVs up to 40 feet (no hookups) and six double sites. Picnic tables and fire grills are provided. Drinking water, flush toilets, and a dump station may be available (call to confirm); there is usually a camp host. Supplies and a boat ramp are nearby. Some facilities are wheelchair-accessible. Leashed pets are permitted.

**Reservations, fees:** Reservations are accepted at 877/444-6777 ($10 reservation fee) or www.recreation.gov ($9 reservation fee). Sites are $20-35 per night, plus $6 per night for each additional vehicle. Open mid-May through mid-September.

**Directions:** From Redding, drive west on Highway 299 to Weaverville. In Weaverville, turn right (north) on Highway 3 and drive 19.5 miles, approximately three miles past the Mule Creek Ranger Station. Turn right at the signed access road for Hayward Flat and drive about three miles to the campground at the end of the road.

**Contact:** Shasta-Trinity National Forest, Weaverville Ranger Station, 530/623-2121, www.fs.usda.gov/stnf; Shasta Recreation Company, 530/275-8113.

# 89 ALPINE VIEW

### Scenic rating: 9

on Trinity Lake in Shasta-Trinity National Forest

**Map 2.4 Trinity Lake, page 111**

This is an attractive area on the shore of Trinity Lake at a creek inlet. The boat ramp nearby provides a bonus. It's a very pretty spot, with views to the west across the lake arm and to the Trinity Alps, featuring Granite Peak. The Forest Service occasionally runs tours from the campground to historic Bowerman Barn, which was built in 1894. The elevation is 2,400 feet.

**Campsites, facilities:** There are 53 sites for tents or RVs up to 32 feet (no hookups). Picnic tables and fire grills are provided. Drinking water and flush toilets are available. Some facilities are wheelchair-accessible. The Bowerman boat ramp is nearby. Leashed pets are permitted.

**Reservations, fees:** Reservations are not accepted. Sites are $20-35 per night, plus $6 per night for each additional vehicle. Open mid-May through mid-September.

**Directions:** From Redding, drive west on Highway 299 to Weaverville. In Weaverville, turn right (north) on Highway 3 and drive 22.5 miles to Covington Mill (south of Trinity Center). Turn right (south) on Guy Covington Drive and drive three miles to the camp (one mile past Bowerman boat ramp) on the right side of the road.

**Contact:** Shasta-Trinity National Forest, Weaverville Ranger Station, 530/623-2121, www.fs.usda.gov/stnf; Shasta Recreation Company, 530/275-8113.

# 90 CAPTAINS POINT BOAT-IN

### Scenic rating: 7

on Trinity Lake in Shasta-Trinity National Forest

**Map 2.4 Trinity Lake, page 111**

The Trinity River arm of Trinity Lake is a massive piece of water, stretching north from the giant Trinity Dam for nearly 20 miles. This camp is the only boat-in camp along this entire stretch of shore, and it is situated at a prominent spot, where a peninsula juts well into the main lake body. This is a perfect boat-in site for water-skiers or anglers. The fishing is often excellent for smallmouth bass in the cove adjacent to Captain's Point, using grubs. The elevation is 2,400 feet.

**Campsites, facilities:** There are three tent sites. Picnic tables and fire grills are provided. Vault toilets are available. No drinking water is available. Garbage must be packed out. Several boat ramps are available at campgrounds and private resorts at Trinity Lake. Leashed pets are permitted.

**Reservations, fees:** Reservations are not accepted. There is no fee for camping. Open year-round.

**Directions:** From Redding, drive west on Highway 299 to Weaverville. In Weaverville, turn right (north) on Highway 3 and drive about seven miles to the signed turnoff on the right side of the road for the Trinity Alps Marina. Turn right and drive approximately 10 miles to the marina and boat ramp. Launch your boat and cruise north about four miles up

# SHASTA LAKE

Shasta Lake is one of America's top recreation lakes and the boating capital of the West. The massive reservoir boasts 370 miles of shoreline; more than a dozen each of campgrounds, boat launches, and marinas; lakeshore lodging; and 400 houseboat and cabin rentals. A remarkable 22 species of fish live in the lake. Many of the campgrounds feature lake views. In addition, getting here is easy—it's a straight shot off I-5. There is a $12 boat launch fee.

the main Trinity River arm of the lake. Look for Captains Point on the left side of the lake.
**Contact:** Shasta-Trinity National Forest, Weaverville Ranger Station, 530/623-2121, www.fs.usda.gov/stnf.

## 91 ANTLERS RV PARK & CAMPGROUND

**Scenic rating: 7**

on Shasta Lake

**Map 2.4 Shasta Lake, page 111**

Antlers Park is along the Sacramento River arm of Shasta Lake at 1,116 feet. The 20-acre park has shady sites. This is a full-service spot for campers, boaters, and anglers, with access to the beautiful Sacramento River arm. The camp often fills in summer, including on weekdays.
**Campsites, facilities:** There are 70 sites with full hookups (30 and 50 amps) for RVs of any length (several are pull-through), 40 sites for tents, and several rental trailers. Picnic tables and fire rings or fire grills are provided. Tent sites also have food lockers. Amenities include restrooms with showers, a seasonal convenience store and snack bar, ice, coin laundry, Sunday pancake breakfasts, cable TV hookups, video games, playground, volleyball court, table tennis, horseshoes, basketball, Wi-Fi, and a seasonal swimming pool. Boat rentals, houseboats, moorage, and a complete marina with recreation room are adjacent to the park. Some facilities are wheelchair-accessible. Leashed pets are permitted, with a limit of two.
**Reservations, fees:** Reservations are

recommended. RV sites are $30-45.80 per night, tent sites are $21-31.20 per night, plus $4.40 per person per night for more than two people and $2 per pet per night. Some credit cards are accepted. Open year-round.
**Directions:** From Redding, drive north on I-5 for 24 miles to the Lakeshore Drive/Antlers Road exit in Lakehead. Take that exit, turn right at the stop sign, and drive a short distance to Antlers Road. At Antlers Road, turn right and drive 1.5 miles south to the campground on the left. Check traffic reports as bridge work is ongoing in this area.
**Contact:** Antlers RV Park & Campground, 20682 Antlers Road, Lakehead, 530/238-2322 or 800/642-6849, www.antlersrvpark.com.

## 92 ANTLERS

**Scenic rating: 7**

on Shasta Lake in Shasta-Trinity National Forest

**Map 2.4 Shasta Lake, page 111**

Antlers is a well-known spot on the primary Sacramento River inlet of giant Shasta Lake that attracts returning campers and boaters year after year. It is the farthest upstream marina/camp on the lake. Lake levels can fluctuate greatly from spring through fall, and the operators will move their docks to compensate. Easy access off I-5 is a big plus for boaters.
Note: Caltrans has been replacing Antlers Bridge on I-5 over the Sacramento River arm of Shasta Lake near Lakehead. Another 0.4-mile section of I-5 south of the bridge will

be realigned (thanks to a high accident rate). Traffic will continue on Antlers Bridge during construction with a new "parallel alignment," so expect some inconvenience and plan your time accordingly. Antlers Boat Ramp will remain open, as will lake access.

**Campsites, facilities:** There are 41 individual sites and 18 double sites for tents or RVs up to 35 feet (no hookups). Picnic tables, food lockers, and fire grills are provided. Drinking water and flush and vault toilets are available. A boat ramp, amphitheater with summer interpretive programs, grocery store, and coin laundry are nearby. Some facilities are wheelchair-accessible. Leashed pets are permitted.

**Reservations, fees:** Reservations are accepted May through September at 877/444-6777 ($10 reservation fee) or www.recreation.gov ($9 reservation fee). Sites are $20 per night, double sites are $35 per night, plus $6 per night for each additional vehicle. Open year-round.

**Directions:** From Redding, drive north on I-5 for 24 miles to the Lakeshore Drive/Antlers Road exit in Lakehead. Take that exit, turn right at the stop sign, and drive a short distance to Antlers Road. At Antlers Road, turn right and drive one mile south to the campground.

**Contact:** Shasta-Trinity National Forest, Shasta Lake Ranger District, 530/275-1587, www.fs.usda.gov/stnf; Shasta Lake Visitor Center, 530/275-1589; Shasta Recreation Company, 530/275-8113.

## 93 GREGORY CREEK

### Scenic rating: 7

on Shasta Lake in Shasta-Trinity National Forest

**Map 2.4 Shasta Lake, page 111**

Gregory Creek Campground closes every year from late winter through early summer for bald eagle nesting. Until the birds leave the nest, the campground remains closed. When open, it is one of the more secluded Forest Service campgrounds on Shasta Lake, and it has become extremely popular with the younger crowd. It is just above lakeside, on the eastern shore of the northern Sacramento River arm of the lake. When the lake is fullest in the spring and early summer, this is a great spot.

**Campsites, facilities:** There are 18 sites for tents or RVs up to 16 feet (no hookups). Picnic tables and fire grills are provided. Drinking water and flush toilets are available. Leashed pets are permitted.

**Reservations, fees:** Reservations are not accepted. Sites are $10 per night, plus $6 per night for each additional vehicle. Usually open July through September; call to verify current status.

**Directions:** From Redding, drive north on I-5 for 21 miles to the Salt Creek/Gilman Road exit. Take that exit and drive over the freeway to Gregory Creek Road. Turn right and drive 10 miles to the campground at the end of the road. Check traffic reports as bridge work is ongoing in this area.

**Contact:** Shasta-Trinity National Forest, Shasta Lake Ranger District, 530/275-1587, www.fs.usda.gov/stnf; Shasta Lake Visitor Center, 530/275-1589; Shasta Recreation Company, 530/275-8113.

## 94 LAKESHORE VILLA RV PARK

### Scenic rating: 7

on Shasta Lake

**Map 2.4 Shasta Lake, page 111**

This is a large campground with level, shaded sites for RVs, set near the northern Sacramento River arm of giant Shasta Lake. Most of the campers visiting here are boaters coming for the water sports—waterskiing, wakeboarding, or tubing. The sites are level and graveled.

**Campsites, facilities:** There are 91 sites for tents or RVs up to 45 feet with full or partial hookups (20, 30, and 50 amps); some sites are pull-through. There are also two RV rentals. Restrooms with showers, ice, dump station, cable TV, Wi-Fi, playground, and group facilities are available. A boat ramp, store, restaurant, and bar are nearby. Some facilities are wheelchair-accessible. Leashed pets are permitted (bring proof of current rabies shot).

**Reservations, fees:** Reservations are accepted. RV sites are $25-38 per night, tent sites are $18-25 per night, plus $2 per additional vehicle and $1.50 per dog per day. Some credit cards are accepted. Open year-round.

**Directions:** From Redding, drive north on I-5 for 24 miles to Exit 702 for Lakeshore Drive/ Antlers Road in Lakehead. Take that exit, turn left at the stop sign, and drive under the freeway to Lakeshore Drive. Turn left on Lakeshore Drive and drive 0.5 mile to the campground on the right. Check traffic reports as bridge work is ongoing in this area.

**Contact:** Lakeshore Villa RV Park, 20672 Lakeshore Dr., Lakehead, 530/238-8688, www.lakeshorevillarvpark.net.

## 95 LAKESHORE INN & RV

**Scenic rating: 7**

on Shasta Lake

**Map 2.4 Shasta Lake, page 111**

Shasta Lake is a boater's paradise and an ideal spot for campers with boats. Lakeshore Inn & RV is on the Sacramento River arm of Shasta Lake. The nearest marina is 2.75 miles away. Shasta Lake Caverns are 10 miles away, and Shasta Dam tours are available about 20 miles away.

**Campsites, facilities:** There are 40 sites with full or partial hookups (30 and 50 amps) for tents or RVs of any length; some sites are pull-through. Ten cabins are also available. Picnic tables are provided. Restrooms with showers, cable TV, dump station, seasonal swimming pool, playground, video arcade, coin laundry, seasonal bar and restaurant, and a small seasonal convenience store are available. Family barbecues are held on Sunday in season, 5pm-9pm. Live music is scheduled most Friday and

Saturday nights. Some facilities are wheelchair-accessible. Leashed pets are permitted in the campground only.

**Reservations, fees:** Reservations are recommended at 530/238-2003. Sites are $20-37 per night, plus $2.50 per person per night for more than two people and $1 per pet per night. Some credit cards are accepted. Open year-round, with limited winter facilities.

**Directions:** From Redding, drive north on I-5 for 24 miles to Exit 702 for Lakeshore Drive/ Antlers Road in Lakehead. Take that exit, turn left at the stop sign, and drive under the freeway to Lakeshore Drive. Turn left on Lakeshore Drive and drive one mile to the campground. Check the traffic reports because bridge work is ongoing in this area.

**Contact:** Lakeshore Inn & RV, 20483 Lakeshore Dr., Lakehead, 530/238-2003, www.shastacamping.com.

## 96 SHASTA LAKE RV RESORT AND CAMPGROUND

**Scenic rating: 7**

on Shasta Lake

**Map 2.4 Shasta Lake, page 111**

Shasta Lake RV Resort and Campground is one of a series on the upper end of Shasta Lake with easy access off I-5 by car, then easy access by boat to premium trout or bass fishing as well as waterskiing and water sports.

**Campsites, facilities:** There are 50 sites with full hookups (30 amps) for RVs up to 40 feet, 19 tent sites, one trailer rental, and three cabins. Some sites are pull-through. Picnic tables, barbecues, and fire rings are provided. Restrooms with showers, seasonal convenience store, firewood, bait, coin laundry, playground, table tennis, horseshoes, trailer and boat storage, Wi-Fi, and a seasonal swimming pool are available. A private dock has 36 boat slips. Leashed pets are permitted.

**Reservations, fees:** Reservations are accepted

at 800/374-2782. RV sites are $36 per night, tent sites are $26 per night, plus $4 per person per night for more than three people and $2 per pet per night. Some credit cards are accepted. Open year-round.

**Directions:** From Redding, drive north on I-5 for 24 miles to the Lakeshore Drive/Antlers Road exit in Lakehead. Take that exit, turn left at the stop sign, and drive under the freeway to Lakeshore Drive. Turn left on Lakeshore Drive and drive 1.5 miles to the campground on the right. Check traffic reports as bridge work is ongoing in this area.

**Contact:** Shasta Lake RV Resort and Campground, 20433 Lakeshore Dr., 530/238-2370 or 800/374-2782, www.shastalakerv.com.

## 97 LAKESHORE EAST

### Scenic rating: 7

on Shasta Lake in Shasta-Trinity National Forest

**Map 2.4 Shasta Lake, page 111**

Lakeshore East is near the full-service community of Lakehead on the Sacramento arm of Shasta Lake. It's a nice spot, with a good boat ramp and marina nearby at Antlers or Sugarloaf.

**Campsites, facilities:** There are 17 individual sites and six double sites for tents or RVs up to 30 feet (no hookups), as well as three furnished yurts. Picnic tables and fire grills are provided. Drinking water and flush toilets are available. A boat ramp, grocery store, and coin laundry are available nearby. Some facilities are wheelchair-accessible. Leashed pets are permitted.

**Reservations, fees:** Reservations are accepted May through September at 877/444-6777 ($10 reservation fee) or www.recreation.gov ($9 reservation fee). Sites are $20 per night for a single site, $35 for a double site, and $65 per night per yurt, plus $6 per night for each additional vehicle. Open year-round.

**Directions:** From Redding, drive north on I-5 for 24 miles to the Lakeshore Drive/Antlers

Road exit at Lakehead. Take the Antlers exit, turn left at the stop sign, and drive under the freeway to Lakeshore Drive. Turn left on Lakeshore Drive and drive three miles. Look for the campground entrance on the left side of the road.

**Contact:** Shasta-Trinity National Forest, Shasta Lake Ranger District, 530/275-1587, www.fs.usda.gov/stnf; Shasta Lake Visitor Center, 530/275-1589; Shasta Recreation Company, 530/275-8113.

## 98 NELSON POINT AND GROUP CAMP

### Scenic rating: 7

on Shasta Lake in Shasta-Trinity National Forest

**Map 2.4 Shasta Lake, page 111**

This is an easy-to-reach campground, only a few minutes from I-5. It's beside the Salt Creek inlet of Shasta Lake, deep in a cove. In low-water years, or when the lake level is low in the fall and early winter, this camp can seem quite distant from water's edge. This campground can be reserved as a group camp July through September; the rest of the year, sites are available "as-needed."

**Campsites, facilities:** There are eight individual sites for tents or RVs up to 16 feet (no hookups). When used as a group site, it can accommodate up to 60 people. Vault toilets, picnic tables, and fire grills are provided. No drinking water is available. A grocery store and coin laundry are nearby in Lakehead. Leashed pets are permitted.

**Reservations, fees:** Reservations are required for group sites at 877/444-6777 ($10 reservation fee) or www.recreation.gov ($9 reservation fee). Individual sites are $10 per night, plus $6 per night for each additional vehicle. The group site is $100 per night. Open May through early September.

**Directions:** From Redding, drive north on I-5 for about 20 miles to the Salt Creek Road/

Gilman Road exit. Take that exit, turn left and drive 0.25 mile to Gregory Creek Road. Turn right and drive one mile to Conflict Point Road. Turn left and drive one mile to the campground on the left.

**Contact:** Shasta-Trinity National Forest, Shasta Lake Ranger District, 530/275-1587, www.fs.usda.gov/stnf; Shasta Lake Visitor Center, 530/275-1589; Shasta Recreation Company, 530/275-8113.

## 99 GOOSENECK COVE BOAT-IN

### Scenic rating: 4
on Shasta Lake in Shasta-Trinity National Forest

**Map 2.4 Shasta Lake, page 111**

You want a camp all to yourself? There's a good chance of that at Gooseneck Cove, because it is well hidden, set back in a cove on the west side of the Sacramento River arm of giant Shasta Lake. The fishing on the Sacramento River arm of Shasta Lake is very good, both trolling for trout all summer, especially at the headwaters in midsummer, or in the spring, casting with Senkos or grubs (on darthead jigs or rigged Texas-style) for bass. Waterskiing is also excellent, with water temperatures in the high 70s for most of summer.

**Campsites, facilities:** There are 12 boat-in sites for tents. Picnic tables and fire grills are provided. Vault toilets are available. No drinking water is available. Garbage must be packed out. Small stores with supplies are available at Antlers. Leashed pets are permitted.

**Reservations, fees:** Reservations are not accepted. There is no fee for camping. A $12 fee is charged for boat launching. Open year-round.

**Directions:** From Redding, drive north on I-5 for 24 miles to the Lakeshore Drive/Antlers Road exit in Lakehead. Take that exit, turn left at the stop sign, and drive a short distance to Antlers Road. At Antlers Road, turn right and drive one mile south to the campground

and nearby boat launch. Launch your boat and cruise seven miles south to the boat-in campground.

**Contact:** Shasta-Trinity National Forest, Shasta Lake Ranger District, 530/275-1587, www.fs.usda.gov/stnf; Shasta Lake Visitor Center, 530/275-1589.

## 100 MCCLOUD BRIDGE

### Scenic rating: 7
on Shasta Lake in Shasta-Trinity National Forest

**Map 2.4 Shasta Lake, page 111**

Even though reaching this camp requires a long drive, it remains popular. That is because the best shore-fishing access at the lake is available at nearby McCloud Bridge. It is common to see 15 or 20 people shore fishing here for trout on summer weekends. In the fall, big brown trout migrate through this section of lake en route to their upstream spawning grounds.

**Campsites, facilities:** There are 11 individual sites and three double sites for tents or RVs up to 16 feet (no hookups). Picnic tables and fire grills are provided. Drinking water, vault toilets, and a group picnic area are available. Some facilities are wheelchair-accessible. Leashed pets are permitted.

**Reservations, fees:** Reservations are not accepted. Rates are $20 per night for single sights, $35 per night for double sites, plus $6 per night for each additional vehicle. Open early May through September.

**Directions:** From Redding, drive north on I-5 for about 20 miles to the Salt Creek/Gilman exit. Turn right on Gilman Road/County Road 7H009 and drive northeast for 18.5 miles. Cross the McCloud Bridge and drive one mile to the campground entrance on the right.

**Contact:** Shasta-Trinity National Forest, Shasta Lake Ranger District, 530/275-1587, www.fs.usda.gov/stnf; Shasta Lake Visitor Center, 530/275-1589; Shasta Recreation Company, 530/275-8113.

## 101 PINE POINT AND GROUP CAMP

🏊 🚣 🛶 🐴 🚙 ⛺

**Scenic rating: 7**

on Shasta Lake in Shasta-Trinity National Forest

**Map 2.4 Shasta Lake, page 111**

Pine Point is a pretty little camp, set on a ridge above the McCloud Arm of Shasta Lake amid oak trees and scattered ponderosa pines. The view is best in spring, when lake levels are generally highest. Boat-launching facilities are available at Hirz Bay; boaters park their boats on shore below the camp while the rest of their party arrives at the camp by car. That provides a chance not only for camping, but also for boating, swimming, waterskiing, and fishing. Note: From July through September, this campground can be reserved as a group site only. It is also used as a summer overflow camping area on weekends and holidays.

**Campsites, facilities:** There are 14 sites for tents or RVs up to 24 feet (no hookups), which can also be used as a group camp for up to 100 people. Picnic tables, food lockers, and fire rings are provided. Drinking water and vault toilets are available. Leashed pets are permitted.

**Reservations, fees:** Reservations are required for the group site at 877/444-6777 ($10 reservation fee) or www.recreation.gov ($9 reservation fee). Single sites are $20 per night, plus $6 per night for each additional vehicle, and it's $130 per night for the group site. Open May through early September.

**Directions:** From Redding, drive north on I-5 for about 20 miles to the Salt Creek/Gilman exit. Turn right on Gilman Road/County Road 7H009 and drive northeast for 17 miles to the campground entrance road on the right.

**Contact:** Shasta-Trinity National Forest, Shasta Lake Ranger District, 530/275-1587, www.fs.usda.gov/stnf; Shasta Lake Visitor Center, 530/275-1589; Shasta Recreation Company, 530/275-8113.

## 102 ELLERY CREEK

🏊 🚣 🛶 🐴 🚙 ⛺

**Scenic rating: 7**

on Shasta Lake in Shasta-Trinity National Forest

**Map 2.4 Shasta Lake, page 111**

This pretty camp is where Ellery Creek empties into the upper McCloud Arm of Shasta Lake. Several sites are set on the pavement with an unobstructed view of the beautiful McCloud Arm. This stretch of water is excellent for trout fishing in the summer, with bank-fishing access available two miles upstream at the McCloud Bridge. In the spring, there are tons of small spotted bass along the shore from the camp continuing upstream to the inlet of the McCloud River. Boat-launching facilities are available five miles south at Hirz Bay.

**Campsites, facilities:** There are 19 sites for tents or RVs up to 30 feet (no hookups). Picnic tables, food lockers, and fire grills are provided. Drinking water and vault toilets are available. Leashed pets are permitted.

**Reservations, fees:** Reservations are accepted at 877/444-6777 ($10 reservation fee) or www.recreation.gov ($9 reservation fee). Sites are $20 per night, plus $6 per night for each additional vehicle. Open early May through September.

**Directions:** From Redding, drive north on I-5 for about 20 miles to the Salt Creek/Gilman exit. Turn right on Gilman Road/County Road 7H009 and drive northeast for 15 miles to the campground on the right side of the road.

**Contact:** Shasta-Trinity National Forest, Shasta Lake Ranger District, 530/275-1587, www.fs.usda.gov/stnf; Shasta Lake Visitor Center, 530/275-1589; Shasta Recreation Company, 530/275-8113.

## 103 MOORE CREEK AND GROUP CAMP

### Scenic rating: 8

on Shasta Lake in Shasta-Trinity National Forest

**Map 2.4 Shasta Lake, page 111**

The McCloud Arm of Shasta Lake is the most beautiful of the five arms at Shasta, with its emerald-green waters and limestone canyon towering overhead to the east. That beautiful setting is taken advantage of at this camp, with a good view of the lake and limestone, along with good trout fishing on the adjacent section of water. Moore Creek is rented as a group camp most of the summer, except during holidays when individual sites are available on a first-come, first-served basis.

**Campsites, facilities:** There are 12 sites for tents or RVs up to 16 feet (no hookups) that are usually rented as one group site for up to 90 people. Picnic tables and fire grills are provided. Drinking water and vault toilets are available. Leashed pets are permitted.

**Reservations, fees:** Reservations are required for the group site at 877/444-6777 ($10 reservation fee) or www.recreation.gov ($9 reservation fee). Sites are $20 per night for individual sites, plus $6 per night for each additional vehicle, and it's $130 per night for the group site. Open late May through early September.

**Directions:** From Redding, drive north on I-5 for about 20 miles to the Salt Creek/Gilman exit. Take that exit and turn right on Gilman Road/County Road 7H009 and drive northeast for 14 miles to the campground on the right side of the road.

**Contact:** Shasta-Trinity National Forest, Shasta Lake Ranger District, 530/275-1587, www.fs.usda.gov/stnf; Shasta Lake Visitor Center, 530/275-1589; Shasta Recreation Company, 530/275-8113.

## 104 DEKKAS ROCK GROUP CAMP

### Scenic rating: 8

on Shasta Lake in Shasta-Trinity National Forest

**Map 2.4 Shasta Lake, page 111**

The few people who know about this camp love this little spot. It is an ideal group camp, set on a flat above the McCloud Arm of Shasta Lake, shaded primarily by bays and oaks, with a boat ramp two miles to the south at Hirz Bay. The views are pretty, looking across the lake at the limestone ridge that borders the McCloud Arm. In late summer and fall when the lake level drops, it can be a hike from the camp down to water's edge.

**Campsites, facilities:** There is one group site for tents or RVs up to 16 feet (no hookups) that can accommodate up to 60 people. A central meeting area with preparation tables, picnic tables, two pedestal grills, and a large barbecue is provided. Drinking water and vault toilets are available. Leashed pets are permitted.

**Reservations, fees:** Reservations are required at 877/444-6777 ($10 reservation fee) or www.recreation.gov ($9 reservation fee). The camp is $130 per night.

**Directions:** From Redding, drive north on I-5 for about 20 miles to the Salt Creek/Gilman exit. Turn right on Gilman Road/County Road 7H009 and drive northeast for 11 miles to the campground on the right side of the road.

**Contact:** Shasta-Trinity National Forest, Shasta Lake Ranger District, 530/275-1587, www.fs.usda.gov/stnf; Shasta Lake Visitor Center, 530/275-1589; Shasta Recreation Company, 530/275-8113.

## 105 HIRZ BAY 1 AND 2 GROUP CAMPS

🚶 🏊 🛶 ⚓ 🐴 🚐 ⛺

### Scenic rating: 8

on Shasta Lake in Shasta-Trinity National Forest

**Map 2.4 Shasta Lake, page 111**

This is the spot for your own private party, provided you get a reservation, and is set on a point at the entrance of Hirz Bay on the McCloud River arm of Shasta Lake. A boat ramp is only 0.5 mile away on the camp access road, giving access to the McCloud River arm. This is an excellent spot to make a base camp for a fishing trip, with great trolling for trout in this stretch of the lake.

**Campsites, facilities:** There are two group sites for tents or RVs up to 30 feet (no hookups). Hirz Bay 1 can accommodate 120 people; Hirz Bay 2 can accommodate 80 people. Picnic tables and fire grills are provided. Drinking water, vault toilets, and a group picnic area are available. Leashed pets are permitted.

**Reservations, fees:** Reservations are required at 877/444-6777 ($10 reservation fee) or www.recreation.gov ($9 reservation fee). Hirz Bay 1 is $130 per night; Hirz Bay 2 is $100 per night. Open April through late September.

**Directions:** From Redding, drive north on I-5 for about 20 miles to the Salt Creek/Gilman exit. Turn right on Gilman Road/County Road 7H009 and drive northeast for 10 miles to the campground/boat launch access road. Turn right and drive 0.5 mile to the camp on the left side of the road. The group camp is past the family campground.

**Contact:** Shasta-Trinity National Forest, Shasta Lake Ranger District, 530/275-1587, www.fs.usda.gov/stnf; Shasta Lake Visitor Center, 530/275-1589; Shasta Recreation Company, 530/275-8113.

## 106 HIRZ BAY

🚶 🏊 🛶 ⚓ 🏕 ♿ 🚐 ⛺

### Scenic rating: 8

on Shasta Lake in Shasta-Trinity National Forest

**Map 2.4 Shasta Lake, page 111** BEST 🌙

This camp on a point at the entrance of Hirz Bay is an excellent spot to make a base camp for a fishing trip, with great trolling for trout in this stretch of the lake. This is one of three camps in the immediate area (the others are Hirz Bay 1 and 2 Group Camps; see listing in this chapter). All provide nearby access to a boat ramp (0.5 mile down the road) and the McCloud River arm of Shasta Lake.

**Campsites, facilities:** There are 37 individual sites and 11 double sites for tents or RVs up to 30 feet (no hookups). Picnic tables and fire grills are provided. Drinking water and flush toilets are available. A camp host is usually available in the summer. A boat ramp is nearby. Some facilities are wheelchair-accessible. Leashed pets are permitted.

**Reservations, fees:** Reservations are accepted May through September at 877/444-6777 ($10 reservation fee) or www.recreation.gov ($9 reservation fee). Sites are $20 per night, double sites are $35 per night, plus $6 per night for each additional vehicle. Open year-round.

**Directions:** From Redding, drive north on I-5 for about 20 miles to the Salt Creek/Gilman exit. Turn right on Gilman Road/County Road 7H009 and drive northeast for 10 miles to the campground/boat launch access road. Turn right and drive 0.5 mile to the camp on the left side of the road.

**Contact:** Shasta-Trinity National Forest, Shasta Lake Ranger District, 530/275-1587, www.fs.usda.gov/stnf; Shasta Lake Visitor Center, 530/275-1589; Shasta Recreation Company, 530/275-8113.

## 107 MADRONE CAMP

### Scenic rating: 7

on Squaw Creek in Shasta-Trinity National Forest

**Map 2.4 Shasta Lake, page 111**

Tired of people? Then you've come to the right place. This remote camp is set along Squaw Creek, a feeder stream of Shasta Lake, which lies to the southwest. It's way out there, far away from anybody. Even though Shasta Lake is relatively close, about 10 miles away, this is another world. A network of four-wheel-drive roads provides a recreation option, detailed on a map of Shasta-Trinity National Forest.

**Campsites, facilities:** There are 10 sites for tents or RVs up to 16 feet (no hookups). Picnic tables and fire grills are provided. Vault toilets are available. No drinking water is available. Garbage must be packed out. Leashed pets are permitted.

**Reservations, fees:** Reservations are not accepted. There is no fee for camping. Open year-round.

**Directions:** From Redding, drive 31 miles east on Highway 299 to the town of Montgomery Creek. Turn left on Fenders Ferry Road/Forest Road 27 and drive 18 miles to the camp (the road starts as gravel and then becomes dirt). Note: The access road is rough and RVs are not advised.

**Contact:** Shasta-Trinity National Forest, Shasta Lake Ranger District, 530/275-1587, www.fs.usda.gov/stnf; Shasta Lake Visitor Center, 530/275-1589.

## 108 HOLIDAY HARBOR RESORT

### Scenic rating: 7

on Shasta Lake

**Map 2.4 Shasta Lake, page 111 BEST (**

This camp is one of the more popular family-oriented, all-service resorts on Shasta Lake, which has the second-largest dam in the United States. It sits on the lower McCloud Arm of the lake, which is extremely beautiful, with a limestone mountain ridge off to the east. It is an ideal jumping-off point for all water sports, especially waterskiing, houseboating and boating, and fishing. A good boat ramp, boat rentals, and store with all the goodies are bonuses. The place is full service and even offers boat-launching service. Campers staying here also get a 15 percent discount on boat rentals. Another plus is the nearby side trip to Shasta Caverns, a privately guided adventure (fee charged) into limestone caves. This camp often fills in summer, even on weekdays.

**Campsites, facilities:** There are 27 sites with full hookups (50 amps) for RVs up to 40 feet, with tents allowed in several sites. Picnic tables and barbecues are provided. Restrooms with showers, a general store, seasonal café, gift shop, coin laundry, marina, marine repair service, boat moorage, swim area, playground, propane gas, and houseboat and boat and personal watercraft rentals are available. Some facilities are wheelchair-accessible. Leashed pets are permitted.

**Reservations, fees:** Reservations are recommended. Sites are $32.50-42.50 per night, plus $4-5 per person per night for more than two people, $4-5 per night for each additional vehicle, $10.25-15 per night for boat moorage, and $2 per pet per night. Some credit cards are accepted. Open April through October.

**Directions:** From Redding, drive 18 miles north on I-5 to Exit 695 and the O'Brien Road/Shasta Caverns Road exit. Turn right (east) at Shasta Caverns Road and drive one mile to the resort entrance on the right; check in at the store. Check traffic reports as bridge work is ongoing in this area.

**Contact:** Holiday Harbor Resort, 20061 Shasta Caverns Road, Shasta Lake, 530/238-2383 or 800/776-2628, www.lakeshasta.com.

## 109 GREENS CREEK BOAT-IN

### Scenic rating: 10

on Shasta Lake in Shasta-Trinity National Forest

**Map 2.4 Shasta Lake, page 111** BEST

This is one of my favorite spots on the planet on a warm spring day, maybe mid-April, but it is always special. This boat-in campsite provides an exceptional base camp and boat-in headquarters for a recreation paradise. The camp rests at the foot of dramatic limestone formations on the McCloud Arm of Shasta Lake. By boat, this is one of the best fishing spots. The campsites are in a region well wooded and little traveled, with good opportunities in the evening to see wildlife.

**Campsites, facilities:** There are seven boat-in sites for tents. Picnic tables, bear lockers, and fire grills are provided. Vault toilets are available. No drinking water is available. Garbage must be packed out. Supplies are available at Holiday Harbor. Leashed pets are permitted.

**Reservations, fees:** Reservations are not accepted. There is no fee for camping. A $10 fee is charged for boat launching. Open year-round.

**Directions:** From Redding, drive north on I-5 over the Pit River Bridge at Shasta Lake to the O'Brien Road/Shasta Caverns Road exit. Turn east (right) on Shasta Caverns Road and drive 0.25 mile to a signed turnoff for Bailey Cove. Turn right and drive one mile to Bailey Cove boat ramp. Launch your boat and cruise four miles northeast up the McCloud Arm. Land your boat and pick your campsite. Note: The Bailey Cove boat ramp is not usable when the lake level drops more than 50 feet.

**Contact:** Shasta-Trinity National Forest, Shasta Lake Ranger District, 530/275-1587, www.fs.usda.gov/stnf; Shasta Lake Visitor Center, 530/275-1589.

## 110 SKI ISLAND BOAT-IN

### Scenic rating: 8

on Shasta Lake in Shasta-Trinity National Forest

**Map 2.4 Shasta Lake, page 111**

Could there be any secrets left about Shasta Lake? You bet, with boat-in campsites providing the best of all worlds for people willing to rough it just a little. Ski Island is an outstanding place to set up camp and then boat, fish, ski, or explore this giant lake. It is on the Pit River arm of the lake about three miles upstream from the Pit River (I-5) bridge. The closest boat ramp to Ski Island is at Silverthorn Resort, which is in a cove on the Pit River arm of the lake. The closest public boat ramp is at Jones Valley, also on the Pit River arm. This three-acre island has a boat-in campground and several little trails. It is well out of sight, and out of mind for most campers as well. One note: In wet weather, the reddish, iron-based soil on the island will turn the bottom of your boat rust-colored with even a minimum of tracking in.

**Campsites, facilities:** There are 29 boat-in sites for tents. Picnic tables and fire grills are provided. Vault toilets are available. No drinking water is available. Garbage must be packed out. Small stores with supplies are available at Silverthorn Resort and Jones Valley Resort. Leashed pets are permitted.

**Reservations, fees:** Reservations are not accepted. There is no fee for camping. A $10 fee is charged for boat launching. Open year-round.

**Directions:** From Redding, drive north on I-5 for three miles to Exit 682 for Oasis Road. Take that exit and drive to Oasis Road. Turn right on Oasis Road and drive 3.5 miles to Bear Mountain Road. Turn right and drive to Dry Creek Road. Turn left on Dry Creek Road and drive seven miles to a fork in the road. Bear right at the fork and drive to Jones Valley Boat Ramp (a left at the fork takes you to Silverthorn Resort). Launch your boat and head west (to the left) for four miles to Ski Island. Land and pick your campsite.

**Contact:** Shasta-Trinity National Forest, Shasta Lake Ranger District, 530/275-1587, www.fs.usda.gov/stnf; Shasta Lake Visitor Center, 530/275-1589.

## 111 ARBUCKLE FLAT BOAT-IN

🏊 🎣 🚤 🐕 ⛺

### Scenic rating: 9

on Shasta Lake in Shasta-Trinity National Forest

**Map 2.4 Shasta Lake, page 111** **BEST (**

How could anything be secluded on Northern California's most popular recreation lake? Well, here is your answer. Arbuckle Flat is a truly secluded boat-in campground well up the Pit River arm of the lake, set far back in a deep cove. You will feel a million miles away from all the fast traffic back at the main lake body. Specifically, it is five miles east of the Jones Valley Boat Ramp, on the right (south) side. You pay a small price for this seclusion. After landing your boat, you must then carry your gear up a hill to the campsites. When the lake is low, this is like a march up Cardiac Hill. In the spring, when the lake is full, there isn't an issue. The landscape surrounding the campsites is peppered with oak. Fishing is often good in spring for the beautiful Pit River strain of rainbow trout, trolling along the shore. It's also good for bass and crappie in a nearby cove, where so many submerged trees stick up out of the water that the lake looks like it needs a shave.

**Campsites, facilities:** There are 11 boat-in sites for tents. Picnic tables and fire grills are provided. Vault toilets are available. No drinking water is available. Garbage must be packed out. Small stores with supplies are available at Silverthorn Resort and Jones Valley Resort. Leashed pets are permitted.

**Reservations, fees:** Reservations are not accepted. There is no fee for camping. A $10 fee is charged for boat launching. Open year-round.

**Directions:** From Redding, drive north on

I-5 for three miles to Exit 682 for Oasis Road. Take that exit and drive to Oasis Road. Turn right on Oasis Road and drive 3.5 miles to Bear Mountain Road. Turn right and drive to Dry Creek Road. Turn left on Dry Creek Road and drive seven miles to a fork in the road. Bear right at the fork and drive to Jones Valley Boat Ramp (a left at the fork takes you to Silverthorn Resort). Launch your boat and head east (to the right) for five miles. The last major arm off to your right hides the campground at the back of the cove, in the oaks above the shore. Land and pick your campsite.

**Contact:** Shasta-Trinity National Forest, Shasta Lake Ranger District, 530/275-1587, www.fs.usda.gov/stnf; Shasta Lake Visitor Center, 530/275-1589.

## 112 JONES VALLEY INLET

🚶 🚴 🏊 🛶 🚤 🐕 🚐 ⛺

### Scenic rating: 4

on Shasta Lake in Shasta-Trinity National Forest

**Map 2.4 Shasta Lake, page 111**

This is one of the few primitive camp areas on Shasta Lake, set on the distant Pit River arm of the lake. It is an ideal camp for hiking and biking, with nearby Clickapudi Trail routed for miles along the lake's shore, in and out of coves, and then entering the surrounding foothills and oak/bay woodlands. The camp is pretty, if a bit exposed, with two nearby resorts, Jones Valley and Silverthorn, providing boat rentals and supplies.

**Campsites, facilities:** There is an area for dispersed, primitive camping for tents or RVs up to 30 feet (no hookups). Drinking water, portable toilets, and trash service are available. During fire season, a free California campfire permit is required. A boat ramp at Jones Valley is two miles from camp. Groceries are available nearby. Leashed pets are permitted.

**Reservations, fees:** Reservations are not accepted. Sites are $10 per vehicle per night. Open March through October.

**Directions:** From Redding, turn east on Highway 299 and drive 7.5 miles just past the town of Bella Vista. At Dry Creek Road turn left and drive nine miles to a Y intersection. Bear right at the Y (left will take you to Silverthorn Resort) and drive a short distance to the campground entrance on the left side of the road.

**Contact:** Shasta-Trinity National Forest, Shasta Lake Ranger District, 530/275-1587, www.fs.usda.gov/stnf; Shasta Lake Visitor Center, 530/275-1589; Shasta Recreation Company, 530/275-8113.

## 113 UPPER AND LOWER JONES VALLEY CAMPS

**Scenic rating: 3**

on Shasta Lake in Shasta-Trinity National Forest

**Map 2.4 Shasta Lake, page 111**

Lower Jones is a small camp along a deep cove in the remote Pit River arm of Shasta Lake. The advantage of Lower Jones Valley is that it is closer to the lake than Upper Jones Valley. A trailhead at the camp provides access to Clickapudi Trail, a great hiking and biking trail that traces the lake's shore, routed through woodlands. Two nearby resorts, Jones Valley and Silverthorn, provide boat rentals and supplies.

**Campsites, facilities:** There are 18 sites and three double sites for tents or RVs up to 16 feet (no hookups) in two adjacent campgrounds. Picnic tables and fire grills are provided. Drinking water, food lockers, and vault toilets are available. A boat ramp at Jones Valley is two miles from camp. Some facilities are wheelchair-accessible. Leashed pets are permitted.

**Reservations, fees:** Reservations are not accepted. Upper Jones sites are $20 per night. Lower Jones single sites are $20 per night or $30 per night for a double site, plus $6 per night for each additional vehicle. Lower Jones is open year-round. Upper Jones is open May through September.

**Directions:** From Redding, turn east on Highway 299 and drive 7.5 miles just past the town of Bella Vista. At Dry Creek Road, turn left and drive nine miles to a Y intersection. Bear right at the Y (left will take you to Silverthorn Resort) and drive a short distance to the campground entrances, on the left side for Lower Jones and the right side for Upper Jones.

**Contact:** Shasta-Trinity National Forest, Shasta Lake Ranger District, 530/275-1587, www.fs.usda.gov/stnf; Shasta Lake Visitor Center, 530/275-1589; Shasta Recreation Company, 530/275-8113.

## 114 SHASTA

**Scenic rating: 6**

on the Sacramento River in Shasta-Trinity National Forest

**Map 2.4 Shasta Lake, page 111**

You cross Shasta Dam to reach this site, which doubles as a staging area for the nearby Chappie-Shasta OHV Area, one of the few in the north of the state. Expect to see lots of quads and dirt bikes—loud and wild and hey, it's a perfect spot for them. Because of past mining in the area, it's barren with almost no shade, but the views of the river and Shasta Dam are incredible. Nearby dam tours are unique and memorable.

**Campsites, facilities:** There are 22 sites for tents or RVs up to 30 feet (no hookups). Picnic tables and fire rings are provided. Drinking water and vault toilets are available. A boat ramp is nearby. Groceries and bait are available in Shasta Lake City. Leashed pets are permitted.

**Reservations, fees:** Reservations are not accepted. Sites are $10 per night, plus $5 per night for each additional vehicle. Open year-round.

**Directions:** From I-5 in Redding, drive north for three miles to the exit for the town of Shasta Lake City and Shasta Dam Boulevard. Take that exit and bear west on Shasta Dam Boulevard and drive three miles to Lake Boulevard. Turn right on Lake Boulevard and drive two miles. Cross Shasta Dam and continue four miles to the signed campground. Check traffic reports as bridge work is ongoing in this area.

There is a security checkpoint at the dam. Make sure you have proper ID and current registration for all vehicles (or you may be subject to a search). The dam is closed 10pm-6am.

**Contact:** Bureau of Land Management Redding Field Office 530/224-2100, www.blm.gov/ca.

## 115 FAWNDALE OAKS RV PARK

### Scenic rating: 5

near Shasta Lake

**Map 2.4 Shasta Lake, page 111**

This RV park sits on 40 acres with shaded sites. It is midway between Shasta Lake and Redding, so it's close to many recreational activities. Toward Redding, the options include Turtle Bay Exploration Park, WaterWorks Park, public golf courses, and Sacramento River trails, which are paved, making them accessible for wheelchairs and bicycles. Toward Shasta Lake, there are tours of Shasta Caverns, via a short drive to Holiday Harbor.

**Campsites, facilities:** There are 10 tent sites and 15 sites with full hookups (30 and 50 amps) and cable TV for RVs up to 45 feet. Some sites are pull-through. A cabin and trailer are also available for rent. Picnic tables are provided, and some sites have barbecues. Wi-Fi, coin laundry, boat and RV storage, a general store, picnic area, playground, seasonal swimming pool, club room, game room, propane, and group facilities are available. Some facilities are wheelchair-accessible. Leashed pets are permitted.

**Reservations, fees:** Reservations are accepted by telephone or online. RV sites are $30-35 per night for two people, tent sites are $23 per night for a family of four, plus $2 per person per night for any additional people, $1 per pet per night,

and $3 per night for each additional vehicle. Weekly and monthly rates are available. Some credit cards are accepted. Open year-round.

**Directions:** From Redding, drive north on I-5 for nine miles to the Fawndale Road exit (Exit 689). Take that exit and turn right (east) on Fawndale Road. Drive 0.5 mile to the second RV park at the end of the road at 15015 Fawndale Road.

**Contact:** Fawndale Oaks RV Park, 15015 Fawndale Road, Redding, 530/275-0764 or 888/838-2159, www.fawndaleoaks.com.

## 116 BEAR MOUNTAIN RV RESORT AND CAMPGROUND

### Scenic rating: 5

near Shasta Lake

**Map 2.4 Shasta Lake, page 111**

This is a privately operated 52-acre park in the remote Jones Valley area five miles from Shasta Lake. A hiking trail leaves from the campground, rises up a hill, and provides a great view of Redding. The resort emphasizes that there is no train noise here, as there often is at campgrounds closer to Shasta Lake.

**Campsites, facilities:** There are 70 sites with full or partial hookups (30 amps) for RVs up to 40 feet, 14 tent sites, and four park-model cabins. Some RV sites are pull-through. Picnic tables and fire rings are provided. Drinking water, restrooms with flush toilets and coin showers, coin laundry, dump station, a seasonal swimming pool, table tennis, playground, volleyball, and horseshoe pit are available. A boat ramp is within three miles. Leashed pets are permitted.

**Reservations, fees:** Reservations are accepted. RV sites are $18-24 per night, tent sites are $14 per night, plus $2 per person per night for more than two people. Weekly and monthly rates are available. Some credit cards are accepted. Open year-round.

**Directions:** From Redding, drive north on

I-5 for three miles to Exit 682 for Oasis Road. Take that exit and drive to Oasis Road. Turn right on Oasis Road and drive 3.5 miles to Bear Mountain Road. Turn right on Bear Mountain Road and drive 3.5 miles to the campground on the left.

Note: Do not use GPS or mapping sites to reach this area.

**Contact:** Bear Mountain RV Resort and Campground, 14216 Bear Mountain Road, Redding, 530/275-4728, www.campshasta.net.

# 117 EAST WEAVER

### Scenic rating: 6

on the east branch of Weaver Creek in Shasta-Trinity National Forest

**Map 2.4, page 110**

This camp is along East Weaver Creek. Another mile to the west on East Weaver Road, the road dead-ends at a trailhead, a good side trip. From here, the hiking trail is a significant four-mile climb to tiny East Weaver Lake, southwest of Monument Peak (elevation 7,771 feet). The elevation at East Weaver is 2,700 feet.

**Campsites, facilities:** There are 10 sites for tents or RVs up to 25 feet (no hookups). Picnic tables and fire grills are provided. Drinking water (summer only) and vault toilets are available. Supplies and a coin laundry are available in Weaverville. Leashed pets are permitted.

**Reservations, fees:** Reservations are not accepted. Sites are $15 per night or $8 per night in the winter, plus $6 for additional vehicles. Open year-round.

**Directions:** From Redding, drive west on Highway 299 to Weaverville. In Weaverville, turn right (north) on Highway 3 and drive about two miles to East Weaver Road. Turn left on East Weaver Road and drive 3.5 miles to the campground.

**Contact:** Shasta-Trinity National Forest, Weaverville Ranger Station, 530/623-2121, www.fs.usda.gov/stnf.

# 118 DOUGLAS CITY AND STEINER FLAT

### Scenic rating: 7

on the Trinity River

**Map 2.4, page 110**

If you want to camp along this stretch of the main Trinity River, these camps are your best bet (they're along the river about two miles from each other). They are off the main road, near the river, with good bank fishing access (the prime season is from mid-August through winter for salmon and steelhead). There's paved parking, a group picnic site, and two beaches at Douglas City. Steiner Flat, a more primitive camp, provides better access for fishing. This can be a good base camp for an off-season fishing trip on the Trinity River or a lounging spot during the summer. The elevation is 1,700 feet.

**Campsites, facilities:** Douglas City has 20 sites for tents or RVs up to 28 feet (no hookups). Picnic tables and fire grills are provided. Drinking water and restrooms with sinks and flush toilets are available. Steiner Flat has dispersed camping for 22 tents and RVs up to 40 feet (no hookups). Picnic tables and fire grills are provided. Vault toilets are available. There is no drinking water. Supplies are available within one mile in the town of Douglas City. Leashed pets are permitted at both sites.

**Reservations, fees:** Reservations are not accepted. Sites at Douglas City are $10 per night, plus $5 per additional vehicle. There is no fee for camping at Steiner Flat. Douglas City is open mid-May through November; Steiner Flat is open year-round, weather permitting.

**Directions:** From Redding, turn on Highway 299 west and drive west (toward Weaverville). Continue over the bridge at the Trinity River near Douglas City to Steiner Flat Road. Turn left on Steiner Flat Road and drive 0.5 mile to Douglas City campground on the left. To reach Steiner Flat, continue two more miles and look for the campground on the left.

**Contact:** Bureau of Land Management,

Redding Field Office, 530/224-2100, www.blm.gov/ca.

## 119 STEEL BRIDGE

### Scenic rating: 7

on the Trinity River

**Map 2.4, page 110**

Very few people know of this camp, yet it can be a prime spot for anglers and campers; it's one of the better stretches of water in the area for steelhead, with good shore-fishing access (the prime time is from October through December). In the summer, the shade of conifers will keep you cool. Don't forget to bring your own water. The elevation is 1,700 feet.

**Campsites, facilities:** There are 12 sites for tents or RVs up to 20 feet (no hookups). Picnic tables and fire grills are provided. Vault toilets are available. No drinking water is available. Supplies are available within three miles in Douglas City. Some facilities are wheelchair-accessible. Leashed pets are permitted.

**Reservations, fees:** Reservations are not accepted. Sites are $5 per night, plus $5 per additional vehicle. Open mid-May through winter, weather permitting.

**Directions:** From Redding, turn west on Highway 299 and drive over Buckhorn Summit. Continue toward Douglas City to Steel Bridge Road (if you reach Douglas City, you have gone 2.3 miles too far). At Steel Bridge Road, turn right and drive about two miles to the campground at the end of the road.

**Contact:** Bureau of Land Management, Redding Field Office, 530/224-2100, www.blm.gov/ca.

## 120 OLD LEWISTON BRIDGE RV RESORT

### Scenic rating: 7

on the Trinity River

**Map 2.4, page 110**

This is a popular spot for calm-water kayaking, rafting, and fishing. Though much of the water from Trinity and Lewiston Lakes is diverted via tunnel to Whiskeytown Lake (en route to the valley and points south), enough escapes downstream to provide a viable stream here near the town of Lewiston. This upstream section below Lewiston Lake is prime in the early summer for trout, particularly the chance for a huge brown trout (special regulations in effect). A fishing shuttle service is available. The campground is in a hilly area but has level sites, with nearby Lewiston Lake also a major attraction. Some sites are occupied by long-term renters.

**Campsites, facilities:** There are 52 sites with full hookups (30 amps) for RVs up to 45 feet, a separate area for tents, and five rental trailers. Picnic tables and fire rings are provided. Restrooms with showers, coin laundry, grocery store, ice, bait and tackle, and propane gas refills are available. A group picnic area is available by reservation. A restaurant is within 0.5 mile. Leashed pets are permitted.

**Reservations, fees:** Reservations are accepted by phone or website. Sites are $30 per night for RVs, $15 per night per vehicle for tent campers, plus $2 per person per night for more than two people. Weekly and monthly rates are available. Some credit cards are accepted. Open year-round.

**Directions:** From Redding, turn on Highway 299 and drive west over Buckhorn Summit, then continue for five miles to Trinity Dam Boulevard. Turn right on Trinity Dam Boulevard and drive four miles to Lewiston, then continue north to Rush Creek Road. Turn left (west) on Rush Creek Road and drive 0.25 mile to the resort on the left.

**Contact:** Old Lewiston Bridge RV Resort,

Rush Creek Road, Lewiston, 530/778-3894 or 800/922-1924, www.lewistonbridgerv.com.

## 121 TRINITY RIVER RESORT AND RV PARK

### Scenic rating: 7

on the Trinity River

**Map 2.4, page 110**

For many, this privately operated park has an ideal location. You get level, grassy sites with shade trees along the Trinity River, yet it is just a short drive north to Lewiston Lake or a bit farther to giant Trinity Lake. Lake or river, take your pick. The resort covers nearly 14 acres, and about half the sites are rented for the entire summer.

**Campsites, facilities:** There are 52 sites with full hookups (30 and 50 amps) for RVs up to 40 feet, five tent sites, and one rental travel trailer. Restrooms with showers, a coin laundry, cable TV, Wi-Fi, recreation room, lending library, a clubhouse with big screen (seats 4), athletic field, propane gas, camp store, ice, firewood, boat and trailer storage, horseshoes, and picnic area are available. Some facilities are wheelchair-accessible. Leashed pets are permitted.

**Reservations, fees:** Reservations are recommended. RV sites are $32 per night; tent sites are $22 per night. Weekly and monthly rates are available. Some credit cards are accepted. Open year-round. Pets on leash are permitted.

**Directions:** From Redding, turn on Highway 299 west and drive west over Buckhorn Summit. Continue for five miles to Trinity Dam Boulevard. Turn right on Trinity Dam Boulevard and drive four miles to Lewiston. Continue on Trinity Dam Boulevard to Rush Creek Road. Turn left on Rush Creek Road and drive 2.3 miles to the campground on the left.

**Contact:** Trinity River Lodge RV Resort, 7420 Rush Creek Road, Lewiston, 530/778-3791, www.trinityriverresort.com.

## 122 MARY SMITH

### Scenic rating: 10

on Lewiston Lake in Shasta-Trinity National Forest

**Map 2.4, page 110**      **BEST (**

This is one of the prettiest spots you'll ever see, set along the southwestern shore of Lewiston Lake. When you wake up and peek out of your sleeping bag, the natural beauty of this serene lake can take your breath away. Hand-launched boats, such as kayaks and canoes, are ideal here, and the lake speed limit is 10 mph. The lake has 15 miles of shoreline. Although swimming is allowed, the water is too cold for most people. Bird-watching is good. The best fishing is from Lakeview Terrace and the tules upstream to just below Trinity Dam. The elevation is 2,000 feet.

**Campsites, facilities:** There are 11 sites for tents only; some require a very short walk. There are also six "glampsites"—each has a large tent on a raised platform with a futon bed and down comforter inside and an exterior deck with chairs. Picnic tables and fire grills are provided. Drinking water and flush and vault toilets are available. Boat launching and rentals are available nearby at Pine Cove Marina. Supplies and a coin laundry are available in Lewiston. Leashed pets are permitted.

**Reservations, fees:** Reservations are not accepted. Tent sites are $20 per night; glampsites are $85 per night. Open early May through mid-September.

**Directions:** From Redding, turn on Highway 299 west and drive west over Buckhorn Summit. Continue for five miles to Trinity Dam Boulevard. Turn right on Trinity Dam Boulevard and drive four miles to Lewiston, and then continue on Trinity Dam Boulevard for 2.5 miles to the campground.

**Contact:** Shasta-Trinity National Forest, Weaverville Ranger Station, 530/623-2121, www.fs.usda.gov/stnf; Shasta Recreation Company, 530/275-8113; Pine Cove Marina, 530/778-3878.

## 123 COOPER GULCH

### Scenic rating: 8

on Lewiston Lake in Shasta-Trinity National Forest

**Map 2.4, page 110**

Here is a nice spot along a beautiful lake, featuring a short trail to Baker Gulch, where a pretty creek enters Lewiston Lake. The trout fishing is good on the upper end of the lake (where the current starts) and upstream. The lake speed limit is 10 mph. Swimming is allowed, although the water is cold because it flows in from the bottom of Trinity Lake. The lake is designated a wildlife-viewing area, with large numbers of waterfowl and other birds often spotted near the tules off the shore of Lakeview Terrace. Bring all of your own supplies and plan on hunkering down awhile.

**Campsites, facilities:** There are five sites for tents or RVs up to 16 feet (no hookups). Picnic tables and fire grills are provided. Drinking water and vault toilets are available. Boat launching and rentals are nearby at Pine Cove Marina. Supplies and a coin laundry are available in Lewiston. Some facilities are wheelchair-accessible. Leashed pets are permitted.

**Reservations, fees:** Reservations are not accepted. Sites are $15 per night, plus $6 per night per additional vehicle. Open early April through late October.

**Directions:** From Redding, turn on Highway 299 west and drive west over Buckhorn Summit. Continue for five miles to Trinity Dam Boulevard. Turn right on Trinity Dam Boulevard, drive four miles to Lewiston, and then continue on Trinity Dam Boulevard another four miles north to the campground.

**Contact:** Shasta-Trinity National Forest, Weaverville Ranger Station, 530/623-2121, www.fs.usda.gov/stnf; Shasta Recreation Company, 530/275-8113; Pine Cove Marina, 530/778-3878.

## 124 LAKE VIEW TERRACE RESORT

### Scenic rating: 8

on Lewiston Lake

**Map 2.4, page 110**

This might be your Golden Pond. It's a terraced RV park—with cabin rentals also available—overlooking Lewiston Lake, one of the prettiest drive-to lakes in the region. Fishing for trout is excellent from Lakeview Terrace continuing upstream toward the dam. Lewiston Lake is perfect for fishing, with a 10-mph speed limit in effect (all the hot boats go to nearby Trinity Lake), along with excellent prospects for rainbow and brown trout. Other fish species include brook trout and kokanee salmon. The topper is that Lewiston Lake is always full to the brim, just the opposite of the up-and-down nightmare of its neighboring big brother, Trinity.

**Campsites, facilities:** There are 40 sites with full hookups (50 amps) for tents or RVs up to 40 feet; some sites are pull-through. Cabins are also available. Picnic tables and barbecues are provided. Restrooms with showers, coin laundry, seasonal heated pool, propane gas, ice, horseshoes, playground, boat, kayak, and patio-boat rentals are available. Supplies are available within five miles. Leashed pets are permitted.

**Reservations, fees:** Reservations are recommended. Sites are $30 per night, plus $3 per person per night for more than two people and $2 per additional vehicle per night. Weekly and monthly rates are available. Some credit cards are accepted. Open year-round.

**Directions:** From Redding, turn on Highway 299 west and drive west over Buckhorn Summit. Continue for five miles to Trinity Dam Boulevard. Turn right on Trinity Dam Boulevard and drive 10 miles (5 miles past Lewiston) to the resort on the left side of the road.

**Contact:** Lake View Terrace Resort, 530/778-3803, www.lakeviewterraceresort.com.

## 125 TUNNEL ROCK

### Scenic rating: 7

on Lewiston Lake in Shasta-Trinity National Forest

**Map 2.4, page 110**

This is a very small, primitive alternative to Ackerman (see listing in this chapter), which is more developed and another mile up the road to the north. The proximity to the Pine Cove boat ramp and fish-cleaning station, less than two miles to the south, is a primary attraction. Pine Cove Marina is full service and rents fishing boats. The elevation is 1,700 feet.

**Campsites, facilities:** There are four sites for tents or RVs up to 15 feet (no hookups). Picnic tables and fire grills are provided. Vault toilets are available. There is no drinking water. Leashed pets are permitted.

**Reservations, fees:** Reservations are not accepted. Sites are $10 per night, plus $5 per additional vehicle. Open year-round.

**Directions:** From Redding, turn on Highway 299 west and drive over Buckhorn Summit. Continue for five miles to County Road 105/ Trinity Dam Road. Turn right on Trinity Dam Road and drive four miles to Lewiston, and then continue another seven miles north on Trinity Dam Boulevard to the campground.

**Contact:** Shasta-Trinity National Forest, Weaverville Ranger Station, 530/623-2121, www.fs.usda.gov/stnf; Shasta Recreation Company, 530/275-8113.

## 126 ACKERMAN

### Scenic rating: 7

on Lewiston Lake in Shasta-Trinity National Forest

**Map 2.4, page 110**

Of the camps and parks at Lewiston Lake, Ackerman is closest to the lake's headwaters. This stretch of water below Trinity Dam is the best area for trout fishing on Lewiston Lake.

Nearby Pine Cove boat ramp, two miles south of the camp, offers the only boat launch on Lewiston Lake with docks and a fish-cleaning station—a popular spot for anglers. When the Trinity powerhouse is running, trout fishing is excellent in this area. The elevation is 2,000 feet.

**Campsites, facilities:** There are 51 sites for tents or RVs up to 40 feet (no hookups). Picnic tables and fire grills are provided. Non-potable water, flush toilets, and a dump station are available. Leashed pets are permitted.

**Reservations, fees:** Reservations are not accepted. Sites are $20-35 per night ($9 per night during the winter). Open year-round.

**Directions:** From Redding, turn on Highway 299 west and drive west over Buckhorn Summit. Continue for five miles to Trinity Dam Boulevard. Turn right on Trinity Dam Boulevard and drive four miles to Lewiston. Continue north on Trinity Dam Boulevard for eight miles to the campground.

**Contact:** Shasta-Trinity National Forest, Weaverville Ranger Station, 530/623-2121, www.fs.usda.gov/stnf; Shasta Recreation Company, 530/275-8113.

## 127 OAK BOTTOM

### Scenic rating: 7

on Whiskeytown Lake in Whiskeytown National Recreation Area

**Map 2.4, page 110**

The prettiest hiking trails at Whiskeytown Lake are at the far western end of the reservoir, and this camp provides excellent access to them. One hiking and biking trail skirts the north shoreline of the lake and is routed to the lake's inlet at the Judge Carr Powerhouse. The other, with the trailhead just a short drive to the west, is routed along Mill Creek, a pristine, clear-running stream with the trail jumping over the water many times. The campground sites seem a little close, but the camp is next to a beach area. There are junior ranger programs, and evening ranger programs at the Oak Bottom Amphitheater are available several nights per week from mid-June through Labor Day. A self-guided nature trail is five miles away at the visitors center.

**Campsites, facilities:** There are 98 walk-in tent sites and 22 sites for RVs up to 32 feet (no hookups) in a large parking area near the launch ramp. Picnic tables and fire grills are provided. Drinking water, restrooms with flush toilets and coin showers, storage lockers, a convenience store, ice, firewood, a dump station, a boat ramp, and boat rentals are available. Some facilities are wheelchair-accessible. Leashed pets are permitted.

**Reservations, fees:** Reservations are accepted mid-May through mid-September at 530/359-2269. Mid-October through mid-April, sites are first-come, first-served. Mid-April through mid-October, RV sites are $20, shore-side tents are $25, and all remaining tent sites are $23 per night. Mid-October through mid-April, tent and RV sites are $11 per night. There is a pet fee of $2 per night per pet. A park-use permit is $5 per day, $10 per week, or $25 per year. Open year-round.

**Directions:** From Redding, turn on Highway 299 west and drive west for 15 miles (past the visitors center) to the campground entrance road on the left. Turn left and drive a short distance to the campground.

**Contact:** Forever Resorts, 530/359-2269, www.whiskeytownmarinas.com; Whiskeytown National Recreation Area, 530/242-3400 or 530/242-3412, www.nps.gov/whis; Whiskeytown Visitor Center, 530/246-1225; Oak Bottom Campground Store, 530/359-2269.

## 128 SHEEP CAMP
🕅 5% 🏕

### Scenic rating: 8
in Whiskeytown National Recreation Area

**Map 2.4, page 110**

Sheep Camp is a tiny, primitive camp often overlooked in Whiskeytown National

Recreation Area, near a cliff with great views; you will likely have it to yourself. One of the highlights is the nearby hike to Brandy Creek Falls, a series of pools-and-drops that pours into a big pool. From the trailhead, it's a 1.5-mile one-way trip.

**Campsites, facilities:** There are four sites for tents only. Picnic tables, food lockers, and fire pits are provided. Vault toilets are available, but there is no drinking water except at the Whiskeytown Visitor Center. Garbage must be packed out.

**Reservations, fees:** Reservations are not accepted. Sites are $15 per night. A backcountry use permit is required and may be obtained from the visitors center. A Whiskeytown park-use permit is also required ($5 per day, $10 per week, or $25 annually). Open seasonally, weather permitting; closed midwinter.

**Directions:** From Redding, turn west on Highway 299 and drive west for 10 miles to the visitors center on the left and get your permits. From the visitors center, continue south on Kennedy Memorial Drive to a fork. Bear right at the fork, cross over the dam, and continue past the Brandy Creek campground area to Shasta Bally Road. Turn left and drive about eight miles to the campground.

**Contact:** Whiskeytown National Recreation Area, 530/242-3412, www.nps.gov/whis; Whiskeytown Visitor Center, 530/246-1225.

## 129 DRY CREEK GROUP CAMP

### Scenic rating: 7
on Whiskeytown Lake in Whiskeytown National Recreation Area

**Map 2.4, page 110**

If you're in a group and take the time to reserve this spot, you'll be rewarded with some room and the quiet that goes along with it. This is the most remote drive-to camp at Whiskeytown Lake. A boat ramp is about two miles away (to the east) at Brandy Creek. You'll pass it on the way in. Note: Reservations are an absolute must, and can be made five months in advance.

**Campsites, facilities:** Two tent-only group sites can accommodate up to 50 people each. Picnic tables and fire grills are provided. Drinking water, food storage lockers, and vault toilets are available. Leashed pets are permitted.

**Reservations, fees:** Reservations required during summer at 877/444-6777 or www.recreation.gov ($9 reservation fee). Sites are $80 per night. A Whiskeytown day-use pass is required ($5 per day, $10 per week, $25 annually). Open early April through October.

**Directions:** From Redding, drive west on Highway 299 for 10 miles to the visitors center and Kennedy Memorial Drive. Turn left and drive six miles to the campground on the right side of the road.

**Contact:** Whiskeytown National Recreation Area, 530/242-3400 or 530/242-3412, www. nps.gov/whis; Whiskeytown Visitor Center, 530/246-1225.

## 130 BRANDY CREEK

### Scenic rating: 7

on Whiskeytown Lake in Whiskeytown National Recreation Area

**Map 2.4, page 110**

For campers with boats, this is the best place to stay at Whiskeytown, as there is a boat ramp less than 0.25 mile away. Whiskeytown Lake has 36 miles of shoreline and is popular for sailing and sailboarding; it gets a lot more wind than other lakes in the region. (Personal watercraft have been banned from this lake.) Fishing for kokanee salmon is good in the early morning before the wind comes up; trout fishing is pretty good as well.

**Campsites, facilities:** There are 37 sites for RVs up to 35 feet (no hookups) and two primitive tent sites (site #2 is on a steep downhill road). A dump station is available. There are

no restrooms or potable water. Leashed pets are permitted.

**Reservations, fees:** Reservations are not accepted. Sites are $15 per night for tent or RV, or $7 per night during the off-season. A Whiskeytown day-use pass is required ($5 per day, $10 per week, $25 annually). Closed in winter.

**Directions:** From Redding, drive west on Highway 299 for eight miles to the visitors center and Kennedy Memorial Drive. Turn left at the visitors center (Kennedy Memorial Drive) and drive five miles to the campground entrance road on the right. Turn right and drive a short distance to the camp.

**Contact:** Whiskeytown National Recreation Area, 530/242-3400 or 530/242-3412, www. nps.gov/whis; Whiskeytown Visitor Center, 530/246-1225.

## 131 PELTIER BRIDGE

### Scenic rating: 7

below the dam on Clear Creek in Whiskeytown National Recreation Area

**Map 2.4, page 110**

This is a small, pretty, and virtually secret campground located on Clear Creek in Whiskeytown National Recreation Area. Secret? That's right—rangers request its exact location not be revealed. Only when you get your permit at the visitors center overlooking Whiskeytown Lake will they provide specific directions. The camp is in the woods and requires a short hike to get there. I can tell you that Clear Creek is stocked with rainbow trout in the 6- to 8-inch class.

**Campsites, facilities:** There are nine sites for tents only. Picnic tables, food lockers, and fire pits are provided. Vault toilets are available, but there is no drinking water except at the Whiskeytown Visitor Center. Garbage must be packed out.

**Reservations, fees:** Reservations are not accepted. Sites are $15 per night. A backcountry use permit is required and may be obtained from the visitors center. A Whiskeytown day-use pass is also required ($5 per day, $10 per week, $25 annually). Open seasonally, weather permitting.

**Directions:** From Redding, turn on Highway 299 west and drive west for 10 miles to the visitors center. Rangers will provide specific directions to the campground at that time.

**Contact:** Whiskeytown National Recreation Area, 530/242-3412, www.nps.gov/whis; Whiskeytown Visitor Center, 530/246-1225.

## **132** HORSE CAMP

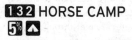

### Scenic rating: 6
in Whiskeytown National Recreation Area

#### Map 2.4, page 110

This is the only campground in Whiskeytown National Recreation Area where horse camping is permitted. Horse Camp is on a well-maintained dirt road and is accessible to vehicles pulling horse trailers.

**Campsites, facilities:** There are two sites for tents only. Picnic tables, food lockers, and fire pits are provided. Vault toilets and drinking water (summer only) are available. Garbage must be packed out.

**Reservations, fees:** Reservations are not accepted. Sites are $15 per night. A backcountry use permit is required and may be obtained from the visitors center. A Whiskeytown day-use pass is also required ($5 per day, $10 per week, $25 annually). Open seasonally, weather permitting.

**Directions:** From Redding, turn west on Highway 299 and drive west for 10 miles to the visitors center. Note that campers with horses must register at the visitors center to get permits and directions to the horse camp.

**Contact:** Whiskeytown National Recreation Area, 530/242-3412, www.nps.gov/whis; Whiskeytown Visitor Center, 530/246-1225.

## **133** PREMIER RV RESORTS

### Scenic rating: 2
in Redding

#### Map 2.4, page 110

If you're stuck with no place to go, this large park could be your savior. Nearby recreation options include a waterslide park and the Turtle Bay Museum and Exploration Park on the Sacramento River. Sundial Bridge, with its glass walkway that allows users to look down into the river, is a stunning feat of architecture where the experience simulates walking on air. In addition, Whiskeytown Lake is nearby to the west, and Shasta Lake lies to the north. A casino and several golf courses are nearby.

**Campsites, facilities:** There are 120 sites with full or partial hookups (30 and 50 amps) for RVs of any length, a cabin, and two yurts. A flat cut-out area on a hillside provides space for dispersed tent sites. Picnic tables and fire grills are provided. Drinking water, restrooms with flush toilets and showers, playground, seasonal swimming pool, coin laundry, dump station, satellite TV hookups, Wi-Fi, a convenience store, propane gas, and a recreation room are available. Some facilities are wheelchair-accessible. Leashed pets are permitted.

**Reservations, fees:** Reservations are accepted. RV sites are $45-55 per night, tent sites are $37 per night, yurts are $52 per night, and it's $3 per person per night for more than two people over age five. Weekly and monthly rates, as well as group rates, are available. Some credit cards are accepted. Open year-round.

**Directions:** In Redding, drive north on I-5 to the Lake Boulevard/Burney-Alturas exit. Turn west (left) on Lake Boulevard and drive 0.25 mile to North Boulder Drive. Turn right (north) on North Boulder Drive and drive one block to the resort on the left.

**Contact:** Premier RV Resorts, 530/246-0101 or 888/710-8450, www.premierrvresorts.com.

## 134 MARINA RV PARK

### Scenic rating: 6

on the Sacramento River

**Map 2.4, page 110**

The riverside setting is a highlight here, with the Sacramento River providing relief from the dog days of summer. An easy, paved walking and biking trail is available nearby at the Sacramento River Parkway, providing river views and sometimes a needed breeze on hot summer evenings. It is two miles away from the Turtle Bay Museum and close to a movie theater. A golf driving range is nearby. This park includes an area with long-term RV renters.

**Campsites, facilities:** There are 42 sites with full or partial hookups (30 amps) for RVs up to 40 feet. Picnic tables, restrooms with showers, a coin laundry, small store, Wi-Fi, seasonal swimming pool, spa, boat ramp, and a dump station are available. Leashed pets are permitted.

**Reservations, fees:** Reservations are accepted. Sites are $36 per night, plus $2 per person per night for more than two people. Weekly and monthly rates are available. Open year-round.

**Directions:** In Redding, turn west on Highway 44 and drive 1.5 miles to the exit for Convention Center/Marina Park Drive. Take that exit, turn left, and drive over the highway to a stoplight and Marina Park Drive. Turn left (south) on Marina Park Drive and drive 0.8 mile to the park on the left.

**Contact:** Marina RV Park, 530/241-4396, www.marinarvpark.com.

## 135 SACRAMENTO RIVER RV PARK

### Scenic rating: 7

south of Redding

**Map 2.4, page 110**

This makes a good headquarters for a fall fishing trip on the Sacramento River, where the salmon come big from August through October. In the summer, trout fishing is very good from this area as well, but a boat is a must. No problem; there's a boat ramp at the park. In addition, you can hire fishing guides who launch from here daily. The park is open year-round, and if you want to stay close to home, a three-acre pond with bass, bluegill, and perch is also available at the resort. You also get great long-distance views of Mount Shasta and Mount Lassen.

**Campsites, facilities:** There are 140 sites with full hookups (30 and 50 amps) for RVs of any length and 10 sites for tents in a shaded grassy area. Some RV sites are pull-through. Picnic tables, restrooms with showers, coin laundry, dump station, cable TV, Wi-Fi, bait, boat launch, playground, two tennis courts, basketball hoops, horseshoes, golf driving range, and a large seasonal swimming pool are available. A clubhouse is available by reservation. Some facilities are wheelchair-accessible. Leashed pets are permitted.

**Reservations, fees:** Reservations are accepted. RV sites are $38 per night; tent sites are $18 per night. Some credit cards are accepted. Open year-round.

**Directions:** From Redding, drive south on I-5 for five miles to the Knighton Road exit. Turn west (right) and drive a short distance to Riverland Drive. Turn left on Riverland Drive and drive two miles to the park at the end of the road.

**Contact:** Sacramento River RV Resort, 530/365-6402, www.sacramentoriverrvresort.com.

## 136 DEERLICK SPRINGS

### Scenic rating: 7

on Browns Creek in Shasta-Trinity National Forest

**Map 2.4, page 110**

It's a long, twisty drive to this remote and

primitive camp on the edge of the Chanchelulla Wilderness in the transition zone where the valley's oak grasslands give way to conifers. This quiet little spot is along Browns Creek. A trailhead just north of camp provides a stream-side walk. The elevation is 3,100 feet.

**Campsites, facilities:** There are 13 sites for tents only. Picnic tables and fire grills are provided. Vault toilets are available. No drinking water is available. Garbage must be packed out. Leashed pets are permitted.

**Reservations, fees:** Reservations are not accepted. There is no fee for camping. Open May through October.

**Directions:** From Red Bluff, turn west on Highway 36 (very twisty) and drive to the Forest Service ranger station in Platina. In Platina, turn right (north) on Harrison Gulch Road and drive 10 miles to the campground on the left.

**Contact:** Shasta-Trinity National Forest, Harrison Gulch Ranger Station, 530/352-4211, www.fs.usda.gov/stnf.

## 137 BASIN GULCH

### Scenic rating: 5
in Shasta-Trinity National Forest

**Map 2.4, page 110**

This little-known campground rarely gets much use. A trail out of this camp climbs Noble Ridge, eventually rising to a good lookout at 3,933 feet, providing sweeping views of the north valley. Of course, you could also just drive there, taking a dirt road out of Platina. There are many backcountry Forest Service roads in the area, so your best bet is to get a Shasta-Trinity National Forest map, which details the roads. The elevation is 2,700 feet.

**Campsites, facilities:** There are 13 sites for tents or RVs up to 20 feet (no hookups). Picnic tables and fire grills are provided. Vault toilets are available. No drinking water is available. Leashed pets are permitted.

**Reservations, fees:** Reservations are not

accepted. Sites are $10 per night. Open May through October.

**Directions:** From Red Bluff, drive about 45 miles west on Highway 36 to the Yolla Bolly District Ranger Station. From the ranger station, turn south on Stuart Gap Road and drive two miles to the campground on the left.

**Contact:** Shasta-Trinity National Forest, Harrison Gulch Ranger Station, 530/352-4211, www.fs.usda.gov/stnf.

## 138 SYCAMORE GROVE AND CAMP DISCOVERY

### Scenic rating: 6
on the Sacramento River in Red Bluff Recreation Area

**Map 2.4, page 110**

Lake Red Bluff is a seasonal lake created by the Red Bluff Diversion Dam on the Sacramento River, and waterskiing, bird-watching, hiking, and fishing are the most popular activities. A three-mile-long paved trail parallels the river, and cycling and skating are allowed. It has become a backyard swimming hole for local residents in the summer when the temperatures reach the high 90s and low 100s almost every day. In early September, the Bureau of Reclamation raises the gates at the diversion dam to allow migrating salmon an easier course on the upstream journey, and in the process, Lake Red Bluff reverts to its former self as the Sacramento River.

**Campsites, facilities:** The Sycamore Grove Camp has 30 sites for tents or RVs up to 40 feet, some with partial hookups. Camp Discovery is a group site with 11 screened cabins and can accommodate up to 100 people and RVs to 35 feet. Drinking water, restrooms with coin showers, flush and vault toilets, picnic areas, visitors center, two boat ramps, and a fish-viewing plaza are available. There are two large barbecues, electrical outlets, lockable storage, five large picnic tables, a restroom with showers and sinks, and an amphitheater in the group camp area. Some facilities are wheelchair-accessible. Leashed pets are permitted.

**Reservations, fees:** Reservations for Sycamore Grove are accepted at 877/444-6777 ($10 reservation fee) or www.recreation.gov ($9 reservation fee). Sites are $16-30 per night. Reservations for Camp Discovery are required at 530/527-1196. The group camp is $175 per night. Open March through November.

**Directions:** From I-5 at Red Bluff, turn east on Highway 36 and drive 100 yards to the first turnoff at Sale Lane. Turn right (south) on Sale Lane and drive 2.5 miles to the campground at the end of the road.

**Contact:** Mendocino National Forest, Red Bluff Recreation Area, 530/527-2813, www.fs.fed.us; Discovery Center, 530/527-1196.

## 139 TOMHEAD SADDLE

### Scenic rating: 4

in Shasta-Trinity National Forest

**Map 2.4, page 110**

This one is way out there in remote wildlands. Little known and rarely visited, it's primarily a jumping-off point for ambitious backpackers. The camp is on the edge of the Yolla Bolly-Middle Eel Wilderness. A trailhead leads to the South Fork of Cottonwood Creek, a trek that entails hiking eight miles in dry, hot terrain. The elevation is 5,700 feet.

**Campsites, facilities:** There are five sites for tents only. Picnic tables and fire grills are provided. Vault toilets and a horse corral and are available. There is no drinking water and garbage must be packed out. Leashed pets are permitted.

**Reservations, fees:** Reservations are not accepted. There is no fee for camping. Open late June through mid-September, weather permitting.

**Directions:** From I-5 in Red Bluff, turn west on Highway 36 and drive about 13 miles to Cannon Road. Turn left on Cannon Road and drive about five miles to Pettyjohn Road. Turn west on Pettyjohn Road and drive to Saddle Camp and Forest Road 27N06. Turn south on Forest Road 27N06 and drive three miles to the campground on the left. It is advisable to obtain a map of Shasta-Trinity National Forest.

**Contact:** Shasta-Trinity National Forest, Harrison Gulch Ranger Station, 530/352-4211, www.fs.usda.gov/stnf.

# LASSEN AND MODOC

© DREAMSTIME.COM

At 10,457 feet, Mount Lassen's domed summit is visible for more than 100 miles. It blew its top in 1914, with continuing eruptions through 1918. Now dormant, the volcanic-based geology–pumice boulders, volcanic rock, and spring-fed streams from underground lava tubes–dominates this landscape. Lassen Volcanic National Park is one of the few national parks where you can enjoy the wilderness in relative solitude. The best hikes are the Summit Climb and Bumpass Hell. Highlights include canoeing and fly-fishing at Fall River, Big Lake, and Ahjumawi State Park. McArthur-Burney Falls State Park, along with the Pit River and Lake Britton, make the best destinations for families. In remote Modoc County, Lava Beds National Monument boasts caves and lava tubes, including the 6,000-foot Catacomb Tunnel. Nearby is pretty Medicine Lake, formed in a caldera, which provides good exploring.

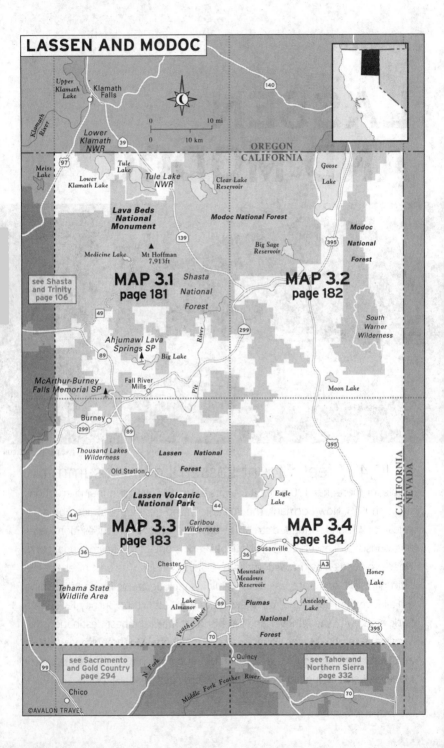

# LASSEN AND MODOC

Upper Klamath Lake

Klamath Falls

Klamath River

Lower Klamath NWR

140

0      10 mi
0      10 km

OREGON
CALIFORNIA

Meiss Lake

97

Tule Lake

Lower Klamath Lake

Tule Lake NWR

Clear Lake Reservoir

Goose Lake

395

**Lava Beds National Monument**

*Modoc National Forest*

Medicine Lake

139

▲ Mt Hoffman 7,913ft

Big Sage Reservoir

**Modoc National Forest**

see Shasta and Trinity page 106

# MAP 3.1
## page 181

*Shasta National Forest*

# MAP 3.2
## page 182

South Warner Wilderness

49

*Ahjumawi Lava Springs SP*

River

Big Lake

299

Moon Lake

*McArthur-Burney Falls Memorial SP* ▲

Fall River Mills

89

Pit River

Burney

299

89

*Thousand Lakes Wilderness*

395

**Lassen   National   Forest**

Old Station

Eagle Lake

**Lassen Volcanic National Park**

44

# MAP 3.3
## page 183

*Caribou Wilderness*

44

36

Chester

36    Susanville

# MAP 3.4
## page 184

A3

Honey Lake

*Tehama State Wildlife Area*

Mountain Meadows Reservoir

Lake Almanor

89

*Plumas*

Antelope Lake

Feather River

70

*National*

*Forest*

395

CALIFORNIA
NEVADA

see Sacramento and Gold Country page 294

99

Quincy

N. Fork

Chico

Middle Fork Feather River

see Tahoe and Northern Sierra page 332

70

©AVALON TRAVEL

# Map 3.1

## Sites 1-16
## Pages 185-192

3.2

3.3

1 2
3 4

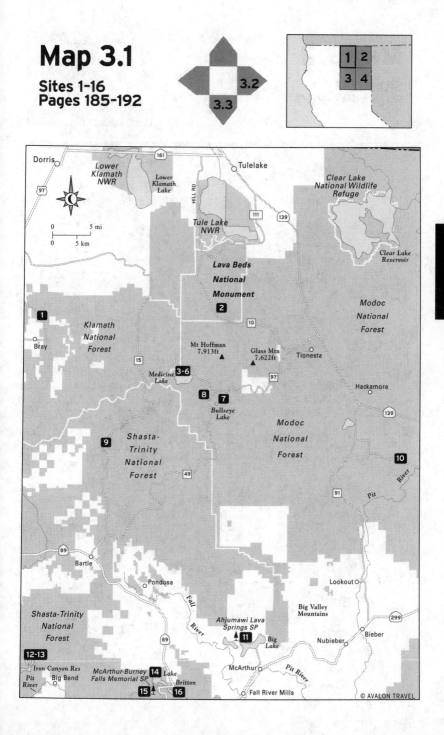

Dorris

161

Tulelake

Lower Klamath NWR

Lower Klamath Lake

Clear Lake National Wildlife Refuge

97

HILL RD

Tule Lake NWR

111

139

Clear Lake Reservoir

0    5 mi
0    5 km

Lava Beds National Monument

**2**

10

Modoc National Forest

**1**

Bray

Klamath National Forest

Mt Hoffman 7,913ft ▲

Glass Mtn 7,622ft ▲

Tionesta

Hackamore

139

15

Medicine Lake

**3-6**

97

**8**   **7**

Bullseye Lake

Modoc National Forest

**9**

Shasta-Trinity National Forest

49

**10**

River

91

Pit

89

Bartle

Pondosa

Fall River

Lookout

Big Valley Mountains

299

Shasta-Trinity National Forest

89

Ahjumawi Lava Springs SP

**11**

Big Lake

Nubieber   Bieber

**12-13**

Iron Canyon Res

Pit River   Big Bend

McArthur-Burney Falls Memorial SP

**14**   Lake

Britton

**15**   **16**

McArthur

Fall River Mills

Pit River

© AVALON TRAVEL

# Map 3.2

**Sites 17-32**
**Pages 193-200**

3.1 · 3.4

| 1 | 2 |
|---|---|
| 3 | 4 |

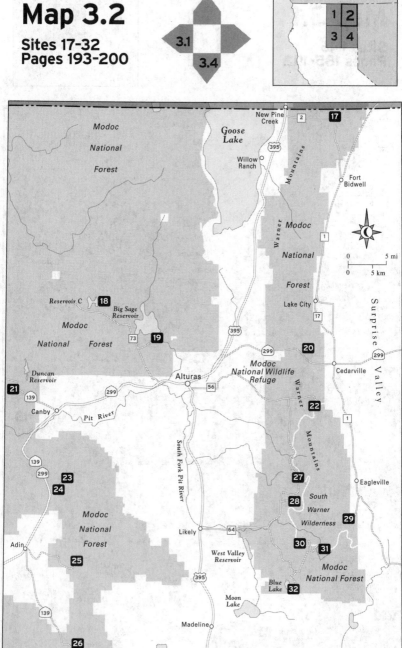

# Map 3.3

**Sites 33-84
Pages 200-224**

3.1
3.4

1 2
3 4

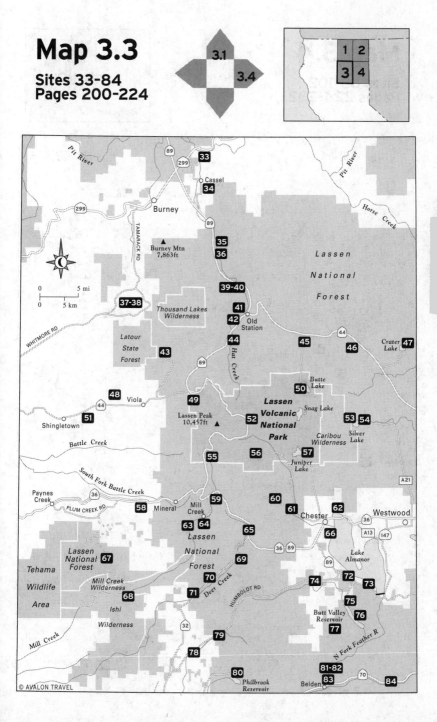

# Map 3.4
## Sites 85-102
## Pages 224-232

3.2
3.3

1 2
3 **4**

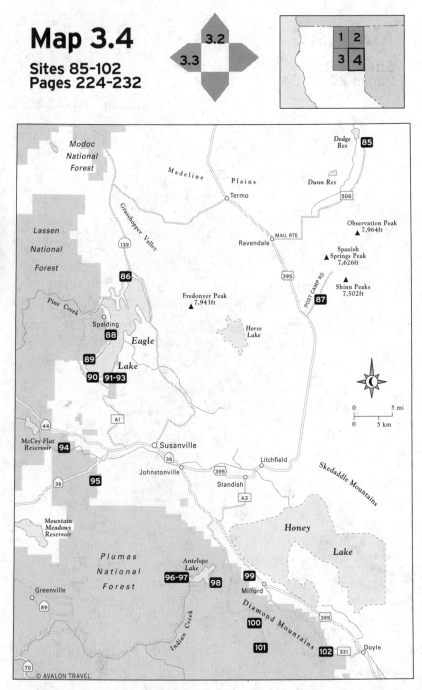

Modoc National Forest

Madeline Plains

Dodge Res

**85**

Dunn Res

Termo

506

Lassen National Forest

Grasshopper Valley

139

Ravendale

MAIL RTE

Observation Peak
▲ 7,964ft

Spanish Springs Peak
▲ 7,626ft

395

POST CAMP RD

**87**

Shinn Peaks
▲ 7,502ft

**86**

Pine Creek

Spalding

**88**

Eagle

**89**

Lake

**90** **91-93**

Fredonyer Peak
▲ 7,943ft

Horse Lake

A1

44

McCoy Flat Reservoir
**94**

○ Susanville

36

**95**

36

Johnstonville

Litchfield

Skedaddle Mountains

395

Standish

A3

Mountain Meadows Reservoir

Honey

Lake

Plumas

National

Forest

Antelope Lake

**96-97**

**98**

**99**

Milford

Greenville

89

Indian Creek

**100**

Diamond Mountains

395

**101**

**102** 331

Doyle

70

© AVALON TRAVEL

0        5 mi
0        5 km

# ■ SHAFTER

### Scenic rating: 4

in Klamath National Forest

**Map 3.1, page 181**

This little-used camp offers trout fishing at nearby Butte Creek for small rainbows, primarily 6- to 8-inchers. Little Orr Lake, about a 10-minute drive away on the southwest flank of Orr Mountain, provides fishing for bass and larger rainbow trout, 10- to 12-inchers, as well as a sprinkling of smaller brook trout. This camp is primitive and not well known, set in a juniper- and sage-filled landscape. The elevation is 4,300 feet. A great side trip is to the nearby Orr Mountain Lookout, where there are spectacular views of Mount Shasta. The road adjacent to the campground is paved, keeping the dust down—a Forest Service touch that is like gold in the summer.

**Campsites, facilities:** There are 10 sites for tents or RVs up to 40 feet (no hookups). Picnic tables and fire grills are provided. Drinking water and vault toilets are available. A boat ramp is available at Orr Lake. Garbage must be packed out. Leashed pets are permitted.

**Reservations, fees:** Reservations are not accepted. Sites are $10 per night. Open year-round, with limited services in winter.

**Directions:** From Redding, drive north on I-5 to Weed and the exit for Central Weed/Highway 97. Take that exit, turn right at the stop sign, drive through Weed and bear right (north) on Highway 97, and then drive 40 miles to Ball Mountain Road. Turn right at Ball Mountain Road and drive 2.5 miles to a T junction with Old State Highway 97. Turn right and drive 4.25 miles (crossing railroad tracks) to the campground on the right side of the road.

**Contact:** Klamath National Forest, Goosenest Ranger District, 530-398-4391, www.fs.usda. gov/klamath.

# ■ INDIAN WELL

### Scenic rating: 9

in Lava Beds National Monument

**Map 3.1, page 181**

Lava Beds National Monument is a one-in-a-million spot, with more than 500 lava-tube caves, Schonchin Butte (a cinder cone with a hiking trail), Mammoth Crater, Native American petroglyphs and pictographs, battlefields and campsites from the Modoc War, and wildlife overlooks of Tule Lake. After winter's first snow, this is one of the best places in the West to photograph deer. Nearby is Klamath National Wildlife Refuge, the largest bald eagle wintering area in the lower 48. If you are new to the outdoors, an interpretive center is available to explain it all to you through informative displays. The visitors center is open year-round.

**Campsites, facilities:** There are 43 sites for tents or RVs up to 30 feet (no hookups) and a group site for up to 40 people. Picnic tables, fire rings, and cooking grills are provided. Drinking water and flush toilets are available. Some facilities are wheelchair-accessible. Supplies are available in the town of Tulelake (30 miles north). Leashed pets are permitted in the campground and on the roads only.

**Reservations, fees:** Reservations are not accepted for the individual sites but are required for the group site at 530/667-8113. Individual sites are $10 per night, with a maximum of eight campers per site. The group site is $3 per person per night ($45-60 total per night). The park entrance fee is $15. Free backcountry camping is allowed; check at the visitors center. Open year-round.

**Directions:** From Redding, drive north on I-5 to the Central Weed/Highway 97 exit. Take that exit, turn right and continue for one mile to U.S. 97. Drive north on U.S. 97 for 54 miles to Highway 161. Turn east on Highway 161 and drive 20 miles to Hill Road. Turn right (south) and drive 18 miles to the visitors center and the campground entrance on the left. Turn left and drive 0.25 mile to the campground.

**Contact:** Lava Beds National Monument Visitor Center, 530/667-8113, www.nps.gov/labe.

## 3 MEDICINE

🚶 🏊 🛶 🚣 🐴 ♿ 🚐 ⛺

### Scenic rating: 7
on Medicine Lake in Modoc National Forest

**Map 3.1, page 181**

Lakeside campsites tucked away in conifers make this camp a winner. Medicine Lake, at 640 acres, was formed in the crater of an old volcano and is surrounded by lodgepole pine and fir trees. The lake is stocked with rainbow and brook trout in the summer, gets quite cold in the fall, and freezes over in winter. All water sports are permitted. Many side trips are possible, including nearby Bullseye and Blanche Lakes and Ice Caves (both signed and off the access road) and Lava Beds National Monument just 15 miles north. At 6,700 feet, temperatures can drop in summer and the season is short.

**Campsites, facilities:** There are 22 sites for tents or RVs up to 30 feet (no hookups). Picnic tables and fire grills are provided. Drinking water and vault toilets are available. Ranger-guided cave tours, walks, and talks are available during the summer. A boat ramp is nearby. A café and bar are in Bartle; otherwise, no supplies are available within an hour's drive. Some facilities are wheelchair-accessible. Leashed pets are permitted.

**Reservations, fees:** Reservations are not accepted. Sites are $14 per vehicle per night. Open late May through early October, weather permitting.

**Directions:** From Redding, drive north on I-5 past Dunsmuir to Highway 89. Turn east on Highway 89 and drive 28 miles (just past Bartle) to Forest Road 15/Harris Springs Road. Turn left on Forest Road 15 and drive approximately five miles to the Y intersection with Forest Road 49/Medicine Lake Road. Turn right on Forest Road 49 and drive approximately 26 miles to the lake and campground access road.

**Contact:** Modoc National Forest, Doublehead Ranger District, 530/667-2246, www.fs.usda.gov/modoc.

## 4 A. H. HOGUE

🚶 🏊 🛶 🚣 🐴 ♿ 🚐 ⛺

### Scenic rating: 7
on Medicine Lake in Modoc National Forest

**Map 3.1, page 181**

This camp was created in 1990 when the original Medicine Lake Campground was divided in half. (For more information, see the Medicine listing.)

**Campsites, facilities:** There are 24 sites for tents or RVs up to 30 feet (no hookups). Picnic tables and fire grills are provided. Drinking water and vault toilets are available. A boat ramp is nearby. Some facilities are wheelchair-accessible. Leashed pets are permitted. A café and bar are in Bartle; otherwise, no supplies are available within an hour's drive.

**Reservations, fees:** Reservations are not accepted. Sites are $14 per vehicle per night. Open late May through early October, weather permitting.

**Directions:** From Redding, drive north on I-5 past Dunsmuir to Highway 89. Turn east on Highway 89 and drive 28 miles (just past Bartle) to Forest Road 15/Harris Springs Road. Turn left on Forest Road 15 and drive approximately five miles to the Y intersection with Forest Road 49/Medicine Lake Road. Turn right on Forest Road 49 and drive approximately 26 miles to the lake and campground access road.

**Contact:** Modoc National Forest, Doublehead Ranger District, 530/667-2246, www.fs.usda.gov/modoc.

## 5 HEMLOCK

### Scenic rating: 7
on Medicine Lake in Modoc National Forest

**Map 3.1, page 181**

This is one in a series of campgrounds on Medicine Lake operated by the Forest Service. A special attraction at Hemlock is the natural sand beach. (For more information, see the Medicine listing in this chapter.)

**Campsites, facilities:** There are 22 sites for tents or RVs up to 22 feet (no hookups). Picnic tables and fire grills are provided. Drinking water and vault toilets are available. A boat ramp is available nearby. Some facilities are wheelchair-accessible. Leashed pets are permitted. A café and bar are in Bartle; otherwise, no supplies are available within an hour's drive.

**Reservations, fees:** Reservations are not accepted. Sites are $14 per vehicle per night. Open late May through early October, weather permitting.

**Directions:** From Redding, drive north on I-5 past Dunsmuir to Highway 89. Turn east on Highway 89 and drive 28 miles (just past Bartle) to Forest Road 15/Harris Springs Road. Turn left on Forest Road 15 and drive approximately five miles to the Y intersection with Forest Road 49/Medicine Lake Road. Turn right on Forest Road 49 and drive approximately 26 miles to the lake and campground access road.

**Contact:** Modoc National Forest, Doublehead Ranger District, 530/667-2246, www.fs.usda.gov/modoc.

## 6 HEADQUARTERS

### Scenic rating: 7
on Medicine Lake in Modoc National Forest

**Map 3.1, page 181**

This is one of four campgrounds beside Medicine Lake. There is no lake access from this camp because of private property between the lake and campground. The elevation is 6,700 feet. (For more information, see the Medicine listing in this chapter.)

**Campsites, facilities:** There are 16 sites for tents or RVs up to 18 feet (no hookups). Picnic tables and fire grills are provided. Vault toilets are available. There is no drinking water. A boat ramp is nearby. A café and bar are in Bartle; otherwise, no supplies are available within an hour's drive. Some facilities are wheelchair-accessible. Leashed pets are permitted.

**Reservations, fees:** Reservations are not accepted. Sites are $14 per vehicle per night. Open late May through early October, weather permitting.

**Directions:** From Redding, drive north on I-5 past Dunsmuir to Highway 89. Turn east on Highway 89 and drive 28 miles (just past Bartle) to Forest Road 15/Harris Springs Road. Turn left on Forest Road 15 and drive approximately five miles to the Y intersection with Forest Road 49/Medicine Lake Road. Turn right on Forest Road 49 and drive approximately 26 miles to the lake and campground access road.

**Contact:** Modoc National Forest, Doublehead Ranger District, 530/667-2246, www.fs.usda.gov/modoc.

## 7 BULLSEYE LAKE

### Scenic rating: 7
near Medicine Lake in Modoc National Forest

**Map 3.1, page 181**

This tiny lake gets overlooked every year, mainly because of its proximity to nearby Medicine Lake. Bullseye Lake is shallow, but because snow keeps it locked up until late May or early June, the water stays plenty cold for small trout through July. It is stocked with just 750 six- to eight-inch rainbow trout, not much to crow about—or to catch, for that matter. No boat motors are allowed. Nearby are some ice caves, created by ancient volcanic action. The place is small, quiet, and pretty, but most of all, small. This camp is at an elevation of 6,500 feet.

**Campsites, facilities:** There are six sites for

tents or RVs up to 22 feet (no hookups). Picnic tables and fire grills are provided. A vault toilet is available. There is no drinking water. Garbage must be packed out. Supplies are available in McCloud. A café and bar are in Bartle; otherwise, no supplies are available within an hour's drive. Leashed pets are permitted.

**Reservations, fees:** Reservations are not accepted. There is no fee for camping. Open late May through October, weather permitting.

**Directions:** From Redding, drive north on I-5 past Dunsmuir to Highway 89. Turn east on Highway 89 and drive 28 miles (just past Bartle) to Forest Road 15/Harris Springs Road. Turn left on Forest Road 15 and drive approximately five miles to the Y intersection with Forest Road 49/Medicine Lake Road. Turn right on Forest Road 49 and drive approximately 24 miles to the Bullseye Lake access road (if you reach Medicine Lake, you have gone about two miles too far). Turn right at the Bullseye Lake access road and drive a short distance past Blanche Lake, then turn right and drive a short distance to the lake.

**Contact:** Modoc National Forest, Doublehead Ranger District, 530/667-2246, www.fs.usda. gov.modoc.

## 8 PAYNE SPRINGS
🥾 🏕️ 🚐 ⛺

### Scenic rating: 8
near Medicine Lake in Modoc National Forest

Map 3.1, page 181

This camp is by a small spring in a very pretty riparian area. It's small, but it is special.

**Campsites, facilities:** There are five dispersed sites for tents or RVs up to 20 feet (no hookups). Picnic tables and fire grills are provided. A vault toilet is available. No drinking water is available. Garbage must be packed out. A café and bar are in Bartle. Supplies are available in Tionesta, a 30-minute drive, or McCloud. Leashed pets are permitted.

**Reservations, fees:** Reservations are not

accepted. There is no fee for camping. Open late May through October, weather permitting.

**Directions:** From Redding, drive north on I-5 past Dunsmuir to Highway 89. Turn east on Highway 89 and drive 28 miles (just past Bartle) to Forest Road 15/Harris Springs Road. Turn left on Forest Road 15 and drive approximately five miles to the Y intersection with Forest Road 49/Medicine Lake Road. Turn right on Forest Road 49 and drive 30 miles (0.2 mile past the Bullseye Lake access road) to the Payne Springs access road (if you reach Medicine Lake, you have gone too far). Turn left on the Payne Springs access road and drive a short distance to the campground.

**Contact:** Modoc National Forest, Doublehead Ranger District, 530/667-2246, www.fs.usda. gov/modoc.

## 9 HARRIS SPRINGS
🥾 🦌 🚐 ⛺

### Scenic rating: 3
in Shasta-Trinity National Forest

Map 3.1, page 181

This camp is a hidden spot in remote Shasta-Trinity National Forest, nestled in the long, mountainous ridge that runs east from Mount Shasta to Lava Beds National Monument. The camp, at 4,800 feet, is very popular with deer hunters in the fall. The Harris Spring Guard station, built in 1929, is 0.25 mile on the opposite side of the access road (but is no longer staffed). The area is best explored by four-wheel drive, venturing to a series of small buttes, mountaintops, and lookouts in the immediate area. A map of Shasta-Trinity National Forest is a must.

**Campsites, facilities:** There are 15 sites for tents or RVs up to 32 feet (no hookups). Picnic tables and fire grills are provided. There is no drinking water. Vault toilets are available. Garbage must be packed out. Leashed pets are permitted.

**Reservations, fees:** Reservations are not accepted. There is no fee for camping. Open late May through early October, weather permitting.

**Directions:** From Redding, drive north on I-5 past Dunsmuir to the junction with Highway 89. Turn east on Highway 89 and drive 28 miles (just past Bartle) to Forest Road 15/ Harris Springs Road. Bear left on Forest Road 15 and drive five miles to the Y intersection with Harris Springs Road and Medicine Lake Road/Forest Road 49. Bear left at the Y, staying on Harris Springs Road/Forest Road 15, and drive 12 miles to a junction with a forest road signed for the Harris Springs Guard Station. Turn right and drive a short distance, and look for the campground entrance on the right side of the road.

**Contact:** Shasta-Trinity National Forest, McCloud Ranger District, 530/964-2184, www. fs.usda.gov/stnf.

## 10 COTTONWOOD FLAT

**Scenic rating: 6**

in Modoc National Forest

**Map 3.1, page 181**

The camp is wooded and shady, set at 4,700 feet elevation in the rugged and remote Devil's Garden area of Modoc National Forest. The region is known for large mule deer, and Cottonwood Flat is well situated as a base camp for a hunting trip in the fall. The weather can get extremely cold early and late in the season.

**Campsites, facilities:** There are 10 sites for tents or RVs up to 16 feet (no hookups). Picnic tables and fire grills are provided. There is no drinking water. Vault toilets are available. Garbage must be packed out. Supplies are available within 10 miles in Canby. Leashed pets are permitted.

**Reservations, fees:** Reservations are not accepted. There is no fee for camping. Open May through October, weather permitting.

**Directions:** From Redding, drive east on Highway 299 for about 100 miles to the town of Adin. Continue on Highway 299 for about 20

miles to the Canby Bridge at the Pit River and the junction with Forest Road 84. Turn left on Forest Road 84 and drive about eight miles to Forest Road 42N95. Turn right and drive 0.5 mile to the campground entrance on the left side of the road. Note: The access road is not recommended for RVs longer than 16 feet.

**Contact:** Modoc National Forest, Devil's Garden Ranger District, 530/233-5811, www. fs.usda.gov/modoc.

## 11 AHJUMAWI LAVA SPRINGS BOAT-IN

**Scenic rating: 8**

at Big Lake in Ahjumawi Lava Springs State Park

**Map 3.1, page 181**

This is a one-of-a-kind boat-in camp on Big Lake and connecting Horr Pond in the Fall River matrix of streams. Ahjumawi means "where the waters come together," and it was named by the Pit River Native Americans who inhabit the area near the confluence of Big Lake, Tule River, Ja She Creek, Lava Creek, and Fall River. Together the waters form one of the largest freshwater springs in the world. Springs flowing from the lava are prominent along the shoreline. This is a place of exceptional and primeval scenery. Much of the land is covered with lava flows, including vast areas of jagged black basalt, along with lava tubes and spattercone and conic depressions. There are brilliant aqua bays and, for campers, peace and quiet. However, you may be joined on land by armies of mosquitoes in the spring; they're not so bad while you're on the water.

Access is by boat only, ideal for canoes, and, in addition, the lake is not well known outside of the region. Expert fly fishers try for giant but elusive rainbow trout, best in the early morning at the springs. Because of high water clarity, long leaders and perfect casts are essential. There are also nesting areas around the lake for bald eagles, ospreys, and blue herons, and this park is considered a stellar habitat for bird-watching. A series of connecting trails are accessible from camp. The park is a wilderness area, covering 6,000 acres, and most of it is extremely rugged lava rock. The many signs of this area's ancient past include bedrock mortars, ceremonial sites, and prehistoric rockfish traps. Herds of large mule deer forage through much of the park. Bears also roam this area. Finally, there are magnificent views of Mount Shasta, Lassen Peak, and other mountains.

**Campsites, facilities:** There are nine boat-in sites. Picnic tables, food lockers, and fire pits are provided. Vault toilets are available. No drinking water is available. Garbage must be packed out. Leashed pets are permitted.

**Reservations, fees:** Reservations are not accepted. Sites are $15 per night. Open year-round, weather permitting.

**Directions:** From Redding, drive east on Highway 299 for 73 miles to McArthur. Turn left on Main Street and drive 3.5 miles (becomes a dirt road) to the Rat Farm boat launch at Big Lake. Launch boat and proceed by boat 1-3 miles to one of the nine boat-in campsites. (As you head out from Rat Farm, the campsites are on the right side of the lake, tucked along the shore.)

**Contact:** Ahjumawi Lava Springs State Park, c/o McArthur-Burney Falls Memorial State Park, 530/335-2777, www.parks.ca.gov.

## 12 DEADLUN
🥾 🛶 🎣 🚣 🐾 🚐 ⛺

### Scenic rating: 7
on Iron Canyon Reservoir in Shasta-Trinity National Forest

**Map 3.1, page 181**

Deadlun is a pretty, forested campground, shaded and quiet, with a five-minute walk or one-minute drive to the Deadlun Creek arm of Iron Canyon Reservoir. If you have a canoe to launch or fishing equipment to carry, driving is the choice. Trout fishing is good in April and May and then again in October and early

November. One downer is that the shoreline is often very muddy in March and early April. Because of an engineering error with the dam, the lake never fills completely, causing the lakeshore to be strewn with stumps and quite muddy after spring rains and snowmelt.

**Campsites, facilities:** There are 25 sites for tents or RVs up to 24 feet (no hookups). Picnic tables and fire grills are provided. Vault toilets are available. No drinking water is available. A small boat ramp is available one mile from the camp. Garbage must be packed out. Leashed pets are permitted.

**Reservations, fees:** Reservations are not accepted. There is no fee for camping. Open year-round.

**Directions:** From Redding, drive east on Highway 299 for 37 miles to Big Bend Road/County Road 7M01. Turn left and drive 17 miles to the town of Big Bend. Continue for five miles to the lake, bearing right at the T intersection, and continue for two miles (past the boat-launch turnoff) to the campground turnoff on the left side of the road. Turn left and drive one mile to the campground.

**Contact:** Shasta-Trinity National Forest, Shasta Lake Ranger District, 530/275-1587, www.fs.usda.gov/recarea/stnf; Shasta Lake Visitor Center, 530/275-1589.

## 13 HAWKINS LANDING
🥾 🛶 🎣 🚣 🚤 🐾 🚐 ⛺

### Scenic rating: 7
on Iron Canyon Reservoir

**Map 3.1, page 181**

The adjacent boat ramp makes Hawkins Landing the better of the two camps at Iron Canyon Reservoir for campers with trailered boats (though Deadlun is far more secluded). Iron Canyon, with 15 miles of shoreline, provides good fishing for trout and has a resident bald eagle or two. One problem with this lake is the annual drawdown in late fall, which causes the shoreline to be extremely muddy in the spring. The lake usually rises high enough to make the boat ramp functional by mid-April. The best spot for swimming is near the earth dam, which is also a good put-in area for kayaks and canoes. Elevation is 2,700 feet.

**Campsites, facilities:** There are 10 sites for tents or RVs up to 30 feet (no hookups). Picnic tables and fire grills are provided. Drinking water, vault toilets, and a small boat ramp are available. Supplies can be obtained in Big Bend. Leashed pets are permitted.

**Reservations, fees:** Reservations are not accepted. Sites are $10 per night, plus $1 per pet per night, $3 per night for each additional vehicle, and $8 per night for additional RV. Open mid-April through Labor Day weekend, weather permitting.

**Directions:** From Redding, drive east on Highway 299 for 37 miles to Big Bend Road. At Big Bend Road turn left and drive 15.2 miles to the town of Big Bend. Continue for 2.1 miles to Forest Road 38N11. Turn left and drive 3.3 miles to the Iron Canyon Reservoir Spillway. Turn right and drive 1.1 miles to a dirt road. Turn left and drive 0.3 mile to the campground.

**Contact:** PG&E Land Projects, 916/386-5164, www.pge.com/recreation.

## 14 NORTHSHORE

🏊 🚤 🚣 🦌 🚐 ⛺

**Scenic rating: 8**

on Lake Britton

**Map 3.1, page 181**

In 2016, an algae alert was issued for Lake Britton stating that "harmful algae may be present in these waters." Contact PG&E for algae alerts before planning a trip here.

This peaceful campground among the woodlands near the shore of Lake Britton is directly across the lake from McArthur-Burney Falls Memorial State Park. Boating, fishing, and kayaking are popular. Boat rentals are available near the boat ramp. The lake has fair prospects for trout and smallmouth bass and is sometimes excellent for crappie. The elevation is 2,800 feet.

For side trips, the best trout fishing in the area is on the Pit River near Powerhouse Number Three. A hot spring is available in Big Bend, about a 30-minute drive from camp. The nearby town of Burney has great restaurants, annual events, and shopping. Note: This is a bald eagle nesting area, and some areas are closed in spring when an active nest is verified. Don't be surprised if a beautiful eagle swoops down and visits you.

**Campsites, facilities:** There are 30 sites for tents or RVs up to 30 feet (no hookups). Picnic tables and fire grills are provided. Drinking water and vault toilets are available. Coin showers with hot water (provided by solar panels) and flush toilets are near the camp entrance. An unimproved boat ramp is near the camp and an improved boat ramp is available in McArthur-Burney Falls State Park (about four miles away). Supplies can be obtained in Fall River Mills or Burney. Leashed pets are permitted.

**Reservations, fees:** Reservations are not accepted. Sites are $22 per night, plus $3 per night for each additional car, $8 per night per additional RV, and $1 per pet per night. There is a $7 boat-launch fee. Open mid-April through mid-September, weather permitting.

**Directions:** From Redding, drive east on Highway 299 to Burney and then continue for five miles to Highway 89. Turn left (north) and drive 9.7 miles (past the state park entrance and over the Lake Britton Bridge) to Clark Creek Road. Turn left (west) and drive about a mile to the camp access road. Turn left and drive one mile to the camp.

**Contact:** PG&E Land Projects, 916/386-5164, www.pge.com/recreation.

## 15 MCARTHUR-BURNEY FALLS MEMORIAL STATE PARK

### Scenic rating: 9
in McArthur-Burney Falls Memorial State Park

**Map 3.1, page 181**

McArthur-Burney Falls Memorial State Park was originally formed by volcanic activity and features 910 acres of forest and five miles of stream and lake shore. The Headwaters horse camp is three miles from the main campground. (Non-equestrian campers may stay at the horse camp, but only tents are allowed.) The campground is pretty and set amid large ponderosa pines. Camping-style cabins were installed in 2008 and have been a hit since.

Burney Falls is a 129-foot waterfall, a beautiful cascade split at the top by a little grove of trees, with small trickles oozing and falling out of the adjacent moss-lined wall. Since it is fed primarily by a spring, it runs strong and glorious most of the year, producing 100 million gallons of water every day. The Headwaters Trail provides an outstanding hike to see the waterfall and Burney Creek, as well as for an easy adventure and fishing access to the stream. An excellent fly-fishing section of the Pit River is below the dam.

**Campsites, facilities:** There are 128 sites for tents or RVs up to 32 feet (no hookups), six horse-camp sites, one hike-in/bike-in site, and 24 wood camping cabins. Picnic tables, food lockers, and fire grills are provided. Drinking water, restrooms with flush toilets and showers, and a dump station are available. Vault toilets and a small horse corral are available at the horse camp. Wi-Fi is available within 150 feet of the visitors center. A grocery/gift store and boat rentals are available in the summer. Some facilities are wheelchair-accessible. Leashed pets are permitted, except on the trails and the beach.

**Reservations, fees:** Reservations are accepted seasonally for RV sites, tent sites, and camping cabins at 800/444-7275 or www.reserveamerica.com ($8 reservation fee). Sites are $30-35 per night, plus $10 per night for each additional vehicle; primitive sites are $15-30 per night for primitive sites; it's $5 per person per night for the hike-in/bike-in site. Camping cabins start at $71.50 per night. Reservations are not accepted for equestrian sites. The horse camp is $15 per night, plus $10 per night per additional vehicle and $2 per night per horse. Boat launching is $8 per day. Open year-round.

**Directions:** From Redding, drive east on Highway 299 to Burney and then continue for five miles to the junction with Highway 89. At Highway 89, turn north (left) and drive six miles to the campground entrance on the left side of the road.

**Contact:** McArthur-Burney Falls State Park, 530/335-2777, www.parks.ca.gov.

## 16 DUSTY CAMPGROUND

### Scenic rating: 8
on Lake Britton

**Map 3.1, page 181**

In 2016, an algae alert was issued for Lake Britton stating that "harmful algae may be present in these waters." Contact PG&E for algae alerts before planning a trip.

This is one in a series of campgrounds near the north shore of Lake Britton, which has 18 miles of shoreline. (See Northshore listing in this chapter for more information.) The elevation is 2,800 feet. It provides an alternative to nearby McArthur-Burney Falls Memorial State Park, which is far more popular.

**Campsites, facilities:** There are seven sites for tents or RVs up to 30 feet (no hookups); two of the sites can accommodate groups of up to 12 people each. Fire rings are provided. Vault toilets are available. Drinking water is not available. Garbage must be packed out in winter. Some facilities are wheelchair-accessible. Leashed pets are permitted.

**Reservations, fees:** Reservations are not accepted. Single sites are $8 per night, doubles sites are $16, plus $3 per night for each additional vehicle, $8 per night per additional RV, and $1 per pet per night. Fees are collected mid-April through early November. Open year-round.

**Directions:** From Redding, drive east on Highway 299 to Burney and continue for five miles to the junction with Highway 89. Turn left (north) and drive 7.5 miles (past the state park entrance and over the Lake Britton Bridge) to the campground access road on the right (it will be confusing because the campground is on the left). Turn right and drive 0.75 mile (in the process crossing the highway) to the campground.

**Contact:** PG&E Land Projects, 916/386-5164, www.pge.com/recreation.

## 17 CAVE LAKE

**Scenic rating: 8**

in Modoc National Forest

**Map 3.2, page 182**

A pair of lakes can be discovered out here in the middle of nowhere, with Cave Lake on one end and Lily Lake on the other. Together they make a nice set, very quiet, extremely remote, with good fishing for rainbow trout and brook trout. A canoe, pram, or float tube can be ideal. No motors are permitted. Of the two lakes, it is nearby Lily Lake that is prettier and provides the better fishing. Cave Lake is at 6,600 feet. By camping here, you become a member of the 5 Percent Club; that is, the 5 percent of campers who know of secret, isolated little spots such as this one.

**Campsites, facilities:** There are six sites for tents or RVs up to 15 feet (no hookups); trailers are not advised because of the steep access road. Picnic tables and fire grills are provided. Drinking water and vault toilets are available. Garbage must be packed out. Motors (including electric) are prohibited on the lake. Supplies are available in New Pine Creek and Davis Creek. Leashed pets are permitted.

**Reservations, fees:** Reservations are not accepted. There is no fee for camping. Open July through October, weather permitting.

**Directions:** From Redding, drive east on Highway 299 for 146 miles to Alturas and U.S. 395. Turn north on U.S. 395 and drive 40 miles to Forest Road 2 (if you reach the town of New Pine Creek on the Oregon/California border, you have driven a mile too far). Turn right on Forest Road 2 (a steep dirt road—trailers are not recommended) and drive six miles to the campground entrance on the left side of the road, just beyond the Lily Lake picnic area.

**Contact:** Modoc National Forest, Warner Mountain Ranger District, 530/279-6116, www.fs.usda.gov/modoc.

## 18 RESERVOIR C

**Scenic rating: 6**

near Alturas in Modoc National Forest

**Map 3.2, page 182**

It is one great adventure to explore the "alphabet lakes" in the remote Devil's Garden area of Modoc County. Reservoir C and Reservoir F provide the best of the lot, but the success can go up and down like a yo-yo, just like the water levels in the lakes. Reservoir C is stocked with both Eagle Lake trout and brown trout. A sidelight to this area is the number of primitive roads that are routed through Modoc National Forest, perfect for four-wheel-drivers. The elevation is 4,900 feet.

**Campsites, facilities:** There is a dispersed camping area for tents or RVs up to 22 feet (no hookups). Picnic tables and fire grills are provided. There are no toilets. A primitive boat ramp is available. No drinking water is available. Garbage must be packed out. Leashed pets are permitted.

**Reservations, fees:** Reservations are not accepted. There is no fee for camping. Open May through September.

**Directions:** From Alturas, drive west on Highway 299 for three miles to Crowder Flat Road/County Road 73. Turn right on Crowder

Flat Road and drive 9.5 miles to Triangle Ranch Road/Forest Road 43N18. Turn left on Triangle Ranch Road and drive seven miles to Forest Road 44N32. Turn right on Forest Road 44N32, drive 0.5 mile, turn right on the access road for the lake and campground, and drive 0.5 mile to the camp at the end of the road.

**Contact:** Modoc National Forest, Devil's Garden Ranger District, 530/233-5811, www.fs.usda.gov/modoc.

## 19 BIG SAGE RESERVOIR

### Scenic rating: 5

in Modoc National Forest

**Map 3.2, page 182**

This is a do-it-yourself camp: pick your own spot, bring your own water, and don't expect to see anybody else. This camp is set along Big Sage Reservoir—that's right, sagebrush country at 5,100 feet elevation. It is a big lake, covering 5,000 surface acres, and a boat ramp is adjacent to the campground. This is one of the better bass lakes in Modoc County. Catfish and crappie are also here. Water sports are allowed, except for personal watercraft. Swimming is not recommended because of algae growth in mid-summer, murky water, and muddy shoreline. Water levels can fluctuate greatly.

**Campsites, facilities:** There are 11 sites for tents or RVs up to 22 feet (no hookups). Picnic tables and fire grills are provided. Vault toilets are available. There is no drinking water. Some facilities are wheelchair-accessible. Garbage must be packed out. A boat ramp is available nearby. Leashed pets are permitted. Supplies can be obtained in Alturas, about eight miles away.

**Reservations, fees:** Reservations are not accepted. There is no fee for camping. Open May through September.

**Directions:** From Alturas, drive west on Highway 299 for three miles to Crowder Flat Road/County Road 73. Turn right on Crowder Flat Road and drive about five miles to County

Road 180. Turn right on County Road 180 and drive four miles. Turn left at the access road for the campground and boat ramp and drive a short distance to the camp on the left side of the road.

**Contact:** Modoc National Forest, Doublehead Ranger District, 530/667-2246, www.fs.usda.gov/modoc.

## 20 STOUGH RESERVOIR

### Scenic rating: 8

in Modoc National Forest

**Map 3.2, page 182**

Stough Reservoir looks like a large country pond where cattle might drink. You know why? Because it once actually was a cattle pond on a family ranch that has since been converted to Forest Service property. It is in the north Warner Mountains (not to be confused with the South Warner Wilderness), which feature many back roads and remote four-wheel-drive routes. The elevation is 6,200 feet. Note that you may find this campground named "Stowe Reservoir" on some maps and in previous editions of this book. The name is now officially spelled "Stough Reservoir," after the family that originally owned the property.

**Campsites, facilities:** There are 14 sites for tents or RVs up to 22 feet (no hookups). Picnic tables and fire grills are provided. Drinking water and vault toilets are available. Garbage must be packed out. Leashed pets are permitted. Supplies can be obtained in Cedarville, six miles away.

**Reservations, fees:** Reservations are not accepted. There is no fee for camping. Open late May through early October, weather permitting.

**Directions:** From Redding, drive east on Highway 299 to Alturas. In Alturas, continue north on Highway 299/U.S. 395 for five miles to the split-off for Highway 299. Turn right on Highway 299 and drive about 12 miles (just past Cedar Pass). Look for the signed entrance road on the left side of the road. Turn left and drive one mile to the campground on the left side of the road.

**Contact:** Modoc National Forest, Warner Mountain Ranger District, 530/279-6116, www.fs.usda.gov/modoc.

# 21 HOWARD'S GULCH

### Scenic rating: 6

near Duncan Reservoir in Modoc National Forest

**Map 3.2, page 182**

This is the nearest campground to Duncan Reservoir, three miles to the north and stocked with trout each year by the Department of Fish and Wildlife. The camp sits in the typically sparse woods of Modoc National Forest, but a beautiful grove of aspens is three miles west on Highway 139, on the left side of the road. By the way, Highway 139 isn't much of a highway at all, but it is paved and will get you there. The elevation is 4,700 feet.

**Campsites, facilities:** There are 11 sites for tents or RVs up to 22 feet (no hookups). Picnic tables and fire grills are provided. Drinking water and vault toilets are available. Some facilities are wheelchair-accessible. Supplies are available within five miles in Canby. Leashed pets are permitted.

**Reservations, fees:** Reservations are not accepted. Sites are $12 per night. Open May through October, weather permitting.

**Directions:** From Redding, drive east on Highway 299 for about 100 miles to Adin. Continue on Highway 299 for about 25 miles to Highway 139. Turn left (northwest) on Highway 139 and drive six miles to the campground on the left side of the road.

**Contact:** Modoc National Forest, Devil's Garden Ranger District, 530/233-5811, www.fs.usda.gov/modoc.

# 22 PEPPERDINE AND HORSE CAMP

### Scenic rating: 5

in Modoc National Forest

**Map 3.2, page 182**

This camp is outstanding for hikers planning a backpacking trip into the adjacent South Warner Wilderness. The camp is at 6,680 feet, set along the south side of tiny Porter Reservoir, with horse corrals within walking distance. A trailhead out of camp provides direct access to the Summit Trail, the best hike in the South Warner Wilderness.

**Campsites, facilities:** There are four sites for tents or RVs up to 16 feet (no hookups) in the family camp and six sites for RVs up to 25 feet (no hookups) in the horse camp. Picnic tables and fire grills are provided. Drinking water and vault toilets are available. Corrals are available with water for stock. Garbage must be packed out. Supplies are available in Cedarville or Alturas. Some facilities are wheelchair-accessible. Leashed pets are permitted.

**Reservations, fees:** Reservations are not accepted. There is no fee for camping. Open July through October, weather permitting.

**Directions:** In Alturas, drive south on U.S. 395 to the southern end of town and County Road 56. Turn left on County Road 56 and drive 13 miles to the Modoc Forest boundary and the junction with Parker Creek Road. Bear left on Parker Creek Road and continue for six miles to the signed campground access road on the right. Turn right and drive 0.5 mile to the campground on the left side of the road.

**Contact:** Modoc National Forest, Warner Mountain Ranger District, 530/279-6116, www.fs.usda.gov/modoc.

## 23 UPPER RUSH CREEK

### Scenic rating: 8

in Modoc National Forest

**Map 3.2, page 182**

Upper Rush Creek is a pretty campground along Rush Creek, a quiet, wooded spot that gets little use. It sits in the shadow of nearby Manzanita Mountain (elevation 7,036 feet) to the east, where there is a Forest Service lookout for a great view. To reach the lookout, drive back toward Highway 299, and when you reach the paved road, County Road 198, turn left and drive 0.5 mile to Forest Road 22. Turn left on Forest Road 22 and head up the hill. One mile from the summit, turn left at a four-way junction and drive to the top. You get dramatic views of the Warm Springs Valley to the north and the Likely Flats to the east, looking across miles and miles of open country.

**Campsites, facilities:** There are 13 sites for tents or RVs up to 22 feet (no hookups), but Lower Rush Creek (see listing in this chapter) is better for trailers. Picnic tables and fire grills are provided. Vault toilets are available, but there is no drinking water. Garbage must be packed out. Supplies can be obtained about nine miles away in Adin. Leashed pets are permitted.

**Reservations, fees:** Reservations are not accepted. There is no fee for camping. Open May through October, weather permitting.

**Directions:** From Redding, turn east on Highway 299 and drive to Adin. Continue east on Highway 299 for about seven miles to a signed campground turnoff on the right side of the road. Turn right and drive to the junction with Forest Road 40N05. Turn left and drive 2.5 miles to the campground at the end of the road.

**Contact:** Modoc National Forest, Big Valley Ranger District, 530/299-3215, www.fs.usda.gov/modoc.

## 24 LOWER RUSH CREEK

### Scenic rating: 6

on Rush Creek in Modoc National Forest

**Map 3.2, page 182**

This is one of two obscure campgrounds a short distance from Highway 299 on Rush Creek in southern Modoc County. Lower Rush Creek is the first camp you will come to, with flat campsites surrounded by an outer fence and set along Rush Creek. This little-known and little-used camp is better suited for trailers than the one at Upper Rush Creek. Elevation is 4,400 feet.

**Campsites, facilities:** There are 10 sites for tents or RVs up to 22 feet (no hookups). Picnic tables and fire grills are provided. Vault toilets are available, but there is no drinking water. Garbage must be packed out. Supplies are available in Adin. Leashed pets are permitted.

**Reservations, fees:** Reservations are not accepted. There is no fee for camping. Open May through October, weather permitting.

**Directions:** From Redding, turn east on Highway 299 and drive to Adin. Continue east on Highway 299 for about seven miles to a signed campground turnoff on the right side of the road. Turn right and drive to the junction with Forest Road 40N05. Turn left and drive one mile to the campground on the right.

**Contact:** Modoc National Forest, Big Valley Ranger District, 530/299-3215, www.fs.usda.gov/modoc.

## 25 ASH CREEK

### Scenic rating: 7

in Modoc National Forest

**Map 3.2, page 182**

This starkly beautiful, remote camp at 4,800 feet sits along Ash Creek, a stream with small trout. This region of Modoc National Forest has an extensive network of backcountry roads, popular with deer hunters in the fall. The Ash Creek Wildlife Area is about 10 miles west of camp. Summer comes relatively late out here, and it can be cold and wet even in early June. Stash some extra clothes, just in case. That will probably guarantee nice weather.

**Campsites, facilities:** There is a small area for dispersed camping. The site is no longer maintained by the Forest Service, and facilities are limited. There is an old vault toilet but no drinking water, and garbage must be packed out. Supplies can be obtained in Adin. Leashed pets are permitted.

**Reservations, fees:** Reservations are not accepted. There is no fee for camping. Open May through October, weather permitting.

**Directions:** From Redding, turn east on Highway 299 and drive to Adin and Ash Valley Road. Turn right on Ash Valley Road/County Road 88/527 and drive eight miles. Turn left at the signed campground turnoff and drive a mile to the campground on the right side of the road.

**Contact:** Modoc National Forest, Big Valley Ranger District, 530/299-3215; Ash Creek Wildlife Area, 530/294-5824.

## 26 WILLOW CREEK

### Scenic rating: 7

in Modoc National Forest

**Map 3.2, page 182**

This remote camp and picnic area along little Willow Creek rests amid pines, aspens, and willows. On the north side of the campground is Lower McBride Springs. Elevation is 5,200 feet.

**Campsites, facilities:** There are eight sites for tents or RVs up to 28 feet (no hookups). Picnic tables and fire grills are provided. Drinking water and vault toilets are available. Some facilities are wheelchair-accessible. Leashed pets are permitted.

**Reservations, fees:** Reservations are not accepted. Sites are $12 per night. Open May through October, weather permitting.

**Directions:** From Redding, drive east on

Highway 299 to Adin and Highway 139. Turn right on Highway 139 and drive 14 miles to the campground on the left side of the road.

**Contact:** Modoc National Forest, Big Valley Ranger District, 530/299-3215, www.fs.usda.gov/modoc.

## 27 SOUP SPRINGS

### Scenic rating: 8

in Modoc National Forest

**Map 3.2, page 182**

This is a beautiful, quiet, wooded campground at a trailhead into the South Warner Wilderness. Soup Creek originates at Soup Springs in the meadow adjacent to the campground. The trail leads two miles into the wilderness, where it junctions with the Mill Creek Trail. At the junction, turn left for a beautiful walk along Mill Creek and into Mill Creek Meadow, an easy yet pristine stroll that can provide a serene experience. The elevation is 6,800 feet.

**Campsites, facilities:** There are eight sites for tents or RVs up to 22 feet (no hookups). Picnic tables and fire grills are provided. Drinking water and vault toilets are available. Garbage must be packed out. There are three corrals at the trailhead. Supplies can be obtained in Likely. Leashed pets are permitted.

**Reservations, fees:** Reservations are not accepted. Sites are $12 per night. Open June through October, weather permitting.

**Directions:** From Alturas, drive south on U.S. 395 for 17 miles to the town of Likely, where you'll come to Jess Valley Road. Turn left on Jess Valley Road/County Road 64 and drive nine miles to the fork. Bear left on West Warner Road/Forest Road 5 and go 4.5 miles to Soup Loop Road. Turn right on Soup Loop Road/Forest Road 40N24 and continue on that gravel road for six miles to the campground entrance on the right.

**Contact:** Modoc National Forest, Warner

Mountain Ranger District, 530/279-6116, www. fs.usda.gov/modoc.

## 28 MILL CREEK FALLS
🏃 🏕 ♿ 🚐 ⛺

### Scenic rating: 9
in Modoc National Forest

**Map 3.2, page 182**

This nice, wooded campground is a good base camp for a backpacking trip into the South Warner Wilderness. The camp is set on Mill Creek at 5,700 feet elevation. To see Mill Creek Falls, take the trail out of camp and bear left at the Y. To enter the interior of the South Warner Wilderness, bear right at the Y, after which the trail passes Clear Lake, heads to Poison Flat and Poison Creek, and then reaches a junction. Left will take you to the Mill Creek Trail; right will take you up to the Summit Trail. Take your pick; you can't go wrong.

**Campsites, facilities:** There are 19 sites for tents or RVs up to 22 feet (no hookups). Picnic tables and fire grills are provided. Drinking water and vault toilets are available. Supplies are available in Likely. Some facilities are wheelchair-accessible. Leashed pets are permitted.

**Reservations, fees:** Reservations are not accepted. Sites are $12 per night. Open June through October, weather permitting.

**Directions:** From Alturas drive 17 miles south on U.S. 395 to the town of Likely, where you'll come to Jess Valley Road. Turn left on Jess Valley Road/County Road 64 and drive nine miles to the fork. Bear left on West Warner Road/Forest Road 5 and drive 2.5 miles to Forest Road 40N46. Turn right on Forest Road 40N46 and drive two miles to the campground entrance at the end of the road.

**Contact:** Modoc National Forest, Warner Mountain Ranger District, 530/279-6116, www. fs.usda.gov/modoc.

## 29 EMERSON
🏃 🏊 🏕 🐾 5% 🚐 ⛺

### Scenic rating: 6
in Modoc National Forest

**Map 3.2, page 182**

This tiny camp is virtually unknown, nestled at 6,000 feet on the eastern boundary of the South Warner Wilderness. Big alkali lakes and miles of the Nevada flats can be seen on the other side of the highway as you drive along the entrance road to the campground. A trailhead at this primitive setting is used by hikers and backpackers. Note that hitting the trail is a steep, sometimes wrenching climb for 4.5 miles to North Emerson Lake (poor to fair fishing). For many, this hike is a true butt-kicker.

**Campsites, facilities:** There are three sites for tents or RVs up to 16 feet (no hookups) and one walk-in site. Picnic tables and fire grills are provided. A campfire permit, available at the ranger station, is required to use a camp stove or barbecue. Vault toilets are available. No drinking water is available. Garbage must be packed out. Supplies can be obtained in Cedarville. Leashed pets are permitted.

**Reservations, fees:** Reservations are not accepted. There is no fee for camping. Open July through October, weather permitting.

**Directions:** From Alturas, drive north on U.S. 395/Highway 299 for about five miles to the junction with Highway 299. Turn right on Highway 299 and drive to Cedarville and County Road 1. Turn south on County Road 1 and drive to Eagleville. From Eagleville, continue south on County Road 1 for 1.5 miles to Forest Road 40N43/County Road 40. Turn right and drive three miles to the campground at the end of the road. The access road is steep, narrow, and very slick in wet weather. Trailers are not recommended.

**Contact:** Modoc National Forest, Warner Mountain Ranger District, 530/279-6116, www. fs.usda.gov/modoc.

# 30 EAST CREEK

### Scenic rating: 7

near South Warner Wilderness in Modoc
National Forest

**Map 3.2, page 182**

This pretty little camp sits in the trees adjacent
to a meadow at the edge of the South Warner
Wilderness. The equestrian sites here replace
those formerly at Patterson, which no longer
permits horse camping. Though the campground was untouched, the surrounding area
was torched by the 2001 Blue Fire. The area is
slowly transitioning back to forest with lots of
heavy brush undergrowth. East Creek Trail
is subject to hazardous snags that still stand
from the fire. A connecter trail leaves camp
and meets with the Summit Trail just north of
Patterson.

**Campsites, facilities:** There are 10 sites for
tents or RVs up to 36 feet (no hookups); five
sites have horse corrals. Picnic tables and fire
grills are provided. Drinking water and vault
toilets are available. Garbage must be packed
out. Leashed pets are permitted.

**Reservations, fees:** Reservations are not accepted. There is no fee for camping. Open May
through October, weather permitting.

**Directions:** From Alturas, drive 17 miles south
on U.S. 395 to the town of Likely. Turn left on
Jess Valley Road/County Road 64 and drive
nine miles to the fork. Bear right on Forest
Road 64 and drive 14 miles to the campground
on the left. East Creek is approximately two
miles west of Patterson campground.

**Contact:** Modoc National Forest, Warner
Mountain Ranger District, 530/279-6116, www.
fs.usda.gov/modoc.

# 31 PATTERSON

### Scenic rating: 4

in Modoc National Forest

**Map 3.2, page 182**

Patterson is set at 7,200 feet amid a landscape
recovering from a big forest fire. The 2001
Blue Fire enveloped 35,000 acres in the South
Warners. Since then, vegetation growth has improved and the area is now covered by thick
brush.

There are both positives and negatives to
the burn of 2001. On the positive side, there is
a chance for much wider and longer views, as
well as the opportunity to watch the evolution
of the landscape in a post-fire setting. On the
negative side, tree skeletons (snags) jut out of
the brush. The most affected area is to the east,
especially on East Creek Trail, currently closed,
which rises through the burned area to a high,
barren mountain rim. The Summit Trail just
north of camp remains open.

**Campsites, facilities:** There are 15 sites for
tents or RVs up to 16 feet (no hookups). Picnic
tables and fire grills are provided. Vault toilets
are available. Drinking water may be available
seasonally; call to confirm. Garbage must be
packed out. Supplies are available in Likely or
Cedarville. Leashed pets are permitted.

**Reservations, fees:** Reservations are not accepted. There is no fee for camping. Open mid-
May through October, weather permitting.

**Directions:** From Alturas drive 17 miles south
on U.S. 395 to the town of Likely. Turn left on
Jess Valley Road/County Road 64 and drive
nine miles to the fork. Bear right on Forest
Road 64 and drive for 16 miles to the campground on the left.

**Contact:** Modoc National Forest, Warner
Mountain Ranger District, 530/279-6116, www.
fs.usda.gov/modoc.

## 32 BLUE LAKE

🚶‍♂️ 🏊 🎣 🚣 🛶 🚴 🏕️ ♿ 🚐 ⛺

### Scenic rating: 6

in Modoc National Forest

**Map 3.2, page 182**

This is a strange scene: a somewhat wooded campground (with some level campsites) near the shore of Blue Lake, with nearby slopes still showing damage from a 2001 forest fire. The lake covers 160 acres and provides fishing for large brown trout and rainbow trout. A 5-mph speed limit assures quiet water for small boats and canoes. A trail circles the lake and takes less than an hour to hike. The elevation is 6,000 feet. Bald eagles have been spotted. While their presence negates year-round use of six campsites otherwise available, the trade-off is an unprecedented opportunity to view the national bird. The Blue Fire of 2001 burned 35,000 acres in this area, including the east and west slopes adjoining Blue Lake. Yet get this: The campground was untouched.

**Campsites, facilities:** There are 48 sites for tents or RVs up to 32 feet (no hookups) and one group site for up to 30 people. Picnic tables and fire grills are provided. Drinking water and vault toilets are available. Some facilities are wheelchair-accessible, including a paved boat launch and fishing pier. Supplies are available in Likely. Leashed pets are permitted.

**Reservations, fees:** Reservations are not accepted. Sites are $14 per night. The group site is $42-70 per night. Open mid-May through October, weather permitting.

**Directions:** From Alturas, drive south on U.S. 395 for seven miles to the town of Likely, where you'll come to Jess Valley Road. Turn left on Jess Valley Road/County Road 64 and drive nine miles to the fork. At the fork, bear right on Forest Road 64 and drive seven miles to Forest Road 38N30. Turn right on Forest Road 38N30 and drive two miles to the campground.

**Contact:** Modoc National Forest, Warner Mountain Ranger District, 530/279-6116, www.fs.usda.gov/modoc.

## 33 PIT RIVER

🚶‍♂️ 🎣 🏕️ ♿ 🚐 ⛺

### Scenic rating: 6

on the Pit River

**Map 3.3, page 183**

Very few out-of-towners know about this hidden campground along the Pit River. It can provide a good base camp for a fishing trip adventure. The best stretch of trout water on the Pit is near Powerhouse Number Three. In addition to fishing there are many other recreation options. A parking area and trail along Hat Creek are available where the Highway 299 bridge crosses Hat Creek. Baum Lake, Crystal Lake, and the Cassel section of Hat Creek are all within five miles of this camp.

**Campsites, facilities:** There are eight sites for tents or RVs up to 40 feet (no hookups) and one group site for up to eight people. Picnic tables and fire rings are provided. Vault toilets, a wheelchair-accessible fishing pier, and a small-craft launch ramp are available. No drinking water is available. Garbage must be packed out. There are supplies and a coin laundry in Fall River Mills. Some facilities are wheelchair-accessible. Leashed pets are permitted.

**Reservations, fees:** Reservations are not accepted. Sites are $8 per night, and it's $12 per night for the double site. Open May through November.

**Directions:** From Redding, drive east on Highway 299 to Burney and continue for five miles to the junction with Highway 89. At the junction, continue straight on Highway 299, cross the Pit River Bridge, and drive about three miles to Pit One Powerhouse Road. Turn right and drive down the hill to the Pit River Lodge. Turn right and drive 0.5 mile to the campground.

**Contact:** Bureau of Land Management, Alturas Field Office, 530/233-4666, www.blm.gov/ca.

# 34 CASSEL

**Scenic rating: 8**

on Hat Creek

### Map 3.3, page 183

This camp at 3,200 feet nestles in the beautiful Hat Creek Valley. It is an outstanding location for a fishing trip base camp, with nearby Crystal Lake, Baum Lake, and Hat Creek (all in the Hat Creek Valley) providing trout fishing. This section of Hat Creek is well known for its challenging fly-fishing. A good source of fishing information is Vaughn's Sporting Goods in Burney. Baum Lake is ideal for car-top boats with electric motors.

**Campsites, facilities:** There are 27 sites for tents or RVs up to 30 feet (no hookups). Picnic tables and fire grills are provided. Drinking water and vault toilets are available. Some facilities are wheelchair-accessible. Leashed pets are permitted.

**Reservations, fees:** Reservations are accepted at online at www.pge.com/recreation ($1.50 reservation fee per day). Sites are $22 per night, plus $5 per night for each additional vehicle, $10 per night per additional RV, and $2 per pet per night. Open early to mid-April through early to mid-November, weather permitting.

**Directions:** From Redding, drive east on Highway 299 to Burney and continue for five miles to the junction with Highway 89. At the junction, continue straight on Highway 299 for two miles to Cassel Road. At Cassel Road, turn right and drive 3.6 miles to the campground entrance on the left.

**Contact:** PG&E Land Projects, 916/386-5164, www.pge.com/recreation.

# 35 HAT CREEK HEREFORD RANCH RV PARK AND CAMPGROUND

**Scenic rating: 8**

near Hat Creek

### Map 3.3, page 183

This privately operated campground is set in a working cattle ranch. Campers are not allowed near the cattle pasture or cattle. Fishing is available in Hat Creek or in the nearby stocked trout pond. Swimming is also allowed in the pond. Sightseeing is excellent, with Burney Falls, Lassen Volcanic National Park, and Subway Caves all within 30 miles.

**Campsites, facilities:** There are 40 tent sites and 50 RV sites with full or partial hookups (30 amps); some sites are pull-through. Picnic tables and fireplaces are provided. Restrooms with showers, a dump station, coin laundry, playground, swimming beach, horseshoes, table tennis, group pavilion, stocked fishing pond, Wi-Fi, and a convenience store are available. Some facilities are wheelchair-accessible. Leashed pets are permitted.

**Reservations, fees:** Reservations are recommended and can be made by telephone or online; all sites require a deposit. RV sites are $31-35 per night and tent sites are $26-29 per night, plus $3 per night for more than two people and $1 per night per pet. Some credit cards are accepted. Open April through October.

**Directions:** From Redding, drive east on Highway 299 to Burney and continue for five miles to the junction with Highway 89. Turn right (south) on Highway 89 and drive 12 miles to the second Doty Road Loop exit. Turn left and drive 0.5 mile to the park entrance on the right.

**Contact:** Hat Creek Hereford Ranch RV Park and Campground, 530/335-7171 or 877/459-9532, www.hatcreekherefordrv.com.

## 36 HONN

### Scenic rating: 7

on Hat Creek in Lassen National Forest

**Map 3.3, page 183**

This primitive, tiny campground is near the point where Honn Creek enters Hat Creek, at 3,400 feet elevation in Lassen National Forest. The creek is extremely pretty, shaded by trees and flowing emerald green. The camp provides streamside access for trout fishing, though this stretch of creek is sometimes overlooked by the Department of Fish and Wildlife in favor of stocking the creek at the more popular Cave Camp and Bridge Camp. (See listings in this chapter for more information.)

**Campsites, facilities:** There are six tent sites. Picnic tables and fire grills are provided. Vault toilets are available. Drinking water is not available. A grocery store, coin laundry, and propane gas are nearby. Leashed pets are permitted.

**Reservations, fees:** Reservations are not accepted. Sites are $10 per night, plus $5 per night for more than two vehicles. Open late April through October, weather permitting.

**Directions:** From Redding, drive east on Highway 299 to Burney and continue for five miles to the junction with Highway 89. Turn right (south) on Highway 89 and drive 15 miles to the campground entrance on the left side of the road.

**Contact:** Lassen National Forest, Hat Creek Ranger District, 530/336-5521, www.fs.usda.gov/lassen; Department of Fish and Wildlife fishing information, 530/225-2146.

## 37 OLD COW MEADOWS

### Scenic rating: 7

in Latour Demonstration State Forest

**Map 3.3, page 183**

Nobody finds this campground without this book. You want quiet? You don't want to be bugged by anyone? This tiny camp, virtually unknown, is set at 5,900 feet in a wooded area along Old Cow Creek. Recreation options include all-terrain-vehicle use on existing roads and walking the dirt roads that crisscross the area.

**Campsites, facilities:** There are three sites for tents or RVs up to 25 feet (no hookups). Picnic tables and fire grills are provided. Vault toilets and drinking water are available. Garbage must be packed out. Some facilities are wheelchair-accessible. Leashed pets are permitted.

**Reservations, fees:** Reservations are not accepted. There is no fee for camping. Open June through October, weather permitting.

**Directions:** In Redding, turn east on Highway 44 and drive about 9.5 miles to Millville Road. Turn left on Millville Road and drive 0.5 mile to the intersection of Millville Road and Whitmore Road. Turn right on Whitmore Road and drive 13 miles, through Whitmore, until Whitmore Road becomes Tamarack Road. Continue for one mile to a fork at Bateman Road. Take the right fork on Bateman Road, drive 3.5 miles (where the road turns to gravel), and then continue 10 miles to Huckleberry Road. Turn right on Huckleberry Road and drive two miles to the campground.

**Contact:** Latour Demonstration State Forest, 530/225-2438, www.fire.ca.gov.

## 38 SOUTH COW CREEK

### Scenic rating: 6

in Latour Demonstration State Forest

**Map 3.3, page 183**

This camp is set at 5,600 feet in a pretty, wooded area next to a small meadow along South Cow Creek. It's used mostly in the fall for hunting, with off-highway-vehicle use on the surrounding roads in the summer. If you want to get away from it all without leaving your vehicle, this is one way to do it. The creek is a reliable water source, providing you use a water filtration pump.

Latour has two other small, little-known campgrounds: Old Station, with three campsites, and Butcher Gulch, with two campsites.

**Campsites, facilities:** There are four sites for tents or RVs up to 30 feet (no hookups). Picnic tables and fire grills are provided. Vault toilets and drinking water are available. Garbage must be packed out. Some facilities are wheelchair-accessible. Leashed pets are permitted.

**Reservations, fees:** Reservations are not accepted. There is no fee for camping. Open June through October, weather permitting.

**Directions:** In Redding, turn east on Highway 44 and drive about 9.5 miles to Millville Road. Turn left on Millville Road and drive 0.5 mile to the intersection of Millville Road and Whitmore Road. Turn right on Whitmore Road and drive 13 miles, through Whitmore, until Whitmore Road becomes Tamarack Road. Continue for one mile to the fork at Bateman Road. Take the right fork on Bateman Road, drive 3.5 miles (where the road turns to gravel), and then continue for 11 miles to South Cow Creek Road. Turn right (east) and drive one mile to the campground.

**Contact:** Latour Demonstration State Forest, 530/225-2438, www.fire.ca.gov.

# 39 BRIDGE CAMP

### Scenic rating: 7
on Hat Creek in Lassen National Forest

**Map 3.3, page 183**

This camp is one of four along Highway 89 in the area along Hat Creek. It is at 4,000 feet elevation, with shaded sites and the stream within very short walking distance. Trout are stocked on this stretch of the creek, with fishing access available out of camp, as well as at Rocky and Cave Camps to the south and Honn to the north. In one weekend, anglers might hit all four.

**Campsites, facilities:** There are 25 sites for tents or RVs up to 22 feet (no hookups). Picnic tables and fire grills are provided. There is

no drinking water. Vault toilets are available. A grocery store and propane gas are nearby. Leashed pets are permitted.

**Reservations, fees:** Reservations are not accepted. Sites are $10 per night, plus $5 per night for more than two vehicles. Open late April to mid-October, weather permitting.

**Directions:** From Redding, drive east on Highway 299 to Burney and continue for five miles to the junction with Highway 89. Turn right (south) on Highway 89 and drive 19 miles to the campground entrance on the right side of the road. If you reach Old Station, you have gone five miles too far.

**Contact:** Lassen National Forest, Hat Creek Ranger District, 530/336-5521, www.fs.usda.gov/lassen; Department of Fish and Wildlife fishing information, 530/225-2146.

# 40 ROCKY CAMP

### Scenic rating: 7
on Hat Creek in Lassen National Forest

**Map 3.3, page 183**

This small, primitive camp along Hat Creek on Highway 89 is usually a third choice for campers if nearby Cave and Bridge Camps are full. Streamside fishing access is a plus, with this section of stream stocked with rainbow trout. The elevation is 4,000 feet. (See the Cave Camp listing for more information.)

**Campsites, facilities:** There are eight tent sites. Picnic tables and fire grills are provided. Vault toilets are available. No drinking water is available. A grocery store and propane gas are nearby. Leashed pets are permitted.

**Reservations, fees:** Reservations are not accepted. Sites are $10 per night, plus $5 per night for more than two vehicles. Open late April through October, weather permitting.

**Directions:** From Redding, drive east on Highway 299 to Burney and continue for five miles to the junction with Highway 89. Turn right (south) on Highway 89 and drive 20 miles to the campground entrance on the right side of the road. If you reach Old Station, you have gone four miles too far.

**Contact:** Lassen National Forest, Hat Creek Ranger District, 530/336-5521, www.fs.usda.gov/lassen; Department of Fish and Wildlife fishing information, 530/225-2146.

of the road. If you reach Old Station, you have gone one mile too far.

**Contact:** Lassen National Forest, Hat Creek Ranger District, 530/336-5521, www.fs.usda.gov/lassen; Department of Fish and Wildlife fishing information, 530/225-2146.

## 41 CAVE CAMP

### Scenic rating: 7
on Hat Creek in Lassen National Forest

**Map 3.3, page 183**

Cave Camp is right along Hat Creek, with easy access off Highway 89 and an anglers' trail available along the stream. This stretch of Hat Creek is planted with rainbow trout twice per month by the Department of Fish and Wildlife, starting with the opening of trout season on the last Saturday of April. Nearby side trips include Lassen Volcanic National Park, about a 15-minute drive to the south on Highway 89, and Subway Caves (turn left at the junction just across the road from the campground). A rare bonus is that wheelchair-accessible fishing is available.

**Campsites, facilities:** There are 46 sites for tents or RVs up to 22 feet (no hookups). Picnic tables and fire grills are provided. Drinking water and flush toilets are available in summer; vault toilets are available year-round. Supplies can be obtained in Old Station. Some facilities are wheelchair-accessible. Leashed pets are permitted.

**Reservations, fees:** Reservations are not accepted. Sites are $16 per night, plus $5 per night for more than two vehicles in summer; sites are $10 per night during winter. Of the 46 campsites, 16 are open year-round; the remaining 30 sites are open late April through mid-October, weather permitting.

**Directions:** From Redding, drive east on Highway 299 to Burney and continue for five miles to the junction with Highway 89. Turn right (south) on Highway 89 and drive 23 miles to the campground entrance on the right side

## 42 HAT CREEK

### Scenic rating: 7
on Hat Creek in Lassen National Forest

**Map 3.3, page 183**

This is one in a series of Forest Service camps set beside beautiful Hat Creek, a good trout stream stocked regularly by the Department of Fish and Wildlife. The elevation is 4,300 feet. The proximity to Lassen Volcanic National Park to the south is a big plus. Supplies are available in the little town of Old Station one mile to the north.

**Campsites, facilities:** There are 75 sites for tents or RVs up to 30 feet, and three group camps for tents or RVs up to 30 feet that can accommodate up to 50 people each (no hookups). Picnic tables and fire grills are provided. Drinking water and flush toilets are available in summer, and vault toilets year-round. A grocery store, dump station, coin laundry, and propane gas are nearby. There is an accessible fishing platform. Leashed pets are permitted.

**Reservations, fees:** Tent and RV sites are first-come, first-served. Reservations are required for group sites at 877/444-6777 ($10 reservation fee) or www.recreation.gov ($9 reservation fee). Tent and RV sites are $16 per night, plus $5 per night for each additional vehicle, and it's $80 per night for group camps. Open late April through October, weather permitting.

**Directions:** From Redding, drive east on Highway 44 to the junction with Highway 89 (near the entrance to Lassen Volcanic National Park). Turn left (north) on Highway 89 and drive about 12 miles to the campground

entrance on the left side of the road. Turn left and drive a short distance to the campground.
**Contact:** Lassen National Forest, Hat Creek Ranger District, 530/336-5521, www.fs.usda.gov/lassen; Department of Fish and Wildlife fishing information, 530/225-2146.

## 43 NORTH BATTLE CREEK RESERVOIR

**Scenic rating: 7**

on Battle Creek Reservoir

**Map 3.3, page 183**

This little-known lake is at 5,600 feet in elevation, largely surrounded by Lassen National Forest. No gas engines are permitted on the lake, making it ideal for canoes, rafts, and car-top aluminum boats equipped with electric motors. When the lake level is up in early summer, it is a pretty setting with good trout fishing.

**Campsites, facilities:** There are 15 sites for tents or RVs up to 30 feet (no hookups) and five walk-in tent sites. Picnic tables and fire grills are provided. Drinking water and vault toilets are available. A car-top boat launch is nearby. Leashed pets are permitted.

**Reservations, fees:** Reservations are accepted online at www.pge.com/recreation ($1.50 reservation fee per day). Sites are $22 per night, plus $5 per night for each additional vehicle, $10 per additional RV per night, and $2 per pet per night. Open mid-May through mid-September, weather permitting.

**Directions:** From Redding, drive east on Highway 44 to Viola. From Viola, continue east for 3.5 miles to Forest Road 32N17. Turn left on Forest Road 32N17 and drive five miles to Forest Road 32N31. Turn left and drive four miles to Forest Road 32N18. Turn right and drive 0.5 mile to the reservoir and the campground on the right side of the road.

**Contact:** PG&E Land Projects, 916/386-5164, www.pge.com/recreation.

## 44 BIG PINE CAMP

**Scenic rating: 7**

on Hat Creek in Lassen National Forest

**Map 3.3, page 183**

This campground is on the headwaters of Hat Creek, a pretty spot amid ponderosa pines. The elevation is 4,500 feet. A dirt road out of camp parallels Hat Creek, providing access for trout fishing. A great vista point is on the highway, a mile south of the campground entrance road. It is only a 10-minute drive south to the Highway 44 entrance station for Lassen Volcanic National Park.

**Campsites, facilities:** There are 19 sites for tents or RVs up to 22 feet (no hookups). Picnic tables and fire grills are provided. Drinking water (at two hand pumps) and vault toilets are available. A dump station, grocery store, and propane gas are nearby. Leashed pets are permitted.

**Reservations, fees:** Reservations are not accepted. Sites are $12 per night, plus $5 per night for more than two vehicles. Open May through October, weather permitting.

**Directions:** From Redding, drive east on Highway 44 to the junction with Highway 89 (near the entrance to Lassen Volcanic National Park). Turn left (north) on Highway 89 and drive about eight miles (one mile past the vista point) to the campground entrance on the right side of the road. Turn right and drive 0.5 mile to the campground.

**Contact:** Lassen National Forest, Hat Creek Ranger District, 530/336-5521, www.fs.usda.gov/lassen; Department of Fish and Wildlife fishing information, 530/225-2146.

## 45 BUTTE CREEK

**Scenic rating: 6**

in Lassen National Forest

**Map 3.3, page 183**

This primitive, little-known spot on little Butte

Creek is just three miles from the northern boundary of Lassen Volcanic National Park. The elevation is 5,600 feet. It is a four-mile drive south out of camp on Forest Road 18 to Butte Lake in Lassen Park and to the trailhead for a great hike up to the Cinder Cone (6,907 feet), with dramatic views of the Lassen wilderness.

**Campsites, facilities:** There are 10 dispersed camping sites for tents or RVs up to 22 feet (no hookups). There is no drinking water and no restrooms available. Garbage must be packed out. Leashed pets are permitted.

**Reservations, fees:** Reservations are not accepted. There is no fee for camping. Open May through October, weather permitting.

**Directions:** From Redding, drive east on Highway 44 to the junction with Highway 89 (near the entrance to Lassen Volcanic National Park). Turn north on Highway 89 and drive to Highway 44. Turn east (right) on Highway 44 and drive 11 miles to Forest Road 18. Turn right at Forest Road 18 and drive three miles to the campground on the left side of the road.

**Contact:** Lassen National Forest, Eagle Lake Ranger District, 530/257-4188, www.fs.usda.gov/lassen.

## 46 BOGARD

### Scenic rating: 6

in Lassen National Forest

**Map 3.3, page 183**

This little camp is along Pine Creek, which flows through Pine Creek Valley at the foot of the Bogard Buttes. It is a relatively obscure camp that gets missed by many travelers. Beautiful aspens are breathtaking in fall. To the nearby west is a network of Forest Service roads, and beyond is the Caribou Wilderness.

**Campsites, facilities:** There are 11 dispersed camping sites for tents or RVs up to 25 feet (no hookups). Picnic tables and fire grills are provided. Drinking water (hand pumped) and vault toilets are available. Leashed pets are permitted.

**Reservations, fees:** Reservations are not accepted. There is no fee. Open May through October, weather permitting.

**Directions:** From Redding, drive east on Highway 44 to the junction with Highway 89 (near the entrance to Lassen Volcanic National Park). Turn north on Highway 89 and drive to Highway 44. Turn east on Highway 44 and drive to the Bogard Work Center (about seven miles past Poison Lake) and the adjacent rest stop. Continue east on Highway 44 for two miles to a gravel road on the right side of the road (Forest Road 31N26). Turn right on Forest Road 31N26 and drive two miles. Turn right on Forest Road 31N21 and drive 0.5 mile to the campground at the end of the road.

**Contact:** Lassen National Forest, Eagle Lake Ranger District, 530/257-4188, www.fs.usda.gov/lassen.

## 47 CRATER LAKE

### Scenic rating: 8

in Lassen National Forest

**Map 3.3, page 183**

This hideaway near Crater Lake rests at 6,800 feet elevation in remote Lassen National Forest, just below Crater Mountain (that's it up there to the northeast at 7,420 feet). This 27-acre lake provides trout fishing, boating (gas motors are discouraged), and, if you can stand the ice-cold water, a quick dunk on warm summer days.

**Campsites, facilities:** There are 17 sites for tents. Picnic tables and fire grills are provided. Drinking water (hand pumped) and vault toilets are available. Leashed pets are permitted.

**Reservations, fees:** Reservations are not accepted. Sites are $10 per night. Open June through October, weather permitting.

**Directions:** From Redding, drive east on Highway 44 to the junction with Highway 89 (near the entrance to Lassen Volcanic National Park). Turn north on Highway 89 and drive to Highway 44. Turn east on Highway 44 (right) and drive to the Bogard Work Center and adjacent rest stop. Turn left at Forest Road 32N08 (signed Crater Lake) and drive one mile to a T intersection. Bear right and continue on Forest Road 32N08 for six miles (including two hairpin left turns) to the campground on the left side of the road. Note: Forest Road 32N08 is a rough washboard road.

**Contact:** Lassen National Forest, Eagle Lake Ranger District, 530/257-4188, www.fs.usda.gov/lassen.

## 48 MACCUMBER RESERVOIR

### Scenic rating: 7

on MacCumber Reservoir

**Map 3.3, page 183**

Here's a small lake, easy to reach from Redding, that is little known and rarely visited. MacCumber Reservoir is at 3,500 feet and is stocked with rainbow trout each year, providing fair fishing. No gas motors are permitted. That's fine—it guarantees quiet, calm water, ideal for car-top boats: prams, canoes, rafts, and small aluminum boats.

**Campsites, facilities:** There are nine sites for tents or RVs up to 30 feet (no hookups) and five walk-in tent sites. Picnic tables and fire grills are provided. Drinking water and vault toilets are available. Leashed pets are permitted.

**Reservations, fees:** Reservations are accepted online at www.pge.com/recreation ($1.50 reservation fee per day). Sites are $18 per night, plus $5 per night for each additional vehicle, $10 per night per additional RV, and $2 per pet per night. Open mid-April through mid-September, weather permitting.

**Directions:** In Redding, turn east on Highway 44 and drive toward Viola to Lake MacCumber Road (if you reach Viola, you have gone four miles too far). Turn left at Lake MacCumber Road and drive two miles to the reservoir and campground.

**Contact:** PG&E Land Projects, 916/386-5164, www.pge.com/recreation.

## 49 MANZANITA LAKE

### Scenic rating: 9

in Lassen Volcanic National Park

**Map 3.3, page 183**

Manzanita Lake, at 5,890 feet, is one of the prettiest lakes in Lassen Volcanic National Park, and evening walks around the lake are beautiful. The campground, among towering Ponderosa pines, is often crowded due to this great natural beauty. Manzanita Lake provides good catch-and-release trout fishing for experienced fly fishers in prams and other non-powered boats. Fishing regulations prohibit bait and lures with barbs. This is no place for a dad, mom, and a youngster to fish from shore with Power Bait; you'll end up with a citation. Swimming is permitted, but there are few takers. Note that there have been mountain lion sightings at various locations in the park.

**Campsites, facilities:** There are 179 sites for tents or RVs up to 35 feet (no hookups) and five group sites (in Loop B) for up to 25 people each. Note that Loop D is tent-only. Twenty rustic cabins sleep 2-6 people each. Picnic tables, fire grills, and bear-proof food lockers are provided. Drinking water (until mid-October) and flush and vault toilets are available. A museum, visitors center, and small store, as well as propane gas, groceries, coin showers, dump station, and coin laundry, are nearby. Ranger programs are offered in the summer. A boat launch is also nearby (no motors are permitted on boats at Manzanita Lake). Some facilities are wheelchair-accessible. Leashed pets are permitted at campsites only.

**Reservations, fees:** Reservations for individual sites (Loops A and C) are accepted May to October and are required for group sites at 877/444-6777 or www.recreation.gov ($9 reservation fee). Sites in Loops B (except group sites) and D are first-come, first-served. Sites are $15-24 per night, group sites are $70 per night, cabins are $63-89 per night, and there's a $20 per vehicle park entrance fee. Some credit cards are accepted. Open late May through late

November, weather permitting. (In fall, it's open without drinking water at a reduced rate until the camp is closed by snow.)

**Directions:** From Redding, drive east on Highway 44 to the junction with Highway 89. Turn right (south) on Highway 89 and drive one mile to the entrance station to Lassen Volcanic National Park (the state highway becomes Lassen Park Highway/Main Park Road). Continue a short distance on Lassen Park Highway/Main Park Road to the campground entrance road. Turn right and drive 0.5 mile to the campground.

**Contact:** Lassen Volcanic National Park, 530/595-4444, www.nps.gov/lavo.

## 50 BUTTE LAKE

🚶 🏊 🛶 🛥 🚐 🦌 ♿ 🚙 ⛺

### Scenic rating: 9

in Lassen Volcanic National Park

**Map 3.3, page 183**

Butte Lake campground is situated in an open, volcanic setting with a sprinkling of lodgepole pines. The contrast of the volcanics against the emerald green of the lake is beautiful and memorable; the Cinder Cone Trail can provide an even better look. The trailhead is near the boat launch area, and it's a strenuous hike involving a climb of 800 feet over the course of two miles to the top of the Cinder Cone. The footing is often loose because of volcanic pebbles. At the rim, you can peer inside the Cinder Cone, as well as be rewarded with lake views and a long-distance vista. Trout fishing is poor at Butte Lake, as at nearly all the lakes at this park, because trout have not been planted for years. The elevation is 6,100 feet, and the lake covers 212 acres.

**Campsites, facilities:** There are 101 sites for tents or RVs up to 35 feet (no hookups), one equestrian camp for up to 10 people, and six group tent sites that can accommodate 10-25 people each. Some sites are pull-through. Picnic tables, fire rings, and bear-proof food lockers are provided. Drinking water (through

mid-September) and flush and vault toilets are available. Corrals and watering stations are available at the equestrian camp. A boat ramp is nearby. No motors are permitted on the lake. Some facilities are wheelchair-accessible. Leashed pets are permitted at campsites only.

**Reservations, fees:** Reservations are accepted for individual sites (Loop B) and are required for group and equestrian sites at 877/444-6777 or www.recreation.gov ($9 reservation fee). Sites in Loop A are first-come, first-served. Tent and RV sites are $20 per night, or $15 per night when there's no water; the equestrian camp is $35 per night; group sites are $70 per night; and the park entrance fee is $20 per vehicle. Open mid-June through October, weather permitting.

**Directions:** From Redding, drive east on Highway 44 to the junction with Highway 89. Bear north on Highway 89/44 and drive 13 miles to Old Station. Just past Old Station, turn right (east) on Highway 44 and drive 10 miles to Forest Road 32N21/Butte Lake Road. Turn right and drive six miles on a gravel road to the campground.

**Contact:** Lassen Volcanic National Park, 530/595-4444, www.nps.gov/lavo.

## 51 MOUNT LASSEN/ SHINGLETOWN KOA

🚶 🏊 🛶 🏠 🚵 🚐 ⛺

### Scenic rating: 6

near Lassen Volcanic National Park

**Map 3.3, page 183**

This popular KOA camp is 14 miles from the entrance of Lassen Volcanic National Park and has pretty, wooded sites. Location is always the critical factor on vacations, and this park is set up perfectly for launching trips into Lassen Volcanic National Park. Hat Creek provides trout fishing along Highway 89, and just inside the Highway 44 entrance station at Lassen is Manzanita Lake, providing good fishing and hiking.

**Campsites, facilities:** There are 30 sites with

full or partial hookups (30 and 50 amps) for tents or RVs up to 60 feet, including some pull-through sites, and 10 cabins. Picnic tables and fire grills are provided. Restrooms with flush toilets and showers, a playground, basketball and volleyball half-courts, tetherball, heated pool (summer only), a dump station, a convenience store, ice, firewood, coin laundry, a recreation room, Wi-Fi, a dog run, and propane gas are available. Leashed pets are permitted, with certain restrictions.

**Reservations, fees:** Reservations are accepted with a deposit at 800/562-3403. RV sites are $38-64 per night, tent sites are $32-50 per night, cabins are $70-160, plus $5 per person per night for more than two people. Some credit cards are accepted. Open April through October.

**Directions:** From Redding, turn east on Highway 44 and drive to Shingletown. In Shingletown, continue east for four miles and look for the park entrance on the right (signed KOA).

**Contact:** Mount Lassen/Shingletown KOA, 530/474-3133, www.koa.com.

## 52 SUMMIT LAKE: NORTH, SOUTH, AND STOCK CORRAL

🥾🏊🚴🚣🐴♿🚐⛺

### Scenic rating: 9

in Lassen Volcanic National Park

**Map 3.3, page 183**      BEST (

Summit Lake is a beautiful spot where deer often visit in the evening on the adjacent meadow just east of the campgrounds. The lake is small, just 15 acres, and since trout plants were suspended it has been fished out. Summit Lake is the most popular lake for swimming in the park. Evening walks around the lake are perfect for families. A more ambitious trail is routed out of camp and leads past lavish wildflower displays in early summer to a series of wilderness lakes. The campgrounds are at an elevation of 6,695 feet.

**Campsites, facilities:** There are 46 sites for tents or RVs up to 35 feet at North Summit; 48 sites for tents or RVs up to 30 feet at South Summit (Loop E is tent-only); and one equestrian site for tents or RVs up to 35 feet that can accommodate up to 10 people and eight horses (no hookups). Picnic tables, fire rings, and bear-proof food lockers are provided. Drinking water and toilets (flush toilets at North Summit; pit toilets at South Summit; vault toilets at the equestrian site) are available. Water for stock corral campers is available at both Summit Lake campgrounds. Ranger programs are sometimes offered in summer. Some facilities are wheelchair-accessible. Leashed pets are permitted at campsites only.

**Reservations, fees:** Reservations are accepted at 877/444-6777 or www.recreation.gov ($9 reservation fee). North Summit sites are $22 per night; Loop A sites are first-come, first-served, while Loop B sites are available by reservation. South Summit sites are $20 per night; Loop C and D sites are available by reservation, while Loop A sites are first-come, first-served for tents only. South Summit is first-come, first-served after mid-September, when sites are $10 per night. The equestrian site is $35 per night. There is a $20 park entrance fee per vehicle. Some credit cards are accepted. Open late June through October, weather permitting.

**Directions:** From Redding, drive east on Highway 44 to the junction with Highway 89. Turn south on Highway 89 and drive one mile to the entrance station to Lassen Volcanic National Park (where the state highway becomes Lassen Park Highway/Main Park Road). Continue on Lassen Park Highway/Main Park Road for 12 miles to the campground entrance on the left side of the road. The horse camp is across the street from the other campsites.

**Contact:** Lassen Volcanic National Park, 530/595-4444, www.nps.gov/lavo.

## 53 SILVER BOWL

**Scenic rating: 7**

on Silver Lake in Lassen National Forest

**Map 3.3, page 183**

Pretty Silver Lake, at 6,400 feet elevation, sits at the edge of the Caribou Wilderness. There is an unimproved boat ramp at the southern end of the lake. It is occasionally planted by the Department of Fish and Wildlife with Eagle Lake trout and brown trout, which provide a summer fishery for campers. A trailhead from adjacent Caribou Lake is routed west into the wilderness, with routes available both to Emerald Lake to the northwest and to Betty, Trail, and Shotoverin Lakes nearby to the southeast.

**Campsites, facilities:** There are 18 sites for tents or RVs up to 25 feet (no hookups). Picnic tables and fire grills are provided. Drinking water and vault toilets are available. Leashed pets are permitted.

**Reservations, fees:** Reservations are not accepted. Sites are $12 per night. Open late May through October, weather permitting.

**Directions:** From Red Bluff, drive east on Highway 36 to the junction with Highway 89. Continue east on Highway 36 past Lake Almanor to Westwood. In Westwood, turn left on County Road A21 and drive 12.5 miles to Silver Lake Road. Turn left on Silver Lake Road/County Road 110 and drive 8.5 miles north to Silver Lake. At Silver Lake, turn right and drive 0.75 mile to the campground.

**Contact:** Lassen National Forest, Almanor Ranger District, 530/258-2141, www.fs.usda.gov/lassen.

## 54 ROCKY KNOLL

**Scenic rating: 7**

on Silver Lake in Lassen National Forest

**Map 3.3, page 183**

This is one of two camps at pretty Silver Lake, set at 6,400 feet elevation at the edge of the Caribou Wilderness. The other camp is Silver Bowl nearby to the north, which is larger and provides better access for hikers. This camp, however, is closer to the boat ramp, which is at the south end of the lake. Silver Lake provides a good summer fishery for campers.

**Campsites, facilities:** There are 18 sites for tents or RVs up to 27 feet (no hookups). Picnic tables and fire grills are provided. Vault toilets are available, but there is no drinking water. Leashed pets are permitted.

**Reservations, fees:** Reservations are not accepted. There is no fee for camping. Open late May through early November, weather permitting.

**Directions:** From Red Bluff, drive east on Highway 36 to the junction with Highway 89. Continue east on Highway 36 past Lake Almanor to Westwood. In Westwood, turn left on County Road A21 and drive 12.5 miles to Silver Lake Road. Turn left (west) on Silver Lake Road/County Road 110 and drive 8.5 miles to Silver Lake. At Silver Lake, turn left and drive 300 yards to the campground.

**Contact:** Lassen National Forest, Almanor Ranger District, 530/258-2141, www.fs.usda.gov/lassen.

## 55 SOUTHWEST WALK-IN

**Scenic rating: 8**

in Lassen Volcanic National Park

**Map 3.3, page 183**

This pretty campground (elevation 6,700 feet) is east of the Kohm Yah-mah-nee Visitors Center parking area near the southwest entrance station. Just taking the short walk required to reach the camp will launch you into an orbit beyond most of the highway cruisers visiting Lassen. The 4.6-mile hike to Mill Creek Falls, the park's highest waterfall, begins at the campground. The Sulphur Works and Brokeoff Mountain Trailheads are nearby, as is the visitors center. One must-see is Bumpass Hell. The trail is about seven miles north of the campground on the right side of the Lassen Park Highway/Main Park Road. This easy hike takes you past steam vents and boiling mud pots, all set in prehistoric-looking volcanic rock. Ranger-led programs are sometimes offered.

**Campsites, facilities:** There are 21 walk-in tent sites and a large parking lot available for RVs of any length (no hookups). Picnic tables, fire rings, and bear-proof food lockers are provided. Drinking water and restrooms with flush toilets (in the visitors center) are available in summer. Leashed pets are permitted in the campground only.

**Reservations, fees:** Reservations are not accepted. Sites are $16 per night for tent campers, and it's $10 per night for RV parking, plus a $20 per vehicle park entrance fee. Open year-round, weather permitting.

**Directions:** From Red Bluff, take Highway 36 east for 48 miles to the junction with Highway 89. Turn left on Highway 89 (becomes Lassen Park Highway/Main Park Road) and drive to the park's entrance. Just after passing through the park entrance gate, look for the camp parking area on the right side of the road.

**Contact:** Lassen Volcanic National Park, 530/595-4444, www.nps.gov/lavo.

## 56 WARNER VALLEY

🥾 🛶 🐾 ⛺

### Scenic rating: 7

on Hot Springs Creek in Lassen Volcanic National Park

**Map 3.3, page 183**

Lassen is one of the great national parks of the West, yet it gets surprisingly little use compared to Yosemite, Sequoia, and Kings Canyon National Parks. This campground gets overlooked because of its remote access out of Chester. The camp is set along Hot Springs Creek at 5,650 feet. The best hike is the 2.5-mile walk out to the unique Devil's Kitchen geothermal area. Other options are a 2.5-mile hike—with an 800-foot climb—to Drake

Lake, and a three-mile hike to Boiling Springs Lakes. It's also a good horseback-riding area. The Drakesbad Resort, where securing reservations is about as difficult as finding Bigfoot, is near the campground.

**Campsites, facilities:** There are 18 tent sites. RVs and trailers are not recommended because of road conditions. Picnic tables, food lockers, and fire rings are provided. Drinking water (until mid-September) and pit toilets are available. Leashed pets are permitted in the campground only.

**Reservations, fees:** Reservations are not accepted. Sites are $16 per night or $12 per night after mid-September. There is a park entrance fee of $20 per vehicle. Open June through late September, weather permitting (with no water from mid-September due to snow closure).

**Directions:** From Red Bluff, take Highway 36 east for 44 miles to the junction with Highway 89 (do not turn left, or north, on Highway 89 to Lassen Volcanic National Park entrance, as signed). Continue east on Highway 36/89 to Chester and Feather River Drive. Turn left (north) on Feather River Drive (Warner Valley Road) and drive 0.75 mile to County Road 312. Bear left and drive six miles to Warner Valley Road. Turn right and drive 11 miles to the campground on the right. Note: The last 3.5 miles are unpaved, and there is one steep hill that can be difficult to climb for large or underpowered RVs, or if you are towing a trailer.

**Contact:** Lassen Volcanic National Park, 530/595-4444, www.nps.gov/lavo.

## 57 JUNIPER LAKE

🥾 🏊 🛶 🐾 ⛺

### Scenic rating: 10

in Lassen Volcanic National Park

**Map 3.3, page 183**

This pretty spot is on the eastern shore of Juniper Lake, at an elevation of 6,792 feet. It is far from the busy Lassen Park Highway/Main Park Road (Highway 89) corridor that is routed through central Lassen Volcanic National Park.

From the north end of the lake, a great side trip is to make the 0.5-mile, 400-foot climb to Inspiration Point, which provides a panoramic view of the park's backcountry. A two-mile hike up Mount Harkness begins from camp. Since no drinking water is provided, it is critical to bring a water purification pump or plenty of bottled water.

**Campsites, facilities:** There are 18 tent sites, an equestrian site, and two group tent sites that can accommodate 10-15 people each (no hookups). Picnic tables, fire rings, and bear-proof food lockers are provided. Vault toilets are available. Drinking water is not available. Leashed pets are permitted in the campground only.

**Reservations, fees:** Reservations are not accepted for individual sites but are required for the group site at 877/444-6777 or www.recreation.gov ($9 reservation fee). Reservations are also required for the equestrian site at 530/335-7029. Single sites are $10 per night, group sites $30 per night, and the equestrian site is $10 plus $4 per horse per night. Park entrance fee per vehicle is $20. Open late June through late September, weather permitting.

**Directions:** From Red Bluff, take Highway 36 east for 44 miles to the junction with Highway 89 (do not turn left, or north, on Highway 89 to Lassen Volcanic National Park entrance, as signed). Continue east on Highway 36/89 to Chester and Feather River Drive. Turn left (north) on Feather River Drive and drive 0.75 mile to the Y and the junction for County Road 318. Bear right (marked for Juniper Lake) on County Road 318 and drive 11 miles to the campground on the right, set along the east side of the lake. Note: This is a very rough dirt road; RVs and trailers are not recommended.

**Contact:** Lassen Volcanic National Park, 530/595-4444, www.nps.gov/lavo.

## 58 BATTLE CREEK

**Scenic rating: 7**

on Battle Creek in Lassen National Forest

**Map 3.3, page 183**

This pretty spot offers easy access and streamside camping along Battle Creek. The trout fishing can be good in May, June, and early July, when the creek is stocked with trout by the Department of Fish and Wildlife. Many people drive right by without knowing there is a stream here and that the fishing can be good. The elevation is 4,800 feet.

**Campsites, facilities:** There are 50 sites for tents or RVs up to 30 feet (no hookups). Picnic tables and fire grills are provided. Drinking water, flush and vault toilets, and a day-use picnic area are available. Supplies can be obtained in the town of Mineral. Leashed pets are permitted.

**Reservations, fees:** Reservations are not accepted. Sites are $18 per night. Open late April through early November, weather permitting.

**Directions:** From Red Bluff, turn east on Highway 36 and drive 39 miles to the campground (if you reach Mineral, you have gone two miles too far).

**Contact:** Lassen National Forest, Almanor Ranger District, 530/258-2141, www.fs.usda.gov/lassen; Department of Fish and Wildlife fishing information, 530/225-2146.

## 59 THE VILLAGE AT CHILDS MEADOW

**Scenic rating: 7**

near Mill Creek

**Map 3.3, page 183**

The Village at Childs Meadow is an 18-acre resort set at 5,000 feet elevation. It features many recreation options, including catch-and-release fishing one mile away at Mill Creek. Trails for horseback riding are nearby. The trailhead for Spencer Meadow Trail is just east of the resort along Highway 36. The trail provides a 12-mile route (one-way) to Spencer Meadow and an effervescent spring that is the source of Mill Creek.

**Campsites, facilities:** There are seven tent sites and 21 sites with full hookups (50 amps) for RVs of any length; most are pull-through. Cabins, park-model cabins, and a motel are also available. Picnic tables and fire rings are provided. Drinking water and restrooms with flush toilets and showers are available. A coin laundry, store, restaurant, Wi-Fi, group picnic area, meeting room, and horseshoes are on-site. Groups can be accommodated. Leashed pets are permitted.

**Reservations, fees:** Reservations are accepted at 888/595-3383. RV sites are $35 per night, while tent sites are $25 per night. Some credit cards are accepted. Open mid-May through October, weather permitting.

**Directions:** From Red Bluff, drive east on Highway 36 for 43 miles to the town of Mineral. Continue east on Highway 36 for 10 miles to the resort on the left.

**Contact:** The Village at Childs Meadow, 530/595-3383, www.thevillageatchildsmeadow.com.

## 60 DOMINGO SPRINGS
🚶 🛶 🐕 🚙 ⛺

### Scenic rating: 7
in Lassen National Forest

**Map 3.3, page 183**

This camp is named after a spring adjacent to the site. It is a small fountain that pours into the headwaters of the North Fork Feather River, a good trout stream. The Pacific Crest Trail is routed from this camp north for four miles to Little Willow Lake and the southern border of Lassen Volcanic National Park. The elevation is 5,060 feet.

**Campsites, facilities:** There are 18 sites for tents or RVs up to 27 feet (no hookups). Picnic tables and fire grills are provided. Drinking

water and vault toilets are available. Leashed pets are permitted.

**Reservations, fees:** Reservations are not accepted. Sites are $14 per night. Open late May through early November, weather permitting.

**Directions:** From Red Bluff, take Highway 36 east to Chester and Feather River Drive. Turn left on Feather River Drive and drive 0.75 mile to County Road 312. Bear left and drive five miles to the Y with County Road 311 and County Road 312. Bear left on County Road 311 and drive two miles to the campground entrance road on the left.

**Contact:** Lassen National Forest, Almanor Ranger District, 530/258-2141, www.fs.usda.gov/lassen.

## 61 HIGH BRIDGE
🚶 🛶 🐕 🚙 ⛺

### Scenic rating: 8
on the North Fork of the Feather River in Lassen National Forest

**Map 3.3, page 183**

This camp (elevation 5,200 feet), near where the South Cascades meet the North Sierra, is ideal for many people. The result is that it is often full in July and August. The payoff includes a pretty, adjacent trout stream, the headwaters of the North Fork Feather. Trout fishing is often good, including some rare large brown trout, a surprise considering the relatively small size of the stream. Nearby access to the Warner Valley/Drakesbad entrance of Lassen Volcanic National Park provides a must-do side trip. The area is wooded and the road dusty.

**Campsites, facilities:** There are 11 sites for tents and one site that can accommodate an RV up to 20 feet (no hookups). Picnic tables and fire grills are provided. Drinking water and vault toilets are available. Groceries and propane gas are available in Chester. Leashed pets are permitted.

**Reservations, fees:** Reservations are not accepted. Sites are $14 per night. Open late May through early November, weather permitting.

**Directions:** From Red Bluff, take Highway 36 east to Chester and Feather River Drive. Turn left on Feather River Drive and drive 0.75 mile to County Road 312. Bear left and drive five miles to the campground entrance road on the left.

**Contact:** Lassen National Forest, Almanor Ranger District, 530/258-2141, www.fs.usda. gov/lassen; Department of Fish and Wildlife fishing information, 530/225-2146.

## 62 LAST CHANCE CREEK

### Scenic rating: 7

near Lake Almanor

**Map 3.3, page 183**

This secluded camp at 4,500 feet is adjacent to where Last Chance Creek empties into the north end of Lake Almanor. It is an unpublicized PG&E camp that is known primarily by locals and gets missed almost every time by out-of-towners. The adjacent lake area is a breeding ground in the spring for white pelicans, and the beauty of these birds in large flocks can be extraordinary.

**Campsites, facilities:** There are 12 sites for tents or RVs up to 30 feet (no hookups), and three group camps can accommodate up to 100 people (total). Picnic tables and fire grills are provided. Drinking water and vault toilets are available. Some facilities are wheelchair-accessible. Leashed pets are permitted.

**Reservations, fees:** Reservations are accepted online at www.pge.com/recreation ($1.50 reservation fee per day) for individual sites and are required for the group camps. Sites are $22 per night for individual sites, plus $5 per night for each additional vehicle and $10 per night for each additional RV; group sites are $85-169 per night (includes reservation fee). Pet fee is $2 per pet per night. Group sites require a two-night minimum stay and a three-night minimum on holidays. Open mid-May through September, weather permitting.

**Directions:** From Red Bluff, take Highway

36 east to Chester and continue for two miles over the causeway (at the north end of Lake Almanor). About 0.25 mile after crossing the causeway, turn left on the campground access road and drive 3.5 miles to the campground.

**Contact:** PG&E Land Projects, 916/386-5164, www.pge.com/recreation.

## 63 HOLE-IN-THE-GROUND

### Scenic rating: 8

on Mill Creek in Lassen National Forest

**Map 3.3, page 183**

This is one of two campgrounds set along Mill Creek at 4,300 feet. Take your pick. The highlight here is a trail that follows along Mill Creek for many miles; it provides good fishing access. Rules mandate the use of artificials with a single barbless hook, as well as catch-and-release; check current fishing regulations. The result is a challenging but quality wild-trout fishery. Another option is to drive 0.5 mile to the end of the Forest Service road, where there is a parking area for a trail that leads downstream along Mill Creek and into a state game refuge. To keep things easy, obtain a map of Lassen National Forest that details the recreational opportunities.

**Campsites, facilities:** There are 13 sites for tents or RVs up to 24 feet (no hookups). Picnic tables and fire grills are provided. Drinking water and vault toilets are available. Supplies are available in Mineral. Leashed pets are permitted.

**Reservations, fees:** Reservations are not accepted. Sites are $12 per night. Open late April through early November, weather permitting.

**Directions:** From Red Bluff, drive 43 miles east on Highway 36 to the town of Mineral and the junction with Highway 172. Turn right on Highway 172 and drive six miles to the town of Mill Creek. In Mill Creek, turn south onto Forest Road 28N06 (signed) and drive five miles to the campground access road. Turn left and drive 0.25 mile to the camp.

**Contact:** Lassen National Forest, Almanor Ranger District, 530/258-2141, www.fs.usda. gov/lassen.

# 64 MILL CREEK RESORT

### Scenic rating: 7

on Mill Creek near Lassen National Forest

**Map 3.3, page 183**

This is a great area, surrounded by Lassen National Forest and within close range of the southern Highway 89 entrance to Lassen Volcanic National Park. It is at 4,800 feet along oft-bypassed Highway 172. A highlight is Mill Creek (to reach it, turn south on the Forest Service road in town and drive to a parking area at the end of the road along the stream), where there is a great easy walk along the stream and fair trout fishing. Note that about half the campsites are taken by longterm renters.

**Campsites, facilities:** There are 14 sites for tents or self-contained RVs up to 35 feet and eight RV sites with full hookups (30 amps). There are also 11 cabins are available. Picnic tables and fire rings are provided. Drinking water, vault toilets, seasonal showers, coin laundry, a playground, a small grocery store, post office, and a restaurant are also available. Some facilities are wheelchair-accessible. Leashed pets are permitted.

**Reservations, fees:** Reservations are recommended. RV sites are $30 per night, tent sites are $16 per night, and cabins are $85-120 per night. Campsites are open May through October. Cabins are available year-round.

**Directions:** From Red Bluff, drive 43 miles east on Highway 36 to the town of Mineral and the junction with Highway 172. Turn right and drive six miles to the town of Mill Creek. In Mill Creek, look for the sign for Mill Creek Resort on the right side of the road.

**Contact:** Mill Creek Resort, 530/595-4449 or 888/595-4449, www.millcreekresort.net.

# 65 GURNSEY AND GURNSEY CREEK GROUP

### Scenic rating: 7

in Lassen National Forest

**Map 3.3, page 183**

This camp is (elevation 5,000 feet) in Lassen National Forest has extremely easy access off Highway 36. It is on the headwaters of little Gurnsey Creek, a highlight of the surrounding Lost Creek Plateau. Gurnsey Creek runs downstream and pours into Deer Creek, a good trout stream with access along narrow, winding Highway 32 to the nearby south. The group camps are ideal spots for a Scout troop.

**Campsites, facilities:** There are 30 sites for tents or RVs up to 30 feet (no hookups). There are two group camps that can accommodate up to 56 people and 112 people respectively with tents or RVs up to 30 feet (no hookups); larger groups may reserve both camps together. Picnic tables and fire grills are provided. Drinking water and vault toilets are available. Supplies are available in Mineral. Some facilities are wheelchair-accessible. Leashed pets are permitted.

**Reservations, fees:** Reservations are not accepted for individual sites but are required for the group sites at 877/444-6777 ($10 reservation fee) or www.recreation.gov ($9 reservation fee). Tent and RV sites are $14 per night. Group Site 1 is $56 per night or $392 per week. Group Camp 2 is $112 per night or $784 per week, with a two-night minimum stay required. Open May through October, weather permitting.

**Directions:** From Red Bluff, drive east on Highway 36 for 55 miles (five miles east of Childs Meadow). Turn left at the campground entrance road and drive a short distance to the campground.

**Contact:** Lassen National Forest, Almanor Ranger District, 530/258-2141, www.fs.usda. gov/lassen.

## 66 NORTH SHORE CAMPGROUND

### Scenic rating: 7

on Lake Almanor

**Map 3.3, page 183**

This is a large, privately developed park on the northern shoreline of beautiful Lake Almanor. The park has 37 acres and a mile of shoreline. The camp is set amid pine tree cover, and most of the sites are lakefront or lake-view. About half of the sites are filled with seasonal renters. The lending library here was once the original Chester jail, built in 1925. Alas, the jail itself busted out during a storm a few years ago and was found washed ashore at this campground, which converted it to its new use.

**Campsites, facilities:** There are 34 tent sites and 94 sites with partial hookups (30 amps) for RVs up to 40 feet; a few are pull-through. Five log cabins are also available. Picnic tables and fire rings are provided. Drinking water, restrooms with showers and flush toilets, coin laundry, general store, playground, lending library, Wi-Fi, propane, dump station, fish-cleaning station, horseshoes, boat ramp, boat dock, boat slips, and boat rentals are available. Leashed pets are permitted.

**Reservations, fees:** Reservations are accepted by phone. RV sites are $46-56 per night, tent sites are $36 per night, plus $5 per person per night for more than four people at tent sites (up to six maximum) and $5 per night per additional vehicle. Monthly and seasonal rates are available. Some credit cards are accepted. Open May through October.

**Directions:** From Red Bluff, take Highway 36 east for 44 miles to the junction with Highway 89. Drive east on Highway 36/89; the camp is two miles past Chester on the right.

**Contact:** North Shore Campground, 530/258-3376, www.northshorecampground.com.

## 67 SOUTH ANTELOPE

### Scenic rating: 6

near the eastern edge of the Ishi Wilderness

**Map 3.3, page 183**

This primitive campsite is for visitors who want to explore the Ishi Wilderness without an extensive drive (compared to other camps in the wilderness here). The South Fork of Antelope Creek runs west from the camp and provides an off-trail route for the ambitious. For easier hikes, trailheads along Ponderosa Way provide access into the eastern flank of the Ishi. The best nearby trail is Lower Mill Creek Trail, with the trailhead eight miles south at Black Rock.

**Campsites, facilities:** There is dispersed camping for tents only. Picnic tables and fire pits are provided. There is no drinking water and no toilets. Garbage must be packed out. Leashed pets are permitted.

**Reservations, fees:** Reservations are not accepted. There is no fee for camping. A campfire permit is required. Open year-round.

**Directions:** From Red Bluff, drive east on Highway 36 for about 35 miles to the town of Paynes Creek and Plum Creek Road. Turn right (south) on Plum Creek Road and drive two miles to Ponderosa Way. Turn right (south) and continue for nine miles to the campground on the right. Note: The road is rough and only vehicles with high clearance are advised. No RVs or trailers are allowed.

**Contact:** Lassen National Forest, Almanor Ranger District, 530/258-2141, www.fs.usda.gov/lassen.

## 68 BLACK ROCK

### Scenic rating: 7

on the eastern edge of the Ishi Wilderness

**Map 3.3, page 183**

This remote, primitive camp is at the base of the huge, ancient Black Rock, one of the oldest geological points in Lassen National Forest. A bonus is that Mill Creek runs adjacent to the sites, providing a water source. This is the edge of the Ishi Wilderness, where remote hiking in solitude is possible without venturing to high mountain elevations; a campfire permit is required for overnight use by backpackers. A trailhead is available right out of the camp. The trail leads downstream along Mill Creek, extending five miles into the Ishi Wilderness, downhill all the way. Be prepared when hiking in this area because the heat can be almost intolerable at times, often passing the 100°F mark for days on end.

**Campsites, facilities:** There are six tent sites. Picnic tables and fire pits are provided. A vault toilet is available. No drinking water is available. Mill Creek is adjacent to the camp and is a viable water source; remember to filter stream water. Garbage must be packed out. Leashed pets are permitted.

**Reservations, fees:** Reservations are not accepted. There is no fee for camping. Open year-round, weather permitting.

**Directions:** From Red Bluff, drive east on Highway 36 for about 35 miles to the town of Paynes Creek and Plum Creek Road. Turn right (south) on Plum Creek Road and drive two miles to Ponderosa Way. Turn right (south) and continue for 16 miles to the campground on the right. Note: The road is rough and only vehicles with high clearance are advised. No RVs or trailers are allowed.

**Contact:** Lassen National Forest, Almanor Ranger District, 530/258-2141, www.fs.usda.gov/lassen.

## 69 ELAM

### Scenic rating: 7

on Deer Creek in Lassen National Forest

**Map 3.3, page 183**

Of the campgrounds on Deer Creek along Highway 32, Elam gets the most use. It is the first stopping point visitors arrive at while heading west on narrow, curvy Highway 32,

and it has an excellent day-use picnic area available. The stream is stocked with rainbow trout in late spring and early summer, with good access for fishing. It is a pretty area where Elam Creek enters Deer Creek. A Forest Service Information Center is nearby in Chester. If the camp has too many people to suit your style, consider other more distant and primitive camps downstream on Deer Creek. The elevation is 4,600 feet.

**Campsites, facilities:** There are 15 sites for tents or RVs up to 30 feet (no hookups). Picnic tables and fire grills are provided. Drinking water and vault toilets are available. Leashed pets are permitted.

**Reservations, fees:** Reservations are not accepted. Sites are $14 per night, plus $3 per night for each additional vehicle. Open mid-April through October, weather permitting.

**Directions:** From Red Bluff, take Highway 36 east for 44 miles to the junction with Highway 89. Continue east on Highway 36/89 to the junction with Highway 32. Turn south on Highway 32 and drive three miles to the campground on the right side of the road. Trailers are not recommended.

**Contact:** Lassen National Forest, Almanor Ranger District, 530/258-2141, www.fs.usda.gov/lassen.

## 70 ALDER CREEK

### Scenic rating: 7

on Deer Creek in Lassen National Forest

**Map 3.3, page 183**

Deer Creek is a great little trout stream that runs along Highway 32. Alder Creek is one of three camps set along Highway 32 with streamside access; this one is at 3,900 feet elevation, near where both Alder Creek and Round Valley Creek pour into Deer Creek. The stream's best stretch of trout water is from here to Elam, upstream.

**Campsites, facilities:** There are six tent sites. Trailers and RVs are not recommended. Picnic tables and fire grills are provided. Vault toilets are available. No drinking water is available; stream water should be purified before use. Leashed pets are permitted.

**Reservations, fees:** Reservations are not accepted. Sites are $10 per night. Open mid-May through mid-October, weather permitting.

**Directions:** From Red Bluff, take Highway 36 east for 44 miles to the junction with Highway 89. Continue east on Highway 36/89 to the junction with Highway 32. Turn south on Highway 32 and drive eight miles to the campground on the right side of the road.

**Contact:** Lassen National Forest, Almanor Ranger District, 530/258-2141, www.fs.usda. gov/lassen.

# 71 POTATO PATCH

### Scenic rating: 7
on Deer Creek in Lassen National Forest

**Map 3.3, page 183**

You get good hiking and fishing at this camp beside Deer Creek at 3,400 feet elevation. It has good access for trout fishing. This is a wild trout stream in this area, and the use of artificials with a single barbless hook and catch-and-release are required along most of the river; check DFG regulations. An excellent anglers'/ swimmers' trail is available along the river.

**Campsites, facilities:** There are 32 sites for tents or RVs up to 27 feet (no hookups). Picnic tables and fire grills are provided. Drinking water and vault toilets are available. Some facilities are wheelchair-accessible. Leashed pets are permitted.

**Reservations, fees:** Reservations are not accepted. Sites are $14 per night. Open early April through early November, weather permitting.

**Directions:** From Red Bluff, take Highway 36 east for 44 miles to the junction with Highway 89. Continue east on Highway 36/89 to the junction with Highway 32. Turn south on Highway 32 and drive 11 miles to the campground on the right side of the road.

**Contact:** Lassen National Forest, Almanor Ranger District, 530/258-2141, www.fs.usda. gov/lassen; Department of Fish and Wildlife, 530/225-2146.

# 72 ROCKY POINT CAMPGROUND

### Scenic rating: 7
on Lake Almanor

**Map 3.3, page 183**

What you get here is a series of four campgrounds along the southwest shore of Lake Almanor, provided by PG&E as mitigation for its hydroelectric activities on the Feather River system. The camps are upstream from the dam, with boat ramps available on each side of the dam. This is a pretty spot, with giant Almanor ringed by lodgepole pines and firs. The lake is usually full, or close to it, well into summer, with Mount Lassen in the distance to the north—bring your camera. The lake is 13 miles long and all water sports are permitted. Though it can take a day or two to find the fish, once that effort is made, fishing is good for large trout and salmon in the spring and fall and for smallmouth bass in the summer.

**Campsites, facilities:** There are 130 sites for tents or RVs up to 30 feet (no hookups), five overflow units, and two group sites (North and South) with 5 and 19 sites respectively. Picnic tables and fire grills are provided. Drinking water, vault toilets, and a dump station are available. Some facilities are wheelchair-accessible. Leashed pets are permitted.

**Reservations, fees:** Reservations are accepted online at www.pge.com/recreation for most of the individual sites (spaces 1-109) and are required for the group sites. Sites are $25 per night ($1.50 reservation fee per night) for up to six people; the North group site is $142 per night and the South group site is $561 per night (includes reservation fee); it's $5 per night for each additional vehicle, $10 per night per additional RV, and $2 per pet per night. Weekend and weekly rates are available. Open May through October.

**Directions:** From Red Bluff, take Highway 36 east for 44 miles to the junction with Highway 89. Continue east on Highway 36/89 to Lake Almanor and the next junction with Highway 89 (two miles before reaching Chester). Turn right on Highway 89 and drive eight miles to the southwest end of Lake Almanor. Turn left at your choice of four campground entrances.

**Contact:** PG&E Land Projects, 916/386-5164 or 530/284-1785, www.pge.com/recreation.

# 73 ALMANOR NORTH, SOUTH, AND LEGACY
🥾🚲🚊🛶🚗🐕♿🚐⛺

### Scenic rating: 8
on Lake Almanor in Lassen National Forest

**Map 3.3, page 183**   BEST (

This is one of Lake Almanor's best-known and most popular Forest Service campgrounds, set along the western shore of beautiful Almanor at 4,550 feet elevation directly across from the beautiful Almanor Peninsula. There are two linked campgrounds—North and South—and a new first-come, first-served RV campground at Legacy. There is an excellent view of Mount Lassen to the north, along with gorgeous sunrises. A 10-mile recreation trail runs right through the campground and is excellent for biking or hiking. This section of the lake provides good fishing for smallmouth bass in the summer. Fishing in this lake is also good for rainbow trout, brown trout, and lake-raised salmon.

**Campsites, facilities:** There are 104 sites for tents or RVs up to 25 or 40 feet (no hookups) at Almanor North and South. Almanor Legacy has 13 sites for tents or RVs (partial hookups). There is also a group camp for tents or RVs up to 60 feet that can accommodate up to 100 people. Picnic tables and fire grills are provided. Drinking water and vault toilets are available. A dump station, boat ramp, and beach area are nearby. Some facilities

are wheelchair-accessible. Leashed pets are permitted.

**Reservations, fees:** Reservations are accepted for individual sites at Almanor North and South and are required for the group camp at 877/444-6777 ($10 reservation fee) or www.recreation.gov ($9 reservation fee). Reservations are not accepted for Almanor Legacy. North and South sites are $18 per night for single sites, $36 per night for the double site, $30 per night for Almanor Legacy sites, and $100 per night for the group camp. Open May through September, weather permitting.

**Directions:** From Red Bluff, take Highway 36 east for 44 miles to the junction with Highway 89. Continue east on Highway 36/89 to Lake Almanor and the next junction with Highway 89 (two miles before reaching Chester). Turn right on Highway 89 and drive six miles to County Road 310. (The group camp is on the left side of Highway 89 at the CR 310 intersection.) Turn left on County Road 310 and drive 0.25 mile to the campground.

**Contact:** Lassen National Forest, Almanor Ranger District, 530/258-2141, www.fs.usda.gov/lassen.

# 74 SOLDIER MEADOWS
🛶🐕🚐⛺

### Scenic rating: 7
on Soldier Creek in Lassen National Forest

**Map 3.3, page 183**

This primitive camp is little known and is used primarily by anglers and hunters in season. The campsites are shaded, set in forest on the edge of meadows and near a stream. The latter is Soldier Creek, which is stocked with trout by the Department of Fish and Wildlife; check fishing regulations. In the fall, early storms can drive deer through this area on their annual migration to their wintering habitat in the valley, making this a decent base camp for hunters. However, no early storms often means no deer. The elevation is 4,890 feet.

**Campsites, facilities:** There are 15 sites for

tents or RVs up to 25 feet (no hookups). Picnic tables and fire rings are provided. Vault toilets are available. No drinking water is available. Leashed pets are permitted.

**Reservations, fees:** Reservations are not accepted. Sites are $10 per night. Open late May through early November, weather permitting.

**Directions:** From Chester, drive south on Highway 89 for approximately six miles to Humboldt Road. Turn right on Humboldt Road and drive one mile, bear right at the fork, and continue five more miles to the intersection at Fanani Meadows. Turn right and drive one mile to the campground on the left.

**Contact:** Lassen National Forest, Almanor Ranger District, 530/258-2141, www.fs.usda.gov/lassen.

## 75 PONDEROSA FLAT

Scenic rating: 7

on Butt Valley Reservoir

**Map 3.3, page 183**

This camp is at the north end of Butt Valley Reservoir (more commonly called Butt Lake), the little brother to nearby Lake Almanor. It is a fairly popular camp, with the boat ramp a prime attraction, allowing campers/anglers a lakeside spot with easy access. Technically, Butt is the "afterbay" for Almanor, fed by a four-mile-long pipe with water from Almanor. What occurs is that pond smelt from Almanor get ground up in the Butt Lake powerhouse, providing a large amount of feed for trout at the head of the lake; that's why the trout often get huge at Butt Lake. The one downer is that lake drawdowns are common, exposing tree stumps. In 2012, a large forest fire burned the slopes above the far side of the lake.

**Campsites, facilities:** There are 63 sites, including three double sites, for tents or RVs up to 30 feet (no hookups), as well as an over-flow camping area. Picnic tables and fire grills are provided. Drinking water, vault toilets, and a boat ramp are available. Some facilities

are wheelchair-accessible. Leashed pets are permitted.

**Reservations, fees:** Reservations are accepted online at www.pge.com/recreation ($1.50 reservation fee per night) for most of the individual sites (spaces 24-63) and are required for the group sites (call for rates). Sites are $25 per night for up to six people, plus $5 per night for each additional vehicle, $10 per night for each additional RV, and $2 per pet per night. Open May through October, weather permitting.

**Directions:** From Red Bluff, take Highway 36 east for 44 miles to the junction with Highway 89. Continue east on Highway 36/89 to Lake Almanor and the next junction with Highway 89 (two miles before reaching Chester). Turn right on Highway 89 and drive about seven miles to Butt Valley Road. Turn right on Butt Valley Road and drive 3.2 miles to the campground on the right side of the road.

**Contact:** PG&E Land Projects, 916/386-5164 or 530/284-1785, www.pge.com/recreation.

## 76 COOL SPRINGS

Scenic rating: 7

on Butt Valley Reservoir

**Map 3.3, page 183**

One of two camps at Butt Lake (officially known as Butt Valley Reservoir), Cool Springs is about midway down the lake on its eastern shore, 2.5 miles south of Ponderosa Flat. Cool Springs Creek enters the lake near the camp. (See the Ponderosa Flat listing for more information about Butt Lake.)

**Campsites, facilities:** There are 25 sites for tents or RVs up to 30 feet (no hookups) and five walk-in tent sites. Picnic tables and fire grills are provided. Drinking water, vault toilets, and a boat ramp are available. Some facilities are wheelchair-accessible. Leashed pets are permitted.

**Reservations, fees:** Reservations are accepted online at www.pge.com/recreation ($1.50 reservation fee per night). Sites are $22 per night for up to six people, plus $5 per night for each additional vehicle, $10 per night per additional RV, and $2 per pet per night. Open mid-May to mid-September, weather permitting.

**Directions:** From Red Bluff, take Highway 36 east for 44 miles to the junction with Highway 89. Continue east on Highway 36/89 to Lake Almanor and the next junction with Highway 89 (two miles before reaching Chester). Turn right on Highway 89 and drive about seven miles to Butt Valley Road. Turn right on Butt Valley Road and drive 5.7 miles to the campground on the right side of the road.

**Contact:** PG&E Land Projects, 916/386-5164, www.pge.com/recreation.

## 77 YELLOW CREEK

### Scenic rating: 8

in Humbug Valley

**Map 3.3, page 183**

Yellow Creek is one of Cal Trout's pet projects. It's a beautiful stream for fly fishers, demanding the best from skilled anglers. This camp at 4,400 feet in Humbug Valley provides access to this stretch of water. Another option is to fish Butt Creek, which has much easier fishing for small, planted rainbow trout; access is along the road on the way in.

**Campsites, facilities:** There are 11 sites for tents or RVs up to 30 feet (no hookups). Picnic tables and fire grills are provided. Drinking water and vault toilets are available. Leashed pets are permitted.

**Reservations, fees:** Reservations are not accepted. Sites are $22 per night, plus $5 per night for each additional vehicle, $10 per night per additional RV, and $2 per pet per night. Open mid-May to mid-September.

**Directions:** From Red Bluff, take Highway 36 east for 44 miles to the junction with Highway 89. Continue east on Highway 36/89 for eight miles to Humbug Road. Turn right and drive 0.6 mile and bear left to stay on Humbug Road.

Continue for 1.2 miles and bear right (signed for Longville) to stay on Humbug Road. Continue for 5.4 miles to Humbug Valley and a road intersection. Turn left to stay on Humbug Road and drive 1.2 miles (passing the Soda Springs Historic Site) to a fork. Bear right to stay on Humbug Road and drive 0.3 mile to the campground.

**Contact:** PG&E Land Projects, 916/386-5164, www.pge.com/recreation.

## 78 BUTTE MEADOWS

### Scenic rating: 6

on Butte Creek in Lassen National Forest

**Map 3.3, page 183**

On hot summer days, when a cold stream sounds even better than a cold drink, Butte Meadows provides a hideout in the national forest east of Chico. This is a summer camp situated along Butte Creek, which is stocked with rainbow trout by the Department of Fish and Wildlife. Nearby Doe Mill Ridge and the surrounding Lassen National Forest can provide good side-trip adventures. Camp elevation is 4,600 feet.

**Campsites, facilities:** There are 13 sites for tents or RVs up to 25 feet (no hookups). Fire grills and picnic tables are provided. Drinking water and vault toilets are available. Supplies are available in Butte Meadows. Leashed pets are permitted.

**Reservations, fees:** Reservations are not accepted. Sites are $12 per night. Open late April through early November, weather permitting.

**Directions:** From Chico, drive about 15 miles northeast on Highway 32 to the town of Forest Ranch. Continue on Highway 32 for another nine miles. Turn right on Humboldt Road and drive five miles to Butte Meadows.

**Contact:** Lassen National Forest, Almanor Ranger District, 530/258-2141, www.fs.usda.gov/lassen; Department of Fish and Wildlife fishing information, 530/225-2146.

## 79 CHERRY HILL

### Scenic rating: 7

on Butte Creek in Lassen National Forest

**Map 3.3, page 183**

The camp is along little Butte Creek at the foot of Cherry Hill, just downstream from the confluence of Colby Creek and Butte Creek. It is also on the western edge of the alpine zone in Lassen National Forest. A four-mile drive to the north, much of it along Colby Creek, will take visitors to the Colby Mountain Lookout at 6,002 feet for a dramatic view of the Ishi Wilderness to the west. Nearby to the south is Philbrook Reservoir.

**Campsites, facilities:** There are six walk-in tent sites and 19 sites for tents or RVs up to 30 feet (no hookups). Picnic tables and fire grills are provided. Drinking water and vault toilets are available. Supplies are available in the town of Butte Meadows. Leashed pets are permitted.

**Reservations, fees:** Reservations are not accepted. Sites are $14 per night. Open late April through early November, weather permitting.

**Directions:** From Chico, drive northeast on Highway 32 for approximately 24 miles to the junction with Humboldt Road (well past the town of Forest Ranch). Turn right and drive five miles to Butte Meadows. Continue on Humboldt Road for three miles to the campground on the right side of the road.

**Contact:** Lassen National Forest, Almanor Ranger District, 530/258-2141, www.fs.usda.gov/lassen.

## 80 PHILBROOK RESERVOIR

### Scenic rating: 7

in Lassen National Forest

**Map 3.3, page 183**

Philbrook Reservoir is at 5,600 feet on the western mountain slopes above Chico, on the southwest edge of Lassen National Forest. It is a pretty lake, though subject to late-season drawdowns, with a scenic lookout a short distance from camp. Swimming beaches and a picnic area are bonuses. The lake is loaded with small trout—a dink here, a dink there, a dink everywhere.

**Campsites, facilities:** There are 20 sites for tents or RVs up to 30 feet (no hookups), as well as an overflow camping area. Picnic tables and fire grills are provided. Drinking water and vault toilets are available. Trailer and car-top boat launches are available. Some facilities are wheelchair-accessible. Leashed pets are permitted.

**Reservations, fees:** Reservations are accepted online at www.pge.com/recreation ($1.50 reservation fee per night). Sites are $22 per night, plus $5 per night for each additional vehicle, $10 per night per additional RV, and $2 per pet per night. Open May through September (opening date subject to change).

**Directions:** At Orland on I-5, take the Highway 32/Chico exit and drive to Chico and the junction with Highway 99. Turn south on Highway 99 and drive to Skyway Road/Paradise (in south Chico). Turn east on Skyway Road, drive through Paradise, and continue for 27 miles to Humbug Summit Road. Turn right and drive two miles to Philbrook Road. Turn right and drive 3.1 miles to the campground entrance road. Turn right and drive 0.5 mile to the campground. Note: Access roads are unpaved and often rough.

**Contact:** PG&E Land Projects, 916/386-5164, www.pge.com/recreation.

## 81 QUEEN LILY

### Scenic rating: 7

on the North Fork of the Feather River in Plumas National Forest

**Map 3.3, page 183**

The North Fork Feather River is a prime destination for camping and trout fishing, especially for families. This is one of three camps along the river on Caribou Road. This stretch of river is well stocked. Insider's note: The first 150 yards of river below the dam at Caribou typically have large but elusive trout.

**Campsites, facilities:** There are 12 sites for tents or RVs up to 30 feet (no hookups). Picnic tables, bear-proof lockers, and fire grills are provided. Drinking water and flush toilets are available. A grocery store and coin laundry are within three miles. Leashed pets are permitted.

**Reservations, fees:** Reservations are not accepted. Sites are $25 per night. Open May through September.

**Directions:** From Oroville, drive north on Highway 70 to Caribou Road (two miles past Belden). Turn left on Caribou Road and drive about three miles to the campground on the left side of the road.

**Contact:** Plumas National Forest, Mt. Hough Ranger District, 530/283-0555, www.fs.usda. gov/plumas or www.royalelkparkmanagement. com.

## 82 NORTH FORK

### Scenic rating: 7

on the North Fork of the Feather River in Plumas National Forest

**Map 3.3, page 183**

This camp is between Queen Lily nearby to the north and Gansner Bar camp nearby to the south; all three are on the North Fork Feather River. The elevation is 2,600 feet. Fishing access is good and trout plants are decent, making for a good fishing/camping trip. Note: All three camps are extremely popular on summer weekends.

**Campsites, facilities:** There are 19 sites for tents or RVs up to 32 feet (some electric sites). Picnic tables, bear-proof lockers, and fire grills are provided. Drinking water and flush toilets are available. A grocery store and coin laundry are available within three miles. Leashed pets are permitted.

**Reservations, fees:** Reservations are not

accepted. Sites are $25-30 per night. Open May through September.

**Directions:** From Oroville, drive north on Highway 70 to Caribou Road (two miles past Belden at Gansner Ranch Ranger Station). Turn left on Caribou Road and drive about two miles to the campground on the left side of the road.

**Contact:** Plumas National Forest, Mt. Hough Ranger District, 530/283-0555, www.fs.usda. gov/plumas or www.royalelkparkmanagement. com.

## 83 GANSNER BAR

### Scenic rating: 7

on the North Fork of the Feather River in Plumas National Forest

**Map 3.3, page 183**

Gansner Bar is the first of three camps along Caribou Road, which runs parallel to the North Fork Feather River. Of the three, this one receives the highest trout stocks of rainbow trout in the 10- to 12-inch class. Caribou Road runs upstream to Caribou Dam, with stream and fishing access along almost all of it. The camps often fill on summer weekends.

**Campsites, facilities:** There are 16 sites for tents or RVs up to 30 feet (no hookups). Picnic tables, bear-proof lockers, and fire grills are provided. Drinking water and flush toilets are available. A grocery store and coin laundry are available within one mile. Some facilities are wheelchair-accessible. Leashed pets are permitted.

**Reservations, fees:** Reservations are not accepted. Sites are $25 per night. Open April through October.

**Directions:** From Oroville, drive northeast on Highway 70 to Caribou Road (two miles past Belden). Turn left on Caribou Road and drive a short distance to the campground on the left side of the road.

**Contact:** Plumas National Forest, Mt. Hough Ranger District, 530/283-0555, www.fs.usda.

gov/plumas or www.royalelkparkmanagement.
com.

## 84 HALLSTED

### Scenic rating: 7

on the North Fork of the Feather River in
Plumas National Forest

**Map 3.3, page 183**

Easy highway access and a pretty trout stream
right alongside have made this an extremely
popular campground. It typically fills on summer weekends. Hallsted is on the East Branch
North Fork Feather River at 2,800 feet elevation. The river is stocked with trout by the
Department of Fish and Wildlife. This campground closed in 2012 for major construction,
reopening in 2013 with new restrooms with
showers and with partial hookups available at
some campsites.

**Campsites, facilities:** There are 20 sites for
tents or RVs up to 30 feet (some hookups for
water and electricity). Picnic tables and fire
grills are provided. Drinking water and flush
toilets are available. A grocery store is within
a quarter mile. Some facilities are wheelchair-
accessible. Leashed pets are permitted.

**Reservations, fees:** Reservations are accepted at 877/444-6777 ($10 reservation fee)
or www.recreation.gov ($9 reservation fee).
Sites are $25-30 per night. Open May through
September.

**Directions:** From Oroville, drive northeast on
Highway 70 to Belden. Continue past Belden
for about 12 miles to the campground entrance
on the right side of the road. Turn right and
drive 0.25 mile to the campground.

**Contact:** Plumas National Forest, Mt. Hough
Ranger District, 530/283-0555, www.fs.usda.
gov/plumas or www.royalelkparkmanagement.
com.

## 85 DODGE RESERVOIR

### Scenic rating: 6

near Ravendale

**Map 3.4, page 184**

This remote, little-used camp is set at 5,735 feet
elevation near Dodge Reservoir. The lake covers 400 acres and is stocked with Eagle Lake
trout. Those who know of this lake feel as if
they know a secret, because the limit is two at
Eagle Lake itself, but it is five here. Small boats
can be launched from the shoreline, and though
it can be windy, mornings are usually calm,
ideal for canoes. The surrounding hillsides are
sprinkled with sage and juniper. This camp is
also popular with hunters who get drawn in
the annual DFG lottery for tags for this zone.
There is a very good chance that, along the entire length of road from the Madeline Plain into
Dodge Reservoir, you'll see some wild horses.
There's no sight quite like them. They are considered to be wild, but some will stay close to
the road, while others will come no closer than
300 yards.

**Campsites, facilities:** There are 11 sites for
tents or RVs up to 35 feet (no hookups). Picnic
tables and fire pits are provided. A vault toilet is available. No drinking water is available.
Garbage must be packed out. There is no developed boat ramp, but hand-launched boats
are permitted. Some facilities are wheelchair-
accessible. Leashed pets are permitted.

**Reservations, fees:** Reservations are not accepted. There is no fee for camping, but donations are encouraged. Open year-round,
weather permitting.

**Directions:** From Susanville, drive north on
U.S. 395 for 54 miles to Ravendale and County
Road 502. Turn right on County Road 502
(Mail Route) and drive four miles, then bear
left to stay on County Road 502. Continue
four miles, then bear right to stay on County
Road 502. Drive two miles to County Road 526.
Continue straight onto County Road 526 and
drive 4.5 miles to County Road 504. Turn left
and drive two miles to County Road 506. Turn

right and drive 7.5 miles to the access road for Dodge Reservoir. Turn left on the access road and drive one mile to the lake and camp. Note: The last mile of road before the turnoff to Dodge Reservoir can become impassable with just a small amount of rain or snow.

**Contact:** Bureau of Land Management, Eagle Lake Field Office, 530/257-0456, www.blm. gov/ca.

## 86 NORTH EAGLE LAKE

**Scenic rating: 7**

on Eagle Lake

**Map 3.4, page 184**

This camp provides direct access in the fall to the fishing area of Eagle Lake. When the weather turns cold, the population of Eagle Lake trout migrates to its favorite haunts just outside the tules, often in water only 5-8 feet deep. A boat ramp is about 1.5 miles southwest on Stone Road. In the summer this area is quite exposed and the lake can be hammered by west winds, which can howl from midday to sunset. A recent drawdown has also left boat ramps and marinas high and dry. The elevation is 5,100 feet.

**Campsites, facilities:** There are 20 sites for tents or RVs up to 35 feet (no hookups). Picnic tables and fire grills are provided. Drinking water and vault toilets are available. A boat ramp is nearby. A private dump station is within 1.5 miles. Leashed pets are permitted.

**Reservations, fees:** Reservations are not accepted. Sites are $8 per night. Open Memorial Day through mid-November, weather permitting.

**Directions:** From Red Bluff, drive east on Highway 36 to Susanville. In Susanville, turn left (north) on Highway 139 and drive 29 miles to County Road A1. Turn left at County Road

A1 and drive 0.5 mile to the campground on the right.

**Contact:** Bureau of Land Management, Eagle Lake Field Office, 530/257-0456, www.blm. gov/ca.

## 87 RAMHORN SPRINGS

**Scenic rating: 3**

south of Ravendale

**Map 3.4, page 184**

This camp is not even three miles off the biggest state highway in northeastern California, yet it feels remote and is little known. It is way out in Nowhere Land, near the flank of Shinn Peaks (7,502 feet). There are large numbers of antelope in the area, along with a sprinkling of large mule deer. Hunters lucky enough to get a deer tag can use this camp for their base in the fall. It is also popular for upland game hunters in search of sage grouse and chukar.

**Campsites, facilities:** There are 10 sites for tents or RVs up to 35 feet (no hookups). Picnic tables and fire grills are provided. Vault toilets and a horse corral are available. There is no drinking water, although spring water, which can be filtered, is available. Some facilities are wheelchair-accessible. Leashed pets are permitted.

**Reservations, fees:** Reservations are not accepted. There is no fee for camping, but donations are encouraged. Open year-round, weather permitting.

**Directions:** From Red Bluff, drive east on Highway 36 to Susanville. Past Susanville, turn north on U.S. 395 and drive 45 miles to Post Camp Road. Turn right on Post Camp Road (unmarked except for a small recreation sign) and drive 2.5 miles east to the campground.

**Contact:** Bureau of Land Management, Eagle Lake Field Office, 530/257-0456, www.blm. gov/ca.

## 88 EAGLE LAKE RV PARK

### Scenic rating: 7

near Susanville

**Map 3.4, page 184**

Eagle Lake RV Park has become something of a headquarters for anglers in pursuit of Eagle Lake trout, which typically range 18-22 inches. A nearby boat ramp provides access to Pelican Point and Eagle Point, where the fishing is often best in the summer. In the fall, the north end of the lake provides better prospects (see the North Eagle Lake listing in this chapter). This RV park has all the amenities, including a small store. That means no special trips into town, just vacation time, lounging beside Eagle Lake, maybe catching a big trout now and then. One downer: The wind typically howls most summer afternoons. When the whitecaps are too big to deal with and surface conditions become choppy, get off the water; it can be dangerous. Resident deer, including bucks with spectacular racks, can be like pets on late summer evenings.

**Campsites, facilities:** There are 65 RV sites with full hookups (30 amps), including some pull-through sites; a separate grassy area for tents only; and cabin and RV rentals. Picnic tables and fire grills are provided. Restrooms with showers, a coin laundry, satellite TV hookups, Wi-Fi, a dump station, convenience store, propane gas, diesel, bait and tackle, video rentals, RV supplies, firewood, and recreation room are available. A boat ramp, dock, and boat slips are nearby. Some facilities are wheelchair-accessible. Leashed pets are permitted.

**Reservations, fees:** Reservations are recommended. RV sites are $36.50-38.50 per night, tent sites are $25 per night, plus $5 per night for each additional person for more than four people and $1 per pet per night. Cabins and trailers are also available. Some credit cards are accepted. Open late May through early November, weather permitting.

**Directions:** From Red Bluff, drive east on Highway 36 toward Susanville. Just before reaching Susanville, turn left on County Road A1 and drive approximately 25 miles to County Road 518 near Spalding Tract. Turn right on County Road 518 and drive through a small neighborhood to The Strand (the lake frontage road). Turn right on The Strand and drive about eight blocks to Palmetto Way and the entrance to the store and the park entrance at 687-125 Palmetto Way. Register at the store.

**Contact:** Eagle Lake RV Park, 530/825-3133, www.eaglelakeandrv.com.

## 89 CHRISTIE

### Scenic rating: 7

on Eagle Lake in Lassen National Forest

**Map 3.4, page 184**

This camp is set along the southern shore of Eagle Lake at 5,100 feet. Eagle Lake, with 100 miles of shoreline, is well known for its big trout (hooray) and big winds (boo). The camp offers some protection from the north winds. Its location is also good for seeing osprey in the Osprey Management Area, which covers a six-mile stretch of shoreline just two miles to the north above Wildcat Point. A nearby resort is a bonus. The nearest boat ramp is at Gallatin Marina. A five-mile-long paved trail runs from Christie to Aspen Grove Walk-In (see listing in this chapter), perfect for hiking, cycling, and horseback riding.

**Campsites, facilities:** There are 69 individual sites and 10 double sites for tents or RVs up to 50 feet (no hookups). Picnic tables and fire grills are provided. Drinking water and restrooms with electricity and flush toilets are available. Some facilities are wheelchair-accessible. A grocery store is nearby. A dump station is 2.5 miles away at Merrill Campground. Leashed pets are permitted. A campground host is on-site.

**Reservations, fees:** Reservations are accepted at 877/444-6777 ($10 reservation fee) or www.recreation.gov ($9 reservation fee). Single sites are $20 per night, double sites are $30 per night, plus $3-5 per night for each additional vehicle. Open May through October, weather permitting.

**Directions:** From Red Bluff, drive east on Highway 36 toward Susanville. Three miles before Susanville turn left on Eagle Lake Road/County Road A1 and drive 19.5 miles to the campground on the right side of the road.

**Contact:** Lassen National Forest, Eagle Lake Ranger District, 530/257-4188, www. fs.usda.gov/lassen (Nov.-Apr.); Lassen Cougar Enterprises, 530/825-3454 (May-Oct.).

## 90 MERRILL

### Scenic rating: 8
on Eagle Lake in Lassen National Forest

**Map 3.4, page 184**

This is one of the largest, most developed Forest Service campgrounds in the entire county. It is along the southern shore of Eagle Lake at 5,100 feet. The nearest boat launch is at Gallatin Marina, where there is a developed swim beach.

**Campsites, facilities:** There are 300 individual sites and two double sites with full or partial hookups (30 and 50 amps) for tents or RVs up to 50 feet. Picnic tables and fire rings are provided. Drinking water and flush toilets are available. A camp host is on-site. A grocery store, Wi-Fi access, a dump station, and a boat ramp are nearby. Some facilities are wheelchair-accessible. Leashed pets are permitted.

**Reservations, fees:** Reservations are accepted at 877/444-6777 ($10 reservation fee) or www. recreation.gov ($9 reservation fee). Single sites are $20 per night and double sites are $30 per night (no hookups); it's $30 per night for sites with partial hookups and $35 per night for sites with full hookups; group sites with partial hookups are $60 per night; and it costs $3-5 per night for each additional vehicle. Open May through October, weather permitting.

**Directions:** From Red Bluff, drive east on Highway 36 toward Susanville. Three miles before Susanville, turn left on Eagle Lake Road/County Road A1 and drive 17.5 miles to the campground on the right side of the road.

**Contact:** Lassen National Forest, Eagle Lake Ranger District, 530/257-4188, www. fs.usda.gov/lassen (Nov.-Apr.); Lassen Cougar Enterprises, 530/825-3454 (May-Oct.); camp host 530/825-3450.

## 91 ASPEN GROVE WALK-IN

### Scenic rating: 7
on Eagle Lake in Lassen National Forest

**Map 3.4, page 184**

Eagle Lake is known as one of the great trout lakes in California, producing the fast-growing and often huge Eagle Lake rainbow trout. All water sports are allowed and, with 100 miles of shoreline, there's plenty of room for everyone—just be prepared for cold water. This camp is one of four at the south end of the lake and is a popular choice for anglers, with a boat ramp adjacent to the campground. A bonus is a good chance to see bald eagles and ospreys. A five-mile-long paved, wheelchair-accessible recreation trail runs from this campground to Christie Campground and then continues to other campgrounds.

One problem with Eagle Lake is the wind, which can whip the shallow lake into a froth in the early summer. (It is imperative that anglers/boaters get on the water early, and then get back to camp early, with the fishing for the day often done by 10:30am.) A newer problem is the recent drawdown; the lake has been drawn down to the point that several boat ramps and marinas are high and dry.

**Campsites, facilities:** There are 28 tent sites. Picnic tables and fire grills are provided. Drinking water and flush toilets are available. A boat ramp is nearby. There are no wheelchair facilities for campers. Leashed pets are permitted.

**Reservations, fees:** Reservations are accepted for some sites at 877/444-6777 ($10 reservation fee) or www.recreation.gov ($9 reservation fee).

Sites are $20 per night. Open May through September.

**Directions:** From Red Bluff, drive east on Highway 36 toward Susanville. Three miles before Susanville, turn left on Eagle Lake Road/County Road A1 and drive 15.5 miles to County Road 231. Turn right on County Road 231 and drive two miles to the campground on the left side of the road. Walk a short distance to the campsites.

**Contact:** Lassen National Forest, Eagle Lake Ranger District, 530/257-4188, www. fs.usda.gov/lassen (Nov.-Apr.); Lassen Cougar Enterprises, 530/825-3454 (May-Oct.).

## 92 WEST EAGLE GROUP CAMPS

### Scenic rating: 9

on Eagle Lake in Lassen National Forest

**Map 3.4, page 184**

If you are coming in a big group to Eagle Lake, you'd better get on the telephone first and reserve this camp. Then you can have your own private slice of solitude along the southern shore of Eagle Lake. Bring your boat; the Gallatin Marina and a swimming beach are only about a mile away. The elevation is 5,100 feet.

**Campsites, facilities:** There are two group camps for tents or RVs up to 35 feet (no hookups) that can accommodate 75 and 100 people, respectively. Picnic tables and fire grills are provided. Drinking water, flush toilets, electricity, and picnic areas may be available. (The water system was under repair at time of publication.) A grocery store, dump station, and boat ramp are nearby. Some facilities are wheelchair-accessible. Leashed pets are permitted.

**Reservations, fees:** Reservations are required at 877/444-6777 ($10 reservation fee) or www. recreation.gov ($9 reservation fee). Sites are $125 per night. Open May through October, weather permitting.

**Directions:** From Red Bluff, drive east on Highway 36 toward Susanville. Three miles before Susanville, turn left on Eagle Lake Road/County Road A1 and drive 15.5 miles to County Road 231. Turn right on County Road 231 and drive 0.25 mile to the campground on the left side of the road.

**Contact:** Lassen National Forest, Eagle Lake Ranger District, 530/257-4188, www. fs.usda.gov/lassen (Nov.-Apr.); Lassen Cougar Enterprises, 530/825-3454 (May-Oct.).

## 93 EAGLE

### Scenic rating: 8

on Eagle Lake in Lassen National Forest

**Map 3.4, page 184**

Eagle is set just up the road from Aspen Grove Walk-In, which is more popular because of the boat ramp nearby. The elevation is 5,100 feet. (See the Aspen Grove Walk-In listing in this chapter for information about Eagle Lake.)

**Campsites, facilities:** There are 50 individual sites and two double sites for tents or RVs up to 25 feet and two accessible sites with hookups. Picnic tables and fire grills are provided. Drinking water and flush toilets are available. Some facilities are wheelchair-accessible. There is a boat launch nearby at Gallatin Marina. Leashed pets are permitted.

**Reservations, fees:** Reservations are accepted at 877/444-6777 ($10 reservation fee) or www. recreation.gov ($9 reservation fee). Single sites are $20 per night, double sites are $30 per night, accessible sites are $35 per night, and it's $5 per night for each additional vehicle. Open May through October, weather permitting.

**Directions:** From Red Bluff, drive east on Highway 36 toward Susanville. Three miles before Susanville, turn left on Eagle Lake Road/County Road A1 and drive 15.5 miles to County Road 231. Turn right and drive 0.5 mile to the campground on the left side of the road.

**Contact:** Lassen National Forest, Eagle Lake Ranger District, 530/257-4188, www.

fs.usda.gov/lassen (Nov.-Apr.); Lassen Cougar Enterprises, 530/825-3454 (May-Oct.).

# 94 GOUMAZ

### Scenic rating: 7
on the Susan River in Lassen National Forest

Map 3.4, page 184

This camp is beside the Susan River, adjacent to the historical Bizz Johnson Trail, a former route for a rail line that has been converted to a 25-mile trail. The trail runs from Susanville to Westwood, but this section provides access to many of its prettiest and most remote stretches as it runs in a half circle around Pegleg Mountain (7,112 feet) to the east. It is an outstanding route for biking, hiking, and horseback riding in the summer and cross-country skiing in the winter. Equestrian campers are welcome. Elevation is 5,200 feet.

**Campsites, facilities:** There are five sites for tents or RVs up to 25 feet (no hookups). Picnic tables and fire grills are provided. Drinking water and vault toilets are available. Leashed pets are permitted.

**Reservations, fees:** Reservations are not accepted. There is no fee for camping. Open May through October, weather permitting.

**Directions:** From Red Bluff, drive east on Highway 36 past Lake Almanor to the junction with Highway 44. Turn west on Highway 44 and drive six miles (one mile past the Worley Ranch) to Goumaz Road/Forest Road 30N08. Turn left on Goumaz Road and drive about five miles to the campground entrance road on the right.

**Contact:** Lassen National Forest, Eagle Lake Ranger District, 530/257-4188, www.fs.usda. gov/lassen.

# 95 ROXIE PECONOM WALK-IN

### Scenic rating: 5
in Lassen National Forest

Map 3.4, page 184

This small camp, at 4,800 feet elevation, is next to Willard Creek, a seasonal stream in eastern Lassen National Forest. It's shaded and quiet. The camp requires only about a 100-foot walk from the parking area. The best nearby recreation is the Bizz Johnson Trail, with a trailhead on Highway 36 (two miles east) at a parking area on the left side of the highway. This is an outstanding biking and hiking route.

**Campsites, facilities:** There are 10 walk-in tent sites. Picnic tables and fire rings are provided. Drinking water and vault toilets are available. Garbage must be packed out. Leashed pets are permitted.

**Reservations, fees:** Reservations are not accepted. There is no fee for camping. Open May through October, weather permitting.

**Directions:** From Red Bluff, drive east on Highway 36 past Lake Almanor and continue past Fredonyer Pass for three miles to Forest Road 29N03 on the right. Turn right and drive two miles to the campground parking area on the right. Park and walk 100 feet to the campground.

**Contact:** Lassen National Forest, Eagle Lake Ranger District, 530/257-4188, www.fs.usda. gov/lassen.

# 96 BOULDER CREEK

### Scenic rating: 7
at Antelope Lake in Plumas National Forest

Map 3.4, page 184

Antelope Lake is a pretty mountain lake circled by conifers, with nice campsites and good trout fishing. It is at 5,000 feet elevation in remote eastern Plumas National Forest, far enough away so the marginally inclined never make the trip. Campgrounds are at each end of the lake (this one is just north of Lone Rock at the north end), with a boat ramp at Lost Cove on the east side of the lake. All water sports are permitted, and swimming is best near the campgrounds. The lake isn't huge, but it is big enough, with 15 miles of shoreline and little islands, coves, and peninsulas to give it an intimate feel.

**Campsites, facilities:** There are 70 sites for tents or RVs up to 40 feet (no hookups). Picnic tables and fire grills are provided. Drinking water and vault toilets are available. Some facilities are wheelchair-accessible. Leashed pets are permitted.

**Reservations, fees:** Reservations are accepted at 877/444-6777 ($10 reservation fee) or www. recreation.gov ($9 reservation fee). Standard sites are $23 per night; lakeside sites are $25 per night. There is a $7 boat launch fee. Open May through early September.

**Directions:** From Red Bluff, drive east on Highway 36 to Susanville and U.S. 395. Turn south on U.S. 395 and drive about 10 miles (one mile past Janesville) to County Road 208. Turn right on County Road 208 (signed Antelope Lake) and drive about 15 miles to a Y (one mile before Antelope Lake). Turn left at the Y and drive four miles to the campground entrance on the right side of the road (on the northwest end of the lake).

**Contact:** Plumas National Forest, Mt. Hough Ranger District, 530/283-0555, www.fs.usda. gov/plumas or www.royalelkparkmanagement. com.

## 97 LONE ROCK

Scenic rating: 9

at Antelope Lake in Plumas National Forest

Map 3.4, page 184

This camp provides an option to nearby Boulder Creek, to the immediate north at the northwest shore of Antelope Lake. (See the Boulder Creek listing for more information.) The elevation is 5,000 feet. Campfire programs are offered in the summer at the on-site amphitheater.

**Campsites, facilities:** There are 87 sites for tents or RVs up to 40 feet (no hookups). Picnic tables and fire grills are provided. Drinking water and vault toilets are available. Some facilities are wheelchair-accessible. Leashed pets are permitted.

**Reservations, fees:** Reservations are accepted at 877/444-6777 ($10 reservation fee) or www. recreation.gov ($9 reservation fee). Sites are $23-25 per night. There is a $7 boat launch fee. Open May through October.

**Directions:** From Red Bluff, drive east on Highway 36 to Susanville and U.S. 395. Go south on U.S. 395 and drive about 10 miles (one mile past Janesville) to County Road 208. Turn right on County Road 208 (signed Antelope Lake) and drive about 15 miles to a Y (one mile before Antelope Lake). Turn left at the Y and drive three miles to the campground entrance on the right side of the road (on the northwest end of the lake).

**Contact:** Plumas National Forest, Mt. Hough Ranger District, 530/283-0555, www.fs.usda. gov/plumas or www.royalelkparkmanagement. com.

## 98 LONG POINT

Scenic rating: 7

at Antelope Lake in Plumas National Forest

Map 3.4, page 184

Long Point is a pretty camp on a peninsula that extends well into Antelope Lake, facing Lost Cove. The lake's boat ramp is at Lost Cove, a three-mile drive around the northeast shore. Fishing is often good for both rainbow and brown trout, and there is a nature trail. A group campground is within this campground.

**Campsites, facilities:** There are 38 sites for tents or RVs up to 30 feet, along with four group sites for tents or RVs up to 35 feet that can accommodate up to 25 people each (no hookups). Picnic tables and fire grills are provided.

Drinking water and vault toilets are available. A boat ramp is nearby. Some facilities are wheelchair-accessible. Leashed pets are permitted.

**Reservations, fees:** Reservations are accepted for individual sites and required for the group sites at 877/444-6677 ($10 reservation fee) or www.recreation.gov ($9 reservation fee). Single sites are $25 per night, double sites are $50 per night, and it's $75 per night for group sites. Open May through October.

**Directions:** From Red Bluff, drive east on Highway 36 to Susanville and U.S. 395. Go south on U.S. 395 and drive about 10 miles (one mile past Janesville) to County Road 208. Turn right on County Road 208 (signed Antelope Lake) and drive about 15 miles to a Y (one mile before Antelope Lake). Turn right at the Y and drive one mile to the campground entrance on the left side of the road.

**Contact:** Plumas National Forest, Mt. Hough Ranger District, 530/283-0555, www.fs.usda.gov/plumas or www.royalelkparkmanagement.com.

## 99 HONEY LAKE CAMPGROUND

### Scenic rating: 4

near Milford

**Map 3.4, page 184**

Honey Lake is a strange-looking place—a vast, shallow lake set on the edge of the desert of the Great Basin. The campground is at 4,385 feet elevation and covers 30 acres, most of it overlooking the lake. There are a few pine trees in the campground, and a waterfowl management area is along the north shore of the lake. This campground is popular with hunters. Equestrian facilities, including a corral and exercise ring, are available. There are north and south entrances with easy access. The lake is 26 miles across, and on rare flat calm evenings, the sunsets are spectacular.

**Campsites, facilities:** There are 44 sites: Some are pull-through sites for tents or RVs of any length, and most have full or partial hookups (30 amps). There are also 25 mobile homes and trailers. Picnic tables are provided. Amenities include restrooms with showers, a coin laundry, dump station, propane gas, gift and grocery store, playground, ice, and video rentals. Some facilities are wheelchair-accessible. Leashed pets are permitted.

**Reservations, fees:** Reservations are not accepted. RV sites are $21-39.95 per night, tent sites are $17-24 per night per night, and it's $2.50-3.50 per person per night for more than two people. Long-term rentals are available. Some credit cards are accepted. Open year-round.

**Directions:** From Susanville on U.S. 395, drive 17 miles south (if you reach Milford, you have gone two miles too far) to the campground on the west side of the highway. It is 65 miles north of Reno.

**Contact:** Honey Lake Campground, 530/253-2508.

## 100 LAUFMAN

### Scenic rating: 5

in Plumas National Forest

**Map 3.4, page 184**

Laufman is an extremely remote and little-known campground along little Willow Creek at an elevation of 5,100 feet. Though U.S. 395 is a high-use highway between Susanville and Reno, this small camp is overlooked. The shoulder seasons in spring and fall are cold, while spring and early summer can be windy.

**Campsites, facilities:** There are six sites for tents or RVs up to 25 feet (no hookups). Picnic tables and fire grills are provided. Vault toilets are available. No drinking water is available. Garbage must be packed out. Leashed pets are permitted.

**Reservations, fees:** Reservations are not accepted. There is no fee for camping. Open May through September, weather permitting.

**Directions:** From Susanville on U.S. 395, drive

south for 24 miles to Milford. In Milford turn right (southeast) on County Road 336 and drive about four miles to the campground on the right.

**Contact:** Plumas National Forest, Beckwourth Ranger District, 530/836-2575, www.fs.usda. gov/plumas.

## 101 CONKLIN PARK

### Scenic rating: 4

on Willow Creek in Plumas National Forest

**Map 3.4, page 184**

This camp is along little Willow Creek on the northeastern border of the Dixie Mountain State Game Refuge. The campground is little known, primitive, rarely used, and is not likely to change any time soon. The elevation is 5,900 feet.

**Campsites, facilities:** There are nine sites for tents or RVs up to 25 feet (no hookups). Picnic tables and fire grills are provided. Vault toilets are available. No drinking water is available. Garbage must be packed out. Leashed pets are permitted.

**Reservations, fees:** Reservations are not accepted. There is no fee for camping. Open May through October, weather permitting.

**Directions:** From Susanville on U.S. 395, drive south for 24 miles to Milford. In Milford turn right on County Road 336 and drive about four miles to a Y. Bear to the right on Forest Road 70/26N70 and drive three miles. Turn right at the bridge at Willow Creek, turn left on Forest Road 70 (now paved), and drive three miles to the camp entrance road on the left side.

**Contact:** Plumas National Forest, Beckwourth

Ranger District, 530/836-2575, www.fs.usda. gov/plumas.

## 102 MEADOW VIEW EQUESTRIAN

### Scenic rating: 6

near Little Last Chance Creek in Plumas National Forest

**Map 3.4, page 184**

This little-known, primitive camp is set along the headwaters of Little Last Chance Creek, along the eastern border of the Dixie Mountain State Game Refuge. The access road continues along the creek and connects with primitive roads that enter the interior of the game refuge. Side-trip options include Frenchman Lake to the south and the drive up to Dixie Mountain, at 8,323 feet elevation. The camp elevation is 6,100 feet.

**Campsites, facilities:** There are six sites for tents or RVs up to 30 feet (no hookups). Picnic tables and fire grills are provided. Vault toilets are available. No drinking water is available. A horse corral is available across the road from the campground. Garbage must be packed out. Leashed pets are permitted.

**Reservations, fees:** Reservations are not accepted. There is no fee for camping. Open May through October, weather permitting.

**Directions:** From Reno, drive north on U.S. 395 for 43 miles to Doyle. At Doyle, turn west on Doyle Grade Road/County Road 331 (a dirt road most of the way) and drive seven miles to the campground.

**Contact:** Plumas National Forest, Beckwourth Ranger District, 530/836-2575, www.fs.usda. gov/plumas.

# MENDOCINO AND WINE COUNTRY

The Mendocino coast is dramatic and remote with several stellar state parks, while Sonoma Valley produces some of the most popular wines in the world. The Mendocino coast features a series of romantic hideaways and excellent adventuring and hiking. The Fort Bragg area has three state parks, with outstanding recreation, including several easy hikes, many amid redwoods and along pretty streams. Reservations are required far in advance for a campsite at a state park on a summer weekend. A driving tour of Highway 1 along this section of the coast is the fantasy of many. Along the twists and turns of the road are dozens of hidden beaches and untouched coastline to stop and explore. The prize spots are MacKerricher State Park, Salt Point State Park, and Anchor Bay. Inland via U.S. 101 are family-friendly campgrounds at Clear Lake, Lake Berryessa, and Blue Lakes.

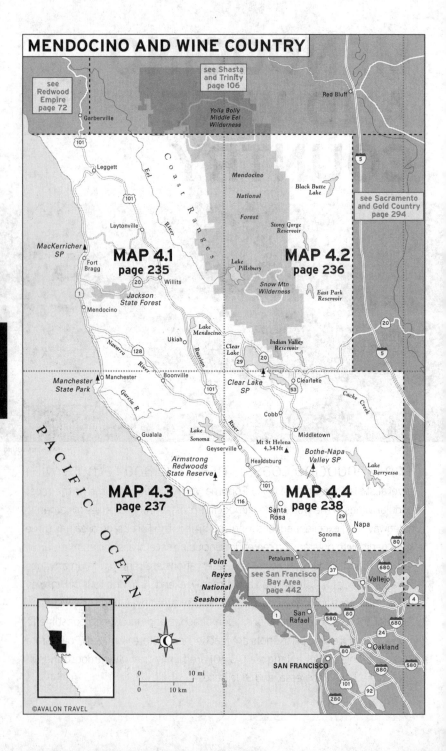

# MENDOCINO AND WINE COUNTRY

see Redwood Empire page 72

see Shasta and Trinity page 106

Garberville

Red Bluff

Yolla Bolly Middle Eel Wilderness

Leggett

Mendocino

National

Forest

Black Butte Lake

see Sacramento and Gold Country page 294

Laytonville

Stony Gorge Reservoir

MacKerricher SP

Fort Bragg

**MAP 4.1 page 235**

Lake Pillsbury

**MAP 4.2 page 236**

Willits

Snow Mtn Wilderness

East Park Reservoir

Jackson State Forest

Mendocino

Lake Mendocino

Ukiah

Clear Lake

Indian Valley Reservoir

Manchester State Park

Manchester

Boonville

Clear Lake SP

Clearlake

Cache Creek

Gualala

Lake Sonoma

Cobb

Middletown

Geyserville

Mt St Helena 4,343ft

Bothe-Napa Valley SP

Lake Berryessa

**MAP 4.3 page 237**

Armstrong Redwoods State Reserve

Healdsburg

**MAP 4.4 page 238**

PACIFIC OCEAN

Santa Rosa

Sonoma

Napa

Point Reyes National Seashore

Petaluma

see San Francisco Bay Area page 442

Vallejo

San Rafael

Oakland

SAN FRANCISCO

0        10 mi
0        10 km

©AVALON TRAVEL

# Map 4.1

## Sites 1-36
## Pages 239-256

4.2

4.3

1 2
3 4

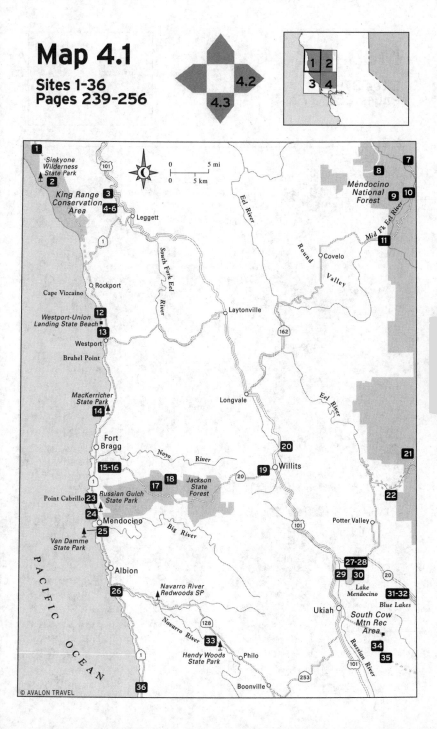

# Map 4.2

## Sites 37-69
## Pages 257-272

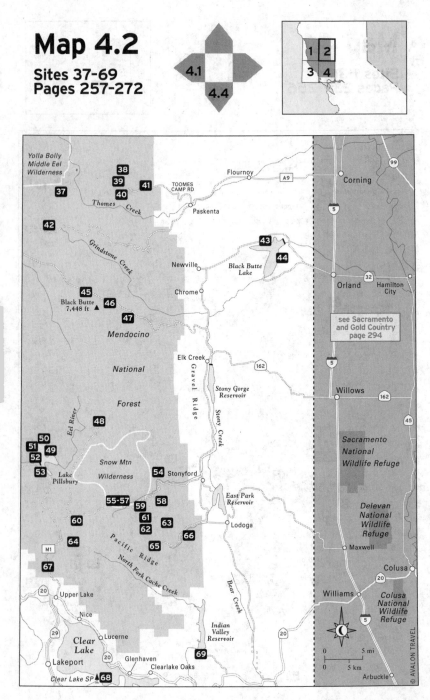

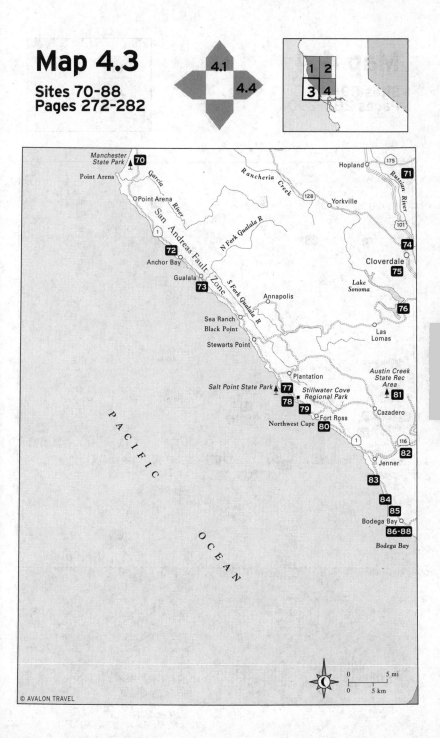

# Map 4.3

**Sites 70-88**
**Pages 272-282**

4.1

4.4

1 2
3 4

Manchester State Park ▲ 70
Point Arena

Rancheria Creek

Hopland
175

71

Russian River

Point Arena

128

Yorkville

Garcia River

San Andreas Fault Zone

101

72
Anchor Bay

N Fork Gualala R

74

Cloverdale

75

Gualala
73

S Fork Gualala R

Annapolis

Lake Sonoma

76

Sea Ranch
Black Point

Las Lomas

Stewarts Point

Austin Creek State Rec Area

Plantation

Salt Point State Park ▲ 77
78

Stillwater Cove Regional Park

▲ 81

Cazadero

79
Northwest Cape

80
Fort Ross

1

116

82

PACIFIC

Jenner

83

84

85
Bodega Bay

86-88

OCEAN

Bodega Bay

N

0        5 mi
0        5 km

© AVALON TRAVEL

# Map 4.4

**Sites 89-104
Pages 283-290**

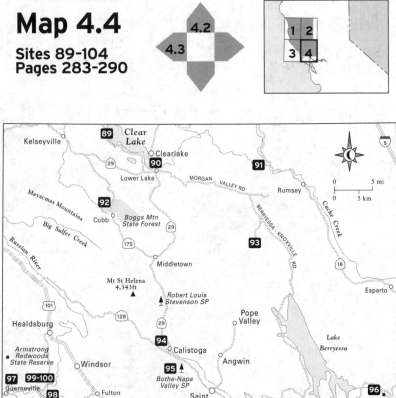

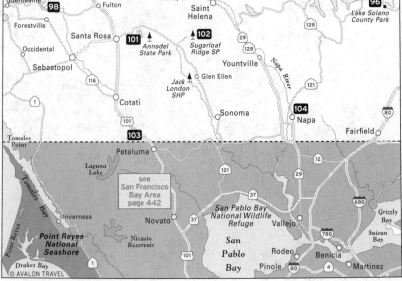

# 1 NADELOS AND WAILAKI

### Scenic rating: 7

in the King Range

**Map 4.1, page 235**

Nadelos and Wailaki campgrounds are a short distance apart at 1,840 feet elevation near the South Fork Bear Creek at the southern end of the King Range National Conservation Area. This provides access to a rare geographic dynamic, where mountains and coast adjoin. Nearby Chemise Mountain, elevation 2,598 feet, is one of the highest points in California within two miles of the sea, and it provides a dramatic lookout on clear days. Nadelos is also one of the few camps with individual sites that can be reserved by a group.

**Campsites, facilities:** There are 13 trailer sites at Nadelos, which is also available as a group site for 20-60 people. There are 13 sites for tents or RVs up to 20 feet (no hookups) at Wailaki. Picnic tables and fire grills are provided. Drinking water and vault toilets are available. Some facilities are wheelchair-accessible. Leashed pets are permitted.

**Reservations, fees:** Reservations for individual sites are not accepted. Reservations for group camping at Nadelos are accepted at 707/986-5400. Individual sites are $8 per night; group sites are $85 per night. Open year-round.

**Directions:** From Eureka, drive 60 miles south on U.S. 101 to the Redway exit. Take the Redway/Shelter Cove exit onto Redwood Drive into the town of Redway. Drive 2.5 miles (look on the right for the King Range Conservation Area sign) to Briceland-Thorne Road. Turn right on Briceland-Thorne Road (which will become Shelter Cove Road) and drive 17 miles to Chemise Mountain Road. Turn left (south) on Chemise Mountain Road and drive one mile to Nadelos Campground on the right. To reach Wailaki Campground from Nadelos, continue 0.4 mile to the camp on the right.

**Contact:** Bureau of Land Management, Arcata Field Office, 707/825-2300, www.blm.gov/ca.

# 2 SINKYONE WILDERNESS

### Scenic rating: 10

in Sinkyone Wilderness State Park

**Map 4.1, page 235**

This is a great jumping-off point for a backpacking trip in the Sinkyone Wilderness on the Lost Coast, one of the few wilderness areas where a trip can be made any month of the year. The terrain is primitive, steep, and often wet, but it provides a rare coastal wilderness experience. Starting at the northern trailhead at Orchard Camp, or the southern trailhead at the Usal Beach campground, it's an ambitious weekend tromp of 17 miles. This is a unique 7,367-acre park that is named after the Sinkyone tribe, which once lived in this area. It is called the Lost Coast because no highways provide direct access. Regardless, it has become surprisingly popular for backpackers on the California Coastal Trail. Annual rainfall is up to 80 inches per year, mostly between November and May. Summer temperatures range 45-75°F, with morning and evening fog common.

**Campsites, facilities:** At Usal Beach, there are 35 tent sites. Picnic tables and fire rings are provided. Pit toilets are provided. No drinking water is available, and garbage must be packed out. Between Bear Harbor and Jones Beach there are 23 tent sites with picnic tables, fire rings, and pit toilets (bring your own toilet paper). Drinking water is available at the Needle Rock Visitor Center where there is a single developed campsite. Pets are not permitted at campsites.

**Reservations, fees:** Reservations are not accepted. Sites are $25 per night, the site at Needle Rock Visitor Center is $35 per night, it's $3 per night for each additional vehicle, and trail camp walk-in sites are $5 per night. Open year-round, weather permitting (but roads may be impassable in wet weather).

**Directions:** To reach the northern boundary of the Sinkyone Wilderness from U.S. 101 north of Garberville, take the Redway exit, turn west on Briceland Road, and drive 17 miles to Whitethorn. From Whitethorn continue six more miles to the four-corners fork. Drive straight ahead to the middle left fork and continue 3.5 miles on a dirt road to the Needle Rock Visitor Center (the last nine miles are unpaved).

To reach the southern boundary of the Sinkyone Wilderness from Leggett on U.S. 101, turn southwest on Highway 1 (toward Fort Bragg) and drive 14.66 miles to mile marker 90.88 at County Road 431. Turn right on County Road 431 (a dirt road, often unsigned) and drive six miles to the Usal Beach Campground. Note: The roads can be quite rough and impassable in wet weather. Trailers and RVs are not recommended.

**Contact:** Sinkyone Wilderness State Park, 707/986-7711 or 707/247-3318, www.parks. ca.gov.

## 3 REDWOODS RIVER RESORT

### Scenic rating: 8

on the Eel River

**Map 4.1, page 235**

This resort is situated in a 21-acre grove of redwoods on U.S. 101 and features 1,500 feet of river access, including a sandy beach and two swimming holes. Many of the campsites are shaded. A hiking trail leads from the resort to the Eel River, a walk of just over a quarter mile. This is one in a series of both public and private campgrounds along the highway between Leggett and Garberville. Steelhead and salmon fishing are popular in winter, and the resort provides nearby access to state parks. The elevation is 700 feet.

**Campsites, facilities:** There are 14 tent sites and 27 sites with full hookups (30 amps) for RVs of any length; some sites are pull-through. Eight cabins and eight lodge rooms are also available. At campsites, picnic tables and fire rings are provided. Restrooms with showers, a seasonal heated swimming pool, playground,

recreation room, Wi-Fi, mini mart, coin laundry, group kitchen, dump station, table tennis, basketball, volleyball, badminton, horseshoes, shuffleboard, group facilities, seasonal organized activities, and a seasonal evening campfire are available. Some facilities are wheelchair-accessible. Leashed pets are permitted, with breed restrictions, except in buildings.

**Reservations, fees:** Reservations are recommended in summer. RV sites with full hookups are $35-60 per night, RV sites with partial hookups are $30-38 per night, tent sites are $27-60 per night, rates vary for multi-person sites, and each pet is $2 per night. Camping cabins, standard cabins, motel rooms, and vacation rentals are also available. Off-season discounts are available. Some credit cards are accepted. Open year-round.

**Directions:** From the junction of U.S. 101 and Highway 1 in Leggett, drive north on U.S. 101 for seven miles to the campground entrance on the left.

**Contact:** Redwoods River Resort, 707/925-6249, www.redwoodriverresort.com.

## 4 REDWOOD CAMPGROUND

### Scenic rating: 8

in Standish-Hickey State Recreation Area

**Map 4.1, page 235**

Standish-Hickey covers 1,012 acres in an inland river canyon; the South Fork Eel provides two miles of river frontage. The park is known as "the gateway to the tall trees country" and the Grove Trail contains one of the few virgin stands of redwoods in this area. This is one of three camps in Standish-Hickey State Recreation Area, and it is by far the most unusual. Reaching Redwood Campground requires driving over a temporary "summer bridge," which provides access to a pretty spot along the South Fork Eel River. In early September, out comes the bridge and up comes the river. Redwood Campground is open only in summer and rangers consider it a "premium" camp. There are two other campgrounds at this park (see listings for Rock Creek and Hickey in this chapter). The elevation is 800 feet.

**Campsites, facilities:** There are 63 sites for tents or RVs up to 18 feet (no hookups). No trailers, including pop-up tent trailers, are permitted. Picnic tables, food lockers, and fire rings are provided. Drinking water and restrooms with coin showers and flush toilets are available. Some facilities are wheelchair-accessible. Leashed pets are permitted.

**Reservations, fees:** Reservations are not accepted. Tent sites are $25-75 per night, RV sites are $30-69, and group sites are $169-178 per night. There is a $6 fee for each extra person, and it's $8 per night for each additional vehicle. Open July through Labor Day weekend.

**Directions:** From the junction of U.S. 101 and Highway 1 in Leggett, drive north on U.S. 101 for one mile. The park entrance is on the west (left) side of the road.

**Contact:** Standish-Hickey State Recreation Area, 707/925-6482, www.parks.ca.gov.

## 5 ROCK CREEK

### Scenic rating: 8
in Standish-Hickey State Recreation Area

**Map 4.1, page 235**

This is one of two main campgrounds (the other is Hickey, see listing in this chapter) set in a mixed redwood grove at Standish-Hickey State Recreation Area. This is a classic state park camp, with numbered sites, flat tent spaces, picnic tables, and food lockers. There are 12 miles of hiking trails in the park. Hiking is only fair, but most people enjoy the short tromp down to the nearby South Fork Eel River. In the winter, steelhead migrate through the area. (See the Redwood Campground listing for more details on this park.)

**Campsites, facilities:** There are 35 sites for tents or RVs up to 27 feet (no hookups) and for trailers up to 24 feet; there is one hike-in/bike-in site. Picnic tables, food lockers, and fire rings

are provided. Drinking water and restrooms with coin showers and flush toilets are available. Some facilities are wheelchair-accessible. Leashed pets are permitted.

**Reservations, fees:** Reservations are not accepted at this time. Sites are $35 per night, plus $8 per night for each additional vehicle, and it's $5 per person per night for the hike-in/bike-in site. Open year-round.

**Directions:** From the junction of U.S. 101 and Highway 1 in Leggett, drive north on U.S. 101 for one mile. The park entrance is on the west (left) side of the road.

**Contact:** Standish-Hickey State Recreation Area, 707/925-6482, www.parks.ca.gov.

## 6 HICKEY

### Scenic rating: 8
on the Eel River in Standish-Hickey State Recreation Area

**Map 4.1, page 235**

This is an ideal layover for U.S. 101 cruisers yearning to spend a night in the redwoods. The park is best known for its campsites amid redwoods and for the nearby South Fork Eel River with its steelhead fishing in the winter. The elevation is 800 feet. Insider's tip: There's a great swimming hole on the Eel River in the summer. (See details about Standish-Hickey State Recreation Area in the Redwood Campground listing in this chapter.)

**Campsites, facilities:** There are 63 sites for tents or RVs up to 16 feet (no hookups) and trailers up to 24 feet. Picnic tables, food lockers, and fire rings are provided. Drinking water and restrooms with showers and flush toilets are available. A grocery store is available nearby. Some facilities are wheelchair-accessible. Leashed pets are permitted.

**Reservations, fees:** Reservations are not accepted at this time. Sites are $35 per night, plus $8 per night for each additional vehicle. Hike-in/bike-in sites are $5 per night. Open year-round.

**Directions:** From the junction of U.S. 101 and Highway 1 in Leggett, drive north on U.S. 101 for one mile. The park entrance is on the west (left) side of the road.

**Contact:** Standish-Hickey State Recreation Area, 707/925-6482, www.parks.ca.gov.

## 7 HAMMERHORN

### Scenic rating: 7
on Hammerhorn Lake in Mendocino National Forest

**Map 4.1, page 235**

Hammerhorn Lake is obscure and hidden: a veritable dot of a lake, just five acres, set at 3,500 feet in Mendocino National Forest. The lake is too small for motorized boats, but swimming is allowed. There is a spring at the south end of the lake; if you go out of the camp and hike along the edge of the lake, you can often hear the water running out of the pipe before you see it. The lake is near the border of the Yolla Bolly Wilderness, with Green Springs Trailhead a few miles away to the northeast. A great side trip is the drive up to Anthony Peak.

**Campsites, facilities:** There are nine sites for tents or RVs up to 16 feet (no hookups). Picnic tables and fire grills are provided. Drinking water, vault toilets, and fishing piers are available. Garbage must be packed out. Supplies are available in Covelo. Some facilities are wheelchair-accessible, including two fishing piers. Leashed pets are permitted.

**Reservations, fees:** Reservations are not accepted. Sites are $8 per night. Open May to November.

**Directions:** From Willits, drive north on U.S. 101 for 13 miles to Longvale and the junction with Highway 162. Turn northeast on Highway 162 and drive to Covelo. Continue east on Highway 162 for 12 miles to the Eel River Bridge. After crossing the bridge, turn left on Forest Road M1 and drive about 17 miles to Forest Road M21. Turn right and drive one mile to the campground entrance.

**Contact:** Mendocino National Forest, Covelo Ranger District, 707/983-6118, www.fs.usda.gov/mendocino.

## 8 RATTLESNAKE CREEK

### Scenic rating: 7
in Mendocino National Forest

**Map 4.1, page 235**

This camp is so small and secret that it is not even listed on the Forest Service website. It has only two tent sites and is located relatively near Green Springs Camp (at the southern end of the Yolla Bolly Wilderness). The secret at Rattlesnake Creek is that a swimming hole is just upstream of the bridge near the campground. Very few people know about this, or the campground either. The elevation is 4,000 feet.

**Campsites, facilities:** There are two primitive sites for tents only. There is no drinking water, and garbage must be packed out.

**Reservations, fees:** Reservations are not accepted. There is no fee for camping.

**Directions:** From Willits, drive north on U.S. 101 for 13 miles to Longvale and the junction with Highway 162. Turn northeast on Highway 162 and drive to Covelo. Continue east on Highway 162 for 12 miles to the Eel River Bridge. Drive across the bridge and turn left on Forest Service Road M1/Indian Dick Road. Drive about 17 miles on Forest Service Road M1/Indian Dick Road to Forest Service Road M21. From that junction, drive north on Indian Dick Road for five miles. Cross the cement bridge at Rattlesnake Creek and turn left to the camp.

**Contact:** Mendocino National Forest, Covelo Ranger District, 707/983-6118, www.fs.usda.gov/mendocino.

# 9 HOWARD MEADOWS AND HOWARD LAKE

**Scenic rating: 8**

near Howard Lake in Mendocino National Forest

**Map 4.1, page 235**

Howard Lake is a small lake deep in Mendocino National Forest. It is pretty and larger than Hammerhorn Lake to the north. If the tiny campground at Howard Lake is occupied, the camp at Howard Meadows is within walking distance. The elevation is 3,500 feet.

**Campsites, facilities:** There are four sites for tents or small RVs at Howard Lake; one site is wheelchair-accessible. There are six sites for tents or small RVs at Howard Meadows. Picnic tables and fire rings are provided. Vault toilets are available, but there is no drinking water. Garbage must be packed out.

**Reservations, fees:** Reservations are not accepted. Sites are $6 per night. Open mid-May to November.

**Directions:** From Willits, drive north on U.S. 101 for 13 miles to Longvale and the junction with Highway 162. Turn northeast on Highway 162 and drive 29 miles to Covelo. Continue east on Highway 162 and drive nine miles to the Eel River Bridge. After crossing the bridge, turn left on Forest Service Road M1/Indian Dick Road. Drive 12 miles to the campground.

**Contact:** Mendocino National Forest, Covelo Ranger District, 707/983-6118, www.fs.usda. gov/mendocino.

# 10 LITTLE DOE

**Scenic rating: 5**

near Howard Lake in Mendocino National Forest

**Map 4.1, page 235**

Little Howard Lake is tucked deep in the interior of Mendocino National Forest between Espee Ridge to the south and Little Doe Ridge to the north, at an elevation of 3,600 feet. For a drive-to lake, it is surprisingly remote and provides fair trout fishing, primitive camping, and an opportunity for car-top boating. The lake covers 15-20 acres, and swimming is allowed. Side trips include Hammerhorn Lake, about six miles away, and several four-wheel-drive roads that allow you to explore the area. A Forest Service map is recommended.

**Campsites, facilities:** There are 13 sites for tents or RVs up to 16 feet (no hookups). Picnic tables and fire pits are provided. Vault toilets are available. No drinking water is available. Garbage must be packed out. No gas motors are allowed. Supplies are available in Covelo, 25 miles away. Leashed pets are permitted.

**Reservations, fees:** Reservations are not accepted. Sites are $6 per night. Open mid-May to November.

**Directions:** From Willits, drive north on U.S. 101 for 13 miles to Longvale and the junction with Highway 162. Turn northeast on Highway 162 and drive 29 miles to Covelo. Continue east on Highway 162 and drive nine miles to the Eel River Bridge. After crossing the bridge, turn left on Forest Road M1/Indian Dick Road and drive 14 miles to the campground.

**Contact:** Mendocino National Forest, Covelo Ranger District, 707/983-6118, www.fs.usda. gov/mendocino.

# 11 EEL RIVER

**Scenic rating: 8**

in Mendocino National Forest

**Map 4.1, page 235**

This little-known spot sits in oak woodlands at the confluence of the Middle Fork of the Eel River and Black Butte River. The elevation is 1,500 feet, and it's often extremely hot in summer. Eel River is an ancient Native American campsite and a major archaeological site. For this reason restoration has been limited and at times the camp is overgrown and weedy. Who cares, though? After all, you're camping.

**Campsites, facilities:** There are 15 sites for tents or RVs up to 21 feet (no hookups). Picnic tables and fire grills are provided. Drinking water (seasonally) and vault toilets are available. Garbage must be packed out. Leashed pets are permitted.

**Reservations, fees:** Reservations are not accepted. Sites are $8 per night. Open mid-May to November.

**Directions:** From Willits, drive north on U.S. 101 for 13 miles to Longvale and the junction with Highway 162. Turn northeast on Highway 162 and drive to Covelo. Continue east on Highway 162 for 13 miles to the campground.

**Contact:** Mendocino National Forest, Covelo Ranger District, 707/983-6118, www.fs.usda.gov/mendocino.

## 12 WESTPORT-UNION LANDING STATE BEACH

**Scenic rating: 8**

near Westport overlooking the Pacific Ocean

**Map 4.1, page 235**

This campground is considered primitive by state park standards. Sites are set on an ocean bluff and it can get windy, but the reward is the view. This park covers more than three miles of rugged and scenic coastline. Splendid views, colorful sunsets, and tree-covered mountains provide great photo opportunities. Several small sandy beaches and one large beach at the mouth of Howard Creek provide some good spots for surf fishing. Several species of rockfish and abalone can be taken when tides and ocean conditions are right. But note that the surf can surge, discouraging all but the hardy. The park was named for two early-day communities, Westport and Union Landing—settlements well known for lumber and rail ties. The northern Mendocino coast is remote, beautiful,

and gets far less people pressure than the Fort Bragg area. That is the key to its appeal.

**Campsites, facilities:** There are 85 sites for tents or RVs of any length (no hookups); eight people maximum per site. Dispersed hike-in/bike-in sites are also available. Picnic tables and fire rings are provided. Drinking water and chemical flush toilets are available. Call before planning a trip, though, as some services may be reduced or eliminated. A grocery store is nearby. Leashed pets are permitted.

**Reservations, fees:** Reservations are not accepted. Sites are $25 per night, plus $8 per night for each additional vehicle, and hike-in/bike-in sites are $5 per night. Open year-round.

**Directions:** From Fort Bragg, drive north on Highway 1 to Westport. In Westport, continue north on Highway 1 for three miles to the campground entrance on the west side of the road.

**Contact:** California State Parks, Mendocino District, 707/937-5804, www.parks.ca.gov.

## 13 WESTPORT BEACH RV PARK AND CAMPGROUND

**Scenic rating: 8**

near Westport overlooking the Pacific Ocean

**Map 4.1, page 235**

Westport Beach campground sits above the beach near the mouth of Wages Creek, with both creekside and beach sites. The 30-acre campground has a quarter mile of beach frontage. As you venture north from Fort Bragg, the number of vacationers in the area falls way off, providing a chance for quiet beaches and serene moments. The best nearby hiking is to the north out of the trailhead for the Sinkyone Wilderness.

**Campsites, facilities:** There are 75 sites for RVs of any length with full hookups (20, 30, and 50 amps), seven sites for RVs of any length (no hookups), 50 sites for tents only, and five group sites for tents or RVs (no hookups) that can accommodate 12-50 people each. Some RV sites are pull-through. Beach camping is possible. A cabin, cottage, and tepee are also available. Picnic tables and fire rings are provided at most sites. Drinking water, restrooms with flush toilets and coin showers, a convenience store, coin laundry, telephone, Wi-Fi, playground, volleyball, shuffleboard, horseshoes, firewood, and ice are available. Some facilities are wheelchair-accessible. Leashed pets are permitted.

**Reservations, fees:** Reservations are accepted at 707/964-2964 or online at www.westport-beachrvpark.com. RV sites are $56 per night (full or partial hookups), tent sites are $42 per night, and group sites are $140 per night (for up to eight people). Cabins are $185 per night; the tepee is $80 per night. There is a fee of $5-7 per night per person for more than two people, and each pet is $2 per night. Some credit cards are accepted. Open year-round.

**Directions:** From Fort Bragg, drive north on Highway 1 to Westport. In Westport, continue north on Highway 1 for 0.5 mile to the campground entrance on the west side of the highway.

**Contact:** Westport Beach RV Park and Campground, 707/964-2964, www.westport-beachrvpark.com.

## 14 MACKERRICHER STATE PARK

### Scenic rating: 9

north of Fort Bragg overlooking the Pacific Ocean

**Map 4.1, page 235**

MacKerricher is a beautiful park on the Mendocino coast, a great destination for adventure and exploration. The camps are set in a coastal forest, with gorgeous walk-in sites. Nearby features include a small beach, great tidepools, a rocky point where harbor seals hang out in the sun, a small lake (Cleone) with trout fishing, a great bike trail, and outstanding short hikes. The short jaunt around little Cleone Lake has many romantic spots, often tunneling through vegetation then emerging for lake views. The coastal walk to the point to see seals and tidepools is equally captivating. For wheelchair users, a wheelchair-accessible trail leads to Laguna Point and a raised boardwalk runs halfway around Cleone Lake, a former tidal lagoon. This park covers more than 1,530 acres of beach, bluff, headlands, dune, forest, and wetlands. That diverse landscape provides habitat for more than 90 species of birds, most in the vicinity of Cleone Lake. The headland supplies a prime vantage point for whale-watching in winter and spring.

**Campsites, facilities:** There are 140 sites for tents or RVs up to 35 feet (no hookups), 10 walk-in sites, and two group sites for up to 40-60 people each. Picnic tables, fire rings, and food lockers are provided. Drinking water, restrooms with flush toilets and coin showers, a picnic area, Wi-Fi, and a dump station are available. A seasonal junior ranger program with nature walks, campfire programs, and exhibits may be offered. Call before planning a trip, though, as some services may be reduced or eliminated. Some facilities are wheelchair-accessible.

**Reservations, fees:** Reservations are accepted at 800/444-7275 ($10 reservation fee) or www.reserveamerica.com ($9 reservation fee); family campsites are now site-specific. Drive-in sites are $35 per night, plus $8 per night for each additional vehicle; walk-in tent sites are $25 per night; hike-in/bike-in sites are $5 per night. Group sites are $200-260 per night. Open year-round.

**Directions:** From Fort Bragg, drive north on Highway 1 for three miles to the campground entrance on the left side of the road.

**Contact:** MacKerricher State Park, 707/964-9112; Mendocino District, 707/937-5804, www.parks.ca.gov.

## 15 FORT BRAGG LEISURE TIME RV PARK

🏃 🚴 ⛵ 🐾 ♿ 🚐 ⛺

**Scenic rating: 5**

in Fort Bragg

**Map 4.1, page 235**

This privately operated park adjoins Jackson State Forest, with easy access for hiking and cycling trails. The park offers horseshoes, badminton, and a covered group picnic area. The drive from Willits to Fort Bragg on Highway 20 is always a favorite, a curving two-laner through redwoods—not too slow, not too fast, best seen from the saddle of a Harley-Davidson. At the end of it is the coast, and just three miles inland is this campground in the sunbelt, said to be out of the fog by breakfast. Within short drives are Noyo Harbor in Fort Bragg, Russian Gulch State Park, Mendocino to the south, and MacKerricher State Park to the north. In fact, there's so much in the area, you could explore for days. Note that about 10 percent of the sites are filled with permanent or long-term renters.

**Campsites, facilities:** There are 70 sites, many with full or partial hookups (30 amps), for tents or RVs up to 40 feet; some sites are pull-through. Picnic tables and fire rings are provided. Restrooms with coin showers, satellite TV, Wi-Fi, a dump station, a fish-cleaning station, horseshoes, RV storage, and a coin laundry are available. Some facilities are wheelchair-accessible. Leashed pets are permitted.

**Reservations, fees:** Reservations are accepted at 800/700-8542. RV sites with full hookups are $35 per night, partial hookup sites are $34 per night, and tent sites are $25 per night, plus $5 per person per night for more than two people, $3 per night for each additional vehicle, $3 per night for first pet, and $2 per night for an additional pet (some breed restrictions). Group rates are available. Monthly and seasonal rates are available. Some credit cards are accepted. Open year-round.

**Directions:** In Fort Bragg at the junction of Highway 1 and Highway 20, turn east on Highway 20 and drive 2.5 miles to the campground entrance on the right side of the road.

**Contact:** Fort Bragg Leisure Time RV Park, 30801 Hwy. 20, 707/964-5994, www.fortbragg-gltrvpark.com.

## 16 POMO RV PARK AND CAMPGROUND

⛵ 🐾 ♿ 🚐 ⛺

**Scenic rating: 7**

in Fort Bragg

**Map 4.1, page 235**

This park covers 17 acres of lush, native vegetation, including rhododendrons, near the ocean. It is one of several camps on the Fort Bragg and Mendocino coast, and groups are welcome. Nearby Noyo Harbor offers busy restaurants, deep-sea fishing, a boat ramp, harbor, and a nice walk out to the Noyo Harbor jetty. Huckleberry picking is also an option. Many of the RV spaces are quite wide at this park.

**Campsites, facilities:** There are 94 sites with full or partial hookups (30 and 50 amps) for RVs of any length and 30 sites for tents. Some sites are pull-through. Picnic tables and fire rings are provided. Restrooms with coin showers, cable TV hookups, Wi-Fi, a convenience store, firewood, ice, RV supplies, propane gas, coin laundry, dump station, fish-cleaning table, group meeting room, horseshoe pits, and a large grass playing field are available. Some facilities are wheelchair-accessible. Leashed pets are permitted.

**Reservations, fees:** Reservations are recommended in the summer. RV sites with hookups are $45-47 per night, tent sites are $30 per night, plus $3-15 per person per night for more than two people and $1 per pet per night. Open year-round.

**Directions:** In Fort Bragg at the junction of Highway 1 and Highway 20, drive south on Highway 1 for one mile to Tregoning Lane. Turn left (east) and drive a short distance to the park at the end of the road.

**Contact:** Pomo RV Park and Campground,

17999 Tregoning Lane, 707/964-3373, www.pomorv.com.

## 17 JACKSON DEMONSTRATION STATE FOREST, CAMP 1

🚶 🐕 ♿ 5% 🚐 ⛺

### Scenic rating: 7

near Fort Bragg

**Map 4.1, page 235**

Primitive campsites set in a vast forest of redwoods and Douglas firs are the prime attraction at Jackson Demonstration State Forest. Even though Highway 20 is a major connecting link to the coast in the summer, these camps get bypassed because they are primitive and largely unknown. Why? Because reaching them requires driving on dirt roads sometimes frequented by logging trucks, and there are few campground signs along the highway. This camp features lots of tree cover, with oaks, redwoods, and madrones. Most of the campsites are adjacent to the south fork of the north fork of the Noyo River, well known among locals but completely missed by most others. A one-mile trail circles the campground; the trailhead is at the day-use area. A DFG hatchery is next to the campground, but note that no fishing is permitted in the river.

**Campsites, facilities:** There are 32 sites for tents or RVs up to 27 feet (no hookups). Tilley, a group site for tents or RVs up to 45 feet, can accommodate 25-150 people. Picnic tables and fire pits are provided. Pit toilets are available. No drinking water is available. A camp host is on-site. Some facilities are wheelchair-accessible. Leashed pets are permitted.

**Reservations, fees:** Reservations are accepted only for the group site at 707/964-5674; advance payment is required. Sites are $15 per night, plus $5 per night for an additional vehicle, and the group site is $50 per night. A camping permit is required and can be obtained from the camp host. Campers are limited to 30 days per year and no more than 14 consecutive days. Open late May through September.

**Directions:** From Willits on U.S. 101, turn west on Highway 20 and drive 27 miles to Forest Road 350 (at mile marker 5.9). Turn right (north) and drive 1.3 miles to the campground.

**Contact:** Jackson Demonstration State Forest, 707/964-5674, www.fire.ca.gov.

## 18 JACKSON DEMONSTRATION STATE FOREST, CAMP 20

🚶 🚴 🐕 5% 🚐 ⛺

### Scenic rating: 6

near Fort Bragg

**Map 4.1, page 235**

A highlight of Jackson Demonstration Forest is a 50-foot waterfall on Chamberlain Creek. Set in a steep canyon at the east end of the forest, amid giant firs and redwoods, it can be reached with a 10-minute walk. Extensive logging roads are good yet challenging for mountain biking. What to do first? Get a map from the State Forestry Department. For driving, the roads are extremely dusty in summer and muddy in winter.

**Campsites, facilities:** There are 30 sites for tents or RVs up to 16 feet (no hookups) and two group sites: Redtail and Horse Camp. Picnic tables and fire rings are provided. Vault toilets are available. No drinking water is available. Corrals are available only at Horse Camp. A camp host is on-site. Leashed pets are permitted.

**Reservations, fees:** Reservations are not accepted for individual sites but are required for group sites at 707/964-5674. Sites are $15 per night, plus $5 per night for each additional vehicle, and the group sites are $50 per night. A camping permit is required and can be obtained from the camp host or the State Department of Forestry and Fire Protection office (802 N. Main St./Hwy 1, Fort Bragg). Campers are limited to 30 days per year and no more than 14 consecutive days. Open late May through September.

**Directions:** From Willits on U.S. 101, turn west on Highway 20 and drive 17 miles. At mile marker 16.9 (just past the Chamberlain Bridge) continue driving for about 0.25 mile to the Dunlap camp entrance on the left.

**Contact:** Jackson Demonstration State Forest, 707/964-5674, www.fire.ca.gov.

## 19 WILLITS-UKIAH KOA

### Scenic rating: 3

near Willits

**Map 4.1, page 235**

This is an ideal spot to park your RV if you plan on taking the Skunk Train west to Fort Bragg. A depot for the train is within walking distance of the campground, and tickets are available at KOA. The campground, which has a western theme, also offers nightly entertainment in summer. The elevation is 1,377 feet.

**Campsites, facilities:** There are 21 sites for tents and 50 sites with full or partial hookups (30 and 50 amps) for RVs of any length. Many sites are pull-through. Twelve cabins and two lodges are also available, as are tepees and rental RVs. Groups can be accommodated. Picnic tables and fire rings are provided. Drinking water, restrooms with flush toilets and showers, Wi-Fi, a playground, seasonal heated swimming pool, mini golf, basketball, volleyball, fishing pond, convenience store, RV supplies, coin laundry, hot tubs, and a dump station are available. Some facilities are wheelchair-accessible. Leashed pets are permitted, with certain restrictions.

**Reservations, fees:** Reservations are accepted at 800/562-8542. RV sites with partial or full hookups are $53-65, tent sites are $40-75 per night, plus $3-4 per person per night for more than two people. Teepees and cabins are $65-135 per night; camping lodges are $60 per night. Monthly rates are available off-season,

and other discounts are available. Some credit cards are accepted. Open year-round.

**Directions:** From Willits at the junction of U.S. 101 and Highway 20, turn west on Highway 20 and drive 1.5 miles to the campground on the right.

**Contact:** Willits-Ukiah KOA, 1600 Hwy. 20, 707/459-6179, www.willitskoa.com or www.koa.com.

## 20 CREEKSIDE CABINS AND RV RESORT

### Scenic rating: 5

north of Willits

**Map 4.1, page 235**

The privately operated park is in a pretty valley, primarily oak/bay woodlands with a sprinkling of conifers. It was previously known as Hidden Valley Campground. The most popular nearby recreation option is taking the Skunk Train in Willits for the ride out to the coast at Fort Bragg. There are two golf courses within six miles. Note that about half of the sites are occupied by long-term renters.

**Campsites, facilities:** There are 50 sites, including 35 with full or partial hookups (20, 30, or 50 amps), for tents or RVs up to 50 feet. Picnic tables are provided, and some sites provide satellite TV, telephone, and Wi-Fi access. Restrooms with showers, ice, a coin laundry, and a dump station are available. Some facilities are wheelchair-accessible. Leashed pets are permitted.

**Reservations, fees:** Reservations are accepted. RV sites with full hookups are $45 per night, RV sites with partial hookups are $35 per night, tent sites are $25 per night, plus $3 per person per night for more than two people. Open year-round.

**Directions:** From Willits on U.S. 101, drive north for 6.5 miles on U.S. 101 to the campground on the east (right) side of the road.

**Contact:** Creekside Cabins and RV Resort, 29801 N. U.S. 101, Willits, 707/459-2521.

## 21 POGIE POINT

### Scenic rating: 7

on Lake Pillsbury in Mendocino National Forest

Map 4.1, page 235

This camp is beside Lake Pillsbury in Mendocino National Forest, in the back of a cove at the lake's northwest corner. When the lake is full, this spot is quite pretty. A boat ramp is about a quarter mile to the south, a bonus. The elevation is 1,900 feet. (For more information about Lake Pillsbury, see the Fuller Grove listing in this chapter.)

**Campsites, facilities:** There are 50 sites for tents or RVs up to 16 feet (no hookups). Picnic tables and fire grills are provided. Drinking water and vault toilets are available. Some facilities are wheelchair-accessible. Leashed pets are permitted.

**Reservations, fees:** Reservations are not accepted. Sites are $16 per night, plus $3 per night for each additional vehicle and $1 per pet per night. Open May through October.

**Directions:** From Ukiah on U.S. 101, drive north to the junction with Highway 20. Turn east (right) on Highway 20 and drive five miles. Turn northeast on East Potter Valley Road toward Lake Pillsbury. Drive 5.9 miles to the town of Potter Valley. Continue on East Potter Valley Road to Eel River Road. Turn right and drive 15 miles to the Eel River Information Kiosk at Lake Pillsbury. Continue for two miles to the campground access road. Turn right and drive a short distance to the campground.

**Contact:** Mendocino National Forest, Upper Lake Ranger District, 707/275-2361, www.fs.usda.gov/mendocino; PG&E Land Services, 916/386-5164, www.pge.com/recreation.

## 22 TROUT CREEK

### Scenic rating: 7

near East Van Arsdale Reservoir

Map 4.1, page 235

Relatively few campers know about this spot. Most others looking over this area are setting up shop at nearby Lake Pillsbury to the east. But if you like to watch the water roll by, this could be your port of call since it sits at the confluence of Trout Creek and the Eel River (not far from the East Van Arsdale Reservoir). Boats can be hand-launched. Insider's tip: Nearby in Potter Valley to the south, the East Fork Russian River (Cold Creek) is stocked with trout during the summer. The elevation is 1,500 feet.

**Campsites, facilities:** There are 17 single sites for tents or RVs up to 30 feet (no hookups), one double site, and three walk-in tent sites. Trailers are not allowed in the lower loop. Fire grills and picnic tables are provided. Drinking water and vault toilets are available. Leashed pets are permitted.

**Reservations, fees:** Reservations are accepted online at www.pge.com/recreation. Sites are $16 per night, plus $5 per night for each additional vehicle and $2 per pet per night. Open mid-April through early September, weather permitting.

**Directions:** From Ukiah on U.S. 101, drive north to the junction with Highway 20. Turn east (right) on Highway 20 and drive five miles to East Potter Valley Road (M8/Eel River Road). Turn northeast on East Potter Valley Road toward Lake Pillsbury and drive 5.9 miles to the town of Potter Valley. Continue on East Potter Valley Road to Eel River Road. Turn right and drive 4.5 miles to the Eel River Bridge. From the bridge, continue two miles to the campground entrance.

**Contact:** PG&E Land Services, 916/386-5164, www.pge.com/recreation.

## 23 CASPAR BEACH RV PARK

### Scenic rating: 8

near Mendocino

**Map 4.1, page 235**

This privately operated park has opportunities for beachcombing, kayaking, fishing, abalone and scuba diving, and good lookouts for whale-watching. The park is across the road from the ocean and somewhat wooded, with a small, year-round creek running behind it. The park is about midway between Fort Bragg and Mendocino, with Fort Bragg five miles to the north. Note that some of the sites are filled with long-term renters.

**Campsites, facilities:** There are 59 sites with full or partial hookups (30 amps) for RVs up to 50 feet, 30 tent sites, and two group tent sites that can accommodate up to 20 people each. Some sites are pull-through. Picnic tables and fire rings are provided. Cable TV, Wi-Fi, restrooms with flush toilets and coin showers, a dump station, a fish-cleaning station, a convenience store, firewood, propane, a playground, a video arcade, video rentals, and a coin laundry are available. Surfboards, boogie boards, and kayaks are available to rent. Some facilities are wheelchair-accessible. Leashed pets are permitted.

**Reservations, fees:** Reservations are accepted. RV sites with full hookups are $46-59 per night, RV sites with partial hookups are $42 per night, tent sites are $38-42 per night, plus $3-5 per person per night for more than two people and $2 per pet per night. Group tent sites are $85 per night and $3-5 per person per night for more than six people. Monthly rates are available. Some credit cards are accepted. Open year-round.

**Directions:** From Mendocino on Highway 1, drive north for 3.5 miles to the Point Cabrillo exit. Turn west on Point Cabrillo Drive and continue 0.75 mile to the campground on the left at 14441 Point Cabrillo Drive.

From Fort Bragg on Highway 1, drive south for 4.5 miles to Point Cabrillo Drive (mile marker 54.6). Turn right and continue 0.75 mile to the campground.

**Contact:** Caspar Beach RV Park, 707/964-3306, www.casparbeachrvpark.com.

## 24 RUSSIAN GULCH STATE PARK

### Scenic rating: 9

north of Mendocino near the Pacific Ocean

**Map 4.1, page 235**

Russian Gulch State Park is near some of California's most beautiful coastline, but the camp speaks to the woods, not the water, with the campsites set in a wooded canyon. They include some of the prettiest and most secluded drive-in sites available on the Mendocino coast. There is a great hike, an easy hour-long walk to Russian Gulch Falls, a wispy 36-foot waterfall that cascades into a rock basin. While it's always pretty, it's awesome in late winter. Much of the route is accessible by bicycle, with a bike rack available where the trail narrows and turns to dirt. In addition, there are many more miles of hiking trails and a few miles of trails for cycling. The park covers more than 1,100 acres with about 1.5 miles of ocean frontage, its rugged headlands thrusting into the Pacific. It rivals Point Lobos for coastal beauty. And yet the park is better known for its heavily forested canyon, Russian Gulch Creek Canyon, and a headland that features the Devil's Punchbowl, a 100-foot-wide and 60-foot-deep blowhole where one can look right in and watch the sea surge. Swim, dive, deep-sea fish for rockfish, or explore the tidepools on the beach.

**Campsites, facilities:** There are 27 sites for tents or RVs up to 24 feet (no hookups), one hike-in/bike-in site, four equestrian sites, and one group site for up to 40 people. Picnic tables, fire grills, and food lockers are provided. Drinking water, coin showers, and flush toilets are available. A seasonal junior ranger program with nature walks, campfire programs, and exhibits is also available. A day-use picnic area, beach access, and recreation hall are nearby. Call before planning a trip, though, as some services may be reduced or eliminated. Some facilities are wheelchair-accessible. Leashed pets are permitted in the campground and on some trails.

**Reservations, fees:** Reservations are accepted at 800/444-7275 ($10 reservation fee) or www. reserveamerica.com ($9 reservation fee). Call 707/937-5804 for equestrian sites. Individual and equestrian sites are $35-45 per night, plus $8 per night for each additional vehicle; the hike-in/bike-in site is $5 per night per person; and the group site is $140 per night. Open mid-March through October, weather permitting, with a two-night maximum stay for hike-in/ bike-in campers.

**Directions:** From Mendocino, drive two miles north on Highway 1 to the campground entrance on the west side of the highway.

**Contact:** Russian Gulch State Park, 707/937-4296; Mendocino District, 707/937-5804, www. parks.ca.gov.

## 25 VAN DAMME STATE PARK

### Scenic rating: 10

near Mendocino

**Map 4.1, page 235**

The campsites at Van Damme are extremely popular, usually requiring reservations, but with a bit of planning your reward is a base of operations in a beautiful park with redwoods and a remarkable fern understory. The hike-in site (about 1.75 miles) on Fern Canyon Trail is perfectly situated for those wishing to take one of the most popular hikes in the Mendocino area, with the trail crossing the Little River several times and weaving among old trees. Just across from the entrance to the park is a small but beautiful coastal bay with a pretty beach,

ideal for launching sea kayaks. The park covers 1,831 acres. A sidelight is the Pygmy Forest, where mature cone-bearing cypress and pine trees are only six inches to eight feet tall. Another favorite is the Bog Trail, where skunk cabbage grows in abundance, most striking when seen in May and June. Ten miles of trails extend through the Little River's fern-rich canyon, and a paved road is popular with cyclists and joggers. Abalone divers explore the waters off the beach. Kayak tours may be available at the beach parking lot in the summer.

**Campsites, facilities:** There are 63 sites for tents or RVs up to 35 feet (no hookups), five for tents only, nine primitive environmental sites, one hike-in/bike-in site, and one group campsite for up to 50 people. Picnic tables, food lockers, and fire grills are provided. Drinking water, restrooms with flush toilets and coin showers, Wi-Fi, and a dump station are available. A seasonal junior ranger program with nature walks, campfire programs, and exhibits is also available. A grocery store and propane gas are nearby. Some facilities are wheelchair-accessible. Leashed pets are permitted at campsites but not in environmental sites.

**Reservations, fees:** Reservations are recommended at 800/444-7275 ($10 reservation fee) or www.reserveamerica.com ($9 reservation fee). Sites are $35-45 per night, plus $8 per night for each additional vehicle; environmental sites are $25 per night; the hike-in/bike-in site is $5 per night per person; and the group site is $160 per night. Open year-round for family camping; group sites are open mid-March through August only.

**Directions:** From Mendocino on Highway 1, drive south for three miles to the town of Little River and the park entrance road on the left (east) side of the road.

**Contact:** Van Damme State Park, 707/937-0851; Mendocino District, 707/937-5804, www. parks.ca.gov.

## 26 NAVARRO BEACH CAMPGROUND

### Scenic rating: 6

near the mouth of the Navarro River in Navarro River Redwoods State Park

**Map 4.1, page 235**

Navarro Beach is a primitive campground that can bail out drivers stuck for a night without a spot. It is small and open, with no tree cover, set near the ocean and the Navarro River. The camp is just south of the Navarro River Bridge.

**Campsites, facilities:** There are 10 sites for tents or RVs up to 30 feet (no hookups). Picnic tables and fire grills are provided. Pit toilets are available, but there is no drinking water. Leashed pets are permitted.

**Reservations, fees:** Reservations are not accepted. Sites are $25 per night, plus $8 per night for each additional vehicle. Open year-round.

**Directions:** From Mendocino, drive 11 miles south on Highway 1 to the junction with Highway 128. Continue 0.8 mile south on Highway 1 and, almost immediately, take the exit for Navarro Bluffs Road. Drive a short distance on Navarro Bluffs Road to the campground (on the south side of the Navarro River Bridge).

**Contact:** Navarro River Redwoods State Park, c/o Hendy Woods State Park, 707/895-3141; Mendocino District, 707/937-5804, www.parks.ca.gov.

## 27 BUSHAY

### Scenic rating: 7

at Lake Mendocino

**Map 4.1, page 235**

Bushay, on the northeast end of Lake Mendocino, is on a point that provides a pretty southern exposure when the lake is full. The lake is five miles long and one mile wide. It offers fishing for striped bass, largemouth bass, smallmouth bass, crappie, catfish, and bluegill,

as well as waterskiing and powerboating. A nearby visitors center features exhibits of local Native American history. The elevation is 750 feet, and the lake covers 1,750 acres and has 15 miles of shoreline. (For more information about Lake Mendocino, see the Chekaka listing in this chapter.)

**Campsites, facilities:** There are 130 sites for tents or RVs up to 35 feet (no hookups). There are three group sites for 80-120 people. Picnic tables, fire rings, and lantern holders are provided. Drinking water, restrooms with showers and vault toilets, a playground (in the adjacent day-use area), group facilities, a dump station, and horse staging facilities are available. The boat ramp is two miles from camp near Kyen Campground. Some facilities are wheelchair-accessible. Leashed pets are permitted.

**Reservations, fees:** Reservations are accepted at 877/444-6777 ($10 reservation fee) or www.recreation.gov ($9 reservation fee). Sites are $25-35 per night, and group sites are $235 per night. Boat launching is free with a camping pass. Open May through September.

**Directions:** From Ukiah, drive north on U.S. 101 for five miles to the Highway 20 turn-off. Drive five miles east on Highway 20. Just after crossing the Russian River bridge, turn left (Inlet Road) and drive approximately one mile to the campground.

**Contact:** U.S. Army Corps of Engineers, Lake Mendocino, 707/467-4200 or 707/462-7581, www.recreation.gov.

## 28 KYEN

### Scenic rating: 7

at Lake Mendocino

**Map 4.1, page 235**

This camp is on the north shore of Lake Mendocino. With the access road off Highway 20 instead of U.S. 101 (as with Chekaka), Kyen can be overlooked by newcomers. A nearby boat ramp makes it especially attractive. (For more information, see the Bushay and Chekaka listings in this chapter.)

**Campsites, facilities:** There are 93 sites for tents or RVs up to 30 feet (no hookups). Picnic tables, fire grills, and lantern holders are provided. Restrooms with showers and flush toilets, a playground (in the adjacent day-use area), a dump station, and a boat ramp are available. Some facilities are wheelchair-accessible. Leashed pets are permitted, except in some day-use areas.

**Reservations, fees:** Reservations are accepted at 877/444-6777 ($10 reservation fee) or www. recreation.gov ($9 reservation fee). Sites are $25-50 per night. Boat launching is free with a camping pass. Open year-round with limited winter facilities.

**Directions:** From Ukiah, drive north on U.S. 101 for five miles to the Highway 20 turnoff. Drive east on Highway 20 to Marina Drive. Turn right and drive 200 yards (past the boat ramp) to the campground.

**Contact:** U.S. Army Corps of Engineers, Lake Mendocino, 707/462-7581, www.recreation.gov.

## 29 CHEKAKA

### Scenic rating: 7

at Lake Mendocino

**Map 4.1, page 235**

Lake Mendocino is known for good striped-bass fishing, waterskiing, and boating. Nearby, upstream of the lake, are Potter Valley and the East Fork Russian River (also called Cold Creek), which provides trout fishing in the summer. A boat ramp adjacent to the dam is a bonus. The elevation is 750 feet. This campground sits beside the dam at the south end of Lake Mendocino, and the Kaweyo Trailhead is nearby. Insider's tip: An 18-hole Frisbee-golf course is at the Chekaka overlook.

**Campsites, facilities:** There are 22 sites for tents or RVs up to 35 feet (no hookups) and one group site for up to 50 people. Picnic tables, lantern hangers, and fire grills are provided.

Drinking water, vault toilets, disc golf, a horse staging area, and a playground are available. A boat ramp is nearby. Some facilities are wheelchair-accessible. Leashed pets are permitted.

**Reservations, fees:** Reservations are accepted at 877/444-6777 ($10 reservation fee) or www. recreation.gov ($9 reservation fee). Single sites are $20 per night; the group site is $40 per night. Boat launching is free with a camping pass. Open early April through September.

**Directions:** From Ukiah, drive north on U.S. 101 to Lake Mendocino Drive. Exit right on Lake Mendocino Drive and continue to the first stoplight. Turn left on North State Street and drive to the next stoplight. Turn right (which will put you back on Lake Mendocino Drive) and drive about two miles to the signed entrance to the campground at Coyote Dam.

**Contact:** U.S. Army Corps of Engineers, Lake Mendocino, 707/462-7581.

## 30 MITI BOAT-IN/HIKE-IN

### Scenic rating: 7

on Lake Mendocino

**Map 4.1, page 235**

This is one of several campgrounds on the north end of Lake Mendocino. Boat ramps are at Kyen at the north end of the lake and at Chekaka at the south end of the lake. The north ramp (Marina Drive off Highway 20) is open 24 hours; the south ramp closes at night.

**Campsites, facilities:** There are 15 boat-in/hike-in sites for tents only. Picnic tables, fire rings, and lantern holders are provided. Vault toilets are available. No drinking water is available. Garbage must be packed out. Leashed pets are permitted.

**Reservations, fees:** Reservations are not accepted. Sites are $8 per night, plus a one-time $3 boat launch fee. Open April through September, weather permitting. (Some sites may be flooded in the spring.)

**Directions:** From Ukiah, drive north on U.S. 101 to the Highway 20 turnoff. For boat-in campers: Drive east on Highway 20 to Marina Drive. Turn right and drive to the north boat ramp of the lake. The campground is approximately one mile by water.

For hike-in campers: Drive five miles east on Highway 20. Just after crossing the Russian River bridge, turn left (Inlet Road) and drive approximately one mile to the Bu-Shay Ranger Station. Park and hike two miles to the campground.

**Contact:** U.S. Army Corps of Engineers, Lake Mendocino, 707/462-7581.

## 31 PINE ACRES BLUE LAKES RESORT

**Scenic rating: 8**

on Upper Blue Lake

**Map 4.1, page 235**

The Blue Lakes are often overlooked because of their proximity to Clear Lake. These lovely lakes offer good fishing for trout, especially in spring and early summer on Upper Blue Lake. (Note: All boats must be certified mussel-free before launching.) Other fish species are bass, crappie, catfish, and bluegill. With a 5-mph speed limit in place, quiet boating is the rule. Lake frontage sites are available, and other bonuses are a sandy beach and a good swimming area. A lawn area is available for tent camping. Note that the RV sites are spaced very close together.

**Campsites, facilities:** There are 17 sites with full or partial hookups (30 amps) for RVs up to 40 feet, a lawn area for dispersed tent camping, six cabins, and four lodge rooms. Two RV sites are pull-through. Rooms and cottages are also available. Picnic tables and barbecues are provided. Restrooms with flush toilets and coin showers, a dump station, group facilities, boat rentals, boat launching, moorings, boat ramp, fish-cleaning station, horseshoes, convenience store, fishing supplies, and lake frontage sites are available. Paddleboats, rowboats, and kayaks are available to rent. Leashed pets are permitted, with certain restrictions.

**Reservations, fees:** Reservations are recommended. RV sites with full hookups are $37-46 per night, tent sites are $37 per night, plus $10 per person per night for more than two people, $8 per night for each additional vehicle, and $2 per pet per night. Boat launching is free for campers. There's a two-night minimum on weekends. Some credit cards are accepted. Open year-round.

**Directions:** From Ukiah, drive north on U.S. 101 for five miles to the junction with Highway 20. Turn east on Highway 20 and drive about 13 miles to Irvine Avenue. Turn right on Irvine Avenue and drive one block to the end of the road and Blue Lakes Road. Turn right and drive a short distance to the resort on the right.

**Contact:** Pine Acres Blue Lakes Resort, 5328 Blue Lakes Road, 707/275-2811, www.bluelakepineacres.com.

## 32 NARROWS LODGE RESORT

**Scenic rating: 8**

on Upper Blue Lake

**Map 4.1, page 235**

One of several campgrounds in the immediate vicinity at Blue Lakes, this is a good fish camp with boat docks and a fish-cleaning station. (Note: All boats must be certified mussel-free before launching.) The Blue Lakes are often overlooked because of their proximity to Clear Lake, but they are a quiet and pretty alternative, with good trout fishing in the spring and early summer, and decent prospects year-round. The lakes are long and narrow with a primarily forested shoreline, and the elevation is 1,400 feet.

**Campsites, facilities:** There are 30 sites with full or partial hookups (50 amps) for tents or RVs of any length, three park-model cabins, two cabins, and 14 motel rooms. Picnic tables are provided. Restrooms with flush toilets and showers, a dump station, Wi-Fi, a recreation room, boat rentals, a pier, a boat ramp, boat slips, fishing supplies, a picnic area, and ice are available. Leashed pets are allowed.

**Reservations, fees:** Reservations are accepted at 800/476-2776. RV and tent sites are $30-45 per night, depending on view and whether hookups are partial or full. There are fees of $5 per person per night for more than two people, $3 per night for each additional vehicle, and $3 per pet per night. Some credit cards are accepted. Open year-round.

**Directions:** From Ukiah, drive north on U.S. 101 for five miles to the junction with Highway 20. Turn east on Highway 20 and drive about 13 miles to Blue Lakes Road. Turn right and drive one mile to the resort.

**Contact:** Narrows Lodge Resort, 5690 Blue Lakes Rd., 707/275-2718 or 800/476-2776, www.thenarrowsresort.com.

## 33 HENDY WOODS STATE PARK

### Scenic rating: 7

near Boonville

**Map 4.1, page 235**

This is a remarkable setting where the flora changes from open valley grasslands and oaks to a cloaked redwood forest with old growth, as if you had waved a magic wand. The campsites are in the forest, with a great trail routed among the old redwoods and up to the Hermit Hut (a fallen redwood stump covered with branches), where a hobo lived for 18 years. No, it wasn't me. There are two virgin redwood groves in the park: Big Hendy (80 acres with a self-guided discovery trail available) and Little Hendy (20 acres). The Navarro River runs the park's length, but note that fishing is forbidden in the park and that catch-and-release fishing is the law from the bridge at the park entrance on downstream; check regulations. The park is in the middle of the Anderson Valley wine district, which will at first seem an unlikely place

to find an 845-acre redwood park, and is not as cold and foggy as the coastal redwood parks.

**Campsites, facilities:** There are 92 sites for tents or RVs up to 35 feet (no hookups), two hike-in/bike-in sites, and three cabins. Picnic tables, food lockers, and fire grills are provided. Drinking water, flush toilets, coin showers, and a dump station are available. A seasonal junior ranger program with nature walks, campfire programs, and exhibits are also available. A grocery store and propane gas station are nearby. Some facilities are wheelchair-accessible. Leashed pets are permitted.

**Reservations, fees:** Reservations are accepted February through August at 877/444-6777 ($10 reservation fee) or www.recreation.gov ($9 reservation fee). September through January, sites are first-come, first-served. Sites are $35-45 per night, plus $10 per night for each additional vehicle; hike-in/bike-in sites are $5 per person per night; and cabins are $50-70 per night. The maximum per site is eight people. Open year-round.

**Directions:** From Cloverdale on U.S. 101, turn northwest on Highway 128 and drive about 35 miles to Philo Greenwood Road. Turn left on Philo Greenwood Road and drive 0.5 mile to the park entrance on the left.

**Contact:** Hendy Woods State Park, 707/895-3141; Mendocino District, 707/937-5804, www.parks.ca.gov.

## 34 RED MOUNTAIN

### Scenic rating: 3

near Ukiah

**Map 4.1, page 235**

Like Mayacmus (see listing in this chapter), this camp is in the Cow Mountain area east of Ukiah. But be forewarned: With 120 miles of trails in the Cow Mountain area, this is a popular spot for off-highway motorcycles. If you don't like bikes, go to the other camp. Besides motorcycle trails, there are opportunities for hiking and hunting. Horseback riding is an option in the northern part of the recreation area.

**Campsites, facilities:** There are 11 tent sites. Picnic tables and fire grills are provided. Vault toilets are available, but there is no drinking water. Leashed pets are permitted.

**Reservations, fees:** Reservations are not accepted. There is no fee for camping. There is a 14-day stay limit. Open year-round, weather permitting.

**Directions:** From U.S. 101 in Ukiah, turn east on Talmage Road and drive 1.5 miles to Eastside Road. Turn right and drive a short distance to Mill Creek Road. Turn left and drive seven miles to the campground entrance road on the right. Turn right and drive 0.25 mile to the campground.

**Contact:** Bureau of Land Management, Ukiah Field Office, 707/468-4000, www.blm.gov/ca.

## 35 MAYACMUS
🏃🐕⛺

### Scenic rating: 5
near Ukiah

**Map 4.1, page 235**

This campground is within the Cow Mountain Recreation Area on the slopes of Cow Mountain, the oft-overlooked wild region east of Ukiah. The primitive area is ideal for hiking and horseback riding. In the fall, it is a popular hunting area as well, for the few who know of it. This section of the recreation area is quiet, with hiking on Mayacmus Trail providing access to Willow Creek, Mill Creek, and several overlooks of Clear Lake to the south. The flora is chaparral and oak/bay grasslands, and the weather is extremely hot in the summer. By the way, off-highway vehicles frequent the southern part of the recreation area but are prohibited in this immediate region.

**Campsites, facilities:** There are six tent sites. Picnic tables and fire grills are provided (sometimes stolen or vandalized). Pit toilets are available. No drinking water is available, but there

is water for animals. Garbage must be packed out. Leashed pets are permitted.

**Reservations, fees:** Reservations are not accepted. There is no fee for camping. Stay limit is 14 days. Open year-round, weather permitting.

**Directions:** From U.S. 101 in Ukiah, turn east on Talmage Road and drive 1.5 miles to Eastside Road. Turn right and drive 0.25 mile to Mill Creek Road. Turn left and drive three miles (just beyond Mill Creek County Park) to the sign for North Cow Mountain at Mendo Rock Road. Turn left and drive five miles to a Y intersection with the campground access road. Bear left and drive one mile to the campground.

**Contact:** Bureau of Land Management, Ukiah Field Office, 707/468-4000, www.blm.gov/ca.

## 36 MANCHESTER BEACH KOA
🏃🏊🎣🐕🔥♿🚐⛺

### Scenic rating: 7
north of Point Arena at Manchester State Beach

**Map 4.1, page 235**

This is a privately operated KOA park beside Highway 1 near the beautiful Manchester State Beach. The cute little log cabins, complete with electric heat, are a great plus. They can provide a great sense of privacy, and after a good sleep, campers are ready to explore the adjacent state park.

**Campsites, facilities:** There are 57 tent sites and 43 sites with full or partial hookups (30 and 50 amps) for tents or RVs (up to 65 feet). There are also two cottages, 27 cabins, and trailers available to rent. Picnic tables, barbecues, and fire rings are provided. Drinking water, restrooms with flush toilets and showers, Wi-Fi, cable TV, heated seasonal pool, spa, disc golf, recreation room, playground, dump station, convenience store, group facilities, ice, firewood, coin laundry, and propane gas are available. Some facilities are wheelchair-accessible.

Leashed pets are permitted, with certain breeds prohibited; call for details.

**Reservations, fees:** Reservations are accepted at 800/562-4188. RV sites are $55 per night, tent sites are $40 per night, plus $3-5 per person per night for more than two people. Groups of 18 or more can reserve sites for $4-13 per person per night, $3 per pet per night. Cabins are $75-197 per night. Hike-in/bike-in sites are $10 per night. Some credit cards are accepted. Open year-round.

**Directions:** From U.S. 101 in Petaluma, take the Washington Street exit. Turn west on Washington Street, drive through Petaluma (Washington Street becomes Bodega Highway), and continue for 17 miles to Highway 1. Continue straight (west) on Highway 1 for eight miles to Bodega Bay. Turn north on Highway 1 and drive 66 miles to Point Arena. Continue north on Highway 1 for about six miles to Kinney Road. Turn west (toward the ocean) and drive one mile to the campground.

**Contact:** Manchester Beach KOA, 44330 Kinney Rd., 707/882-2375, www.manchester-beachkoa.com.

## 37 GREEN SPRINGS FAMILY AND EQUESTRIAN CAMP

🧑‍🤝‍🧑 5% 🚐 ⛺

**Scenic rating: 7**

in Mendocino National Forest

### Map 4.2, page 236

Green Springs is a wilderness trailhead camp and staging area at the southern border for the Yolla Bolly Wilderness. Green Springs is not a destination camp, but rather a launch point. From here, you can head north along the ridge into the Yolla Bolly, what is called the Eel Divide: All water running off the slope to the west runs into the Eel River watershed; all water running to the east runs into the Sacramento River watershed. This is a land of little-known peaks, small creeks, and few people. The elevation is 6,000 feet. There is a good swimming hole at nearby Rattlesnake Creek camp (see listing in this chapter).

**Campsites, facilities:** There are four primitive sites for tents or small RVs. Picnic tables and fire rings are provided. Vault toilets are available, but there is no drinking water. Water is available from a spring but must be boiled or treated before use. Horse corrals are available on a first-come, first-served basis. Garbage must be packed out.

**Reservations, fees:** Reservations are not accepted. There is no fee for camping.

**Directions:** From Willits, drive north on U.S. 101 for 13 miles to Longvale and the junction with Highway 162. Turn northeast on Highway 162 and drive to Covelo. Continue east on Highway 162 for 12 miles to the Eel River Bridge. Drive across the bridge and turn left on Forest Service Road M1/Indian Dick Road. Drive about 17 miles on Forest Service Road M1/Indian Dick Road to Forest Service Road M21. Turn right and drive seven miles to Forest Service Road M2. Turn left on Forest Service Road M2 and drive 1.5 miles to the Green Springs Trailhead on the left.

**Contact:** Mendocino National Forest, Yolla Bolly-Middle Eel Wilderness, 707/983-6118, www.fs.usda.gov/mendocino.

## 38 THREE PRONG

🧑‍🤝‍🧑 5% 🚐 ⛺

**Scenic rating: 6**

in Mendocino National Forest

### Map 4.2, page 236

Three Prong is a remote and primitive campground situated near a large meadow. You'll have a view of fir and pine trees. It gets little use, except in fall as a base camp for hunters. That's about it. The elevation is 5,800 feet.

**Campsites, facilities:** There are six sites for tents or small RVs. Picnic tables and fire rings are provided. Vault toilets are available, but there is no drinking water. Garbage must be packed out.

**Reservations, fees:** Reservations are not

accepted. There is no fee for camping. Open June through October, weather permitting.

**Directions:** From Corning, take County Road A9 west for 20 miles to Paskenta and Forest Road 23N01. Turn west on Forest Road 23N01 and drive to Forest Road 24N13. Turn left on Forest Road 24N13 and drive to the campground.

**Contact:** Mendocino National Forest, Grindstone Ranger District, 530/934-3316; Paskenta Work Center, 530/833-5544, www. fs.usda.gov/mendocino.

## 39 KINGSLEY GLADE

**Scenic rating: 6**

in Mendocino National Forest

**Map 4.2, page 236**

Kingsley Grade is west of Paskenta and Red Bluff. You know what that means, right? Right—it gets smoking hot out here in summer. Like nearby Sugarfoot to the south, this is primarily a base camp for hunters working the eastern slopes of the Eel Divide in the fall. It is in the transition zone where oaks give way to pines. The elevation is 4,500 feet.

**Campsites, facilities:** There are six sites for tents or small RVs. Picnic tables and fire rings are provided. Vault toilets are available, but there is no drinking water. Garbage must be packed out.

**Reservations, fees:** Reservations are not accepted. There is no fee for camping. Open June through October, weather permitting.

**Directions:** From Corning, take County Road A9 west for 20 miles to Paskenta and Forest Road M2/Thomes Road. Turn west on Forest Road M2/Thomes Road (Forest Road 23N01) and drive 18 miles to Forest Road 24N01. Turn left on Forest Road 24N01 and drive 4.3 miles to the campground.

**Contact:** Mendocino National Forest, Grindstone Ranger District, 530/934-3316; Paskenta Work Station, 530/833-5544, www. fs.usda.gov/mendocino.

## 40 SUGARFOOT GLADE

**Scenic rating: 6**

in Mendocino National Forest

**Map 4.2, page 236**

On the east-facing slopes of the Eel Divide, tiny campgrounds are sprinkled in national forest land west of Paskenta and the Sacramento Valley. This one is small, primitive, and so remote that it seems to be in the middle of nowhere. Actually, that is perfect in the fall when hunters use it as a base camp. A small seasonal creek runs through the camp amid a landscape of ponderosa pines and oak trees.

**Campsites, facilities:** There are six sites for tents or small RVs. Picnic tables and fire rings are provided. Vault toilets are available, but there is no drinking water. Garbage must be packed out.

**Reservations, fees:** Reservations are not accepted. There is no fee for camping. Open mid-May to mid-November.

**Directions:** From Corning, take County Road A9 west for 20 miles to Paskenta and Forest Road 23N01. Turn west on Forest Road 23N01 and drive 18 miles to Forest Road 24N01. Turn left on Forest Road 24N01 and drive past Kingsley Glade Campground to Sugarfoot Glade Campground.

**Contact:** Mendocino National Forest, Grindstone Ranger District, 530/934-3316; Paskenta Work Center, 530/833-5544, www. fs.usda.gov/mendocino.

## 41 WHITLOCK

**Scenic rating: 4**

in Mendocino National Forest

**Map 4.2, page 236**

This obscure Forest Service camp is often empty or close to it. It is at 4,300 feet elevation, where conifers have taken over from the valley grasslands to the nearby east. The camp is situated amid good deer range and makes a good hunting base camp in the fall, with a network of Forest Service roads in the area. It is advisable to obtain a Forest Service map.

**Campsites, facilities:** There are five sites for tents or RVs up to 16 feet (no hookups). Picnic tables and fire grills are provided. Vault toilets are available. Drinking water is not available. Garbage must be packed out. Leashed pets are permitted.

**Reservations, fees:** Reservations are not accepted. There is no fee for camping. Open late May through October.

**Directions:** From Corning on I-5, turn west onto County Road A9/Corning Road and drive 20 miles to Paskenta and Toomes Camp Road/County Road 122. Turn right (north) on Toomes Camp Road/County Road 122 and drive 14 miles to the campground on the right.

**Contact:** Mendocino National Forest, 530/934-3316, www.fs.usda.gov/mendocino; Paskenta Work Center, 530/833-5544.

## 42 WELLS CABIN

### Scenic rating: 6

in Mendocino National Forest

**Map 4.2, page 236**

You'll join the 5 Percent Club when you reach this spot. It is one mile from Anthony Peak Lookout (6,900 feet), where, on a clear day, you can get great views all the way to the Pacific Ocean and sweeping views of the Sacramento Valley to the east. This campground is hardly used during the summer and often provides a cool escape from the heat of the valley. The elevation is 6,300 feet.

**Campsites, facilities:** There are 25 sites for tents or small RVs up to 16 feet (no hookups). Picnic tables, grills, and fire rings are provided. Vault toilets are available. Drinking water is not available. Garbage must be packed out. Leashed pets are permitted.

**Reservations, fees:** Reservations are not accepted. There is no fee for camping. Open late June through October, weather permitting.

**Directions:** From Corning on I-5, turn west on County Road A9 and drive 20 miles to Paskenta and Forest Road M4. Turn west on Forest Road M4 and drive to the junction with Forest Road 23N16. Turn right (north) and drive three miles to the campground.

**Contact:** Mendocino National Forest, 530/934-3316, www.fs.usda.gov/mendocino; Paskenta Work Center, 530/833-5544.

## 43 BUCKHORN

### Scenic rating: 5

on Black Butte Lake

**Map 4.2, page 236**  **BEST (**

Black Butte Lake is in the foothills of the north Sacramento Valley at 500 feet. The bad news: In summer, the lack of trees and shade coupled with very hot weather equals temps capable of hitting 100°F for days on end. The good news: The lake is one of the 10 best lakes in Northern California for crappie, best in spring. There can also be good fishing for largemouth, smallmouth, and spotted bass; channel catfish; bluegill; and sunfish. Recreation options include powerboating, sailboating, and sailboarding. A one-mile interpretive trail is available.

**Campsites, facilities:** There are 87 sites for tents or RVs up to 35 feet (no hookups), five walk-in sites, and a group site for 25-80 people. Picnic tables and fire grills are provided. Drinking water, restrooms with flush toilets and showers, a dump station, a fish-cleaning station, and a playground are available. A boat ramp is nearby. Some facilities are wheelchair-accessible. Leashed pets are permitted.

**Reservations, fees:** Reservations are accepted at 877/444-6777 or www.recreation.gov ($9 reservation fee). Individual sites, including walk-in sites, are $16 per night. The group site is $175 per night. Open year-round.

**Directions:** From I-5 in Orland, take the Black Butte Lake exit. Drive about 15 miles west on Road 200/Newville Road to Buckhorn Road.

Turn left and drive a short distance to the campground on the north shore of the lake.

**Contact:** Black Butte Lake, U.S. Army Corps of Engineers, 530/865-4781.

## 44 ORLAND BUTTES

### Scenic rating: 5

on Black Butte Lake

**Map 4.2, page 236**

Black Butte Lake isn't far from I-5, but a lot of campers zoom right by it. The lake has 40 miles of shoreline at 500 feet in elevation. All water sports are allowed. The prime time to visit is in late spring and early summer, when the bass and crappie fishing can be quite good. Three self-guided nature trails are in the immediate area, including Paul Thomas Trail, a short 0.25-mile walk to an overlook. (See the Buckhorn listing for more information.) Note: In late winter and early spring, this area is delightful as spring arrives. But from mid-June through August, expect very hot, dry weather.

**Campsites, facilities:** There are 35 sites for tents or RVs up to 35 feet (no hookups) and a group site for 15-50 people. Picnic tables and fire grills are provided. Drinking water, flush toilets, showers, boat ramp, fish-cleaning station, disc golf course, and a dump station are available. Leashed pets are permitted.

**Reservations, fees:** Reservations are accepted at 877/444-6777 or www.recreation.gov ($9 reservation fee). Sites are $18 per night, and the group site is $100 per night. Open April through early September.

**Directions:** From I-5 in Orland, take the Black Butte Lake exit. Drive west on Road 200/Newville Road for six miles to Road 206. Turn left and drive three miles to the camp entrance on the right.

**Contact:** Black Butte Lake, U.S. Army Corps of Engineers, 530/865-4781.

## 45 MASTERSON GROUP CAMP

### Scenic rating: 5

near Plaskett Lakes in Mendocino National Forest

**Map 4.2, page 236**

This is a group camp only. It is just a half mile away from the Plaskett Lakes, two small lakes of three and four acres set at 6,000 feet and surrounded by a mixed conifer forest. No motors are permitted at either lake, and swimming is not recommended because it is mucky and weedy. It is advisable to obtain a map of Mendocino National Forest, which details nearby streams, lakes, and hiking trails. One notable trail is the Black Butte Trail.

**Campsites, facilities:** This group camp has 20 tent or RV sites (no hookups) for up to 75 people. Fire grills and picnic tables are provided. Drinking water and vault toilets are available. Leashed pets are permitted.

**Reservations, fees:** Reservations are required at 877/444-6777 or www.recreation.gov ($9 reservation fee). Sites are $75 per night. Open mid-May through mid-October.

**Directions:** In Willows on I-5, turn west on Highway 162 and drive toward the town of Elk Creek. Just after crossing the Stony Creek Bridge, turn north on County Road 306 and drive four miles to Alder Springs Road/Forest Highway 7. Turn left and drive 31 miles to the camp on the right.

**Contact:** Mendocino National Forest, Grindstone Ranger District, Stonyford Work Center, 530/963-3128, www.fs.usda.gov/mendocino.

## 46 PLASKETT MEADOWS

### Scenic rating: 7

in Mendocino National Forest

**Map 4.2, page 236**

This is a little-known camp in the mountains

near Plaskett Lakes, a pair of connected dot-sized mountain lakes that form the headwaters of little Plaskett Creek. Trout fishing is best at the westernmost of the two lakes. No motors are permitted in the lakes and swimming is not recommended. The camp is at an elevation of 6,000 feet. It is advisable to obtain a map of Mendocino National Forest, which details nearby streams, lakes, and hiking trails.

**Campsites, facilities:** There are 31 sites for tents or RVs up to 26 feet (no hookups). Fire grills and picnic tables are provided. Drinking water and vault toilets are available. Garbage must be packed out. Some facilities are wheelchair-accessible. Leashed pets are permitted.

**Reservations, fees:** Reservations are not accepted. Sites are $10 per night. Open mid-May through mid-October.

**Directions:** In Willows on I-5, turn west on Highway 162 and drive toward the town of Elk Creek. Just after crossing the Stony Creek Bridge, turn north on County Road 306 and drive four miles to Alder Springs Road/Forest Highway 7. Turn left and drive 31 miles to the campground on the left.

**Contact:** Mendocino National Forest, Grindstone Ranger District, 530/934-3316; Stonyford Work Center, 530/963-3128, www.fs.usda.gov/mendocino.

## **47** ATCHISON CAMP

### Scenic rating: 5

in Mendocino National Forest

**Map 4.2, page 236**

Very few people know about this little spot. Atchison Camp is at an elevation of 4,500 feet in a remote national forest in an area that is hot and dry all summer long. A network of four-wheel-drive roads crisscrosses the area. Hunters use this camp as a base in the fall, then drive around in ATVs or pickup trucks looking for deer or places to hunt.

**Campsites, facilities:** There are six sites for tents or small RVs. Picnic tables and fire rings

are provided. Vault toilets are available, but there is no drinking water. Garbage must be packed out.

**Reservations, fees:** Reservations are not accepted. There is no fee for camping.

**Directions:** In Willows, take Highway 162 west to the town of Elk Creek. Just after crossing the Stony Creek Bridge, turn north on County Road 306 and drive four miles to Alder Springs Road/Forest Highway 7. Turn left onto Alder Springs Road/Forest Highway 7 and drive about 26 miles to the campground.

**Contact:** Mendocino National Forest, Covelo Ranger District, 707/983-6118, www.fs.usda.gov/mendocino.

## **48** LOWER NYE

### Scenic rating: 8

in Mendocino National Forest

**Map 4.2, page 236**

This camp is on the northern border of the Snow Mountain Wilderness. It is a good jumping-off point for backpackers, or a spot for folks who don't want to be bugged by anybody. It is at 3,300 feet on Skeleton Creek near the Eel River. Be sure to obtain a detailed USGS topographic map.

**Campsites, facilities:** There are six sites for tents or RVs up to 16 feet (no hookups). There are no tables, grills, toilets, or drinking water available. Garbage must be packed out. Leashed pets are permitted.

**Reservations, fees:** Reservations are not accepted. There is no fee for camping. Open May to November, weather permitting.

**Directions:** From Ukiah on U.S. 101, drive north to the junction of Highway 20. Turn east on Highway 20 and drive to the town of Upper Lake and to Elk Mountain Road. Turn left on Elk Mountain Road (which becomes Forest Road M1) and drive 17 miles to Forest Road M10/Bear Creek Road. Turn right (dirt road) on Forest Road M10/Bear Creek Road and drive seven miles to Forest Road 18N04/

Rice Creek Road. Turn north on Forest Road 18N04/Rice Creek Road and drive 14 miles to the campground.

**Contact:** Mendocino National Forest, Upper Lake Ranger District, 707/275-2361, www. fs.usda.gov/mendocino.

## 49 SUNSET POINT CAMPGROUND

**Scenic rating: 7**

on Lake Pillsbury in Mendocino National Forest

**Map 4.2, page 236**

This camp is on the northeast corner of Lake Pillsbury, and Pillsbury Pines boat launch and picnic area are less than a quarter mile to the south. Lakeshore Trail, an adjacent designated nature trail along the shore of the lake here, is accessible to hikers, equestrians, and bicyclists. However, a section of the trail is covered with water when the lake is full. The surrounding national forest offers side-trip possibilities.

**Campsites, facilities:** There are 54 sites, including 14 double sites, for tents or small-to-medium RVs (no hookups). Picnic tables, grills, and some fire grills are provided. Drinking water and vault toilets are available. A boat ramp is nearby. Leashed pets are permitted.

**Reservations, fees:** Reservations are not accepted. Sites are $16 per night, plus $5 per night for each additional vehicle and $2 per pet per night. Open mid-April through early September.

**Directions:** From Ukiah on U.S. 101, drive north to the junction with Highway 20. Turn east (right) on Highway 20 and drive five miles. Turn northeast on East Potter Valley Road toward Lake Pillsbury. Drive 5.9 miles to the town of Potter Valley. Continue on East Potter Valley Road to Eel River Road. Turn right and drive 15 miles to the Eel River Information Kiosk at Lake Pillsbury. Continue east for 4.1 miles to Lake Pillsbury and the junction with Hall Mountain Road. Turn right and drive three miles to the camp entrance.

**Contact:** Mendocino National Forest, Upper Lake Ranger District, 707/275-2361, www. fs.usda.gov/mendocino; PG&E Land Services, 916/386-5164, www.pge.com/recreation; Sunset Point Campground, 707/743-1513.

## 50 OAK FLAT

**Scenic rating: 6**

near Lake Pillsbury in Mendocino National Forest

**Map 4.2, page 236**

This primitive camp provides an option if Lake Pillsbury's other camps are full. It is at 1,850 feet elevation near the north shore of Lake Pillsbury in the heart of Mendocino National Forest. Nearby trails leading into the backcountry are detailed on a Forest Service map.

**Campsites, facilities:** There are 18 sites for tents or RVs up to 16 feet (no hookups). Picnic tables and fire grills are provided. Drinking water and vault toilets are available. Garbage must be packed out. A campfire permit is required. A boat ramp is at the lake. Leashed pets are permitted.

**Reservations, fees:** Reservations are not accepted. Sites are $10 per night. Open year-round.

**Directions:** From Ukiah on U.S. 101, drive north to the junction with Highway 20. Turn east (right) on Highway 20 and drive five miles to East Potter Valley Road. Turn northeast on East Potter Valley Road toward Lake Pillsbury and drive 5.9 miles to the town of Potter Valley. Continue on East Potter Valley Road to Eel River Road. Turn right and drive 15 miles to the Eel River Information Kiosk at Lake Pillsbury. Continue for four miles around the north end of the lake and look for the camp entrance on the right side of the road.

**Contact:** Mendocino National Forest, Upper Lake Ranger District, 707/275-2361, www. fs.usda.gov/mendocino.

## 51 NAVY CAMP

### Scenic rating: 7
on Lake Pillsbury in Mendocino National Forest

Map 4.2, page 236

This camp is used primarily as an overflow area, and is usually open on busy weekends and holidays. When Lake Pillsbury is full of water, this is an attractive camp. However, when the lake level is down, as is common in the fall, it can seem as if the camp is on the edge of a dust bowl. The camp is in the lake's north cove, sheltered from north winds. Although the setting is pretty, there is little shade and a lot of poison oak.

**Campsites, facilities:** There are 20 sites for tents or RVs up to 16 feet (no hookups). Picnic tables are provided. Drinking water and vault toilets are available. A boat ramp is nearby at Fuller Grove. Some facilities are wheelchair-accessible. Leashed pets are permitted.

**Reservations, fees:** Reservations are not accepted. Sites are $16 per night, plus $3 per night for each additional vehicle and $1 per pet per night. Open Memorial Day weekend through October for overflow camping.

**Directions:** From Ukiah on U.S. 101, drive north to the junction with Highway 20. Turn east (right) on Highway 20 and drive five miles to East Potter Valley Road. Turn northeast on East Potter Valley Road toward Lake Pillsbury and drive 5.9 miles to the town of Potter Valley. Continue on East Potter Valley Road to Eel River Road. Turn right and drive 15 miles to the Eel River Information Kiosk at Lake Pillsbury. Continue for four miles around the north end of the lake and look for the campground entrance on the right side of the road. The campground is on the north shore, just west of Oak Flat Camp.

**Contact:** Mendocino National Forest, Upper Lake Ranger District, 707/275-2361, www.fs.usda.gov/mendocino.

## 52 FULLER GROVE AND FULLER GROVE GROUP CAMP

### Scenic rating: 7
on Lake Pillsbury in Mendocino National Forest

Map 4.2, page 236

This is one of several campgrounds bordering Lake Pillsbury, which, at 2,000 acres, is the largest lake in Mendocino National Forest. Set at an elevation of 1,800 feet, Pillsbury is big and pretty when full, with 65 miles of shoreline. It has lakeside camping, good boat ramps, and good fishing for trout in spring and bass in the warmer months. This camp is along the northwest shore of the lake, with a boat ramp only about a quarter mile away to the north. There are numerous backcountry roads in the area, which provide access to a state game refuge to the north and the Snow Mountain Wilderness to the east.

For something different, consider spending the night at 4,400 feet in the old Pine Mountain Fire Lookout, seven miles southwest. It can be rented out for overnight stays.

**Campsites, facilities:** There are 30 sites for tents or RVs up to 22 feet (no hookups) and a group tent area for up to 60 people. Picnic tables, food lockers, and fire grills are provided. Drinking water and vault toilets are available. A boat ramp is nearby. Leashed pets are permitted.

**Reservations, fees:** Reservations are not accepted for individual sites but are required for the group site at 916/386-5164. Sites are $16 per night, plus $3 per night for each additional vehicle and $1 per pet per night. The group site is $133 per night with a two-night minimum stay ($20 reservation fee). Nearby Pine Mountain Lookout can be reserved at 877/444-6777 ($10 reservation fee) or www.recreation.gov ($9 reservation fee) for $50 per night (two-night minimum). Weekly rates are available. Open May through October.

**Directions:** From Ukiah on U.S. 101, drive north to the junction with Highway 20. Turn east (right) on Highway 20 and drive five miles to East Potter Valley Road. Turn northeast on East Potter Valley Road toward Lake Pillsbury and drive 5.9 miles to the town of Potter Valley. Continue on East Potter Valley Road to Eel River Road. Turn right and drive 15 miles to the Eel River Information Kiosk at Lake Pillsbury. Continue for 2.2 miles to the campground access road. Turn right and drive 0.25 mile to the campground; the group camp is adjacent to the boat ramp. Call Upper Lake Ranger Station for access to the fire lookout.

**Contact:** Mendocino National Forest, Upper Lake Ranger District, 707/275-2361, www. fs.usda.gov/mendocino; PG&E Land Services, 916/386-5164, www.pge.com/recreation.

## 53 LAKE PILLSBURY RESORT

**Scenic rating: 6**

on Lake Pillsbury in Mendocino National Forest

**Map 4.2, page 236**

This is a pretty spot beside the shore of Lake Pillsbury in the heart of Mendocino National Forest. It can be headquarters for a vacation involving boating, fishing, waterskiing, or exploring the surrounding national forest. A boat ramp, small marina, and full facilities make this place a prime attraction in a relatively remote location. This is the only resort on the lake that accepts reservations, and it has some lakefront sites.

**Campsites, facilities:** There are 39 sites for tents or RVs up to 26 feet (no hookups) and two sites with full hookups (30 amps). Ten cabins are also available. Picnic tables and fire pits are provided. Drinking water, restrooms with flush toilets and coin showers, a playground, boat rentals, fuel, boat dock, fishing supplies, and a small marina are available. Leashed pets are permitted.

**Reservations, fees:** Reservations are recommended. RV sites with full hookups are $40 per night, tent sites are $30 per night, plus $8 per

person per night for more than six people, $8 per night for each additional vehicle, and $9 per pet per night. Boat launching is $7 per day. Weekly rates are available. Some credit cards are accepted. Open May through October.

**Directions:** From Ukiah on U.S. 101, drive north to the junction with Highway 20. Turn east (right) on Highway 20 and drive five miles to East Potter Valley Road (toward Lake Pillsbury). Turn left (northeast) on East Potter Valley Road and drive 5.9 miles to the town of Potter Valley. Continue on East Potter Valley Road to Eel River Road. Turn right and drive 11 miles (unpaved road) to the stop sign. Turn right (still Eel River Road) and drive 0.2 mile to Kapranos Road. Turn left and drive about 1.5 miles to the resort.

**Contact:** Lake Pillsbury Resort, 2756 Kapranos Rd., 707/743-9935, www.lprandm.com or www. lakepillsburyresort.com.

## 54 NORTH FORK

**Scenic rating: 2**

on Stony Creek in Mendocino National Forest

**Map 4.2, page 236**

This primitive camp at 1,700 feet elevation sits at the confluence of the north, south, and middle forks of Stony Creek. There are many trailheads for hiking in the area, within a few miles of the Snow Mountain Wilderness, but none at this camp. There are great views of St. John Mountain and Snow Mountain. (See the Mill Creek listing in this chapter for additional information.) Off-highway-vehicle use is possible from camp.

**Campsites, facilities:** There are five tent sites. Picnic tables and fire grills are provided. Vault toilets are available. No drinking water is available. Garbage must be packed out. Leashed pets are permitted.

**Reservations, fees:** Reservations are not accepted. Sites are $5 per night. Open May through October.

**Directions:** From I-5 at Maxwell, turn west on

Maxwell-Sites Road and drive to Sites. Turn left on Sites-Lodoga Road and continue to Lodoga and Lodoga-Stonyford Road. Turn right on Lodoga-Stonyford Road and loop around East Park Reservoir to reach Stonyford and Fouts Springs Road. Turn west on Fouts Springs Road/Forest Road M10 and drive about nine miles to Forest Road 18N03. Turn right on Forest Road 18N03 and drive two miles to the campground on the right.

**Contact:** Mendocino National Forest, Grindstone Ranger District, Stonyford Work Center, 530/963-3128, www.fs.usda.gov/mendocino.

## 55 FOUTS AND SOUTH FORK
🚶 🐕 ♿ 🚐 ⛺

### Scenic rating: 1
on Stony Creek in Mendocino National Forest

**Map 4.2, page 236**

These two adjoining camps are in a designated off-highway-vehicle (OHV) area and are used primarily by dirt bikers. So if you're looking for quiet, these camps are not for you. Several OHV trails are nearby—North Fork, South Fork, and Mill Creek—and campers can ride their OHVs directly out of camp. To the west is the Snow Mountain Wilderness and excellent hiking trails; to the south is an extensive Forest Service road and OHV trail network. The elevation is 1,700 feet.

**Campsites, facilities:** There are nine sites for tents or RVs up to 16 feet at Fouts (no hookups); there are several dispersed sites at South Fork. Picnic tables and fire grills are provided. Both sites have vault toilets; only Fouts has drinking water. Garbage must be packed out. Some facilities are wheelchair-accessible. Leashed pets are permitted.

**Reservations, fees:** Reservations are not accepted. Sites are $5 per night. Open year-round, although trails may be closed during wet weather.

**Directions:** From I-5 at Maxwell, turn west on Maxwell-Sites Road and drive to Sites. Turn left on Sites-Lodoga Road and continue to Lodoga. Turn right on Lodoga-Stonyford Road and loop around East Park Reservoir to reach Stonyford. From Stonyford, turn west on Fouts Springs Road/County Road M10 and drive about eight miles. Turn right (north) on Forest Road 18N03 and drive one mile to the campgrounds on your right.

**Contact:** Mendocino National Forest, Grindstone Ranger District, 530/934-3316; Stonyford Work Center, 530/963-3128, www.fs.usda.gov/mendocino.

## 56 GRAY PINE GROUP CAMP
🚶 🐕 🚐 ⛺

### Scenic rating: 1
in Mendocino National Forest

**Map 4.2, page 236**

Similar to Fouts Campground, Gray Pine is in a forested area with many OHV trails nearby. It is near (but not on) Stony Creek. (See the Fouts and South Fork listing for additional information.)

**Campsites, facilities:** There is one group site for tents or RVs up to 26 feet (no hookups) that can accommodate up to 75 people. Picnic tables and fire rings are provided. Drinking water, vault toilets, and a group barbecue grill are available. Leashed pets are permitted.

**Reservations, fees:** Reservations are required at 877/444-6777 ($10 reservation fee) or www.recreation.gov ($9 reservation fee). The fee is $75 per night. Open year-round, weather permitting.

**Directions:** From I-5 at Maxwell, turn west on Maxwell-Sites Road and drive to Sites. Turn left on Sites-Lodoga Road and continue to Lodoga. Turn right on Lodoga-Stonyford Road and loop around East Park Reservoir to reach Stonyford. From Stonyford, turn west on Fouts Springs Road/County Road M10 and drive about nine miles. Turn right on Forest Road 18N03 and drive less than a mile to the campground on your right.

**Contact:** Mendocino National Forest,

Grindstone Ranger District, 530/934-3316; Stonyford Work Center, 530/963-3128, www. fs.usda.gov/mendocino.

## 57 DAVIS FLAT
🏃🏻 🐕 ♿ �-road 🔼

### Scenic rating: 1
in Mendocino National Forest

**Map 4.2, page 236**

Davis Flat is across the road from Fouts and South Fork campgrounds. All three campgrounds are in a designated off-highway-vehicle area, so expect OHVers, especially in the winter; campers are allowed to ride their OHVs from the campground. This isn't the quietest camp around, but there is some good hiking in the area to the immediate west in the Snow Mountain Wilderness. The elevation is 1,700 feet.

**Campsites, facilities:** There is dispersed camping for tents or RVs of any length (no hookups). Twenty picnic tables and fire grills are provided. Drinking water, vault toilets, and a dump station are available. Some facilities are wheelchair-accessible. Leashed pets are permitted.

**Reservations, fees:** Reservations are not accepted. Sites are $5 per night. There is a $5 dump station fee. Open year-round, weather permitting.

**Directions:** From I-5 at Maxwell, turn west on Maxwell-Sites Road and drive to Sites. Turn left on Sites-Lodoga Road and continue to Lodoga. Turn right on Lodoga-Stonyford Road and loop around East Park Reservoir to reach Stonyford. From Stonyford, turn west on Fouts Springs Road/County Road M10 and drive about nine miles to Forest Road 18N03. Turn right and drive one mile to the campground on your left.

**Contact:** Mendocino National Forest, Grindstone Ranger District, 530/934-3316,

Stonyford Work Center, 530/963-3128, www. fs.usda.gov/mendocino.

## 58 MILL CREEK
🏃🏻 🏊 🐕 🔼

### Scenic rating: 3
in Mendocino National Forest

**Map 4.2, page 236**

This campground is beside Mill Creek near Fouts Springs at the southeastern boundary of the Snow Mountain Wilderness. A nearby trailhead, a mile to the west, provides a hiking route into the wilderness that connects along Trout Creek, a great little romp. Mill Creek is quite pretty in the late spring, but by late summer the flow drops way down. Elevation is 1,700 feet. Expect heavy off-highway-vehicle use October through May. Fouts Springs/Davis Flat is an OHV staging area. OHV riders are allowed to ride from camp.

**Campsites, facilities:** There are five tent sites. Picnic tables and fire rings are provided. Vault toilets are available. Creek water must be treated before drinking. Leashed pets are permitted.

**Reservations, fees:** Reservations are not accepted. Sites are $5 per night. Open year-round, weather permitting.

**Directions:** From I-5 at Maxwell, turn west on Maxwell-Sites Road and drive to Sites. Turn left on Sites-Lodoga Road and continue to Lodoga. Turn right on Lodoga-Stonyford Road and loop around East Park Reservoir to reach Stonyford. From Stonyford, turn west on Fouts Springs Road/Forest Road M10 and drive about 8.5 miles to the campground entrance on the right.

**Contact:** Mendocino National Forest, Grindstone Ranger District, Stonyford Work Center, 530/963-3128, www.fs.usda.gov/ mendocino.

## 59 DIXIE GLADE HORSE CAMP

🏇 �car 🏕

**Scenic rating: 6**

near the Snow Mountain Wilderness in Mendocino National Forest

**Map 4.2, page 236**

Got a horse who likes to tromp? No? Then take a pass on this one. Yes? Then sign right up, because this is a trailhead camp for people preparing to head north by horseback into the adjacent Snow Mountain Wilderness.

**Campsites, facilities:** There are seven sites for tents or RVs up to 26 feet (no hookups). Picnic tables and fire grills are provided. Vault toilets are available. No drinking water is available. Garbage must be packed out. A horse corral and hitching rack are available. Water in horse troughs is usually available; check current status. Leashed pets are permitted.

**Reservations, fees:** Reservations are not accepted. Sites are $5 per night. Open April through November, weather permitting.

**Directions:** From I-5 at Maxwell, turn west on Maxwell-Sites Road and drive to Sites and Sites-Lodoga Road. Turn left on Sites-Lodoga Road and continue to Lodoga and Lodoga-Stonyford Road. Turn right on Lodoga-Stonyford Road and loop around East Park Reservoir to reach Stonyford and Fouts Springs Road. Turn west on Fouts Springs Road/County Road M10 and drive 13 miles to the camp on the right side of the road.

**Contact:** Mendocino National Forest, Grindstone Ranger District, 530/934-3316; Stonyford Work Center, 530/963-3128, www.fs.usda.gov/mendocino.

## 60 BEAR CREEK CAMPGROUND

🥾 🛶 🏇 5% �car 🏕

**Scenic rating: 7**

in Mendocino National Forest

**Map 4.2, page 236**

This campground is a primitive spot out in the boondocks of Mendocino National Forest, at 2,000 feet elevation. It's a pretty spot, too, beside Bear Creek near its confluence with Blue Slides Creek. Trout fishing can be good. It's about a 10-minute drive to Summit Springs Trailhead at the southern end of the Snow Mountain Wilderness. There are numerous OHV roads in this region.

**Campsites, facilities:** There are 16 sites for tents or RVs up to 22 feet (no hookups). Picnic tables and fire grills are provided. Vault toilets are available. No drinking water is available. Garbage must be packed out. Leashed pets are permitted.

**Reservations, fees:** Reservations are not accepted. There is no fee for camping. Open year-round, weather permitting, but the camp closes when the creek is too high to ford.

**Directions:** From Ukiah on U.S. 101, drive north to the junction with Highway 20 at Calpella. Turn east on Highway 20 and drive to the town of Upper Lake and Mendenhall Avenue. Turn left on Mendenhall Avenue (which becomes Forest Road M1) and drive one mile to the stop sign and Forest Road M1/Elk Mountain Road. Bear left on Forest Road M1/Elk Mountain Road and drive 16 miles (the latter stretch is extremely twisty) to Forest Road M10. Turn right (east) and drive eight miles to the campground entrance road on the left. Turn left and continue 0.5 mile to the camp. Note: Approximately five miles along Forest Road M10, the Rice Fork of the Eel River must be forded. Access can be dangerous and sometimes impossible when the water is high; call for road conditions. High-clearance vehicles are recommended.

**Contact:** Mendocino National Forest, Upper

Lake Ranger District, 707/275-2361, www.
fs.usda.gov/mendocino.

## 61 MILL VALLEY

### Scenic rating: 5
near Letts Lake in Mendocino National Forest

**Map 4.2, page 236**

This camp is beside Lily Pond, a little, teeny guy, with larger Letts Lake just a mile away. Since Lily Pond does not have trout and Letts Lake does, this camp gets far less traffic than its counterpart. The area is crisscrossed with numerous creeks, OHV routes, and Forest Service roads, making it a great adventure for owners of four-wheel drives, who are allowed to drive their OHVs from the campground. The elevation is 4,200 feet.

**Campsites, facilities:** There are 15 sites for tents or RVs up to 18 feet (no hookups). Picnic tables and fire grills are provided. Vault toilets and drinking water are available. Garbage must be packed out. Leashed pets are permitted.

**Reservations, fees:** Reservations are not accepted. Sites are $10 per night. Open mid-May through November, weather permitting.

**Directions:** From I-5 at Maxwell, turn west on Maxwell-Sites Road and drive to Sites and Sites-Lodoga Road. Turn left on Sites-Lodoga Road and continue to Lodoga and Lodoga-Stonyford Road. Turn right on Lodoga-Stonyford Road and loop around East Park Reservoir to reach Stonyford and Fouts Springs Road. Turn west on Fouts Springs Road/County Road M10 and drive about 16 miles into national forest (where the road becomes Forest Service 17N02) to the camp access road on the left. Turn left and drive 0.25 mile to the camp.

**Contact:** Mendocino National Forest, Grindstone Ranger District, 530/934-3316; Stonyford Work Center, 530/963-3128; www. fs.usda.gov/mendocino.

## 62 LETTS LAKE COMPLEX

### Scenic Rating: 9
in Mendocino National Forest

**Map 4.2, page 236**

An increasingly popular spot is Letts Lake, a 35-acre, spring-fed lake set in a mixed conifer forest at 4,500 feet just south of the Snow Mountain Wilderness. There are four main loops, each with a separate campground: Main, Stirrup, Saddle, and Spillway. The complex is on the east side of the lake. No motors are allowed at Letts Lake, making it ideal for canoes, rafts, and float tubes. Swimming is allowed, although the shoreline is rocky. This lake is stocked with rainbow trout in early summer and is known also for black bass. It's a designated historical landmark, the site where the homesteaders known as the Letts brothers were murdered. While that may not impress you, the views to the north of the Snow Mountain Wilderness will. In addition, several natural springs can be fun to hunt up. By the way, after such a long drive to get here, don't let your eagerness cause you to stop at Lily Pond (on the left, one mile before reaching Letts Lake), because there are no trout in it.

**Campsites, facilities:** There are four campgrounds with 42 sites for tents or RVs up to 24 feet (no hookups). Picnic tables and fire rings are provided. Drinking water and vault toilets are available. A picnic area is nearby. Some facilities, including a fishing pier, are wheelchair-accessible. Leashed pets are permitted.

**Reservations, fees:** Reservations are not accepted. Sites are $12 per night and there is a 14-day limit. Open May through October.

**Directions:** From I-5 at Maxwell, turn west on Maxwell-Sites Road and drive to Sites and Sites-Lodoga Road. Turn left on Sites-Lodoga Road and continue to Lodoga and Lodoga-Stonyford Road. Turn right on Lodoga-Stonyford Road and loop around East Park Reservoir to reach Stonyford and Fouts Springs Road. Turn west on Fouts Springs Road/County Road M10 and drive 19 miles into national forest (where the road becomes Forest Service 17N02) to the campground on the east side of Letts Lake.

**Contact:** Mendocino National Forest, Grindstone Ranger District, Stonyford Work Center, 530/963-3128, www.fs.usda.gov/mendocino.

## 63 OLD MILL

### Scenic rating: 5
near Mill Creek in Mendocino National Forest

**Map 4.2, page 236**

Little known and little used, this camp is at 3,700 feet amid a mature stand of pine and fir on Trough Spring Ridge. It's at the site of—guess what?—an old mill. Expect some OHV company as drivers of OHVs are allowed to ride from camp.

**Campsites, facilities:** There are eight sites for tents or RVs up to 16 feet (no hookups). Note that the access road is poor for RVs. Picnic tables and fire rings are provided. A vault toilet is available. No drinking water is available. Garbage must be packed out. Leashed pets are permitted.

**Reservations, fees:** Reservations are not accepted. There is no fee for camping. Open May through October.

**Directions:** From I-5 at Maxwell, turn west on Maxwell-Sites Road and drive to Sites and Sites-Lodoga Road. Turn left on Sites-Lodoga Road and continue to Lodoga and Lodoga-Stonyford Road. Turn right on Lodoga-Stonyford Road and loop around East Park Reservoir to reach Stonyford and Fouts Springs Road. Turn west on Fouts Springs Road/County Road M10 and drive about six miles to Forest Road M5. Turn left on Forest Road M5/Trough Springs Road and drive 7.5 miles on a narrow road to the campground on your right. (The access road is not recommended for RVs.)

**Contact:** Mendocino National Forest, Grindstone Ranger District, Stonyford Work Center, 530/963-3128, www.fs.usda.gov/mendocino.

## 64 DEER VALLEY CAMPGROUND

### Scenic rating: 4
in Mendocino National Forest

**Map 4.2, page 236**

This one is way out there. It is used primarily in summer by OHV enthusiasts and in the fall by deer hunters. It is set at 3,700 feet in Deer Valley, about five miles from the East Fork of Middle Creek.

**Campsites, facilities:** There are seven sites for tents or RVs up to 16 feet (no hookups). Picnic tables and fire grills are provided. Vault toilets are available. No drinking water is available. Garbage must be packed out. Leashed pets are permitted.

**Reservations, fees:** Reservations are not accepted. Sites are $6 per night. Open April through October, weather permitting.

**Directions:** From Ukiah on U.S. 101, drive north to the junction with Highway 20. Turn east on Highway 20 and drive to the town of Upper Lake and Mendenhall Avenue. Turn left on Mendenhall Avenue (which becomes Forest Road M1) and drive 17 miles (the latter stretch is extremely twisty) to Forest Road 16N01. Turn right on Forest Road 16N01 and drive about four miles to the campground.

**Contact:** Mendocino National Forest, Upper Lake Ranger District, 707/275-2361, www.fs.usda.gov/mendocino.

## 65 CEDAR CAMP

### Scenic rating: 6
in Mendocino National Forest

**Map 4.2, page 236**

This camp is at 4,300 feet elevation, just below Goat Mountain (6,121 feet) to the west about a mile away. Why did anybody decide to build a campground way out here? Because a small spring starts nearby, creating a trickle that runs into the nearby headwaters of Little Stony

Creek. The campground connects to the OHV trail system.

**Campsites, facilities:** There are five sites for tents or RVs up to 16 feet (no hookups). Note that the access road is poor for trailers. Picnic tables and fire grills are provided. A vault toilet is available. No drinking water is available. Garbage must be packed out. Leashed pets are permitted.

**Reservations, fees:** Reservations are not accepted. There is no fee for camping. Open May to November, weather permitting.

**Directions:** From I-5 at Maxwell, turn west on Maxwell-Sites Road and drive to Sites and Sites-Lodoga Road. Turn left on Sites-Lodoga Road and continue to Lodoga and Lodoga-Stonyford Road. Turn right on Lodoga-Stonyford Road and loop around East Park Reservoir to reach Stonyford and Fouts Springs Road. Turn west on Fouts Springs Road/County Road M10 and drive about six miles to County Road M5. Turn left on Forest Road M5 (Trough Springs Road) and drive 13 miles to the campground on your right.

**Contact:** Mendocino National Forest, Grindstone Ranger District, Stonyford Work Center, 530/963-3128, www.fs.usda.gov/mendocino.

## 66 LITTLE STONY CAMPGROUND

🏞 🚣 ♿ 🐕 🚐 ⛺

### Scenic rating: 7

on Little Stony Creek in Mendocino National Forest

**Map 4.2, page 236**

This pretty spot is in Little Stony Canyon, beside Little Stony Creek at 1,500 feet. Very few people know of the place, and you will find it is appropriately named: It is little, it is stony, and the little trout amid the stones fit right in. The camp provides streamside access and, with Goat Mountain Road running along most of the stream, it is easy to fish much of this creek

in an evening. Expect heavy OHV use from fall through spring.

**Campsites, facilities:** There are eight sites for tents or RVs up to 16 feet (no hookups). Picnic tables and fire grills are provided. Vault toilets are available. No drinking water is available. Garbage must be packed out. A day-use area is nearby. Leashed pets are permitted.

**Reservations, fees:** Reservations are not accepted. Sites are $5 per night. Open year-round.

**Directions:** From I-5 at Maxwell, turn west on Maxwell-Sites Road and drive to Sites. Turn left on Sites-Lodoga Road and continue to where the road crosses Stony Creek. Just after the bridge, turn left on Goat Mountain Road and drive four miles (a rough county road) to the campground on the left.

**Contact:** Mendocino National Forest, Grindstone Ranger District, 530/934-3316; Stonyford Work Center, 530/963-3128, www.fs.usda.gov/mendocino.

## 67 MIDDLE CREEK CAMPGROUND

🐕 🚐 ⛺

### Scenic rating: 6

in Mendocino National Forest

**Map 4.2, page 236**

Middle Creek campground—some call it CC Camp—is not widely known, but it's known well enough as an off-highway-vehicle staging area. An easy track for beginners on dirt bikes and OHVs is located here. The camp is at 2,000 feet at the confluence of the West and East Forks of Middle Creek.

**Campsites, facilities:** There are 23 sites, including two double sites, for tents or RVs up to 30 feet (no hookups). Picnic tables and fire grills are provided. Drinking water and vault toilets are available. Leashed pets are permitted.

**Reservations, fees:** Reservations are not accepted. Sites are $8 per night, double sites are $12 per night, plus $2 per night for each additional vehicle. Open year-round.

**Directions:** From Ukiah on U.S. 101, drive

north to the junction with Highway 20. Turn east on Highway 20 and drive to the town of Upper Lake and Mendenhall Avenue. Turn left on Mendenhall Avenue (which becomes Forest Road M1) and drive eight miles to the camp on the right.

**Contact:** Mendocino National Forest, Upper Lake Ranger District, 707/275-2361, www.fs.usda.gov/mendocino.

## 68 CLEAR LAKE STATE PARK

🚶 🚴 🏊 ⛴ 🏄 🎣 🐕 ♿ 🚐 ⛺

### Scenic rating: 9

in Kelseyville at Clear Lake

**Map 4.2, page 236**

If you have fallen in love with Clear Lake and its surrounding oak woodlands, it is difficult to find a better spot than at Clear Lake State Park. It is on the western shore of Clear Lake, and though the oak woodlands flora means you can seem quite close to your camping neighbors, the proximity to quality boating, water sports, and fishing makes the lack of privacy worth it. Reservations are a necessity in summer. That stands to reason, with excellent bass fishing from boats beside a tule-lined shoreline near the park and good catfishing in the sloughs that run through the park. Some campsites have water frontage. The elevation is 1,500 feet. Clear Lake is the largest natural freshwater lake within California state borders, and it has 150 miles of shoreline. Despite its name, the lake is not clear but green and, in late summer, rather soupy with algae and water grass in certain areas. The high nutrients in the lake give rise to a flourishing aquatic food chain. With that comes the highest number of large bass of any lake in Northern California. A few short hiking trails are also available at the park. The self-guided Indian Nature Trail passes through the site of what was once a Pomo village. Rangers are friendly, helpful, and provide reliable fishing information. Junior ranger programs and guided walks for bird and flower identification are also available. Note: All boats must be certified mussel-free before launching.

**Campsites, facilities:** There are 147 sites for tents or RVs up to 35 feet (no hookups), two group sites for up to 40 people each, and two hike-in/bike-in sites. Eight cabins are also available. Picnic tables and fire rings are provided. Drinking water, restrooms with coin showers and flush toilets, and a dump station are available. A boat ramp, dock, fish-cleaning stations, boat battery charging station, visitors center, Wi-Fi, and swimming beach are nearby. A grocery store, coin laundry, propane gas, restaurant, and gas station are within three miles. Some facilities, including the boat ramp, are wheelchair-accessible. Leashed pets are permitted in the campgrounds.

**Reservations, fees:** Reservations are accepted at 877/444-6777 ($10 reservation fee) or www.recreation.gov ($9 reservation fee). Drive-in sites at Cole Creek are $30 per night, drive-in sites at Kelsey Creek are $30 per night, premium sites at Lakeview are $35 per night, premium sites at Kelsey Creek and Lakeside are $45 per night, plus $5 per night for each additional vehicle. It's $75 per night for group sites, and hike-in/bike-in sites are $5 per person per night. Boat launching is $5 per day. Open year-round.

**Directions:** From Vallejo, drive north on Highway 29 to Lower Lake. Turn left on Highway 29 and drive seven miles to Soda Bay Road. Turn right on Soda Bay Road and drive 11 miles to the park entrance on the right side of the road.

From Kelseyville on Highway 29, take the Kelseyville exit and turn north on Main Street. Drive a short distance to State Street. Turn right and drive 0.25 mile to Gaddy Lane. Turn right on Gaddy Lane and drive about two miles to Soda Bay Road. Turn right and drive one mile to the park entrance on the left.

**Contact:** Clear Lake State Park, 707/279-4293 or 707/279-2267, www.parks.ca.gov.

## 69 BLUE OAK

🏃🏊🚣⛵🚤🐕 5%🚐 ⛺

### Scenic rating: 7

at Indian Valley Reservoir

**Map 4.2, page 236**

Indian Valley Reservoir is kind of like an ugly dog that you love more than anything because inside beats a heart that will never betray you. The camp is out in the middle of nowhere in oak woodlands, about a mile from the dam. It is primitive and little known. For many, that kind of isolation is perfect. The lake has 41 miles of shoreline, is long and narrow, and is set at 1,500 feet elevation. The boat speed limit is 10 mph. While there are good trails nearby, it is the outstanding fishing for bass, bluegill, and some kokanee salmon at the lake every spring and early summer that is the key reason to make the trip. In addition, in the spring, there is a great variety of wildflowers in and around the campground. A detailed map is available from the BLM. Note: All boats must be certified mussel-free before launching. Inspections are not available at the reservoir; they are instead available at Clear Lake.

**Campsites, facilities:** There are six sites for tents or RVs up to 20 feet (no hookups). Picnic tables and fire grills are provided. Vault toilets are available, but there is no drinking water. Leashed pets are permitted.

**Reservations, fees:** Reservations are not accepted. There is no fee for camping. There is a 14-day stay limit. Open year-round, weather permitting.

**Directions:** From Williams on I-5, turn west on Highway 20 and drive 25 miles into the foothills to Walker Ridge Road. Turn north (right) on Walker Ridge Road (a dirt road) and drive north for about four miles to a "major" intersection of two dirt roads. Turn left and drive about 2.5 miles toward the Indian Valley Dam. The Blue Oak campground is just off the road on the right, about 1.5 miles from Indian Valley Reservoir.

**Contact:** Bureau of Land Management, Ukiah

Field Office, 707/468-4000, www.blm.gov/ca; Yolo County Flood Control, 530/662-0265.

## 70 MANCHESTER STATE PARK

🏃🏊�־🐕🚐⛺

### Scenic rating: 8

near Point Arena

**Map 4.3, page 237**

Due to service reductions, the park is open to camping in summer only. Call the Mendocino District Office to confirm opening dates, site availability, and services.

Manchester State Park is a beautiful park on the Sonoma coast, near the Garcia River with the nearby town of Point Arena providing supplies. The park features 760 acres of beach, sand dunes, and grasslands, with 18,000 feet of ocean frontage and five miles of gentle sandy beach stretching southward toward the Point Arena Lighthouse. Alder Creek Trail is a great hike, routed north along beachfront to the mouth of Alder Creek and its beautiful coastal lagoon. This is where the San Andreas Fault heads off from land into the sea. In winter, the main attraction is steelhead fishing in the Garcia River. Spring and early summer see a variety of coastal wildflowers and the park provides habitat for tundra swans.

**Campsites, facilities:** When open, there are 18-40 sites for tents or RVs up to 30 feet and one group site for 40 people. The walk-in campground has closed. Service reductions are in place.

**Reservations, fees:** Seasonal reservations for the group site are accepted at 800/444-7275 or online at www.reserveamerica.com. All other sites are first-come first-served. Sites are $25 per night, plus $8 per night for each additional vehicle; the group site is $100 per night. Open summer only with service reductions in place.

**Directions:** On U.S. 101 north of Santa Rosa, turn west on River Road and drive 16 miles to Guerneville and Highway 116. Continue west on Highway 116 and drive about 20 miles to

Highway 1 at Jenner. Turn north on Highway 1 and drive 55 miles to Point Arena. From Point Arena, continue north about five miles to Kinney Lane. Turn left and drive one mile to the campground entrance on the right.

**Contact:** Manchester State Park, 707/882-2463; Mendocino District, 707/937-5804, www.parks.ca.gov.

## 71 SHELDON CREEK

### Scenic rating: 3

near Hopland

**Map 4.3, page 237**

Only the locals know about this spot, and hey, there aren't a lot of locals around. The camp is set amid rolling hills, grasslands, and oaks along little Sheldon Creek. It is pretty and quiet in the spring when the hills have greened up, but hot in the summer. Recreational possibilities include hiking and, in the fall, hunting.

**Campsites, facilities:** There are five sites for tents only. Picnic tables and fire grills are provided. Vault toilets are available. No drinking water is available. Garbage must be packed out. Leashed pets are permitted.

**Reservations, fees:** Reservations are not accepted. There is no fee for camping. There is a 14-day stay limit. Open year-round, weather permitting.

**Directions:** From Santa Rosa on U.S. 101, drive north to Hopland and the junction with Highway 175. Turn east on Highway 175 and drive three miles to Old Toll Road. Turn right on Old Toll Road and drive eight miles to the camp.

**Contact:** Bureau of Land Management, Ukiah Field Office, 707/468-4000, www.blm.gov/ca.

## 72 ANCHOR BAY CAMPGROUND

### Scenic rating: 8

near Gualala

**Map 4.3, page 237**

This is a quiet and beautiful stretch of California coast. The six-acre campground is on the ocean side of Highway 1 north of Gualala, with sites set at ocean level as well as amid trees—take your pick. Nearby Gualala Regional Park, six miles to the south, provides an excellent easy hike, the headlands-to-beach loop with coastal views, a lookout of the Gualala River, and many giant cypress trees. In winter, the nearby Gualala River attracts large but elusive steelhead.

**Campsites, facilities:** There are 30 sites for tents or RVs up to 40 feet; 12 sites have partial hookups (15 amps). Picnic tables and fire pits are provided. Drinking water, restrooms with flush toilets and coin showers, Wi-Fi, fish-cleaning room, dive-gear washroom, ice, bait, firewood, picnic area, and a dump station are available. Some facilities are wheelchair-accessible. Leashed pets are permitted, with certain restrictions, at a maximum of two per site.

**Reservations, fees:** Reservations are recommended at 707/884-4222 ($10 reservation fee). Base rates for all sites are $42-54 per night, plus $20 per night for a second vehicle (free if towed by RV), $3-5 per person per night for more than two people, and $3 per pet per day. Boat launching is $5 per day. Some credit cards are accepted. Off-season and senior discounts are available. Open year-round.

**Directions:** From San Francisco, take U.S. 101 north to Cotati/Rhonert Park and the exit for Highway 116. Take that exit to Highway 116 West and drive 14 miles to River Road/Main Street (still Highway 116). Turn left and drive 12 miles to Highway 1 at Jenner. Turn north on Highway 1 and drive 38 miles to Gualala. Continue four miles north on Highway 1 to the campground on the left (west) side of the road.

**Contact:** Anchor Bay Campground, 707/884-4222, www.abcamp.com.

## 7.3 GUALALA POINT REGIONAL PARK

🚶 🚴 🏊 🎣 🐕 ♿ 🚐 ⛺

**Scenic rating: 8**

at Sonoma County Regional Park

**Map 4.3, page 237**

This is a dramatic spot near the ocean, close to the mouth of the Gualala River. The campground is on the east side of the highway, about 0.3 mile from the ocean. A trail along the bluff provides an easy hiking adventure; on the west side of the highway other trails to the beach are available.

**Campsites, facilities:** There are 23 sites for tents or RVs up to 25 feet (no hookups) and one hike-in/bike-in site. Picnic tables and fire rings are provided. Drinking water, restrooms with flush toilets and coin showers, dump station, and firewood are available. Some facilities are wheelchair-accessible. Leashed pets are permitted with valid rabies certificate.

**Reservations, fees:** Reservations are accepted on weekdays at 707/565-2267 ($9.50 reservation fee). Sites are $35 per night, plus $7 per night for each additional vehicle; the hike-in/bike-in site is $5 per night; and it's $2 per pet per night. Open year-round.

**Directions:** On U.S. 101 north of Santa Rosa, turn west on River Road and drive 16 miles to Guerneville and Highway 116. Continue west on Highway 116 and drive about 20 miles to Highway 1 at Jenner. Turn north on Highway 1 and drive 38 miles to Gualala. Turn right at the park entrance (a day-use area is on the west side of the highway).

**Contact:** Gualala Point Regional Park 707/785-2377, www.sonomacounty.ca.gov or http://parks.sonomacounty.ca.gov.

## 7.4 CLOVERDALE/ HEALDSBURG KOA

🚶 🏊 🎣 🎣 🐕 🛶 ♿ 🚐 ⛺

**Scenic rating: 7**

near the Russian River

**Map 4.3, page 237**

This KOA campground is just above the Russian River in the Alexander Valley wine country, just south of Cloverdale. The park is both rustic and tidy. The hillside pool has a nice view. In addition, a fishing pond is stocked with largemouth bass, bluegill, and catfish. On moonless nights, this is a great place for stargazing. Bird-watching is another pastime in this area. The nearby Russian River is an excellent beginner's route in an inflatable kayak or canoe. The nearby wineries in Asti make for a popular side trip.

**Campsites, facilities:** There are 75 sites with full hookups (30 and 50 amps) for RVs of any length, 42 sites for tents, 18 cabins, and 10 lodges. Some sites are pull-through. Picnic tables and fire rings and barbecues are provided. Restrooms with flush toilets and showers, Wi-Fi, solar-heated swimming pool, gymnastic playground, dump station, coin laundry, recreation room, mini golf, spa and hot tub, nature trails, catch-and-release fish pond, weekend entertainment in the summer, and a convenience and gift store are available. Some facilities are wheelchair-accessible. Leashed pets are permitted, with certain restrictions.

**Reservations, fees:** Reservations are accepted at 800/562-4042. RV sites with full hookups are $60-75 (pull-through, view, and 50 amps), tent sites are $63-82 (with electricity), plus $10 per person per night for more than two people. Camping cabins are $76-86 per night, and lodges are $150-215 per night. Some credit cards are accepted. Open year-round.

**Directions:** From Cloverdale on U.S. 101, take the Central Cloverdale exit, which puts you on Asti Road. Drive straight on Asti Road to 1st Street. Turn right (east) and drive a short distance to River Road. Turn right (south) and drive four miles to Asti Ridge Road. Turn left and drive to the campground entrance.

In summer/fall: South of Cloverdale on U.S. 101, take the Asti exit to Asti Road. Turn right (south) on Asti Road and drive 1.5 miles to Washington School Road. Turn left (east) and drive 1.5 miles to Asti Ridge Road. Turn right and drive to the campground entrance. Note: This route is usually open Memorial Day weekend through late November, when a seasonal bridge is in place. Both routes are well signed.

**Contact:** Cloverdale KOA, 707/894-3337 or 800/562-4042, www.winecountrykoa.com.

## 75 DUTCHER CREEK RV PARK & CAMPGROUND

🏊 🦌 🚐 ⛺

### Scenic rating: 6

in the Alexander Valley

**Map 4.3, page 237**

This RV park is set in foothill-style oak woodlands and provides a layover spot for those touring the Alexander Valley wine country. The Russian River is nearby, running north to south through Cloverdale, the valley, and on to Healdsburg.

**Campsites, facilities:** There are 10 RV sites available with full hookups (30 and 50 amp) and four tent sites. One site is pull-through. Picnic tables are provided. Drinking water, a swimming pool, a coin laundry, and restrooms with flush toilets and showers are available. Leashed pets are permitted.

**Reservations, fees:** Reservations are accepted. Tent sites are $40 per night and RV sites are $60 per night, with weekly and monthly rates available. Credit cards are accepted online only. Open year-round.

**Directions:** From U.S. 101 south of Cloverdale, take the Dutcher Creek Road exit and drive 0.2 mile to Theresa Drive. Turn west on Theresa Drive and drive 0.3 mile to the campground.

**Contact:** Dutcher Creek RV Park &

Campground, 707/894-4829, www.dutchercreekrv.com.

## 76 LAKE SONOMA RECREATION AREA

🚶 🏊 🛶 🎣 🐕 ♿ 🚐 ⛺

### Scenic rating: 8

near Healdsburg

**Map 4.3, page 237**    **BEST (**

Lake Sonoma is one of the best weekend vacation sites for Bay Area campers. The developed campground (Liberty Glen) is fine for car campers, but the boat-in sites are ideal for folks who desire a quiet and pretty lakeside setting. This is a big lake, extending nine miles north on the Dry Creek arm and four miles west on the Warm Springs Creek arm. An adjacent 8,000-acre wildlife area was set aside to protect nesting peregrine falcons. Forty miles of hiking trails traverse the area. The lake elevation is 450 feet, with 53 miles of shoreline and hundreds of hidden coves. A sandy swimming beach is available at Yorty Creek, but there is no lifeguard. The water-skier versus angler conflict has been resolved by limiting high-speed boats to specified areas. Laws are strictly enforced, making this lake excellent for either sport. Wildlife-watching includes wild pigs, wild turkeys, blacktail deer, and river otters. The best fishing is in the protected coves of the Warm Springs and Dry Creek arms of the lake. Fish species include bass, catfish, rainbow trout, crappie, and sunfish. The visitors center is adjacent to a public fish hatchery. Steelhead come to spawn from the Russian River between late December and late March.

**Campsites, facilities:** There are 103 primitive boat-in/hike-in sites around the lake and 95 tent and RV sites (no hookups). There are also five group sites, including two boat-in, one equestrian, and two drive-in at Liberty Glen Campground (2.5 miles from the lake). Picnic tables, fire grills, vault toilets, lantern poles, and garbage bins are provided at the primitive sites, but no drinking water is available. Picnic tables, fire rings, and lantern holders are provided at Liberty Glen, and showers and flush toilets are also available. A boat ramp and houseboat and boat rentals are nearby. Saturday night campfire talks are held at an amphitheater during the summer. Campsites have limited facilities in winter. Some facilities are wheelchair-accessible. Leashed pets are permitted.

**Reservations, fees:** Reservations are accepted at 877/444-6777 ($10 reservation fee) or www.recreation.gov ($9 reservation fee). Reservations for equestrian sites are accepted at 707/431-4590. Single sites are $24-50 per night (non-electric). Group and equestrian group sites are $50-100 per night. Open year-round.

**Directions:** From Santa Rosa, drive north on U.S. 101 to Healdsburg. In Healdsburg, take the Dry Creek Road exit, turn left, and drive northwest for 11 miles. After you cross a small bridge, the visitors center will be on your right.

To reach the Yorty Creek Boat Ramp: On U.S. 101 at the south end of Cloverdale, take the Cloverdale Boulevard exit to Cloverdale Boulevard. Turn right on Cloverdale Boulevard and drive one block to Treadway Street. Turn left and drive two blocks to Foothill Boulevard. Turn right and drive 0.75 mile to Hot Springs Road. Turn left and drive about five miles to the boat launch. Note: Hot Springs Road is narrow with many hairpin turns. Trailers are prohibited, but the launch provides access for canoes, kayaks, and car-top boats to boat-in sites nearby.

**Contact:** U.S. Army Corps of Engineers, Lake Sonoma Visitor Center, 707/431-4533; headquarters, 707/431-4590; Lake Sonoma Marina, 707/433-2200.

## 77 SALT POINT STATE PARK

### Scenic rating: 9

near Fort Ross

**Map 4.3, page 237**

This is a gorgeous piece of Sonoma coast, highlighted by Fisk Mill Cove, inshore kelp beds, outstanding short hikes, and abalone diving. In fact, this is one of the finest diving areas for red abalone in the state. There is also an underwater reserve for divers, which is a protected area. Unfortunately, diving accidents do occur because of the occasional large surf, strong currents, and rocky shoreline. There are two campgrounds, Gerstle Cove Campground and the much larger Woodside Campground. Great hikes include Bluff Trail and Stump Beach Trail (great views). During abalone season, this is one of the best and most popular spots on the Northern California coast; note that new regulations require a review to ensure no diving in closed areas. The Kruse Rhododendron Reserve is within the park and definitely worth the stroll. This 317-acre conservation reserve features second-growth redwoods, Douglas firs, tanoaks, and many rhododendrons, with five miles of hiking trails. After the fall rains, this area is popular for mushroom hunters (the Kruse Rhododendron Reserve is closed to mushroom picking). Mushroom hunters must park in the area open to picking and are limited to five pounds per day. Of course, this can be a dangerous hobby; eat only mushrooms you can identify as safe. But you knew that, right?

**Campsites, facilities:** At Gerstle Cove Campground, there are 30 sites for tents or RVs up to 31 feet (no hookups). At Woodside Campground, there are 79 sites for tents or RVs up to 31 feet (no hookups), 20 walk-in tent sites (about a 300-yard walk), 10 hike-in/bike-in sites, a group site that can accommodate up to 40 people, and a primitive overflow area for self-contained vehicles. Picnic tables and fire rings are provided. Drinking water and flush toilets are available. Summer interpretive programs may be offered; firewood is available for purchase. Call before planning a trip, as services may be reduced or closed. The picnic area and one hiking trail are wheelchair-accessible. Leashed pets are permitted, except on trails.

**Reservations, fees:** Reservations are accepted at 877/444-6777 ($10 reservation fee) or www.recreation.gov ($9 reservation fee). Sites at Gerstle Cove and Woodside are $35 per night, plus $8 per night for each additional vehicle; Woodside's tent-only sites are $25 per night, hike-in/bike-in sites are $5 per person per night, and the group site is $200 per night. The park is open year-round; some campsites may close seasonally.

**Directions:** On U.S. 101 north of Santa Rosa, turn west on River Road and drive 16 miles to Guerneville and Highway 116. Continue west on Highway 116 and drive 13.1 miles to Highway 1 at Jenner. Turn north on Highway 1 and drive about 20 miles to the park entrance; Woodside Campground is on the right and Gerstle Cove is on the left.

**Contact:** Salt Point State Park, 707/847-3221; Russian River District, 707/865-2391, www.parks.ca.gov.

## 78 OCEAN COVE CAMPGROUND

### Scenic rating: 8

near Fort Ross

**Map 4.3, page 237**

The highlights here are the campsites on a bluff overlooking the ocean. Alas, it can be foggy during the summer. A good side trip is to Fort Ross, with a stellar easy hike available on the Fort Ross Trail, which features a walk through an old colonial fort as well as great coastal views, excellent for whale-watching. There is also excellent hiking at Stillwater Cove Regional Park, just a mile to the south off Highway 1.

**Campsites, facilities:** There are 125 pull-through sites for tents or RVs of any length (no hookups) and three large group sites. Picnic tables and fire grills are provided. Drinking water, chemical toilets, and coin showers are available. A boat launch, grocery store, fishing supplies, and diving-gear sales are nearby. Leashed pets are permitted.

**Reservations, fees:** Reservations are not accepted for individual sites but are required for group sites. Sites are $26 per night per vehicle,

plus $2 per pet per night and $8 per day for boat launching. The group site is $260 per night for up to 10 vehicles, plus $26 per night per each additional vehicle. Some credit cards are accepted. Open April through November.

**Directions:** From San Francisco, take U.S. 101 north to Cotati/Rohnert Park and the exit for Highway 116. Take that exit to Highway 116 west and drive 14 miles to River Road/Main Street (still Highway 116). Turn left and drive 12 miles to Highway 1 at Jenner. Turn north on Highway 1 and drive 17 miles north on Highway 1 (five miles north of Fort Ross) to the campground entrance on the left.

**Contact:** Ocean Cove Campground, 707/847-3422, www.oceancove.org.

## 79 STILLWATER COVE REGIONAL PARK

### Scenic rating: 8

near Fort Ross

**Map 4.3, page 237**

Stillwater Cove has a dramatic rock-strewn cove and sits on a classic chunk of Sonoma coast. The campground is sometimes overlooked, since it is a county-operated park and not on the state park reservation system. One of the region's great hikes is Stockoff Creek Loop, with the trailhead at the day-use parking lot. In a little more than a mile, the trail is routed through forest with both firs and redwoods, and then along a pretty stream. To get beach access, you must cross Highway 1 and then drop to the cove.

**Campsites, facilities:** There are 20 sites for tents or RVs up to 30 feet (no hookups), as well as a hike-in/bike-in site. Picnic tables and fire rings are provided. Drinking water, restrooms with flush toilets and coin showers, firewood, and a dump station are available. Supplies can be obtained in Ocean Cove (one mile north) and Fort Ross. Some facilities are wheelchair-accessible. Leashed pets are permitted with a valid rabies certificate.

**Reservations, fees:** Reservations are accepted at 707/565-2267 on weekdays ($9.50 reservation fee). Sites are $35 per night, plus $7 per night for each additional vehicle; the hike-in/bike-in site is $5 per night; pets cost $2 per night. Environmental campsites are $20 per night, and group sites are $225 per night. Open year-round.

**Directions:** From San Francisco, take U.S. 101 north to Cotati/Rohnert Park and the exit for Highway 116. Take that exit to Highway 116 west and drive 14 miles to River Road/Main Street (still Highway 116). Turn left and drive 12 miles to Highway 1 at Jenner. Turn north on Highway 1 and drive 16 miles north on Highway 1 (four miles north of Fort Ross) to the park entrance.

**Contact:** Stillwater Cove Regional Park, Sonoma County, 707/847-3245; Sonoma County Regional Parks, 707/565-2041, www.sonomacounty.ca.gov.

## 80 REEF

### Scenic rating: 8

at Fort Ross State Historic Park

**Map 4.3, page 237**

The campground at Fort Ross is two miles south of the north entrance station, less than a quarter mile from the ocean. The privacy and beauty of the campsites vary as much as in any state park in California. Some redwoods and pines provide cover, and some sites are open. The sites at the end of the road fill up very quickly. Though the weather is relatively benign, tents are needed for protection against moisture from fog. From camp, a trail leads down to a beach, more rocky than sandy, and a one-mile trail leads to the fort.

Fort Ross is just as its name announces: an old fort—in this case, an old Russian fort from 1812. As a destination site, Fort Ross is known as a popular abalone diving spot, with the best areas below the campground and at nearby Reef Terrace. It also provides good, easy hikes amid

its 3,386 acres. The park features a museum in the visitors center, which is always a must-see for campers making the tour up Highway 1.

**Campsites, facilities:** There are 21 sites for tents or RVs up to 18 feet (no hookups). Picnic tables, food lockers, and fire rings are provided. Drinking water and flush toilets are available. Call before planning a trip, as services may be reduced or closed. A visitors center and guided tours and programs are available. Some facilities are wheelchair-accessible. Leashed pets are permitted.

**Reservations, fees:** Reservations are not accepted. Sites are $25 per night, plus $8 per night for each additional vehicle. Senior discounts are available. Open April through November, weather permitting.

**Directions:** On U.S. 101 north of Santa Rosa, turn west on River Road and drive 16 miles to Guerneville and Highway 116. Continue west on Highway 116 and drive about 13 miles to Highway 1 at Jenner. Turn north on Highway 1 and drive 10 miles to the (Fort Ross Reef) campground entrance. To reach the main state park entrance, drive north for two miles.

**Contact:** Fort Ross State Historic Park, 707/847-3286 or 707/847-3708, www.parks.ca.gov or www.fortrossstatepark.org.

## 81 BULLFROG POND

### Scenic rating: 7

in Austin Creek State Recreation Area near the Russian River

**Map 4.3, page 237**

Austin Creek State Recreation Area and Armstrong Redwoods State Reserve together form 7,000 acres of continuous parkland. Bullfrog Pond is in Austin Creek SRA, set near a pond and in an open landscape featuring woodlands and foothills; the rugged topography provides a sense of isolation. The highlight is a system of 22 miles of hiking trails leading to a series of small creeks: Schoolhouse Creek, Gilliam Creek, and Austin Creek. The hikes involve steep climbs, and in the summer it's hot—with temperatures occasionally exceeding 100°F—so plan accordingly. All of the park's trails are open to horses, and horseback-riding rentals are available in adjacent Armstrong Redwoods State Park. There are many attractive side-trip possibilities, including Armstrong Redwoods, of course, but also canoeing on the Russian River (3.5 miles away), fishing (smallmouth bass in summer, steelhead in winter), and wine-tasting. Annual winter rainfall often exceeds 50 inches. Elevations range 150-1,900 feet on Marble Mine Ridge.

**Campsites, facilities:** There are 23 sites for tents or RVs up to 20 feet (no hookups or trailers) and three backcountry campsites (requiring a hike of 3.5-5.1 miles) at Tom King and Manning Flat. Picnic tables and fire grills are provided. Drinking water and flush toilets are available; only vault toilets are available at the backcountry sites, and there is no drinking water. Some facilities are wheelchair-accessible. Leashed pets are permitted at the main campground only.

**Reservations, fees:** Reservations are not accepted. A backcountry permit is required for the backcountry sites. Sites are $25 per night, plus $8 per night for each additional vehicle. Group reservations are available for $35 per night. Open year-round, but expect occasional fire closures during summer.

**Directions:** On U.S. 101 north of Santa Rosa, turn west on River Road and drive 15 miles to Guerneville and Armstrong Woods Road. Turn right and drive 2.5 miles to the entrance of Armstrong Redwoods State Park. Check in at the kiosk, and continue 3.5 miles through Armstrong Redwoods to Austin Creek State Recreation Area and the campground. The final 2.5 miles are steep and narrow, and no trailers, towed vehicles, or vehicles over 20 feet are permitted.

**Contact:** Austin Creek State Recreation Area, 707/869-2015 or 707/865-2391, www.parks.ca.gov; Stewards of the Coast and Redwoods, 707/869-9177, www.stewardsofthecoastandredwoods.org.

## 82 CASINI RANCH FAMILY CAMPGROUND

**Scenic rating: 8**

on the Russian River

**Map 4.3, page 237**

Woods and water—this campground has both, with sites near the Russian River in both sun-filled and shaded areas. Its location on the lower river makes a side trip to the coast easy, with Sonoma Coast State Beach about a 15-minute drive to the west. No long-term rentals are available.

**Campsites, facilities:** There are 225 sites for tents or RVs of any length; many have full or partial hookups (30 amps), and some sites are pull-through. Group and youth group camping and cabins (no pets) are also available. Picnic tables and fire grills are provided. Restrooms with flush toilets and showers, a playground, a dump station, coin laundry, cable TV, Wi-Fi, game arcade, boat and canoe rentals, propane gas, group facilities, seasonal activities, and a convenience store are available. Some facilities are wheelchair-accessible. Leashed pets are permitted.

**Reservations, fees:** Reservations are accepted at 800/451-8400. RV sites with full hookups are $58-66 per night, RV sites with partial hookups are $53-66 (riverfront) per night, tent sites are $52-59 per night, plus $5-14 per person per night for more than two people and $2 per pet per night. Group camping is $225-275 per night. Weekly and monthly rates are available. Discounts are available weekdays and in the off-season. Some credit cards are accepted. Open year-round.

**Directions:** On U.S. 101 north of Santa Rosa, turn west on River Road and drive 16 miles to Guerneville and Highway 116. Continue west on Highway 116 and drive eight miles to Duncan Mills and Moscow Road. Turn left (southeast) on Moscow Road and drive 0.6 mile to the campground on the left.

**Contact:** Casini Ranch Family Campground Store, 707/865-2255, www.casiniranch.com.

## 83 WRIGHTS BEACH

### Scenic rating: 8

in Sonoma Coast State Park

**Map 4.3, page 237**

This park provides more than its share of heaven and hell. This state park campground is at the north end of a beach that stretches south for about a mile, yet to the north it is steep and rocky. The campsites are considered a premium because of their location next to the beach. Because the campsites are often full, a key plus is an overflow area available for self-contained vehicles. Sonoma Coast State Beach stretches from Bodega Head to Vista Trail for 17 miles, separated by rock bluffs and headlands that form a series of beaches. More than a dozen access points from the highway allow you to reach the beach. There are many excellent side trips. The best is to the north, where you can explore dramatic Shell Beach (the turnoff is on the west side of Highway 1) or take Pomo Trail (the trailhead is on the east side of the highway, across from Shell Beach) up the adjacent foothills for sweeping views of the coast. That's the heaven. Now for the hell: Dozens of people have drowned here. Wrights Beach is not for swimming; rip currents, heavy surf, and surprise rogue waves can make even playing in the surf dangerous. Many rescues are made each year. The bluffs and coastal rocks can also be unstable and unsafe for climbing. Got it? 1) Stay clear of the water. 2) Don't climb the bluffs. Now it's up to you to get it right.

**Campsites, facilities:** There are 29 sites for tents or RVs up to 27 feet (no hookups), with a limit of eight people per site, and an overflow area for self-contained vehicles. Picnic tables, food lockers, and fire rings are provided. Garbage must be packed out. Call before planning a trip, as services may be reduced or closed. Showers and a dump station are available at nearby Bodega Dunes Campground. Some facilities are wheelchair-accessible. Leashed pets are permitted in the campground and on the beach.

**Reservations, fees:** Reservations are recommended at 877/444-6777 ($10 reservation fee) or www.recreation.gov ($9 reservation fee). Developed sites are $35 per night, premium sites are $45 per night, plus $8 per night for each additional vehicle. Open year-round, weather permitting.

**Directions:** In Petaluma on U.S. 101, take the East Washington exit and turn west (this street becomes Bodega Avenue). Drive west through Petaluma and continue for 17 miles to Highway 1. Turn right (north) on Highway 1 and drive nine miles to Bodega Bay. From Bodega Bay, continue north for six miles to the campground entrance.

**Contact:** Sonoma Coast State Park, 707/875-3483, www.parks.ca.gov.

## 84 BODEGA BAY RV PARK

### Scenic rating: 8

in Bodega Bay

**Map 4.3, page 237**

Bodega Bay RV Park is one of the oldest RV parks in the state, and there are few north-state coastal destinations better than Bodega Bay. Excellent seafood restaurants are five minutes away, and some of the best deep-sea fishing is available out of Bodega Bay Sportfishing. In addition, there is a great view of the ocean at nearby Bodega Head to the west. It is a 35-minute walk from the park to the beach.

**Campsites, facilities:** There are 72 sites, most with full hookups (30 and 50 amps), for RVs of any length; some sites are pull-through. No tents are permitted. Picnic tables are provided. Drinking water and restrooms with flush toilets and showers are available. Coin laundry, restaurant, group facilities, horseshoes, video arcade, bocce ball, Wi-Fi, and cable TV are available. Some facilities are wheelchair-accessible. Leashed pets are permitted.

**Reservations, fees:** Reservations are recommended at 800/201-6864. RV sites with full hookups are $46 per night, RV sites without hookups are $35 per night, plus $5 per person per night for more than four people. Group discounts are available. Some credit cards are accepted. Open year-round.

**Directions:** In Petaluma on U.S. 101, take the East Washington exit and turn west (this street becomes Bodega Avenue). Drive west through Petaluma and continue for 17 miles to Highway 1. Turn right (north) on Highway 1 and drive nine miles to Bodega Bay. In Bodega Bay, continue north for two miles to the RV park on the left.

**Contact:** Bodega Bay RV Park, 2001 Hwy. 1, 707/875-3701, www.bodegabayrvpark.com.

## 85 BODEGA DUNES

### Scenic rating: 8

in Sonoma Coast State Park

**Map 4.3, page 237**

Sonoma Coast State Park features several great campgrounds, and if you like beaches, this one rates high. Bodega Dunes campground is near Salmon Creek Beach, the closest beach to the campground and far safer than Wrights Beach. The beach stretches for miles, providing stellar beach walks and excellent beach-combing during low tides. For some campers, a foghorn sounding repeatedly through the night can make sleep difficult. The quietest sites are among the dunes. A day-use area includes a wheelchair-accessible boardwalk that leads out to a sandy beach. In summer, campfire programs and junior ranger programs are often offered. To the nearby south is Bodega Bay, with a major deep-sea sportfishing operation—crowned by often excellent salmon fishing; check current fishing regulations. The town of Bodega Bay offers a full marina and restaurants.

**Campsites, facilities:** There are 98 sites for tents or RVs up to 31 feet (no hookups) and one hike-in/bike-in site. Picnic tables, food lockers, and fire grills are provided. Drinking water, restrooms with flush toilets and showers, and

a dump station may be available. Call before planning a trip, as services may be limited or closed. Laundry facilities, supplies, and horse rentals are less than a mile away. Some facilities, including a boardwalk to the beach, are wheelchair-accessible. Leashed pets are permitted at the campsites only.

**Reservations, fees:** Reservations are accepted at 877/444-6777 ($10 reservation fee) or www.recreation.gov ($9 reservation fee). Sites are $35 per night, plus $8 per night for each additional vehicle; the hike-in/bike-in site is $5 per person per night. Open year-round.

**Directions:** In Santa Rosa on U.S. 101, turn west on Highway 12 and drive 10 miles to Sebastopol (Highway 12 becomes Bodega Highway). Continue straight (west) for 10 miles to Bodega. Continue for 0.5 mile to Highway 1. Turn right (north) on Highway 1 and drive five miles to Bodega Bay. Continue 0.5 mile north to the campground entrance on the left (west).

**Contact:** Sonoma Coast State Park, 707/875-3483, www.parks.ca.gov.

## 86 WESTSIDE REGIONAL PARK

### Scenic rating: 7

on Bodega Bay

**Map 4.3, page 237**

This campground is on the west shore of Bodega Bay. One of the greatest boat launches on the coast is adjacent to the park on the south, providing access to prime fishing waters. Salmon fishing is excellent from mid-June through August; check current fishing regulations. A small, protected beach (where kids can dig in the sand and wade) is at the end of the road beyond the campground. The state beach nearby has hiking trails.

**Campsites, facilities:** There are 45 sites for tents or RVs of any length (no hookups); most sites are pull-through. Picnic tables and fire grills are provided. Drinking water, restrooms with flush toilets and coin showers, a fish-cleaning station, a boat rinsing station, firewood, a dump station, and a boat ramp are available. Supplies can be obtained in Bodega Bay. Some facilities are wheelchair-accessible. Leashed pets are permitted with a valid rabies certificate.

**Reservations, fees:** Reservations are accepted on weekdays at 707/565-2267 ($9.50 reservation fee). Sites are $35 per night, plus $7 per night for each additional vehicle and $2 per pet per night. Open year-round.

**Directions:** In Petaluma on U.S. 101, take the East Washington exit and turn west (this street becomes Bodega Avenue). Drive west through Petaluma and continue for 17 miles to Highway 1 north. Merge right onto Highway 1 and drive north nine miles to Bodega Bay. In Bodega Bay, continue north to Eastshore Road. Turn left and drive one block to Bay Flat Road. Turn right and drive (becomes Westshore Road) two miles to the park on the left, 0.5 mile past Spud Point Marina.

**Contact:** Westside Regional Park, Sonoma County Parks Department, 707/875-3540 or 707/565-2041, www.sonomacounty.ca.gov.

## 87 PORTO BODEGA MARINA & RV PARK

🏊 📷 🐕 🚐

### Scenic rating: 7
in Bodega Bay

Map 4.3, page 237

This RV park is a short distance from Bodega Bay. The sites are open, most with full hookups, and the park is designed as a base to launch get-aways. Fishing is often excellent out of Bodega Bay, and charter boat operations and an excellent marina and boat ramp are nearby. Nearby Bodega Head is an excellent spot for short walks or to watch the sunset.

**Campsites, facilities:** There are 58 sites for RVs up to 42 feet, 18 of which have full hookups (20, 30, and 50 amp). Picnic tables and fire pits are provided. Drinking water, restrooms with flush toilets, showers, boat launch, cable

TV hookups, and a dump station are available. Restaurants and grocery stores are nearby. Leashed pets are permitted.

**Reservations, fees:** Reservations are recommended at 707/875-2354. Sites with hookups are $57-62 per night ($45 per night without hookups).

**Directions:** From U.S. 101 in Santa Rosa, drive west on Highway 12 to Sebastopol, where Highway 12 becomes Bodega Highway. Continue west on Bodega Highway 11 miles to where Bodega Highway ends at Highway 1. Turn right and drive five miles into Bodega Bay. Turn left on Eastshore Road and drive one block to the intersection with Bay Flat Road. Drive straight through the intersection and bear right to the campground.

**Contact:** Porto Bodega Marina & RV Park, 1500 Bay Flat Rd., 707/875-2354, www.porto-bodega.com.

## 88 DORAN REGIONAL PARK

🏊 📷 🐕 ♿ 🚐 ⛺

### Scenic rating: 7
on Bodega Bay

Map 4.3, page 237

This campground is beside Doran Beach on Bodega Bay, which offers complete fishing and marina facilities. In season, it's also a popular clamming and crabbing spot. This park has a wide, somewhat sheltered sandy beach. Salmon fishing is often excellent during the summer at the Whistle Buoy offshore from Bodega Head, and rock fishing is good year-round offshore. Fishing is also available off the rock jetty in the park.

**Campsites, facilities:** There are 132 sites for tents or RVs of any length (no hookups), one group tent site for up to 50 people, and one hike-in/bike-in site. Picnic tables and fire grills are provided. Drinking water, restrooms with flush toilets and coin showers, dump stations, fish-cleaning station, and a boat ramp are available. Some facilities are wheelchair-accessible. Supplies can be obtained in Bodega

Bay. Leashed pets are permitted with a valid rabies certificate.

**Reservations, fees:** Reservations are accepted on weekdays at 707/565-2267 ($9.50 reservation fee). Sites are $32 per night, plus $7 per night for each additional vehicle and $2 per pet per night; the hike-in/bike-in site is $5 per night. The group site is $225 per night. Environmental sites are $20 per night. Open year-round.

**Directions:** In Petaluma on U.S. 101, take the East Washington exit and turn west (this street becomes Bodega Avenue). Drive west through Petaluma and continue for 17 miles to Highway 1. Merge right (north) on Highway 1 and drive toward Bodega Bay and Doran Park Road. Turn left onto the campground entrance road. If you reach the town of Bodega Bay, you have gone a mile too far.

**Contact:** Sonoma County Parks Department, 707/875-3540 or 707/565-2041, www.sonoma-county.org.

## 89 EDGEWATER RESORT AND RV PARK

**Scenic rating: 7**

on Clear Lake

**Map 4.4, page 238**

Soda Bay is one of Clear Lake's prettiest and most intimate spots, and this camp provides excellent access. It also provides friendly, professional service. Both waterskiing and fishing for bass and bluegill are excellent in this part of the lake. The resort has 600 feet of lake frontage, including a 300-foot swimming beach and a 230-foot fishing pier. This resort specializes in groups and family reunions. Wine-tasting, casinos, and golfing are nearby. Insider's tip: This park is very pet friendly and has occasional doggie socials. Note: All boats must be certified mussel-free before launching.

**Campsites, facilities:** There are 61 sites with full hookups (20, 30, and 50 amps) for tents or RVs of any length, and eight cabins. Picnic tables and fire grills are provided. Restrooms

with showers, cable TV, Wi-Fi, a clubhouse, group facilities, a general store, a coin laundry, a seasonal heated swimming pool, horseshoes, volleyball, and table tennis are available. A seasonal swimming beach, pet station, dog run, boat ramp, fishing pier, boat docking, fish-cleaning station, bait and tackle, and watercraft rentals are on the premises. Firewood is available for purchase. Leashed pets are permitted.

**Reservations, fees:** Reservations are accepted at 800/396-6224. Gold sites for RVs or tents are $45 per night, Silver sites are $40 per night, and standard sites are $35 per night, plus $5 per person per night for more than two people and $5 per pet per night. Boat launching is $10 per day and includes slip and trailer parking. RVs and tents cannot occupy the same site. Group rates are available. Holiday rates are higher. Winter discounts and weekly rates are available. Some credit cards are accepted. Open year-round.

**Directions:** In Kelseyville on Highway 29, take the Merritt Road exit and drive on Merritt Road for two miles (it becomes Gaddy Lane) to Soda Bay Road. Turn right on Soda Bay Road and drive three miles to the campground entrance on the left.

**Contact:** Edgewater Resort and RV Park, 6420 Soda Bay Rd., 707/279-0208, www.edgewater-resort.net.

## 90 SHAW'S SHADY ACRES

**Scenic rating: 7**

on Cache Creek

**Map 4.4, page 238**

Shaw's Shady Acres is beside Cache Creek, just south of Clear Lake. Canoeing and kayaking are popular. The fishing for catfish is often quite good on summer nights in Cache Creek, a deep, green, slow-moving water that looks more like a slough in a Mississippi bayou than a creek. Waterfront campsites with scattered walnut, ash, and oak trees are available. Clear Lake (the lake, not the town) is a short drive to the north, and a state park is across the creek, an excellent destination for kayaking. In addition to the campsites, there are an additional 36 long-term or permanent sites. Note: All boats must be certified mussel-free before launching.

**Campsites, facilities:** There are six RV sites with full hookups (30 amps) and 10 tent sites. Picnic tables and barbecues are provided. Restrooms with showers, a fishing dock, fishing boat rentals, a boat ramp, coin laundry, swimming pool (seasonal), fishing supplies, and a convenience store are available. Leashed pets are allowed, with certain restrictions.

**Reservations, fees:** Reservations are recommended. Sites are $30 per night, plus $4 per person per night for more than two people. Boat launching is free for campers. Open year-round.

**Directions:** From the town of Lower Lake, drive north on Highway 53 for 1.3 miles to Old Highway 53. Turn left on Old Highway 53 and then almost immediately you will arrive at Cache Creek Way. Turn left and drive 0.25 mile to the park entrance.

**Contact:** Shaw's Shady Acres, 7805 Cache Creek Way, 707/994-2236, www.shadyacres-clearlake.com.

## 91 CACHE CREEK REGIONAL PARK

**Scenic rating: 7**

near Rumsey

**Map 4.4, page 238**

This is the best campground in Yolo County, yet it's known by few out-of-towners. It is at 1,300 feet elevation beside Cache Creek, which is the river closest to the Bay Area that provides white-water rafting opportunities. This section of river features primarily Class I and II water, ideal for inflatable kayaks and overnight trips. One rapid, Big Mother, is sometimes considered Class III, though that might be a stretch. Of course, drought conditions may change this. For current water levels, contact Yolo County

Flood Control and Water Conservation District (530/662-0265, www.yolocounty.org).

**Campsites, facilities:** There are 45 sites for tents or RVs up to 42 feet (no hookups), including some pull-through sites, and four group sites that can accommodate 20-30 people. Picnic tables, barbecue pits, and fire rings are provided. Drinking water, restrooms with flush toilets, a playground, and a dump station are available. Some facilities are wheelchair-accessible. Leashed pets are permitted.

**Reservations, fees:** Reservations are accepted for the group sites and for some of the individual sites at 530/406-4880. Sites are $25 per night, plus $6 per night for each additional vehicle and $2 per pet per night. Group sites are $115-165 per night. Hike-in/bike-in sites are $25. Off-season discounts are available. Yolo County residents get a discount. Open year-round.

**Directions:** From Vacaville on I-80, turn north on I-505 and drive 21 miles to Madison and the junction with Highway 16 West. Turn northwest on Highway 16 and drive northwest for about 35 miles to the town of Rumsey. From Rumsey, continue west on Highway 16 for five miles to the park entrance on the left.

**Contact:** Cache Creek Regional Park, 1475 Hwy. 16, 530/406-4880, www.yolocounty.org.

## 92 BOGGS MOUNTAIN DEMONSTRATION STATE FOREST

**Scenic rating: 5**

near Middletown

**Map 4.4, page 238**

This overlooked spot is in a state forest that covers 3,500 acres of pine and Douglas fir. There are two adjoining campgrounds. This is a popular destination for the region's equestrians, with numerous trails for horses, hikers, and bikers. Remember: Equestrians have the right of way over hikers and bikers, and hikers have the right of way over bikers. Got it? The

International Mountain Biking Association has chosen this as one of the top 10 riding areas in the country. A 14-mile trail system started as a series of hand-built fire lines. Note that in early fall, this area is open to deer hunting. Boggs is one of nine state forests managed with the purpose of demonstrating economical forest management, which means there is logging along with compatible recreation.

**Campsites, facilities:** There are 19 sites for tents or RVs up to 22 feet (no hookups). No drinking water is available. Picnic tables and fire pits are provided. Vault toilets are available. Garbage must be packed out. A coin laundry, pizza parlor, and gas station are within two miles. Horses and leashed pets are permitted.

**Reservations, fees:** Reservations are not accepted. Sites are $10 per night; group sites are $25 per night. Self-registration is required. Open year-round.

**Directions:** From Vallejo, drive north on Highway 29 past Calistoga to Middletown and the junction with Highway 175. Turn left (north) on Highway 175 and drive seven miles (through the town of Cobb) to Forestry Road. Turn right and drive one mile to the campground on the left.

**Contact:** Boggs Mountain Demonstration State Forest, 707/928-4378, www.fire.ca.gov or www.boggsmountain.net.

## 93 LOWER HUNTING CREEK

### Scenic rating: 4

near Lake Berryessa

**Map 4.4, page 238**

This little-known camp might seem, to the folks who wind up here accidentally, as if it's out in the middle of nowhere, and it turns out that it is. If you plan on spending a few days here, it's advisable to get information or a map of the surrounding area from the Bureau of Land Management before your trip. There are about 25 miles of trails for off-highway-vehicle exploration on the surrounding lands. In the

fall, the area provides access for deer hunting with generally poor to fair results.

**Campsites, facilities:** There are five sites for tents or RVs up to 20 feet (no hookups) and an overflow area. Picnic tables and fire grills are provided. Shade shelters, garbage cans, and vault toilets are available, but there is no drinking water. Leashed pets are permitted.

**Reservations, fees:** Reservations are not accepted. There is no fee for camping. There is a 14-day stay limit. Open year-round.

**Directions:** In Lower Lake on Highway 29, turn southeast on Morgan Valley Road/Berryessa-Knoxville Road and drive 15 miles to Devilhead Road. Turn south and drive two miles to the campground.

**Contact:** Bureau of Land Management, Ukiah District, 707/468-4000, www.blm.gov/ca.

## 94 CALISTOGA RV AND CAMPGROUND

### Scenic rating: 3

in Calistoga

**Map 4.4, page 238**

What this really is, folks, is just the Napa County Fairgrounds converted into an RV park. It is open year-round, except when the county fair is in progress. Who knows, maybe you can win a stuffed bear. What is more likely, of course, is that you have come for the health spas, with great natural hot springs, mud baths, and assorted goodies at the resorts in Calistoga. Downtown Calistoga is within walking distance, and nearby parks include Bothe-Napa Valley and Robert Louis Stevenson State Parks. Cycling, wine-tasting, and hot-air balloon rides are also popular.

**Campsites, facilities:** There are 69 sites with partial or full hookups (30 and 50 amps) for RVs. Some sites are pull-through. Group sites are available by reservation only with a 10-vehicle minimum. Restrooms with flush toilets and showers, a picnic area, Wi-Fi, and a dump station are available. No fires are permitted. Picnic tables are available for a fee ($10). A nine-hole golf course is adjacent to the campground area. Some facilities are wheelchair-accessible. Leashed pets are permitted.

**Reservations, fees:** Reservations are accepted and are required for groups at 707/942-5221 or online. RV sites with full hookups are $50-60 per night, RV sites with partial hookups are $37-47 per night, plus $5 per person for more than two people and $2 per pet per night. Some credit cards are accepted. Open year-round.

**Directions:** From Napa on Highway 29, drive north to Calistoga, turn right on Lincoln Avenue, and drive four blocks to Fairway. Turn left and drive about four blocks to the end of the road to the campground.

**Contact:** Calistoga RV and Campground, 707/942-5221, www.calistogacampground.org.

## 95 BOTHE-NAPA VALLEY STATE PARK

**Scenic rating: 7**

near Calistoga

**Map 4.4, page 238**

It's always a stunner for newcomers to discover this beautiful park with redwoods and a pretty stream so close to the Napa Valley wine and spa country. Though the campsites are relatively exposed, they are set beneath a pretty oak/bay/madrone forest, with trailheads for hiking nearby. One trail is routed south from the day-use parking lot for 1.8 miles to the restored Bale Grist Mill, a giant waterwheel on a pretty creek. Weekend tours of the Bale Grist Mill are available in summer. Another, more scenic route, the Redwood Trail, heads up Ritchey Canyon, amid redwoods and towering Douglas firs, and along Ritchey Creek, all of it beautiful and intimate. The park covers 2,000 acres. Most of it is rugged, with elevations ranging from 300 to 2,000 feet. In summer, temperatures can reach the hundreds, which is why finding a redwood grove can be stunning. The park has more than 10 miles of trails. Those who explore will find

that the forests are on the north-facing slopes while the south-facing slopes tend to be brushy. The geology is primarily volcanic, yet vegetation hides most of it. Bird-watchers will note that this is one of the few places where you can see six species of woodpeckers, including the star of the show, the pileated woodpecker (the size of a crow).

**Campsites, facilities:** There are 45 sites for tents or a few RVs up to 31 feet and trailers up to 24 feet (no hookups). There are also nine walk-in (up to 50 feet) tent sites, one hike-in/bike-in site, one group tent site for up to 30 people, and three yurts. Picnic tables and fire rings are provided. Drinking water, restrooms with flush toilets and coin showers, and a seasonal swimming pool are available. Supplies can be obtained four miles away in Calistoga. Some facilities are wheelchair-accessible. Leashed pets are permitted, but not on trails.

**Reservations, fees:** Reservations are recommended at 800/444-7275 ($10 reservation fee) or www.reserveamerica.com ($9 reservation fee). Sites are $35 per night, plus $8 per night for each additional vehicle; the group site is $125 per night, hike-in/bike-in sites are $5 per person, and yurts are $70 per night. Cabins are $225 per night. Open year-round.

**Directions:** From Napa on Highway 29, drive north to St. Helena and continue north for five miles (one mile past the entrance to Bale Grist Mill State Park) to the park entrance road on the left.

**Contact:** Bothe-Napa Valley State Park, 707/942-4575, www.parks.ca.gov.

## 96 LAKE SOLANO PARK

**Scenic rating: 6**

near Lake Berryessa

**Map 4.4, page 238**

Lake Solano provides a low-pressure option to nearby Lake Berryessa. It is a long, narrow lake below the outlet at Monticello Dam at Lake Berryessa, technically called the afterbay.

Compared to Berryessa, life here moves at a much slower pace, and some people prefer it. The water temperature at Lake Solano is also much cooler than at Berryessa. The lake has fair trout fishing in the spring, and it is known among Bay Area anglers as the closest fly-fishing spot for trout in the region. No motors, including electric motors, are permitted on boats at the lake. The park covers 177 acres along the river. A swimming pond is available in summer, and a children's fishing pond (trout and bass) is open year-round. The gate closes at night; check in before dusk.

**Campsites, facilities:** There are 56 sites for tents or RVs (no hookups) and 36 sites for tents or RVs (water and electricity, 30 amps) up to 38 feet; some sites are pull-through. Picnic tables and fire grills are provided. Drinking water, restrooms with flush toilets and showers, one dump station, a picnic area, a boat ramp, and boat rentals (summer weekends only) are available. A grocery store is within walking distance, and firewood and ice are sold on the premises. Some facilities are wheelchair-accessible. Leashed pets are permitted in the campground only.

**Reservations, fees:** Reservations are accepted and recommended at least 14 days in advance at 530/795-2990 or online at www.co.solano.ca.us ($9 reservation fee). Tent sites are $21 per night, RV sites with water and electricity are $30 per night, plus $10 per night for each additional vehicle and $1 per pet per night. Some credit cards are accepted. Open year-round.

**Directions:** In Vacaville, turn north on I-505 and drive 11 miles to the junction of Highway 128. Turn west on Highway 128 and drive about five miles (past Winters) to Pleasant Valley Road. Turn left on Pleasant Valley Road (well signed) and drive into the park.

**Contact:** Lake Solano Park, 8685 Pleasant Valley Rd., 530/795-2990, www.co.solano.ca.us.

## 97 JOHNSON'S BEACH & RESORT

**Scenic rating: 7**

on the Russian River in Guerneville

**Map 4.4, page 238**

Johnson's is on the north bank of the Russian River in Guerneville. The resort offers canoes, kayaks, and pedal boats for rent, as well as beach chairs and a boat launch. This is often a good fishing spot for steelhead in early winter.

**Campsites, facilities:** There are 37 sites for tents only. Picnic tables and fire rings are provided. Restrooms with flush toilets, coin showers, a dump station, a laundry room, a game room, and a sandy beach are available.

**Reservations, fees:** Reservations are accepted. Tent sites are $40 per night for two people and one vehicle, $5 per night per each additional person (maximum 4 people). Open mid-May to mid-October with a two-night minimum required.

**Directions:** From Santa Rosa, take U.S. 101 north to River Road. Turn left (west) on River Road and drive 15 miles to Church Street in Guerneville. Turn left (south) on Church Street and drive one block to the campground at the corner of Church and First Streets.

**Contact:** Johnson's Beach & Resort, 707/869-2022, www.johnsonsbeach.com.

## 98 SCHOOLHOUSE CANYON PARK

**Scenic rating: 7**

near Guerneville on the Russian River

**Map 4.4, page 238**

Schoolhouse Canyon Park offers a step back in time on the banks of the Russian River. Just two miles outside Guerneville, this 30-acre heritage park rolls out the welcome mat for families.

**Campsites, facilities:** There are 25 sites for tents or RVs up to 25 feet (some partial hookups). Picnic tables and fire pits are provided.

Restrooms with flush toilets and coin showers are available. Leashed pets are permitted with some restrictions.

**Reservations, fees:** Reservations are accepted. RV sites (with hookups) are $55 per night, tent sites are $40 per night for two people, plus $5 for each additional person, $5 per night for each additional vehicle, and $5 per pet per night. Cash only. Open May to September.

**Directions:** From Santa Rosa, take U.S. 101 north to River Road. Turn left (west) on River Road and drive about 11.5 miles to Schoolhouse Canyon Park.

**Contact:** Schoolhouse Canyon Park, 12600 River Rd., Guerneville, 707/869-2311, www. schoolhousecanyon.com.

## 99 BURKE'S CANOE TRIPS

**Scenic rating: 7**

on the Russian River near Guerneville

**Map 4.4, page 238**

Burke's Canoe Trips is one of the major canoe rental businesses on the Russian River. Their campground is set amid redwoods along the Russian River and provides a great base for canoe trips, including shuttle rides. Canoe and kayak rentals ($65 per canoe trip, $40 per kayak trip, no dogs allowed on trips) include shuttle and equipment for a great paddle through the redwoods to Guerneville. For RV camping, try Mirabel Trailer Park (707/887-2383) next door, but be aware there are many permanent residents—not always a positive thing (and because of that, they do not qualify as a true campground for this book). Because groups come to Burke's for canoe and kayak trips, at times they can turn camping into a loud party into the night.

**Campsites, facilities:** There are 30 sites for tents only and a group site for 75 people. Picnic tables and fire rings are provided. Drinking water and restrooms with flush toilets and showers are available. Canoe and kayak rentals

are available, with shuttle provided for easy return to camp. Pets are not permitted.

**Reservations, fees:** Reservations are highly recommended. Tent sites are $10 per person per night. Call for rates for the group site. Open seasonally May to September, weather permitting.

**Directions:** From Santa Rosa, take U.S. 101 north to River Road. Turn left (west) on River Road and drive 8.2 miles to Burke's, just past the Mirabel Trailer Park and one mile north of Forestville.

**Contact:** Burke's Canoe Trips, 8600 River Rd., 707/887-1222, www.burkescanoetrips.com.

## 100 RIVER BEND RESORT

**Scenic rating: 7**

on the Russian River near Guerneville

**Map 4.4, page 238**

River Bend Resort provides direct access to the Russian River and has a small beach for swimming. Burke's Canoe Trips is nearby, and Korbel Champagne Cellars is adjacent to the property. Guerneville is four miles away.

**Campsites, facilities:** There are 26 tent sites and 62 RV sites (most with full hookups). Picnic tables, fire pits, water, and electricity are provided. Restrooms with flush toilets, showers, a dog walk, a general store, propane, a playground, Wi-Fi, and a sport court are available. Leashed pets are permitted with some restrictions.

**Reservations, fees:** Reservations are required. RV sites with full hookups are $45-55 (riverfront) per night, tent sites are $32-43 per night for four people, plus $5 for each additional person, $5 per night for an additional vehicle, and $5 per pet per night. Open year-round.

**Directions:** From Santa Rosa, take U.S. 101 north to River Road. Turn left (west) on River Road and drive about 11 miles to River Bend Resort.

**Contact:** River Bend Resort, 11820 River Rd., 707/887-7662, www.riverbendresort.net.

## 101 SPRING LAKE REGIONAL PARK

**Scenic rating: 6**

at Spring Lake near Santa Rosa

**Map 4.4, page 238**

Spring Lake is one of the few lakes in the greater Bay Area that provide lakeside camping. No gas-powered boats are permitted on this small, pretty lake, which keeps things fun and quiet for everybody. An easy trail along the west shore of the lake to the dam, then into adjoining Howarth Park, provides a pleasant evening stroll. This little lake is where a 24-pound world-record bass was reportedly caught, a story taken as a hoax by nearly all anglers.

**Campsites, facilities:** There are 26 sites for tents or RVs up to 40 feet (no hookups), four hike-in sites, and one group site for up to 75 people and 15 vehicles. Several sites are pull-through. Picnic tables and fire grills are provided. Drinking water, restrooms with flush toilets and showers, a dump station, a boat ramp (no gas-powered motorboats), and boat rentals (in summer) are available. A grocery store, coin laundry, firewood, and propane gas are available within five minutes. Some facilities are wheelchair-accessible. Leashed pets are permitted.

**Reservations, fees:** Reservations are accepted on weekdays at 707/565-2267 ($9.50 reservation fee). Sites are $35 per night, plus $7 per night for each additional vehicle; hike-in/bike-in sites are $5 per night. Each pet is $2 per night. The group site is $225 per night. There is a 10-day camping limit. Open daily from May through September and on weekends and holidays only during the off-season.

**Directions:** From Santa Rosa on U.S. 101, turn east on Highway 12 and drive two miles to the junction with Hoen Avenue. Continue straight (east) onto Hoen Avenue and drive one mile (crossing Summerfield Road) to Newanga Avenue. Turn left and drive 0.5 mile to the park entrance.

**Contact:** Spring Lake Regional Park, 5585 Newanga Ave., 707/539-8092; Sonoma County Parks, 707/565-2041, www.sonoma-county.org.

## 102 SUGARLOAF RIDGE STATE PARK

**Scenic rating: 5**

near Santa Rosa

**Map 4.4, page 238**

Sugarloaf Ridge State Park is a perfect example of a place that you can't make a final judgment about from your first glance. Your first glance will lead you to believe that this is just hot foothill country, with old ranch roads set in oak woodlands for horseback riding and sweaty hiking or biking. A little discovery here, however, is that a half-mile walk off the Canyon Trail will lead you to a 25-foot waterfall, beautifully set in a canyon, complete with a redwood canopy. A shortcut to this waterfall is off the south side of the park's entrance road. Otherwise, it can be a long, hot, and challenging hike. In all, there are 25 miles of trails for hikers and equestrians. Hikers planning for a day of it should leave early, wear a hat, and bring plenty of water. Rangers report that some unprepared hikers have suffered heatstroke in summer, and many others have just plain suffered. In the off-season, when the air is cool and clear, the views from the ridge are eye-popping—visitors can see the Sierra Nevada, Golden Gate, and a thousand other points of scenic beauty from the top of Bald Mountain at 2,769 feet. For the less ambitious, a self-guided nature trail along Sonoma Creek begins at the campground.

**Campsites, facilities:** There are 49 sites for tents or RVs up to 27 feet (no hookups) and one group site for tents only for up to 50 people. Picnic tables, food lockers, and fire grills are provided. Drinking water, coin showers, and flush toilets are available. Leashed pets are permitted in campsites only.

**Reservations, fees:** Reservations are recommended at 800/444-7275 ($10 reservation fee) or www.reserveamerica.com ($9 reservation fee). Sites are $35 per night, plus $8 per night for each additional vehicle, and the group site is $165 per night. Open year-round.

**Directions:** From Santa Rosa on U.S. 101, turn east on Highway 12 and drive seven miles to Adobe Canyon Road. Turn left and drive 3.5 miles to the park entrance at the end of the road.

**Contact:** Sugarloaf Ridge State Park, 707/833-5712, www.parks.ca.gov or http://sugarloaf-park.org.

## 103 SAN FRANCISCO NORTH/PETALUMA KOA

### Scenic rating: 3

near Petaluma

**Map 4.4, page 238**

This campground is less than a mile from U.S. 101, yet it has a rural feel in a 60-acre farm setting. It's a good base camp for folks who require some quiet mental preparation before heading south to the Bay Area or to the nearby wineries, redwoods, and Russian River. The big plus is that this KOA has the cute log cabins called "Kamping Kabins," providing privacy for those who want it. There are recreational activities and live music on Saturdays in summer. During October, a pumpkin patch and corn maze are open across the street from the park.

**Campsites, facilities:** There are 312 sites for RVs or tents, most with full or partial hookups (30 and 50 amps), 34 cabins, 11 lodges, and four studio lodges. Most sites are pull-through. Picnic tables and fire pits are provided. Restrooms with flush toilets and showers, cable TV hookups, free Wi-Fi, dump station, playground, recreation rooms, basketball, volleyball, heated seasonal swimming pool, hot tub, sauna, petting farm, horseshoes, bocce ball,

coin laundry, propane gas, and a convenience store are available. Some facilities are wheelchair-accessible. Leashed pets are permitted, with certain restrictions.

**Reservations, fees:** Reservations are accepted at 800/562-1233 or through the website. RV sites with full hookups are $80 per night, RV sites with partial hookups are $59 per night, tent sites are $59-60 per night, plus $5-7 per person per night for more than two people. Camping cabins are $86-90 per night, and lodges are $161 per night. Some credit cards are accepted. Open year-round.

**Directions:** From Petaluma on U.S. 101 north, take the Penngrove exit and drive west for 0.25 mile on Petaluma Boulevard to Stony Point Road. Turn right (north) on Stony Point Road and drive 0.25 mile to Rainsville Road. Turn left (west) on Rainsville Road and drive a short distance to the park entrance.

**Contact:** San Francisco North/Petaluma KOA, 20 Rainsville Rd., 707/763-1492, www.petaluma-koa.com.

## 104 NAPA VALLEY EXPOSITION RV PARK

### Scenic rating: 2

in Napa

**Map 4.4, page 238**

This RV park is directly adjacent to the Napa Valley Exposition. In July, when the fair is in operation, the campground closes. The rest of the year it is simply an RV parking area, and it can come in handy.

**Campsites, facilities:** There are 28 sites with full hookups (30 and 50 amps) for RVs of any length and a grassy area for at least 100 self-contained RVs. Some sites are pull-through. Picnic tables, restrooms with showers, coin laundry, free Wi-Fi, and a dump station are available. A camp host is on-site. A restaurant is within walking distance. Some facilities are wheelchair-accessible. Leashed pets are permitted.

**Reservations, fees:** Reservations are recommended for individual sites and are required for groups at 707/253-4900, ext. 102. RV sites with full hookups are $50 per night. Open year-round, except during the fair.

**Directions:** From Napa on Highway 29, drive to the Napa/Lake Berryessa exit. Take that exit, turn right (east), and drive about one mile to Silverado/Highway 121. Turn right and drive less than one mile to the fairgrounds entrance on the left.

**Contact:** Napa Valley Exposition, 707/253-4900, ext. 102, www.napavalleyexpo.com.

# SACRAMENTO AND GOLD COUNTRY

© DREAMSTIME.COM

The Sacramento Valley is a landscape filled with rivers—the Sacramento, Feather, Yuba, American, and Mokelumne—providing both recreation and habitat for wildlife refuges. This is an area for California history buffs, with Placerville KOA and nearby Malakoff Diggins State Historic Park in the center of some of the state's most extraordinary history: the gold rush era. The highlight of foothill country is its series of great lakes—Camanche, Rollins, Oroville—for water sports, fishing, and recreation. In the Mother Lode country, three lakes—Camanche, Amador, and Pardee—are outstanding for fishing. Spring and fall are gorgeous, as are summer evenings, but there are always periods of 100°F-plus temperatures in the summer. But that's what gives these lakes and rivers such appeal. On a hot day, jumping into a cool lake is more valuable than gold.

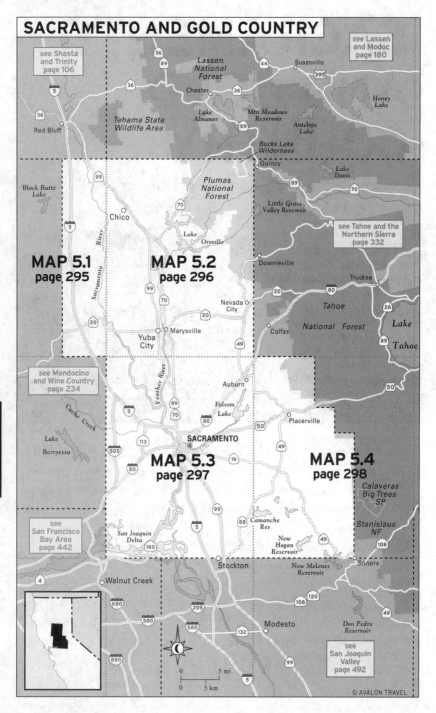

# SACRAMENTO AND GOLD COUNTRY

see Shasta
and Trinity
page 106

see Lassen
and Modoc
page 180

Lassen
National
Forest

Susanville

Chester

Honey
Lake

Red Bluff

Tehama State
Wildlife Area

Lake
Almanor

Mtn Meadows
Reservoir

Antelope
Lake

Bucks Lake
Wilderness

Quincy

Black Butte
Lake

Plumas
National
Forest

Lake
Davis

see Tahoe and the
Northern Sierra
page 332

Chico

Little Grass
Valley Reservoir

Lake
Oroville

## MAP 5.1
page 295

## MAP 5.2
page 296

Downieville

Truckee

Tahoe

National   Forest

Lake

Nevada
City

Tahoe

see Mendocino
and Wine Country
page 234

Yuba
City

Marysville

Colfax

Cache Creek

Auburn

Lake
Berryessa

Folsom
Lake

Placerville

SACRAMENTO

## MAP 5.3
page 297

## MAP 5.4
page 298

Calaveras
Big Trees
SP

see
San Francisco
Bay Area
page 442

San Joaquin
Delta

Camanche
Res

New
Hogan
Reservoir

Stanislaus
NF

Stockton

New Melones
Reservoir

Sonora

Walnut Creek

Modesto

Don Pedro
Reservoir

see
San Joaquin
Valley
page 492

0       5 mi

0       5 km

© AVALON TRAVEL

# Map 5.1

**Sites 1-2
Page 299**

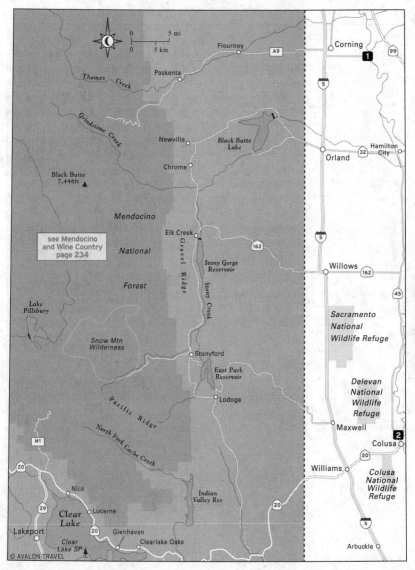

# Map 5.2

### Sites 3-33
### Pages 300-314

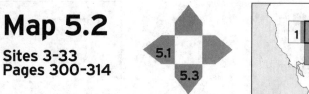

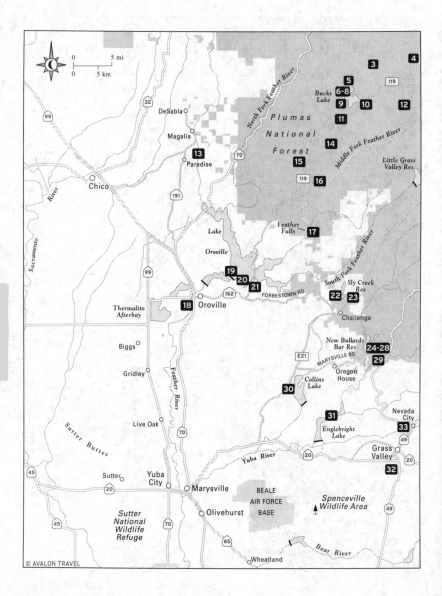

© AVALON TRAVEL

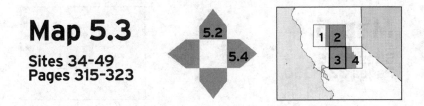

# Map 5.3

## Sites 34-49
## Pages 315-323

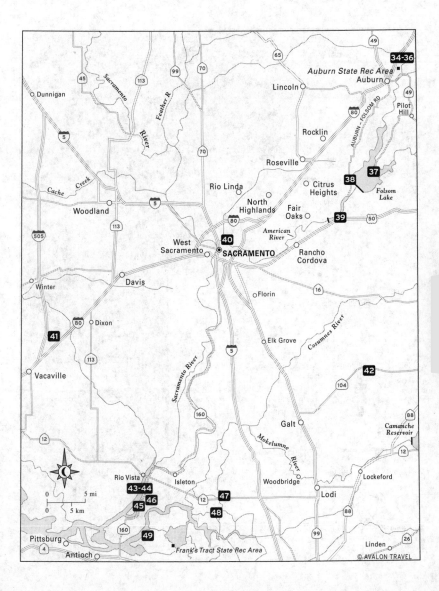

# Map 5.4

**Sites 50-62
Pages 323-330**

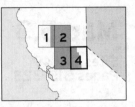

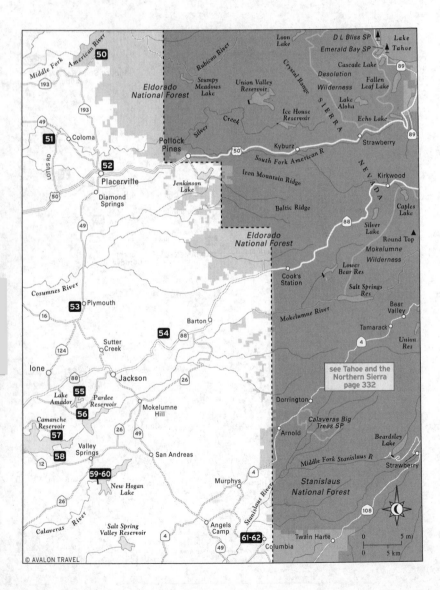

see Tahoe and the
Northern Sierra
page 332

# 1 WOODSON BRIDGE STATE RECREATION AREA

🚶 🏊 🛶 ⛵ 🚣 🐴 🚐 ⛺

### Scenic rating: 7

on the Sacramento River

**Map 5.1, page 295**

The campground at Woodson Bridge features direct access to the Sacramento River. The preserve itself is 328 acres of thick, riparian forest, including some of the only virgin habitat left on this 400-mile length of the Sacramento River. Boat-in sites, designed as camping spots for kayakers and canoeists, and a nearby boat ramp provide easy access for water sports, making this an ideal spot for campers with trailered boats. Note that waterskiing and personal watercraft are discouraged on this section of the river.

There are about two miles of hiking trails in the park; a beach is nearby. In June, the nearby Tehama Riffle is one of the best spots on the entire river for shad fishing. By mid-August, salmon start arriving, en route to their spawning grounds. Summer weather is hot, with high temperatures commonly 85-100°F. In winter, look for bald eagles; in summer, the yellow-billed cuckoo builds nests here.

**Campsites, facilities:** There are 35 sites for tents or RVs up to 31 feet (no hookups) and one boat-in site. One group site for up to 40 people is available. Picnic tables and fire grills are provided. Drinking water, coin showers, flush toilets, and boat launch (across the street) are available, and there is a camp host. Leashed pets are permitted.

**Reservations, fees:** Reservations are accepted May through September at 800/444-7275 or www.reserveamerica.com ($8 reservation fee). In April and October sites are first-come, first-served. Sites are $31 per night, plus $8 per night for each additional vehicle; it's $165 per night for the group camp. Open April through October.

**Directions:** From Corning, take the South Avenue exit off I-5 and drive six miles east to the campground on the left.

**Contact:** Woodson Bridge State Recreation Area, 530/839-2112, www.parks.ca.gov; American Land and Leisure, 800/342-2267, www.americanll.com.

# 2 COLUSA-SACRAMENTO RIVER STATE RECREATION AREA

🛶 🚐 🐴 ♿ 🚐 ⛺

### Scenic rating: 5

near Colusa

**Map 5.1, page 295**

This region of the Sacramento Valley is well known as a high-quality habitat for birds. This park covers 67 acres and features great bird-watching opportunities. Nearby Delevan and Colusa National Wildlife Refuges are outstanding destinations for wildlife-viewing as well, and they provide good duck hunting in December. In summer, the nearby Sacramento River is a bonus, with shad fishing in June and July, salmon fishing from August through October, sturgeon fishing in the winter, and striped-bass fishing in the spring. (Call to confirm that the boat channel is passable.) The landscape features cottonwoods and willows along the Sacramento River.

**Campsites, facilities:** There are 10 sites for tents, four sites for tents or RVs up to 30 feet (no hookups), and one group site for 10-100 people. Picnic tables and barbecues are provided. Drinking water, restrooms with flush toilets and coin showers, a boat ramp, Wi-Fi, and a dump station are available. Some facilities are wheelchair-accessible. A grocery store, restaurant, gas station, tackle shop, and coin laundry are within three blocks. Leashed pets are permitted.

**Reservations, fees:** Reservations for individual sites are accepted at 800/444-7275 or www.reserveamerica.com ($8 reservation fee). Group reservations are accepted at Colusa City Hall (530/458-4740, ext. 106). Sites are $15-28 per night, plus $6 per night for each additional vehicle. The group site is $135 per night, plus

$6 per vehicle for more than 10 vehicles. Open year-round.

**Directions:** In Williams, at the junction of I-5 and Highway 20, drive east on Highway 20 for nine miles to the town of Colusa. Turn north (straight ahead) on 10th Street and drive two blocks, just over the levee, to the park.

**Contact:** Colusa City Hall, 530/458-4740, ext. 106, www.cityofcolusa.com; Colusa-Sacramento River State Recreation Area, 530/458-4927, www.parks.ca.gov.

## 3 SILVER LAKE

**Scenic rating: 8**

in Plumas National Forest

**Map 5.2, page 296**

While tons of people go to Bucks Lake for the great trout fishing and lakeside camps, nearby Silver Lake gets little attention despite great natural beauty, good hiking, decent trout fishing, and a trailhead to the Bucks Lake Wilderness. The camp is at the north end of the lake, at 5,800 feet elevation, a primitive and secluded spot. No powerboats (or swimming) are allowed on Silver Lake, which makes it ideal for canoes and rafts. The lake has lots of small brook trout. The Pacific Crest Trail is routed on the ridge above the lake, skirting past Mount Pleasant (6,924 feet) to the nearby west.

**Campsites, facilities:** There are seven tent sites. Picnic tables and fire grills are provided. Vault toilets are available. Garbage must be packed out. No drinking water is available. Leashed pets are permitted.

**Reservations, fees:** Reservations are not accepted. There is no fee for camping. Open May through October, weather permitting.

**Directions:** From Oroville, drive north on Highway 70 to the junction with Highway 89. Turn south on Highway 89/70 and drive 11 miles to Quincy and Bucks Lake Road. Turn right at Bucks Lake Road and drive west for

nine miles to Silver Lake Road. Turn right and drive seven miles to the campground at the north end of the lake.

**Contact:** Plumas National Forest, Mt. Hough Ranger District, 530/283-0555, www.fs.usda.gov/plumas.

## 4 SNAKE LAKE

**Scenic rating: 8**

in Plumas National Forest

**Map 5.2, page 296**

Snake Lake is a rarity in the northern Sierra, a mountain lake that has bass, catfish, and bluegill. That is because it is a shallow lake at 5,800 feet elevation in Plumas National Forest. The camp is on the west shore. Motors of up to 5 horsepower are allowed. A road that circles the lake provides a good bicycle route for youngsters. A side trip to the nearby north is Smith Lake, about a five-minute drive, with the Butterfly Valley Botanical Area bordering it.

**Campsites, facilities:** There are 17 sites for tents. Picnic tables and fire grills are provided. Campfire permits are required when campfires are allowed. Vault toilets are available. No drinking water is available. Garbage must be packed out. Leashed pets are permitted.

**Reservations, fees:** Reservations are not accepted. There is no fee for camping. Open May through October, weather permitting.

**Directions:** From Oroville, drive north on Highway 70 to the junction with Highway 89. Turn south on Highway 89/70 and drive 11 miles to Quincy and Bucks Lake Road. Turn right at Bucks Lake Road and drive five miles to County Road 422. Turn right and drive two miles to the Snake Lake access road. Turn right and drive one mile to the campground on the right.

**Contact:** Plumas National Forest, Mt. Hough Ranger District, 530/283-0555, www.fs.usda.gov/plumas.

# 5 MILL CREEK

## Scenic rating: 7

at Bucks Lake in Plumas National Forest

**Map 5.2, page 296**

When Bucks Lake is full, this is one of the prettiest spots on the lake. The camp is set deep in Mill Creek Cove, adjacent to where Mill Creek enters the northernmost point of Bucks Lake. A boat ramp is a half mile away to the south, providing boat access to one of the better trout fishing spots at the lake. Unfortunately, when the lake level falls, this camp is left high and dry, some distance from the water. All water sports are permitted on this 1,800-acre lake. The elevation is 5,200 feet.

**Campsites, facilities:** There are 19 sites for tents or RVs up to 27 feet (no hookups) and two walk-in tent sites. Picnic tables, food lockers, and fire grills are provided. Drinking water and vault toilets are available. Showers are available a half mile away at Sandy Point boat launch. Groceries are available within five miles. Leashed pets are permitted.

**Reservations, fees:** Reservations are not accepted. Sites are $25 per night. Open mid-May through September, weather permitting.

**Directions:** From Oroville, drive north on Highway 70 to the junction with Highway 89. Turn south on Highway 89/70 and drive 11 miles to Quincy. In Quincy, turn right at Bucks Lake Road and drive 17 miles to Bucks Lake and the junction with Bucks Lake Dam Road/ Forest Road 33. Turn right, drive around the lake, cross over the dam, and continue for about three miles to the campground.

**Contact:** Plumas National Forest, Mt. Hough Ranger District, 530/283-0555, www.fs.usda. gov/plumas; Royal Elk Park Management, 707/799-4453, www.royalelkparkmanagement.com.

# 6 SUNDEW

## Scenic rating: 7

on Bucks Lake in Plumas National Forest

**Map 5.2, page 296**

Sundew Camp is on the northern shore of Bucks Lake, just north of Bucks Lake Dam. A boat ramp is about two miles north at Sandy Point Day Use Area at the Mill Creek Cove, providing access to one of the better trout spots on the lake. You want fish? At Bucks Lake you can get fish—it's one of the state's top mountain trout lakes. Fish species include rainbow, brown, and Mackinaw trout. Sunrises are often spectacular from this camp, with the light glowing on the lake's surface.

**Campsites, facilities:** There are 22 sites for tents or RVs up to 35 feet (no hookups). Picnic tables, food lockers, and fire grills are provided. Drinking water and vault toilets are available. Leashed pets are permitted.

**Reservations, fees:** Reservations are not accepted. Sites are $25 per night. Open mid-May through September, weather permitting.

**Directions:** From Oroville, drive north on Highway 70 to the junction with Highway 89. Turn south on Highway 89/70 and drive 11 miles to Quincy. In Quincy, turn right at Bucks Lake Road and drive 17 miles to Bucks Lake and the junction with Bucks Lake Dam Road/ Forest Road 33. Turn right, drive around the lake, cross over the dam, continue for 0.5 mile, and turn right at the campground access road.

**Contact:** Plumas National Forest, Mt. Hough Ranger District, 530/283-0555, www.fs.usda. gov/plumas; Royal Elk Park Management, 707/799-4453, www.royalelkparkmanagement.com.

# 7 HUTCHINS GROUP CAMP

### Scenic rating: 6

near Bucks Lake in Plumas National Forest

**Map 5.2, page 296**

This is a prime spot for a Scout outing or for any other large group that would like a pretty spot. An amphitheater is available. It is at 5,200 feet elevation near Bucks and Lower Bucks Lakes. (For more information, see the Sundew, Lower Bucks, and Haskins Valley listings in this chapter.)

**Campsites, facilities:** There are three group sites for tents or RV up to 35 feet (no hookups) that can accommodate up to 25 people each. Picnic tables, food lockers, and fire grills are provided. Drinking water and vault toilets are available. A boat ramp is available. Some facilities are wheelchair-accessible. Leashed pets are permitted.

**Reservations, fees:** Reservations are required at 877/444-6777 ($10 reservation fee) or www.recreation.gov ($9 reservation fee). The group camp is $70-75 per night. Open May through October.

**Directions:** From Oroville, drive north on Highway 70 to the junction with Highway 89. Turn south on Highway 89/70 and drive 11 miles to Quincy and Bucks Lake Road. Turn right at Bucks Lake Road and drive 17 miles to Bucks Lake and the junction with Bucks Lake Dam Road/Forest Road 33. Turn right, drive around the lake, cross over the dam, continue for a short distance, and turn right. Drive 0.5 mile, cross the stream (passing an intersection), and continue straight for 0.5 mile to the campground.

**Contact:** Plumas National Forest, Mt. Hough Ranger District, 530/283-0555, www.fs.usda.gov/plumas; Royal Elk Park Management, 707/799-4453, www.royalelkparkmanagement.com.

# 8 LOWER BUCKS

### Scenic rating: 7

on Lower Bucks Lake in Plumas National Forest

**Map 5.2, page 296**

This camp is on Lower Bucks Lake—actually the afterbay for Bucks Lake—below the Bucks Lake Dam. It is a small, primitive, and quiet spot that is often overlooked because it is not on the main lake.

**Campsites, facilities:** There are seven sites for tents or self-contained RVs up to 26 feet (no hookups). Picnic tables and fire rings are provided. Vault toilets are available. There is no drinking water. Leashed pets are permitted.

**Reservations, fees:** Reservations are not accepted. Sites are $20 per night. Open May through October.

**Directions:** From Oroville, drive north on Highway 70 to the junction with Highway 89. Turn south on Highway 89/70 and drive 11 miles to Quincy and Bucks Lake Road. Turn right at Bucks Lake Road and drive 17 miles to Bucks Lake and the junction with Bucks Lake Dam Road/Forest Road 33. Turn right and drive four miles around the lake, cross over the dam, drive 0.25 mile, and then turn left on the campground entrance road.

**Contact:** Plumas National Forest, Mt. Hough Ranger District, 530/283-0555, www.fs.usda.gov/plumas; Royal Elk Park Management, 707/799-4453, www.royalelkparkmanagement.com.

# 9 HASKINS VALLEY

### Scenic rating: 7

on Bucks Lake

**Map 5.2, page 296**

This is the biggest and most popular of the campgrounds at Bucks Lake, a pretty alpine lake with excellent trout fishing and clean campgrounds. A boat ramp is available nearby to the north, along with Bucks Lodge. This camp is deep in a cove at the extreme south end of the lake, where the water is quiet and sheltered from north winds. Bucks Lake, at 5,200 feet elevation, is well documented for excellent fishing for rainbow and Mackinaw trout, with high catch rates of rainbow trout and lake records in the 16-pound class. Insider's tip: This is the best lake in the region for sailboarding.

**Campsites, facilities:** There are 65 sites for tents or RVs up to 40 feet (no hookups). Picnic tables and fire grills are provided. Drinking water and vault toilets are available. A dump station and boat ramp are nearby. Some facilities are wheelchair-accessible. Leashed pets are permitted.

**Reservations, fees:** Reservations are not accepted. Sites are $25 per night, plus $5 per night for each additional vehicle, $2 per pet per night, and $10 for boat launching. Open May to early October, weather permitting.

**Directions:** From Oroville, drive north on Highway 70 to the junction with Highway 89. Turn south on Highway 89/70 and drive 11 miles to Quincy. In Quincy, turn right at Bucks Lake Road and drive 16.5 miles to the campground entrance on the right side of the road.

**Contact:** PG&E Land Services, 916/386-5164, www.pge.com/recreation.

## 10 WHITEHORSE
🏃🏊🎣🚣🐕🚐⛺

### Scenic rating: 7
near Bucks Lake in Plumas National Forest

**Map 5.2, page 296**

This campground along Bucks Creek is about two miles from the boat ramps and south shore concessions at Bucks Lake. The trout fishing can be quite good at Bucks Lake. The elevation is 5,200 feet. (For more information, see the Haskins Valley listing.)

**Campsites, facilities:** There are 19 sites for tents or RVs up to 27 feet (no hookups). Picnic tables and fire grills and bear boxes are provided. Drinking water and vault toilets are

available. A grocery store and coin laundry are within five miles. Leashed pets are permitted.

**Reservations, fees:** Reservations are accepted at 877/444-6777 ($10 reservation fee) or www.recreation.gov ($9 reservation fee). Sites are $23 per night. Open June through September.

**Directions:** From Oroville, drive north on Highway 70 to the junction with Highway 89. Turn south on Highway 89/70 and drive 11 miles to Quincy and Bucks Lake Road. Turn right at Bucks Lake Road and drive 14.5 miles to the campground entrance on the right side of the road.

**Contact:** Plumas National Forest, Mt. Hough Ranger District, 530/283-0555, www.fs.usda.gov/plumas; Royal Elk Park Management, 530/283-3732, www.royalelkparkmanagement.com.

## 11 GRIZZLY CREEK
🏊🚣🚐🐕🚐⛺

### Scenic rating: 4
near Bucks Lake in Plumas National Forest

**Map 5.2, page 296**

This is an alternative to the more developed, more crowded campgrounds at Bucks Lake. It is a small, primitive camp set near Grizzly Creek at 5,400 feet elevation. Nearby Bucks Lake provides good trout fishing, resorts, and boat rentals.

**Campsites, facilities:** There are 11 sites for tents or RVs up to 35 feet (no hookups). Picnic tables and fire grills are provided. Drinking water and vault toilets are available. A boat ramp is available at Bucks Lake. Leashed pets are permitted.

**Reservations, fees:** Reservations are not accepted. Sites are $20 per night. Open June through October.

**Directions:** From Oroville, drive north on Highway 70 to the junction with Highway 89. Turn south on Highway 89/70 and drive 11 miles to Quincy and Bucks Lake Road. Turn right at Bucks Lake Road and drive 17 miles to Bucks Lake and the junction with Bucks Lake

Dam Road/Forest Road 33. Turn right and drive one mile to the junction with Oroville-Quincy Road/Forest Road 36. Bear left and drive one mile to the campground on the right side of the road.

**Contact:** Plumas National Forest, Mt. Hough Ranger District, 530/283-0555, www.fs.usda.gov/plumas.

## 12 DEANES VALLEY

### Scenic rating: 5

on Rock Creek in Plumas National Forest

**Map 5.2, page 296**

This secret spot is on South Fork Rock Creek, deep in a valley at an elevation of 4,400 feet in Plumas National Forest. The trout are very small natives. If you want a pure, quiet spot, great; if you want good fishing, not so great. The surrounding region has a network of backcountry roads, including routes passable only by four-wheel-drive vehicles; to explore these roads, get a map of Plumas National Forest.

**Campsites, facilities:** There are seven sites for tents or RVs up to 24 feet (no hookups). Picnic tables and fire grills are provided. Vault toilets are available. There is no drinking water. Garbage must be packed out. Leashed pets are permitted.

**Reservations, fees:** Reservations are not accepted. There is no fee for camping. Open April through October, weather permitting.

**Directions:** From Oroville, drive north on Highway 70 to the junction with Highway 89. Turn south on Highway 89/70 and drive 11 miles to Quincy and Bucks Lake Road. Turn right at Bucks Lake Road and drive 3.5 miles to Forest Road 24N28. Turn left and drive seven miles to the campground on the left.

**Contact:** Plumas National Forest, Mt. Hough Ranger District, 530/283-0555, www.fs.usda.gov/plumas.

## 13 QUAIL TRAILS VILLAGE RV AND MOBILE HOME PARK

### Scenic rating: 4

near Paradise

**Map 5.2, page 296**

This is a rural motor-home campground near the west branch of the Feather River, with nearby Lake Oroville as the feature attraction. The Lime Saddle section of the Lake Oroville State Recreation Area is three miles away, with a beach, boat-launching facilities, and concessions. Note: About one-third of the sites are taken by long-term rentals.

**Campsites, facilities:** There are 20 pull-through sites with full hookups (30 amps) for RVs of any length, along with five tent sites. Picnic tables are provided. Wi-Fi, restrooms with showers, and a coin laundry are available. All facilities are wheelchair-accessible. Leashed pets up to 30 pounds are permitted.

**Reservations, fees:** Reservations are accepted. RV sites are $32 per night; tent sites are $20 per night. Weekly and monthly rates are available. Open year-round.

**Directions:** From Oroville, drive north on Highway 70 for six miles to Pentz Road. Turn left and drive six miles south to the park on the left.

**Contact:** Quail Trails Village RV and Mobile Home Park, 5110 Pentz Rd., 530/877-6581, www.quailtrailsvillage.com.

## 14 LITTLE NORTH FORK

### Scenic rating: 7

on the Middle Fork of the Feather River in Plumas National Forest

**Map 5.2, page 296**

Guaranteed quiet? You've got it. This is a primitive camp in the outback that few know of. It is along the Little North Fork of the Middle Fork of the Feather River at 4,000 feet elevation. The surrounding backcountry of Plumas National Forest features an incredible number of roads, giving four-wheel-drive owners a chance to get so lost they'll need this camp. Instead, get a map of Plumas National Forest before venturing out.

**Campsites, facilities:** There are six sites for tents or RVs up to 16 feet (no hookups). Picnic tables and fire grills are provided. Drinking water and vault toilets are available. Garbage must be packed out. Some facilities are wheelchair-accessible. Leashed pets are permitted.

**Reservations, fees:** Reservations are not accepted. There is no fee for camping. Open May through October.

**Directions:** From Oroville, turn east on Highway 162/Oroville-Quincy Highway and drive 26.5 miles to the Brush Creek Work Center. Continue northeast on Oroville-Quincy Highway for about six miles to County Road 60. Turn right and drive about eight miles to the campground entrance road on the left side of the road. Turn left and drive 0.25 mile to the campground. Note: This route is long, twisty, bumpy, and narrow for most of the way.

**Contact:** Plumas National Forest, Feather River Ranger District, 530/534-6500, www.fs.usda.gov/plumas.

## 15 ROGERS COW CAMP

### Scenic rating: 4

in Plumas National Forest

**Map 5.2, page 296**

This remote camp is at 4,000 feet elevation in Plumas National Forest near the headwaters of Coon Creek. The drive to get here is along the Oroville-Quincy "Highway," a long and curvy but paved Forest Service road; this backcountry route connects Oroville to Quincy and passes Lake Oroville and Bucks Lake in the process. It can still put you way out there in no-man's land. You want quiet, you've got it. There are no other natural destinations in the area; I'm not saying Coon Creek is anything to see, though.

Obtain a map of Plumas National Forest, which details all backcountry roads.

**Campsites, facilities:** There are six sites for tents or RVs up to 16 feet (no hookups). Picnic tables and fire grills are provided. Drinking water and vault toilets are available. Garbage must be packed out. Some facilities are wheelchair-accessible. Leashed pets are permitted.

**Reservations, fees:** Reservations are not accepted. There is no fee for camping. Open year-round, weather permitting.

**Directions:** In Oroville, drive east on Highway 162/Oroville-Quincy Highway for 26.5 miles to the Brush Creek Work Center. Continue on Oroville-Quincy Highway for eight miles to the campground entrance road on the left side of the road. Turn left and drive a short distance to the camp.

**Contact:** Plumas National Forest, Feather River Ranger District, 530/534-6500, www.fs.usda.gov/plumas.

## 16 MILSAP BAR

### Scenic rating: 8

on the Middle Fork of the Feather River in Plumas National Forest

**Map 5.2, page 296**

Milsap Bar is a well-known access point to the Middle Fork Feather River. This river country features a deep canyon and beautiful surroundings. Access is excellent for fly-fishing for trout. Your best bet is heading upstream from the bridge; a tributary that enters the main stem on the left is the best spot to start. On the far side of the campground is a feeder stream with a pool-and-drop. Insider's note: Locals often turn this campground into a party pad on Friday or Saturday night; weeknights in spring and fall are best. The elevation is 1,600 feet.

**Campsites, facilities:** There are 12 sites for tents or RVs up to 16 feet (no hookups). Picnic tables and fire grills are provided. Vault toilets are available. No drinking water is available.

Garbage must be packed out. Leashed pets are permitted.

**Reservations, fees:** Reservations are not accepted. There is no fee for camping. Open May through September.

**Directions:** In Oroville, drive east on Highway 162/Oroville-Quincy Highway for 26.5 miles to the Brush Creek Work Center and Bald Rock Road. Turn right on Bald Rock Road and drive for about 0.5 mile to Forest Road 22N62/Milsap Bar Road. Turn left and drive eight miles to the campground (a narrow, steep, mountain dirt road).

**Contact:** Plumas National Forest, Feather River Ranger District, 530/534-6500, www. fs.usda.gov/plumas.

## 17 FEATHER FALLS TRAILHEAD CAMPGROUND

### Scenic rating: 7

Feather Falls Scenic Area in Plumas National Forest

**Map 5.2, page 296**

This small campground is at the trailhead for the fantastic hike to 410-foot Feather Falls. This is one of California's greatest hikes, a 9.5-mile round-trip loop leading past Native American grinding mortars to a viewing deck perched on a knife-edge outcrop for a full frontal view of the waterfall. In addition, the creek canyon is the winter home for millions of ladybugs.

**Campsites, facilities:** There are five sites for tents or RVs up to 16 feet (no hookups). Picnic tables and fire grills are provided. Drinking water and vault toilets are available. Garbage service is available; when cans are full, garbage must be packed out. Leashed pets are permitted.

**Reservations, fees:** Reservations are not accepted. There is no fee for camping. A 14-day maximum stay rule is in place. Open May through September, weather permitting.

**Directions:** From Oroville, drive east on

Oroville Dam Boulevard to Olive Highway. Turn right on Olive Highway and drive five miles to Forbestown Road. Turn right on Forbestown Road and drive seven miles to Lumpkin Road. Turn left on Lumpkin Road and drive 12 miles to the trailhead turnoff. Turn left at the turnoff and drive 1.5 miles to the parking area. Campsites are at the beginning of the parking area, while the trailhead is at the far end.

**Contact:** Plumas National Forest, Feather River Ranger District, 530/534-6500, www. fs.usda.gov/plumas.

## 18 DINGERVILLE USA

### Scenic rating: 3

near Oroville

**Map 5.2, page 296**

You're right, they thought of this name all by themselves, needed no help. It is an RV park in the Oroville foothill country—hot and dry in the summer, but with side trips nearby. It is adjacent to a wildlife area and the Feather River and within short range of Lake Oroville and the Thermalito Afterbay for boating, water sports, and fishing. The RV park is a clean, quiet campground with easy access from the highway. Some of the sites are occupied by long-term renters.

**Campsites, facilities:** There are 40 pull-through sites with full hookups (30 amps) for RVs of any length. No tents are permitted. Picnic tables are provided. Restrooms with showers, cable TV, a seasonal swimming pool, coin laundry, horseshoe pit, a dog park, and a nine-hole executive golf course are available. Some facilities are wheelchair-accessible. Leashed pets are permitted.

**Reservations, fees:** Reservations are recommended. Sites are $36 per night. Some credit cards are accepted. Open year-round.

**Directions:** From Oroville, drive south on Highway 70 to the second Pacific Heights Road turnoff. Turn right at Pacific Heights Road and drive less than one mile to the campground on the left.

From Marysville, drive north on Highway 70 to Palermo-Welsh Road. Turn left on Palermo-Welsh Road and drive to Pacific Heights Road. Turn left (north) on Pacific Heights Road and drive 0.5 mile to the campground entrance on the right.

**Contact:** Dingerville USA, 530/533-9343, www.dingervilleusa.com.

## 19 LAKE OROVILLE BOAT-IN AND FLOATING CAMPS

**Scenic rating: 10**

on Lake Oroville

**Map 5.2, page 296**

It doesn't get any stranger than this, and for those who have tried, it doesn't get any better. We're talking about the double-decker floating camps at Lake Oroville, along with the great boat-in sites. The floating camps look like giant patio boats and sleep 15 people. There are also dispersed boat-in camps around the lake, which are particularly excellent in the spring and early summer, when the water level at the lake is high. In late summer, when the lake level drops, it can be a fair hike up the bank to the campsites, and, in addition, if the water drops quickly, your boat can be left sitting on the bank; it can be quite an effort to get it back in the water. Oroville is an outstanding lake for water sports, with warm water and plenty of room, and also with excellent bass fishing, especially in the spring.

**Campsites, facilities:** There are four dispersed boat-in camps, one group boat-in site (Bloomer) for up to 75 people, and 10 boat-in floating camps for up to 15 people. Picnic tables, sinks, food lockers, garbage cans, and propane barbecues are provided. Vault toilets are available. There is no drinking water. Some facilities are wheelchair-accessible. Leashed pets are permitted, except on trails or beaches.

**Reservations, fees:** Reservations are accepted at 800/444-7275 or www.reserveamerica.com ($8 reservation fee). Floating camps are $175 per night, individual boat-in sites are $20 per night, and the group boat-in site is $135 per night. Open year-round.

**Directions:** From Oroville, drive east on Oroville Dam Boulevard/Highway 162 (becomes the Olive Highway) for 5.5 miles to Canyon Drive. Turn left and drive two miles to Oroville Dam. Turn left and drive over the dam to the spillway parking lot at the end of the road. Register at the entrance station. Boats can be launched from this area.

**Contact:** Lake Oroville State Recreation Area, 530/538-2200; Lake Oroville Visitor Center, 530/538-2219, www.parks.ca.gov.

## 20 BIDWELL CANYON

**Scenic rating: 7**

on Lake Oroville

**Map 5.2, page 296**

Bidwell Canyon is a major destination at giant Lake Oroville because the campground is near a major marina and boat ramp. It is along the southern shore of the lake, on a point directly adjacent to the massive Oroville Dam to the west. Many campers use this spot for boating headquarters. Lake Oroville is created from the tallest earth-filled dam in the country, rising 770 feet above the streambed of the Feather River. It creates a huge reservoir when full. It is popular for waterskiing, as the water is warm enough in the summer for all water sports, and there is enough room for both anglers and water-skiers. Fishing is excellent for spotted bass. What a lake—there are even floating toilets here (imagine that!). It is very hot in midsummer, with high temperatures ranging from the mid-80s to the low 100s. The area has four distinct seasons—spring is quite beautiful with many wildflowers and greenery. A must-see is the view from the 47-foot tower using the high-powered telescopes, where there is a panoramic view of the lake, Sierra Nevada, valley, foothills, and the Sutter Buttes. The Feather River Hatchery is nearby.

**Campsites, facilities:** There are 75 sites with full hookups (30 amps) for tents or RVs up to 40 feet and trailers up to 31 feet (including boat trailers). Picnic tables and fire grills are provided. Drinking water, flush toilets, and coin showers are available. Boat rentals are available on the lake. A grocery store, boat ramp, marina with fuel and boat pumping station, snack bar, and propane gas are within two miles. Leashed pets are permitted, except on trails or beaches.

**Reservations, fees:** Reservations are accepted at 800/444-7275 or www.reserveamerica.com ($8 reservation fee). Sites are $45 per night, plus $4 per night for each additional vehicle. Open year-round.

**Directions:** From Oroville, drive east on Oroville Dam Boulevard/Highway 162 (becomes the Olive Highway) for 6.8 miles to Kelly Ridge Road. Turn left (north) on Kelly Ridge Road and drive 1.5 miles to Arroyo Drive. Turn right and drive 0.25 mile to the campground.

**Contact:** Lake Oroville State Recreation Area, 530/538-2200; Lake Oroville Visitor Center, 530/538-2219, www.parks.ca.gov.

## 21 LOAFER CREEK FAMILY, GROUP, AND EQUESTRIAN CAMPS

🚶 🏞 🏊 🚤 🐎 ⛷ ♿ 🚐 ⛺

**Scenic rating: 7**

on Lake Oroville

**Map 5.2, page 296**

These are three different campground areas that are linked, designed for individual use, groups, and equestrians, respectively. The camps are just across the water at Lake Oroville from Bidwell Canyon, but campers come here for more spacious sites. It's also a primary option for campers with boats, with the Loafer Creek boat ramp one mile away. So hey, this spot is no secret. A bonus is an extensive equestrian trail system right out of camp.

**Campsites, facilities:** There are 137 sites for

tents or RVs up to 40 feet (no hookups) and trailers to 31 feet (including boat trailers), 15 equestrian sites with a two-horse limit per site, and six group sites for up to 25 people each. Picnic tables and fire grills are provided. Drinking water, restrooms with flush toilets and coin showers, laundry tubs, Wi-Fi, and a dump station are available. A tethering and feeding station is near each site for horses, and a horse-washing station is provided. Some facilities are wheelchair-accessible. Propane, groceries, boat rentals, and a boat ramp are nearby. Leashed pets are permitted, but not on trails or beaches.

**Reservations, fees:** Reservations are accepted at 800/444-7275 or www.reserveamerica.com ($8 reservation fee). Sites are $35 per night for single sites, plus $4 per night for each additional vehicle; $125 per night for group sites; and $45 per night for equestrian sites. Open year-round.

**Directions:** From Oroville, drive east on Oroville Dam Boulevard/Highway 162 (becomes the Olive Highway) for approximately eight miles to the signed campground entrance on the left.

**Contact:** Lake Oroville State Recreation Area, 530/538-2200; Lake Oroville Visitor Center, 530/538-2219, www.parks.ca.gov.

## 22 SLY CREEK

🏞 🏊 🚤 🐎 ♿ 🚐 ⛺

**Scenic rating: 7**

on Sly Creek Reservoir in Plumas National Forest

**Map 5.2, page 296**

Sly Creek Camp is on Sly Creek Reservoir's southwestern shore near Lewis Flat, with a boat ramp about a mile to the north. Both camps at this lake are well situated for campers and anglers. This camp provides direct access to the lake's main body, with good trout fishing well upstream on the main lake arm. You get quiet water and decent fishing. The elevation is 3,530 feet.

**Campsites, facilities:** There are 23 sites for tents or RVs up to 40 feet (no hookups). Picnic tables and fire grills are provided. Drinking water and vault toilets are available. A car-top boat launch and fish-cleaning stations are available on Sly Creek Reservoir. Some facilities are wheelchair-accessible. Leashed pets are permitted.

**Reservations, fees:** Reservations are not accepted. Sites are $20 per night. Open late April through mid-October, weather permitting.

**Directions:** From Oroville, drive east on Highway 162/Oroville Dam Boulevard for about eight miles (becomes the Olive Highway) to Forbestown Road. Turn right and drive through Forbestown to Challenge and LaPorte Road. Turn left on LaPorte Road and drive 15 miles to Forest Road 16 (signed for Sly Creek Reservoir). Turn left on Forest Road 16 and drive 4.5 miles to the campground on the eastern end of the lake.

**Contact:** Plumas National Forest, Feather River Ranger District, 530/534-6500, www. fs.usda.gov/plumas.

## 23 STRAWBERRY
🏊 🎣 🚤 🐴 🚐 ⛺

### Scenic rating: 7

on Sly Creek Reservoir in Plumas National Forest

Map 5.2, page 296

Sly Creek Reservoir is a long, narrow lake in western Plumas National Forest. There are two campgrounds on opposite ends of the lake, with different directions to each. This camp is set in the back of a cove on the lake's eastern arm at an elevation of 3,530 feet, with a boat ramp nearby. This is a popular lake for trout fishing in the summer.

**Campsites, facilities:** There are 17 sites for tents or RVs up to 40 feet (no hookups). Picnic tables and fire grills are provided. Drinking water and vault toilets are available. A car-top boat launch and fish-cleaning station are available on Sly Creek Reservoir. Leashed pets are permitted.

**Reservations, fees:** Reservations are not accepted. Sites are $20 per night. Open mid-May to early October, weather permitting.

**Directions:** From Oroville, drive east on Highway 162/Oroville Dam Boulevard for about eight miles (becomes the Olive Highway) to Forbestown Road. Turn right and drive through Forbestown to Challenge and LaPorte Road. Turn left on LaPorte Road and drive 15 miles to Forest Road 16 (signed for Sly Creek Reservoir). Turn left on Forest Road 16 and drive two miles to the campground on the eastern end of the lake.

**Contact:** Plumas National Forest, Feather River Ranger District, 530/534-6500, www. fs.usda.gov/plumas.

## 24 GARDEN POINT BOAT-IN
🏊 🛶 🚤 🐴 5% ⛺

### Scenic rating: 8

on Bullards Bar Reservoir

Map 5.2, page 296   BEST (

Bullards Bar Reservoir is one of the few lakes in the Sierra Nevada to offer boat-in camping at developed boat-in sites and to allow boaters to create their own primitive sites anywhere along the lake's shoreline when permitted. A chemical toilet is required gear for boat-in shoreline camping at some sites. Garden Point Boat-In is on the western shore of the northern Yuba River arm. This lake provides plenty of recreation options, including good fishing for kokanee salmon and small spotted bass, water-skiing, and many coves for playing in the water. All water sports are allowed.

**Campsites, facilities:** There are 12 single and four double tent sites accessible by boat only. Picnic tables and fire grills are provided. Vault toilets are available. No drinking water is available. Garbage must be packed out. Supplies and boat rentals are available at the Emerald Cove Marina. Leashed pets are permitted.

**Reservations, fees:** Reservations and a

camping permit are required from Emerald Cove Marina at 530/692-3200 ($7.50 reservation fee). Single sites are $22 per night; double sites are $44 per night. Open mid-April to mid-October, weather permitting.

**Directions:** From Marysville, drive northeast on Highway 20 to Marysville Road. Turn north at Marysville Road (signed Bullards Bar Reservoir) and drive about 12 miles to Old Marysville Road. Turn right and drive 14 miles to reach the Cottage Creek launch ramp and the marina (turn left just before the dam).

To reach the Dark Day boat ramp, continue over the dam and drive four miles, turn left on Dark Day Road, and continue to the ramp. From the boat launch, continue to the campground on the northwest side.

**Contact:** Emerald Cove Marina, 530/692-3200; Tahoe National Forest, Yuba River Ranger District, North, 530/288-3231, www.bullardsbar.com, www.fs.usda.gov/plumas.

## 25 DARK DAY WALK-IN

**Scenic rating: 8**

on Bullards Bar Reservoir

**Map 5.2, page 296**

Along with Schoolhouse, this is a car-accessible camping area at Bullards Bar Reservoir with direct shoreline access. You park in a central area and then walk a short distance to the campground. The lake is a very short walk beyond that. Bullards Bar is a great camping lake, pretty, with 55 miles of shoreline and several lake arms and good fishing for kokanee salmon (as long as you have a boat) and bass. It is set at 2,000 feet elevation in the foothills, like a silver dollar in a field of pennies. A bonus at Bullards Bar is that there is never a charge for day use, parking, or boat launching.

**Campsites, facilities:** There are 10 walk-in tent sites (some are double or triple sites). Picnic tables and fire pits are provided. Drinking water and vault toilets are available. Garbage must be packed out. A boat ramp is nearby,

and supplies and boat rentals are available at Emerald Cove Marina. Leashed pets are permitted.

**Reservations, fees:** Reservations and a camping permit are required from Emerald Cove Marina at 530/692-3200 ($7.50 reservation fee). Sites are $22 per night, double sites are $44 per night, and triple sites are $66 per night. Open mid-April through mid-October, weather permitting.

**Directions:** From Marysville, drive northeast on Highway 20 to Marysville Road. Turn north at Marysville Road (signed Bullards Bar Reservoir) and drive about 12 miles to Old Marysville Road. Turn right, drive 14 miles, and continue over the dam for four miles to Dark Day Road. Turn left and drive past the boat launch to the campground on the northwest side of the lake.

**Contact:** Emerald Cove Marina, 530/692-3200; Tahoe National Forest, Yuba River Ranger District, North, 530/288-3231, www.bullardsbar.com, www.fs.usda.gov/plumas.

## 26 SHORELINE CAMP BOAT-IN

**Scenic rating: 8**

on Bullards Bar Reservoir

**Map 5.2, page 296** **BEST (**

There are two boat-in campgrounds on Bullards Bar Reservoir, but another option is to throw all caution to the wind and just head out on your own, camping wherever you want. Bring a large tarp for sun protection, and, of course, plenty of water or a water purification pump. This is a big, beautiful lake, with good trolling for kokanee salmon. Rainbow trout are also here. Note: A portable chemical toilet and a camping permit are required.

**Campsites, facilities:** Boaters may choose their own primitive campsite anywhere on the shore of Bullards Bar Reservoir, with a maximum of six people per site. Garbage must be packed out. Supplies and boat rentals are available at Emerald Cove Marina. Leashed pets are permitted.

**Reservations, fees:** Reservations and a camping permit are required from Emerald Cove Marina at 530/692-3200 ($7.50 reservation fee). Sites are $22 per night. Open mid-April through mid-October, weather permitting.

**Directions:** From Marysville, drive east on Highway 20 for 12 miles to Marysville Road. Turn left on Marysville Road (signed Bullards Bar Reservoir) and drive 12 miles to Old Marysville Road. Turn right on Old Marysville Road and drive 14 miles to the Cottage Creek Launch Ramp (turn left just before the dam). To reach the boat launch, continue to the campgrounds on the west side.

**Contact:** Emerald Cove Marina, 530/692-3200; Tahoe National Forest, Yuba River Ranger District, North, 530/288-3231, www.bullards-bar.com, www.fs.usda.gov/plumas.

## 27 MADRONE COVE BOAT-IN

**Scenic rating: 8**

on Bullards Bar Reservoir

Map 5.2, page 296                              BEST (

This is one of two boat-in campgrounds at Bullards Bar Reservoir. It is on the main Yuba River arm of the lake, along the western shore. This is a premium boat-in site. The elevation is 2,000 feet.

**Campsites, facilities:** There are 10 tent sites, accessible by boat only. Picnic tables and fire grills are provided. Vault toilets are available. No drinking water is available. Garbage must be packed out. Supplies and boat rentals are available at the marina. Leashed pets are permitted.

**Reservations, fees:** Reservations and a camping permit are required from Emerald Cove Marina at 530/692-3200 ($7.50 reservation fee). Sites are $22 per night. Open mid-April through mid-October.

**Directions:** From Marysville, drive east on Highway 20 for 12 miles to Marysville Road

(signed Bullards Bar Reservoir). Turn left at Marysville Road and drive 12 miles to Old Marysville Road. Turn right on Old Marysville Road and drive 14 miles to reach the Cottage Creek Launch Ramp and the marina (turn left just before the dam). To reach the ramp, continue over the dam, drive four miles to Dark Day Road, turn left, and continue to the ramp. From the boat launch, continue to the campground on the west side.

**Contact:** Emerald Cove Marina, 530/692-3200; Tahoe National Forest, Yuba River Ranger District, North, 530/288-3231, www.bullards-bar.com, www.fs.usda.gov/plumas.

## 28 SCHOOLHOUSE

**Scenic rating: 7**

on Bullards Bar Reservoir

Map 5.2, page 296

Bullards Bar Reservoir is one of the better lakes in the Sierra Nevada for camping, primarily because the lake level tends to be higher than at many other lakes. The camp is on the southeast shore, with a trail out of the camp to a beautiful lookout of the lake. Bullards Bar is known for good fishing for trout and kokanee salmon, waterskiing, and all water sports. A concrete boat ramp is to the south at Cottage Creek. Boaters should consider the special boat-in camps at the lake. The elevation is 2,200 feet.

**Campsites, facilities:** There are 56 sites for tents or RVs of any length (no hookups). Single sites accommodate six people, double sites accommodate 12 people, and triple sites hold up to 18 people. Picnic tables, food lockers, and fire rings are provided. Drinking water and flush and vault toilets are available. A boat ramp and boat rentals are nearby. Some facilities are wheelchair-accessible. Supplies are available in North San Juan, Camptonville, Dobbins, and at the marina. Leashed pets are permitted.

**Reservations, fees:** Reservations and a camping permit are required from Emerald Cove

Marina at 530/692-3200 ($7.50 reservation fee). Single sites are $22 per night, double sites are $44 per night, and triple sites are $66 per night. Open mid-April through mid-October.

**Directions:** From Marysville, drive east on Highway 20 for 12 miles to Marysville Road (signed Bullards Bar Reservoir). Turn left on Marysville Road and drive 12 miles to Old Marysville Road. Turn right on Old Marysville Road and drive 14 miles to the dam, then continue three miles to the campground entrance road on the left.

**Contact:** Emerald Cove Marina, 530/692-3200; Tahoe National Forest, Yuba River Ranger District, North, 530/288-3231, www.bullards-bar.com, www.fs.usda.gov/plumas.

## 29 HORNSWOGGLE GROUP CAMP

### Scenic rating: 7

on Bullards Bar Reservoir in Tahoe National Forest

**Map 5.2, page 296**

This camp is designed for group use. A concrete boat ramp is one mile north at the Dark Day Picnic Area. (For information about family campgrounds and boat-in sites, see the listings in this chapter that are located on Bullards Bar Reservoir.)

**Campsites, facilities:** There are five 25-person group sites and one 50-person group site for tents or RVs up to 50 feet (no hookups). Picnic tables, food lockers, and fire grills are provided. Drinking water and flush and vault toilets are available. A boat ramp is nearby. Supplies and boat rentals are available at the marina. Leashed pets are permitted.

**Reservations, fees:** Reservations and a camping permit are required from Emerald Cove Marina at 530/692-3200 ($7.50 reservation fee). Sites are $80-140 per night. Open April to mid-October.

**Directions:** From Auburn, drive north on Highway 49 to Nevada City and continue for

17 miles through the town of North San Juan. Continue on Highway 49 for approximately eight miles to Marysville Road. Turn left on Marysville Road and drive approximately five miles to the campground on the left.

**Contact:** Emerald Cove Marina, 530/692-3200; Tahoe National Forest, Yuba River Ranger District, North, 530/288-3231, www.bullards-bar.com, www.fs.usda.gov/plumas.

## 30 COLLINS LAKE RECREATION AREA

### Scenic rating: 8

near Marysville on Collins Lake

**Map 5.2, page 296**

Collins Lake is in the foothill country east of Marysville at 1,200 feet elevation, ideal for the camper, boater, and angler. I counted 45 campsites near the lakefront. This lake is becoming known as an outstanding destination for trophy-sized trout, especially in late spring through early summer, though fishing is often good year-round for know-hows. Other fish species are bass, crappie, bluegill, and catfish. Guide Larry Hemphill has made it a habit to catch big bass here. The lake has 12 miles of shoreline and is quite pretty. In summer, warm water makes the lake exceptional for waterskiing (permitted from May through mid-October). There is a marina adjacent to the campground, and farther south is a 60-foot-wide swimming beach and boat ramp. Bonuses for anglers: No personal watercraft are allowed on the lake, and a weekly fishing report is available at the camp's website. Insider's tip: Lakefront sites fill quickly; book early.

**Campsites, facilities:** There are 150 sites with full or partial hookups (30 amps) for RVs or tents, 134 sites with no hookups for tents or RVs, four group tent sites, one group RV site, and a large overflow camping area. Some sites are pull-through. Four rental trailers and five cabins are also available. Picnic tables and barbecues are provided. Restrooms with flush toilets and coin showers, drinking water, portable toilets, dump station, playground, marina, boat ramp, boat rentals, berths, sandy swimming beach, beach volleyball, three group picnic areas, convenience store, coin laundry, firewood, ice, and propane gas are available. RV storage is also available. Some facilities are wheelchair-accessible. Leashed pets are permitted.

**Reservations, fees:** Reservations are accepted up to one year in advance (two-night minimum, $10 nonrefundable reservation deposit required). Tent sites are $28 per night, RV sites without hookups are $30-40 per night, RV sites with hookups are $44-60 per night, lakefront RV sites are $40 (no hookups) and $60 (full hookups) per night, plus $13 per night per additional vehicle and $4 per night per additional person age 13 and older. There is an open area for tent camping at $28 per night and an open parking area for self-contained RVs at $38 per night. Boat launching is $9 per day with campsite. Weekly and monthly rates are available. Some credit cards are accepted. Open year-round.

**Directions:** From Marysville, drive east on Highway 20 for about 12 miles to Marysville Road/Road E-21. Turn left (north) and drive approximately 10 miles to the recreation area entrance road on the right. Turn right, drive 0.3 mile to the entrance station and store, and then continue to the campground. (For detailed directions from other areas, visit the website.)

**Contact:** Collins Lake Recreation Area, 530/692-1600 or 800/286-0576, www.collinslake.com.

## 31 ENGLEBRIGHT LAKE BOAT-IN

**Scenic rating: 8**

near Marysville

**Map 5.2, page 296**      **BEST**

Englebright Lake is an outstanding destination for boat-in camping, fishing, and waterskiing—remember this place. It always seems to have plenty of water, and there are more developed boat-in campsites along its 19 miles of shoreline than at any other lake in California. The lake looks like a huge water snake, long and narrow, set in the Yuba/Nevada Canyon at 520 feet elevation. In summer, it is a waterskiing mecca, with warm, calm water. All water sports are allowed. Trout fishing is good on the upper end of the lake, where waterskiing is prohibited year-round. Rangers say people show up every week with tents or RVs, but all sites are boat-in only!

**Campsites, facilities:** There are 96 spacious boat-in sites (no hookups) along the shores of Englebright Lake. Picnic tables, fire grills, and lantern hangers are provided. Pit toilets are available. Two boat ramps are on either side of Skippers Cove. Drinking water is available at the Narrows day-use area and at the marina. Boat rentals (including houseboats), mooring, fuel dock, and groceries are available at the marina. Leashed pets are permitted.

**Reservations, fees:** Reservations are not accepted. Boat-in sites are $20 per night, and group sites are $50-72 per night. Open year-round.

**Directions:** From Auburn, drive north on Highway 49 to Grass Valley and the junction with Highway 20. Turn west on Highway 20 and drive to Mooney Flat Road (if you reach Smartville, you have gone a mile too far). Turn right on Mooney Flat Road and drive three miles to the entrance for the Narrows Recreation Area. Continue 0.5 mile to Joe Miller Road and the entrance to Skipper's Cove Marina on the left.

**Contact:** U.S. Army Corps of Engineers, Sacramento District, Englebright Lake, 530/432-6427; Skippers Cove, concessionaire, 530/432-6302, www.englebrightlake.com.

## 32 NEVADA COUNTY FAIRGROUNDS

🏊 🐕 ♿ 🚐

### Scenic rating: 6

near Grass Valley

**Map 5.2, page 296**

The motto here is "California's Most Beautiful Fairgrounds," and that's right. The area is at 2,300 feet in the Sierra foothills, with a good number of pines sprinkled about. The park is adjacent to the fairgrounds, and even though the fair runs for a week every August, the park is open year-round. However, check status before planning a trip because the campground is sometimes closed for scheduled activities. A caretaker at the park is available to answer any questions. Kids can fish at a small lake nearby. The Draft Horse Classic is held every September, and a country Christmas Faire is held Thanksgiving weekend.

**Campsites, facilities:** There are 144 sites with full or partial hookups (50 amps) for RVs of any length, as well as an open dirt and grassy area with no hookups available as an overflow area. No tents are permitted. Two dump stations, drinking water, restrooms with showers and flush toilets, Wi-Fi, and group facilities are available. Some facilities are wheelchair-accessible. Leashed pets are permitted.

**Reservations, fees:** Reservations are recommended. RV sites are $27-35 per night, and showers are $10 per person. A seven-day limit is enforced. Some credit cards are accepted. Open year-round; however, it may book up during events.

**Directions:** From Auburn, drive north on Highway 49 to Grass Valley and the McKnight Way exit. Take that exit and turn left on McKnight Way. Drive over the freeway to Freeman Lane (just past the shopping center on the left). Turn right on Freeman Lane and drive to the second stop sign and McCourtney Road. Continue straight on McCourtney Road and drive two blocks to the fairgrounds on the right. Continue to Gate 4.

**Contact:** Nevada County Fairgrounds, 530/273-6217, www.nevadacountyfair.com.

## 33 INNTOWN CAMPGROUND

🏕 🐕 ♿ 🚐 ⛺

### Scenic rating: 6

in Nevada City

**Map 5.2, page 296**

Campsites close to Nevada City have been thin on the ground, with the sole exception of the nearby Nevada County Fairgrounds. No more. With the opening of the 15-acre InnTown Campground in 2016, happy campers now have a wealth of options to choose from—tent sites, RV sites, and comfy tent cabins—all within two miles of downtown Nevada City. Nestled in the woods next to the Narrow Gauge Railroad Museum, this clean, compact campground has it all: modern restrooms with showers, wash basins, well-lit walking paths, and a popular commons area for cooking, reading, and riding out the wet weather. For an added bit of luxury, spring for one of the homey tent cabins—complete with heated mattress pads and quaint Gold Country touches.

**Campsites, facilities:** There are 40 tent sites and 18 RV sites (up to 55 feet), some with full hookups and some with water and electric only. Some sites are walk-in (wagons available). There are also 15 "glamping" tent cabins with electricity, lights, beds with heated mattress pads, and linens and towels. Picnic tables are provided. Restrooms with showers and flush toilets, drinking water, wash stations, and a dump station are available. A commons building holds a camp store, kitchen, laundry, TV area, Wi-Fi, and outdoor barbecue. The Narrow Gauge Railroad Museum is next door, and a historic Chinese cemetery is on-site. Some facilities are wheelchair-accessible. Two dogs maximum per site are welcome for a fee.

**Reservations, fees:** Tent sites are $45-50 per night, RV sites with hookups are $50-65 per night, tent cabins are $90-100 per night, plus $10 each additional vehicle and $5-10 per dog (maximum two). Open year-round with a two-night minimum Friday-Saturday April-October.

**Directions:** From Auburn, drive north for 27 miles on Highway 49 to Nevada City and the Gold Flat Road exit. Take that exit and turn right on Gold Flat Road and then immediately turn left onto Hollow Way. Drive 0.2 mile and turn right onto Bost Avenue. Drive straight and turn left onto Kidder Court. Drive past the Narrow Gauge Railroad Museum to enter the campground at 9 Kidder Court.

**Contact:** InnTown Campground, 530/265-9900, http://inntowncampground.com.

## 34 LAKE CLEMENTINE BOAT-IN

🚶 🚴 🏊 🛶 🚣 🏄 ⛺

### Scenic rating: 8

in Auburn State Recreation Area near Auburn

| Map 5.3, page 297 | BEST ( |

This boat-in campground is on Lower Lake Clementine, a long and narrow 3.5-mile lake. It is a great, remote place to camp with kayaking and boat-in camping, with pristine, glasslike water. All water sports are allowed, with a boat limit of 25 boats per day—and the quota is reached every day on summer weekends. Auburn State Recreation Area is a jewel in the valley foothill country, covering more than 42,000 acres along the North and Middle Forks of the American River. The Auburn SRA is composed of land set aside for the Auburn Dam, consisting of 40 miles along two forks of the American River. Formerly the domain of gold miners, the area is now home to wildlife as well as a wide variety of recreational opportunities. The American River runs through the park, offering visitors opportunities to fish, boat, kayak, and raft. In addition, there are more than 100 miles of hiking, biking, and horseback-riding trails.

Note that there is a very sharp hairpin turn on the road that makes it difficult to get trailered boats in, especially those towed by trucks with long wheelbases. Trailers over 24 feet are not advised.

**Campsites, facilities:** There are 15 boat-in sites (eight people per site). Picnic tables, fire grills, and pit toilets are provided. A marina and boat launch are available. There is no drinking water. Garbage must be packed out.

**Reservations, fees:** Reservations are accepted at 800/444-7275 or www.reserveamerica.com ($8 reservation fee). Boat-in sites are $38 per night, plus $10 per extra vehicle and a $10 fee for boat launch. Open mid-May to mid-September.

**Directions:** From I-80 at Auburn, take the Auburn Ravine/Foresthill exit to Foresthill Road. Turn right and drive on Foresthill Road for two miles to Lake Clementine Road. Turn left (road narrows) and drive 2.5 miles (with a sharp hairpin turn that is very difficult to negotiate by trucks with trailered boats) to the boat launch. After launching, cruise by boat 1.5 miles northeast to the boat-in campgrounds.

**Contact:** Auburn State Recreation Area, 530/885-4527, www.parks.ca.gov; marina, 530/885-5097.

## 35 MINERAL BAR

🚶 🚴 🏊 🛶 🚐 🐕 🚙 ⛺

### Scenic rating: 8

in Auburn State Recreation Area near Colfax

| Map 5.3, page 297 | BEST ( |

Mineral Bar is a primitive camp situated near the American River in the Auburn State Recreation Area, a 42,000-acre park. This recreational mecca is paradise for hikers and boaters, and is especially popular for white-water rafting.

**Campsites, facilities:** There are 18 sites for tents or RVs up to 24 feet (no hookups). Picnic tables and fire grills are provided. Chemical toilets are available. No drinking water is available. Leashed pets are permitted.

**Reservations, fees:** Reservations are not accepted. Sites are $28 per night, plus $10 per night for each additional vehicle. Open year-round, with limited winter facilities.

**Directions:** From I-80 in Auburn, drive east for 15 miles to Colfax and the Canyon Way/Placer Hills Drive exit. Take that exit and turn left on Canyon Way, then drive one mile to Iowa Hill Road. Turn right and drive three miles on a narrow paved road to the campground.

**Contact:** Auburn State Recreation Area, 530/885-4527, www.parks.ca.gov.

## 36 RUCK-A-CHUCKY

### Scenic rating: 8
in Auburn State Recreation Area near Auburn

Map 5.3, page 297 | **BEST (**

Ruck-A-Chucky is a small primitive camp in the Auburn State Recreation Area; it is one of two primitive camps at the park. Auburn State Recreation Area covers more than 42,000 acres along the North and Middle Forks of the American River and is home to wildlife as well as a wide variety of recreational opportunities.

**Campsites, facilities:** There are five sites for tents only. Picnic tables and fire grills are provided. Chemical toilets are available. No drinking water is available. Leashed pets are permitted.

**Reservations, fees:** Reservations are not accepted. Sites are $28 per night, plus $10 per night for each additional vehicle. Open spring through fall, weather permitting.

**Directions:** From I-80 in Auburn, take the Auburn Ravine/Foresthill Road exit to Foresthill Road. Turn right and drive for seven miles to Drivers Flat Road. Turn right and drive 2.8 miles on a dirt road to the campground on the right. Vehicles with high clearance are recommended.

**Contact:** Auburn State Recreation Area, 530/885-4527, www.parks.ca.gov.

## 37 PENINSULA

### Scenic rating: 6
in Folsom Lake State Recreation Area

Map 5.3, page 297

This is one of the big camps at Folsom Lake, but it is also more remote than the other camps, requiring a circuitous drive. It is on the peninsula on the northeast shore, right where the North Fork American River arm of the lake enters the main lake area. A nearby boat ramp, marina, and boat rentals make this a great weekend spot. Fishing for bass and trout is often quite good in spring and early summer, and other species include catfish and perch. Waterskiing and wakeboarding are popular in the hot summer, and all water sports are allowed.

Note: Due to fluctuating water levels, the launch ramps at the Peninsula Campground may be inoperable when the lake level falls below 430 feet. Check online (http://cdec.water.ca.gov) to confirm levels.

**Campsites, facilities:** There are 100 sites for tents or RVs up to 32 feet (no hookups). Picnic tables and fire grills are provided. Drinking water and restrooms with flush toilets are available. A bike path is nearby. Boat rentals, moorings, snack bar, ice, and bait and tackle are available at the Folsom Lake Marina. Some facilities, including the Oaks Nature Trail, are wheelchair-accessible. Leashed pets are permitted.

**Reservations, fees:** Reservations are accepted at 800/444-7275 or www.reserveamerica.com ($8 reservation fee). Sites are $28-33 per night, plus $12 per night for each additional vehicle. Open March through October.

**Directions:** From Placerville, drive east on U.S. 50 to the Spring Street/Highway 49 exit. Turn north on Highway 49 (toward the town of Coloma) and continue 8.3 miles into the town of Pilot Hill and Rattlesnake Bar Road. Turn left on Rattlesnake Bar Road and drive nine miles to the end of the road and the park entrance.

**Contact:** Folsom Lake State Recreation Area,

916/988-0205 or 916/933-6108 (kiosk), www. parks.ca.gov.

## 38 BEAL'S POINT

### Scenic rating: 6

in Folsom Lake State Recreation Area

**Map 5.3, page 297**

Folsom Lake State Recreation Area is Sacramento's backyard vacation spot, a huge lake covering about 18,000 acres with 75 miles of shoreline, which means plenty of room for boating, waterskiing, fishing, and sunning. This camp is on the lake's southwest side, just north of the dam, with a boat ramp nearby at Granite Bay. The lake has a productive trout fishery in the spring, a fast-growing population of kokanee salmon, and good prospects for bass in late spring and early summer. By summer, wakeboarders and water-skiers usually take over the lake each day by about 10am. One problem with this lake is that a minor water drawdown can cause major amounts of shoreline to become exposed on its upper arms. There are opportunities for hiking, biking, running, picnics, and horseback riding. A paved 32-mile-long trail, the American River Parkway, connects Folsom Lake with many Sacramento County parks before reaching Old Sacramento. This trail is outstanding for family biking and inline skating. Summers are hot and dry. The camp is close to the city of Folsom, with restaurants and shops only 15 minutes away.

Note: Due to fluctuating water levels, the launch ramps at the Peninsula Campground may be inoperable when the lake level falls below 430 feet. Check online (http://cdec.water. ca.gov) to confirm levels.

**Campsites, facilities:** There are 64 sites for tents or RVs of any length; some sites have full hookups (30 and 50 amps). Picnic tables and fire grills are provided. Drinking water, restrooms with flush toilets and showers, and a dump station are available. A bike path and horseback-riding facilities are nearby. Some facilities are wheelchair-accessible. There are boat rentals, moorings, a summer snack bar, ice, and bait and tackle at the Folsom Lake Marina. Leashed pets are permitted.

**Reservations, fees:** Reservations are accepted at 800/444-7275 or www.reserveamerica.com ($8 reservation fee). Tent sites are $33 per night, RV sites (hookups) are $58 per night, and it's $12 per night for each additional vehicle. Discounts are available in the off-season. Open year-round.

**Directions:** From Sacramento, drive east on U.S. 50 to the Folsom Boulevard exit. Take that exit to the stop sign and Folsom Boulevard. Turn left and continue north on Folsom Boulevard for 3.5 miles (road name changes to Folsom-Auburn Road) to the park entrance on the right.

**Contact:** Folsom Lake State Recreation Area, 916/988-0205; Beal's Point Campground, 916/791-1531 or 916/791-1531 (kiosk), www. parks.ca.gov.

## 39 NEGRO BAR GROUP CAMP

### Scenic rating: 8

in Folsom Lake State Recreation Area

**Map 5.3, page 297**

Lake Natoma is pretty and quiet, compared to nearby Folsom, with no parties, mayhem, or water sports. Natoma is the afterbay for Folsom Lake, located directly below Folsom Dam. It is comparatively small with 13 miles of shoreline, very narrow instead of wide, with cold water instead of warm. This camp is at the head of the lake on the northern shore, with an adjacent boat ramp. Lake Natoma is popular for crew races, sailing, kayaking, and other aquatic sports. A 5-mph speed limit is enforced on the lake, and swimming is allowed. The Folsom Lake entrance is a 10-minute drive from Lake Natoma. The Sacramento River Parkway runs nearby.

**Campsites, facilities:** Three group tent sites

can accommodate 25-50 people each. Picnic tables and fire grills are provided. Drinking water and restrooms with flush toilets are available. A bike path and canoe and kayak rentals are available nearby. Leashed pets are permitted.

**Reservations, fees:** Reservations are accepted at 800/444-7275 or www.reserveamerica.com ($8 reservation fee). Negro Bar A and B are $195 per night; Negro Bar C is $115 per night. Open year-round.

**Directions:** From I-80 north of Sacramento, take the Douglas Boulevard exit and head east for five miles to Auburn-Folsom Road. Turn right on Auburn-Folsom Road and drive south for six miles to Greenback Lane. Turn right on Greenback Lane and merge immediately into the left lane. The park entrance is approximately 0.2 mile on the left.

**Contact:** Folsom Lake State Recreation Area, 916/988-0205 or 916/988-6923 (kiosk), www.parks.ca.gov.

## 40 SACRAMENTO WEST/ OLD TOWN KOA

### Scenic rating: 2

in West Sacramento

**Map 5.3, page 297**

This is the choice of car and RV campers touring California's capital and looking for a layover spot. It is in West Sacramento not far from the Capitol building, the railroad museum, Sutter's Fort, Old Sacramento, Crocker Museum, and shopping.

**Campsites, facilities:** There are 95 pull-through sites with full or partial hookups (30 and 50 amps) for RVs (up to 105 feet) and 21 tent sites. Twelve cabins, three cottages, three park models, and a group camping area are also available. Restrooms with flush toilets and showers, Wi-Fi, cable TV, playground, fishing pond, seasonal swimming pool, coin laundry, dump station, propane gas, firewood, and a convenience and gift store are available. Some

facilities are wheelchair-accessible. Leashed pets are permitted, with certain restrictions.

**Reservations, fees:** Reservations are accepted at 800/562-2747. RV sites are $50-55 per night; tent sites are $40-45 per night. Off-season discounts are available. Some credit cards are accepted. Open year-round.

**Directions:** From Sacramento, drive west on I-80 about four miles to the West Capitol Avenue exit. Exit and turn left onto West Capitol Avenue, going under the freeway to the second stoplight and the intersection with Lake Road. Turn left onto Lake Road and continue a half block to the camp on the right.

**Contact:** Sacramento West/Old Town KOA, 3951 Lake Rd., 916/371-6771, www.sacwestrvpark.com.

## 41 VINEYARD RV PARK

### Scenic rating: 2

in Vacaville

**Map 5.3, page 297**

This is one of two privately operated parks in the area set up primarily for RVs. It is in a eucalyptus grove, with clean, well-kept sites. If you are heading to the Bay Area, it is late in the day, and you don't have your destination set, this spot offers a chance to hole up for the night and formulate your travel plans. Note that about half of the sites are long-term rentals.

**Campsites, facilities:** There are 110 sites with full hookups (30 and 50 amps) for RVs of any length. Some sites are pull-through. RV and tent cabin rentals are also available. Picnic tables are provided. Restrooms with flush toilets and showers, Wi-Fi, a seasonal swimming pool, coin laundry, enclosed dog walk, and ice are available. Some facilities are wheelchair-accessible. Leashed pets are permitted, with certain restrictions.

**Reservations, fees:** Reservations are recommended at 866/447-8797. RV sites are $55-65 per night, tent cabins are $45-75 per night, plus $1 per pet per night. Weekly and monthly rates are available. Some credit cards are accepted. Open year-round.

**Directions:** From Vacaville on I-80, turn north on I-505 and drive three miles to Midway Road. Turn right (east) on Midway Road and drive 0.5 mile to the second campground on the left.

**Contact:** Vineyard RV Park, 4985 Midway Rd., 866/447-8797, www.vineyardrvpark.com.

## 42 RANCHO SECO RECREATION AREA

**Scenic rating: 6**

near Sacramento

**Map 5.3, page 297**   **BEST (**

There is a shortage of campgrounds close to Sacramento, so this one about 35 miles from the state capital comes in handy. This public facility has a 160-acre lake surrounded by 400 acres of open space and includes trails for walking and bicycling. The centerpiece of this recreation area is the lake, which is especially popular for fishing and sailboarding. The lake is stocked with rainbow trout, and fishing derbies are held during the winter. Other fish species include bass, bluegill, redear sunfish, crappie, and catfish. Live bait is prohibited and only electric motors are allowed. A bonus is that the lake level remains constant year-round, and since the lake is fed by the Folsom South Canal, the water is warm in summer. Swimming is popular and there is a large sandy beach with summer lifeguard service. Pedal boats and kayaks can also be rented on weekends in summer. Tent sites are situated along the lake and a seven-mile nature trail loop is also next to the lake. The Amanda Blake Memorial Wildlife Refuge is here, and visitors can observe exotic captive wildlife that has been rescued from circuses and other performing groups. Migratory birds, including bald eagles, winter at the lake. What are those two large towers? They're remnants of the now-closed Rancho Seco nuclear power-generating station.

**Campsites, facilities:** There are 32 tent sites, 18 sites with partial hookups (30 amps) for RVs of any length, and two group tent sites that can accommodate up to 250 people each. A couple of sites are pull-through. Picnic tables and fire grills are provided. Drinking water, restrooms with coin showers, dump station, swimming beach, six fishing piers, picnic areas, coin laundry, fish-cleaning station, horseshoe pit, recreation room, seasonal general store, weekend boat rentals, and boat launch are available. Supplies are available in Galt. Some facilities are wheelchair-accessible, including some fishing piers. Leashed pets are permitted.

**Reservations, fees:** Reservations are accepted at 800/416-6992. Tent sites are $15-25 per night; RV sites are $20-30 per night. Rates include eight people, three tents, and one vehicle per night. Two group sites are $200 per night each. Pets are $3 per night, and it's $10 per each additional vehicle per night. Boat launch fees are $5. There is a 14-day maximum stay. Open year-round; discounts are available.

**Directions:** From Sacramento, drive south on Highway 99 for approximately 25 miles to the Twin Cities Road/Highway 104 exit. Take that exit and drive east for 13 miles, past the two towers, to the Rancho Seco Park exit. Turn right and continue to the lake and campground.

**Contact:** Rocky Mountain Recreation Co., 800/416-6992 or 661/702-1420, www.rocky-mountainrec.com.

## 43 SANDY BEACH REGIONAL PARK

**Scenic rating: 6**

on the Sacramento River

**Map 5.3, page 297**

This is a surprisingly little-known park, especially considering it provides beach access to the Sacramento River. The actual campground consists of what are called "utility parking spots"; that is, drive-in parking with water and electricity. The park has a sandy beach stretching for more than a half mile, fairly unique for the lower Delta and Sacramento River. In winter and spring, it is one of the few viable spots where you can fish from the shore for sturgeon. It also provides outstanding boating access to the Sacramento River, including one of the best fishing spots for striped bass in the fall and again in spring (usually best near the Rio Vista Bridge). Windy summer days provide good windsurfing, though the water can be a bit choppy.

**Campsites, facilities:** There are 42 sites with partial hookups (30 amps) for tents or RVs of any length. Picnic tables and fire pits are provided. Drinking water, restrooms with flush toilets and showers, a dump station, picnic areas, volleyball, horseshoes, firewood, and a boat ramp are available. A camp host is onsite. Some facilities are wheelchair-accessible. Supplies can be obtained within a mile. Leashed pets are permitted in the campground only.

**Reservations, fees:** Reservations are accepted online at www.solanocounty.com/park ($9 reservation fee). Tent and RV sites (water and electricity) are $30-34 per night, plus $10 per night for each additional vehicle and $1 per pet per night. Some credit cards are accepted. Open year-round.

**Directions:** From I-80 in Fairfield, take the Highway 12 exit and drive southeast for 14 miles to Rio Vista and the intersection with Main Street. Turn right on Main Street and drive a short distance to 2nd Street. Turn right and drive 0.5 mile to Beach Drive. Turn left (west) and drive 0.5 mile to the park.

**Contact:** Sandy Beach Regional Park, 707/374-2097, www.solanocounty.com/park.

## 44 DELTA MARINA YACHT HARBOR AND RV PARK

🏊 🍴 🚿 🦌 🎣 ♿ 🚐

**Scenic rating: 6**

on the Sacramento River Delta

**Map 5.3, page 297**

This is a prime spot for boat campers. Summers are hot and breezy, and waterskiing is popular on the nearby Sacramento River. From November to March, the striped-bass fishing is quite good, often as close as just a half mile upriver at the Rio Vista Bridge. The boat launch at the harbor is a bonus, especially with night lighting. Some campsites have river frontage, and some sites are filled with long-term renters.

**Campsites, facilities:** There are 25 sites with full hookups (30 and 50 amps) for RVs up to 40 feet. No tents are permitted. Picnic tables and fire grills are provided. Restrooms with showers, cable TV, Wi-Fi, coin laundry, playground, boat ramp, fishing pier, marine repair service, pet restroom, restaurant, marine supplies and gift store, ice, and propane gas are available. Fuel is available 24 hours. Boat launching is free for RV guests. Some facilities are wheelchair-accessible. Leashed pets are permitted.

**Reservations, fees:** Reservations are accepted at 866/774-2315. RV sites are $38-48 per night, plus $5 per night per person for more than four people. Maximum is two pets. There is a two-week maximum stay in summer. Some credit cards are accepted. Open year-round.

**Directions:** From Fairfield on I-80, take the Highway 12 exit and drive southeast for 14 miles to Rio Vista and the intersection with Main Street. Take the Main Street exit and drive a short distance to 2nd Street. Turn right on 2nd Street and drive to Marina Drive. Turn left on Marina Drive and continue a short distance to the harbor.

**Contact:** Delta Marina Yacht Harbor and RV Park, 707/374-2315, www.deltamarina.com.

## 45 BRANNAN ISLAND STATE RECREATION AREA

🚶 🚴 🏊 🛶 🚤 🚐 🦌 🐕 ♿ 🚐 ⛺

**Scenic rating: 7**

on the Sacramento River

**Map 5.3, page 297**          **BEST (**

This state park is perfectly designed for boaters, set in the heart of the Delta's vast waterways. You get year-round adventure: waterskiing, wakeboarding, and fishing for catfish are popular in the summer, and in the winter the immediate area is often good for striped-bass fishing. The proximity of the campgrounds to the boat launch deserves a medal. What many people do is tow a boat here, launch it, keep it docked, and then return to their site and set up; this allows them to come and go as they please, boating, fishing, and exploring in the Delta. A six-lane boat ramp provides access to a maze of waterways amid many islands, marshes, sloughs, and rivers. Day-use areas include the Windy Cove sailboarding area. Though striped bass in winter and catfish in summer are the most favored fish, sturgeon, bluegill, perch, bullhead, and bass are also caught. Some sections of the San Joaquin Delta are among the best bass fishing spots in California. A hiking/biking trail circles the park.

**Campsites, facilities:** There are 102 sites (12 sites with hookups) for tents or RVs up to 36 feet, 13 walk-in sites, and six group sites for up to 30 people each. Picnic tables and fire rings are provided. Drinking water, restrooms with coin showers (at campground and boat launch), boat berths, a dump station, and a boat launch are available. Supplies can be obtained three miles away in Rio Vista. Some facilities are wheelchair-accessible. Leashed pets are permitted.

**Reservations, fees:** Reservations are accepted at 800/444-7275 or www.reserveamerica.com ($8 reservation fee). Tent and RV sites (no hookups) are $36-49 per night, RV sites (with hookups) are $49 per night, cabins are $56 per night, plus $10 per night for each additional vehicle. Group camping is $100 per night. Boat launching is $5 per day. Open year-round.

**Directions:** In Fairfield on I-80, take the Highway 12 exit, drive southeast 14 miles to Rio Vista, and continue to Highway 160. Turn right on Highway 160 and drive three miles to the park entrance on the left.

**Contact:** Brannan Island State Recreation Area, 916/777-6671; Entrance Kiosk, 916/777-7701, www.parks.ca.gov; American Land and Leisure, 800/342-2267, www.americanll.com.

## 46 SNUG HARBOR RESORT

**Scenic rating: 7**

near Rio Vista

Map 5.3, page 297     **BEST (**

This year-round resort is an ideal resting place for families who enjoy waterskiing, wakeboarding, boating, biking, swimming, and fishing. After the ferry ride, it is only a few minutes to Snug Harbor, a gated marina resort on eight acres with a campground, RV hookups, and a separate area with cabins and cottages. Some say that the waterfront sites with docks give the place the feel of a Louisiana bayou, yet everything is clean and orderly, including a full-service marina, a store, and all facilities—and an excellent location to explore the boating paradise of the Delta. Anglers will find good prospects for striped bass, black bass, bluegill, steelhead, sturgeon, and catfish. The waterfront sites with docks are a bonus.

**Campsites, facilities:** There are 38 waterfront sites with docks available with full or partial hookups (30 and 50 amps) for RVs of any length, including four pull-through waterview sites with full or partial hookups for RVs. There are also 10 tent sites (tents are allowed at some RV sites), two double sites for RVs, and 12 park-model cabins. Barbecues or burn barrels are provided. Restrooms with key-accessible showers, a dump station, Wi-Fi, a small convenience store, swimming beach, children's play area, volleyball, croquet, bocce ball, badminton, horseshoes, boat launch, and a covered-berth marina are available. Some facilities are wheelchair-accessible. Dogs are permitted on leash at some sites.

**Reservations, fees:** Reservations are recommended. RV and tent sites are $50-65 per night, double sites are $100-110, plus $10 per night for each additional vehicle and $2 per pet per night. Cottages are $100-550 per night. Boat launching is available for a one-time fee of $10. Some credit cards are accepted. Open year-round.

**Directions:** From Fairfield, take Highway 12 east to Rio Vista and Front Street. Turn left on Front Street (before crossing the bridge) and drive under the bridge to River Road. Turn right on River Road and drive two miles to the Rio Vista/Real McCoy Ferry (signed Ryer Island). Take the ferry (free) across the Sacramento River to Ryer Island and Levee Road. Turn right on Levee Road and drive 4.5 miles to the Snug Harbor entrance on the right.

**Contact:** Snug Harbor Resort, 916/775-1455, www.snugharbor.net.

## 47 WESTGATE LANDING COUNTY PARK

### Scenic rating: 6

on the San Joaquin River Delta near Stockton

**Map 5.3, page 297**

Summer temperatures typically reach the high 90s and low 100s here, and this county park provides a little shade and boating access to the South Fork Mokelumne River. On hot summer nights, some campers stay up late and night fish for catfish. Between storms in winter, the area typically gets smothered in dense fog. The sites are not pull-through but semicircles, which work nearly as well for RV drivers.

**Campsites, facilities:** There are 14 sites for tents or RVs up to 32 feet (no hookups). Picnic tables and barbecues are provided. Drinking water and flush toilets are available. Groceries and propane gas are nearby. A fishing pier, 24 boat slips, and boat docking are available. Some facilities are wheelchair-accessible. Leashed pets are permitted, with a limit of two.

**Reservations, fees:** Reservations are accepted at least two weeks in advance at 209/953-8800 ($10 reservation fee). Less than two weeks, sites are first come, first served. Sites are $20 per night, plus $5 per night for each additional vehicle and $1 per pet per night. Boat slips cost $20 per day. Open year-round.

**Directions:** From Stockton, drive 13.5 miles north on I-5 to Highway 12. Take Highway 12 west and drive about five miles to Glasscock

Road. Turn right and drive about a mile to the park.

**Contact:** San Joaquin County Parks Department, 209/953-8800 or 209/331-7400, www.sjparks.com or www.mgzoo.com.

## 48 STOCKTON DELTA KOA

### Scenic rating: 6

near Stockton

**Map 5.3, page 297**

Some people may remember this campground by its previous name: Tower Park Resort. This huge resort is ideal for boat-in campers who desire a full-facility marina. The camp is on Little Potato Slough near the Mokelumne River. In the summer, this is a popular waterskiing area. Some hot weekends are like a continuous party. Note that tents are now allowed.

**Campsites, facilities:** There are 352 sites with full hookups (30-50 amps) for RVs up to 78 feet, 50 tent sites, and 21 park-model cabins. Picnic tables are provided. Restrooms with showers, a dump station, pavilion, banquet room, boat rentals, overnight boat slips, boat storage, double boat launch, playground, swimming pool, spa, water slides, gas station, restaurant, coin laundry, Wi-Fi, gift shop, store, ice, and propane gas are available. Leashed pets are permitted, with certain restrictions.

**Reservations, fees:** Reservations are available at 800/562-0913, with a three-night minimum on summer holidays. RV sites are $48-88 per night, tent sites are $68 per night, with a maximum of six people per site. Some credit cards are accepted. Open year-round.

**Directions:** From Stockton, drive 13.5 miles north on I-5 to Highway 12. Take Highway 12 west and drive about five miles to Tower Park Way (before the first bridge). Turn left and drive a short distance to the park.

**Contact:** Stockton Delta KOA, 209/369-1041, www.koa.com or http://koa.com/campgrounds/stockton.

## 49 EDDOS HARBOR AND RV PARK

**Scenic rating: 6**

on the San Joaquin River Delta

**Map 5.3, page 297**                          **BEST (**

This is an ideal spot for campers with boats. Eddos is on the San Joaquin River and Gallagher Slough, upstream of the Antioch Bridge, in an outstanding region for fishing, powerboating, wakeboarding, and waterskiing. In summer, boaters have access to 1,000 miles of Delta waterways, with the best of them in a nearby spider web of rivers and sloughs off the San Joaquin to False River, Frank's Tract, and Old River. Hot weather and sheltered sloughs make this ideal for waterskiing. In the winter, a nearby fishing spot and the mouth of the False River attract striped bass. Many of the sites are occupied by seasonal renters; plan well ahead for the summer.

**Campsites, facilities:** There are 42 sites with full hookups (30 and 50 amps) for RVs up to 40 feet. Picnic tables are provided. Restrooms with flush toilets and showers, a launch ramp, boat storage, fuel dock, Wi-Fi, coin laundry, propane, and a small grocery store are available. Some facilities are wheelchair-accessible. Leashed pets are permitted, with some breed restrictions.

**Reservations, fees:** Reservations are recommended. Sites are $35-38 per night. Weekly and monthly rates are available. Some credit cards are accepted. Open year-round.

**Directions:** In Fairfield on I-80, take the Highway 12 exit and drive 14 miles southeast to Rio Vista and continue three miles to Highway 160 (at the signal just after the bridge). Turn right on Highway 160 and drive three miles to Sherman Island/East Levee Road, at the end of the drawbridge. Turn left on East Levee Road and drive 5.5 miles to the campground along the San Joaquin River. Note: If arriving by boat, look for the camp adjacent to Light 21.

**Contact:** Eddos Harbor and RV Park, 925/757-5314, www.eddosharbor.com.

## 50 DRU BARNER EQUESTRIAN CAMP

**Scenic rating: 7**

near Georgetown in Eldorado National Forest

**Map 5.4, page 298**

This camp, at 3,200 feet elevation in an area of pine and fir, is ideal for horses; there are miles of equestrian trails. Please note that wheat straw is not allowed at this campground.

**Campsites, facilities:** There are 48 sites for tents or RVs up to 35 feet (no hookups). Picnic tables and fire rings are provided. Drinking water and flush and vault toilets are available. Five stock troughs and four hitching posts are also available. Some facilities are wheelchair-accessible. Leashed pets are permitted.

**Reservations, fees:** Reservations are not accepted. Sites are $8 per night. Open year-round.

**Directions:** From Sacramento, take I-80 east to the north end of Auburn and the exit for Elm Avenue. Take that exit and turn left on Elm Avenue, then drive about 0.1 mile to High Street. Turn left on High Street, drive through the signal that marks the continuation of High Street as Highway 49, and drive 3.5 miles on Highway 49 to the bridge. Turn right over the bridge and drive 2.5 miles into the town of Cool and Georgetown Road/Highway 193. Turn left and drive 14 miles into Georgetown to a four-way stop at Main Street. Turn left on Main Street and drive 5.5 miles (the road becomes Georgetown-Wentworth Springs Road/Forest Road 1) to Bottle Hill Bypass Road. Turn left on Bottle Hill Bypass Road and drive about a mile to the campground on the left.

**Contact:** Eldorado National Forest, Georgetown Ranger District, 530/333-4312, www.fs.usda.gov/eldorado.

## 51 CAMP LOTUS

### Scenic rating: 7

on the American River near Coloma

**Map 5.4, page 298**          **BEST (**

This is a great area with a half mile of frontage on the South Fork of the American River. During spring and summer you'll see plenty of white-water rafters and kayakers because this is a popular place for outfitters to put in and take out. Several swimming holes are in the immediate vicinity. The camp is situated on 23 acres at 700 feet elevation. Trees at Camp Lotus include pines, oaks, willows, and cottonwoods. Coloma, two miles away, is where you'll find the Marshall Gold Discovery Site. Gold was discovered there in 1848, and the site features displays and exhibits on gold rush-era mining methods and the history of the California gold rush. Wineries are nearby, and gold panning, hiking, and fishing are also popular.

**Campsites, facilities:** There are 30 tent sites and 10 sites with partial hookups (20 and 30 amps) for tents or RVs of any length. A tepee, three lodge rooms, and three cabins are also available for rent. Picnic tables and fire grills are provided. Drinking water, restrooms with showers, Wi-Fi, dump station, general store with deli, volleyball, horseshoes, and raft and kayak put-in and take-out areas are available. Groups can be accommodated. Limited supplies are available in Coloma. Some facilities are wheelchair-accessible. Dogs are not permitted.

**Reservations, fees:** Reservations are accepted and required for weekends. Sites are $27-36 per night, plus $9-12 per person for more than three people. Credit cards are accepted. Open February through October.

**Directions:** From Sacramento, drive east on U.S. 50 for approximately 30 miles (past Cameron Park) to Exit 37, the Ponderosa Road exit. Take that exit and drive north over the freeway to North Shingle Road. Turn right and drive 10 miles (the road becomes Lotus Road) to Bassi Road. Turn left and drive one mile to the campground entrance on the right.

**Contact:** Camp Lotus, 530/622-8672, www.camplotus.com.

## 52 PLACERVILLE KOA

### Scenic rating: 5

near Placerville

**Map 5.4, page 298**

This is a classic KOA campground, complete with the cute little log cabins KOA calls "Kamping Kabins." The location of this camp is ideal for many, set near U.S. 50 in the Sierra foothills, the main route up to South Lake Tahoe. Nearby is Apple Hill, which from September to November is a popular tourist attraction, when the local ranches and orchards sell produce and crafts, often with live music. In addition, the Marshall Gold Discovery Site is 10 miles north, where gold was discovered in 1848, setting off the 1849 gold rush. Whitewater rafting and gold panning are popular on the nearby American River.

**Campsites, facilities:** There are 70 sites with full or partial hookups (30 and 50 amps) for RVs (up to 100 feet); 14 tent sites, including eight with electricity; 20 sites for tents or RVs; and eight cabins. Some sites are pull-through. Picnic tables and barbecues are provided. Restrooms with flush toilets and showers, drinking water, dump station, cable TV, Wi-Fi, recreation room, seasonal swimming pool, spa (some restrictions apply), playground, video arcade, basketball courts, 18-hole miniature golf course, convenience store, snack bar, dog run, petting zoo, fishing pond, bike rentals, pavilion cooking facilities, volleyball court, and horseshoe pits are available. Some facilities are wheelchair-accessible. Leashed pets are permitted, with certain restrictions.

**Reservations, fees:** Reservations are accepted at 800/562-4197. RV sites are $66-71 per night; tent sites are $48-51 per night. Some credit cards are accepted. Open year-round.

**Directions:** From U.S. 50 west of Placerville, take the exit for Shingle Springs Drive/Exit 39 (not the Shingle Springs/Ponderosa Road exit). Drive one block to Rock Barn Road. Turn left and drive 0.5 mile to the campground at the end of the road.

**Contact:** Placerville KOA, 800/562-4197 or 530/676-2267, www.koa-placerville.com.

## 53 FAR HORIZONS 49ER VILLAGE RV RESORT

### Scenic rating: 4

in Plymouth

**Map 5.4, page 298**

This is the granddaddy of RV parks, on 23 acres in the heart of the Gold Country 40 miles east of Stockton and Sacramento. It is rarely crowded and offers warm pools and a huge spa. A bonus is the year-round heated, covered swimming pool. This resort is pet-friendly, and dogs receive a free Milk-Bone at check-in. Wineries are nearby. Note that renters occupy about one-fourth of the sites.

**Campsites, facilities:** There are 329 sites with full hookups (30 and 50 amps) for RVs up to 40 feet and 15 park-model cabins. Some sites are pull-through. Restrooms with flush toilets and showers, cable TV, dump station, playground, two heated swimming pools, indoor spa, recreation room, TV lounge, recreation complex, Wi-Fi, business services, organized activities, café, gift shop, coin laundry, propane gas, and a general store are available. Some facilities are wheelchair-accessible. Leashed pets are permitted.

**Reservations, fees:** Reservations are recommended at 800/339-6981. Sites are $43-80 per night (holiday rates higher), plus $5 per night for each additional person, $2 per night for each additional vehicle, and $3 per night per pet. Winter discounts are available. Some credit cards are accepted. Open year-round.

**Directions:** From Sacramento, drive east on U.S. 50 to Watt Avenue. Turn south on Watt Avenue and drive to Highway 16. Turn left (east) on Highway 16/Jackson Road and drive approximately 30 miles to Highway 49 north/Jackson Road. Merge north on Highway 49 and drive two miles to the resort on the left side of the road at 18265 Highway 49. Note: This is a mile south of Main Street in Plymouth.

**Contact:** Far Horizons 49er Village RV Resort, 209/245-6981, www.49ervillage.com.

## 54 INDIAN GRINDING ROCK STATE HISTORIC PARK

### Scenic rating: 7

near Jackson

**Map 5.4, page 298**

This park is like a living history lesson. Indian Grinding Rock covers 135 acres in the Sierra foothills at an elevation of 2,400 feet. Set in a small valley of meadows and oaks, the park contains the most remarkable limestone bedrock mortars in California, as well as a reconstructed Miwok village with petroglyphs, a museum, and two nature trails; one massive table rock has hundreds of mortars. (If it looks familiar, you may recognize it from a TV show I shot here.) Interpretive talks are offered for groups (by reservation).

Local Native Americans schedule several ceremonies each year, including the Acorn Harvest Thanksgiving in September. In summer, expect warm and dry temperatures, often exceeding 90°F. Spring and fall are ideal, with winters cool, often right on the edge of snow (a few times) and rain (mostly) during storms.

**Campsites, facilities:** There are 23 sites for tents or RVs up to 27 feet (no hookups), and a group camp for up to 44 people includes bark houses. Picnic tables, fire grills, and food lockers are provided. Drinking water and restrooms with flush toilets and coin showers are available. Some facilities are wheelchair-accessible. Leashed pets are permitted.

**Reservations, fees:** Reservations are accepted at www.reserveamerica.com or 800/444-7275

($8 reservation fee). To reserve the bark houses, call 209/296-7488. Tent and RV sites are $30-35 per night (up to 8 people per campsite), plus $10 per night for each additional vehicle. It's $85 per night for the group camp. Open year-round.

**Directions:** From Jackson, drive east on Highway 88 for 11 miles to Pine Grove-Volcano Road. Turn left on Pine Grove-Volcano Road and drive 1.75 miles to the campground on the left.

**Contact:** Indian Grinding Rock State Historic Park, 209/296-7488, www.parks.ca.gov.

## 55 LAKE AMADOR RECREATION AREA

### Scenic rating: 7

near Stockton

**Map 5.4, page 298**

Lake Amador is in the foothill country east of Stockton at an elevation of 485 feet, covering 400 acres with 13 miles of shoreline. Everything is set up for fishing, with large trout stocks from winter through late spring and the chance for huge bass. The lake record bass weighed 17 pounds, 1.25 ounces. The Carson Creek arm and Jackson Creek arm are the top spots. Night fishing is available. Waterskiing and personal watercraft are prohibited, and the speed limit is 5 mph. A bonus is a swimming pond. About half of the sites are lakefront with full hookups.

**Campsites, facilities:** There are 186 sites for tents or RVs of any length and 13 group sites for 5-30 vehicles each; some sites have full hookups (30 and 50 amps). Picnic tables and fire grills are provided. Drinking water, restrooms with showers, a dump station, boat ramp, boat rentals, fishing supplies (including bait and tackle), seasonal café, convenience store, propane gas, swimming pond with water slide, pool tables, horseshoe pits, two disc-golf courses, and a playground are available. Some facilities are wheelchair-accessible. Leashed pets are permitted.

**Reservations, fees:** Reservations are accepted February through August ($5 reservation fee). Tent sites are $30 per night per vehicle, plus $1 per person for more than four people; RV sites are $40 per night. Boat launching is $7 per day and fishing is $5 per day. Some credit cards are accepted. Open year-round.

**Directions:** From Stockton, turn east on Highway 88 and drive 24 miles to Clements. Just east of Clements, bear left on Highway 88 and drive nine miles to Jackson Valley Road. Turn right (well signed) and drive five miles to Lake Amador Drive. Turn right and drive over the dam to the campground office.

**Contact:** Lake Amador Recreation Area, 209/274-4739, www.lakeamador.com.

## 56 LAKE PARDEE MARINA

### Scenic rating: 7

on Pardee Reservoir

**Map 5.4, page 298**     **BEST (**

Many people think that Pardee is the prettiest lake in the Mother Lode country; it's a big lake covering 2,257 acres with 37 miles of shoreline. It is a beautiful sight in the spring when the lake is full and the surrounding hills are green and glowing. Waterskiing, personal watercraft, swimming, and all water/body contact are prohibited at the lake; it is set up expressly for fishing, with high catch rates for rainbow trout and kokanee salmon. During hot weather, attention turns to bass, both smallmouth and largemouth, as well as catfish and sunfish. The lake speed limit is 25 mph. All of the money collected from the daily fishing fee is used to purchase and stock rainbow trout.

**Campsites, facilities:** There are 190 sites for tents or RVs up to 42 feet (no hookups) and 12 sites with full hookups (50 amps) for RVs. Picnic tables and fire grills are provided. Drinking water, restrooms with showers (in the hookup section), chemical toilets (in the no-hookup campground), dump station, full-service marina, fish-cleaning station, boat ramp, boat rentals, coin laundry, café, gas station, convenience store, propane gas, RV and boat storage, wading pool, and a seasonal swimming pool are available. Some facilities are wheelchair-accessible. Leashed pets are permitted.

**Reservations, fees:** Reservations are accepted ($9 registration fee). RV sites with full hookups are $36 per night and tent sites are $26-50 per night, plus $9.50 per night for each additional vehicle and $5 per pet per night. Boat launching is $8.50 per day. There is a daily fishing fee of $5.50. Monthly and seasonal rates are available. Some credit cards are accepted. Open February through October.

**Directions:** From Stockton, drive east on Highway 88/Waterloo Road for 17 miles to the town of Clements. One mile east of Clements, bear left on Highway 88 and drive 11 miles to Jackson Valley Road. Turn right and drive 3.4 miles to a four-way stop sign at Buena Vista. Turn right and drive 3.1 miles to Stony Creek Road. Turn left and drive a mile to the campground on the right. (Driving directions from other areas are available on the marina's website.)

**Contact:** Lake Pardee Marina, 209/772-1472, www.pardeelakerecreation.com.

## 57 CAMANCHE LAKE NORTH

### Scenic rating: 7

on Camanche Lake

**Map 5.4, page 298**    **BEST (**

The sites at North Shore feature grassy spots with picnic tables set above the lake, and though there are few trees and the sites seem largely exposed, the lake view is quite pretty. In spring, this site rates much higher. The lake will beckon you and is excellent for boating and all water sports, with a full-service marina. The warm, clean waters make for good waterskiing and wakeboarding (in specified areas), along with fishing for trout in spring, bass in early summer, and crappie, bluegill, and catfish in summer. There are five miles of hiking and equestrian trails. Note: All boats must be certified mussel-free before launching.

**Campsites, facilities:** There are 219 sites for tents or RVs of any length (no hookups) and four group sites for 12-72 people. There are also seven boat-in sites at Eagle Beach Campground, 15 cottages, and motel rooms available. Picnic tables and fire grills are provided. Restrooms with showers, drinking water, dump station, boat ramp, boat rentals, coin laundry, convenience store, café, tennis courts, basketball court, volleyball, horseshoe pits, and a playground are available. Some facilities are wheelchair-accessible. Leashed pets are permitted.

**Reservations, fees:** Reservations are accepted at 866/763-5121 ($10.50 reservation fee). Tent sites are $8-35 per night, premium tent sites and boat-in sites are $8.25-35 per night, and RV sites are $48-53 per night, plus $12 per day for additional vehicles. Car and boat access is $13.50-17, fishing is $5 per day, boat launch is $10 per day, and pets cost $5 each per day. Group rates are available on a sliding scale. Discounts are available off-season. Some credit cards are accepted. Open year-round.

**Directions:** From Stockton, drive east on Highway 88/Waterloo Road for 17 miles to Clements. One mile east of Clements, bear left on Highway 88 and drive six miles to Liberty Road/North Camanche Parkway. Turn right and drive six miles to Camanche Road. Turn right and drive to the Camanche North Shore entrance gate.

**Contact:** Camanche Lake North, 866/763-5123 ext 3 or 209/763-5121, www.camancherecreation.com or www.lakecamancheresort.com.

## 58 CAMANCHE LAKE SOUTH AND EQUESTRIAN

### Scenic rating: 7

on Camanche Lake

**Map 5.4, page 298**

Camanche Lake is a huge, multifaceted facility, covering 7,700 acres with 53 miles of shoreline, set in the foothills east of Lodi at 325 feet elevation. It is the number one recreation lake for waterskiing, wakeboarding, and personal watercraft (in specified areas), as well as swimming. In the spring and summer, it provides outstanding fishing for bass, trout, crappie, bluegill, and catfish. There are two campgrounds at the lake, and both have boat ramps nearby and full facilities. A new equestrian campground is open, and it's about one mile from the main campground area. This one at South Shore has a large but exposed overflow area for camping, a way to keep from getting stuck for a spot on popular weekends. Note: All boats must be certified mussel-free before launching.

**Campsites, facilities:** There are 149 sites for tents or RVs of any length (no hookups), including 35 double sites and 35 group sites for up to 16 people. Seven cottages are also available. Turkey Hill Equestrian Camp can accommodate groups of up to 32 people, as well as their horses and trailers. Picnic tables and fire grills are provided. Drinking water, restrooms with flush toilets and showers, chemical toilets, dump station, trout pond, marina, boat ramp, boat rentals, coin laundry, amphitheater with seasonal movies, basketball, tennis courts, volleyball, horseshoe pits, playground, and a convenience store are available. Some facilities are wheelchair-accessible. Leashed pets are permitted.

**Reservations, fees:** Reservations are accepted at 866/763-5178 ($9 reservation fee). Tent sites are $8-28 per night, premium tent sites and boat-in sites are $8.25-35 per night, RV sites are $47.50-53 per night, equestrian sites range $25-155 for 8-32 people, plus $5 per pet per day. Car and boat access is $12, fishing access is $5 per day, a boat launch is $10 per day. Group rates are available on a sliding scale. Monthly rates are available with a six-month limit. Discounts are available off-season. Some credit cards are accepted. Open year-round.

**Directions:** From Stockton, drive east on Highway 88/Waterloo Road for 17 miles to Clements. One mile east of Clements, continue east on Highway 12 and drive six miles to South Camanche Parkway at Wallace. Continue straight and drive five miles to the entrance gate.

**Contact:** Camanche Lake South, 209/763-5178, www.camancherecreation.com.

## 59 OAK KNOLL CAMPGROUND AND COYOTE POINT GROUP CAMP

**Scenic rating: 7**

at New Hogan Lake

Map 5.4, page 298

This is one of two camps at New Hogan Lake. The reservoir was created by an Army Corps of Engineers dam project on the Calaveras River. (See the Acorn Camp and Deer Flat Boat-In listing for more information.)

**Campsites, facilities:** There are 49 sites for tents or RVs of any length and a group site for tents or RVs of any length that can accommodate up to 50-60 people (no hookups). Fire grills and picnic tables are provided. Drinking water, vault toilets, and coin showers are available. A dump station, a fish-cleaning station, and a four-lane boat ramp (at Fiddleneck) are nearby. A grocery store and propane gas are within five miles. Some facilities are wheelchair-accessible. Leashed pets are permitted.

**Reservations, fees:** Reservations are accepted at 877/444-6777 or www.recreation.gov ($9 reservation fee). Sites are $20 per night, and the group site is $125 per night. Open May through early September.

**Directions:** From Stockton, drive east on Highway 26 for about 30 miles to Valley Springs and Hogan Dam Road. Turn right and drive 1.5 miles to Hogan Parkway. Turn left and drive one mile to South Petersburg Road. Turn left and drive 0.5 mile to the campground on the right (adjacent to Acorn Camp).

**Contact:** U.S. Army Corps of Engineers, Sacramento District, 209/772-1343.

## 60 ACORN CAMP AND DEER FLAT BOAT-IN

**Scenic rating: 7**

at New Hogan Lake

**Map 5.4, page 298**

New Hogan is a big lake in the foothill country east of Stockton, at an elevation of 680 feet and covering 4,000 acres, with 50 miles of shoreline. Acorn is on the lake and operated by the Army Corps of Engineers. Boaters might also consider boat-in sites near Deer Flat on the eastern shore, and there is a group camp at Coyote Point. Boating and waterskiing are popular here, and all water sports are allowed. It's a decent lake for fishing, with a unique opportunity for striped bass, and it's OK for largemouth bass. Other species are crappie, bluegill, and catfish. There are bicycle trails and an eight-mile equestrian trail. An interpretive trail below the dam is worth checking out. Insider's tip: This is a wintering area for bald eagles.

**Campsites, facilities:** There are 128 sites for tents or RVs of any length (no hookups) and 30 boat-in sites. Fire pits and picnic tables are provided. Drinking water, restrooms with flush toilets and coin showers, pay telephones, a fish-cleaning station, an amphitheater, and a dump station are available. A two-lane, paved boat ramp and an 18-hole disc golf course are nearby. Nature walks and ranger programs are sometimes available. Groceries, a restaurant, and propane gas are within two miles. Some facilities are wheelchair-accessible. Leashed pets are permitted.

**Reservations, fees:** Reservations are accepted for the Acorn campsites at 877/444-6777 or www.recreation.gov ($9 reservation fee) and at 800/444-7275 or www.reserveamerica.com. Sites are $16-20 per night, and boat-in sites are $12 per night. Some credit cards are accepted. Open year-round, with reduced sites in winter; boat-in sites are open May through September.

**Directions:** From Stockton, drive east on Highway 26 for about 30 miles to Valley Springs and Hogan Dam Road. Turn right and drive 1.5 miles to Hogan Parkway. Turn left and drive one mile to South Petersburg Road. Turn left and drive 0.25 mile to the campground on the right.

**Contact:** U.S. Army Corps of Engineers, Sacramento District, 209/772-1343.

## 61 49ER RV RANCH

**Scenic rating: 6**

near Columbia

**Map 5.4, page 298**

This historic ranch/campground was originally built in 1852 as a dairy farm. Several original barns are still standing. The place has been brought up to date, of course, with a small store on the property providing last-minute supplies. Location is a plus, with the Columbia State Historic Park only a half mile away and the Stanislaus River arm of New Melones Lake within a five-minute drive. Live theater and wineries are nearby. The elevation is 2,100 feet. Note that there is a separate mobile home park on the premises.

**Campsites, facilities:** There are 42 sites with full hookups (50 amps) for trailers and RVs up to 50 feet. Picnic tables and cable TV are provided. Restrooms with showers, drinking water, coin laundry, convenience store, dump station, Wi-Fi, propane gas, and a large barn for group or club activities are available. Twenty-four hour security is provided. A hospitality hut provides evening campfires and morning coffee and tea. Some facilities are wheelchair-accessible. Leashed pets are permitted.

**Reservations, fees:** Reservations are accepted by phone or website. RV sites are $49 per night, plus $2.50 per night per additional person and $3 per night for each additional vehicle. Group and senior rates are available. Open year-round.

**Directions:** From Sonora, turn north on Highway 49 and drive for 2.5 miles to Parrotts Ferry Road. Turn right and drive 1.7 miles to Columbia Street. Turn right and drive 0.4 mile to Pacific Street. Turn left and drive a block to Italian Bar Road. Turn right and drive 0.5 mile to the campground on the right.

**Contact:** 49er RV Ranch, 209/532-4978, www.49errvpark.com.

## 62 MARBLE QUARRY RV PARK
🏃🏊🚣🐕🏕️♿🚐⛺

### Scenic rating: 6

near Columbia

**Map 5.4, page 298**

This is a family-oriented RV park set at 2,100 feet elevation in the Gold Country, within range of several adventures. A 0.25-mile trail leads directly to Columbia State Historic Park, and the Stanislaus River arm of New Melones Lake is only five miles away.

**Campsites, facilities:** There are 85 sites with full or partial hookups (30 and 50 amps) for RVs up to 45 feet, a small area for tents, and three cabins of different sizes, including mid-size and executive cabins with kitchenettes. A few sites are pull-through. Picnic tables are provided. Restrooms with showers, satellite TV, a seasonal swimming pool, coin laundry, Wi-Fi, convenience store, dump station, playground, two clubhouses, reading/TV room, group facilities, and propane gas are available. Some facilities are wheelchair-accessible. Leashed pets are permitted.

**Reservations, fees:** Reservations are accepted at 866/677-8464 or www.marblequarryrvpark. com. RV sites are $40-52 per night, tent sites are $25-30 per night, plus $4 per person per night for more than four people (over age 6); cabins are $49-168. Discounts are available for seniors and military and in the off-season. Some credit cards are accepted. Open year-round.

**Directions:** From Sonora, turn north on Highway 49 and drive 2.5 miles to Parrotts Ferry Road (stop sign). Bear right on Parrotts Ferry Road and drive 1.5 miles to Columbia Street. Turn right and drive a short distance to Jackson Street. Turn right on Jackson Street and drive 0.25 mile (becomes Yankee Hill Road) to the campground on the right.

**Contact:** Marble Quarry RV Park, 11551 Yankee Hill Rd., 866/677-8464 or 209/532-9539, www.marblequarryrvpark.com.

# TAHOE AND THE NORTHERN SIERRA

Mount Tallac affords a view across Lake Tahoe like no other: a cobalt-blue expanse of water bordered by mountains that span miles of Sierra wildlands. This area has the widest range and largest number of campgrounds in California. Tahoe and the Northern Sierra feature hundreds of lakes. The best for scenic beauty are Echo Lakes, Donner, Fallen Leaf, Sardine, Caples, Loon, and Union Valley. The north end of the Northern Sierra starts near Bucks Lake and extends to Bear River Canyon. In between are the Lakes Basin Recreation Area in southern Plumas County; the Crystal Basin in the Sierra foothills west of Tahoe; Lake Davis near Portola; and the Carson River Canyon and Hope Valley south of Tahoe. It's true that people come here in droves, but if you're willing to hunt a bit, there are spots you can share with only chipmunks.

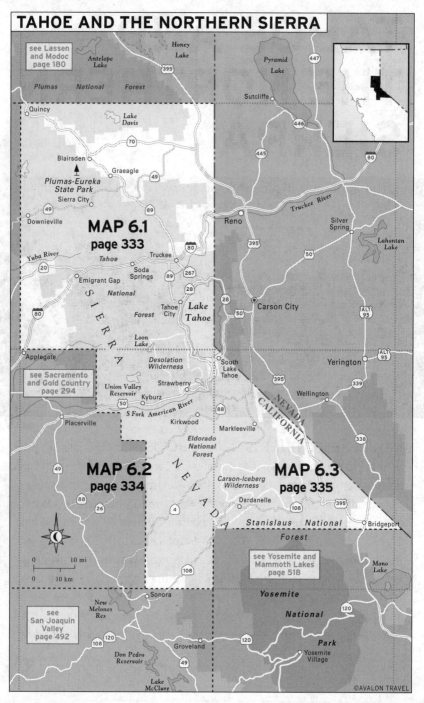

# TAHOE AND THE NORTHERN SIERRA

see Lassen and Modoc page 180

Honey Lake

Antelope Lake

Pyramid Lake

447

395

Sutcliffe

Plumas National Forest

Quincy

Lake Davis

70

446

445

Blairsden

Graeagle

49

Plumas-Eureka State Park

Sierra City

89

Reno

80

Truckee River

Silver Spring

49

Downieville

395

50

Lahontan Lake

## MAP 6.1
### page 333

Yuba River

Tahoe

Truckee

80

20

Soda Springs

Emigrant Gap

89

267

National

28

28

50

Carson City

ALT 95

Forest

Tahoe City

Lake Tahoe

Loon Lake

Applegate

80

Desolation Wilderness

South Lake Tahoe

Yerington

ALT 95

see Sacramento and Gold Country page 294

Union Valley Reservoir

Strawberry

395

Wellington

339

50

Kyburz

S Fork American River

88

NEVADA CALIFORNIA

Placerville

Kirkwood

Markleeville

338

Eldorado National Forest

## MAP 6.2
### page 334

49

Carson-Iceberg Wilderness

## MAP 6.3
### page 335

88

26

NEVADA

Dardanelle

108

395

Bridgeport

4

Stanislaus National

0      10 mi

Forest

Mono Lake

0      10 km

108

see Yosemite and Mammoth Lakes page 518

Sonora

Yosemite

New Melones Res

120

see San Joaquin Valley page 492

108

120

Groveland

49

120

National

120

Park

Don Pedro Reservoir

Yosemite Village

Lake McClure

©AVALON TRAVEL

# Map 6.1

**Sites 1-102**
**Pages 337-383**

6.2

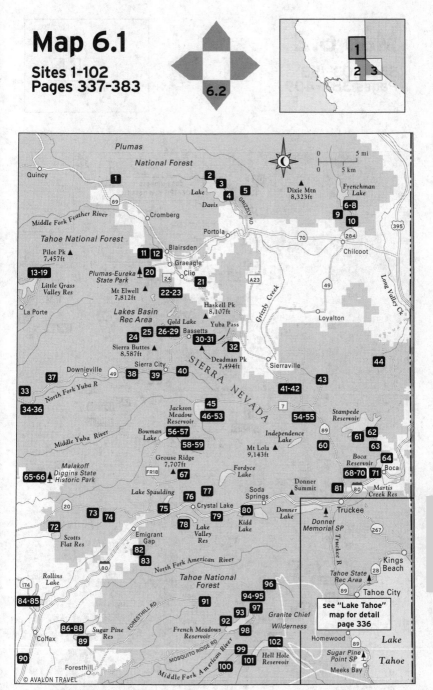

# Map 6.2

**Sites 103-158**
**Pages 383-409**

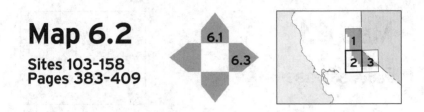

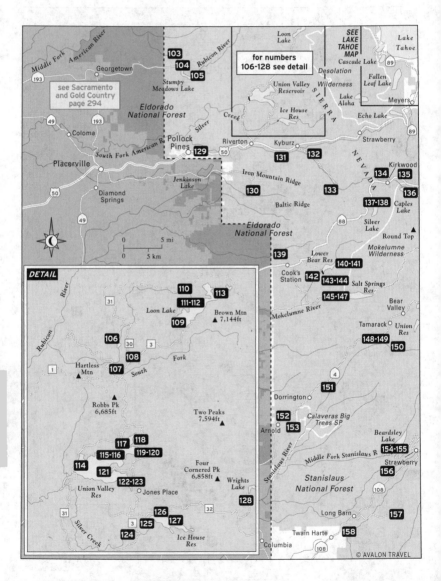

for numbers
106-128 see detail

# Map 6.3

**Sites 159-201**
**Pages 409-428**

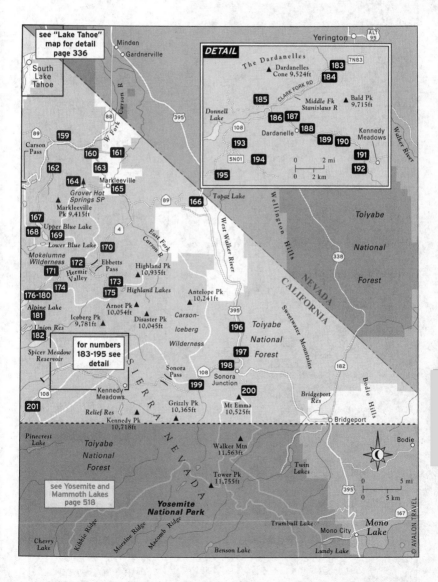

# LAKE TAHOE
## Sites 202-221  Pages 429-438

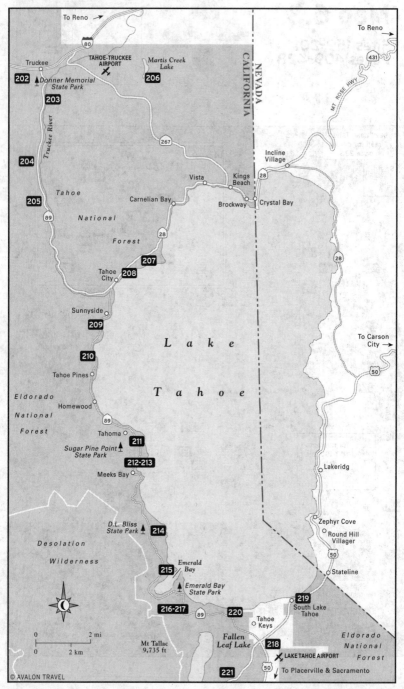

# 1 BRADY'S CAMP

### Scenic rating: 4

on Pine Creek in Plumas National Forest

**Map 6.1, page 333**

Don't expect much company here. This is a tiny, little-known, primitive camp near Pine Creek, at roughly 7,000 feet elevation. A side trip is to make the half-mile drive up to Argentine Rock (7,209 feet) for a lookout onto this remote forest country. To the east are many miles of national forest accessible by vehicle.

**Campsites, facilities:** There are six tent sites. Picnic tables and fire grills are provided. Vault toilets are available. No drinking water is available. Garbage must be packed out. Leashed pets are permitted.

**Reservations, fees:** Reservations are not accepted. There is no fee for camping. Open May through October, weather permitting.

**Directions:** From Oroville, drive north on Highway 70 to the junction with Highway 89. Turn south on Highway 89/70 and drive 11 miles to Quincy. In Quincy, continue on Highway 89/70 for six miles to Squirrel Creek Road. Turn left and drive seven miles (after two miles bear right at the Y) to Forest Road 25N29. Turn left and drive one mile to the campground on the right side of the road.

**Contact:** Plumas National Forest, Mt. Hough Ranger District, 530/283-0555, www.fs.usda.gov/plumas.

# 2 LIGHTNING TREE

### Scenic rating: 7

on Lake Davis in Plumas National Forest

**Map 6.1, page 333**

Lightning Tree campground is near the shore of Lake Davis. Davis is a good-sized lake, with 32 miles of shoreline, set high in the northern Sierra at 5,775 feet. Lake Davis is one of the top mountain lakes in California for fishing, with large rainbow trout in the early summer and fall. This camp is perfectly situated for a fishing trip. It is at Lightning Tree Point on the lake's remote northeast shore, directly across the lake from Freeman Creek, one of the better spots for big trout. This lake is famous for pike; the Department of Fish and Game has twice poisoned the lake to kill them. In turn, the biggest trout plants in California history have been made here. There are three boat ramps on the lake.

**Campsites, facilities:** There are 19 single and 21 double sites for tents or RVs up to 50 feet (no hookups). Vault toilets and drinking water are available. A dump station and a car-top boat launch are nearby. Some facilities are wheelchair-accessible. Leashed pets are permitted.

**Reservations, fees:** Reservations are accepted at 877/444-6777 ($10 reservation fee) or www.recreation.gov ($9 reservation fee). Sites are $23 per night or $46 per night for a double site, plus $3 per pet per night. Open May through October, weather permitting.

**Directions:** From Truckee, turn north on Highway 89 and drive to Sattley and County Road A23. Turn right on County Road A23 and drive 13 miles to Highway 70. Turn left on Highway 70 and drive one mile to Grizzly Road. Turn right on Grizzly Road and drive about six miles to Lake Davis. Continue north on Lake Davis Road along the lake's east shore and drive about five miles to the campground entrance on the left side of the road.

**Contact:** Plumas National Forest, Beckwourth Ranger District, 530/836-2575, Lake Davis Recreation Area, www.fs.usda.gov/plumas; Thousand Trails, 530/832-1076.

# 3 GRASSHOPPER FLAT

### Scenic rating: 7

on Lake Davis in Plumas National Forest

**Map 6.1, page 333**

Grasshopper Flat provides a nearby alternative to Grizzly at Lake Davis, with the boat ramp at adjacent Honker Cove a primary attraction for campers with trailered boats for fishing. The camp is on the southeast end of the lake, at 5,800 feet elevation. Lake Davis is known for its large rainbow trout; they bite best in early summer and fall. Swimming and powerboats are allowed, but no waterskiing or personal watercraft are permitted.

**Campsites, facilities:** There are 69 sites for tents or RVs up to 35 feet (no hookups) and one group site for up to 25 people. Picnic tables and fire grills are provided. Drinking water and restrooms with flush toilets and coin showers are available. A boat ramp, grocery store, and a dump station are nearby. Some facilities are wheelchair-accessible. Leashed pets are permitted.

**Reservations, fees:** Reservations are accepted at 877/444-6777 ($10 reservation fee) or www.recreation.gov ($9 reservation fee). Sites are $23 per night for single sites, $100 per night for the group site, $3 per pet per night. Open May through October, weather permitting.

**Directions:** From Truckee, turn north on Highway 89 and drive to Sattley and County Road A23. Turn right on County Road A23 and drive 13 miles to Highway 70. Turn left on Highway 70 and drive one mile to Grizzly Road. Turn right on Grizzly Road and drive about six miles to Lake Davis. Continue north on Lake Davis Road for a mile (just past Grizzly) to the campground entrance on the left side of the road.

**Contact:** Plumas National Forest, Beckwourth Ranger District, 530/836-2575, Lake Davis Recreation Area, www.fs.usda.gov/plumas; Thousand Trails, 530/832-1076.

## 4 CROCKER

### Scenic rating: 5

in Plumas National Forest

**Map 6.1, page 333**

Even though this camp is just four miles east of Lake Davis, it is little known and little used since there are three lakeside camps close by. It

is in Plumas National Forest at 5,900 feet elevation, and it is about a 15-minute drive north to the border of the Dixie Mountain State Game Refuge.

**Campsites, facilities:** There are 10 sites for tents or RVs up to 16 feet (no hookups). Picnic tables and fire grills are provided. Vault toilets are available. No drinking water is available. Garbage must be packed out. Leashed pets are permitted.

**Reservations, fees:** Reservations are not accepted. There is no fee for camping. Open May through October, weather permitting.

**Directions:** From Reno, drive north on U.S. 395 to the junction with Highway 70. Turn west on Highway 70 and drive to Beckwourth and County Road 111/Beckwourth-Genessee Road. Turn right on County Road 111 and drive six miles to the campground on the left side of the road.

**Contact:** Plumas National Forest, Beckwourth Ranger District, 530/836-2575, www.fs.usda.gov/plumas.

## 5 GRIZZLY

### Scenic rating: 7

on Lake Davis in Plumas National Forest

**Map 6.1, page 333**

This is one of the better developed campgrounds at Lake Davis and is a popular spot for camping anglers. Its proximity to the Grizzly Store, just over the dam to the south, makes getting last-minute supplies a snap. In addition, a boat ramp is to the north in Honker Cove, providing access to the southern reaches of the lake, including the island area, where trout trolling is good in early summer and fall. Elevation is 5,800 feet.

**Campsites, facilities:** There are 56 sites for tents or RVs up to 35 feet (no hookups). Picnic tables and fire grills are provided. Drinking water and flush toilets are available. A boat ramp, grocery store, and a dump station are nearby. Some facilities are wheelchair-accessible. Leashed pets are permitted.

**Reservations, fees:** Reservations are accepted for some sites at 877/444-6777 ($10 reservation fee) or www.recreation.gov ($9 reservation fee). Sites are $23 per night, plus $3 per pet per night. Open late May through mid-October, weather permitting.

**Directions:** From Truckee, turn north on Highway 89 and drive to Sattley and County Road A23. Turn right on County Road A23 and drive 13 miles to Highway 70. Turn left on Highway 70 and drive one mile to Grizzly Road. Turn right on Grizzly Road and drive about six miles to Lake Davis. Continue north on Lake Davis Road for less than a mile to the campground entrance on the left side of the road.

**Contact:** Plumas National Forest, Beckwourth Ranger District, Lake Davis Recreation Area, 530/836-2575, www.fs.usda.gov/plumas; Thousand Trails, 530/ 832-1076.

# 6 BIG COVE
🚶‍♀️🏊‍♂️🚣‍♂️🚐🏠🐕‍🦺♿🚍⛺

### Scenic rating: 7
at Frenchman Lake in Plumas National Forest

**Map 6.1, page 333**

Big Cove is one of four camps at the southeastern end of Frenchman Lake, with a boat ramp available about a mile away near the Frenchman and Spring Creek camps. (For more information, see the Frenchman listing in this chapter.) A trail from the campground leads to the lakeshore. Another trail connects to the Spring Creek campground, a walk of 0.5 mile. The elevation is 5,800 feet.

**Campsites, facilities:** There are 42 sites, including 10 doubles, for tents or RVs up to 50 feet (no hookups). Picnic tables and fire rings are provided. Drinking water, flush toilets, and hot showers are available. A boat ramp and dump station are nearby. A grocery store and propane gas are seven miles away. Some facilities are wheelchair-accessible. Leashed pets are permitted.

**Reservations, fees:** Reservations are accepted for some sites at 877/444-6777 ($10 reservation fee) or www.recreation.gov ($9 reservation fee). Sites are $23-46 per night, plus $3 per pet per night. Open May through October, weather permitting.

**Directions:** From Reno, drive north on U.S. 395 to the junction with Highway 70. Turn west on Highway 70 and drive to Chilcoot and the junction with Frenchman Lake Road. Turn right on Frenchman Lake Road and drive nine miles to the lake and to a Y. At the Y, turn right and drive two miles to Forest Road 24N01. Turn left and drive a short distance to the campground entrance on the left side of the road (on the east side of the lake).

**Contact:** Plumas National Forest, Beckwourth Ranger District, 530/836-2575, www.fs.usda.gov/plumas; Thousand Trails, 530/258-7606.

# 7 SPRING CREEK
🚶‍♀️🏊‍♂️🚣‍♂️🚐🏠🐕‍🦺♿🚍⛺

### Scenic rating: 7
on Frenchman Lake in Plumas National Forest

**Map 6.1, page 333**

Frenchman Lake is set at 5,800 feet elevation, on the edge of high desert to the east and forest to the west. The lake has 21 miles of shoreline and is surrounded by a mix of sage and pines. All water sports are allowed. This camp is on the southeast end of the lake, where there are three other campgrounds, including a group camp and a boat ramp. The lake provides good fishing for stocked rainbow trout—best in the cove near the campgrounds. Trails lead out from the campground: One heads 0.25 mile to the Frenchman campground; the other is a 0.5-mile route to Big Cove campground.

**Campsites, facilities:** There are 32 sites for tents or RVs up to 35 feet (no hookups). Picnic tables and fire grills are provided. Drinking water and vault toilets are available. Some facilities are wheelchair-accessible. A boat ramp and dump station are nearby. Leashed pets are permitted for a fee.

**Reservations, fees:** Reservations are accepted for some sites at 877/444-6777 ($10 reservation fee) or www.recreation.gov ($9 reservation fee). Sites are $23 per night, plus $3 per pet per night. Open May through October, weather permitting.

**Directions:** From Reno, drive north on U.S. 395 to the junction with Highway 70. Turn west on Highway 70 and drive to Chilcoot and the junction with Frenchman Lake Road. Turn right on Frenchman Lake Road and drive nine miles to the lake and to a Y. At the Y, turn right and drive two miles to the campground on the left side of the road.

**Contact:** Plumas National Forest, Beckwourth Ranger District, 530/836-2575, www.fs.usda.gov/plumas; Thousand Trails, 530/258-7606.

## 8 FRENCHMAN

### Scenic rating: 7
on Frenchman Lake in Plumas National Forest

**Map 6.1, page 333**

This camp is on the southeast end of the lake, where there are three other campgrounds, including a group camp and a boat ramp. The best trout fishing is in the cove near the campgrounds and the two inlets, one along the west shore and one at the head of the lake. The proximity to Reno, only 35 miles away, keeps gambling in the back of the minds of many anglers. Because of water demands downstream, the lake often drops significantly by the end of summer. A trail from camp is routed 0.25 mile to the Spring Creek campground.

**Campsites, facilities:** There are 37 sites for tents or RVs up to 35 feet (no hookups). Picnic tables and fire grills are provided. Drinking water and vault toilets are available. A dump station and boat ramp are nearby. Some facilities are wheelchair-accessible. Leashed pets are permitted.

**Reservations, fees:** Reservations are accepted at 877/444-6777 ($10 reservation fee) or www.recreation.gov ($9 reservation fee). Sites are $23

per night, plus $3 per pet per night. Open May through October, weather permitting.

**Directions:** From Reno, drive north on U.S. 395 to the junction with Highway 70. Turn west on Highway 70 and drive to Chilcoot and the junction with Frenchman Lake Road. Turn right on Frenchman Lake Road and drive nine miles to the lake and to a Y. At the Y, turn right and drive 1.5 miles to the campground on the left side of the road.

**Contact:** Plumas National Forest, Beckwourth Ranger District, 530/836-2575, www.fs.usda.gov/plumas; Thousand Trails, 530/258-7606.

## 9 COTTONWOOD SPRINGS

### Scenic rating: 7
near Frenchman Lake in Plumas National Forest

**Map 6.1, page 333**

Cottonwood Springs, elevation 5,800 feet, is largely an overflow camp at Frenchman Lake. It is the only camp at the lake with a group site. The more popular Frenchman, Big Cove, and Spring Creek camps are along the southeast shore of the lake near a boat ramp.

**Campsites, facilities:** There are 20 sites for tents or RVs up to 50 feet (no hookups) and two group sites for tents or RVs up to 35 feet that can accommodate up to 25 and 50 people respectively. Picnic tables and fire rings are provided. Drinking water and flush toilets are available. Some facilities are wheelchair-accessible. A boat ramp and dump station are nearby. Leashed pets are permitted.

**Reservations, fees:** Reservations are accepted for individual sites and are required for group sites at 877/444-6777 ($10 reservation fee) or www.recreation.gov ($9 reservation fee). Sites are $23 per night, group sites are $100-140 per night, and $3 per pet per night. Open May through October, weather permitting.

**Directions:** From Reno, drive north on U.S. 395 to the junction with Highway 70. Turn west on Highway 70 and drive to Chilcoot and the junction with Frenchman Lake Road. Turn right on Frenchman Lake Road and drive nine miles to the lake and to a Y. At the Y, turn left and drive 1.5 miles to the campground on the right side of the road.

**Contact:** Plumas National Forest, Beckwourth Ranger District, 530/836-2575, www.fs.usda. gov/plumas; Thousand Trails, 530/258-7606.

## 10 CHILCOOT

### Scenic rating: 7

on Little Last Chance Creek in Plumas National Forest

**Map 6.1, page 333**

This small camp along Little Last Chance Creek at 5,400 feet elevation is about three miles downstream from Frenchman Lake. The stream provides good trout fishing, but access can be difficult at some spots because of brush.

**Campsites, facilities:** There are 40 sites for tents or RVs up to 35 feet (no hookups) and five walk-in sites for tents only. Picnic tables and fire rings are provided. Drinking water and flush toilets are available. Some facilities are wheelchair-accessible. A boat ramp, grocery store, and dump station are nearby. Leashed pets are permitted.

**Reservations, fees:** Reservations are accepted for some sites at 877/444-6777 ($10 reservation fee) or www.recreation.gov ($9 reservation fee). Sites are $23 per night, plus $3 per pet per night. Open May through October, weather permitting.

**Directions:** From Reno, drive north on U.S. 395 to the junction with Highway 70. Turn west on Highway 70 and drive to Chilcoot and the junction with Frenchman Lake Road. Turn right on Frenchman Lake Road and drive six miles to the campground on the left side of the road.

**Contact:** Plumas National Forest, Beckwourth Ranger District, 530/836-2575, www.fs.usda. gov/plumas; Thousand Trails, 530/258-7606.

## 11 LITTLE BEAR RV PARK

### Scenic rating: 7

on the Feather River

**Map 6.1, page 333**

This is a privately operated RV park near the Feather River. Nearby destinations include Plumas-Eureka State Park and the Lakes Basin Recreation Area. The elevation is 4,300 feet. About half of the sites are taken by full-season rentals.

**Campsites, facilities:** There are 100 sites with full or partial hookups (30 amps and 50 amps) for RVs of any length, along with 10 sleeping cabins. Picnic tables and fire rings are provided. Drinking water, restrooms with showers and flush toilets, coin laundry, convenience store, satellite TV, Wi-Fi, RV storage, propane, and ice are available. Amenities include a dump station, clubhouse, table tennis, shuffleboard, and horseshoes.

**Reservations, fees:** Reservations are recommended. RV sites with hookups are $36-45, plus $4-6 per person per night for more than two people and $1 per pet per night. Camping cabins are $48-58 per night. Weekly and monthly rates are available. Open mid-April through late October.

**Directions:** From Truckee, drive northwest on Highway 89 to Graeagle. Continue north on Highway 89 for one mile to Little Bear Road. Turn left on Little Bear Road and drive a short distance to the campground on the right.

**Contact:** Little Bear RV Park, 530/836-2774, www.littlebearrvpark.com.

## 12 MOVIN' WEST RV PARK

### Scenic rating: 5

in Graeagle

**Map 6.1, page 333**

This RV park began life as a mobile home park. Approximately half of the sites are for permanent residents; the other half are for vacationers, with about half of those rented for the summer. The park has also become very popular with golfers. A nine-hole golf course is across the road and five other golf courses are within five miles. The elevation is 4,300 feet.

**Campsites, facilities:** There are 51 sites for RVs of any length with full (30 amps), partial, or no hookups, including five pull-through sites. There are also two tent sites and two cabins. Picnic tables and fire rings are provided. Drinking water, restrooms with flush toilets and showers, cable TV, Wi-Fi, and a coin laundry are available. Propane gas, a nine-hole golf course, swimming pond, horse stable, and mini golf are nearby. Leashed pets are permitted.

**Reservations, fees:** Reservations are recommended. RV sites with hookups are $41-43 per night, tent sites are $38 per night, cabins are $50 per night, plus $4 per person per night for more than two people. Weekly rates are available. Open May through October.

**Directions:** From Truckee, drive northwest on Highway 89 about 50 miles to Graeagle. Continue just past Graeagle to County Road A14 (Graeagle-Johnsville Road). Turn left and drive 0.25 mile northwest to the campground on the left.

**Contact:** Movin' West RV Park, 530/836-2614.

choose from at the lake, all on the opposite eastern shore.

**Campsites, facilities:** There are 20 walk-in sites (of a few yards to 0.1 mile) for tents. There is also a parking lot for overflow camping for RVs up to 35 feet. Picnic tables and fire grills are provided. Drinking water, vault toilets, and a fish-cleaning station are available. A dump station, boat ramp, and grocery store are nearby. Some facilities are wheelchair-accessible. Leashed pets are permitted.

**Reservations, fees:** Reservations are not accepted. Sites are $23 per night. Open May through September, weather permitting.

**Directions:** From Oroville, drive east on Highway 162/Oroville Dam Boulevard for about eight miles (becomes the Olive Highway) to Forbestown Road. Turn right and drive through Forbestown to Challenge and LaPorte Road. Turn left on LaPorte Road and drive to LaPorte. Continue two miles past LaPorte to the junction with County Road 514/Little Grass Valley Road. Turn left and drive about five miles to the campground access road on the west side of the lake. Turn right on the access road and drive 0.25 mile to the campground.

**Contact:** Plumas National Forest, Feather River Ranger District, 530/534-6500, www.fs.usda.gov/plumas.

## 13 BLACK ROCK WALK-IN AND OVERFLOW

🏃 🏊 🎣 🚐 🐕 ♿ 🚗 ⛺

### Scenic rating: 7

on Little Grass Valley Reservoir in Plumas National Forest

**Map 6.1, page 333**

This is the only campground on the west shore of Little Grass Valley Reservoir, with an adjacent boat ramp making it an attractive choice for anglers. The lake is at 5,060 feet elevation in Plumas National Forest and provides lakeside camping and decent fishing for rainbow trout and kokanee salmon. If you don't like the company, there are seven other camps to

## 14 HORSE CAMPGROUND

🏃 🏊 🎣 🚐 🐕 ♿ 🚗 ⛺

### Scenic rating: 7

on Little Grass Valley Reservoir in Plumas National Forest

**Map 6.1, page 333**

This camp is reserved for equestrians only and thus it gets low use. This is a high-country forested campground near Little Grass Valley Reservoir, but there is no lake view because of tree cover. Several trails are accessible from the campground, including the Pacific Crest Trail and Lakeshore Trail, as well as access to Bald Mountain (6,255 feet). The elevation at camp is 5,060 feet.

**Campsites, facilities:** There are 10 sites for tents or RVs up to 25 feet (no hookups) available for equestrian campers only. Picnic tables and fire grills are provided. Vault toilets are available. No drinking water is available. Hitching posts, a wheelchair-accessible mounting rack, and a fish-cleaning station are available. A restaurant and deli are available five miles away in LaPorte. Leashed pets are permitted.

**Reservations, fees:** Reservations are accepted at 877/444-6777 ($10 reservation fee) or www. recreation.gov ($9 reservation fee). Sites are $23 per night. Open June through September.

**Directions:** From Oroville, drive east on Highway 162/Oroville Dam Boulevard for about eight miles (becomes the Olive Highway) to Forbestown Road. Turn right and drive through Forbestown to Challenge and LaPorte Road. Turn left on LaPorte Road and drive to LaPorte. Continue on County Road 512 (which becomes County Road 514/Little Grass Valley Road) for three miles to Forest Road 22N57. Turn right and drive four miles (cross the bridge) to the campground on the left.

**Contact:** Plumas National Forest, Feather River Ranger District, 530/534-6500, www. fs.usda.gov/plumas.

## 15 PENINSULA TENT

**Scenic rating: 9**

on Little Grass Valley Reservoir in Plumas National Forest

**Map 6.1, page 333**

This camp, at 5,060 feet in elevation, is exceptional in that most of the campsites provide views of Little Grass Valley Reservoir, a pretty lake in the national forest. The fishing can be excellent, especially for rainbow trout, brown trout, and kokanee salmon. The camp gets moderate use, and it is a pretty site with tents sprinkled among white fir and pine. This is a good family campground. A 13.5-mile hiking trail circles the lake.

**Campsites, facilities:** There are 25 sites for

tents. Picnic tables and fire rings are provided. Drinking water and flush toilets are available. A boat launch, fish-cleaning station, and a swimming beach are nearby. Some facilities are wheelchair-accessible. Leashed pets are permitted.

**Reservations, fees:** Reservations are not accepted. Sites are $23 per night. Open Memorial Day weekend through September, weather permitting.

**Directions:** From Oroville, drive east on Highway 162/Oroville Dam Boulevard for about eight miles (becomes the Olive Highway) to Forbestown Road. Turn right and drive through Forbestown to Challenge and LaPorte Road. Turn left on LaPorte Road and drive to LaPorte. Continue on County Road 512 (which becomes County Road 514/Little Grass Valley Road) for three miles to Forest Road 22N57. Continue on Forest Road 514 for one mile to the campground entrance on the right. Turn right and drive 0.25 mile to the campground.

**Contact:** Plumas National Forest, Feather River Ranger District, 530/534-6500, www. fs.usda.gov/plumas.

## 16 RUNNING DEER

**Scenic rating: 7**

on Little Grass Valley Reservoir in Plumas National Forest

**Map 6.1, page 333**

Little Grass Valley Reservoir is a pretty mountain lake set at 5,060 feet elevation in Plumas National Forest, providing lakeside camping, boating, and fishing for rainbow trout and kokanee salmon. Looking straight north from the camp is a spectacular view, gazing across the water and up at Bald Mountain, at 6,255 feet elevation. One of seven campgrounds on the eastern shore, this one is on the far northeastern end of the lake. A trailhead for the Pacific Crest Trail is nearby at little Fowler Lake about four miles north of Little Grass Valley Reservoir. Note that fish-cleaning stations are not available at Running Deer, but there is one nearby at Little Beaver.

**Campsites, facilities:** There are 41 sites for tents or RVs up to 40 feet (no hookups). Picnic tables and fire rings are provided. Drinking water and flush toilets are available. A fish-cleaning station, boat ramp, grocery store, and dump station are nearby. Leashed pets are permitted.

**Reservations, fees:** Reservations are accepted at 877/444-6777 ($10 reservation fee) or www.recreation.gov ($9 reservation fee). Sites are $23-25 per night. Open late May through September.

**Directions:** From Oroville, drive east on Highway 162/Oroville Dam Boulevard for about eight miles (becomes the Olive Highway) to Forbestown Road. Turn right and drive through Forbestown to Challenge and LaPorte Road. Turn left on LaPorte Road and drive to LaPorte. Continue on County Road 512 (which becomes County Road 514/Little Grass Valley Road) for three miles to Forest Road 22N57. Turn right and drive three miles to the campground on the left.

**Contact:** Plumas National Forest, Feather River Ranger District, 530/534-6500, www.fs.usda.gov/plumas.

## 17 WYANDOTTE

### Scenic rating: 8

on Little Grass Valley Reservoir in Plumas National Forest

**Map 6.1, page 333**

Of the eight camps on Little Grass Valley Reservoir, this is the favorite. It is set at 5,100 feet elevation on a small peninsula that extends well into the lake, with a boat ramp nearby. All water sports are allowed. (For more information, see the Running Deer listing in this chapter.)

**Campsites, facilities:** There are 28 individual sites (including two double sites) for tents or RVs up to 40 feet (no hookups). Picnic tables

and fire rings are provided. Drinking water and flush toilets are available. A dump station, boat ramp, fish-cleaning station, and grocery store are nearby. Leashed pets are permitted.

**Reservations, fees:** Reservations are not accepted. Single sites are $23 per night. Open late May through mid-October, weather permitting.

**Directions:** From Oroville, drive east on Highway 162/Oroville Dam Boulevard for about eight miles (becomes the Olive Highway) to Forbestown Road. Turn right and drive through Forbestown to Challenge and LaPorte Road. Turn left on LaPorte Road and drive to LaPorte. Continue two miles past LaPorte to the junction with County Road 514/Little Grass Valley Road. Turn left and drive one mile to a junction. Turn left and drive one mile to the campground entrance road on the right.

**Contact:** Plumas National Forest, Feather River Ranger District, 530/534-6500, www.fs.usda.gov/plumas.

## 18 LITTLE BEAVER

### Scenic rating: 7

on Little Grass Valley Reservoir in Plumas National Forest

**Map 6.1, page 333**

This is one of eight campgrounds on Little Grass Valley Reservoir, set at 5,060 feet elevation. Take your pick. (For more information, see the Running Deer listing in this chapter.)

**Campsites, facilities:** There are 120 sites for tents or RVs up to 40 feet (no hookups). Picnic tables and fire rings are provided. Drinking water and flush toilets are available. A grocery store, dump station, fish-cleaning station, and boat ramp are nearby. Some facilities are wheelchair-accessible. Leashed pets are permitted.

**Reservations, fees:** Reservations are accepted at 877/444-6777 ($10 reservation fee) or www.recreation.gov ($9 reservation fee). Sites are $23-25 per night. Open June through mid-September, weather permitting.

**Directions:** From Oroville, drive east on Highway 162/Oroville Dam Boulevard for about eight miles (becomes the Olive Highway) to Forbestown Road. Turn right and drive through Forbestown to Challenge and LaPorte Road. Turn left on LaPorte Road and drive to LaPorte. Continue two miles past LaPorte to the junction with County Road 514/Little Grass Valley Road. Turn left and drive one mile to a junction. Turn right and drive two miles to the campground entrance road on the left.

**Contact:** Plumas National Forest, Feather River Ranger District, 530/534-6500, www.fs.usda.gov/plumas.

## 19 RED FEATHER CALIFORNIA

🥾 ♒ ⛵ 🎣 🚣 🐴 🚐 ⛺

### Scenic rating: 7

on Little Grass Valley Reservoir in Plumas National Forest

**Map 6.1, page 333**

This camp is well developed and popular, set on the eastern shore of Little Grass Valley Reservoir, just south of Running Deer and just north of Little Beaver. Bears frequent this area, so be sure to properly store your food and avoid scented products. (For more information, see the Running Deer listing in this chapter.)

**Campsites, facilities:** There are 59 sites for tents or RVs up to 40 feet (no hookups). Picnic tables and fire rings are provided. Drinking water and flush toilets are available. A dump station, boat ramp, fish-cleaning station, and grocery store are nearby. Leashed pets are permitted.

**Reservations, fees:** Reservations are accepted at 877/444-6777 ($10 reservation fee) or www.recreation.gov ($9 reservation fee). Sites are $23-25 per night. Open late June through September, weather permitting.

**Directions:** From Oroville, drive east on Highway 162/Oroville Dam Boulevard for about eight miles (becomes the Olive Highway) to Forbestown Road. Turn right and drive

through Forbestown to Challenge and LaPorte Road. Turn left on LaPorte Road and drive to LaPorte. Continue two miles past LaPorte to the junction with County Road 514/Little Grass Valley Road. Turn left and drive one mile to a junction. Turn right and drive three miles to the campground entrance road on the left.

**Contact:** Plumas National Forest, Feather River Ranger District, 530/534-6500, www.fs.usda.gov/plumas.

## 20 JAMISON CREEK CAMPGROUND

🥾 ♒ 🐴 ♿ 🚐 ⛺

### Scenic rating: 9

in Plumas-Eureka State Park

**Map 6.1, page 333**

Plumas-Eureka State Park is a beautiful chunk of parkland, featuring great hiking, a pretty lake, and a well-maintained campground. For newcomers to the area, Jamison Camp at the southern end of the park makes for an excellent first stop. So does the nearby hike to Grass Lake, a first-class tromp that takes about two hours and features a streamside walk along Little Jamison Creek, with the chance to take a five-minute cutoff to see 40-foot Jamison Falls. A historical mine, park museum, blacksmith shop, stable, and stamp mill are also here, with campers allowed free admission to the museum. Other must-see destinations in the park include Eureka Lake, and from there, the 1,100-foot climb to Eureka Peak (7,447 feet) for a dramatic view of all the famous peaks in this region. Camp elevation is 5,200 feet and the park covers 5,500 acres. Fishing opportunities include Madora and Eureka Lakes and Jamison Creek, best in May and June. The visitors center was originally constructed as a bunkhouse for miners; more than $8 million in gold was mined here. In winter, enjoy the solitude of several cross-country ski or snowshoe trails.

**Campsites, facilities:** Upper Jamison Creek Campground has 67 sites for tents or RVs up to 30 feet (no hookups). Picnic tables, food lockers, and fire rings are provided. Drinking water and restrooms with flush toilets and free showers are available. A dump station is nearby, and a grocery store, coin laundry, and propane gas are available within five miles. Some facilities are wheelchair-accessible. Leashed pets are permitted.

**Reservations, fees:** Reservations are accepted for the summer season at 800/444-7275 or www.reserveamerica.com ($8 reservation fee). Sites are $35 per night plus $8 per night for each additional vehicle. Open mid-May through September, weather permitting.

**Directions:** In Truckee, drive north on Highway 89 to Graeagle. Just after passing Graeagle (one mile from the junction of Highway 70) turn left on County Road A14/Graeagle-Johnsville Road and drive west for about five miles to the park entrance on the left.

**Contact:** Plumas-Eureka State Park, 530/836-2380, www.parks.ca.gov; Plumas-Eureka State Park Association, www.plumas-eureka.org.

## 21 CLIO'S RIVERS EDGE RV PARK

### Scenic rating: 7

on the Feather River

**Map 6.1, page 333**

This is a giant RV park adjacent to a pretty and easily accessible stretch of the Feather River. There are many possible side-trip destinations, including Plumas-Eureka State Park, Lakes Basin Recreation Area, several nearby golf courses, and a horseback-riding facility. The elevation is about 4,500 feet. Many of the sites are rented for the entire summer season.

**Campsites, facilities:** There are 220 sites with full hookups (50 amps) for RVs of any length. Some sites are pull-through. Picnic tables are provided. Drinking water, restrooms with flush toilets and coin showers, coin laundry, Wi-Fi (some sites), and cable TV are available. A grocery store is within three miles. Some facilities

are wheelchair-accessible. Leashed pets are permitted, with certain restrictions.

**Reservations, fees:** Reservations are accepted. RV sites with hookups are $40-50 per night, plus $5 per person per night for more than two people, $2 per night per additional vehicle, and $2-5 per pet per night. Weekly and monthly rates are available. Some credit cards are accepted. Open mid-April through October.

**Directions:** From Truckee, drive north on Highway 89 toward Graeagle and Blairsden. Near Clio (4.5 miles south of Highway 70 at Blairsden), look for the campground entrance on the right (0.2 mile south of Graeagle).

**Contact:** Clio's River's Edge, 530/836-2375, www.riversedgervpark.net.

## 22 LAKES BASIN GROUP CAMP

### Scenic rating: 8

in Plumas National Forest

**Map 6.1, page 333**

This is a Forest Service group camp that is ideal for Boy and Girl Scouts. It is at 6,400 feet elevation, just a short drive from the trailhead to beautiful Frazier Falls, and also near Gold Lake, Little Bear Lake, and 15 lakes below nearby Mount Elwell.

**Campsites, facilities:** This group camp is for tents only and can accommodate up to 25 people. Fire grills are provided. Drinking water and vault toilets are available. Supplies are available in Graeagle. Some facilities are wheelchair-accessible. Leashed pets are permitted.

**Reservations, fees:** Reservations are required at 877/444-6777 or www.recreation.gov ($9 reservation fee). The group site is $80 per night, plus $3 per pet per night. Open June through October, weather permitting.

**Directions:** From Truckee, drive north on Highway 89 toward Graeagle to the Gold Lake Highway (one mile before reaching Graeagle).

Turn left on the Gold Lake Highway and drive about seven miles to the campground.

**Contact:** Plumas National Forest, Beckwourth Ranger District, 530/836-2575, www.fs.usda.gov/plumas; Thousand Trails, 530/832-1076.

## 23 LAKES BASIN

### Scenic rating: 8

in Plumas National Forest

**Map 6.1, page 333**

This camp is a great location for a base camp to explore the surrounding Lakes Basin Recreation Area. From nearby Gold Lake or Elwell Lodge, there are many short hikes to small pristine lakes. The trailhead to climb Mount Elwell is also at the camp, and there is a short hike to beautiful Long Lake. In early summer, a must-do trip is the easy hike to Frazier Falls, only a mile round-trip to see the spectacular 176-foot waterfall, though the trail is crowded during the middle of the day. The trail to this waterfall is paved and is wheelchair-accessible. The camp elevation is 6,400 feet.

**Campsites, facilities:** There are 23 sites for tents or RVs up to 30 feet (no hookups). Fire grills are provided, but there are no picnic tables. Drinking water and vault toilets are available. Supplies are available in Graeagle. Some facilities are wheelchair-accessible. Leashed pets are permitted.

**Reservations, fees:** Reservations are accepted at 877/444-6777 ($10 reservation fee) or www.recreation.gov ($9 reservation fee). Single sites are $20 per night and double sites are $40 per night, plus $3 per pet per night. Open June through October, weather permitting.

**Directions:** From Truckee, drive north on Highway 89 toward Graeagle to the Gold Lake Highway (one mile before reaching Graeagle). Turn left on the Gold Lake Highway and drive about seven miles to the campground.

**Contact:** Plumas National Forest, Beckwourth Ranger District, 530/836-2575, www.fs.usda.gov/plumas; Thousand Trails, 530/832-1076.

## 24 PACKSADDLE

### Scenic rating: 6

near Packer Lake in Tahoe National Forest

**Map 6.1, page 333**

Packsaddle is a Forest Service site about 0.5 mile from Packer Lake, with an additional 15 lakes within a five-mile radius. The trailhead to climb Sierra Buttes—one of America's truly great hiking trails—is just up the road. Sierra Buttes features a climb of 2,369 feet over the course of five miles, highlighted by a stairway with 176 steps that literally juts into open space. All of this is crowned by an astounding view for hundreds of miles in all directions. Packer Lake, at 6,218 feet elevation, is nearby and has log cabins, trout fishing, and low-speed boating. The campground elevation is 6,000 feet.

**Campsites, facilities:** There are 16 sites for tents or RVs up to 35 feet (no hookups). Vault toilets and drinking water are available. Pack and saddle animals are permitted, and corrals and hitching rails are available. Supplies are available in Bassetts and Sierra City. Some facilities are wheelchair-accessible. Leashed pets are permitted.

**Reservations, fees:** Reservations are accepted at 877/444-6777 ($10 reservation fee) or www.recreation.gov ($9 reservation fee). Sites are $24 per night, plus $5 per night for each additional vehicle. Open late May through September, weather permitting.

**Directions:** From Truckee, turn north on Highway 89 and drive 22 miles to Sierraville and Highway 49. Turn left on Highway 49 and drive about 18 miles to the Bassetts Store and the Gold Lakes Highway. Turn right on Gold Lakes Highway and drive 1.5 miles to Packer Lake Road. Turn left and drive a short distance to a fork. Bear right at the fork (signed for Packer Lake) and drive 2.5 miles to the campground on the left.

**Contact:** Tahoe National Forest, Yuba River Ranger District, North, 530/288-3231, www.fs.usda.gov/tahoe.

## 25 BERGER

### Scenic rating: 6

in Tahoe National Forest

**Map 6.1, page 333**

Berger Camp provides an overflow alternative to nearby Diablo, which is also extremely primitive. On busy summer weekends, when an open campsite can be difficult to find at a premium location in the Lakes Basin Recreation Area, these two camps provide a safety valve to keep you from being stuck for the night. Nearby are Packer Lake, the trail to the Sierra Buttes, Sardine Lakes, and Sand Pond, all excellent destinations. The elevation is 5,900 feet.

**Campsites, facilities:** There are nine sites for tents or RVs up to 16 feet (no hookups). Picnic tables and fire grills are provided. Vault toilets and garbage bins are available. No drinking water is available. Supplies are available in Bassetts and Sierra City. Leashed pets are permitted.

**Reservations, fees:** Reservations are accepted at 877/444-6777 ($10 reservation fee) or www.recreation.gov ($9 reservation fee). Sites are $20 per night, plus $5 per night for each additional vehicle. Open late May through September, weather permitting.

**Directions:** From Truckee, turn north on Highway 89 and drive 22 miles to Sierraville and Highway 49. Turn left on Highway 49 and drive about 18 miles to the Bassetts Store and the Gold Lakes Highway. Turn right on Gold Lakes Highway and drive 1.5 miles to Packer Lake Road. Turn left, drive a short distance, bear right at the fork, and drive two miles to the campground on the left.

**Contact:** Tahoe National Forest, Yuba River Ranger District, North, 530/288-3231, www.fs.usda.gov/tahoe.

## 26 SNAG LAKE

### Scenic rating: 8

in Tahoe National Forest

**Map 6.1, page 333**

Snag Lake is an ideal little lake for camping anglers with canoes. There are no boat ramps and you can have the place virtually to yourself. It is at 6,000 feet in elevation, an easy-to-reach lake in the Lakes Basin Recreation Area. Trout fishing is only fair, as in fair numbers and fair size, mainly rainbow trout in the 10- to 12-inch class. Note that campers here must provide their own drinking water.

**Campsites, facilities:** There are 12 sites for tents or RVs up to 16 feet (no hookups). Picnic tables and fire grills are provided. Vault toilets are available. No drinking water is available. Garbage must be packed out. Only hand boat launching is allowed. Supplies are available in Bassetts and Sierra City. Leashed pets are permitted.

**Reservations, fees:** Reservations are not accepted. There is no fee for camping. Open June through October, weather permitting.

**Directions:** From Truckee, turn north on Highway 89 and drive 22 miles to Sierraville and Highway 49. Turn left on Highway 49 and drive about 18 miles to the Bassetts Store and the Gold Lakes Highway. Turn right on Gold Lakes Highway and drive five miles to the campground on the left.

**Contact:** Tahoe National Forest, Yuba River Ranger District, North, 530/288-3231, www.fs.usda.gov/tahoe.

## 27 DIABLO

### Scenic rating: 8

on Packer Creek in Tahoe National Forest

**Map 6.1, page 333**

This is a developed camping area on Packer Creek, about two miles from Packer Lake. This area is extremely beautiful with several lakes nearby, including the Sardine Lakes and Packer Lake, and this camp provides an overflow area when the more developed campgrounds have filled.

**Campsites, facilities:** There are 18 sites for tents or RVs up to 30 feet (no hookups). Picnic tables and fire rings are provided. Vault toilets are available. No drinking water is available. Supplies are available in Bassetts and Sierra City. Leashed pets are permitted.

**Reservations, fees:** Reservations are accepted at 877/444-6777 ($10 reservation fee) or www. recreation.gov ($9 reservation fee). Sites are $18 per night, plus $5 per night for each additional vehicle. Open late May through September, weather permitting.

**Directions:** From Truckee, turn north on Highway 89 and drive 22 miles to Sierraville and Highway 49. Turn left on Highway 49 and drive about 18 miles to the Bassetts Store and the Gold Lakes Highway. Turn right on Gold Lakes Highway and drive 1.5 miles to Packer Lake Road. Turn left, drive a short distance, bear right at the fork, and drive one mile to the campground on the right side of the road.

**Contact:** Tahoe National Forest, Yuba River Ranger District, North, 530/288-3231, www. fs.usda.gov/tahoe.

## 28 SALMON CREEK

### Scenic rating: 9

in Tahoe National Forest

**Map 6.1, page 333**

This campground is at the confluence of Packer and Salmon Creeks, at 5,800 feet elevation, with easy access off the Gold Lakes Highway. It is near the Lakes Basin Recreation Area, with literally dozens of small lakes within five miles, plus great hiking, fishing, and low-speed boating.

**Campsites, facilities:** There are 32 sites for tents or RVs up to 30 feet (no hookups). Picnic tables and fire grills are provided. Drinking water and vault toilets are available. Supplies

and a coin laundry are available in Sierra City. Leashed pets are permitted.

**Reservations, fees:** Reservations are accepted at 877/444-6777 ($10 reservation fee) or www. recreation.gov ($9 reservation fee). Sites are $24 per night, plus $5 per night for each additional vehicle. Open June through October.

**Directions:** From Truckee, turn north on Highway 89 and drive 22 miles to Sierraville and Highway 49. Turn left on Highway 49 and drive about 18 miles to the Bassetts Store and the Gold Lakes Highway. Turn right on Gold Lakes Highway and drive two miles to the campground on the left side of the road.

**Contact:** Tahoe National Forest, Yuba River Ranger District, North, 530/288-3231, www. fs.usda.gov/tahoe.

## 29 SARDINE LAKES

### Scenic rating: 8

in Tahoe National Forest

**Map 6.1, page 333**

This campground is in the Tahoe National Forest near Sand Pond and about a mile from Lower Sardine Lake. Lower Sardine Lake is a jewel below the Sierra Buttes, one of the prettiest settings in California. A great hike is routed along the shore of Lower Sardine Lake to a hidden waterfall (in spring) that feeds the lake, and ambitious hikers can explore beyond and discover Upper Sardine Lake. Trout fishing is excellent in Lower Sardine Lake, with a primitive boat ramp available for small boats. The speed limit and small size of the lake keep boaters slow and quiet. A small marina and boat rentals are available. Nearby is the beautiful Sand Pond Interpretive Trail.

**Campsites, facilities:** There are 27 sites for tents or RVs up to 22 feet (no hookups). Picnic tables and fire grills are provided. Drinking water and vault toilets are available. Limited supplies are available at the Sardine Lake Lodge or in Bassetts. Leashed pets are permitted.

**Reservations, fees:** Reservations are accepted

at 877/444-6777 ($10 reservation fee) or www.recreation.gov ($9 reservation fee). Single sites are $24 per night, double sites are $48 per night, plus $5 per night for each additional vehicle. Open June through October, weather permitting.

**Directions:** From Truckee, turn north on Highway 89 and drive 22 miles to Sierraville and Highway 49. Turn left on Highway 49 and drive about 18 miles to the Bassetts Store and the Gold Lakes Highway. Turn right on Gold Lakes Highway and drive 1.5 miles to Packer Lake Road. Turn left, drive a short distance, then bear left at the fork (signed) and drive 0.5 mile to the campground on the left.

**Contact:** Tahoe National Forest, Yuba River Ranger District, North, 530/288-3231, www.fs.usda.gov/tahoe.

## 30 CHAPMAN

### Scenic rating: 8

on the North Yuba River in Tahoe National Forest

**Map 6.1, page 333**

This campground is along Chapman Creek at 6,000 feet, just across the highway from where it enters the North Yuba River. A good side trip is to hike Chapman Creek Trail, which leads out of camp to Beartrap Meadow or to Haskell Peak (8,107 feet).

**Campsites, facilities:** There are 24 sites for tents or RVs up to 22 feet (no hookups). Picnic tables and fire grills are provided. Drinking water may be available and vault toilets are available. Supplies are available in Bassetts. Leashed pets are permitted.

**Reservations, fees:** Reservations are accepted at 877/444-6777 ($10 reservation fee) or www.recreation.gov ($9 reservation fee). Sites are $20 per night, $5 per night for each additional vehicle. Open June through October, weather permitting.

**Directions:** From Truckee, turn north on

Highway 89 and drive 20 miles to Sierraville. At Sierraville, turn left on Highway 49, drive over Yuba Pass, and continue for four miles to the campground on the right.

**Contact:** Tahoe National Forest, Yuba River Ranger District, North, 530/288-3231, www.fs.usda.gov/tahoe.

## 31 SIERRA

### Scenic rating: 7

on the North Yuba River in Tahoe National Forest

**Map 6.1, page 333**

This is an easy-to-reach spot along the North Yuba River, used primarily as an overflow area from nearby Chapman (a mile upstream). Nearby recreation options include Chapman Creek Trail, several waterfalls (see the Wild Plum listing in this chapter), and the nearby Lakes Basin Recreation Area to the north off the Gold Lake Highway. The elevation is 5,600 feet. Note: Bring your own drinking water.

**Campsites, facilities:** There are 17 sites for tents or RVs up to 22 feet (no hookups). Picnic tables and fire rings are provided. Vault toilets are available. No drinking water is available. Supplies are available in Bassetts. Leashed pets are permitted.

**Reservations, fees:** Reservations are accepted at 877/444-6777 ($10 reservation fee) or www.recreation.gov ($9 reservation fee). Sites are $18 per night, plus $5 per night for each additional vehicle. Open June through October, weather permitting.

**Directions:** From Truckee, turn north on Highway 89 and drive 20 miles to Sierraville. At Sierraville, turn left on Highway 49 and drive over Yuba Pass. Continue for five miles to the campground on the left side of the road.

**Contact:** Tahoe National Forest, Yuba River Ranger District, North, 530/288-3231, www.fs.usda.gov/tahoe.

## 32 YUBA PASS

### Scenic rating: 6

in Tahoe National Forest

**Map 6.1, page 333**

This camp is right at Yuba Pass at an elevation of 6,700 feet. In the winter, the surrounding area is a Sno-Park, which gives it an unusual look in summer. Yuba Pass is a popular bird-watching area in the summer.

**Campsites, facilities:** There are 20 sites for tents or RVs up to 22 feet (no hookups). Picnic tables and fire grills are provided. Drinking water and vault toilets are available. Supplies are available at Bassetts. Leashed pets are permitted.

**Reservations, fees:** Reservations are accepted at 877/444-6777 ($10 reservation fee) or www.recreation.gov ($9 reservation fee). Sites are $24 per night, plus $5 per night for each additional vehicle. Open late June through October, weather permitting.

**Directions:** From Truckee, drive north on Highway 89 past Sattley to the junction with Highway 49. Turn west on Highway 49 and drive about six miles to the campground on the left side of the road.

**Contact:** Tahoe National Forest, Yuba River Ranger District, North, 530/288-3231, www.fs.usda.gov/tahoe.

## 33 CARLTON/CAL-IDA

### Scenic rating: 7

on the North Yuba River in Tahoe National Forest

**Map 6.1, page 333**

Carlton is on the North Yuba River, and Cal-Ida is across the road. Both are right next door to Fiddle Creek. (For more information, see the Fiddle Creek listing in this chapter.)

**Campsites, facilities:** There are 21 sites at Carlton and 19 sites at Cal-Ida for tents or RVs up to 28 feet (no hookups). Picnic tables and fire grills are provided. Drinking water and vault toilets are available. Some facilities are wheelchair-accessible. Some supplies are available at the Indian Valley Outpost nearby. Leashed pets are permitted.

**Reservations, fees:** Reservations are accepted at 877/444-6777 ($10 reservation fee) or www.recreation.gov ($9 reservation fee). Sites are $24 per night, plus $5 per night for each additional vehicle. Open mid-April through November, weather permitting.

**Directions:** From Auburn, take Highway 49 north to Nevada City and continue on Highway 49 (the road jogs left, then narrows) to Camptonville. Continue northeast for nine miles to the campground entrance. The camping area at Carlton is one mile northeast of the Highway 49 bridge at Indian Valley. The camping area at Cal-Ida is just east of the Indian Valley Outpost on the Cal-Ida Road.

**Contact:** Tahoe National Forest, Yuba River Ranger District, North, 530/288-3231, www.fs.usda.gov/tahoe.

## 34 FIDDLE CREEK

### Scenic rating: 7

on the North Yuba River in Tahoe National Forest

**Map 6.1, page 333**

This camp is situated on the North Yuba River along Highway 49 in a quiet, forested area. This is a beautiful river, one of the prettiest to flow westward out of the Sierra Nevada, with deep pools and miniature waterfalls. It is popular for rafting out of Goodyears Bar, and if you can stand the cold water, there are many good swimming holes along Highway 49. It's at 2,200 feet elevation. There are several other campgrounds along this stretch of the Yuba River. Fiddle Creek Ridge Trail starts across the highway on Cal-Ida Road and is routed out to Indian Rock.

**Campsites, facilities:** There are 16 tent sites. Picnic tables and fire rings are provided.

Drinking water and vault toilets are available. Limited supplies are nearby at the Indian Valley Outpost. Some facilities are wheelchair-accessible, including a paved trail to the Yuba River. Leashed pets are permitted.

**Reservations, fees:** Reservations are accepted at 877/444-6777 ($10 reservation fee) or www.recreation.gov ($9 reservation fee). Sites are $24 per night, plus $5 per night for each additional vehicle. Open April to November, weather permitting.

**Directions:** From Auburn, take Highway 49 north to Nevada City and continue on Highway 49 (the road jogs left, then narrows) to Camptonville. Continue northeast for 9.5 miles to the campground entrance on the right.

**Contact:** Tahoe National Forest, Yuba River Ranger District, North, 530/288-3231, www. fs.usda.gov/tahoe.

## 35 INDIAN VALLEY

🥾 🏊 ➡️ 🐕 🚐 ⛺

### Scenic rating: 7

on the North Yuba River in Tahoe National Forest

**Map 6.1, page 333**

This is an easy-to-reach spot set at 2,200 feet beside the North Yuba River. Highway 49 runs adjacent to the Yuba River for miles eastward, providing easy access to the river in many areas. There are several other campgrounds in the immediate area (see the listings in this chapter for Fiddle Creek and Carlton/Cal-Ida, both within a mile).

**Campsites, facilities:** There are 17 sites for tents or RVs up to 22 feet (no hookups). Picnic tables and fire grills are provided. Drinking water and vault toilets are available. Limited supplies are available nearby at the Indian Valley Outpost. Leashed pets are permitted.

**Reservations, fees:** Reservations are accepted at 877/444-6777 ($10 reservation fee) or www. recreation.gov ($9 reservation fee). Single sites are $24 per night, double sites are $48 per night,

plus $5 per night for each additional vehicle. Open year-round.

**Directions:** From Auburn, take Highway 49 north to Nevada City and continue on Highway 49 (the road jogs left, then narrows) to Camptonville. Drive 10 miles to the camp entrance on the right.

**Contact:** Tahoe National Forest, Yuba River Ranger District, North, 530/288-3231, www. fs.usda.gov/tahoe.

## 36 ROCKY REST

🥾 🏊 ➡️ 🐕 🚐 ⛺

### Scenic rating: 7

on the North Yuba River in Tahoe National Forest

**Map 6.1, page 333**

This is one in a series of campgrounds set at streamside on the North Yuba River. The elevation is 2,200 feet. A footbridge crosses the North Yuba River and provides an outstanding seven-mile hike.

**Campsites, facilities:** There are 10 dispersed camping sites for tents and RVs up to 16 feet (no hookups). Picnic tables and fire grills are provided. Drinking water and vault toilets are available. Limited supplies are nearby at the Indian Valley Outpost. Leashed pets are permitted.

**Reservations, fees:** Reservations are accepted at 877/444-6777 ($10 reservation fee) or www. recreation.gov ($9 reservation fee). Sites are $24 per night, plus $5 per night for each additional vehicle. Open mid-April through November, weather permitting.

**Directions:** From Auburn, take Highway 49 north to Nevada City and continue (the road jogs left, then narrows) to Camptonville. Continue on Highway 49 for 10 miles to the campground entrance on the right.

**Contact:** Tahoe National Forest, Yuba River Ranger District, North, 530/288-3231, www. fs.usda.gov/tahoe.

## 37 RAMSHORN

🏃 🏊 🎣 🐕 🚐 ⛺

**Scenic rating: 7**

on the North Yuba River in Tahoe National Forest

**Map 6.1, page 333**

This camp is on Ramshorn Creek, just across the road from the North Yuba River. It's one in a series of camps on this stretch of the beautiful North Yuba River. One mile east is a well-known access point for white-water rafting trips on the Yuba. The camp's elevation is 2,200 feet.

**Campsites, facilities:** There are 16 sites for tents or RVs up to 22 feet (no hookups). Picnic tables and fire grills are provided. Vault toilets and drinking water are available. Supplies are available in Downieville. Leashed pets are permitted.

**Reservations, fees:** Reservations are accepted at 877/444-6777 ($10 reservation fee) or www.recreation.gov ($9 reservation fee). Sites are $24 per night, plus $5 per night for each additional vehicle. Open year-round.

**Directions:** From Auburn, take Highway 49 north to Nevada City and continue on Highway 49 (the road jogs left, then narrows) to Camptonville. Drive 15 miles north to the campground entrance on the left.

**Contact:** Tahoe National Forest, Yuba River Ranger District, North, 530/288-3231, www.fs.usda.gov/tahoe.

## 38 UNION FLAT

🏃 🏊 🎣 🐕 ♿ 🚐 ⛺

**Scenic rating: 8**

on the North Yuba River in Tahoe National Forest

**Map 6.1, page 333**

Of all the campgrounds on the North Yuba River along Highway 49, Union Flat has the best swimming. The camp has a nice swimming hole next to it, and the water is cold. The Goodyears Bar Run is a highly popular one-day eight-mile rafting trip, primarily Class III-IV, with an outrageous Class V rapid (Class VI means risk of death) that newcomers can portage. The put-in is at Union Flat Campground and the take-out is at Fiddle Creek Campground. Recreational mining is also an attraction here. The elevation is 3,400 feet.

**Campsites, facilities:** There are 11 sites for tents or RVs up to 35 feet (no hookups). Picnic tables and fire grills are provided. Drinking water and vault toilets are available. Some facilities are wheelchair-accessible. Supplies are available in Downieville. Leashed pets are permitted.

**Reservations, fees:** Reservations are accepted at 877/444-6777 ($10 reservation fee) or www.recreation.gov ($9 reservation fee). Single sites are $24 per night, double sites are $48 per night, plus $5 per night for each additional vehicle. Open May through October, weather permitting.

**Directions:** From Auburn, take Highway 49 north to Nevada City and continue (the road jogs left, then narrows) to Downieville. Drive six miles east to the campground entrance on the right.

**Contact:** Tahoe National Forest, Yuba River Ranger District, North, 530/288-3231, www.fs.usda.gov/tahoe.

## 39 LOGANVILLE

🏃 🏊 🎣 🐕 🚐 ⛺

**Scenic rating: 8**

on the North Yuba River in Tahoe National Forest

**Map 6.1, page 333**

Sierra City is only two miles away, meaning you can make a quick getaway for a prepared meal or any food or drink you may need to add to your camp. Loganville is on the North Yuba River, elevation 4,200 feet. It offers a good stretch of water in this region for trout fishing, with many pools below miniature waterfalls.

**Campsites, facilities:** There are 19 sites for tents or RVs up to 22 feet (no hookups). Picnic

tables and fire grills are provided. Drinking water and vault toilets are available. Garbage bins are at the visitors center. Supplies and a coin laundry are available in Sierra City. Leashed pets are permitted.

**Reservations, fees:** Reservations are accepted at 877/444-6777 ($10 reservation fee) or www.recreation.gov ($9 reservation fee). Sites are $24 per night, plus $5 per night for each additional vehicle. Open May through October, weather permitting.

**Directions:** From Auburn, take Highway 49 north to Nevada City and continue on Highway 49 (the road jogs left, then narrows) to Downieville. Drive 12 miles east to the campground entrance on the right (two miles west of Sierra City).

**Contact:** Tahoe National Forest, Yuba River Ranger District, North, 530/288-3231, www.fs.usda.gov/tahoe.

## 40 WILD PLUM

### Scenic rating: 8

on Haypress Creek in Tahoe National Forest

**Map 6.1, page 333**

This popular Forest Service campground is on Haypress Creek at 4,400 feet. Several hidden waterfalls in the area make this a popular camp for the people who know of them. A scenic hike up Haypress Trail goes past a waterfall to Haypress Valley. Two other nearby waterfalls are Loves Falls (on the North Yuba on Highway 49 two miles east of Sierra City) and Hackmans Falls (remote, set in a ravine one mile south of Sierra City; no road access).

**Campsites, facilities:** There are 47 sites for tents or RVs up to 22 feet (no hookups). Picnic tables, food lockers, and fire grills are provided. Drinking water and vault toilets are available. Supplies and a coin laundry are available in Sierra City. Leashed pets are permitted.

**Reservations, fees:** Reservations are accepted at 877/444-6777 ($10 reservation fee) or www.

recreation.gov ($9 reservation fee). Sites are $24 per night, plus $5 per night for each additional vehicle. Open May through October, weather permitting.

**Directions:** From Auburn, take Highway 49 north to Nevada City and continue (the road jogs left, then narrows) past Downieville to Sierra City and Wild Plum Road. Turn right on Wild Plum Road and drive two miles to the campground entrance road on the right.

**Contact:** Tahoe National Forest, Yuba River Ranger District, North, 530/288-3231, www.fs.usda.gov/tahoe.

## 41 COLD CREEK

### Scenic rating: 8

in Tahoe National Forest

**Map 6.1, page 333**

There are four small campgrounds along Highway 89 between Sierraville and Truckee, all within close range of side trips to Webber Lake, Independence Lake, and Sierra Hot Springs in Sierraville. Cold Creek is just upstream of the confluence of Cottonwood Creek and Cold Creek, at 5,800 feet elevation.

**Campsites, facilities:** There are six sites for tents or RVs up to 22 feet (no hookups). Picnic tables and fire rings are provided. Drinking water and vault toilets are available. Supplies are available in Sierraville. Leashed pets are permitted.

**Reservations, fees:** Reservations are accepted at 877/444-6777 ($10 reservation fee) or www.recreation.gov ($9 reservation fee). Sites are $16 per night, plus $5 per night for each additional vehicle. Open May through October.

**Directions:** From Truckee, drive north on Highway 89 for about 20 miles to the campground on the left side of the road. If you reach Sierraville, you have gone five miles too far.

**Contact:** Tahoe National Forest, Sierraville Ranger District, 530/994-3401, www.fs.usda.gov/tahoe.

## 42 COTTONWOOD CREEK

**Scenic rating: 7**

in Tahoe National Forest

Map 6.1, page 333

This camp sits beside Cottonwood Creek at 5,800 feet elevation. An interpretive trail starts at the upper camp and makes a short loop, and there are several nearby side-trip options, including trout fishing on the Little Truckee River to the south, visiting the Sierra Hot Springs out of Sierraville to the north, or venturing into the surrounding Tahoe National Forest.

**Campsites, facilities:** There are 48 sites for tents or RVs up to 30 feet (no hookups). Picnic tables and fire rings are provided. Drinking water and vault toilets are available. Supplies are available in Sierraville. Leashed pets are permitted.

**Reservations, fees:** Reservations are accepted at 877/444-6777 ($10 reservation fee) or www. recreation.gov ($9 reservation fee). Sites are $20 per night, plus $5 per night for each additional vehicle. Open mid-May through early October, weather permitting.

**Directions:** From Truckee, drive north on Highway 89 for about 20 miles to the campground entrance road on the right (0.5 mile past Cold Creek Camp).

**Contact:** Tahoe National Forest, Sierraville Ranger District, 530/994-3401, www.fs.usda. gov/tahoe.

## 43 BEAR VALLEY

**Scenic rating: 7**

on Bear Valley Creek in Tahoe National Forest

Map 6.1, page 333

The surrounding national forest land was largely burned by the historic Cottonwood Fire of 1994, but the camp itself was saved. It is at 6,700 feet elevation, with a spring adjacent to the campground. The road leading southeast out of camp is routed to Sardine Peak Look-Out (8,134 feet), where there is a dramatic view of the region. There is an 18-mile loop OHV trail across the road from the campground.

**Campsites, facilities:** There are 10 sites for tents or RVs up to 16 feet (no hookups). Picnic tables and fire rings are provided. Vault toilets and bear boxes are available. There is no drinking water. Garbage must be packed out. Supplies are available in Sierraville. Leashed pets are permitted.

**Reservations, fees:** Reservations are not accepted. There is no fee for camping. Open May through October, weather permitting.

**Directions:** From Truckee, drive north on Highway 89 for about 17 miles. Turn right on County Road 451 and drive northeast about six miles to the campground entrance on the right.

**Contact:** Tahoe National Forest, Sierraville Ranger District, 530/994-3401, www.fs.usda. gov/tahoe.

## 44 LOOKOUT

**Scenic rating: 4**

in Humboldt-Toiyabe National Forest

Map 6.1, page 333

This primitive camp is set in remote country near the California/Nevada border at 6,700 feet elevation. It is a former mining site, and the highlight is a quartz crystal mine a short distance from the campground. Stampede Lake provides a side-trip option, about 10 miles to the southwest, over the rough dirt Henness Pass Road.

**Campsites, facilities:** There are 17 sites for tents or RVs up to 35 feet (no hookups). Picnic tables and fire grills are provided. Vault toilets are available. There is no drinking water. Garbage must be packed out. Leashed pets are permitted.

**Reservations, fees:** Reservations are not accepted; sites are first-come, first-served. Sites are $6 per night, plus $6 per night for each extra vehicle. Open June through September.

**Directions:** From Truckee on I-80, drive east across the state line into Nevada to Verdi. Take the Verdi exit and drive north through town to Bridge Street and then to Old Dog Valley Road. Drive north on Old Dog Valley Road for 11 miles to the campground.

**Contact:** Humboldt-Toiyabe National Forest, Carson Ranger District, 775/882-2766, www. fs.usda.gov/htnf.

## 45 LITTLE LASIER MEADOWS EQUESTRIAN

### Scenic rating: 7

near Jackson Meadow Reservoir

**Map 6.1, page 333**

This is the best camp in the area for those with horses. Little Lasier Meadows has open sites in the forest, adjacent to a meadow, and has a horse corral. Best of all, there is direct access to the Pacific Crest Trail. Nearby Jackson Meadow Reservoir is very pretty and provides boating, fishing, and swimming.

**Campsites, facilities:** There are 11 sites for tents or RVs. Drinking water and vault toilets are available. Picnic tables, fire rings, horse corrals, and tie rails are provided. Corrals and water for horses are available.

**Reservations, fees:** Reservations are required at 877/444-6777 ($10 reservation fee) or www. recreation.gov ($9 reservation fee). Sites are $24 per night, plus $5 each additional vehicle per night. Open year-round, weather permitting.

**Directions:** From Truckee, drive north 17.5 miles on Highway 89 to Forest Road 7/ Fiberboard Road. Turn left and drive 15 miles to the East Meadows turnoff. Cross the metal bridge and take the first left turn. Drive approximately two miles to the campground.

**Contact:** Tahoe National Forest, Sierraville Ranger District, 530/994-3401, www.fs.usda. gov/tahoe.

## 46 SILVER TIP GROUP CAMP

### Scenic rating: 7

at Jackson Meadow Reservoir in Tahoe National Forest

**Map 6.1, page 333**

This group camp is on the southwest edge of Jackson Meadow Reservoir at 6,100 feet elevation, in a pretty area with pine forest, high meadows, and the trademark granite look of the Sierra Nevada. A boat ramp and swimming beach are nearby at Woodcamp. (For more information, see the Woodcamp listing in this chapter.)

**Campsites, facilities:** There are two group sites for tents or RVs up to 22 feet (no hookups) that can accommodate up to 25 people each. Picnic tables and fire rings are provided. Drinking water and vault toilets are available. Obtain supplies in Truckee or Sierraville. A boat ramp is nearby. Leashed pets are permitted.

**Reservations, fees:** Reservations are accepted at 530/265-5302. The camps are $88 per night. Open June through October, weather permitting.

**Directions:** From Truckee, drive north on Highway 89 for 17 miles to Forest Road 7. Turn left on Forest Road 7 and drive 16 miles to Jackson Meadow Reservoir. At the lake, continue across the dam around the west shoreline and then turn left at the campground access road. The entrance is on the right just after the Woodcamp campground.

**Contact:** Nevada Irrigation District, 530/265-5302; Tahoe National Forest, Sierraville Ranger District, 530/994-3401, www.fs.usda.gov/tahoe.

## 47 WOODCAMP

### Scenic rating: 7

at Jackson Meadow Reservoir in Tahoe
National Forest

**Map 6.1, page 333**

Woodcamp and Pass Creek are the best camps
for boaters at Jackson Meadow Reservoir because each is directly adjacent to a boat ramp.
That is critical because fishing is far better by
boat here than from shore, with a good mix of
both rainbow and brown trout. The camp is at
6,700 feet elevation along the lake's southwest
shore, in a pretty spot with a swimming beach
and short interpretive hiking trail nearby. All
water sports are allowed. This is a beautiful lake
in the Sierra Nevada, complete with pine forest
and a classic granite backdrop.

**Campsites, facilities:** There are 16 sites for
tents or RVs up to 22 feet (no hookups). Picnic
tables and fire rings are provided. Drinking
water, flush and vault toilets, food lockers, and
firewood (fee) are available. Supplies are available in Truckee or Sierraville. A boat ramp is
adjacent to the camp and a dump station is
nearby. Leashed pets are permitted.

**Reservations, fees:** Reservations are accepted
at 877/444-6777 ($10 reservation fee) or www.
recreation.gov ($9 reservation fee). Sites are $24
per night, plus $5 per night for each additional
vehicle. Rates are higher on holidays. Open
June through October, weather permitting.

**Directions:** From Truckee, drive north on
Highway 89 for 17 miles to Forest Road 7. Turn
left on Forest Road 7 and drive 16 miles to
Jackson Meadow Reservoir. At the lake, continue across the dam around the west shoreline
and then turn left at the campground access
road. The entrance is on the right just before
the Woodcamp boat ramp.

**Contact:** Nevada Irrigation District, 530/265-
5302; Tahoe National Forest, Sierraville Ranger
District, 530/994-3401, www.fs.usda.gov/tahoe.

## 48 FIR TOP

### Scenic rating: 7

at Jackson Meadow Reservoir in Tahoe
National Forest

**Map 6.1, page 333**

Jackson Meadow is a great destination for a
short vacation, and that's why there are so
many campgrounds available; it's not exactly
a secret. This camp is above the lake, less than
a mile from a boat ramp near Woodcamp. (See
the Woodcamp and Pass Creek listings in this
chapter for more information.) The elevation
is 6,200 feet.

**Campsites, facilities:** There are 10 sites for
tents or RVs up to 22 feet (no hookups). Picnic
tables and fire rings are provided. Drinking
water, flush and vault toilets, and food lockers
are available. Supplies are available in Truckee
or Sierraville. Leashed pets are permitted.

**Reservations, fees:** Reservations are accepted
at 877/444-6777 ($10 reservation fee) or www.
recreation.gov ($9 reservation fee). Sites are $24
per night, plus $5 per night for each additional
vehicle. Rates are higher on holidays. Open
June through November, weather permitting.

**Directions:** From Truckee, drive north on
Highway 89 for 17.5 miles to Forest Road 7.
Turn left on Forest Road 7 and drive 16 miles
to Jackson Meadow Reservoir. Continue across
the dam and around the lake to the west side.
Turn left at the campground access road. The
campground entrance is on the right across
from the entrance to the Woodcamp Picnic
Area.

**Contact:** Nevada Irrigation District, 530/265-
5302; Tahoe National Forest, Sierraville Ranger
District, 530/994-3401, www.fs.usda.gov/tahoe.

## 49 FINDLEY

**Scenic rating: 7**

at Jackson Meadow Reservoir in Tahoe National Forest

**Map 6.1, page 333**

Findley is near Woodcamp Creek, a quarter mile from where it pours into Jackson Meadow Reservoir. Though it is not a lakeside camp, it is quite pretty just the same, and within a mile of the boat ramp near Woodcamp. It is at 6,300 feet elevation. This is one of several camps at the lake.

**Campsites, facilities:** There are 11 sites for tents or RVs up to 22 feet (no hookups). Picnic tables and fire rings are provided. Drinking water, flush and vault toilets, and food lockers are available. Supplies are available in Truckee or Sierraville. A boat ramp is nearby. Some facilities are wheelchair-accessible. Leashed pets are permitted.

**Reservations, fees:** Reservations are accepted at 877/444-6777 ($10 reservation fee) or www. recreation.gov ($9 reservation fee). Sites are $24 per night, plus $5 per night for each additional vehicle. Open May through October.

**Directions:** From Truckee, drive north on Highway 89 for 17 miles to Forest Road 7. Turn left on Forest Road 7 and drive 16 miles to Jackson Meadow Reservoir. Continue across the dam around the lake to the west side. Turn left at the campground access road and drive about 0.25 mile to the entrance on the left.

**Contact:** Nevada Irrigation District, 530/265-5302; Tahoe National Forest, Sierraville Ranger District, 530/994-3401, www.fs.usda.gov/tahoe.

## 50 JACKSON POINT BOAT-IN

**Scenic rating: 10**

at Jackson Meadow Reservoir in Tahoe National Forest

**Map 6.1, page 333**

This is one of the few boat-in camps available anywhere in the high Sierra. The gorgeous spot is situated on the end of a peninsula that extends from the east shore of Jackson Meadow Reservoir. Small and primitive, it's the one place at the lake where you can gain entry into the 5 Percent Club. From the point, there is a spectacular view of the Sierra Buttes. Because the lake levels are kept near full all summer, this boat-in camp is doubly appealing. The elevation is 6,200 feet.

**Campsites, facilities:** There are 12 tent sites. Picnic tables and fire rings are provided. Vault toilets are available. There is no drinking water; reservoir water must be purified before drinking. Garbage must be packed out. Supplies are available in Truckee or Sierraville. Leashed pets are permitted.

**Reservations, fees:** Reservations are not accepted. There is no fee for camping. Open June through September, weather permitting.

**Directions:** From Truckee, drive north on Highway 89 for 17 miles to Forest Road 7. Turn left on Forest Road 7 and drive 16 miles to Jackson Meadow Reservoir. Drive to Pass Creek and the boat launch (on the left at the north end of the lake). Launch your boat and cruise 0.5 mile south to Jackson Point and the boat-in campsites.

**Contact:** Nevada Irrigation District, 530/265-5302; Tahoe National Forest, Sierraville Ranger District, 530/994-3401, www.fs.usda.gov/tahoe.

## 51 PASS CREEK

**Scenic rating: 7**

at Jackson Meadow Reservoir in Tahoe National Forest

**Map 6.1, page 333**

This is the premium campground at Jackson Meadow Reservoir, a developed site with water, a concrete boat ramp, a swimming beach nearby at Aspen Creek Picnic Area, and access to the Pacific Crest Trail 0.5 mile to the east (you'll pass it on the way in). This lake has the trademark look of the high Sierra, and the bonus is that lake levels are often kept higher than at other reservoirs on the western slopes of the Sierra Nevada. Trout stocks are excellent, with rainbow and brown trout planted each summer after ice-out. The elevation is 6,100 feet.

**Campsites, facilities:** There are 25 sites for tents or RVs up to 22 feet (no hookups). Picnic tables and fire rings are provided. Drinking water, flush and vault toilets, and food lockers are available. A dump station and boat ramp are nearby. Supplies are available in Truckee or Sierraville. Some facilities are wheelchair-accessible. Leashed pets are permitted.

**Reservations, fees:** Reservations are accepted at 877/444-6777 ($10 reservation fee) or www. recreation.gov ($9 reservation fee). Sites are $24 per night, plus $5 per night for each additional vehicle. Rates are higher on holidays. Open May through October, weather permitting.

**Directions:** From Truckee, drive north on Highway 89 for 17 miles to Forest Road 7. Turn left on Forest Road 7 and drive 16 miles to Jackson Meadow Reservoir; the campground is on the left at the north end of the lake.

**Contact:** Nevada Irrigation District, 530/265-5302; Tahoe National Forest, Sierraville Ranger District, 530/994-3401, www.fs.usda.gov/tahoe.

## 52 EAST MEADOWS

### Scenic rating: 7

at Jackson Meadow Reservoir in Tahoe National Forest

**Map 6.1, page 333**

This camp is in a beautiful setting on the northeast side of Jackson Meadow Reservoir, on the edge of a sheltered cove. The Pacific Crest Trail passes right by camp, providing access for a day trip, though no stellar destinations are on this stretch of the PCT. The nearest boat ramp is at Pass Creek, two miles away. The elevation is 6,200 feet.

**Campsites, facilities:** There are 44 sites for tents or RVs up to 40 feet (no hookups). Picnic

tables and fire rings are provided. Drinking water, flush and vault toilets, food lockers, a camp store, and firewood (fee) are available. A dump station and boat ramp are near Pass Creek. Supplies are available in Truckee or Sierraville. Some facilities are wheelchair-accessible. Leashed pets are permitted.

**Reservations, fees:** Reservations are accepted at 877/444-6777 ($10 reservation fee) or www.recreation.gov ($9 reservation fee). Single sites are $24 per night, double sites are $48 per night, plus $5 per night for each additional vehicle. Open May through October, weather permitting.

**Directions:** From Truckee, drive north on Highway 89 for 17 miles to Forest Road 7. Turn left on Forest Road 7 and drive 15 miles to the campground entrance road on the left (if you reach Pass Creek, you have gone too far). Turn left and drive a mile to the campground on the right.

**Contact:** Nevada Irrigation District, 530/265-5302; Tahoe National Forest, Sierraville Ranger District, 530/994-3401, www.fs.usda.gov/tahoe.

## 53 ASPEN GROUP CAMP

### Scenic rating: 7

at Jackson Meadow Reservoir in Tahoe National Forest

**Map 6.1, page 333**

A boat ramp and easy access to adjacent Jackson Meadow Reservoir make this a premium group camp. The elevation is 6,100 feet.

**Campsites, facilities:** There are three group sites for tents or RVs up to 40 feet (no hookups) that can accommodate 25-50 people each. Picnic tables and fire grills are provided. Drinking water, vault toilets, food lockers, firewood (fee), and a campfire circle are available. Some facilities are wheelchair-accessible. A dump station is nearby. There is a boat ramp nearby at Pass Creek. Supplies are available in Truckee or Sierraville. Leashed pets are permitted.

**Reservations, fees:** Reservations are accepted at Nevada Irrigation District (530/265-5302). Sites are $80-131.82 per night. Open mid-May through October, weather permitting.

**Directions:** From Truckee, drive north on Highway 89 for 17.5 miles to Forest Road 7. Turn left on Forest Road 7 and drive 16 miles (a mile past Pass Creek) to the campground entrance on the right.

**Contact:** Tahoe National Forest, Sierraville Ranger District, 530/994-3401, www.fs.usda.gov/tahoe.

## 54 UPPER LITTLE TRUCKEE

### Scenic rating: 7

on the Little Truckee River in Tahoe National Forest

**Map 6.1, page 333**

This camp is along the Little Truckee River at 6,100 feet. The Little Truckee is a pretty trout stream, with easy access not only from this campground, but also from another three miles northward along Highway 89, then from another seven miles to the west along Forest Road 7, the route to Webber Lake. It is only about a 10-minute drive from this camp to reach Stampede Lake to the east.

**Campsites, facilities:** There are 21 sites for tents or RVs up to 30 feet (no hookups) and one group site for up to 25 people. Picnic tables and fire rings are provided. Drinking water and vault toilets are available. Supplies are available in Sierraville. Leashed pets are permitted.

**Reservations, fees:** Reservations are accepted at 877/444-6777 ($10 reservation fee) or www.recreation.gov ($9 reservation fee). Sites are $20 per night, the group site is $65 per night, plus $5 per night for each additional vehicle. Open mid-May through October, weather permitting.

**Directions:** From Truckee, drive north on Highway 89 for about 11 miles to the campground on the left, a short distance beyond Lower Little Truckee Camp.

**Contact:** Tahoe National Forest, Sierraville Ranger District, 530/994-3401, www.fs.usda.gov/tahoe.

## 55 LOWER LITTLE TRUCKEE

### Scenic rating: 7

on the Little Truckee River in Tahoe National Forest

**Map 6.1, page 333**

This pretty camp is along Highway 89 and the Little Truckee River at 6,200 feet. (For more information, see the Upper Little Truckee listing in this chapter.)

**Campsites, facilities:** There are 12 sites for tents or RVs up to 20 feet (no hookups) and two walk-in tent sites. Picnic tables and fire grills are provided. Drinking water and vault toilets are available. Supplies are available in Sierraville or Truckee. Leashed pets are permitted.

**Reservations, fees:** Reservations are accepted at 877/444-6777 ($10 reservation fee) or www.recreation.gov ($9 reservation fee). Sites are $20 per night, plus $5 per night for each additional vehicle. Open May through October, weather permitting.

**Directions:** From Truckee, drive north on Highway 89 for about 12 miles to the campground on the left. If you reach Upper Little Truckee Camp, you have gone 0.5 mile too far.

**Contact:** Tahoe National Forest, Sierraville Ranger District, 530/994-3401, www.fs.usda.gov/tahoe.

## 56 JACKSON CREEK

### Scenic rating: 7

near Bowman Lake in Tahoe National Forest

**Map 6.1, page 333**

This primitive campground is at 5,600 feet elevation, adjacent to Jackson Creek, a primary feeder stream to Bowman Lake to the nearby west. There are several lakes within a five-mile radius, including Bowman Lake, Jackson Meadow Reservoir, Sawmill Lake (private), and Faucherie Lake. A trailhead is available a mile south (on the right side of the road) at the north end of Sawmill Lake. The trail is routed to a series of pretty Sierra lakes to the west of Haystack Mountain (7,391 feet).

**Campsites, facilities:** There are 14 primitive tent sites. Picnic tables and fire grills are provided. Vault toilets are available. No drinking water is available; stream water must be purified before drinking. Garbage must be packed out. Leashed pets are permitted.

**Reservations, fees:** Reservations are not accepted. There is no fee for camping. Open June through October, weather permitting.

**Directions:** From Sacramento, drive east on I-80 past Emigrant Gap to Highway 20. Turn west on Highway 20 and drive to Bowman Road/Forest Road 18. Turn right and drive about 16 miles to Bowman Lake (much of the road is quite rough), then continue for four miles east of the lake to the campground. High-clearance vehicles are required and four-wheel-drive vehicles are recommended.

**Contact:** Nevada Irrigation District, 530/265-5302; Tahoe National Forest, Yuba River Ranger District, South, 530/265-4531, www.fs.usda.gov/tahoe.

## 57 BOWMAN LAKE

🚶 🏊 🏖 🛥 🎣 🐕 ⛰

**Scenic rating: 8**

in Tahoe National Forest

**Map 6.1, page 333**

Bowman is a sapphire jewel set in Sierra granite at 5,568 feet elevation, extremely pretty and ideal for campers with car-top boats. Pine trees surround the lake, and the shoreline is sprinkled with large granite slabs. Swimming is allowed, and the boat speed limit is 10 mph. There is no boat ramp (you wouldn't want to trailer a boat on the access road anyway), but there are lots of small rainbow trout that are

eager to please during the evening bite. The camp is on the eastern end of the lake, just below where Jackson Creek pours in. The lake is flanked by Bowman Mountain (7,392 feet) and Red Hill (7,075 feet) to the south and Quartz Hill (7,025 feet) to the north.

**Campsites, facilities:** There are seven primitive tent sites. Vault toilets are available. No drinking water is available. Garbage must be packed out. Leashed pets are permitted.

**Reservations, fees:** Reservations are not accepted. There is no fee for camping. Open mid-June through October, weather permitting.

**Directions:** From Sacramento, drive east on I-80 past Emigrant Gap to Highway 20. Turn west on Highway 20 and drive to Bowman Road/Forest Road 18. Turn right and drive about 16 miles (much of the road is quite rough) to Bowman Lake and the campground on the right side of the road at the head of the lake. High-clearance vehicles are required and four-wheel-drive vehicles are recommended.

**Contact:** Nevada Irrigation District, 530/265-5302; Tahoe National Forest, Yuba River Ranger District, South, 530/265-4531, www.fs.usda.gov/tahoe.

## 58 FAUCHERIE GROUP CAMP

🚶 🏊 🏖 🛥 🎣 🐕 🚐 ⛰

**Scenic rating: 7**

near Bowman Lake in Tahoe National Forest

**Map 6.1, page 333**

Faucherie Lake is the kind of place that most people believe can be reached only by long, difficult hikes with a backpack. Guess again: Here it is, set in Sierra granite at 6,100 feet elevation, quiet and pristine, a classic alpine lake. It is ideal for car-top boating and has decent fishing for both rainbow and brown trout. This group camp is on the lake's northern shore, a prime spot, with the outlet creek nearby.

**Campsites, facilities:** There are two group camps for tents or RVs up to 22 feet (no hookups) that can accommodate up to 25 people each. Picnic tables and fire grills are provided.

Vault toilets and garbage bins are available. No drinking water is available; stream water must be purified before drinking. A primitive boat ramp is nearby. Leashed pets are permitted.

**Reservations, fees:** Reservations are accepted at Nevada Irrigation District (530/265-5302). The camp is $50 per night. Open June through October, weather permitting.

**Directions:** From Sacramento, drive east on I-80 past Emigrant Gap to Highway 20. Turn west on Highway 20 and drive to Bowman Road/Forest Road 18. Turn right and drive about 16 miles (much of the road is quite rough) to Bowman Lake and continue four miles to a Y. Bear right at the Y and drive about three miles to the campground at the end of the road. Four-wheel-drive vehicles are advised.

**Contact:** Nevada Irrigation District, 530/265-5302; Tahoe National Forest, Yuba River Ranger District, South, 530/265-4531, www.fs.usda.gov/tahoe.

# 59 CANYON CREEK

### Scenic rating: 6

near Faucherie Lake in Tahoe National Forest

**Map 6.1, page 333**

This pretty spot is at 6,000 feet elevation in Tahoe National Forest, a mile from Sawmill Lake (which you pass on the way in) and a mile from pretty Faucherie Lake. It is along Canyon Creek, the stream that connects those two lakes. Of the two, Faucherie provides better fishing, and because of that there are fewer people at Sawmill. Take your pick. A trail at the north end of Sawmill Lake leads to several small alpine lakes, a great day hike or overnight backpacking trip.

**Campsites, facilities:** There are 16 sites for tents or RVs up to 16 feet (no hookups). Picnic tables and fire grills are provided. Vault toilets and food-storage lockers are available. No drinking water is available; stream water must be purified before drinking. Garbage must be packed out. Leashed pets are permitted.

**Reservations, fees:** Reservations are not accepted. There is no fee for camping. Open June through October, weather permitting.

**Directions:** From Sacramento, drive east on I-80 to Emigrant Gap. Take the off-ramp and head north on the short connector road to Highway 20. Turn west on Highway 20 and drive four miles to Bowman Road/Forest Road 18. Turn right and drive about 16 miles (nine of these miles are paved, but the rest is quite rough) to Bowman Lake and continue four miles to a Y. Bear right at the Y and drive about two miles to the campground on the right side of the road. High-clearance vehicles are required and four-wheel-drive vehicles are recommended.

**Contact:** Nevada Irrigation District, 530/265-5302; Tahoe National Forest, Yuba River Ranger District, South, 530/265-4531, www.fs.usda.gov/tahoe.

# 60 SAGEHEN CREEK

### Scenic rating: 7

in Tahoe National Forest

**Map 6.1, page 333**

This is a small, primitive camp at 6,500 feet elevation beside little Sagehen Creek, just north of a miniature mountain range called the Sagehen Hills, which top out at 7,707 feet. Sagehen Creek provides an option when the camps along Highway 89 and at Stampede, Boca, and Prosser Creek have filled. In the fall, it is popular as a base camp.

**Campsites, facilities:** There are 11 sites for tents or RVs up to 16 feet (no hookups). Picnic tables and fire grills are provided. Vault toilets are available. No drinking water is available. Garbage must be packed out. Leashed pets are permitted.

**Reservations, fees:** Reservations are not accepted. There is no fee for camping. Open mid-May to mid-October, weather permitting.

**Directions:** From Truckee, drive 8.5 miles north on Highway 89 to Sagehen Summit Road on the left. Turn left and drive four miles to the campground.

**Contact:** Tahoe National Forest, Truckee Ranger District, 530/587-3558, www.fs.usda. gov/tahoe.

## 61 LOGGER

**Scenic rating: 7**

at Stampede Lake in Tahoe National Forest

**Map 6.1, page 333**

Covering 3,400 acres and with 25 miles of shoreline, Stampede Lake is a huge lake by Sierra standards—the largest in the region after Lake Tahoe. It is set at 6,000 feet, surrounded by Sierra granite and pines, and on days when the wind is down, it's quite beautiful. The campground is also huge, set along the lake's southern shore, a few minutes' drive from the Captain Roberts boat ramp. This camp is ideal for campers, boaters, and anglers. The lake is becoming one of the top fishing lakes in California for kokanee salmon (which can be caught only by trolling), and it also has some large Mackinaw trout and a sprinkling of planter-sized rainbow trout. All water sports are allowed. One problem at Stampede is receding water levels from midsummer through fall, a real pain, which puts the campsites some distance from the lake. Even when the lake is full, there are only a few "lakeside" campsites. However, the boat ramp has been extended to assist boaters during drawdowns.

**Campsites, facilities:** There are 200 sites for tents or RVs up to 32 feet (no hookups), including some double and triple sites. Picnic tables and fire rings are provided. Drinking water, vault toilets, and a dump station are available. A concrete boat ramp is one mile from camp. Some facilities are wheelchair-accessible. Leashed pets are permitted.

**Reservations, fees:** Reservations are accepted at 877/444-6777 ($10 reservation fee) or www. recreation.gov ($9 reservation fee). Single sites are $26 per night, double sites are $52 per night,

and triple sites are $78 per night, plus $5 per night for each additional vehicle. Open May through October.

**Directions:** From Truckee, drive east on I-80 for seven miles to the Boca-Hirschdale/County Road 270 exit. Take that exit and drive north on County Road 270 for about seven miles (past Boca Reservoir) to the junction with County Road S261 on the left. Turn left and drive 1.5 miles to the campground on the right.

**Contact:** Tahoe National Forest, Truckee Ranger District, 530/587-3558, www.fs.usda. gov/tahoe.

## 62 EMIGRANT GROUP

**Scenic rating: 7**

at Stampede Lake in Tahoe National Forest

**Map 6.1, page 333**

Note: The campground has a planned closure for the 2018 season while the dam undergoes renovations.

Emigrant Group is at a beautiful spot on Stampede Lake, near a point along a cove on the southeastern corner of the lake. There is a beautiful view of the lake from the point, and a boat ramp is two miles to the east. Elevation is 6,000 feet. (See the Logger listing in this chapter for more information.)

**Campsites, facilities:** There are four group sites for tents and RVs up to 32 feet (no hookups): Two sites can accommodate 25 people each and two sites can accommodate up to 50 people each. Picnic tables and fire grills are provided. Drinking water and vault toilets are available. Bring your own firewood. Horseshoe pits and a three-lane concrete boat ramp are available. Some facilities are wheelchair-accessible. Leashed pets are permitted.

**Reservations, fees:** Reservations are required at 877/444-6777 ($10 reservation fee) or www. recreation.gov ($9 reservation fee). Group sites are $97-201 per night. Open May through September, weather permitting.

**Directions:** From Truckee, drive east on I-80

for seven miles to the Boca-Hirschdale/County Road 270 exit. Take that exit and drive north on County Road 270 for about seven miles (past Boca Reservoir) to the junction with County Road S261 on the left. Turn left and drive 1.5 miles to the campground access road on the right. Turn right and drive one mile to the camp on the left.

**Contact:** Tahoe National Forest, Truckee Ranger District, 530/587-3558, www.fs.usda.gov/tahoe.

# 63 BOYINGTON MILL

### Scenic rating: 7

on the Little Truckee River in Tahoe National Forest

**Map 6.1, page 333**

Boyington Mill is a little Forest Service camp set between Boca Reservoir to the south and Stampede Lake to the north, along a small inlet creek to the adjacent Little Truckee River. Though open all summer, it is most often used as an overflow camp when lakeside campsites at Boca, Stampede, and Prosser have already filled. The elevation is 5,700 feet.

**Campsites, facilities:** There are 11 sites for tents or RVs up to 32 feet (no hookups). Picnic tables and fire rings are provided. Vault toilets are available. No drinking water is available. Leashed pets are permitted.

**Reservations, fees:** Reservations are accepted at 877/444-6777 ($10 reservation fee) or www.recreation.gov ($9 reservation fee). Sites are $20 per night, plus $5 per night for each additional vehicle. Open May through October, weather permitting.

**Directions:** From Truckee, drive east on I-80 for seven miles. Take the Boca-Hirschdale exit and drive north on County Road 270 for four miles (past Boca Reservoir) to the campground.

**Contact:** Tahoe National Forest, Truckee Ranger District, 530/587-3558, www.fs.usda.gov/tahoe.

# 64 BOCA REST CAMPGROUND

### Scenic rating: 7

on Boca Reservoir in Tahoe National Forest

**Map 6.1, page 333**

The Boca Dam faces I-80, so the lake is out of sight of the zillions of highway travelers who would otherwise certainly stop here. Those who do stop find that the lake is very pretty, set at 5,700 feet elevation and covering 1,000 acres with deep, blue water and 14 miles of shoreline. All water sports are allowed. This camp is on the lake's northeastern shore, not far from the inlet to the Little Truckee River. The boat ramp is some distance away.

**Campsites, facilities:** There are 20 sites for tents or RVs up to 22 feet (no hookups) and three sites for tents only. Picnic tables and fire grills are provided. Drinking water and vault toilets are available. A hand-launch boat ramp is also available. A concrete boat ramp is three miles away on the southwest shore of Boca Reservoir. Leashed pets are permitted.

**Reservations, fees:** Reservations are accepted at 877/444-6777 ($10 reservation fee) or www.recreation.gov ($9 reservation fee). Sites are $20 per night, plus $5 per night for each additional vehicle. Open May through October, weather permitting.

**Directions:** From Truckee, drive east on I-80 for seven miles to the Boca-Hirschdale exit. Take that exit and drive north on County Road 270 for about 2.5 miles to the campground on the left side of the road.

**Contact:** Tahoe National Forest, Truckee Ranger District, 530/587-3558, www.fs.usda.gov/tahoe.

## 65 MALAKOFF DIGGINS STATE HISTORIC PARK

🏃 🐎 � 🏕️

### Scenic rating: 6

near Nevada City

**Map 6.1, page 333**

This camp at 3,400 feet elevation sits near a small lake in the park, but the main attraction of the area is its gold-mining past. A trip here is like a walk through history. Gold-mining efforts at this site washed away entire mountains with powerful streams of water, leaving behind enormous cliffs. This practice began in the 1850s and continued for many years. Several major gold-mining operations combined hydraulic mining with giant sluice boxes. Hydraulic mining was a scourge to the land, of course, and was eventually put to an end due to litigation between mine operators and landowners downstream. Though the remains of the state's biggest hydraulic mine are now closed to the public, visitors can view exhibits on mining life. The park also contains a 7,847-foot bedrock tunnel that served as a drain. Although this tunnel is not open to the public, a shorter tunnel is available for viewing.

**Campsites, facilities:** There are 30 sites for tents or RVs up to 24 feet (no hookups), three cabins, and one group tent site for up to 50 people. Picnic tables and fire rings are provided. Drinking water and flush toilets (March to mid-September) are available. Leashed pets are permitted.

**Reservations, fees:** Reservations are accepted at 877/444-6777 or www.recreation.gov ($8 reservation fee). Sites are $35 per night, plus $8 per night for each additional vehicle, $165 per night for the group site, and $40 per night for the cabins. Open year-round.

**Directions:** From Auburn, drive north on Highway 49 to Nevada City and continue 11 miles to the junction of Tyler Foote Crossing Road. Turn right and drive approximately 11 miles (in the process the road changes names to Cruzon Grade and Back Bone Road) to Der Bec Road. Turn right on Der Bec Road and drive one mile to North Bloomfield Road. Turn right and drive two miles to the entrance on the right. The route is well signed; the last two miles are quite steep.

**Contact:** California State Parks, 530/265-2740, www.parks.ca.gov.

## 66 SOUTH YUBA

🏃 🏊 ⚓ 🛶 ♿ � 🏕️

### Scenic rating: 7

near the Yuba River

**Map 6.1, page 333**

This little-known BLM camp is next to where little Kenebee Creek enters the Yuba River. The Yuba is about a mile away, with some great swimming holes and evening trout-fishing spots to explore. A good side trip is to nearby Malakoff Diggins State Historic Park and the town of North Bloomfield (about a 10-minute drive to the northeast on North Bloomfield Road), which is being completely restored to its 1850s character. Twelve-mile-long South Yuba Trail begins at the state park and features outstanding spring wildflower blooms. The elevation is 2,600 feet.

**Campsites, facilities:** There are 16 sites for tents or RVs up to 27 feet (no hookups). Picnic tables and fire grills are provided. Drinking water and pit toilets are available. Some facilities are wheelchair-accessible. Leashed pets are permitted.

**Reservations, fees:** Reservations are not accepted. Sites are $5 per night. Open April through mid-October, weather permitting.

**Directions:** From Auburn, turn north on Highway 49, drive to Nevada City, and then continue on Highway 49 (the highway jogs left in town) a short distance to North Bloomfield Road. Turn right and drive 10 miles to the one-lane bridge at Edward's Crossing. Cross the bridge and continue 1.5 miles to the campground on the right side of the road (the road becomes quite rough). This route is not recommended for RVs or trailers.

Alternative route for RVs or vehicles with

trailers: From Auburn turn north on Highway 49 to Nevada City and continue on Highway 49 (the highway jogs left in town) to Tyler Foote Crossing Road. Turn right and drive to Grizzly Hills Road (just past North Columbia). Turn right and drive two miles to North Bloomfield Road. Bear right on North Bloomfield Road and drive 0.5 mile to the campground on the left.

**Contact:** Bureau of Land Management, Mother Lode Field Office, 916/941-3101, www. blm.gov/ca.

# 67 GROUSE RIDGE

### Scenic rating: 7
near Bowman Lake in Tahoe National Forest

Map 6.1, page 333

Grouse Ridge, at 7,520 feet elevation, is at the gateway to beautiful hiking country filled with small high Sierra lakes. The camp is primarily used as a trailhead and jumping-off point, not as a destination itself. The closest hike is the 0.5-mile tromp up to Grouse Ridge Lookout, at 7,707 feet, which provides a spectacular view to the north of this area and its many small lakes. As you hike north, the trail passes Round Lake (to the left) in the first mile and Middle Lake (on the right) two miles later, with opportunities to take cutoff trails on either side of the ridge to visit numerous other lakes.

**Campsites, facilities:** There are nine sites for tents only. Picnic tables and fire grills are provided. Vault toilets are available. No drinking water is available. Garbage must be packed out. Leashed pets are permitted.

**Reservations, fees:** Reservations are not accepted. There is no fee for camping. Open June through October, weather permitting.

**Directions:** From Sacramento, drive east on I-80 past Emigrant Gap to Highway 20. Turn west on Highway 20 and drive to Bowman Road/Forest Road 18. Turn north on Bowman Road and drive five miles to Grouse Ridge Road. Turn right on Grouse Ridge Road and drive six miles on rough gravel to the campground. High-clearance vehicles are required and four-wheel-drive vehicles are recommended.

**Contact:** Tahoe National Forest, Yuba River Ranger District, South, 530/265-4531, www. fs.usda.gov/tahoe.

# 68 LAKESIDE

### Scenic rating: 7
on Prosser Creek Reservoir in Tahoe National Forest

Map 6.1, page 333

This primitive camp is in a deep cove in the northwestern end of Prosser Creek Reservoir, near the lake's headwaters. It is a gorgeous lake, at 5,741 feet elevation, and a 10-mph speed limit keeps the fast boats out. The adjacent shore is decent for hand-launched, car-top boats, providing the lake level is up, and a concrete boat ramp is a mile down the road. Lots of trout are stocked every year. The trout fishing is often quite good after the ice breaks up in late spring. Sound perfect? Unfortunately for many, the Prosser OHV Park is nearby and can be noisy.

**Campsites, facilities:** There are 32 sites for tents or RVs up to 33 feet (no hookups). Drinking water and vault toilets are available. A boat ramp is nearby. Some facilities are wheelchair-accessible. Leashed pets are permitted.

**Reservations, fees:** Reservations are accepted at 877/444-6777 ($10 reservation fee) or www.recreation.gov ($9 reservation fee; search for Lakeside in Truckee). Sites are $20 per night, plus $5 per night for each additional vehicle. Open June through October, weather permitting.

**Directions:** From Truckee, drive north on Highway 89 for three miles to the campground entrance road on the right. Turn right and drive less than a mile to the campground.

**Contact:** Tahoe National Forest, Truckee Ranger District, 530/587-3558, www.fs.usda. gov/tahoe.

## 69 PROSSER RANCH CAMPGROUND

**Scenic rating: 9**

at Prosser Reservoir

**Map 6.1, page 333**

This camp is at an elevation of 5,800 feet on the west shore peninsula of Prosser Reservoir. Though water levels can be an issue in late summer and fall, it is gorgeous in late spring and early summer. The landscape consists of Sierra granite sprinkled with pines, and the contrast of the emerald water, granite shore, and cobalt sky can be very special. In spring and fall, look for rainbow trout up to 18 inches. In summer, anglers have a shot at 10- to 12-inch planters. A 10-mph speed limit for boaters keeps it quiet.

**Campsites, facilities:** There are 29 sites for tents and small RVs, along with one group site for tents only that can accommodate up to 50 people. Drinking water and vault toilets are available. Picnic tables and fire grills are provided. A boat ramp is nearby.

**Reservations, fees:** Reservations are accepted for individual sites (search for Prosser Family) and are required for the group site (search for Prosser Ranch Group) at 877/444-6777 ($10 reservation fee) or www.recreation.gov ($9 reservation fee). Sites are $20 per night; the group site is $143 per night and allows 10 vehicles; plus $5 each additional vehicle per night. A maximum stay of 14 days is enforced. Open late May through early September.

**Directions:** From Truckee, drive north on Highway 89 for four miles and turn right onto the access road to Prosser Reservoir. This campground is past Lakeside Campground.

**Contact:** Tahoe National Forest, Truckee Ranger District, 530/587-3558, www.fs.usda.gov/tahoe.

## 70 BOCA SPRING CAMPGROUND AND GROUP CAMP

**Scenic rating: 7**

in Tahoe National Forest

**Map 6.1, page 333**

Boca Spring is just past the north end of Boca Lake, near the Little Truckee River and a short way beyond Lakeside Campground. Boca is known for good trolling for trout and large kokanee salmon. A forest road provides access to a good stretch of the Little Truckee River, which can also provide good fishing for small trout. The elevation is 5,800 feet.

**Campsites, facilities:** There are seven tent sites, eight sites for tents or RVs, and one group site for up to 25 people. Some sites are pull-through. Drinking water and vault toilets are available. Fire grills are provided. Horses are permitted in the campground; a watering trough and hitching posts are provided. Some facilities are wheelchair-accessible.

**Reservations, fees:** Reservations are accepted at 877/444-6777 ($10 reservation fee) or www.recreation.gov ($9 reservation fee). Sites are $20 per night, the group site is $66 per night, plus $5 for each additional vehicle. A maximum stay of 14 days is enforced. Open mid-May through September.

**Directions:** From Truckee, drive north on Highway 89 for four miles and turn right onto the access road to Prosser Reservoir. This campground is past Lakeside Campground.

**Contact:** Tahoe National Forest, Truckee Ranger District, 530/587-3558, www.fs.usda.gov/tahoe.

## 71 BOCA

**Scenic rating: 7**

on Boca Reservoir in Tahoe National Forest

**Map 6.1, page 333**

Boca Reservoir is known as a "big fish factory,"

with some huge but rare brown trout and rainbow trout sprinkled among a growing fishery for kokanee salmon. The lake is set at 5,700 feet amid a few sparse pines. While the surrounding landscape is not in the drop-dead beautiful class, the lake can still seem a Sierra gem on a windless dawn out on a boat. It is within a few miles of I-80. The camp is the best choice for anglers/boaters, with a launch ramp just down from the campground.

**Campsites, facilities:** There are 23 sites for tents or RVs up to 16 feet (no hookups). Picnic tables and fire grills are provided. Vault toilets are available. No drinking water is available. A concrete boat ramp is north of the campground on Boca Reservoir. Truckee is the nearest place for telephones and supplies. Leashed pets are permitted.

**Reservations, fees:** Reservations are accepted at 877/444-6777 ($10 reservation fee) or www. recreation.gov ($9 reservation fee). Sites are $20 per night, plus $5 per night for each additional vehicle. Open May through October, weather permitting.

**Directions:** From I-80 in Truckee, take the exit for Highway 89 north. At the stoplight, turn left onto Highway 89 north and drive approximately one mile to Prosser Dam Road. Turn right and drive 4.5 miles to Prosser-Boca Road. Turn right and drive approximately four miles to the camp on the left.

**Contact:** Tahoe National Forest, Truckee Ranger District, 530/587-3558, www.fs.usda. gov/tahoe.

## 72 SCOTTS FLAT LAKE RECREATION AREA

🏊 🚣 🛶 🎣 🐴 🚶 ♿ 🚐 ⛺

### Scenic rating: 8

near Grass Valley

**Map 6.1, page 333**

At 3,100 feet elevation, Scotts Flat Lake is shaped like a large teardrop and is one of the prettier lakes in the Sierra foothills, with 7.5 miles of shoreline circled by forest. Rules prohibiting personal watercraft keep the place sane. The camp is on the lake's north shore, largely protected from spring winds and within short range of the marina and one of the lake's two boat launches. Trout fishing is good in the spring and early summer. When the lake heats up, waterskiing and powerboating become more popular. Sailing and sailboarding are also good during afternoon winds.

**Campsites, facilities:** There are 187 sites for tents or RVs up to 35 feet (no hookups). Picnic tables and fire pits are provided. Restrooms with flush toilets and coin showers, coin laundry, and a dump station are provided. A general store, bait and tackle, boat rentals, boat ramp, and a playground are also available. Groups can be accommodated. Some facilities are wheelchair-accessible. Leashed pets are permitted.

**Reservations, fees:** Reservations are recommended in the summer at 530/265-5302. Tent sites are $25-30 per night, RV sites are $25-35 per night, lakefront sites are $30-35 per night; it's $10 per night for each additional vehicle, $2 per additional person per night, $3 per pet per night, and $6 for boat launching ($13 if not camping). Maximum stay is 14 days. Group rates are $90-300 per night. Discount rates are available mid-October to mid-April. Some credit cards are accepted. Open year-round, weather permitting.

**Directions:** From Auburn, drive north on Highway 49 to Nevada City and the junction with Highway 20. Continue straight onto Highway 20 and drive five miles east to Scotts Flat Road. Turn right and drive four miles to the camp entrance road on the right (on the north shore of the lake).

**Contact:** Scotts Flat Lake Recreation Area, 530/265-5302 or 530/265-8861, www.scotts-flatlake.net.

## 73 WHITE CLOUD

### Scenic rating: 5

in Tahoe National Forest

**Map 6.1, page 333**

This camp is along historic Pioneer Trail, which has turned into one of the top mountain-bike routes in the Sierra Nevada—easy and fast. The trail traces the route of the first wagon road opened by emigrants and gold seekers in 1850. It is best suited for mountain biking, with a lot of bikers taking the one-way downhill ride (with an extra car for a shuttle ride) from Bear Valley to Lone Grave. The Omega Overlook is the highlight, with dramatic views of granite cliffs and the Yuba River. The elevation is 4,200 feet.

**Campsites, facilities:** There are 46 sites for tents or RVs of any length (no hookups). Picnic tables and fire grills are provided. Drinking water, flush toilets, and vault toilets are available. Leashed pets are permitted.

**Reservations, fees:** Reservations are accepted for 15 sites at 877/444-6777 ($10 reservation fee) or www.recreation.gov ($9 reservation fee). The remaining 31 sites are first-come, first-served. Sites are $24-48 per night, plus $5 per night for each additional vehicle. Open May through September, weather permitting.

**Directions:** From Sacramento, drive east on I-80 to Emigrant Gap. Take the off-ramp and then head north on the short connector road to Highway 20. Turn west on Highway 20 and drive about 15 miles to the campground entrance on the left.

**Contact:** Tahoe National Forest, Yuba River Ranger District, South, 530/265-4531, www.fs.usda.gov/tahoe; Big Bend Visitor's Center, 530/426-3609.

## 74 SKILLMAN FAMILY, EQUESTRIAN, AND GROUP CAMP

### Scenic rating: 5

in Tahoe National Forest

**Map 6.1, page 333**

Skillman Group Camp is at 4,400 feet, on a loop access road just off Highway 20, and historic Pioneer Trail runs right through it. (See the White Cloud listing in this chapter for more information.)

**Campsites, facilities:** There are 12 sites for tents or RVs up to 25 feet (no hookups). This campground can also be used as a group camp for tents or RVs up to 25 feet and can accommodate up to 36 people and 12 horses. Picnic tables and fire grills are provided. Vault toilets are available; drinking water may be available (call to confirm). Horse corrals, tie rails, troughs, and stock water are available. Leashed pets are permitted.

**Reservations, fees:** Reservations are accepted at 877/444-6777 ($10 reservation fee) or www.recreation.gov ($9 reservation fee). Single sites are $18-24 per night, and the group site is $110 per night; the entire campground is available for $300 per night. Open May through October, weather permitting.

**Directions:** From Sacramento, drive east on I-80 past Emigrant Gap to Highway 20. Turn west on Highway 20 and drive 12 miles to the campground entrance on the left.

**Contact:** Tahoe National Forest, Yuba River Ranger District, South, 530/265-4531, www.fs.usda.gov/tahoe.

## 75 LAKE SPAULDING

### Scenic rating: 8

near Emigrant Gap

**Map 6.1, page 333**

Lake Spaulding is set at 5,000 feet elevation in the Sierra Nevada, complete with huge boulders and a sprinkling of conifers. Its clear, pure, very cold water has startling effects on swimmers. The 772-acre lake is extremely pretty, with the Sierra granite backdrop looking as if it has been cut, chiseled, and smoothed. Just one problem: There's not much of a lake view from the campground, although there are a few sites with filtered views. In fact, the lake is about a quarter mile from the campground. The drive here is nearly a straight shot up I-80, so there will be plenty of company at the campground. All water sports are allowed, except personal watercraft. Fishing for kokanee salmon and rainbow trout is often good, as well as fishing for trout at the nearby South Fork Yuba River. There are many other lakes in the mountain country to the immediate north that make for excellent side trips, including Bowman, Weaver, and Faucherie Lakes.

**Campsites, facilities:** There are 25 sites (13 are walk-in) for tents or RVs up to 30 feet (no hookups) and an overflow area. Picnic tables and fire grills are provided. Drinking water, vault toilets, and picnic areas are available. A boat ramp is nearby. Supplies are available in Nevada City. Some facilities are wheelchair-accessible. Leashed pets are permitted.

**Reservations, fees:** Reservations are accepted. Sites are $22 per night, plus $5 per night for each additional vehicle, $2 per pet per night, and $10 per day for boat launching. Open mid-May through late October, weather permitting.

**Directions:** From Sacramento, drive east on I-80 past Emigrant Gap to Highway 20. Drive west on Highway 20 for 2.3 miles to Lake Spaulding Road. Turn right on Lake Spaulding Road and drive 0.5 mile to the campground.

**Contact:** Lake Spaulding Campground, 530/389-2236; PG&E Land Projects, 916/386-5164, www.pge.com/recreation.

## 76 INDIAN SPRINGS

### Scenic rating: 8
near the Yuba River in Tahoe National Forest

**Map 6.1, page 333**

The camp is easy to reach from I-80 yet is in a beautiful setting at 5,600 feet along the South Fork Yuba River. This is a gorgeous stream, running deep blue-green and pure through granite, complete with giant boulders and beautiful pools. Trout fishing is fair. A small swimming beach is nearby, though the water is cold. There are also several lakes in the vicinity.

**Campsites, facilities:** There are 28 sites for tents or RVs up to 26 feet (no hookups) and seven walk-in tent sites. Picnic tables and fire grills are provided. Drinking water and vault toilets are available. A grocery store and propane gas are nearby. Leashed pets are permitted.

**Reservations, fees:** Reservations are accepted at 877/444-6777 ($10 reservation fee) or www.recreation.gov ($9 reservation fee). Sites are $24 per night, plus $5 per night for each additional vehicle. Open June through September, weather permitting.

**Directions:** From Sacramento, drive east on I-80 to Yuba Gap and continue for about three miles to the Eagle Lakes exit. Head north on Eagle Lakes Road for a mile to the campground on the left side of the road.

**Contact:** Tahoe National Forest, Yuba River Ranger District, South, 530/265-4531, www.fs.usda.gov/tahoe.

## 77 WOODCHUCK

### Scenic rating: 8
on Rattlesnake Creek in Tahoe National Forest

**Map 6.1, page 333**

This small camp is only a few miles from I-80, but it is quite obscure and little known to most travelers. It is on Rattlesnake Creek at 6,300 feet in Tahoe National Forest, at the threshold of some great backcountry and four-wheel-drive roads that lead to many beautiful lakes. To explore, a map of Tahoe National Forest is a must.

**Campsites, facilities:** There are eight sites for tents. Picnic tables and fire grills are provided. Vault toilets are available. No drinking water is available; stream water must be purified before drinking. Garbage must be packed out. A grocery store and propane gas are nearby. Leashed pets are permitted.

**Reservations, fees:** Reservations are not accepted. Sites are $18 per night, plus $5 per night for each additional vehicle. Open June through October, weather permitting.

**Directions:** From Sacramento, drive east on I-80 to Yuba Gap and continue for about four miles to the Cisco Grove exit north. Take that exit, turn left on the frontage road, and drive a short distance to the stop sign and Rattlesnake Road/frontage road. Turn left on the frontage road/Rattlesnake Road and drive a short distance. Turn right and continue on Rattlesnake Road (gravel, steep, and curvy; trailers not recommended) and drive four miles to the campground on the right.

**Contact:** Tahoe National Forest, Yuba River Ranger District, South, 530/265-4531, www.fs.usda.gov/tahoe; Big Bend Visitor's Center, 530/426-3609.

## 78 LODGEPOLE

### Scenic rating: 8
on Lake Valley Reservoir in Tahoe National Forest

**Map 6.1, page 333**

Lake Valley Reservoir is at 5,786 feet elevation and covers 300 acres. It is gorgeous when full, its shoreline sprinkled with conifers and boulders. The lake provides decent results for anglers, who have the best luck while trolling. A 15-mph speed limit prohibits waterskiing and personal watercraft, and that keeps the place quiet and peaceful. The camp is about a quarter mile from the lake's southwest shore and

two miles from the boat ramp on the north shore. A trailhead from camp leads south up Monumental Ridge and to Monumental Creek (three miles, one-way) on the northwestern flank of Quartz Mountain (6,931 feet).

**Campsites, facilities:** There are 214 sites for tents or RVs up to 42 feet (no hookups). Picnic tables and fire grills are provided. Drinking water and flush toilets are available. A boat ramp is nearby. Supplies can be obtained off I-80. Some facilities are wheelchair-accessible. Leashed pets are permitted.

**Reservations, fees:** Reservations are accepted online at www.pge.com/recreation. Sites are $25 per night, $5 per night for each additional vehicle, $2 per pet per night. Open late May through September, weather permitting.

**Directions:** From I-80, take the Yuba Gap exit and drive south for 0.4 mile to Lake Valley Road. Turn right on Lake Valley Road and drive for 1.2 miles until the road forks. Bear right and continue for 1.5 miles to the campground entrance road to the right on another fork.

**Contact:** Lodgepole, 530/389-2236; PG&E Land Projects, 916/386-5164, www.pge.com/recreation.

## 79 HAMPSHIRE ROCKS

### Scenic rating: 8
on the Yuba River in Tahoe National Forest

**Map 6.1, page 333**

This camp sits along the South Fork of the Yuba River at 5,800 feet elevation, with easy access off I-80 and a nearby Forest Service information center. Fishing for trout is fair. There are some swimming holes, but the water is often very cold. Nearby lakes that can provide side trips include Sterling and Fordyce Lakes (drive-to) to the north, and the Loch Leven Lakes (hike-to) to the south.

**Campsites, facilities:** There are 30 sites for tents or RVs up to 22 feet (no hookups) and five walk-in tent sites. Picnic tables and fire grills are provided. Drinking water and vault toilets are available. A convenience store, restaurant, and propane gas are nearby. Leashed pets are permitted.

**Reservations, fees:** Reservations are accepted at 877/444-6777 ($10 reservation fee) or www.recreation.gov ($9 reservation fee). Sites are $24 per night, $5 per night for each additional vehicle. Open June through September, weather permitting.

**Directions:** From Sacramento, drive east on I-80 to Cisco Grove and continue for a mile to the Big Bend exit. Take that exit (remaining just south of the highway), then turn left on the frontage road and drive east for two miles to the campground on the right.

**Contact:** Tahoe National Forest, Yuba River Ranger District, South, 530/265-4531, www.fs.usda.gov/tahoe.

## 80 KIDD LAKE GROUP CAMP

### Scenic rating: 7

west of Truckee

**Map 6.1, page 333**

Kidd Lake is one of four lakes bunched along the access road just south of I-80. It is in the northern Sierra's high country, at 6,750 feet, and gets loaded with snow every winter. In late spring and early summer, always call ahead for conditions on the access road. The fishing is frustrating, consisting of a lot of tiny brook trout. Only car-top boats are permitted on Kidd Lake, with a primitive area available for launching. The camp is just northeast of the lake, within walking distance of the shore. It features 10 small group sites that can accommodate 100 people when reserved together.

**Campsites, facilities:** There are 10 group tent sites for up to 10 people each. Picnic tables and fire grills are provided. Drinking water and vault toilets are available. Supplies are available in Truckee. Leashed pets are permitted.

**Reservations, fees:** Reservations are required online at www.pge.com/recreation. Group sites are $50-175 per site per night, plus $2 per pet

per night and $5 per each additional vehicle. Open June through mid-October, weather permitting.

**Directions:** From Sacramento, drive east on I-80 toward Truckee. Take the Norden/Soda Springs exit, drive a short distance, turn south on Soda Springs Road, and drive 0.8 mile to Pahatsi Road. Turn right and drive two miles. When the road forks, bear right and drive a mile to the campground entrance road on the left.

**Contact:** Kidd Lake Group Camp, 530/389-2236; PG&E Land Projects, 916/386-5164, www.pge.com/recreation.

## 81 COACHLAND RV PARK

### Scenic rating: 6

in Truckee

**Map 6.1, page 333**

Truckee is the gateway to recreation at North Tahoe. Within minutes are Donner Lake, Prosser Creek Reservoir, Boca Reservoir, Stampede Lake, the Truckee River, and ski resorts. Squaw Valley is a short distance to the south off Highway 89, and Northstar is just off Highway 267. Coachland RV Park is in a wooded area near I-80, providing easy access. The downtown Truckee area (with restaurants) is a half mile away. This is one of the few parks in the area open year-round. The elevation is 6,000 feet. One problem: Only 25 of the 131 sites are available for overnighters, with the rest taken by long-term rentals.

**Campsites, facilities:** There are 131 pull-through sites with full hookups (30 amps; 13 sites provide 50 amps) for trailers or RVs up to 40 feet. Picnic tables are provided. Restrooms with showers, coin laundry, cable TV, Wi-Fi, playground, horseshoes, athletic field, tetherball, clubhouse, and propane are available. Some facilities are wheelchair-accessible. Leashed pets are permitted.

**Reservations, fees:** Reservations are recommended. RV sites are $44-54 per night, plus

$4 per person (over age 17) per night for more than two people and $2 per night for each additional vehicle. Weekly and monthly rates are available. Some credit cards are accepted. Open year-round.

**Directions:** From eastbound I-80 in Truckee, take Exit 188A to Donner Pass Road. Turn north on Donner Pass Road and drive one block to Pioneer Trail. Turn left and drive a short distance to the park at 10100 Pioneer Trail on the left side of the road.

From westbound I-80 in Truckee, take Exit 188 to Highway 89. Turn right on Highway 89 and drive north one block to Donner Pass Road. Turn left and drive one block to Pioneer Trail. Turn right and continue to the park.

**Contact:** Coachland RV Park, 530/587-3071, www.coachlandrvpark.com.

## 82 NORTH FORK

### Scenic rating: 7

on the North Fork of the American River in Tahoe National Forest

**Map 6.1, page 333**

This is gold-mining country, and this camp is along the Little North Fork of the North Fork American River at 4,400 feet in elevation, where you might still find a few magic gold flecks. Unfortunately, they will probably be fool's gold, not the real stuff. This feeder stream is small and pretty, and the camp is fairly remote and overlooked by most. It is on the edge of a network of backcountry Forest Service roads. To explore them, a map of Tahoe National Forest is a must.

**Campsites, facilities:** There are 15 sites for tents or RVs up to 16 feet (no hookups) and two sites for tents only. Picnic tables and fire grills are provided. Drinking water and vault toilets are available. Supplies are available at Emigrant Gap, Cisco Grove, and Soda Springs. Leashed pets are permitted.

**Reservations, fees:** Reservations are accepted at 877/444-6777 ($10 reservation fee) or www.

recreation.gov ($9 reservation fee). Sites are $24 per night, plus $5 per night for each additional vehicle. Open June through October, weather permitting.

**Directions:** From Sacramento, drive east on I-80 to the Emigrant Gap exit. Take that exit and drive south a short distance to Texas Hill Road/Forest Road 19. Turn right and drive about seven miles to the camp on the right.

**Contact:** Tahoe National Forest, Yuba River Ranger District, South, 530/265-4531, www.fs.usda.gov/tahoe.

## 83 TUNNEL MILLS GROUP CAMP

### Scenic rating: 7

on the North Fork of the American River in Tahoe National Forest

**Map 6.1, page 333**

This is a good spot for a Boy or Girl Scout camp-out. It's a rustic, quiet group camp set all by itself along the (take a deep breath) East Fork of the North Fork of the North Fork of the American River (whew). (See the North Fork listing in this chapter for more recreation information.) The elevation is 4,400 feet.

**Campsites, facilities:** Two group sites can accommodate up to 30 people each: One site is for tents only and the other is for tents or RVs up to 40 feet (no hookups). Picnic tables and fire grills are provided. Vault toilets are available. No drinking water is available. Supplies are available at the Nyack exit near Emigrant Gap. Leashed pets are permitted.

**Reservations, fees:** Reservations are required at 877/444-6777 ($10 reservation fee) or www.recreation.gov ($9 reservation fee). The camp is $99 per night. Open June through September, weather permitting.

**Directions:** From Sacramento, drive east on I-80 to the Emigrant Gap exit. Drive south for a short distance to Texas Hill Road/Forest Road 19. Turn right and drive about nine miles to the campground on the right side of the road.

**Contact:** Tahoe National Forest, Yuba River Ranger District, South, 530/265-4531, www.fs.usda.gov/tahoe.

## 84 ORCHARD SPRINGS RESORT

🏊 🛶 ⛵ 🐕 ♿ 🚐 ⛺

**Scenic rating: 7**

on Rollins Lake

**Map 6.1, page 333**

Orchard Springs Resort is on the shore of Rollins Lake among pine, oak, and cedar trees in the Sierra Nevada foothills. The summer heat makes the lake excellent for waterskiing, boating, and swimming. Spring and fall are great for trout and bass fishing.

**Campsites, facilities:** There are 70 tent sites and 13 sites with full hookups (30 amps) for tents or RVs up to 40 feet. Two sites are pull-through. Four camping cabins are also available. Picnic tables, fire rings, and some barbecues are provided. Drinking water, restrooms with flush toilets and showers, launch ramp, boat rentals, slips, bait and tackle, swimming beach, group picnic area, and a convenience store are available. Some facilities are wheelchair-accessible. Leashed pets are permitted.

**Reservations, fees:** Reservations are accepted. RV sites (hookups) are $39 per night, water-view tent sites are $29-33 per night, plus $10 per night for each additional vehicle unless towed, $6.50 per boat per night, $3 per pet per night, and $25 daily boat slip rental. Camping cabins are $59 per night. Some credit cards are accepted. Open year-round.

**Directions:** From Auburn, drive northeast on I-80 for about 20 miles to the Colfax/Grass Valley exit. Take that exit and loop back over the freeway to the stop sign. Turn right and drive a short distance to Highway 174. Turn right and drive north on Highway 174 (a winding, two-lane road) for 3.7 miles (bear left at Giovanni's Restaurant) to Orchard Springs Road. Turn right on Orchard Springs Road and drive 0.5 mile to the road's end. Turn right at the gatehouse and continue to the campground.
**Contact:** Orchard Springs Resort, 530/346-2212, www.osresort.net.

## 85 PENINSULA CAMPING AND BOATING RESORT

🏊 🛶 ⛵ 🐕 🚐 ⛺

**Scenic rating: 8**

on Rollins Lake

**Map 6.1, page 333**

Peninsula Campground sits on a point that extends into Rollins Lake, flanked on each side by two sprawling lake arms. The resort has 280 acres and 1.5 miles of lake frontage. A bonus is that you can boat directly from some of the lakefront sites. If you like boating, waterskiing, or swimming, you'll definitely like this place in the summer. All water sports are allowed. Fishing is available for rainbow and brown trout, small- and largemouth bass, perch, crappie, and catfish. This is a family-oriented campground with lots of youngsters on summer vacation. In summer, the lake is crowded and water sports dominate.

**Campsites, facilities:** There are 70 sites for tents or RVs up to 40 feet (no hookups) and two group sites for 24-40 people. Three cabins are also available. Picnic tables and fire pits are provided. Restrooms with flush toilets and showers, drinking water, Wi-Fi, dump station, boat rentals (fishing boats, patio boats, canoes, and kayaks), boat ramp, fish-cleaning station, swimming beach, horseshoes, volleyball, and a convenience store are available. Marine gas is available on the lake. Leashed pets are permitted, but call for current status.

**Reservations, fees:** Reservations are accepted by phone or online ($5-20 fee). Single sites are $32.50-36.50 per night, double sites are $65-80 per night, plus $10 per night for each additional vehicle and $6 per pet per night; the group sites are $125-175 per night, and cabins are $55 per night. Maximum 14-day stay. Some credit cards are accepted. Open mid-April through September.

**Directions:** From Auburn, drive northeast on I-80 for about 20 miles to the Colfax/Grass Valley exit. Take that exit and loop back over the freeway to the stop sign. Turn right and drive a short distance to Highway 174. Turn right and drive north on Highway 174 (a winding, two-lane road) for eight miles to You Bet Road. Turn right, drive 4.3 miles (turning right again to stay on You Bet Road), and continue another 3.1 miles to the campground entrance at the end of the road.

**Contact:** Peninsula Camping and Boating Resort, 530/477-9413 or 866/469-2267), www.penresort.com.

# 86 GIANT GAP

### Scenic rating: 7

on Sugar Pine Reservoir in Tahoe National Forest

#### Map 6.1, page 333

This is a lakeside spot along the western shore of Sugar Pine Reservoir at 4,000 feet elevation in Tahoe National Forest. There is a ramp on the south shore for boaters. A 10-mph speed limit is the law, making this lake ideal for anglers in search of quiet water. Other recreation notes: There's a little less than a mile of paved trail, which goes through the day-use area. Big Reservoir (also known as Morning Star Lake), five miles to the east, is the only other lake in the region and also has a campground. The trout and bass fishing at Sugar Pine is fair—not usually great, not usually bad. Swimming is allowed; kayaking and canoeing are also popular.

**Campsites, facilities:** There are 20 sites for tents or RVs of any length (no hookups) and five sites for tents only. Picnic tables and fire grills are provided. Drinking water and vault toilets are available. Some facilities are wheelchair-accessible. A dump station and boat ramp are on the south shore. Supplies can be obtained in Foresthill. Leashed pets are permitted.

**Reservations, fees:** Reservations are accepted at 877/444-6777 ($10 reservation fee) or www.recreation.gov ($9 reservation fee). Single sites are $24 per night, double sites are $48 per night, plus $5 per night for additional vehicle. Open May to mid-October, weather permitting.

**Directions:** From Sacramento, drive east on I-80 to the north end of Auburn and the Foresthill Road exit. Take that exit and drive east for 20 miles to Foresthill. Drive through Foresthill (road changes to Foresthill Divide Road) and continue for eight miles to Sugar Pine Road. Turn left and drive five miles to a fork. Turn right and drive one mile to the campground.

**Contact:** Tahoe National Forest, American River Ranger District, Foresthill Ranger Station, 530/367-2224, www.fs.usda.gov/tahoe.

# 87 SHIRTTAIL CREEK

### Scenic rating: 7

on Sugar Pine Reservoir in Tahoe National Forest

#### Map 6.1, page 333

This camp is near the little creek that feeds into the north end of Sugar Pine Reservoir. The boat ramp is all the way around the south side of the lake, near Forbes Creek Group Camp. (For recreation information, see the Giant Gap listing in this chapter.)

**Campsites, facilities:** There are 30 sites for tents or RVs of any length (no hookups; double and triple sites are available). Picnic tables and fire grills are provided. Drinking water and vault toilets are available. Some facilities are wheelchair-accessible. A dump station and boat ramp are on the south shore. Supplies can be obtained in Foresthill. Leashed pets are permitted.

**Reservations, fees:** Reservations are accepted at 877/444-6777 ($10 reservation fee) or www.recreation.gov ($9 reservation fee). Single sites are $24 per night, double sites are $48 per night, and triple sites are $72 per night. Open May through mid-October, weather permitting.

**Directions:** From Sacramento, drive east on I-80 to the north end of Auburn and the Foresthill Road exit. Take that exit and drive east for 20 miles to Foresthill. Drive through Foresthill (road changes to Foresthill Divide Road) and continue for eight miles to Sugar Pine Road. Turn left and drive five miles to the campground access road. Turn right (signed) and drive to the campground.

**Contact:** Tahoe National Forest, American River Ranger District, Foresthill Ranger Station, 530/367-2224, www.fs.usda.gov/tahoe.

## 88 BIG RESERVOIR/ MORNING STAR LAKE

### Scenic rating: 7
on Big Reservoir in Tahoe National Forest

**Map 6.1, page 333**

Here's a quiet lake where no boat motors are allowed. That makes it ideal for canoeists, rowboaters, and tube floaters who don't like the idea of having to dodge water-skiers. The lake is stocked with rainbow trout; fishing permits are required and can be obtained at the campground. Big Reservoir (also known as Morning Star Lake) is quite pretty with a nice beach and some lakefront campsites. Elevation is 4,000 feet.

**Campsites, facilities:** There are 106 sites for tents or RVs up to 40 feet (no hookups) and two group sites for 40-60 people. Picnic tables and fire grills are provided. Drinking water, vault toilets, showers, dump station, and firewood (fee) are available. Some facilities are wheelchair-accessible. Leashed pets are permitted.

**Reservations, fees:** Reservations are accepted at 530/367-2129. Single sites are $25-35 per night, plus $6 per night per extra vehicle, and the group sites are $100-180 per night. Fishing fees are $12 for campers and $25 per day for day-use. Open Memorial Day through September, weather permitting.

**Directions:** From Sacramento, drive east on I-80 to Auburn and the Foresthill Road exit. Take that exit and drive east for 26 miles. Turn left at Sugar Pine Recreation Area and drive 3.5 miles to a junction in the road. Keep right onto Forest Road 24 (signed Big Reservoir). Drive 2.5 miles to the campground entrance road on the right.

**Contact:** Tahoe National Forest, American River Ranger District, Foresthill Ranger Station, 530/367-2224, www.fs.usda.gov/tahoe; concessionaire: DeAnza Placer Gold Mining Company, 530/367-2129.

## 89 FORBES CREEK GROUP CAMP

### Scenic rating: 7
on Sugar Pine Reservoir in Tahoe National Forest

**Map 6.1, page 333**

The boat launch is nearby, but note: A 10-mph speed limit is the law. That makes for quiet water, perfect for anglers, canoeists, and other small boats. A paved trail circles the 160-acre lake. (For more information see the Giant Gap listing in this chapter.)

**Campsites, facilities:** There are two group campsites, Madrone and Rocky Ridge, for tents or RVs up to 45 feet (no hookups) that can accommodate up to 50 people each. Picnic tables and fire grills are provided. Drinking water and vault toilets are available. Some facilities are wheelchair-accessible. A campfire circle, central parking area, dump station, and a boat ramp are available nearby. Supplies can be obtained in Foresthill. Leashed pets are permitted.

**Reservations, fees:** Reservations are accepted at 877/444-6777 ($10 reservation fee) or www.recreation.gov ($9 reservation fee). Sites are $132 per night. Open May through mid-October, weather permitting.

**Directions:** From Sacramento, drive east on I-80 to the north end of Auburn and the

Foresthill Road exit. Take that exit and drive east for 20 miles to Foresthill. Drive through Foresthill (road changes to Foresthill Divide Road) and continue for eight miles to Sugar Pine Road/Forest Road 10. Turn left and drive five miles to the fork in the road (still Sugar Pine Road/Forest Road 10). Bear left and drive approximately 4.5 miles to the boat ramp (still Sugar Pine Road/Forest Road 10). Turn right, head up the hill, and drive approximately seven miles to the camp.

**Contact:** Tahoe National Forest, American River Ranger District, Foresthill Ranger Station, 530/367-2224, www.fs.usda.gov/tahoe.

## 90 BEAR RIVER CAMPGROUND

**Scenic rating: 7**

near Colfax on Bear River

**Map 6.1, page 333**

This RV park is set in the Sierra foothills at 1,800 feet, near Bear River, and features riverfront campsites. The park covers 200 acres, offers five miles of hiking trails, and is right on the Placer and Nevada County lines. It fills up on weekends and is popular with both locals and out-of-towners. In the spring, when everything is green, it can be a gorgeous landscape. Fishing is OK for rainbow and brown trout, smallmouth bass, and bluegill. Noncommercial gold panning is permitted, and some rafting is popular on the river. A 14-day maximum stay is enforced. No amplified music is allowed at any time—yes!

**Campsites, facilities:** There are 23 sites for tents or small RVs up to 30 feet (no hookups) and two group sites for tents or RVs up to 35 feet for 50-100 people. Picnic tables and fire rings are provided. Vault toilets are available. There is no drinking water. Supplies are available within five miles in Colfax or Bowman. Leashed pets are permitted.

**Reservations, fees:** Reservations are accepted for the group sites at 530/886-4901 ($5 reservation fee). Sites are $10 per night, plus $2 per night for each additional vehicle and $1 per pet per night; the group sites are $40-75 per night. A certificate of insurance and a security deposit are required for group sites. Open April through October, weather permitting.

**Directions:** From Sacramento, drive east on I-80 east of Auburn to West Weimar Crossroads exit. Take that exit onto Weimar Cross Road and drive north for 1.5 miles to Placer Hills Road. Turn right and drive 2.5 miles to Plum Tree Road. Turn left and drive one mile to the campground on the left. The access road is steep and narrow.

**Contact:** Bear River Campground, Placer County Facilities Services, 530/886-4901, www.placer.ca.gov.

## 91 ROBINSONS FLAT

**Scenic rating: 5**

near French Meadows Reservoir in Tahoe National Forest

**Map 6.1, page 333**

This camp is set at 6,800 feet elevation in remote Tahoe National Forest, on the eastern flank of Duncan Peak (7,116 feet), with a two-mile drive south to Duncan Peak Lookout (7,182 feet). A trail out of camp follows along a small stream, a fork to Duncan Creek, in Little Robinsons Valley. French Meadows Reservoir is 15 miles southeast. An equestrian camp with seven sites is also available.

**Campsites, facilities:** There are seven sites for tents or RVs up to 25 feet, plus an equestrian camp with seven sites for tents or RVs up to 45 feet (no hookups). Picnic tables and fire grills are provided. Drinking water (from a hand pump in the equestrian section) and vault toilets are available. Garbage must be packed out. Supplies are available in Foresthill. Some facilities are wheelchair-accessible. Leashed pets are permitted.

**Reservations, fees:** Reservations are not

accepted. There is no fee for camping. Open mid-May through October, weather permitting.

**Directions:** From Sacramento, drive east on I-80 to the north end of Auburn and the Foresthill Road exit. Take that exit and drive east to Foresthill (the road name changes to Foresthill Divide Road) and continue northeast (the road is narrow and curvy) for 27 miles to the junction with County Road 43. The campground is at the junction.

**Contact:** Tahoe National Forest, American River Ranger District, Foresthill Ranger Station, 530/367-2224, www.fs.usda.gov/tahoe.

## 92 POPPY HIKE-IN/BOAT-IN

Scenic rating: 10

on French Meadows Reservoir in Tahoe National Forest

**Map 6.1, page 333**

This camp is on the north side of French Meadows Reservoir, about midway along the lake's shore. It can be reached only by boat or on foot, supplying a great degree of privacy compared to the other camps on this lake. A trail along the north shore of the reservoir runs right through the camp, providing two different trailhead access points, as well as a good side-trip hike. The lake is quite big, covering nearly 2,000 acres when full, at 5,300 feet elevation on a dammed-up section of the Middle Fork American River. It is stocked with rainbow trout but also has prime habitat for brown trout, and big ones are sometimes caught by surprise.

**Campsites, facilities:** There are 12 tent sites, accessible by boat or by a mile-long foot trail from McGuire boat ramp. Picnic tables and fire grills are provided. Vault toilets are available. No drinking water is available. Garbage must be packed out. Supplies are available in Foresthill. Leashed pets are permitted.

**Reservations, fees:** Reservations are not accepted. Sites are $18 per night. Open May through October, weather permitting.

**Directions:** From Sacramento, drive east on I-80 to the north end of Auburn and the Foresthill Road exit. Take that exit and drive east to Foresthill and Mosquito Ridge Road (Forest Road 96). Turn right (east) and drive 40 miles (curvy) to French Meadows Reservoir Dam and to a junction. Turn left (still Mosquito Ridge Road) and continue for three miles to the lake and campground.

**Contact:** Tahoe National Forest, American River Ranger District, Foresthill Ranger Station, 530/367-2224, www.fs.usda.gov/tahoe.

## 93 LEWIS AT FRENCH MEADOWS

Scenic rating: 7

on French Meadows Reservoir in Tahoe National Forest

**Map 6.1, page 333**

This camp is not right at lakeside but is just across the road from French Meadows Reservoir. It is still quite pretty, set along a feeder creek near the lake's northwest shore. A boat ramp is available only a half mile to the south, and the adjacent McGuire boat ramp area has a trailhead that is routed along the lake's northern shoreline. This lake is big (2,000 acres) and pretty, created by a dam on the Middle Fork American River, with good fishing for rainbow trout.

**Campsites, facilities:** There are 40 sites for tents or RVs up to 45 feet (no hookups). Picnic tables and fire grills are provided. Drinking water, bear boxes, and flush and vault toilets are available. A concrete boat ramp is one mile away. Supplies are available in Foresthill. Some facilities are wheelchair-accessible. Leashed pets are permitted.

**Reservations, fees:** Reservations are accepted at 877/444-6777 ($10 reservation fee) or www.recreation.gov ($9 reservation fee). Sites are $20 per night, plus $5 per night per additional vehicle. Open mid-May through early September.

**Directions:** From Sacramento, drive east

on I-80 to the north end of Auburn and the Foresthill Road exit. Take that exit and drive east to Foresthill and Mosquito Ridge Road (Forest Road 96). Turn right (east) and drive 40 miles (curvy) to Anderson Dam and to a junction. Turn left (still Mosquito Ridge Road) and then continue along the southern shoreline of French Meadows Reservoir for five miles to a fork at the head of the lake. Bear left at the fork and drive 0.5 mile to the camp on the right side of the road.

**Contact:** Tahoe National Forest, American River Ranger District, Foresthill Ranger Station, 530/367-2224, www.fs.usda.gov/tahoe.

## 94 AHART

**Scenic rating: 7**

near French Meadows Reservoir in Tahoe National Forest

**Map 6.1, page 333**

This camp is a mile north of French Meadows Reservoir near where the Middle Fork of the American River enters the lake. It is on the Middle Fork and is primarily used for campers who would rather camp near this river than French Meadows Reservoir. Note: This is bear country in the summer.

**Campsites, facilities:** There are 12 sites for tents or RVs up to 40 feet (no hookups). Picnic tables and fire grills are provided. Vault toilets are available. No drinking water is available. Supplies are available in Foresthill. Leashed pets are permitted.

**Reservations, fees:** Reservations are not accepted. Sites are $20 per night, plus $5 per night per additional vehicle. Open late May through October, weather permitting.

**Directions:** From Sacramento, drive east on I-80 to the north end of Auburn and the Foresthill Road exit. Take that exit and drive east to Foresthill and Mosquito Ridge Road (Forest Road 96). Turn right (east) and drive 40 miles (curvy) to Anderson Dam and to a junction. Turn left (still Mosquito Ridge Road) and

then continue along the southern shoreline of French Meadows Reservoir for seven miles.

**Contact:** Tahoe National Forest, American River Ranger District, Foresthill Ranger Station, 530/367-2224, www.fs.usda.gov/tahoe.

## 95 GATES GROUP CAMP

**Scenic rating: 7**

on the North Fork of the American River in Tahoe National Forest

**Map 6.1, page 333**

This group camp is well secluded along the North Fork American River, just upstream from where it pours into French Meadows Reservoir. (For recreation options, see the French Meadows, Lewis at French Meadows, and Coyote Group Camp listings in this chapter.)

**Campsites, facilities:** There are two group sites for tents or RVs of any length (no hookups) that can accommodate up to 25 people or 75 people. Picnic tables and fire grills are provided. Drinking water, vault toilets, central parking, and a campfire circle are available. Obtain supplies in Foresthill. Leashed pets are permitted.

**Reservations, fees:** Reservations are required at 877/444-6777 ($10 reservation fee) or www.recreation.gov ($9 reservation fee). Sites are $82-165 per night. Open mid-May through October, weather permitting.

**Directions:** From Sacramento, drive east on I-80 to the north end of Auburn and the Foresthill Road exit. Take that exit and drive east to Foresthill and Mosquito Ridge Road (Forest Road 96). Turn right (east) and drive 40 miles (curvy) to Anderson Dam and to a junction. Turn left (still Mosquito Ridge Road) and continue along the southern shoreline of French Meadows Reservoir for five miles to a fork at the head of the lake. Bear left at the fork (Forest Road 68) and drive a mile to the camp at the end of the road.

**Contact:** Tahoe National Forest, American

River Ranger District, Foresthill Ranger Station, 530/367-2224, www.fs.usda.gov/tahoe.

## 96 TALBOT

🏃 🏊 🛶 🏕 ♿ ⛺

### Scenic rating: 7

on the Middle Fork of the American River in Tahoe National Forest

**Map 6.1, page 333**

Talbot camp is at 5,600 feet elevation along the Middle Fork of the American River, primarily used as a trailhead camp for backpackers heading into the Granite Chief Wilderness. The trail is routed along the Middle Fork American River, turning south into Picayune Valley, flanked by Needle Peak (8,971 feet), Granite Chief (9,886 feet), and Squaw Peak to the east, then beyond to connect with the Pacific Crest Trail. The nearby trailhead has stock trailer parking. Hitching rails are available at the trailhead.

**Campsites, facilities:** There are five tent sites. Picnic tables and fire grills are provided. Vault toilets are available. No drinking water is available; river water must be purified before drinking. Garbage must be packed out. Supplies are available in Foresthill. The camp is within a state game refuge and no firearms are permitted. Some facilities are wheelchair-accessible. Leashed pets are permitted.

**Reservations, fees:** Reservations are not accepted. There is no fee for camping. Open June through October, weather permitting.

**Directions:** From Sacramento, drive east on I-80 to the north end of Auburn and the Foresthill Road exit. Take that exit and drive east to Foresthill and Mosquito Ridge Road (Forest Road 96). Turn right (east) and drive 40 miles (curvy) to Anderson Dam and to a junction. Turn left (still Mosquito Ridge Road) and then continue along the southern shoreline of French Meadows Reservoir for four miles (road turns into dirt) and continue four more miles to the campground.

**Contact:** Tahoe National Forest, American

River Ranger District, Foresthill Ranger Station, 530/367-2224, www.fs.usda.gov/tahoe.

## 97 COYOTE GROUP CAMP

🏃 🏊 🛶 🚤 🏕 ♿ 🚙 ⛺

### Scenic rating: 6

on French Meadows Reservoir in Tahoe National Forest

**Map 6.1, page 333**

This group camp is right at the head of French Meadows Reservoir, at 5,300 feet elevation. A boat ramp is two miles to the south, just past Lewis on the lake's north shore. (For recreation options, see the Poppy Hike-In/Boat-In and French Meadows listings in this chapter.)

**Campsites, facilities:** There are four group sites for tents or RVs of any length (no hookups): Three can accommodate up to 25 people and one can accommodate up to 50 people. Picnic tables and fire grills are provided. Drinking water and vault toilets are available. A campfire circle and central parking area are also available. Supplies are available in Foresthill. Black Bear is the largest camp and has wheelchair-accessible facilities. Leashed pets are permitted.

**Reservations, fees:** Reservations are required at 877/444-6777 ($10 reservation fee) or www.recreation.gov ($9 reservation fee). Sites are $82-143 per night. Open mid-May through October.

**Directions:** From Sacramento, drive east on I-80 to the north end of Auburn and the Foresthill Road exit. Take that exit and drive east to Foresthill and Mosquito Ridge Road (Forest Road 96). Turn right (east) and drive 40 miles (curvy) to Anderson Dam and to a junction. Turn left (still Mosquito Ridge Road) and then continue along the southern shoreline of French Meadows Reservoir for five miles to a fork at the head of the lake. Bear left at the fork and drive 0.5 mile to the camp on the left side of the road.

**Contact:** Tahoe National Forest, American

River Ranger District, Foresthill Ranger Station, 530/367-2224, www.fs.usda.gov/tahoe.

## 98 FRENCH MEADOWS

### Scenic rating: 7

on French Meadows Reservoir in Tahoe National Forest

**Map 6.1, page 333**

The nearby boat launch makes this the choice for boating campers. The camp is on French Meadows Reservoir at 5,300 feet elevation. It is on the lake's southern shore, with the boat ramp about a mile to the south (you'll see the entrance road on the way in). This is a big lake set in remote Tahoe National Forest in the North Fork American River Canyon with good trout fishing. All water sports are allowed. The lake level often drops in late summer, and then a lot of stumps and boulders start poking through the lake surface. This creates navigational hazards for boaters and water-skiers, but it also makes it easier for the anglers to know where to find the fish. If the fish don't bite, boaters should make the nearby side trip to pretty Hell Hole Reservoir to the south.

**Campsites, facilities:** There are 75 sites for tents or RVs up to 45 feet (no hookups). Picnic tables and fire grills are provided. Vault toilets are available. Potable water is not always available; check with the ranger station. Some facilities are wheelchair-accessible. A concrete boat ramp is nearby. Supplies are available in Foresthill. Leashed pets are permitted.

**Reservations, fees:** Reservations are accepted at 877/444-6777 ($10 reservation fee) or www.recreation.gov ($9 reservation fee). Sites are $24 per night, plus $5 per night for each additional vehicle. Open late May through October, weather permitting.

**Directions:** From Sacramento, drive east on I-80 to the north end of Auburn and the Foresthill Road exit. Take that exit and drive east to Foresthill and Mosquito Ridge Road (Forest Road 96). Turn right (east) and drive 40 miles (curvy) to Anderson Dam and to a junction. Turn left (still Mosquito Ridge Road) and then continue along the southern shoreline of French Meadows Reservoir for four miles to the campground.

**Contact:** Tahoe National Forest, American River Ranger District, Foresthill Ranger Station, 530/367-2224, www.fs.usda.gov/tahoe.

## 99 BIG MEADOWS

### Scenic rating: 7

near Hell Hole Reservoir in Eldorado National Forest

**Map 6.1, page 333**

Note: This campground sustained damage from a wildfire and was closed for repairs at time of publication. Contact the ranger station for current conditions.

This camp sits on a meadow near the ridge above Hell Hole Reservoir, which is about two miles away. (For more information, see the Hell Hole listing in this chapter.)

**Campsites, facilities:** There are 54 sites available, including six tent sites and 45 sites for tents or RVs up to 50 feet (no hookups). Picnic tables are provided. Drinking water and flush and vault toilets are available. A boat ramp is nearby. Some facilities are wheelchair-accessible. Leashed pets are permitted.

**Reservations, fees:** Reservations are not accepted. Single sites are $10 per night, double sites are $20, plus $5 per night for each additional vehicle. Open late May through early November, weather permitting.

**Directions:** From Sacramento, drive east on I-80 to the north end of Auburn. Take the Elm Avenue exit and turn left at the first stoplight onto Elm Avenue. Drive 0.1 mile, turn left on High Street, and continue through the signal where High Street merges with Highway 49. Continue on Highway 49 for about 3.5 miles, turn right over the bridge, and drive about 2.5 miles into the town of Cool. Turn left on Georgetown Road/Highway 193 and drive about 14 miles into Georgetown. At the four-way stop turn left on Main Street (which becomes Wentworth Springs/Forest Road 1) and drive about 25 miles. Turn left on Forest Road 2 and drive 21 miles to the campground on the left.

**Contact:** Eldorado National Forest, Georgetown Ranger District, 530/333-4312, www.fs.usda.gov/eldorado.

## 100 MIDDLE MEADOWS GROUP CAMP

### Scenic rating: 7

on Long Canyon Creek in Eldorado National Forest

**Map 6.1, page 333**

This group camp is within range of several adventures. To the nearby east is Hell Hole Reservoir (you'll need a boat to do it right), and to the nearby north is French Meadows Reservoir (you'll drive past the dam on the way in). Unfortunately, there isn't a heck of a lot to do at this camp other than watch the water flow by on adjacent Long Canyon Creek.

**Campsites, facilities:** There are two walk-in group sites for tents only that can accommodate up to 25 people and 50 people. RVs up to 16 feet can park in the spaces adjacent to the sites. Picnic tables and fire grills are provided. Vault toilets are available. The drinking water system is under repair. Supplies can be obtained in Foresthill. Some facilities are wheelchair-accessible. Leashed pets are permitted.

**Reservations, fees:** Reservations are accepted at 877/444-6777 ($10 reservation fee) or www.recreation.gov ($9 reservation fee). The sites are $12.50-25 per night. Open mid-May through mid-September, weather permitting.

**Directions:** From Sacramento, drive east on I-80 to the north end of Auburn. Take the Elm Avenue exit and turn left at the first stoplight onto Elm Avenue. Drive 0.1 mile, turn left on High Street, and continue through the signal where High Street merges with Highway 49.

Travel on Highway 49 for about 3.5 miles, turn right over the bridge, and drive about 2.5 miles into the town of Cool. Turn left on Georgetown Road/Highway 193 and drive about 14 miles into Georgetown. At the four-way stop turn left on Main Street (which becomes Wentworth Springs/Forest Road 1) and drive about 25 miles. Turn left on Forest Road 2 and drive 19 miles to the campground on the right.

**Contact:** Eldorado National Forest, Georgetown Ranger District, 530/333-4312, www.fs.usda.gov/eldorado.

## 101 HELL HOLE

### Scenic rating: 8

near Hell Hole Reservoir in Eldorado National Forest

**Map 6.1, page 333**

Hell Hole is a mountain temple with sapphire-blue water. For the most part, there is limited bank access because of its granite-sculpted shore, and that's why there are no lakeside campsites. This is the closest drive-to camp at Hell Hole Reservoir, about a mile away with a boat launch nearby. All water sports are allowed. Be sure to bring a boat and then enjoy the scenery while you troll for kokanee salmon, brown trout, Mackinaw trout, and a sprinkling of rainbow trout. This is a unique fishery compared to the put-and-take rainbow trout at so many other lakes. The lake has 15 miles of shoreline, and the elevation is 4,700 feet; the camp elevation is 5,200 feet. Note that afternoon winds can make the water choppy.

**Campsites, facilities:** There are 10 sites for tents only. Picnic tables and fire rings are provided. Vault toilets are available. Supplies can be obtained in Georgetown. A boat launch is nearby at the reservoir. Leashed pets are permitted.

**Reservations, fees:** Reservations are not accepted. Sites are $10 per night. Open late May through early November, weather permitting.

**Directions:** From Sacramento, drive east on

I-80 to the north end of Auburn. Take the Elm Avenue exit and turn left at the first stoplight onto Elm Avenue. Drive 0.1 mile, turn left on High Street, and continue through the signal where High Street merges with Highway 49. Continue on Highway 49 for about 3.5 miles, turn right over the bridge, and drive about 2.5 miles into the town of Cool. Turn left on Georgetown Road/Highway 193 and drive about 14 miles into Georgetown. At the four-way stop turn left on Main Street (which becomes Wentworth Springs/Forest Road 1) and drive about 25 miles. Turn left on Forest Road 2 and drive about 22 miles to the campground on the left.

**Contact:** Eldorado National Forest, Georgetown Ranger District, 530/333-4312, www.fs.usda.gov/eldorado.

## 102 UPPER HELL HOLE WALK-IN/BOAT-IN

### Scenic rating: 10

on Hell Hole Reservoir in Eldorado National Forest

**Map 6.1, page 333**

When the lake is full, this is a beautiful spot, set on the southern shore at the upper end of Hell Hole Reservoir in remote national forest seen by relatively few people. Getting here requires a boat-in or three-mile walk on a trail routed along the southern edge of the lake overlooking Hell Hole. The trail's short rises and falls feel longer than five miles and can tire you out on a hot day—bring plenty of water. When the lake level is high, an access road on the opposite side of the lake leads to a put-in for kayaks and canoes that can shorten the trip. You'll arrive at this little trail camp, ready to explore onward the next day into the Granite Chief Wilderness or just do nothing except enjoy adjacent Buck Meadow, the lake's headwaters, and the paradise you have discovered. Note that bears frequent this area, so store your food properly and avoid scented products.

**Campsites, facilities:** There are 15 tent sites accessible by trail or boat only. Picnic tables and fire grills are provided. Pit toilets are available. There is no drinking water, so bring a water filter. Garbage must be packed out. A boat launch is at the reservoir and the camp can be reached by boat, but low water levels during August and September can make passage difficult or impossible; call for current status. Supplies can be obtained in Georgetown. Leashed pets are permitted.

**Reservations, fees:** Reservations are not accepted. There is no fee for camping. Campfire permits are required from the Forest Service. Open May to mid-September, weather permitting.

**Directions:** From Sacramento, drive east on I-80 to the north end of Auburn. Take the Elm Avenue exit and turn left at the first stoplight onto Elm Avenue. Drive 0.1 mile, turn left on High Street, and continue through the signal where High Street merges with Highway 49. Continue on Highway 49 for about 3.5 miles, turn right over the bridge, and drive about 2.5 miles into the town of Cool. Turn left on Georgetown Road/Highway 193 and drive about 14 miles into Georgetown. At the four-way stop turn left on Main Street (which becomes Wentworth Springs/Forest Road 1) and drive about 25 miles. Turn left on Forest Road 2 and drive about 23 miles (a mile past the Hell Hole Campground access road) to the parking area at the boat ramp. From the trailhead, hike three miles to the camp.

**Contact:** Eldorado National Forest, Georgetown Ranger District, 530/333-4312, www.fs.usda.gov/eldorado.

## 103 PONDEROSA COVE

### Scenic rating: 8

near Stumpy Meadows Lake in Eldorado National Forest

**Map 6.2, page 334**

Sitting at 4,400 feet, this group camp is true to

its name, featuring huge and fragrant ponderosa pines. The campground is east of the dam right across the road from Stumpy Meadows Lake.

**Campsites, facilities:** There is one group site for RVs up to 45 feet (no hookups) that can accommodate 75 people. Walk-in tent sites have parking along the spur. Picnic tables and fire grills are provided. Drinking water and vault toilets are available. A boat ramp and a dump station are nearby. Leashed pets are permitted.

**Reservations, fees:** Reservations are accepted at 877/444-6777 ($10 reservation fee) or www. recreation.gov ($9 reservation fee). The group site is $170 per night, and boat launch is $8 per day. Open mid-May through mid-September, weather permitting.

**Directions:** From Placerville, take Highway 49N for 0.5 mile and turn right on Highway 193 to Georgetown. Turn right onto Main Street and drive 14 miles to the campground, just north of the Stumpy Boat Ramp.

**Contact:** Eldorado National Forest, Georgetown Ranger District, 530/333-4312, www.fs.usda.gov/eldorado.

## 104 STUMPY MEADOWS

### Scenic rating: 9

on Stumpy Meadows Lake in Eldorado National Forest

**Map 6.2, page 334**

This is the camp of choice for visitors to Stumpy Meadows Lake. Visitors first notice the huge ponderosa pine trees, noted for their distinctive, mosaiclike bark. The lake is at 4,400 feet elevation in Eldorado National Forest and covers 320 acres with water that is cold and clear; this is one of the prettiest lakes you can reach on pavement in the region. The lake has both rainbow and brown trout, and in the fall provides good fishing for big browns (they move up into the head of the lake, near where Pilot Creek enters).

**Campsites, facilities:** There are 29 sites for tents or RVs up to 28 feet length (no hookups). Two sites are double units and 10 sites are for tents only. (If you are new to maneuvering RVs around huge trees, go for sites 3-16.) Picnic tables and fire grills are provided. Drinking water and vault toilets are available. A boat ramp and a dump station are nearby. Some facilities are wheelchair-accessible. Leashed pets are permitted.

**Reservations, fees:** Reservations are accepted at 877/444-6777 ($10 reservation fee) or www. recreation.gov ($9 reservation fee). Single sites are $24 per night, $48 per night for double sites, $7 per night for each additional vehicle, boat launch is $8 per day. Open May through mid-October, weather permitting.

**Directions:** From Sacramento on I-80, drive east to the north end of Auburn. Turn left on Elm Avenue and drive about 0.1 mile. Turn left on High Street and drive through the signal that marks the continuation of High Street as Highway 49. Drive 3.5 miles on Highway 49, turn right over the bridge, and drive 2.5 miles into the town of Cool. Turn left on Georgetown Road/Highway 193 and drive 14 miles into Georgetown. At the four-way stop, turn left on Main Street, which becomes Georgetown-Wentworth Springs Road/Forest Road 1. Drive about 18 miles to Stumpy Meadows Lake. Continue about a mile and turn right into Stumpy Meadows campground.

**Contact:** Eldorado National Forest, Georgetown Ranger District, 530/333-4312, www.fs.usda.gov/eldorado.

## 105 BLACK OAK GROUP CAMP

### Scenic rating: 8

near Stumpy Meadows Lake in Eldorado National Forest

**Map 6.2, page 334**

This group camp is directly adjacent to Stumpy Meadows Campground. (See the Stumpy Meadows listing in this chapter for more information.) The boat ramp for the lake is just south of the Mark Edson Dam, near the picnic area. The elevation is 4,400 feet.

**Campsites, facilities:** There are two group sites for tents only that can accommodate 10-50 people, a tent site for 10-25 people, and one group site for RVs of any length (no hookups) that can accommodate 75 people. Picnic tables and fire grills are provided. Drinking water and vault toilets are available. A boat ramp and a dump station are nearby. Leashed pets are permitted.

**Reservations, fees:** Reservations are accepted at 877/444-6777 ($10 reservation fee) or www.recreation.gov ($9 reservation fee). Tent sites are $50-85 per night, the group RV site is $100-110 per night, and boat launch is $7 per day. Open mid-May through mid-September, weather permitting.

**Directions:** From Sacramento on I-80, drive east to the north end of Auburn. Turn left on Elm Avenue and drive about 0.1 mile. Turn left on High Street and drive through the signal that marks the continuation of High Street as Highway 49. Drive 3.5 miles on Highway 49, turn right over the bridge, and drive 2.5 miles into the town of Cool. Turn left on Georgetown Road/Highway 193 and drive 14 miles into Georgetown. At the four-way stop, turn left on Main Street, which becomes Georgetown-Wentworth Springs Road/Forest Road 1. Drive about 18 miles to Stumpy Meadows Lake, and then continue for two miles to the north shore of the lake and the campground entrance road on the right.

**Contact:** Eldorado National Forest, Georgetown Ranger District, 530/333-4312, www.fs.usda.gov/eldorado.

## 106 GERLE CREEK

**Scenic rating: 7**

on Gerle Creek Reservoir in Eldorado National Forest

**Map 6.2, page 334**

This is a small, pretty, but limited spot along the northern shore of little Gerle Creek Reservoir at 5,231 feet elevation. This camp was renovated in 2012. The lake is ideal for canoes or other small boats because no motors are permitted and no boat ramp is available. That makes for quiet water. It is in Gerle Creek Canyon, which feeds into the South Fork Rubicon River. No trout plants are made at this lake, and fishing can be correspondingly poor. A wild brown trout population lives here, though. A network of Forest Service roads to the north can provide great exploring. A map of Eldorado National Forest is a must.

**Campsites, facilities:** There are 19 sites for tents and RVs up to 40 feet (no hookups) and 31 sites for tents only. Picnic tables and fire grills are provided. Drinking water and vault toilets are available. Wheelchair-accessible trails and fishing pier are available nearby. Leashed pets are permitted.

**Reservations, fees:** Reservations are accepted at 877/444-6777 ($10 reservation fee) or www. recreation.gov ($9 reservation fee). Sites are $28-50 per night, plus $7 per night for each additional vehicle. Open mid-May through mid-October, weather permitting.

**Directions:** From Placerville, drive east on U.S. 50 for 23 miles to Riverton and the junction with Ice House Road/Forest Road 3. Turn north and drive 27 miles (past Union Valley Reservoir) to a fork with Forest Road 30. Turn left, drive two miles, bear left on the campground entrance road, and drive a mile to the campground.

**Contact:** Eldorado National Forest, Pacific Ranger District, 530/644-2349, www.fs.usda. gov/eldorado.

## 107 SOUTH FORK GROUP CAMP

### Scenic rating: 8

on the South Fork of the Rubicon River in Eldorado National Forest

**Map 6.2, page 334**

This primitive national forest camp sits alongside the South Fork Rubicon River, just over a mile downstream from the outlet at Gerle Creek Reservoir. Trout fishing is fair and there are several side trips available. These include Loon Lake (eight miles to the northeast), Gerle Creek Reservoir (to the nearby north), and Union Valley Reservoir (to the nearby south). The elevation is 5,200 feet.

**Campsites, facilities:** The group camp is for tents only and can accommodate up to 125 people. Picnic tables and fire grills are provided. Vault toilets are available. No drinking water is available; stream water must be purified before drinking. Garbage must be packed out. Leashed pets are permitted.

**Reservations, fees:** Reservations are required at 877/444-6777 ($10 reservation fee) or www.recreation.gov ($9 reservation fee). The camp is $100 per night. Open late May through early September.

**Directions:** From Placerville, drive east on U.S. 50 for 23 miles to Riverton and the junction with Ice House Road/Forest Road 3. Turn north and drive about 23 miles to the junction with Forest Road 13N28 (3.5 miles past Union Valley Reservoir). Bear left on Forest Road 13N28 and drive two miles to the campground entrance on the right.

**Contact:** Eldorado National Forest, Pacific Ranger District, 530/644-2349, www.fs.usda.gov/eldorado.

## 108 AIRPORT FLAT

### Scenic rating: 6

near Loon Lake in Eldorado National Forest

**Map 6.2, page 334**

Loon Lake is a gorgeous mountain lake in the Crystal Basin. Airport Flat provides an overflow area when the camps at Loon Lake (see listing in this chapter) are full. Trout fishing is good, and Loon Lake, along with Ice House Reservoir, is a favorite spot whether for a weekend or a week. Smaller Gerle Creek Reservoir and Union Valley Reservoir are also in the area. The elevation is 5,300 feet.

**Campsites, facilities:** There are 16 sites for tents or RVs. Vault toilets, picnic tables, fire rings, and bear-proof boxes are provided. No drinking water is available. Garbage must be packed out. All sites are wheelchair-accessible. Leashed pets are allowed.

**Reservations, fees:** Reservations are not accepted. There is no fee for camping. Open Memorial Day weekend to mid-October.

**Directions:** From Placerville, drive east on U.S. 50 for 23 miles to Riverton and the junction with Ice House Road/Forest Road 3. Turn north and drive 27 miles (past Union Valley Reservoir) to a fork with Forest Road 30. Turn left toward Gerle Creek Reservoir and the campground is about three miles from the fork, on the right.

**Contact:** Eldorado National Forest, Pacific Ranger District, 530/644-2349, www.fs.usda.gov/eldorado; Crystal Basin, 530/293-3510.

## 109 LOON LAKE

### Scenic rating: 9

in Eldorado National Forest

**Map 6.2, page 334**

Loon Lake is near the Sierra crest at 6,400 feet, covering 600 acres with depths up to 130 feet. This is the lake's primary campground, and it is easy to see why, with a picnic area, beach (includes a small unit for changing clothes), and boat ramp adjacent to the camp. The lake provides good trout fishing, and the lake is stocked on a regular basis once the access road is clear of snow. Afternoon winds drive anglers off the lake but are cheered by sailboarders. An excellent trail leads along the lake's eastern shore to Pleasant Hike-In/Boat-In, where there's a trailhead for the Desolation Wilderness.

**Campsites, facilities:** There are 53 sites for tents or RVs up to 40 feet, nine equestrian sites, two group sites for 25 and 50 people respectively, and one group equestrian site for tents or RVs up to 40 feet that can accommodate up to 25 people (no hookups). A chalet with a kitchen and electric heat holds up to 20 people (it's 1.5 miles west of the campground). Picnic tables and fire grills are provided. Drinking water and vault toilets are available. Tie lines are available for horses. A boat ramp and swimming beach are nearby. A dump station is two miles away. Some facilities are wheelchair-accessible. Leashed pets are permitted.

**Reservations, fees:** Reservations are accepted at 877/444-6777 ($10 reservation fee) or www.recreation.gov ($9 reservation fee). Single sites are $28 per night, double sites are $56 per night, plus $7 per night for each additional vehicle; group sites are $130-160 per night, and the chalet is $100 per night. The campground is open June through mid-October, weather permitting; the chalet is open year-round.

**Directions:** From Placerville, drive east on U.S. 50 for 23 miles to Riverton and the junction with Ice House Road/Forest Road 3. Turn left and drive 34 miles to a fork at the foot of Loon Lake. Turn right and drive one mile to the Loon Lake Picnic Area or boat ramp.

**Contact:** Eldorado National Forest, Pacific Ranger District, 530/644-2349, www.fs.usda.gov/eldorado; American Land and Leisure, 530/293-0827.

## 110 WENTWORTH SPRINGS FOUR-WHEEL DRIVE

### Scenic rating: 7
near Loon Lake in Eldorado National Forest

**Map 6.2, page 334**

There is one reason people come here: to set up a base camp for an OHV adventure, whether they are the owners of four-wheel drives, all-terrain vehicles, or dirt bikes. These vehicles traverse a network of roads leading from the camp; these roads would flat-out destroy your average car. The camp is deep in Eldorado National Forest, at 6,200 feet elevation. While the north end of Loon Lake is a mile to the east, the road there is extremely rough (perfect, right?). The road is gated along the lake, preventing access to this camp for those who drive directly to Loon Lake.

**Campsites, facilities:** There are eight sites for tents only. Picnic tables and fire grills are provided. Vault toilets are available. No drinking water is available. Garbage must be packed out. Leashed pets are permitted.

**Reservations, fees:** Reservations are not accepted. There is no fee for camping. Open June through October, weather permitting.

**Directions:** From Placerville, drive east on U.S. 50 for 23 miles to Riverton and the junction with Ice House Road/Forest Road 3. Turn left and drive 30 miles to the junction with Forest Road 30. Bear left and drive 3.5 miles to Forest Road 33. Turn right and drive seven miles to the campground on the left side of the road. (The access road is suitable for four-wheel-drive vehicles and off-highway motorcycles only.)

**Contact:** Eldorado National Forest, Pacific Ranger District, 530/644-2349, www.fs.usda.gov/eldorado.

## 111 NORTHSHORE

### Scenic rating: 9

on Loon Lake in Eldorado National Forest

**Map 6.2, page 334**

The waterfront sites are in an extremely pretty setting on the northwestern shore of Loon Lake. There are few facilities, though, and no boat ramp; the boat ramp is near the Loon Lake campground and picnic area at the south end of the lake. (For more information, see the Loon Lake and Pleasant Hike-In/Boat-In listings.)

**Campsites, facilities:** There are 15 sites for tents or RVs up to 35 feet (no hookups). Picnic tables and fire grills are provided. Vault toilets are available. There is no drinking water. Some facilities are wheelchair-accessible. Leashed pets are permitted.

**Reservations, fees:** Reservations are not accepted. Sites are $10 per night, plus $5 per night for each additional vehicle. Open June through September, weather permitting.

**Directions:** From Placerville, drive east on U.S. 50 for 23 miles to Riverton and the junction with Ice House Road/Forest Road 3. Turn left and drive 34 miles to a fork at the foot of Loon Lake. Turn left and drive three miles to the campground.

**Contact:** Eldorado National Forest, Pacific Ranger District, 530/644-2349, www.fs.usda.gov/eldorado.

## 112 RED FIR GROUP CAMP

### Scenic rating: 6

on Loon Lake in Eldorado National Forest

**Map 6.2, page 334**

This is a pretty, wooded camp, ideal for medium-sized groups. It is across the road from the 600-acre lake, offering a secluded, quiet spot. Lake access is a short hike away. All water sports are allowed on Loon Lake. (See the Loon Lake and Northshore listings in this chapter for more information.) Elevation is 6,500 feet.

**Campsites, facilities:** This tent-only group site can accommodate up to 25 people. Drinking water, vault toilets, fire rings, and grills are available. Some facilities are wheelchair-accessible. Leashed pets are permitted.

**Reservations, fees:** Reservations are required at 877/444-6777 ($10 reservation fee) or www.recreation.gov ($9 reservation fee). The camp is $40 per night. Open mid-June through mid-October, weather permitting.

**Directions:** From Placerville, drive east on U.S. 50 for 23 miles to Riverton and the junction with Ice House Road/Forest Road 3. Turn left and drive 34 miles to a fork at the foot of Loon Lake. Turn left and drive three miles to the campground (just beyond the Loon Lake Northshore camp).

**Contact:** Eldorado National Forest, Pacific Ranger District, 530/644-2349, www.fs.usda.gov/eldorado.

## 113 PLEASANT HIKE-IN/BOAT-IN

### Scenic rating: 10

on Loon Lake in Eldorado National Forest

**Map 6.2, page 334**      **BEST**

This premium Sierra camp, hike-in or boat-in only, is on the remote northeast shore of Loon Lake at 6,378 feet elevation. In many ways this makes for a perfect short vacation. A trail is routed east from the camp for four miles past Buck Island Lake (6,436 feet) and Rockbound Lake (6,529 feet), just inside the northern border of the Desolation Wilderness. When the trail is clear of snow, this makes for a fantastic day hike; a wilderness permit is required if staying overnight inside the wilderness boundary.

**Campsites, facilities:** There are 10 boat-in or hike-in tent sites. Picnic tables and fire rings are provided. A free California Campfire permit, available at any Forest Service office, is required for campfires. No drinking water or toilets are available. Garbage must be packed out. The camp is accessible by boat or trail only. Leashed pets are permitted.

**Reservations, fees:** Reservations are not accepted. There is no fee for camping. Open mid-June to mid-October, weather permitting.

**Directions:** From Placerville, drive east on U.S. 50 for 23 miles to Riverton and the junction with Ice House Road/Forest Road 3. Turn left and drive 34 miles to a fork at the foot of Loon Lake. Turn right and drive a mile to the Loon Lake Picnic Area or boat ramp. Either hike or boat 2.5 miles to the campground on the northeast shore of the lake.

**Contact:** Eldorado National Forest, Pacific Ranger District, 530/644-2349, www.fs.usda. gov/eldorado; Crystal Basin, 530/293-3510.

## 114 WEST POINT

Scenic rating: 9

at Union Valley Reservoir in Eldorado National Forest

**Map 6.2, page 334**

West Point is a pretty, primitive campground on the northwest shore of little Union Valley Reservoir. This is a pretty spot in the Crystal Basin that sometimes gets overlooked in the shadow of Loon Lake and Ice House Reservoir. But the camping, low-speed boating, and trout fishing can be excellent. Some surprise giant Mackinaw trout and brown trout can provide a fish of a lifetime when the lake first opens in late spring. The elevation is 4,875 feet.

**Campsites, facilities:** There are eight sites for tents or RVs. Vault toilets and a boat launch are available. Fire rings are provided, but there are no grills or picnic tables. Drinking water is not available. Garbage must be packed out.

**Reservations, fees:** Reservations are not accepted. There is no fee for camping.

**Directions:** From Placerville, drive east on U.S. 50 for 23 miles to Riverton and the junction with Ice House Road/Forest Road 3. Turn north on Ice House Road and drive seven miles to Peavine Ridge Road. Turn left on Peavine

Ridge Road and drive east for three miles to Bryant Springs Road. Turn right on Bryant Springs Road and drive north five miles to just past West Point Boat Ramp on the right.

**Contact:** Eldorado National Forest, Pacific Ranger District, 530/644-2349, www.fs.usda. gov/eldorado; Crystal Basin, 530/293-3510.

## 115 WOLF CREEK AND WOLF CREEK GROUP

Scenic rating: 9

on Union Valley Reservoir in Eldorado National Forest

**Map 6.2, page 334**

Wolf Creek Camp is on the north shore of Union Valley Reservoir. Listen up. Notice that it's quieter? Yep. That's because there are not as many water-skiers in the vicinity. Why? The nearest boat ramp is three miles away. The view of the Crystal Range from the campground is drop-dead gorgeous. The elevation is 4,900 feet.

**Campsites, facilities:** There are 42 sites for tents or RVs up to 40 feet (no hookups). There are also three group sites for tents or RVs up to 40 feet that can accommodate 13, 25, and 50 people respectively and one group site for tents only that can accommodate 25 people. Picnic tables and fire grills are provided. Drinking water and vault toilets are available. Some facilities are wheelchair-accessible. A boat ramp is three miles away at the campground at Yellowjacket. Leashed pets are permitted (fee).

**Reservations, fees:** Reservations are accepted for individual sites and required for group sites at 877/444-6777 ($10 reservation fee) or www. recreation.gov ($9 reservation fee). Single sites are $28 per night, $56 per night for a double site, plus $7 per night for each additional vehicle. Group sites are $110-160 per night. Open mid-May through mid-September, weather permitting.

**Directions:** From Placerville, drive east on U.S. 50 for 23 miles to Riverton and the junction with Ice House Road/Forest Road 3. Turn left (north) and drive 19 miles to Forest Road 12N78/Union Valley Road (at the head of Union Valley Reservoir). Turn left (west) and drive two miles to the campground.

**Contact:** Eldorado National Forest, Pacific Ranger District, 530/644-2349, www.fs.usda. gov/eldorado.

## 116 CAMINO COVE

### Scenic rating: 10

on Union Valley Reservoir in Eldorado National Forest

**Map 6.2, page 334**          **BEST (**

Camino Cove Camp is the nicest spot at Union Valley Reservoir, a slam dunk. It is set at the north end of the lake on a peninsula, absolutely beautiful, a tree-covered landscape and yet with sweeping views of the Crystal Basin. Since the campground is free, however, it has become very popular with the 20-something crowd. When school is out, and especially on weekends, be prepared for a bit of noise. The nearest boat ramp is 1.5 miles to the west at West Point. If this camp is full, there is a small camp at West Point, with just eight sites. The elevation is 4,900 feet.

**Campsites, facilities:** There are 32 sites for tents or RVs up to 30 feet (no hookups). Fire rings are provided. Vault toilets are available. No drinking water is available. Garbage must be packed out. A swimming beach is nearby and a boat ramp is 1.5 miles away at the campground at West Point. Some facilities are wheelchair-accessible. Leashed pets are permitted.

**Reservations, fees:** Reservations are not accepted. There is no fee for camping. Open early May through October, weather permitting.

**Directions:** From Placerville, drive east on U.S. 50 for 23 miles to Riverton and the junction with Ice House Road/Forest Road 3. Turn north on Ice House Road and drive seven miles to Peavine Ridge Road. Turn left and drive three miles to Bryant Springs Road. Turn right and drive five miles north past the West Point

boat ramp, then continue 1.5 miles east to the campground entrance on the right.

**Contact:** Eldorado National Forest, Pacific Ranger District, 530/644-2349, www.fs.usda. gov/eldorado.

## 117 YELLOWJACKET

### Scenic rating: 8

on Union Valley Reservoir in Eldorado National Forest

**Map 6.2, page 334**

The camp is at 4,900 feet elevation on the north shore of gorgeous Union Valley Reservoir. A boat launch adjacent to the camp makes this an ideal destination for trout-angling campers with boats. Union Valley Reservoir, a popular weekend destination for campers from the Central Valley, is stocked with brook trout and rainbow trout by the Department of Fish and Game.

**Campsites, facilities:** There are 40 sites for tents or RVs up to 30 feet (no hookups). Picnic tables and fire rings are provided. Drinking water and flush and vault toilets are available. A boat ramp and dump station are nearby. Leashed pets are permitted for a fee.

**Reservations, fees:** Reservations are accepted at 877/444-6777 ($10 reservation fee) or www. recreation.gov ($9 reservation fee). Sites are $28 per night, plus $7 per night for each additional vehicle. Open mid-May through mid-September, weather permitting.

**Directions:** From Placerville, drive east on U.S. 50 for 23 miles to Riverton and the junction with Ice House Road/Forest Road 3. Turn left (north) and drive 19 miles to Forest Road 12N78/Union Valley Road (at the head of Union Valley Reservoir). Turn left (west) and drive one mile to Forest Road 12N33. Turn left (south) and drive 0.5 mile to the campground.

**Contact:** Eldorado National Forest, Pacific Ranger District, 530/644-2349, www.fs.usda. gov/eldorado; American Land and Leisure, 530/293-0827.

## 118 WENCH CREEK AND WENCH CREEK GROUP

**Scenic rating: 7**

on Union Valley Reservoir in Eldorado National Forest

Map 6.2, page 334

Wench Creek is on the northeast shore of Union Valley Reservoir. (For more information, see the Jones Fork and Peninsula Recreation Area listings in this chapter.) The elevation is 4,900 feet.

**Campsites, facilities:** There are 100 sites for tents or RVs up to 25 feet (no hookups) and two group tent sites for up to 50 people each. Picnic tables and fire grills are provided. Drinking water and vault toilets are available. A boat ramp is three miles away at the Yellowjacket campground. Leashed pets are permitted.

**Reservations, fees:** Reservations are not accepted for individual sites but are accepted for group sites at 877/444-6777 ($10 recreation fee) or www.recreation.gov ($9 reservation fee). Sites are $25 per night, plus $7 per night for each additional vehicle. The group sites are $160 per night. Open mid-May through September.

**Directions:** From Placerville, drive east on U.S. 50 for 23 miles to Riverton and the junction with Ice House Road/Forest Road 3. Turn left and drive 15 miles to the campground entrance road (four miles past the turnoff for Sunset Camp). Turn left and drive a mile to the campground at the end of the road.

**Contact:** Eldorado National Forest, Pacific Ranger District, 530/644-2349, www.fs.usda.gov/eldorado; American Land and Leisure, 530/293-0827.

## 119 BIG SILVER GROUP CAMP

**Scenic rating: 7**

on Big Silver Creek in Eldorado National Forest

Map 6.2, page 334

This camp was built along the Union Valley bike trail, less than a mile from Union Valley Reservoir. The paved bike trail stretches for miles both north and south of the campground and is wheelchair-accessible. It's a classic Sierra forest setting, with plenty of ponderosa pine on the north side of Big Silver Creek.

**Campsites, facilities:** There is one group site for tents or RVs up to 50 feet (no hookups) that can accommodate up to 50 people. Picnic tables and fire grills are provided. Vault toilets are available. No drinking water is available; stream water must be purified before drinking. There is also a group kitchen area with pedestal grills. Some facilities are wheelchair-accessible. Leashed pets are permitted.

**Reservations, fees:** Reservations are required at 877/444-6777 ($10 reservation fee) or www.recreation.gov ($9 reservation fee). The camp is $50 per night. Open late May through mid-October, weather permitting.

**Directions:** From Placerville, drive east on U.S. 50 for 23 miles to Riverton and the junction with Ice House Road/Forest Road 3. Turn left (north) and drive about 16 miles to the campground.

**Contact:** Eldorado National Forest, Pacific Ranger District, 530/644-2349, www.fs.usda.gov/eldorado.

## 120 AZALEA COVE HIKE-IN/BOAT-IN

**Scenic rating: 9**

on Union Valley Reservoir in Eldorado National Forest

Map 6.2, page 334    BEST (

Union Valley Reservoir, at 4,900 feet elevation,

has 4.5 miles of bike trail on its shores, in addition to boating and fishing activities. The distance to the campsite is less than a half mile by trail and approximately one mile by boat. (For additional information, see the Wench Creek and Peninsula Recreation Area listings in this chapter.)

**Campsites, facilities:** There are 10 sites for tents only. Picnic tables and fire rings are provided. Vault toilets are available. There is no drinking water. Garbage must be packed out. Some facilities are wheelchair-accessible. Leashed pets are permitted.

**Reservations, fees:** Reservations are not accepted. There is no fee for camping. Open mid-June through mid-October, weather permitting.

**Directions:** From Placerville, drive east on U.S. 50 for 23 miles to Riverton and the junction with Ice House Road/Forest Road 3. Turn left (north) and drive about 16 miles to the Big Silver Group Campground parking lot. Park and then hike or cycle approximately 0.5 mile to Azalea Cove Campground. To reach Azalea Cove Campground by boat, continue for three miles on Ice House Road to Forest Road 12N78. Turn left (west) and drive one mile to Forest Road 12N33. Turn left (south) and drive 0.5 mile to Yellowjacket Campground. Park and boat approximately one mile to Azalea Cove Campground.

**Contact:** Eldorado National Forest, Pacific Ranger District, 530/644-2349, www.fs.usda. gov/eldorado; Crystal Basin, 530/293-3510.

## 121 PENINSULA RECREATION AREA

🏊 🚣 🛶 🎣 🐕 ♿ 🚐 ⛺

### Scenic rating: 8

on Union Valley Reservoir in Eldorado National Forest

**Map 6.2, page 334**

The two campgrounds here, Sunset and Fashoda, are the prettiest of all the camps at Union Valley Reservoir, set at the eastern tip of the peninsula that juts into the lake at the mouth of Jones Fork. A nearby boat ramp (you'll see it on the left on the way in) is a big plus, along with a picnic area and beach. All water sports are allowed. The lake has decent trout fishing, with brook, brown, rainbow, and Mackinaw trout; kokanee salmon; and smallmouth bass. The place is gorgeous, set at 4,900 feet elevation in the Sierra Nevada. Note that sections of Sunset Camp are closed when bald eagles are nesting (usually early summer).

**Campsites, facilities:** There are 131 sites for tents or RVs up to 50 feet (no hookups) at Sunset Camp and 30 walk-in tent sites at Fashoda Camp. Picnic tables, fire rings, and fire grills are provided. Drinking water, coin showers (at Fashoda), vault toilets, boat ramp, and a dump station are available. Some facilities are wheelchair-accessible. Leashed pets are permitted for a fee.

**Reservations, fees:** Reservations are accepted at 877/444-6777 ($10 reservation fee) or www. recreation.gov ($9 reservation fee, look for Sunset-Union Valley or Fashoda). Single sites are $28 per night, double sites are $56 per night, plus $7 per night for each additional vehicle. Open late May through late September, weather permitting.

**Directions:** From Placerville, drive east on U.S. 50 for 23 miles to Riverton and the junction with Ice House Road/Forest Road 3. Turn left and drive 14 miles to the campground entrance road (a mile past the turnoff for Jones Fork Camp). Turn left and drive 1.5 miles to the campground at the end of the road.

**Contact:** Eldorado National Forest, Pacific Ranger District, 530/644-2349, www.fs.usda. gov/eldorado; American Land and Leisure, 530/293-0827.

## 122 JONES FORK

### Scenic rating: 7

on Union Valley Reservoir in Eldorado National Forest

**Map 6.2, page 334**

The Crystal Basin Recreation Area is the most popular backcountry region for campers from the Sacramento area, and Union Valley Reservoir is the centerpiece. The area gets its name from the prominent granite Sierra ridge, which looks like crystal when it is covered with frozen snow. This is a big lake, set at 4,900 feet elevation, with numerous lakeside campgrounds and three boat ramps providing access. This is the first camp you will arrive at, set at the mouth of the Jones Fork Cove.

**Campsites, facilities:** There are 10 sites for tents or RVs up to 25 feet (no hookups). Picnic tables and fire rings are provided. Vault toilets are available. No drinking water is available. Some facilities are wheelchair-accessible. Leashed pets are permitted.

**Reservations, fees:** Reservations are not accepted. Sites are $10 per night, plus $5 per night for each additional vehicle. Open June through October.

**Directions:** From Placerville, drive east on U.S. 50 for 23 miles to Riverton and the junction with Ice House Road/Forest Road 3. Turn left and drive 14 miles to the campground entrance road on the left (at the south end of Union Valley Reservoir). Turn left and drive 0.5 mile to the campground.

**Contact:** Eldorado National Forest, Pacific Ranger District, 530/644-2349, www.fs.usda. gov/eldorado.

## 123 LONE ROCK

### Scenic rating: 9

near Union Valley Reservoir in Eldorado National Forest

**Map 6.2, page 334**

This is a hike-in, bike-in, or boat-in spot at Union Valley Reservoir. It is little known, but once you claim it, it will always be on your list. Lake views and quiet tent sites in a primitive do-it-yourself setting make this a winner for those who know of it. The elevation is 4,800 feet.

**Campsites, facilities:** There are five sites for tents only that can only be accessed by bike, trail, or boat. Vault toilets are available. Picnic tables, fire rings, and a bike rack are provided. There is no drinking water.

**Reservations, fees:** Reservations are not accepted. There is no fee for camping.

**Directions:** From Placerville, drive east on U.S. 50 for 23 miles to Riverton and the junction with Ice House Road/Forest Road 3. If hiking or biking, turn left and drive 14 miles to the Jones Fork campground entrance and begin there. For boat-in camping, drive 14 miles to the Sunset Camp entrance to launch from there.

**Contact:** Eldorado National Forest, Pacific Ranger District, 530/644-2349, www.fs.usda. gov/eldorado; Crystal Basin, 530/293-3510.

## 124 SILVER CREEK GROUP

### Scenic rating: 5

near Ice House Reservoir in Eldorado National Forest

**Map 6.2, page 334**

Silver Creek is a pretty spot at 5,200 feet elevation. Ice House is only two miles north, and Union Valley Reservoir is four miles north. Either bring your own drinking water or bring a water filtration pump for stream water. Note: RVs and trailers are not allowed.

**Campsites, facilities:** One group tent site

can accommodate up to 40 people. Picnic tables and fire rings are provided. Vault toilets are available. No drinking water is available; stream water must be purified before drinking. Leashed pets are permitted.

**Reservations, fees:** Reservations are required at 877/444-6777 ($10 reservation fee) or www.recreation.gov ($9 reservation fee). The site is $113 per night. Open June through October, weather permitting.

**Directions:** From Placerville, drive east on U.S. 50 for 23 miles to Riverton and the junction with Ice House Road/Forest Road 3. Turn north and drive about nine miles on Forest Road 3 to the campground entrance road on the left.

**Contact:** Eldorado National Forest, Pacific Ranger District, 530/644-2349, www.fs.usda.gov/eldorado.

## 125 ICE HOUSE UPPER AND LOWER

🧍 🚲 🛶 ⛵ 🚤 🐕 ♿ 🚙 ⛺

### Scenic rating: 8
on Ice House Reservoir in Eldorado National Forest

**Map 6.2, page 334**

Along with Loon Lake and Union Valley Reservoir, Ice House Reservoir is a feature destination in the Crystal Basin Recreation Area. Ice House gets most of the anglers and Union Valley gets most of the campers. All water sports are allowed at Ice House, though. The camp is set on the lake's northwestern shore, at 5,500 feet elevation, just up from the dam and adjacent to the lake's boat ramp. The lake, created by a dam on South Fork Silver Creek, covers 650 acres, with the deepest spot about 130 feet deep. It is stocked with rainbow trout, brook trout, and brown trout. A 2.5-mile bike trail connects Ice House to Northwind and Strawberry Point campgrounds.

**Campsites, facilities:** There are 83 sites for tents or RVs up to 30 feet (no hookups). Picnic tables and fire grills are provided. Drinking

water, vault toilets, boat ramp, and a dump station are available. Some facilities are wheelchair-accessible. Leashed pets are permitted for a fee.

**Reservations, fees:** Reservations are accepted at 877/444-6777 ($10 reservation fee) or www.recreation.gov ($9 reservation fee). Single sites are $28 per night, double sites are $56 per night, plus $7 per night for each additional vehicle. Open late May through mid-October, weather permitting.

**Directions:** From Placerville, drive east on U.S. 50 for 23 miles to Riverton and the junction with Ice House Road/Forest Road 3. Turn left (north) and drive 11 miles to Forest Road 32/Ice House/Wrights Tie Road. Turn right (east) and drive 1.5 miles to the campground access road on the right.

**Contact:** Eldorado National Forest, Pacific Ranger District, 530/644-2349, www.fs.usda.gov/eldorado; American Land and Leisure, 530/293-0827.

## 126 NORTHWIND

🧍 🚲 🛶 ⛵ 🚤 🐕 ♿ 🚙 ⛺

### Scenic rating: 7
on Ice House Reservoir in Eldorado National Forest

**Map 6.2, page 334**

This camp sits on the north shore of Ice House Reservoir. It is slightly above the reservoir, offering prime views. A 2.5-mile bike trail connects Northwind with Ice House and Strawberry Point campgrounds. (See the Ice House Upper and Lower listing for more information.)

**Campsites, facilities:** There are eight single sites and one double site for tents or RVs up to 40 feet (no hookups). Picnic tables and fire grills are provided. Vault toilets are available. No drinking water is available; lake water must be purified before drinking. Some facilities are wheelchair-accessible. Leashed pets are permitted.

**Reservations, fees:** Reservations are not

accepted. Sites are $10 per night, plus $5 per night for each additional vehicle. Open May through mid-October, weather permitting.

**Directions:** From Placerville, drive east on U.S. 50 for 23 miles to Riverton and the junction with Ice House Road/Forest Road 3. Turn left (north) and drive 11 miles to Forest Road 32/Ice House/Wrights Tie Road. Turn right (east) and drive three miles (two miles past the boat ramp) to the campground access road on the right.

**Contact:** Eldorado National Forest, Pacific Ranger District, 530/644-2349, www.fs.usda.gov/eldorado.

## 127 STRAWBERRY POINT
🚶 🚴 🏊 🛶 🚤 🐴 ♿ 🚐 ⛺

**Scenic rating: 7**
on Ice House Reservoir in Eldorado National Forest

### Map 6.2, page 334

This camp is on the north shore of Ice House Reservoir, at 5,400 feet elevation. A 2.5-mile bike trail connects Strawberry Point with Northwind and Ice House campgrounds. (For more information, see the Ice House Upper and Lower listing in this chapter.)

**Campsites, facilities:** There are 10 sites for tents or RVs up to 40 feet (no hookups). Picnic tables and fire grills are provided. Vault toilets are available. No drinking water is available; lake water must be purified before drinking. Some facilities are wheelchair-accessible. Leashed pets are permitted.

**Reservations, fees:** Reservations are not accepted. Sites are $10 per night, plus $5 per night for each additional vehicle. Open May through December, weather permitting.

**Directions:** From Placerville, drive east on U.S. 50 for 23 miles to Riverton and the junction with Ice House Road/Forest Road 3. Turn left (north) and drive 11 miles to Forest Road 32/Ice House/Wrights Tie Road. Turn right (east) and drive three miles (three miles past

the boat ramp) to the campground access road on the road.

**Contact:** Eldorado National Forest, Pacific Ranger District, 530/644-2349, www.fs.usda.gov/eldorado.

## 128 WRIGHTS LAKE AND EQUESTRIAN
🚶 🏊 🛶 🚤 🐴 ♿ 🚐 ⛺

**Scenic rating: 8**
in Eldorado National Forest

### Map 6.2, page 334

This high mountain lake (7,000 feet) has shoreline picnicking and good fishing and hiking. There is no boat ramp, and the rules do not permit motors, so it is ideal for canoes, rafts, prams, and people who like quiet. Swimming is allowed. Fishing is fair for both rainbow trout and brown trout. This is a classic alpine lake, though small (65 acres), with a trailhead for the Desolation Wilderness at its north end. It is only a three-mile hike to the beautiful Twin Lakes and Island Lake, on the western flank of Mount Price (9,975 feet).

**Campsites, facilities:** There are 72 sites for tents or RVs up to 50 feet (no hookups) and 15 sites at the equestrian camp. Picnic tables and fire grills are provided. Drinking water and vault toilets are available. Some facilities are wheelchair-accessible, including a boat dock. Leashed pets are permitted.

**Reservations, fees:** Reservations are accepted and are required for some sites in July and August at 877/444-6777 ($10 reservation fee) or www.recreation.gov ($9 reservation fee). Single sites are $20 per night, $36 per night for a double site, plus $5 per night for each additional vehicle. Open late June through mid-October, weather permitting.

**Directions:** From Placerville, drive east on U.S. 50 for 23 miles to Riverton and the junction with Ice House Road/Forest Road 3. Turn left (north) and drive 11 miles to Forest Road 32/Ice House/Wrights Tie Road. Turn right (east) and drive nine miles to Forest Road 4/

Wrights Lake Road. Turn left (north) and drive two miles to the campground on the right side of the road.

**Contact:** Eldorado National Forest, Pacific Ranger District, 530/644-2349, www.fs.usda.gov/eldorado.

## 129 SLY PARK RECREATION AREA

**Scenic rating: 7**

on Jenkinson Lake

**Map 6.2, page 334**

Sly Park and Jenkinson Lake are at 3,500 feet elevation in the lower reaches of Eldorado National Forest, with a climate that is perfect for summer camping, fishing, and water sports. The best campsites are 10, 12, 14-16, 67-70, 133-134, and 140. Sly Park publishes a special reader on camping etiquette, and I'd like to see more of that across the state. Jenkinson Lake covers 640 acres and features eight miles of forested shoreline. Participants of water sports get along, with most water-skiers/wakeboarders motoring around the lake's main body, while anglers head upstream into the Hazel Creek arm of the lake for trout (in the spring) and bass (in the summer). Good news for anglers: Personal watercraft are not permitted. More good news: This is one of the better lakes in the Sierra for brown trout. There is a boat ramp at the campground and another one on the southwest end of the lake. The area also has several hiking trails, and the lake is good for swimming. There are nine miles of trails available for hiking, biking, and equestrians; an equestrian trail circles the lake. The Black Oak Equestrian group camp is available for visitors with horses, complete with riding trails, hitching posts, and corrals. Note: No pets or babies with diapers are allowed in the lake.

**Campsites, facilities:** There are 191 sites for tents or RVs up to 40 feet (no hookups). Five group sites can accommodate 50-100 people. An equestrian camp called Black Oak has 12 sites and two youth-group areas. Picnic tables, fire rings, and barbecues are provided. Drinking water, vault toilets, boat rentals, and firewood are available. Two boat ramps are available nearby. Some facilities are wheelchair-accessible. A grocery store, snack bar, dump station, bait, and propane gas are available nearby. Leashed pets are permitted.

**Reservations, fees:** Reservations are accepted at least seven days in advance at 866/759-7275 or 530/644-2792 ($9 reservation fee). Standard tent sites are $33 per night, premium sites are $50-80 per night, Black Oak Equestrian sites are $40 per night, plus $15 per night per additional vehicle, $4 per night for each additional person, and $5 per pet per day. Group sites are $250-330 per night ($20 reservation fee) for up to 50 people. Boat launching is $9 per day. Reduced rates are available for seniors and in winter. Some credit cards are accepted during the summer season. Open year-round.

**Directions:** From Sacramento, drive east on U.S. 50 to Pollock Pines and take the exit for Sly Park Road. Drive south for 4.5 miles to Jenkinson Lake and the campground entrance.

**Contact:** Sly Park Recreation Area, El Dorado Irrigation District, 530/295-6824, www.eid.org.

## 130 CAPPS CROSSING GROUP CAMP

**Scenic rating: 7**

on the North Fork of the Cosumnes River in Eldorado National Forest

**Map 6.2, page 334**

This camp is out in the middle of nowhere along the North Fork of the Cosumnes River. It's a primitive spot that doesn't get much use. This camp is in the western reaches of a vast number of backcountry Forest Service roads. A map of Eldorado National Forest is a must to explore them. The elevation is 5,200 feet.

**Campsites, facilities:** There is one group tent site for up to 42 people. Single sites are available if the camp is not reserved by a group. Picnic tables and fire grills are provided. Drinking water and vault toilets are available. Leashed pets are permitted for a fee.

**Reservations, fees:** Reservations are required for groups at 877/444-6777 ($10 reservation fee) or www.recreation.gov ($9 reservation fee). The group camp is $105 per night, single sites are $20 per night, and double sites are $46 per night. Open mid-May through mid-September, weather permitting.

**Directions:** From Sacramento, drive east on U.S. 50 to Placerville and continue for 12 miles to the Sly Park Road exit. Turn right and drive about six miles to the Mormon Emigrant Trail/Forest Road 5. Turn left on Mormon Emigrant Trail and drive about 13 miles to North-South Road/Forest Road 6. Turn right (south) on North-South Road and drive about six miles to the campground on the left side of the road.

**Contact:** Eldorado National Forest, Placerville Ranger District, 530/644-2324, www.fs.usda.gov/eldorado.

## 131 SAND FLAT-AMERICAN RIVER

### Scenic rating: 7

on the South Fork of the American River in Eldorado National Forest

**Map 6.2, page 334**

This first-come, first-served campground often gets filled up by U.S. 50 travelers. And why not? You get easy access, a well-signed exit, and a nice setting on the South Fork of the American River. The elevation is 3,900 feet. The river is very pretty, but fishing is often poor. In winter, the snow level usually starts just a few miles uphill.

**Campsites, facilities:** There are 29 sites for tents or RVs of any length (no hookups) and four walk-in tent sites. Picnic tables and fire grills are provided. Drinking water and vault toilets are available. Groceries, restaurant, and gas are nearby. Some facilities are wheelchair-accessible. Leashed pets are permitted.

**Reservations, fees:** Reservations are not accepted. Single sites are $20 per night, double sites are $40 per night, plus $7 per night for each additional vehicle. Open May through late October, weather permitting.

**Directions:** From Sacramento, drive east on U.S. 50 to Placerville and then continue 28 miles to the campground on the right. (If you reach the Kyburz store, you have driven about one mile too far.)

**Contact:** Eldorado National Forest, Placerville Ranger District, 530/644-2324, www.fs.usda.gov/eldorado.

## 132 CHINA FLAT

### Scenic rating: 7

on the Silver Fork of the American River in Eldorado National Forest

**Map 6.2, page 334**

China Flat sits across the road from the Silver Fork American River, with a nearby access road that is routed along the river for a mile. This provides access for fishing, swimming, gold panning, and exploring. The elevation is 4,800 feet. The camp feels far off the beaten path, even though it is only five minutes from that parade of traffic on U.S. 50.

**Campsites, facilities:** There are 19 sites for tents or RVs of any length (no hookups). Picnic tables and fire grills are provided. Drinking water and vault toilets are available. Some facilities are wheelchair-accessible. Leashed pets are permitted.

**Reservations, fees:** Reservations are not accepted. Single sites are $20 per night, double sites are $40 per night, plus $7 per night for each additional vehicle. Open May through October, weather permitting.

**Directions:** From Sacramento, drive east on U.S. 50 to Kyburz and Silver Fork Road. Turn right and drive three miles to the campground on the right side of the road.

**Contact:** Eldorado National Forest, Placerville

Ranger District, 530/644-2324, www.fs.usda. gov/eldorado.

# 133 SILVER FORK

### Scenic rating: 7
on the Silver Fork of the American River in Eldorado National Forest

**Map 6.2, page 334**

The tons of vacationers driving U.S. 50 along the South Fork American River always get frustrated when they try to fish or camp, because there are precious few opportunities for either. But, just 20 minutes off the highway, you can find both at Silver Fork Camp. The access road provides many fishing opportunities and the stream is stocked with rainbow trout by the state. The camp is set right along the river, at 5,500 feet elevation, in Eldorado National Forest.

**Campsites, facilities:** There are 35 sites for tents or RVs of any length (no hookups) and four double sites. Picnic tables and fire grills are provided. Drinking water and vault toilets are available. Some of the facilities are wheelchair-accessible. Leashed pets are permitted.

**Reservations, fees:** Reservations are not accepted. Single sites are $20 per night, double sites are $40 per night, plus $7 per night for each additional vehicle. Open May through October, weather permitting.

**Directions:** From Sacramento, drive east on U.S. 50 to Kyburz and Silver Fork Road. Turn right and drive eight miles to the campground on the right side of the road.

**Contact:** Eldorado National Forest, Placerville Ranger District, 530/644-2324, www.fs.usda. gov/eldorado.

# 134 KIRKWOOD LAKE

### Scenic rating: 8
in Eldorado National Forest

**Map 6.2, page 334**

Little Kirkwood Lake is in a beautiful Sierra setting, with good shoreline access, fishing for small rainbow trout, and quiet water. Despite that, it is often overlooked in favor of nearby Silver Lake and Caples Lake along Highway 88. No boat motors are allowed, but swimming is permitted. Nearby Kirkwood Ski Resort stays open all summer and offers excellent opportunities for horseback riding, hiking, and meals. The elevation is 7,600 feet. Note: The access road is too narrow for trailers.

**Campsites, facilities:** There are 12 sites for tents only. Picnic tables and fire grills are provided. Drinking water, vault toilets, and food lockers are available. Some facilities are wheelchair-accessible. Leashed pets are permitted.

**Reservations, fees:** Reservations are not accepted. Sites are $22-44 per night, plus $5 per night for each additional vehicle. Open June through mid-October, weather permitting.

**Directions:** From Jackson, drive east on Highway 88 for 60 miles (four miles past Silver Lake) to the campground entrance road on the left (if you reach the sign for Kirkwood Ski Resort, you have gone 0.5 mile too far). Turn left and drive 0.25 mile (road not suitable for trailers or large RVs) to the campground on the left.

**Contact:** Eldorado National Forest, Amador Ranger District, 209/295-4251, www.fs.usda. gov/eldorado.

# 135 CAPLES LAKE

### Scenic rating: 8
in Eldorado National Forest

**Map 6.2, page 334**

Caples Lake, in the high country at 7,800 feet, is a pretty lake right along Highway 88. It covers

600 acres, has a 5-mph speed limit, and provides good trout fishing and excellent hiking terrain. Swimming is allowed. The camp is across the highway (a little two-laner) from the lake, with the Caples Lake Resort, boat rentals, and a boat launch nearby. There is a parking area at the west end of the lake, where you can begin a great 3.5-mile hike to Emigrant Lake, in the Mokelumne Wilderness on the western flank of Mount Round Top (10,310 feet).

**Campsites, facilities:** There are 30 sites for tents or RVs up to 35 feet (no hookups), along with seven walk-in tent sites (requiring a 200-foot walk). Picnic tables and fire grills are provided. Drinking water and vault toilets are available. Groceries, propane gas, boat ramp, and boat rentals are nearby. Some facilities are wheelchair-accessible. Leashed pets are permitted.

**Reservations, fees:** Reservations are not accepted. Single sites are $24 per night, double sites are $48 per night, plus $5 per night for each additional vehicle. Open June through mid-October, weather permitting.

**Directions:** From Jackson, drive east on Highway 88 for 63 miles (one mile past the entrance road to Kirkwood Ski Area) to the camp entrance road on the left.

**Contact:** Eldorado National Forest, Amador Ranger District, 209/295-4251, www.fs.usda.gov/eldorado; Caples Lake Resort, 209/258-8888, http://capleslakeresort.com.

## 136 WOODS LAKE

### Scenic rating: 9
in Eldorado National Forest

**Map 6.2, page 334**      **BEST (**

Woods Lake is only two miles from Highway 88, yet it can provide campers the feeling of visiting a far-off land. It is a small but beautiful lake in the granite backdrop of the high Sierra, set at 8,200 feet elevation near Carson Pass. Boats with motors are not permitted, making it ideal for canoes and rowboats. Trout fishing

is fair. A great three-mile loop hike heads to little Round Top Lake and Winnemucca Lake (twice the size of Woods Lake) and back. They are on the northern flank of Mount Round Top (10,310 feet).

**Campsites, facilities:** There are 25 tent sites. Picnic tables and fire rings are provided. Drinking water and vault toilets are available. Groceries and propane gas are available within five miles. Some facilities are wheelchair-accessible. Leashed pets are permitted.

**Reservations, fees:** Reservations are not accepted. Single sites are $24 per night, double sites are $48 per night, plus $5 per night for each additional vehicle. Open late June through October, weather permitting.

**Directions:** From Jackson, drive east on Highway 88 to Caples Lake and continue for a mile to the Woods Lake turnoff on the right (two miles west of Carson Pass). Turn south and drive a mile to the campground on the right (trailers and RVs are not recommended).

**Contact:** Eldorado National Forest, Amador Ranger District, 209/295-4251, www.fs.usda.gov/eldorado.

## 137 SILVER LAKE WEST

### Scenic rating: 9
on Silver Lake in Eldorado National Forest

**Map 6.2, page 334**      **BEST (**

The Highway 88 corridor provides access to three excellent lakes: Lower Bear River Reservoir, Silver Lake, and Caples Lake. Silver Lake is difficult to pass by, with cabin rentals, pretty campsites, decent trout fishing, and excellent hiking. The lake is at 7,200 feet elevation in a classic granite cirque just below the Sierra ridge. This camp is on the west side of Highway 88, across the road from the lake. A great hike starts at the trailhead on the east side of the lake, a two-mile tromp to little Hidden Lake, one of several nice hikes in the area. In addition, horseback riding is available nearby at Plasse's Resort. Note that bears frequent this campground, so store food properly and avoid scented products.

**Campsites, facilities:** There are 42 sites for tents or RVs up to 24 feet (no hookups). Picnic tables, food lockers, and fire pits are provided. Vault toilets and drinking water are available. A boat ramp and boat rentals are nearby. Leashed pets are permitted. There is a maximum of six people and two pets per site.

**Reservations, fees:** Reservations are not accepted. Sites are $25 per night, plus $10 per night for each additional vehicle and $3 per pet per night. Boat launch is $10. Open Memorial Day weekend through October, weather permitting.

**Directions:** From Jackson, drive east on Highway 88 for 50 miles (to the north end of Silver Lake) to the campground entrance road on the left.

**Contact:** Eldorado Irrigation District, 530/295-6824, www.eid.org.

## 138 SILVER LAKE EAST

### Scenic rating: 7
in Eldorado National Forest

**Map 6.2, page 334**

Silver Lake is an easy-to-reach alpine lake at 7,200 feet, providing a beautiful setting, good trout fishing, and hiking. This camp is on the northeast side of the lake, with a boat ramp nearby. (See the Silver Lake West listing in this chapter for more information.)

**Campsites, facilities:** There are 48 sites for tents or RVs up to 40 feet (no hookups) and 14 walk-in tent sites. Picnic tables, food lockers, and fire grills are provided. Drinking water and flush and vault toilets are available. A grocery store, boat rentals, boat ramp, and propane gas are nearby. Leashed pets are permitted.

**Reservations, fees:** Reservations are accepted at 877/444-6777 ($10 reservation fee) or www. recreation.gov ($9 reservation fee). Single sites are $24 per night, double sites are $48 per night, plus $5 per night for each additional vehicle and

$3 per pet per night. Open June through mid-October, weather permitting.

**Directions:** From Jackson, drive east on Highway 88 for 50 miles (to the north end of Silver Lake) to the campground entrance road on the right.

**Contact:** Eldorado National Forest, Amador Ranger District, 209/295-4251, www.fs.usda. gov/eldorado.

## 139 PIPI

### Scenic rating: 7
on the Middle Fork of the Cosumnes River in Eldorado National Forest

**Map 6.2, page 334**

PiPi (pronounced pie-pie) is far enough out of the way to get missed by most campers. It is beside the Middle Fork of the Cosumnes River at 4,100 feet elevation. There are some good swimming holes in the area, but the water is cold and swift in early summer (after all, it's snowmelt). A trail/boardwalk along the river is wheelchair-accessible. Several sites border a pretty meadow in the back of the camp. This is also a gateway to a vast network of Forest Service roads to the north in Eldorado National Forest.

**Campsites, facilities:** There are 51 sites for tents or RVs up to 42 feet (no hookups), including two double sites and one triple site. Picnic tables and fire grills are provided. Drinking water and vault toilets are available. Some facilities are wheelchair-accessible. Leashed pets are permitted.

**Reservations, fees:** Reservations are accepted at 877/444-6777 ($10 reservation fee) or www. recreation.gov ($9 reservation fee). It's $22 per night for single sites, $44 per night for double sites, $66 per night for the triple site, and $5 per night for each additional vehicle. Open May through mid-November, weather permitting.

**Directions:** From Jackson, drive east on Highway 88 to Pioneer and continue for nine miles to Omo Ranch Road. Turn left and drive

0.8 mile to North-South Road/Forest Road 6. Turn right and drive 5.9 miles to the campground on the right side of the road.

**Contact:** Eldorado National Forest, Amador Ranger District, 209/295-4251, www.fs.usda.gov/eldorado.

## 140 BEAR RIVER GROUP CAMP

### Scenic rating: 6

on Bear River Reservoir in Eldorado National Forest

**Map 6.2, page 334**

This is a group camp near Bear River Reservoir, a pretty lake that provides powerboating and trout fishing. (See the listing in this chapter for South Shore, which is just a mile from this camp.)

**Campsites, facilities:** Three group sites for tents only can accommodate 25 people each, and one group site holds 25-50 people. Picnic tables, fire grills, and group cooking facilities are provided. Drinking water, vault toilets, coin showers, food lockers, and wash racks are available. A grocery store, propane gas, a boat ramp, and boat rentals are nearby. Leashed pets are permitted.

**Reservations, fees:** Reservations are required at 877/444-6777 ($10 reservation fee) or www.recreation.gov ($9 reservation fee). Sites are $75-150 per night. Open mid-June through mid-September, weather permitting.

**Directions:** From Stockton, drive east on Highway 88 for about 80 miles to the lake entrance on the right side of the road (well signed). Turn right and drive five miles (past the dam) to the campground entrance on the left side of the road.

**Contact:** Eldorado National Forest, Amador Ranger District, 209/295-4251, www.fs.usda.gov/eldorado.

## 141 BEAR RIVER LAKE RESORT

### Scenic rating: 8

on Bear River Reservoir

**Map 6.2, page 334**

Bear River Lake Resort is a complete vacation service lodge, with everything you could ask for. A lot of people have been asking in recent years, making this a popular spot that often requires a reservation. The resort also sponsors fishing derbies in the summer and sweetens the pot considerably by stocking exceptionally large rainbow trout. Other fish species include brown trout and Mackinaw trout. The resort is at 6,000 feet. The lake freezes over in the winter. (See the South Shore listing in this chapter for more information about Bear River Reservoir.)

**Campsites, facilities:** There are 152 sites with partial hookups (15 amps) for tents or RVs up to 35 feet, a group site for up to 60 people, and seven cabins. Picnic tables and fire pits are provided. Restrooms with flush toilets and coin showers, drinking water, a dump station, boat ramp, boat rentals, berthing, bait and tackle, fishing licenses, playground, firewood, ice, propane gas, coin laundry, Wi-Fi, pay phone, restaurant and cocktail lounge, and grocery store are available. ATVs are permitted, but no motorcycles are allowed. Some facilities are wheelchair-accessible. Leashed pets are permitted at campsites but not in lodging units.

**Reservations, fees:** Reservations are recommended. Tent and RV sites (water and electricity) are $33 per night, extra-large sites are $50 per night, plus $5 for each additional vehicle with a maximum of two vehicles. The one-time pet fee is $5. It's $255 per night for the group site and $117 per night for cabins. Monthly rates are available. Some credit cards are accepted. Open May through October.

**Directions:** From Stockton, drive east on Highway 88 for about 80 miles to the lake entrance on the right side of the road, 42 miles east of Jackson. Turn right and drive 2.5 miles to a junction (if you pass the dam, you have gone 0.25 mile too far). Turn left and drive 0.5 mile to the campground entrance on the right side of the road.

**Contact:** Bear River Lake Resort, 209/295-4868, www.bearrivercampground.com.

## 142 SUGAR PINE POINT

### Scenic rating: 7

near Bear River Reservoir in Eldorado National Forest

**Map 6.2, page 334**

This camp is similar in nature to Pardoes Point (see listing in this chapter), with one exception: It is directly across the lake—on the other shoreline, that is, from Pardoes.

**Campsites, facilities:** There are eight sites for tents only, including two double sites. Picnic tables and fire rings are provided. Vault toilets are available. Drinking water is not available; lake water must be purified before drinking. Nearby Bear River Resort offers groceries, showers, and potable water. Some facilities are wheelchair-accessible. Leashed pets are permitted.

**Reservations, fees:** Reservations are not accepted. Single sites are $20 per night, double sites are $40 per night, plus $5 each additional vehicle per night. Open from May to mid-November.

**Directions:** From Stockton, drive east on Highway 88 for about 80 miles to Bear River Road. Turn right and drive 2.5 miles south on Bear River Road to Forest Road 8N20. Turn right on Forest Road 8N20 and drive three miles to the campground.

**Contact:** Eldorado National Forest, Amador Ranger District, 209/295-4251, www.fs.usda.gov/eldorado.

## 143 PARDOES POINT

### Scenic rating: 7

in Eldorado National Forest

**Map 6.2, page 334**

There are several camps at Bear River Reservoir—Bear River Lake Resort is the most popular because you can see the lake, it has a boat ramp, and you can get supplies. Pardoes Point is located near the lower end of the reservoir. It's not a true "lakeside" camp, though you can get glimpses of the lake from some sites. Bear River Reservoir often provides good fishing. The elevation is 6,000 feet, and ice-outs occur earlier than at Silver Lake and Caples Lake farther up Highway 88.

**Campsites, facilities:** There are 10 tent sites, including one double site. Picnic tables and fire rings are provided. Drinking water and vault toilets are available. Some facilities are wheelchair-accessible. Leashed pets are permitted.

**Reservations, fees:** Reservations are not accepted. Single sites are $22 per night, double sites are $44 per night, plus $5 per each additional vehicle per night. Open from May to mid-November.

**Directions:** From Stockton, drive east on Highway 88 for about 80 miles to Bear River Road. Turn right and drive south on Bear River Road for four miles to the campground.

**Contact:** Eldorado National Forest, Amador Ranger District, 209/295-4251, www.fs.usda.gov/eldorado.

## 144 SOUTH SHORE

### Scenic rating: 7

on Bear River Reservoir in Eldorado National Forest

**Map 6.2, page 334**

Bear River Reservoir is at 5,900 feet, which means it becomes ice-free earlier in the spring than its uphill neighbors to the east, Silver Lake and Caples Lake. It is a good-sized lake—725 acres—and cold and deep, too. All water sports are allowed. It gets double-barreled trout stocks, receiving fish from the state and from the operator of the lake's marina and lodge. This campground is on the lake's southern shore, just east of the dam. Explorers can drive south for five miles to Salt Springs Reservoir, which has a trailhead and parking area on the north side of the dam for a great day hike along the lake.

**Campsites, facilities:** There are 22 sites for tents or RVs up to 35 feet (no hookups). Picnic tables and fire grills are provided. Drinking water and vault toilets are available. A boat ramp, grocery store, boat rentals, and propane gas are available at nearby Bear River Lake Resort. Some facilities are wheelchair-accessible. Leashed pets are permitted.

**Reservations, fees:** Reservations are accepted at 877/444-6777 ($10 reservation fee) or www.recreation.gov ($9 reservation fee). Single sites are $22 per night, double sites are $44 per night, triple sites are $66 per night, plus $5 per each additional vehicle per night. Open mid-May through mid-October, weather permitting.

**Directions:** From Stockton, drive east on Highway 88 for about 80 miles to the lake entrance on the right side of the road (well signed). Turn right and drive four miles (past the dam) to the campground entrance on the right side of the road.

**Contact:** Eldorado National Forest, Amador Ranger District, 209/295-4251, www.fs.usda.gov/eldorado.

## 145 WHITE AZALEA

### Scenic rating: 7

on the Mokelumne River in Eldorado National Forest

**Map 6.2, page 334**

Out here in the remote Mokelumne River Canyon are three primitive camps set on the Mokelumne's North Fork. White Azalea, at 3,500 feet elevation, is the closest of the three

to Salt Springs Reservoir, the prime recreation destination. It's about a three-mile drive to the dam and an adjacent parking area for a wilderness trailhead for the Mokelumne Wilderness. This trail makes a great day hike, routed for four miles along the north shore of Salt Springs Reservoir to Blue Hole at the head of the lake.

**Campsites, facilities:** There are six tent sites. Portable toilets are provided. No drinking water is available; river water must be purified before drinking. Garbage must be packed out. Leashed pets are permitted.

**Reservations, fees:** Reservations are not accepted. There is no fee for camping. Open year-round, weather permitting.

**Directions:** From Jackson, drive east on Highway 88 to Pioneer and then continue for 18 miles to Ellis Road/Forest Road 92 (78 miles from Jackson), at a signed turnoff for Lumberyard Campground. Turn right on Ellis Road and drive 12 miles to Salt Springs Road (Forest Road 9). Turn left, cross the Bear River, and continue for three miles to the campground on the right. The road is steep, narrow, and curvy in spots, not good for RVs or trailers.

**Contact:** Eldorado National Forest, Amador Ranger District, 209/295-4251, www.fs.usda.gov/eldorado.

## 146 MOORE CREEK

### Scenic rating: 7

on the Mokelumne River in Eldorado National Forest

**Map 6.2, page 334**

This camp is at 3,200 feet elevation on little Moore Creek, a feeder stream to the nearby North Fork Mokelumne River. It's one of three primitive camps within two miles. (See the White Azalea listing for more information.)

**Campsites, facilities:** There are eight tent sites. Picnic tables are provided at some sites. Vault toilets are available. No drinking water is available; river water must be purified before drinking. Garbage must be packed out. Leashed pets are permitted.

**Reservations, fees:** Reservations are not accepted. There is no fee for camping. Open year-round, weather permitting.

**Directions:** From Jackson, drive east on Highway 88 to Pioneer and then continue for 18 miles to Ellis Road/Forest Road 92 (78 miles from Jackson), at a signed turnoff for Lumberyard Campground. Turn right on Ellis Road and drive 12 miles to Salt Springs Road (Forest Road 9). Turn right and drive 2.5 miles, cross the bridge over the Mokelumne River, and turn right on the campground entrance road. Drive 0.25 mile to the campground on the right. The road is steep, narrow, and winding in spots—not good for RVs or trailers.

**Contact:** Eldorado National Forest, Amador Ranger District, 209/295-4251, www.fs.usda. gov/eldorado.

## 147 MOKELUMNE
🏊 ⛵ 🐕 🚐 ⛺

### Scenic rating: 7
on the Mokelumne River in Eldorado National Forest

**Map 6.2, page 334**

This primitive spot is beside the Mokelumne River at 3,200 feet elevation, one of three primitive camps in the immediate area. There are some good swimming holes nearby. Fishing is fair, with the trout on the small side. (See the White Azalea listing in this chapter for more information.)

**Campsites, facilities:** There are 13 sites for tents and RVs up to 40 feet (no hookups). Vault toilets and some picnic tables are provided. No drinking water is available; river water must be purified before drinking. Garbage must be packed out (it is occasionally serviced in summer). Leashed pets are permitted.

**Reservations, fees:** Reservations are not accepted. There is no fee for camping. Open year-round, weather permitting.

**Directions:** From Jackson, drive east on

Highway 88 to Pioneer and then continue for 18 miles to Ellis Road/Forest Road 92 (78 miles from Jackson), at a signed turnoff for Lumberyard Campground. Turn right on Ellis Road and drive 12 miles to Salt Springs Road (Forest Road 9). Turn right and drive 2.5 miles to the campground on the left side of the road (at the Mokelumne River).

**Contact:** Eldorado National Forest, Amador Ranger District, 209/295-4251, www.fs.usda. gov/eldorado.

## 148 BIG MEADOW AND BIG MEADOW GROUP CAMP
🐕 🚐 ⛺

### Scenic rating: 5
in Stanislaus National Forest

**Map 6.2, page 334**

Big Meadow, elevation 6,460 feet, sits on the western slopes of the Sierra Nevada. Recreation attractions nearby include the North Fork Stanislaus River two miles to the south in a national forest (see the Sand Flat Four-Wheel Drive listing in this chapter), with access available from a four-wheel-drive road just east of camp or on Spicer Reservoir Road (see the Stanislaus River listing in this chapter). Lake Alpine, a pretty lake popular for trout fishing, is nine miles east on Highway 4. Three mountain reservoirs—Spicer, Utica, and Union—are all within a 15-minute drive. Big Meadow is also a good base camp for hunting.

**Campsites, facilities:** There are 65 sites for tents or RVs up to 27 feet (no hookups), along with one group tent site (requires a walk-in of 100 feet) that can accommodate 25-50 people. Picnic tables and fire grills are provided. Drinking water and vault toilets are available. Groceries, coin laundry, and propane gas are within five miles. Leashed pets are permitted.

**Reservations, fees:** Reservations are not accepted. Sites are $19 per night, and the group camp is $50 per night. Open June through October, weather permitting.

**Directions:** From Angels Camp on Highway

49, turn east on Highway 4 and drive about 30 miles (three miles past Ganns Meadows) to the campground on the right.

**Contact:** Stanislaus National Forest, Calaveras Ranger District, 209/795-1381, www.fs.usda/stanislaus.

## 149 SAND FLAT FOUR-WHEEL DRIVE

### Scenic rating: 7

on the Stanislaus River in Stanislaus National Forest

**Map 6.2, page 334**

This one is for four-wheel-drive cowboys who want to carve out a piece of the Sierra Nevada wildlands for themselves. It is set at 5,900 feet elevation on the North Fork Stanislaus River, where there is decent fishing for small trout, with the fish often holding right where white water runs into pools. You won't get bugged by anyone at this tiny, primitive camp, named for the extensive sandy flat on the south side of the river. The access road is steep and often rough. Trailers are not allowed.

**Campsites, facilities:** There are 10 sites for tents only. Picnic tables and fire rings are provided. Pit toilets are available. No drinking water is available. Garbage must be packed out. Leashed pets are permitted.

**Reservations, fees:** Reservations are not accepted. There is no fee for camping. Free campfire permits are required. Open June through October, weather permitting.

**Directions:** From Angels Camp on Highway 49, turn east on Highway 4 and drive about 25 miles to a dirt/gravel road on the right. Turn right and drive two miles on a steep, unimproved road (four-wheel drive required).

**Contact:** Stanislaus National Forest, Calaveras Ranger District, 209/795-1381, www.fs.usda/stanislaus.

## 150 STANISLAUS RIVER

### Scenic rating: 8

in Stanislaus National Forest

**Map 6.2, page 334**

As you might figure from its name, this camp provides excellent access to the adjacent North Fork Stanislaus River. The elevation is 6,200 feet, with timbered sites and the river just south of camp.

**Campsites, facilities:** There are 25 sites for tents or RVs up to 35 feet (no hookups). Fire grills and picnic tables are provided. Drinking water and vault toilets are available. Garbage must be packed out. Supplies are available in Bear Valley. Leashed pets are permitted.

**Reservations, fees:** Reservations are not accepted. Sites are $12 per night. Open June through October, weather permitting.

**Directions:** From Angels Camp on Highway 49, turn east on Highway 4 and drive about 44 miles to Spicer Reservoir Road. Turn right and drive four miles to the campground on the right side of the road.

**Contact:** Stanislaus National Forest, Calaveras Ranger District, 209/795-1381, www.fs.usda.gov.

## 151 WA KA LUU HEP YOO

### Scenic rating: 8

on the Stanislaus River in Stanislaus National Forest

**Map 6.2, page 334**

This riverside Forest Service campground provides good trout fishing on the Stanislaus River and a put-in for white-water rafting. The highlight for most is the fishing—it's one of the best spots on the Stanislaus, stocked by Fish and Game, and good for rainbow, brook, and brown trout. It is four miles downstream of Dorrington and was first opened in 1999 as part of the Sourgrass Recreation Complex. There are cultural sites and preserved artifacts, such as grinding rocks. It is a pretty streamside spot, with ponderosa pines and black oaks providing good screening. A wheelchair-accessible trail runs along the stream. The camp is at an elevation of 3,900 feet, but it feels higher. By the way, I was told that the Miwuk term *"wa ka luu"* means river, and *"hep yoo"* describes an untamed or wild force of nature.

**Campsites, facilities:** There are 49 sites for tents or RVs up to 50 feet (no hookups). Picnic tables and fire grills are provided. Drinking water and restrooms with hot showers and flush and vault toilets are available. Some facilities are wheelchair-accessible. Leashed pets are permitted.

**Reservations, fees:** Reservations are not accepted. Sites are $20 per night. Free campfire permits are required. Open Memorial Day weekend through October, weather permitting.

**Directions:** From Angels Camp, drive east on Highway 4, past Arnold to Dorrington and Board's Crossing-Sourgrass Road. Turn right and drive four miles to the campground on the left (just before the bridge that crosses the Stanislaus River).

**Contact:** Stanislaus National Forest, Calaveras Ranger District, 209/795-1381, www.fs.usda/stanislaus.

## 152 GOLDEN PINES RV RESORT AND CAMPGROUND

🏃 🏊 🏠 🐕 👩‍🦽 🚐 ⛺

**Scenic rating: 6**

near Arnold

**Map 6.2, page 334**

This is a privately operated park at 5,800 feet elevation on the slopes of the Sierra Nevada. The resort is surrounded by 400 acres of forest and has a self-guided nature trail. Nearby destinations include Stanislaus National Forest, the North Stanislaus River, and Calaveras Big Trees State Park (two miles away). The latter features 150 giant sequoias, along with the biggest stump you can imagine, and two easy hikes; one passes through the North Grove, another through the South Grove. The Bear Valley/Mount Reba ski resort is nearby. Note that about half the sites are long-term vacation leases.

**Campsites, facilities:** There are 33 sites with full or partial hookups (30 amps) for RVs up to 42 feet and 40 sites for tents only. Cabins and trailer rentals are also available. Picnic tables, fire pits, and barbecues are provided. Drinking water, restrooms with showers, a seasonal heated swimming pool, playground, horseshoes, table tennis, volleyball, group facilities, pay phone, coin laundry, and propane gas are available. Some facilities are wheelchair-accessible. Leashed pets are permitted.

**Reservations, fees:** Reservations are recommended. RV sites with full hookups are $45-50 per night, tent sites are $40 per night, plus $5 per night for more than two people, $5 per night for each additional vehicle, and a $5 one-time fee per pet. Cabins are $55-75 per night. Some credit cards are accepted. Weekly and monthly rates are available. Open year-round.

**Directions:** From Angels Camp, turn northeast on Highway 4 and drive 22 miles to Arnold. Continue for seven miles to the campground entrance on the left.

**Contact:** Golden Pines RV Resort and Campground, 209/795-2820, www.golden-pinesresort.com.

## 153 CALAVERAS BIG TREES STATE PARK

🏃 🚲 🏊 🏕 ❄️ 🐕 👩‍🦽 🚐 ⛺

**Scenic rating: 7**

near Arnold

**Map 6.2, page 334**

Calaveras Big Trees State Park is known for its two groves of giant sequoias and an epic stump. (Giant sequoias are known for their massive diameter rather than height, as is the case with coast redwoods.) The park covers 6,500 acres, preserving the extraordinary North Grove of giant sequoias, which includes the Discovery

Tree. Through the years, additional acreage surrounding the grove has been added, providing a mixed conifer forest as a buffer around the giant sequoias. The North Grove Loop is an easy 1.5-mile walk that is routed among 150 sequoias; the sweet fragrance of the huge trees fills the air. Another hike, a five-miler, is in the South Grove, where the park's two largest sequoias (the Agassiz Tree and the Palace Hotel Tree) can be seen on a spur trail. A visitors center is open during peak periods, offering exhibits on the giant sequoia and natural history.

The North Fork Stanislaus River runs near Highway 4, providing trout-fishing access. The Stanislaus (near the bridge) and Beaver Creek (about 10 miles away) are stocked with trout in late spring and early summer. In the winter, this is a popular spot for cross-country skiing and snowshoeing. The elevation is 4,800 feet.

**Campsites, facilities:** The North Grove Campground has 51 sites for tents, 48 sites for RVs up to 30 feet (no hookups), five hike-in environmental sites, and two group sites for 40 and 60 people respectively. The Oak Hollow Campground has 33 sites for tents only and 18 sites for RVs up to 30 feet (no hookups). Picnic tables, fire rings, and food lockers are provided. Drinking water, restrooms with flush toilets and coin showers, and firewood are available. A dump station is in North Grove. No bicycles are allowed on the paths, but they are permitted on fire roads and paved roads. Some facilities are wheelchair-accessible, including a nature trail and exhibits. Leashed pets are permitted, but not on trails.

**Reservations, fees:** Reservations are accepted May through September at 800/444-7275 or www.reserveamerica.com ($8 reservation fee). Sites are first-come, first-served October through April. Sites are $35 per night, $10 per night for each additional vehicle, $70-135 per night for group sites, and $25 per night for environmental sites. Cabins are $165-185 per night. Open year-round, with 12 sites available in winter.

**Directions:** From Angels Camp, drive east on Highway 4 for 23 miles to Arnold and then continue another four miles to the park entrance on the right.

**Contact:** Calaveras Big Trees State Park, 209/795-2334; Columbia State Park, 209/544-9128, www.parks.ca.gov.

## 154 BEARDSLEY DAM

**Scenic rating: 6**

at Beardsley Reservoir in Stanislaus National Forest

**Map 6.2, page 334**

This lake is set in a deep canyon with a paved ramp, a nice picnic area, and a fair beach. It is often an outstanding fishery early in the season for brown trout, and then, once planted, good for catches of hatchery fish during the evening bite. In winter and spring, as soon as the gate is opened to the boat ramp access road, the fishing is best when the wind blows. This lake allows powerboats and all water sports. The water is generally warm enough for swimmers by midsummer. The camp is at 3,400 feet elevation, but because it is near the bottom of the lake canyon, it actually feels much higher. Since the lake is a reservoir, it is subject to severe drawdowns in late summer. Bonus: There is more fishing nearby on the Middle Fork of the Stanislaus.

**Campsites, facilities:** There are 16 sites for tents or RVs up to 22 feet (no hookups). Fire rings are provided. Vault toilets are available. No drinking water is available. Garbage must be packed out. Leashed pets are permitted.

**Reservations, fees:** Reservations are not accepted. Sites are $20 per night. Open May through October, weather permitting (the road is often gated at the top of the canyon when the boat ramp road at lake level is iced over).

**Directions:** From Sonora, drive east on Highway 108 for about 25 miles to Strawberry and the turnoff for Beardsley Reservoir/Forest Road 52. Turn left and drive seven miles to Beardsley Dam. Continue for 0.25 mile past the dam to the campground.

**Contact:** Stanislaus National Forest, Summit Ranger District, 209/965-3434, www.fs.usda/ stanislaus.

## 155 BLACK OAK FLAT/ TELELI PULAYA

🚶 🏊 🎣 🚗 🐕 🚐 ⛺

### Scenic rating: 7

near Beardsley Reservoir in Stanislaus National Forest

**Map 6.2, page 334**

TeleLi puLaya ("black oak") offers nice, shaded sites amid conifers with plenty of privacy between sites. There's also a really nice panoramic view of the Middle Fork of the Stanislaus River canyon off to the southwest.

**Campsites, facilities:** There are 22 sites for tents or RVs up to 40 feet (no hookups); two can be used as group sites. Picnic tables and fire rings are provided. Drinking water and vault toilets are available. Leashed pets are permitted.

**Reservations, fees:** Reservations are not accepted. Sites are $20 per night or $30 for a group site, plus $5 per extra vehicle. Open May to mid-September.

**Directions:** From Sonora, drive east on Highway 108 for about 25 miles to Strawberry and the turnoff for Beardsley Reservoir/Forest Road 52. Turn left and drive four miles to campground on right.

**Contact:** Stanislaus National Forest, Summit Ranger District, 209/965-3434, www.fs.usda/ stanislaus.

## 156 FRASER FLAT

🏊 🐕 ♿ 🚐 ⛺

### Scenic rating: 7

on the South Fork of the Stanislaus River in Stanislaus National Forest

**Map 6.2, page 334**

This camp is along the South Fork of the Stanislaus River at an elevation of 4,800 feet.

If the fish aren't biting, a short side trip via Forest Service roads will route you north into the main canyon of the Middle Fork Stanislaus. A map of Stanislaus National Forest is required for this adventure.

**Campsites, facilities:** There are 38 sites for tents or RVs up to 22 feet (no hookups), including some double sites. Picnic tables and fire grills are provided. Drinking water, vault toilets, and a wheelchair-accessible fishing pier are available. Some facilities are wheelchair-accessible. A grocery store and propane gas are nearby. Leashed pets are permitted.

**Reservations, fees:** Reservations are not accepted. Sites are $19-38 per night, plus $5 per night for each additional vehicle. Open May through October, weather permitting.

**Directions:** From Sonora, drive east on Highway 108 to Long Barn. Continue east for six miles to Spring Gap Road/Forest Road 4N01. Turn left and drive three miles to the campground on the left side of the road.

**Contact:** Stanislaus National Forest, Mi-Wok Ranger District, 209/586-3234, www. fs.usda/stanislaus; Dodge Ridge Corporation, 209/965-3116.

## 157 HULL CREEK

🐕 ♿ 🚐 ⛺

### Scenic rating: 7

in Stanislaus National Forest

**Map 6.2, page 334**

This obscure camp borders little Hull Creek (too small for trout fishing) at 5,600 feet elevation in Stanislaus National Forest. This is a good spot for those wishing to test out four-wheel-drive vehicles, with an intricate set of Forest Service roads available to the east. To explore that area, a map of Stanislaus National Forest is essential.

**Campsites, facilities:** There are 19 sites for tents or RVs up to 22 feet (no hookups). Picnic tables and fire grills are provided. Drinking water and vault toilets are available. Some facilities are wheelchair-accessible. Leashed pets are permitted.

**Reservations, fees:** Reservations are not accepted. Sites are $12 per night. Open May through October, weather permitting.

**Directions:** From Sonora, drive east on Highway 108 to Long Barn and the Long Barn Fire Station and a signed turnoff for the campground at Road 31/Forest Road 3N01. Turn right and drive 12 miles to the campground on the left side of the road.

**Contact:** Stanislaus National Forest, Mi-Wok Ranger District, 209/586-3234, www.fs.usda/stanislaus.

## 158 SUGAR PINE RV PARK

### Scenic rating: 5

in Twain Harte

**Map 6.2, page 334**

Twain Harte is a beautiful little town, right at the edge of the snow line in winter, and right where pines take over the alpine landscape. This park is at the threshold of mountain country, with Pinecrest, Dodge Ridge, and Beardsley Reservoir nearby. It sits on 15 acres and features several walking paths. Note that only 17 of the RV sites are available for overnight campers; the other sites are rented as annual vacation leases. RVs and mobile homes are also for sale at the park.

**Campsites, facilities:** There are 78 sites with full hookups (20, 30, and 50 amps) for RVs up to 40 feet, 15 tent sites, and three park-model cabins. Picnic tables are provided. Restrooms with showers, cable TV, Wi-Fi, playground, seasonal swimming pool, horseshoes, volleyball, badminton, tetherball, basketball, coin laundry, group facilities, and convenience store are available. Some facilities are wheelchair-accessible. Leashed pets are permitted.

**Reservations, fees:** Reservations are accepted. Sites are $45 per night, plus $5 per pet and $4 per night for each additional guest or vehicle. The group site is $64 per night. Some credit cards are accepted. Open year-round.

**Directions:** From Sonora, drive east on Highway 108 for 17 miles to the park on the right side of the road, three miles east of Twain Harte.

**Contact:** Sugar Pine RV Park, 209/586-4631, www.sugarpinervpark.com.

## 159 KIT CARSON

### Scenic rating: 8

on the West Fork of the Carson River in Humboldt-Toiyabe National Forest

**Map 6.3, page 335**

This is one in a series of pristine, high-Sierra camps along the West Fork of the Carson River. There's good trout fishing, thanks to regular stocks from the Department of Fish and Game. This is no secret, however, and the area from the Highway 89 bridge on downstream gets a lot of fishing pressure. The elevation is 6,900 feet.

**Campsites, facilities:** There are 12 sites for tents or RVs up to 22 feet (no hookups). Picnic tables and fire grills are provided. Drinking water and vault toilets are available. Leashed pets are permitted.

**Reservations, fees:** Reservations are not accepted. Sites are $18 per night, plus $5 per night per extra vehicle. Open late-May through mid-September, weather permitting.

**Directions:** From Sacramento, drive east on U.S. 50 to the junction with Highway 89. Turn south on Highway 89 and drive over Luther Pass to the junction with Highway 88. Turn left and drive a mile to the campground on the left side of the road.

From Jackson, drive east on Highway 88 over Carson Pass and to the junction with Highway 89 and then continue for a mile to the campground on the left side of the road.

**Contact:** Humboldt-Toiyabe National Forest, Carson Ranger District, 775/882-2766, www.

fs.usda/htnf; WestTrek Services, 760/932-7092, www.westrekservices.com.

## 160 CRYSTAL SPRINGS

**Scenic rating: 8**

on the West Fork of the Carson River in Humboldt-Toiyabe National Forest

**Map 6.3, page 335**

For many people, this camp is an ideal choice. It is at an elevation of 6,000 feet, right alongside the West Fork of the Carson River. This stretch of water is stocked with trout by the Department of Fish and Game. Crystal Springs is easy to reach, just off Highway 88, and supplies can be obtained in nearby Woodfords or Markleeville. Grover Hot Springs State Park makes a good side-trip destination.

**Campsites, facilities:** There are 19 sites for tents or RVs up to 35 feet (no hookups). Picnic tables and fire grills are provided. Drinking water and vault toilets are available. Some facilities are wheelchair-accessible. Leashed pets are permitted.

**Reservations, fees:** Reservations are not accepted. Sites are $18 per night, plus $5 per night for extra vehicle. Open late April to early October, weather permitting.

**Directions:** From Sacramento, drive east on U.S. 50 to the junction with Highway 89. Turn south on Highway 89 and drive over Luther Pass to the junction with Highway 88. Turn left (east) and drive 4.5 miles to the campground on the right side of the road.

From Jackson, drive east on Highway 88 over Carson Pass to the junction with Highway 89 and continue for 4.5 miles to the campground on the right side of the road.

**Contact:** Humboldt-Toiyabe National Forest, Carson Ranger District, 775/882-2766, www.fs.usda/htnf; WestTrek Services, 760/932-7092, www.westrekservices.com.

## 161 INDIAN CREEK RECREATION AREA

**Scenic rating: 10**

near Indian Creek Reservoir and Markleeville

**Map 6.3, page 335**

This beautiful campground is set amid sparse pines near Indian Creek Reservoir, elevation 5,600 feet. The campground is popular and often fills to capacity. This is an excellent lake for trout fishing, and the nearby Carson River is managed as a trophy trout fishery. The lake covers 160 acres, with a maximum speed for boats on the lake set at 5 mph. Sailing, sailboarding, and swimming are allowed. There are several good hikes in the vicinity as well. The best is a short trek, a one-mile climb to Summit Lake, with scenic views of the Indian Creek area. Summers are dry and warm, with high temperatures typically in the 80s, and nights cool and comfortable. (There is little shade in the summer at the group site.) Bears occasionally visit. The lake freezes over in winter. It is about 35 miles to Carson City, Nevada, and two miles to Markleeville.

**Campsites, facilities:** There are 19 sites for tents or RVs up to 30 feet (no hookups), 10 walk-in sites for tents only, and a group tent site for up to 40 people. Picnic tables and fire grills are provided. Drinking water, restrooms with flush toilets and showers, and a dump station are available. A boat ramp is nearby. Some facilities are wheelchair-accessible. Leashed pets are permitted.

**Reservations, fees:** Reservations are not accepted for individual sites but are required for the group tent site at 775/885-6000. Single sites are $20 per night, double sites are $32 per night, walk-in sites are $14 per night, and the group site is $50 per night. Open late April through mid-November, weather permitting.

**Directions:** From Sacramento, drive east on U.S. 50 over Echo Summit to Meyers and Highway 89. Turn south on Highway 89 and drive to Highway 88. Turn left (east) on Highway 88/89 and drive six miles to

Woodfords and Highway 89. Turn right (south) on Highway 89 and drive about four miles to Airport Road. Turn left on Airport Road and drive four miles to Indian Creek Reservoir. At the fork, bear left and drive to the campground on the west side of the lake.

From Markleeville, drive north on Highway 89 for about four miles to Airport Road. Turn right on Airport Road and drive about four miles to Indian Creek Reservoir. At the fork, bear left and drive to the campground on the west side of the lake.

**Contact:** Bureau of Land Management, Carson City Field Office, 775/885-6000, www.blm.gov/nv.

## 162 HOPE VALLEY

### Scenic rating: 7

near the Carson River in Humboldt-Toiyabe National Forest

**Map 6.3, page 335**

The West Fork of the Carson River runs right through Hope Valley, a pretty trout stream with a choice of four streamside campgrounds. Trout stocks are made near the campgrounds during summer. The campground at Hope Valley is just east of Carson Pass, at 7,300 feet elevation, in a very pretty area. A trailhead for the Pacific Crest Trail is three miles south of the campground. The primary nearby destination is Blue Lakes, about a 10-minute drive away. Insider's note: Little Tamarack Lake, just beyond the turnoff for Lower Blue Lake, is excellent for swimming.

**Campsites, facilities:** There are 13 single sites for tents or RVs up to 22 feet and six group sites (two sites are tent only) that can accommodate up to 12 people each (no hookups). Picnic tables and fire grills are provided. Drinking water and vault toilets are available. Some facilities are wheelchair-accessible. Leashed pets are permitted.

**Reservations, fees:** Reservations are accepted at 877/444-6777 ($10 reservation fee) or www.

recreation.gov ($9 reservation fee). Sites are $22 per night, group sites are $40 per night, plus $5 per night for each extra vehicle. Open June through September.

**Directions:** From Sacramento, drive east on U.S. 50 to the junction with Highway 89. Turn south on Highway 89 and drive over Luther Pass to the junction with Highway 88. Turn right (west) and drive two miles to Blue Lakes Road. Turn left (south) and drive 1.5 miles to the campground on the right side of the road.

From Jackson, drive east on Highway 88 over Carson Pass and continue east for five miles to Blue Lakes Road. Turn right (south) and drive 1.5 miles to the campground on the right side of the road.

**Contact:** Humboldt-Toiyabe National Forest, Carson Ranger District, 775/882-2766, www.fs.usda/htnf; WestTrek Services, 760/932-7092, www.westrekservices.com.

## 163 TURTLE ROCK PARK

### Scenic rating: 5

near Woodfords

**Map 6.3, page 335**

Because it is administered at the county level, this pretty, wooded campground, set at 6,000 feet elevation, gets missed by a lot of folks. Most vacationers want the more pristine beauty of the nearby camps along the Carson River. But it doesn't get missed by mountain bikers, who travel here every July for the "Death Ride," a wild ride over several mountain passes. The camp always fills for this event. (If it snows, it closes, so call ahead if you're planning an autumn visit.) Nearby side trips include Grover Hot Springs and the hot springs in Markleeville.

**Campsites, facilities:** There are 26 sites for trailers or RVs up to 34 feet (no hookups) and 12 tent sites. Picnic tables and fire grills are provided. Drinking water, flush toilets, and a shower are available. A camp host is on-site. A recreation building is available for rent; tennis and basketball courts, a disc golf course, and horseshoe pits are available. Coin laundry, groceries, and propane gas are available within two miles. Some facilities are wheelchair-accessible. Leashed pets are permitted.

**Reservations, fees:** Reservations are not accepted. Tent sites are $10 per night, drive-in sites are $15 per night, plus $3 per night for each additional vehicle. Monthly and senior rates are available. Open May through mid-October, weather permitting.

**Directions:** From Sacramento, drive east on U.S. 50 to the junction with Highway 89. Turn south on Highway 89 and drive over Luther Pass to the junction with Highway 88. Turn left (east) and drive to Woodfords and the junction with Highway 89. Turn south on Highway 89 and drive 4.5 miles to the park entrance on the right side of the road.

**Contact:** Alpine County Public Works, 530/694-2140, www.alpinecountyca.gov.

## 164 GROVER HOT SPRINGS STATE PARK

**Scenic rating: 8**

near Markleeville

**Map 6.3, page 335**

This is a famous spot for folks who like the rejuvenating powers of hot springs. Some say they feel a glow about them for weeks after soaking here. When touring the South Tahoe/Carson Pass area, many vacationers take part of a day to make the trip to the hot springs. This park is set in alpine meadow at 5,900 feet elevation on the east side of the Sierra at the edge of the Great Basin, and it's surrounded by peaks that top 10,000 feet. The landscape is primarily pine forest and sagebrush. It is well known for the great fluctuations in weather, from serious blizzards to intense, dry heat, and from mild nights to awesome rim-rattling thunderstorms. High winds are occasional but legendary. The hot

springs are green because of the mineral deposits at the bottom of the pools. During thunderstorms, the hot springs pools close because of the chance of lightning strikes. Yet they remain open in snow, even blizzards, when it can be a euphoric experience to sit in the steaming water.

Note that the pools are closed for maintenance for two weeks in September. A 2.4-mile round-trip hike starts from the campground and continues to a series of small waterfalls. Side-trip options include a nature trail in the park and driving to the Carson River (where the water is a mite cooler) and fishing for trout.

**Campsites, facilities:** There are 26 sites for tents and 50 sites for tents or RVs up to 27 feet (no hookups) and trailers up to 24 feet. Picnic tables, fire grills, and food lockers are provided. Restrooms with flush toilets and coin showers (summer only), drinking water, a hot springs pool with wheelchair access, and a heated swimming pool are available. A visitors center is opposite the campground entrance. A grocery store is four miles away, and a coin laundry is within 10 miles. Leashed pets are permitted.

**Reservations, fees:** Reservations are accepted at 800/444-7275 or www.reserveamerica.com ($8 reservation fee). Sites are $35 per night, plus $8 per night for each additional vehicle, and pool fees are $5-7 per person per day. Open year-round, with reduced facilities in winter; closed Wednesdays in winter.

**Directions:** From Sacramento, drive east on U.S. 50 to the junction with Highway 89. Turn south on Highway 89 and drive over Luther Pass to the junction with Highway 88. Turn left and drive to Woodfords and the junction with Highway 89. Turn right (south) and drive six miles to Markleeville and the junction with Hot Springs Road. Turn right and drive four miles to the park entrance.

**Contact:** Grover Hot Springs State Park, 530/694-2248; Sierra District, 530/525-7232, www.parks.ca.gov; pool information, 530/525-7232.

## 165 MARKLEEVILLE

### Scenic rating: 7

on Markleeville Creek in Humboldt-Toiyabe National Forest

**Map 6.3, page 335**

This is a pretty, streamside camp at 5,500 feet along Markleeville Creek, a mile from the East Fork of the Carson River. The trout here are willing, but alas, are dinkers. This area is the transition zone where high mountains to the west give way to the high desert to the east. The hot springs in Markleeville and Grover Hot Springs State Park provide good side trips.

**Campsites, facilities:** There are 10 sites for tents or RVs up to 24 feet (no hookups). Trailers are not recommended because of road conditions. Picnic tables and fire grills are provided. Drinking water and vault toilets are available. A grocery store and restaurant are nearby. Leashed pets are permitted.

**Reservations, fees:** Reservations are not accepted. Sites are $18 per night, plus $5 per night for extra vehicle. Open late April through September, weather permitting.

**Directions:** From Sacramento, drive east on U.S. 50 to the junction with Highway 89. Turn south on Highway 89 and drive over Luther Pass to the junction with Highway 88. Turn left and drive to Woodfords and the junction with Highway 89. Turn south, drive six miles to Markleeville, and continue for 0.5 mile to the campground on the left side of the highway.

**Contact:** Humboldt-Toiyabe National Forest, Carson Ranger District, 775/882-2766, www.fs.usda/htnf.

## 166 TOPAZ LAKE RV PARK

### Scenic rating: 6

on Topaz Lake, near Markleeville

**Map 6.3, page 335**

At 5,000 feet elevation, Topaz Lake is one of the hidden surprises for California anglers. The surprise is the size of the rainbow trout, with one of the highest rates of 15- to 18-inch trout of any lake in the mountain country. All water sports are allowed on this 2,400-acre lake, and there is a swimming area. The campground itself is attractive, with shade trees. The setting is on the edge of barren high desert, which also serves as the border between California and Nevada. Wind is a problem for small boats, especially in the early summer. Some of the sites are rented for the entire season.

**Campsites, facilities:** There are 59 sites with full hookups (50 amps) for RVs up to 42 feet. Some sites are pull-through. Tents are allowed with RVs only, though tent-only sites are allowed during nonpeak season. Picnic tables, Wi-Fi, and cable TV are provided. Restrooms with coin showers, a coin laundry, propane gas, a small grocery store, mailboxes, a fish-cleaning station, and horseshoe pits are available. A 40-boat marina with courtesy launch and boat-trailer storage is available at lakeside. Some facilities are wheelchair-accessible. Leashed pets are permitted.

**Reservations, fees:** Reservations are recommended. RV sites (full hookups) are $36 per night, plus $3.50 per person for more than two people. Discounts and monthly rates are available. Some credit cards are accepted. Open March through early October, weather permitting.

**Directions:** From Carson City, drive south on U.S. 395 for 45 miles to Topaz Lake and the campground on the left side of the road.

From Bridgeport, drive north on U.S. 395 for 45 miles to the campground on the right side of the road (0.3 mile south of the California/Nevada border).

**Contact:** Topaz Lake RV Park, 530/495-2357, www.topazlakervpark.com.

## 167 UPPER BLUE LAKE DAM AND EXPANSION

🚶 🏊 🚣 ⛵ 🎣 🐕 🚙 ⛺

### Scenic rating: 7

near Carson Pass

**Map 6.3, page 335**

These two camps sit across the road from each other along Upper Blue Lake, and are two of five camps in the area. The trout fishing is usually quite good in early summer. (See the Lower Blue Lake listing in this chapter for more information.) These camps are three miles past the Lower Blue Lake campground. The elevation is 8,400 feet.

**Campsites, facilities:** There are 32 sites at Upper Blue Lake Dam and 15 sites at the expansion area for tents or RVs up to 25 feet. Picnic tables and fire grills are provided at Upper Blue Lake Dam only. Drinking water and vault toilets are available. Leashed pets are permitted.

**Reservations, fees:** Reservations are not accepted. Sites are $23 per night, plus $5 per night for each additional vehicle and $2 per pet per night. Open June through mid-October, weather permitting.

**Directions:** From Sacramento, drive east on U.S. 50 to the junction with Highway 89. Turn south on Highway 89 and drive over Luther Pass to the junction with Highway 88. Turn right and drive 2.5 miles to Blue Lakes Road. Turn left and drive 12 miles to the junction at the south end of Lower Blue Lake. Turn right and drive three miles to the Upper Blue Lake Dam campground on the left side of the road or the expansion area on the right.

From Jackson, drive east on Highway 88 over Carson Pass and continue east for five miles to Blue Lakes Road. Turn right (south) and drive 12 miles to a junction at the south end of Lower Blue Lake. Turn right and drive three miles to the Upper Blue Lake Dam campground on the left side of the road or the expansion area on the right.

**Contact:** PG&E Land Projects, 916/386-5164, www.pge.com/recreation.

## 168 MIDDLE CREEK AND EXPANSION

🚶 🏊 🎣 🐕 ♿ 🚙 ⛺

### Scenic rating: 7

near Carson Pass and Blue Lakes

**Map 6.3, page 335**

This tiny, captivating spot, set along the creek that connects Upper and Lower Blue Lakes, provides a take-your-pick deal for anglers. PG&E has expanded this facility and now offers a larger camping area about 200 yards from the original campground. (See the Lower Blue Lake listing in this chapter for more information.) The elevation is 8,200 feet.

**Campsites, facilities:** There are five sites for tents or RVs up to 30 feet at Middle Creek and 35 sites for tents or RVs up to 45 feet at the expansion area (no hookups). Picnic tables and fire grills are provided. Drinking water and vault toilets are available at the expansion area. Some facilities are wheelchair-accessible. Leashed pets are permitted.

**Reservations, fees:** Reservations are not accepted. Sites are $23 per night, plus $5 per night for each additional vehicle and $2 per pet per night. Open late May to mid-October, weather permitting.

**Directions:** From Sacramento, drive east on U.S. 50 to the junction with Highway 89. Turn south on Highway 89 and drive over Luther Pass to the junction with Highway 88. Turn right and drive 2.5 miles to Blue Lakes Road. Turn left and drive 12 miles to a junction at the south end of Lower Blue Lake. Turn right and drive 1.5 miles to the Middle Creek campground on the left side of the road and continue another 200 yards to reach the expansion area.

From Jackson, drive east on Highway 88 over Carson Pass and continue east for five miles to Blue Lakes Road. Turn right (south) and drive 12 miles (road becomes dirt) to a junction at the south end of Lower Blue Lake. Turn right and drive 1.5 miles to the Middle Creek campground on the left side of the road and continue another 200 yards to reach the expansion area.

**Contact:** PG&E Land Projects, 916/386-5164, www.pge.com/recreation.

## 169 LOWER BLUE LAKE
🥾 🏊 🎣 🚣 🦌 🚐 ⛺

**Scenic rating: 7**

near Carson Pass

**Map 6.3, page 335**

This is the high country, at 8,400 feet, where the terrain is stark and steep and edged by volcanic ridgelines, and where the deep blue-green hue of lake water brightens the landscape. Lower Blue Lake provides a popular trout fishery, with rainbow, brook, and cutthroat trout all stocked regularly. The boat ramp is adjacent to the campground. The access road crosses the Pacific Crest Trail, providing a route to a series of small, pretty, hike-to lakes just outside the edge of the Mokelumne Wilderness.

**Campsites, facilities:** There are 16 sites for tents or RVs up to 25 feet (no hookups). Picnic tables and fire grills are provided. Drinking water and vault toilets are available. Leashed pets are permitted.

**Reservations, fees:** Reservations are not accepted. Sites are $23 per night, plus $5 per night for each additional vehicle and $2 per pet per night. There's a 14-day occupancy limit. Open June through mid-October, weather permitting.

**Directions:** From Sacramento, drive east on U.S. 50 to the junction with Highway 89. Turn south on Highway 89 and drive over Luther Pass to the junction with Highway 88. Turn right and drive 2.5 miles to Blue Lakes Road. Turn left and drive 12 miles to a junction at the south end of Lower Blue Lake. Turn right and drive a short distance to the campground on the left side of the road.

From Jackson, drive east on Highway 88 over Carson Pass and continue east for five miles to Blue Lakes Road. Turn right (south) and drive 12 miles to a junction at the south end of Lower

Blue Lake. Turn right and drive a short distance to the campground on the left.

**Contact:** PG&E Land Projects, 916/386-5164, www.pge.com/recreation.

## 170 SILVER CREEK
🥾 🎣 🦌 🚐 ⛺

**Scenic rating: 6**

in Humboldt-Toiyabe National Forest

**Map 6.3, page 335**

This pretty spot near Silver Creek has easy access from Highway 4 and, in years without washouts, good fishing in early summer for small trout. It is in the remote high Sierra, east of Ebbetts Pass. A side trip to Ebbetts Pass features Kinney Lake, Pacific Crest Trail access, and a trailhead at the north end of the lake (on the west side of Highway 4) for a mile hike to Lower Kinney Lake. No bikes are permitted on the trails. The elevation is 6,800 feet.

**Campsites, facilities:** There are 22 sites for tents or RVs up to 22 feet (no hookups). Picnic tables and fire grills are provided. Drinking water, vault toilets, and garbage service are available. Leashed pets are permitted.

**Reservations, fees:** Reservations are accepted at 877/444-6777 ($10 reservation fee) or www.recreation.gov ($9 reservation fee). Sites are $18-34 per night, plus $6 per night for each extra vehicle. Open late May through early September, weather permitting.

**Directions:** From Angels Camp, drive east on Highway 4 all the way over Ebbetts Pass and continue for about six miles to the campground.

From Markleeville, drive south on Highway 89 to the junction with Highway 4. Turn west on Highway 4 (steep and winding) and drive about five miles to the campground.

**Contact:** Humboldt-Toiyabe National Forest, Carson Ranger District, 775/882-2766, www.fs.usda/htnf.

## 171 MOSQUITO LAKE

### Scenic rating: 10

at Mosquito Lake in Stanislaus National Forest

**Map 6.3, page 335**

Mosquito Lake is in a pristine Sierra setting at 8,260 feet elevation, presenting remarkable beauty for a place that can be reached by car. Most people believe that Mosquito Lake is for day-use only, and that's why they crowd into nearby Lake Alpine Campground. But it's not just for day-use, and this camp is often overlooked because it is about a mile west of the little lake. The lake is small, a pretty emerald green, and even has a few small trout in it. The camp provides a few dispersed sites.

**Campsites, facilities:** There are 11 sites for tents or RVs up to 16 feet (no hookups). Picnic tables and fire grills are provided. Vault toilets are available. No drinking water is available. Garbage must be packed out. Leashed pets are permitted.

**Reservations, fees:** Reservations are not accepted. Sites are $8 per night. A free campfire permit is required from the district office. Open June through September, weather permitting.

**Directions:** From Angels Camp, drive east on Highway 4 to Lake Alpine and continue for about six miles to the campground on the left side of the road.

**Contact:** Stanislaus National Forest, Calaveras Ranger District, 209/795-1381, www.fs.usda.gov/stanislaus.

## 172 HERMIT VALLEY

### Scenic rating: 8

in Stanislaus National Forest

**Map 6.3, page 335**

This tiny, remote, little-known spot is near the border of the Mokelumne Wilderness near where Grouse Creek enters the Mokelumne River, at 7,100 feet elevation. Looking north, there is a good view into Deer Valley. A primitive road, a half mile west of camp, is routed through Deer Valley north for six miles to the Blue Lakes. On the opposite (south) side of the road from the camp, a little-traveled hiking trail meanders up Grouse Creek to Beaver Meadow and Willow Meadow near the border of the Carson-Iceberg Wilderness.

**Campsites, facilities:** There are 25 sites for tents or RVs of any length (no hookups). Vault toilets are available. No drinking water is available. Garbage must be packed out. Leashed pets are permitted.

**Reservations, fees:** Reservations are not accepted. There is no fee for camping. A free campfire permit is required from the district office. Open June through October, weather permitting.

**Directions:** From Angels Camp, drive east on Highway 4 to Lake Alpine and continue for about nine miles to the campground on the left side of the road (just east of the Mokelumne River Bridge). Note: Trailers are not recommended because of the steep access road.

**Contact:** Stanislaus National Forest, Calaveras Ranger District, 209/795-1381, www.fs.usda.gov/stanislaus.

## 173 BLOOMFIELD

### Scenic rating: 7

in Stanislaus National Forest

**Map 6.3, page 335**

This is a primitive and little-known camp set at 7,800 feet elevation near Ebbetts Pass. The North Fork Mokelumne River runs right by the camp, with good stream access for about a mile on each side of the camp. The access road continues south to Highland Lakes, a destination that provides car-top boating, fair fishing, and trailheads for hiking into the Carson-Iceberg Wilderness.

**Campsites, facilities:** There are 20 sites for tents or RVs up to 16 feet (no hookups). Picnic tables and fire rings are provided. Drinking water and vault toilets are available. Garbage must be packed out. Facilities and supplies are available at Lake Alpine Lodge, 25 minutes away. Leashed pets are permitted.

**Reservations, fees:** Reservations are not accepted. Sites are $12 per night. A free campfire permit is required from the district office. Open June through October, weather permitting.

**Directions:** From Angels Camp, drive east on Highway 4 to Lake Alpine and continue for about 15 miles to Forest Road 8N01 on the right side of the road (1.5 miles west of Ebbetts Pass). Turn right and drive two miles to the campground on the right side of the road. Note: Access roads are rough and not recommended for trailers.

**Contact:** Stanislaus National Forest, Calaveras Ranger District, 209/795-1381, www.fs.usda. gov/stanislaus.

## 174 PACIFIC VALLEY
🥾🐕🚐🏕

### Scenic rating: 7
in Stanislaus National Forest overlooking Pacific Creek

Map 6.3, page 335

This is a do-it-yourself special; that is, more of a general area for camping than a campground, set up for backpackers heading out on expeditions into the Carson-Iceberg Wilderness to the south. It is set at 7,600 feet elevation along Pacific Creek, a tributary to the Mokelumne River. The landscape is an open lodgepole forest with nearby meadow and a small stream. The trail from camp heads south and reaches three forks within two miles. The best is routed deep into the wilderness, flanking Hiram Peak (9,760 feet), Airola Peak (9,938 feet), and Iceberg Peak (9,781 feet).

**Campsites, facilities:** There are 15 sites for tents or RVs up to 16 feet (no hookups). Picnic tables and fire grills are provided. Vault toilets are available. Drinking water is sometimes available. Garbage must be packed out. Equestrians with horse trailers may camp at

the southern end of the campground, near the trailhead. Leashed pets are permitted.

**Reservations, fees:** Reservations are not accepted. Sites are $10 per night when water is available, $5 per night with no water. A free campfire permit is required from the district office. Open June through October, weather permitting.

**Directions:** From Angels Camp, drive east on Highway 4 to Lake Alpine and continue for eight miles to a dirt road. Turn right (south) and drive about 0.5 mile to the campground. Note: Trailers are not recommended because of the rough roads.

**Contact:** Stanislaus National Forest, Calaveras Ranger District, 209/795-1381, www.fs.usda. gov/stanislaus.

## 175 UPPER AND LOWER HIGHLAND LAKES
🥾🏊🛶�🚐🐕♿🚌🏕

### Scenic rating: 9
in Stanislaus National Forest

Map 6.3, page 335

This camp is between Upper and Lower Highland Lakes, two beautiful alpine ponds that offer good fishing for small brook trout as well as spectacular panoramic views. The boat speed limit is 5 mph, and a primitive boat ramp is at Upper Highland Lake; gas motors are discouraged. Swimming is allowed, although the water is very cold. The elevation at this campground is 8,600 feet, with Hiram Peak (9,760 feet) looming to the nearby south. Several great trails are available from this camp. Day hikes include up Boulder Creek and Disaster Creek. For overnight backpacking, a trail starts at the north end of Highland Lakes (a parking area is available) and leads east for two miles to Wolf Creek Pass, where it connects with the Pacific Crest Trail; from there, turn left or right—you can't lose. The access road is not recommended for trailers or large RVs.

**Campsites, facilities:** There are 35 sites for tents or RVs up to 16 feet (no hookups). Picnic

tables and fire grills are provided. Drinking water and vault toilets are available. Garbage must be packed out. Some facilities are wheelchair-accessible. Leashed pets are permitted.

**Reservations, fees:** Reservations are not accepted. Sites are $12 per night. Open July through September, weather permitting.

**Directions:** From Angels Camp, drive east on Highway 4 to Arnold, past Lake Alpine, and continue for 14.5 miles to Forest Road 8N01 (one mile west of Ebbetts Pass). Turn right and drive 7.5 miles to the campground on the right side of the road. Note: The roads are rough and trailers are not recommended.

**Contact:** Stanislaus National Forest, Calaveras Ranger District, 209/795-1381, www.fs.usda. gov/stanislaus.

## 176 LODGEPOLE GROUP LAKE ALPINE

### Scenic rating: 6
near Lake Alpine in Stanislaus National Forest

**Map 6.3, page 335**

What to do when all the campgrounds at Lake Alpine are full? Gather together your friends and family and head to this group site just two miles west of the lake. Set in an undeveloped plain at 7,290 feet, the camp is large, flat, and open, but with Lake Alpine so close, there are plenty of opportunities for hiking, fishing, and boating.

**Campsites, facilities:** There are two group sites for up to 50 people each with tents or RVs (no hookups). Picnic tables and fire grills are provided. Drinking water and vault toilets are available. A grocery store, restaurant, coin showers, and a coin laundry are nearby. Some facilities are wheelchair-accessible. Leashed pets are permitted.

**Reservations, fees:** Reservations are required at 877/444-6777 ($10 reservation fee) or www. recreation.gov ($9 reservation fee) and must be made at least four days in advance. Sites are $100 per night. Open mid-June through early September, weather permitting.

**Directions:** From Angels Camp, drive east on Highway 4 for 50 miles to Lake Alpine. Lodgepole Group is two miles west of Lake Alpine, near Bear Valley.

**Contact:** Stanislaus National Forest, Calaveras Ranger District, 209/795-1381, www.fs.usda. gov/stanislaus.

## 177 SILVERTIP

### Scenic rating: 6
near Lake Alpine in Stanislaus National Forest

**Map 6.3, page 335**

This camp is just over a half mile from the shore of Lake Alpine at an elevation of 7,350 feet. Why then would anyone camp here when there are campgrounds right at the lake? Two reasons: 1) Those lakeside camps are often full on summer weekends; 2) Highway 4 is snowplowed to this campground entrance, but not beyond. So in big snow years when the road is still closed in late spring and early summer, you can park your rig here to camp, then hike in to the lake. In the fall, it also makes for a base camp for hunters. (See the Lake Alpine Campground listing in this chapter for more information.)

**Campsites, facilities:** There are 23 sites for tents or RVs up to 27 feet (no hookups). Picnic tables and fire grills are provided. Drinking water and restrooms with flush toilets are available. A boat launch is about a mile away. A grocery store, coin laundry, and coin showers are nearby. Some facilities are wheelchair-accessible. Leashed pets are permitted.

**Reservations, fees:** Reservations are not accepted. Sites are $25 per night. Open June through early October, weather permitting.

**Directions:** From Angels Camp, drive east on Highway 4 to Arnold and continue for 29 miles to Lake Alpine. A mile before reaching the lake (adjacent to the Bear Valley/Mount

Reba turnoff), turn right at the campground entrance on the right side of the road.
**Contact:** Stanislaus National Forest, Calaveras Ranger District, 209/795-1381, www.fs.usda. gov/stanislaus.

## 178 LAKE ALPINE CAMPGROUND

**Scenic rating: 8**

on Lake Alpine in Stanislaus National Forest

**Map 6.3, page 335**                    **BEST (**

Lake Alpine is one of the prettiest lakes you can drive to, set at 7,300 feet elevation amid pines and Sierra granite. This is the campground that is in the greatest demand at Lake Alpine, and it is easy to see why. It is very small, a boat ramp is adjacent to the camp, you can get supplies at a small grocery store within walking distance, and during the evening rise you can often see the jumping trout from your campsite. A trailhead out of nearby Silver Valley Camp provides a two-mile hike to pretty Duck Lake and beyond into the Carson-Iceberg Wilderness.
**Campsites, facilities:** There are 25 sites for tents or RVs up to 27 feet (no hookups). Picnic tables and fire grills are provided. Drinking water, restrooms with flush toilets, and a boat launch are available. A grocery store, restaurant, coin showers, and a coin laundry are nearby. Some facilities are wheelchair-accessible. Leashed pets are permitted.
**Reservations, fees:** Reservations are not accepted. Sites are $25 per night. Open June through October, weather permitting.
**Directions:** From Angels Camp, drive east on Highway 4 to Arnold and continue east for 29 miles to Lake Alpine. Just before reaching the lake turn right and drive 0.25 mile to the campground on the left.
**Contact:** Stanislaus National Forest, Calaveras

Ranger District, 209/795-1381, www.fs.usda. gov/stanislaus.

## 179 PINE MARTEN

**Scenic rating: 8**

near Lake Alpine in Stanislaus National Forest

**Map 6.3, page 335**

Lake Alpine is a beautiful Sierra lake surrounded by granite and pines and set at 7,300 feet, just above where the snowplows stop in winter. This camp is on the northeast side, about a quarter mile from the shore. Fishing for rainbow trout is good in May and early June, before the summer crush. Despite the long drive to get here, the lake is becoming better known for its beauty, camping, and hiking. Lake Alpine has 180 surface acres and a 10-mph speed limit. A trailhead out of nearby Silver Valley Camp provides a two-mile hike to pretty Duck Lake and beyond into the Carson-Iceberg Wilderness.
**Campsites, facilities:** There are 32 sites for tents or RVs up to 27 feet (no hookups). Picnic tables and fire grills are provided. Drinking water and flush toilets are available. A boat ramp is nearby. A grocery store, propane gas, and coin laundry are nearby. Some facilities are wheelchair-accessible. Leashed pets are permitted.
**Reservations, fees:** Reservations are not accepted. Sites are $25 per night. Open June through early October, weather permitting.
**Directions:** From Angels Camp, drive east on Highway 4 to Arnold and continue east for 29 miles to Lake Alpine. Drive to the northeast end of the lake to the campground entrance on the right side of the road.
**Contact:** Stanislaus National Forest, Calaveras Ranger District, 209/795-1381, www.fs.usda. gov/stanislaus.

## 180 SILVER VALLEY

### Scenic rating: 8

on Lake Alpine in Stanislaus National Forest

**Map 6.3, page 335**

This is one of four camps at Lake Alpine. Silver Valley is on the northeast end of the lake at 7,400 feet elevation, with a trailhead nearby that provides access to the Carson-Iceberg Wilderness. (For recreation information, see the Pine Marten listing in this chapter.)

**Campsites, facilities:** There are 21 sites for tents or RVs up to 16 feet (no hookups). Picnic tables and fire grills are provided. Drinking water and restrooms with flush toilets are available. Some facilities are wheelchair-accessible. A boat launch, grocery store, and coin laundry are nearby. Leashed pets are permitted.

**Reservations, fees:** Reservations are not accepted. Sites are $25 per night. A free campfire permit is required. Open June through October, weather permitting.

**Directions:** From Angels Camp, drive east on Highway 4 to Arnold and continue east for 29 miles to Lake Alpine. Drive to the northeast end of the lake to the campground entrance on the right side of the road. Turn right and drive 0.5 mile to the campground.

**Contact:** Stanislaus National Forest, Calaveras Ranger District, 209/795-1381, www.fs.usda.gov/stanislaus.

## 181 UTICA AND UNION RESERVOIRS

### Scenic rating: 10

northeast of Arnold in Stanislaus National Forest

**Map 6.3, page 335**

These twin reservoirs are set in Sierra granite at 6,850 feet. Union is a beautiful and quiet lake that is kept that way with rules that mandate a 5-mph speed limit. Utica does not allow motors of any kind. Most of the campsites provide lakeside views. Fishing is often good—trolling for kokanee salmon—but you need a boat. The setting is great, especially for canoes or other small boats. This area was once a secret, but alas the secret is out and there are now three new, small campgrounds around the water's edge.

**Campsites, facilities:** There are four campgrounds for tents only (RVs are not recommended); sites are a mixture of walk-in and standard sites. Utica has two campgrounds: Sandy Flat with 11 sites and Rocky Point with 12 sites. Union Reservoir also has two campgrounds: Union West has 18 sites and Union East 11 sites. Vault toilets are available. There is no drinking water. Garbage must be packed out. A boat ramp is nearby. Leashed pets are permitted.

**Reservations, fees:** Reservations are not accepted. Sites are $16 per night. Open June through September, weather permitting.

**Directions:** From Angels Camp, drive east on Highway 4 for about 32 miles to Spicer Reservoir Road. Turn right and drive east for about seven miles to Forest Road 7N75 and turn left. To reach Utica, continue two miles and turn left onto Forest Road 7N17; continue one mile to Utica Reservoir on the right. To reach Union Reservoir, stay on Forest Road 7N75 for approximately three miles. Each camp is visible from the road.

**Contact:** Stanislaus National Forest, Calaveras Ranger District, 209/795-1381, www.fs.usda.gov/stanislaus.

## 182 SPICER RESERVOIR AND GROUP CAMP

### Scenic rating: 8

near Spicer Reservoir in Stanislaus National Forest

**Map 6.3, page 335**

Set at 6,200 feet elevation and covering only 227 acres, Spicer Reservoir isn't big by reservoir standards, but it is surrounded by canyon walls and is quite pretty from a boat. Good trout fishing adds to the beauty. A boat ramp is available near the campground, and the lake speed limit is 10 mph. The east end of the lake is in the Carson-Iceberg Wilderness; no motors are allowed past the buoy marker. A trail links the east end of Spicer Reservoir to the Summit Lake Trailhead, with the route bordering the north side of the reservoir. Note: This area can really get hammered with snow in big winters, so always check for access conditions in the spring and early summer before planning a trip.

**Campsites, facilities:** There are 60 sites for tents or RVs up to 50 feet (no hookups). One group site for tents or RVs up to 28 feet (no hookups) can accommodate up to 75 people. Picnic tables and fire grills are provided. Drinking water and vault toilets, group facilities, and a primitive amphitheater are available. A boat ramp is nearby. Some facilities are wheelchair-accessible. Leashed pets are permitted.

**Reservations, fees:** Reservations are not accepted for individual sites but are required for the group site at 209/296-8895. Sites are $24 per night, and the group site is $140 per night. Open June through October, weather permitting.

**Directions:** From Angels Camp, drive east on Highway 4 for about 32 miles to Spicer Reservoir Road/Forest Road 7N01. Turn right, drive seven miles, bear right at a fork with a sharp right turn, and drive a mile to the campground at the west end of the lake.

**Contact:** Stanislaus National Forest, Calaveras Ranger District, 209/795-1381, www.fs.usda.gov/stanislaus or www.srmgocamping.com.

## 183 SAND FLAT-STANISLAUS RIVER

🏃 🏊 ⛵ 🐕 ♿ 🚐 ⛺

### Scenic rating: 7

on the Clark Fork of the Stanislaus River in Stanislaus National Forest

**Map 6.3, page 335**

Sand Flat campground, at 6,200 feet, is only three miles (by vehicle on Clark Fork Road) from an outstanding trailhead for the Carson-Iceberg Wilderness. The camp is used primarily by late-arriving backpackers who camp for the night, get their gear in order, then head off on the trail. The trail is routed out of Iceberg Meadow, with a choice of heading north to Paradise Valley (unbelievably green and loaded with corn lilies along a creek) and onward to the Pacific Crest Trail, or east to Clark Fork and upstream to Clark Fork Meadow below Sonora Peak. Two choices, both winners.

**Campsites, facilities:** There are 68 sites for tents or RVs up to 22 feet (no hookups) and 15 walk-in tent sites. Picnic tables and fire grills are provided. Drinking water and vault toilets are available. You can buy supplies in Dardanelle. Some facilities are wheelchair-accessible. Leashed pets are permitted.

**Reservations, fees:** Reservations are not accepted. Sites are $19 per night per vehicle. Open May through early October, weather permitting.

**Directions:** From Sonora, drive east on Highway 108 past the town of Strawberry to Clark Fork Road. Turn left on Clark Fork Road and drive six miles to the campground entrance on the right side of the road.

**Contact:** Stanislaus National Forest, Summit Ranger District, 209/965-3434, www.fs.usda.gov/stanislaus.

## 184 CLARK FORK AND CLARK FORK HORSE

### Scenic rating: 8

on the Clark Fork of the Stanislaus River in Stanislaus National Forest

**Map 6.3, page 335**

Clark Fork borders the Clark Fork of the Stanislaus River and is used by both drive-in vacationers and backpackers. A trailhead for hikers is a quarter mile away on the north side of Clark Fork Road (a parking area is available). The trail travels along Arnot Creek, skirting between Iceberg Peak on the left and Lightning Mountain on the right, for eight miles to Wolf Creek Pass and the junction with the Pacific Crest Trail. (For another nearby trailhead, see the Sand Flat-Stanislaus River listing in this chapter.)

**Campsites, facilities:** There are 88 sites for tents or RVs up to 40 feet and, at an adjacent area, 14 equestrian sites for tents or RVs up to 22 feet (no hookups). Picnic tables and fire grills are provided. Drinking water, vault and flush toilets, and a dump station are available. At the equestrian site, no drinking water is available, but there are water troughs. Supplies are available in Dardanelle. Some facilities are wheelchair-accessible. Leashed pets are permitted.

**Reservations, fees:** Reservations are not accepted. Single sites are $20 per night, double sites are $38-40 per night, the horse camp is $17-60 per night, plus $5 per night for each additional vehicle. Open May through October, weather permitting.

**Directions:** From Sonora, drive east on Highway 108 past the town of Strawberry to Clark Fork Road. Turn left, drive five miles, turn right, and drive 0.5 mile to the campground entrance on the right side of the road.

**Contact:** Stanislaus National Forest, Summit Ranger District, 209/965-3434, www.fs.usda.gov/stanislaus.

## 185 FENCE CREEK

### Scenic rating: 4

near the Middle Fork of the Stanislaus River in Stanislaus National Forest

**Map 6.3, page 335**

Fence Creek is a feeder stream to Clark Fork, which runs a mile downstream and joins with the Middle Fork Stanislaus River en route to Donnells Reservoir. The camp sits along little Fence Creek, at 5,600 feet elevation. Fence Creek Road continues east for another nine miles to an outstanding trailhead at Iceberg Meadow on the edge of the Carson-Iceberg Wilderness.

**Campsites, facilities:** There are 37 sites for tents or RVs up to 22 feet (no hookups). Picnic tables and fire grills are provided. Vault toilets are available. No drinking water is available. Supplies are available in Pinecrest about 10 miles away. Some facilities are wheelchair-accessible. Leashed pets are permitted.

**Reservations, fees:** Reservations are not accepted. Sites are $10 per night. Open May through mid-October, weather permitting.

**Directions:** From Sonora, drive east on Highway 108 about 50 miles to Clark Fork Road. Turn left and drive a mile to Forest Road 6N06. Turn left again and drive 0.5 mile to the campground on the right.

**Contact:** Stanislaus National Forest, Summit Ranger District, 209/965-3434, www.fs.usda.gov/stanislaus.

## 186 BOULDER FLAT

### Scenic rating: 7

near the Middle Fork of the Stanislaus River in Stanislaus National Forest

**Map 6.3, page 335**

You want camping on the Stanislaus River? As you drive east on Highway 108, this is the first in a series of campgrounds along the Middle Fork Stanislaus. Boulder Flat is set at 5,600 feet elevation and offers easy access off the highway. Here's another bonus: This stretch of river is stocked with trout.

**Campsites, facilities:** There are 20 sites for tents or RVs up to 22 feet (no hookups). Picnic tables and fire grills are provided. Drinking water and vault toilets are available. You can buy supplies in Dardanelle. Some facilities are wheelchair-accessible. Leashed pets are permitted.

**Reservations, fees:** Reservations are not accepted. Sites are $15-30 per night, plus $5 per night for each additional vehicle. Open May through October, weather permitting.

**Directions:** From Sonora, drive east on Highway 108 past the town of Strawberry to Clark Fork Road. At Clark Fork Road, continue east on Highway 108 for a mile to the campground on the left side of the road.

**Contact:** Stanislaus National Forest, Summit Ranger District, 209/965-3434, www.fs.usda. gov/stanislaus; Dodge Ridge Corporation, 209/965-3116.

## 187 BRIGHTMAN FLAT

### Scenic rating: 7
on the Middle Fork of the Stanislaus River in Stanislaus National Forest

**Map 6.3, page 335**

This camp is on the Middle Fork of the Stanislaus River at 5,700 feet elevation, a mile east of Boulder Flat and two miles west of Dardanelle. (For recreation options, see the Pigeon Flat listing in this chapter.)

**Campsites, facilities:** There are 32 sites for tents or RVs up to 22 feet (no hookups). Picnic tables and fire grills are provided. Vault toilets are available. There is no drinking water, although untreated water may be available from the stream. You can buy supplies in Dardanelle. Some facilities are wheelchair-accessible. Leashed pets are permitted.

**Reservations, fees:** Reservations are not

accepted. Sites are $15 per night, plus $5 per night for each additional vehicle. Open May through October, weather permitting.

**Directions:** From Sonora, drive east on Highway 108 past the town of Strawberry to Clark Fork Road. At Clark Fork Road, continue east on Highway 108 for two miles to the campground entrance on the left side of the road.

**Contact:** Stanislaus National Forest, Summit Ranger District, 209/965-3434, www.fs.usda. gov/stanislaus; Dodge Ridge Corporation, 209/965-3116.

## 188 DARDANELLE

### Scenic rating: 7
on the Middle Fork of the Stanislaus River in Stanislaus National Forest

**Map 6.3, page 335**

This Forest Service camp is within walking distance of supplies in Dardanelle and is also right alongside the Middle Fork Stanislaus River. This section of river is stocked with trout by the Department of Fish and Game. The trail to see Columns of the Giants is just 1.5 miles to the east out of Pigeon Flat.

**Campsites, facilities:** There are 28 sites for tents or RVs up to 28 feet (no hookups). Picnic tables and fire grills are provided. Drinking water and vault toilets are available. You can buy supplies in Dardanelle. Leashed pets are permitted.

**Reservations, fees:** Reservations are not accepted. Sites are $19-38 per night, plus $5 per night for each additional vehicle. Open May through October, weather permitting.

**Directions:** From Sonora, drive east on Highway 108 past Strawberry to Dardanelle and the campground on the left side of the road.

**Contact:** Stanislaus National Forest, Summit Ranger District, 209/965-3434, www.fs.usda. gov/stanislaus; Dodge Ridge Corporation, 209/965-3116.

# 189 PIGEON FLAT

### Scenic rating: 7

on the Middle Fork of the Stanislaus River in Stanislaus National Forest

**Map 6.3, page 335**

The prime attraction at Pigeon Flat is the short trail to Columns of the Giants, a rare example of columnar hexagonal rock, similar to the phenomenon at Devils Postpile near Mammoth Lakes. In addition, the camp is adjacent to the Middle Fork Stanislaus River; trout are small and get fished hard. Supplies are available within walking distance in Dardanelle. The elevation is 6,000 feet.

**Campsites, facilities:** There are seven walk-in tent sites. Picnic tables and fire grills are provided. Vault toilets are available. No drinking water is available. You can buy supplies in Dardanelle. Leashed pets are permitted.

**Reservations, fees:** Reservations are not accepted. Sites are $11 per night, plus $5 per night for each additional vehicle. Open May through October, weather permitting.

**Directions:** From Sonora, drive east on Highway 108 past the town of Strawberry to Dardanelle. Continue 1.5 miles east to the campground on the right side of the road, next to the Columns of the Giants Interpretive Site.

**Contact:** Stanislaus National Forest, Summit Ranger District, 209/965-3434, www.fs.usda. gov/stanislaus; Dodge Ridge Corporation, 209/965-3116.

# 190 EUREKA VALLEY

### Scenic rating: 8

on the Middle Fork of the Stanislaus River in Stanislaus National Forest

**Map 6.3, page 335**

There are about a half dozen campgrounds on this stretch of the Middle Fork Stanislaus River near Dardanelle, at 6,100 feet elevation. The river runs along two sides of this campground, making it quite pretty. This stretch of river is planted with trout by the Department of Fish and Game, but it is hit pretty hard despite its relatively isolated location. A good short and easy hike is to Columns of the Giants, accessible on a 0.25-mile-long trail out of Pigeon Flat, a mile to the west.

**Campsites, facilities:** There are 28 sites for tents or RVs up to 22 feet (no hookups). Picnic tables and fire grills are provided. Drinking water and vault toilets are available. You can buy supplies in Dardanelle. Leashed pets are permitted.

**Reservations, fees:** Reservations are not accepted. Sites are $18 per night, plus $5 per night for each additional vehicle. Open May through October, weather permitting.

**Directions:** From Sonora, drive east on Highway 108 past the town of Strawberry to Dardanelle. Continue three miles east to the campground on the right.

**Contact:** Stanislaus National Forest, Summit Ranger District, 209/965-3434, www.fs.usda. gov/stanislaus; Dodge Ridge Corporation, 209/965-3116.

# 191 BAKER

### Scenic rating: 7

on the Middle Fork of the Stanislaus River in Stanislaus National Forest

**Map 6.3, page 335**

Baker lies at the turnoff for the well-known and popular Kennedy Meadow Trailhead for the Emigrant Wilderness. The camp is set along the Middle Fork Stanislaus River, at 6,200 feet elevation, downstream a short way from the confluence with Deadman Creek. The trailhead, with a nearby horse corral, is another two miles farther on the Kennedy Meadow access road. From here it is a 1.5-mile hike to a fork in the trail; right will take you two miles to Relief Reservoir, 7,226 feet, and left will route you up Kennedy Creek for five miles to pretty Kennedy Lake, just north of Kennedy Peak (10,716 feet).

**Campsites, facilities:** There are 44 sites for tents or RVs up to 22 feet (no hookups). Picnic tables and fire grills are provided. Drinking water and vault toilets are available. Groceries, a restaurant, and showers are available at nearby Kennedy Meadows Pack Station. Leashed pets are permitted.

**Reservations, fees:** Reservations are not accepted. Sites are $20-40 per night, plus $5 per night for each additional vehicle. Open May through mid-October, weather permitting.

**Directions:** From Sonora, drive east on Highway 108 past Strawberry to Dardanelle. From Dardanelle, continue 5.5 miles east to the campground on the right side of the road at the turnoff for Kennedy Meadow.

**Contact:** Kennedy Meadows Pack Station Resort, 209/965-3900; Stanislaus National Forest, Summit Ranger District, 209/965-3434, www.fs.usda.gov/stanislaus.

## 192 DEADMAN

### Scenic rating: 7
on the Middle Fork of the Stanislaus River in Stanislaus National Forest

**Map 6.3, page 335**

This is a popular trailhead camp and an ideal jumping-off point for backpackers heading into the adjacent Emigrant Wilderness. The elevation is 6,200 feet. The camp is a short distance from Baker (see the Baker listing in this chapter for hiking destinations). Groceries, a restaurant, and showers are available at nearby Kennedy Meadows Pack Station.

**Campsites, facilities:** There are 17 sites for tents or RVs up to 22 feet (no hookups). Picnic tables and fire grills are provided. Drinking water and vault toilets are available. You can buy supplies in Dardanelle. Some facilities are wheelchair-accessible. Leashed pets are permitted.

**Reservations, fees:** Reservations are not accepted. Sites are $20-40 per night, plus $5 per

night for each additional vehicle. Open May through early October, weather permitting.

**Directions:** From Sonora, drive east on Highway 108 past the town of Strawberry to Dardanelle. From Dardanelle, continue 5.5 miles east to the Kennedy Meadow turnoff. Drive a mile on Kennedy Meadow Road to the campground, which is opposite the parking area for Kennedy Meadow Trail.

**Contact:** Kennedy Meadows Pack Station Resort, 209/965-3900; Stanislaus National Forest, Summit Ranger District, 209/965-3434, www.fs.usda.gov/stanislaus.

## 193 NIAGARA CREEK

### Scenic rating: 6
in Stanislaus National Forest

**Map 6.3, page 335**

This camp is beside Niagara Creek at 6,600 feet elevation, high in Stanislaus National Forest on the western slopes of the Sierra. It provides direct access to a network of roads in national forest, including routes to Double Dome Rock and another to Eagle Meadows. So if you have a four-wheel-drive vehicle or dirt bike, this is the place to come.

**Campsites, facilities:** There are nine sites for tents or RVs up to 22 feet (no hookups); some are walk-in sites. Picnic tables and fire grills are provided. A vault toilet is available. No drinking water is available. You can buy supplies in Pinecrest about 10 miles away. Leashed pets are permitted.

**Reservations, fees:** Reservations are not accepted. Sites are $10 per vehicle per night. Open May through October, weather permitting.

**Directions:** From Sonora, drive east on Highway 108 to the town of Strawberry and continue for about 15 miles to Eagle Meadows Road/Forest Road 5N01 on the right. Turn right and drive 0.5 mile to the campground on the left.

**Contact:** Stanislaus National Forest, Summit

Ranger District, 209/965-3434, www.fs.usda.
gov/stanislaus.

## 194 NIAGARA CREEK OFF-HIGHWAY VEHICLE

🚶 🏊 🐕 🚐 ▲

### Scenic rating: 6

on Niagara Creek in Stanislaus National Forest

**Map 6.3, page 335**

This small, primitive camp along Niagara Creek is designed primarily for people with off-highway vehicles. Got it? It is on Niagara Creek near Donnells Reservoir. The elevation is 6,600 feet.

**Campsites, facilities:** There are 12 sites for tents or RVs up to 22 feet (no hookups). Picnic tables and fire grills are provided. A vault toilet is available. No drinking water is available. You can buy supplies in Pinecrest about 10 miles away. Leashed pets are permitted.

**Reservations, fees:** Reservations are not accepted. Sites are $10 per vehicle per night. Open May through October, weather permitting.

**Directions:** From Sonora, drive east on Highway 108 to Strawberry and continue for about 15 miles to Eagle Meadows Road/Forest Road 5N01. Turn right and drive 1.5 miles to the campground on the left (just after crossing the bridge at Niagara Creek).

**Contact:** Stanislaus National Forest, Summit Ranger District, 209/965-3434, www.fs.usda. gov/stanislaus.

## 195 MILL CREEK

🚶 🏊 🐕 🚐 ▲

### Scenic rating: 7

on Mill Creek in Stanislaus National Forest

**Map 6.3, page 335**

This pretty little camp along Mill Creek is at 6,200 feet elevation, high in Stanislaus National Forest, near a variety of outdoor recreation options. The camp is near the Middle Fork Stanislaus River, which is stocked with trout near Donnells. For hiking, there is an outstanding trailhead at Kennedy Meadow (east of Donnells). For fishing, both Beardsley Reservoir (boat necessary) and Pinecrest Lake (shoreline prospects fair) provide two nearby alternatives.

**Campsites, facilities:** There are 17 sites for tents or RVs up to 22 feet (no hookups). Picnic tables and fire grills are provided. Vault toilets and garbage service are available. There is no drinking water. Leashed pets are permitted.

**Reservations, fees:** Reservations are not accepted. Sites are $10 per night. Open May through mid-October, weather permitting.

**Directions:** From Sonora, drive east on Highway 108 to Strawberry. From Strawberry continue east on Highway 108 about 13 miles to Forest Road 5N21. Turn right on Forest Road 5N21 and drive 0.1 mile to the campground access road (Forest Road 5N26) on the left.

**Contact:** Stanislaus National Forest, Summit Ranger District, 209/965-3434, www.fs.usda. gov/stanislaus.

## 196 BOOTLEG

🏊 🐕 🚐 ▲

### Scenic rating: 6

on the Walker River in Humboldt-Toiyabe National Forest

**Map 6.3, page 335**

Location is always key, and easy access off U.S. 395, the adjacent West Walker River, and good trout stocks in summer make this a popular spot. Note that this camp is on the west side of the highway, and anglers have to cross the road to gain fishing access. The elevation is 6,600 feet. (See the Chris Flat and Sonora Bridge listings in this chapter for more information.)

**Campsites, facilities:** There are 63 sites for tents or RVs up to 35 feet (no hookups). Picnic tables and fire grills are provided. Drinking water and flush toilets are available. Leashed pets are permitted.

**Reservations, fees:** Reservations are not

accepted. Sites are $20 per night, plus $5 per night for each additional vehicle. Open early May through mid-September, weather permitting.

**Directions:** From Carson City, drive south on U.S. 395 to Coleville and then continue south for 13 miles to the campground on the west side of the highway (six miles north of the junction of U.S. 395 and Highway 108).

**Contact:** Humboldt-Toiyabe National Forest, Bridgeport Ranger District, 760/932-7070, www.fs.usda.gov/htnf or www.westrekservices.com.

## 197 CHRIS FLAT

### Scenic rating: 7

on the Walker River in Humboldt-Toiyabe National Forest

**Map 6.3, page 335**

This is one of two campgrounds along U.S. 395 next to the West Walker River, a pretty trout stream with easy access and good stocks of rainbow trout. The plants are usually made at two campgrounds, resulting in good prospects at Chris Flat and west on Highway 108 at Sonora Bridge. The elevation is 6,600 feet.

**Campsites, facilities:** There are 14 sites for tents or RVs up to 30 feet (no hookups). Picnic tables and fire grills are provided. Drinking water (shut off during freezing temperatures) and vault toilets are available. Leashed pets are permitted.

**Reservations, fees:** Reservations are not accepted. Sites are $20 per night, plus $6 per night for each additional vehicle. Open April through mid-November, weather permitting.

**Directions:** From Carson City, drive south on U.S. 395 to Coleville and then continue south for 15 miles to the campground on the east side

of the road (four miles north of the junction of U.S. 395 and Highway 108).

**Contact:** Humboldt-Toiyabe National Forest, Bridgeport Ranger District, 760/932-7070, www.fs.usda.gov/htnf or www.westrekservices.com.

## 198 SONORA BRIDGE

### Scenic rating: 7

near the Walker River in Humboldt-Toiyabe National Forest

**Map 6.3, page 335**

The West Walker River is a pretty stream, flowing over boulders and into pools, and each year this stretch of river is well stocked with rainbow trout by the Department of Fish and Game. One of several campgrounds near the West Walker, Sonora Bridge is set at 6,800 feet elevation, about 0.5 mile from the river. The setting is in the transition zone from high mountains to high desert on the eastern edge of the Sierra Nevada.

**Campsites, facilities:** There are 23 sites for tents or RVs up to 35 feet (no hookups). Picnic tables and fire grills are provided. Drinking water and vault toilets are available. Leashed pets are permitted.

**Reservations, fees:** Reservations are not accepted. Sites are $12 per night, plus $5 per night for each additional vehicle. Open mid-May through mid-October, weather permitting.

**Directions:** From north of Bridgeport, at the junction of U.S. 395 and Highway 108, turn west on Highway 108 and drive one mile to the campground on the left.

**Contact:** Humboldt-Toiyabe National Forest, Bridgeport Ranger District, 760/932-7070, www.fs.usda.gov/htnf or www.westrekservices.com.

## 199 LEAVITT MEADOWS

🚶🏊🎣🐎♿🚐⛺

### Scenic rating: 9

on the Walker River in Humboldt-Toiyabe
National Forest

**Map 6.3, page 335**

While Leavitt Meadows sits right beside
Highway 108, a little winding two-laner, several
nearby off-pavement destinations make this
camp a winner. The camp is in the high eastern
Sierra, east of Sonora Pass at 7,000 feet elevation, where Leavitt Creek and Brownie Creek
enter the West Walker River. There is a pack
station for horseback riding nearby. For four-
wheel-drive owners, the most popular side trip
is driving four miles west on Highway 108, then
turning south and driving four miles to Leavitt
Lake, where the trout fishing is sometimes
spectacular, if you're trolling a gold Cripplure.

**Campsites, facilities:** There are 16 sites for
tents or RVs up to 30 feet (no hookups). Picnic
tables, food lockers, and fire grills are provided.
Drinking water and vault toilets are available.
Some facilities are wheelchair-accessible.
Leashed pets are permitted.

**Reservations, fees:** Reservations are not accepted. Sites are $20 per night, plus $6 per night
for each additional vehicle. Open April through
mid-October, weather permitting.

**Directions:** From the junction of Highway 108
and U.S. 395 north of Bridgeport, turn west on
Highway 108 and drive approximately seven
miles to the campground on the left side of the
road.

**Contact:** Humboldt-Toiyabe National Forest,
Bridgeport Ranger District, 760/932-7070,
www.fs.usda.gov/htnf.

## 200 OBSIDIAN

🚶🏊🎣🐎🚐⛺

### Scenic rating: 6

on Molybdenite Creek in Humboldt-Toiyabe
National Forest

**Map 6.3, page 335**

This primitive, little-known camp at 7,800
feet elevation is set up for backpackers, with
an adjacent trailhead providing a jumping-
off point into the wilderness; wilderness permits are required. The trail is routed up the
Molybdenite Creek drainage and into the
Hoover Wilderness.

**Campsites, facilities:** There are 12 sites for
tents or RVs up to 30 feet (no hookups). Picnic
tables and fire grills are provided. Vault toilets
are available. No drinking water is available.
Garbage must be packed out. Leashed pets are
permitted.

**Reservations, fees:** Reservations are not accepted. Sites are $12 per night, plus $5 per night
for each additional vehicle. Open June through
October, weather permitting.

**Directions:** At the junction of U.S. 395 and
Highway 108 (13 miles north of Bridgeport),
drive south a short distance on U.S. 395 to an
improved dirt road and a sign that reads Little
Walker River Road. Turn west and drive four
miles to the campground.

**Contact:** Humboldt-Toiyabe National Forest,
Bridgeport Ranger District, 760/932-7070,
www.fs.usda.gov/htnf or www.westrekser-
vices.com.

## 201 CASCADE CREEK

🐕🚐⛺

### Scenic rating: 6

in Stanislaus National Forest

**Map 6.3, page 335**

This campground is set along Cascade Creek at
an elevation of 6,000 feet. A Forest Service road
about a quarter mile west of camp on the south
side of the highway provides a side trip three
miles up to Pikes Peak, at 7,236 feet.

**Campsites, facilities:** There are 14 sites for tents or RVs up to 22 feet (no hookups). Picnic tables and fire rings are provided. Vault toilets are available. No drinking water is available. Garbage must be packed out. Supplies are available in Dardanelle. Leashed pets are permitted.

**Reservations, fees:** Reservations are not accepted. Sites are $10 per night. Open May through October, weather permitting.

**Directions:** From Sonora, drive east on Highway 108 to Strawberry and continue for 11 miles to the campground on the left side of the road.

**Contact:** Stanislaus National Forest, Summit Ranger District, 209/965-3434, www.fs.usda.gov/stanislaus.

## 202 DONNER MEMORIAL STATE PARK

**Scenic rating: 9**

on Donner Lake

Lake Tahoe map, page 336

The remarkable beauty of Donner Lake often evokes a deep, heartfelt response. Nearly everybody passing by from nearby I-80 has looked down and seen it. The lake is big, three miles long and three-quarters of a mile wide, gemlike blue, and set near the Sierra crest at 5,900 feet. The area is well developed, with a number of cabins and access roads, and this state park is the feature destination. Along the southeastern end of the lake, it is extremely pretty, but the campsites are set in forest, not along the lake. Fishing is good (typically only in the early morning), trolling for kokanee salmon or rainbow trout, with big Mackinaw and brown trout providing wild cards. The park features more than three miles of frontage of Donner Creek and Donner Lake, with 2.5 miles of hiking trails. Donner Lake itself has 7.5 miles of shoreline. The lake is open to all water sports, but there is no boat launch at the park; a public ramp is available in the northwest corner of the lake. Campers get free admission to Emigrant Trail Museum. Note: All boats must be certified mussel-free before launching.

**Campsites, facilities:** There are 138 sites for tents or RVs up to 28 feet (no hookups) and trailers up to 24 feet, along with two hike-in/bike-in sites. Picnic tables, food lockers, and fire pits are provided. Drinking water, coin showers, vault toilets, a picnic area, and an interpretive trail are available. Supplies are available one mile away in Truckee. Some facilities are wheelchair-accessible. Leashed pets are permitted.

**Reservations, fees:** Reservations are accepted at 800/444-7275 or www.reserveamerica.com ($8 reservation fee). Sites are $35 per night, plus $8 per night for each additional vehicle and $7 per person per night for hike-in/bike-in sites (two-night maximum). Open late May to late October, weather permitting.

**Directions:** From Auburn, drive east on I-80 just past Donner Lake to the Donner State Park exit. Take that exit and turn south (right) on Donner Pass Road and drive 0.5 mile to the park entrance on the left at the southeast end of the lake.

**Contact:** Donner Memorial State Park, 530/582-7892 or 530/582-7894, www.parks.ca.gov; for boat-launching info, call 530/582-7720.

## 203 GRANITE FLAT

**Scenic rating: 6**

on the Truckee River in Tahoe National Forest

Lake Tahoe map, page 336

This camp is along the Truckee River at 5,800 feet elevation. The area is known for a ton of traffic on adjacent Highway 89, as well as decent trout fishing and, in the spring and early summer, rafting. It is about a 15-minute drive to Squaw Valley or Lake Tahoe. A bike route travels along the Truckee River out of Tahoe City.

**Campsites, facilities:** There are 51 sites for tents or RVs up to 40 feet (no hookups), several doubles, and seven walk-in tent sites. Picnic tables and fire grills are provided. Drinking water and vault toilets are available. Some facilities are wheelchair-accessible. Leashed pets are permitted.

**Reservations, fees:** Reservations are accepted at 877/444-6777 ($10 reservation fee) or www.recreation.gov ($9 reservation fee). Sites are $22-44 per night, plus $5 per night for each additional vehicle. Open May through October, weather permitting.

**Directions:** From Truckee, drive south on Highway 89 for 1.5 miles to the campground entrance on the left.

**Contact:** Tahoe National Forest, Truckee Ranger District, 530/587-3558, www.fs.usda.gov/tahoe.

## 204 GOOSE MEADOWS

### Scenic rating: 6
on the Truckee River in Tahoe National Forest

**Lake Tahoe map, page 336**

There are three campgrounds along the Truckee River off Highway 89 between Truckee and Tahoe City. Goose Meadows provides good fishing access with decent prospects, despite the high number of vehicles roaring past on the adjacent highway. This stretch of river is also popular for rafting. Elevation is 5,800 feet.

**Campsites, facilities:** There are 21 sites for tents or RVs up to 30 feet (no hookups). Picnic tables and fire grills are provided. Drinking water and vault toilets are available. Supplies are available in Truckee and Tahoe City. Some facilities are wheelchair-accessible. Leashed pets are permitted.

**Reservations, fees:** Reservations are accepted at 877/444-6777 ($10 reservation fee) or www.recreation.gov ($9 reservation fee). Sites are $22 per night, plus $5 per night for each additional

vehicle. Open May through October, weather permitting.

**Directions:** From Truckee, drive south on Highway 89 for four miles to the campground entrance on the left (river) side of the highway.

**Contact:** Tahoe National Forest, Truckee Ranger District, 530/587-3558, www.fs.usda.gov/tahoe.

## 205 SILVER CREEK

### Scenic rating: 8
on the Truckee River in Tahoe National Forest

**Lake Tahoe map, page 336**

This pretty campground is near where Silver Creek enters the Truckee River. The trout fishing is often good in this area. This is one of three campgrounds along Highway 89 and the Truckee River between Truckee and Tahoe City. The elevation is 6,000 feet.

**Campsites, facilities:** There are 11 sites for tents or RVs up to 40 feet (no hookups), five sites for tents only, and seven walk-in tent sites. Picnic tables and fire grills are provided. Drinking water and vault toilets are available. Supplies are available in Truckee and Tahoe City. Some facilities are wheelchair-accessible. Leashed pets are permitted.

**Reservations, fees:** Reservations are accepted at 877/444-6777 ($10 reservation fee) or www.recreation.gov ($9 reservation fee). Sites are $20 per night, plus $5 per night for each additional vehicle. Open June through September, weather permitting.

**Directions:** From Truckee, drive south on Highway 89 for six miles to the campground entrance on the river side of the highway.

**Contact:** Tahoe National Forest, Truckee Ranger District, 530/587-3558, www.fs.usda.gov/tahoe.

## 206 MARTIS CREEK LAKE

### Scenic rating: 7

near Truckee

Lake Tahoe map, page 336

If only this lake weren't so often windy in the afternoon, it would be heaven to fly fishers in float tubes. To some it's heaven anyway, with Lahontan cutthroat trout growing to 25 inches here. This is a special catch-and-release fishery where anglers are permitted to use only artificial lures with single, barbless hooks. The setting is somewhat sparse and open—a small lake, 70 acres, on the eastern edge of the Martis Valley. No motors are permitted at the lake, making it ideal (when the wind is down) for float tubes or prams. Sailing, sailboarding, and swimming are permitted. There is no boat launch, but small boats can be hand-launched. The lake level can fluctuate daily, which, along with the wind, can be frustrating for those who show up expecting automatic perfection; that just isn't the way it is out there. At times, the lake level can be very low. The elevation is 5,800 feet.

**Campsites, facilities:** There are 25 sites for tents or RVs of any length (no hookups). Some sites are pull-through. Picnic tables and fire grills are provided. Drinking water, vault toilets, tent pads, firewood, and pay phones are available. Supplies are available in Truckee. Some facilities are wheelchair-accessible. Leashed pets are permitted.

**Reservations, fees:** Reservations are accepted for wheelchair-accessible sites only at 530/587-8113. Sites are $18 per night. Open mid-May through mid-October, weather permitting.

**Directions:** From Truckee, drive south on Highway 267 for about three miles (past the airport) to the lake entrance road on the left. Turn left and drive another 2.5 miles to the campground at the end of the road.

**Contact:** U.S. Army Corps of Engineers, Sacramento District, 530/587-8113.

## 207 LAKE FOREST CAMPGROUND

### Scenic rating: 8

on Lake Tahoe

Lake Tahoe map, page 336

The north shore of Lake Tahoe provides beautiful lookouts and excellent boating access. The latter is a highlight of this camp, with a boat ramp nearby. From here it is a short cruise to Dollar Point and around the corner north to Carnelian Bay, one of the better stretches of water for trout fishing. The elevation is 6,200 feet. There is a 10-day camping limit. Note: All boats must be certified mussel-free before launching.

**Campsites, facilities:** There are 20 sites for tents or RVs up to 25 feet (no hookups). Picnic tables and fire grills are provided. Drinking water and vault toilets are available. Some facilities are wheelchair-accessible. A grocery store, coin laundry, and propane gas are available within four miles. Leashed pets are permitted.

**Reservations, fees:** Reservations are not accepted. Sites are $20 per night. Open May through October, weather permitting.

**Directions:** From Truckee, drive south on Highway 89 through Tahoe City to Highway 28. Bear north on Highway 28 and drive four miles to the campground entrance road (Lake Forest Road) on the right.

**Contact:** Tahoe City Public Utility District, Parks and Recreation, 530/583-3440, ext. 10, www.tahoecitypud.com.

## 208 TAHOE STATE RECREATION AREA

### Scenic rating: 9

on Lake Tahoe

Lake Tahoe map, page 336

This is a popular summer-only campground at the north shore of Lake Tahoe. The Tahoe State Recreation Area covers a large area just west of Highway 28 near Tahoe City. There are opportunities for hiking and horseback riding nearby (though not right at the park). It is also near shopping, restaurants, and, unfortunately, traffic jams in Tahoe City. A boat ramp is two miles to the northwest at nearby Lake Forest, and bike rentals are available in Tahoe City for rides along Highway 89 near the shore of the lake. For a more secluded site nearby at Tahoe, get reservations instead for Sugar Pine Point State Park, 11 miles south on Highway 89. Note: All boats must be certified mussel-free before launching.

**Campsites, facilities:** There are 24 sites for tents or RVs up to 21 feet (no hookups) and trailers up to 15 feet. Picnic tables, food lockers, barbecues, and fire pits are provided. Drinking water, vault toilets, coin showers, and firewood are available. Leashed pets are permitted.

**Reservations, fees:** Reservations are accepted at 800/444-7275 or www.reserveamerica.com ($8 reservation fee). Sites are $35 per night, plus $10 per night for each additional vehicle. Open May through October, weather permitting.

**Directions:** From Truckee, drive south on Highway 89 through Tahoe City. Turn north on Highway 28 and drive 0.9 mile to the campground entrance on the right side of the road.

**Contact:** Tahoe State Recreation Area, 530/583-3074 or 530/525-7982; Sierra District, 530/525-7232, www.parks.ca.gov.

## 209 WILLIAM KENT

### Scenic rating: 8

near Lake Tahoe in the Lake Tahoe Basin

Lake Tahoe map, page 336

William Kent camp is a little pocket of peace near the busy traffic of Highway 89 on the western shore corridor. It is on the west side of the highway, meaning visitors have to cross the highway to get lakeside access. The elevation is 6,300 feet, and the camp is wooded with primarily lodgepole pines. The drive here is awesome or ominous, depending on how you look

at it, with the view of incredible Lake Tahoe to the east, the third-deepest blue lake in North America and the 10th-deepest lake in the world. But you often have a lot of time to look at it, since traffic rarely moves quickly.

**Campsites, facilities:** There are 50 tent sites and 31 sites for RVs up to 40 feet (no hookups). Picnic tables, food lockers, and fire grills are provided. Drinking water, flush toilets, and a dump station are available. A grocery store, coin laundry, and propane gas are nearby. Some facilities are wheelchair-accessible. Leashed pets are permitted, but not on the beach.

**Reservations, fees:** Reservations are accepted at 877/444-6777 ($10 reservation fee) or www. recreation.gov ($9 reservation fee). Sites are $28-30 per night, plus $7 per night for each additional vehicle. Open late May through mid-October, weather permitting.

**Directions:** From Truckee, drive south on Highway 89 to Tahoe City. Turn south on Highway 89 and drive three miles to the campground entrance on the right side of the road.

**Contact:** Lake Tahoe Basin Management Unit, 530/543-2600, www.fs.usda.gov/ltmbu; Taylor Creek Visitor Center, 530/543-2674.

## 210 KASPIAN

### Scenic rating: 7

on Lake Tahoe

Lake Tahoe map, page 336

As gorgeous and as huge as Lake Tahoe is, there are relatively few camps or even restaurants with lakeside settings. Kaspian is one of the few, set along the west shore of the lake at 6,235 feet elevation near the little town of Tahoe Pines. A Forest Service road (Barker Pass Road) adjacent to the camp heads west into national forest to trailheads for Ellis Peak, Twin Peaks, and the Pacific Crest Trail for incredible views of Lake Tahoe.

**Campsites, facilities:** There are nine walk-in sites for tents only. RVs up to 20 feet may use the parking lot on a space-available basis.

Picnic tables and fire grills are provided. Drinking water, food lockers, and flush toilets are available. A grocery store, coin laundry, and propane gas are nearby. Some facilities are wheelchair-accessible. Leashed pets are permitted, but not on the beach.

**Reservations, fees:** Reservations are accepted at 877/444-6777 ($10 reservation fee) or www. recreation.gov ($9 reservation fee). Sites are $20-22 per night, plus $7 per night for each additional vehicle. Open May through September, weather permitting.

**Directions:** From Truckee, drive south on Highway 89 to Tahoe City. Turn south on Highway 89 and drive four miles to the campground (signed) on the west side of the road. The tent sites require a walk-in of 50-100 feet.

**Contact:** Lake Tahoe Basin Management Unit, 530/543-2600, www.fs.usda.gov/ltmbu; Taylor Creek Visitor Center, 530/543-2674; California Land Management, 530/583-3642.

## 211 ED Z'BERG SUGAR PINE POINT STATE PARK

**Scenic rating: 10**

on Lake Tahoe

**Lake Tahoe map, page 336**

This is one of three beautiful and popular state parks on the west shore of Lake Tahoe. It is just north of Meeks Bay on General Creek, with almost two miles of lake frontage available, though the campground is on the opposite side of Highway 89. General Creek, a feeder stream to Lake Tahoe, is one of the clearest streams imaginable. A pretty trail travels seven miles along the creek up to Lost Lake, just outside the northern boundary of the Desolation Wilderness. This stream also provides trout fishing from mid-July to mid-September. This park contains one of the finest remaining natural areas at Lake Tahoe. The park features dense forests of pine, fir, aspen, and juniper, covering more than 2,000 acres of beautiful landscape. There are many hiking trails, a swimming beach, and, in winter, 20 kilometers of cross-country skiing trails and a heated restroom. There is also evidence of occupation by Washoe Indians, with bedrock mortars, or grinding rocks, near the Ehrman Mansion. The elevation is 6,200 feet.

**Campsites, facilities:** There are 125 sites for tents or RVs up to 32 feet and trailers up to 26 feet (no hookups). There are also 10 group sites for up to 40 people each. Picnic tables and fire rings are provided. Drinking water, restrooms with flush toilets and coin showers (except in winter), a dump station, a day-use area, Wi-Fi, and a nature center with bird displays are available. A grocery store and propane gas are available nearby. Some facilities are wheelchair-accessible. Leashed pets are permitted.

**Reservations, fees:** Reservations are accepted at 800/444-7275 or www.reserveamerica.com ($8 reservation fee). Sites are $35 per night, plus $10 per night for each additional vehicle, and it's $165 per night for a group site. Open year-round.

**Directions:** From Truckee, drive south on Highway 89 through Tahoe City. Continue south on Highway 89 and drive 9.3 miles to the campground (signed) on the right (west) side of the road.

**Contact:** Ed Z'berg Sugar Pine Point State Park, 530/525-7982; Sierra District, 530/525-7232, www.parks.ca.gov.

## 212 MEEKS BAY

**Scenic rating: 9**

on Lake Tahoe

**Lake Tahoe map, page 336**

Meeks Bay is a beautiful spot along the western shore of Lake Tahoe. A bicycle trail is available nearby and is routed along the lake's shore, but it requires occasionally crossing busy Highway 89. Note: All boats must be certified mussel-free before launching.

**Campsites, facilities:** There are 20 sites for tents or RVs up to 20 feet (no hookups) and 16 sites for tents only. Picnic tables, food lockers, and fire grills are provided. Drinking water and flush toilets are available. Coin laundry and groceries are available nearby. Some facilities are wheelchair-accessible. Leashed pets are permitted, but not on the beach.

**Reservations, fees:** Reservations are accepted at 877/444-6777 ($10 reservation fee) or www.recreation.gov ($9 reservation fee). Sites are $28-30 per night, plus $7 per night for each additional vehicle. Open mid-May through mid-October, weather permitting.

**Directions:** In South Lake Tahoe at the junction of Highway 89 and U.S. 50, turn north on Highway 89 and drive 17 miles to the campground (signed) on the east side of Highway 89.

**Contact:** Lake Tahoe Basin Management Unit, 530/543-2600, www.fs.usda.gov/ltmbu; Taylor Creek Visitor Center, 530/543-2674.

## 213 MEEKS BAY RESORT AND MARINA

### Scenic rating: 7

on Lake Tahoe

**Lake Tahoe map, page 336**

Prime access for boating makes this a camp of choice for the boater/camper at Lake Tahoe. This campground is extremely popular and often booked well ahead of time for July and August. A boat launch is on the premises, and access to Rubicon Bay and beyond to breathtaking Emerald Bay is possible, a six-mile trip one-way for boats. The resort is adjacent to a 20-mile paved bike trail, with a swimming beach also nearby. A 14-day stay limit is enforced. Note: All boats must be certified mussel-free before launching.

**Campsites, facilities:** There are 22 sites with full hookups (50 amps) for RVs up to 60 feet and 14 sites for tents. Some sites are pull-through. Lodge rooms, cabins, and a house are also available. Picnic tables, bear lockers, and fire grills are provided. Restrooms with showers and flush toilets, a snack bar, a gift shop, and a camp store are available. A boat ramp, boat rentals (kayaks, canoes, and paddle boats), and boat slips are also available.

**Reservations, fees:** Reservations are accepted at 877/326-3357 or www.meeksbayresort.com. RV sites are $30-50 per night, tent sites are $20-30 per night, and it's $60 per night for boat slips plus $25 to launch boats. There is a maximum of six people per site. Some credit cards are accepted. Open May through September.

**Directions:** In South Lake Tahoe at the junction of Highway 89 and U.S. 50, turn north on Highway 89 and drive 17 miles to the campground on the right at 7941 Emerald Bay Road.

**Contact:** Meeks Bay Resort and Marina, 530/525-6946 or 988/326-3357, www.meeksbayresort.com.

## 214 D. L. BLISS STATE PARK

### Scenic rating: 10

on Lake Tahoe

**Lake Tahoe map, page 336**    BEST (

D. L. Bliss State Park is set on one of Lake Tahoe's most beautiful stretches of shoreline, from Emerald Point at the mouth of Emerald Bay northward to Rubicon Point, spanning about three miles. The camp is at the north end of the park, the sites nestled amid pine trees, with 80 percent of the campsites within 0.5-1 mile of the beach. The park is named for a pioneering lumberman, railroad owner, and banker of the region, whose family donated this 744-acre parcel to California in 1929. There are two great easy hiking trails. Rubicon Trail is one of Tahoe's most popular easy hikes, a meandering path just above the southwest shore of Lake Tahoe, wandering through pine, cedar, and fir, with breaks for fantastic panoramas of the lake, as well as spots where you can see nearly 100 feet into the lake. Don't be surprised if you are joined by a chipmunk circus, many begging, sitting upright, hoping for their nut for the day. While this trail is beautiful and solitary at dawn, by noon it can be crowded with hikers and chipmunks alike. Another trail, a great hike for youngsters, is Balancing Rock Trail, just a 0.5-mile romp, where after about 40 yards you arrive at this 130-ton, oblong granite boulder that is set on a tiny perch, and the whole thing seems to defy gravity. Some day it has to fall, right? Not yet. Rubicon Trail runs all the way past Emerald Point to Emerald Bay.

**Campsites, facilities:** There are 147 sites for tents or RVs up to 18 feet (no hookups) and trailers up to 15 feet, two hike-in/bike-in sites, and a group site for up to 50 people. Picnic tables, fire grills, and food lockers are provided. Restrooms have coin showers and flush toilets, and a dump station is available. All water must sometimes be pump-filtered or boiled before use, depending on current water conditions. Some facilities are wheelchair-accessible. Leashed pets are permitted at campsites only.

**Reservations, fees:** Reservations are accepted at 800/444-7275 or www.reserveamerica.com ($8 reservation fee). Sites are $35 per night, premium lakefront sites are $45 per night, plus $10 per night for each additional vehicle. It's $165 per night for the group site and $7 per night for the hike-in/bike-in sites (two-night maximum). Open late May through late September, weather permitting.

**Directions:** In South Lake Tahoe at the junction of Highway 89 and U.S. 50, turn north on Highway 89 and drive 10.5 miles to the state park turnoff on the right side of the road. Turn right (east) and drive to the park entrance. (If arriving from the north, drive from Tahoe City south on Highway 89 for 17 miles to the park entrance road.)

**Contact:** D. L. Bliss State Park, 530/525-7277; Sierra District, 530/525-7232, www.parks.ca.gov.

## 215 EMERALD BAY STATE PARK AND BOAT-IN

**Scenic rating: 10**

on Lake Tahoe

**Lake Tahoe map, page 336**   **BEST (**

Emerald Bay is a place of rare and divine beauty, one of the most striking and popular state parks on the planet. With its deep cobalt-blue waters, awesome surrounding ridgelines, glimpses of Lake Tahoe out the mouth of the bay, and even a little island, there may be no place more perfect to run a boat or kayak.

There are boat-in camps on the northern side of Emerald Bay, set in pine forest with water views. Even when Tahoe is packed, there are times when you can paddle right up and find a site—though a reservation at one of the 20 boat-in sites makes for a sure thing, of course. Drive-in campsites are available near Eagle Point at the mouth of Emerald Bay. Sites are also accessible via the Rubicon Trail from D. L. Bliss State Park.

Emerald Bay is a designated underwater park featuring Fanette Island, Tahoe's only island, and Vikingsholm, one of the greatest examples of Scandinavian architecture in North America. Vikingsholm is located along the shore about a mile's hike from the campground, and tours are very popular. The park also has several short hiking trails. Note: All boats must be certified mussel-free before launching.

**Campsites, facilities:** There are 94 sites for tents or RVs up to 21 feet (no hookups) and trailers up to 18 feet, as well as 20 boat-in sites. Picnic tables and fire grills are provided. Drinking water and restrooms with flush toilets and coin showers are available. At boat-in sites, drinking water and vault toilets are available. Leashed pets are permitted in the campground and on asphalt, but not on trails.

**Reservations, fees:** Reservations are accepted at 800/444-7275 or www.reserveamerica.com ($8 reservation fee). Sites are $35 per night, plus $10 per night for each additional vehicle. It's

$35 per night for boat-in sites. Open early June through mid-September, weather permitting.

**Directions:** In South Lake Tahoe at the junction of Highway 89 and U.S. 50, turn north on Highway 89 and drive 6.5 miles to the state park entrance turnoff on the right side of the road.

**Contact:** Emerald Bay State Park, 530/525-7232 or 530/541-3030 (summer); D. L. Bliss State Park, 530/525-7277, www.parks.ca.gov.

## 216 CAMP SHELLY

**Scenic rating: 7**

near Lake Tahoe in the Lake Tahoe Basin

**Lake Tahoe map, page 336**

This campground is near South Lake Tahoe within close range of an outstanding bicycle trail. The camp is set in the woods, with campfire programs available on Saturday night in summer. Nearby to the west is the drive to Inspiration Point and the incredible lookout of Emerald Bay, as well as the parking area for the short hike to Eagle Falls. Nearby to the east are Fallen Leaf Lake and the south shore of Lake Tahoe. Note: All boats must be certified mussel-free before launching.

**Campsites, facilities:** There are 25 sites for tents or RVs up to 24 feet long and 10.5 feet high (no hookups). Group camping is available; at least five sites must be reserved. Picnic tables, food lockers, and fire grills are provided. Drinking water, restrooms with free showers and flush toilets, horseshoes, table tennis, volleyball, and basketball are available. Some facilities are wheelchair-accessible. Groceries, propane, and a boat ramp are nearby at Camp Richardson. Leashed pets are permitted.

**Reservations, fees:** Reservations can be made in person at the Robert Livermore Community Center (4444 East Ave., Livermore, 9am-4pm Mon.-Fri.). Reservations can also be made by mail, at the campground office (which is intermittently staffed during the season), or by calling 925/960-2400. A reservation form can be downloaded online. Sites are $45 per night, plus $5 per night for each additional vehicle; group sites are an extra $5 per site per night. Open mid-June through Labor Day weekend.

**Directions:** In South Lake Tahoe at the junction of U.S. 50 and Highway 89, turn north on Highway 89, drive 2.5 miles to Camp Richardson, and then continue for 1.3 miles to the sign for Mount Tallac. Turn left at the sign for Mount Tallac Trailhead/Camp Shelly and drive to the campground on the right.

**Contact:** Camp Shelly, 530/541-6985; Livermore Area Recreation and Park District, 925/373-5700 or 925/960-2400, www.larpd.dst. ca.us.

## 217 FALLEN LEAF CAMPGROUND

**Scenic rating: 7**

in the Lake Tahoe Basin

**Lake Tahoe map, page 336**

This is a large camp near the north shore of Fallen Leaf Lake, at 6,337 feet elevation. The lake is big (three miles long), quite deep (430 feet at its deepest point), and almost as blue as nearby Lake Tahoe. A concessionaire operates the campground. Recreational opportunities include boat rentals at the marina and horseback-riding at Camp Richardson Resort. Fishing is best in the fall for kokanee salmon. Because Fallen Leaf Lake is circled by forest—much of it private property—you will need a boat to fish or explore the lake. A visitors center is north of the Fallen Leaf Lake turnoff on Highway 89. Note: All boats must be certified mussel-free before launching.

**Campsites, facilities:** There are 75 sites for tents, 130 sites for tents or RVs up to 40 feet (no hookups), and six yurts. Picnic tables, food lockers, and fire grills are provided. Drinking water, vault toilets, and coin showers are available. A boat ramp, coin laundry, and supplies are nearby. Some facilities are wheelchair-accessible. Leashed pets are permitted.

**Reservations, fees:** Reservations are accepted at 877/444-6777 ($10 reservation fee) or www.recreation.gov ($9 reservation fee). Sites are $33-35 per night, plus $7 per night for each additional vehicle, and it's $84 per night for yurts. Open mid-May through mid-October, weather permitting.

**Directions:** In South Lake Tahoe at the junction of U.S. 50 and Highway 89, turn north on Highway 89 and drive two miles to the Fallen Leaf Lake turnoff. Turn left and drive 1.5 miles to the campground.

**Contact:** Lake Tahoe Basin Management Unit, 530/543-2600, www.fs.usda.gov/ltmbu; Taylor Creek Visitor Center, 530/543-2674.

## 218 TAHOE VALLEY RV RESORT

### Scenic rating: 5

in South Lake Tahoe

**Lake Tahoe map, page 336**

This is a massive, privately operated park near South Lake Tahoe. The nearby attractions include five golf courses, horseback riding, casinos, and, of course, "the Lake." Note that about half of the sites are filled with seasonal renters.

**Campsites, facilities:** There are 439 sites with full or partial hookups (30 and 50 amps) for RVs of any length, 77 sites for tents, and two group sites for up to 100 people. Some RV sites are pull-through. Picnic tables and fire grills are provided. Restrooms with showers, cable TV, Wi-Fi, dump station, coin laundry, seasonal heated swimming pool, playground, tennis courts, grocery store, RV supplies, propane gas, ice, firewood, and a recreation room are available. Some facilities are wheelchair-accessible. Leashed pets are permitted.

**Reservations, fees:** Reservations are recommended at 530/541-2222 or online at www.rvonthego.com and www.reserveamerica.com ($9 reservation fee). RV sites (with hookups) are $46-69 per night, tent sites are $50 per night, plus a $3 resort fee per day. Monthly rates are

available. Credit cards are accepted. Open year-round.

**Directions:** In South Lake Tahoe, at the Y junction of Highway 89 and U.S. 50, drive south for 0.5 mile to C Street. Turn right and drive 1.5 blocks to the campground.

**Contact:** Tahoe Valley RV Resort, 1175 Melba Dr., 530/541-2222 or 877/570-2267.

## 219 CAMPGROUND BY THE LAKE

### Scenic rating: 5

in South Lake Tahoe

**Lake Tahoe map, page 336**

This city-operated campground provides an option at South Lake Tahoe. It is set at 6,200 feet elevation, across the road from the lake, with pine trees and views of the lake. Note: All boats must be certified mussel-free before launching.

**Campsites, facilities:** There are 175 sites for tents or RVs up to 40 feet. Some sites have partial hookups (30 and 50 amps) and/or are pull-through. Five tent cabins are also available. Picnic tables, barbecues, and fire grills are provided. Drinking water, restrooms with flush toilets and showers, a dump station, playground, and boat ramp (check current status) are available. An indoor ice-skating rink and a public indoor heated pool are nearby (fee for access). Some facilities are wheelchair-accessible. Supplies and a coin laundry are nearby. Leashed pets are permitted.

**Reservations, fees:** Reservations are accepted at 530/542-6096 ($7 reservation fee). Sites are $24-29 per night, RV sites (with electricity) are $35-40 per night, plus $6 per night for each additional person, $2 per pet per night, and $6 per night for each additional vehicle. Tent cabins are $49-51 per night. Weekly rates are available. Some credit cards are accepted. Open April through October, with a 14-day maximum stay.

**Directions:** If entering South Lake Tahoe on U.S. 50, drive east on U.S. 50 to Rufus Allen

Boulevard. Turn right and drive 0.25 mile to the campground on the right side of the road.
**Contact:** Campground by the Lake, 530/542-6096; City of South Lake Tahoe, Parks and Recreation Department, 530/542-6055, www.cityslt.us.

## 220 HISTORIC CAMP RICHARDSON RESORT

Scenic rating: 7

on Lake Tahoe

**Lake Tahoe map, page 336**   BEST

Camp Richardson Resort is within minutes of boating, biking, gambling, and, in the winter, skiing and snowboarding. It's a take-your-pick deal. It's a legendary spot, often called "Camp Rich." With cabins, a restaurant, and live music (often nightly in summer) also on the property, this is a place that offers one big package. The campsites are set in the woods, not on the lake itself, but are within a short walking distance of the lake. From here you can gain access to an excellent bike route that runs for three miles, then loops around by the lake for another three miles, most of it flat and easy, all of it beautiful. You can also make the easy, beautiful ride to Fallen Leaf Lake. A marina for boating, water-skiing lessons (I actually did this!), an ice cream parlor, and year-round recreation make Camp Rich a popular winner. The elevation is 6,300 feet. Note: All boats must be certified mussel-free before launching.

**Campsites, facilities:** There are 223 sites for tents and 112 sites with full or partial hook-ups (30 amps) for RVs up to 35 feet, including two pull-through sites. Cabins, duplex units, inn rooms, and hotel rooms are also available. Picnic tables and fire pits are provided. Restrooms with showers and flush toilets, drinking water, dump station, group facilities, and playground are available. A full-service marina, boat ramp, boat rentals, swimming beach, bike rentals, general store, restaurant, ice cream parlor, and propane gas are nearby.

Some facilities are wheelchair-accessible. Pets are not permitted.

**Reservations, fees:** Reservations are accepted at 800/544-1801. RV sites (hookups) are $45-135 per night, tent sites are $35 per night, plus $5 per night for each additional vehicle. Cabins are rented by the week in summer. Some credit cards are accepted. Open June through October, with lodging available year-round.
**Directions:** In South Lake Tahoe at the junction of Highway 89 and U.S. 50, turn north on Highway 89 and drive 2.5 miles to the resort on the right side of the road.
**Contact:** Historic Camp Richardson Resort, 530/541-1801, www.camprichardson.com.

## 221 KOA SOUTH LAKE TAHOE

Scenic rating: 5

near Lake Tahoe

**Lake Tahoe map, page 336**

Like so many KOA camps, this one is on the outskirts of a major destination area—in this case, South Lake Tahoe. It is within close range of gambling, fishing, hiking, and bike rentals. Elevation is 6,300 feet.

**Campsites, facilities:** There are 40 sites with full hookups (30 amps) for RVs up to 36 feet, along with 16 sites with no hookups for tents and RVs. Some sites are pull-through. A lodge, chalet, and chateau are also available. Picnic tables and fire grills are provided. Restrooms with showers, cable TV, Wi-Fi, dump station, recreation room, seasonal heated swimming pool, playground, coin laundry, convenience store, RV supplies, horseshoes, firewood, ice, and propane gas are available. Some facilities are wheelchair-accessible. Leashed pets are permitted.

**Reservations, fees:** Reservations are recommended at 800/562-3477. RV sites (hookups) are $70-108 per night, tent sites are $50-95 per night, plus $5 per person per night for more than two people, $5 per night for each additional vehicle, $15 per boat per night, and $5 per pet per night. Off-season prices are discounted; holiday rates are higher. Weekly and monthly rates are available. Some credit cards are accepted. Open April through mid-October.

**Directions:** From Sacramento, take U.S. 50 and drive east over the Sierra Nevada past Echo Summit to Meyers. As you enter Meyers, it will be the first campground on the right. Turn right and enter the campground.

**Contact:** KOA South Lake Tahoe, 530/577-3693, www.laketahoekoa.com.

# SAN FRANCISCO BAY AREA

© SABRINA YOUNG

The Bay Area is home to 150 significant parks (including 12 with redwoods), 7,500 miles of hiking and biking trails, 45 lakes, 25 waterfalls, 100 miles of coast, mountains with incredible lookouts, bays with islands, and, in all, 1.2 million acres of greenbelt with hundreds of acres being added each year. With unique recreation possibilities come unique campgrounds: boat-in camps at Tomales Bay, ferry-in camps on Angel Island, and hike-in camps at Point Reyes National Seashore, the Marin Headlands, Sunol-Ohlone Wilderness, Butano Redwoods State Park, and Big Basin Redwoods State Park. Demand for all campgrounds is higher, so plan ahead. But if you visit at non-peak times (Sunday through Thursday or spring through fall), it's like having the park to yourself.

# SAN FRANCISCO BAY AREA

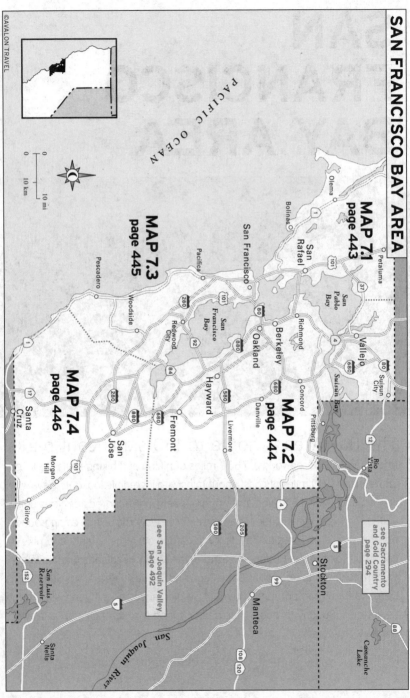

©AVALON TRAVEL

PACIFIC OCEAN

MAP 7.1
page 443

MAP 7.3
page 445

MAP 7.2
page 444

MAP 7.4
page 446

see Sacramento
and Gold Country
page 294

see San Joaquin Valley
page 492

Olema
Bolinas
Petaluma
San Rafael
San Pablo Bay
Vallejo
Suisun City
Suisun Bay
Rio Vista
Camanche Lake
Stockton
Manteca
Santa Nella
San Luis Reservoir
Gilroy
Morgan Hill
Santa Cruz
San Jose
Fremont
Livermore
Danville
Concord
Pittsburg
Hayward
Oakland
Berkeley
Richmond
Redwood City
Woodside
Pescadero
Pacifica
San Francisco
San Francisco Bay

San Joaquin River

0   10 mi
0   10 km

# Map 7.1

### Sites 1-16 Pages 447-455

## NORTH BAY

see Mendocino and Wine Country page 234

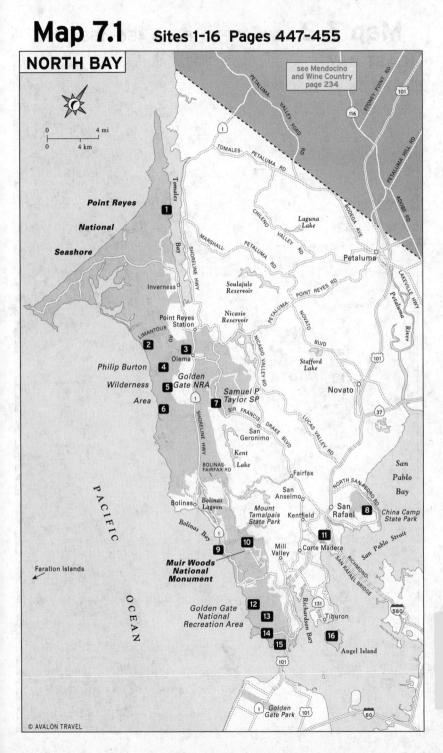

0  4 mi
0  4 km

*Point Reyes*

*National*

*Seashore*

Tomales

PETALUMA VALLEY FORD RD

STONY POINT RD

101

116

TOMALES- PETALUMA RD

PETALUMA HILL RD

ADOBE RD

1

CHILENO VALLEY RD

Laguna Lake

BODEGA AVE

**1**

Inverness

Point Reyes Station

SHORELINE HWY

MARSHALL-

PETALUMA RD

Soulajule Reservoir

POINT REYES RD

PETALUMA

NOVATO

**Petaluma**

LAKEVILLE HWY

Petaluma River

LIMANTOUR RD

**2**

**3**

Olema

**4**

*Golden Gate NRA*

**5**

*Philip Burton*

*Wilderness*

*Area*

**6**

Nicasio Reservoir

NICASIO VALLEY RD

*Samuel P Taylor SP*

**7**

SIR FRANCIS DRAKE BLVD

San Geronimo

Kent Lake

BOLINAS-FAIRFAX RD

BLVD

Stafford Lake

101

37

**Novato**

LUCAS VALLEY RD

Fairfax

San Anselmo

NORTH SAN PEDRO RD

*San Pablo Bay*

**8**

*China Camp State Park*

PACIFIC

Bolinas

*Bolinas Lagoon*

*Bolinas Bay*

1

*Mount Tamalpais State Park*

Kentfield

**San Rafael**

San Pablo Strait

**9**

**10**

Mill Valley

Corte Madera

**11**

RICHMOND-SAN RAFAEL BRIDGE

*Muir Woods National Monument*

*Golden Gate National Recreation Area*

**12**

**13**

**14**

**15**

Richardson Bay

131

Tiburon

**16**

*Angel Island*

580

101

OCEAN

Farallon Islands

1

*Golden Gate Park*

101

80

© AVALON TRAVEL

# Map 7.2 Sites 17-20 Pages 456-458

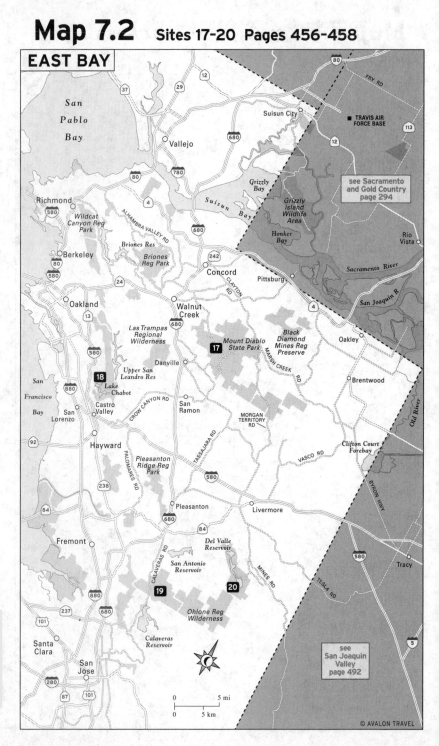

**EAST BAY**

San Pablo Bay

Richmond

Wildcat Canyon Reg Park

Berkeley

Oakland

San Francisco Bay

San Lorenzo

Hayward

Fremont

Santa Clara

San Jose

Vallejo

Suisun City

Suisun Bay

Grizzly Bay

Briones Res

Briones Reg Park

Concord

Walnut Creek

Las Trampas Regional Wilderness

Danville

Upper San Leandro Res

Lake Chabot

Castro Valley

San Ramon

Pleasanton Ridge Reg Park

Pleasanton

**17** Mount Diablo State Park

**18**

**19**

San Antonio Reservoir

Ohlone Reg Wilderness

Calaveras Reservoir

Del Valle Reservoir

**20**

Livermore

Pittsburg

Black Diamond Mines Reg Preserve

Morgan Territory Rd

Clifton Court Forebay

Oakley

Brentwood

Travis Air Force Base

see Sacramento and Gold Country page 294

Rio Vista

Sacramento River

San Joaquin R

Old River

Tracy

see San Joaquin Valley page 492

Grizzly Island Wildlife Area

Honker Bay

0        5 mi
0        5 km

© AVALON TRAVEL

# Map 7.3 Sites 21-27 Pages 459-462

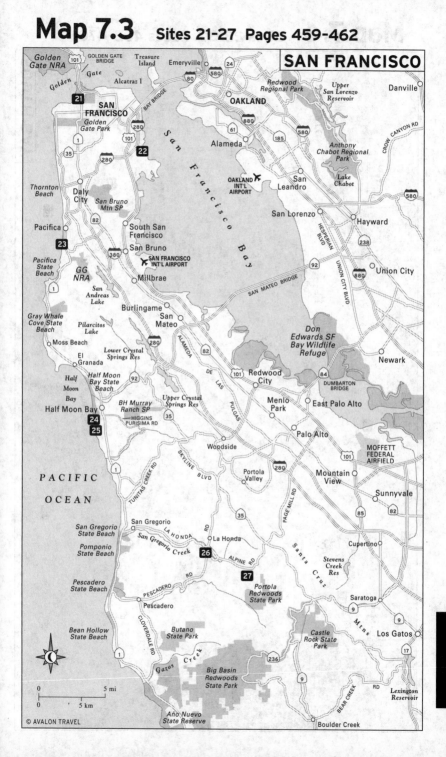

**SAN FRANCISCO**

Golden Gate NRA

GOLDEN GATE BRIDGE

Treasure Island

Emeryville

Redwood Regional Park

Upper San Lorenzo Reservoir

Danville

Golden Gate

Alcatraz I

OAKLAND

**21** SAN FRANCISCO

Golden Gate Park

Anthony Chabot Regional Park

Alameda

San Leandro

Lake Chabot

Thornton Beach

Daly City

San Bruno Mtn SP

OAKLAND INT'L AIRPORT

San Francisco Bay

CROW CANYON RD

Pacifica

South San Francisco

San Bruno

San Lorenzo

Hayward

**23**

SAN FRANCISCO INT'L AIRPORT

HESPERIAN BLVD

UNION CITY BLVD

Pacifica State Beach

GG NRA

Millbrae

SAN MATEO BRIDGE

Union City

San Andreas Lake

Gray Whale Cove State Beach

Pilarcitos Lake

Burlingame

San Mateo

Don Edwards SF Bay Wildlife Refuge

Moss Beach

El Granada

Lower Crystal Springs Res

ALAMEDA

Newark

Half Moon Bay State Beach

Half Moon Bay

Redwood City

DUMBARTON BRIDGE

DE LAS PULGAS

Menlo Park

East Palo Alto

Half Moon Bay

BH Murray Ranch SP

Upper Crystal Springs Res

**24**
**25**

HIGGINS PURISIMA RD

Palo Alto

MOFFETT FEDERAL AIRFIELD

Woodside

SKYLINE BLVD

PACIFIC OCEAN

Portola Valley

Mountain View

Sunnyvale

TUNITAS CREEK RD

PAGE MILL RD

San Gregorio State Beach

San Gregorio

LA HONDA RD

La Honda

Cupertino

Santa Cruz

Stevens Creek Res

Pomponio State Beach

San Gregorio Creek

**26**

ALPINE RD

Pescadero State Beach

PESCADERO RD

**27**

Portola Redwoods State Park

Saratoga

Los Gatos

Pescadero

CLOVERDALE RD

Butano State Park

Castle Rock State Park

Mtns

Bean Hollow State Beach

Gazos Creek

Big Basin Redwoods State Park

BEAR CREEK RD

Lexington Reservoir

0    5 mi
0    5 km

Año Nuevo State Reserve

Boulder Creek

© AVALON TRAVEL

# Map 7.4 Sites 28-39 Pages 462-470

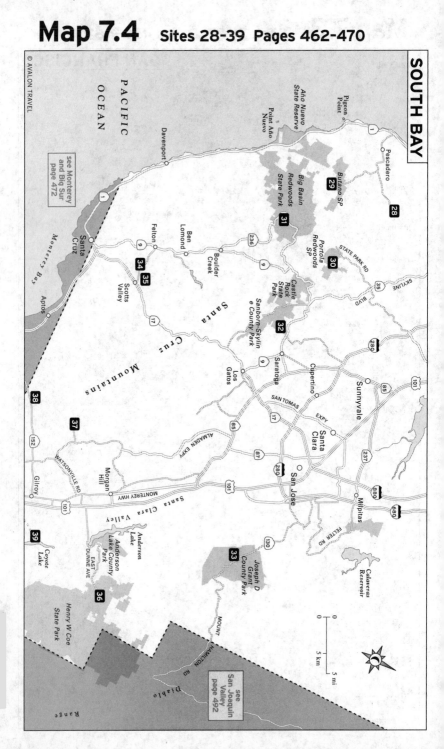

# 1 TOMALES BAY BOAT-IN
🏃🏊🚣🛶🚤 5% ⛺

### Scenic rating: 10
in Point Reyes National Seashore

**Map 7.1, page 443**     **BEST (**

Here is a little slice of paradise secreted away along the west shore of Tomales Bay. Dispersed boat-in camps are set along small, sandy coves along the bases of steep cliffs, from just north of Indian Beach at Tomales Bay State Park all the way north to Tomales Point. Boaters are required to bring portable toilets, and reservations are often a necessity, especially on weekends. Tomales Bay is pretty, quiet, and protected from the onshore coastal winds, and offers outstanding sea kayaking. Note that some spots that appear gorgeous during low tides can be covered by water during high tides, so pick your spot above the tide line. Sightings of elk are common, with a herd of 500 on the Pierce Ranch section of Point Reyes National Seashore. Day hikes are sensational from Pierce Ranch to Tomales Point, and kayaking is outstanding.

**Campsites, facilities:** Twenty permits are issued daily for dispersed boat-in tent sites along the shore of Tomales Bay. Pit toilets are available only at Marshall Beach and Tomales/Kehoe Beach. No drinking water or other facilities are available. Garbage must be packed out. Boaters must bring portable toilets. No wood gathering is permitted.

**Reservations, fees:** Reservations are accepted at 800/444-7275 ($10 reservation fee) or www.recreation.gov ($9 reservation fee). Camping permits are required from the Bear Valley Visitor Center at 415/663-8054 and must be picked up in person (for directions, see the Sky Camp Hike-In listing in this chapter). Single sites are $20 per night, group sites (7-25 people) are $40-50; there's a four-day maximum stay. Open year-round, weather permitting.

**Directions:** To reach the boat launch, drive on U.S. 101 to Petaluma and the East Washington exit. Take that exit and drive west (this street becomes Bodega Avenue) through Petaluma and continue to Highway 1. Turn left (south) on Highway 1 and drive 3.5 miles to the Miller County Park boat launch on the right (0.5 mile before Blakes Landing). Launch your boat and paddle across Tomales Bay to the boat-in campsites along the Point Reyes National Seashore.

**Contact:** Point Reyes National Seashore, 415/464-5100, www.nps.gov/pore.

# 2 COAST CAMP HIKE-IN
🏃 ⛺

### Scenic rating: 7
in Point Reyes National Seashore

**Map 7.1, page 443**

This hike-in camp is set on an open ocean bluff, just above Santa Maria Beach on the Point Reyes National Seashore. It is a 1.8-mile hike to get to this northernmost camp on the Coast Trail. (The complete Coast Trail is a 19-mile trip and one of the best hikes in the Bay Area.) From Coast Camp, you can continue south, where the trail contours south along the bluffs above the beach for 1.4 miles to Sculptured Beach. You'll find a series of odd geologic formations, including caves, tunnels, and sea stacks. A backcountry permit is required. You can also hike up the Woodward Trail for sensational views of Drakes Bay and across the ocean.

**Campsites, facilities:** There are 12 individual and two group hike-in sites. Picnic tables and fire grills are provided. Drinking water is available. Vault toilets are available. Charcoal or gas stoves are allowed, with backpacking stoves recommended for cooking. No wood fires are permitted. Garbage must be packed out. No vehicles or pets are permitted.

**Reservations, fees:** Reservations are accepted at 800/444-7275 ($10 reservation fee) or www.recreation.gov ($9 reservation fee). Camping permits are required from the Bear Valley Visitor Center at 415/663-8054 and must be picked up in person (for directions, see the Sky Camp Hike-In listing in this chapter). Single sites are $20 per night, and group sites (7-25 people) are $40-50; maximum stay is four days. Open year-round.

**Directions:** From U.S. 101 in Marin, take the Sir Francis Drake Boulevard/San Anselmo exit and drive about 20 miles to Highway 1 at Olema. Turn right on Highway 1 and drive a very short distance. Turn left at Bear Valley Road and drive north for two miles to Limantour Road. Turn left at Limantour Road and drive six miles to the access road for the Point Reyes Hostel. Turn left and drive 0.2 mile to the trailhead on the right side of the road. A parking area is a short distance ahead and to the right.

**Contact:** Point Reyes National Seashore, 415/464-5100, www.nps.gov/pore.

## 3 OLEMA RV RESORT & CAMPGROUND

**Scenic rating: 4**

in Olema

Map 7.1, page 443

If location is everything, then this 32-acre campground should be rated a 10. It is set in Olema, in a valley amid Marin's coastal foothills, an ideal jumping-off spot for a Point Reyes adventure. It borders the Point Reyes National Seashore to the west and the Golden Gate National Recreation Area to the east, with Tomales Bay to the nearby north. There are several excellent trailheads within a 10-minute drive along Highway 1 to the south. The campsites are small and tightly placed, and I have received a few complaint letters about the ambience of the place.

**Campsites, facilities:** There are 187 sites, some with full or partial hookups (30 and 50 amps), for tents or RVs of any length, as well as a large area for up to 175 tents. Picnic tables and fire rings are provided. Drinking water, restrooms with showers, dump station, coin laundry, post office, ATM, firewood, ice, playground, RV supplies, propane, horseshoes, volleyball, shuffleboard, badminton, tetherball,

Wi-Fi, meeting facilities, amphitheater, and a recreation hall (for groups of 25 or more only) are available. Some facilities are wheelchair-accessible. Leashed pets are permitted (two pets per site).

**Reservations, fees:** Reservations are accepted at www.olemacampground.net or 800/655-2267. RV sites are $45-63 per night, plus $3 per night for each additional vehicle; tent sites are $40-49, plus $3 per person per night for more than two people. Rates are discounted fall through spring. Weekly rates are available. Most credit cards are accepted. Open year-round.

**Directions:** From U.S. 101 in Marin, take the San Anselmo/Sir Francis Drake Boulevard exit and drive west for about 22 miles to Highway 1 at Olema. Turn north (right) on Highway 1 and drive 0.25 mile to the campground on the left.

**Contact:** Olema RV Resort & Campground, 415/663-8106, www.olemacampground.net.

## 4 SKY CAMP HIKE-IN

**Scenic rating: 7**

in Point Reyes National Seashore

Map 7.1, page 443

Sky Camp is on the western flank of Inverness Ridge at 1,025 feet elevation, with panoramic views of Drakes Bay, Point Reyes, and the Farallon Islands. Hit it right and it will feel like a foothold in the sky. To reach the camp, start at the Sky Trail Trailhead off Limantour Road. The hike starts by climbing a service road, then enters a forest to emerge at Sky Camp in 1.4 miles. Some sites are secluded for privacy, while others are out in the open. Wildflower blooms are exceptional in spring.

**Campsites, facilities:** There are 11 individual sites and a group site (walk-in only) that can accommodate up to 25 people. Permits must be obtained from the Bear Valley Visitor Center before camping. Vault toilets and fire grills (charcoal only, no wood fires) are provided. Drinking water is available intermittently;

check for current status. Garbage must be packed out. No vehicles or pets are allowed.

**Reservations, fees:** Reservations are accepted at 800/444-7275 ($10 reservation fee) or www.recreation.gov ($9 reservation fee). Camping permits are required from the Bear Valley Visitor Center at 415/663-8054 and must be picked up in person. Single sites are $20 per night, group sites (7-25 people) are $40-50; there's a four-day maximum stay. Open year-round.

**Directions:** From U.S. 101 in Marin, take the Sir Francis Drake Boulevard/San Anselmo exit and drive west for about 20 miles to Highway 1 at Olema. Turn north on Highway 1 and drive a very short distance to Bear Valley Road. Turn left at Bear Valley Road and drive north for 0.7 mile to the visitors center road on the left (signed "Seashore Information"). Turn left and drive to the visitors center parking lot and Bear Valley Trailhead.

To reach the trailhead: From Bear Valley Visitor Center, exit the parking lot onto Bear Valley Road. Turn left on Bear Valley Road and drive two miles to Limantour Road. Turn left on Limantour and drive three miles to the signed spur road for Sky Trail Trailhead on the left. Turn left and go a short distance to the parking area and trailhead.

**Contact:** Point Reyes National Seashore, 415/464-5100, www.nps.gov/pore.

# 5 GLEN CAMP HIKE-IN

### Scenic rating: 10
in Point Reyes National Seashore

**Map 7.1, page 443**

Glen Camp Hike-In is set in the coastal foothills of Point Reyes National Seashore and is surrounded by forest. The hike to it starts at the Bear Valley Visitor Center, where you can obtain your backcountry permits and hiking information, and is routed on popular Bear Valley Trail, a wide road made out of compressed rock. It is 1.6 miles to Divide Meadow,

with a modest 215-foot climb, then another 1.6 miles through Bear Valley to Glen Trail. Turn left on Glen Loop Trail and hike 1.4 miles, with the trail moving laterally in and out of two canyons to reach the camp. It is secluded and quiet. Get a map and a permit, and bring everything you need.

**Campsites, facilities:** There are 12 hike-in sites. Picnic tables and fire grills are provided. Vault toilets are available. Drinking water is available intermittently; check for current status. Charcoal or gas stoves are allowed, with backpacking stoves recommended for cooking. No wood fires are permitted. Garbage must be packed out. No vehicles or pets are permitted.

**Reservations, fees:** Reservations are accepted at 800/444-7275 ($10 reservation fee) or www.recreation.gov ($9 reservation fee). Camping permits are required from the Bear Valley Visitor Center at 415/663-8054 and must be picked up in person (for directions, see the Sky Camp Hike-In listing in this chapter). Single sites are $20 per night, group sites (7-25 people) are $40-50; there's a four-day maximum stay. Open year-round.

**Directions:** From U.S. 101 in Marin, take the Sir Francis Drake Boulevard/San Anselmo exit and drive west for about 20 miles to Highway 1 at Olema. Turn north on Highway 1 and drive a very short distance to Bear Valley Road. Turn left at Bear Valley Road and drive north for 0.7 mile to the visitors center road on the left (signed "Seashore Information"). Turn left and drive to the visitors center parking lot and Bear Valley Trailhead. It is a 4.6-mile hike to the camp.

**Contact:** Point Reyes National Seashore, 415/464-5100, www.nps.gov/pore.

# 6 WILDCAT CAMP HIKE-IN

### Scenic rating: 10
in Point Reyes National Seashore

**Map 7.1, page 443**     BEST (

This backpack camp sits in a grassy meadow

near a small stream that flows to the ocean, just above remote Wildcat Beach. From the Palomarin Trailhead, getting to this camp takes you on a fantastic 5.5-mile hike that crosses some of the Bay Area's most beautiful wildlands. The trail is routed along the ocean for about a mile, heads up into the coastal hills, turns left, and skirts past Bass Lake, Crystal Lake, and Pelican Lake, and, ultimately, heads past Alamere Creek to this beautiful camp set on an ocean bluff. A fantastic side trip is to hike along the beach from Wildcat Camp to the south, where you can get a full frontal view of Alamere Falls. It is a dramatic 40-foot free fall, a rare ocean bluff waterfall.

**Campsites, facilities:** There are five individual and three group hike-in sites. Picnic tables and fire grills are provided. Vault toilets are available. Drinking water is available intermittently; check for current status. Charcoal or gas stoves are allowed, with backpacking stoves recommended for cooking. No wood fires are permitted. Garbage must be packed out. No vehicles or pets are permitted.

**Reservations, fees:** Reservations are accepted at 800/444-7275 ($10 reservation fee) or www.recreation.gov ($9 reservation fee). Camping permits are required from the Bear Valley Visitor Center at 415/663-8054 and must be picked up in person (for directions, see the Sky Camp Hike-In listing in this chapter). Single sites are $20 per night, group sites (7-25 people) are $40-50; maximum stay is four days. Open year-round.

**Directions:** From U.S. 101 in Marin, take the Sir Francis Drake Boulevard/San Anselmo exit and drive about 20 miles west on Sir Francis Drake Boulevard to the town of Olema and Highway 1. Turn left on Highway 1 and drive 9.3 miles to Olema-Bolinas Road on the right (look for a white ranch house opposite the turn). Turn right on Olema-Bolinas Road and drive 1.5 miles to Mesa Road. Turn right and drive six miles (past an area known as "The Towers" due to all the antennas) to the parking area and Palomarin Trailhead. It is a 5.6-mile hike to the campground on the Coast Trail.

**Contact:** Point Reyes National Seashore, 415/464-5100 or 415/663-8054, www.nps.gov/pore.

# 7 SAMUEL P. TAYLOR STATE PARK

🚶 🚴 🐕 ♿ 🚐 ⛺

### Scenic rating: 9

near San Rafael

**Map 7.1, page 443**

This is a beautiful park, with campsites set amid redwoods, complete with a babbling brook running nearby. The park covers more than 2,700 acres of wooded countryside in the steep and rolling hills of Marin County and features a unique contrast of coast redwoods with open grassland. Hikers will find 20 miles of trails, a hidden waterfall, and some good mountain-biking routes on service roads. The paved bike path that runs through the park and parallels Lagunitas Creek is a terrific, easy ride. Trees include redwood, Douglas fir, oak, and madrone, and native wildflowers include buttercups, milkmaids, and Indian paintbrush. The section of the park on the north side of Sir Francis Drake has the best hiking in the park. Campsites are on the south side of the park, except for three sites on the north side.

**Campsites, facilities:** There are 25 sites for tents, 35 sites for tents or RVs up to 27 feet (no hookups); some sites may be combined into small group sites. There is also one hike-in/bike-in camp, one group site at Madrone for 50 people, two primitive group sites for up to 10 people each at Devil's Gulch, and one equestrian site with corrals at Devil's Gulch Horse Camp. Cabins are also available. Picnic tables, food lockers, and fire grills are provided. Drinking water, coin showers, flush and pit toilets, and Wi-Fi are available. There is a small store and café two miles away in Lagunitas. Some facilities are wheelchair-accessible. Leashed pets are permitted in campsites only.

**Reservations, fees:** Reservations are not accepted at this time; all sites are first-come, first-served. Sites are $35 per night, plus $8 per night for each additional vehicle, the equestrian camp is $100 per night, and it's $7 per person per night for hike-in/bike-in sites. Devil's Gulch group sites are $50 per night; the Madrone group site is $225 per night. Cabins are $100 per night ($100 deposit). Open year-round.

**Directions:** From U.S. 101 in Marin, take the Sir Francis Drake Boulevard exit and drive west for about 15 miles to the park entrance on the left side of the road.

**Contact:** Samuel P. Taylor State Park, 415/488-9897, www.parks.ca.gov; Marin Sector, 415/898-4362.

## 8 CHINA CAMP STATE PARK
🚶 🚴 🏕 ♿ ⛺

### Scenic rating: 10
on San Pablo Bay near San Rafael

**Map 7.1, page 443**

This is one of the Bay Area's prettiest campgrounds, set in woodlands with a picturesque creek running past. The camps are shaded and sheltered. Directly adjacent to the camp is a meadow, marshland, and then San Pablo Bay. Deer can seem as tame as chipmunks. Hiking is outstanding, taking either Shoreline Trail for a pretty walk near the edge of San Pablo Bay or Bay View Trail for the climb up the ridge that borders the park, in the process gaining spectacular views of the bay and miles of charm. The landscape includes an extensive intertidal salt marsh and meadow and oak habitats. There are five miles of hiking trails, heavily used on spring and summer weekends. A highlight is the China Camp Village, which depicts an early Chinese settlement.

**Campsites, facilities:** There are 30 walk-in tent sites and one hike-in/bike-in site. Picnic tables, food lockers, and fire grills are provided. Drinking water and a restroom with flush toilets and showers are available. Some facilities are wheelchair-accessible. Leashed pets are permitted at the campground and picnic areas.

**Reservations, fees:** Reservations are accepted at 800/444-7275 ($10 reservation fee) or www.reserveamerica.com ($9 reservation fee). Sites are $35 per night, plus $8 per night for each additional vehicle, and $7 per person per night for the hike-in/bike-in site. Open year-round, weather permitting.

**Directions:** From San Francisco, drive north on U.S. 101 to San Rafael and take the North San Pedro Road exit. Drive east on North San Pedro Road for five miles to the Back Ranch Meadows Campground entrance on the right. Turn right and drive a short distance to the campground trailhead at the end of the road. Reaching the sites requires a one- to five-minute walk.

**Contact:** China Camp State Park, 415/456-0766, www.parks.ca.gov; Friends of China Camp, 415/488-5161, www.friendsofchina-camp.org.

## 9 STEEP RAVINE ENVIRONMENTAL CAMPSITES
🚶 🛶 ♿ ⛺

### Scenic rating: 10
in Mount Tamalpais State Park

**Map 7.1, page 443**          **BEST (**

This is one of the most remarkable spots on the California coast. Rustic cabins sit perched on a rocky bluff overlooking the ocean with dramatic views of passing ships, marine birds, migrating whales, and heart-stopping sunsets. There is an easy walk down to secluded Redrock Beach. Just across Highway 1 (with a short jog to the right) is the trailhead for the Steep Ravine Trail up the slopes of Mount Tamalpais. After a stay here, you'll feel like you're a million miles from civilization.

**Campsites, facilities:** There are seven walk-in sites for tents and 10 primitive cabins (also known as environmental sites), each with a wood stove, picnic table, and a flat wood surface for sleeping. At tent sites, picnic tables and fire grills are provided and pit toilets are available. Drinking water is nearby, and wood is available for purchase. No pets are permitted.

**Reservations, fees:** Reservations are accepted at 800/444-7275 ($10 reservation fee) or www.reserveamerica.com ($9 reservation fee). Sites are $25 per night for tent sites, $100 per night for environmental cabins, with one vehicle per cabin and five people maximum per site. Open year-round.

**Directions:** From U.S. 101 in Marin, take the Stinson Beach/Highway 1 exit. Drive west to the stoplight at the T intersection (Highway 1). Turn left on Highway 1 and drive about 11 miles to the gated access road on the left side of the highway at Rocky Point. (The gate lock combination will be provided when reservations are made, or by calling 415/388-2070 up to one week before your stay.)

**Contact:** Mount Tamalpais State Park, 415/388-2070; Marin Sector, 415/898-4362, www.parks.ca.gov.

## 10 PANTOLL WALK-IN, ALICE EASTWOOD, AND FRANK VALLEY

### Scenic rating: 10

in Mount Tamalpais State Park

**Map 7.1, page 443**    **BEST (**

When camping at Pantoll, you are within close range of the divine, including some of the best hiking, best lookouts, and just plain best places to be anywhere in the Bay Area. The camp is in the woods on the western slopes of Mount Tamalpais, which some say is a place of special power, with sensational hiking and trailheads. The walk to the Pantoll Campground can be as short as 100 feet and as long as just over a quarter mile. This landscape is a mix of redwood groves, oak woodlands, and grasslands, and provides drop-dead beautiful views of the ocean nearby as well as a trip into a lush redwood canyon with a stream. Steep Ravine Trail

is routed out of camp to the west into a wondrous gorge filled with redwoods and a stream with miniature waterfalls. It is best seen after a good rain, when everything is dripping with moisture. Another great hike from this camp is on Matt Davis/Coastal Trail, which provides beautiful views of the coast. Another must is the nearby drive to the East Peak Lookout, where the entire world seems within reach. This park provides more than 50 miles of trails for hiking and biking, which in turn link to a network of 200 miles of other trails.

**Campsites, facilities:** There are 16 walk-in tent sites, two group sites for 25 and 75 people each, and one equestrian group site for up to 25 people. Picnic tables, food lockers, and fire grills are provided. Drinking water, flush toilets, and Wi-Fi are available. Firewood is available for purchase. Leashed pets are permitted at campsites only.

**Reservations, fees:** Reservations are accepted at 800/444-7275 ($10 reservation fee) or www.reserveamerica.com ($9 reservation fee). Walk-in sites are $25 per night, the Alice Eastwood Group Camps are $110 and $225 per night, and the Frank Valley Horse Camp is $75 per night (horse required). Open year-round.

**Directions:** From U.S. 101 in Marin, take the Stinson Beach/Highway 1 exit. Drive west to the stoplight at the T intersection for Highway 1. Turn left and drive about four miles uphill to the Panoramic Highway. Bear to the right on Panoramic Highway and continue for 5.5 miles to the Pantoll parking area. Turn left at the Pantoll parking area and ranger station. A 100- to 500-foot walk is required to reach the campground.

Directions to the group site and the combination to the gate lock will be provided when reservations are made; or call 415/388-2070 up to one week before your stay.

**Contact:** Mount Tamalpais State Park, 415/388-2070; Marin Sector, 415/898-4362, www.parks.ca.gov.

## 11 MARIN RV PARK

### Scenic rating: 2

in Greenbrae

**Map 7.1, page 443**

For out-of-towners with RVs, this can make an ideal base camp for Marin County adventures. To the west are Mount Tamalpais State Park, Muir Woods National Monument, Samuel P. Taylor State Park, and Point Reyes National Seashore. To the nearby east is the Loch Lomond Marina on San Pablo Bay, where fishing trips can be arranged for striped bass and sturgeon; phone Loch Lomond Bait Shop (415/456-0321). The park offers complete sightseeing information and easy access to buses and ferry service to San Francisco.

**Campsites, facilities:** There are 86 sites with full hookups (30 and 50 amps) for tents or RVs. Restrooms with showers, coin laundry, Wi-Fi, swimming pool, dump station, and RV supplies are available. Some facilities are wheelchair-accessible. Leashed pets are permitted.

**Reservations, fees:** Reservations are recommended. Sites are $65 per night for two people, $2 per person per night for more than two people, six people maximum per site. Weekly and monthly rates are available in the off-season. Some credit cards are accepted. Open year-round.

**Directions:** From the south: From the Golden Gate Bridge, drive north on U.S. 101 for 10 miles to Lucky Drive (south of San Rafael). Exit and turn left on Redwood Highway (no sign) and drive three blocks north to the park entrance on the right.

From the north: From San Rafael, drive south on U.S. 101 to the Lucky Drive exit (450A). Take that exit to the first light at Tamal Vista. Turn left and drive to the next stoplight and Wornum Avenue. Turn left at Wornum Avenue and drive under the freeway to Redwood Highway (frontage road). Turn left and drive four blocks north to the park entrance.

**Contact:** Marin RV Park, 415/461-5199 or 888/461-5199, www.marinrvpark.com.

## 12 HAYPRESS HIKE-IN

### Scenic rating: 9

in the Marin Headlands

**Map 7.1, page 443**

Nope, your eyes aren't foolin' ya—this is one of three free(!) campgrounds in the Marin Headlands. Haypress campground is on the outskirts of Tennessee Valley at the north end of the Marin Headlands. This is a primitive backpacking campground where you must bring everything you need. Reaching camp requires a 0.75-mile hike from the popular Tennessee Valley trailhead. Yet in just 20-30 minutes, hikers can visit a world that seemingly belongs just to them.

**Campsites, facilities:** There are five tent sites, with a maximum of four people per site. Picnic tables are provided. Portable toilets and food lockers are available. No drinking water is available. No fires are permitted; backpacking stoves are required for cooking. A map/brochure is available at the Marin Headlands Visitor Center or by contacting the Golden Gate National Recreation Area. A detailed hiking map of the area is available for a fee.

**Reservations, fees:** Reservations and a permit are required from the visitors center before camping. There is no fee. Groups up to 20 can reserve any site from November through March. Three sites can be reserved for groups up to 12 from April through October. Open year-round, weather permitting. Maximum stay per season is three nights.

**Directions:** From U.S. 101 in Marin, take the Stinson Beach/Highway 1 exit. Drive 0.6 mile to Tennessee Valley Road. Turn left on Tennessee Valley Road and drive two miles to where the road dead-ends at a parking area and trailhead. Follow the trailhead for Tennessee Valley and hike 0.75 mile to the campground.

**Contact:** Marin Headlands Visitor Center,

Building 948, Fort Barry, Sausalito, 415/331-1540, www.nps.gov/goga.

## 13 HAWK CAMP HIKE-IN

🚶 🏕

### Scenic rating: 10

on Marin Headlands

**Map 7.1, page 443**

This is the most remote of the campgrounds on the Marin Headlands. It is high above Gerbode Valley, requiring a hike of 3.5 miles, climbing much of the way from the parking lot and trailhead at Tennessee Valley. It is a small campground, with three sites and room for no more than four people per site. After parking at Tennessee Valley, take the trailhead for the Old Marincello Vehicle Road/Bobcat Trail. This route climbs in a counterclockwise direction around Mount Vortac; after 1.7 miles you will reach a junction with Mount Vortac Trail. Do not turn at that junction. Continue straight on Bobcat Trail for 0.7 mile to a junction with Hawk Trail. Turn right and hike on the trail for one mile to Hawk Camp, elevation 750 feet. Below you to the southeast is Gerbode Valley.

**Campsites, facilities:** There are three tent sites, with a maximum of four people per site. Picnic tables and food lockers are provided, and chemical toilets are available. There is no drinking water and fires are not permitted. Backpacking stoves are required for cooking. A map/brochure is available at the Marin Headlands Visitor Center or by contacting the Golden Gate National Recreation Area. A detailed hiking map of the area is available for a fee.

**Reservations, fees:** Reservations and a permit are required from the visitors center before camping. There is no fee. All three sites can be reserved by groups of up to 12 from November through March. Open year-round, weather permitting, with a three-night maximum stay per season.

**Directions:** From U.S. 101 in Marin, take the Stinson Beach/Highway 1 exit. Drive 0.6 mile and turn left on Tennessee Valley Road. Drive two miles until the road dead-ends at the parking area and trailhead. Take the trailhead for Old Marincello Vehicle Road/Bobcat Trail and hike 3.5 miles.

**Contact:** Marin Headlands Visitor Center, Building 948, Fort Barry, Sausalito, 415/331-1540, www.nps.gov/goga.

## 14 BICENTENNIAL WALK-IN

🚶 🏕

### Scenic rating: 9

on Marin Headlands

**Map 7.1, page 443**

Of the hike-in campgrounds on the Marin Headlands, Bicentennial Walk-In is the easiest to reach. It is only a 100-yard walk northwest from the parking area near Battery Wallace. This is a small camp with space for just three tents.

**Campsites, facilities:** There are three sites for tents-only; no more than three people per site in one tent. Portable toilets and food lockers are available. Picnic tables and barbecue grills are available 100 yards away at Battery Wallace. Drinking water is available one mile away at the visitor center. Campfires are not allowed; gas stoves may be used for cooking. A map/brochure is available at the Marin Headlands Visitor Center. A detailed hiking map of the area is available for a fee.

**Reservations, fees:** Reservations and a permit from the visitors center are required before camping. There is no fee. Open year-round, weather permitting, with a three-night maximum stay per season.

**Directions:** From San Francisco, drive north on U.S. 101 over the Golden Gate Bridge and into Marin to the Alexander Avenue exit. Take the Alexander Avenue exit and turn left underneath the highway. Take the wide paved road to the right (Conzelman Road, but there is no sign) and look for the Marin Headlands sign. Continue west for 3.5 miles (it becomes a one-way road) to the parking area on your left for

Battery Wallace (on your right). Park and walk 100 yards north to the campground.

**Contact:** Marin Headlands Visitor Center, Building 948, Fort Barry, Sausalito, 415/331-1540, www.nps.gov/goga.

## 15 KIRBY COVE

**Scenic rating: 10**

on Marin Headlands

**Map 7.1, page 443**

Kirby Cove is nestled in a grove of cypress and eucalyptus trees in a stunning setting just west of the Golden Gate Bridge. It is small and pristine, with space for just four sites and restricted parking. Two campsites are perched on a bluff overlooking the beach; the views are drop-dead beautiful of the Golden Gate Bridge, San Francisco Headlands, and the mouth of the bay opening to the Pacific Ocean. Group sites are set amid eucalyptus trees and are a short walk inland. An old concrete military bunker draws curiosity from many.

**Campsites, facilities:** There are four tent sites for no more than 10 people per site. Picnic tables, food lockers, and fire rings/barbecue pits are provided. Vault toilets are available, but there is no drinking water. It is recommended that you bring a backpacking stove because of occasional fire restrictions; wood collecting is not permitted. A map/brochure is available at the Marin Headlands Visitor Center or by contacting the Golden Gate National Recreation Area. A detailed hiking map of the area is available for a fee.

**Reservations, fees:** Reservations are accepted at 800/444-7275 ($10 reservation fee) or www.recreation.gov ($9 reservation fee). Sites are $25 per night for up to three cars and 10 people. Maximum stay of three nights per year. Open April through October.

**Directions:** From San Francisco, drive north on U.S. 101 over the Golden Gate Bridge and into Marin to the Alexander Avenue exit. Take the Alexander Avenue exit and turn left underneath the highway. Take the wide paved road to the right (Conzelman Road, but there is no sign) and look for the Marin Headlands sign. Continue west on Conzelman about 0.25 mile to Kirby Cove Road (the first turn on the left, a dirt road). Bear left and drive to the gate. When you get reservations, you will get the code for the gate. Unlock the gate and drive 0.9 mile to the campground.

**Contact:** Marin Headlands Visitor Center, Building 948, Fort Barry, Sausalito, 415/331-1540, www.nps.gov/goga.

## 16 ANGEL ISLAND STATE PARK WALK-IN/BOAT-IN

**Scenic rating: 10**

on Angel Island

**Map 7.1, page 443**   **BEST (**

Camping at Angel Island is one of the unique adventures in the Bay Area; the only catch is that getting to the campsites requires a ferry boat ride and then a walk of 1-2 miles, or a kayak or boat trip from the mainland directly to the camp. The payoff comes at the end of the day, when all of the park's day visitors depart for the mainland, leaving the entire island to you. Plan far ahead because the sites can book up months in advance. The group camp is popular with kayakers because of beach access. From start to finish, it's a great trip, featuring a private campsite, often with spectacular views of San Francisco Bay, the San Francisco waterfront and skyline, Marin Headlands, and Mount Tamalpais. The tromp up to 798-foot Mount Livermore includes a short, steep stretch, but in return furnishes one of the most spectacular urban lookouts in America. Be ready for cold, foggy weather at night in midsummer. The park features more than 13 miles of trails, including Perimeter Road, a must-do for all avid cyclists. Bikes are also permitted on the park's fire road system. Angel Island has a stunning history, including being used from 1910 to 1940 to process thousands of immigrants as they entered America; historic tram tours are available.

**Campsites, facilities:** There are 10 hike-in sites and one group hike-in/boat-in site for up to 20 people. Picnic tables, barbecues, and food lockers are provided. Drinking water and pit toilets are available. Garbage service is available. No open wood campfires are permitted; only charcoal is allowed. A seasonal café is on the island. Some facilities are wheelchair-accessible.

**Reservations, fees:** Reservations are accepted at 800/444-7275 ($10 reservation fee) or www.reserveamerica.com ($9 reservation fee). Sites are $30 per night (limit eight people per site). The boat-in group site is $50 per night. To avoid park entrance fees, campers must check in at the Ayala Cove kiosk (at Angel Island) and show reservation vouchers to the ferry boat operator. Open year-round, with limited ferry service in winter.

**Directions:** Angel Island can be reached by ferry from San Francisco and Oakland/Alameda; for schedule information, call 415/773-1188 or check www.blueandgoldfleet.com. From Tiburon, contact 415/435-2131 or www.angelislandferry.com for schedule information.

**Contact:** Angel Island State Park, 415/435-5390, www.parks.ca.gov; Marin District 707/769-5665; bike rentals and tram tours, www.angelisland.com.

## 17 MOUNT DIABLO STATE PARK

🚶 🚴 🐴 ♿ 🚐 ⛺

### Scenic rating: 8

east of Oakland

**Map 7.2, page 444**

Mount Diablo, elevation 3,849 feet, provides one of the most all-encompassing lookouts anywhere in America, an awesome 360 degrees on clear mornings. On crystal-clear days you can see the Sierra Nevada and its white, snowbound crest. Some claim to have seen Half Dome in Yosemite with binoculars. The drive to the summit is a must-do trip, and the weekend interpretive center right on top of the mountain is one of the best in the Bay Area. The camps at Mount Diablo are set in foothill/oak grassland country, with some shaded sites. Winter and spring are good times to visit, when the weather is still cool enough for good hiking trips. Most of the trails require long hikes, often including significant elevation gains and losses. No alcohol is permitted in the park. The park offers extensive but challenging hiking, biking, and horseback riding. A museum, visitors center, and gift shop is perched on the Diablo summit. Summers are hot and dry, and in late summer the park can be closed because of fire danger. In winter, snow occasionally falls on the peak—according to my logbook, during the first full moon in February.

**Campsites, facilities:** There are 64 sites in three campgrounds for tents or RVs up to 20 feet long (no hookups) and five group sites for 20-50 people. Barbecue Terrace is a group site for equestrian use with hitching posts and a water trough. Picnic tables and fire grills are provided. Drinking water and flush and vault toilets are available. Showers are available at Juniper campground. Some facilities are wheelchair-accessible. Leashed pets are permitted only in campgrounds and picnic areas.

**Reservations, fees:** Reservations are accepted at 800/444-7275 ($10 reservation fee) or www.reserveamerica.com ($9 reservation fee). Sites are $30 per night, plus $10 per night for each additional vehicle; group sites are $65-165 per night. Open year-round.

**Directions:** From Danville on I-680, take the Diablo Road exit. Turn east on Diablo Road and drive three miles to Mount Diablo Scenic Boulevard. Turn left and continue 3.5 miles (the road becomes South Gate Road) to the park entrance station. Register at the kiosk, obtain a park map, and drive to the designated campground.

**Contact:** Mount Diablo State Park, 925/837-2525 or 925/837-0904; Diablo Vista District, 707/769-5652, www.parks.ca.gov.

## 18 ANTHONY CHABOT REGIONAL PARK

### Scenic rating: 7

near Castro Valley

**Map 7.2, page 444**

The campground at Chabot Regional Park is on a hilltop sheltered by eucalyptus, with good views and trails available. The best campsites are the walk-in units, requiring a walk of only a minute or so. Several provide views of Lake Chabot to the south a half mile away. The 315-acre lake provides good trout fishing in the winter and spring, and a chance for huge but elusive largemouth bass. Huckleberry Trail is routed down from the campground (near walk-in site 20) to the lake at Honker Bay, a good fishing area. There is also a good 12-mile bike ride around the lake. In all, this 5,000-acre park includes 31 miles of hiking, biking, and riding trails. East Bay Skyline Trail runs the length of the park. Boat rentals are available, but no swimming or water-body contact is permitted. Note: All boats must be certified mussel-free before launching. A weekend marksmanship range is available at the park, and a golf course is nearby.

**Campsites, facilities:** There are 75 sites for tents and small RVs, including 11 RV sites with full hookups (30 amps) and 10 walk-in tent sites. Group camping is available for a minimum of 11 people. Picnic tables and fire grills are provided. Restrooms with flush toilets and showers, drinking water, a dump station, an amphitheater, a picnic area, and naturalist-led campfire programs are available. A small marina, boat rentals, snack bar, and bait and tackle are available nearby at Lake Chabot Regional Park. There is no boat launch and gas motors and inflatables are prohibited; canoes and kayaks can be carried about 100 yards and hand launched. Some facilities are wheelchair-accessible. Leashed pets are permitted.

**Reservations, fees:** Reservations are accepted at 888/327-2757, option 2, or www.ebparks.org ($8 reservation fee). Group sites cannot be reserved online. Sites are $25-35 per night, plus $8 per night for each additional vehicle and $2 per pet per night. Group sites are $100 per night. Some credit cards are accepted. Open year-round.

**Directions:** From I-580 in the Oakland hills, drive to the 35th Avenue exit. Take that exit, and at the stop sign, turn east on 35th Avenue and drive up the hill and straight across Skyline Boulevard, where 35th Avenue becomes Redwood Road. Continue on Redwood Road for eight miles to the park and Marciel Road (campground entrance road) on the right.

**Contact:** Regional Park Headquarters, 888/327-2757; Anthony Chabot Regional Park, 510/639-4751; Chabot Equestrian Center, 510/569-4428, www.ebparks.org.

## 19 SUNOL REGIONAL WILDERNESS

### Scenic rating: 7

south of Sunol

**Map 7.2, page 444**

At press time, the Sunol Campground remained closed. The backpack area is open (reservations required). Please contact the park directly before planning a trip.

Sunol Regional Wilderness is set in rolling oak and bay grasslands and is an outstanding park for off-season hiking, camping, wildlife-viewing, and wildflowers. In the spring and early summer, it is one of the best of the 150 parks in the Bay Area to see wildflowers. It is also the home of more nesting golden eagles than anywhere else in the world, with a chance to see falcons and hawks as well. In addition, Alameda Creek in Little Yosemite forms several miniature pool-and-drop waterfalls in the spring and early summer. The Little Yosemite area is a scenic gorge about two miles upstream from the visitors center. Dogs are allowed in the Ohlone Wilderness during the day but are not permitted overnight. No alcohol is permitted in the park, and it is subject to confiscation.

Bicycles and fires are prohibited at the trail and equestrian camps. Temporary closures can occur in late summer because of fire danger. Gates are locked at night; campers must arrive before dusk.

**Campsites, facilities:** The Sunol backpack area is open to overnight camping by reservation and requires a hike of 3.4 miles or longer. There are no other facilities.

**Reservations, fees:** Reservations are accepted at 888/327-2757 (option 2). An Ohlone Wilderness Permit is required. The fee is $5 per night. Open year-round.

**Directions:** From Walnut Creek, take I-680 to Sunol and take the Highway 84/Calaveras Road exit. Turn south on Calaveras and drive four miles to Geary Road. Turn left on Geary Road and drive two miles to the park entrance.

**Contact:** East Bay Regional Park District Headquarters, 888/327-2757; Sunol Regional Wilderness, 925/862-2244, www.ebparks.org/parks.htm.

## 20 DEL VALLE REGIONAL PARK

### Scenic rating: 7

near Livermore

**Map 7.2, page 444**

Of the 65 parks in the East Bay Regional Park District, Del Valle provides the greatest variety of recreation at the highest quality. Del Valle Reservoir is the centerpiece, a five-mile-long, narrow lake that fills a canyon with 16 miles of shoreline, providing a good boat launch for powerboats (10-mph speed limit) and good fishing for trout (stocked), striped bass, panfish, and catfish. Note: All boats must be certified mussel-free before launching. Two swimming beaches are popular in summer, and an excellent mountain-bike ride along the lake starts just north of the marina. The park offers boat tours of the natural history and lake ecology of the area.

The campsites are somewhat exposed because of the grassland habitat, but they fill anyway on most weekends and three-day holidays. Phase 2 campsites are closest to water in a more open area; Phase 4 campsites are inland and more wooded. A trailhead south of the lake provides access to Ohlone Wilderness Trail, and for the well conditioned, there is the 5.5-mile butt-kicker of a climb to Murietta Falls, gaining 1,600 feet in 1.5 miles. Murietta Falls is the Bay Area's highest waterfall, 100 feet tall, though its thin, silvery wisp is only full in late winter after heavy rains when the hills and aquifer are saturated. Riding trails are also available in this 4,000-acre park.

**Campsites, facilities:** There are 150 sites, including some with full or partial (50 amp) hookups, for tents or RVs of any length and one equestrian site (Caballo Loco). There are also two walk-in group areas for 11-75 people, requiring a walk of 0.25-1 mile. Picnic tables and fire grills are provided. Drinking water, restrooms with flush toilets and showers, dump station, full marina, boat and sailboard rentals, seasonal campfire programs, swimming beaches, and a boat launch are available. Some facilities are wheelchair-accessible. Leashed pets are permitted.

**Reservations, fees:** Reservations are accepted at 888/327-2757, option 2, or www.ebparks.org ($8 reservation fee). Sites are $22-45 per night, plus $8 per night for each additional vehicle, $5 per day boat launch fee, and $2 per pet per night; the equestrian site is $100 per night. Some credit cards are accepted. Open year-round.

**Directions:** From I-580 east in Livermore, take the North Livermore Avenue exit and turn south (right if driving from San Francisco). Drive south and proceed through Livermore (road becomes South Livermore Avenue). Continue for 1.5 miles (the road then becomes Tesla Road) to Mines Road. Turn right on Mines Road and drive 3.5 miles to Del Valle Road. Continue straight on Del Valle Road for four miles to the park entrance.

**Contact:** Del Valle Regional Park,

925/373-0332; East Bay Regional Park District, 888/327-2757, www.ebparks.org/parks.htm.

## 21 ROB HILL GROUP WALK-IN

### Scenic rating: 8

in the Presidio in San Francisco

**Map 7.3, page 445**

Rob Hill campground reopened in 2010 with sparkling facilities and upgraded campsites. This is San Francisco's only campground with tent sites, well hidden in the Presidio beneath a canopy of cypress and eucalyptus trees and with a view of Immigrant Point. The Bay Area Ridge Trail passes directly by the camp and Presidio's roads offer popular bike routes. There are two group camps—it's a great spot for a youth group camp—and they are always full. From the limited parking area, it is an uphill climb of 150 feet to the camp. Free shuttle service is available within the Presidio.

**Campsites, facilities:** There are two group tent sites for up to 30 people each. Picnic tables, drinking water, restrooms with flush toilets, barbecue grills, and a community circle are available. Generators and amplified music are prohibited. Parking is limited (parking permit provided with reservation).

**Reservations, fees:** Reservations are required at 415/561-5444 (ask for reservations), or download an application online at www.presidio.gov/explore and fax it to 415/561-7604. Sites are $125 per night with a five-night maximum stay; only credit cards are accepted. Open April through October.

**Directions:** From the south: Take Highway 1 north into San Francisco. Highway 1 becomes 19th Avenue; stay on 19th Avenue and get in the far left lane as it enters Golden Gate Park (at Lincoln). Take the 25th Avenue exit to your left. Stay on 25th Avenue, continuing north for one mile. Turn right onto El Camino del Mar/Lincoln Boulevard. Turn right on Kobbe Avenue, then right onto Washington Avenue.

Drive to Central Magazine and turn left; look for the first service road on the right. Turn right at that service road and park. Walk up the hill 150 feet to the campground.

From the north: Take U.S. 101/Highway 1 south over the Golden Gate Bridge and get in the right lane at the toll plaza ($7 toll). Immediately after the toll plaza, look for Merchant Street on the right. Turn right on Merchant Street and drive up the hill to the stop sign at Lincoln Boulevard. Turn right and drive to Kobbe Avenue. Turn left onto Kobbe Avenue and then right onto Washington Boulevard. Drive to Central Magazine and turn left; look for the first service road on the right. Turn right at that service road and park. Walk up the hill 150 feet to the campsites on the right.

**Contact:** The Presidio Trust, Rob Hill reservations 415/561-4200, www.presidio.gov/explore.

## 22 CANDLESTICK RV PARK

### Scenic rating: 6

in San Francisco

**Map 7.3, page 445**

This RV park is five miles from downtown San Francisco and an ideal destination for out-of-towners who want to explore the city without having to drive, because the park offers tours and inexpensive shuttles to the downtown area. In addition, there are good hiking opportunities along the shoreline of the bay. On summer afternoons, when the wind howls at 20-30 mph here, sailboarders rip by.

**Campsites, facilities:** There are 165 sites with full hookups (30 and 50 amps) for trailers or RVs up to 42 feet, along with 24 tent sites. Some sites are pull-through. Restrooms with showers, coin laundry, Wi-Fi, grocery store, game room, and RV washing are available. Shuttles and bus tours are also available. Some facilities are wheelchair-accessible. A security officer is posted at the entry station at night. Small leashed pets are permitted.

**Reservations, fees:** Reservations are

recommended at 800/888-2267. RV sites are $89-99 per night for two people, plus $5 per person per night for more than two people. Some credit cards are accepted. Open year-round.

**Directions:** From San Francisco on U.S. 101, take Exit 429A to Gilman Avenue. Turn east on Gilman Avenue and drive around the parking lot to Gate 4.

**Contact:** Candlestick RV Park, 415/822-2299 or 800/888-2267, www.sanfranciscorvpark.com.

## 23 SAN FRANCISCO RV RESORT

🏇 🏊 🎣 ⛵ 🐕 ♿ 🚐

Scenic rating: 8

in Pacifica

**Map 7.3, page 445**

This is one of the best RV parks in the Bay Area. It is on the bluffs just above the Pacific Ocean in Pacifica, complete with beach access, a nearby fishing pier, sometimes excellent surf fishing, and the chance for dramatic ocean sunsets. A golf course is nearby. The park is kept clean and in good shape, and though there is too much asphalt, the proximity to the beach overcomes it. It is only 20 minutes from San Francisco.

**Campsites, facilities:** There are 162 sites with full hookups (50 amps) for RVs up to 45 feet. No tents are allowed. Restrooms with showers, heated swimming pool, year-round spa, playground, game room, group facilities, cable TV, Wi-Fi, convenience store, coin laundry, and propane gas are available. Some facilities are wheelchair-accessible. Leashed pets are permitted, with some exceptions.

**Reservations, fees:** Reservations are recommended at 877/570-2267 or 800/822-1250. Sites are $54-95 per night. Weekly and monthly rates are available. Some credit cards are accepted. Open year-round.

**Directions:** From San Francisco, drive south on I-280 to Highway 1. Bear west on Highway 1 and drive into Pacifica to the Palmetto Drive exit. Take that exit and drive south to the stop

sign (you will be on the west side of the highway). Continue straight ahead (the road becomes Palmetto Avenue) for about two blocks and look for the entrance to the park on the right side of the road at 700 Palmetto.

From the south, drive north on Highway 1 into Pacifica. Take the Manor Drive exit. At the stop sign, turn left on Oceana Avenue (you will be on the east side of the highway) and drive a block to another stop sign at Manor Drive. Turn left and drive a short distance over the highway to a stop sign at Palmetto Avenue. Turn left and drive about two blocks to the park on the right.

**Contact:** San Francisco RV Resort, 650/355-7093, www.sanfranciscorvresort.com.

## 24 HALF MOON BAY STATE BEACH

🏇 🚴 🏊 ⛵ 🎣 🏕 🐕 ♿ 🚐 ⛺

Scenic rating: 7

at Half Moon Bay

**Map 7.3, page 445**

In summer, this park often fills to capacity with campers touring Highway 1. The campground has level, grassy sites for tents, a clean parking area for RVs, and a state beach available just a short walk away. The feature is four miles of broad, sandy beaches with three access points with parking. A visitors center is available. This can be the starting point for an outstanding bike ride seven miles north to Pillar Point Marina. Kayak rentals, fishing, and whale-watching trips are available at the harbor. Typical weather is fog in summer, clear days in spring and fall, and wet and windy in the winter—yet occasionally there are drop-dead beautiful days in winter between storms, warm, clear, and windless. Temperatures range from lows in the mid-40s in winter to highs in the mid-60s in fall. One frustrating point: The weekend traffic on Highway 1 up and down the coast here is often jammed, with absolute gridlock during festivals.

**Campsites, facilities:** There are 52 sites for tents or RVs up to 40 feet (no hookups), four hike-in/bike-in sites, and one group site (Sweetwood, two miles north of the main campground) for tents only that can accommodate 9-50 people. Picnic tables, food lockers, and fire grills are provided. Restrooms with flush toilets and coin showers, drinking water, Wi-Fi, pay telephone, and dump station are available. Some facilities are wheelchair-accessible. Leashed pets are permitted, except on the beach.

**Reservations, fees:** Reservations are accepted at 800/444-7275 ($10 reservation fee) or www.reserveamerica.com ($9 reservation fee). Sites are $35-50 per night, plus $8 per night for each additional vehicle; the group site is $165 per night, and it's $7 per person per night for hike-in/bike-in sites. Open year-round.

**Directions:** Drive to Half Moon Bay to the junction of Highway 1 and Highway 92. Turn south on Highway 1 and drive two blocks to Kelly Avenue. Turn right on Kelly Avenue and drive 0.5 mile to the park entrance at the end of the road.

**Contact:** Half Moon Bay State Beach, 650/726-8820 or 650/726-8819; Santa Cruz District, 831/335-6318, www.parks.ca.gov.

## 25 PELICAN POINT RV PARK

### Scenic rating: 7

in Half Moon Bay

**Map 7.3, page 445**

Pelican Point is on an extended bluff near the ocean in a rural area on the southern outskirts of Half Moon Bay. Fog is common on summer mornings. Sites consist of cement slabs with picnic tables; half of the RV sites are monthly rentals. The harbor has an excellent boat launch, a fish-cleaning station, party boat trips for salmon and rockfish and, in the winter, whale-watching trips. A beautiful golf course is nearby.

**Campsites, facilities:** There are 75 sites with full hookups (30 and 50 amps) for RVs up to 40 feet. Picnic tables are provided. Restrooms

with showers, coin laundry, propane gas, small store, clubhouse, and dump station are available. All facilities are nearby, with restaurants in Half Moon Bay and 10 miles north in Princeton at Pillar Point Harbor. Leashed pets are permitted.

**Reservations, fees:** Reservations are accepted. Sites are $84 per night, plus $3.36 per night for each additional vehicle, $1 per person per night for more than two people, and $1 per pet per night. Some credit cards are accepted. Open year-round.

**Directions:** In Half Moon Bay, at the junction of Highway 1 and Highway 92, turn south on Highway 1 and drive 2.5 miles to Miramontes Point Road. Turn right and drive a short distance to the park entrance on the left.

**Contact:** Pelican Point RV Park, 650/726-9100, www.pelicanpointrv.com.

## 26 JACK BROOK HORSE CAMPS

### Scenic rating: 7

in Sam McDonald County Park just outside La Honda

**Map 7.3, page 445**

This is a beautiful horse camp with access to a network of service roads. The park is filled with second-growth redwoods and then feeds north to rolling foothills. You get a mix of moist, cool redwoods in the canyons and rolling grassland foothills on the ridges. From the top, you also get views to the west across Butano Canyon to the coast.

**Campsites, facilities:** There are three group sites: two small sites for up to 10 people each and one larger site for up to 40 people. Some sites have 15- or 20-amp hookups. Picnic tables and barbecues are provided. Drinking water, flush toilets, showers, horse paddocks, tie posts, and a horse-wash rack are available. A shared outdoor kitchen with refrigerator, freezer, and microwave is also provided.

**Reservations, fees:** Reservations are required

at 650/363-4021 ($10 reservation fee) or online ($7 reservation fee). The two smaller sites are $125 per night on weekends, $75 per night Sunday through Thursday; the larger site is $275 per night on weekends, $150 per night Sunday through Thursday. Open May through mid-November, weather permitting.

**Directions:** From the Peninsula, take U.S. 101 or I-280 to Redwood City/Woodside and Highway 84. Take Highway 84 (Woodside-La Honda-San Gregorio Road) west to La Honda and continue one mile to Alpine Road. Turn left on Alpine Road and drive 1.1 miles to a Y with Pescadero Road. Bear right at the Y and drive 0.5 mile to the park entrance on the right.

From Highway 1: Take the Pescadero Road exit. Drive east on Pescadero Creek Road about 11 miles to the Jack Brook entrance or continue to the Sam McDonald Park entrance, where horse trailers can be parked for entrance on horseback.

**Contact:** San Mateo County Parks and Recreation, 650/879-0238 or 650/363-4021, http://parks.smcgov.org.

## 27 MEMORIAL COUNTY PARK

🏃🏊🚐⛺

### Scenic rating: 8

near La Honda

**Map 7.3, page 445**

This beautiful 500-acre redwood park is on the western slopes of the Santa Cruz Mountains, tucked in a pocket between the tiny towns of La Honda and Loma Mar. The park is known for its family camping areas and Tan Oak and Mount Ellen nature trails. The campground features access to a nearby network of 50 miles of trails, with the best hike along the headwaters of Pescadero Creek. In late winter, it is sometimes possible to see steelhead spawn (no fishing permitted, of course). The trails link with others in nearby Portola State Park and Sam McDonald County Park, providing access to a vast recreation land. A swimming hole on Pescadero Creek next to the campground is popular during the summer. The camp is often filled on summer weekends, but the sites are spaced, so it won't cramp your style.

**Campsites, facilities:** There are 158 sites for tents or RVs up to 35 feet, two group sites for tents or RVs up to 35 feet (no hookups) that can accommodate up to 75 people, and two areas for youth groups of up to 50 people. Picnic tables, food lockers, and fire grills are provided. Drinking water, restrooms with coin showers and flush toilets, an amphitheater, a picnic area, summer convenience store, visitors center, summer campfire programs, dump station, and firewood are available. No smoking is allowed.

**Reservations, fees:** Reservations are required at 650/363-4021 ($10 reservation fee) or online ($7 reservation fee). Sites are $25-35 per vehicle per night, plus $10 per night for each additional vehicle. Group sites are $150-175 per night, plus $6 per vehicle per stay. Open year-round.

**Directions:** From Half Moon Bay at the junction of Highway 1 and Highway 92, drive south on Highway 1 for 18 miles to the Pescadero Road exit. Turn left (east) on Pescadero Road and drive about 10.5 miles to the park entrance on the right.

**Contact:** Memorial County Park, 650/879-0238; San Mateo County Parks and Recreation, 650/363-4021, http://parks.smcgov.org.

## 28 PESCADERO CREEK COUNTY PARK

🏃🚴⛺

### Scenic rating: 7

near Pescadero

**Map 7.4, page 446**

The area that comprises Pescadero Creek Park's 8,020 acres includes Sam McDonald, Memorial, and Heritage Grove Parks. But it's Pescadero Creek Park itself that offers solitude and remote access like no other. There are 26 miles of trail suitable for hiking, biking, and horseback riding, but you'll rarely come across another soul. The reason? Pescadero Creek remains undeveloped. There are no paved roads in and access is only through one of the nearby parks or from the Tarwater Trailhead via a single-lane dirt road. So it gets overlooked. Beautiful coast redwoods line Pescadero Creek, but unfortunately there's no fishing. Pescadero Creek is protected steelhead trout habitat. The hike-in backpacking campgrounds here are small and primitive, with no water but plenty of solitude.

**Campsites, facilities:** There are two hike-in campgrounds available for drop-in camping. Shaw Flat offers eight sites and Tarwater Trail has six sites. Drinking water is not provided. Campfires are not permitted, but backpacking stoves are allowed.

**Reservations, fees:** Reservations are not accepted. The Shaw Flat and Tarwater campgrounds are available first-come, first-served. Sites are $10 per night for up to four campers and one vehicle per site. Check-in is at the Memorial State Park Ranger Station. Open year-round; closing times vary.

**Directions:** Take U.S. 101 or I-280 to Redwood City/Woodside and Highway 84. Take Highway 84 (Woodside-La Honda-San Gregorio Road) west to La Honda. Turn left at 0.5 mile past the village center in La Honda on Pescadero Road. Continue six miles on Pescadero Road to the park entrance.

**Contact:** San Mateo County Parks and Recreation, 650/879-0238 or 650/363-4021, http://parks.smcgov.org.

## 29 BUTANO REDWOODS STATE PARK

🥾 🐕 🚐 ⛺

### Scenic rating: 9

near Pescadero

Map 7.4, page 446

The campground at Butano is in a canyon filled with a redwood forest, so pretty and with such good hiking that it has become popular enough to make reservations a must. The reason for its popularity is a series of exceptional hikes, including one to the Año Nuevo Lookout (well, the lookout is now blocked by trees, but there are glimpses of the ocean elsewhere along the way), Mill Ox Loop, and, for the ambitious, 11-mile Butano Rim Loop. The latter has a backpack camp with eight trail campsites (primitive with pit toilets available) requiring a 5.5-mile hike in the park's most remote area, where no drinking water is available. Creek water is within 0.5 mile of the campsites; bring a water purifier. Año Nuevo State Reserve is about 10 miles away and is an excellent side trip during elephant seal mating season (December through February).

**Campsites, facilities:** There are 21 sites for tents or RVs up to 24 feet (no hookups), 18 walk-in sites, and eight hike-in sites (5.5 miles, with a pit toilet available); a camp stove is required. Picnic tables, food lockers, and fire grills are provided. Drinking water and restrooms with flush toilets are available; some services may not be available during drought years. Leashed pets are permitted in campsites, picnic areas, and on paved roads.

**Reservations, fees:** Reservations are accepted at 800/444-7275 ($10 reservation fee) or www.reserveamerica.com ($9 reservation fee). Reservations are not available for hike-in trail sites. Sites are $35 per night, plus $10 per night for each additional vehicle. Open April through November.

**Directions:** In Half Moon Bay, at the junction of Highway 1 and Highway 92, drive south on Highway 1 for 18 miles to the Pescadero Road exit. Turn left on Pescadero Road and drive three miles past the town of Pescadero to Cloverdale Road. Turn right and drive 4.5 miles to the park entrance on the left.

**Contact:** Butano State Park, 650/879-2040; Half Moon Bay State Park, 650/726-8819, www.parks.ca.gov.

## 30 PORTOLA REDWOODS STATE PARK

🚶 🚴 🐕 ♿ 🚐 ⛺

### Scenic rating: 9

near Skyline Ridge

**Map 7.4, page 446**

Portola Redwoods State Park is very secluded since getting here requires travel on an extremely slow and winding series of roads. The park features redwoods and a mixed evergreen and hardwood forest on the western slopes of the Santa Cruz Mountains, the headwaters of Pescadero Creek, and 18 miles of hiking trails. A literal highlight is a 300-foot-high redwood, one of the tallest trees in the Santa Cruz Mountains. In addition to redwoods, there are Douglas firs and live oaks, as well as a riparian zone along the stream. A four-mile hike links up to nearby Pescadero Creek County Park (which, in turn, borders Memorial County Park). At times in the summer, a low fog will move in along the San Mateo coast, and from lookouts near Skyline, visitors can peer to the west at what seems like a pearlescent sea with little islands (hilltops) poking through (this view is available from the access road, not from campsites). Wild pigs are occasionally spotted, with larger numbers at neighboring Pescadero Creek County Park.

**Campsites, facilities:** There are 53 sites for tents or RVs up to 24 feet (no hookups), four hike-in/bike-in sites, four walk-in sites, six hike-in backpack sites (three-mile hike), and four group sites for 25 or 50 people. Picnic tables, storage lockers, and fire grills are provided. Drinking water, restrooms with flush toilets and coin showers, and firewood are available. The nearest gas is 13 miles away. Some facilities are wheelchair-accessible. Leashed pets are permitted on paved surfaces only.

**Reservations, fees:** Reservations are accepted at 800/444-7275 ($10 reservation fee) or www. reserveamerica.com ($9 reservation fee). Sites are $35 per night, plus $10 per night for each additional vehicle; it's $5 per person per night for hike-in/bike-in sites, $35 per night for walk-in sites, $15 per night for hike-in backpack sites, and $165-335 per night for group sites. Reservations for Slate Creek Backpack Camp are accepted through Big Basin Redwoods at 831/338-8861. Open April through November.

**Directions:** From Palo Alto on I-280, turn west on (slow and twisty) Page Mill Road and drive to Skyline Boulevard/Highway 35. Cross Skyline and continue west on Alpine Road (very twisty) for about three miles to Portola State Park Road. Turn left on Portola State Park Road and drive about three miles to the park entrance at the end of the road.

**Contact:** Portola Redwoods State Park, 650/948-9098, www.parks.ca.gov or www. santacruzstateparks.org.

## 31 BIG BASIN REDWOODS STATE PARK

🚶 🐕 ♿ 🚐 ⛺

### Scenic rating: 10

near Santa Cruz

**Map 7.4, page 446**

Big Basin is one of the best state parks in California, featuring giant redwoods near the park headquarters, secluded campsites set in forest, and rare opportunities to stay in a tent cabin or a backpacking trail site. The park covers more than 18,000 acres of redwoods, much of it old-growth, including forest behemoths more than 1,000 years old. It is a great park for hikers, with four waterfalls making for stellar destinations. Sempervirens Falls, a long, narrow, silvery stream, is an easy 1.5 miles round-trip on Sequoia Trail. The famous Berry Creek Falls is a spectacular 70-foot cascade in a beautiful canyon framed by redwoods. For hikers in good condition, figure two hours (4.7 miles) to reach Berry Creek Falls, five hours for the round-trip in and out, and six hours for the complete loop (12 miles) that extends into the park's most remote areas. Other spectacular waterfalls—Silver Falls and Golden Cascade—lie one mile up the canyon from Berry Creek

Falls. An easy nature loop trail near the park headquarters in the valley floor goes past several mammoth redwoods. This is California's oldest state park, established in 1902. It is home to the largest continuous stand of ancient coast redwoods south of Humboldt State Park in far Northern California. There are more than 80 miles of trails with elevations varying from 2,000 feet at the eastern Big Basin Rim on down to sea level. Rainfall averages 60 inches per year, most arriving from December through mid-March.

**Campsites, facilities:** There are 31 sites for tents or RVs up to 27 feet or trailers up to 24 feet (no hookups), 69 sites for tents only, 38 walk-in sites, 36 tent cabins (reservations required), two hike-in/bike-in sites, 52 hike-in campsites, and four group sites for 40-50 people. Picnic tables, food lockers, and fire grills are provided. Drinking water, pit toilets, restrooms with flush toilets and coin showers, a dump station, firewood, and groceries are available. Some facilities are wheelchair-accessible. Leashed pets are allowed in campsites and on paved roads only.

**Reservations, fees:** Reservations are accepted at 800/444-7275 ($10 reservation fee) or www.reserveamerica.com ($9 reservation fee). Search for Big Basin Tent Cabins to reserve a tent cabin. Sites are $35 per night for individual sites and walk-in sites, plus $10 per night for each additional vehicle; it's $35 per night for hike-in sites, $6 per person per night for hike-in/bike-in sites, and $270-335 per night for group sites. The tent cabins are $75 per night. Open year-round.

**Directions:** From Santa Cruz, turn north on Highway 9 and drive 12 miles to Boulder Creek and Highway 236 (signed Big Basin). Turn west on Highway 236 and drive nine miles to the park headquarters.

**Contact:** Big Basin Redwoods State Park, 831/338-8860 or 831/338-8861; Santa Cruz District, 831/335-6318, www.santacruzstateparks.org, www.parks.ca.gov; Big Basin Tent Cabins, 831/338-4745, www.bigbasintentcabins.com.

## 32 SANBORN-SKYLINE COUNTY PARK

**Scenic rating: 8**

near Saratoga

Map 7.4, page 446

This is a pretty camp set in a redwood forest, semi-primitive, but like a world in a different orbit compared to the asphalt of San Jose and the rest of the Santa Clara Valley. These campgrounds get heavy use on summer weekends, of course. This is headquarters for a 3,688-acre park that stretches from the foothills of Saratoga up to the Skyline Ridge in the Santa Cruz Mountains. Fifteen miles of hiking trails are available, with a trailhead at camp. Most trails explore lush wooded slopes, with redwoods and tanoaks. Dogs are prohibited at walk-in sites but are allowed at the RV sites, the main park's grassy area, and day-use areas.

**Campsites, facilities:** There are 15 sites with full hookups (20 and 30 amps) for RVs up to 30 feet at Sanborn, a separate walk-in campground with 33 sites for tents, and a youth group area for up to 35 people. Picnic tables, food lockers, and fire pits are provided. Drinking water, restrooms with flush toilets and coin showers, a dump station, a seasonal youth science center, and a one-mile nature trail are available. Some facilities are wheelchair-accessible. Leashed pets are permitted in RV campground and picnic areas only.

**Reservations, fees:** Reservations are required at 408/355-2290 (Monday through Friday) or at www.parkhere.org or www.gooutsideandplay.org ($6 reservation fee). Walk-in sites are $15 per night, tent sites are $30 per night, and RV sites are $40 per night. The youth group area is $50 for up to 35 people the first night and then $10 per night. Check-in is required before sunset; gates are locked at dusk. Some credit cards are accepted. RV sites are open year-round; walk-in sites are open mid-March through mid-October.

**Directions:** From San Jose, take Highway 17 south for six miles to Highway 9/Saratoga

Avenue. Turn west and drive to Saratoga, then continue on Highway 9 for two miles to Sanborn Road. Turn left and drive one mile to the park on the right. Walk-in sites require a 0.1- to 0.5-mile walk from the parking area.

**Contact:** Sanborn-Skyline County Park, 408/867-9959, www.sccgov.org.

## 33 JOSEPH D. GRANT COUNTY PARK

**Scenic rating: 7**

near San Jose

**Map 7.4, page 446**

Grant Ranch is a great, wild playland covering more than 9,000 acres in the foothills of nearby Mount Hamilton to the east. It features 52 miles of hiking trails (horses permitted), 20 miles of old ranch roads that are perfect for mountain biking, a pretty lake (Grant Lake), and miles of foothills, canyons, oaks, and grasslands. The campground is set amid oak grasslands, is shaded, and can be used as a base camp for planning the day's recreation. The best hikes are to Halls Valley, especially in the winter and spring when there are many secret little creeks and miniature waterfalls in hidden canyons; Hotel Trail; and Cañada de Pala Trail, which drops to San Felipe Creek, the prettiest stream in the park. Warm-water fishing is available in the lake and several smaller ponds. A great side trip is the slow, curvy drive east to the Mount Hamilton Summit and Lick Observatory for great views of the Santa Clara Valley. Wood fires are often banned in summer.

**Campsites, facilities:** There are 40 sites for tents or RVs up to 31 feet (no hookups). Picnic tables, food lockers, and fire pits are provided. Drinking water, restrooms with flush toilets and free showers, and a dump station are available. Some facilities are wheelchair-accessible. Leashed pets are permitted.

**Reservations, fees:** Reservations are required at 408/355-2201 (Monday through Friday) or at www.parkhere.org or www.gooutsideandplay.

org ($8 reservation fee). Tent sites are $24 per night, and RV sites are $30 per night. Off-season rates are lower. Check-in is required before sunset; gates are locked at dusk. The 22 Halls Valley sites are open year-round; the 18 Snell sites are available April through October.

**Directions:** In San Jose at the junction of I-680 and U.S. 101, take I-680 north to the Alum Rock Avenue exit. Turn east and drive four miles to Mount Hamilton Road. Turn right and drive eight miles to the park headquarters entrance on the right side of the road.

**Contact:** Joseph D. Grant County Park, 408/274-6121; Santa Clara County Parks, www.sccgov.org.

## 34 HENRY COWELL REDWOODS STATE PARK

**Scenic rating: 8**

near Santa Cruz

**Map 7.4, page 446**

This state park near Santa Cruz has good hiking, good views, and a chance of fishing in the winter for steelhead. The 1,750-acre park features 20 miles of trails in the forest, where the old-growth redwoods are estimated at 1,400-1,800 years old. One great easy hike is a 15-minute walk to a lookout platform over Santa Cruz and the Pacific Ocean; the trailhead is near campsite 49. Another good hike is Eagle Creek Trail, a three-mile walk that heads along Eagle Creek and the San Lorenzo River, running through a classic redwood canyon. In winter, there is limited steelhead fishing in the San Lorenzo River. A side-trip option is taking the Roaring Camp Big Trees Railroad (831/335-4400), which is adjacent to camp. Insider's tips: Poison oak is prevalent in this park and around the campground. Alcohol is prohibited in the campground but not in the day-use area.

**Campsites, facilities:** There are 111 sites for tents or RVs up to 35 feet (no hookups) and one hike-in/bike-in site for up to eight people. Picnic tables and fire grills are provided.

Drinking water, restrooms with flush toilets and coin showers, and Wi-Fi are available. Some facilities are wheelchair-accessible. A nature center, bookstore, and picnic area are nearby. Leashed pets are permitted but must be kept inside tents or vehicles at night.

**Reservations, fees:** Reservations are accepted at 800/444-7275 ($10 reservation fee) or www.reserveamerica.com ($9 reservation fee). Sites are $35 per night (maximum of eight people). The hike-in/bike-in site is first come, first served and costs $7 per person per night. Open March through October.

**Directions:** In Scotts Valley on Highway 17, take the Mount Hermon Road exit and drive west toward Felton to Lockwood Lane. Turn left on Lockwood Lane and drive about one mile to Graham Hill Road. Turn left on Graham Hill Road and drive 0.5 mile to the campground on the right.

**Contact:** Henry Cowell Redwoods State Park, 831/438-2396 or 831/335-4598, www.santacruzstateparks.org or www.parks.ca.gov.

## 35 SANTA CRUZ RANCH RV PARK

### Scenic rating: 5

near Scotts Valley

**Map 7.4, page 446**

This camp is situated on 6.5 acres and is just a short hop from Santa Cruz and Monterey Bay. There are many side-trip options, making this a prime location for vacationers cruising the California coast. In Santa Cruz there are several quality restaurants, plus fishing trips and boat rentals at Santa Cruz Wharf, as well as the famous Santa Cruz Beach Boardwalk and amusement park. Discount tickets for local attractions are available in the office. Note that most of the sites are filled with long-term renters; a few sites are set aside for overnight vacationers.

**Campsites, facilities:** There are 27 pull-through sites with full hookups (30 amps) for RVs up to 45 feet and five sites for tents. Picnic tables are provided. Restrooms with showers, cable TV, coin laundry, free Wi-Fi, recreation and meeting room, hot tub, and seasonal heated swimming pool are available. No open fires are allowed. Leashed pets are permitted with approval.

**Reservations, fees:** Reservations are recommended. RV sites are $62-76 per night, and tent sites are $58 per night. The first pet is free, and a second pet is $1 per night. Weekly, monthly, and group rates are available. Some credit cards are accepted. Open year-round.

**Directions:** From Santa Cruz, at the junction of Highways 1 and 17, turn north on Highway 17 and drive three miles to the Mount Hermon/Big Basin exit. Take that exit north onto Mount Hermon Road and drive 0.5 mile to Scotts Valley Drive. Turn right and drive 0.7 mile to Disc Drive. Turn right and continue to 917 Disc Drive on the left. Note: Big rigs should use the Granite Creek exit or call for the best route.

**Contact:** Santa Cruz Ranch RV Park, 831/438-1288 or 800/546-1288, www.santacruzranchrv.com.

## 36 UVAS CANYON COUNTY PARK

### Scenic rating: 8

near Morgan Hill

**Map 7.4, page 446**

This lushly wooded park of 1,133 acres nestles on the eastern side of the Santa Cruz Mountains. It has a stunning array of waterfalls that can be reached with short hikes, including Triple Falls, Black Rock Falls, and several others, making for stellar hikes in winter and spring. In all, the park has six miles of trails, including a self-guided interpretive trail. Note that the gate to the campground is locked at sunset. Uvas Reservoir (five miles away) is closed to all boating, including float tubes.

**Campsites, facilities:** There are 25 sites for tents and small RVs. A youth group area has tent sites for up to 40 people. Picnic tables, food lockers, and fire grills (charcoal fires only) are provided; fires may be prohibited during fire season. Drinking water, showers, and flush toilets are available. Some facilities are wheelchair-accessible. Leashed pets are permitted.

**Reservations, fees:** Reservations are required at 408/355-2201 (Monday through Friday) or at www.parkhere.org or www.gooutsideandplay. org ($8 reservation fee). Sites are $15-40 per night; call for group rates. Open year-round. Check-in is required before sunset; gates close at sunset.

**Directions:** From San Jose, take U.S. 101 south through Coyote to the exit for Bailey Avenue. Take that exit, turn right (west) on Bailey, and drive into the foothills to McKean Road. Turn left on McKean (after 2.2 miles the road becomes Uvas Road) and drive to Croy Road. Turn right on Croy Road and drive 4.4 miles (through Sveadal; drive slowly) to the park entrance.

**Contact:** Uvas Canyon County Park, 408/779-9232, www.sccgov.org.

## 37 HENRY W. COE STATE PARK

🚶‍♂️ 🚴 ⛴️ 🐕 5% 🚐 ⛺

### Scenic rating: 8

near Gilroy

**Map 7.4, page 446**

This is the Bay Area's backyard wilderness, with 87,000 acres of wildlands, including a 23,300-acre designated wilderness area. There are more than 100 miles of ranch roads and 300 miles of hiking trails, a remarkable network that provides access to 140 ponds and small lakes, hidden streams, and a habitat that is paradise for fish, wildlife, and wild flora. In 2007, a wildfire burned about half of the park, but this grassland country sprang back to life with heavy rains in spring of 2010. The backcountry lakes filled as well, with good bass fishing in the more remote lakes that see very little fishing pressure.

The best camping introduction is at the drive-in campsites at park headquarters (east of Morgan Hill), set on a hilltop at 2,600 feet elevation that is ideal for stargazing and watching meteor showers. That provides a taste. If you like it, then come back for the full meal. It is at the wilderness hike-in and bike-in sites where you will get the full flavor of the park. Before setting out for the outback, always consult with the rangers—the ambitious plans of many hikers cause them to suffer dehydration and heatstroke. For wilderness trips, the best jumping-off point is Coyote Creek or Hunting Hollow Trailhead upstream of Coyote Reservoir east of Gilroy. The park has excellent pond-style fishing but requires extremely long hikes (typically 10- to 25-mile round-trips) to reach the best lakes, including Mustang Pond, Jackrabbit Lake, Coit Lake, and Mississippi Lake. Expect hot weather in the summer; spring and early summer are the prime times. Even though the park may appear to be 120 square miles of oak foothills, the terrain is often steep, and making ridges often involves climbs of 1,500 feet. There are many great secrets to be discovered, including Rooster Comb and Coyote Creek. At times on spring days, wild pigs seem to be everywhere. Golden eagles are also abundant. Bring a water purifier for hikes because there is no developed drinking water in the outback.

**Campsites, facilities:** There are 10 sites for tents only and 10 sites for tents or RVs up to 24 feet (no hookups). A drive-in equestrian camp has eight sites. There are 82 hike-in/bike-in sites and 11 hike-in group sites for 9-50 people. Picnic tables and fire grills are provided; wood burning may be prohibited during dry conditions. Drinking water and vault toilets are available. Restrooms with flush toilets are available at the visitors center. Some facilities are wheelchair-accessible. Leashed pets are permitted at the campgrounds, on paved roads, and on the trail from the visitors center to the overflow parking lot.

Corrals are available at the equestrian camp. Vault toilets are a short walk from the hike-in/

bike-in sites. No drinking water is available at the hike-in/bike-in site and garbage must be packed out.

**Reservations, fees:** Reservations are accepted at 800/444-7275 ($10 reservation fee) or www.reserveamerica.com ($9 reservation fee). The hike-in/bike-in sites are first-come, first-served; a wilderness permit is required from park headquarters or at the day-use parking lot. Sites are $20 per night, plus $8 per night for each additional vehicle; it's $75 per night for group sites, $25 per night for horse sites, and $5 per person per night for hike-in/bike-in sites. Open year-round.

**Directions:** From Morgan Hill on U.S. 101, take the East Dunne Avenue exit. Turn east and drive 13 miles (including over the bridge at Anderson Lake, then very twisty and narrow) to the park entrance.

**Contact:** Henry W. Coe State Park, 408/779-2728, www.coepark.org or www.parks.ca.gov.

## 38 MOUNT MADONNA COUNTY PARK

🧍 🐕 ♿ 🚐 ⛺

### Scenic rating: 7

between Watsonville and Gilroy

**Map 7.4, page 446**

It's a twisty son-of-a-gun road to reach the top of Mount Madonna, but the views on clear days of Monterey Bay to the west and Santa Clara Valley to the east always make it worth the trip. In addition, a small herd of white deer are protected in a pen near the parking area for a rare chance to see unique wildlife. This 3,688-acre park is dominated by redwood forest, but at the lower slopes of Mount Madonna the landscape changes to oak woodland, dense chaparral, and grassy meadows. Ohlone Indians once lived here.

There are many good hiking trails in the park; the best is Bayview Loop. The 20-mile trail system includes a one-mile self-guided nature trail. Elevation in the park reaches 1,896 feet. Free programs are offered at the amphitheater on Saturday evenings during the summer. Insider's note: Campsite 105 at Valley View is the only pull-through site. While no credit cards are accepted in person, there is a self-pay machine that accepts credit cards—a nice touch. The campsites are dispersed throughout four campgrounds.

**Campsites, facilities:** There are 118 sites with partial hookups (30 amps) for tents or RVs up to 30 feet, five yurts, and two group areas for up to 240 people. One site is pull-through. Five youth-group areas for 40-50 people each are also available; youth groups must have tax-exempt status. Picnic tables, food lockers, and fire pits are provided. Drinking water, restrooms with coin showers and flush toilets, a dump station, seasonal live music, archery range, picnic areas, an amphitheater, and a visitors center are available. Some facilities are wheelchair-accessible. Leashed pets are permitted.

**Reservations, fees:** Reservations are required at 408/355-2201 (Monday through Friday) or at www.parkhere.org or www.gooutsideand-play.org ($8 reservation fee). RV sites are $30 per night, tent sites are $24 per night, and yurts are $35-50 (sleeps 6), $55-70 (sleeps 8), $75-90 (sleeps 10) per night. Group camps are $180-450 per night, and the youth group area is $50 per night. Some credit cards are accepted at a self-serve machine. Open year-round.

**Directions:** From U.S. 101 in Gilroy, take the Hecker Pass Highway/Highway 152 exit west. Drive west seven miles to Pole Line Road and the park entrance on the right.

From Highway 1 in Watsonville, turn east onto Highway 152 and drive about 12 miles east to Pole Line Road and the park entrance on the left.

**Contact:** Mount Madonna County Park, 408/842-2341, www.sccgov.org.

## 39 COYOTE LAKE AND HARVEY BEAR COUNTY PARKS

🚴 🛶 🚤 🎣 🦌 ♿ 🚐 ⛺

### Scenic rating: 8

near Gilroy

**Map 7.4, page 446**

Several campsites here sit on a bluff with a lake view. Where else in the greater Bay Area can you get that? The campground is nestled in oaks, among 796 acres of parkland, furnishing some much-needed shade. Coyote Lake, a long, narrow lake in a canyon just over the ridge east of U.S. 101, is a pretty surprise to newcomers. It covers 635 acres and provides one of the best lakes for bass fishing in the Bay Area. Other species are bluegill and crappie. Both powerboating and non-motorized boating are allowed; the boat launch is one mile north of the visitors center. Swimming is prohibited. There are no longer hiking trails along the lakeshore, but more than 13 miles of multi-use trails (horses and mountain bikes are allowed) are available, along with trails on the adjacent Harvey Bear County Park to the west that overlooks the lake.

Note: If you continue east about four miles on the access road that runs past the lake to the Coe State Park Hunting Hollow entrance, you'll come to two outstanding trailheads (one at a parking area, one at the Coyote Creek gate) into that park's wildlands. Wildlife, including deer and wild turkey, is abundant. Note: All boats must be certified mussel-free before launching.

**Campsites, facilities:** There are 73 pull-through sites for tents or RVs up to 31 feet; 18 sites have partial hookups. Picnic tables, food lockers, and fire pits are provided. Drinking water, flush toilets, showers, and a boat ramp are available. A visitors center is also available. Some facilities are wheelchair-accessible. Leashed pets are permitted.

**Reservations, fees:** Reservations are required at 408/355-2201 (Monday through Friday) or at www.parkhere.org or www.gooutsideandplay.org ($8 reservation fee). Tent sites are $24 per night, RV sites are $30 per night, and it's $6 per day for boat launching plus an inspection fee. Some credit cards are accepted. Open year-round.

**Directions:** Drive on U.S. 101 to Gilroy and Leavesley Road. Take that exit and drive east on Leavesley Road for 1.75 miles to New Avenue. Turn left on New Avenue and drive 0.6 mile to Roop Road. Turn right on Roop Road and drive three miles to Coyote Reservoir Road. Turn left on Coyote Reservoir Road and drive to the campground.

**Contact:** Coyote Lake County Park, 408/842-7800, www.sccgov.org; Coyote Discount Bait and Tackle, 408/463-0711.

# MONTEREY AND BIG SUR

The coast's scenic rock-strewn charm extends from the seaside towns of Santa Cruz and Monterey down Highway 1 to Big Sur and San Simeon. Sea otters play in Monterey Bay and Highway 1 offers one of the most captivating drives anywhere. The inland strip along Highway 1 provides access to state parks, redwoods, coastal streams, Los Padres National Forest, and the Ventana Wilderness. Farther south is a largely untouched coast. During the summer, only the fog on the coast and the intense heat just 10 miles inland keep this region from attaining perfection. At Big Sur, the campgrounds come in a variety of settings: small hideaways in the redwoods, some near Big Sur River, others in the forest. These state park campgrounds are among the most popular in North America. Reservations are required far in advance all summer, even on weekdays. They are always the first to fill on the state's reservation system.

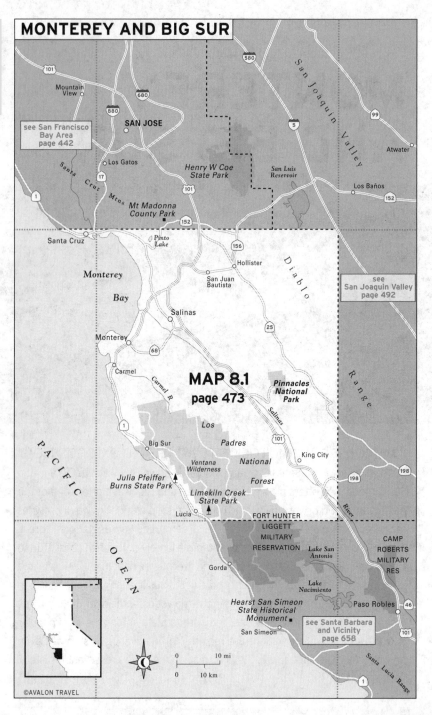

# MONTEREY AND BIG SUR

see San Francisco
Bay Area
page 442

see
San Joaquin Valley
page 492

MAP 8.1
page 473

see Santa Barbara
and Vicinity
page 658

Mountain
View

SAN JOSE

Atwater

Los Gatos

Henry W Coe
State Park

San Luis
Reservoir

Los Baños

Santa Cruz Mtns

Mt Madonna
County Park

Pinto
Lake

Santa Cruz

Monterey
Bay

Hollister

San Juan
Bautista

Salinas

Diablo

Monterey

Carmel

Carmel R

Pinnacles
National
Park

Los

Padres

Salinas

Range

Big Sur

Ventana
Wilderness

National

King City

Julia Pfeiffer
Burns State Park

Forest

Limekiln Creek
State Park

Lucia

PACIFIC

FORT HUNTER
LIGGETT
MILITARY
RESERVATION

Lake San
Antonio

CAMP
ROBERTS
MILITARY
RES

OCEAN

Gorda

Lake
Nacimiento

Paso Robles

Hearst San Simeon
State Historical
Monument

San Simeon

River

Santa Lucia Range

0    10 mi
0    10 km

©AVALON TRAVEL

# Map 8.1

**Sites 1-33**
**Pages 474-489**

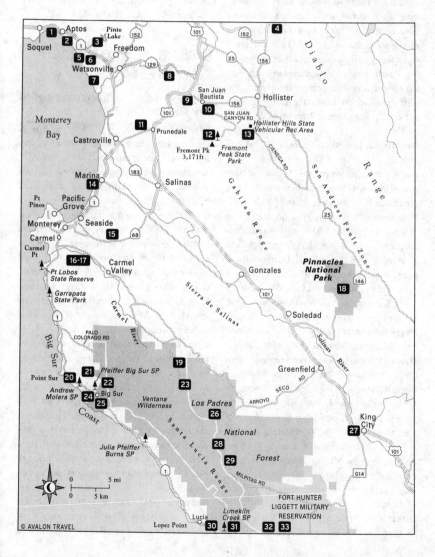

© AVALON TRAVEL

# 1 NEW BRIGHTON STATE BEACH

🏃 🚵 ⛱ 🏊 🎣 🛏 ♿ 🚐 ⛺

**Scenic rating: 10**

near Capitola

**Map 8.1, page 473**

This is one in a series of state park camps set on the bluffs overlooking Monterey Bay. They are among the most popular and in-demand state campgrounds in California. Reservations are a necessity. This camp is near a forest of Monterey pine and live oak. The summer is often foggy and cool, especially in the morning. Beachcombing, swimming, and surf fishing for perch provide recreation options, and skiff rentals are available at the nearby Capitola Wharf. The San Lorenzo River enters the ocean nearby.

**Campsites, facilities:** There are 82 back-in only sites for tents or RVs up to 36 feet; only one RV is permitted per site. Some sites have partial hookups (30 amps). There are also three group sites (9-25 people each) and four hike-in/bike-in sites. Picnic tables, fire rings, and food lockers are provided. Drinking water, restrooms with coin showers and flush toilets, and a visitors center are available. Dump stations, propane gas, groceries, coin laundry, restaurant, and gas station are available within 2.5 miles. Some facilities are wheelchair-accessible. Leashed pets are permitted.

**Reservations, fees:** Reservations are recommended and can be made at 800/444-7275 ($10 reservation fee) or www.reserveamerica.com ($9 reservation fee). Premium sites are $50 per night, RV sites (with hookups) are $50 per night for up to eight people, sites without hookups are $35 per night, plus $10 per night for each additional vehicle. The group site is $185 per night, and hike-in/bike-in camping is $5 per person per night. Maximum stay is two nights per month. Open year-round, weather permitting. Some areas and sites may close for part of the year.

**Directions:** From Santa Cruz, drive south on Highway 1 for about five miles to the Park Avenue exit. Take that exit and turn right on Park Avenue and drive a short distance to McGregor Drive (a four-way stop). Turn left and drive a short distance to the park entrance on the right.

**Contact:** New Brighton State Beach, 831/464-6329; California State Parks, Santa Cruz District, 831/335-6318 or 831/335-3455, www.santacruzstateparks.org or www.parks.ca.gov; Pacific Migrations Visitor Center, 831/464-5620; project office 831/464-6330.

# 2 SEACLIFF STATE BEACH

🏊 ⛱ 🐕 ♿ 🚐

**Scenic rating: 10**

near Santa Cruz

**Map 8.1, page 473**     BEST (

Here is a very pretty spot along Monterey Bay. Beach walks are great, especially for dramatic sunsets on clear evenings, as is swimming and sunbathing on the long stretch of sand backed by coastal bluffs. A visitors center is open in the summer. This is a popular layover for vacationers touring Highway 1 in the summer, but the best weather is from mid-August to early October. A structure many call the "old cement ship" nearby provides some fascination, but for safety reasons visitors are no longer allowed to walk on it. It is actually an old concrete freighter, the *Palo Alto*. Fishing is often good adjacent to the ship.

**Campsites, facilities:** There are 35 sites for self-contained RVs up to 40 feet, and an overflow area can accommodate 21 RVs up to 34 feet (no hookups). Picnic tables and fire grills are provided. Drinking water, restrooms with flush toilets and coin showers, and a picnic area are available. Propane gas, groceries, a coin laundry, and a visitors center are nearby. Some facilities are wheelchair-accessible. Leashed pets are permitted in the camping area and on the beach.

**Reservations, fees:** Reservations are accepted at 800/444-7275 ($10 reservation fee) or www.reserveamerica.com ($9 reservation fee).

Premium sites are $65 per night, sites without hookups are $55 per night, plus $10 per night for each additional vehicle. Open year-round, weather permitting.

**Directions:** From Santa Cruz, drive south on Highway 1 about six miles to State Park Drive/Seacliff Beach exit. Take that exit, turn west (right), and drive a short distance to the park entrance.

**Contact:** Seacliff State Beach, 831/685-6442 or 831/685-6500; California State Parks, Santa Cruz District, 831/429-2851, www.santacruz-stateparks.org or www.parks.ca.gov; visitors center, 831/685-6444.

## 3 PINTO LAKE PARK

**Scenic rating: 7**

near Watsonville

**Map 8.1, page 473**

Pinto Lake can be a real find. Of the nine lakes in the nine Bay Area counties that offer camping, it is the only one where the RV campsites are actually near the lake. For the few who know about it, it's an offer that can't be refused. But note that no tent camping is permitted. The lake is best known as a fishing lake, with trout stocks and a small resident population of crappie and bluegill. Rainbow trout are stocked twice monthly in season. A 5-mph speed limit has been established for boaters, and no swimming or wading is permitted. The leash law for dogs is strictly enforced here.

**Campsites, facilities:** There are 28 sites with full hookups (30 amps) for RVs of any length. No tents are permitted. Picnic tables, cable TV, and barbecues are provided. A boat ramp, boat rentals, Wi-Fi, volleyball, and a softball field are available nearby in the summer. Leashed pets are permitted. Most facilities are wheelchair-accessible. Open year-round.

**Reservations, fees:** Reservations are accepted at 831/728-6194. Sites are $40 per night, plus $2 per night per person for more than two people (children 12 and under are free), $2 per night

for each additional vehicle, and $5 per pet per night (limit two dogs). Credit cards are not accepted.

**Directions:** From Santa Cruz, drive 17 miles south on Highway 1 to the exit for Watsonville/Gilroy-Highway 152. Take that exit onto Main Street, then immediately turn left on Green Valley Road and drive 2.7 miles (0.5 mile past Holohan intersection) to the entrance for the lake and campground on the left.

From Monterey, drive north on Highway 1 to the Green Valley Road exit. Take that exit and turn right at the Green Valley Road and drive 2.7 miles (0.5 mile past the Holohan intersection) to the entrance for the lake and campground.

**Contact:** Pinto Lake Park, 831/722-8139, www.pintolake.com.

## 4 CASA DE FRUTA RV ORCHARD RESORT

**Scenic rating: 3**

near Pacheco Pass

**Map 8.1, page 473**

This 80-acre RV park has a festival-like atmosphere to it, with country music and dancing every weekend in the summer and barbecues on Sunday. The resort is also busy during the Gilroy Garlic Festival in July and the Hollister Independence Rally, a motorcycle event held nearby during the Fourth of July weekend. Huge but sparse San Luis Reservoir is 20 miles to the east.

**Campsites, facilities:** There are 300 sites with full hookups (30 amps) for RVs; some sites are pull-through. Tent sites are also available. Picnic tables are provided. Restrooms with flush toilets and showers, dump station, Wi-Fi, satellite TV, coin laundry, playground, swimming pool, wading pool, outdoor dance floor, horseshoes, volleyball courts, wine- and cheese-tasting room, candy factory, bakery, fruit stand, 24-hour restaurant, motel, gift shop, carousel, narrow-gauge train ride through animal park, and a mini mart are available. Some facilities are wheelchair-accessible. Leashed pets are permitted.

**Reservations, fees:** Reservations are accepted at 800/548-3813. RV sites are $42-50 per night, tent sites are $35 per night, plus $2 per person per night for more than two people and $3 per pet per stay. Some credit cards are accepted. Open year-round.

**Directions:** Drive on U.S. 101 to the junction with Highway 152 (near Gilroy). Take Highway 152 east and drive 13 miles to Casa de Fruta Parkway. Take that exit and drive a short distance to the resort.

**Contact:** Casa de Fruta RV Orchard Resort, 408/842-9316 or 800/548-3813, www.casadefruta.com.

## 5 MANRESA UPLANDS STATE BEACH WALK-IN

### Scenic rating: 10

south of Santa Cruz

**Map 8.1, page 473**

This is a beautiful and extremely popular state park, with the campground on uplands overlooking the Pacific Ocean. Many sites have ocean views; others are set back in a secluded grove of pine and cypress trees. The walk to the campsites is 20-150 yards from a vehicle-unloading zone. There is beach access for fishing, swimming, and surfing. Santa Cruz and Monterey are each a short drive away and offer endless recreation possibilities.

**Campsites, facilities:** There are 64 walk-in sites for tents only. Picnic tables, food lockers, and fire grills are provided. Drinking water, restrooms with flush toilets and coin showers, and firewood are available. Some facilities are wheelchair-accessible. Leashed pets are permitted in the campground and on the beach.

**Reservations, fees:** Reservations are accepted at 800/444-7275 ($10 reservation fee) or www.reserveamerica.com ($9 reservation fee).

Sites are $35 per night. Open March through November.

**Directions:** From Santa Cruz, drive 12 miles southeast on Highway 1 to the San Andreas Road exit. Take that exit south and drive five miles to Sand Dollar Drive. Turn right and drive a short distance to the park entrance on the left. The parking area is about 1,000 yards from the camping area. A 20-minute unloading zone is available within 20-150 yards of the sites.

**Contact:** Manresa Uplands State Beach, 831/761-1795; California State Parks, Santa Cruz District, 831/335-6318, www.santacruzstateparks.org or www.parks.ca.gov.

## 6 SANTA CRUZ KOA

### Scenic rating: 8

near Watsonville

**Map 8.1, page 473**

Bike rentals and nearby access to Manresa State Beach make this KOA campground a winner. The little log cabins are quite cute, and security is first class. It is a popular layover spot and weekend vacation destination. The only downer is the amount of asphalt. In 2012, Santa Cruz KOA won both the KOA President's Award and the Founders Award for exceptional service.

**Campsites, facilities:** There are 180 sites, including five pull-through sites, with full or partial hookups (30 and 50 amps) for RVs of any length, seven sites for tents only, 50 camping cabins, 25 camping lodges, and six Airstream trailers. Picnic tables and fire grills are provided. Restrooms with showers, two dump stations, free Wi-Fi, cable TV, swimming pool, spa, playground, two recreation rooms, bicycle rentals, miniature golf, basketball court, convenience store, and propane gas are available. Some facilities are wheelchair-accessible. Leashed pets are permitted.

**Reservations, fees:** Reservations are advised at 800/562-7701. RV sites are $88-108 per night, tent sites are $62-80 per night. Lodges, airstreams, camp cabins and camping lodges are also available (call for rates). Some credit cards are accepted. Open year-round.

**Directions:** From Santa Cruz, drive 12 miles southeast on Highway 1. Take the San Andreas Road exit and head southwest for 3.5 miles.

**Contact:** Santa Cruz KOA, 1186 San Andreas Road, 831/722-0551, www.santacruzkoa.com or www.koa.com.

## 7 SUNSET STATE BEACH

### Scenic rating: 9

near Watsonville

Map 8.1, page 473

On clear evenings, the sunsets here look as if they are imported from Hawaii. The camp is set on a bluff along Monterey Bay. While there are no ocean views from the campsites, the location makes for easy, short walks down to the beach for beautiful shoreline walks. The beachfront features pine trees, bluffs, and expansive sand dunes. Large agricultural fields border the park. This area was once a good spot for clamming, but the clams have just about been fished out. The best weather is in late summer and fall. Spring can be windy, and early summer is often foggy. Reservations are often needed well in advance to secure a spot.

**Campsites, facilities:** There are 91 sites for tents or RVs up to 31 feet (no hookups), one hike-in/bike-in site, and one group site for 9-50 people. Picnic tables, food lockers, and fire grills are provided. Drinking water, restrooms with flush toilets and coin showers, and firewood are available. Some facilities are wheelchair-accessible. Leashed pets are permitted, except on the beach.

**Reservations, fees:** Reservations are accepted at 800/444-7275 ($10 reservation fee) or www.reserveamerica.com ($9 reservation fee). Sites are $35 per night, plus $10 per night for each additional vehicle. It's $5 per person per night for the hike-in/bike-in site and $335 per night for the group site. South Camp and the group site are open year-round, but Dunes and Pine Hollow campgrounds are only open mid-March through October.

**Directions:** From Highway 1 near Watsonville, take the Riverside Drive exit toward the ocean to Beach Road. Drive 3.5 miles on Beach Road to the San Andreas Road exit. Turn right on San Andreas Road and drive about three miles to Sunset Beach Road. Turn left and drive a short distance to the park entrance.

**Contact:** Sunset State Beach, 831/763-7063; California State Parks, Santa Cruz District, 831/335-6318, www.santacruzstateparks.org or www.parks.ca.gov.

## 8 MCALPINE LAKE AND PARK

### Scenic rating: 5

near San Juan Bautista

Map 8.1, page 473

This is the only privately operated campground in the immediate region that has any spots for tent campers. The camping cabins look like miniature log cabins, quite cute and comfortable. In addition, the park has a 40-foot-deep lake stocked with trout, bass, bluegill, sturgeon, and catfish; no fishing license is required. The swimming pool has been transformed into a trout-fishing pond. Other highlights of the park are its proximity to Mission San Juan Bautista and the relatively short drive to the Monterey-Carmel area.

**Campsites, facilities:** There are 45 sites for tents only, 27 sites with partial hookups (30 amps) for tents or RVs, 14 sites with full hookups (30 amps) for RVs, and four cabins. Picnic tables are provided; small fire pits can be brought in. Restrooms with flush toilets and showers, dump station, group barbecue facilities, fishing pond, bait and tackle, coin laundry, propane gas, and groceries are available at a country store. Some facilities are wheelchair-accessible. Leashed pets are permitted.

**Reservations, fees:** Reservations are accepted. RV sites are $40 per night, tent sites are $32 per night, and it's $10 per person per night for more than four people and $5 per night for each additional vehicle. Some credit cards are accepted. Weekly and monthly rates are available. Open year-round.

**Directions:** On U.S. 101, drive to the Highway 129 exit. Take Highway 129 west and drive 100 feet to Searle Road (frontage road). Turn left onto Searle Road and drive to the stop sign at Anzar. Turn left again on Anzar and drive under the freeway to the park entrance on the left (900 Anzar Road).

**Contact:** McAlpine Lake and Park, 831/623-4263, www.mcalpinelake.com.

## ⑨ MONTEREY VACATION RV PARK

### Scenic rating: 4

near San Juan Bautista

**Map 8.1, page 473**

This RV park has an ideal location for many vacationers. It's a 10-minute drive to San Juan Bautista, 15 minutes to winery tours, 30 minutes to the Monterey Bay Aquarium, and 40 minutes to Monterey's Fisherman's Wharf and Cannery Row. It's in an attractive spot with some trees, but the nearby attractions are what make it a clear winner. The park is next to the old stagecoach trail where famous outlaw Joaquin Murrieta once ambushed travelers. Note that about half of the sites are occupied by long-term renters.

**Campsites, facilities:** There are 88 sites with full hookups (30 amps) for RVs up to 40 feet; many are pull-through. No tents. Picnic tables and barbecues are provided at some sites. Restrooms with flush toilets and showers, a coin laundry, Wi-Fi, and propane gas are available. Some facilities are wheelchair-accessible. Leashed pets up to 40 pounds are permitted, with certain restrictions.

**Reservations, fees:** Reservations are recommended for three-day holiday weekends; rates are $27-35 per night, plus $3 per person per night for more than two people and $1 per pet per night. Some credit cards are accepted (except on discounts). Open year-round.

**Directions:** On U.S. 101, drive toward San Juan Bautista (between Gilroy and Salinas). The park is on U.S. 101 two miles south of the Highway 156/San Juan Bautista exit at 1400 U.S. 101.

**Contact:** Monterey Vacation RV Park, 831/726-9118.

## ⑩ MISSION FARM RV PARK

### Scenic rating: 4

near San Juan Bautista

**Map 8.1, page 473**

The primary appeal of this RV park is that it is within easy walking distance of San Juan Bautista. The park is beside a walnut orchard surrounded by redwood trees—it's a very quiet place. Golfing and fishing are nearby.

**Campsites, facilities:** There are 144 sites with full hookups (30 amps) for RVs up to 33 feet and a grassy area for tents. Picnic tables are provided. Restrooms with flush toilets and showers, coin laundry, and propane gas are available. Some facilities are wheelchair-accessible. Leashed pets are permitted.

**Reservations, fees:** Reservations are recommended. Sites are $37.50 per night, plus $8 per person per night for more than two people and $5 per pet per night. Monthly rates are available. Some credit cards are accepted. Open year-round.

**Directions:** From U.S. 101 near San Juan Bautista, drive three miles east on U.S. 101/Highway 156. Merge onto Highway 156 east toward San Juan Bautista/Hollister and drive three miles to The Alameda. Turn right at The Alameda and drive one block to San Juan-Hollister Road. Turn left and drive 0.25 mile to the campground at 400 San Juan-Hollister Road.

**Contact:** Mission Farm RV Park, 831/623-4456.

## 11 SALINAS/MONTEREY KOA
🏊 🐕 👨‍👩‍👧 ♿ 🚐

**Scenic rating: 3**

near Salinas

Map 8.1, page 473

If Big Sur, Monterey, and Carmel are packed, this RV park provides some overflow space. This KOA is located right by the highway, about a half-hour drive from the Monterey area.

**Campsites, facilities:** There are 79 sites with full or partial hookups (30 amps) for RVs up to 40 feet; some sites are pull-through. There are also 21 cabins. Picnic tables are provided. Restrooms with showers, recreation room, swimming pool (heated and open mid-May to mid-October), playground, cable TV, clubhouse, basketball court, and coin laundry are available. Some facilities are wheelchair-accessible. Pets are permitted, with breed restrictions, and must be attended and leashed at all times.

**Reservations, fees:** Reservations are recommended. RV sites are $49-65 per night, plus $10 per night per each additional vehicle. Some credit cards are accepted. Open year-round.

**Directions:** From Salinas, drive north on U.S. 101 for seven miles to Highway 156 West. Take the exit for Highway 156 West and drive over the overpass 0.2 mile to the Prunedale Road exit. Take that exit to Prunedale North Road. Turn right and drive a short distance to the campground entrance on the left.

**Contact:** Salinas/Monterey KOA, 831/663-2886 or 800/541-0085 (reservations), www.koa.com or www.reynoldsresorts.com.

## 12 FREMONT PEAK STATE PARK
🚶 🐕 🏕 ♿ 🚐 ⛺

**Scenic rating: 7**

near San Juan Bautista

Map 8.1, page 473

Most vacationers in this region are heading to Monterey Bay and the surrounding environs. That's why Fremont Peak State Park is missed by a lot of folks. It is on a ridge (2,900 feet) with great views of Monterey Bay available on the trail going up Fremont Peak (3,169 feet) in the Gavilan Range. An observatory with a 30-inch telescope at the park is open to the public on specified Saturday evenings. There are views of the San Benito Valley, Salinas Valley, and the Santa Lucia Mountains. A picnic is held in the park each April to commemorate Captain John C. Frémont, his expeditions, and his raising of the U.S. flag in defiance of the Mexican government. Note: There is no access from this park to the adjacent Hollister Hills State Vehicular Recreation Area.

**Campsites, facilities:** There are 21 primitive sites for tents or RVs up to 25 feet (no hookups) and one group site for up to 50 people. Picnic tables and fire rings are provided. Drinking water and pit toilets are available. Some facilities are wheelchair-accessible. Leashed pets are permitted.

**Reservations, fees:** Reservations are accepted at 800/444-7275 ($10 reservation fee) or www.reserveamerica.com ($9 reservation fee). Sites are $25 per night, plus $10 per night for each additional vehicle, and it's $100 per night for group site. The Valley View campground is open March through November; Oak Point and the group campgrounds are open year-round.

**Directions:** From Highway 156 in San Juan Bautista, drive to San Juan Canyon Road. Turn south on San Juan Canyon Road (unsigned except for state park directional sign) and drive 11 miles (narrow, twisty, not recommended for vehicles longer than 25 feet) to the park.

**Contact:** Fremont Peak State Park, 831/623-4255; Monterey State Park District, Gavilan

Sector, 831/623-4526, www.parks.ca.gov; observatory, 831/623-2465, www.fpoa.net.

## 13 HOLLISTER HILLS STATE VEHICULAR RECREATION AREA

Scenic rating: 4

near Hollister

**Map 8.1, page 473**

This unique park was designed for off-highway-vehicle (OHV) enthusiasts. It provides 80 miles of trails for motorcycles and 40 miles of trails for four-wheel-drive vehicles. Some of the trails are accessible directly from the campground. All trails close at sunset. Note that there is no direct access to Fremont Peak State Park, bordering directly to the west. Elevations at the park range 800-2,600 feet. Visitors are advised to always call in advance when planning a trip because the area is sometimes closed for special events. A sidelight is that a 288-acre area is set aside for hiking and mountain biking. In addition, a self-guided natural history walk is routed into Azalea Canyon and along the San Andreas Fault.

**Campsites, facilities:** There are seven campgrounds with a total of 125 sites for tents or RVs of any length (no hookups) and group sites for up to 300 people. Picnic tables and fire rings are provided. Drinking water, restrooms with flush toilets and showers, and a camp store are available. Some facilities are wheelchair-accessible. Leashed pets are permitted.

**Reservations, fees:** Reservations are not accepted. Sites are $10 per night per vehicle. Group sites are $250 per night. Open year-round.

**Directions:** From Highway 156 west of Hollister, drive east to Union Road. Turn right (south) on Union Road and drive three miles to Cienega Road. Turn right (south) on Cienega Road and drive five miles to the park on the right.

**Contact:** Hollister Hills State Vehicular Recreation Area, 831/637-3874 or 831/637-8186 (district office), www.parks.ca.gov or www.ohv.parks.ca.gov; Fault Line Power Sports, 831/637-9780, www.faultlinemc.com.

## 14 MARINA DUNES RV PARK

Scenic rating: 4

near Monterey Bay

**Map 8.1, page 473**

This is a popular park for RV cruisers who are touring Highway 1 and want a layover spot near Monterey. This place fills the bill, open all year and in Marina, just a short drive from the many side-trip opportunities available in Monterey and Carmel. It is set in the sand dunes, about 300 yards from the ocean. Horseback riding, boat rentals, and golfing are nearby.

**Campsites, facilities:** There are 65 sites, most with full hookups (30 and 50 amps), for RVs of any length and 10 sites for tents. Picnic tables and barbecue grills are provided. Restrooms with showers, drinking water, coin laundry, cable TV, Wi-Fi, recreation room, playground, volleyball, horseshoes, meeting room, picnic area, RV supplies, gift shop, dump station, and propane are available. Some facilities are wheelchair-accessible. Leashed pets are permitted.

**Reservations, fees:** Reservations are recommended. RV sites are $55-80 per night, and tent sites are $35 per night. Credit cards are accepted. Open year-round.

**Directions:** From Highway 1 in Marina, drive to the Reservation Road exit. Take that exit and drive west a short distance to Dunes Drive. Turn right on Dunes Drive and drive to the end of the road and the park entrance on the right.

**Contact:** Marina Dunes RV Park, 831/384-6914, www.marinadunesrv.com.

## 15 LAGUNA SECA RECREATION AREA

**Scenic rating: 5**

near Monterey

Map 8.1, page 473

This campground is just minutes away from the sights in Monterey and Carmel. It is situated in oak woodlands overlooking the world-famous Laguna Seca Raceway. There are three separate camping areas: Chaparral, Cam-Am Circle, and Grand Prix Campgrounds.

**Campsites, facilities:** There are 172 sites for tents or RVs up to 40 feet; most sites have partial hookups (30 amps). A large overflow area is also available for RVs and tents. Picnic tables and fire pits are provided. Restrooms with showers, dump station, pond, rifle and pistol range, clubhouse, and group camping and meeting facilities are available. Some facilities are wheelchair-accessible. Leashed pets are permitted.

**Reservations, fees:** Reservations are accepted at 888/588-2267 ($9 reservation fee). There are 70 tent and RV sites (no hookups) at Grand Prix for $27-32 per night. RV sites (water and electricity) are available at Chaparral and Cam-Am Circle for $32-37 per night, plus $15 per night for each additional vehicle and $2 per pet per night (maximum two pets). Off-season and group rates are available ($15 fee). Some credit cards are accepted. Open year-round.

**Directions:** From Monterey and U.S. 101, drive east on Highway 68 for 6.5 miles to the park entrance on the left.

**Contact:** Laguna Seca Recreation Area, 831/758-3604 or 888/588-2267, www.co.monterey.ca.us/parks.

## 16 CARMEL BY THE RIVER RV PARK

**Scenic rating: 8**

on the Carmel River

Map 8.1, page 473

Location, location, location. That's what vacationers want. Well, this park is on the Carmel River, minutes away from Carmel, Cannery Row, the Monterey Bay Aquarium, golf courses, and the beach. Hedges and flowers separate each RV site.

**Campsites, facilities:** There are 35 sites with full hookups (30 and 50 amps) for RVs up to 45 feet. No tents are permitted. Restrooms with showers, cable TV, Wi-Fi, recreational cabana, game room with pool tables, barbecue area, and river access are available. A convenience store and propane gas are nearby. Some facilities (and a bathroom) are wheelchair-accessible. Leashed pets are permitted.

**Reservations, fees:** Reservations are accepted for two or more nights. Sites are $65-90 per night, plus $3 per person per night for more than two people over age 12, $5 per night for each additional vehicle, and $2 per pet per night. Open year-round.

**Directions:** In Carmel on Highway 1, drive to Carmel Valley Road. Take Carmel Valley Road southeast and drive 4.5 miles to Schulte Road. Turn right and drive to the end of the road (27680 Schulte Road in Carmel).

**Contact:** Carmel by the River RV Park, 831/624-9329, www.carmelrv.com.

## 17 SADDLE MOUNTAIN RANCH RV PARK AND CAMPGROUND

**Scenic rating: 6**

near the Carmel River

Map 8.1, page 473

This pretty park is about 100 yards from the Carmel River amid a grove of oak trees. The park offers hiking trails, and if you want to make a buyer's swing into Carmel, it's only a five-mile drive. Note: The Carmel River is reduced to a trickle most of the year and can go dry in drought years.

**Campsites, facilities:** There are 28 tent sites and 23 sites with full hookups (30 amps) for RVs up to 40 feet. Picnic tables, cable TV, Wi-Fi, and barbecue grills are provided. Restrooms with flush toilets and showers are available. A seasonal swimming pool, playground, horseshoe pits, badminton, croquet, and a basketball court are nearby. Some facilities are wheelchair-accessible. Leashed pets are permitted in the RV area only; check for current status of pet policy for campground.

**Reservations, fees:** Reservations are accepted. RV sites are $65-72 per night, tent sites are $35-60 per night, plus $5 per person per night for more than two people, $5 per night for each additional vehicle, and $5 per pet. Weekly and monthly rates are available, as well as group rates. Open year-round.

**Directions:** In Carmel on Highway 1 drive to Carmel Valley Road. Take Carmel Valley Road southeast and drive 4.5 miles to Schulte Road. Turn right and drive to the park at the end of the road (27625 Schulte Road in Carmel).

**Contact:** Saddle Mountain RV Park and Campground, 831/624-1617, www.carmel-camping.com.

## 18 PINNACLES CAMPGROUND

🏃 ⛵ 🐎 🔥 ♿ 🚐 ⛺

### Scenic rating: 7
near Pinnacles National Park

**Map 8.1, page 473**

This is the only camp at Pinnacles National Park, where there are more than 30 miles of hiking trails and two sets of talus caves. Pinnacles National Park is like a different planet—it's a 24,000-acre park with volcanic clusters and strange caves, all great for exploring. The jagged pinnacles for which the park was named were formed by the erosion of an ancient volcanic eruption and are popular for rock climbing. This is a popular place for astronomy buffs—ranger-led dark sky viewings are offered occasionally—and condors can sometimes be seen flying in the monument and over the campground. Campfire programs are held in the amphitheater most of the year. If you are planning to stay a weekend in the spring, arrive early on Friday evening to be sure you get a campsite. In the summer, beware of temperatures in the 90s and 100s. Also note that the Bear Gulch Caves can be closed seasonally to protect nesting bat populations; always check with rangers.

**Campsites, facilities:** There are 99 sites for tents, 36 RV sites with partial hookups (30 amps), and 14 group sites for 20 people each. Picnic tables and fire grills are provided. Drinking water, restrooms with flush toilets and showers, dump station, amphitheater, convenience store, and a swimming pool (April through September) are available. Campfires are permitted, but rules are subject to change without warning. Although discouraged, leashed dogs are permitted in the campground. They are not permitted on trails.

**Reservations, fees:** Reservations are accepted at 877/444-6777 ($10 reservation fee) or www.recreation.gov ($9 reservation fee). Tent sites are $23 per night, and RV sites are $36 per night. Group sites are $75 per night for 1-10 people, $110 for 11-20 people. Some credit cards are accepted. There is a park entrance fee of $15. Open year-round, weather permitting.

**Directions:** From Hollister, drive south on Highway 25 for 32 miles to Highway 146 west (signed "Pinnacles"). Take Highway 146 and drive 2.5 miles to the campground on the left.

**Contact:** Pinnacles Campground, www.nps.gov/pinn; Pinnacles Campground Store, 831/389-4538.

## 19 WHITE OAKS

### Scenic rating: 7

on Chews Ridge in Los Padres National Forest

**Map 8.1, page 473**

Note: At time of publication, this campground remained closed due to damage from the 2016 Soberanes Fire. Please contact the ranger station for updates.

This camp is at 4,000 feet elevation near Anastasia Creek, and there's a surprisingly remote feel to the area despite its relative proximity to Carmel Valley. A good hike starts about a mile from the camp and is routed into the Ventana Wilderness. Several backcountry trail camps are also available.

**Campsites, facilities:** There are seven sites for tents or RVs up to 20 feet. Picnic tables and fire grills are provided. Vault toilets are available. There is no drinking water. Campfire permits are required and are available free from the Forest Service. Leashed pets are permitted.

**Reservations, fees:** Reservations are not accepted. Sites are $20 per night, plus $10 per night each additional vehicle. Open year-round, weather permitting.

**Directions:** From Highway 1 in Carmel, drive to Carmel Valley Road. Turn east on Carmel Valley Road and drive about 22 miles to Tassajara Road/County Road 5007. Turn right (south) on Tassajara Road/County Road 5007 and drive eight miles to the campground on the left.

From Salinas, drive south on U.S. 101 to Soledad. Continue south for approximately one mile to the exit for Arroyo Road. Take that exit and drive west on Arroyo Road (becomes Arroyo Seco Road) for 16.5 miles to Carmel Valley Road. Turn right and drive 17.5 miles to Tassajara Road. Turn left and drive eight miles to the campground on the left.

**Contact:** Los Padres National Forest, Monterey Ranger District, 831/385-5434, www.fs.usda.gov/lpnf.

## 20 ANDREW MOLERA STATE PARK WALK-IN

### Scenic rating: 7

in Big Sur

**Map 8.1, page 473**

Considering the popularity and grandeur of Big Sur, some campers might find it hard to believe that any primitive campgrounds are available. Believe it. Fortunately, this park survived the devastating 2016 Soberanes Fire. It offers fairly exposed walk-in sites, and while there's not much privacy, the setting amid beautiful coastal terrain compensates. It is extremely popular and often fills by Thursday. Since all sites are first-come, first-served, plan to arrive on a Wednesday if you hope to score a coveted weekend stay. One of the highlights is a great trail that leads one mile to a beautiful beach. It is part of a trail system that features miles of trails routed through meadows, along beaches, and to hilltops.

**Campsites, facilities:** There are 24 sites for tents limited to four people each; three of these sites are for hike-in/bike-in campers. Picnic tables, food lockers, and fire grills are provided. Drinking water and flush toilets are available. Bring your own firewood; campfires are prohibited during fire season, and smoking is prohibited throughout the park.

**Reservations, fees:** Reservations are not accepted. Tent sites are $25 per night, hike-in/bike-in sites are $5 per person, and additional vehicles are $10 per night per vehicle. Open year-round, weather permitting.

**Directions:** From Carmel, drive 21 miles south on Highway 1 to the park camping lot on the right. Park and walk 150 yards to the camp.

**Contact:** Pfeiffer Big Sur State Park, 831/667-2315; California State Parks, Monterey District, 831/649-2836, www.parks.ca.gov.

## 21 BIG SUR CAMPGROUND AND CABINS

### Scenic rating: 8

on the Big Sur River

Map 8.1, page 473

At this camp is near the Big Sur River on the west side of Highway 1, campers can stay in the redwoods, swim in the river, and explore nearby Pfeiffer Beach. Cruising Highway 1 south to Lucia and back offers endless views of breathtaking coastal scenery.

Note: Due to the 2016 Soberanes Fire, many trails in the adjoining state parks and national forests remain closed. There are no trails out of the campground.

**Campsites, facilities:** There are 35 sites with partial hookups (20 and 30 amps) for RVs up to 40 feet, 35 sites for tents and RVs (no hookups), 16 cabins, and four camping cabins. Picnic tables and fire grills are provided. Restrooms with flush toilets and showers, drinking water, dump station, playground, basketball, inner-tube rentals, convenience store, and coin laundry are available. Leashed pets are permitted at campsites but not in cabins.

**Reservations, fees:** Reservations are recommended. RV sites are $65-90 per night, tent sites are $50-80 per night, plus $5 per person per night for more than two people, $15 per night for each additional vehicle with a maximum of two cars, and $5 per pet per night. Some credit cards are accepted. Open year-round.

**Directions:** From Carmel, drive 25 miles south on Highway 1 to the campground on the right side of the road (two miles north of the state park).

**Contact:** Big Sur Campground and Cabins, 831/667-2322, www.bigsurcamp.com.

## 22 PFEIFFER BIG SUR STATE PARK

### Scenic rating: 10

in Big Sur

Map 8.1, page 473

Note: At time of publication, Pfeiffer Big Sur State Park remained closed to camping due to damage from the 2016 Soberanes Fire. The adjoining Big Sur Lodge offers 26 cottages.

This is one of the most popular state parks in California, and it's easy to see why: fantastic coastal vistas along Highway 1, redwood forests and waterfalls in Julia Pfeiffer Burns State Park (11.5 miles to the south), expansive beaches in Andrew Molera State Park (4.5 miles north), great restaurants such as Ventana Inn (a few miles south), and private, patrolled sites. Reservations are a necessity. The park features 800 acres of alders, conifers, cottonwoods, maples, oaks, redwoods, sycamores, and willows, plus open meadows—just about everything, in other words. Wildlife includes raccoons, skunk, deer, squirrels, occasional bobcats and mountain lions, and many birds, among them water ouzels and belted kingfishers. Wild boar are spotted infrequently.

**Campsites, facilities:** There are 204 sites for tents or RVs up to 32 feet and trailers up to 27 feet and two group sites for up to 35 people each. Picnic tables and fire grills are provided. Fires may be prohibited during fire season. Restrooms with flush toilets and showers, Wi-Fi, a coin laundry, and drinking water are available. Groceries, a café, a dump station, and propane gas are nearby. Some facilities are wheelchair-accessible. Leashed pets are permitted in the campground only. Smoking is prohibited in undeveloped areas, on trails, and in the campgrounds.

**Reservations, fees:** Reservations are accepted at 800/444-7275 ($10 reservation fee) or www.reserveamerica.com ($9 reservation fee). Tent and RV sites are $35 per night, premium sites are $50 per night, plus $10 per night for each additional vehicle. Group sites are $150 per night. Open year-round, pending recovery efforts.

**Directions:** From Carmel, drive 26 miles south on Highway 1 to the park on the left (east side of highway).

**Contact:** Pfeiffer Big Sur State Park, 831/667-2315; California State Parks, Monterey District, 831/649-2836, www.parks.ca.gov; Big Sur Lodge, www.bigsurlodge.com.

## 23 CHINA CAMP

### Scenic rating: 6
on Chews Ridge in Los Padres National Forest

**Map 8.1, page 473**

Note: At time of publication, this campground remained closed due to damage from the 2016 Soberanes Fire. Please contact the ranger station for updates.

A lot of folks might find it difficult to believe that a spot that feels so remote can be so close to the manicured Carmel Valley. But here it is, one of two camps on Tassajara Road at an elevation of 4,500 feet. Tassajara Hot Springs, a private facility, is seven miles away at the end of Tassajara Road.

**Campsites, facilities:** There are nine sites for tents or RVs up to 20 feet (no hookups). Picnic tables and fire grills are provided. Vault toilets are available. No drinking water is available. Leashed pets are permitted.

**Reservations, fees:** Reservations are not accepted. There is no fee for camping. Open April through November, weather permitting.

**Directions:** From Highway 1 in Carmel, turn east on Carmel Valley Road and drive about 22 miles. Turn right (south) on Tassajara Road/County Road 5007 and drive 11 miles to the campground on the right.

From Salinas, drive south on U.S. 101 to Soledad. Continue south for approximately one mile to the exit for Arroyo Road. Take that exit and drive west on Arroyo Road (becomes Arroyo Seco Road) for 16.5 miles to Carmel Valley Road. Turn right and drive 17.5 miles to

Tassajara Road. Turn left and drive 11 miles to the campground on the right.

**Contact:** Los Padres National Forest, Monterey Ranger District, 831/385-5434, www.fs.usda.gov/lpnf.

## 24 RIVERSIDE CAMPGROUND AND CABINS

### Scenic rating: 8
on the Big Sur River

**Map 8.1, page 473**

This is one in a series of privately operated camps designed for Highway 1 cruisers touring the Big Sur area. This camp is set amid redwoods. Side trips include expansive beaches with sea otters playing on the edge of kelp beds (Andrew Molera State Park), redwood forests and waterfalls (Julia Pfeiffer Burns State Park), and several quality restaurants, including Nepenthe for those on a budget and the Ventana Inn for those who can light cigars with $100 bills.

**Campsites, facilities:** There are 35 sites for tents or RVs up to 34 feet; 12 sites have partial hookups (20 amps). Twelve cabins are also available. Picnic tables and fire pits are provided. Restrooms with flush toilets and coin showers are available. A coin laundry and free Wi-Fi and firewood are available. A store is on-site. Leashed pets are permitted at campsites and in most cabins.

**Reservations, fees:** Reservations are recommended at 831/667-2414 or reservations@riversidecampground.com. RV sites are $55-60 per night, tent sites are $50-55 per night, plus $5 per person per night for more than two people over age 6 (maximum of five people), $10 per night for each additional vehicle (maximum of two vehicles), and $5 per pet per night at tent and RV sites and $20 per pet per night in cabins. Some credit cards are accepted. Open year-round, weather permitting.

**Directions:** From Carmel, drive 22 miles south on Highway 1 to the campground on the right.

**Contact:** Riverside Campground and Cabins, tel. 831/667-2414, www.riversidecampground. com.

## 25 FERNWOOD RESORT

Scenic rating: 7

on the Big Sur River

**Map 8.1, page 473**

This resort is snuggled in the beautiful redwoods of Big Sur right on Highway 1. Many of the campsites are close together along the Big Sur River and a bit removed from the highway noise. There are also eight tent cabins behind the restaurant and a roadside motel facing Highway 1. A highlight is the live music on Saturday nights in the adjoining restaurant and bar. Crown your trip with dinner at the onsite Redwood Grill or a hike at nearby Pfeiffer Big Sur State Park.

**Campsites, facilities:** There are 15 sites for tents only, 31 sites with partial hookups (30 amps) for RVs up to 36 feet, 10 tent cabins, and a motel. Fire grills and picnic tables are provided. Restrooms with showers, a grocery store, a restaurant, and a bar are available; Wi-Fi is available in restaurant/bar area. Some facilities are wheelchair-accessible. Leashed pets are permitted.

**Reservations, fees:** Reservations are accepted by phone at 831/667-2422. RV sites are $75 per night, tent sites are 60-75 per night, plus $5 per person per night for more than two people (maximum of six), $5 per night for each additional vehicle, and $5 per pet per night. Tent cabins are $110 per night, plus $10 per person per night for more than two people. Discounts are available in the off-season. Some credit cards are accepted. Open year-round.

**Directions:** From Carmel, drive 26 miles south on Highway 1 to the campground on the right.

**Contact:** Fernwood Resort, 831/667-2422, www.fernwoodbigsur.com.

## 26 ARROYO SECO

Scenic rating: 5

along Arroyo Seco River in Los Padres National Forest

**Map 8.1, page 473**

Note: At time of publication, this campground remained closed due to damage from the 2016 Soberanes Fire. Please contact the ranger station for updates.

This pretty spot near the Arroyo Seco River is just outside the northern border of the Ventana Wilderness. The elevation is 900 feet.

**Campsites, facilities:** There are 49 sites for tents or RVs up to 26 feet, plus a group site for 25-50 people. Picnic tables and fire grills are provided. Drinking water and restrooms with flush toilets and coin showers are available. Firewood is available from the camp host, and a grocery store is within five miles. Some facilities are wheelchair-accessible. Leashed pets are permitted.

**Reservations, fees:** Reservations are accepted for individual sites and required for group sites at 877/444-6777 ($10 reservation fee) or www. recreation.gov ($9 reservation fee). Single sites are $30 per night, double sites are $60 per night, primitive single sites are $25, primitive double sites are $50 per night, plus $10 per night for each additional vehicle, and the group site is $125 per night. Open year-round.

**Directions:** Drive on U.S. 101 to the town of Greenfield and the Arroyo Seco Road/Elm Avenue exit. Turn west on Elm Avenue/Road G16 and drive six miles to Arroyo Seco Road. Turn left and drive 6.5 miles to Carmel Valley Road. Turn right and drive 3.5 miles to the campground.

**Contact:** Los Padres National Forest, Monterey Ranger District, 831/385-5434, www. fs.usda.gov/lpnf; Rocky Mountain Recreation Company, 831/674-5726.

## 27 SAN LORENZO COUNTY PARK

**Scenic rating: 3**

in King City

Map 8.1, page 473

A lot of folks cruising up and down the state on U.S. 101 can underestimate their travel time and find themselves caught out near King City, a small city about midpoint between Northern and Southern California. Well, don't sweat it, because San Lorenzo County Park offers a spot to overnight. It's near the Salinas River, which isn't exactly the Mississippi, but it'll do. A museum complex captures the rural agricultural life of the valley. The park covers 200 acres, featuring playgrounds and ball fields.

**Campsites, facilities:** There are 93 sites with full or partial hookups (30 amps) for tents or RVs of any length; some sites are pull-through. Picnic tables and fire pits are provided. A dump station, restrooms with flush toilets and showers, picnic area, coin laundry, meeting facilities, playgrounds, horseshoes, putting green, volleyball, softball fields, walking trail, and computer kiosks are available. Leashed pets are permitted.

**Reservations, fees:** Reservations are accepted at 888/588-2267 or 831/385-5964 ($9 reservation fee; $15 for groups). Tent sites are $32-35 per night, RV sites (water and electricity) are $37-42 per night, RV sites (full hookups) are $40 per night, plus $15 per night for each additional vehicle and $2 per pet per night. Off-season and group rates are available. Open year-round.

**Directions:** From King City on U.S. 101, take the Broadway exit, turn onto Broadway, and drive to the park at 1160 Broadway.

**Contact:** San Lorenzo County Park, 831/385-5964, www.co.monterey.ca.us/parks.

## 28 ESCONDIDO

**Scenic rating: 6**

in Los Padres National Forest

Map 8.1, page 473

Note: At time of publication, this campground remained closed due to damage from the 2016 Soberanes Fire. Please contact the ranger station for updates.

This camp is at an elevation of 2,300 feet at a trailhead that connects to a network of other trails.

**Campsites, facilities:** There are nine sites for tents only. Picnic tables and fire grills are provided. Vault toilets are available. There is no drinking water. Spring water is available; purify before use. Garbage must be packed out. Leashed pets are permitted.

**Reservations, fees:** Reservations are not accepted. Sites are $20 per night, plus $10 per night for each additional vehicle. Open April through November, weather permitting.

**Directions:** From U.S. 101 in King City, turn south on County Route G14 and drive 18 miles. Turn north on Mission Road and drive six miles. Turn left on Del Venturi-Milpitas Road/Indian Road and drive 20 miles to the campground on the left.

**Contact:** Los Padres National Forest, Monterey Ranger District, 831/385-5434, www.fs.usda.gov/lpnf.

## 29 MEMORIAL PARK

**Scenic rating: 6**

in Los Padres National Forest

Map 8.1, page 473

Note: At time of publication, this campground remained closed due to damage from the 2016 Soberanes Fire. Please contact the ranger station for updates.

This backcountry campground is within the vicinity of the Arroyo Seco River. The elevation is 2,000 feet. Be sure to pack plenty of drinking water for the trail and expect warm, dry conditions, even in spring.

**Campsites, facilities:** There are eight sites for tents only. Picnic tables and fire grills are provided. Vault toilets are available. No drinking water is available. Garbage must be packed out. Leashed pets are permitted.

**Reservations, fees:** Reservations are not accepted. Sites are $20 per night, plus $10 per each additional vehicle. Open year-round, weather permitting.

**Directions:** From U.S. 101 in King City, turn south on County Route G14 and drive 18 miles. Turn north on Mission Road and drive six miles. Turn left on Del Venturi-Milpitas Road/ County Road 4050 and drive 16 miles to the campground on the right.

**Contact:** Los Padres National Forest, Monterey Ranger District, 831/385-5434, www.fs.usda. gov/lpnf.

## 30 KIRK CREEK

### Scenic rating: 8

in Los Padres National Forest near the Pacific Ocean

**Map 8.1, page 473**

This pretty camp is set along Kirk Creek where it empties into the Pacific Ocean. There is beach access through a footpath. Another trail from camp branches north through the Ventana Wilderness, which is sprinkled with little-used, hike-in backcountry campsites. For gorgeous scenery without all the work, a quaint little café in Lucia provides open-air dining on a cliff-top deck, with a dramatic sweeping lookout over the coast.

**Campsites, facilities:** There are 34 sites for tents or RVs up to 30 feet (no hookups). Picnic tables and fire grills are provided. Vault toilets are available. There is no drinking water, but a camp host may have firewood and drinking water for sale. Leashed pets are permitted.

**Reservations, fees:** Reservations are required at least 8 days in advance at 877/444-6777 ($10

reservation fee) or www.recreation.gov ($9 reservation fee). Sites are $35 per night, hike-in/ bike-in sites are $5 per night, plus $10 per each additional vehicle. Open year-round.

**Directions:** From Monterey, drive south on Highway 1 to Lucia. From Lucia, continue south on Highway 1 for four miles to the campground on the right.

**Contact:** Parks Management Company, 805/434-1996, www.campone.com; Los Padres National Forest, Monterey Ranger District, 831/385-5434, www.fs.usda.gov/lpnf.

## 31 LIMEKILN STATE PARK

### Scenic rating: 9

south of Big Sur

**Map 8.1, page 473**

Limekiln State Park reopened in the summer of 2010 to near-full glory. It had closed in 2008 after the Chalk Fire, but the redwoods and the neighboring coastal grasslands are fire resilient. Limekiln provides spectacular views of the coast and is a layover spot for Highway 1 cruisers south of the Big Sur area. Drive-in campsites are near both the beach and the redwoods—take your pick. Several hiking trails are nearby, including one that is routed past some historic lime kilns, which were used in the late 1800s to make cement and bricks. A short rock hop on a spur trail (just off the main trail) leads to gorgeous 100-foot Limekiln Falls. One problem: Parking is limited.

**Campsites, facilities:** There are 13 sites for tents and 11 sites for tents or RVs up to 24 feet (no hookups) and trailers up to 15 feet. Picnic tables and fire grills are provided. Drinking water, restrooms with showers and flush toilets, and firewood are available. Fire restrictions may apply. Some facilities are wheelchair-accessible. Leashed pets are allowed, except on trails.

**Reservations, fees:** Reservations are accepted at 800/444-7275 ($10 reservation fee) or www. reserveamerica.com ($9 reservation fee). Sites are $35 per night, plus $10 per night for each additional vehicle. Some credit cards are accepted for reservations, but not at the park. Open year-round, weather and road conditions permitting.

**Directions:** From Big Sur, drive south on Highway 1 for 32 miles (past Lucia) to the park on the left.

**Contact:** Limekiln State Park, 831/667-2403; California State Parks, Monterey District, 831/649-2836, www.parks.ca.gov; Parks Management Company, 805/434-1996, www.campone.com.

## 32 NACIMIENTO

### Scenic rating: 4

in Los Padres National Forest

**Map 8.1, page 473**

Note: At time of publication, this campground remained closed due to damage from the 2016 Soberanes Fire. Please contact the ranger station for updates.

This little-known spot is near the Nacimiento River at 1,600 feet elevation.

**Campsites, facilities:** There are eight sites for tents or RVs up to 25 feet (no hookups). Picnic tables and fire grills are provided. Vault toilets are available. No drinking water is available. Leashed pets are permitted.

**Reservations, fees:** Reservations are not accepted. Sites are $20 per night, plus $10 per each additional vehicle. Open year-round.

**Directions:** From Monterey, drive south on Highway 1 to Lucia. From Lucia, continue south on Highway 1 for four miles to Nacimiento Road. Turn east (left) on Nacimiento Road and drive 11 winding miles to the campground on the right.

**Contact:** Parks Management Company, 805/434-1996, www.campone.com; Los Padres National Forest, Monterey Ranger District, 831/385-5434, www.fs.usda.gov/lpnf.

## 33 PONDEROSA

### Scenic rating: 4

in Los Padres National Forest

**Map 8.1, page 473**

Note: At time of publication, this campground remained closed due to damage from the 2016 Soberanes Fire. Please contact the ranger station for updates.

This camp is at 1,500 feet elevation in Los Padres National Forest is not far from the border of the Ventana Wilderness and the Hunter Liggett Military Reservation. It is one in a series of small camps on Nacimiento-Ferguson Road.

**Campsites, facilities:** There are 23 sites for tents or RVs up to 35 feet. Picnic tables and fire grills are provided. Vault toilets and drinking water are available. Leashed pets are permitted.

**Reservations, fees:** Reservations are required at least eight days in advance at 877/444-6777 ($10 reservation fee) or www.recreation.gov ($9 reservation fee). Sites are $25 per night, plus $10 per each additional vehicle. Open year-round.

**Directions:** From Monterey, drive south on Highway 1 to Lucia. From Lucia, continue south on Highway 1 for four miles to Nacimiento-Ferguson Road. Turn left on Nacimiento-Ferguson Road and drive about 12 miles to the campground on the right.

**Contact:** Parks Management Company, 805/434-1996, www.campone.com; Los Padres National Forest, Monterey Ranger District, 831/385-5434, www.fs.usda.gov/lpnf.

# SAN JOAQUIN VALLEY

Though the San Joaquin Valley is noted for searing weather all summer long, that is when the lakes in the foothills become a Garden of Eden for boating and water-sports enthusiasts. Some of these lakes are among the best for waterskiing and powerboat recreation—Lake Don Pedro east of Modesto, Bass Lake near Oakhurst, Lake McClure near Merced, Pine Flat Lake east of Fresno, and Lake Kaweah near Visalia. Lake Don Pedro, Pine Flat Lake, and Lake Kaweah are great fishing lakes, while the Kaweah and Kings Rivers boast ideal pocket water for fly fishers. Most campgrounds are family-oriented, and many are on access roads to Yosemite (with lower prices than their counterparts in the park). This region offers many settings in the Sierra foothills, which can serve as launch points into Yosemite, Sequoia, and Kings Canyon National Parks.

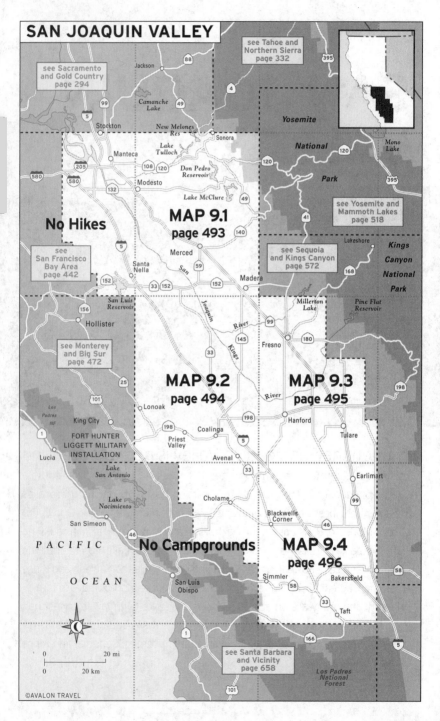

## SAN JOAQUIN VALLEY

see Sacramento and Gold Country page 294

see Tahoe and Northern Sierra page 332

**No Hikes**

**MAP 9.1 page 493**

see San Francisco Bay Area page 442

see Yosemite and Mammoth Lakes page 518

see Sequoia and Kings Canyon page 572

see Monterey and Big Sur page 472

**MAP 9.2 page 494**

**MAP 9.3 page 495**

FORT HUNTER LIGGETT MILITARY INSTALLATION

PACIFIC

OCEAN

**No Campgrounds**

**MAP 9.4 page 496**

see Santa Barbara and Vicinity page 658

0        20 mi
0        20 km

©AVALON TRAVEL

# Map 9.1

## Sites 1-7
## Pages 498-501

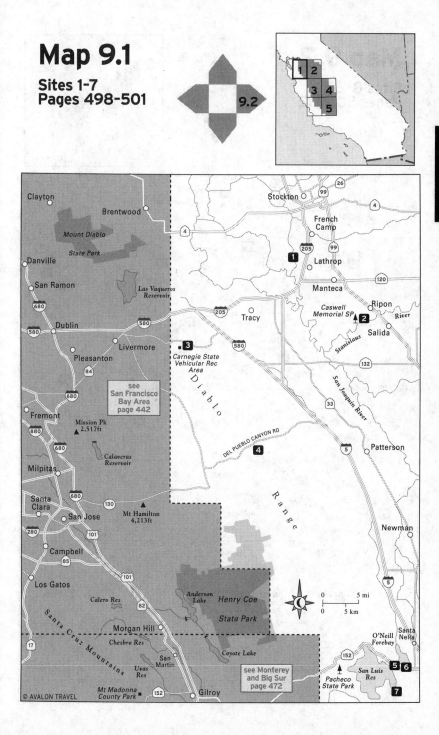

# Map 9.2
## Sites 8-28
## Pages 501-512

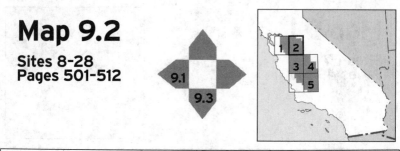

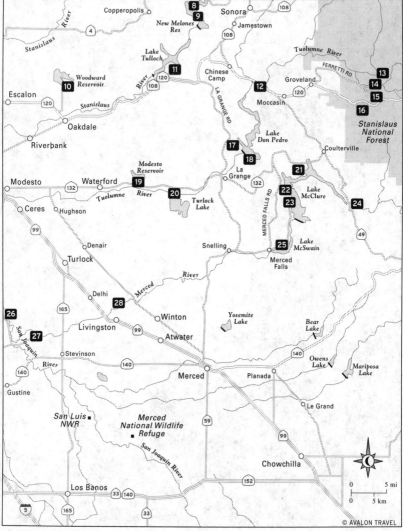

# Map 9.3

**Site 29**
**Page 512**

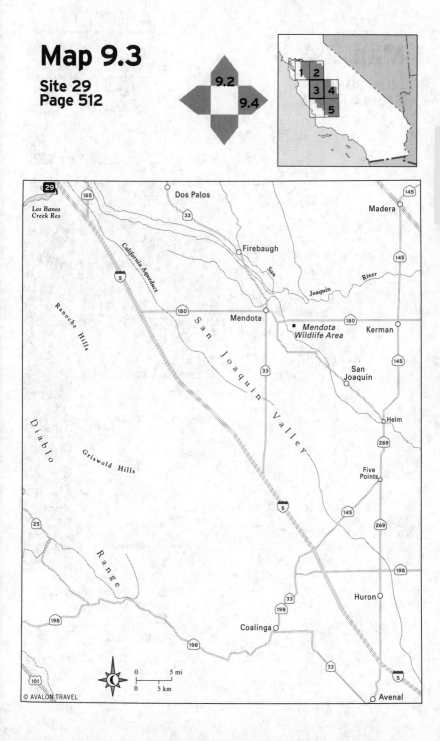

# Map 9.4

## Sites 30-32
## Pages 513-514

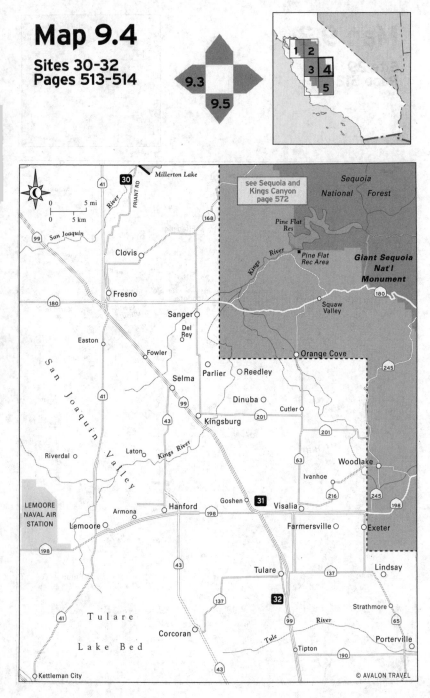

# Map 9.5

### Sites 33-36
### Pages 514-516

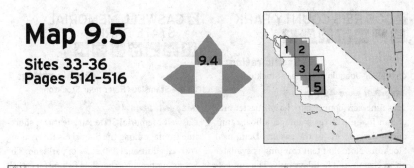

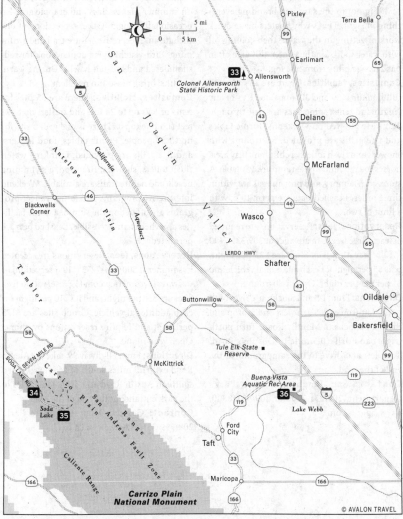

© AVALON TRAVEL

# 1 DOS REIS COUNTY PARK

## Scenic rating: 6

on the San Joaquin River near Stockton

**Map 9.1, page 493**

This nine-acre county park has a quarter mile of San Joaquin River frontage, a boat ramp, and nearby access to the eastern Delta near Stockton. Note that tent camping is available on weekends and holidays only. The sun gets scalding hot in the summer, branding everything in sight. That's why boaters make quick work of getting in the water, then cooling off with water sports. In the winter, this area often has zero visibility from tule fog.

**Campsites, facilities:** There are 26 sites with full hookups (20 and 30 amps) for RVs of any length and tents; some sites are pull-through. Tents are allowed on weekends. Picnic tables and fire grills are provided. Restrooms with showers and flush toilets, a children's play area, horseshoe pits, and a boat ramp are available. A store, coin laundry, and propane gas are within three miles. Leashed pets are permitted, with a limit of two.

**Reservations, fees:** Reservations are required at least three weeks in advance at 209/331-7400 ($10 reservation fee). Sites are $25 per night, plus $5 per night for each additional vehicle and $1 per pet per night. Open year-round.

**Directions:** From I-5 and Stockton, drive south to the Lathrop exit. Turn west on Lathrop and drive 1.5 blocks to Manthy Road. Turn north (right) and drive 0.5 mile to Dos Reis Road. Turn left and drive to the campground at the end of the road.

**Contact:** San Joaquin County Parks Department, 209/331-7400 or 209/953-8800, www.sjparks.com.

# 2 CASWELL MEMORIAL STATE PARK

## Scenic rating: 7

on the Stanislaus River near Stockton

**Map 9.1, page 493**

Caswell Memorial State Park features shoreline frontage along the Stanislaus River, along with an additional 250 acres of parkland. The Stanislaus provides shoreline fishing for catfish on summer nights. Bass and crappie are also occasionally caught. Other recreation options include an interpretive nature trail and swimming. Bird-watching is popular; look for red-shouldered and red-tail hawks. During warm months, bring mosquito repellent.

**Campsites, facilities:** There are 65 sites for tents or RVs up to 24 feet and trailers up to 21 feet (no hookups). There is one group site for up to 50 people. Picnic tables, food lockers, and fire grills are provided. Drinking water, flush toilets, showers, firewood, a swimming beach, and nature trails are available. Weekend interpretive programs and junior ranger programs are offered in the summer. Some facilities are wheelchair-accessible. Leashed pets are permitted.

**Reservations, fees:** Reservations are accepted in summer at 800/444-7275 ($10 reservation) or www.reserveamerica.com ($9 reservation fee). Sites are $30 per night, and it's $10 per night for each additional vehicle. Group sites are $175 per night and require reservations by phone. Open year-round.

**Directions:** From Highway 99, take the Austin Road exit (1.5 miles south of Manteca). Turn south on Austin Road and drive four miles to the park entrance at the end of the road.

**Contact:** Caswell Memorial State Park, 209/599-3810, www.parks.ca.gov.

## 3 CARNEGIE STATE VEHICULAR RECREATION AREA

### Scenic rating: 2

near Tracy

**Map 9.1, page 493**

This is a major state-run off-highway vehicle (OHV) area, with mainly dirt bikes and all-terrain vehicles. Don't show up without one, or its equivalent. This area is barren, ugly, and extremely noisy on weekends. It can get hot, windy, and dusty as well. But that's just what dirt bikers want, and they have it all to themselves. The main campground fills on most weekends from October through May, especially during special events. The area covers 1,500 acres with challenging hill-type trail riding and a professionally designed motocross track. There is also a four-wheel-drive obstacle course. Elevations here rise to 1,800 feet, with summer temperatures peaking at 105°F. Winters are mild.

**Campsites, facilities:** There are 22 sites for tents or RVs of any length (no hookups). Picnic tables, shade ramadas, and fire rings are provided. Coin showers (bring quarters) and flush toilets are available. There is no drinking water; bring bottled water. Cell phone service is not available, but there is a pay phone. Nearest supplies are 14 miles away. Some facilities are wheelchair-accessible. Leashed pets are permitted.

**Reservations, fees:** Reservations are not accepted. Sites are $10 per night. Open year-round, weather permitting.

**Directions:** From I-580 (south of Tracy), drive to Corral Hollow Road. Take that exit and drive west for six miles to the campground on the left.

**Contact:** Carnegie State Vehicular Recreation Area, 925/447-9027; Carnegie Sector Office, 925/447-0426, www.parks.ca.gov.

## 4 DEER CREEK CAMPGROUND

### Scenic rating: 4

in Frank Raines Regional Park near Modesto

**Map 9.1, page 493**

This park is primarily a riding area for folks with dirt bikes, all-terrain vehicles, and dune buggies who take advantage of the rough-terrain riding course. About 850 acres of this 1,500-acre park are reserved for OHV use. Deer and pig hunting in season are also a possibility. A side-trip option is to visit Minniear Park, directly to the east, which is a day-use wilderness park with hiking trails and a creek. This area is very pretty in the spring when the foothills are still green and many wildflowers are blooming.

**Campsites, facilities:** There are 28 sites with full hookups (30 amps) for RVs or tents and 20 sites for tents or RVs (no hookups). Fire grills and picnic tables are provided. Potable water, restrooms with showers and flush toilets, a picnic area, baseball diamond, playground, group facilities, nature trails, and a recreation hall with a full kitchen are available. Some facilities are wheelchair-accessible. Leashed pets are permitted.

**Reservations, fees:** Reservations are accepted at 800/444-7275 ($10 reservation fee) or www.reserveamerica.com ($9 reservation fee). Sites are $30-64 per night, plus $10 per night for each additional vehicle and $3 per pet per night. The OHV fee is $5 per day. OHV recreation is open mid-October through early June. Deer Creek Campground is open year-round, weather permitting.

**Directions:** On I-5, drive to the Patterson exit (south of the junction of I-5 and I-580). Turn west on the Patterson exit and drive onto Diablo Grande Parkway. Continue a short distance under the freeway to Del Puerto Canyon Road. Turn west (right) and drive 16 miles to the park and the campground on the right at 17802 Del Puerto Canyon Road in Patterson.

**Contact:** Frank Raines Regional Park,

209/525-6750; Stanislaus County Parks and Recreation Department, www.stancounty.com.

## 5 SAN LUIS CREEK

### Scenic rating: 5

on San Luis Reservoir

Map 9.1, page 493

San Luis Creek Campground is near San Luis Reservoir. It is one in a series of camps operated by the state in the San Luis Reservoir State Recreation Area, adjacent to the reservoir and O'Neill Forebay, home of many of the biggest striped bass in California, including the world record for landlocked stripers. Note: All boats must be certified mussel-free before launching.

**Campsites, facilities:** There are 53 sites with partial hookups (20 and 30 amps) for tents or RVs up to 30 feet and two group sites for up to 30 and 60 people each. Picnic tables and fire pits are provided. Drinking water, pit toilets, and a dump station are available. Flush toilets, coin showers, and shade ramadas are available in the group sites. A boat ramp is nearby. Some facilities are wheelchair-accessible. Leashed pets are permitted.

**Reservations, fees:** Reservations are accepted at 800/444-7275 ($10 reservation fee) or www.reserveamerica.com ($9 reservation fee). Sites are $40 per night, plus $10 per night for each additional vehicle. Group sites are $200 per night and require reservations by phone. Open year-round.

**Directions:** Drive on Highway 152 to San Luis Reservoir (12 miles west of Los Banos) and the signed campground entrance road (15 miles west of Los Banos). Turn north and drive two miles to the campground on the left.

**Contact:** San Luis Reservoir State Recreation Area, 209/826-1196; Four Rivers Sector, 209/826-1197, www.parks.ca.gov.

## 6 MEDEIROS

### Scenic rating: 5

on O'Neill Forebay near Santa Nella

Map 9.1, page 493

This is a vast, primitive campground set on the stark expanse of foothill country on O'Neill Forebay and near San Luis Reservoir. It is best known for wind in the spring, hot weather in the summer, and low water levels in the fall. Striped-bass fishing is best in the fall when the wind is down and stripers will corral schools of bait fish near the lake surface. Sailboarding is decent. There's a large, developed swimming beach on O'Neill Forebay and boats can be launched four miles west of the campground at San Luis Creek, however there may be problems with launching in low water conditions. The forebay can get congested on weekends and holidays; the reservoir is less crowded. The campground elevation is 225 feet. (See the Basalt listing for more information about San Luis.) Note: All boats must be certified mussel-free before launching and must be removed from the water by sunset.

**Campsites, facilities:** There are 350 primitive sites for tents or RVs of any length (no hookups). Some shaded ramadas with fire grills and picnic tables are available. Drinking water and chemical toilets are available. A boat ramp is four miles away. Leashed pets are permitted.

**Reservations, fees:** Reservations are not accepted. Sites are $20 per night, and each additional vehicle is $10 per night. Boat launching is $7 per day. Open year-round.

**Directions:** Drive on Highway 152 to Highway 33 (about 10 miles west of Los Banos). Turn north (right) on Highway 33 and drive 0.25 mile to the campground entrance on the left.

**Contact:** San Luis Reservoir State Recreation Area, 209/826-1196; Four Rivers Sector, 209/826-1197, www.parks.ca.gov.

## 7 BASALT

**Scenic rating: 5**

on San Luis Reservoir

Map 9.1, page 493

San Luis Reservoir is a huge, man-made lake, covering 13,800 acres with 65 miles of shoreline, developed among stark foothills to provide a storage facility along the California Aqueduct. It fills by late winter and is used primarily by anglers, water-skiers, and sailboarders. When the Sacramento River Delta water pumps take the water, they also take the fish, filling this lake up with both. Striped-bass fishing is best in the fall when the stripers chase schools of bait fish on the lake surface. Spring and early summer can be quite windy, but that makes for good sailboarding. The adjacent O'Neill Forebay is the best recreation bet because of the boat launch and often good fishing. There is a visitors center at the Romero Overlook. Summer temperatures can occasionally exceed 100°F, but evenings are usually pleasant. During winter, tule fog is common. Note that in spring and early summer, it can turn windy very quickly. Warning lights mark several spots at the reservoir and forebay. Note: All boats must be certified mussel-free before launching. The elevation is 575 feet.

**Campsites, facilities:** There are 79 sites for tents or RVs up to 35 feet (no hookups). Picnic tables and fire grills are provided. Drinking water, restrooms with flush toilets and coin showers, a dump station, picnic areas, and a boat ramp are available. A store, coin laundry, gas station, restaurant, and propane gas are nearby (about 1.5 miles away). Some facilities are wheelchair-accessible. Leashed pets are permitted.

**Reservations, fees:** Reservations are accepted at 800/444-7275 ($10 reservation fee) or www.reservationamerica.com ($9 reservation fee). Sites are $30 per night, plus $10 per night for each additional vehicle. Boat launch is $7 per day. Open year-round.

**Directions:** Drive on Highway 152 to San Luis Reservoir (12 miles west of Los Banos) and the Basalt campground entrance road. Turn south on Basalt Road and drive 2.5 miles to the campground on the left.

**Contact:** San Luis Reservoir State Recreation Area, 209/826-1196; Four Rivers Sector, 209/826-1197, www.parks.ca.gov.

## 8 GLORY HOLE

**Scenic rating: 7**

at New Melones Reservoir

Map 9.2, page 494

Glory Hole encompasses both Big Oak and Ironhorse campgrounds. This is one of two major recreation areas on New Melones Reservoir in the Sierra Nevada foothills, a popular spot with a boat ramp nearby for access to outstanding waterskiing and fishing. Campfire programs are often offered at the amphitheater in summer. Camp hosts are usually on-site year-round. (See the Tuttletown Recreation Area listing for more information.)

**Campsites, facilities:** Big Oak has 53 sites for tents or RVs up to 40 feet (no hookups). Ironhorse has 69 sites for tents or RVs of any length; 20 walk-in sites are for tents only. Picnic tables and fire grills are provided. Drinking water, restrooms with flush toilets and showers, marina, boat ramps, houseboat and boat rentals, swimming beach, amphitheater, and playground are available. Some facilities are wheelchair-accessible. Leashed pets are permitted.

**Reservations, fees:** Reservations are accepted at 877/444-6777 ($10 reservation fee) or www.recreation.gov ($9 reservation fee). Sites are $18-22 per night, plus $8 per night per additional vehicle. Open year-round.

**Directions:** From Sonora, drive north on Highway 49 for about 15 miles (Glory Hole Market will be on the left side of the road) to Whittle Ranch Road. Turn left and drive five miles to the campground, with sites on both sides of the road.

**Contact:** U.S. Bureau of Reclamation, New Melones Visitor Center, 209/536-9094; New Melones Lake Marina, 209/785-3300; Glory Hole Sports, 209/736-4333.

## 9 TUTTLETOWN RECREATION AREA

**Scenic rating: 7**

at New Melones Reservoir

Map 9.2, page 494

Here is a mammoth camping area set on the giant New Melones Reservoir in the Sierra Nevada foothills, a beautiful sight when the lake is full. The lake is in the valley foothills between the historic mining towns of Angels Camp and Sonora. New Melones is one of California's top recreation lakes. All water sports are permitted. Waterskiing and houseboating are particularly popular. Tuttletown encompasses three campgrounds (Acorn, Manzanita, and Chamise) and two group camping areas (Oak Knoll and Fiddleneck). Huge New Melones Reservoir covers 12,500 acres and offers more than 100 miles of shoreline and good fishing. The elevation is 1,085 feet. A boat ramp is near camp. Although the lake's main body is huge, the better fishing is well up the lake's Stanislaus River arm (for trout) and in its coves (for bass and bluegill), where there are submerged trees providing perfect aquatic habitat. Trolling for kokanee salmon also has become popular. The lake level often drops dramatically in the fall.

**Campsites, facilities:** Acorn has 69 sites for tents or RVs of any length (no hookups); Chamise has 35 tent sites; Manzanita has 52 sites for tents or RVs of any length and 15 walk-in tent sites; Oak Knoll group site holds up to 50 people; and Fiddleneck group site holds up to 60 people. Picnic tables and fire grills are provided. Drinking water, restrooms with flush toilets and showers, dump station, playground, and boat ramp are available. Some facilities are wheelchair-accessible. Leashed pets are permitted.

**Reservations, fees:** Reservations are accepted at 877/444-6777 ($10 reservation fee) or www.recreation.gov ($9 reservation fee). Sites are $18-22 per night, plus $8 per night per additional vehicle, and the group sites are $125-150 per night. Open year-round.

**Directions:** From Sonora, drive north on Highway 49 to Reynolds Ferry Road. Turn left and drive about two miles to the entrance road to the campgrounds.

**Contact:** U.S. Bureau of Reclamation, New Melones Visitor Center, 209/536-9094.

## 10 WOODWARD RESERVOIR COUNTY PARK

**Scenic rating: 7**

near Oakdale

Map 9.2, page 494

This is one of the best sailing lakes in Northern California. Regattas are held through the year, and it is also very popular for sailboarding. Woodward's nickname, in fact, is "Windward Reservoir." Woodward Reservoir is a large lake covering 2,900 acres with 23 miles of shoreline, set in the rolling foothills just north of Oakdale. It is a good lake for both waterskiing and fishing, with minimal conflict between the two sports. All boating is allowed, and speedboats have the main lake body to let her rip. Trout fishing has improved and they are stocked here in winter. In recent years, the county and local hatcheries began restocking the reservoir, planting redear sunfish, bluegill, largemouth bass, and channel catfish in addition to rainbow trout. Note that because this is one of the largest reservoirs near Modesto and Stockton, it gets lots of local traffic, especially on summer weekends. There are equestrian facilities at this park, and horse camping is permitted in undeveloped sites only (Area A to Area FF).

Note: Seasonally, all body-to-water contact

at the reservoir is prohibited; call ahead to confirm.

**Campsites, facilities:** There are 180 sites for tents and RVs, some with partial hookups, and 40 RV sites with full hookups (30 amps). Primitive camping is available in designated areas. Picnic tables and fire grills are provided. Drinking water, a dump station, picnic shelter, three boat ramps, fish-cleaning station, dry boat storage, restrooms with flush toilets and showers, and some equestrian facilities are available. Some facilities are wheelchair-accessible. Leashed pets are permitted.

**Reservations, fees:** Reservations are accepted at 800/444-7275 ($10 reservation fee) or www.reserveamerica.com ($9 reservation fee). Primitive sites are $20 per night, RV sites (hookups) are $15-35 per night, plus $7 per day boat launch fee, $10 per night per additional vehicle, $3 per pet per night, and $3 per horse per night. Holiday weekend rates are $2 higher. Open year-round.

**Directions:** Drive on Highway 120 to Oakdale (the road becomes Highway 108/120) and the junction with County Road J14/26 Mile Road. Turn left on 26 Mile Road and drive four miles to the park entrance at Woodward Reservoir (14528 26 Mile Road).

**Contact:** Woodward Reservoir County Park, 209/847-3304; Stanislaus County Parks, 209/525-6750, www.stancounty.com/parks.

# 11 LAKE TULLOCH RV CAMPGROUND AND MARINA

🏞️🏊🛶🚐🐕🏇♿🚐⛺

### Scenic rating: 7

on the south shore of Lake Tulloch

**Map 9.2, page 494**

This camp features tons of waterfront on Lake Tulloch, a dispersed tent area, and cabins with direct beach access. Unlike so many reservoirs in the foothill country, this one is nearly always full of water. In addition, it is a place where anglers and water-skiers live in harmony. That is because of the many coves and a six-mile-long arm with an enforced 5-mph speed limit. It's a big lake, shaped like a giant X with extended lake arms adding up to 55 miles of shoreline. The campground features mature oak trees that provide shade to most of the developed sites. A secret at Tulloch is that fishing is also good for crawdads. The elevation is 500 feet.

**Campsites, facilities:** There are 130 sites, including 31 boat sites and 30 with full or partial hookups (30 and 50 amps) for tents or RVs up to 35 feet, a large area for lakefront tent camping and self-contained RVs, and 12 waterfront cabins. Picnic tables and fire grills are provided. Drinking water, restrooms with flush toilets and showers, coin laundry, convenience store, dump station, playground, restaurant, volleyball, horseshoes, tetherball, table tennis, swimming beach, marina, boat rentals, boat slips, fuel dock, and a boat launch are available. Some facilities are wheelchair-accessible. Leashed pets are permitted.

**Reservations, fees:** Reservations are accepted. Sites are $23-45 per night, plus $15 per night for the first additional vehicle, $23 per each additional vehicle, and $3 per pet per night. Cabins are $100-175 per night. Group rates are available. Boat launch fee is $10 (once per weekend). Credit cards are accepted. Open year-round.

**Directions:** From Manteca, drive east on Highway 120 (it becomes Highway 108/120) to Oakdale. Continue east for 13 miles to Tulloch Road on the left. Turn left and drive 4.6 miles to the campground entrance and gatehouse at the south shore of Lake Tulloch.

**Contact:** Lake Tulloch RV Campground and Marina, 209/881-0107 or 800/894-2267, www.laketullochcampground.com; Lake Tulloch Boat Rentals, 209/881-3410 or 866/979-2628.

## **12** MOCCASIN POINT

**Scenic rating: 7**

at Lake Don Pedro

**Map 9.2, page 494**

This camp is at the northeastern end of Lake Don Pedro, adjacent to a boat ramp. Moccasin Point juts well into the lake, directly across from where the major Tuolumne River arm enters the lake. Don Pedro is a giant lake, with extended lake arms and nearly 13,000 surface acres and 160 miles of shoreline. It is one of the best boating and recreation lakes in California, but subject to drawdowns from midsummer through early fall. At different times, fishing is excellent for salmon, trout, or bass. Other species are redear sunfish, catfish, crappie, and bluegill. Houseboating and boat-in camping (bring sunscreen) provide options. The elevation is 800 feet.

**Campsites, facilities:** There are 50 sites for tents, 18 sites with full hookups (20 and 30 amps) for RVs of any length, and an overflow camping area with 28 sites. Some sites are pull-through. Picnic tables, fire rings, food lockers, and barbecue units are provided at all sites. Drinking water, restrooms with showers, dump station, group picnic area, Wi-Fi, fish-cleaning station, propane gas, ice, small store, boat ramp, motorboat and fuel, moorings, and bait and tackle are available. Some facilities are wheelchair-accessible.

**Reservations, fees:** Reservations are accepted for a minimum of two nights (three nights on holidays) at 209/852-2396 or www.donpedrolake.com ($10 reservation fee). RV sites are $22-36 per night, tent sites are $18-28 per night, plus $10 per each additional vehicle per day. Primitive boat-in camping is $8 per night with a $10 day-use fee. Weekend rates are higher. Some credit cards are accepted. Open year-round.

**Directions:** From Manteca, drive east on Highway 120 (it becomes Highway 108/120) for 30 miles to the Highway 120/Yosemite exit. Bear right on Highway 120 and drive 11 miles to Jacksonville Road. Turn left on Jacksonville Road and drive a short distance to the campground on the right.

**Contact:** Don Pedro Recreation Agency, 209/852-2396; Moccasin Point Marina, 209/989-2206, www.donpedrolake.com.

## **13** LUMSDEN BRIDGE

**Scenic rating: 6**

on the Tuolumne River in Stanislaus National Forest

**Map 9.2, page 494**

This is one of three camps along this immediate stretch of the Tuolumne River, one of the best white-water-rafting rivers in California. Note that a permit is required for this activity; contact the Forest Service for details. The camp is at 1,500 feet elevation on the north side of the river, accessible just after crossing the Lumsden Bridge—hence the name.

Note: This campground lies in the 2013 Rim Fire burned area and the surrounding landscape may be unstable. Please exercise caution when hiking on area trails.

**Campsites, facilities:** There are nine walk-in sites for tents only. Picnic tables and fire grills are provided. Vault toilets are available. No drinking water is available; river water must be purified before use. Garbage must be packed out. Leashed pets are permitted.

**Reservations, fees:** Reservations are not accepted. There is no fee for camping. Open April through October, weather permitting.

**Directions:** From Groveland, drive east on Highway 120 for about eight miles (just under a mile beyond County Road J132) to Ferretti Road. Turn left on Ferretti Road and drive to Lumsden Road. Turn right and continue for 5.5 miles to the camp on the left side of the road. (The road is not recommended for RVs or trailers.)

**Contact:** Stanislaus National Forest, Groveland Ranger District, 209/962-7825, www.fs.usda.gov.

## 14 LUMSDEN

**Scenic rating: 7**

on the Tuolumne River in Stanislaus National Forest

**Map 9.2, page 494**          **BEST (**

One of the best access points for white-water rafting on the wild and scenic Tuolumne River, including its premium stretch between Hetch Hetchy Reservoir in Yosemite and Don Pedro Reservoir, is within this campground area. Unless you are an expert rafter, you are advised to attempt running this stretch of river only with a professional rafting company. Note that a permit is required for this activity; contact the Forest Service for details. The camp is at 1,500 feet elevation, just across the road from the river. The access road down the canyon is steep and bumpy.

Note: This campground lies in the 2013 Rim Fire burned area and the surrounding landscape may be unstable. Please exercise caution when hiking on area trails.

**Campsites, facilities:** There are eight sites for tents only. Picnic tables and fire grills are provided. Vault toilets are available. No drinking water is available; river water must be purified before use. Garbage must be packed out. Leashed pets are permitted.

**Reservations, fees:** Reservations are not accepted. There is no fee for camping. Open year-round, weather permitting.

**Directions:** From Groveland, drive east on Highway 120 for about eight miles (just under a mile beyond County Road J132) to Ferretti Road. Turn left on Ferretti Road and drive to Lumsden Road. Turn right and continue for four miles to the camp on the left side of the road. (The road is not recommended for RVs or trailers.)

**Contact:** Stanislaus National Forest, Groveland Ranger District, 209/962-7825, www.fs.usda.gov.

## 15 LOST CLAIM

**Scenic rating: 4**

near the Tuolumne River in Stanislaus National Forest

**Map 9.2, page 494**

This is one in a series of easy-access camps off Highway 120 that provide overflow areas when all the sites are taken in Yosemite National Park to the east. A feeder stream to the Tuolumne River runs by the camp. The elevation is 3,100 feet.

Note: This campground lies in the 2013 Rim Fire burned area and the surrounding landscape may be unstable. Please exercise caution when hiking on area trails.

**Campsites, facilities:** There are 10 sites for tents only. Picnic tables and fire grills are provided. Vault toilets and drinking water are available. A convenience store is nearby. Leashed pets are permitted.

**Reservations, fees:** Reservations are accepted at 877/444-6777 ($10 reservation fee) or www.recreation.gov ($9 reservation fee). Sites are $19 per night. Open May through Labor Day.

**Directions:** From Groveland, drive east on Highway 120 for 12 miles (four miles past the Groveland District Office) to the campground on the left side of the road. (The access road is not recommended for RVs or trailers.)

**Contact:** Stanislaus National Forest, Groveland Ranger District, 209/962-7825, www.fs.usda.gov.

## 16 THE PINES AND PINES GROUP

**Scenic rating: 4**

in Stanislaus National Forest

**Map 9.2, page 494**

The Pines camp is at 3,200 feet elevation on the western edge of Stanislaus National Forest, only 0.5 mile from the Groveland District Office and about five miles from the Tuolumne River (see the Lumsden listing in this chapter). A Forest Service road is routed south of camp for two miles, climbing to Smith Peak Lookout (3,877 feet) and providing sweeping views to the west of the San Joaquin Valley foothills.

**Campsites, facilities:** There are 11 sites for tents or RVs up to 22 feet (no hookups) and a group site for up to 50 people. Picnic tables and fire grills are provided. Drinking water and vault toilets are available. A convenience store is nearby. Some facilities are wheelchair-accessible. Leashed pets are permitted.

**Reservations, fees:** Reservations are required for the group sites only at 877/444-6777 ($10 reservation fee) or www.recreation.gov ($9 reservation fee; look online for Pines Group Stanislaus. Sites are $19 per night, $90 per night for the group site. Open year-round, weather permitting. There is no fee in winter (limited facilities).

**Directions:** From Groveland, drive east on Highway 120 for nine miles (about a mile past the County Road J132 turnoff) to the signed campground entrance road on the right. Turn right onto the campground entrance road and drive a short distance to the camp.

**Contact:** Stanislaus National Forest, Groveland Ranger District, 209/962-7825, www.fs.usda.gov.

## 17 BLUE OAKS

Scenic rating: 7

at Lake Don Pedro

**Map 9.2, page 494**

Blue Oaks is between the dam at Lake Don Pedro and Fleming Meadows. The on-site boat ramp to the east is a big plus here. (See the Fleming Meadows and Moccasin Point listings in this chapter for more information.)

**Campsites, facilities:** There are 196 sites for tents or RVs of any length; some sites have partial hookups (20 and 30 amps) and one is pull-through. Group camping is available for up to 200 people. Picnic tables, fire rings, food lockers, and barbecue units are provided. Drinking water, restrooms with flush toilets and showers, boat launch, fish-cleaning stations, Wi-Fi, and a dump station are available. Some facilities are wheelchair-accessible. A store, coin laundry, and propane gas are nearby at Fleming Meadows Marina. No pets are permitted.

**Reservations, fees:** Reservations are accepted for a minimum of two nights (three nights on holidays) and can be made at 209/852-2396 or www.donpedrolake.com ($10 reservation fee). Tent sites are $24-29 per night, RV sites with partial hookups are $22-35 per night, RV sites with full hookups are $36-41 per night, plus $10 per day for each additional vehicle. Primitive boat-in camping is $8 per night with a $10 day-use fee. The group site is $300 per night. Weekend rates are higher. Some credit cards are accepted. Open year-round.

**Directions:** From Manteca, take Highway 120 east to Oakdale (the road becomes Highway 120/108). Continue east on Highway 108 for 20 miles to La Grange Road/J59 (signed "Don Pedro Reservoir"). Turn right on La Grange Road and drive 10 miles to Bonds Flat Road. Turn left on Bonds Flat Road and drive 0.5 mile to the campground on the left.

**Contact:** Don Pedro Recreation Area, 209/852-2396, www.donpedrolake.com; Lake Don Pedro Marina, 209/852-2369.

## 18 FLEMING MEADOWS

Scenic rating: 7

on Lake Don Pedro

**Map 9.2, page 494**

Fleming Meadows is on the shore of Lake Don Pedro, just east of the dam. A boat ramp is in the campground on the southeast side of the dam. Features include a sandy beach and concession stand. This is a big camp at the foot of a giant lake, where hot weather, warm water, waterskiing, and bass fishing make for weekend vacations. Don Pedro has many extended lake arms, providing 160 miles of shoreline and nearly 13,000 surface acres when full. (See the Moccasin Point listing in this chapter for more information.)

**Campsites, facilities:** There are 172 sites for tents or RVs of any length, including 51 walk-in sites for tents and 90 sites with full hook-ups (20 and 30 amps) for RVs. A few sites are pull-through. Picnic tables, fire rings, food lockers, and barbecues are provided. Drinking water, restrooms with flush toilets and showers, and a dump station are available. A coin laundry, store, ice, snack bar, Wi-Fi, group picnic areas, restaurant, swimming lagoon, amphitheater, softball field, volleyball, bait and tackle, motorboat and houseboat rentals, boat ramp, mooring, boat storage, engine repairs, and propane gas are nearby. Some facilities are wheelchair-accessible.

**Reservations, fees:** Reservations are accepted for a minimum of two nights (three nights on holidays) and can be made at 209/852-2396 or www.donpedrolake.com ($10 reservation fee). Tent sites are $24-29 per night, RV sites with partial hookups are $22-35 per night, RV sites with full hookups are $36-41 per night, plus $10 per day for each additional vehicle. Primitive boat-in camping is $8 per night with a $10 day-use fee. The group site is $300 per night. Weekend rates are higher. Some credit cards are accepted. Open year-round.

**Directions:** From Manteca, take Highway 120 east to Oakdale (the road becomes Highway 120/108). Continue east on Highway 108 for 20 miles to La Grange Road/J59 (signed "Don Pedro Reservoir"). Turn right on La Grange Road and drive 10 miles to Bonds Flat Road. Turn left on Bonds Flat Road and drive 2.5 miles to the campground on the left.

**Contact:** Don Pedro Recreation Area, 209/852-2396; Lake Don Pedro Marina, 209/852-2369, www.donpedrolake.com.

## 19 MODESTO RESERVOIR REGIONAL PARK AND BOAT-IN

**Scenic rating: 7**

on Modesto Reservoir

**Map 9.2, page 494**

Modesto Reservoir is a big lake, at 2,800 acres with 31 miles of shoreline, set in the hot foothill country. That's good because it is a popular place in the summer. Waterskiing is excellent in the main lake body. Sandy swimming beaches are available, and swimming is popular. Anglers head to the southern shore of the lake, which is loaded with submerged trees and coves and is also protected by a 5-mph speed limit. Fishing for bass is good, though the fish are often small. Wildlife viewing is good and waterfowl hunting is available in season. The elevation is 200 feet. All watercraft must be certified free of mussels.

**Campsites, facilities:** There are 134 sites with full hookups (30 amps) for RVs up to 36 feet and 36 tent sites. Picnic tables and fire grills are provided. Drinking water, restrooms with flush toilets and showers, dump station, two boat ramps, store, snack bar, propane, gas, archery range, and radio-controlled glider field are available. Some facilities are wheelchair-accessible. No gas cans are permitted.

**Reservations, fees:** Reservations are accepted at 800/444-7275 or www.reserveamerica.com ($9 reservation fee). Sites are $5-25 per night, plus $10 per night per additional vehicle. Holiday weekend rates are $2 higher. Boat launch is $7 per day. Open year-round.

**Directions:** From Modesto, drive east on Highway 132 for 16 miles past Waterford to Reservoir Road. Turn left and drive to the campground at 18143 Reservoir Road.

**Contact:** Modesto Reservoir Regional Park, 209/525-6750, www.stancounty.com/parks.

## 20 TURLOCK LAKE STATE RECREATION AREA

Scenic rating: 6

east of Modesto

**Map 9.2, page 494**

This campground is on the shady south shore of the Tuolumne River, about one mile from Turlock Lake. Turlock Lake warms to 65-74°F in the summer, cooler than many Central Valley reservoirs, since the water entering this lake is released from the bottom of Don Pedro Reservoir. It often seems just right for boating and all water sports on hot summer days. The lake covers 3,500 surface acres and offers 26 miles of shoreline. A boat ramp is available near the camp, making it ideal for boaters/campers. Bass fishing is fair in the summer. In the late winter and spring, the lake is quite cold, fed by snowmelt from the Tuolumne River. Trout fishing is good year-round as a result. The elevation is 250 feet. The park is bordered by ranches, orchards, and mining tailings along the river.

**Campsites, facilities:** There are 48 sites for tents or RVs up to 27 feet (no hookups), 15 sites for tents, and one hike-in/bike-in site. Picnic tables, fire grills, and food lockers are provided. Drinking water and restrooms with flush toilets and coin showers are available. A swimming beach and boat ramp are nearby. The boat facilities are wheelchair-accessible. Leashed pets are permitted.

**Reservations, fees:** Reservations are accepted at 800/444-7275 ($10 reservation fee) or www.reserveamerica.com ($9 reservation fee). Sites are $36 per night, plus $11 per night for each additional vehicle, and it's $6 per person per night for hike-in/bike-in site. Boat launching is $7 per day. Open year-round.

**Directions:** From Modesto, drive east on Highway 132 for 14 miles to Waterford, then continue eight miles on Highway 132 to Roberts Ferry Road. Turn right (south) and drive one mile to Lake Road. Turn left and drive two miles to the campground on the left.

**Contact:** Turlock Lake State Recreation Area, 209/874-2056 or 209/874-2008, www.parks.ca.gov; American Land and Leisure, 800/342-2267, www.americanll.com.

## 21 HORSESHOE BEND RECREATION AREA

Scenic rating: 7

on Lake McClure

**Map 9.2, page 494**

Lake McClure is a unique, horseshoe-shaped lake in the foothill country west of Yosemite. It adjoins smaller Lake McSwain, connected by the Merced River. McClure is shaped like a giant H, with its lake arms providing 82 miles of shoreline, warm water for waterskiing, and fishing for bass (on the west half of the H near Cotton Creek) and for trout (on the east half of the H). There is a boat launch adjacent to the campground. It's one of four lakes in the immediate area; the others are Don Pedro Reservoir to the north and Modesto Reservoir and Turlock Lake to the west. The elevation is 900 feet.

**Campsites, facilities:** There are 100 sites for tents or RVs of any length, including 35 with partial hookups (30 amps). Picnic tables and barbecues are provided. Restrooms with showers, dump station, boat ramp, fish-cleaning stations, picnic areas, swimming lagoon, store (seasonal), and coin laundry are available. Some facilities are wheelchair-accessible. Leashed pets are permitted.

**Reservations, fees:** Reservations are accepted at 855/800-2267. Tent sites are $22 per night, RV sites (hookups) are $28 per night, plus $8 per night for each additional vehicle and $4 per pet per night. Cabins are $110-155 per night. Boat launch is $8 per day. Senior and extended-stay discounts are available. Some credit cards are accepted. Open year-round.

**Directions:** From Modesto, drive east on Highway 132 for 31 miles to La Grange and then continue for about 17 miles (toward Coulterville) to the north end of Lake McClure and the campground entrance road on the right side of the road. Turn right and drive 0.5 mile to the campground.

**Contact:** Horseshoe Bend Recreation Area, 209/878-3452 or 209/378-2521; Merced Irrigation District, 209/378-2521, www.lakemcclure.com.

## 22 BARRETT COVE RECREATION AREA

**Scenic rating: 7**
on Lake McClure

**Map 9.2, page 494**

Lake McClure is shaped like a giant H, with its lake arms providing 82 miles of shoreline. The lake is popular for water sports, including skiing, wakeboarding, houseboating, and fishing. Although swimming is not prohibited in the lake, you'll rarely see people swimming or playing along the shore, mainly because of the typically steep drop-offs. This camp is on the left side of the H, that is, on the western shore, within a park that provides a good boat ramp. This is the largest in a series of camps on Lake McClure. (See the Horseshoe Bend Recreation Area, McClure Point Recreation Area, and Bagby Recreation Area listings in this chapter for more information.)

**Campsites, facilities:** There are 275 sites for tents or RVs of any length, including 89 with full hookups (30 amps). Picnic tables and barbecues are provided. Restrooms with showers, boat ramps, dump station, swimming lagoon, and playground are available. A convenience store, coin laundry, marina, picnic areas, fish-cleaning stations, boat and houseboat rentals, and propane gas are also on-site. Some facilities are wheelchair-accessible. Leashed pets are permitted.

**Reservations, fees:** Reservations are accepted at 855/800-2267. Tent sites are $22 per night, RV sites (hookups) are $28 per night, plus $8 per night for each additional vehicle and $4 per pet per night. Cabins are $110-155 per night. Boat launch is $8 per day. Senior and extended-stay discounts are available. Some credit cards are accepted. Open year-round.

**Directions:** From Modesto, drive east on Highway 132 for 31 miles to La Grange and continue about eight miles (toward Coulterville) to Merced Falls Road. Turn right and drive three miles to the campground entrance on the left. Turn left and drive a mile to the campground on the left side of the road.

**Contact:** Barrett Cove Recreation Area, 209/378-2611; Merced Irrigation District, 209/378-2521, www.lakemcclure.com.

## 23 MCCLURE POINT RECREATION AREA

**Scenic rating: 7**
on Lake McClure

**Map 9.2, page 494**

McClure Point Recreation Area is the campground of choice for campers/boaters coming from the Turlock and Merced areas. It is a well-developed facility with an excellent boat ramp that provides access to the main body of Lake McClure. This is the best spot on the lake for waterskiing.

**Campsites, facilities:** There are 100 sites for tents or RVs up to 40 feet; 52 sites have partial hookups (30 amps). Picnic tables and barbecues are provided. Restrooms with showers, boat ramps, boat rentals, marina, fish-cleaning stations, picnic areas, swimming lagoon, and a coin laundry are available. A store is nearby. Leashed pets are permitted.

**Reservations, fees:** Reservations are accepted at 855/800-2267. Tent sites are $22 per night, RV sites (hookups) are $28 per night, plus $8 per night for each additional vehicle and $4 per pet per night. Cabins are $110-155 per night. Boat launch is $8 per day. Senior and extended-stay discounts are available. Some credit cards are accepted. Open year-round.

**Directions:** From Turlock, drive east on County Road J16 for 19 miles to the junction with Highway 59. Continue east on Highway 59/County Road J16 for 4.5 miles to Snelling and bear right at Lake McClure Road. Drive approximately two miles to Lake McSwain Dam and continue for seven miles to the campground at the end of the road.

**Contact:** McClure Point and Bagby Recreation Area, 209/378-2521, www.lakemcclure.com.

## 24 BAGBY RECREATION AREA

**Scenic rating: 7**

on upper Lake McClure

**Map 9.2, page 494**

This is the most distant and secluded camp on Lake McClure. It is set near the Merced River as it enters the lake, way up adjacent to the Highway 49 bridge, nearly an hour's drive from the dam. Trout fishing is good in the area, and it makes sense; when the lake heats up in summer, the trout naturally congregate near the cool incoming flows of the Merced River.

**Campsites, facilities:** There are 30 sites for tents or RVs of any length, including 10 sites with partial hookups (30 amps). Drinking water, restrooms with flush toilets and coin showers, picnic areas, and fish-cleaning stations are available. A boat ramp is available unless the lake water level is too low. Some facilities are wheelchair-accessible. Leashed pets are permitted.

**Reservations, fees:** Reservations are accepted at 855/800-2267. Tent sites are $22 per night, RV sites (hookups) are $28 per night, plus $8 per night for each additional vehicle and $4 per pet per night. Cabins are $110-155 per night. Boat launch is $8 per day. Senior and extended-stay discounts are available. Some credit cards are accepted. Open year-round.

**Directions:** From Turlock, drive east on County Road J16 for 19 miles to the junction with Highway 59. Continue east on Highway 59/County Road J16 for 4.5 miles to Snelling and Merced Falls Road (continue straight—it's

well signed). Drive 0.5 mile to Hornitos Road. Turn right and drive eight miles (drive over the bridge) to Hornitos to a Y. Bear left at the Y in Hornitos (signed to Highway 49) and drive 10 miles to Highway 49. Turn left on Highway 49 and drive eight miles to the Bagby Bridge and entrance kiosk on the right.

**Contact:** McClure Point and Bagby Recreation Area, 209/378-2521, www.lakemcclure.com.

## 25 LAKE MCSWAIN RECREATION AREA

**Scenic rating: 7**

near McSwain Dam on the Merced River

**Map 9.2, page 494**

Lake McSwain is actually the afterbay for adjacent Lake McClure, and this camp is near the McSwain Dam on the Merced River. Even though McClure and McSwain sit beside each other, each has its own identity. McSwain is low-key with a 10-mph speed limit. If you have a canoe or car-top boat, this lake is preferable to Lake McClure because waterskiing is not allowed. In terms of size, McSwain is like a pond compared to the giant McClure, but unlike McClure, the water levels are kept up almost year-round at McSwain. The water is cold and trout stocks are good in the spring. The lake is used primarily by anglers, and several fishing derbies are held each year. The shoreline is favorable for swimming, and there is even a good sandy beach.

**Campsites, facilities:** There are 100 sites for tents or RVs up to 40 feet, including 65 with partial hookups (30 amps). The best access sites for large RVs are the pull-through sites in the G Loop. Picnic tables, barbecues, and electrical connections are provided. Drinking water, dump station, restrooms with showers, boat ramp, boat rentals, coin laundry, and a playground are available. A convenience store, marina, snack bar, fish-cleaning stations, picnic area, and propane gas are available nearby.

Some facilities are wheelchair-accessible. Leashed pets are permitted.

**Reservations, fees:** Reservations are accepted at 855/800-2267. Tent sites are $22 per night, RV sites (hookups) are $28, and cabins are $110-155 per night. Open year-round.

**Directions:** From Turlock, drive east on County Road J16 for 19 miles to the junction with Highway 59. Continue east on Highway 59/County Road J16 for 4.5 miles to Snelling. Continue straight ahead to Lake McClure Road and drive seven miles to the campground turn-off on the right.

**Contact:** Lake McSwain Recreation Area, 209/378-2521; Lake McSwain Marina, 209/378-2534, www.lakemcclure.com.

## 26 FISHERMAN'S BEND RIVER CAMPGROUND

**Scenic rating: 5**

on the San Joaquin River

**Map 9.2, page 494**

This small, privately operated campground is along the San Joaquin River on the fork of the San Joaquin and Merced Rivers in the southern outskirts of the San Joaquin Delta country. The park offers shaded sites and direct river access for boaters. This section of river provides fishing for catfish, largemouth bass, and occasionally striped bass and sturgeon. Although many of the sites are rented seasonally or longer, about 10 sites are usually available for overnight campers.

**Campsites, facilities:** There are 38 pull-through sites with full hookups (30 amps) for RVs of any length and 20 sites for tents only. Picnic tables are provided. Drinking water, restrooms with showers, coin laundry, boat ramp, horseshoes, basketball, convenience store, fish-cleaning station, and playground, are available. Some facilities are wheelchair-accessible. Leashed pets are permitted, with certain restrictions.

**Reservations, fees:** Reservations are accepted at 209/862-3731. Sites are $15-25 per night, plus $5 per night per extra vehicle. Weekly and monthly rates are available. Open year-round.

**Directions:** Drive on I-5 to the exit for Newman/Stuhr Road (south of the junction of I-5 and I-580). Take that exit and turn east on County Road J18/Stuhr Road and drive 6.5 miles to Hills Ferry Road. Turn left and drive a mile to River Road. Turn left on River Road and drive to 26836 River Road on the right.

**Contact:** Fisherman's Bend River Campground, 209/862-3731.

## 27 GEORGE J. HATFIELD STATE RECREATION AREA WALK-IN

**Scenic rating: 5**

near Newman

**Map 9.2, page 494**

This is a small state park in the heart of the San Joaquin Valley, near the confluence of the Merced River and the San Joaquin River, well known for hot summer days and foggy winter nights. The park has many trees. Swimming is popular in the summer. Fishing is good for catfish in the summer, and some folks stay up late hoping a big channel catfish will take their bait. During the peak migration from late fall through winter and early spring, there can also be a good number of striped bass in the area. This park is more popular for day use than for camping. The campsites require a walk of about 100 feet.

**Campsites, facilities:** There are 15 walk-in sites for tents and a large group site for tents or RVs up to 25 feet that can accommodate up to 40 people. Picnic tables and fire grills are provided. Chemical toilets are provided. There is no drinking water. Supplies can be obtained in Newman, five miles away. Leashed pets are permitted.

**Reservations, fees:** Reservations are accepted for the group site at 800/444-7275 ($10 reservation fee) or www.reserveamerica.com ($9 reservation fee). Individual sites are first-come, first-served. Sites are $20 per night, plus $10 per night for each additional vehicle, and the group site is $150 per night. Open year-round, weather permitting.

**Directions:** Drive on I-5 to the exit for Newman/Stuhr Road (south of the junction of I-5 and I-580). Take that exit and turn east on County Road J18/Stuhr Road, then drive to Newman and the junction with Highway 33. Continue straight on Stuhr Road for 1.5 miles to Hills Ferry Road. Turn left and drive three miles to the park entrance on the right (just past the bridge over the San Joaquin River).

**Contact:** George J. Hatfield State Recreation Area, 209/632-1852; Four Rivers Sector, 209/826-1197, www.parks.ca.gov.

## 28 MCCONNELL STATE RECREATION AREA
🏊 🚤 🎣 ♿ 🚐 ⛺

### Scenic rating: 6
on the Merced River

**Map 9.2, page 494**

In summer, the weather here is scorching hot. Fortunately, this 74-acre park on the Merced River provides some badly needed relief and a river to cool off in. Fishing is popular for catfish, perch, black bass, and salmon in the fall (California sport-fishing license required). A small loop hosts shaded campsites, an amphitheater, and a trail to the beach.

**Campsites, facilities:** There are 20 sites for tents or RVs up to 30 feet (no hookups) and two tent-only group sites for 20 or 50 people; group sites have an electrical hookup (20 amps). Picnic tables, fire grills, and food lockers are provided. Drinking water, restrooms with flush toilets and coin showers, and a swimming beach are available. Firewood is available for purchase. Supplies can be obtained in Delhi, five miles away. Some facilities are wheelchair-accessible. Leashed pets are permitted.

**Reservations, fees:** Reservations are accepted February through June at 800/444-7275 ($10

reservation fee) or www.reserveamerica.com ($9 reservation fee). Sites are $30 per night, plus $10 per night for each additional vehicle, and it's $100-150 per night for group sites. Open when reservations are accepted; call to confirm.

**Directions:** From Modesto, drive south on Highway 99 to Delhi. Continue south for five miles to the South Avenue exit. Take that exit and turn east on South Avenue and drive 2.7 miles to Pepper Street. Turn right and drive one mile to McConnell Road. Turn right and drive a short distance to the park entrance at the end of the road.

**Contact:** McConnell State Recreation Area, 209/394-7755; Four Rivers Sector, 209/826-1197, www.parks.ca.gov.

## 29 LOS BANOS CREEK RESERVOIR
🏊 🚤 🚤 🎣 🚐 ⛺

### Scenic rating: 6
near Los Banos

**Map 9.3, page 495**

Los Banos Creek Reservoir is set in a long, narrow valley, covering 410 surface acres with 12 miles of shoreline. It provides a smaller, more low-key setting (a 5-mph speed limit is enforced) compared to the nearby giant, San Luis Reservoir. In spring, it can be quite windy and is a popular spot for sailboarding and sailing. It is also stocked with trout in late winter and spring, and some large bass have been caught here. The elevation is 330 feet. Although drinking water is available, campers are advised to bring their own water, as the water supply is limited. Note: All boats must be certified mussel-free before launching.

**Campsites, facilities:** There are 14 sites for tents or RVs up to 30 feet (no hookups). Picnic tables, shade ramadas, and fire grills are provided. Drinking water, chemical toilets (one with wheelchair accessibility), and picnic areas are available. A boat ramp is nearby. Leashed pets are permitted.

**Reservations, fees:** Reservations are not

accepted. Sites are $20 per night, and it's $10 per night for each additional vehicle. Boat launching is $7 per day. Open year-round, weather permitting.

**Directions:** Drive on Highway 152 to Volta Road (five miles west of Los Banos). Turn south on Volta Road and drive about a mile to Pioneer Road. Turn left on Pioneer Road and drive a mile to Canyon Road. Turn south (right) onto Canyon Road and drive about five miles to the park.

**Contact:** San Luis Reservoir State Recreation Area, 209/826-1196; Four Rivers Sector, 209/826-1197, www.parks.ca.gov.

## 30 LOST LAKE

### Scenic rating: 7

on the lower San Joaquin River

**Map 9.4, page 496**

Lost Lake campground is part of a Fresno County park. It is in the foothills of the San Joaquin Valley, at an elevation of about 500 feet, along the lower San Joaquin River. The campground is broken out into two areas, with about half along the river. Many think this park is quite pretty. There is a lot of wildlife at this park, especially birds and deer. A self-guided hiking trail is routed into a nature study area. Easy kayaking and canoeing is a plus, with no powerboats permitted. Trout fishing is available; check fishing regulations.

**Campsites, facilities:** There are 42 sites for tents, with most accessible for self-contained RVs up to 36 feet, and one group site for up to 80 people. Picnic tables and barbecues are provided. Drinking water, flush toilets, volleyball, softball, and a playground are available. A restaurant and store are two miles away in Friant. Some facilities, including a fishing dock, are wheelchair-accessible. Leashed pets are permitted.

**Reservations, fees:** Reservations are accepted for the group site only at 559/600-3004. Sites are $25 per night, plus $5 per night for each additional vehicle, and it's $100-200 per night for the group site (10-vehicle minimum). Open year-round.

**Directions:** From Fresno, drive north on Highway 41 for 24 miles to the first exit for Friant Road. Take that exit and drive 12 miles to the entrance road for Lost Lake. Turn left and drive a short distance to the campground.

**Contact:** Fresno County Parks Department, 559/600-3004, www.co.fresno.ca.us.

## 31 VISALIA/FRESNO SOUTH KOA

### Scenic rating: 3

west of Visalia

**Map 9.4, page 496**

This is a layover spot for Highway 99 cruisers. If you're looking for a spot to park your rig for the night, you can't get too picky around these parts. Most campers are on their way to or from Sequoia and Kings Canyon National Parks. The swimming pool is a great bonus during the summer. Grassy shaded sites are available. Golf and tennis are nearby. (And by the way, Visalia is my favorite town in the San Joaquin Valley.)

**Campsites, facilities:** There are 48 pull-through RV sites with full or partial hookups (30 and 50 amps), 20 sites for tents or RVs with no hookups, 20 sites for tents only, and eight cabins. Restrooms with showers, seasonal heated swimming pool, laundry facilities, playground, recreation room, free Wi-Fi, dog walk, store, gift shop, dump station, and propane gas are available. Leashed pets are permitted, with certain restrictions.

**Reservations, fees:** Reservations are accepted at 800/562-0540. Pull-through RV sites with full hookups (50 amps) are $60.27 per night, pull-through RV sites with water and electricity are $58.27 per night, standard RV sites with full or partial hookups are $35-51 per night, and tent sites are $39-46 per night, plus $5 per person per night for more than two people. Some credit cards are accepted. Open year-round.

**Directions:** From Highway 99 near Visalia, take the Goshen Avenue exit and drive 0.2 mile to Betty Drive/County Road 332. Turn left and drive 0.5 mile to County Road 76. Turn left and drive 0.5 mile (becomes Avenue 308) to the campground.

**Contact:** Visalia-Fresno KOA, 559/651-0544, www.koa.com.

## 32 SUN AND FUN RV PARK

### Scenic rating: 2

near Tulare

**Map 9.4, page 496**

This RV park is just off Highway 99, exactly halfway between San Francisco and Los Angeles. Are you having fun yet? Anybody making the long drive up or down the state on Highway 99 will learn what a dry piece of life the San Joaquin Valley can seem in summer. That's why the swimming pool at this RV park can be a lifesaver. The park has mature trees, providing an opportunity for shade. Note that most of the sites are filled with long-term renters, but a few spaces are reserved for overnight campers.

**Campsites, facilities:** There are 59 sites with full hookups (30 and 50 amps) for RVs up to 45 feet. No tents are allowed. Picnic tables and barbecues are provided at some sites. Restrooms with showers, drinking water, cable TV, dump station, playground, swimming pool, spa, coin laundry, dog runs, and a recreation room are available. A golf course, restaurant, and store are nearby. Some facilities are wheelchair-accessible. Leashed pets are permitted.

**Reservations, fees:** Reservations are accepted during business hours. Sites are $50 per night. Weekly and monthly rates are available. Open year-round.

**Directions:** From Tulare, drive south on Highway 99 for three miles to the Avenue 200 exit. Take Avenue 200 west and drive a short distance to the park.

**Contact:** Sun and Fun RV Park, 1000 East Rankin, 559/686-5779, www.westernm.com/communities.

## 33 COLONEL ALLENSWORTH STATE HISTORIC PARK

### Scenic rating: 2

near Earlimart

**Map 9.5, page 497**

What you have here is the old town of Allensworth, which has been restored as a historical park dedicated to the African American pioneers who founded it with Colonel Allen Allensworth. Allensworth is the sole town in California to be established, financed, and governed by African Americans, and the colonel was the highest-ranking army chaplain of his time. A museum is available at the school, and the colonel's house offers a 30-minute movie on the history of Allensworth. Tours are available by appointment. One frustrating element is that railroad tracks run alongside the park, and it can be disruptive. There can be other problems—very hot weather in the summer and, since it is an open area, the wind can blow dust and sand. Are we having fun yet? One nice touch is the addition of shade ramadas at some campsites, although campsites are on the primitive side.

**Campsites, facilities:** There are 15 sites for tents or RVs up to 35 feet (no hookups). Picnic tables and camp stoves are provided. Restrooms with flush toilets and coin showers, drinking water, dump station, visitors center, and picnic area are available. A store and coin laundry are 12 miles away in Delano. Some facilities are wheelchair-accessible. Leashed pets are permitted.

**Reservations, fees:** Reservations are accepted at 800/444-7275 ($10 reservation fee) or www.reserveamerica.com ($9 reservation fee). Sites are $20 per night. Open year-round, Friday and Saturday only.

**Directions:** From Fresno, drive south on Highway 99 about 60 miles to Earlimart and the Avenue 56 exit. Turn right (west) on Avenue 56 and drive seven miles to the Highway 43 turnoff. Turn left (south) on Highway 43 and drive two miles to Palmer Avenue. Turn right (and drive over the railroad tracks) to the park entrance.

**Contact:** Colonel Allensworth State Historic Park, 661/849-3433 or 661/849-2101, www. parks.ca.gov.

## 34 SELBY

**Scenic rating: 6**

at Carrizo Plain National Monument northeast of San Luis Obispo

**Map 9.5, page 497**

The Carrizo Plain is California's largest nature preserve, but because of its remote location, primitive setting, and lack of recreational lakes and streams, it remains largely unknown and is explored by few people. The feature attraction is to visit Soda Lake in the winter to see flocks of the endangered sandhill crane; the lake is a nesting area for these huge birds with seven-foot wingspans. Selby is a primitive camping area at the base of the Caliente Mountain Range, known for its scorching hot temperatures (hey, after all, "Caliente") during the summer. The top hiking destination in the region is Painted Rock, a 55-foot rock with Chumash pictographs. Other hiking trails are available.

**Campsites, facilities:** This is a primitive camping area with 13 designated sites for tents or RVs up to 25 feet (no hookups). Picnic tables, shade ramadas, and fire rings are provided. Vault toilets and horse corrals are available. No drinking water is available, but there is usually water for livestock. Garbage must be packed out. Nearest services are about 50 miles away. Leashed pets are permitted.

**Reservations, fees:** Reservations are not accepted. There is no fee for camping, but donations are encouraged. Group camping must be authorized by calling 661/391-6048. Open year-round.

**Directions:** From Bakersfield, drive west on Highway 58 for about 30 miles to McKittrick (where Highway 33 merges with Highway 58). Bear left on Highway 58/33, continuing through town, and drive west for approximately 10 miles to Seven-Mile Road. Turn west on Seven-Mile Road and drive seven miles (six miles will be on gravel/dirt road) to Soda Lake Road. Turn left on Soda Lake Road and drive about six miles to the Selby camping area on your right.

**Contact:** Bureau of Land Management, Bakersfield Field Office, 661/391-6000, www. blm.gov/ca.

## 35 KCL

**Scenic rating: 6**

at the Carrizo Plain National Monument, northeast of San Luis Obispo

**Map 9.5, page 497**

KCL is the name of the old ranch headquarters in the Carrizo, of which remain old broken-down outbuildings, a corral, and not much else. Note that the buildings are off-limits to visitors. At least there are some trees (in comparison, there are none at nearby Selby camp). The Carrizo Plain is best known for providing a habitat for many rare species of plants, animals, and insects, in addition to furnishing the winter nesting sites at Soda Lake for the awesome migration of giant sandhill cranes. These birds are often spotted north of this area. This campground is popular with hunters and birders because of its easy access to Soda Lake Road for daily outings. Dispersed camping is allowed throughout the national monument.

**Campsites, facilities:** This is a primitive camping area with 12 sites for tents or RVs up to 25 feet (no hookups). Picnic tables and fire pits are provided. Vault toilets and corrals are available. No drinking water is available, but there is usually water for livestock. Garbage must be packed out. The nearest services are about 50 miles away. Some facilities are wheelchair-accessible. Leashed pets are permitted.

**Reservations, fees:** Reservations are not accepted. There is no fee for camping. Group camping must be authorized by calling 661/391-6048. Open year-round.

**Directions:** From Bakersfield, drive west on Highway 58 for about 30 miles to McKittrick (where Highway 33 merges with Highway 58). Bear left on Highway 58/33, continuing through town, and drive west for about 10 miles to Seven-Mile Road. Turn west on Seven-Mile Road, and drive seven miles (six miles will be on gravel/dirt road) to Soda Lake Road. Turn left on Soda Lake Road and drive 0.5 mile to the entrance of the Carrizo Plains National Monument. Continue about 15 miles to the KCL camping area on your right.

**Contact:** Bureau of Land Management, Bakersfield Field Office, 661/391-6000, www.blm.gov/ca.

## 36 BUENA VISTA AQUATIC RECREATION AREA

### Scenic rating: 6

near Bakersfield

**Map 9.5, page 497**

This is the showpiece of Kern County recreation. Buena Vista is actually two connected lakes fed by the West Side Canal: little Lake Evans to the west and larger Lake Webb to the east. Be certain to know the difference between the two: Lake Webb (875 acres) is open to all boating including personal watercraft, and fast boats towing skiers are a common sight

in designated ski areas. The speed limit is 45 mph. Lake Evans (85 acres) is small, quiet, and has a strictly enforced 5-mph speed limit, an ideal lake for family water play and fishing. Swimming is prohibited at both lakes but is allowed in the lagoons. Lake Webb is a catfish lake, while Lake Evans is stocked in season with trout and also has bass, bluegill, catfish, and crappie. The elevation is 330 feet.

**Campsites, facilities:** There are 112 sites, some with full hookups (30 and 50 amps) for RVs or tents, and an overflow camping area. Picnic tables and fire grills are provided. Restrooms with flush toilets and showers, drinking water, playground, four boat ramps, store, dump station, and picnic shelters are available. Two swimming lagoons, a marina, snack bar, fishing supplies, and groceries are available nearby. A PGA-rated golf course is two miles west. Some facilities are wheelchair-accessible. Leashed pets are permitted.

**Reservations, fees:** Reservations are accepted Monday through Friday at 661/868-7050 ($7 reservation fee). Tent sites are $28-40 per night, RV sites (hookups) are $36-40 per night, plus $12-15 for each additional vehicle, $4 per night per pet, and $7 per night for boats. Group discounts are available. Some credit cards are accepted. Open year-round.

**Directions:** From I-5 just south of Bakersfield, take Highway 119 west and drive two miles to Highway 43. Turn south (left) on Highway 43 and drive two miles to the campground at road's end.

**Contact:** Buena Vista Aquatic Recreation Area, Kern County Parks, 661/868-7000, www.co.kern.ca.us/parks/index.htm; Buena Vista concession, 661/763-1526.

# YOSEMITE AND MAMMOTH LAKES

Some of nature's most perfect artwork exists in Yosemite and the eastern Sierra near Mammoth Lakes. Yosemite Valley is the world's greatest showpiece–it is also highly visited. Though 24,000 people jam into Yosemite Valley each summer day, the park is actually 90 percent wilderness, with 318 lakes, dozens of pristine streams, the Grand Canyon of the Tuolumne River, Matterhorn Peak, Benson Lake, and dozens of waterfalls. Anything in Yosemite is going to be in high demand year-round; the same is true near Mammoth Lakes. Over Tioga Pass lie Tioga Lake, Ellery Lake, Saddlebag Lake, and the eastern Sierra, home to Mono Lake with its weird tufa spires. June Lake Loop and Mammoth Lakes have small lakes with cabins, fishing, hiking, mountain biking, winter sports, and a nearby series of hot springs. Hiking and fishing opportunities abound at Devils Postpile National Monument.

# YOSEMITE AND MAMMOTH LAKES

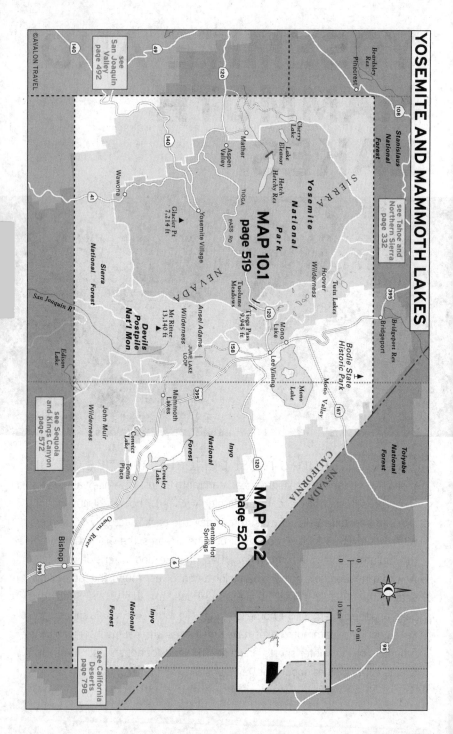

©AVALON TRAVEL

see San Joaquin Valley page 492

see Tahoe and Northern Sierra page 332

see Sequoia and Kings Canyon page 572

see California Deserts page 798

**MAP 10.1**
page 519

**MAP 10.2**
page 520

Stanislaus National Forest

Yosemite National Park

Sierra National Forest

John Muir Wilderness

Ansel Adams Wilderness

Hoover Wilderness

Inyo National Forest

Toiyabe National Forest

Bodie State Historic Park

Glacier Pt 7,214 ft

Mt Ritter 13,140 ft

Devils Postpile Nat'l Mon

Tuolumne Meadows 9,945 ft

Tioga Pass

Yosemite Village

Wawona

Mather

Aspen Valley

Cherry Lake

Eleanor Lake

Hetch Hetchy Res

Mono Lake

Mono Lake

Lee Vining

Bridgeport

Bridgeport Res

Twin Lakes

Mammoth Lakes

Convict Lake

Toms Place

Crowley Lake

Benton Hot Springs

Bishop

Edison Lake

San Joaquin R

Owens River

Beardsley Res

Pinecrest

Mono Valley

JUNE LAKE LOOP

CALIFORNIA

NEVADA

SIERRA NEVADA

TIOGA PASS RD

108

120

140

49

41

140

120

120

158

395

395

395

167

6

95

0    10 km
0    10 mi

# Map 10.1

**Sites 1-69**
**Pages 521-556**

10.2

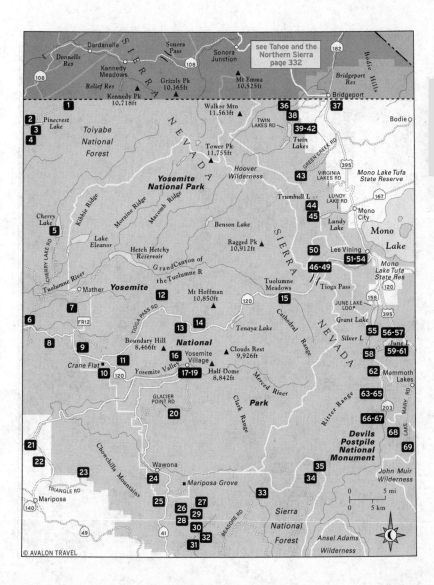

# Map 10.2

## Sites 70-99
## Pages 556-570

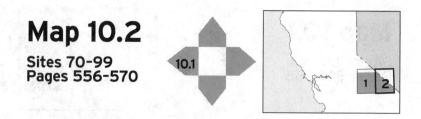

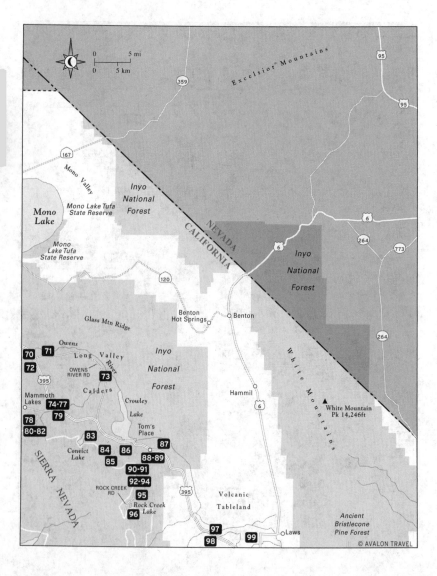

© AVALON TRAVEL

# 1 HERRING RESERVOIR

**Scenic rating: 8**

at Herring Lake in Stanislaus National Forest

**Map 10.1, page 519**

This is a pretty little spot, a rustic campground set near Herring Creek as it enters Herring Lake, at an elevation of 7,350 feet. There is no boat ramp, but hand-launched boats, such as kayaks, canoes, rafts, prams, and float tubes, are ideal. The lake is shallow, with fair fishing for brook trout and rainbow trout. No horses are permitted.

**Campsites, facilities:** There are 42 sites for tents or RVs up to 22 feet (no hookups). Fire rings are provided. Vault toilets are available. No drinking water is available. Garbage must be packed out. Leashed pets are permitted.

**Reservations, fees:** Reservations are not accepted. There is no fee for camping, but donations are accepted. Open May through October, weather permitting.

**Directions:** From Sonora, drive east on Highway 108 for about 25 miles to Strawberry. Continue past Strawberry for two miles to Herring Creek Road/Forest Road 4N12. Turn right and drive seven miles to Hamill Canyon Road/Forest Road 4N12. Bear right and drive 0.25 mile to Herring Creek Reservoir. Continue another 0.25 mile (cross the bridge) and turn right and drive to the campground. The road is rough and not recommended for RVs or low-clearance vehicles.

**Contact:** Stanislaus National Forest, Summit Ranger District, 209/965-3434, www.fs.usda. gov/stanislaus.

# 2 PINECREST

**Scenic rating: 7**

near Pinecrest Lake in Stanislaus National Forest

**Map 10.1, page 519**

This monster-sized Forest Service camp is near Pinecrest Lake. A launch ramp is available, and a 20-mph speed limit is enforced on the lake. A trail circles the lake and also branches off to nearby Catfish Lake. In early summer, there is good fishing for stocked rainbow trout. The elevation is 5,600 feet. Winter camping is allowed near the Pinecrest Day-Use Area. (For details about Pinecrest Lake, see the Meadowview listing in this chapter.)

**Campsites, facilities:** There are 196 sites for tents or RVs up to 22 feet (no hookups). Picnic tables and fire grills are provided. Drinking water and flush toilets are available. Garbage must be packed out. A grocery store, coin laundry, coin showers, boat ramp, and propane gas are nearby at Pinecrest Lake Resort. Some facilities are wheelchair-accessible. Leashed pets are permitted.

**Reservations, fees:** Reservations are required mid-May to mid-September at 877/444-6777 ($10 reservation fee) or www.recreation.gov ($9 reservation fee). Sites are $25 per night. Open May through October, weather permitting.

**Directions:** From Sonora, drive east on Highway 108 for about 30 miles to the signed turn for Pinecrest Lake on the right. Turn right and drive to the access road (0.7 mile past the turnoff signed Pinecrest) for the campground. Turn right and drive a short distance to the campground.

**Contact:** Stanislaus National Forest, Summit Ranger District, 209/965-3434, www.fs.usda. gov/stanislaus; Dodge Ridge Corporation, 209/965-3475, www.dodgeridge.com; Pinecrest campground, 209/965-3116.

# 3 PIONEER TRAIL GROUP CAMP

**Scenic rating: 8**

near Pinecrest Lake in Stanislaus National Forest

**Map 10.1, page 519**

If you're going to Pinecrest Lake with a Scout troop, this is the spot, since it is set up specifically for groups. You get beautiful creek and lake views, with the camp set at an elevation of 5,700 feet. (For recreation information, see the Meadowview listing in this chapter.)

**Campsites, facilities:** There are three group areas for tents or RVs up to 22 feet (no hookups). One site can accommodate 50-100 people and two sites can accommodate up to 50 people each. Picnic tables and fire grills are provided. Drinking water and vault toilets are available. Garbage must be packed out. A grocery store, coin laundry, boat ramp, coin showers, and propane gas are nearby. Some facilities are wheelchair-accessible. Leashed pets are permitted.

**Reservations, fees:** Reservations are required mid-May to mid-September at 877/444-6777 ($10 reservation fee) or www.recreation. gov ($9 reservation fee). Sites are $90-130 per night. Open May through October, weather permitting.

**Directions:** From Sonora, drive east on Highway 108 for about 30 miles to the signed road for Pinecrest Lake. Turn right at the sign and drive 0.5 mile to the signed road for Pinecrest/Dodge Ridge Road. Turn right and drive about a mile to the campground entrance on the left.

**Contact:** Stanislaus National Forest, Summit Ranger District, 209/965-3434, www.fs.usda. gov/stanislaus; Dodge Ridge Corporation, 209/965-3475, www.dodgeridge.com.

# 4 MEADOWVIEW

🚶 🚴 🏊 🛶 🛥 🎣 🐕 ♿ 🚐 ⛺

### Scenic rating: 7
near Pinecrest Lake in Stanislaus National Forest

**Map 10.1, page 519**

No secret here, folks. This camp is one mile from Pinecrest Lake, a popular weekend vacation area (and a trail connects the camp with the town). Pinecrest Lake is at 5,621 feet elevation, covers 300 acres and 2.5 miles of shoreline, has a sandy swimming beach, and has a

20-mph speed limit for boaters. The lake is the centerpiece of a fully developed family vacation area; boat rentals at the small marina are a big bonus. The lake is stocked with rainbow trout and also has a small resident population of brown trout. The easy hike around the lake is a popular walk. If you want something more ambitious, a cutoff on the north side of the lake heads one mile up to little Catfish Lake, which in reality is a set of shallow ponds surrounded by old-growth forest. The Dodge Ridge Ski Area is nearby, with many privately owned cabins in the area.

**Campsites, facilities:** There are 100 sites for tents or RVs up to 22 feet (no hookups). Picnic tables and fire grills are provided. Drinking water and flush toilets are available. A grocery store, coin laundry, boat ramp, boat rentals, coin showers, and propane gas are nearby. Garbage must be packed out. Some facilities are wheelchair-accessible. Leashed pets are permitted.

**Reservations, fees:** Reservations are not accepted. Sites are $23 per night, plus $5 per each additional vehicle per night. Open May through September, weather permitting.

**Directions:** From Sonora, drive east on Highway 108 for about 30 miles to the sign for Pinecrest Lake. Turn right at the sign and drive 0.5 mile to Pinecrest/Dodge Ridge Road. Turn right and drive about 200 yards to the campground entrance on the right side of the road.

**Contact:** Stanislaus National Forest, Summit Ranger District, 209/965-3434, www.fs.usda. gov/stanislaus; Dodge Ridge Corporation, 209/965-3475, www.dodgeridge.com.

# 5 CHERRY VALLEY AND BOAT-IN

🚶 🏊 🛶 🛥 🐕 🚐 ⛺

### Scenic rating: 7
on Cherry Lake in Stanislaus National Forest

**Map 10.1, page 519**

Cherry Lake is a mountain lake surrounded by national forest at 4,700 feet elevation, just outside the western boundary of Yosemite National Park. It is much larger than most people anticipate and provides much better trout fishing than anything in Yosemite. The camp is on the southwest shore of the lake, about a mile ride to the boat launch on the west side of the Cherry Valley Dam. A bonus is that dispersed boat-in camping is allowed on the lake's east side. All water sports are allowed, yet because it takes a considerable drive to reach the lake, you won't find nearly the waterskiing traffic as at other regional lakes. Water levels can fluctuate. The lake is bordered to the east by Kibbie Ridge; just on the other side are Yosemite Park and Lake Eleanor. A campfire permit is required from the Forest Service.

**Campsites, facilities:** There are 45 sites for tents or RVs up to 22 feet (no hookups). Primitive boat-in camping is permitted on the lake's east side. Picnic tables and fire grills are provided. Drinking water and vault toilets are available. A boat ramp is nearby. Leashed pets are permitted.

**Reservations, fees:** Reservations are accepted at 877/444-6777 ($10 reservation fee) or www. recreation.gov ($9 reservation fee). Single sites are $22 per night; double sites are $44 per night. There is no fee for camping. A 14-day limit is enforced. Open May through October, weather permitting.

**Directions:** From Groveland, drive east on Highway 120 for about 15 miles to Forest Road 1N07/Cherry Lake Road. Turn left and drive 20 miles (narrow, curvy, steep in some spots) to Cottonwood Road/Forest Road 1N04. Turn left and drive one mile to the campground entrance road. Turn right and drive one mile to the campground.

**Contact:** Stanislaus National Forest, Groveland Ranger District, 209/962-7825, www.fs.usda.gov/stanislaus.

# 6 SWEETWATER

### Scenic rating: 4

near the South Fork of the Tuolumne River in Stanislaus National Forest

**Map 10.1, page 519**

This camp is at 3,000 feet elevation near the South Fork Tuolumne River, one of several camps along Highway 120 that provide a safety valve for campers who can't find space in Yosemite National Park to the east. Nearby, on the North Fork of the Tuolumne River, is a popular swimming area known as Rainbow Pools, with a waterfall and series of pools created by the river. White-water rafting and kayaking are available a few miles from this camp; a Forest Service permit is required.

This area still has some burned trees from the 2013 Rim Fire. Exercise caution when walking through burned areas, especially on windy days.

**Campsites, facilities:** There are 12 sites for tents or RVs up to 22 feet (no hookups). Picnic tables and fire grills are provided. Drinking water and vault toilets are available. Leashed pets are permitted.

**Reservations, fees:** Reservations are not accepted. Sites are $22 per night. A 14-day limit is enforced. Open April through October, weather permitting.

**Directions:** From Groveland, drive east on Highway 120 for about 15 miles (five miles past the Groveland District Office) to the campground on the left side of the road.

**Contact:** Stanislaus National Forest, Groveland Ranger District, 209/962-7825, www.fs.usda.gov/stanislaus.

# 7 DIMOND "O"

### Scenic rating: 7

in Stanislaus National Forest

**Map 10.1, page 519**

Dimond "O" is at 4,400 feet elevation on the

eastern side of Stanislaus National Forest—just two miles from the western border of Yosemite National Park. This area still has some burned trees from the 2013 Rim Fire. Exercise caution when walking through burned areas, especially on windy days.

**Campsites, facilities:** There are 38 sites for tents or RVs up to 22 feet (no hookups). Picnic tables and fire grills are provided. Drinking water and vault toilets are available. Some facilities are wheelchair-accessible. Leashed pets are permitted.

**Reservations, fees:** Reservations are accepted at 877/444-6777 ($10 reservation fee) or www.recreation.gov ($9 reservation fee). Single sites are $24 per night; double sites are $48 per night. Open April through October, weather permitting.

**Directions:** From Groveland, drive east on Highway 120 for 25 miles to Evergreen Road/Forest Road 12. Turn left on Evergreen Road and drive six miles to the campground.

**Contact:** Stanislaus National Forest, Groveland Ranger District, 209/962-7825, www.fs.usda.gov/stanislaus.

## 8 YOSEMITE LAKES

### Scenic rating: 6

on Tuolumne River at Groveland

**Map 10.1, page 519**

This is a 400-acre park at 3,600 feet elevation along the South Fork Tuolumne River in the Sierra foothills near Groveland. Its proximity to Yosemite National Park, just five miles from the west entrance station, makes it ideal for many. The park is an affiliate of Thousand Trails, whose facilities usually are open only to members, but in this case, it is open to the general public on a limited basis. It is a family-oriented park with a large variety of recreation options and seasonal organized activities. Fishing and swimming are popular, and the river is stocked with trout. A plus is 24-hour security.

**Campsites, facilities:** There are 20 sites with full hookups (30 amps) for RVs of any length and 25 sites for tents available to the public (more sites are available to Thousand Trails members only), as well as cabins, yurts, and a hostel. Picnic tables and fire rings are provided. Restrooms, drinking water, showers, flush toilets, fish-cleaning station, and coin laundry are available. A store, gas station, propane, and firewood are available. The park enforces an annual no-burn status: No ground fires or charcoal are permitted; only propane grills and approved spark-arrester fire pits are allowed. Kayak rentals, pedalboats, inner tubes, and bicycles are for rent. Some facilities are wheelchair-accessible. Leashed pets are permitted.

**Reservations, fees:** Reservations are accepted at 800/533-1001 or 209/962-0108. RV sites are $48 per night; tent sites are $39 per night. Credit cards are accepted. Open year-round, weather permitting.

**Directions:** Drive east on Highway 120 to Groveland. From Groveland, continue east for 18 miles to the entrance road (signed) for Yosemite Lakes on the right. Turn right and drive a short distance to the park.

**Contact:** Yosemite Lakes, 209/962-0121, www. stayatyosemite.com.

## 9 HODGDON MEADOW

### Scenic rating: 7

in Yosemite National Park

**Map 10.1, page 519**

Hodgdon Meadow is on the outskirts of Yosemite, just inside the park's borders at the Big Oak Flat (Highway 120) entrance station, at 4,900 feet in elevation. It is near a small feeder creek to the South Fork Tuolumne River. It is about a 20-minute drive on Highway 120 to a major junction, where a left turn takes you on Tioga Road and to Yosemite's high country, including Tuolumne Meadows, and where staying on Big Flat Road routes you toward Yosemite Valley (25 miles from the camp). Because of the presence of bears, use of bear boxes is required.

**Campsites, facilities:** There are 105 sites for tents or RVs up to 35 feet (no hookups) and four group sites for 13-30 people each (no trailers in group sites). Picnic tables, fire rings, and bear boxes (mandatory) are provided. Drinking water and flush toilets are available. Leashed pets are permitted in the campground but not in group camps or on trails.

**Reservations, fees:** Reservations are accepted and are required mid-April through mid-October at 877/444-6777 ($10 reservation fee) or www.recreation.gov ($9 reservation fee). Sites are $26 per night May through October, $18 the rest of the year, and the group campsite $50 per night, plus $30 park entrance fee per vehicle. Open year-round, except for group sites.

**Directions:** From Groveland, drive east on Highway 120 to the Big Oak Flat entrance station for Yosemite National Park. Just after passing the entrance station, turn left and drive a short distance to the campground on the right.

**Contact:** Yosemite National Park, 209/372-0200 for an automated menu of recorded information, www.nps.gov/yose.

## 10 CRANE FLAT

### Scenic rating: 6

near Tuolumne Grove of Big Trees in Yosemite National Park

**Map 10.1, page 519**

Crane Flat is within a five-minute drive of the Tuolumne Grove of Big Trees and to the Merced Grove to the west. This is the feature attraction in this part of Yosemite National Park, near the western border close to the Big Oak Flat Entrance Station (Highway 120). The elevation is 6,200 feet. Yosemite Valley is about a 25-minute drive away.

**Campsites, facilities:** There are 161 sites for tents or RVs up to 35 feet (no hookups). Picnic tables, fire rings, and bear boxes (mandatory) are provided. Drinking water and flush toilets are available. Groceries, propane gas, and a gas station are nearby. Some facilities are wheelchair-accessible. Leashed pets are allowed in the campground.

**Reservations, fees:** Reservations are required at 877/444-6777 ($10 reservation fee) or www.recreation.gov ($9 reservation fee). Sites are $26 per night, plus a $30 park entrance fee per vehicle. Open July through September, weather permitting.

**Directions:** From Groveland, drive east on Highway 120 to the Big Oak Flat entrance station for Yosemite National Park. After passing through the entrance station, drive about 10 miles to the campground entrance road on the right. Turn right and drive 0.5 mile to the campground.

**Contact:** Yosemite National Park, 209/372-0200 for an automated menu of recorded information, www.nps.gov/yose.

## 11 TAMARACK FLAT

### Scenic rating: 7

on Tamarack Creek in Yosemite National Park

**Map 10.1, page 519**

The road to this campground looks something like the surface of the moon. Then you arrive and find one of the few primitive drive-to camps in Yosemite National Park, at 6,300 feet elevation. From the trailhead at camp, you can link up with El Capitan Trail and then hike across Ribbon Meadow on up to the north valley rim at El Capitan, at 7,569 feet elevation. This is the largest single piece of granite in the world, and standing atop it for both the sensation and the divine view is a breathtaking experience. From camp, Yosemite Valley is 23 miles away.

**Campsites, facilities:** There are 52 sites for tents. RVs and trailers are not recommended. Picnic tables, fire rings, and bear boxes (mandatory) are provided. Vault toilets are available. No drinking water is available.

**Reservations, fees:** Reservations are not accepted. Sites are $12 per night, plus a $30 park entrance fee per vehicle. Open June through September.

**Directions:** From Merced, drive east on Highway 140 to the Arch Rock entrance station. Continue east to the Big Oak Flat Road junction (0.5 mile before entering Yosemite Valley). Turn left and drive 14 miles to Tioga Road. Turn right on Tioga Road and drive three miles to the campground entrance on the right side of the road. Turn right and drive 2.5 miles to the campground at the end of the road. Note that the access road is difficult; trailers and RVs are not advised.

**Contact:** Yosemite National Park, 209/372-0200 for an automated menu of recorded information, www.nps.gov/yose.

## 12 WHITE WOLF

### Scenic rating: 8

in Yosemite National Park

**Map 10.1, page 519**

This is one of Yosemite National Park's prime mountain camps for people who like to hike, either for great day hikes in the immediate area and beyond, or for overnight backpacking trips. The day hike to Lukens Lake is an easy two-mile trip, the payoff being this pretty little alpine lake set amid a meadow, pines, and granite. Just about everybody who camps at White Wolf makes the trip. Backpackers (wilderness permit required) can make the overnight trip into the Ten Lakes Basin, below Grand Mountain and Colby Mountain. Bears are common at this camp, and campers are required to secure food in the bear-proof lockers. The elevation is 8,000 feet.

**Campsites, facilities:** There are 74 sites for tents or RVs up to 27 feet (no hookups). Tent cabins are also available. Picnic tables, fire rings, and bear boxes (mandatory) are provided. Drinking water and flush toilets are available. Evening ranger programs are occasionally offered. A small store with a walk-up window and limited items is nearby. Leashed

pets are permitted in the campground but not on trails.

**Reservations, fees:** Reservations are not accepted. Sites are $18 per night, plus a $30 park entrance fee per vehicle. Open May to early September, weather permitting.

**Directions:** From Merced, drive east on Highway 140 to the Arch Rock entrance station. Continue east to the Big Oak Flat Road junction (0.5 mile before entering Yosemite Valley). Turn left and drive 14 miles to Tioga Road. Turn right and drive 15 miles to White Wolf Road on the left. Turn left and drive a mile to the campground entrance road on the right.

**Contact:** Yosemite National Park, 209/372-0200 for an automated menu of recorded information, www.nps.gov/yose.

## 13 YOSEMITE CREEK

### Scenic rating: 9

on Yosemite Creek in Yosemite National Park

**Map 10.1, page 519**          **BEST (**

This is the most remote drive-to camp in Yosemite National Park, a great alternative to camping in the valley or at Tuolumne Meadows, and the rough, curvy access road keeps many visitors away. It is set along Yosemite Creek at 7,659 feet elevation, with poor trout fishing but a trailhead for a spectacular hike. If you arrange a shuttle ride, you can make a great one-way trip down to the north side of the Yosemite Canyon rim, skirting past the top of Yosemite Falls (a side trip to Yosemite Point is a must!), then tackling the unbelievable descent into the valley, emerging at Camp 4 Walk-In. Note: The narrow entrance road is a remnant of "Old Tioga Road."

**Campsites, facilities:** There are 75 tent sites. RVs and trailers are not allowed. Picnic tables, fire grills, and bear boxes (mandatory) are provided. Vault toilets are available. There is no drinking water. Leashed pets are permitted.

**Reservations, fees:** Reservations are not accepted. Sites are $12 per night, plus a $30 park entrance fee per vehicle. A 14-day stay limit is enforced. Open mid-June through early September, weather permitting.

**Directions:** From Merced, drive east on Highway 140 to the Arch Rock entrance station. Continue east to the Big Oak Flat Road junction (0.5 mile before entering Yosemite Valley). Turn left and drive 14 miles to Tioga Road. Turn right and drive about 30 miles (just beyond the White Wolf turnoff on the left) to Yosemite Creek Campground Road on the right. Turn right and drive five miles to the campground at the end of the road. RVs and trailers are not recommended.

**Contact:** Yosemite National Park, 209/372-0200 for an automated menu of recorded information, www.nps.gov/yose.

## 14 PORCUPINE FLAT

🏞️ 🚐 ⛺

### Scenic rating: 6

near Yosemite Creek in Yosemite National Park

Map 10.1, page 519

Porcupine Flat, at 8,100 feet elevation, is southwest of Mount Hoffman, one of the prominent nearby peaks along Tioga Road in Yosemite National Park. The trailhead for a hike to May Lake, just below Mount Hoffman, is about five miles away on a signed turnoff on the north side of the road. Several little peaks above the lake offer hikers great views, including one of the back side of Half Dome.

**Campsites, facilities:** There are 52 sites for tents or RVs up to 24 feet (no hookups). There is limited RV space. Picnic tables, fire rings, and bear boxes (mandatory) are provided. Vault toilets are available. No drinking water is available.

**Reservations, fees:** Reservations are not accepted. Sites are $12 per night, plus a $30 park entrance fee per vehicle. Open mid-June through mid-October, weather permitting.

**Directions:** From Merced, drive east on Highway 140 to the Arch Rock entrance station.

Continue east to the Big Oak Flat Road junction (0.5 mile before entering Yosemite Valley). Turn left and drive 14 miles to Tioga Road. Turn right and drive about 25 miles to the campground on the left side of the road (16 miles west from Tuolumne Meadows).

**Contact:** Yosemite National Park, 209/372-0200 for an automated menu of recorded information, www.nps.gov/yose.

## 15 TUOLUMNE MEADOWS

🏞️ 🎣 🐕 🚐 ⛺

### Scenic rating: 8

in Yosemite National Park

Map 10.1, page 519                    BEST (

This is Yosemite's biggest camp, and for the variety of nearby adventures, it might also be the best. It is in the high country, at 8,600 feet, and can be used as a base camp for fishing, hiking, and horseback riding, or as a start-up point for a backpacking trip (wilderness permit required). This is one of the top trailheads in North America. There are two outstanding and easy day hikes from here, one heading north on the Pacific Crest Trail for the near-level walk to Tuolumne Falls and Glen Aulin, the other heading south up Lyell Fork (toward Donohue Pass), with good fishing for small brook trout. With a backpack (wilderness permit required), either route can be extended for as long as desired into remote and beautiful country. The campground is huge, and neighbors are guaranteed, but it is well wooded and feels somewhat secluded even with all the RVs and tents. There are lots of food-raiding bears in the area—use of bear boxes is required.

**Campsites, facilities:** There are 304 sites for tents or RVs up to 35 feet (no hookups), four horse camps, and seven group sites that can accommodate 30 people each. There are 25 hike-in sites available for backpackers (no parking is available for backpacker campsites, often reserved for those hiking the Pacific Crest Trail, for which a wilderness permit is required). Picnic tables, fire rings, and bear boxes (mandatory) are provided. Drinking water, flush toilets, and a dump station are available. Showers and groceries are nearby. Leashed pets are permitted, except in group sites, horse camps, and backpacker sites.

**Reservations, fees:** Reservations are accepted for half of the sites at 877/444-6777 ($10 reservation fee) or www.recreation.gov ($9 reservation fee); the remaining sites are first come, first served. Reservations are required for the group and horse camps. Tent and RV sites are $26 per night, walk-in (backpack) sites are $6 per night per person, horse campsites are $30 per night, and group sites are $50 per night, plus a $30 per vehicle park entrance fee. Open early June through late September, weather permitting.

**Directions:** From Merced, drive east on Highway 140 to the Arch Rock entrance station. Continue east to the Big Oak Flat Road junction (0.5 mile before entering Yosemite Valley). Turn left and drive 14 miles to Tioga Road. Turn right and drive 46 miles to the campground on the right side of the road.

From just south of Lee Vining at the junction of U.S. 395 and Highway 120, turn west and drive to the Tioga Pass entrance station for Yosemite National Park. Continue for about eight miles to the campground entrance on the left.

**Contact:** Yosemite National Park, 209/372-0200 for an automated menu of recorded information, www.nps.gov/yose.

## 16 CAMP 4

### Scenic rating: 8
in Yosemite Valley in Yosemite National Park

Map 10.1, page 519

The concept at Camp 4 was to provide a climber's bivouac near the base of El Capitan, and so it is. It has also worked as a walk-in alternative to drive-in camps that sometimes resemble combat zones. The sites are jammed together, and six people will be placed in your site, whether you know them or not. Regardless, the camp is in a great location, within walking distance of Yosemite Falls. It has a view of Leidig Meadow and the southern valley rim, with Sentinel Rock directly across the valley. A trail is routed from camp to Lower Yosemite Fall. In addition, the trailhead for Yosemite Falls Trail is a short distance away, a terrible, butt-kicking climb up Columbia Rock to the rim adjacent to the top of the falls, but providing one of the most incredible views in all the world. Insider's note: After originally being named Camp 4, the park once renamed this campground as "Sunnyside Walk-In." The name was switched back to the original, because climbers never stopped calling it Camp 4.

**Campsites, facilities:** There are 35 walk-in tent sites. Six people are placed in each campsite, regardless of the number of people in each party. Picnic tables, fire pits, and bear boxes (mandatory) are provided. Drinking water and flush toilets are available. A parking area, showers, groceries, and a coin laundry are nearby. No pets are allowed.

**Reservations, fees:** Reservations are not accepted. Sites are $6 per person per night, plus a $30 park entrance fee per vehicle. There is a seven-day limit during the summer. Open year-round.

**Directions:** From Merced, drive east on Highway 140 to the Arch Rock entrance station. Continue east to the Big Oak Flat Road junction (0.5 mile before entering Yosemite Valley). Continue into Yosemite Valley and drive past the chapel to a stop sign. Turn left, cross Sentinel Bridge, and drive one mile to another stop sign. Continue 1.5 miles and look for the large sign marking the parking area for Camp 4 Walk-In on the right (near the base of El Capitan).

**Contact:** Yosemite National Park, 209/372-0200 for an automated menu of recorded information, www.nps.gov/yose.

# HIKING THE JMT:
# TUOLUMNE MEADOWS TO YOSEMITE VALLEY

### 22 MILES ONE-WAY / 2 DAYS

The first glimpses of Yosemite Valley will seem like a privileged view into heaven after having hiked the entire John Muir Trail (JMT) from Mount Whitney. For hikers making only this 22-mile section, the rewards can seem just as profound. The trip starts at **Tuolumne Meadows,** where backpackers can buy a good cheap breakfast, obtain wilderness permits, and camp in a special area set aside for JMT hikers. When you take your first steps away from Tuolumne Meadows, resist the urge to rush to the finish line in order to close out a historic expedition. Instead, relax and enjoy the downhill glide, always remembering that you are in sacred land.

Compared to the rest of the JMT, this leg will come with far less strain, starting with a 3.1-mile tromp past Cathedral Lakes and requiring a 0.5-mile walk on a signed cutoff trail. If you can time it right, this area can make a great layover camp, with deep, emerald-green water and Cathedral Peak in the background. Beyond Cathedral Lakes, the trail makes a relatively short 500-foot climb over Cathedral Pass, skirts Tresidder Peak, and then descends through pristine Long Meadow. After passing Sunrise Trail Camp, a decent layover, the trail picks up little Sunrise Creek and follows it all the way down to Little Yosemite Valley, a popular trail camp. From Cathedral Lakes, it's 14.5 miles to the junction of Half Dome Trail and another 2.2 miles to Little Yosemite.

For JMT hikers, making the climb to the top of Half Dome is a must, even though it often means putting up with a parade of people and even delays waiting for the line to move at the climbing cable. The Half Dome climb starts with a steep hike for the first mile, followed by steep switchbacks across granite on good trail to the foot of Half Dome's back wall. Here you'll find climbing cables to aid your final 300-foot ascent, and as you go, you'll discover breathtaking views of Tenaya Canyon. This is considered one of the world's glamour hikes, and while it turns hiking into an act of faith, I have seen 8-year-olds and 70-year-olds make the cable climb. Adding the Half Dome side trip to the rest of the JMT leg will add a round-trip of 5.2 miles to your hike.

Because of its proximity to Half Dome, the **Little Yosemite Valley Trail Camp** is often crowded. From there, though, it's an easy five-mile hike downhill to Yosemite Valley. From Little Yosemite, the JMT is routed along the Merced River. In a mile, you'll reach Liberty Cap and, shortly later, Nevada Fall. Then down, down you go, with the trail often turning to giant granite steps, down past Emerald Pool and then to Vernal Fall, another spectacular waterfall. Since Vernal Fall is just 1.7 miles from the end of the trail, you'll start meeting lots of day hikers coming from the other direction, many gasping for breath as they make the uphill climb out of Yosemite Valley. Many will ask how far you've hiked; some may even want to take your photograph. It may feel a bit inane, but, hey, enjoy it. After all, you just finished the John Muir Trail, the greatest hiking trail in the world.

## **17** LOWER PINES

🚶 🚲 🏊 🎣 🐕 ♿ 🚐 ⛺

### Scenic rating: 9

in Yosemite Valley in Yosemite National Park

**Map 10.1, page 519**      **BEST** ☾

Lower Pines sits right along the Merced River, quite pretty, in the center of Yosemite Valley. Of course, the tents and RVs are jammed in quite close together. Within walking distance is the trail to Mirror Lake (a zoo on parade), as well as the trailhead at Happy Isles for the hike up to Vernal Fall and Nevada Fall. The park's shuttle bus picks up riders near the camp entrance.

**Campsites, facilities:** There are 60 sites for tents or RVs up to 40 feet, one double site for tents or RVs up to 40 feet, and two group camps for up to 12 people each (no hookups). Fire rings, picnic tables, and bear boxes (mandatory) are provided. Drinking water and flush toilets are available. A grocery store, coin laundry, propane gas, recycling center, dump station, and horse and bike rentals are nearby. Some facilities are wheelchair-accessible. Leashed pets are permitted.

**Reservations, fees:** Reservations are required at 877/444-6777 ($10 reservation fee) or www.recreation.gov ($9 reservation fee). Sites are $26 per night, and it's $36 per night for double or group sites, plus a $30 park entrance fee per vehicle. There is a seven-day limit during the summer. Open late March through October, weather permitting.

**Directions:** From Merced, drive east on Highway 140 to the Arch Rock entrance station. Continue east to the Big Oak Flat Road junction (0.5 mile before entering Yosemite Valley). Continue into Yosemite Valley and drive past Curry Village (on the right) to the campground entrance on the left side of the road (just before Clarks Bridge).

**Contact:** Yosemite National Park, 209/372-0200 for an automated menu of recorded information, www.nps.gov/yose.

## 18 UPPER PINES

### Scenic rating: 9

in Yosemite Valley in Yosemite National Park

**Map 10.1, page 519**    **BEST**

Of the campgrounds in Yosemite Valley, Upper Pines is the closest trailhead to paradise, providing you can get a campsite at the far south end of the camp. From here it is a short walk to Happy Isles Trailhead and with it the chance to hike to Vernal Fall on Mist Trail (steep) or beyond to Nevada Fall (very steep) at the foot of Liberty Cap. But crowded this camp is, and you'd better expect it. People come from all over the world to camp here. Sometimes it appears as if they are from other worlds as well. The elevation is 4,000 feet.

**Campsites, facilities:** There are 238 sites for tents or RVs up to 35 feet (no hookups). Fire rings, picnic tables, and bear boxes

(mandatory) are provided. Drinking water, flush toilets, and dump station are available. A grocery store, coin laundry, propane gas, recycling center, and horse and bike rentals are nearby. Three sites provide wheelchair access. Leashed pets are permitted in the campgrounds but not on trails.

**Reservations, fees:** Reservations are required mid-March through November at 877/444-6777 ($10 reservation fee) or www.recreation.gov ($9 reservation fee). Sites are first-come, first-served December to mid-March. Sites are $26 per night, plus a $30 park entrance fee per vehicle. There is a seven-day limit during the summer. Open year-round.

**Directions:** From Merced, drive east on Highway 140 to the Arch Rock entrance station. Continue east to the Big Oak Flat Road junction (0.5 mile before entering Yosemite Valley). Continue into Yosemite Valley and drive past Curry Village (on the right) to the campground entrance on the right side of the road (just before Clarks Bridge).

**Contact:** Yosemite National Park, 209/372-0200 for an automated menu of recorded information, www.nps.gov/yose.

## 19 NORTH PINES

### Scenic rating: 9

in Yosemite Valley in Yosemite National Park

**Map 10.1, page 519**

North Pines is set along the Merced River. A trail out of camp heads east and links with the paved road/trail to Mirror Lake, a virtual parade of people. If you continue hiking past Mirror Lake, you will get astounding views of Half Dome and then leave the masses behind as you enter Tenaya Canyon. The elevation is 4,000 feet.

**Campsites, facilities:** There are 81 sites for tents or RVs up to 40 feet (no hookups). Picnic tables, fire grills, and bear boxes (mandatory) are provided. Drinking water, flush toilets, and a dump station are available. A grocery store, coin laundry, recycling center, propane gas, and horse and bike rentals are nearby. Some facilities are wheelchair-accessible. Leashed pets are allowed.

**Reservations, fees:** Reservations are required at 877/444-6777 ($10 reservation fee) or www.recreation.gov ($9 reservation fee). Sites are $26 per night, plus a $30 park entrance fee per vehicle. Open April through early November, weather permitting.

**Directions:** From Merced, drive east on Highway 140 to the Arch Rock entrance station. Continue east to the Big Oak Flat Road junction (0.5 mile before entering Yosemite Valley). Continue into Yosemite Valley, drive past Curry Village (on the right), continue past Upper and Lower Pines Campgrounds, and drive over Clarks Bridge to a junction at the horse stables. Turn left at the horse stables and drive a short distance to the campground on the right.

**Contact:** Yosemite National Park, 209/372-0200 for an automated menu of recorded information, www.nps.gov/yose.

## 20 BRIDALVEIL CREEK

### Scenic rating: 10

near Glacier Point in Yosemite National Park

**Map 10.1, page 519**

There may be no better view in the world than the one from Glacier Point, looking down into Yosemite Valley, where Half Dome stands like nature's perfect sculpture. Then there are the perfect views of Yosemite Fall, Nevada Fall, Vernal Fall, and several hundred square miles of Yosemite's wilderness backcountry. This is the closest camp to Glacier Point's drive-to vantage point, but it is also the closest camp to the best day hikes in the entire park. Along Glacier Point Road are trailheads to Sentinel Dome (incredible view of Yosemite Fall) and Taft Point (breathtaking drop, incredible view of El Capitan), and McGurk Meadow (one of the most pristine spots on Earth). At 7,200 feet,

the camp is more than 3,000 feet higher than Yosemite Valley. A good day hike out of camp leads you to Ostrander Lake, just below Horse Ridge.

**Campsites, facilities:** There are 110 sites for tents or RVs up to 35 feet (no hookups), three equestrian sites, and two group sites for 13-30 people each. Picnic tables, fire rings, and bear boxes (mandatory) are provided. Drinking water and flush toilets are available. Leashed pets are permitted, except in group sites.

**Reservations, fees:** Reservations are not accepted for individual sites, but they are required for equestrian sites and group sites at 800/444-6777 ($10 reservation fee) or www.recreation.gov ($9 reservation fee). Sites are $18 per night, equestrian sites are $30 per night, and group sites are $50 per night, plus a $30 park entrance fee per vehicle. A 14-day stay limit is enforced. Open mid-June through early September, weather permitting.

**Directions:** From Merced, drive east on Highway 140 to the Arch Rock entrance station. Continue east (past Big Oak Flat Road junction) to the junction with Wawona Road/Highway 41 (just before Yosemite Valley). Turn right on Highway 41/Wawona Road and drive about 10 miles to Glacier Point Road. Turn left on Glacier Point Road and drive about five miles (a few miles past Badger Pass Ski Area) to Peregoy Meadow and the campground access road on the right. Turn right and drive a short distance to the campground.

**Contact:** Yosemite National Park, 209/372-0200 for an automated menu of recorded information, www.nps.gov/yose.

## 21 MERCED RIVER RECREATION AREA

### Scenic rating: 8

on the Merced River east of Briceburg

**Map 10.1, page 519**     **BEST (**

What a spot: The campsites are along one of the prettiest sections of the Merced River, where you can enjoy great hiking, swimming, rafting, kayaking, and fishing, all on the same day. There are three campgrounds: McCabe Flat, Willow Placer, and Railroad Flat. The access road out of camp leads downstream to the Yosemite Railroad Grade, which has been converted into a great trail. One of the best wildflower blooms anywhere in the Sierra foothills is near here at Red Hills (just outside Chinese Camp), usually best in April. If you don't mind the cold water, swimming in the Merced River's pools can provide relief from summer heat. Evening fly-fishing is good in many of the same spots through July. But the true attraction on the Merced River is rafting and kayaking. An extraordinarily long stretch of river, 29 miles, can be run from the put-in at Red Bud Day-Use Area to the take-out at Bagby. A number of white-water guide companies work this stretch of river.

**Campsites, facilities:** There are 23 walk-in tent sites, nine sites for tents or RVs up to 18 feet (no hookups), and one large group site at Willow Placer campground. Picnic tables, fire grills, and garbage collection are provided. Vault and pit toilets are available. No drinking water is available at the campsites (drinking water is available across from the Briceburg Bridge). Supplies are available in Mariposa. Some facilities are wheelchair-accessible. Leashed pets are permitted.

**Reservations, fees:** Reservations are not accepted. Sites are $10 per night. There is a 14-day limit. Open April through October, weather permitting.

**Directions:** From Merced, turn east on Highway 140 and drive 40 miles to Mariposa. Continue another 15 miles to Briceburg and the Briceburg Visitor Center on the left. Turn left at a road that is signed "BLM Camping Areas" (the road remains paved for about 150 yards). Drive over the Briceburg suspension bridge and turn left, traveling downstream on the road, parallel to the river. Drive 2.5 miles to McCabe Flat, 3.8 miles to Willow Placer, and 4.8 miles to Railroad Flat.

**Contact:** Bureau of Land Management,

Mother Lode Field Office, 916/941-3101, www.blm.gov/ca.

## 22 YOSEMITE WEST-MARIPOSA KOA

### Scenic rating: 7

near Mariposa

**Map 10.1, page 519**

A little duck pond, a swimming pool, and proximity to Yosemite National Park make this one a winner. A shuttle bus service (fee) to the national park is a great bonus. The RV sites are lined up along the entrance road. A 10pm "quiet time" helps ensure a good night's sleep. It's a one-hour drive to Yosemite Valley, and your best bet is to get there early to enjoy the spectacular beauty before the park is packed with people.

**Campsites, facilities:** There are 49 sites with full or partial hookups (30 and 50 amps) for RVs up to 40 feet, 26 tent sites, 12 cabins, and three lodges. Picnic tables and barbecues are provided; no wood fires are allowed. Restrooms with showers, dump station, Wi-Fi, telephone access, coin laundry, convenience store, propane gas, seasonal swimming pool, train caboose with arcade, and playground are available. Some facilities are wheelchair-accessible. Leashed pets are permitted in RV and tent sites only, with certain restrictions.

**Reservations, fees:** Reservations are accepted at 800/562-9391. RV sites are $58-67 per night, tent sites are $40 per night, plus $6 per person per night for more than two people and $2 per pet per night. Call for cabin and lodge prices. Some credit cards are accepted. Open March through October.

**Directions:** From Merced, drive east on Highway 140 to Mariposa. Continue on Highway 140 for seven miles to Midpines and the campground entrance on the left at 6323 Highway 140.

**Contact:** Yosemite-Mariposa KOA, 209/966-2201, www.yosemitekoa.com.

## 23 JERSEYDALE

🚶 🐴 5% 🚐 ⛺

### Scenic rating: 5

in Sierra National Forest

**Map 10.1, page 519**

This little camp gets overlooked by many visitors shut out of nearby Yosemite National Park simply because they don't realize it exists. Jerseydale is southwest of the national park in Sierra National Forest, with two good side trips nearby. If you continue north on Jerseydale Road to its end (about six miles), you will come to a Forest Service road/trailhead that provides access east along a portion of the South Fork of the Merced River, where there is often good fishing, swimming, and rafting. In addition, a dirt road from the camp is routed east for many miles into the Chowchilla Mountains.

**Campsites, facilities:** There are 10 sites for tents or RVs up to 24 feet (no hookups). Picnic tables and fire grills are provided. Vault toilets are available. Water is available but must be boiled before drinking. A few hitching posts are available and horses are permitted at these camps. Leashed pets are permitted.

**Reservations, fees:** Reservations are not accepted. There is no fee for camping. Open May through November.

**Directions:** From Mariposa, drive northeast on Highway 140 for about five miles to Triangle Road (if you reach Midpines, you have gone 1.5 miles too far). Turn right on Triangle Road and drive about six miles to Darrah and Jerseydale Road. Turn left and drive three miles to the campground on the left side of the road (adjacent to the Jerseydale Ranger Station).

**Contact:** Sierra National Forest, Bass Lake Ranger District, 559/877-2218, www.fs.usda.gov/sierra.

## 24 WAWONA

🚶 🏊 🛶 🐴 ♿ 🚐 ⛺

### Scenic rating: 9

on the South Fork of the Merced River in Yosemite National Park

**Map 10.1, page 519**

Wawona is an attractive alternative to the packed camps in Yosemite Valley, providing you don't mind the relatively long drives to the best destinations. The camp is pretty, set along the South Fork of the Merced River, with the sites more spacious than at most other drive-to camps in the park. The nearest attraction is the Mariposa Grove of Giant Sequoias, but get your visit in by 9am, because after that it turns into a zoo, complete with shuttle train. The best nearby hike is a strenuous 10-mile round-trip to Chilnualna Falls, the prettiest sight in the southern region of the park; the trailhead is at the east end of Chilnualna Road in North Wawona. It's a 45-minute drive to either Glacier Point or Yosemite Valley.

**Campsites, facilities:** There are 93 sites for tents or RVs up to 35 feet (no hookups), one group tent site for 13-30 people each, and two horse camps. Picnic tables, fire grills, and bear boxes (mandatory) are provided. Drinking water and flush toilets are available. There are some stock-handling facilities for camping with pack animals; call for further information. A grocery store, dump station, propane gas, gas station, post office, restaurant, and seasonal horseback-riding facilities are nearby. Some facilities are wheelchair-accessible. Leashed pets are permitted but not in group sites, in horse camps, or on trails.

**Reservations, fees:** From mid-April through September, reservations are required at 877/444-6777 ($10 reservation fee) or www.recreation.gov ($9 reservation fee). Online reservations are not accepted for horse sites. Reservations are not needed from October to April. Sites are $26 per night or $18 per night in the off-season, horse campsites are $30 per night, and the group site is $50 per night, plus a $30 park entrance fee is per vehicle. A seven-day camping limit is enforced during the summer. Open year-round, although the horse camp is open April through October only.

**Directions:** From Oakhurst, drive north on Highway 41 to the Wawona entrance of Yosemite National Park. Continue north on Highway 41 past Wawona (golf course on the left) and drive one mile to the campground entrance on the left.

**Contact:** Yosemite National Park, 209/372-0200 for an automated menu of recorded information, www.nps.gov/yose.

## 25 SUMMERDALE

### Scenic rating: 7
on the South Fork of the Merced River in Sierra National Forest

**Map 10.1, page 519**

You can't get much closer to Yosemite National Park. This camp is within a mile of the Wawona entrance to Yosemite, about a five-minute drive to the Mariposa Grove. If you don't mind its proximity to the highway, this is a pretty spot in its own right, set along Big Creek, a feeder stream to the South Fork Merced River. Some good swimming holes are in this area. The elevation is 5,000 feet.

**Campsites, facilities:** There are 29 sites for tents or RVs up to 24 feet (no hookups). Picnic tables and fire grills are provided. Vault toilets are available. Water is available but must be boiled before drinking. A grocery store is nearby (within one mile). Some facilities are wheelchair-accessible. Leashed pets are permitted.

**Reservations, fees:** Reservations are accepted at 877/444-6777 ($10 reservation fee) or www.recreation.gov ($9 reservation fee). Sites are $30 per night, plus $7 per night for each additional vehicle. Open May through September, weather permitting.

**Directions:** From Oakhurst, drive north on Highway 41 to Fish Camp and continue for one mile to the campground entrance on the left side of the road.

**Contact:** Sierra National Forest, Bass Lake Ranger District, 559/877-2218, www.fs.usda.gov/sierra.

## 26 BIG SANDY

### Scenic rating: 7
on Big Creek in Sierra National Forest

**Map 10.1, page 519**

It's only six miles from the highway and just eight miles from the southern entrance to Yosemite National Park. So when Wawona is full in southern Yosemite, this camp provides a much-needed option. It's a pretty camp on Big Creek in the Sierra National Forest, one of two camps in the immediate area. The elevation is 5,800 feet. If you head into Yosemite for the tour of giant sequoias in Wawona, get there early, by 7:30 or 8:30am, when the grove is still quiet and cool, and you will have the old, mammoth trees practically to yourself.

**Campsites, facilities:** There are 18 sites for tents or RVs up to 20 feet (no hookups). Picnic tables and fire grills are provided. Vault toilets are available. No drinking water is available. Leashed pets are permitted.

**Reservations, fees:** Reservations are not accepted. Single sites are $26.22 per night, double sites are $48 per night, and it's $7 per night for each additional vehicle. Open May through September, weather permitting.

**Directions:** From Oakhurst drive north on Highway 41 for 15 miles to Forest Road 6S07 (one mile before reaching Marriotts). Turn right on Forest Road 6S07 and drive about six miles (a slow, rough road) to the camp.

**Contact:** Sierra National Forest, Bass Lake Ranger District, 559/877-2218, www.fs.usda.gov/sierra.

## 27 FRESNO DOME

### Scenic rating: 7
on Big Creek in Sierra National Forest

**Map 10.1, page 519**

This camp is named after nearby Fresno Dome to the east, at 7,540 feet elevation the dominating feature in the surrounding landscape. The trailhead for a mile hike to its top is two miles curving down the road to the east. This camp is at 6,400 feet on Big Creek in Sierra National Forest, a good option to nearby Yosemite National Park.

**Campsites, facilities:** There are 15 sites for tents or RVs up to 20 feet (no hookups). Picnic tables and fire grills are provided. Vault toilets are available. No drinking water is available. Garbage service is located near the entrance to the campground. Leashed pets are permitted.

**Reservations, fees:** Reservations are not accepted. Single sites are $26.22 per night, double sites are $48 per night, and it's $7 per night for each additional vehicle. A 14-day limit is enforced. Open June through mid-October, weather permitting.

**Directions:** From Oakhurst, drive north on Highway 41 approximately five miles to Sky Ranch Road/Forest Road 6S10. Turn right and drive 12 miles to the campground on the left.

**Contact:** Sierra National Forest, Bass Lake Ranger District, 559/877-2218, www.fs.usda. gov/sierra.

## 28 NELDER GROVE

### Scenic rating: 7
in Sierra National Forest

**Map 10.1, page 519**

Nelder Grove is a primitive spot, also pretty, yet it is a camp that is often overlooked. It is set amid the Nelder Grove of giant sequoias, the majestic mountain redwoods. There are two interpretive trails, each about a two-mile walk. Since the southern entrance to Yosemite National Park is just 10 miles away, Nelder Grove is overshadowed by Yosemite's Wawona Grove. The elevation is 5,300 feet.

**Campsites, facilities:** There are seven sites for tents or RVs up to 20 feet (no hookups). Picnic tables and fire grills are provided. Vault toilets are available. No drinking water is available. Garbage must be packed out. Leashed pets are permitted.

**Reservations, fees:** Reservations are not accepted. There is no fee for camping. Open May through October, weather permitting.

**Directions:** From Fresno, drive north on Highway 41 for 46 miles to the town of Oakhurst. Continue north on Highway 41 for five miles to Sky Ranch Road/Forest Road 6S10. Turn right (northeast) and drive about eight miles to Forest Road 6S47Y. Turn left and drive a short distance to the campground.

**Contact:** Sierra National Forest, Bass Lake Ranger District, 559/877-2218, www.fs.usda. gov/sierra.

## 29 KELTY MEADOW AND EQUESTRIAN CAMP

### Scenic rating: 6
on Willow Creek in Sierra National Forest

**Map 10.1, page 519**

This primitive campground is often used by campers with horses. It is at Kelty Meadow by Willow Creek. Side-trip options feature nearby Fresno Dome, the Nelder Grove of giant sequoias, and, of course, the southern entrance to nearby Yosemite National Park. The elevation is 5,800 feet.

**Campsites, facilities:** There are 11 sites for tents or RVs up to 20 feet. Fire grills and picnic tables are provided. Vault toilets and hitching posts are available. No drinking water is available. Garbage service is located near the entrance to the campground. Leashed pets are permitted.

**Reservations, fees:** Reservations are required at 877/444-6777 ($10 reservation fee) or www.

recreation.gov ($9 reservation fee). Single sites are $24-48 per night, plus $7 per night for each additional vehicle. There is a two-night minimum stay on weekends and a three-night minimum on holidays. Open June through September, weather permitting.

**Directions:** From Oakhurst on Highway 41, drive five miles north to Sky Ranch Road/Forest Road 6S10. Turn left (northeast) and drive approximately 10 miles to the campground.

**Contact:** Sierra National Forest, Bass Lake Ranger District, 559/877-2218, www.fs.usda. gov/sierra.

## 30 SOQUEL

### Scenic rating: 7

on the North Fork of Willow Creek in Sierra National Forest

**Map 10.1, page 519**

Soquel is at 5,400 feet elevation on the North Fork of Willow Creek, an alternative to nearby Grey's Mountain in Sierra National Forest. When the camps are filled at Bass Lake, these two camps provide overflow areas as well as more primitive settings for those who are looking for more of a wilderness experience.

**Campsites, facilities:** There are 11 sites for tents or RVs up to 20 feet (no hookups). Picnic tables and fire grills are provided. Vault toilets are available. There is no drinking water. Leashed pets are permitted.

**Reservations, fees:** Reservations are accepted at 877/444-6777 ($10 reservation fee) or www. recreation.gov ($9 reservation fee). Single sites are $23.62 per night, plus $7 per night for each additional vehicle. Open May through October, weather permitting.

**Directions:** From Fresno, drive north on Highway 41 for 46 miles to the town of Oakhurst. Continue north on Highway 41 for five miles to Sky Ranch Road/Forest Road 6S10. Turn right (east) and drive approximately five miles to Forest Road 6S40. Turn right and drive about 0.75 mile to the campground.

**Contact:** Sierra National Forest, Bass Lake Ranger District, 559/877-2218, www.fs.usda. gov/sierra.

## 31 GREY'S MOUNTAIN

### Scenic rating: 7

on Willow Creek in Sierra National Forest

**Map 10.1, page 519**

This is a small, primitive campground to keep in mind when all the campgrounds are filled at nearby Bass Lake. It is one of a series of campgrounds on Willow Creek. The elevation is 5,400 feet, just below Sivels Mountain to the east at 5,813 feet.

**Campsites, facilities:** There are 26 sites for tents or RVs up to 20 feet (no hookups). Picnic tables and fire grills are provided. Vault toilets are available. No drinking water is available. Leashed pets are permitted.

**Reservations, fees:** Reservations are not accepted. Single sites are $26.22 per night, double sites are $52.54 per night, and it's $7 per night for each additional vehicle. Open May through November, weather permitting.

**Directions:** From Oakhurst, drive north on Highway 41 for approximately five miles to Sky Ranch Road/Forest Road 6S10. Turn right and drive five miles to Forest Road 6S40. Turn right and drive 0.75 mile to Forest Road 6S08 and the camp.

**Contact:** Sierra National Forest, Bass Lake Ranger District, 559/877-2218, www.fs.usda. gov/sierra.

## 32 TEXAS FLAT GROUP CAMP

### Scenic rating: 5

on the North Fork of Willow Creek in Sierra National Forest

**Map 10.1, page 519**

If you are on your honeymoon, this definitely

ain't the place to be. Unless you like the smell of horses, that is. It's a pretty enough spot along the North Fork of Willow Creek, but the camp is primitive and designed for groups with horses. This camp is 15 miles from the south entrance of Yosemite National Park and 15 miles north of Bass Lake. The elevation is 5,400 feet.

**Campsites, facilities:** There are four group sites for tents or RVs up to 20 feet (no hookups) that can accommodate up to 30 people each. Picnic tables and fire grills are provided. Vault toilets and a corral are available. There is no drinking water. Leashed pets are permitted.

**Reservations, fees:** Reservations are accepted at 877/444-6777 ($10 reservation fee) or www.recreation.gov ($9 reservation fee). Sites are $88-133.20 per night. A 14-day limit is enforced. Open June through November.

**Directions:** From Fresno, drive about 52 miles north on Highway 41 to Sky Ranch Road/County Road 632. Turn right (east) on Sky Ranch Road/Forest Road 6S10 and drive approximately five miles to Forest Road 6S40. Turn right and drive about 0.75 mile to Forest Road 6S08. Turn left and drive 2.5 miles to Forest Road 6S38 and the campground.

**Contact:** Sierra National Forest, Bass Lake Ranger District, 559/877-2218, www.fs.usda.gov/sierra.

## 33 UPPER CHIQUITO

### Scenic rating: 7

on Chiquito Creek in Sierra National Forest

**Map 10.1, page 519**

Upper Chiquito is at 6,800 feet elevation on a major access road to Sierra National Forest and the western region of the Ansel Adams Wilderness, about 15 miles to the east. The camp is on Upper Chiquito Creek. About a mile down the road (southwest) is a Forest Service spur road (turn north) that provides access to a trail that meanders up Chiquito Creek for three miles to gorgeous Chiquita Lake (another route

with a longer drive and shorter hike is available out of Fresno Dome).

**Campsites, facilities:** There are 20 sites for tents or RVs up to 20 feet (no hookups). Picnic tables and fire rings are provided. Vault toilets are available. No drinking water is available. Garbage service is located at the entrance to the campground. Leashed pets are permitted.

**Reservations, fees:** Reservations are not accepted. There is no fee for camping. Open July through October, weather permitting.

**Directions:** From Fresno, drive north on Highway 41 for 50 miles to Yosemite Forks and County Road 222. Turn right on County Road 222 (keeping to the right at each of two Y intersections) and drive six miles to Pines Village and Beasore Road. Turn left onto Beasore Road and drive 16 miles to the campground.

**Contact:** Sierra National Forest, Bass Lake Ranger District, 559/877-2218, www.fs.usda.gov/sierra.

## 34 CLOVER MEADOW

### Scenic rating: 8

in Sierra National Forest

**Map 10.1, page 519**

This is one of two excellent jumping-off camps in the area for backpackers; the other is Granite Creek. The camp, at 7,000 feet elevation, is adjacent to the Clover Meadow Ranger Station, where backcountry information is available. While a trail is available from camp heading east into the Ansel Adams Wilderness, most hikers drive about three miles farther northeast on Minarets Road to a trailhead for a five-mile hike to Cora Lakes. Bring mosquito repellent.

**Campsites, facilities:** There are seven sites for tents or RVs up to 20 feet (no hookups). Picnic tables and fire rings are provided. Drinking water and vault toilets are available. Garbage must be packed out. Leashed pets are permitted.

**Reservations, fees:** Reservations are not

accepted. There is no fee for camping. Open June through October, weather permitting.

**Directions:** From Fresno, drive north on Highway 41 for about 25 miles to North Fork Road/County Road 200. Turn right and drive northeast for 17.5 miles to Auberry Road/County Road 222. Turn left (north) and drive one mile to the town of North Fork and Mammoth Pool Road. Turn right and drive 1.5 miles to County Road 225 (still Mammoth Pool Road). Turn right and drive (the road eventually becomes Minarets Road) to the junction with Forest Road 4S81. Bear left (north) on Forest Road 4S81 and drive to the campground entrance road. Bear left (signed "Clover Meadow") and drive to the campground, adjacent to the Clover Meadow Ranger Station. The total distance from North Fork to the entrance road is about 63 miles; it's 20 miles north of the well-signed Mammoth Pool Reservoir on Minarets Road.

**Contact:** Sierra National Forest, Bass Lake Ranger District, 559/877-2218, www.fs.usda.gov/sierra.

## 35 GRANITE CREEK AND EQUESTRIAN CAMP

### Scenic rating: 6

in Sierra National Forest

**Map 10.1, page 519**

This camp is a good jumping-off point for backpackers since a trail from camp leads north for five miles to Cora Lakes in the Ansel Adams Wilderness, with the option of continuing to more remote wilderness. In addition, the upper half of this campground is available for equestrians. Note that nearby Clover Meadow camp (see listing in this chapter) may be more desirable because it has both drinking water to tank up your canteens and a ranger station to obtain the latest trail information. The elevation is 6,900 feet.

**Campsites, facilities:** There are 14 sites for tents or RVs up to 20 feet (no hookups). Picnic

tables and fire rings are provided. Vault toilets are available. A horse corral is in the upper loop. No drinking water is available. Garbage must be packed out. Leashed pets are permitted.

**Reservations, fees:** Reservations are not accepted. There is no fee for camping. Open June through October, weather permitting.

**Directions:** From Fresno, drive north on Highway 41 for about 25 miles to North Fork Road/County Road 200. Turn right and drive northeast for 17.5 miles to Auberry Road/County Road 222. Turn left (north) and drive one mile to the town of North Fork and Mammoth Pool Road. Turn right and drive 1.5 miles to County Road 225 (still Mammoth Pool Road). Turn right and drive (the road eventually becomes Minarets Road) to the junction with Forest Road 4S81. Bear left (north) on Forest Road 4S81 and drive to the campground entrance road. Turn left (signed "Granite Creek") and drive 3.5 miles to the campground. (The total distance from North Fork to the entrance road is about 66.5 miles; it's 23.5 miles north of Mammoth Pool Reservoir on the well-signed Minarets Road.)

**Contact:** Sierra National Forest, Bass Lake Ranger District, 559/877-2218, www.fs.usda.gov/sierra.

## 36 BUCKEYE

### Scenic rating: 8

near Buckeye Creek in Humboldt-Toiyabe National Forest

**Map 10.1, page 519**

Here's a little secret: A two-mile hike out of camp heads to the undeveloped Buckeye Hot Springs. That is what inspires campers to bypass the fishing at nearby Robinson Creek (three miles away) and Twin Lakes (six miles away). The camp feels remote and primitive, set at 7,000 feet elevation on the eastern slope of the Sierra near Buckeye Creek. Another secret is that rainbow trout are planted at the little bridge that crosses Buckeye Creek near the campground. A trail starts near camp and travels through Buckeye Canyon and into the Hoover Wilderness.

**Campsites, facilities:** There are 68 sites for tents or RVs up to 35 feet (no hookups). Picnic tables and fire grills are provided. Vault and flush toilets are available. There is no drinking water. Some facilities are wheelchair-accessible. Leashed pets are permitted.

**Reservations, fees:** Reservations are not accepted. Sites are $18 per night, plus $6 per night for each additional vehicle. Open May to mid-October, weather permitting.

**Directions:** On U.S. 395, drive to Bridgeport and the junction with Twin Lakes Road. Turn west and drive seven miles to Buckeye Road. Turn right (north) on Buckeye Road (dirt, often impassable when wet) and drive 3.5 miles to the campground.

**Contact:** Humboldt-Toiyabe National Forest, Bridgeport Ranger District, 760/932-7070, www.fs.usda.gov/htnf.

## 37 WILLOW SPRINGS MOTEL AND RV PARK

### Scenic rating: 6

near Bridgeport

**Map 10.1, page 519**

Willow Springs RV Park is set at 6,800 feet elevation along U.S. 395, which runs along the eastern Sierra from Carson City south to Bishop and beyond to Lone Pine. The park is one mile from the turnoff to Bodie ghost town. A nice touch to the place is a central campfire that has been in place for more than 50 years. The country is stark here on the edge of the high Nevada desert, but there are many side trips that give the area life. The most popular destinations are to the nearby south: Mono Lake, with its tufa towers and incredible populations of breeding gulls and waterfowl, and the Bodie ghost town. For trout fishing, there's Bridgeport Reservoir to the north (good trolling) and downstream to

the East Walker River (fly-fishing), both excellent destinations, as well as Twin Lakes to the west (huge brown trout).

**Campsites, facilities:** There are 25 sites with full hookups (30 amps) for RVs of any length. A motel is also available. Picnic tables are provided. Restrooms with showers, coin laundry, and campfires are sometimes available. A restaurant is within walking distance. Leashed pets are permitted.

**Reservations, fees:** Reservations are accepted. Sites are $40 per night, plus $5 per person per night for more than two people. Open May through October.

**Directions:** From Bridgeport on U.S. 395, drive five miles south to the park, which is on the east side of the highway.

**Contact:** Willow Springs Motel and RV Park, 760/932-7725, www.willowspringsbridgeport.com.

## 38 HONEYMOON FLAT

### Scenic rating: 8

on Robinson Creek in Humboldt-Toiyabe National Forest

**Map 10.1, page 519**

This camp beside Robinson Creek at 7,000 feet elevation sits in the transition zone between the Sierra Nevada range to the west and the high desert to the east. It is easy to reach on the access road to Twin Lakes, only three miles farther. The lake is famous for occasional huge brown trout. However, the fishing at Robinson Creek is also often quite good, thanks to large numbers of trout planted each year.

**Campsites, facilities:** There are 35 sites for tents or RVs up to 35 feet (no hookups). Picnic tables, fire grills, and bear boxes and are provided. Drinking water and vault toilets are available. Some facilities are wheelchair-accessible. Leashed pets are permitted.

**Reservations, fees:** Reservations are accepted for 10 sites at 877/444-6777 ($10 reservation fee) or www.recreation.gov ($9 reservation fee).

Sites are $18 per night, double sites are $40 per night, and it's $6 per night for each additional vehicle. Open mid-April through September.

**Directions:** On U.S. 395, drive to Bridgeport and the junction with Twin Lakes Road. Turn west and drive eight miles to the campground.

**Contact:** Humboldt-Toiyabe National Forest, Bridgeport Ranger District, 760/932-7070, www.fs.usda.gov/htnf or www.westrekservices.com.

## 39 PAHA

### Scenic rating: 8
near Twin Lakes in Humboldt-Toiyabe National Forest

**Map 10.1, page 519**

This is one in a series of camps near Robinson Creek and within close range of Twin Lakes. The elevation at the camp is 7,000 feet. (See the Lower Twin Lake and Honeymoon Flat listings in this chapter for more information.)

**Campsites, facilities:** There are 22 sites for tents or RVs up to 35 feet (no hookups) and one yurt. Picnic tables and fire grills are provided. Drinking water, flush toilets, and garbage bins are available. Two boat launches, a store, coin showers, and a coin laundry are available at Twin Lakes Resort. Some facilities are wheelchair-accessible. Leashed pets are permitted.

**Reservations, fees:** Reservations are accepted at 877/444-6777 ($10 reservation fee) or www.recreation.gov ($9 reservation fee). Sites are $22 per night, double sites are $40 per night, and it's $6 per night for each additional vehicle. The yurt is $100 per night with a two-night minimum; it's $45 for each additional night or $250 per week. Open May through October, weather permitting.

**Directions:** On U.S. 395, drive to Bridgeport and the junction with Twin Lakes Road. Turn west and drive 10 miles to the campground.

**Contact:** Humboldt-Toiyabe National Forest, Bridgeport Ranger District, 760/932-7070, www.fs.usda.gov/htnf or www.westrekservices.com.

## 40 ROBINSON CREEK: NORTH & SOUTH

### Scenic rating: 9
near Twin Lakes in Humboldt-Toiyabe National Forest

**Map 10.1, page 519**

This campground, one of a series in the area, is set at 7,000 feet elevation on Robinson Creek, not far from Twin Lakes. The campground is divided into two areas, North and South. (For recreation options, see the Lower Twin Lake and Honeymoon Flat listings in this chapter.)

**Campsites, facilities:** The South campground has 26 sites and the North campground has eight sites; all are for tents or RVs up to 35 feet (no hookups). Picnic tables, fire rings, and bear boxes (mandatory) are provided. Drinking water and flush and vault toilets are available. Boat launches, a store, coin laundry, and coin showers are nearby at Twin Lakes Resort. An amphitheater is nearby. Some facilities are wheelchair-accessible. Leashed pets are permitted.

**Reservations, fees:** Reservations are accepted at 877/444-6777 ($10 reservation fee) or www.recreation.gov ($9 reservation fee). Sites are $23 per night, double sites are $42 per night, and it's $6 per night for each additional vehicle. Open mid-April through October, weather permitting. The North campground closes two weeks after the South campground closes.

**Directions:** On U.S. 395, drive to Bridgeport and the junction with Twin Lakes Road. Turn west and drive 10 miles to the campground.

**Contact:** Humboldt-Toiyabe National Forest, Bridgeport Ranger District, 760/932-7070, www.fs.usda.gov/htnf or www.westrekservices.com.

## 41 CRAGS CAMPGROUND

### Scenic rating: 8

on Robinson Creek in Humboldt-Toiyabe
National Forest

**Map 10.1, page 519**

Crags Campground, at 7,100 feet elevation in
the Sierra, is one of a series of campgrounds
along Robinson Creek near Lower Twin Lake.
While this camp does not offer direct access
to Lower Twin, home of giant brown trout, it
is very close. (See the Lower Twin Lake and
Honeymoon Flat listings in this chapter.)

**Campsites, facilities:** There are 46 single, six
double, and three triple sites for tents or RVs
up to 45 feet (no hookups) and a group site for
up to 45 people. Picnic tables, fire rings, and
bear boxes (mandatory) are provided. Drinking
water and flush toilets are available. Some facilities are wheelchair-accessible. A boat launch
(at Lower Twin Lake), store, coin laundry, and
coin showers are within a half mile. Leashed
pets are permitted.

**Reservations, fees:** Reservations are accepted
for some sites at 877/444-6777 ($10 reservation
fee) or www.recreation.gov ($9 reservation fee).
Single sites are $23 per night, double sites are
$44 per night, triple sites are $50 per night, and
it's $5 per night for each additional vehicle. The
group site is $125 per night. Open mid-May
through September, weather permitting.

**Directions:** On U.S. 395, drive to Bridgeport
and the junction with Twin Lakes Road. Turn
west and drive 11 miles to South Twin Road
(just before reaching Lower Twin Lake). Turn
left and drive over the bridge at Robinson Creek
to another road on the left. Turn left and drive
a short distance to the campground.

**Contact:** Humboldt-Toiyabe National Forest,
Bridgeport Ranger District, 760/932-7070,
www.fs.usda.gov/htnf or www.westrekser-
vices.com.

## 42 LOWER TWIN LAKE

### Scenic rating: 9

in Humboldt-Toiyabe National Forest

**Map 10.1, page 519**

The Twin Lakes are actually two lakes, set high
in the eastern Sierra at 7,000 feet elevation.
Each lake is unique. Lower Twin, known as
the fishing lake, with a 5-mph speed limit, has
a full resort, marina, boat ramp, and some of
the biggest brown trout in the West. The state-
record brown—26.5 pounds—was caught here
in 1985. Of course, most of the trout are your
typical 10- to 12-inch planted rainbow trout,
but nobody seems to mind, with the chance of
a true monster-sized fish always in the back of
the minds of anglers. Upper Twin Lake, with
a resort and marina, is a primary destination
for boaters, personal watercraft riders, water-
skiers, swimmers, and sailboarders. These
lakes are very popular in summer. An option
for campers is an excellent trailhead for hiking
near Mono Village at the head of Upper Twin
Lake. Barney Lake Trail leads up the headwaters of Robinson Creek, steeply at times, to
Barney Lake, an excellent day hike.

**Campsites, facilities:** There are 14 sites for
tents or RVs up to 35 feet (no hookups). Picnic
tables, fire grills, and bear boxes (mandatory)
are provided. Drinking water and flush toilets
are available. A boat launch, store, coin showers, and a coin laundry are nearby. Leashed pets
are permitted.

**Reservations, fees:** Reservations are accepted
at 877/444-6777 ($10 reservation fee) or www.
recreation.gov ($9 reservation fee). Sites are $26
per night, plus $6 per night for each additional
vehicle. Open early May through mid-October,
weather permitting.

**Directions:** On U.S. 395, drive to Bridgeport
and the junction with Twin Lakes Road. Turn
west and drive 11 miles to South Twin Road
(just before reaching Lower Twin Lake). Turn
left and drive over the bridge at Robinson Creek
and to the campground entrance road on the
right.

**Contact:** Humboldt-Toiyabe National Forest, Bridgeport Ranger District, 760/932-7070, www.fs.usda.gov/htnf or www.westrekservices.com.

## 43 GREEN CREEK
🏃🏊⛵🐕🚐⛺

### Scenic rating: 7
in Humboldt-Toiyabe National Forest

**Map 10.1, page 519**

This camp is ideal for backpackers or campers who like to fish for trout in streams. That is because it is at 7,500 feet, with a trailhead that leads into the Hoover Wilderness and to several high mountain lakes, including Green Lake, West Lake, and East Lake; the ambitious can hike beyond in remote northeastern Yosemite National Park. The camp is set along Green Creek, a fair trout stream with small rainbow trout.

**Campsites, facilities:** There are 10 sites for tents or RVs up to 35 feet, three double sites, and two group sites for tents or RVs of any length that can accommodate 25 and 30 people respectively (no hookups). Picnic tables and fire grills are provided. Drinking water and vault toilets are available. Leashed pets are permitted.

**Reservations, fees:** Reservations are not accepted for individual sites but are required for group sites at 877/444-6777 ($10 reservation fee) or www.recreation.gov ($9 reservation fee). Sites are $20 per night, plus $5 per night for each additional vehicle, and the group site is $60-75 per night. Open mid-May through early October, weather permitting.

**Directions:** From Bridgeport, drive south on U.S. 395 for four miles to Green Lakes Road (dirt). Turn right and drive seven miles to the campground.

**Contact:** Humboldt-Toiyabe National Forest, Bridgeport Ranger District, 760/932-7070,

www.fs.usda.gov/htnf or www.westrekservices.com.

## 44 TRUMBULL LAKE
🏃🏊⛵🐕♿🚐⛺

### Scenic rating: 8
in Humboldt-Toiyabe National Forest

**Map 10.1, page 519**

This is a high-mountain camp (9,500 feet) at the gateway to a beautiful Sierra basin. Little Trumbull Lake is the first lake on the north side of Virginia Lakes Road, with Virginia Lakes nearby, along with the Hoover Wilderness and access to many other small lakes by trail. A trail passes just north of Blue Lake, and then it leads west to Frog Lake, Summit Lake, and beyond into a remote area of Yosemite National Park. If you don't want to rough it, cabins, boat rentals, and a restaurant are available at Virginia Lakes Resort. No gas motors, swimming, or water/body contact is permitted at Virginia Lakes.

**Campsites, facilities:** There are 33 sites for tents or RVs up to 40 feet (no hookups). Picnic tables and fire grills are provided. Drinking water, garbage bins, and vault toilets are available. A store is nearby at the resort. Some facilities are wheelchair-accessible. Leashed pets are permitted.

**Reservations, fees:** Reservations are accepted at 877/444-6777 ($10 reservation fee) or www.recreation.gov ($9 reservation fee). Single sites are $22 per night, double sites are $40 per night, triple sites are $51 per night, and it's $6 per night for each additional vehicle. Open June through September, weather permitting.

**Directions:** From Bridgeport, drive south on U.S. 395 for 13.5 miles to Virginia Lakes Road. Turn right on Virginia Lakes Road and drive 6.5 miles to the campground entrance road.

**Contact:** Humboldt-Toiyabe National Forest, Bridgeport Ranger District, 760/932-7070, www.fs.usda.gov/htnf or www.westrekservices.com.

## 45 LUNDY CANYON CAMPGROUND

### Scenic rating: 7

near Lundy Lake

**Map 10.1, page 519**

This camp is set high in the eastern Sierra at 7,400 feet elevation along pretty Lundy Creek, the mountain stream that feeds Lundy Lake and then runs downhill, eventually joining other creeks on its trip to nearby Mono Lake. Nearby Lundy Lake (at 7,800 feet elevation) is a long, narrow lake with good fishing for rainbow trout and brown trout. The water is clear and cold, even through the summer. A trailhead just west of the lake ascends steeply up into the Hoover Wilderness to several small pretty lakes, passing two waterfalls about two miles in. A must-do side trip is visiting Mono Lake and its spectacular tufa towers, best done at the Mono Lake Tufa State Reserve along the southern shore of the lake.

**Campsites, facilities:** There are 37 sites for tents or RVs up to 35 feet (no hookups). Picnic tables and fire rings are provided. Pit toilets and bear boxes are available. There is no drinking water. Supplies are available in Lee Vining, 8.5 miles away. Some facilities are wheelchair-accessible. Leashed pets are permitted.

**Reservations, fees:** Reservations are not accepted. Sites are $16 per night, limit two vehicles and six people per site. Monthly rates are available. Open mid-April through mid-November, weather permitting.

**Directions:** From Lee Vining, drive north on U.S. 395 for seven miles to Lundy Lake Road. Turn left and drive a short distance to the campground.

**Contact:** Mono County Public Works, 760/932-5440, www.mono.ca.gov/facilities.

## 46 TIOGA LAKE

### Scenic rating: 9

in Inyo National Forest

**Map 10.1, page 519**

Tioga Lake is a dramatic sight, with gemlike blue waters encircled by Sierra granite at 9,700 feet elevation. Together with adjacent Ellery Lake, it makes a pair of gorgeous waters with near-lake camping, trout fishing (stocked with rainbow trout), and access to Yosemite National Park and Saddlebag Lake. Conditions here are much like those at neighboring Ellery Lake. The only downers: It can get windy here (no foolin'!) and the camps fill quickly from the overflow crowds at Tuolumne Meadows. (See the Ellery Lake listing for more information.)

**Campsites, facilities:** There are 13 sites for tents or RVs up to 30 feet (no hookups). Picnic tables, fire rings, and bear boxes (mandatory) are provided. Drinking water and pit toilets are available. Some facilities are wheelchair-accessible. Leashed pets are permitted.

**Reservations, fees:** Reservations are not accepted. Sites are $21 per night, plus $5 per each additional vehicle. Open early June through mid-October, weather permitting.

**Directions:** On U.S. 395, drive to just south of Lee Vining and the junction with Highway 120. Turn west on Highway 120 and drive about 11 miles (just past Ellery Lake) to the campground on the left side of the road.

From Merced, drive east on Highway 140 to the Arch Rock entrance station. Continue east to the Big Oak Flat Road junction (0.5 mile before entering Yosemite Valley). Turn left and drive 14 miles to Tioga Road. Turn right and drive about 65 miles (past Tuolumne Meadows) and through the Tioga Pass entrance station. Continue one mile to the campground entrance road on the right side of the road.

**Contact:** Inyo National Forest, Mono Basin Scenic Area Ranger Station and Visitor Center, 760/647-3044, www.fs.usda.gov/inyo; Inyo Recreation, 760/934-5795.

## 47 ELLERY LAKE

### Scenic rating: 9

in Inyo National Forest

**Map 10.1, page 519**

Ellery Lake offers all the spectacular beauty of Yosemite but is two miles outside park borders. That means it is stocked with trout by the Department of Fish and Game (no lakes in Yosemite are planted, hence the lousy fishing). Just like at neighboring Tioga Lake, here are deep-blue waters set in rock in the 9,500-foot-elevation range, one of the most pristine highway-access lake settings anywhere. Although there is no boat ramp, boats with small motors are allowed and can be hand-launched. Nearby Saddlebag Lake, the highest drive-to lake in California, is a common side trip. Whenever Tuolumne Meadows fills in Yosemite, this camp fills shortly thereafter. Camp elevation is 9,500 feet.

**Campsites, facilities:** There are 21 sites for tents or RVs up to 30 feet (no hookups). Picnic tables and fire grills are provided. Drinking water, pit toilets, and bear boxes are available. A grocery store is nearby. Some facilities are wheelchair-accessible. Leashed pets are permitted.

**Reservations, fees:** Reservations are not accepted. Sites are $21 per night, plus $5 for each additional vehicle. Open early June through mid-October, weather permitting.

**Directions:** On U.S. 395, drive to just south of Lee Vining and the junction with Highway 120. Turn west on Highway 120 and drive about 10 miles to the campground on the left side of the road.

From Merced, drive east on Highway 140 to the Arch Rock entrance station. Continue east to the Big Oak Flat Road junction (0.5 mile before entering Yosemite Valley). Turn left and drive 14 miles to Tioga Road. Turn right and drive about 65 miles (past Tuolumne Meadows) and through the Tioga Pass entrance station. Continue four miles to the campground entrance road on the right.

**Contact:** Inyo National Forest, Mono Basin Scenic Area Ranger Station and Visitor Center, 760/647-3044, www.fs.usda.gov/inyo; Inyo Recreation, 760/934-5795.

## 48 JUNCTION

### Scenic rating: 7

near Ellery and Tioga Lakes in Inyo National Forest

**Map 10.1, page 519**

Which way do you go? From Junction, any way you choose, you can't miss. Two miles to the north is Saddlebag Lake, the highest drive-to lake (10,087 feet) in California. Directly across the road is Ellery Lake and a mile to the south is Tioga Lake, two beautiful, pristine waters with trout fishing. To the east is Mono Lake, and to the west is Yosemite National Park. From camp, it is a one-mile hike to Bennetville, a historical camp. Take your pick. Camp elevation is 9,600 feet.

**Campsites, facilities:** There are 13 sites for tents or RVs up to 30 feet (no hookups). Picnic tables, fire rings, and bear boxes (mandatory) are provided. Vault toilets are available. There is no drinking water. Some facilities are wheelchair-accessible. Leashed pets are permitted.

**Reservations, fees:** Reservations are not accepted. Sites are $16 per night, plus $5 for each additional vehicle. Open early June through mid-October, weather permitting.

**Directions:** On U.S. 395, drive to just south of Lee Vining and the junction with Highway 120. Turn west on Highway 120 and drive about 10 miles to Saddlebag Road and the campground on the right side of the road.

From Merced, drive east on Highway 140 to the Arch Rock entrance station. Continue east to the Big Oak Flat Road junction (0.5 mile before entering Yosemite Valley). Turn left and drive 14 miles to Tioga Road. Turn right and drive about 65 miles (past Tuolumne Meadows) and through the Tioga Pass entrance station. Continue two miles to Saddlebag Lake Road and the campground on the left side of the road.

**Contact:** Inyo National Forest, Mono Basin Scenic Area Ranger Station and Visitor Center, 760/647-3044, www.fs.usda.gov/inyo; Inyo Recreation, 760/934-5795.

## 49 SAWMILL WALK-IN
🏃 🐕 🏕️

### Scenic rating: 8

near Ellery and Tioga Lakes in Inyo National Forest

**Map 10.1, page 519**

This walk-in tent campground features sites peppered above Sawmill Valley and Lee Vining Creek. The first site is a short walk from the parking lot; sites 11 and 12 (next to the Harvey Monroe Hall National Area border) are 0.2 mile away. Solitude, breathtaking vistas, and hiking opportunities make a stay here an awesome experience. Yosemite National Park and Mono Basin Scenic Area offer nearby side trips. The elevation is 9,700 feet.

**Campsites, facilities:** There are 12 tent sites. Picnic tables, fire rings, and bear boxes (mandatory) are provided. Vault toilets are available. There is no drinking water available. Nearby Tioga Pass Resort has limited groceries and supplies. Leashed pets are permitted.

**Reservations, fees:** Reservations are not accepted. Sites are $16 per night, plus $5 for each additional vehicle. Open early June through mid-October, weather permitting.

**Directions:** From Lee Vining, take U.S. 395 south 0.3 mile to the sign for Tioga Pass. Turn right onto Highway 120 and drive west 10.2 miles to Saddlebag Road. Turn left onto Saddlebag Road (gravel) and drive 1.6 miles to the campground on the left.

**Contact:** Inyo National Forest, Mono Basin Scenic Area Ranger Station and Visitor Center, 760/647-3044, www.fs.usda.gov/inyo; Inyo Recreation, 760/934-5795.

## 50 SADDLEBAG LAKE AND TRAILHEAD GROUP
🏃 🚣 ⛴️ 🏕️ 🐕 ♿ 🚐 🏕️

### Scenic rating: 10

in Inyo National Forest

**Map 10.1, page 519**          **BEST (**

This camp is in spectacular high country above the tree line, the highest drive-to camp and lake in California, at 10,087 feet elevation. The camp is about a quarter mile from the lake, within walking range of the little store and boat rentals, and a one-minute drive for launching a boat at the ramp. The scenery is stark; everything is granite, ice, or water, with only a few lodgepole pines managing precarious toeholds, sprinkled across the landscape on the access road. From the excellent trailhead, the best hike heads out past little Hummingbird Lake to Lundy Pass. A hikers' shuttle boat to ferry you across the lake is a nice plus. Note that with the elevation and the high mountain pass, it can be windy and cold, and some people find it difficult to catch their breath on simple hikes. In addition, RV users should note that level sites are extremely hard to come by.

**Campsites, facilities:** There are 19 sites for tents or RVs up to 30 feet (no hookups) at Saddlebag Lake, and one group tent site holds up to 25 people at Trailhead. Drinking water, fire grills, and picnic tables are provided. Flush toilets, boat rentals, and a primitive boat launch are available. A grocery store is nearby. Some facilities are wheelchair-accessible. Leashed pets are permitted.

**Reservations, fees:** Reservations are not accepted for individual sites but are required for the group site (listed as Trailhead Group) at 877/444-6777 ($10 reservation fee) or www.recreation.gov ($9 reservation fee). Sites are $21 per night, the group site is $94 per night, and it's $5 for each additional vehicle. Open late June through early September, weather permitting.

**Directions:** On U.S. 395, drive 0.5 mile south of Lee Vining and the junction with Highway 120. Turn west and drive about 11 miles to

Saddlebag Lake Road. Turn right and drive 2.5 miles to the campground on the right.

From Merced, drive east on Highway 140 to the Arch Rock entrance station. Continue east to the Big Oak Flat Road junction (0.5 mile before entering Yosemite Valley). Turn left and drive 14 miles to Tioga Road. Turn right and drive about 65 miles (past Tuolumne Meadows) and through the Tioga Pass entrance station. Continue two miles to Saddlebag Lake Road. Turn left and drive 2.5 miles (rough road) to the campground on the right.

**Contact:** Inyo National Forest, Mono Basin Scenic Area Ranger Station and Visitor Center, 760/647-3044, www.fs.usda.gov/inyo; Inyo Recreation, 760/934-5795.

# 51 BIG BEND

### Scenic rating: 8
on Lee Vining Creek in Inyo National Forest

**Map 10.1, page 519**

This camp is set in sparse but beautiful country along Lee Vining Creek at 7,800 feet elevation. Ancient pine trees are on-site. It is an excellent bet for an overflow camp if Tuolumne Meadows in nearby Yosemite is packed. The view from the camp to the north features Mono Dome (10,614 feet) and Lee Vining Peak (11,691 feet).

**Campsites, facilities:** There are 17 sites for tents or RVs up to 30 feet (no hookups). Picnic tables, fire rings, and bear boxes (mandatory) are provided. Drinking water and vault toilets are available. Some facilities are wheelchair-accessible. Leashed pets are permitted.

**Reservations, fees:** Reservations are not accepted. Sites are $21 per night, plus $5 for each additional vehicle. A 14-day limit is enforced. Open late April through mid-October, weather permitting.

**Directions:** On U.S. 395, drive to just south of Lee Vining and the junction with Highway 120. Turn west on Highway 120 and drive about 3.5 miles to Poole Power Plant Road and the signed campground access road on the right. Turn right and drive a short distance to the camp.

**Contact:** Inyo National Forest, Mono Basin Scenic Area Ranger Station and Visitor Center, 760/647-3044, www.fs.usda.gov/inyo.

# 52 ASPEN GROVE

### Scenic rating: 8
on Lee Vining Creek

**Map 10.1, page 519**

This high-country, primitive camp is along Lee Vining Creek at 7,500 feet elevation, on the eastern slopes of the Sierra just east of Yosemite National Park. Take the side trip to moonlike Mono Lake, best seen at the south shore's Tufa State Reserve.

**Campsites, facilities:** There are 56 sites for tents or RVs up to 40 feet (no hookups). Picnic tables and fire rings are provided. Drinking water and vault toilets are available. You can buy supplies in Lee Vining. Leashed pets are permitted.

**Reservations, fees:** Reservations are not accepted. Sites are $14 per night, plus $5 for each additional vehicle. A 14-day limit is enforced. Open May through October, weather permitting.

**Directions:** On U.S. 395, drive to just south of Lee Vining and the junction with Highway 120. Turn west on Highway 120 and drive about 3.5 miles. Exit onto Poole Power Plant Road. Turn left and drive about four miles west to the campground on the left.

**Contact:** Inyo National Forest, Mono Basin Scenic Area Ranger Station and Visitor Center, 760/647-3044, www.fs.usda.gov/inyo.

## 53 MORAINE CAMP

🚶 🎣 🐕 🚐 ⛺

**Scenic rating: 7**

near Lee Vining

**Map 10.1, page 519**

This camp provides an alternative to Yosemite National Park. (For more information, see the Lower Lee Vining Camp listing in this chapter.)

**Campsites, facilities:** There are 20 sites for tents or RVs up to 40 feet (no hookups). Picnic tables and fire rings are provided. Pit toilets are available. There is no drinking water. You can buy supplies in Lee Vining (about two miles away). Leashed pets are permitted.

**Reservations, fees:** Reservations are not accepted. Sites are $14 per night, plus $5 for each additional vehicle. Open May through October, weather permitting.

**Directions:** On U.S. 395, drive to just south of Lee Vining and the junction with Highway 120. Turn west on Highway 120 and drive 3.5 miles to Poole Power Plant Road. Exit left onto Poole Power Plant Road and drive 0.25 mile to the campground entrance at the end of the road.

**Contact:** Inyo National Forest, Mono Basin Scenic Area Ranger Station and Visitor Center, 760/647-3044, www.fs.usda.gov/inyo.

## 54 LOWER LEE VINING CAMP

🚶 🎣 🐕 🚐 ⛺

**Scenic rating: 7**

near Lee Vining

**Map 10.1, page 519**

This former Mono County camp and its neighboring camps—Moraine, Aspen, and Big Bend—can be a godsend for vacationers who show up at Yosemite National Park and make the discovery that there are no sites left, a terrible experience for some late-night arrivals. But these Forest Service campgrounds provide a great safety valve, even if they are extremely primitive, on the edge of timber. Lee Vining Creek is the highlight, flowing right past the campgrounds along Highway 120, bound for Mono Lake to the nearby east. It is stocked regularly during the fishing season. A must-do side trip is venturing to the south shore of Mono Lake to walk amid the bizarre yet beautiful tufa towers. There is good rock-climbing and hiking in the area. Although sunshine is the norm, be prepared for all kinds of weather: It can snow every month of the year. Short but lively thunderstorms are common in early summer. Other nearby trips are to Mammoth Lakes, June Lake, and Bodie State Park.

**Campsites, facilities:** There are 53 sites for tents or RVs up to 40 feet (no hookups). Picnic tables, fire rings, and bear boxes (mandatory) are provided. Vault toilets are available. There is no drinking water. Supplies are available in Lee Vining (about two miles away). Leashed pets are permitted.

**Reservations, fees:** Reservations are not accepted. Sites are $14 per night, plus $5 for each additional vehicle. Open May through October, weather permitting.

**Directions:** On U.S. 395, drive to just south of Lee Vining and the junction with Highway 120. Turn west on Highway 120 and drive about 2.5 miles. Turn left into the campground entrance.

**Contact:** Inyo National Forest, Mono Basin Scenic Area Ranger Station and Visitor Center, 760/647-3044, www.fs.usda.gov/inyo.

## 55 SILVER LAKE

🚶 🎣 🛶 🏠 ♿ 🚐 ⛺

**Scenic rating: 9**

in Inyo National Forest

**Map 10.1, page 519**

Silver Lake, at 7,200 feet elevation, is an 80-acre lake in the June Lake Loop with Carson Peak looming in the background. Boat rentals, fishing for trout at the lake, a beautiful trout stream (Rush Creek) next to the camp, and a nearby trailhead for wilderness hiking and horseback riding (rentals available) are the highlights. The camp is largely exposed and vulnerable to winds, the only downer. Within walking distance to the south is Silver Lake, always a pretty sight, especially when afternoon winds cause the lake surface to sparkle. The lake speed limit is 10 mph. Swimming is not recommended because of the rocky shoreline. Just across the road from the camp is a great trailhead for the Ansel Adams Wilderness, with a two-hour hike that climbs to pretty Agnew Lake overlooking the June Lake basin; a wilderness permit is required for overnight use.

**Campsites, facilities:** There are 63 sites for tents or RVs up to 40 feet (no hookups). Picnic tables, fire rings, and bear boxes (mandatory) are provided. Drinking water, flush toilets, and horseback-riding facilities are available. A grocery store, coin laundry, motorboat rentals, boat ramp, bait, café, boat fuel, and propane gas are nearby. Some facilities are wheelchair-accessible. Leashed pets are permitted.

**Reservations, fees:** Reservations are accepted at 877/444-6777 ($10 reservation fee) or www.recreation.gov ($9 reservation fee). Sites are $22-39.29 per night, plus $5 per night for extra vehicles. A 14-day limit is enforced. Open late April through early November, weather permitting.

**Directions:** From Lee Vining on U.S. 395, drive south for six miles to the first Highway 158 north/June Lake Loop turnoff. Turn west (right) and drive nine miles (past Grant Lake) to Silver Lake. Just as you arrive at Silver Lake (a small store is on the right), turn left at the campground entrance.

**Contact:** Inyo National Forest, Mono Basin Scenic Area Ranger Station and Visitor Center, 760/647-3044, www.fs.usda.gov/inyo; Inyo Recreation, 760/934-5795.

## 56 OH! RIDGE

### Scenic rating: 8

on June Lake in Inyo National Forest

**Map 10.1, page 519**

This is the largest of the campgrounds on June Lake. However, it is not the most popular since it is not right on the lakeshore but back about a quarter mile or so from the north end of the lake. Regardless, it has the best views of the lake, with the ridge of the high Sierra providing a backdrop. The lake is a good one for trout fishing. The elevation is 7,600 feet.

**Campsites, facilities:** There are 144 sites for tents or RVs up to 40 feet (no hookups). Picnic tables, fire grills, and bear boxes (mandatory) are provided. Drinking water, flush toilets, and a swimming beach are available. A grocery store, coin laundry, volleyball, amphitheater, boat ramp, boat and tackle rentals, moorings, and propane gas are nearby. Some facilities are wheelchair-accessible. Leashed pets are permitted.

**Reservations, fees:** Reservations are accepted at 877/444-6777 ($10 reservation fee) or www.recreation.gov ($9 reservation fee). Sites are $22.32-24.11 per night, plus $5 per night for extra vehicles. Open late April through early November, weather permitting.

**Directions:** From Lee Vining, drive south on U.S. 395 (past the first Highway 158/June Lake Loop turnoff) to June Lake Junction (a gas station/store is on the west side of the road) and Highway 158 south. Turn west on Highway 158 south and drive two miles to Oh! Ridge Road. Turn right and drive a mile to the campground access road (signed). Turn left and drive to the campground.

**Contact:** Inyo National Forest, Mono Basin Scenic Area Ranger Station and Visitor Center, 760/647-3044, www.fs.usda.gov/inyo; Inyo Recreation, 760/934-5795.

## 57 PINE CLIFF RESORT

### Scenic rating: 7

at June Lake

**Map 10.1, page 519**      **BEST (**

You'll find "kid heaven" at Pine Cliff Resort. This camp is in a pretty setting along the north shore of June Lake (7,600 feet elevation), the feature lake among four in the June Lake Loop. The campsites are nestled in pine trees, designed so each site accommodates different-sized rigs and families, and the campground is about a quarter mile from June Lake. This is the only camp at June Lake Loop that has a swimming beach. The landscape is a pretty one, with the lake set below snowcapped peaks. The bonus is that June Lake gets large numbers of trout plants each summer, making it extremely popular with anglers. Of the lakes in the June Lake Loop, this is the one that has the most of everything—the most beauty, the most fish, the most developed accommodations, and, alas, the most people. This resort has been operated as a family business for more than 50 years.

**Campsites, facilities:** There are 154 sites with full hookups (20 and 30 amps) for RVs, 17 sites with partial hookups (20 and 30 amps) for tents or RVs, and 55 sites for tents; a few sites are pull-through. There are also 14 rental trailers. Picnic tables and fire rings are provided. Restrooms with flush toilets and coin showers, drinking water, coin laundry, basketball, volleyball, tetherball, horseshoes, convenience store, and propane gas are available. Some facilities are wheelchair-accessible. A primitive boat ramp, fish-cleaning facilities, and fuel are nearby. Leashed pets are permitted, with a maximum of two per site.

**Reservations, fees:** Reservations are recommended. Sites are $25-35 per night, plus $5 per night for each additional vehicle and $1 per person per night for more than four people. The first pet is free, and the second pet is $1 per night. Open mid-April through October.

**Directions:** From Lee Vining, drive south on U.S. 395 (passing the first Highway 158 north/June Lake Loop turnoff) to June Lake Junction (a sign is posted for "June Lake Village") and Highway 158 south. Turn right (west) on Highway 158 south and drive two miles to North Shore Drive (a sign is nearby for Pine Cliff Resort). Turn right and drive 0.5 mile to Pine Cliff Road. Turn left and drive 0.5 mile to the resort store on the right (route is well signed).

**Contact:** Pine Cliff Resort, 760/648-7558.

## 58 GULL LAKE

### Scenic rating: 8

in Inyo National Forest

**Map 10.1, page 519**

Little Gull Lake, just 64 acres, is the smallest of the lakes on the June Lake Loop, but to many it is the prettiest. It is set at 7,600 feet, just west of June Lake, and with Carson Peak looming on the Sierra crest to the west, it is a dramatic and intimate setting. The lake is stocked with trout each summer, providing good fishing. A boat ramp is on the lake's southwest corner. Insider's tip: Youngsters love the rope swing at Gull Lake.

**Campsites, facilities:** There are 11 sites for tents or RVs up to 30 feet (no hookups). Drinking water, fire grills, bear boxes (mandatory), and picnic tables are provided. Flush toilets are available. A grocery store, coin laundry, boat ramp, and propane gas are nearby. Some facilities are wheelchair-accessible. Leashed pets are permitted.

**Reservations, fees:** Reservations are not accepted. Sites are $22 per night, plus $5 each additional vehicle per night. Open late April through early November, weather permitting.

**Directions:** From Lee Vining, drive south on U.S. 395 (past the first Highway 158/June Lake Loop turnoff) to June Lake Junction (a gas station/store is on the west side of the road) and Highway 158. Turn west on Highway 158 and drive three miles to the campground entrance on the right side of the road.

**Contact:** Inyo National Forest, Mono Basin Scenic Area Ranger Station and Visitor Center, 760/647-3044, www.fs.usda.gov/inyo; Inyo Recreation, 760/934-5795.

## 59 REVERSED CREEK

### Scenic rating: 6

in Inyo National Forest

**Map 10.1, page 519**

This camp is at 7,600 feet elevation near pretty Reversed Creek, the only stream in the region that flows toward the mountains, not away from them. It is a small, tree-lined stream that provides decent trout fishing. The campsites are sheltered in a grove of aspens but are close enough to the road that you can still hear highway traffic. There are cabins available for rent nearby. Directly opposite the camp, on the other side of the road, is Gull Lake and the boat ramp. Two miles to the west, on the west side of the road, is the trailhead for the hike to Fern Lake on the edge of the Ansel Adams Wilderness, a little butt-kicker of a climb.

**Campsites, facilities:** There are 17 sites for tents or RVs up to 30 feet (no hookups). Picnic tables and fire grills are provided. Drinking water and flush toilets are available. A grocery store, coin laundry, and propane gas are nearby. Boating is available at nearby Silver Lake, two miles away. Some facilities are wheelchair-accessible. Leashed pets are permitted.

**Reservations, fees:** Reservations are accepted at 877/444-6777 ($10 reservation fee) or www.recreation.gov ($9 reservation fee). Sites are $19.64-21.43 per night, plus $5 per night for extra vehicles. Open mid-May through October, weather permitting.

**Directions:** From Lee Vining, drive south on U.S. 395 (past the first Highway 158/June Lake Loop turnoff) to June Lake Junction (a gas station/store is on the west side of the road) and Highway 158 south. Turn right (west) on Highway 158 south and drive three miles to the campground on the left side of the road (across from Gull Lake).

**Contact:** Inyo National Forest, Mono Basin Scenic Area Ranger Station and Visitor Center, 760/647-3044, www.fs.usda.gov/inyo; Inyo Recreation, 760/934-5795.

## 60 JUNE LAKE

### Scenic rating: 9

in Inyo National Forest

**Map 10.1, page 519**

June Lake gets the highest use of all the lakes in the June Lakes Loop, and it has the best swimming, best fishing, and best sailboarding. There are three campgrounds at pretty June Lake; this is one of the two operated by the Forest Service (the other is Oh! Ridge). This one is on the northeast shore of the lake at 7,600 feet elevation, a pretty spot with all supplies available just two miles south in the town of June Lake. The nearest boat launch is north of town. This is a good lake for trout fishing, receiving high numbers of stocked trout each year. A 10-mph speed limit is enforced.

**Campsites, facilities:** There are 28 sites for tents or RVs up to 32 feet (no hookups). Picnic tables, fire grills, and bear boxes (mandatory use) are provided. Drinking water, restrooms with flush toilets, and a boat ramp are available. A grocery store, coin laundry, boat and tackle rentals, moorings, and propane gas are nearby. Leashed pets are permitted.

**Reservations, fees:** Reservations are accepted at 877/444-6777 ($10 reservation fee) or www. recreation.gov ($9 reservation fee). Sites are $19.64-21.43 per night, plus $5 per night for extra vehicles. Open late April through early November, weather permitting.

**Directions:** From Lee Vining, drive south on U.S. 395 (passing Highway 158 north) for 20 miles (six miles past Highway 158 north) to June Lake Junction (signed "June Lake Village") and Highway 158 south. Turn west (right) on Highway 158 south and drive two miles to June Lake. Turn right (signed) and drive a short distance to the campground.

**Contact:** Inyo National Forest, Mono Basin Scenic Area Ranger Station and Visitor Center, 760/647-3044, www.fs.usda.gov/inyo; Inyo Recreation, 760/934-5795.

## 61 HARTLEY SPRINGS

### Scenic rating: 8

in Inyo National Forest

**Map 10.1, page 519**

Even though this camp is only a five-minute drive from U.S. 395, those five minutes will take you into another orbit. It is in a forest of Jeffrey pine and has the feel of a remote, primitive camp, set in a high-mountain environment at an elevation of 8,400 feet. About two miles to the immediate north, at 8,611 feet, is Obsidian Dome "Glass Flow," a craggy geologic formation that some people enjoy scrambling around on and exploring; pick your access point carefully.

**Campsites, facilities:** There are 20 sites for tents or RVs up to 40 feet (no hookups). Picnic tables and fire grills are provided. Vault toilets are available. No drinking water is available. Garbage must be packed out. Leashed pets are permitted.

**Reservations, fees:** Reservations are not accepted. There is no fee for camping. Open late May through early November, weather permitting.

**Directions:** From Lee Vining, drive south on U.S. 395 (passing the first Highway 158/June Lake Loop turnoff) for 10 miles to June Lake Junction. Continue south on U.S. 395 for six miles to Glass Creek Road (a dirt road on the west side of the highway). Turn west (right) and drive two miles to the campground entrance road on the left.

**Contact:** Inyo National Forest, Mono Basin Scenic Area Ranger Station and Visitor Center, 760/647-3044, www.fs.usda.gov/inyo.

## 62 AGNEW MEADOWS EQUESTRIAN CAMP

### Scenic rating: 9

in Inyo National Forest

**Map 10.1, page 519**

Note: At time of publication, this campground remained closed due to severe damage from a wind storm. Horse corrals are under reconstruction, but the campground will remain closed through 2017 and facilities may change. For base camp access to the PCT, see the listings for Pumice Flat and Upper Soda Springs in this chapter.

This is a perfect camp to use as a launching pad for a backpacking trip or day of fly-fishing for trout. It is along the Upper San Joaquin River at 8,400 feet, with a trailhead for the Pacific Crest Trail near camp. You can hike seven miles to the gorgeous Thousand Island Lake, a beautiful lake sprinkled with islands set below Banner and Ritter Peaks in the spectacular Minarets. For day hiking, walk the River Trail, which is routed from Agnew Meadows along the San Joaquin. The trail provides access to excellent fishing with a chance at the grand slam of California trout—four species in a single day (though the trout are small).

**Campsites, facilities:** Four group equestrian sites for tents or RVs up to 45 feet (no hookups) can accommodate 10-20 people each. Picnic tables and fire grills are provided. Drinking water, vault toilets, and hitching racks are available. Supplies can be obtained at the Reds Meadow Resort store. Some facilities are wheelchair-accessible. Leashed pets are permitted.

**Reservations, fees:** Reservations are required at 877/444-6777 ($10 reservation fee) or www.recreation.gov ($9 reservation fee). Sites are $34-75 per night, plus $24 per night for an equestrian site and a $10 per vehicle Reds Meadow/Agnew Meadows access fee. Open mid-June through mid-September, weather permitting.

**Directions:** On U.S. 395, drive to Mammoth Junction/Highway 203. Turn west on Highway

---

## HIKING THE JMT/PCT: AGNEW MEADOWS TO TUOLUMNE MEADOWS

**28 MILES ONE-WAY / 3 DAYS**

This section of the JMT/PCT features breathtaking views of the Minarets, many glacial-cut lakes, and the wondrous descent into Yosemite. The PCT starts here by leaving Reds Meadow, an excellent place to arrange a food drop. The trail heads out into the most beautiful section of Inyo National Forest and the Ansel Adams Wilderness. All in a row, the PCT passes Rosalie, Shadow, Garnet, and **Thousand Island Lakes.** If they look like Ansel Adams's pictures in real life, it's because they are. The background setting of Banner and Ritter Peaks is among the most beautiful anywhere. From Thousand Island Lake, the PCT makes a fair climb over Island Pass (10,200 feet), then drops down into the headwaters of Rush Creek, where emerald green flows swirl over boulders, pouring like a wilderness fountain. From here, it's a decent, steady ascent back above tree line to Donohue Pass (11,056 feet), the southern wilderness border of Yosemite National Park. It was here, while munching on a trail lunch, that we saw a huge landslide on the westward canyon wall. A massive amount of rock material fell in just a few seconds—an unforgettable show of natural forces. The trail becomes quite blocky at Donohue Pass, and you rock hop your way down to the headwaters of Lyell Fork, a pretzel-like stream that meanders through the meadows. It pours all the way to **Tuolumne Meadows,** and, following it, the trail is nearly flat for more than four miles. At Tuolumne Meadows you can resupply—and get a cheeseburger.

---

203 and drive four miles, through the town of Mammoth Lakes to Minaret Road (still Highway 203). Turn right and drive five miles to Minaret Station (past the Mammoth Mountain Ski Area). Continue for 2.6 miles to the campground entrance road on the right. Turn right and drive just under a mile to the campground. The access road to the group sites is steep and narrow.

Note: From June to September, Highway 203 west from Mammoth Mountain Main Lodge is only accessible to private vehicles that are camping. All other visitors must use the Reds Meadow Shuttle Bus (7am-7:30pm daily, $7 per person) to access Reds Meadow Valley and Devils Postpile National Monument.

**Contact:** Inyo National Forest, 760/873-2400, www.fs.usda.gov/inyo; CLM Services, 650/322-1181, www.clm-services.com.

## 63 PUMICE FLAT

**Scenic rating: 8**

on the San Joaquin River in Inyo National Forest

**Map 10.1, page 519**

Pumice Flat (7,700 feet elevation) provides roadside camping within short range of several adventures. A trail out of camp links with the Pacific Crest Trail, where you can hike along the Upper San Joaquin River for miles, with excellent access for fly-fishing, and head north into the Ansel Adams Wilderness. Devils Postpile National Monument is just two miles south, along with the trailhead for Rainbow Falls.

**Campsites, facilities:** There are 17 sites for tents or RVs up to 45 feet (no hookups). Picnic tables, fire grills, and bear boxes are provided. Drinking water, vault toilets, and horseback-riding facilities are available. Limited supplies are available at a small store, or buy full supplies in Mammoth Lakes. Leashed pets are permitted.

**Reservations, fees:** Reservations are not accepted. Single sites are $22 per night, plus a $10 per vehicle Reds Meadow/Agnew Meadows access fee. Open mid-June through mid-September, weather permitting.

**Directions:** On U.S. 395, drive to Mammoth Junction/Highway 203. Turn west on Highway 203 and drive four miles, through the town of Mammoth Lakes to Minaret Road (still Highway 203). Turn right and drive five miles to Minaret Station (past the Mammoth Mountain Ski Area). Continue for 5.1 miles to the campground on the right.

Note: From June to September, Highway 203 west from Mammoth Mountain Main Lodge is only accessible to private vehicles that are camping. All other visitors must use the Reds Meadow Shuttle Bus (7am-7:30pm daily, $7 per person) to access Reds Meadow Valley and Devils Postpile National Monument.

**Contact:** Inyo National Forest, 760/873-2400, www.fs.usda.gov/inyo; CLM Services, 650/322-1181, www.clm-services.com.

## 64 UPPER SODA SPRINGS

**Scenic rating: 8**

on the San Joaquin River in Inyo National Forest

| Map 10.1, page 519 | BEST ( |
| --- | --- |

This is a premium location within earshot of the Upper San Joaquin River and within minutes of many first-class recreation options. The river is stocked with trout at this camp, with several good pools within short walking distance. Farther upstream, accessible by an excellent trail, are smaller wild trout that provide good fly-fishing prospects. Devils Postpile National Monument, a massive formation of ancient columnar jointed rock, is only three miles to the south. The Pacific Crest Trail passes right by the camp, providing a trailhead for access to numerous lakes in the Ansel Adams Wilderness. The elevation is 7,700 feet.

**Campsites, facilities:** There are 28 sites for tents or RVs up to 36 feet (no hookups). Picnic tables, fire grills, and bear boxes are provided. Drinking water, flush toilets, and horseback-riding facilities are available. Limited supplies can be obtained at the Red's Meadow Resort store. Leashed pets are permitted.

**Reservations, fees:** Reservations are not accepted. Sites are $22 per night, plus a $10 per vehicle Reds Meadow/Agnew Meadows access fee. Open mid-June through mid-September, weather permitting.

**Directions:** On U.S. 395, drive to Mammoth Junction/Highway 203. Turn west on Highway 203 and drive four miles, through the town of Mammoth Lakes to Minaret Road (still Highway 203). Turn right and drive five miles to Minaret Station (past the Mammoth Mountain Ski Area). Continue for 5.1 miles to the campground entrance road on the right. Turn right and drive 0.25 mile to the campground.

Note: From June to September, Highway 203 west from Mammoth Mountain Main Lodge is only accessible to private vehicles that are camping. All other visitors must use the Reds Meadow Shuttle Bus (7am-7:30pm daily, $7 per person) to access Reds Meadow Valley and Devils Postpile National Monument.

**Contact:** Inyo National Forest, 760/873-2400, www.fs.usda.gov/inyo; CLM Services, 650/322-1181, www.clm-services.com.

## 65 PUMICE FLAT GROUP CAMP

**Scenic rating: 6**

on the San Joaquin River in Inyo National Forest

| Map 10.1, page 519 |
| --- |

Pumice Flat Group Camp is at 7,700 feet elevation near the Upper San Joaquin River, adjacent to Pumice Flat. (For recreation information, see the Pumice Flat listing in this chapter.)

**Campsites, facilities:** There are four group sites for tents or RVs up to 45 feet (no hookups) that can accommodate 20-50 people each. Picnic tables and fire grills are provided. Drinking water, flush toilets, and horseback-riding facilities are available. You can buy supplies in Mammoth Lakes. Leashed pets are permitted.

**Reservations, fees:** Reservations are accepted at 877/444-6777 ($10 reservation fee) or www.recreation.gov ($9 reservation fee). Sites are $75-188 per night per group, plus a $10 per vehicle Reds Meadow/Agnew Meadows access fee. Open mid-June through mid-September, weather permitting.

**Directions:** On U.S. 395, drive to Mammoth Junction/Highway 203. Turn west on Highway 203 and drive four miles, through the town of Mammoth Lakes to Minaret Road (still Highway 203). Turn right and drive five miles to Minaret Station (past the Mammoth Mountain Ski Area). Continue for 5.1 miles to the campground on the left side of the road.

Note: From June to September, Highway 203 west from Mammoth Mountain Main Lodge is only accessible to private vehicles that are camping. All other visitors must use the Reds Meadow Shuttle Bus (7am-7:30pm daily, $7 per person) to access Reds Meadow Valley and Devils Postpile National Monument.

**Contact:** Inyo National Forest, 760/873-2400, www.fs.usda.gov/inyo; CLM Services, 650/322-1181, www.clm-services.com.

## 66 MINARET FALLS

### Scenic rating: 8

on the San Joaquin River in Inyo National Forest

**Map 10.1, page 519**

This camp has one of the prettiest settings of the series of camps along the Upper San Joaquin River and near Devils Postpile National Monument. It is at 7,600 feet elevation near Minaret Creek, across from where beautiful Minaret Falls pours into the San Joaquin River. Devils Postpile National Monument, one of the best examples in the world of hexagonal, columnar jointed rock, is less than a mile from camp, where there is also a trail to awesome Rainbow Falls. The Pacific Crest Trail runs right through this area as well, and if you hike to the south, there is excellent streamside fishing access.

**Campsites, facilities:** There are 27 sites for tents or RVs up to 47 feet (no hookups). Picnic tables and fire grills are provided. Drinking water and vault toilets are available. Horseback-riding facilities are nearby. You can buy limited supplies at the Red's Meadow Resort store, or all supplies in Mammoth Lakes. Some facilities are wheelchair-accessible. Leashed pets are permitted.

**Reservations, fees:** Reservations are not accepted. Sites are $22 per night, plus a $10 per vehicle Reds Meadow/Agnew Meadows access fee. Open mid-June through mid-September, weather permitting.

**Directions:** On U.S. 395, drive to Mammoth Junction/Highway 203. Turn west on Highway 203 and drive four miles, through the town of Mammoth Lakes to Minaret Road (still Highway 203). Turn right and drive five miles to Minaret Station (past the Mammoth Mountain Ski Area). Continue for six miles to the campground entrance road on the right. Turn right and drive 0.25 mile to the campground.

Note: From June to September, Highway 203 west from Mammoth Mountain Main Lodge is only accessible to private vehicles that are camping. All other visitors must use the Reds Meadow Shuttle Bus (7am-7:30pm daily, $7 per person) to access Reds Meadow Valley and Devils Postpile National Monument.

**Contact:** Inyo National Forest, 760/873-2400, www.fs.usda.gov/inyo; CLM Services, 650/322-1181, www.clm-services.com

## 67 DEVILS POSTPILE NATIONAL MONUMENT

### Scenic rating: 9
near the San Joaquin River

**Map 10.1, page 519**

Devils Postpile is a spectacular and rare example of hexagonal, columnar jointed rock that looks like posts—hence the name. The camp is at 7,600 feet elevation and provides nearby access for the easy hike to the Postpile (guided walks are offered during the summer). If you keep walking, it is a 2.5-mile walk to Rainbow Falls, a breathtaking 101-foot cascade that produces rainbows in its floating mist, seen only from the trail alongside the waterfall looking downstream. The camp is also adjacent to the Middle Fork San Joaquin River and the Pacific Crest Trail. The John Muir and Pacific Crest Trails join into one trail in the monument.

Bicyclists may access the monument at no charge or use the fee-based shuttle bus, which can carry up to three bikes. Bicycles must stay on trails; mountain biking is permitted on the Starkwater Trail only after the shuttle has stopped running for the season.

**Campsites, facilities:** There are 21 sites for tents or RVs up to 25 feet (no hookups). Picnic tables, fire rings, and bear boxes (mandatory) are provided. Drinking water and flush toilets are available. Some facilities are wheelchair-accessible. Leashed pets are permitted. Leashed pets are allowed on the trails and on the shuttle bus.

**Reservations, fees:** Reservations are not accepted. Sites are $20 per night, plus a $4-7 per person Reds Meadow/Devils Postpile access fee ($10 per vehicle with no shuttle). Open mid-June through mid-October, weather permitting, with a two-week maximum stay. Note: National Parks Passes and Golden Passports are not accepted.

**Directions:** On U.S. 395, drive to Mammoth Junction/Highway 203. Turn west on Highway 203 and drive four miles, through the town of Mammoth Lakes to Minaret Road (still Highway 203). Turn right and drive five miles to Minaret Station (past the Mammoth Mountain Ski Area). Continue for nine miles to the campground entrance road on the right.

Note: From June to September, Highway 203 west from Mammoth Mountain Main Lodge is only accessible to private vehicles that are camping. All other visitors must use the Reds Meadow Shuttle Bus (7am-7:30pm daily, $7 per person) to access Reds Meadow Valley and Devils Postpile National Monument.

**Contact:** Devils Postpile National Monument, 760/934-2289, www.nps.gov/depo.

## 68 REDS MEADOW

### Scenic rating: 6
in Inyo National Forest

**Map 10.1, page 519**

Reds Meadow is situated in a lodgepole forest next to Reds Creek in the Inyo National Forest. The campground serves as a perfect base for day trips into Devils Postpile National Monument, Rainbow Falls, Minaret Falls, the JMT, and the PCT, and is the closest campground to Red's Meadow Resort & Pack Station (no affiliation), one of the best outfitters for horseback-riding trips. The pack station leads day rides to Rainbow Falls and multiday trips into the Ansel Adams Wilderness on the Pacific Crest Trail. The nearby San Joaquin River provide recreation options. The elevation is 7,600 feet.

**Campsites, facilities:** There are 52 sites for tents or RVs up to 30 feet (no hookups). Picnic tables, fire rings, and bear boxes (mandatory) are provided. Drinking water, flush toilets, horseback riding, and natural hot springs are available. You can buy limited supplies at a small store. Leashed pets are permitted.

**Reservations, fees:** Reservations are not accepted. Sites are $22 per night, plus a $10 per vehicle Reds Meadow/Agnew Meadows access fee. Open mid-June through mid-September, weather permitting.

**Directions:** On U.S. 395, drive to Mammoth Junction/Highway 203. Turn west on Highway 203 and drive four miles, through the town of Mammoth Lakes to Minaret Road (still Highway 203). Turn right and drive five miles to Minaret Station (past the Mammoth Mountain Ski Area). Continue for 7.4 miles to the campground entrance on the left.

Note: From June to September, Highway 203 west from Mammoth Mountain Main Lodge is only accessible to private vehicles that are camping. All other visitors must use the Reds Meadow Shuttle Bus (7am-7:30pm daily, $7 per person) to access Reds Meadow Valley and Devils Postpile National Monument.

**Contact:** Inyo National Forest, 760/873-2400, www.fs.usda.gov/inyo; CLM Services, 650/322-1181, www.clm-services.com.

## 69 LAKE GEORGE

### Scenic rating: 8

in Inyo National Forest

**Map 10.1, page 519**

The sites here have views of Lake George, a beautiful lake in a rock basin below the spectacular Crystal Crag. Lake George is at 9,000 feet elevation, a small lake fed by creeks coming from both Crystal Lake and TJ Lake. TJ Lake is only about a 20-minute walk from the campground, and Crystal Lake is about a 45-minute romp; both make excellent short hiking trips. Trout fishing at Lake George is decent—not great, not bad, but decent. Swimming is not allowed, but boats with small motors are permitted.

**Campsites, facilities:** There are 16 sites for tents or RVs up to 25 feet (no hookups). Picnic tables, fire grills, and bear boxes (mandatory) are provided. Drinking water and flush toilets are available. A grocery store, coin laundry, coin showers, primitive boat launch, and propane gas are nearby. Leashed pets are permitted.

**Reservations, fees:** Reservations are not

accepted. Sites are $23 per night with a seven-day limit. Open mid-June through mid-September, weather permitting.

**Directions:** From Lee Vining on U.S. 395, drive south for 25 miles to Mammoth Junction and Highway 203/Minaret Summit Road. Turn west on Highway 203 and drive four miles to Lake Mary Road. Continue straight through the intersection and drive four miles to Lake Mary Loop Drive. Turn left and drive 0.3 mile to Lake George Road. Turn right and drive 0.5 mile to the campground.

**Contact:** Inyo National Forest, Mammoth Lakes Visitor Center, 760/924-5500, www.fs.usda.gov/inyo; Inyo Recreation, 760/934-5795.

## 70 GLASS CREEK

### Scenic rating: 5

in Inyo National Forest

**Map 10.2, page 520**

This primitive camp is along Glass Creek at 7,600 feet elevation, about a mile from Obsidian Dome to the nearby west. A trail follows Glass Creek past the southern edge of the dome, a craggy, volcanic formation that tops out at 8,611 feet elevation. That trail continues along Glass Creek, climbing to the foot of San Joaquin Mountain for a great view of the high desert to the east. Insider's tip: The Department of Fish and Game stocks Glass Creek with trout just once each June, right at the camp.

**Campsites, facilities:** There are 50 sites for tents or RVs up to 40 feet (no hookups). Picnic tables and fire grills are provided. Vault toilets are available. No drinking water is available. Some facilities are wheelchair-accessible. Leashed pets are permitted.

**Reservations, fees:** Reservations are not accepted. There is no fee for camping. A 14-day limit is enforced. Open late April through early November, weather permitting.

**Directions:** From Lee Vining, drive south on U.S. 395 (past the first Highway 158/June

Lake Loop turnoff) for 11 miles to June Lake Junction. Continue south on U.S. 395 for six miles to a Forest Service road (Glass Creek Road). Turn west (right) and drive 0.25 mile to the camp access road on the right. Turn right and continue 0.5 mile to the main camp at the end of the road. Two notes: 1) A primitive area with large RV sites can be used as an overflow area on the right side of the access road. 2) If arriving from the south on U.S. 395, a direct left turn to Glass Creek Road is impossible. Heading north you will pass the CalTrans Crestview Maintenance Station on the right. Continue north, make a U-turn when possible, and follow the above directions.

**Contact:** Inyo National Forest, Mono Basin Scenic Area Ranger Station and Visitor Center, 760/647-3044, www.fs.usda.gov/inyo.

## 7.1 BIG SPRINGS

### Scenic rating: 5
on Deadman Creek in Inyo National Forest

Map 10.2, page 520

Big Springs, at 7,300 feet elevation, is on the edge of the high desert on the east side of U.S. 395. The main attractions are Deadman Creek, which runs right by the camp, and Big Springs, just on the opposite side of the river. The hot springs in the area are best reached by driving south on U.S. 395 to the Mammoth Lakes Airport and turning left on Hot Creek Road. As with all hot springs, use at your own risk.

**Campsites, facilities:** There are 26 sites for tents or RVs up to 40 feet (no hookups). Picnic tables and fire grills are provided. Vault toilets are available. No drinking water is available. Leashed pets are permitted.

**Reservations, fees:** Reservations are not accepted. There is no fee for camping. A 21-day limit is enforced. Open late April through early November, weather permitting.

**Directions:** From Lee Vining, drive south on U.S. 395 (past the first Highway 158/June Lake

Loop turnoff) to June Lake Junction. Continue south for about seven miles to Owens River Road. Turn east (left) and drive two miles to a fork. Bear left at the fork and drive 0.25 mile to the camp on the left side of the road.

**Contact:** Inyo National Forest, Mono Basin Scenic Area Ranger Station and Visitor Center, 760/647-3044, www.fs.usda.gov/inyo.

## 7.2 DEADMAN AND OBSIDIAN FLAT GROUP

### Scenic rating: 5
on Deadman Creek in Inyo National Forest

Map 10.2, page 520

This little-known camp at 7,800 feet elevation along little Deadman Creek is primitive and dusty in the summer, cold in the early summer and fall. From camp, hikers can drive west for three miles to the headwaters of Deadman Creek and to a trailhead for a route that runs past San Joaquin Mountain and beyond to little Yost Lake, a one-way hike of four miles.

**Campsites, facilities:** There are 30 sites for tents or RVs up to 30 feet. Nearby Obsidian Flat Group Camp can accommodate tents or RVs of any length and up to 50 people (no hookups). Picnic tables and fire grills are provided. Bear boxes are provided at Obsidian. Vault toilets are available. There is no drinking water. Garbage must be packed out. Leashed pets are permitted.

**Reservations, fees:** Reservations are not accepted at Deadman and there is no fee for camping. Reservations are required at Obsidian Flat Group at 877/444-6777 ($10 reservation fee) or www.recreation.gov ($9 reservation fee); the group site is $20 per night. Open late May through early November, weather permitting.

**Directions:** From Lee Vining, drive south on U.S. 395 (past the first Highway 158/June Lake Loop turnoff) to June Lake Junction. Continue south for 6.5 miles to a Forest Service road (Deadman Creek Road) on the west (right) side of the road. Turn west (right)

and drive two miles to the camp access road on the right. Turn right and drive 0.5 mile to the camp. Note: If you are arriving from the south on U.S. 395 and you reach the CalTrans Crestview Maintenance Station on the right, you have gone one mile too far; make a U-turn when possible and return for access.

**Contact:** Inyo National Forest, Mono Basin Scenic Area Ranger Station and Visitor Center, 760/647-3044, www.fs.usda.gov/inyo.

## 73 BROWN'S OWENS RIVER CAMPGROUND

### Scenic rating: 7

near the Owens River

**Map 10.2, page 520**

This camp along the upper Owens River is well situated for hiking, mountain biking, fishing, and swimming. The campground landscape is fairly sparse, so the campground can seem less intimate than those set in a forest. But this makes for great long-distance views of the White Mountains and for taking in those sunsets.

**Campsites, facilities:** There are 75 sites for tents or RVs of any length (no hookups). Some trailer rentals with full hookups are available. Picnic tables and fire rings are provided. Drinking water, flush and pit toilets, coin showers, coin laundry, and a convenience store are available. Some facilities are wheelchair-accessible. Leashed pets are permitted.

**Reservations, fees:** Reservations are accepted by phone only. Sites are $24 per night. Open late April through late September.

**Directions:** From Mammoth Lakes on Highway 395/203, drive south on Highway 395 to Benton Crossing Road. Turn left and drive five miles to campground.

**Contact:** Brown's Owens River Campground, 760/920-0971, www.brownscampgrounds.com.

## 74 PINE GLEN

### Scenic rating: 6

in Inyo National Forest

**Map 10.2, page 520**

Note: Pine Glen will close for the 2017 season while the water system is replaced. The Forest Service plans to reopen it for the 2018 season.

This is a well-situated base camp for several side trips. The most popular is the trip to Devils Postpile National Monument, with a shuttle ride from the Mammoth Ski Area. Other nearby trips include exploring Inyo Craters and Mammoth Lakes. The elevation is 7,800 feet.

**Campsites, facilities:** There are 10 sites (used as overflow from Old Shady Rest and New Shady Rest campgrounds) and nine group sites for tents or RVs up to 55 feet (no hookups) that can accommodate 15-30 people each. Picnic tables and fire grills are provided; bear boxes are at the group site only. Drinking water, flush toilets, and a dump station are available. A grocery store, coin laundry, propane gas, and horseback-riding facilities are nearby in Mammoth Lakes. Leashed pets are permitted.

**Reservations, fees:** Reservations are accepted for individual sites but are required for group sites at 877/444-6777 ($10 reservation fee) or www.recreation.gov ($9 reservation fee). Sites are $18.58-20.35 per night, group sites are $49.58-99.56 per night, and it's $5 per night for each additional vehicle. Open late May through September, weather permitting.

**Directions:** From Lee Vining on U.S. 395, drive south for 25 miles to Mammoth Junction and Highway 203/Minaret Summit Road. Turn west on Highway 203 and drive about three miles to the Mammoth Lakes Visitor Center. Just past the visitor center, turn right on Old Sawmill Road and drive a short distance to the campground on the right.

**Contact:** Inyo National Forest, Mammoth Lakes Visitor Center, 760/924-5500, www.fs.usda.gov/inyo; Inyo Recreation, 760/934-5795.

## 75 NEW SHADY REST

🥾 🛶 🐎 🚙 ⛺

**Scenic rating: 6**

in Inyo National Forest

**Map 10.2, page 520**

This easy-to-reach camp is at 7,800 feet elevation, not far from the Mammoth Mountain Ski Area. The surrounding Inyo National Forest provides many side-trip opportunities, including Devils Postpile National Monument (by shuttle available from near the Mammoth Mountain Ski Area), the Upper San Joaquin River, and the Inyo National Forest backcountry trails, streams, and lakes.

**Campsites, facilities:** There are 92 sites for tents or RVs up to 38 feet (no hookups). Picnic tables, fire grills, and bear boxes (mandatory) are provided. Drinking water and flush toilets are available. A dump station, playground, grocery store, coin laundry, and propane gas are nearby. Up to two leashed pets per site are permitted.

**Reservations, fees:** Reservations are accepted at 877/444-6777 ($10 reservation fee) or www. recreation.gov ($9 reservation fee). Sites are $19.47-21.44 per night, plus $5 per night for each additional vehicle and a $10 dump station fee. Open mid-May through October with a 14-day limit, weather permitting.

**Directions:** From Lee Vining on U.S. 395, drive south for 25 miles to Mammoth Junction and Highway 203/Minaret Summit Road. Turn west on Highway 203 and drive about three miles to the Mammoth Lakes Visitor Center. Just past the visitors center, turn right on Old Sawmill Road and drive a short distance to the campground on the right.

**Contact:** Inyo National Forest, Mammoth Lakes Visitor Center, 760/924-5500, www.fs.usda.gov/inyo; Inyo Recreation, 760/934-5795.

## 76 OLD SHADY REST

🥾 🛶 🐎 🚙 ⛺

**Scenic rating: 6**

in Inyo National Forest

**Map 10.2, page 520**

Names such as "Old Shady Rest" are usually reserved for mom-and-pop RV parks. The Forest Service respected tradition in officially naming this park what the locals have called it all along. Like New Shady Rest, this camp is near the Mammoth Lakes Visitor Center, with the same side trips available. It is one of three camps in the immediate vicinity. The elevation is 7,800 feet.

**Campsites, facilities:** There are 47 sites for tents or RVs up to 55 feet (no hookups). Picnic tables and fire grills are provided. Drinking water and flush toilets are available. A dump station, playground, grocery store, coin laundry, and propane gas are nearby. Leashed pets are permitted.

**Reservations, fees:** Reservations are not accepted. Sites are $19.47-21.44 per night. Open mid-June through early September, weather permitting.

**Directions:** From Lee Vining on U.S. 395, drive south for 25 miles to Mammoth Junction and Highway 203/Minaret Summit Road. Turn west on Highway 203 and drive about three miles to the Forest Service Visitor Center. Just past the visitors center, turn right and drive 0.3 mile to the campground on the left.

**Contact:** Inyo National Forest, Mammoth Lakes Visitor Center, 760/924-5500, www.fs.usda.gov/inyo; Inyo Recreation, 760/934-5795.

## 77 MAMMOTH MOUNTAIN RV PARK

🏊 🥾 🐎 🚴 ♿ 🚙 ⛺

**Scenic rating: 6**

near Mammoth Lakes

**Map 10.2, page 520**

This RV park is just across the street from the

Forest Service Visitor Center. Got a question? Someone there has got an answer. This camp is open year-round, making it a great place to stay for a ski trip.

**Campsites, facilities:** There are 179 sites, some with full hookups (50 amps), for tents or RVs up to 45 feet, and two group tent sites for at least 17 people (minimum). Two cabins are also available. Picnic tables are provided. Fire pits are provided at some sites. Restrooms with showers, drinking water, cable TV, dump station, coin laundry, heated year-round swimming pool, seasonal recreation room, playground, RV supplies, and a spa are available. Some facilities are wheelchair-accessible. Supplies can be obtained in Mammoth Lakes, 0.25 mile away. Leashed pets are permitted, with certain restrictions.

**Reservations, fees:** Reservations are accepted at 800/582-4603 and www.mammothrv.com. RV sites are $45-52 per night, tent sites are $31-36 per night, plus $3 per person per night for more than two people, $2 per night for each additional vehicle, and $2 per pet per night (three pets max). The group site is $25 per night (minimum of 17 people) with an additional fee of $5 per each person. Some credit cards are accepted. Open year-round.

**Directions:** From Lee Vining on U.S. 395, drive south for 25 miles to Mammoth Junction and Highway 203. Turn west on Highway 203 and drive three miles to the park on the left.

From Bishop, drive 40 miles north on Highway 395 to the Mammoth Lakes exit. Turn west on Highway 203, go under the overpass, and drive three miles to the park on the left.

**Contact:** Mammoth Mountain RV Park, 760/934-3822, www.mammothrv.com.

## 78 TWIN LAKES

**Scenic rating: 8**

in Inyo National Forest

Map 10.2, page 520

From Twin Lakes, you can look southwest

and see pretty Twin Falls, a wide cascade that runs into the head of upper Twin Lake. There are actually two camps here, one on each side of the access road, at 8,600 feet. Lower Twin Lake is a favorite for fly fishers in float tubes. Powerboats, swimming, and sailboarding are not permitted. Use is heavy at the campground. Often there will be people lined up waiting for another family's weeklong vacation to end so theirs can start. Excellent hiking trails are in the area.

**Campsites, facilities:** There are 92 sites for tents or RVs up to 40 feet (no hookups). Picnic tables, fire grills, and bear boxes (mandatory use) are provided. Drinking water, flush toilets, and a boat launch are available. A grocery store, coin laundry, coin showers, and propane gas are nearby. Some facilities are wheelchair-accessible. Leashed pets are permitted.

**Reservations, fees:** Reservations are accepted at 877/444-6777 ($10 reservation fee) or www. recreation.gov ($9 reservation fee). Sites are $20.35-22.12 per night, $5 per night for each additional vehicle. Open mid-May through late October, weather permitting.

**Directions:** From Lee Vining on U.S. 395, drive south for 25 miles to Mammoth Junction and Highway 203/Minaret Summit Road. Turn west on Highway 203 and drive four miles to Lake Mary Road. Continue straight through the intersection and drive 2.3 miles to Twin Lakes Loop Road. Turn right and drive 0.5 mile to the campground.

**Contact:** Inyo National Forest, Mammoth Lakes Visitor Center, 760/924-5500, www.fs.usda.gov/inyo; Inyo Recreation, 760/934-5795.

## 79 SHERWIN CREEK

**Scenic rating: 7**

in Inyo National Forest

Map 10.2, page 520

This camp is along little Sherwin Creek, at 7,600 feet elevation, a short distance from the town of Mammoth Lakes. If you drive a mile east on Sherwin Creek Road, then turn right at the short spur road, you will find a trailhead for a six-mile hike to Valentine Lake in the John Muir Wilderness, on the northwest flank of Bloody Mountain.

**Campsites, facilities:** There are 70 sites for tents or RVs up to 34 feet (no hookups) and 15 walk-in tent sites. Picnic tables, fire grills, and bear boxes (mandatory) are provided. Drinking water and flush toilets are available. Leashed pets are permitted.

**Reservations, fees:** Reservations are accepted at 877/444-6777 ($10 reservation fee) or www.recreation.gov ($9 reservation fee). Sites are $19.47-22.24 per night, plus $5 per night for each additional vehicle. Open early May through mid-September, weather permitting.

**Directions:** From Lee Vining on U.S. 395, drive south for 25 miles to Mammoth Junction and Highway 203/Minaret Summit Road. Turn west on Highway 203 and drive about three miles to the Mammoth Lakes Visitor Center and continue a short distance to Old Mammoth Road. Turn left and drive about a mile to Sherwin Creek. Turn south and drive two miles on largely unpaved road to the campground on the left side of the road.

**Contact:** Inyo National Forest, Mammoth Lakes Visitor Center, 760/924-5500, www.fs.usda.gov/inyo; Inyo Recreation, 760/934-5795.

## 80 LAKE MARY

**Scenic rating: 9**

in Inyo National Forest

**Map 10.2, page 520**

Lake Mary is the star of the Mammoth Lakes region. Of the 11 lakes in the area, this is the largest and most developed. It provides a resort, boat ramp, and boat rentals, and it receives the highest number of trout stocks. No waterbody contact, including swimming, is allowed, and the speed limit is 10 mph. It is set at 8,900

feet elevation in a place of incredible natural beauty, one of the few spots that literally have it all. Of course, that often includes quite a few other people. If there are too many for you, an excellent trailhead at nearby Coldwater camp leads up to Emerald Lake.

**Campsites, facilities:** There are 41 sites for tents or RVs up to 30 feet (no hookups). Picnic tables, fire rings, and bear boxes (mandatory) are provided. Drinking water and flush toilets are available. A grocery store, coin laundry, and propane gas are nearby. Two leashed pets per site are permitted.

**Reservations, fees:** Reservations are accepted at 877/444-6777 ($10 reservation fee) or www.recreation.gov ($9 reservation fee). Sites are $20.35-23.12 per night, plus $5 per night for each additional vehicle. Open early June through mid-September with a 14-day limit, weather permitting.

**Directions:** Take U.S. 395 to Mammoth Junction and Highway 203. Turn west on Highway 203 and drive through the town of Mammoth Lakes to the junction of Minaret Road/Highway 203 and Lake Mary Road. Continue straight through the intersection and drive 3.6 miles to Lake Mary Loop Drive. Turn right and drive 0.5 mile to the campground entrance.

**Contact:** Inyo National Forest, Mammoth Lakes Visitor Center, 760/924-5500, www.fs.usda.gov/inyo; Inyo Recreation, 760/934-5795.

## 81 PINE CITY

**Scenic rating: 7**

near Lake Mary in Inyo National Forest

**Map 10.2, page 520**

This camp is at the edge of Lake Mary at an elevation of 8,900 feet. It's popular for both families and fly fishers with float tubes. Swimming is not permitted.

**Campsites, facilities:** There are 10 sites for tents or RVs up to 40 feet (no hookups). Picnic

tables, fire grills, and bear boxes (mandatory) are provided. Drinking water and flush toilets are available. A grocery store, coin laundry, boat launch, boat rentals, and propane gas are nearby. Some facilities are wheelchair-accessible. Leashed pets are permitted.

**Reservations, fees:** Reservations are not accepted. Sites are $23 per night. Open early June through mid-September.

**Directions:** Take U.S. 395 to Mammoth Junction and Highway 203. Turn west on Highway 203 and drive through the town of Mammoth Lakes to the junction of Minaret Road/Highway 203 and Lake Mary Road. Continue straight through the intersection and drive 3.6 miles to Lake Mary Loop Drive. Turn left and drive 0.25 mile to the campground.

**Contact:** Inyo National Forest, Mammoth Lakes Visitor Center, 760/924-5500, www.fs.usda.gov/inyo; Inyo Recreation, 760/934-5795.

supplies in Mammoth Lakes. Two leashed pets per site are permitted.

**Reservations, fees:** Reservations are accepted at 877/444-6777 ($10 reservation fee) or www.recreation.gov ($9 reservation fee). Sites are $20.35-22.12 per night, plus $5 per night for each additional vehicle, with a 14-day limit. Open mid-June through mid-September.

**Directions:** From Lee Vining on U.S. 395, drive south for 25 miles to Mammoth Junction and Highway 203/Minaret Summit Road. Turn west on Highway 203 and drive four miles to Lake Mary Road. Continue straight through the intersection and drive 3.6 miles to Lake Mary Loop Drive. Turn left and drive 0.6 mile to the camp entrance road.

**Contact:** Inyo National Forest, Mammoth Lakes Visitor Center, 760/924-5500, www.fs.usda.gov/inyo; Inyo Recreation, 760/934-5795.

## 82 COLDWATER

**Scenic rating: 7**

on Coldwater Creek in Inyo National Forest

**Map 10.2, page 520**

While this camp is not the first choice of many simply because there is no lake view, it has a special attraction all its own. First, it is a two-minute drive from the campground to Lake Mary, which has a boat ramp, rentals, and good trout fishing. Second, at the end of the campground access road is a trailhead for two outstanding hikes. From the Y at the trailhead, if you head right, you will travel up Coldwater Creek to Emerald Lake, a great little hike. If you head to the left, you will have a more ambitious trip to Arrowhead, Skelton, and Red Lakes, all within three miles. The elevation is 8,900 feet.

**Campsites, facilities:** There are 77 sites for tents or RVs up to 50 feet (no hookups). Picnic tables, fire grills, and bear boxes (mandatory) are provided. Drinking water, flush toilets, and horse facilities are available. You can buy

## 83 CONVICT LAKE

**Scenic rating: 7**

in Inyo National Forest

**Map 10.2, page 520**     **BEST (**

This is the most popular camp in the Mammoth area and it is frequently full. While the lake rates a 10 for scenic beauty, the camp itself is in a stark desert setting, out of sight of the lake, and it can get windy and cold due to the exposed sites. After driving on U.S. 395 to get here, it is always astonishing to clear the rise and see Convict Lake (7,583 feet) and its gemlike waters set in a mountain bowl beneath a back wall of high, jagged wilderness peaks. The camp is right beside Convict Creek, about a quarter mile from Convict Lake. Both provide very good trout fishing, including some rare monster-sized brown trout below the Convict Lake outlet. Fishing is often outstanding in Convict Lake, with a chance of hooking a 10- or 15-pound trout. The lake speed limit is 10 mph, and although swimming is allowed, it is not popular because of the cold, often choppy water. A trail is routed around the lake, providing a nice day hike. A bonus is an outstanding resort with a boat launch, boat rentals, cabin rentals, small store, restaurant, and bar. Horseback rides and hiking are also available, with a trail routed along the north side of the lake, then along upper Convict Creek (a stream crossing is required about three miles in) and into the John Muir Wilderness.

**Campsites, facilities:** There are 85 sites for tents or RVs up to 40 feet (no hookups). Rental cabins are also available through Convict Lake Resort. Picnic tables, fire grills, and bear boxes (mandatory) are provided. Drinking water, coin showers, and flush toilets are available. A dump station, boat ramp, store, restaurant, and horseback-riding facilities are nearby. Some facilities are wheelchair-accessible. Leashed pets are permitted.

**Reservations, fees:** Reservations are accepted at 877/444-6777 ($10 reservation fee) or www.recreation.gov ($9 reservation fee). For cabin reservations, call 800/992-2260. Sites are $23 per night, plus $5 per night for each additional vehicle. Open mid-April through October, weather permitting; the cabins are open year-round.

**Directions:** From Lee Vining on U.S. 395, drive south for 31 miles (five miles past Mammoth Junction) to Convict Lake Road (adjacent to Mammoth Lakes Airport). Turn west (right) on Convict Lake Road and drive three miles to Convict Lake. Cross the dam and drive a short distance to the campground entrance road on the left. Turn left and drive 0.25 mile to the campground.

From Bishop, drive north on U.S. 395 for 35 miles to Convict Lake Road. Turn west (left) and drive three miles to the lake and campground.

**Contact:** Inyo National Forest, Mammoth Lakes Visitor Center, 760/924-5500, www.fs.usda.gov/inyo; Convict Lake Resort and Cabins, 800/992-2260, www.convictlake.com.

## 84 MCGEE CREEK RV PARK

**Scenic rating: 6**

near Crowley Lake

**Map 10.2, page 520**

This is a popular layover spot for folks visiting giant Crowley Lake. Crowley Lake is still one of the better lakes in the Sierra for trout fishing, with good prospects for large rainbow trout and brown trout, though the 20-pound brown trout that once made this lake famous are now mainly a legend. McGee Creek runs through the campground, and trout fishing is popular. Several trout ponds are also available; call for fees. Beautiful Convict Lake provides a nearby side-trip option. It is about nine miles to Rock Creek Lake, a beautiful high-mountain destination. Note: All boats must be certified mussel-free before launching. The elevation is 7,000 feet.

**Campsites, facilities:** There are 40 sites with full (50 amps), partial, or no hookups for tents or RVs up to 40 feet; some sites are pull-through. Picnic tables are provided and there are fire pits at some sites. Drinking water and restrooms with showers and flush toilets are available. Leashed pets are permitted.

**Reservations, fees:** Reservations are accepted. Sites are $25-35 per night, plus $3 per person per night for more than two people age 16 and over. Weekly and monthly rates are available. Open late April through September, weather permitting.

**Directions:** From the junction of U.S. 395 and Highway 203 (the Mammoth Lakes turnoff), drive south on U.S. 395 for eight miles to the turnoff for McGee Creek Road. Take that exit and look for the park entrance on the left.

**Contact:** McGee Creek RV Park, 760/935-4233, www.mcgeecreekrv-campground.com.

## 85 MCGEE CREEK

### Scenic rating: 7

in Inyo National Forest

**Map 10.2, page 520**

This is a Forest Service camp at an elevation of 7,600 feet, set along little McGee Creek, a good location for fishing and hiking. There are few trees. The stream is stocked with trout, and a trailhead is just up the road. From here you can hike along upper McGee Creek and into the John Muir Wilderness.

**Campsites, facilities:** There are 28 sites for tents or RVs up to 25 feet (no hookups). Picnic tables and fire grills are provided. Drinking water, flush and vault toilets, and shade structures are available. Horseback-riding facilities are nearby. Some facilities are wheelchair-accessible. Leashed pets are permitted.

**Reservations, fees:** Reservations are accepted at 877/444-6777 ($10 reservation fee) or www.recreation.gov ($9 reservation fee). Sites are $21 per night, plus $7 per night for additional vehicle. Open mid-May through mid-October, weather permitting.

**Directions:** From Mammoth Lakes at the junction of U.S. 395 and Highway 203, drive south on U.S. 395 for 8.5 miles to McGee Creek Road (signed). Turn right (toward the Sierra) and drive 1.5 miles on a narrow, windy road to the campground.

**Contact:** Inyo National Forest, White Mountain Ranger District, 760/873-2500, www.fs.usda.gov/inyo; McGee Creek Pack Station, 760/935-4324.

## 86 CROWLEY LAKE

### Scenic rating: 5

near Crowley Lake

**Map 10.2, page 520**

This large BLM camp is across U.S. 395 from the south shore of Crowley Lake. The surroundings are fairly stark and the elevation is 6,800 feet. For many, that is of little concern. Crowley is the trout-fishing capital of the eastern Sierra, with the annual opener (the last Saturday in April) a great celebration. Though the trout fishing can go through a lull in midsummer, it can become excellent again in the fall when the lake's population of big brown trout heads up to the top of the lake at the mouth of the Owens River. This is a large lake with 45 miles of shoreline. In the summer, water sports include swimming, waterskiing, wakeboarding, personal watercraft riding, and sailboarding. Note: All boats must be certified mussel-free before launching.

**Campsites, facilities:** There are 47 sites for tents or RVs of any length (no hookups). Picnic tables and fire grills are provided. Drinking water and vault toilets are available. Floating chemical toilets are available on the lake. A grocery store, boat ramp, boat rentals, and horseback-riding facilities are nearby. Leashed pets are permitted.

**Reservations, fees:** Reservations are not accepted. Sites are $5 per night, and season passes are available for $300. There is a 14-day limit. Open late April through October, weather permitting.

**Directions:** Drive on U.S. 395 to the Crowley Lake Road exit (30 miles north of Bishop). Take that exit west (toward the Sierra) to Crowley Lake Road. Turn right on Crowley Lake Road and drive northwest for three miles to the campground entrance on the left (well signed).

**Contact:** Bureau of Land Management, Bishop Field Office, 760/872-5008, www.blm.gov/ca; McGee Creek Pack Station, 760/935-4324.

## 87 TUFF

### Scenic rating: 5

near Crowley Lake in Inyo National Forest

**Map 10.2, page 520**

Easy access off U.S. 395 makes this camp a winner, though it is not nearly as pretty as those up Rock Creek Road to the west of Tom's Place.

The fact that you can get in and out of here quickly makes it ideal for campers planning fishing trips to nearby Crowley Lake. The elevation is 7,000 feet. Note: All boats must be certified mussel-free before launching.

**Campsites, facilities:** There are 34 sites for tents or RVs up to 45 feet (no hookups). Picnic tables, fire grills, and bear boxes (mandatory) are provided. Drinking water and flush toilets are available. Some facilities are wheelchair-accessible. Leashed pets are permitted.

**Reservations, fees:** Reservations are accepted at 877/444-6777 ($10 reservation fee) or www. recreation.gov ($9 reservation fee). Sites are $21 per night, plus $7 per additional vehicle. A 21-day limit is enforced. Open late April through mid-October, weather permitting.

**Directions:** From Mammoth Lakes at the junction of U.S. 395 and Highway 203, drive south on U.S. 395 for 15.5 miles (one mile north of Tom's Place) to Rock Creek Road. Turn left (east) on Rock Creek Road and drive 0.5 mile to the campground.

**Contact:** Inyo National Forest, White Mountain Ranger District, 760/873-2500, www. fs.usda.gov/inyo.

## 88 FRENCH CAMP

### Scenic rating: 5

on Rock Creek near Crowley Lake in Inyo National Forest

**Map 10.2, page 520**

French Camp is just a short hop from U.S. 395 and Tom's Place, right where the high Sierra turns into high plateau country. Side-trip opportunities include boating and fishing on giant Crowley Lake and, to the west on Rock Creek Road, visiting little Rock Creek Lake 10 miles away. The elevation is 7,500 feet.

**Campsites, facilities:** There are 86 sites for tents or RVs up to 40 feet (no hookups). Picnic tables, fire grills, and bear boxes (mandatory) are provided. Drinking water, flush toilets, and

a dump station are available. Leashed pets are permitted.

**Reservations, fees:** Reservations are accepted at 877/444-6777 ($10 reservation fee) or www. recreation.gov ($9 reservation fee). Sites are $23 per night, plus $7 per additional vehicle. Open early May through October, weather permitting.

**Directions:** From Mammoth Lakes at the junction of U.S. 395 and Highway 203, drive south on U.S. 395 for 15 miles to Tom's Place and Rock Creek Road. Turn right (toward the Sierra) at Rock Creek Road and drive 0.25 mile to the campground on the right.

**Contact:** Inyo National Forest, White Mountain Ranger District, 760/873-2500, www. fs.usda.gov/inyo.

## 89 HOLIDAY CAMPGROUND

### Scenic rating: 5

near Crowley Lake in Inyo National Forest

**Map 10.2, page 520**

There's a story behind every name. Holiday is a group camp that is opened as an overflow camp when needed. It is near Rock Creek, not far from Crowley Lake, with surroundings far more stark than the camps to the west on Rock Creek Road. The elevation is 7,500 feet.

**Campsites, facilities:** There are 35 sites for tents or RVs up to 16 feet (no hookups) or groups up to 100 people. Picnic tables and fire grills are provided. Drinking water (summer only) and vault toilets are available. Some facilities are wheelchair-accessible. Leashed pets are permitted.

**Reservations, fees:** Reservations are not accepted. Sites are $22 per night (rate for group camping varies based on size). Open year-round; winter use is free with no water, garbage service, or snow removal.

**Directions:** From Mammoth Lakes at the junction of U.S. 395 and Highway 203, drive south on U.S. 395 for 15 miles south to Tom's Place and Rock Creek Road. Turn right (toward the

Sierra) and drive 0.5 mile to the campground on the left.

**Contact:** Inyo National Forest, White Mountain Ranger District, 760/873-2500, www. fs.usda.gov/inyo.

# 90 ASPEN GROUP CAMP

### Scenic rating: 7
near Crowley Lake in Inyo National Forest

**Map 10.2, page 520**

This small group campground on Rock Creek is primarily a base camp for anglers and campers heading to nearby Crowley Lake or venturing west to Rock Creek Lake.

**Campsites, facilities:** There is one group camp for tents or RVs up to 25 feet (no hookups) that can accommodate up to 25 people. Picnic tables, fire grills, and bear boxes (mandatory) are provided. Drinking water and flush toilets are available. Limited supplies are available in Tom's Place, three miles away. Some facilities are wheelchair-accessible. Leashed pets are permitted.

**Reservations, fees:** Reservations are required at 877/444-6777 ($10 reservation fee) or www. recreation.gov ($9 reservation fee). The group fee is $73 per night. Open mid-May through mid-October, weather permitting.

**Directions:** From Mammoth Lakes at the junction of U.S. 395 and Highway 203, drive south on U.S. 395 for 15 miles south to Tom's Place and Rock Creek Road. Turn right (toward the Sierra) at Rock Creek Road and drive three miles to the campground.

**Contact:** Inyo National Forest, White Mountain Ranger District, 760/873-2500, www. fs.usda.gov/inyo.

# 91 IRIS MEADOW

### Scenic rating: 5
near Crowley Lake in Inyo National Forest

**Map 10.2, page 520**

Iris Meadow, at 8,300 feet elevation on the flank of Red Mountain (11,472 feet), is the first in a series of five Forest Service camps set near Rock Creek Canyon on the road leading from Tom's Place up to pretty Rock Creek Lake. A bonus is that some of the campsites are next to the creek. Rock Creek is stocked with trout, and nearby Rock Creek Lake also provides fishing and boating for hand-launched boats. Note: All boats must be certified mussel-free before launching at Crowley Lake. This camp also has access to a great trailhead for wilderness exploration.

**Campsites, facilities:** There are 14 sites for tents or RVs up to 40 feet (no hookups). Picnic tables, fire grills, and bear boxes (mandatory) are provided. Drinking water and flush toilets are available. Limited supplies are available in Tom's Place, three miles away. Some facilities are wheelchair-accessible. Leashed pets are permitted.

**Reservations, fees:** Reservations are not accepted. Sites are $23 per night. Open late May through mid-September, weather permitting.

**Directions:** From Mammoth Lakes at the junction of U.S. 395 and Highway 203, drive south on U.S. 395 for 15 miles to Tom's Place and Rock Creek Road. Turn right (toward the Sierra) at Rock Creek Road and drive three miles to the campground.

**Contact:** Inyo National Forest, White Mountain Ranger District, 760/873-2500, www. fs.usda.gov/inyo.

## 92 BIG MEADOW

### Scenic rating: 8

near Crowley Lake in Inyo National Forest

**Map 10.2, page 520**

This is a smaller, quieter camp in the series of campgrounds along Rock Creek. Some of the campsites are along the creek. Beautiful Rock Creek Lake provides a nearby side trip. In the fall, turning aspens make for spectacular colors. The elevation is 8,600 feet.

**Campsites, facilities:** There are 11 sites for tents or RVs up to 22 feet (no hookups). Picnic tables, fire grills, and bear boxes (mandatory) are provided. Drinking water and flush toilets are available. Limited supplies are available in Tom's Place, four miles away. Some facilities are wheelchair-accessible. Leashed pets are permitted.

**Reservations, fees:** Reservations are not accepted. Sites are $23 per night. Open early May through late October.

**Directions:** From Mammoth Lakes at the junction of U.S. 395 and Highway 203, drive south on U.S. 395 for 15 miles south to Tom's Place and Rock Creek Road. Turn right (toward the Sierra) at Rock Creek Road and drive four miles to the campground.

**Contact:** Inyo National Forest, White Mountain Ranger District, 760/873-2500, www. fs.usda.gov/inyo.

## 93 PALISADE GROUP

### Scenic rating: 8

in Rock Creek Canyon in Inyo National Forest

**Map 10.2, page 520**

This shoe might just fit. Palisade, formerly a tiny family campground, now provides a pretty spot for group camping along Rock Creek at 8,600 feet elevation, with many side-trip options. The closest is fishing for small trout on Rock Creek and at Rock Creek Lake up the road to the west. Another option is horseback riding, and horse rentals are in the area. The area is loaded with aspens. Some of the campsites are directly on the creek.

**Campsites, facilities:** There is a group site for tents only for up to 25 people. Picnic tables, fire grills, and bear boxes (mandatory) are provided. Horseback-riding facilities are nearby. Limited supplies are available in Tom's Place, five miles away. Leashed pets are permitted.

**Reservations, fees:** Reservations are required at 877/444-6777 ($10 reservation fee) or www. recreation.gov ($9 reservation fee). The site is $73 per night. Open mid-May through mid-September, weather permitting.

**Directions:** From Mammoth Lakes at the junction of U.S. 395 and Highway 203, drive south on U.S. 395 for 15 miles south to Tom's Place and Rock Creek Road. Turn right (toward the Sierra) at Rock Creek Road and drive five miles to the campground.

**Contact:** Inyo National Forest, White Mountain Ranger District, 760/873-2500, www. fs.usda.gov/inyo; Rock Creek Pack Station, 760/935-4493, www.rockcreekpackstation.com.

## 94 EAST FORK

### Scenic rating: 8

in Rock Creek Canyon in Inyo National Forest

**Map 10.2, page 520**

This is a beautiful, popular campground along East Fork Rock Creek at 9,000 feet elevation. The camp is only three miles from Rock Creek Lake, where there's an excellent trailhead. Mountain biking is popular in this area, and Lower Rock Creek and Sand Canyon have two of the most difficult and desirable trails around; they're suggested for experienced riders only.

**Campsites, facilities:** There are 133 sites for tents or RVs up to 40 feet (no hookups). Picnic tables, fire grills, and bear boxes (mandatory) are provided. Drinking water and flush toilets are available. Limited supplies are available in

Tom's Place and at Rock Creek Lakes Resort. Leashed pets are permitted.

**Reservations, fees:** Reservations are accepted at 877/444-6777 ($10 reservation fee) or www.recreation.gov ($9 reservation fee). Sites are $23 per night, plus $7 per night for each additional vehicle. Open early May through October.

**Directions:** From Mammoth Lakes at the junction of U.S. 395 and Highway 203, drive south on U.S. 395 for 15 miles south to Tom's Place and Rock Creek Road. Turn right (toward the Sierra) at Rock Creek Road and drive five miles to the campground access road on the left.

**Contact:** Inyo National Forest, White Mountain Ranger District, 760/873-2500, www.fs.usda.gov/inyo.

## 95 PINE GROVE AND UPPER PINE GROVE

### Scenic rating: 8

in Rock Creek Canyon in Inyo National Forest

**Map 10.2, page 520**

Pine Grove is one of the smaller camps in the series of campgrounds along Rock Creek. Of the five camps in this canyon, this one is the closest to Rock Creek Lake, just a two-mile drive away (Rock Creek Lake Campground is closer, of course). The aspens are stunning in September, when miles of mountains turn to shimmering golds. Some of the campsites are along the creek. The elevation is 9,300 feet.

**Campsites, facilities:** There are 19 sites for tents or RVs up to 16 feet (no hookups). Picnic tables, fire grills, and bear boxes (mandatory) are provided. Drinking water and vault toilets are available. Horseback-riding facilities are nearby. Limited supplies can be obtained in Tom's Place and at Rock Creek Lakes Resort. Leashed pets are permitted.

**Reservations, fees:** Reservations are not accepted. Sites are $23 per night. Open mid-May through mid-October.

**Directions:** From Mammoth Lakes at the junction of U.S. 395 and Highway 203, drive south

on U.S. 395 for 15 miles south to Tom's Place and Rock Creek Road. Turn right (toward the Sierra) at Rock Creek Road and drive seven miles to the campground.

**Contact:** Inyo National Forest, White Mountain Ranger District, 760/873-2500, www.fs.usda.gov/inyo.

## 96 ROCK CREEK LAKE

### Scenic rating: 9

in Inyo National Forest

**Map 10.2, page 520**

Small but beautiful Rock Creek Lake, at an elevation of 9,600 feet, features cool, clear water, small trout, and a great trailhead for access to the adjacent John Muir Wilderness, with 50 other lakes within a two-hour hike. The setting is drop-dead beautiful, hence the high rating for scenic beauty, but note that the campsites are set close together, side by side, in a paved parking area. This 63-acre lake has a 5-mph speed limit and swimming is allowed. The lake is stocked with Alpers trout, and they are joined by resident brown trout in the 10- to 16-pound class. At times, especially afternoons in late spring, winds out of the west can be cold and pesky. If this campground is full, the nearby Mosquito Flat walk-in campground provides an option. Note that Mosquito Flat has a limit of one night and is designed as a staging area for wilderness backpacking trips, with tent camping only. Insider's tip: Rock Creek Lakes Resort has mouthwatering homemade pie available in the café.

**Campsites, facilities:** There are 28 sites for tents or RVs up to 22 feet (no hookups) and one group tent site for up to 25 people; some of the sites require a short walk in. Picnic tables and fire grills are provided. Drinking water, flush toilets, an unimproved boat launch, and boat rentals are available. Horseback-riding facilities and a café are nearby. Limited supplies can be obtained in Tom's Place and at Rock Creek Lakes Resort. Leashed pets are permitted.

**Reservations, fees:** Reservations are accepted for individual sites and required for group sites at 877/444-6777 ($10 reservation fee) or www.recreation.gov ($9 reservation fee). Sites are $22 per night, and the group site is $73 per night. Open mid-May through October, weather permitting.

**Directions:** From the junction of U.S. 395 and Highway 203 (the Mammoth Lakes turnoff), drive 15 miles south on U.S. 395 to Tom's Place. Turn right (toward the Sierra) at Rock Creek Road and drive seven miles to the campground.

**Contact:** Inyo National Forest, White Mountain Ranger District, 760/873-2500, www.fs.usda.gov/inyo; Rock Creek Pack Station, 760/935-4493, www.rockcreekpackstation.com.

## 97 PLEASANT VALLEY

🏃 🛶 🏕 ♿ 🚐 ⛺

### Scenic rating: 7

near Pleasant Valley Reservoir

Map 10.2, page 520

Pleasant Valley County Campground is near long, narrow Pleasant Valley Reservoir, created by the Owens River. A 15-minute walk from camp takes you to the lake. It is east of the Sierra range in the high desert plateau country; the elevation is 4,200 feet. That makes it available for year-round fishing, and trout are stocked. The Owens River passes through the park, providing wild trout fishing, with most anglers practicing catch-and-release fly-fishing. This is also near a major jumping-off point for hiking, rock-climbing, and wilderness fishing at the Bishop Pass area to the west.

**Campsites, facilities:** There are 200 sites for tents or RVs of any length (no hookups). Picnic tables and fire grills are provided. Drinking water (hand-pumped well water) and vault toilets are available. Groups can be accommodated. Some facilities are wheelchair-accessible. Leashed pets are permitted.

**Reservations, fees:** Reservations are not accepted. Sites are $14 per night per vehicle. Open year-round.

**Directions:** Drive on U.S. 395 to Pleasant Valley Road (seven miles north of Bishop) on the east side of the road. Turn northeast and drive one mile to the park entrance.

**Contact:** Inyo County Parks Department, 760/873-5577, www.inyocountycamping.com.

## 98 PLEASANT VALLEY PIT CAMPGROUND

🏃 🚴 🐕 🚐 ⛺

### Scenic rating: 6

near Bishop off U.S. 395

Map 10.2, page 520

This camp is set in a rocky desert area just south of Pleasant Valley Reservoir. It's a good spot for kids, with boulder scrambling the primary recreation, and is also a good area to see a variety of raptors. Few travelers on U.S. 395 know about the campground, operated by the Bureau of Land Management.

**Campsites, facilities:** There are 75 sites for tents or RVs (no hookups). Vault toilets and a dumpster are provided. There is a campground host, as well as law enforcement patrols, and the campground sees regular maintenance. Fires, charcoal grills, and portable stoves outside developed campgrounds require a permit, when allowed. Leashed pets are permitted.

**Reservations, fees:** Reservations are not accepted. Sites are $2 per night. There is a 60-day limit. Open November to early May, weather permitting.

**Directions:** From Bishop, drive north on U.S. 395 for about five miles to Pleasant Valley Road. Turn right on Pleasant Valley Road and proceed approximately 0.5 mile to the gravel road on the left (west) side of the road. Turn left on the gravel road and drive to the Pleasant Valley Pit Campground.

**Contact:** Bureau of Land Management, Bishop Field Office, 760/872-5008, www.blm.gov/ca.

## 99 HIGHLANDS RV PARK

🐕 ♿ 🚐

### Scenic rating: 3

near Bishop

**Map 10.2, page 520**

This privately operated RV park near Bishop is set up for U.S. 395 cruisers. There is a casino in town. A great side trip is up two-lane Highway 168 to Lake Sabrina. The elevation is 4,300 feet. Note that a few sites are occupied by long-term renters.

**Campsites, facilities:** There are 103 sites with full hookups (30 and 50 amps) for RVs of any length; many sites are pull-through. No tents are permitted. Picnic tables and cable TV are provided. Drinking water, restrooms with flush toilets and showers, dump station, social room with pool table, free Wi-Fi, propane gas, ice, fish-cleaning station, and coin laundry are available. Supplies are available nearby. Some facilities are wheelchair-accessible. Leashed pets are permitted.

**Reservations, fees:** Reservations are recommended. Sites are $43 per night, plus $1 per person per night for more than two people. Weekly and monthly rates are available. Some credit cards are accepted. Open year-round.

**Directions:** From Bishop, drive two miles north on U.S. 395/North Sierra Highway to the campground on the right (east side of road) at 2275 North Sierra Highway.

**Contact:** Highlands RV Park, 760/873-7616, www.highlandsrvpark.com.

# SEQUOIA AND KINGS CANYON

© DREAMSTIME.COM

There is no place like the high Sierra, from Mount Whitney north through Sequoia and Kings Canyon National Parks. This is a paradise filled with deep canyons, high peaks, natural beauty, and groves of the largest living things on earth—giant sequoias. The most popular campsites are in the vicinity of Sequoia and Kings Canyon National Parks, or on the parks' access roads. But this region has wonderful secrets aside from the parks. The Muir Trail Ranch near Florence Lake is set in the John Muir Wilderness and reachable only by foot, boat, or horse. The western slopes of the Sierra have pretty lakes with good trout fishing, while the eastern slopes offer a series of small streams and great wilderness trailheads. The remote Golden Trout Wilderness is one of the most pristine areas in California. In the Kernville area, campgrounds along the Kern River offer access to outstanding white-water rafting and kayaking.

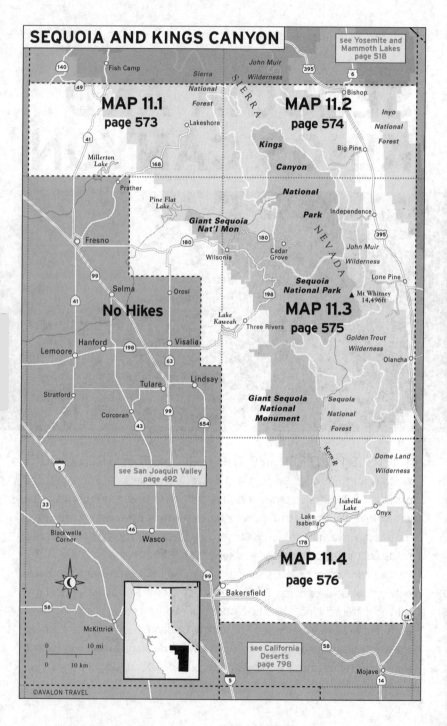

# SEQUOIA AND KINGS CANYON

see Yosemite and Mammoth Lakes page 518

Fish Camp

John Muir Wilderness

**MAP 11.1 page 573**

Sierra National Forest

**MAP 11.2 page 574**

Bishop

Lakeshore

Inyo National Forest

*Kings*

Big Pine

*Canyon*

Millerton Lake

Prather

*National*

Independence

Pine Flat Lake

Giant Sequoia Nat'l Mon

Cedar Grove

*Park*

Fresno

Wilsonia

John Muir Wilderness

Selma

**No Hikes**

Orosi

Lone Pine

Mt Whitney 14,496ft

*Sequoia National Park*

**MAP 11.3 page 575**

Lake Kaweah

Three Rivers

Golden Trout Wilderness

Hanford

Lemoore

Visalia

Olancha

Stratford

Tulare

Lindsay

*Giant Sequoia National Monument*

*Sequoia National Forest*

Corcoran

see San Joaquin Valley page 492

*Dome Land Wilderness*

Kern R.

Isabella Lake

Blackwells Corner

Wasco

Lake Isabella

Onyx

**MAP 11.4 page 576**

Bakersfield

see California Deserts page 798

McKittrick

0    10 mi
0    10 km

Mojave

©AVALON TRAVEL

# Map 11.1

## Sites 1-41
## Pages 578-597

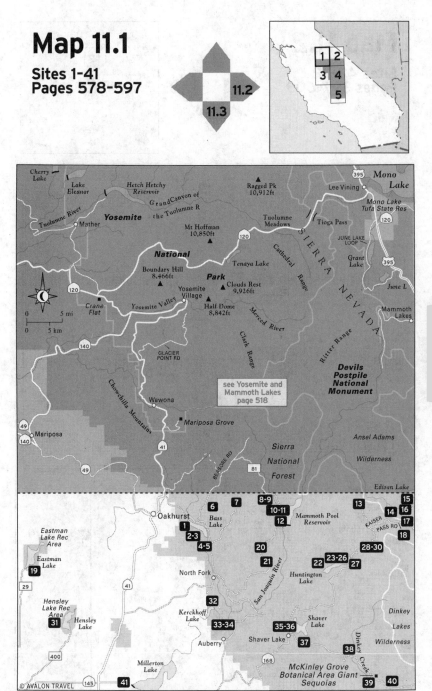

# Map 11.2

**Sites 42-72**
**Pages 597-609**

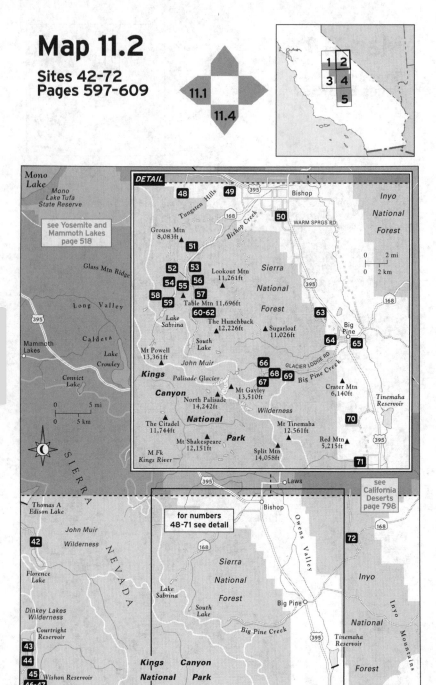

© AVALON TRAVEL

# Map 11.3
## Sites 73-81
## Pages 610-614

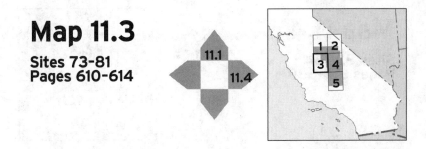

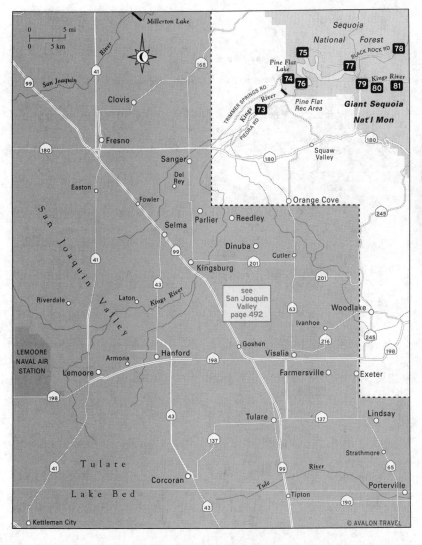

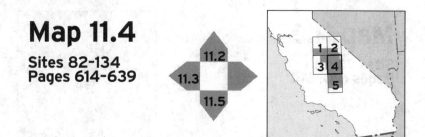

# Map 11.4

## Sites 82-134
## Pages 614-639

11.2

11.3

11.5

1  2
3  4
5

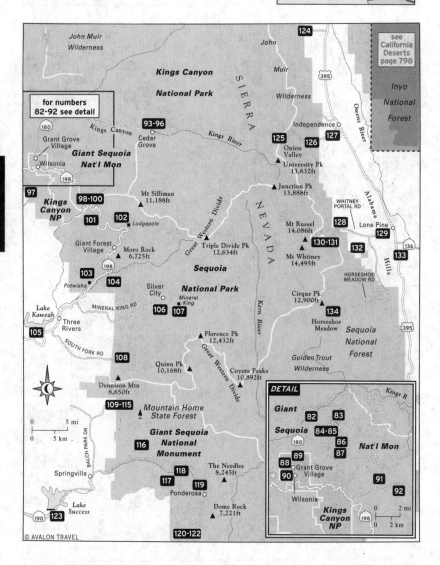

see California Deserts page 798

John Muir Wilderness

Kings Canyon

National Park

SIERRA

John

Muir

Wilderness

124

395

Inyo

National

Forest

Owens River

for numbers 82-92 see detail

93-96

180

Kings Canyon

Cedar Grove

Kings River

125

Independence

126  127

Onion Valley

University Pk 13,632ft

Grant Grove Village

Wilsonia

Giant Sequoia Nat'l Mon

198

97

Kings Canyon NP

98-100

101  102

Mt Silliman 11,188ft

Lodgepole

Great Western Divide

NEVADA

Junction Pk 13,888ft

WHITNEY PORTAL RD

128  Lone Pine

Mt Russel 14,086ft

130-131

129

136

Giant Forest Village

Moro Rock 6,725ft

103

198

104

Potwisha

Triple Divide Pk 12,634ft

Sequoia

National Park

Silver City

106  107

Mineral King

Mt Whitney 14,495ft

132

133

Alabama Hills

HORSESHOE MEADOW RD

Cirque Pk 12,900ft

134

Horseshoe Meadow

Sequoia

National

Forest

395

Lake Kaweah

105

Three Rivers

MINERAL KING RD

SOUTH FORK RD

Kern River

108

Florence Pk 12,432ft

Quinn Pk 10,168ft

Coyote Peaks 10,892ft

Great Western Divide

Golden Trout Wilderness

Dennison Mtn 8,650ft

109-115

Mountain Home State Forest

BALCH PARK DR

0    5 mi
0    5 km

116

Giant Sequoia National Monument

117  118

119

Ponderosa

The Needles 8,245ft

Springville

Dome Rock 7,221ft

190  123

Lake Success

120-122

DETAIL

Giant

Sequoia

Kings R

82   83

84-85

180

86

87

Nat'l Mon

89

88

90

Grant Grove Village

91

92

Wilsonia

198

Kings Canyon NP

0    2 mi
0    2 km

© AVALON TRAVEL

# Map 11.5

**Sites 135-171**
**Pages 640-656**

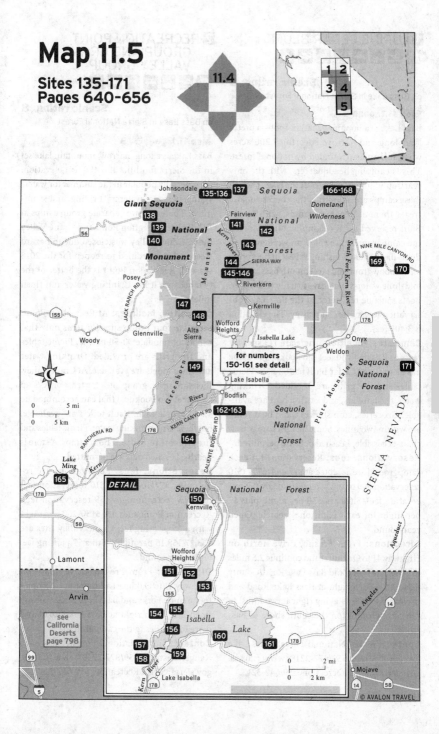

© AVALON TRAVEL

# 1 LUPINE CEDAR BLUFF

## Scenic rating: 8

on Bass Lake in Sierra National Forest

### Map 11.1, page 573

Bass Lake is a popular vacation spot—a pretty lake, long and narrow, covering 1,200 acres when full and surrounded by national forest. This is camping headquarters, with the only year-round individual sites at the lake. Though these camps are adjoining, the concessionaire treats them as separate camps, with Cedar Bluff reserved for RV camping only. Most of the campgrounds are filled on weekends and three-day holidays. Fishing is best in the spring for rainbow trout and largemouth bass, and by mid-June water-skiers have usually taken over. Boats must be registered at the Bass Lake observation tower after launching. The elevation is 3,400 feet.

**Campsites, facilities:** There are 113 sites for tents or RVs up to 40 feet (no hookups): Lupine has 51 sites and Cedar Bluff has 62 sites. Picnic tables and fire grills are provided. Drinking water, flush toilets, and a camp host are available. Groceries, coin showers, and boat ramp are within two miles. Some facilities are wheelchair-accessible. Leashed pets are permitted.

**Reservations, fees:** Reservations for each campground are accepted at 877/444-6777 ($10 reservation fee) or www.recreation.gov ($9 reservation fee). Sites are $30 per night, plus $7 per night for each additional vehicle. Open year-round.

**Directions:** From Fresno, drive north on Highway 41 to Oakhurst and continue 2.5 miles to Yosemite Forks and Bass Lake Road/County Road 222. Turn right at Bass Lake Road and drive eight miles (staying right at two forks) to the campground (on the south shore of Bass Lake).

**Contact:** Sierra National Forest, Bass Lake Ranger District, 559/877-2218, www.fs.usda.gov/sierra; Sierra Recreation, 559/642-3212.

# 2 RECREATION POINT GROUP AND CRANE VALLEY GROUP

## Scenic rating: 8

on Bass Lake in Sierra National Forest

### Map 11.1, page 573

Bass Lake is a long, narrow, mountain lake set in the Sierra foothills at 3,400 feet elevation. It's especially popular in the summer for water-skiing, personal watercraft riding, and swimming. There are two separate group camps at Bass Lake: Recreation Point and Crane Valley (note: Crane Valley was closed due to hazard trees and is scheduled to reopen for the 2018 season). Recreation Point is the better of the two because it has drinking water and flush toilets.

**Campsites, facilities:** At Recreation Point, there are four group sites for tents only that can accommodate 30-50 people. Picnic tables and fire grills are provided. Drinking water and flush toilets are available. At Crane Valley, there are seven group sites for tents or RVs up to 40 feet (no hookups) that can accommodate 12-30 people each. Vault toilets are available, but there is no drinking water. Picnic tables and fire grills are provided at both camps. A store is nearby. Leashed pets are permitted.

**Reservations, fees:** Reservations are required at 877/444-6777 ($10 reservation fee) or www.recreation.gov ($9 reservation fee). Recreation Point sites are $150-250 per night with a $5 parking fee; Crane Valley sites are $63.27-158.15 per night with a $7 parking fee. Open year-round.

**Directions:** From Fresno, drive north on Highway 41 to Oakhurst and continue 2.5 miles to Yosemite Forks and Bass Lake Road/County Road 222. Turn right at Bass Lake Road and drive four miles to the campground.

**Contact:** Sierra National Forest, Bass Lake Ranger District, 559/877-2218, www.fs.usda.gov/sierra; Sierra Recreation, 559/642-3212.

## 3 FORKS

🏃 🏊 🎣 ⛴ 🚣 🐕 ♿ 🚐 ⛺

### Scenic rating: 8
on Bass Lake in Sierra National Forest

**Map 11.1, page 573**

Bass Lake is set in a canyon. It's a long, narrow, deep lake that is popular for fishing in the spring and waterskiing in the summer. It's a pretty spot at 3,400 feet elevation in the Sierra National Forest. This is one of several camps at the lake. Boats must be registered at the Bass Lake observation tower after launching.

**Campsites, facilities:** There are 20 sites for tents or RVs up to 40 feet (no hookups) and eight sites for tents only. Picnic tables and fire grills are provided. Drinking water, bear boxes (mandatory), flush and vault toilets, and a camp host are available. A store, dump station, and coin laundry are nearby. Some facilities are wheelchair-accessible. Leashed pets are permitted.

**Reservations, fees:** Sites are $31.08 per night, plus $7 per night for each additional vehicle. Open May through September.

**Directions:** From Fresno, drive north on Highway 41 to Oakhurst and continue 2.5 miles to Yosemite Forks and Bass Lake Road/County Road 222. Turn right at Bass Lake Road and drive six miles (staying right at two forks) to the campground (on the south shore of Bass Lake). Note: The road is narrow and curvy.

**Contact:** Sierra National Forest, Bass Lake Ranger District, 559/877-2218, www.fs.usda.gov/sierra.

## 4 SPRING COVE

🏃 🏊 🎣 ⛴ 🚣 🐕 ♿ 🚐 ⛺

### Scenic rating: 8
on Bass Lake in Sierra National Forest

**Map 11.1, page 573**

Note: The campground was closed at time of publication due to hazard trees. It is scheduled to reopen for the 2017 season.

This is one of several camps beside Bass Lake, a long, narrow reservoir in the Sierra foothill country. A bonus here is that the shoreline is quite sandy nearly all around the lake. That makes for good swimming and sunbathing. Expect hot weather in the summer. Boats must be registered at the Bass Lake observation tower after launching. The elevation is 3,400 feet.

**Campsites, facilities:** There are 61 sites for tents or RVs up to 35 feet (no hookups); large RVs are not recommended. Picnic tables and fire grills are provided. Drinking water, flush toilets, and a camp host are available. Groceries and a boat ramp are nearby. Some facilities are wheelchair-accessible. Leashed pets are permitted.

**Reservations, fees:** Reservations are accepted at 877/444-6777 ($10 reservation fee) or www.recreation.gov ($9 reservation fee). Sites are $30 per night, plus $7 per night for each additional vehicle. Fees increase on holiday weekends. Open May through August.

**Directions:** From Fresno, drive north on Highway 41 to Oakhurst and continue 2.5 miles to Yosemite Forks and Bass Lake Road/County Road 222. Turn right at Bass Lake Road and drive 8.5 miles (staying right at two forks) to the campground (on the south shore of Bass Lake).

**Contact:** Sierra National Forest, Bass Lake Ranger District, 559/877-2218, www.fs.usda.gov/sierra; Sierra Recreation, 559/642-3212.

## 5 WISHON POINT

🏃 🏊 🎣 ⛴ 🚣 🐕 ♿ 🚐 ⛺

### Scenic rating: 9
on Bass Lake in Sierra National Forest

**Map 11.1, page 573**

This camp on Wishon Point is the smallest, and many say the prettiest, of the camps at Bass Lake. The elevation is 3,400 feet.

**Campsites, facilities:** There are 47 sites for tents or RVs up to 30 feet (no hookups). Some sites are pull-through. Picnic tables and fire grills are provided. Drinking water and flush toilets are available. Groceries and a boat ramp are nearby. Some facilities are wheelchair-accessible. Leashed pets are permitted.

**Reservations, fees:** Reservations are accepted at 877/444-6777 ($10 reservation fee) or www.recreation.gov ($9 reservation fee). Sites are $33-66 per night, plus $7 per night for additional vehicle. Fees increase on holiday weekends. Open late April to early September.

**Directions:** From Fresno, drive north on Highway 41 to Oakhurst and continue 2.5 miles to Yosemite Forks and Bass Lake Road/County Road 222. Turn right at Bass Lake Road and drive nine miles (staying right at two forks) to the campground (on the south shore of Bass Lake).

**Contact:** Sierra National Forest, Bass Lake Ranger District, 559/877-2218, www.fs.usda.gov/sierra; Sierra Recreation, 559/642-3212.

# 6 CHILKOOT

### Scenic rating: 7
near Bass Lake in Sierra National Forest

**Map 11.1, page 573**

A lot of people have heard of Bass Lake, but only the faithful know about Chilkoot Creek. That's where this camp is, but it's just two miles from Bass Lake. It provides a primitive option to use either as an overflow area for Bass Lake or for folks who don't want to get jammed into one of the Bass Lake campgrounds on a popular weekend. The elevation is 4,600 feet.

**Campsites, facilities:** There are 14 sites for tents or RVs up to 20 feet (no hookups). Picnic tables and fire grills are provided. Vault toilets are available. There is no drinking water. Groceries and a coin laundry are available at Bass Lake. Leashed pets are permitted.

**Reservations, fees:** Reservations are accepted at 877/444-6777 ($10 reservation fee) or www.recreation.gov ($9 reservation fee). Sites are $26.22-48 per night, plus $7 per night for each additional vehicle. Holiday weekends are an extra $2. Open early May through early September.

**Directions:** From Fresno, drive north on Highway 41 to Oakhurst and continue 2.5 miles to Yosemite Forks and Bass Lake Road/County Road 222. Turn right at Bass Lake Road and drive six miles to the town of Bass Lake and Beasore Road. Turn left at Beasore Road and drive 4.5 miles to the campground.

**Contact:** Sierra National Forest, Bass Lake Ranger District, 559/877-2218, www.fs.usda.gov/sierra; Sierra Recreation, 559/642-3212.

# 7 GAGGS CAMP

### Scenic rating: 7
in Sierra National Forest

**Map 11.1, page 573**

The masses are not exactly beating a hot trail to this camp. It's a small, remote, and primitive spot, set along a little creek at 5,700 feet elevation, deep in the interior of Sierra National Forest. A Forest Service map is advisable. With that in hand, you can make the three-mile drive to Little Shuteye Pass, where the road is often gated in the winter (the gate is open when the lookout station is staffed); from here it is a three-mile trip to Shuteye Peak, at 8,351 feet, where there is a drop-dead gorgeous view of the surrounding landscape.

**Campsites, facilities:** There are 12 sites for tents or RVs up to 16 feet (no hookups). Picnic tables and fire grills are provided. Vault toilets are available. No drinking water is available. Garbage bins are located at the campground entrance. Leashed pets are permitted.

**Reservations, fees:** Reservations are not accepted. Sites are $26.22 per night, plus $7 per night for each additional vehicle. Open June through October, weather permitting.

**Directions:** From Fresno, drive north on Highway 41 for about 25 miles to North Fork Road/County Road 200. Turn right and drive northeast for 17.5 miles to Auberry Road/County Road 222. Turn left (north) and drive one mile to the town of North Fork and Mammoth Pool Road. Turn right and drive

0.5 mile to Malum Ridge Road/County Road 274. Turn left (north) and drive 4.5 miles to Central Camp Road/Forest Road 6S42. Turn right and drive 11.5 miles (narrow, dirt road) to the campground on the right.

**Contact:** Sierra National Forest, Bass Lake Ranger District, 559/877-2218, www.fs.usda. gov/sierra; Sierra Recreation, 559/642-3212.

## 8 SODA SPRINGS

### Scenic rating: 7

on the West Fork of Chiquito Creek in Sierra National Forest

**Map 11.1, page 573**

Soda Springs is at 4,400 feet elevation on West Fork Chiquito Creek, about five miles from Mammoth Pool Reservoir. It is used primarily as an overflow area if the more developed camps with drinking water have filled up. As long as you remember that the camp is primitive, it is a good overflow option.

**Campsites, facilities:** There are 18 sites for tents or RVs up to 40 feet (no hookups). Picnic tables and fire grills are provided. Vault toilets are available. No drinking water is available. A store and boat ramp are nearby. Leashed pets are permitted.

**Reservations, fees:** Reservations are not accepted. Sites are $26.22-52.44 per night, plus $7 per night for each additional vehicle. Open May through September, weather permitting.

**Directions:** From Fresno, drive north on Highway 41 for about 25 miles to North Fork Road/County Road 200. Turn right and drive northeast for 17.5 miles to Auberry Road/ County Road 222. Turn left (north) and drive one mile to the town of North Fork and Mammoth Pool Road. Turn right and drive 1.5 miles to County Road 225 (still Mammoth Pool Road). Turn right and drive 35 miles (the road

becomes Minarets Road/Forest Road 81) to the campground.

**Contact:** Sierra National Forest, Bass Lake Ranger District, 559/877-2218, www.fs.usda. gov/sierra; Sierra Recreation, 559/642-3212.

## 9 LOWER CHIQUITO

### Scenic rating: 7

on Chiquito Creek in Sierra National Forest

**Map 11.1, page 573**

Lower Chiquito is a primitive, little-known, pretty camp in Sierra National Forest, about eight miles from Mammoth Pool Reservoir. Mosquitoes can be abundant in summer. The elevation is 4,900 feet, with a very warm climate in summer. Note that Lower Chiquito is a long distance (a twisting, 30- to 40-minute drive) from Upper Chiquito, despite the similarity in names and streamside settings along the same creek.

**Campsites, facilities:** There are seven sites for tents or RVs up to 28 feet (no hookups). Picnic tables and fire grills are provided. Vault toilets are available. No drinking water is available. Leashed pets are permitted.

**Reservations, fees:** Reservations are not accepted. Sites are $26.22-48 per night, plus $7 per night for each additional vehicle. Open June through September, weather permitting.

**Directions:** From the town of North Fork (south of Bass Lake), drive east on Mammoth Pool Road/County Road 225 (it becomes Minarets Road/Forest Road 4S81). Bear left (north, still Minarets Road/Forest Road 4S81) and drive to Forest Road 6S71. Turn left on Forest Road 6S71 and drive three miles to the campground. (The distance is about 40 miles from North Fork.)

**Contact:** Sierra National Forest, Bass Lake Ranger District, 559/877-2218, www.fs.usda. gov/sierra; Sierra Recreation, 559/642-3212.

## 10 PLACER

### Scenic rating: 7

near Mammoth Pool Reservoir on Chiquito
Creek in Sierra National Forest

**Map 11.1, page 573**

Note: At time of publication, Placer
Campground was closed due to hazard trees.
It is expected to reopen in 2018.

This little camp is just three miles from
Mammoth Pool Reservoir. With Forest Road
access and a pretty setting along Chiquito
Creek, it is one of the better campgrounds
used as an overflow area for Mammoth Pool
visitors. The elevation is 4,100 feet. (For more
information, see the Mammoth Pool listing in
this chapter.)

**Campsites, facilities:** There are eight sites for
tents or RVs up to 24 feet. Picnic tables and fire
grills are provided. Vault toilets are available.
No drinking water is available. Leashed pets
are permitted.

**Reservations, fees:** Reservations are not accepted. Sites are $26.22-52.44 per night, plus $7
per night for each additional vehicle. Open May
through September.

**Directions:** From Fresno, drive north on
Highway 41 for about 25 miles to North Fork
Road/County Road 200. Turn right and drive
northeast for 17.5 miles to Auberry Road/
County Road 222. Turn left (north) and
drive one mile to the town of North Fork and
Mammoth Pool Road. Turn right and drive 1.5
miles to County Road 225 (still Mammoth Pool
Road). Turn right and drive about 37 miles (the
road becomes Minarets Road/Forest Road 81)
to a junction. Bear right (still Mammoth Pool
Road) and drive one mile to the campground
on the right. The drive from North Fork takes
1.5-2 hours.

**Contact:** Sierra National Forest, Bass Lake
Ranger District, 559/877-2218, www.fs.usda.
gov/sierra; Sierra Recreation, 559/642-3212.

## 11 SWEETWATER

### Scenic rating: 6

near Mammoth Pool Reservoir on Chiquito
Creek in Sierra National Forest

**Map 11.1, page 573**

Sweetwater is small and primitive, but if the
camp at Mammoth Pool Reservoir is filled
up, this spot provides an alternative. It is on
Chiquito Creek, just a mile from the lake. The
elevation is 3,800 feet. (See the Mammoth Pool
listing in this chapter for more information.)

**Campsites, facilities:** There are seven sites for
tents or RVs up to 20 feet (no hookups). Picnic
tables and fire grills are provided. Vault toilets
are available. No drinking water is available.
A store and boat ramp are within 1.5 miles.
Leashed pets are permitted.

**Reservations, fees:** Reservations are accepted at 877/444-6777 ($10 reservation fee)
or www.recreation.gov ($9 reservation fee).
Sites are $26.22 per night, plus $7 per night per
additional vehicle. Open mid-May through
mid-September.

**Directions:** From Fresno, drive north on
Highway 41 for about 25 miles to North Fork
Road/County Road 200. Turn right and drive
northeast for 17.5 miles to Auberry Road/
County Road 222. Turn left (north) and
drive one mile to the town of North Fork and
Mammoth Pool Road. Turn right and drive 1.5
miles to County Road 225 (still Mammoth Pool
Road). Turn right and drive about 37 miles (the
road becomes Minarets Road/Forest Road 81)
to a junction. Bear right (still Mammoth Pool
Road) and drive 1.5 miles to the campground
on the right. The drive from North Fork takes
1.5-2 hours.

**Contact:** Sierra National Forest, Bass Lake
Ranger District, 559/877-2218, www.fs.usda.
gov/sierra; Sierra Recreation, 559/642-3212.

# 12 MAMMOTH POOL

🏊 🛶 🎣 🦌 🚐 ⛺

### Scenic rating: 7

near Mammoth Pool Reservoir in Sierra
National Forest

**Map 11.1, page 573**

Note: At time of publication, this campground
was closed due to hazard trees. It is expected to
reopen in 2018.

Mammoth Pool was created by a dam in the
San Joaquin River gorge, a steep canyon, resulting in a long, narrow lake with steep, high
walls. The lake seems much higher than its
official elevation of 3,330 feet, but that is because of the high ridges. This is the only drive-
in camp at the lake, though there is a boat-in
camp, China Camp, on the lake's upper reaches.
Trout fishing can be good in the spring and
early summer, with waterskiing dominant during warm weather. All water sports are allowed
during part of the season, but get this: Water
sports are restricted from May 1 to June 15 because of deer migrating across the lake—that's
right, swimming—but the campgrounds are
still open. Note that the water level can drop
significantly by late summer.

**Campsites, facilities:** There are 47 sites for
tents or RVs up to 30 feet (no hookups). Picnic
tables and fire grills are provided. Drinking
water and vault toilets are available. A store
and boat ramp are within a mile. Leashed pets
are permitted.

**Reservations, fees:** Reservations are accepted
at 877/444-6777 ($10 reservation fee) or www.
recreation.gov ($9 reservation fee). Sites are
$26.22 per night, double sites are $48 per night,
plus $7 per night per additional vehicle. Open
June through October.

**Directions:** From Fresno, drive north on
Highway 41 for about 25 miles to North Fork
Road/County Road 200. Turn right and drive
northeast for 17.5 miles to Auberry Road/
County Road 222. Turn left (north) and
drive one mile to the town of North Fork and
Mammoth Pool Road. Turn right and drive 1.5
miles to County Road 225 (still Mammoth Pool

Road). Turn right and drive about 37 miles (the
road becomes Minarets Road/Forest Road 81)
to a junction. Bear right (still Mammoth Pool
Road) and drive three miles to Mammoth Pool
Reservoir and the campground. The drive from
North Fork takes 1.5-2 hours.

**Contact:** Sierra National Forest, Bass Lake
Ranger District, 559/877-2218, www.fs.usda.
gov/sierra; Sierra Recreation, 559/642-3212.

# 13 SAMPLE MEADOW

🥾 🐎 🚐 ⛺

### Scenic rating: 7

on Kaiser Creek in Sierra National Forest

**Map 11.1, page 573**

This is a pretty, secluded spot set at 7,800 feet
elevation along Kaiser Creek, with nearby
trailheads available for backpackers. While
there is a trail out of camp, most hikers drive
a mile down Forest Road 80 to the Rattlesnake
Parking Area, from where one trail leads three
miles southwest to Kaiser Ridge and Upper and
Lower Twin Lakes in the Kaiser Wilderness,
a great hike. Another trail is routed north for
three miles to Rattlesnake Creek and then enters the western slopes of the Ansel Adams
Wilderness, with this section featuring a series
of canyons, streams, and very few people. Horse
camping is permitted.

**Campsites, facilities:** There are 16 sites for
tents or RVs up to 16 feet (no hookups). Picnic
tables and fire grills are provided. Vault toilets
are available. No drinking water is available.
Garbage must be packed out. Leashed pets are
permitted.

**Reservations, fees:** Reservations are not accepted. There is no fee for camping. Open June
through October, weather permitting.

**Directions:** From Fresno, drive east on
Highway 168 to Shaver Lake, and then continue
21 miles to Huntington Lake and Kaiser Pass
Road/Forest Road 80. Bear right on Forest Road
80 and drive eight miles to a fork with Forest
Road 7505. Turn left on Forest Road 7505 and
drive 3.5 miles to a fork with the campground

entrance road. Bear left at the campground entrance road and drive 0.25 mile to the campground. The road is narrow and curvy, with blind turns.

**Contact:** Sierra National Forest, High Sierra Ranger District, 559/855-5355, www.fs.usda.gov/sierra.

## 14 PORTAL FOREBAY

### Scenic rating: 8

on Forebay Lake in Sierra National Forest

**Map 11.1, page 573**

This small, primitive camp along the shore of little Forebay Lake is at 7,200 feet elevation. The camp is pretty and provides a good hiking option, with a trailhead near the camp that is routed up Camp 61 Creek and then to Mono Creek, with a ford of Mono Creek required about two miles in. Another side trip is visiting Mono Hot Springs about five miles to the east, just off the road to Lake Edison.

**Campsites, facilities:** There are 11 sites for tents or RVs up to 16 feet (no hookups). Picnic tables and fire grills are provided. Vault toilets are available. No drinking water is available. Groceries are available nearby at Mono Hot Springs. Leashed pets are permitted.

**Reservations, fees:** Reservations are not accepted. Sites are $22-44 per night, rates increase $2 on holiday weekends, and it's $7 per night per each additional vehicle. Open June through October.

**Directions:** From Fresno, drive east on Highway 168 to Shaver Lake and then continue 21 miles to Huntington Lake and Kaiser Pass Road/Forest Road 80. Bear right on Forest Road 80 and drive eight miles to a fork with Forest Road 5. Stay right at the fork on Forest Road 80 and continue five miles to the campground entrance on the left. The road is narrow and curvy, with blind turns.

**Contact:** Sierra National Forest, High Sierra Ranger District, 559/855-5355, www.fs.usda.

gov/sierra; California Land Management, 559/893-2111.

## 15 VERMILLION

### Scenic rating: 8

on Edison Lake in Sierra National Forest

**Map 11.1, page 573**

If you don't mind the drive, Edison Lake is a premium vacation destination. It is a large, high-mountain camp just a few miles from the border of the John Muir Wilderness. A 15-mph speed limit on the lake guarantees quiet water, and trout fishing is often quite good in early summer, with occasionally huge brown trout hooked. Swimming is allowed. A day-trip option is to hike the trail from the camp out along the north shore of Edison Lake for five miles to Quail Meadows, where it intersects with the Pacific Crest Trail in the John Muir Wilderness. A lodge at the lake provides meals and supplies, with a hikers' boat shuttle available to the head of the lake. Hang out for long and you are bound to see John Muir Trail hikers taking a break. Note that the drive in is long and extremely twisty on a narrow road. Also note that the lake level can drop dramatically by late summer. The elevation is 7,700 feet.

**Campsites, facilities:** There are 31 sites for tents or RVs up to 25 feet (no hookups). Picnic tables, fire grills, and food lockers are provided. Vault toilets are available. Drinking water is on-site, but boiling it is recommended. A boat ramp, boat rentals, bait and tackle, horseback-riding facilities, convenience store, and restaurant are nearby. Leashed pets are permitted.

**Reservations, fees:** Reservations are accepted at 877/444-6777 ($10 reservation fee) or www.recreation.gov ($9 reservation fee). Sites are $26-48 per night, rates increase $2 on holiday weekends, plus $7 per night for each additional vehicle. Open June through October.

**Directions:** From the town of Shaver Lake, drive east on Highway 168 for 21 miles to Kaiser Pass Road. Bear northeast on Kaiser

# HIKING THE JMT/PCT:
# EDISON LAKE TO AGNEW MEADOWS

**38 MILES ONE-WAY/3 DAYS**
The world is not perfect, but the scene from Silver Pass comes close. At 10,900 feet, you scan a bare, high-granite landscape sprinkled with alpine lakes. Just north of the pass are five small lakes: Chief, Papoose, Warrior, Squaw, and Lake of the Lone Indian. This is the highlight on this 38-mile section of the Pacific Crest Trail. The trip starts at **Mono Creek,** with a good resupply point at **Edison Lake** (7,650 feet), just two miles away. From the Mono Creek junction, you head north toward Silver Pass, climbing along Silver Pass Creek much of the way. Before you get to Silver Pass, there's a stream crossing that can be dangerous in high-runoff conditions. Top Silver Pass at 10,900 feet, and enjoy a five-mile descent and then a quick ascent to Tully Hole (9,250 feet). Climbing north, you pass Deer Creek, Purple Lake, and Lake Virginia. You head up to Red Cones and then make a steady descent toward **Devils Postpile National Monument.** A good resupply point is at nearby Red's Meadow Resort & Pack Station.

Pass Road/Forest Road 80 (slow and curvy) to Mono Hot Springs (the road becomes Edison Lake Road). Continue on Kaiser Pass/Edison Lake Road for five miles to the campground. It is about 0.25 mile from the west shore of Edison Lake. Be warned that the access road is narrow with many blind turns and may be difficult for RVs.

**Contact:** Sierra National Forest, High Sierra Ranger District, 559/855-5355, www.fs.usda. gov/sierra; California Land Management, 559/893-2111.

## 16 MONO HOT SPRINGS
🏃 🏊 🎣 〰️ 🐕 🚐 ⛺

**Scenic rating: 8**
on the San Joaquin River in Sierra National Forest

**Map 11.1, page 573**

This campground in the Sierra at 7,400 feet elevation along the San Joaquin River sits directly adjacent to the Mono Hot Springs Resort. The hot springs are typically 104°F, with public pools (everybody wears swimming suits) just above the river on one side and the private resort (rock cabins available) with its private baths on the other. A small convenience store and excellent restaurant are available at the lodge. Many find the hot springs perfect, but for some the water is too hot. No problem; the best swimming lake in the Sierra Nevada, Dorris Lake, is a 15-minute walk past the lodge. Dorris is clear, clean, and not too cold since it too is fed by hot springs. There are walls on one side for fun jumps into deep water. The one downer: The drive in to the campground is long, slow, and hellacious, with many blind corners in narrow sections.

**Campsites, facilities:** There are 22 sites for tents or RVs up to 25 feet (no hookups). Picnic tables and fire grills are provided. Vault toilets are available. Drinking water is not available. You can buy supplies in Mono Hot Springs. Leashed pets are permitted.

**Reservations, fees:** Reservations are accepted at 877/444-6777 ($10 reservation fee) or www. recreation.gov ($9 reservation fee). Sites are $26-52 per night, rates increase $2 on holiday weekends, and it's $7 per night for each additional vehicle. Open June through mid-September, weather permitting.

**Directions:** From the town of Shaver Lake, drive east on Highway 168 for 21 miles to Kaiser Pass Road. Bear northeast on Kaiser Pass Road/Forest Road 80 (slow and curvy) to Mono Hot Springs Campground Road (signed). Turn left and drive a short distance to the campground.

Be warned that the access road is narrow with many blind turns and may be difficult for RVs. **Contact:** Sierra National Forest, High Sierra Ranger District, 559/855-5355, www.fs.usda.gov/sierra; California Land Management, 559/893-2111.

## 17 MONO CREEK

### Scenic rating: 7

near Lake Edison in Sierra National Forest

**Map 11.1, page 573**

Here's a beautiful spot in the forest near Mono Creek that makes for an overflow campground when the camps at Mono Hot Springs and Lake Edison are filled, or when you want a quieter, more remote spot. The camp is at 7,400 feet elevation about three miles from Lake Edison, via a twisty and bumpy road. Edison has good evening trout fishing and a small restaurant. For side trips, the Mono Hot Springs Resort is three miles away (slow, curvy, and bumpy driving), and there are numerous trails nearby into the backcountry. A camp host is on-site.

**Campsites, facilities:** There are 14 sites for tents or RVs up to 25 feet (no hookups). Picnic tables, fire grills, and food lockers are provided. Vault toilets are available. Drinking water is not available. Limited supplies and small restaurants are at Lake Edison and Mono Hot Springs. Some facilities are wheelchair-accessible. Leashed pets are permitted.

**Reservations, fees:** Reservations are accepted at 877/444-6777 ($10 reservation fee) or www.recreation.gov ($9 reservation fee). Sites are $26-52 per night, rates increase $2 on holiday weekends, and it's $7 per night for each additional vehicle. Open June through October, weather permitting.

**Directions:** From the town of Shaver Lake, drive east on Highway 168 for 21 miles to Kaiser Pass Road. Bear northeast on Kaiser Pass Road/Forest Road 80 (slow and curvy) to Mono Hot Springs (the road becomes Edison

Lake Road). Continue on Kaiser Pass/Edison Lake Road for three miles to the campground on the left.

**Contact:** Sierra National Forest, High Sierra Ranger District, 559/855-5355, www.fs.usda.gov/sierra; California Land Management, 559/893-2111.

## 18 BOLSILLO

### Scenic rating: 4

on Bolsillo Creek in Sierra National Forest

**Map 11.1, page 573**

This tiny camp at 7,400 feet elevation along Bolsillo Creek has many first-class bonuses. It is just three miles by car to Mono Hot Springs and seven miles to Lake Edison. A trailhead out of camp provides the chance for a three-mile hike south, climbing along Bolsillo Creek and up to small, pretty Corbett Lake on the flank of nearby Mount Givens, at 10,648 feet.

**Campsites, facilities:** There are three tent sites. Picnic tables, fire grills, and bear boxes are provided. Drinking water and vault toilets are available. Garbage must be packed out. You can buy supplies in Mono Hot Springs. Leashed pets are permitted.

**Reservations, fees:** Reservations are not accepted. There is no fee for camping. Open June through October, weather permitting.

**Directions:** From Fresno, drive east on Highway 168 to Shaver Lake, then continue 21 miles to Huntington Lake and Kaiser Pass Road/Forest Road 80. Bear right on Forest Road 80 and drive eight miles to a fork with Forest Road 5. Stay right on Forest Road 80 and drive seven miles (two miles past Portal Forebay) to the campground entrance on the right. The road is narrow and curvy with blind turns, and RVs and trailers are not recommended.

**Contact:** Sierra National Forest, High Sierra Ranger District, 559/855-5355, www.fs.usda.gov/sierra.

## 19 CODORNIZ RECREATION AREA

🚶 🚴 ⛰️ 🏊 🛶 ⛵ 🐕 🎿 ♿ 🚐 ⛺

**Scenic rating: 6**

on Eastman Lake

**Map 11.1, page 573**

Eastman Lake provides relief on your typical 90- or 100-degree summer day out here. It is tucked in the foothills of the San Joaquin Valley at an elevation of 650 feet and covers 1,800 surface acres. Shade shelters have been added at 12 of the more exposed campsites, a big plus. The warm water in summer makes it a good spot for a dip, thus it is a favorite for waterskiing, swimming, and, in the spring, fishing. Swimming is best at the large beach on the west side. The Department of Fish and Game has established a trophy bass program, and fishing can be good in the appropriate season for rainbow trout, catfish, bluegill, and redear sunfish. Check fishing regulations, posted on all bulletin boards. The lake is also a designated "Watchable Wildlife" site; it is home to 163 species of birds and a nesting pair of bald eagles. A small area near the upper end of the lake is closed to boating to protect a bald eagle nest site. Some may remember the problem that Eastman Lake had with hydrilla, an invasive weed. The problem has been largely solved, and a buoy line has been placed at the mouth. No water activities are allowed upstream of this line. Mild winter temperatures are a tremendous plus at this lake.

**Campsites, facilities:** There are 81 sites for tents or RVs of any length (some have full hookups—50 amps—and one is pull-through), three group sites for 40-160 people, three equestrian sites, and one group equestrian site. Picnic tables and fire grills are provided. Drinking water, flush toilets with showers, dump station, playground, horseshoe pits, volleyball court, Frisbee golf course, and two boat ramps are available. An equestrian staging area is available for overnight use, and there are seven miles of hiking, biking, and equestrian trails. Some facilities are wheelchair-accessible. Leashed pets are permitted.

**Reservations, fees:** Reservations are accepted at 877/444-6777 ($10 reservation fee) or www.recreation.gov ($9 reservation fee). Sites are $20-30 per night, group sites are $80-100 per night, and equestrian sites are $20-60 per night. Open year-round.

**Directions:** Drive on Highway 99 to Chowchilla and the Avenue 26 exit. Take that exit and drive east for 17 miles to County Road 29. Turn left (north) on County Road 29 and drive eight miles to the lake.

**Contact:** U.S. Army Corps of Engineers, Sacramento District, Eastman Lake, 559/689-3255.

## 20 ROCK CREEK

🚶 🐕 🚐 ⛺

**Scenic rating: 6**

in Sierra National Forest

**Map 11.1, page 573**

Note: At time of publication, this campground was closed due to hazard trees. It is expected to reopen in 2018.

Drinking water is the big bonus here. It's easier to live with than the no-water situation at Fish Creek, the other camp in the immediate area. It is also why this camp tends to fill up on weekends. A side trip is the primitive road that heads southeast out of camp. It has a series of sharp turns as it heads east and drops down the canyon near where pretty Aspen Creek feeds into Rock Creek. The elevation at camp is 4,300 feet. (For the best camp in the immediate region, see the Mammoth Pool listing in this chapter.)

**Campsites, facilities:** There are 18 sites for tents or RVs up to 30 feet (no hookups). Picnic tables and fire grills are provided. Drinking water and vault toilets are available. A camp host is on-site. Leashed pets are permitted.

**Reservations, fees:** Reservations are accepted at 877/444-6777 ($10 reservation fee) or www.recreation.gov ($9 reservation fee). Sites are

$26.22 per night, double sites are $56.44 per night, and it's $7 per night per each additional vehicle. Open mid-May through September, weather permitting.

**Directions:** From Fresno, drive north on Highway 41 for about 25 miles to North Fork Road/County Road 200. Turn right and drive northeast for 17.5 miles to Auberry Road/County Road 222. Turn left (north) and drive one mile to the town of North Fork and Mammoth Pool Road. Turn right and drive 1.5 miles to County Road 225 (still Mammoth Pool Road). Turn right and drive about 25 miles (the road becomes Minarets Road/Forest Road 81) to the campground on the right.

**Contact:** Sierra National Forest, Bass Lake Ranger District, 559/877-2218, www.fs.usda. gov/sierra; Sierra Recreation, 559/642-3212.

## 21 FISH CREEK

### Scenic rating: 6

in Sierra National Forest

**Map 11.1, page 573**

Note: At time of publication, this campground was closed due to hazard trees. It may reopen in 2018.

This is a small, primitive camp along Fish Creek at 4,600 feet elevation in the Sierra National Forest. It's a nearby option to Rock Creek; both are on the access road to Mammoth Pool Reservoir.

**Campsites, facilities:** There are seven sites for tents or RVs up to 20 feet (no hookups). Picnic tables and fire grills are provided. Vault toilets are available. No drinking water is available. Leashed pets are permitted.

**Reservations, fees:** Reservations are accepted at 877/444-6777 ($10 reservation fee) or www. recreation.gov ($9 reservation fee). Sites are $26.22 per night, plus $7 per night per each additional vehicle. Open June through November, weather permitting.

**Directions:** From Fresno, drive north on Highway 41 for about 25 miles to North Fork

Road/County Road 200. Turn right and drive northeast for 17.5 miles to Auberry Road/County Road 222. Turn left (north) and drive one mile to the town of North Fork and Mammoth Pool Road. Turn right and drive 1.5 miles to County Road 225 (still Mammoth Pool Road). Turn right and drive about 21 miles (the road becomes Minarets Road/Forest Road 81) to the campground on the right.

**Contact:** Sierra National Forest, Bass Lake Ranger District, 559/877-2218, www.fs.usda. gov/sierra; Sierra Recreation, 559/642-3212.

## 22 UPPER AND LOWER BILLY CREEK

### Scenic rating: 8

on Huntington Lake in Sierra National Forest

**Map 11.1, page 573**

Huntington Lake is at an elevation of 7,000 feet in the Sierra Nevada. These camps are at the west end of the lake along the north shore, where Billy Creek feeds the lake. Of these two adjacent campgrounds, Lower Billy Creek is smaller than Upper Billy and has lakeside sites. The lake is four miles long and a half mile wide, with 14 miles of shoreline, several resorts, boat rentals, and a trailhead for hiking into the Kaiser Wilderness.

**Campsites, facilities:** Upper Billy has 44 sites for tents or RVs up to 30 feet. Lower Billy has 13 sites for tents or RVs up to 30 feet (no hookups). Picnic tables, fire grills, and bear boxes are provided. Drinking water may be available; Lower Billy has had intermittent quality issues, so check postings at the campground before drinking. Vault toilets are available at both camps; Upper Billy also has flush toilets. A camp host is on-site. Campfire programs are often available. A small store is nearby. Leashed pets are permitted.

**Reservations, fees:** Reservations are accepted at 877/444-6777 ($10 reservation fee) or www. recreation.gov ($9 reservation fee). Single sites are $30-56 per night, plus $7 per night for each additional vehicle. Open June through October, weather permitting.

**Directions:** From Fresno, drive east on Highway 168 to Shaver Lake, then continue 21 miles to Huntington Lake and Huntington Lake Road. Turn left on Huntington Lake Road and drive about five miles to the campgrounds on the left.

**Contact:** Sierra National Forest, High Sierra Ranger District, 559/855-5355, www.fs.usda. gov/sierra; California Land Management, 559/893-2111.

## 23 CATAVEE

### Scenic rating: 7
on Huntington Lake in Sierra National Forest

**Map 11.1, page 573**

Catavee is one of three camps in the immediate vicinity, set on the north shore at the eastern end of Huntington Lake. The camp sits near where Bear Creek enters the lake. Huntington Lake is a scenic, High Sierra Ranger District lake at 7,000 feet elevation, where visitors can enjoy fishing, hiking, and sailing. Sailboat regattas take place regularly during the summer. All water sports are allowed. Nearby resorts offer boat rentals and guest docks, and a boat ramp is nearby. Tackle rentals and bait are also available. A trailhead near camp offers access to the Kaiser Wilderness.

**Campsites, facilities:** There are 23 sites for tents or RVs up to 30 feet (no hookups). Picnic tables, fire grills, and bear boxes are provided. Drinking water and flush toilets are available. A camp host is on-site. Horseback-riding facilities and a small store are nearby. Some facilities are wheelchair-accessible. Leashed pets are permitted.

**Reservations, fees:** Reservations are accepted at 877/444-6777 ($10 reservation fee) or www. recreation.gov ($9 reservation fee). Sites are $30-60 per night, plus $7 per night for each additional vehicle. Open June through October, weather permitting.

**Directions:** From Fresno, drive east on Highway 168 to Shaver Lake, then continue 21 miles to Huntington Lake and Huntington Lake Road. Turn left on Huntington Lake Road and drive one mile (just past Kinnikinnick) to the campground on the right.

**Contact:** Sierra National Forest, High Sierra Ranger District, 559/855-5355, www.fs.usda. gov/sierra; California Land Management, 559/893-2111.

## 24 KINNIKINNICK

### Scenic rating: 7
on Huntington Lake in Sierra National Forest

**Map 11.1, page 573**

Flip a coin; there are three camps in the immediate vicinity on the north shore of the east end of Huntington Lake, and, with a boat ramp nearby, they are all favorites. Kinnikinnick is set between Catavee and Deer Creek Campgrounds. The elevation is 7,000 feet.

**Campsites, facilities:** There are 27 sites for tents or RVs up to 40 feet (no hookups). Picnic tables, fire grills, and bear boxes are provided. Drinking water and flush toilets are available. Horseback-riding facilities and a store are nearby. Some facilities are wheelchair-accessible. Leashed pets are permitted.

**Reservations, fees:** Reservations are accepted at 877/444-6777 ($10 reservation fee) or www.recreation.gov ($9 reservation fee). Sites are $30-60 per night, $7 per night for each additional vehicle. Open June through October, weather permitting.

**Directions:** From Fresno, drive east on Highway 168 to Shaver Lake, then continue 21 miles to Huntington Lake and Huntington Lake Road. Turn left on Huntington Lake Road and drive one mile to the campground on the right.

**Contact:** Sierra National Forest, High Sierra Ranger District, 559/855-5355, www.fs.usda. gov/sierra; California Land Management, 559/893-2111.

## 25 DEER CREEK

**Scenic rating: 8**

on Huntington Lake in Sierra National Forest

Map 11.1, page 573

This is one of the best camps at Huntington Lake, set near lakeside at Bear Cove with a boat ramp nearby. It is on the north shore of the lake's eastern end. Huntington Lake is four miles long and half a mile wide, with 14 miles of shoreline, several resorts, boat rentals, and a trailhead for hiking into the Kaiser Wilderness. Two other campgrounds are nearby.

**Campsites, facilities:** There are 28 sites for tents or RVs up to 40 feet (no hookups). Picnic tables, fire grills, and bear boxes are provided. Drinking water and flush toilets are available. A store and propane gas are nearby. Some facilities are wheelchair-accessible. Leashed pets are permitted.

**Reservations, fees:** Reservations are accepted at 877/444-6777 ($10 reservation fee) or www. recreation.gov ($9 reservation fee). Sites are $30-60 per night, plus $7 per night for each additional vehicle. Open June through October, weather permitting.

**Directions:** From Fresno, drive east on Highway 168 to Shaver Lake, then continue 21 miles to Huntington Lake and Huntington Lake Road. Turn left on Huntington Lake Road and drive one mile to the campground entrance road on the left.

**Contact:** Sierra National Forest, High Sierra Ranger District, 559/855-5355, www.fs.usda. gov/sierra; California Land Management, 559/893-2111.

## 26 COLLEGE

**Scenic rating: 7**

on Huntington Lake in Sierra National Forest

Map 11.1, page 573

College is a beautiful site along the shore of the northeastern end of Huntington Lake, at 7,000 feet elevation. This camp is close to a small store in the town of Huntington Lake.

**Campsites, facilities:** There are 11 sites for tents or RVs up to 30 feet (no hookups). Picnic tables and fire grills are provided. Vault and flush toilets, drinking water, and a camp host are available. Interpretive programs are offered. Horseback-riding facilities, a store, and propane gas are nearby. Leashed pets are permitted.

**Reservations, fees:** Reservations are accepted at 877/444-6777 ($10 reservation fee) or www. recreation.gov ($9 reservation fee). Sites are $30-60 per night, plus $7 per night for each additional vehicle. Open June through mid-September, weather permitting.

**Directions:** From Fresno, drive east on Highway 168 to Shaver Lake, then continue 21 miles to Huntington Lake and Huntington Lake Road. Turn left on Huntington Lake Road and drive 0.5 mile to the campground.

**Contact:** Sierra National Forest, High Sierra Ranger District, 559/855-5355, www.fs.usda. gov/sierra; California Land Management, 559/893-2111.

## 27 RANCHERIA

**Scenic rating: 8**

on Huntington Lake in Sierra National Forest

Map 11.1, page 573

This is the granddaddy of the camps at Huntington Lake, and also the easiest to reach. It is along the shore of the lake's eastern end. A bonus is nearby Rancheria Falls National Recreation Trail, which provides access to beautiful Rancheria Falls. Another side trip is the 15-minute drive to Bear Butte (the access road is across from the campground entrance) at 8,598 feet elevation, providing a sweeping view of the lake below. The elevation at camp is 7,000 feet.

**Campsites, facilities:** There are 127 sites for tents or RVs up to 40 feet (no hookups) and one triple site for up to 18 people that has electrical and water hookups. Picnic tables and fire grills are provided. Drinking water and flush and vault toilets are available. A camp host is on-site. Interpretive programs are offered. A store and propane gas are nearby. Leashed pets are permitted.

**Reservations, fees:** Reservations are accepted at 877/444-6777 ($10 reservation fee) or www.recreation.gov ($9 reservation fee). Sites are $30-60 per night and the triple site is $83 per night, plus $7 per night for each additional vehicle. Open June through October, weather permitting.

**Directions:** From Fresno, drive east on Highway 168 to Shaver Lake, then continue 20 miles to Huntington Lake and the campground on the left.

**Contact:** Sierra National Forest, High Sierra Ranger District, 559/855-5355, www.fs.usda. gov/sierra; California Land Management, 559/893-2111.

## 28 BADGER FLAT

### Scenic rating: 7
on Rancheria Creek in Sierra National Forest

**Map 11.1, page 573**

This camp is a good launching pad for backpackers. It is at 8,200 feet elevation along Rancheria Creek. The trail leading out of the camp heads into the Kaiser Wilderness to the north and Dinkey Lakes Wilderness to the south. Horses are permitted, but there are no equestrian amenities.

**Campsites, facilities:** There are 15 sites for tents or RVs up to 25 feet (no hookups). Fire grills and picnic tables are provided. Vault toilets are available. There is no drinking water. Leashed pets are permitted.

**Reservations, fees:** Reservations are not accepted. Sites are $22 per night, plus $7 per night for each additional vehicle. Fees increase on holidays. Open June through October, weather permitting.

**Directions:** From Fresno, drive east on

Highway 168 to Shaver Lake, then continue 21 miles to Huntington Lake and Kaiser Pass Road/Forest Road 80. Turn right and drive four miles to the campground.

**Contact:** Sierra National Forest, High Sierra Ranger District, 559/855-5355, www.fs.usda. gov/sierra; California Land Management, 559/893-2111.

## 29 MIDGE CREEK GROUP

### Scenic rating: 7
near Huntington Lake in Sierra National Forest

**Map 11.1, page 573**

This is a good spot to be if you want to avoid the crowds at nearby Rancheria but still be near Huntington Lake. Originally set up to house firefighters, the camp eventually became a permanent facility. It's set in a large, open area shaded by fir trees. Seasonal Midge Creek is nearby.

**Campsites, facilities:** There is one group site for tents or RVs up to 40 feet (no hookups) that can accommodate 25-50 people. There are also six single sites for use as a tent-only group site for up to 36 people. Picnic tables and fire grills are provided. Vault toilets are available. There is no drinking water. Garbage must be packed out. A store and propane gas are nearby. Leashed pets are permitted.

**Reservations, fees:** Reservations are accepted at 559/893-2111. Group sites are $151, single sites are $20 per night, plus $5 per night for each additional vehicle. Open June through October, weather permitting.

**Directions:** From Fresno, drive east for 50 miles on Highway 168 to Shaver Lake, then continue 20 miles northeast to Huntington Lake. At Eastwood Visitors Center turn right, drive 1.2 miles east on Kaiser Pass Road to the campground.

**Contact:** Sierra National Forest, High Sierra Ranger District, 559/855-5355, www.fs.usda. gov/sierra; California Land Management, 559/893-2111.

## 30 BADGER FLAT GROUP AND HORSE CAMP

### Scenic rating: 7

on Rancheria Creek in Sierra National Forest

**Map 11.1, page 573**

Badger Flat is a primitive site along Rancheria Creek at 8,200 feet elevation, about five miles east of Huntington Lake. Though it does not have equestrian amenities, this is still a popular horse camp and a good jumping-off spot for wilderness trekkers. A trail that passes through camp provides two options: Head south for three miles to enter the Dinkey Lakes Wilderness, or head north for two miles to enter the Kaiser Wilderness.

**Campsites, facilities:** There is one group site for tents or RVs up to 35 feet (no hookups) that can accommodate up to 100 people. Picnic tables, fire grills, and food lockers are provided. Vault toilets are available. No drinking water is available. A store is nearby. Leashed pets are permitted.

**Reservations, fees:** Reservations are required at 877/444-6777 ($10 reservation fee) or www.recreation.gov ($9 reservation fee). The group site is $300 per night. Open June through October, weather permitting.

**Directions:** From Fresno, drive east on Highway 168 to Shaver Lake, then continue 21 miles to Huntington Lake and Kaiser Pass Road/Forest Road 80. Turn right and drive five miles to the campground on the right.

**Contact:** Sierra National Forest, High Sierra Ranger District, 559/855-5355, www.fs.usda.gov/sierra; California Land Management, 559/893-2111.

## 31 HIDDEN VIEW

### Scenic rating: 5

north of Fresno on Hensley Lake

**Map 11.1, page 573**

Hensley Lake is popular with water-skiers and personal watercraft users in spring and summer, and it has good prospects for bass fishing as well. Hensley covers 1,500 surface acres with 24 miles of shoreline and, as long as water levels are maintained, makes for a wonderful water playland. Swimming is good, with the best spot at Buck Ridge on the east side of the lake, where there are picnic tables and trees for shade. The reservoir was created by a dam on the Fresno River. A nature trail offers a nice walk. The elevation is 540 feet.

**Campsites, facilities:** There are 55 sites for tents or RVs of any length, some with electrical hookups (30 amps), and two group sites for 50 people each. Picnic tables and fire grills are provided. Restrooms with flush toilets and showers, drinking water, dump station, playground, and boat ramp are available. Some facilities are wheelchair-accessible. Leashed pets are permitted.

**Reservations, fees:** Reservations are accepted at 877/444-6777 ($10 reservation fee) or www.recreation.gov ($9 reservation fee). Sites are $20-30 per night, group sites are $100 per night, plus $4 per night per additional vehicle. Boat launching is free for campers. Open year-round.

**Directions:** From Madera, drive northeast on Highway 145 for about six miles to County Road 400. Bear left on County Road 400 and drive to County Road 603 below the dam. Turn left and drive about two miles on County Road 603 to County Road 407. Turn right on County Road 407 and drive 0.5 mile to the campground.

**Contact:** U.S. Army Corps of Engineers, Sacramento District, Hensley Lake, 559/673-5151.

## 32 SMALLEY COVE

### Scenic rating: 7

on Kerckhoff Reservoir near Madera

**Map 11.1, page 573**

Kerckhoff Reservoir can get so hot that it might

seem as though you could fry an egg on the rocks. Campers should be certain to have some kind of tarp they can set up as a sunscreen. The lake is small and remote, and the use of boat motors more than five horsepower is prohibited. Most campers bring rafts or canoes, and there is a good swimming beach near the picnic area and campground. Fishing is not so good. The elevation is 1,000 feet.

**Campsites, facilities:** There are five sites for tents only. Picnic tables and fire grills are provided. Drinking water and vault toilets are available. Five group picnic sites are available. Supplies are available in Auberry. Some facilities are wheelchair-accessible. Leashed pets are permitted.

**Reservations, fees:** Reservations are not accepted. Sites are $14 per night, plus $3 per night for each additional vehicle and $1 per pet per night. Open year-round.

**Directions:** From Fresno, take Highway 41 north for three miles to the exit for Highway 168 east. Take that exit and drive east on Highway 168 for about 22 miles to Auberry Road. Turn left (north) and drive 2.8 miles to Powerhouse Road. Turn left and drive 8.5 miles to the campground.

**Contact:** PG&E Land Services, 916/386-5164, www.pge.com/recreation; Bass Lake Ranger Station, 559/877-2218.

## 33 YEH-GUB-WEH-TUH CAMPGROUND

🏃 🛶 🐴 ♿ ⛺

### Scenic rating: 8

on the San Joaquin River

**Map 11.1, page 573**

Not many folks know about this spot. It's a primitive setting, but it has some bonuses. For one thing, there's access to the San Joaquin River if you drive to the fishing access trailhead at the end of the road. From there, you get great views of the San Joaquin River Gorge. The camp is a trailhead for two excellent hiking and equestrian trails. Note that the terrain is steep and can be difficult to traverse. Also, this area has poison oak and rattlesnakes. And one more thing: It can get very hot in summer. Are we having fun yet? The setting is primarily oaks, gray pines, and chaparral. Beautiful wildflower displays are highlights in the late winter and spring.

**Campsites, facilities:** There are six walk-in sites for tents only, including two double sites and one triple site for up to 24 people. Drinking water and vault toilets are available. A camp host is on-site. Bring your own firewood. Supplies are available in Auberry. Some facilities are wheelchair-accessible. Leashed pets are permitted.

**Reservations, fees:** Reservations are not accepted. Single sites are $10 per night; double sites are $15 per night. Open year-round.

**Directions:** From Fresno, take Highway 41 north for three miles to the exit for Highway 168 east. Take that exit and drive east on Highway 168 for about 22 miles to Auberry Road. Turn left and drive 2.8 miles to Powerhouse Road. Turn left and drive two miles to Smalley Road (signed "Smalley Road and San Joaquin River Gorge Management Area"). Turn left and drive four miles to the campground on the right.

**Contact:** San Joaquin River Gorge Management Area, 559/855-3492; Bureau of Land Management, Bakersfield Field Office, 661/391-6000, www.blm.gov/ca.

## 34 AHOLUL GROUP AND EQUESTRIAN CAMP

🏃 🛶 🐴 ♿ ⛺

### Scenic rating: 8

on the San Joaquin River

**Map 11.1, page 573**

Aholul is near Yeh-gub-weh-tuh Campground and is the group site option. We have no idea how you pronounce Aholul or Yeh-gub-weh-tuh, and the kind fellow at BLM refused to try. Heh, heh.

**Campsites, facilities:** There is one group site for tents only that can accommodate up to

250 people and an equestrian camp for family camping. A large paved parking lot at Aholul can accommodate RVs and large trailers. Stock water (bring your own bucket) and vault toilets are available. Bring your own drinking water and firewood. Horse corrals are available and are very popular; call 559/855-3492 for availability. Supplies are available in Auberry. Some facilities are wheelchair-accessible. Leashed pets are permitted.

**Reservations, fees:** Reservations are required at 661/391-6000. The group fee is $175 per night; equestrian sites are $25 per night. Open year-round.

**Directions:** From Fresno, take Highway 41 north for three miles to the exit for Highway 168 east. Take that exit and drive east on Highway 168 for about 22 miles to Auberry Road. Turn left and drive 2.8 miles to Powerhouse Road. Turn left and drive two miles to Smalley Road (signed "Smalley Road and San Joaquin River Gorge Management Area"). Turn left and drive four miles to the campground on the right.

**Contact:** San Joaquin River Gorge Management Area, 559/855-3492; Bureau of Land Management, Bakersfield Field Office, 661/391-6000, www.blm.gov/ca.

# 35 CAMP EDISON

**Scenic rating: 8**

on Shaver Lake

**Map 11.1, page 573**

Camp Edison is the best camp at Shaver Lake, set on a peninsula along the lake's western shore, with a boat ramp and marina. The lake is at an elevation of 5,370 feet in the Sierra, a pretty area that has become popular for its calm, warm days and cool water. Boat rentals and bait and tackle are available at the marina. Newcomers with youngsters will discover that the best area for swimming and playing in the water is on the east side of the lake. Though more distant, this part of the lake offers sandy beaches rather than rocky drop-offs.

**Campsites, facilities:** There are 252 sites for RVs or tents, including 11 group sites; some sites have full or partial hookups (20, 30, and 50 amps). During the summer season, six tent trailers also are available. Picnic tables, fire rings, and barbecues are provided. Restrooms with flush toilets and pay showers, drinking water, cable TV, Wi-Fi, general store, dump station, laundry, marina, boat ramp, and horseback-riding facilities are available. Some facilities are wheelchair-accessible. Leashed pets are permitted.

**Reservations, fees:** Reservations are required and can be made online at www.sce.com/campedison. Standard sites are $32 per night, preferred sites are $41 per night, paved sites are $42 per night, RV sites with full hookups are $53 per night, lakeside sites are $50 per night, premium front sites are $73 per night, plus $6 per night for each additional vehicle, $5 per person per night for more than four people, $6 per day for boat launching, and $6 per pet per night. Winter rates are $35 per night. Group sites are $150-389 per night. Open year-round with limited winter services.

**Directions:** From Fresno, take the exit for Highway 41 north and drive north on Highway 41 to the exit for Highway 180 east. Take that exit and drive east on Highway 180 to Highway 168 east. Take that exit and drive east on Highway 168 to the town of Shaver Lake. Continue one mile on Highway 168 to the campground entrance road on the right. Turn right and drive to the campground on the west shore of Shaver Lake.

**Contact:** Camp Edison, P.O. Box 600, 42696 Tollhouse Road, Shaver Lake, CA 93664; Southern California Edison, 559/841-3134, www.sce.com/campedison.

## 36 DORABELLE

### Scenic rating: 7

on Shaver Lake in Sierra National Forest

**Map 11.1, page 573**

This is one of the few Forest Service camps in the state that is set up more for RVers than for tenters. The camp is along a long cove at the southwest corner of the lake, well protected from winds out of the northwest. Several hiking trails are available. Shaver Lake is a popular lake for vacationers, and waterskiing and wakeboarding are extremely popular. It is well stocked with trout and kokanee salmon. Boat rentals and bait and tackle are available at the nearby marina. The elevation is 5,400 feet.

**Campsites, facilities:** There are 67 sites for tents or RVs up to 40 feet (no hookups). Picnic tables and fire grills are provided. Drinking water and vault toilets are available. A store is nearby. Leashed pets are permitted.

**Reservations, fees:** Reservations are accepted at 877/444-6777 ($10 reservation fee) or www.recreation.gov ($9 reservation fee). Sites are $30-60 per night, plus $7 per night for each additional vehicle. Open May through September, weather permitting.

**Directions:** From Fresno, drive east on Highway 168 to Dorabelle Road (on the right just as you enter the town of Shaver Lake). Turn right on Dorabelle Road and drive one mile to the campground at the southwest end of Shaver Lake.

**Contact:** Sierra National Forest, High Sierra Ranger District, 559/855-5355, www.fs.usda.gov/sierra; California Land Management, 559/893-2111.

## 37 SWANSON MEADOW

### Scenic rating: 4

near Shaver Lake in Sierra National Forest

**Map 11.1, page 573**

This is the smallest and most primitive of the camps near Shaver Lake; it is used primarily as an overflow area if lakeside camps are full. It is about two miles south of Shaver Lake at an elevation of 5,600 feet.

**Campsites, facilities:** There are eight sites for tents or RVs up to 25 feet (no hookups). Picnic tables and fire grills are provided. Vault toilets are available. No drinking water is available. A camp host is on-site and a store is nearby. Leashed pets are permitted.

**Reservations, fees:** Reservations are not accepted. Sites are $22-44 per night, plus $5 per night for each additional vehicle. Open May through October, weather permitting.

**Directions:** From Fresno, drive east on Highway 168 to Dinkey Creek Road (on the right just as you enter the town of Shaver Lake). Turn right and drive three miles to the campground entrance road on the left. Turn left and drive a short distance to the campground.

**Contact:** Sierra National Forest, High Sierra Ranger District, 559/855-5355, www.fs.usda.gov/sierra; California Land Management, 559/893-2111.

## 38 DINKEY CREEK AND GROUP CAMP

### Scenic rating: 7

in Sierra National Forest

**Map 11.1, page 573**

This is a huge Forest Service camp set along Dinkey Creek at 5,700 feet elevation, well in the interior of Sierra National Forest. It is a popular camp for anglers who take the trail and hike upstream along the creek for small-trout fishing in a pristine setting. Backpackers occasionally lay over here before driving on to the Dinkey Lakes Parking Area, for hikes to Mystery Lake, Swede Lake, South Lake, and others in the nearby Dinkey Lakes Wilderness.

**Campsites, facilities:** There are 123 sites for tents or RVs up to 35 feet (no hookups) and one group site for up to 50 people. Picnic tables and fire grills are provided. Drinking water, flush and vault toilets, coin showers, interpretive programs, and a camp host are available. Horseback-riding facilities are nearby. You can buy supplies in Dinkey Creek. Some facilities are wheelchair-accessible. Leashed pets are permitted.

**Reservations, fees:** Reservations are required for the group site at 877/444-6777 ($10 reservation fee) or www.recreation.gov ($9 reservation fee). Single sites are $30-60 per night, plus $7 per night for each additional vehicle. The group site is $200 per night. Open May through September, weather permitting.

**Directions:** From Fresno, drive east on Highway 168 to Dinkey Creek Road (on the right just as you enter the town of Shaver Lake). Turn right and drive 13 miles to the campground. A map of Sierra National Forest is advised.

**Contact:** Sierra National Forest, High Sierra Ranger District, 559/855-5355, www.fs.usda. gov/sierra; California Land Management, 559/893-2111.

## 39 GIGANTEA

### Scenic rating: 7
on Dinkey Creek in Sierra National Forest

**Map 11.1, page 573**

This primitive campground is along Dinkey Creek adjacent to the McKinley Grove Botanical Area, which features a little-known grove of giant sequoias. The campground is on a short loop spur road, and day visitors are better off stopping at the McKinley Grove Picnic Area. The elevation is 6,400 feet.

**Campsites, facilities:** There are 10 sites for tents or RVs up to 35 feet (no hookups). Picnic tables and fire grills are provided. Vault toilets are available. No drinking water is available. Supplies are available in Dinkey Creek. Leashed pets are permitted.

**Reservations, fees:** Reservations are not

accepted. Sites are $22 per night, plus $7 per night for each additional vehicle. Open May through October, weather permitting.

**Directions:** From Fresno, drive east on Highway 168 to Dinkey Creek Road (on the right just as you enter the town of Shaver Lake). Turn right and drive 13 miles to McKinley Grove Road/Forest Road 40. Turn right and drive 6.5 miles to the campground.

**Contact:** Sierra National Forest, High Sierra Ranger District, 559/855-5355, www.fs.usda. gov/sierra; California Land Management, 559/893-2111.

## 40 BUCK MEADOW

### Scenic rating: 7
on Deer Creek in Sierra National Forest

**Map 11.1, page 573**

This is one of the three little-known, primitive camps in the area. It's at 6,800 feet elevation along Deer Creek, about seven miles from Wishon Reservoir, a more popular destination.

**Campsites, facilities:** There are 10 sites for tents or RVs up to 35 feet (no hookups). Picnic tables and fire grills are provided. Vault toilets and drinking water are available. Garbage must be packed out. Some facilities are wheelchair-accessible. Leashed pets are permitted.

**Reservations, fees:** Reservations are not accepted. Sites are $22 per night, plus $7 per night for each additional vehicle. Open May through October, weather permitting.

**Directions:** From Fresno, drive east on Highway 168 to Dinkey Creek Road (on the right just as you enter the town of Shaver Lake). Turn right and drive 13 miles to McKinley Grove Road (Forest Road 40). Turn right and drive eight miles to the campground.

**Contact:** Sierra National Forest, High Sierra Ranger District, 559/855-5355, www.fs.usda. gov/sierra; California Land Management, 559/893-2111.

## 41 MILLERTON LAKE STATE RECREATION AREA

**Scenic rating: 6**

near Madera

**Map 11.1, page 573**

As the temperature gauge goes up in the summer, the value of Millerton Lake increases at the same rate. The lake is at 578 feet in the foothills of the San Joaquin Valley, and the water is like gold. The campground and recreation area are set on a peninsula along the north shore of the lake; there are sandy beach areas on both sides of the lake with boat ramps near the campgrounds. It's a big lake, with 43 miles of shoreline, from a narrow lake inlet extending to an expansive main lake body. The irony at Millerton is that when the lake is filled to the brim, the beaches are covered, so ideal conditions are actually when the lake level is down a bit, typically from early summer on. Fishing for bass can be good in spring. Catfish are popular for shoreliners on summer evenings. Waterskiing is very popular in summer, of course. Anglers head upstream, water-skiers downstream. The lake's south side has a huge day-use area. During winter, boat tours are available to view bald eagles. A note of history: The original Millerton County Courthouse, built in 1867, is in the park.

**Campsites, facilities:** There are 148 sites, 27 with full hookups for tents or RVs up to 36 feet, three boat-in sites, and two group sites for 45-75 people. Picnic tables and fire grills are provided. Drinking water, restrooms with flush toilets and coin showers, dump station, picnic areas, full-service marina, snack bar, boat rentals, and boat ramps are available. You can buy supplies in Friant. Some facilities are wheelchair-accessible. Leashed pets are permitted.

**Reservations, fees:** Reservations are accepted at 800/444-7275 ($10 reservation fee) or www.reserveamerica.com ($9 reservation fee). Drive-in sites are $30 per night, RV sites (hookups) are $40 per night, plus $8 per night for each additional vehicle. It's $11 for boat-in sites and $200 per night for group sites. Boat launching is $7 per day. Open year-round.

**Directions:** Drive on Highway 99 to Madera at the exit for Highway 145 east. Take that exit east and drive on Highway 145 for 22 miles (six miles past the intersection with Highway 41) to the park entrance on the right.

**Contact:** Millerton Lake State Recreation Area, 559/822-2332, www.parks.ca.gov.

## 42 JACKASS MEADOW

**Scenic rating: 7**

on Florence Lake in Sierra National Forest

**Map 11.2, page 574**

Jackass Meadow is a pretty spot adjacent to Florence Lake, near the Upper San Joaquin River. There are good canoeing, rafting, and float-tubing possibilities, all high-Sierra style, and swimming is allowed. The boat speed limit is 15 mph. The elevation is 7,200 feet. The lake is remote and can be reached only after a long, circuitous drive on a narrow road with many blind turns. A trailhead at the lake offers access to the wilderness and the John Muir Trail. A hikers' water taxi is available.

**Campsites, facilities:** There are 42 sites for tents or RVs up to 25 feet (no hookups). Picnic tables and fire grills are provided. Vault toilets are available, but there is no drinking water. A boat launch, fishing boat rentals, and wheelchair-accessible fishing pier are nearby. Leashed pets are permitted.

**Reservations, fees:** Reservations are accepted at 877/444-6777 ($10 reservation fee) or www.recreation.gov ($9 reservation fee). Sites are $26-52 per night, plus $7 per night for each additional vehicle. Open June through October, weather permitting.

**Directions:** From the town of Shaver Lake, drive east on Highway 168 for 21 miles to Kaiser Pass Road. Bear northeast on Kaiser Pass Road/Forest Road 80 (slow and curvy) to a junction (left goes to Mono Hot Springs and Lake Edison) with Florence Lake Road. Bear right at the junction and drive seven miles to the campground.

**Contact:** Sierra National Forest, High Sierra Ranger District, 559/855-5355, www.fs.usda.gov/sierra; California Land Management, 559/893-2111.

## 43 TRAPPER SPRINGS

### Scenic rating: 8

on Courtright Reservoir in Sierra National Forest

#### Map 11.2, page 574

Trapper Springs is on the west shore of Courtright Reservoir, at 8,200 feet elevation on the west slope of the Sierra. Courtright is a great destination, with excellent camping, boating, fishing, and hiking into the nearby John Muir Wilderness. A 15-mph speed limit makes the lake ideal for fishing, canoeing, and rafting. Swimming is allowed, but the water is very cold. The lake level can drop dramatically by late summer. One mile north of the camp, a trailhead leads around the north end of the lake to a fork. To the left is the Dinkey Lakes Wilderness. To the right, it goes to the head of the lake then follows Dusy Creek in a long climb into spectacular country in the John Muir Wilderness.

**Campsites, facilities:** There are 70 sites for tents or RVs up to 35 feet (no hookups). Picnic tables and fire grills are provided. Drinking water and vault toilets are available. A boat ramp is nearby. Some facilities are wheelchair-accessible. Leashed pets are permitted.

**Reservations, fees:** Reservations are not accepted. Sites are $24 per night, plus $9 per night for an additional RV, $5 per night for each additional vehicle, and $2 per pet per night. Open mid-June through mid-October.

**Directions:** From Fresno, drive east on Highway 168 to Dinkey Creek Road (on the right just as you enter the town of Shaver Lake). Turn right and drive 13 miles to McKinley Grove Road/Forest Road 40. Turn right and drive 14 miles to Courtright Road. Turn left (north) and drive 12 miles to the campground entrance road on the right.

**Contact:** Sierra National Forest, High Sierra Ranger District, 559/855-5355, www.fs.usda.gov/sierra; PG&E Land Services, 916/386-5164, www.pge.com/recreation.

## 44 MARMOT ROCK

### Scenic rating: 8

on Courtright Reservoir in Sierra National Forest

#### Map 11.2, page 574

Courtright Reservoir is in the high country at 8,200 feet elevation. Marmot Rock is at the southern end of the lake, with a boat ramp nearby. This pretty Sierra lake provides options for boaters and hikers. Trout fishing can also be good. Boaters must observe a 15-mph speed limit, which makes for quiet water. The drive to this lake is very long, slow, and twisty.

**Campsites, facilities:** There are 15 sites for tents or small RVs; most sites are walk-in. Picnic tables, bear boxes, and fire grills are provided. Vault toilets and drinking water are available. A boat ramp is nearby. Leashed pets are permitted.

**Reservations, fees:** Reservations are not accepted. Sites are $24 per night when water is available, $18 per night with no water, plus $5 per night per each additional vehicle and $2 per pet per night. Overflow parking is $18 per night. Open mid-June through mid-October.

**Directions:** From Fresno, drive east on Highway 168 to Dinkey Creek Road (on the right just as you enter the town of Shaver Lake). Turn right and drive 13 miles to McKinley Grove Road/Forest Road 40. Turn right and drive 14 miles to Courtright Road. Turn left (north) and drive 10 miles to the campground entrance road on the right (on the south shore of the lake). Park and walk a short distance to the campground.

**Contact:** PG&E Land Services, 916/386-5164,

www.pge.com/recreation; Sierra National Forest, High Sierra Ranger District, 559/855-5355, www.fs.usda.gov/sierra.

## 45 WISHON VILLAGE RV RESORT

Scenic rating: 7

near Wishon Reservoir

**Map 11.2, page 574**

This privately operated mountain park is near the shore of Wishon Reservoir, about one mile from the dam. Trout stocks often make for good fishing in early summer, and anglers with boats love the 15-mph speed limit, which keeps personal watercraft off the water. Backpackers and hikers can find a great trailhead at the south end of the lake at Coolidge Meadow, where a trail leads to the Woodchuck Creek drainage and numerous lakes in the John Muir Wilderness. The elevation is 6,772 feet.

**Campsites, facilities:** There are 97 sites with full hookups (50 amps) for RVs up to 45 feet, along with 26 sites for tents. Two rental trailers are also available. Picnic tables and fire pits are provided. Restrooms with coin showers, drinking water, a general store, Wi-Fi, and Sunday church services are available. Coin laundry, ice, boat ramp, motorboat and pontoon rentals, bait and tackle, boat slips, volleyball, horseshoes, and propane gas are nearby. Leashed pets are permitted.

**Reservations, fees:** Reservations are recommended. RV sites are $42-54 per night, tent sites are $31-39 per night, plus $3 per person per night for more than two people, $5 per night per additional vehicle, and $3 per pet per night. Weekly and monthly rates are available. Open May through September.

**Directions:** From Fresno, drive east on Highway 168 to Dinkey Creek Road (on the right just as you enter the town of Shaver Lake). Turn right and drive 13 miles to McKinley Grove Road (Forest Road 40). Turn right and

drive 15 miles to the park (66500 McKinley Grove Road/Forest Road 40).

**Contact:** Wishon Village RV Resort, 559/865-5361, www.wishonvillage.com.

## 46 LILY PAD

Scenic rating: 7

near Wishon Reservoir in Sierra National Forest

**Map 11.2, page 574**

This is the smallest of the three camps at Wishon Reservoir, set along the southwest shore at 6,500 feet elevation, about a mile from both the lake and a good boat ramp. A 15-mph speed limit ensures quiet water, making this an ideal destination for families with canoes or rafts. The conditions at this lake are similar to those at Courtright Reservoir. The drive to the lake is very long, slow, and twisty.

**Campsites, facilities:** There are 15 sites for tents or RVs up to 35 feet (no hookups) and four hike-in sites. Picnic tables, bear boxes, and fire grills are provided. Vault toilets are available, but there is no drinking water. Groceries, boat rentals, boat ramp, and propane gas are nearby. Some facilities are wheelchair-accessible. Leashed pets are permitted.

**Reservations, fees:** Reservations are not accepted. Sites are $24 per night, plus $7 per night for additional RV, $5 per night for each additional vehicle, and $2 per pet per night. Open late May through mid-October, weather permitting.

**Directions:** From Fresno, drive east on Highway 168 to Dinkey Creek Road (on the right just as you enter the town of Shaver Lake). Turn right and drive 13 miles to McKinley Grove Road (Forest Road 40). Turn right and drive 16 miles to the campground on the right.

**Contact:** Sierra National Forest, High Sierra Ranger District, 559/855-5355, www.fs.usda.gov/sierra; PG&E Land Services, 916/386-5164, www.pge.com/recreation.

## 47 UPPER KINGS RIVER GROUP CAMP

### Scenic rating: 8

on Wishon Reservoir

**Map 11.2, page 574**

Wishon Reservoir is a great place for a camping trip. When the lake is full, which is not often enough, the place has great natural beauty, set at 6,400 feet elevation and surrounded by national forest. The fishing is fair enough on summer evenings, and a 15-mph speed limit keeps the lake quiet. Swimming is allowed, but the water is very cold. The drive to the lake is long, slow, and twisty. A side-trip option is hiking from the trailhead at Woodchuck Creek, which within the span of a one-day hike takes you into the John Muir Wilderness and past three lakes—Woodchuck, Chimney, and Marsh.

**Campsites, facilities:** A group site for tents or RVs up to 40 feet (no hookups) can accommodate up to 50 people. Picnic tables and fire grills are provided. Drinking water and vault toilets are available. Leashed pets are permitted.

**Reservations, fees:** Reservations are required at 916/386-5164. Sites are $200 per night or $1,400 per week, with a two-night minimum (three-night minimum on holidays). Open late June through early October, weather permitting.

**Directions:** From Fresno, drive east on Highway 168 to Dinkey Creek Road (on the right just as you enter the town of Shaver Lake). Turn right and drive 13 miles to McKinley Grove Road/Forest Road 40. Turn right and drive to the Wishon Dam. The campground is near the base of the dam.

**Contact:** PG&E Land Services, 916/386-5164, www.pge.com/recreation.

## 48 HORTON CREEK

### Scenic rating: 7

near Bishop

**Map 11.2, page 574**

This little-known, primitive BLM camp along Horton Creek, northwest of Bishop, can make a good base camp for hunters in the fall, with wild, rugged country to the west. The elevation is 4,975 feet.

**Campsites, facilities:** There are 49 sites for tents or RVs up to 30 feet (no hookups). Picnic tables and fire grills are provided. Drinking water, lantern holders, vault toilets, and garbage containers are available. Leashed pets are permitted.

**Reservations, fees:** Reservations are not accepted. Sites are $5 per night; LTVA (Long Term Visitor Area) season passes are available for $300. There is a 14-day stay limit. Open early May through October, weather permitting.

**Directions:** Drive on U.S. 395 to Sawmill Road (eight miles north of Bishop). Turn left (northwest, toward the Sierra) and drive a very short distance to Round Valley Road. Turn right and drive approximately five miles to the campground entrance on the left.

**Contact:** Bureau of Land Management, Bishop Field Office, 760/872-4881, www.blm.gov/ca.

## 49 BROWN'S MILLPOND CAMPGROUND

### Scenic rating: 6

near Bishop

**Map 11.2, page 574**

This privately operated camp is adjacent to the Millpond Recreation Area, which offers ball fields, playgrounds, and a swimming lake. No powerboats are allowed. There are opportunities for sailing, archery, tennis, horseshoe games, and fishing.

**Campsites, facilities:** There are 72 sites for

tents or RVs of any length; some sites have partial hookups (30 amps). Picnic tables and fire grills are provided. Restrooms with flush toilets and coin showers, drinking water, and coin laundry are available. Some facilities are wheelchair-accessible. A limit of one vehicle per site is enforced. Leashed pets are permitted.

**Reservations, fees:** Reservations are accepted. Sites are $23-28 per vehicle per night, plus $5 for each additional vehicle. Open March through October.

**Directions:** Drive on U.S. 395 to a road signed "Millpond/County Park" (seven miles north of Bishop). Turn southwest (toward the Sierra) at that road (Ed Powers Road) and drive 0.2 mile to Sawmill Road. Turn right and drive 0.8 mile to Millpond Road. Turn left and drive a short distance to the campground.

**Contact:** Brown's Millpond Campground, 760/873-5342, www.brownscampgrounds.com.

## 50 BROWN'S TOWN

### Scenic rating: 5

near Bishop

**Map 11.2, page 574**

This privately operated campground is one of several in the vicinity of Bishop. It's all shade and grass and it's next to the golf course.

**Campsites, facilities:** There are 103 sites with no hookups for tents or RVs of any length and 47 sites with partial hookups (30 amps) for tents or RVs. Some sites are pull-through. Picnic tables are provided, and fire grills are provided at most sites. Restrooms with flush toilets and coin showers, drinking water, cable TV at 12 sites, coin laundry, dump station, museum, convenience store, and snack bar are available. Leashed pets are permitted.

**Reservations, fees:** Reservations are accepted; in March, sites are first-come, first-served. RV sites are $30 per night, tent sites are $25 per night, plus $1 per person per night for

more than four people and $10 per night per additional vehicle. Stays are limited to 14 days per season. Some credit cards are accepted. Open March through Thanksgiving, weather permitting.

**Directions:** From U.S. 395, drive to Schober Lane (one mile south of Bishop) and the campground entrance. Turn northwest (toward the Sierra) and into the campground.

**Contact:** Brown's Town, 760/873-8522, www.brownscampgrounds.com.

## 51 BITTERBRUSH

### Scenic rating: 6

near Bishop in the Inyo National Forest

**Map 11.2, page 574**

Bitterbrush is situated along Bishop Creek with piñon pines and sagebrush providing the scenery. In the fall, the aspens are spectacular in the canyon between here and beautiful Lake Sabrina. This is a popular winter site as it is frequently below the snow line. The elevation is 7,350 feet.

**Campsites, facilities:** There are 30 sites for tents or RVs to 40 feet (no hookups). Picnic tables, bear-proof lockers, and fire rings are provided. Drinking water (seasonal) and vault toilets are available. A dump station is nearby at Fort Jeffrey Campground. Some facilities are wheelchair-accessible. Leashed pets are permitted.

**Reservations, fees:** Reservations are not accepted. Sites are $24 per night but are free in winter months when there is no water or garbage service. There is a 14-day stay limit. Open year-round, weather permitting.

**Directions:** From Bishop, drive west on Highway 168 for nine miles to the campground.

**Contact:** Inyo National Forest, White Mountain Ranger District, 760/873-2500, www.fs.usda.gov.

## 52 FORKS

### Scenic rating: 7

near South Lake in Inyo National Forest

**Map 11.2, page 574**

After a visit here, it's no mystery how the Forest Service named this camp. It is at the fork in the road, which gives you two options: You can turn south on South Lake Road and drive along the South Fork of Bishop Creek up to pretty South Lake, or you can keep driving on Highway 168 to another beautiful lake, Lake Sabrina, where hikers will find a trailhead that offers access to the John Muir Wilderness. The elevation is 7,800 feet.

**Campsites, facilities:** There are 21 sites for RVs up to 30 feet (no hookups). Picnic tables and fire grills are provided. Drinking water and flush toilets are available. Some facilities are wheelchair-accessible. Supplies are available in Bishop. Leashed pets are permitted.

**Reservations, fees:** Reservations are not accepted. Single sites are $24 per night, double sites are $48 per night, plus $5 per night per additional vehicle. Open late April through October, weather permitting.

**Directions:** Drive on U.S. 395 to Bishop and Highway 168. Turn west (toward the Sierra) on Highway 168 and drive 14 miles to South Lake Road. Turn left and drive 0.25 mile to the campground entrance on the right.

**Contact:** Inyo National Forest, White Mountain Ranger District, 760/873-2500, www.fs.usda.gov; Rainbow Pack Outfitters, 760/873-8877.

## 53 BIG TREES

### Scenic rating: 8

on Bishop Creek in Inyo National Forest

**Map 11.2, page 574**

This is a small Forest Service camp on Bishop Creek at 7,500 feet elevation. This section of the stream is stocked with small trout by the

Department of Fish and Game. Both South Lake and Lake Sabrina are about 10 miles away.

**Campsites, facilities:** There are 16 sites for tents or RVs up to 30 feet (no hookups). Picnic tables, bear boxes (mandatory), and fire grills are provided. Drinking water and flush toilets are available. A dump station is two miles away at Four Jeffrey. Horseback-riding facilities are approximately seven miles away. Supplies are available in Bishop. Leashed pets are permitted.

**Reservations, fees:** Reservations are not accepted. Sites are $24 per night. Open late April through October, weather permitting.

**Directions:** Drive on U.S. 395 to Bishop and Highway 168. Turn west (toward the Sierra) on Highway 168 and drive 11 miles to the campground access road on the left. Turn left and drive two miles on a dirt road to the campground.

**Contact:** Inyo National Forest, White Mountain Ranger District, 760/873-2500, www.fs.usda.gov; Rainbow Pack Outfitters, 760/873-8877.

## 54 BISHOP PARK AND GROUP

### Scenic rating: 6

near Lake Sabrina in Inyo National Forest

**Map 11.2, page 574**

Bishop Park Camp is one in a series of camps along Bishop Creek. This one is just behind the summer community of Aspendell. It is about two miles from Lake Sabrina, an ideal day trip or jumping-off spot for a backpacking expedition into the John Muir Wilderness. The elevation is 8,400 feet.

**Campsites, facilities:** There are 13 sites for tents or RVs up to 22 feet (no hookups), eight sites for tents only, and a group tent site for up to 25 people. Picnic tables, fire grills, and food lockers are provided. Drinking water and flush toilets are available. Horseback-riding facilities are nearby. Supplies are available in

Bishop. Some facilities are wheelchair-accessible. Leashed pets are permitted.

**Reservations, fees:** Reservations are not accepted for the family sites but are required for the group site at 877/444-6777 ($10 reservation fee) or www.recreation.gov ($9 reservation fee). Sites are $24 per night, plus $73 per night for the group site. Open mid-May through mid-October, weather permitting.

**Directions:** Drive on U.S. 395 to Bishop and Highway 168. Turn west (toward the Sierra) on Highway 168 and drive 15 miles to the campground.

**Contact:** Inyo National Forest, White Mountain Ranger District, 760/873-2500, www. fs.usda.gov/inyo; Rainbow Pack Outfitters, 760/873-8877.

## 55 INTAKE AND INTAKE WALK-IN

**Scenic rating: 7**

on Sabrina Creek in Inyo National Forest

Map 11.2, page 574

This small camp, set at 8,200 feet elevation at a tiny reservoir on Bishop Creek, is about three miles from Lake Sabrina, where a trailhead leads into the John Muir Wilderness. Nearby North Lake and South Lake provide side-trip options. All three are beautiful alpine lakes.

**Campsites, facilities:** There are 11 sites for tents or RVs up to 40 feet (no hookups) and five walk-in tent sites on the west shore. Picnic tables, food lockers, and fire grills are provided. Drinking water and flush toilets are available. A dump station is 1.5 miles away at Four Jeffrey. Supplies are available in Bishop. Some facilities are wheelchair-accessible. Leashed pets are permitted.

**Reservations, fees:** Reservations are not accepted. Sites are $24 per night. Open April through October, weather permitting.

**Directions:** Drive on U.S. 395 to Bishop and Highway 168. Turn west (toward the Sierra) on

Highway 168 and drive 14.5 miles to the campground entrance.

**Contact:** Inyo National Forest, White Mountain Ranger District, 760/873-2500, www. fs.usda.gov/inyo.

## 56 FOUR JEFFREY

**Scenic rating: 8**

near South Lake in Inyo National Forest

Map 11.2, page 574

The camp is on the South Fork of Bishop Creek at 8,100 feet elevation, about four miles from South Lake. If you can arrange a trip in the fall, make sure you visit this camp. The fall colors are spectacular, with the aspen trees exploding in yellows and oranges. It is also the last camp on South Lake Road to be closed in the fall, and though nights are cold, it is well worth the trip. This is by far the largest of the Forest Service camps in the vicinity. There are three lakes in the area: North Lake, Lake Sabrina, and South Lake. South Lake is stocked with trout and has a 5-mph speed limit.

**Campsites, facilities:** There are 106 sites for tents or RVs up to 30 feet (no hookups). Picnic tables, food lockers, and fire grills are provided. Drinking water, flush toilets, and a dump station are available. Horseback-riding facilities are nearby. A café, a small store, and fishing-boat rentals are available at South Lake. Supplies are available in Bishop. Some facilities are wheelchair-accessible. Leashed pets are permitted.

**Reservations, fees:** Reservations are accepted at 877/444-6777 ($10 reservation fee) or www. recreation.gov ($9 reservation fee). Sites are $24 per night. Open mid-April through October, weather permitting.

**Directions:** Drive on U.S. 395 to Bishop and Highway 168. Turn west (toward the Sierra) on Highway 168 and drive 14 miles to South Lake Road. Turn left and drive 0.5 mile to the campground.

**Contact:** Inyo National Forest, White

Mountain Ranger District, 760/873-2500, www.fs.usda.gov/inyo; Rainbow Pack Outfitters, 760/873-8877, www.rainbow.zb-net.com.

## 57 CREEKSIDE RV PARK

**Scenic rating: 7**

on the South Fork of Bishop Creek

**Map 11.2, page 574**

This privately operated park in the high country is set up primarily for RVs. A lot of folks are surprised to find it here. The South Fork of Bishop Creek runs through the park. A bonus is a fishing pond stocked with Alpers trout. North, Sabrina, and South Lakes are in the area. The elevation is 8,300 feet.

**Campsites, facilities:** There are 45 sites with full or partial hookups (20 and 30 amps) for RVs up to 35 feet, along with four sites for tents. Fourteen rental trailers are also available. Restrooms with flush toilets and coin showers, drinking water, convenience store, propane, horseshoes, and fish-cleaning facilities are available. Leashed pets are permitted.

**Reservations, fees:** Reservations are accepted. RV sites are $48 per night, tent sites are $35 per night, plus $1 per person per night for more than two people, $5 per night for each additional vehicle, and $5 per pet per night. Open April through October or later, weather permitting. Some credit cards are accepted.

**Directions:** Drive on U.S. 395 to Bishop and Highway 168. Turn west (toward the Sierra) on Highway 168 and drive 14 miles to South Lake Road. Turn left and drive two miles to the campground entrance on the left (1949 South Lake Road).

**Contact:** Creekside RV Park, 760/873-4483, www.bishopcreeksidervpark.com.

## 58 NORTH LAKE

**Scenic rating: 8**

on Bishop Creek near North Lake in Inyo National Forest

**Map 11.2, page 574**

North Lake is a beautiful Sierra lake surrounded by beautiful aspens at an elevation of 9,500 feet, with good trout fishing much of the season. No motors are allowed on this 13-acre lake. The camp is on the North Fork of Bishop Creek near North Lake and close to a trailhead that offers access to numerous lakes in the John Muir Wilderness and eventually connects with the Pacific Crest Trail. An outstanding trailhead leads to several small alpine lakes in the nearby John Muir Wilderness for day hikes or all the way up to Bishop Pass and Dusy Basin.

**Campsites, facilities:** There are 11 sites for tents only. Picnic tables, bear boxes, and fire grills are provided. Vault toilets are available. There is no drinking water. Horseback-riding facilities are nearby. Supplies are available in Bishop. Leashed pets are permitted.

**Reservations, fees:** Reservations are not accepted. Sites are $24 per night. Open early June through mid-September, weather permitting.

**Directions:** Drive on U.S. 395 to Bishop and Highway 168. Turn west (toward the Sierra) on Highway 168 and drive 17 miles to Forest Road 8S02 (signed "North Lake"). Turn right (north) on Forest Road 8S02 and drive two miles to the campground.

**Contact:** Inyo National Forest, White Mountain Ranger District, 760/873-2500, www.fs.usda.gov/inyo; Bishop Pack Outfitters, 760/873-4785.

## 59 SABRINA

**Scenic rating: 8**

near Lake Sabrina in Inyo National Forest

**Map 11.2, page 574**

You get the best of both worlds at this camp. It

is at 9,000 feet elevation on Bishop Creek, just 0.5 mile from 200-acre Lake Sabrina, one of the prettiest alpine lakes in California that you can reach by car. A 10-mph boat speed limit is in effect. Sabrina is stocked with trout, including some big Alpers trout. Trails nearby are routed into the high country of the John Muir Wilderness. Take your pick. Whatever your choice, it's a good one. By the way, Sabrina is pronounced "sa-BRY-na," not "sa-BREE-na."

**Campsites, facilities:** There are 11 sites for tents or RVs up to 30 feet (no hookups) and seven sites for tents only. Picnic tables and fire grills are provided. Drinking water and pit toilets are available. A boat ramp and rentals are nearby. Supplies are available in Bishop. Some facilities are wheelchair-accessible. Leashed pets are permitted.

**Reservations, fees:** Reservations are not accepted. Sites are $24 per night. Open mid-May through mid-September, weather permitting.

**Directions:** Drive on U.S. 395 to Bishop and Highway 168. Turn west (toward the Sierra) on Highway 168 and drive 17 miles (signed "Lake Sabrina" at a fork) to the campground.

**Contact:** Inyo National Forest, White Mountain Ranger District, 760/873-2500, www.fs.usda.gov/inyo; Bishop Pack Outfitters, 760/873-4785.

# 60 WILLOW

### Scenic rating: 8

on Bishop Creek in Inyo National Forest

**Map 11.2, page 574**

This is one in a series of pretty Forest Service camps along the south fork of Bishop Creek. Willow is near Mountain Glen (see listing in this chapter) at an elevation of 9,000 feet. Primitive and beautiful, this is a favorite. Just up the road is the trailhead to the Chocolate Lakes and Bishop Pass, as well as low-speed boating and fishing at Lake Sabrina and South Lake. A good spot to set up shop.

**Campsites, facilities:** There are 10 sites for tents only. Picnic tables, bear boxes, and fire rings are provided. Vault toilets are available. There is no drinking water. Leashed pets are permitted.

**Reservations, fees:** Reservations are not accepted. Sites are $23 per night. There is a seven-day stay limit. Open late May to late September.

**Directions:** From Bishop, drive 13 miles west on Highway 168 to South Lake Road. Turn left and drive 5.5 miles to the campground.

**Contact:** Inyo National Forest, White Mountain Ranger District, 760/873-2500, www.fs.usda.gov/inyo.

# 61 TABLE MOUNTAIN GROUP

### Scenic rating: 8

on Bishop Creek in Inyo National Forest

**Map 11.2, page 574**

Just a short walk down an easy trail leads to another of the pleasant hidden campgrounds along Bishop Creek. This group camp at an elevation of 8,500 feet sits amid a nice mix of aspen and Jeffrey pine and makes a great base camp for hiking, fishing, or just chilling out. Less than one mile up the road is the Tyee Lakes Trailhead, which climbs the flank of Table Mountain and provides fabulous views of the Inconsolable Range and the peaks near South Lake.

**Campsites, facilities:** One group site for tents only accommodates up to 25 people. Picnic tables, bear boxes (mandatory), and fire rings are provided. Vault toilets are available. There is no drinking water. Leashed pets are permitted.

**Reservations, fees:** Reservations are required at 877/444-6777 ($10 reservation fee) or www.recreation.gov ($9 reservation fee). The site is $73 per night with a seven-day stay limit. Open late May to late September.

**Directions:** From Bishop, drive 13 miles west on Highway 168 to South Lake Road. Turn left and drive 4.3 miles to the campground.

**Contact:** Inyo National Forest, White

Mountain Ranger District, 760/873-2500, www.fs.usda.gov/inyo.

## 62 MOUNTAIN GLEN

### Scenic rating: 8

on Bishop Creek in Inyo National Forest

**Map 11.2, page 574**

Mountain Glen rests along the south fork of Bishop Creek. Jeffrey pines, piñon pines, aspens, and sagebrush green the campground, but come in mid-September when the aspens explode in a riot of colors, bringing the canyon to life. You can often have this place to yourself then. Little Bishop Creek is nearby and is stocked with small trout. The elevation is 8,200 feet.

**Campsites, facilities:** There are five sites for tents only. Picnic tables, bear-proof lockers, and fire rings are provided. Vault toilets are available. There is no drinking water. Leashed pets are permitted.

**Reservations, fees:** Reservations are not accepted. Sites are $21 per night. There is a seven-day stay limit. Open late May to late September.

**Directions:** From Bishop drive west 13 miles on Highway 168 to South Lake Road. Turn left and drive three miles to the campground.

**Contact:** Inyo National Forest, White Mountain Ranger District, 760/873-2500, www.fs.usda.gov/inyo.

## 63 KEOUGH'S HOT SPRINGS

### Scenic rating: 5

in Owens Valley on U.S. 395

**Map 11.2, page 574**

This private facility is the site of the eastern Sierra's largest natural hot springs pool. The landscape is the stark high desert, but it makes for sensational sunsets with colors sometimes refracting across what seems an infinite sky.

With the public springs at Hot Creek now off limits, Keough's is a very good choice.

**Campsites, facilities:** There are 10 tent sites and 10 sites for RVs up to 40 feet (partial 30-amp hookups), plus four furnished tent cabins. Picnic tables are provided, and campers can bring their own above-ground fire pit. Drinking water, flush toilets, coin showers, a snack bar, and a gift shop are available. Leashed pets are permitted.

**Reservations, fees:** Reservations are accepted. Sites are $28-33 per night, plus $1 per person per night for more than two people. Maximum stay is 14 days. Open year-round, weather permitting.

**Directions:** From Bishop, drive south on Highway 395 for seven miles to Keough's Hot Springs Road. Turn right on Keough's Hot Springs Road and drive one mile to the resort.

**Contact:** Keough's Hot Springs, 760/872-4670, www.keoughshotsprings.com.

## 64 BAKER CREEK CAMPGROUND

### Scenic rating: 4

near Big Pine

**Map 11.2, page 574**

Because this is a county-operated RV park, it is often overlooked by campers who consider only camps on reservations systems. That makes this a good option for cruisers touring the eastern Sierra on U.S. 395. It's ideal for a quick overnighter, with easy access from Big Pine. The camp is set along Baker Creek at 4,000 feet elevation in the high plateau country of the eastern Sierra. An option is fair trout fishing during the evening bite on the creek.

**Campsites, facilities:** There are 70 sites for tents or RVs up to 30 feet (no hookups). Picnic tables and fire grills are provided. Vault toilets and hand-pumped well water are available. You can buy supplies about 1.5 miles away in Big Pine. Leashed pets are permitted.

**Reservations, fees:** Reservations are not

accepted. Sites are $14 per vehicle per night via automated pay stations that accept credit cards. Open year-round, weather permitting.

**Directions:** Drive on U.S. 395 to Big Pine and Baker Creek Road. Turn west (toward the Sierra) on Baker Creek Road and drive a mile to the campground.

**Contact:** Inyo County Parks Department, 760/873-5577, www.inyocountycamping.com.

## 65 GLACIER VIEW

### Scenic rating: 4

near Big Pine

Map 11.2, page 574

This is one of two county camps near the town of Big Pine, providing U.S. 395 cruisers with two options. The camp is along the Big Pine Canal at 3,900 feet elevation. It is owned by the county but operated by a concessionaire, Brown's, which runs five small campgrounds in the area: Glacier View, Keough's Hot Springs, Millpond, Brown's Owens River, and Brown's Town.

**Campsites, facilities:** There are 40 sites for tents or RVs of any length; some sites have partial hookups (30 amps) and/or are pull-through. Picnic tables and fire grills are provided. Restrooms with flush toilets and coin showers and drinking water are available. There is no dump station. Supplies are available in Big Pine. Leashed pets are permitted.

**Reservations, fees:** Reservations are not accepted. Tent sites are $15 per night; RV sites are $15 per night (no hookups) or $20 per night (electric and water). Open year-round.

**Directions:** Drive on U.S. 395 to the park entrance (0.5 mile north of Big Pine) on the southeast side of the road. Turn east (away from the Sierra) and enter the park.

**Contact:** Inyo County Parks Department, 760/872-6911, www.inyocountycamping.com.

## 66 PALISADE GLACIER AND CLYDE GLACIER GROUP CAMPS

### Scenic rating: 6

on Big Pine Creek in Inyo National Forest

Map 11.2, page 574

This trailhead camp, also known as Big Pine Canyon Group Camp, is popular with groups planning to rock-climb the Palisades. This climbing trip is for experienced mountaineers only; it's a dangerous expedition where risk of life can be included in the bargain. Safer options include exploring the surrounding John Muir Wilderness. Still, it's great as a base camp, even though highway sounds can be heard. The elevation is 7,600 feet.

**Campsites, facilities:** Each campground has two tent-only group sites that can accommodate up to 20 and 25 people respectively. Picnic tables and fire grills are provided. Drinking water and vault toilets are available. Some facilities are wheelchair-accessible. Leashed pets are permitted.

**Reservations, fees:** Reservations are required at 877/444-6777 ($10 reservation fee) or www.recreation.gov ($9 reservation fee). Note that www.recreation.gov lists both of these campgrounds under Big Pine Canyon. Sites are $73 per night. Open mid-May through mid-October.

**Directions:** Drive on U.S. 395 to Big Pine and Crocker Street/Glacier Lodge Road. Turn west (toward the Sierra) and drive nine miles (it becomes Glacier Lodge Road) to the campground on the left.

**Contact:** Inyo National Forest, White Mountain Ranger District, 760/873-2500, www.fs.usda.gov/inyo.

## 67 BIG PINE CREEK

**Scenic rating: 8**

in Inyo National Forest

**Map 11.2, page 574**

This is another good spot for backpackers to launch a multiday trip. The camp is set along Big Pine Creek at 7,700 feet elevation, with trails near the camp that are routed to the numerous lakes in the high country of the John Muir Wilderness.

**Campsites, facilities:** There are 30 sites for tents or RVs up to 22 feet (no hookups). Picnic tables, food lockers, and fire grills are provided. Drinking water and vault toilets are available. Some facilities are wheelchair-accessible. Leashed pets are permitted.

**Reservations, fees:** Reservations are accepted at 877/444-6777 ($10 reservation fee) or www.recreation.gov ($9 reservation fee). Sites are $23 per night. Open early May through October, weather permitting.

**Directions:** Drive on U.S. 395 to Big Pine and Crocker Street/Glacier Lodge Road. Turn west (toward the Sierra) and drive nine miles (it becomes Glacier Lodge Road) to the campground.

**Contact:** Inyo National Forest, White Mountain Ranger District, 760/873-2500, www.fs.usda.gov/inyo or www.camprrm.com.

## 68 UPPER SAGE FLAT

**Scenic rating: 8**

on Big Pine Creek in Inyo National Forest

**Map 11.2, page 574**

This is one in a series of Forest Service camps in the area set up primarily for backpackers taking off on wilderness expeditions. Several nearby trails lead into the John Muir Wilderness. The best of these is routed west past several lakes to the base of the Palisades and beyond to John Muir Trail. Even starting at 7,600 feet, expect a steep climb.

**Campsites, facilities:** There are 21 sites for tents or RVs up to 25 feet (no hookups). Picnic tables, food lockers, and fire grills are provided. Drinking water and vault toilets are available. Some facilities are wheelchair-accessible. Leashed pets are permitted.

**Reservations, fees:** Reservations are accepted at 877/444-6777 ($10 reservation fee) or www.recreation.gov ($9 reservation fee). Sites are $23 per night. Open late April through mid-September, weather permitting.

**Directions:** Drive on U.S. 395 to Big Pine and Crocker Street/Glacier Lodge Road. Turn west (toward the Sierra) and drive 8.5 miles (it becomes Glacier Lodge Road) to the campground.

**Contact:** Inyo National Forest, White Mountain Ranger District, 760/873-2500, www.fs.usda.gov/inyo or www.camprrm.com.

## 69 SAGE FLAT

**Scenic rating: 8**

on Big Pine Creek near Big Pine in Inyo National Forest

**Map 11.2, page 574**

This camp, like the others in the immediate vicinity, is set up primarily for backpackers who are getting ready to head out on multiday expeditions into the nearby John Muir Wilderness. The trail heads west past several lakes to the base of the Palisades and beyond to John Muir Trail. The hike begins with a steep climb from the trailhead at 7,600 feet elevation. The camp is along Big Pine Creek, which is stocked with small trout.

**Campsites, facilities:** There are 28 sites for tents or RVs up to 35 feet (no hookups). Picnic tables, food lockers, and fire grills are provided. Drinking water and vault toilets are available. Some sites are wheelchair-accessible. Leashed pets are permitted.

**Reservations, fees:** Reservations are not accepted. Sites are $22 per night. Open late April through mid-September, weather permitting.

**Directions:** Drive on U.S. 395 to Big Pine and Crocker Street/Glacier Lodge Road. Turn west

(toward the Sierra) and drive eight miles (it becomes Glacier Lodge Road) to the campground.
**Contact:** Inyo National Forest, White Mountain Ranger District, 760/873-2500, www.fs.usda.gov/inyo or www.camprrm.com.

## 70 TINNEMAHA CAMPGROUND

### Scenic rating: 6

near Big Pine

**Map 11.2, page 574**

This primitive, little-known (to out-of-towners) county park campground is on Tinnemaha Creek at 4,400 feet elevation. The creek is stocked with Alpers trout. Horse camping is allowed, but call ahead.

**Campsites, facilities:** There are 55 sites for tents or RVs of any length (no hookups). Picnic tables and fire grills are provided. Vault toilets are available. There is no drinking water, so bring your own. Stream water is available and must be boiled or pump-filtered before use. Leashed pets are permitted.

**Reservations, fees:** Reservations are not accepted. Sites are $14 per vehicle per night. Open year-round.

**Directions:** Drive on U.S. 395 to Tinnemaha Creek Road (seven miles south of Big Pine and 19.5 miles north of Independence). Turn west (toward the Sierra) on Fish Springs Road and drive 0.5 mile to Tinnemaha Creek Road. Turn west (left) and drive two miles to the park on the right.

**Contact:** Inyo County Parks Department, 760/873-5577, www.inyocountycamping.com.

## 71 TABOOSE CREEK CAMPGROUND

### Scenic rating: 4

near Big Pine

**Map 11.2, page 574**

The eastern Sierra is stark country, but this little spot provides a stream (Taboose Creek) and a few aspens near the campground. The setting is high desert, with a spectacular view to the west of the high Sierra rising up from sagebrush. There is an opportunity for trout fishing—fair, not spectacular. The easy access off U.S. 395 is a bonus. The hike up to Taboose Pass from here is one of the steepest grinds in the Sierra. Only the deranged need apply—which is why I did it, of course. The route provides one-day access to the interior of the John Muir Wilderness. The elevation is 3,900 feet.

**Campsites, facilities:** There are 50 sites for tents or RVs up to 40 feet (no hookups). Picnic tables and fire grills are provided. Drinking water (hand-pumped from a well) and vault toilets are available. Supplies are available in Big Pine or Independence. Leashed pets are permitted.

**Reservations, fees:** Reservations are not accepted. Sites are $14 per vehicle per night. Open year-round.

**Directions:** Drive on U.S. 395 to Taboose Creek Road (11 miles south of Big Pine and 14 miles north of Independence). Turn west (toward the Sierra) on Taboose Creek Road and drive 2.5 miles to the campground (straight in).

**Contact:** Inyo County Parks Department, 760/873-5577, www.inyocountycamping.com.

## 72 GRANDVIEW

### Scenic rating: 6

near Big Pine in Inyo National Forest

**Map 11.2, page 574**

This is a primitive and little-known camp in the White Mountains east of Bishop at 8,600 feet elevation along White Mountain Road. The road borders the Ancient Bristlecone Pine Forest to the east and leads north to jumping-off spots for hikers heading up Mount Barcroft (13,023 feet) or White Mountain (14,246 feet, the third-highest mountain in California). A trail out of the camp leads up to an old mining site. The folks who find this area earn their solitude.

**Campsites, facilities:** There are 26 sites for tents or RVs up to 35 feet (no hookups), but the access road may be challenging for larger RVs. Picnic tables and fire grills are provided. Vault toilets are available. No drinking water is available. Garbage must be packed out. Some facilities are wheelchair-accessible. Leashed pets are permitted.

**Reservations, fees:** Reservations are not accepted. Sites are $5 per night. Open year-round, weather permitting.

**Directions:** From Big Pine on U.S. 395, turn east on Highway 168 and drive 13 miles. Turn north on White Mountain/Bristlecone Forest Road (Forest Road 4S01) and drive 5.5 miles to the campground.

**Contact:** Inyo National Forest, White Mountain Ranger District, 760/873-2500, www.fs.usda.gov/inyo.

## 7.3 CHOINUMNI

**Scenic rating: 7**

on lower Kings River

Map 11.3, page 575

This campground is set in the San Joaquin foothills on the Kings River, a pretty area. Since the campground is operated by Fresno County, it is off the radar of many visitors. Fishing, rafting, canoeing, and hiking are popular. The elevation is roughly 1,000 feet, surrounded by a landscape of oak woodlands and grassland foothills. The park is about 33 miles east of Fresno.

**Campsites, facilities:** There are 75 sites for tents or RVs of any length (no hookups) and one group site for up to 75 people. Some sites are pull-through. Picnic tables and fire rings are provided. Drinking water, flush toilets, and a dump station are available. Canoe rentals are available nearby. There are no facilities within 10 miles. Leashed pets are permitted.

**Reservations, fees:** Reservations are accepted for the group site only. Sites are $18 per night, plus $5 per night for each additional vehicle, and $110 per night for the group site. Open year-round.

**Directions:** From Fresno, drive east on Highway 180 for 17.5 miles to Piedra Road. Turn left on Piedra Road and drive eight miles to Trimmer Springs Road. Turn right on Trimmer Springs Road and drive one mile to Pine Flat Road. Turn right and drive 100 yards to the camp entrance on the right.

**Contact:** Fresno County Parks Department, 559/488-3004, www2.co.fresno.ca.us.

## 7.4 ISLAND PARK

**Scenic rating: 7**

on Pine Flat Lake

Map 11.3, page 575

This is one of two Army Corps of Engineer campgrounds available at Pine Flat Lake, a popular lake in the foothill country east of Fresno. When Pine Flat is full, or close to full, it is very pretty. The lake is 21 miles long with 67 miles of shoreline and 5,900 surface acres. Right—a big lake with unlimited potential. Because the temperatures get warm in spring, then smoking hot in summer, the lake is like Valhalla for boating and water sports. The fishing for white bass is often excellent in late winter and early spring, and after that, conditions are ideal for water sports. The elevation is 1,000 feet.

**Campsites, facilities:** There are 97 sites for tents or RVs of any length (some hookups) and two group sites for tents or RVs up to 45 feet for 80 people each. Lakeside camping may not be available due to lake levels. Picnic tables and fire grills are provided. Restrooms with flush toilets and coin showers, drinking water, pay telephone, boat ramp, fish-cleaning station, and dump station are available. There is a seasonal store at the campground entrance. Boat rentals are available within five miles. Some facilities are wheelchair-accessible. Leashed pets are permitted.

**Reservations, fees:** Reservations are accepted for individual sites and required for the group sites at 877/444-6777 ($10 reservation fee) or www.recreation.gov ($9 reservation fee). Tent sites are $20-30 per night, RV sites are $20-60 per night (includes two vehicles), plus $4 per each additional vehicle, and the group site is $100 per night. Open year-round.

**Directions:** From Fresno, drive east on Highway 180 for 17.5 miles to Trimmer Springs Road. Turn left and drive eight miles to the town of Piedra. Continue on Trimmer Springs Road for one mile to Pine Flat Road. Turn right and drive 0.25 mile to the park entrance (signed "Island Park").

**Contact:** U.S. Army Corps of Engineers, Sacramento District, Pine Flat Field Office, 559/787-2589.

## 75 TRIMMER

**Scenic rating: 7**

on Pine Flat Lake in Kings Canyon

**Map 11.3, page 575**

Trimmer is a small campground on the shore of Pine Flat Lake. The lake spans 20 miles and offers 67 miles of shoreline; recreation opportunities include fishing for trout and bass, boating, and wildlife watching for the occasional bobcat or hawk. The nearby Kings River offers whitewater rafting. When the lake level is high, this camp rates much higher for scenic beauty, but the lake level often falls by midsummer.

**Campsites, facilities:** There are 10 sites for tents or RVs up to 30 feet (no hookups). Picnic tables and fire grills are provided. Drinking water and restrooms with flush toilets and free showers are available. A boat ramp (seasonal)

and dock are adjacent to the campground and a marina is nearby. Some facilities are wheelchair-accessible. Leashed pets are permitted.

**Reservations, fees:** Reservations are accepted at 877/444-6777 ($10 reservation fee) or www.recreation.gov ($9 reservation fee). Sites are $20 per night, plus $4 per each additional vehicle. Open year-round, weather permitting.

**Directions:** From Fresno, drive east on Highway 180/Kings Canyon Highway to the Clovis Avenue exit. Turn right onto North Clovis Avenue and then immediately turn left on East Belmont Avenue. After about 13 miles the road veers left and becomes East Trimmer Springs Road. Continue traveling on this road for 18 miles; the entrance to Trimmer Recreation Area is on the right.

**Contact:** U.S. Army Corps of Engineers, Sacramento District, Pine Flat Field Office, 559/787-2589.

## 76 LAKERIDGE CAMPING AND BOATING RESORT

**Scenic rating: 7**

on Pine Flat Lake

**Map 11.3, page 575**

Pine Flat Lake is a 20-mile-long reservoir with seemingly unlimited recreation potential. It is an excellent lake for all water sports. It is in the foothills east of Fresno at 970 feet elevation, covering 4,912 surface acres with 67 miles of shoreline. The lake's proximity to Fresno has made it a top destination for boating and water sports. Fishing for white bass can be excellent in the spring and early summer. There are also rainbow trout, largemouth bass, smallmouth bass, bluegill, catfish, and black crappie. Note: A downer is that there are only a few sandy beaches, and the lake level can drop to as low as 20 percent full.

**Campsites, facilities:** There are 107 sites with full or partial hookups (50 amps) for tents or RVs up to 40 feet. Picnic tables and barbecue grills are available at some sites. Restrooms with showers, Wi-Fi, coin laundry, dump station, ice, horseshoes, and pay phone are available. A convenience store and boat rentals are nearby. Leashed pets are permitted.

**Reservations, fees:** Reservations are recommended at 877/787-2260. RV sites are $35-40 per night, tent sites are $25-30 per night, plus $5 per night per each additional guest. Weekly and monthly rates are available. Some credit cards are accepted. Open year-round.

**Directions:** From Fresno, drive east on Highway 180 for 17.5 miles to Trimmer Springs Road. Turn left and drive eight miles to the town of Piedra. Continue on Trimmer Springs Road for four miles to Sunnyslope Road. Turn right and drive one mile to the resort on the right.

**Contact:** Lakeridge Camping and Boating Resort, 877/787-2260, www.lakeridgecampground.com; Pine Flat Marina, 559/787-2506, www.pineflatlakemarina.com.

## **77** KIRCH FLAT

### Scenic rating: 8
on the Kings River in Sierra National Forest

**Map 11.3, page 575**                    **BEST (**

Kirch Flat is on the Kings River, about five miles from the head of Pine Flat Lake. This campground is a popular take-out spot for rafters and kayakers running the Middle Kings, putting in at Garnet Dike dispersed camping area and then making the 10-mile, Class III run downstream to Kirch Flat. The camp is in the foothill country at 1,100 feet elevation, where the temperatures are often hot and the water cold.

**Campsites, facilities:** There are 17 sites for tents or RVs up to 30 feet (no hookups) and one group camp for up to 50 people and RVs to 35 feet. Picnic tables and fire grills are provided. Vault toilets are available. No drinking water is available. Some facilities are wheelchair-accessible. Leashed pets are permitted.

**Reservations, fees:** Reservations are not

accepted for individual sites but are required for the group site at 559/855-5355. There is no fee for camping. Reservation applications are open March through July with a lottery to select the winners. Open year-round.

**Directions:** From Fresno, drive east on Highway 180 for 17.5 miles to Trimmer Springs Road. Turn left and drive 28 miles to Trimmer. Continue east on Trimmer Springs Road (along the north shore of Pine Flat Lake) and drive 18 miles to the campground on the right.

**Contact:** Sierra National Forest, High Sierra Ranger District, 559/855-5355, www.fs.usda.gov/sierra.

## **78** BLACK ROCK

### Scenic rating: 7
on Black Rock Reservoir in Sierra National Forest

**Map 11.3, page 575**

Little Black Rock Reservoir is a little-known spot that can provide a quiet respite compared to the other big-time lakes and camps in the region. The camp is near the outlet stream on the west end of the lake, created from a small dam on the North Fork Kings River at 4,200 feet elevation.

**Campsites, facilities:** There are 10 sites for tents or small RVs. Picnic tables and fire grills are provided. Vault toilets are available. There is no drinking water. Garbage must be packed out. Bear boxes are not provided; food and garbage must be stored properly. Leashed pets are permitted.

**Reservations, fees:** Reservations are not accepted. Sites are $14 per night, plus $7 per night per additional RV, $5 per night for additional vehicle, and $2 per pet per night. Open year-round, weather permitting.

**Directions:** From Fresno, drive east on Highway 180 for 17.5 miles to Trimmer Springs Road. Turn left and drive 28 miles to Trimmer. Continue east on Trimmer Springs Road (along the north shore of Pine Flat Lake) and drive

18 miles to Black Road. Turn left and drive 10 miles to the campground.

**Contact:** Sierra National Forest, High Sierra Ranger District, 559/855-5355, www.fs.usda. gov/sierra; PG&E Land Services, 916/386-5164, www.pge.com/recreation.

## 79 CAMP 4 1/2

### Scenic rating: 7
on the Kings River in Sequoia National Forest

Map 11.3, page 575

On my visit to this primitive camp, I found five sites, not "four and a half." This Sequoia National Forest campground is small, primitive, and usually hot. The elevation is 1,000 feet. It is one in a series of camps just east of Pine Flat Lake along the Kings River, primarily used for rafting access. (See the Kirch Flat and Mill Flat listings in this chapter for more information.)

**Campsites, facilities:** A dispersed area can accommodate up to five sites for tents only. There are no other services or facilities. Garbage must be packed out. Leashed pets are permitted.

**Reservations, fees:** Reservations are not accepted. There is no fee for camping. Open year-round.

**Directions:** From Fresno, drive east on Highway 180 for 17.5 miles to Trimmer Springs Road. Turn left and drive 28 miles to Trimmer. Continue east on Trimmer Springs Road (along the north shore of Pine Flat Lake) and drive 18 miles (it becomes Forest Road 11S12) to Forest Road 12S01 (crossing the river). Take Forest Road 12S01 for one mile (along the river) to a dirt road on the right (at the junction of the second bridge). Turn right (still Forest Road 12S01) and drive 0.7 mile to the campground. Not advised for trailers or large RVs.

**Contact:** Sequoia National Forest, Hume Lake Ranger District, 559/338-2251, www.fs.usda. gov/sequoia.

## 80 CAMP 4

### Scenic rating: 7
on the Kings River in Sequoia National Forest

Map 11.3, page 575

This is one in a series of camps set on the Kings River upstream from Pine Flat Lake, a popular access point for rafters and kayakers. The Kings River is well known for providing some of the best rafting and kayaking water in California. The weather gets so hot that many take a dunk in the river on purpose; nonrafters had better bring a cooler stocked with ice and drinks. Camp 4 is a mile from Mill Creek Flat.

**Campsites, facilities:** There are five sites for tents only. Picnic tables and fire grills are provided. Vault toilets are available. No drinking water is available. Garbage must be packed out. Leashed pets are permitted.

**Reservations, fees:** Reservations are not accepted. There is no fee for camping. Open year-round.

**Directions:** From Fresno, drive east on Highway 180 for 17.5 miles to Trimmer Springs Road. Turn left and drive 28 miles to Trimmer. Continue east on Trimmer Springs Road (along the north shore of Pine Flat Lake) and drive 18 miles (it becomes Forest Road 11S12) to Forest Road 12S01 (crossing the river). Take Forest Road 12S01 for one mile (along the river) to a dirt road on the right (at the junction of the second bridge). Turn right (still Forest Road 12S01) and drive 1.5 miles to the campground (on the south side of the river). Not advised for trailers and large RVs.

**Contact:** Sequoia National Forest, Hume Lake Ranger District, 559/338-2251, www.fs.usda. gov/sequoia.

# 81 MILL FLAT

🏃 ⛵ 🐾 ⛺

### Scenic rating: 7

on the Kings River in Sequoia National Forest

**Map 11.3, page 575**

This camp is on the Kings River at the confluence of Mill Creek. It's a small, primitive spot that gets very hot in the summer. The elevation is 1,100 feet. Rafters sometimes use this as an access point for trips down the Kings River. This is best in spring and early summer, when melting snow from the high country fills the river with water.

**Campsites, facilities:** There are five sites for tents only. Picnic tables and fire grills are provided. Vault toilets are available. No drinking water is available. Garbage must be packed out. Leashed pets are permitted.

**Reservations, fees:** Reservations are not accepted. There is no fee for camping. Open year-round.

**Directions:** From Fresno, drive east on Highway 180 for 17.5 miles to Trimmer Springs Road. Turn left and drive 28 miles to Trimmer. Continue east on Trimmer Springs Road (along the north shore of Pine Flat Lake) and drive 18 miles (it becomes Forest Road 11S12) to Forest Road 12S01 (crossing the river). Take Forest Road 12S01 for one mile (along the river) to a dirt road on the right (at the junction of the second bridge). Turn right (still Forest Road 12S01) and drive 2.5 miles to the campground (on the south side of the river). Not advised for trailers and large RVs.

**Contact:** Sequoia National Forest, Hume Lake Ranger District, 559/338-2251, www.fs.usda.gov/sequoia.

# 82 PRINCESS

🐾 🚐 ⛺

### Scenic rating: 7

on Princess Meadow in Sequoia National Forest

**Map 11.4, page 576**

This mountain camp is at 5,900 feet elevation. It is popular because of its proximity to both Hume Lake and the star attractions at Kings Canyon National Park. Hume Lake is just four miles from the camp. The Grant Grove entrance to Kings Canyon National Park is only six miles away to the south, while continuing east on Highway 180 will take you into the heart of Kings Canyon.

**Campsites, facilities:** There are 19 sites for tents only and 69 sites for tents or RVs up to 22 feet (no hookups). Picnic tables and fire grills are provided. Only locally obtained firewood is allowed for use in campfires. Drinking water, vault toilets, an amphitheater, and a dump station are available. A store is four miles away at Hume Lake. Leashed pets are permitted.

**Reservations, fees:** Reservations are accepted at 877/444-6777 ($10 reservation fee) or www.recreation.gov ($9 reservation fee). Sites are $25-54 per night, plus $7 per night for each additional vehicle. A $30 national park entrance fee applies. Prices are higher on holiday weekends. Open May through September, weather permitting.

**Directions:** From Fresno, drive east on Highway 180 for 55 miles to the Big Stump Entrance Station at Sequoia and Kings Canyon National Parks. Continue 1.5 miles to a junction (signed left for Grant Grove). Turn left and drive 1.5 miles to Grant Grove Village, then continue for 4.5 miles to the campground on the right.

**Contact:** Sequoia National Forest, Hume Lake Ranger District, 559/338-2251, www.fs.usda.gov/sequoia; California Land Management, 559/335-2232.

## 83 HUME LAKE

### Scenic rating: 8

in Sequoia National Forest

**Map 11.4, page 576**

For newcomers, Hume Lake is a surprise: a pretty lake, with great summer camps for teenagers. Canoeing and kayaking are excellent, and so is the trout fishing, especially near the dam. Swimming is allowed. A 5-mph speed limit is in effect on this 85-acre lake, and only electric motors are permitted. Another surprise is the adjacent religious camp center. The nearby access to Kings Canyon National Park adds a bonus. The elevation is 5,200 feet.

**Campsites, facilities:** There are 14 sites for tents only and 50 sites for tents or RVs up to 22 feet (no hookups), including a few doubles. Picnic tables and fire grills are provided. Only locally obtained firewood is allowed for use in campfires. Drinking water and flush toilets are available. A store, café, bicycle rentals, Wi-Fi, and boat rentals are nearby. Leashed pets are permitted.

**Reservations, fees:** Reservations are accepted at 877/444-6777 ($10 reservation fee) or www. recreation.gov ($9 reservation fee). Sites are $25-54 per night, plus $7 per night for each additional vehicle. A $30 national park entrance fee applies. Rates are higher on holiday weekends. Open mid-May through September, weather permitting.

**Directions:** From Fresno, drive east on Highway 180 for 55 miles to the Big Stump Entrance Station at Sequoia and Kings Canyon National Parks. Continue 1.5 miles to a junction (signed left for Grant Grove). Turn left and drive six miles to the Hume Lake Road junction. Turn right and drive three miles to Hume Lake and the campground entrance road. Turn right and drive 0.25 mile to the campground on the left.

**Contact:** Sequoia National Forest, Hume Lake Ranger District, 559/338-2251, www.fs.usda. gov/sequoia; California Land Management, 559/335-2232.

## 84 ASPEN HOLLOW GROUP CAMP

### Scenic rating: 6

near Hume Lake in Sequoia National Forest

**Map 11.4, page 576**

This large group camp is at 5,200 feet elevation about a mile south of Hume Lake near a feeder to Tenmile Creek, the inlet stream to Hume Lake. Entrances to Kings Canyon National Park are nearby.

**Campsites, facilities:** This is a group camp for tents or RVs of any length (no hookups) that can accommodate up to 100 people. Picnic tables, food lockers (mandatory), and fire grills are provided. Drinking water is not always available; bring your own. Vault toilets are available. Only locally obtained firewood is allowed for use in campfires. A store and laundry facilities are nearby. Some facilities are wheelchair-accessible. Leashed pets are permitted.

**Reservations, fees:** Reservations are required at 877/444-6777 ($10 reservation fee) or www. recreation.gov ($9 reservation fee). The camp is $350 per night. A $30 national park entrance fee applies. Open mid-May through mid-September, weather permitting.

**Directions:** From Fresno, drive east on Highway 180 for 55 miles to the Big Stump Entrance Station at Sequoia and Kings Canyon National Parks. Continue 1.5 miles to a junction (signed left for Grant Grove). Turn left and drive six miles to the Hume Lake Road junction. Turn right and drive three miles to Hume Lake and the campground entrance road. Turn right and drive around Hume Lake. Continue south one mile (past the lake) to the campground entrance road.

**Contact:** Sequoia National Forest, Hume Lake Ranger District, 559/338-2251, www.fs.usda. gov/sequoia; California Land Management, 559/335-2232.

## 85 LOGGER FLAT GROUP CAMP

🏊 🦌 ♿ 🚐 ⛺

### Scenic rating: 7

on Tenmile Creek in Giant Sequoia National Monument

**Map 11.4, page 576**

This is the group-site alternative to Landslide campground. This camp is near the confluence of Tenmile Creek and Landslide Creek at 5,300 feet elevation, about two miles upstream from Hume Lake. (For more information, see the Landslide listing in this chapter.)

**Campsites, facilities:** This is a group camp-site for tents or RVs of any length (no hookups) that can accommodate up to 50 people. Picnic tables, food lockers, and fire ring are provided. Only locally obtained firewood is allowed for use in campfires. Drinking water and vault toilets are available. A store is nearby. Some facilities are wheelchair-accessible. Leashed pets are permitted.

**Reservations, fees:** Reservations are required at 877/444-6777 ($10 reservation fee) or www.recreation.gov ($9 reservation fee). The camp is $175 per night. A $30 national park entrance fee applies. Open mid-May through mid-September, weather permitting.

**Directions:** From Fresno, drive east on Highway 180 for 55 miles to the Big Stump Entrance Station at Sequoia and Kings Canyon National Parks. Continue 1.5 miles to a junction (signed left for Grant Grove). Turn left and drive six miles to the Hume Lake Road junction. Turn right and drive three miles to Hume Lake and the campground entrance road. Turn right and drive around Hume Lake to Tenmile Road. Continue south three miles to the campground entrance on the right.

**Contact:** Sequoia National Forest, Hume Lake Ranger District, 559/338-2251, www.fs.usda.gov/sequoia.

## 86 LANDSLIDE

🏊 🦌 🚐 ⛺

### Scenic rating: 7

on Landslide Creek in Giant Sequoia National Monument

**Map 11.4, page 576**

If you want quiet, you've got it; few folks know about this camp. If you want a stream nearby, you've got it; Landslide Creek runs right beside the camp. If you want a lake nearby, you've got it; Hume Lake is just to the north. If you want a national park nearby, you've got it; Kings Canyon National Park is nearby. Add it up: You've got it. The elevation is 5,800 feet.

**Campsites, facilities:** There are nine sites for tents only and one site for RVs up to 22 feet (no hookups). Picnic tables and fire grills are provided. Only locally obtained firewood is allowed for use in campfires. Drinking water, bear boxes (mandatory), and vault toilets are available. A store is nearby. Leashed pets are permitted.

**Reservations, fees:** Reservations are not accepted. Sites are $18 per night, doubles sites are $36 per night, plus $5 per night for each additional vehicle. A $30 national park entrance fee applies. Open May through September, weather permitting.

**Directions:** From Fresno, drive east on Highway 180 for 55 miles to the Big Stump Entrance Station at Sequoia and Kings Canyon National Parks. Continue 1.5 miles to a junction (signed left for Grant Grove). Turn right at Generals Highway and drive three miles to Hume Lake Road/Tenmile Road (Forest Road 13S09). Turn left and drive about seven miles (past Tenmile campground) to the campground on the left.

**Contact:** Sequoia National Forest, Hume Lake Ranger District, 559/338-2251, www.fs.usda.gov/sequoia.

## 87 TENMILE

### Scenic rating: 7

on Tenmile Creek in Giant Sequoia National Monument

**Map 11.4, page 576**

This is one of three small, primitive campgrounds along Tenmile Creek south (and upstream) of Hume Lake. RV campers are advised to use the lower campsites because they are larger. This one is about four miles from the lake at 5,800 feet elevation. It provides an alternative to camping in nearby Kings Canyon National Park.

**Campsites, facilities:** There are 13 sites for tents or RVs up to 22 feet (no hookups). Picnic tables and fire grills are provided. Only locally obtained firewood is allowed for use in campfires. Vault toilets are available. No drinking water is available. Some facilities are wheelchair-accessible. Leashed pets are permitted.

**Reservations, fees:** Reservations are not accepted. Sites are $18 per night, double sites are $36 per night, plus $5 per night for each additional vehicle. A $30 national park entrance fee applies. Camping fees are higher on holiday weekends. Open May through mid-September, weather permitting.

**Directions:** From Fresno, drive east on Highway 180 for 55 miles to the Big Stump Entrance Station at Sequoia and Kings Canyon National Parks. Continue 1.5 miles to a junction (signed left for Grant Grove). Turn right at Generals Highway and drive three miles to Hume Lake Road/Tenmile Road (Forest Road 13S09). Turn left and drive about five miles to the campground on the left.

**Contact:** Sequoia National Forest, Hume Lake Ranger District, 559/338-2251, www.fs.usda.gov/sequoia.

## 88 AZALEA

### Scenic rating: 7

in the Grant Grove area of Kings Canyon National Park

**Map 11.4, page 576**

This camp is tucked just inside the western border of Kings Canyon National Park, a mere six miles from the Big Stump entrance. The General Grant Grove of giant sequoias is only a one-mile hike away, and services at Grant Grove Village are right across the highway. The spectacular Kings Canyon, one of the deepest gorges in North America, is farther north on Highway 180. The elevation is 6,600 feet.

**Campsites, facilities:** There are 110 sites for tents or RVs up to 30 feet (no hookups). Picnic tables, food lockers, and fire grills are provided. Drinking water and flush toilets are available. Evening ranger programs are often offered. Horseback-riding facilities are nearby. Supplies and showers are available in Grant Grove Village during the summer. Some facilities are wheelchair-accessible. Leashed pets are permitted, except on trails.

**Reservations, fees:** Reservations are not accepted. Sites are $18 per night. A $30 national park entrance fee applies. Open year-round.

**Directions:** From Fresno, drive east on Highway 180 for 55 miles to the Big Stump Entrance Station at Sequoia and Kings Canyon National Parks. Continue 1.5 miles to a junction (signed left for Grant Grove). Turn left and drive 1.5 miles to Grant Grove Village, then continue for 0.7 mile to the campground entrance on the left.

**Contact:** Sequoia and Kings Canyon National Parks, 559/565-3341, www.nps.gov/seki; Kings Canyon Visitor Center, 559/565-4307; Grant Grove Horse Stables, 559/335-9292.

## 89 CRYSTAL SPRINGS

### Scenic rating: 5

in the Grant Grove area of Kings Canyon
National Park

**Map 11.4, page 576**

Crystal Springs lies across the road from
the Azalea campground in the Grant Grove
area. This small, yet sprawling campground
is shaded by evergreens and caters primarily
to groups, with little privacy between sites.
Directly south is Grant Grove Village and its
visitors center. Across Highway 180 lies the
trailhead for the Grant Grove of giant sequoias.

**Campsites, facilities:** There are 36 sites for
tents or RVs up to 22 feet (no hookups) and
13 group sites for 7-15 people each. Picnic tables, food lockers, and fire grills are provided.
Drinking water and flush toilets are available.
Horseback-riding facilities are nearby. Evening
ranger programs are often offered in the summer. Supplies and showers are available in
Grant Grove Village during the summer season. Some facilities are wheelchair-accessible.
Leashed pets are permitted, except on trails.

**Reservations, fees:** Reservations are not accepted. Sites are $18 per night. Group sites are
$35 per night. A $30 national park entrance fee
applies. Open mid-May through mid-September, weather permitting.

**Directions:** From Fresno, drive east on
Highway 180 for 55 miles to the Big Stump
Entrance Station at Sequoia and Kings Canyon
National Parks. Continue 1.5 miles to a junction (signed left for Grant Grove). Turn left and
drive 1.5 miles to Grant Grove Village, then
continue for 0.7 mile to the campground entrance on the right.

**Contact:** Sequoia and Kings Canyon National
Parks, 559/565-3341; Kings Canyon Visitor
Center, 559/565-4307, www.nps.gov/seki.

## 90 SUNSET

### Scenic rating: 7

in the Grant Grove area of Kings Canyon
National Park

**Map 11.4, page 576**

This is the biggest of the three camps just inside the Kings Canyon National Park boundaries near Grant Grove Village, at 6,600 feet
elevation. The nearby General Grant Grove of
giant sequoias is the main attraction. There are
many short, easy walks among the sequoias,
each breathtakingly beautiful. They include Big
Stump Trail, Sunset Trail, North Grove Loop,
General Grant Tree, Manzanita and Azalea
Loop, and Panoramic Point and Park Ridge
Trail. Seeing the General Grant Tree is a rite of
passage for newcomers; after a half-hour walk
you arrive at a sequoia that is approximately
1,800 years old, 107 feet in circumference, and
267 feet tall.

**Campsites, facilities:** There are 157 sites for
tents or RVs up to 30 feet (no hookups) and
two group sites for 15-30 people each. Picnic
tables, food lockers, and fire grills are provided.
Drinking water and flush toilets are available.
In the summer, evening ranger programs are
often available. Horseback-riding facilities are
nearby. Supplies and showers are available in
Grant Grove Village during the summer. Some
facilities are wheelchair-accessible. Leashed
pets are permitted, except on trails.

**Reservations, fees:** Reservations are accepted
July-September at 877/444-6777 ($10 reserva-
tion fee) or www.recreation.gov ($9 reservation
fee). Reservations for the group sites are accepted late May-early September. Sites are $22
per night. Group sites are $40 per night. A $30
per national park entrance fee applies. Open
late May through mid-September, weather
permitting.

**Directions:** From Fresno, drive east on
Highway 180 for 55 miles to the Big Stump
Entrance Station at Sequoia and Kings Canyon
National Parks. Continue 1.5 miles to a junc-
tion (signed left for Grant Grove). Turn left

(still Highway 180) and drive one mile to the campground entrance (0.5 mile before reaching Grant Grove Village).

**Contact:** Sequoia and Kings Canyon National Parks, 559/565-3341; Kings Canyon Visitor Center, 559/565-4307, www.nps.gov/seki.

## 91 BUCK ROCK

### Scenic rating: 4

near Big Meadows Creek in Giant Sequoia National Monument

**Map 11.4, page 576**

This remote camp provides a little-known option to nearby Sequoia and Kings Canyon National Parks. If the national parks are full and you're stuck, this camp offers an insurance policy. The elevation is 7,500 feet.

**Campsites, facilities:** There are five primitive sites for tents or RVs up to 25 feet (no hookups). Picnic tables and fire grills are provided. Only locally obtained firewood is allowed for use in campfires. Toilets are available, but there is no drinking water. Leashed pets are permitted.

**Reservations, fees:** Reservations are not accepted. There is no fee for camping. A $30 national park entrance fee applies. Open May to early September, weather permitting.

**Directions:** From Fresno, drive east on Highway 180 for 55 miles to the Big Stump Entrance Station at Sequoia and Kings Canyon National Parks. Continue 1.5 miles to a junction (signed left for Grant Grove). Turn right at Generals Highway and drive about five miles to Big Meadows Road/Forest Road 14S11. Turn left on Big Meadows Road and drive five miles to the campground entrance road on the left. Turn left and drive a short distance to the campground.

**Contact:** Sequoia National Forest, Hume Lake Ranger District, 559/338-2251, www.fs.usda.gov/sequoia.

## 92 BIG MEADOWS

### Scenic rating: 7

on Big Meadows Creek in Giant Sequoia National Monument

**Map 11.4, page 576**

This primitive, high-mountain camp (7,600 feet) is beside little Big Meadows Creek. Backpackers can use this as a launching pad, with the nearby trailhead (one mile down the road to the west) leading to the Jennie Lake Wilderness. Kings Canyon National Park, only a 12-mile drive away, is a nearby side trip.

**Campsites, facilities:** There are 45 sites along Big Meadows Creek and Big Meadows Road for tents or RVs up to 22 feet (no hookups). Picnic tables and fire grills are provided. Only locally obtained firewood is allowed for use in campfires. Vault toilets are available. No drinking water is available. Leashed pets are permitted.

**Reservations, fees:** Reservations are not accepted. There is no fee for camping. A $30 national park entrance fee applies. Open May through early October, weather permitting.

**Directions:** From Fresno, drive east on Highway 180 for 55 miles to the Big Stump Entrance Station at Sequoia and Kings Canyon National Parks. Continue 1.5 miles to a junction (signed left for Grant Grove). Turn right at Generals Highway and drive about five miles to Big Meadows Road/Forest Road 14S11. Turn left on Big Meadows Road and drive five miles to the camp.

**Contact:** Sequoia National Forest, Hume Lake Ranger District, 559/338-2251, www.fs.usda.gov/sequoia.

## 93 SENTINEL

### Scenic rating: 8

in the Cedar Grove area of Kings Canyon National Park

**Map 11.4, page 576**

The Kings Canyon Scenic Byway provides

stunning rim-of-the-world views of Kings Canyon before dropping right along the Kings River to dead-end in one of the deepest gorges in North America. Sentinel is one of four campgrounds in Cedar Grove; it sits adjacent to the Cedar Grove Visitor center and is only a 0.25-mile walk to Cedar Grove Village. It tends to fill quickly in summer. The elevation is 4,600 feet.

Hiking and trout fishing are excellent. One of the best hikes, but also the most demanding, is the 13-mile round-trip to Lookout Peak, out of the Cedar Grove Village area. It involves a 4,000-foot climb to 8,531 feet elevation, and with it a breathtaking view of Sierra ridges, Cedar Grove far below, and Kings Canyon.

**Campsites, facilities:** There are 82 sites for tents or RVs up to 30 feet (no hookups). Picnic tables, food lockers, and fire grills are provided. Restrooms with flush toilets and drinking water are available. A store, coin showers, coin laundry, riding stables, and snack bar are nearby. Some facilities are wheelchair-accessible. Leashed pets are permitted.

**Reservations, fees:** Reservations are not accepted. Sites are $18 per night. A $30 national park entrance fee applies. Open early July through mid-November, weather permitting.

**Directions:** From Fresno, drive east on Highway 180 for 55 miles to the Big Stump Entrance Station at Sequoia and Kings Canyon National Parks. Continue 1.5 miles to a junction (signed left for Grant Grove). Turn left and drive 32 miles to the campground entrance on the left (near Cedar Grove Village).

**Contact:** Sequoia and Kings Canyon National Parks, 559/565-3341; Cedar Grove Visitor Center, 559/565-3793, www.nps.gov/seki.

## 94 SHEEP CREEK

### Scenic rating: 8

in the Cedar Grove area of Kings Canyon National Park

**Map 11.4, page 576**

Sheep Creek is the largest of four campgrounds in the Cedar Grove area, situated between Highway 180 and the creek after which the campground is named. It's a pretty spot and just a short walk from Cedar Grove Village and it fills quickly on summer weekends. The elevation is 4,600 feet.

**Campsites, facilities:** There are 111 sites for tents or RVs up to 30 feet (no hookups). Picnic tables and fire grills are provided. Restrooms with flush toilets and drinking water are available. A store, coin laundry, snack bar, and coin showers are available nearby. Leashed pets are permitted.

**Reservations, fees:** Reservations are not accepted. Sites are $18 per night. A $30 national park entrance fee applies. Open late May through mid-October.

**Directions:** From Fresno, drive east on Highway 180 for 55 miles to the Big Stump Entrance Station at Sequoia and Kings Canyon National Parks. Continue 1.5 miles to a junction (signed left for Grant Grove). Turn left and drive 31.5 miles to the campground entrance on the left (near Cedar Grove Village).

**Contact:** Sequoia and Kings Canyon National Parks, 559/565-3341; Cedar Grove Visitor Center, 559/565-3793, www.nps.gov/seki.

## 95 CANYON VIEW GROUP CAMP

### Scenic rating: 8

in the Cedar Grove area of Kings Canyon National Park

**Map 11.4, page 576**    **BEST (**

If it weren't for this group camp in the Cedar Grove Village area, large gatherings wishing to camp together in Kings Canyon National Park would be out of luck. The access road leads to dramatic views of the deep Kings River Canyon, one of the deepest gorges in North America. The camp elevation is 4,600 feet.

**Campsites, facilities:** The 23 tent-only sites accommodate up to six people per site. The 12 midsized group sites accommodate 7-15 people, and the four large group sites accommodate 20-40 people. Picnic tables, food lockers, and fire grills are provided. Drinking water and flush toilets are available. Coin showers, store, snack bar, and coin laundry are nearby. Leashed pets are permitted.

**Reservations, fees:** Reservations are not accepted for individual or midsized group sites, but they are required for the large group sites at 877/444-6777 ($10 reservation fee) or www. recreation.gov ($9 reservation fee). Sites are $18 per night, the group sites are $35-40 per night. A $30 national park entrance fee applies. Open late May through September, weather permitting.

**Directions:** From Fresno, drive east on Highway 180 for 55 miles to the Big Stump Entrance Station at Sequoia and Kings Canyon National Parks. Continue 1.5 miles to a junction (signed left for Grant Grove). Turn left and drive 32.5 miles to the campground entrance (0.5 mile past the ranger station, near Cedar Grove Village).

**Contact:** Sequoia and Kings Canyon National Parks, 559/565-3341; Cedar Grove Visitor Center, 559/565-3793, www.nps.gov/seki.

## 96 MORAINE

### Scenic rating: 8

in the Cedar Grove area of Kings Canyon National Park

**Map 11.4, page 576**

This is one in a series of camps in the Cedar Grove Village area of Kings Canyon National Park. This camp is used only as an overflow area. Hikers should drive past the Cedar Grove Ranger Station to the end of the road at Copper Creek, a prime jumping-off point for a spectacular hike. The elevation is 4,600 feet.

**Campsites, facilities:** There are 120 sites for tents or RVs up to 30 feet (no hookups). Picnic tables and fire grills are provided. Drinking water and flush toilets are available. Coin

showers, a store, snack bar, and coin laundry are nearby. Leashed pets are permitted.

**Reservations, fees:** Reservations are not accepted. Sites are $18 per night. A $30 national park entrance fee applies. Open late May through early September, weather permitting.

**Directions:** From Fresno, drive east on Highway 180 for 55 miles to the Big Stump Entrance Station at Sequoia and Kings Canyon National Parks. Continue 1.5 miles to a junction (signed left for Grant Grove). Turn left and drive 33 miles to the campground entrance (one mile past the ranger station, near Cedar Village).

**Contact:** Sequoia and Kings Canyon National Parks, 559/565-3341; Cedar Grove Visitor Center, 559/565-3793, www.nps.gov/seki.

## 97 ESHOM

### Scenic rating: 7

on Eshom Creek in Giant Sequoia National Monument

**Map 11.4, page 576**

The campground at Eshom Creek is just two miles outside the boundaries of Sequoia National Park. It is well hidden and a considerable distance from the crowds and sights in the park interior. It is set along Eshom Creek at an elevation of 4,800 feet. Many campers at Eshom Creek hike straight into the national park, with a trailhead at Redwood Saddle (just inside the park boundary) providing a route to see the Redwood Mountain Grove, Fallen Goliath, Hart Tree, and Hart Meadow in a sensational loop hike.

**Campsites, facilities:** There are 24 sites for tents or RVs up to 22 feet (no hookups) and five group sites for up to 12 people each. Picnic tables and fire grills are provided. Only locally obtained firewood is allowed for use in campfires. Drinking water and vault toilets are available. Leashed pets are permitted.

**Reservations, fees:** Reservations are accepted at 877/444-6777 ($10 reservation fee) or www.

recreation.gov ($9 reservation fee). Sites are $23 per night, plus $7 per night for each additional vehicle, and it's $50 per night for group site. Camping fees are higher on holiday weekends. Open May through early October, weather permitting.

**Directions:** Drive on Highway 99 to Visalia and the exit for Highway 198 east. Take that exit and drive east on Highway 198 for 11 miles to Highway 245. Turn left (north) on Highway 245 and drive 18 miles to Badger and County Road 465. Turn right and drive eight miles to the campground.

**Contact:** Sequoia National Forest, Hume Lake Ranger District, 559/338-2251, www.fs.usda. gov/sequoia; California Land Management, 559/335-2232.

## 98 FIR GROUP CAMPGROUND
🏃 🛶 🐕 🚐 ⛺

### Scenic rating: 6
near Stony Creek in Giant Sequoia National Monument

**Map 11.4, page 576**

This is one of two large group camps in the Stony Creek area.

**Campsites, facilities:** This group camp for tents or RVs up to 30 feet (no hookups) can accommodate up to 100 people. Picnic tables, bear boxes (mandatory), and fire grills are provided. Only locally obtained firewood is allowed for use in campfires. Drinking water and vault toilets are available. A store and coin laundry are nearby. Leashed pets are permitted.

**Reservations, fees:** Reservations are required at 877/444-6777 ($10 reservation fee) or www. recreation.gov ($9 reservation fee). The camp is $350 per night. A $30 national park entrance fee applies. Fees are higher on holiday weekends. Open mid-May through mid-September, weather permitting.

**Directions:** From Fresno, drive east on Highway 180 for 55 miles to the Big Stump Entrance Station at Sequoia and Kings Canyon National Parks. Continue 1.5 miles to a junction (signed left for Grant Grove). Turn right at Generals Highway and drive about 14 miles to the campground entrance on the left.

**Contact:** Sequoia National Forest, Hume Lake Ranger District, 559/338-2251, www.fs.usda. gov/sequoia.

## 99 STONY CREEK
🏃 🛶 🐕 🚐 ⛺

### Scenic rating: 6
in Giant Sequoia National Monument

**Map 11.4, page 576**

Stony Creek Camp provides a good option if the national park camps are filled. It is creekside at 6,400 feet elevation. Sequoia and Kings Canyon National Parks are nearby.

**Campsites, facilities:** There are 26 sites for tents or RVs up to 22 feet (no hookups), 19 sites for tents only, and two walk-in tent sites. Picnic tables and fire grills are provided. Only locally obtained firewood is allowed for use in campfires. Drinking water, bear boxes (mandatory use), flush toilets, and an amphitheater are available. A store and coin laundry are nearby. Leashed pets are permitted.

**Reservations, fees:** Reservations are accepted at 877/444-6777 ($10 reservation fee) or www. recreation.gov ($9 reservation fee). Sites are $25-54 per night, plus $5 per night for each additional vehicle. A $30 national park entrance fee applies. Fees are higher on holiday weekends. Open May through early September, weather permitting.

**Directions:** From Fresno, drive east on Highway 180 for 55 miles to the Big Stump Entrance Station at Sequoia and Kings Canyon National Parks. Continue 1.5 miles to a junction (signed left for Grant Grove). Turn right at Generals Highway and drive about 13 miles to the campground entrance on the right.

**Contact:** Sequoia National Forest, Hume Lake Ranger District, 559/338-2251, www.fs.usda. gov/sequoia.

## 100 COVE GROUP CAMP

### Scenic rating: 6

near Stony Creek in Giant Sequoia National Monument

**Map 11.4, page 576**

This large group camp is beside Stony Creek. The elevation is 6,500 feet.

**Campsites, facilities:** There is one group site for tents or RVs up to 25 feet (no hookups) that accommodates up to 50 people. Picnic tables, bear boxes (mandatory), and fire grills are provided. Only locally obtained firewood is allowed for use in campfires. Drinking water, vault toilets, a store, coin showers, a dump station, and coin laundry are eight miles away. Some facilities are wheelchair-accessible. Leashed pets are permitted.

**Reservations, fees:** Reservations are required at 877/444-6777 ($10 reservation fee) or www. recreation.gov ($9 reservation fee). The camp is $175 per night. A $30 national park entrance fee applies. Fees are higher on holiday weekends. Open mid-May through mid-September, weather permitting.

**Directions:** From Fresno, drive east on Highway 180 for 55 miles to the Big Stump Entrance Station at Sequoia and Kings Canyon National Parks. Continue 1.5 miles to a junction (signed left for Grant Grove). Turn right at Generals Highway and drive about 14 miles to the campground entrance on the left (just past Fir Group Campground).

**Contact:** Sequoia National Forest, Hume Lake Ranger District, 559/338-2251, www.fs.usda. gov/sequoia.

## 101 DORST CREEK

### Scenic rating: 7

on Dorst Creek in Sequoia National Park

**Map 11.4, page 576**     **BEST (**

This is one in a series of popular camps in Sequoia National Park and is a favorite with families. The campground is huge, with spacious sites beneath a forest canopy. There is plenty of room to run around and youngsters are apt to make friends with kids from other sites. An easy hike to the Muir Grove of giant sequoias is nearby. The elevation is 6,700 feet.

Bear visits are common. Campers must keep food in a bear-proof food locker or they will get a ticket. Why? Things that go bump in the night swing through Dorst Creek camp all summer long. That's right; Mr. Bear, along with many friends, makes food raids like a UPS driver on a pickup route. That's why keeping your food in a bear-proof locker is not only a must, it's the law.

**Campsites, facilities:** There are 218 sites for tents or RVs up to 30 feet (no hookups) and four group sites for 25-50 people each. Picnic tables and fire grills are provided. Drinking water, flush toilets, and a dump station are available. A store, coin showers, and coin laundry are eight miles away. Some facilities are wheelchair-accessible. Leashed pets are permitted.

**Reservations, fees:** Reservations are accepted at 877/444-6777 ($10 reservation fee) or www. recreation.gov ($9 reservation fee). Check current status; due to water shortages, some sites may be unavailable. Sites are $22 per night (includes reservation fee), group sites are $40-60 per night. A $30 national park entrance fee applies. Open Memorial Day through Labor Day, weather permitting.

**Directions:** From Fresno, drive east on Highway 180 for 55 miles to the Big Stump Entrance Station at Sequoia and Kings Canyon National Parks. Continue 1.5 miles to a junction (signed left for Grant Grove). Turn right at Generals Highway and drive about 25.5 miles to the campground entrance on the right.

**Contact:** Sequoia and Kings Canyon National Parks, 559/565-3341; Lodgepole Visitor Center, 559/565-4436, www.nps.gov/seki.

## 102 LODGEPOLE

🚶 🚣 📷 🐕 🚐 ⛺

### Scenic rating: 8

on the Marble Fork of the Kaweah River in Sequoia National Park

**Map 11.4, page 576**

This giant, pretty camp on the Marble Fork of the Kaweah River is typically crowded thanks to its convenient location near the amenities of Lodgepole Village. The free Sequoia Shuttle to the Giant Forest stops in the campground, saving you the drive, and an excellent trailhead leads into the backcountry of Sequoia National Park. The elevation is 6,700 feet.

**Campsites, facilities:** There are 214 sites for tents or RVs up to 42 feet (no hookups). In fall and spring, 16 walk-in tent sites are available. Picnic tables and fire grills are provided. Restrooms with flush toilets, drinking water, dump station, gift shop, and evening ranger programs are available. A store, deli, coin showers, and coin laundry are nearby. Leashed pets are permitted.

**Reservations, fees:** Reservations are accepted at 877/444-6777 (March through October, $10 reservation fee), 888/448-1474 (November-February), or www.recreation.gov ($9 reservation fee). Sites are $22 per night (includes reservation fee). A $30 national park entrance fee applies. Open mid-April through late October, with limited winter services, weather permitting.

**Directions:** From Fresno, drive east on Highway 180 for 55 miles to the Big Stump Entrance Station at Sequoia and Kings Canyon National Parks. Continue 1.5 miles to a junction (signed left for Grant Grove). Turn right at Generals Highway and drive about 25 miles to Lodgepole Village and the turnoff for Lodgepole Campground. Turn left and drive 0.25 mile (past Lodgepole Village) to the campground.

**Contact:** Sequoia and Kings Canyon National Parks, 559/565-3341, www.nps.gov/seki; Lodgepole Visitor Center, 559/565-4436; Mineral King Ranger Station, 559/565-3135.

## 103 POTWISHA

🚶 🚣 📷 🐕 ♿ 🚐 ⛺

### Scenic rating: 7

in the Foothills Area of Sequoia National Park

**Map 11.4, page 576**

This pretty spot on the Marble Fork of the Kaweah River is one of Sequoia National Park's smaller drive-to campgrounds. By looking at maps, newcomers may think it is a very short drive farther into the park to see the General Sherman Tree, Giant Forest, and the famous trailhead for the walk up Moro Rock. Nope. It's a slow, twisty drive, but with many pullouts for great views. A few miles east of the camp, visitors can find Buckeye Flat and a trail along Paradise Creek.

**Campsites, facilities:** There are 42 sites for tents or RVs up to 40 feet (no hookups). Picnic tables, food lockers, and fire grills are provided. Drinking water, flush toilets, dump station, and evening ranger programs are available. Some facilities are wheelchair-accessible. Leashed pets are permitted.

**Reservations, fees:** Reservations are accepted at 877/444-6777 (March through October, $10 reservation fee), 888/448-1474 (November through February), or www.recreation.gov ($9 reservation fee). Sites are $22 per night. A $30 national park entrance fee applies. Open year-round.

**Directions:** From Visalia, drive east on Highway 198 for 36 miles to the Ash Mountain entrance station to Sequoia and Kings Canyon National Parks. Continue into the park (the road becomes Generals Highway) and drive four miles to the campground on the left. Vehicles of 22 feet or longer are not advised on Generals Highway from Potwisha to Giant Forest Village and are advised to use Highway 180 through the Big Stump entrance station.

**Contact:** Sequoia and Kings Canyon National Parks, 559/565-3341; Lodgepole Visitor Center, 559/565-4436, www.nps.gov/seki.

# 104 BUCKEYE FLAT

**Scenic rating: 8**

in the Foothills Area of Sequoia National Park

**Map 11.4, page 576**

In any big, popular national park such as Sequoia, the smaller the campground, the better. Well, Buckeye Flat is one of the smaller ones, set on the Middle Fork of the Kaweah River with a trail just south of camp that runs beside pretty Paradise Creek.

**Campsites, facilities:** There are 28 tent sites. Picnic tables, food lockers, and fire grills are provided. Drinking water and flush toilets are available. Some facilities are wheelchair-accessible. Leashed pets are permitted.

**Reservations, fees:** Reservations are accepted at 877/444-6777 (March through October, $10 reservation fee), 888/448-1474 (November through February), or www.recreation.gov ($9 reservation fee). Sites are $22 per night. A $30 national park entrance fee applies. Open mid-April through late September, weather permitting.

**Directions:** From Visalia, drive east on Highway 198 for 36 miles to the Ash Mountain entrance station to Sequoia and Kings Canyon National Parks. Continue into the park (the road becomes Generals Highway) and drive 6.2 miles to the turnoff (across from Hospital Rock) for Buckeye Flat Campground. Turn right and drive 0.6 mile to the campground. Vehicles of 22 feet or longer are not advised on Generals Highway from Potwisha to Giant Forest Village and are advised to use Highway 180 through the Big Stump entrance station.

**Contact:** Sequoia and Kings Canyon National Parks, 559/565-3341; Lodgepole Visitor Center, 559/565-4436, www.nps.gov/seki.

# 105 HORSE CREEK

**Scenic rating: 6**

on Lake Kaweah

**Map 11.4, page 576**

Lake Kaweah is a big lake, covering nearly 2,000 acres with 22 miles of shoreline. This camp is on the southern shore of the lake. In the spring when the lake is full and the surrounding hills are green, you may even think you have found Valhalla. With such hot weather in the San Joaquin Valley, it's a boater's heaven, ideal for water-skiers. In spring, when the water is too cool for water sports, anglers can have the lake to themselves for good bass fishing. Other species include trout, catfish, and crappie. By early summer, it's crowded with personal watercraft and ski boats. The lake level fluctuates and flooding is a potential problem in some years. Another problem is that the water level drops a great deal during late summer, as thirsty farms suck up every drop they can get, killing prospects of developing beaches for swimming and wading. The elevation is 300 feet.

**Campsites, facilities:** There are 76 sites for tents or RVs up to 30 feet (no hookups), including four equestrian sites with horse corrals. Picnic tables and fire grills are provided. Restrooms with flush toilets and showers, drinking water, playground, and a dump station are available. Two paved boat ramps are available at Kaweah Recreation Area and Lemon Hill Recreation Area. A store, coin laundry, boat and water-ski rentals, ice, snack bar, restaurant, gas station, and propane gas are nearby. Some facilities are wheelchair-accessible. Leashed pets are permitted.

**Reservations, fees:** Reservations are accepted at 877/444-6777 ($10 reservation fee) or www.recreation.gov ($9 reservation fee). Sites are $20-25 per night; equestrian sites are $20-40 per night. Some credit cards are accepted. Open year-round.

**Directions:** From Visalia, drive east on Highway 198 for 25 miles to Lake Kaweah's south shore and the camp on the left.

**Contact:** U.S. Army Corps of Engineers, Lake Kaweah, 559/597-2301; Kaweah Heritage Visitors Center, 559/597-2005.

## 106 ATWELL MILL

🚶 🐕 ♿ ⛺

### Scenic rating: 7

in the Mineral King area of Sequoia National Park

**Map 11.4, page 576**

This small, pretty camp in Sequoia National Park is on Atwell Creek near the East Fork of the Kaweah River, at an elevation of 6,650 feet. While the road in is paved, it is slow and twisty, with many blind turns. The terrain in this canyon is open and dry, overlooking the East Fork Kaweah River well below. A trail at camp is routed south for a mile down to the Kaweah River, then climbs out of the canyon and along Deer Creek for another two miles through the East Fork Grove, an outstanding day hike.

**Campsites, facilities:** There are 21 tent sites; no RVs or trailers are permitted. Picnic tables, food lockers, and fire grills are provided. Drinking water (until mid-October) and pit toilets are available. A small store is nearby. Some facilities are wheelchair-accessible. Leashed pets are permitted.

**Reservations, fees:** Reservations are not accepted. Sites are $12 per night. A $30 national park entrance fee applies. Open late May through October, weather permitting; mid-late October only dry camping is allowed.

**Directions:** From Visalia, drive east on Highway 198 for 36 miles to the town of Three Rivers. Continue east for three miles to Mineral King Road. Turn right on Mineral King Road and drive 19 miles (slow, steep, narrow, and twisty, with blind curves) to the campground. RVs and trailers are not recommended.

**Contact:** Sequoia and Kings Canyon National Parks, 559/565-3341; Lodgepole Visitor Center, 559/565-4436, www.nps.gov/seki.

## 107 COLD SPRINGS

🚶 🏊 🐕 ⛺

### Scenic rating: 9

in the Mineral King area of Sequoia National Park

**Map 11.4, page 576**

This high-country camp at Sequoia National Park is at 7,500 feet elevation on the East Fork of the Kaweah River. The trailhead just west of the camp promises a stellar hike south along Mosquito Creek, then climbing over the course of about three miles to the pretty Mosquito Lakes, four small, beautiful lakes on the north flank of Hengst Peak (11,127 feet). At road's end, there are two wilderness trailheads for sensational hikes, including one out to the Great Western Divide. The Mineral King area is marmot central; those little guys are everywhere.

**Campsites, facilities:** There are 40 tent sites. Picnic tables, food lockers, and fire grills are provided. Drinking water (until mid-October) and pit toilets are available. A store is nearby. Leashed pets are permitted.

**Reservations, fees:** Reservations are not accepted. Sites are $12 per night. A $30 national park entrance fee applies. Open May through October.

**Directions:** From Visalia, drive east on Highway 198 for 36 miles to the town of Three Rivers. Continue east for three miles to Mineral King Road. Turn right on Mineral King Road and drive 23 miles (slow, steep, narrow, and twisty, with blind curves) to the campground. RVs and trailers are not recommended.

**Contact:** Sequoia and Kings Canyon National Parks, 559/565-3341; Lodgepole Visitor Center, 559/565-4436, www.nps.gov/seki.

## 108 SOUTH FORK

**Scenic rating: 7**

in the Foothills area of Sequoia National Park

Map 11.4, page 576

The smallest developed camp in Sequoia National Park might be just what you're looking for. It is at 3,650 feet elevation on the South Fork of the Kaweah River, just inside the southwestern border of Sequoia and Kings Canyon National Parks. While it is technically in the park, it is nothing like at the Giant Forest. Instead, the road in is twisty and slow, the landscape open and hot. A trail heads east from the camp and traverses Dennison Ridge, eventually leading to Hockett Lakes, a long, demanding overnight trip. This is black-bear habitat, so proper food storage is required.

**Campsites, facilities:** There are 10 sites for tents only. Picnic tables, food lockers, and fire grills are provided. Check for current fire restrictions. Pit toilets are available. No drinking water is available. Leashed pets are permitted, except on trails.

**Reservations, fees:** Reservations are not accepted. Sites are $12 per night from May through October; there is no fee in other months. The national park entrance fee is $30 per vehicle. Open year-round.

**Directions:** From Visalia, drive east on Highway 198 for 35 miles to South Fork Road (one mile before reaching the town of Three Rivers). Turn right on South Fork Road and drive 13 miles to the campground (the road is dirt for the last four miles).

**Contact:** Sequoia and Kings Canyon National Parks, 559/565-3341; Lodgepole Visitor Center, 559/565-4436, www.nps.gov/seki.

## 109 BALCH PARK

**Scenic rating: 6**

near Mountain Home Demonstration State Forest

Map 11.4, page 576

Balch Park is surrounded by Mountain Home Demonstration State Forest and Giant Sequoia National Monument. A nearby grove of giant sequoias is a feature attraction. The elevation is 6,500 feet. Two stocked fishing ponds are also available.

**Campsites, facilities:** There are 71 sites for tents or RVs up to 40 feet (no hookups); some sites are pull-through. Picnic tables and fire grills are provided. Drinking water and flush toilets are available. Leashed pets are permitted.

**Reservations, fees:** Reservations are not accepted. Sites are $16 per night, plus $5 per night for each additional vehicle and $3 per pet per night. Open May through late October.

**Directions:** From Porterville, drive east on Highway 190 for 19 miles (a mile past the town of Springville) to Balch Park Road. Turn left (north) at Balch Park Road and drive three miles to Bear Creek Road. Turn east (right) and drive 15 miles (extremely slow and curvy) to the campground (RVs not recommended).

Alternative route for RV drivers: After turning north onto Balch Park Road, drive 40 miles (long and curvy) to the park.

**Contact:** Balch Park, Tulare County, 559/539-3896, www.tularecountytreasures.org.

## 110 HIDDEN FALLS WALK-IN

**Scenic rating: 7**

on the Tule River in Mountain Home State Forest

Map 11.4, page 576

This small, quiet camp at 5,900 feet elevation along the Tule River near Hidden Falls is one of the prettier camps in Mountain Home State

Forest. It is remote and overlooked by all but a handful of insiders who know its qualities.

**Campsites, facilities:** There are eight walk-in sites for tents only. Picnic tables, food lockers, and fire grills are provided. Drinking water and pit toilets are available. Leashed pets are permitted.

**Reservations, fees:** Reservations are not accepted. Sites are $15 per night, plus $5 per night for additional vehicle. No trailers are permitted. Open mid-May through early October, weather permitting.

**Directions:** From Porterville, drive east on Highway 190 for 19 miles (a mile past the town of Springville) to Balch Park Road. Turn left (north) at Balch Park Road and drive about 23 miles to the Mountain Home State Forest sign. Continue on Balch Park Road (the road is long and twisty) and follow the signs to the State Forest Headquarters (where free forest maps are available). From this point, the campgrounds are well signed.

**Contact:** Mountain Home State Forest, 559/539-2321 (summer) or 559/539-2855 (winter), www.tularecountytreasures.org.

## 111 MOSES GULCH

### Scenic rating: 7

on the Tule River in Mountain Home State Forest

**Map 11.4, page 576**

Obscure Moses Gulch sits on the Tule River in a canyon below Moses Mountain (9,331 feet) to the nearby north. A trailhead at the eastern end of the state forest provides access both north and south along the North Fork of the Middle Fork Tule River for a scenic hike. The elevation is 5,400 feet. Mountain Home State Forest is surrounded by Sequoia National Forest.

**Campsites, facilities:** There are 10 sites for tents only. Picnic tables, food lockers, and fire grills are provided. Drinking water and vault toilets are available. Leashed pets are permitted.

**Reservations, fees:** Reservations are not

accepted. Sites are $15 per night, plus $5 per night for additional vehicle. No trailers are permitted. Open mid-May through October, weather permitting.

**Directions:** From Porterville, drive east on Highway 190 for 19 miles (a mile past the town of Springville) to Balch Park Road. Turn left (north) at Balch Park Road and drive about 23 miles to the Mountain Home State Forest sign. Continue on Balch Park Road (the road is long and twisty) and follow the signs to the State Forest Headquarters (where free forest maps are available). The campgrounds are well signed from this point.

**Contact:** Mountain Home State Forest, 559/539-2321 (summer) or 559/539-2855 (winter), www.tularecountytreasures.org.

## 112 FRAZIER MILL

### Scenic rating: 8

in Mountain Home State Forest

**Map 11.4, page 576**

Abundant old-growth sequoias are the prime attraction at this remote camp. The Wishon Fork of the Tule River is the largest of the several streams passing through this forest.

**Campsites, facilities:** There are 46 sites for tents, with a few of these sites also for RVs up to 35 feet (no hookups). Picnic tables and fire grills are provided. Drinking water, food lockers, and vault toilets are available. Some facilities are wheelchair-accessible. Leashed pets are permitted.

**Reservations, fees:** Reservations are not accepted, except for the site that is wheelchair-accessible. Sites are $15 per night, plus $5 per night for additional vehicle. Open mid-May through early October, weather permitting.

**Directions:** From Porterville, drive east on Highway 190 for 19 miles (a mile past the town of Springville) to Balch Park Road. Turn left (north) at Balch Park Road and drive about 23 miles to the Mountain Home State Forest sign. Continue on Balch Park Road (the road is long and twisty) and follow the signs to the State Forest Headquarters (where free forest maps are available). The campgrounds are well signed from this point.

**Contact:** Mountain Home State Forest, 559/539-2321 (summer) or 559/539-2855 (winter), www.tularecountytreasures.org.

## 113 SHAKE CAMP
🚶‍♂️🐕♿🚐⛺️

### Scenic rating: 6
in Mountain Home State Forest

**Map 11.4, page 576**

This is a little-known spot for horseback riding. Horses can be rented for the day, hour, or night. The camp is at 6,500 feet elevation and there's a trailhead for trips into the adjoining Sequoia National Forest and beyond to the east into the Golden Trout Wilderness. Hikers should note that the Balch Park Pack Station, a commercial outfitter, is nearby, so you can expect horse traffic on the trail.

**Campsites, facilities:** There are 11 sites for tents or RVs up to 20 feet (no hookups). Picnic tables and fire grills are provided. Drinking water, food lockers, and vault toilets are available. A public pack station with corrals is nearby. Some facilities are wheelchair-accessible. Leashed pets are permitted.

**Reservations, fees:** Reservations are not accepted. Sites are $15 per night, plus $5 per night for additional vehicle. Open mid-May through early October, weather permitting.

**Directions:** From Porterville, drive east on Highway 190 for 19 miles (a mile past the town of Springville) to Balch Park Road. Turn left (north) at Balch Park Road and drive about 23 miles to the Mountain Home State Forest sign. Continue on Balch Park Road (the road is long and twisty) and follow the signs to the State Forest Headquarters (where free forest maps are available). The campgrounds are well signed from this point.

**Contact:** Mountain Home State Forest, 559/539-2321 (summer) or 559/539-2855 (winter), www.tularecountytreasures.org; Balch Park Pack Station, 559/539-2227.

## 114 HEDRICK POND
🚶‍♂️🛶🐕♿🚐⛺️

### Scenic rating: 6
in Mountain Home State Forest

**Map 11.4, page 576**

Mountain Home State Forest is highlighted by giant sequoias, and Hedrick Pond provides a fishing opportunity, as it's stocked occasionally in summer with rainbow trout. This camp is at 6,200 feet elevation, one of five campgrounds in the immediate region. (See the Methuselah Group Camp listing in this chapter for recreation options.)

**Campsites, facilities:** There are 14 sites for tents or RVs up to 20 feet (no hookups). Picnic tables, food lockers, and fire grills are provided. Drinking water and vault toilets are available. Some facilities are wheelchair-accessible. Leashed pets are permitted.

**Reservations, fees:** Reservations are not accepted. Sites are $15 per night, plus $5 per night for additional vehicle. Open mid-May through October, weather permitting.

**Directions:** From Porterville, drive east on Highway 190 for 19 miles (a mile past the town of Springville) to Balch Park Road. Turn left (north) at Balch Park Road and drive about 23 miles to the Mountain Home State Forest sign. Continue on Balch Park Road (the road is long and twisty) and follow the signs to the State Forest Headquarters (where free forest maps are available). The campgrounds are well signed from this point.

**Contact:** Mountain Home State Forest, 559/539-2321 (summer) or 559/539-2855 (winter), www.tularecountytreasures.org.

## 115 METHUSELAH GROUP CAMP

### Scenic rating: 6

in Mountain Home State Forest

**Map 11.4, page 576**

This is a primitive group camp for tents or a few self-contained RVs. Mountain Home State Forest is known for its remoteness and old-growth giant sequoias. Methuselah, a well-known giant sequoia, is 24 feet in diameter and 197 feet tall. Trails provide access to small streams and horseback trips into the surrounding Sequoia National Forest. The elevation is 5,900 feet.

**Campsites, facilities:** There is one group site for tents or 1-2 RVs up to 20 feet (no hookups) that can accommodate 20-80 people. Fire grills and picnic tables are provided. Vault toilets are available. Garbage collection and food lockers are available, but there is no drinking water. Leashed pets are permitted.

**Reservations, fees:** Reservations are required at 559/539-2855. The fee is $50 per night. Open mid-May through early October, weather permitting.

**Directions:** From Porterville, drive east on Highway 190 for 19 miles (a mile past the town of Springville) to Balch Park Road. Turn left (north) at Balch Park Road and drive about 23 miles to the Mountain Home State Forest sign. Continue on Balch Park Road (the road is long and twisty) and follow the signs to the State Forest Headquarters (where free forest maps are available). The campgrounds are well signed from this point.

**Contact:** Mountain Home State Forest, 559/539-2321 (summer) or 559/539-2855 (winter), www.tularecountytreasures.org.

## 116 WISHON

### Scenic rating: 8

on the Tule River in Giant Sequoia National Monument

**Map 11.4, page 576**

Wishon Camp is set at 3,900 feet elevation on the Middle Fork of the North Fork Tule River, just west of the Doyle Springs Summer Home Tract. Just down the road to the east, on the left side, is a parking area for a trailhead. The hike makes its way one mile to the Tule River and then runs along the stream for about five miles to Mountain Home State Forest.

**Campsites, facilities:** There are 31 single sites and four double sites for tents or RVs up to 24 feet (no hookups). Picnic tables and fire grills are provided. Drinking water and vault toilets are available; however, there is no water in winter. Leashed pets are permitted.

**Reservations, fees:** Reservations are accepted at 877/444-6777 ($10 reservation fee) or www.recreation.gov ($9 reservation fee). Sites are $23-50 per night, plus $7 per night for each additional vehicle. Fees are higher on holiday weekends. Open year-round.

**Directions:** From Porterville, drive east on Highway 190 for 25 miles to County Road 209/Wishon Drive. Turn left at County Road 208/Wishon Drive and drive 3.5 miles (narrow and curvy—RVs not advised).

**Contact:** Sequoia National Forest and Giant Sequoia National Monument, Western Divide Ranger District, 559/539-2607, www.fs.usda.gov/sequoia.

## 117 COY FLAT

### Scenic rating: 4

in Giant Sequoia National Monument

**Map 11.4, page 576**

Coy Flat is between Coy Creek and Bear Creek, small forks of the Tule River, at 5,000 feet elevation. The road out of camp travels five miles (through Rogers' Camp, which is private property) to the Black Mountain Grove of redwoods, with some giant sequoias just inside the border of the neighboring Tule River Indian Reservation. From camp, a hiking trail (Forest Trail 31S31) goes east for two miles through the Belknap Camp Grove of sequoias and then turns and heads south for four miles to Slate Mountain, where it intersects with Summit National Recreation Trail, a steep butt-kicker of a hike that tops out at over 9,000 feet elevation.

**Campsites, facilities:** There are 19 single sites and one double site for tents or RVs up to 24 feet (no hookups). Picnic tables and fire grills are provided. Drinking water is not available in drought years. Vault toilets are available. Leashed pets are permitted.

**Reservations, fees:** Reservations are accepted at 877/444-6777 ($10 reservation fee) or www. recreation.gov ($9 reservation fee). Sites are $23-50 per night, plus $7 per night for each additional vehicle. Open mid-April through mid-November.

**Directions:** From Porterville, drive east on Highway 190 for 34 miles to Camp Nelson and Coy Flat Road. Turn right on Coy Flat Road and drive one mile to the campground.

**Contact:** Sequoia National Forest and Giant Sequoia National Monument, Western Divide Ranger District, 559/539-2607, www.fs.usda. gov/sequoia.

## 118 BELKNAP

🚶🛶🐕🔺

### Scenic rating: 7
on the South Fork of Middle Fork Tule River in Giant Sequoia National Monument

**Map 11.4, page 576**

The groves of sequoias in this area are a highlight wherever you go. This camp is on the South Fork of the Middle Fork Tule River near McIntyre Grove and Belknap Camp Grove; a trail from camp heads east for three miles through Wheel Meadow Grove to the junction with Summit National Recreation Trail at

Quaking Aspen camp. The elevation is 5,000 feet.

**Campsites, facilities:** There are 15 sites for tents only. Picnic tables and fire grills are provided. Drinking water and vault toilets are available. A store is nearby. Leashed pets are permitted.

**Reservations, fees:** Reservations are accepted at 877/444-6777 ($10 reservation fee) or www.recreation.gov ($9 reservation fee). Sites are $23-25 per night, plus $7 per night for each additional vehicle. Fees are higher on holiday weekends. Open mid-April through mid-November.

**Directions:** From Porterville, drive east on Highway 190 for 34 miles to Camp Nelson and Nelson Drive. Turn right on Nelson Drive and continue one mile to the camp.

**Contact:** Sequoia National Forest and Giant Sequoia National Monument, Western Divide Ranger District, 559/539-2607, www.fs.usda. gov/sequoia.

## 119 QUAKING ASPEN AND GROUP

🚶🛶🏠♿🚐🔺

### Scenic rating: 4
in Giant Sequoia National Monument

**Map 11.4, page 576**

Quaking Aspen sits at a junction of Forest Service roads at 7,000 feet elevation, near the headwaters of Freeman Creek. A trailhead for Summit National Recreation Trail runs right through camp; it's a popular trip on horseback, heading deep into Sequoia National Forest. Another trailhead is 0.5 mile away on Forest Road 21S50. This hike is routed east along Freeman Creek and reaches the Freeman Grove of sequoias in four miles. The elevation is 7,000 feet.

**Campsites, facilities:** There are 32 sites for tents or RVs up to 24 feet (no hookups), three group sites for up to 12 people, and 5 yurts. There are also two group sites for 25 people and two group sites for 50 people; these group sites are for tents only. Picnic tables and fire grills are provided. Drinking water and vault toilets are available. An amphitheater is available. A store is nearby. Some facilities are wheelchair-accessible. Leashed pets are permitted.

**Reservations, fees:** Reservations are accepted at 877/444-6777 ($10 reservation fee) or www. recreation.gov ($9 reservation fee). Single sites are $23-25 per night, group sites are $42-175 per night, yurts are $75 per night, plus $7 per night for each additional vehicle. Open mid-May through mid-November, weather permitting.

**Directions:** From Porterville, drive east on Highway 190 for 34 miles to Camp Nelson. Continue east on Highway 190 for 11 miles to the campground on the right.

**Contact:** Sequoia National Forest and Giant Sequoia National Monument, Western Divide Ranger District, 559/539-2607, www.fs.usda. gov/sequoia.

## 120 HOLEY MEADOW GROUP CAMP

🏃 🛖 🚐 ⛰️

### Scenic rating: 7

on Double Bunk Creek in Giant Sequoia National Monument

**Map 11.4, page 576**

Holey Meadow is set at 6,400 feet elevation on the western slopes of the Sierra, near Redwood and Long Meadow. Parker Pass is a mile to the west, and if you drive on the Forest Service road over the pass, continue southwest (four miles from camp) to Cold Springs Saddle, and then turn east on the Forest Service spur road, it will take you two miles to Starvation Creek and the Starvation Creek Grove.

**Campsites, facilities:** There are six sites for tents only; they can be reserved as a group site for up to 36 people. Fire grills and picnic tables are provided. Vault toilets are available. There is no drinking water; water is available 2.5 miles away at Redwood Meadow campground. Leashed pets are permitted.

**Reservations, fees:** Reservations are accepted

at 877/444-6777 ($10 reservation fee) or www. recreation.gov ($9 reservation fee). Single sites are $21-23 per night, and the group site is $90 per night. Open June through October.

**Directions:** Drive on Highway 99 to Earlimart (about eight miles north of Delano) and the exit for Avenue 56/County Road J22. Take that exit east and drive 39 miles to the town of California Hot Springs and Parker Pass Road/County Road M50. Turn left on Parker Pass Road and drive 12 miles to Western Divide Highway/County Road M107. Turn left on Western Divide Highway and drive 0.5 mile to the campground entrance.

**Contact:** Sequoia National Forest and Giant Sequoia National Monument, Western Divide Ranger District, 559/539-2607, www.fs.usda. gov/sequoia.

## 121 REDWOOD MEADOW

🏃 🐕 ♿ 🚐 ⛰️

### Scenic rating: 7

near Parker Meadow Creek in Giant Sequoia National Monument

**Map 11.4, page 576**

The highlight here is the 1.5-mile Trail of the Hundred Giants, which passes through a grove of giant sequoias and is accessible for wheelchair hikers. This is the site where President Clinton proclaimed the Giant Sequoia National Monument in 2000. The camp is near Parker Meadow Creek at 6,100 feet elevation. Despite its remoteness, this has become a popular place.

**Campsites, facilities:** There are 15 sites for tents or RVs up to 16 feet (no hookups) and six furnished yurts that sleep up to five people each. Picnic tables and fire grills are provided. Drinking water and vault toilets are available. Some facilities are wheelchair-accessible. Leashed pets are permitted.

**Reservations, fees:** Reservations are accepted at 877/444-6777 ($10 reservation fee) or www.recreation.gov ($9 reservation fee). Sites are $25-27 per night, yurts are $75 per night, plus $7 per night for each additional vehicle.

Open mid-May through October, weather permitting.

**Directions:** Drive on Highway 99 to Earlimart (about eight miles north of Delano) and the exit for Avenue 56/County Road J22. Take that exit east and drive 39 miles to the town of California Hot Springs and Parker Pass Road/County Road M50. Turn left on Parker Pass Road and drive 12 miles to Western Divide Highway/County Road M107. Turn left on Western Divide Highway and drive three miles to the campground entrance.

**Contact:** Sequoia National Forest and Giant Sequoia National Monument, Western Divide Ranger District, 559/539-2607, www.fs.usda.gov/sequoia.

## 122 LONG MEADOW GROUP CAMP

### Scenic rating: 8
in Giant Sequoia National Monument

Map 11.4, page 576

Long Meadow is on little Long Meadow Creek at an elevation of 6,000 feet, within a mile of the remote Cunningham Grove of redwoods to the east. Note that Redwood Meadow is just one mile to the west, where the Trail of the Hundred Giants is a feature attraction.

**Campsites, facilities:** There is one group site for tents or RVs up to 16 feet (no hookups) that can accommodate up to 36 people. Picnic tables and fire grills are provided. Vault toilets are available. No drinking water is available. Leashed pets are permitted.

**Reservations, fees:** Reservations are required at 877/444-6777 ($10 reservation fee) or www.recreation.gov ($9 reservation fee). The camp is $126 per night. Open mid-May through mid-November.

**Directions:** Drive on Highway 99 to Earlimart (about eight miles north of Delano) and the exit for Avenue 56/County Road J22. Take that exit east and drive 39 miles to the town of California Hot Springs and Parker Pass Road/

County Road M50. Turn left on Parker Pass Road and drive 12 miles to Western Divide Highway/County Road M107. Turn left on Western Divide Highway and drive four miles to the campground entrance.

**Contact:** Sequoia National Forest and Giant Sequoia National Monument, Western Divide Ranger District, 559/539-2607, www.fs.usda.gov/sequoia.

## 123 TULE

### Scenic rating: 7
on Lake Success

Map 11.4, page 576

Lake Success is a big lake with many arms, providing 30 miles of shoreline and making the place seem like a dreamland for boaters on hot summer days. The lake is set in the foothill country, at an elevation of 650 feet, where day after day of 100-degree summer temperatures is common. That is why boating, waterskiing, and personal-watercraft riding are so popular—anything to get wet. In the winter and spring, fishing for trout and bass is good, including the chance for largemouth bass. No beaches are developed for swimming because of fluctuating water levels, though the day-use area has a decent sloped stretch of shore that is good for swimming. Lake Success is much shallower than most reservoirs, and the water can fluctuate from week to week, with major drawdowns during the summer. The wildlife area along the west side of the lake is worth exploring, and there is a nature trail below the dam. The campground is the centerpiece of the Tule Recreation Area.

**Campsites, facilities:** There are 103 sites for tents or RVs of any length; some sites have electrical hookups (30 and 50 amps) and some are pull-through. Picnic tables and fire grills are provided. Restrooms with flush toilets and showers, a dump station, picnic areas, and a playground are available. A store, marina, boat ramp, houseboat rentals, boat and water-ski rentals, bait and tackle, propane gas, restaurant, and gas station are nearby. Some facilities are wheelchair-accessible. Leashed pets are permitted.

**Reservations, fees:** Reservations are accepted at 877/444-6677 ($10 reservation fee) or www.recreation.gov ($9 reservation fee). Sites are $20-30 per night. Open year-round.

**Directions:** Drive on Highway 65 to Porterville and the junction with Highway 190. Turn east on Highway 190 and drive eight miles to Lake Success and the campground entrance on the left.

**Contact:** U.S. Army Corps of Engineers, Sacramento District, 559/784-0215; Success Marina, 559/781-2078.

## 124 GOODALE CREEK

🏞 🛶 🐕 🚐 ⛺

### Scenic rating: 6

near Independence

**Map 11.4, page 576**

This obscure BLM camp is along little Goodale Creek at 4,000 feet elevation. It is a good layover spot for U.S. 395 cruisers heading north. In hot summer months, snakes are occasionally spotted near this campground.

**Campsites, facilities:** There are 62 sites for tents or RVs up to 30 feet (no hookups); some sites are pull-through. Picnic tables and fire rings are provided. Vault toilets are available. Check for water availability. Horses and horse trailers are prohibited. Leashed pets are permitted.

**Reservations, fees:** Reservations are not accepted. Sites are $5 per night. Maximum stay is 14 days. An LTVA (Long Term Visitor Area) permit ($300) allows all-season access to this and two other BLM campgrounds—Tuttle Creek (see listing in this chapter) and Crowley. Open early April through October, weather permitting.

**Directions:** Drive on U.S. 395 to Aberdeen Road (12 miles north of Independence). Turn

west (toward the Sierra) on Aberdeen Road and drive two miles to the campground on the left.

**Contact:** Bureau of Land Management, Bishop Field Office, 760/872-4881, www.blm.gov/ca.

## 125 ONION VALLEY

🏞 🐕 🦽 🚐 ⛺

### Scenic rating: 8

in Inyo National Forest

**Map 11.4, page 576**    BEST (

Onion Valley is one of the best trailhead camps for backpackers in the Sierra. The camp is set at 9,200 feet elevation, and from here it's a 2,600-foot climb over the course of about three miles to awesome Kearsarge Pass (11,823 feet). From there you can camp at the Kearsarge Lakes, explore the Kearsarge Pinnacles, or join the John Muir Trail and venture to your choice of many wilderness lakes. This is also the fastest launch point over Kearsarge, then Glen Pass to Rae Lakes, in Kings Canyon National Park. A wilderness map and a wilderness permit are your passports to the high country from this camp. For backpackers, trailhead reservations are required. Note: Bears frequent this camp almost every night of summer. Do not keep your food in your vehicle. Many cars have been severely damaged by bears. Use bear-proof food lockers at the campground and parking area, or use bear-proof food canisters as required in the adjacent wilderness area.

**Campsites, facilities:** There are 29 sites for tents or RVs up to 16 feet (no hookups). Picnic tables and fire grills are provided. Drinking water and vault toilets are available. Some facilities are wheelchair-accessible. Leashed pets are permitted.

**Reservations, fees:** Reservations are accepted at 877/444-6677 ($10 reservation fee) or www.recreation.gov ($9 reservation fee). Sites are $19 per night, plus $7 per night for each additional vehicle. Maximum stay is 14 days. Open late May through September, weather permitting.

**Directions:** Drive on U.S. 395 to Independence and Market Street. Turn west (toward the

Sierra) at Market Street (becomes Onion Valley Road) and drive 15 miles to the campground at the road's end.

**Contact:** Inyo National Forest, Mount Whitney Ranger District, 760/876-6200, www.fs.usda.gov/inyo; Interagency Visitor Center, 760/876-6222.

## 126 UPPER AND LOWER GRAY'S MEADOW

### Scenic rating: 6

on Independence Creek in Inyo National Forest

**Map 11.4, page 576**

Gray's Meadow provides two adjacent camps along Independence Creek. Upper Gray's is at an elevation of 6,200 feet; Lower Gray's is 200 feet lower down the canyon. The creek is stocked with small trout by the Department of Fish and Game. The highlight in the immediate area is the trailhead at the end of the road at Onion Valley camp. For U.S. 395 cruisers looking for a spot, this is a pretty alternative to the camps in Bishop.

**Campsites, facilities:** Lower Gray's has 52 sites for tents or RVs up to 34 feet (no hookups). Upper Gray's has 35 sites for tents or RVs. Picnic tables, food lockers, and fire grills are provided. Drinking water and flush toilets are available. Supplies and a coin laundry are in Independence. Leashed pets are permitted.

**Reservations, fees:** Reservations are accepted at 877/444-6777 ($10 reservation fee) or www.recreation.gov ($9 reservation fee; look for Grays Meadow). Sites are $19 per night, plus $7 per night for additional vehicle. Open late March through mid-October, with a 14-day limit.

**Directions:** Drive on U.S. 395 to Independence and Market Street. Turn west (toward the Sierra) at Market Street (becomes Onion Valley Road) and drive five miles to the campground on the right.

**Contact:** Inyo National Forest, Mount Whitney Ranger District, 760/876-6200, www.fs.usda.gov/inyo; Interagency Visitor Center, 760/876-6222.

## 127 INDEPENDENCE CREEK

### Scenic rating: 4

in Independence

**Map 11.4, page 576**

This unpublicized county park is often overlooked by U.S. 395 cruisers. It is at 3,900 feet elevation, one mile outside the town of Independence, which is spiraling downward into something resembling a ghost town. True to form, maintenance is sometimes lacking. Independence Creek runs through the campground and a museum is within walking distance. At the rate it's going, the whole town could be a museum.

**Campsites, facilities:** There are 25 sites for tents or RVs up to 30 feet (no hookups). Picnic tables and fire grills are provided. Drinking water and vault toilets are available. Some facilities are wheelchair-accessible. Supplies and a coin laundry are available in Independence. Leashed pets are permitted.

**Reservations, fees:** Reservations are not accepted. Sites are $14 per vehicle per night. Open year-round.

**Directions:** Drive on U.S. 395 to Independence and Market Street. Turn west (toward the Sierra) at Market Street and drive one mile (outside the town limits) to the campground.

**Contact:** Inyo County Parks Department, 760/873-5577, www.inyocountycamping.com.

## 128 LONE PINE AND LONE PINE GROUP

### Scenic rating: 8

near Mount Whitney in Inyo National Forest

**Map 11.4, page 576**

This is an alternative for campers preparing to hike Mount Whitney or start the John Muir

Trail. It is at 6,000 feet elevation, 2,000 feet below Whitney Portal (the hiking jumping-off spot), providing a lower-elevation location for hikers to acclimate themselves to the altitude. The camp is set on Lone Pine Creek, with decent fishing and spectacular views of Mount Whitney. Because of its exposure to the east, there are also beautiful sunrises, especially in fall.

**Campsites, facilities:** There are 43 sites for tents or RVs up to 35 feet (no hookups), along with one tent-only group site for up to 15 people. Picnic tables and fire grills are provided; some sites have stone ovens. Drinking water and flush toilets are available. Supplies are available in Lone Pine. Some facilities are wheelchair-accessible. Leashed pets are permitted.

**Reservations, fees:** Reservations are accepted at 877/444-6777 ($10 reservation fee) or www.recreation.gov ($9 reservation fee). Sites are $20 per night, plus $5 per night per each additional vehicle, and it's $63 per night for the group site. Open late April through mid-October, with a 14-day limit.

**Directions:** From U.S. 395, drive to Lone Pine and Whitney Portal Road. Turn west (toward the Sierra) on Whitney Portal Road and drive six miles to the campground on the left.

**Contact:** Inyo National Forest, Mount Whitney Ranger District, 760/876-6200, www.fs.usda.gov/inyo; Interagency Visitor Center, 760/876-6222.

## 129 PORTAGEE JOE CAMPGROUND

### Scenic rating: 4

near Lone Pine

**Map 11.4, page 576**

This small, little-known county park provides an option for both Mount Whitney hikers and U.S. 395 cruisers. The sparse setting is high desert sprinkled with a few aspens, with Mount Whitney and the Sierra crest looming

high to the west. The camp is about five miles from Diaz Lake, set on a small creek at 3,750 feet. Very few out-of-towners know about this spot, a nice insurance policy if you find yourself stuck for a campsite in this region.

**Campsites, facilities:** There are 15 sites for tents or RVs up to 30 feet (no hookups). Picnic tables and fire grills are provided. Vault toilets and well water are available. Supplies and a coin laundry are available in Lone Pine. Leashed pets are permitted.

**Reservations, fees:** Reservations are not accepted. Sites are $14 per vehicle per night. Open year-round.

**Directions:** From U.S. 395, drive to Lone Pine and Whitney Portal Road. Turn west (toward the Sierra) on Whitney Portal Road and drive one mile to Tuttle Creek Road. Turn left (south) at Tuttle Creek Road and drive 0.1 mile to the campground on the right.

**Contact:** Inyo County Parks Department, 760/878-0272 or 760/873-5577, www.inyocountycamping.com.

## 130 WHITNEY TRAILHEAD WALK-IN

### Scenic rating: 9

in Inyo National Forest

**Map 11.4, page 576**      **BEST (**

If Whitney Portal is full (common for this world-class trailhead), this camp at 8,300 feet elevation can be reached by hiking in 0.25 mile. Reservations for the summit hike are required. That accomplished, this hike-in camp is an excellent spot for spending a day to become acclimated to the high altitude. The trailhead to the Mount Whitney summit (14,497 feet) is nearby. Mount Whitney is the beginning of the 211-mile John Muir Trail to Yosemite Valley. Food-raiding bears are a common problem. Campers are required to use bear-proof food lockers or food canisters. There is a one-night stay limit. For information on backcountry permits, call the ranger district.

**Campsites, facilities:** There are 10 walk-in tent sites. Picnic tables and fire grills are provided. Drinking water and vault toilets are available. Garbage must be packed out. Supplies are available in Lone Pine. Some facilities are wheelchair-accessible. Leashed pets are permitted.

**Reservations, fees:** Reservations are not accepted. Sites are $13 per night. Open mid-May through late October, with a one-night stay limit.

**Directions:** Drive on U.S. 395 to Lone Pine and Whitney Portal Road. Turn west (toward the Sierra) and drive 13 miles to the parking lot at Whitney Portal. Park and hike 0.25 mile to the campground.

**Contact:** Inyo National Forest, Mount Whitney Ranger District, 760/876-6200, www.fs.usda.gov/inyo; Interagency Visitor Center, 760/876-2222.

## 131 WHITNEY PORTAL AND GROUP
🚶 🐕 🚗 ⛺

**Scenic rating: 9**

near Mount Whitney in Inyo National Forest

Map 11.4, page 576

This camp is home to a world-class trailhead. It is regarded as the number-one jumping-off spot for the hike to the top of Mount Whitney, the highest spot in the continental United States, at 14,497.6 feet, as well as the start of the 211-mile John Muir Trail from Mount Whitney to Yosemite Valley. Hikers planning to scale the summit must have a wilderness permit, available by reservation at the Forest Service office in Lone Pine. The camp is at 8,000 feet elevation, and virtually everyone staying here plans to make the trek to the Whitney summit, a climb of 6,500 feet over the course of 10 miles. The trip includes an ascent over 100 switchbacks (often snow-covered in early summer) to top Wotan's Throne and reach Trail Crest (13,560 feet). Here you turn right and take Summit Trail, where the ridge is cut by huge notch windows providing a view down more than 10,000 feet to the little town of Lone Pine and the Owens Valley. When you sign the logbook on top, don't be surprised if you see my name in the registry. A plus at the campground is watching the JMT hikers arrive who are just finishing the trail from north to south—that is, from Yosemite to Whitney. There is no comparing the happy look of success when they drop their packs for the last time, head into the little store, and pick a favorite refreshment for celebration.

**Campsites, facilities:** There are 43 sites for tents or RVs up to 22 feet (no hookups), along with three group sites for up to 15 people each. Picnic tables, food lockers, and fire grills are provided. Drinking water and flush toilets are available. Supplies are available in Lone Pine. Leashed pets are permitted.

**Reservations, fees:** Reservations are accepted at 877/444-6777 ($10 reservation fee) or www.recreation.gov ($9 reservation fee). Sites are $22 per night, plus $7 per night per each additional vehicle, and it's $73 per night for a group site. There's a one-night limit for walk-in tent sites and a seven-day stay limit for the group site. Open late May through mid-October.

**Directions:** Drive on U.S. 395 to Lone Pine and Whitney Portal Road. Turn west (toward the Sierra) on Whitney Portal Road (expect road construction delays through 2017) and drive 13 miles to the campground on the left.

**Contact:** Inyo National Forest, Mount Whitney Ranger District, 760/876-6200; Interagency Visitor Center, 760/876-2222, www.fs.usda.gov/inyo; California Land Management, 760/937-6070.

## 132 TUTTLE CREEK
🚶 🐕 🚗 ⛺

**Scenic rating: 4**

near Mount Whitney

Map 11.4, page 576

This primitive BLM camp is set at the base of Mount Whitney along Tuttle Creek at 5,120 feet

# HIKING THE JMT:
# WHITNEY PORTAL TO LAKE EDISON

## 112 MILES ONE-WAY/11 DAYS

You can have a foothold in the sky with every step on the **John Muir Trail** (JMT). This part of the trail is shared with the **Pacific Crest Trail** (PCT) and starts at practically the tip-top of North America—Mount Whitney—and takes you northward across a land of 12,000-foot passes and Ansel Adams-style panoramas.

From the trailhead at **Whitney Portal,** the hike climbs more than 6,100 feet over the course of 11 miles to reach Whitney's summit at 14,505 feet. That includes an ascent of more than 100 switchbacks, which are often snow covered even late in summer, to reach Trail Crest (13,560 feet). Here you turn right and take Summit Trail. In the final stretch to the top, the ridge is cut by huge notched windows in the rock; you look through, and the bottom drops out more than 10,000 feet to the town of Lone Pine below, at an elevation of 3,800 feet. Finally you make it to the top and notice how the surrounding giant blocks of rock look as if they were sculpted with a giant hammer and chisel. From here, the entire Western Divide is visible, and to the north, rows of mountain peaks are lined up for miles to the horizon. Be sure to sign your name in the register, kept in a lightning-proof metal box. You may feel a bit dizzy from the altitude, but you'll know you're someplace very special.

The journey farther north is just as captivating. The route drops into Sequoia National Park, then climbs above timberline for almost a day's worth of hiking as it nears Forester Pass (13,180 feet). It's not only the highest point on the PCT, it's the most dangerous section of trail on the entire route as well. The trail is narrow and steep, cut into a high vertical slab of rock, and is typically icy, with an iced-over snowfield near the top that's particularly treacherous. An ice ax is an absolute must. If you slip here, you could fall thousands of feet.

Once through Forester, the trail heads onward into the John Muir Wilderness along Bubbs Creek, with great wildflowers at nearby Vidette Meadow. Then it's up and over Kearsarge Pass (10,710 feet), and after a short drop, you're back climbing again, this time over Glen Pass (11,978 feet)—a spectacular, boulder-strewn ridge with great views to the north looking into Kings Canyon National Park. Just two miles from Glen Pass is **Rae Lakes,** a fantasy spot for camping (one-night limit), with pristine meadows, shoreline campsites, and lots of eager brook trout.

The JMT then heads through Kings Canyon National Park by following sparkling streams much of the way, finally climbing up and over Pinchot Pass (12,130 feet), then back down along the upper Kings River for a long, steady ascent over Mather Pass (12,100 feet). The wonders continue as you hike along Palisade Lakes, then down into LeConte Canyon, followed by an endless climb up to Muir Pass (11,965 feet). In early summer, snowfields are common, and this can be difficult and trying, especially if your boots keep post-holing through the snow. The country near Muir Pass is extremely stark—nothing but sculpted granite, ice, and a few small turquoise lakes—crowned by the stone Muir Hut at the pass, where hikers can duck in and hide for safety from sudden afternoon thunderstorms and lightning bolts.

The views astound many visitors as the trail drops into Evolution Valley. You finally leave Kings Canyon National Park, following the headwaters of the San Joaquin River into Sierra National Forest. After bottoming out at 7,890 feet, the trail rises steeply in switchback after switchback as it enters the John Muir Wilderness. Finally you top Selden Pass (10,900 feet), take in an incredible view, then make the easy one-mile descent to a pretty campsite at **Marie Lakes.**

The final push on this section of the JMT is climbing up Bear Mountain, then down a terrible, toe-jamming stretch to Mono Creek. Here you make a left turn and continue for two more miles until you come to **Edison Lake,** an excellent place to have a food stash waiting.

elevation and is shadowed by several impressive peaks (Mount Whitney, Lone Pine Peak, and Mount Williamson). It is often used as an overflow area if the camps farther up Whitney Portal Road are full. Note: This campground is often confused with a small county campground also on Tuttle Creek Road just off Whitney Portal Road.

**Campsites, facilities:** There are 83 sites for tents or RVs up to 30 feet (no hookups); some sites are pull-through. A group site holds up to 25 people. Picnic tables and fire rings are provided. Vault toilets are available. Drinking water is available seasonally; a dump station is available when water is available. There are two horse corrals; however, horses are not encouraged. Supplies are available in Lone Pine. Leashed pets are permitted.

**Reservations, fees:** Reservations are not accepted for single sites but are required for the group site at 760/872-5008. Single sites are $5 per night, the group site is $30 per night, and season passes are $300. Open year-round.

**Directions:** Drive on U.S. 395 to Lone Pine and Whitney Portal Road. Turn west (toward the Sierra) on Whitney Portal Road and drive 3.5 miles to Horseshoe Meadow Road. Turn left and drive 1.5 miles to Tuttle Creek Road and the campground entrance (a dirt road) on the right.

**Contact:** Bureau of Land Management, Bishop Field Office, 760/872-4881, www.blm.gov/ca.

## 133 DIAZ LAKE

🏊 ⛵ 🚴 🚐 🐎 🚶 ♿ 🚙 ⛺

### Scenic rating: 7

near Lone Pine

Map 11.4, page 576

Diaz Lake, at 3,650 feet elevation in the Owens Valley, is sometimes overlooked by visitors to nearby Mount Whitney. It's a small lake—just 85 acres—popular for trout fishing in the spring when a speed limit of 15 mph is enforced. The lake is stocked with Alpers trout and also has a surprise population of bass. From May through October, when hot weather takes over and the speed limit is bumped up to 35 mph, you can say *adios* to the anglers and *hola* to water-skiers. The lake is extremely popular for waterskiing and swimming and is sunny most of the year. A 20-foot limit is enforced for boats. A nine-hole golf course is nearby. Boats must be inspected for quagga mussels prior to launching; the launch is closed on Monday and Tuesday.

**Campsites, facilities:** There are 200 sites for tents or RVs of any length; some have partial hookups. Picnic tables and fire grills are provided. Restrooms with flush and vault toilets, drinking water (from a well), a playground, and a boat ramp are available. Supplies and a coin laundry are in Lone Pine. Some facilities are wheelchair-accessible. Leashed pets are permitted.

**Reservations, fees:** Reservations are accepted at 760/873-5577. Sites are $14 per vehicle per night, plus $3 per additional person, and the boat launch fee is $10. Open year-round.

**Directions:** From U.S. 395, drive three miles south of Lone Pine to the Diaz Lake entrance on the west side of the road.

**Contact:** Inyo County Parks Department, 760/876-4700, www.inyocountycamping.com.

## 134 HORSESHOE MEADOW WALK-IN AND EQUESTRIAN

🚶 🐎 ⛺

### Scenic rating: 8

near the John Muir Wilderness in Inyo National Forest

Map 11.4, page 576

Horseshoe Meadow features three trailhead camps, remote and choice, for backpackers heading into the adjacent John Muir Wilderness and Golden Trout Wilderness. The three camps are Cottonwood Pass Walk-In, Cottonwood Lakes Walk-In, and Horseshoe Meadow Equestrian. The camps are at 10,000 feet elevation near the wilderness border, one of the highest trailheads and drive-to campgrounds in the state. Several trails lead out of camp. The best heads west through Horseshoe Meadow and along a creek, then rises steeply for four miles to Cottonwood Pass, where it intersects with the Pacific Crest Trail. From here backpackers can hike north on the Pacific Crest Trail to Chicken Spring Lake to set up camp, a rewarding overnighter, or drop into Big Whitney Meadow in the Golden Trout Wilderness. Some use this camp as a starting point to climb Mount Whitney from its back side (via Guitar Lake). Trailhead reservations are required. There is a one-night stay limit. Food-raiding bears mean that campers are required to use bear-proof food lockers or canisters. The drive in is one of the most spectacular anywhere, with the access road following a cliff edge much of the way and a 6,000-foot drop to the Owens Valley below. You will also pass fantastic volcanics, the site of many movie settings, including *Star Trek* with Captain Kirk and a lizard creature. (Can you remember the old episode? My kids, Jeremy and Kris, could, and they simulated a scene playing on the rocks.)

**Campsites, facilities:** Cottonwood Pass has 18 walk-in sites, Cottonwood Lakes has 12 walk-in sites, and Horseshoe Meadow Equestrian has 10 sites (no hookups). Picnic tables and fire grills are provided. Vault toilets and drinking water are available. A pack station and horse facilities are also available at the equestrian camp; campers are encouraged to pack out all livestock waste. Leashed pets are permitted.

**Reservations, fees:** Reservations are not accepted. Sites are $6 per night for walk-in sites and $12 per night for equestrian sites (limit four per site). Open late May through mid-October, with a one-night stay limit.

**Directions:** Drive on U.S. 395 to Lone Pine and Whitney Portal Road. Turn west (toward the Sierra) on Whitney Portal Road and drive 3.5 miles to Horseshoe Meadows Road. Turn left on Horseshoe Meadows Road and drive 19 miles to the end of the road (a nearly 7,000-foot climb) and the parking area. Park and walk a short distance to the campground.

**Contact:** Inyo National Forest, Mount Whitney Ranger District, 760/876-6200, www.fs.usda.gov/inyo; Interagency Visitor Center, 760/876-2222.

## 135 UPPER PEPPERMINT DISPERSED

### Scenic rating: 6

on Peppermint Creek in Giant Sequoia National Monument

**Map 11.5, page 577**

This is one of two primitive campgrounds at Peppermint Creek, but a road does not directly connect the two camps. Several backcountry access roads snake throughout the area, as detailed on a Forest Service map, and exploring them can make for some self-styled fortune hunts. For the ambitious, hiking the two-mile trail at the end of nearby Forest Road 21S05 leads to a fantastic lookout at The Needles (8,245 feet). The camp elevation is 7,100 feet. There is fire damage in some of the surrounding area.

**Campsites, facilities:** There is dispersed camping for tents or RVs up to 24 feet (no hookups). There is one picnic table for the campground. There is no drinking water or toilets. Garbage must be packed out. A lodge with limited supplies is nearby. Leashed pets are permitted.

**Reservations, fees:** Reservations are not accepted. There is no fee for camping. A campfire permit is required. Open June through September, weather permitting.

**Directions:** From Porterville, drive east on Highway 190 for 34 miles to Camp Nelson. Continue east on Highway 190 for 15 miles to the campground entrance road.

**Contact:** Sequoia National Forest and Giant Sequoia National Monument, Western Divide Ranger District, 559/539-2607, www.fs.usda.gov/sequoia.

## 136 LOWER PEPPERMINT

### Scenic rating: 6

in Giant Sequoia National Monument

**Map 11.5, page 577**

This is a little-known camp in Sequoia National Forest, set along Peppermint Creek at 5,300 feet elevation. This area has a vast network of backcountry roads, which are detailed on a Forest Service map.

**Campsites, facilities:** There are 17 sites for tents or RVs up to 16 feet (no hookups). Picnic tables and fire grills are provided. Drinking water and vault toilets are available. Leashed pets are permitted.

**Reservations, fees:** Reservations are not accepted. Sites are $17 per night. Open June through September.

**Directions:** From Bakersfield, drive east on Highway 178 for 40 miles to the town of Lake Isabella and Highway 155/Burlando Way. Turn left (north) and drive 10 miles to Kernville Sierra Way. Turn (north) and drive 24 miles to Johnsondale and Forest Road 22S82/Lloyd Meadow Road. Turn right and drive about 10.5 miles (paved road) to the campground.

**Contact:** Sequoia National Forest and Giant Sequoia National Monument, Western Divide Ranger District, 559/539-2607, www.fs.usda.gov/sequoia.

## 137 LIMESTONE

### Scenic rating: 5

on the Kern River in Sequoia National Forest

**Map 11.5, page 577**

Set deep in the Sequoia National Forest at 3,800 feet, Limestone is a small campground along the Kern River, fed by snowmelt from Mount Whitney. This stretch of the Kern is extremely challenging and sensational for white-water rafting, with cold water and many of the rapids rated Class IV and Class V—for experts with guides only. The favored put-in is at the Johnsondale Bridge, for a 21-mile run to Kernville. The river pours into Isabella Lake many miles later. Two sections are unrunnable: Fairview Dam (mile 2.5) and Salmon Falls (mile 8). For nonrafters, South Creek Falls provides a side trip, one mile to the west. There is fire damage in some of the surrounding area.

**Campsites, facilities:** There are 20 sites for tents or RVs up to 30 feet (no hookups). Picnic tables and fire grills are provided. Vault toilets are available. No drinking water is available. Supplies and a coin laundry are in Kernville. Leashed pets are permitted.

**Reservations, fees:** Reservations are accepted at 877/444-6777 ($10 reservation fee) or www.recreation.gov ($9 reservation fee). Sites are $21-23 per night, plus $7 per night for each additional vehicle. Open April through November, weather permitting.

**Directions:** From Bakersfield, drive east on Highway 178 for about 40 miles to the town of Lake Isabella and Highway 155/Burlando Way. Turn left (north) and drive 10 miles to Kernville and the Kern River Highway/Sierra Way. Turn left on the Kern River Highway and drive 19 miles (two miles past Fairview) to the campground entrance.

**Contact:** Sequoia National Forest, Kern River Ranger District, Kernville Office, 760/376-3781, www.fs.usda.gov/sequoia.

## 138 LEAVIS FLAT

### Scenic rating: 7

on Deer Creek in Giant Sequoia National Monument

**Map 11.5, page 577**

Leavis Flat is just inside the western border of Sequoia National Forest along Deer Creek, at an elevation of 3,000 feet. The highlight here is the adjacent California Hot Springs.

**Campsites, facilities:** There are nine sites for tents or RVs up to 16 feet (no hookups). Picnic tables and fire grills are provided. Vault toilets are available, but there is no drinking water.

A store, coin laundry, and propane gas can be found nearby. Leashed pets are permitted.

**Reservations, fees:** Reservations are not accepted. There is no fee for camping. Open year-round.

**Directions:** Take Highway 99 to Earlimart (about eight miles north of Delano) and the exit for Avenue 56/County Road J22. Take that exit east and drive 39 miles to the town of California Hot Springs and the campground.

**Contact:** Sequoia National Forest and Giant Sequoia National Monument, Western Divide Ranger District, 559/539-2607, www.fs.usda. gov/sequoia.

## 139 WHITE RIVER
🚶 🏊 🐕 🚐 ⛺

### Scenic rating: 7
in Giant Sequoia National Monument

**Map 11.5, page 577**

White River is set at 4,000 feet elevation, on the White River near where little Dark Canyon Creek enters it. A trail from camp follows downstream along the White River to the west for three miles, dropping into Ames Hole and Cove Canyon. The region's hot springs are about a 10-minute drive away to the north.

**Campsites, facilities:** There are 12 sites for tents or RVs up to 16 feet (no hookups). Picnic tables and fire grills are provided. Drinking water and vault toilets are available. Leashed pets are permitted.

**Reservations, fees:** Reservations are accepted at 877/444-6777 ($10 reservation fee) or www. recreation.gov ($9 reservation fee). Sites are $22 per night, plus $7 per night for each additional vehicle. Open mid-April through mid-October.

**Directions:** Drive on Highway 99 to Delano and the exit for Highway 155. Take that exit and drive east for about 40 miles to Jack Ranch Road (just west of Glennville). Turn left on Jack Ranch Road and drive about four miles to White River Road/Sugarloaf Drive. Turn right and drive 1.5 miles to Forest Road 24S05. Bear left and drive 0.75 mile to Idlewild, and

continue (on this dirt road) for six miles to the campground.

**Contact:** Sequoia National Forest and Giant Sequoia National Monument, Western Divide Ranger District, 559/539-2607, www.fs.usda. gov/sequoia.

## 140 FROG MEADOW DISPERSED
🚶 🏕 5% 🚐 ⛺

### Scenic rating: 6
near Giant Sequoia National Monument

**Map 11.5, page 577**

This small, primitive camp near Tobias Creek at 7,500 feet elevation is in the center of a network of Forest Service roads that explore the surrounding Sequoia National Forest. The nearby feature destination is the Tobias Peak Lookout (8,284 feet), two miles directly south of the camp.

**Campsites, facilities:** There are 10 sites for tents or RVs up to 16 feet (no hookups). There is no drinking water and there are no toilets. Garbage must be packed out. Leashed pets are permitted.

**Reservations, fees:** Reservations are not accepted. There is no fee for camping. Open June through September, weather permitting.

**Directions:** Drive on Highway 99 to Delano and the exit for Highway 155. Take that exit and drive east for about 40 miles to Jack Ranch Road (just west of Glennville). Turn left on Jack Ranch Road and drive about four miles to White River Road/Sugarloaf Drive. Turn right on Sugarloaf Drive and drive 4.5 miles to Guernsey Mill/Sugarloaf Drive. Continue on Sugarloaf Road/Forest Road 23S16 for about seven miles to Forest Road 24S50 (a dirt road). Turn left on Forest Road 24S50 and drive four miles to Frog Meadow and the campground. The route is long, slow, and circuitous. A map of Sierra National Forest is required.

**Contact:** Sequoia National Forest and Giant Sequoia National Monument, Western Divide

Ranger District, 559/539-2607, www.fs.usda.gov/sequoia.

## 141 FAIRVIEW

**Scenic rating: 4**
on the Kern River in Sequoia National Forest

**Map 11.5, page 577**      **BEST (**

Fairview is one of six campgrounds on the Upper Kern River above Isabella Lake and adjacent to the Kern River, one of the prime rafting and kayaking rivers in California. This camp sits at 3,500 feet elevation. Many of the rapids are rated Class IV and Class V—for experts with guides only. The favored put-in is at the Johnsondale Bridge for a 21-mile run to Kernville. The river eventually pours into Isabella Lake. Two sections are unrunnable: Fairview Dam (Mile 2.5) and Salmon Falls (Mile 8). There is fire damage in some of the surrounding area.

**Campsites, facilities:** There are 55 sites for tents or RVs up to 45 feet (no hookups). Picnic tables and fire grills are provided. Drinking water, vault toilets, and a dump station are available. Supplies and a coin laundry are available in Kernville. Some facilities are wheelchair-accessible. Leashed pets are permitted. No glass of any kind is allowed in the campground.

**Reservations, fees:** Reservations are accepted at 877/444-6777 ($10 reservation fee) or www.recreation.gov ($9 reservation fee). Sites are $25-27 per night, plus $7 per night for each additional vehicle. Camping fees are higher on holiday weekends. Open April through October, weather permitting.

**Directions:** From Bakersfield, drive east on Highway 178 for about 40 miles to the town of Lake Isabella and Highway 155/Burlando Way. Turn left (north) and drive 10 miles to Kernville and the Kern River Highway/Sierra Way. Turn left on the Kern River Highway and drive 18 miles to the town of Fairview. Continue to the north end of town to the campground entrance.

**Contact:** Sequoia National Forest, Kern River Ranger District, Kernville Office, 760/376-3781, www.fs.usda.gov/sequoia.

## 142 HORSE MEADOW

**Scenic rating: 8**
on Salmon Creek in Sequoia National Forest

**Map 11.5, page 577**

This is a little-known spot along Salmon Creek at 7,600 feet elevation. It is a region known for big meadows, forests, backcountry roads, and plenty of horses. It is just west of the Dome Land Wilderness, and there are three public pastures for horses in the area, as well as trails ideal for horseback riding. From camp, one trail follows along Salmon Creek to the west to Salmon Falls, a favorite for the few who know of it. A more popular overnight trip is to head to a trailhead about five miles east, which provides a route to Manter Meadows in the Dome Lands.

**Campsites, facilities:** There are 41 sites for tents or RVs up to 22 feet (no hookups). Picnic tables and fire grills are provided. There is no drinking water. Vault toilets are available. Garbage must be packed out. Leashed pets are permitted.

**Reservations, fees:** Reservations are not accepted. Sites are $17 per night, plus $5 per night for each additional vehicle. Open June through October, weather permitting.

**Directions:** From Bakersfield, drive east on Highway 178 for about 40 miles to the town of Lake Isabella and Highway 155/Burlando Way. Turn left (north) and drive 10 miles to Kernville and the Kern River Highway/Sierra Way. Turn left on the Kern River Highway for about 20 miles to Sherman Pass Road (signed "Highway 395/Black Rock Ranger Station"). Make a sharp right on Sherman Pass Road and drive about 6.5 miles to Cherry Hill Road/Forest Road 22S12 (a green gate has a sign that says "Horse Meadow/Big Meadow"). Turn right and drive about four miles (the road becomes dirt) and continue for another three miles (follow the signs) to the campground entrance road.

**Contact:** Sequoia National Forest, Kern River Ranger District, Kernville Office, 760/376-3781, www.fs.usda.gov/sequoia.

## 143 GOLDLEDGE

### Scenic rating: 7
on the Kern River in Sequoia National Forest

**Map 11.5, page 577**

This is another in the series of camps on the Kern River north of Isabella Lake. Swimming is not recommended as the currents are very swift. The elevation is 3,200 feet.

**Campsites, facilities:** There are 24 sites for tents or RVs up to 30 feet (no hookups) and nine walk-in tent sites. Picnic tables and fire grills are provided. Drinking water and vault toilets are available. Supplies and a coin laundry are available in Kernville. Leashed pets are permitted. No glass of any kind is allowed in the campground.

**Reservations, fees:** Reservations are accepted at 877/444-6777 ($10 reservation fee) or www. recreation.gov ($9 reservation fee). Sites are $25-27 per night, plus $7 per night for each additional vehicle. Camping fees are higher on holiday weekends. Open May through August.

**Directions:** From Bakersfield, drive east on Highway 178 for about 40 miles to the town of Lake Isabella and Highway 155/Burlando Way. Turn left (north) and drive 10 miles to Kernville and the Kern River Highway/Sierra Way. Turn left on the Kern River Highway and drive 10 miles to the campground.

**Contact:** Sequoia National Forest, Kern River Ranger District, Kernville Office, 760/376-3781, www.fs.usda.gov/sequoia; California Land Management, 559/335-2232.

## 144 HOSPITAL FLAT

### Scenic rating: 8
on the North Fork of the Kern River in Sequoia National Forest

**Map 11.5, page 577**

It's kind of like the old shell game, trying to pick the best of the campgrounds along the North Fork of the Kern River. This one is seven miles north of Isabella Lake. The elevation is 2,800 feet. (For information on rafting on the Kern River, see the Fairview listing in this chapter.)

**Campsites, facilities:** There are 24 sites for tents or RVs up to 30 feet (no hookups) and four walk-in tent sites for up to 10 people per site. Picnic tables and fire grills are provided. Drinking water and vault toilets are available. Supplies and a coin laundry are available in Kernville. Some facilities are wheelchair-accessible. Leashed pets are permitted. No glass of any kind is allowed in the campground.

**Reservations, fees:** Reservations are accepted at 877/444-6777 ($10 reservation fee) or www. recreation.gov ($9 reservation fee). Sites are $25-108 per night, plus $7 per night for each additional vehicle. Camping fees are higher on holiday weekends. Open May through August.

**Directions:** From Bakersfield, drive east on Highway 178 for about 40 miles to the town of Lake Isabella and Highway 155/Burlando Way. Turn left (north) and drive 10 miles to Kernville and the Kern River Highway/Sierra Way. Turn left on the Kern River Highway and drive 6.5 miles to the campground.

**Contact:** Sequoia National Forest, Kern River Ranger District, Kernville Office, 760/376-3781, www.fs.usda.gov/sequoia; California Land Management, 559/335-2232.

## 145 CAMP THREE

### Scenic rating: 9

on the North Fork of the Kern River in Sequoia National Forest

**Map 11.5, page 577**

This is the second in a series of camps along the North Fork Kern River north of Isabella Lake (in this case, five miles north of the lake). If you don't like this spot, Hospital Flat is just two miles upriver and Headquarters is just one mile downriver. The camp elevation is 2,800 feet.

**Campsites, facilities:** There are 50 sites for tents or RVs up to 30 feet (no hookups) and two group sites for up to 20 people. Picnic tables and fire grills are provided. Drinking water and vault toilets are available. A store and coin laundry are available in Kernville. Some facilities are wheelchair-accessible. Leashed pets are permitted. No glass of any kind is allowed in the campground.

**Reservations, fees:** Reservations are accepted for individual sites and required for the group sites at 877/444-6777 ($10 reservation fee) or www.recreation.gov ($9 reservation fee). Sites are $25-27 per night, plus $7 per night for each additional vehicle, and it's $105 per night for the group sites. Camping fees are higher on holiday weekends. Open May through August.

**Directions:** From Bakersfield, drive east on Highway 178 for about 40 miles to the town of Lake Isabella and Highway 155/Burlando Way. Turn left (north) and drive 10 miles to Kernville and the Kern River Highway/Sierra Way. Turn left on the Kern River Highway and drive five miles to the campground.

**Contact:** Sequoia National Forest, Kern River Ranger District, Kernville Office, 760/376-3781, www.fs.usda.gov/sequoia.

## 146 HEADQUARTERS

### Scenic rating: 8

on the North Fork of the Kern River in Sequoia National Forest

**Map 11.5, page 577**

As you head north from Isabella Lake on Sierra Way, this is the first in a series of Forest Service campgrounds from which to take your pick, all set along the North Fork of the Kern River. The North Fork Kern is best known for offering prime white water for rafting and kayaking. The elevation is 2,800 feet.

**Campsites, facilities:** There are 21 sites for RVs up to 27 feet (no hookups), two for tents or RVs, and 12 sites for tents only. Picnic tables and fire grills are provided. Drinking water and vault toilets are available. Some facilities are wheelchair-accessible. Supplies and a coin laundry are available in Kernville. No glass of any kind is allowed in the campground. Leashed pets are permitted.

**Reservations, fees:** Reservations are accepted at 877/444-6777 ($10 reservation fee) or www.recreation.gov ($9 reservation fee). Sites are $25-79 per night, yurts are $75 per night, plus $7 per night for each additional vehicle. Camping fees are higher on holiday weekends. Open year-round.

**Directions:** From Bakersfield, drive east on Highway 178 for about 40 miles to the town of Lake Isabella and Highway 155/Burlando Way. Turn left (north) and drive 10 miles to Kernville and the Kern River Highway/Sierra Way. Turn left on the Kern River Highway and drive three miles to the campground.

**Contact:** Sequoia National Forest, Kern River Ranger District, Kernville Office, 760/376-3781, www.fs.usda.gov/sequoia.

## 147 CEDAR CREEK

### Scenic rating: 7

in Sequoia National Forest

**Map 11.5, page 577**

This is a little-known, primitive Forest Service camp set at 4,800 feet elevation on the southwest flank of Sequoia National Forest, right along little Cedar Creek, with easy access off Highway 155. Greenhorn Mountain Park and Alder Creek provide nearby alternatives.

**Campsites, facilities:** There are 11 sites for tents only. Picnic tables and fire grills are provided. Vault toilets are available. There is no drinking water. Garbage must be packed out. Leashed pets are permitted.

**Reservations, fees:** Reservations are not accepted. There is no fee for camping. Open May through October.

**Directions:** Drive on Highway 99 to Delano and the exit for Highway 155. Take that exit and drive east on Highway 155 for 41 miles to Glennville. Continue east for nine miles to the campground.

**Contact:** Sequoia National Forest, Kern River Ranger District, Lake Isabella Office, 760/379-5646, www.fs.usda.gov/sequoia.

## 148 GREENHORN MOUNTAIN PARK

### Scenic rating: 7

near Shirley Meadows

**Map 11.5, page 577**

This county campground is near the Shirley Meadows Ski Area, a small ski park open on weekends in winter when there is sufficient snow. Greenhorn Mountain Park covers 160 acres at 6,000 feet elevation. The region is filled with a network of Forest Service roads, detailed on a map of Sequoia National Forest. Isabella Lake is a 15-minute drive to the east. The Greenhorn Summit Amphitheater, set among cedars, pines, and black oaks, is a short walk from Greenhorn Mountain Park Campground.

**Campsites, facilities:** There are 70 sites for tents or RVs up to 24 feet (no hookups) and 17 cabins available as a group rental. Picnic tables and fire pits or fire rings are provided. Check for current fire restrictions. Drinking water, restrooms with flush toilets and showers, and a dump site are available. Leashed pets are permitted.

**Reservations, fees:** Reservations are accepted for groups of at least 40 people. Sites are $18 per night, plus $10 per night for each additional vehicle and $4 per night per pet (limit two). Fees are lower mid-October to mid-March. Open spring through fall, weather permitting.

**Directions:** From Bakersfield, drive east on Highway 178 for about 40 miles to the town of Lake Isabella and Highway 155/Burlando Way. Turn left (north) and drive six miles to Wofford Heights. Turn left (west) on Highway 155 and drive 10 miles to the park on the left.

**Contact:** Kern County Parks, 661/868-7000, www.co.kern.ca.us/parks.

## 149 EVANS FLAT

### Scenic rating: 4

in Sequoia National Forest

**Map 11.5, page 577**

Evans Flat is an obscure campground in the southwest region of Sequoia National Forest, about 10 miles west of Isabella Lake, with no other camps in the vicinity. You have to earn this one, but if you want solitude, Evans Flat can provide it. It is set at 6,100 feet elevation, with Woodward Peak a half mile to the east. A natural spring is east of camp within walking distance.

**Campsites, facilities:** There are 20 sites for tents or RVs up to 20 feet (no hookups). Fire grills and picnic tables are provided. A vault toilet is available. No drinking water is available. Garbage must be packed out. Leashed pets are permitted.

**Reservations, fees:** Reservations are not accepted. There is no fee for camping. Open May through October.

**Directions:** From Bakersfield, drive east on Highway 178 for about 40 miles to the town of Lake Isabella and Highway 155. Turn left (north) and drive six miles to Wofford Heights. Turn left (west) on Highway 155 and drive seven miles to Rancheria Road. Turn left and drive 8.3 miles (first paved, then dirt) to the campground.

**Contact:** Sequoia National Forest, Kern River Ranger District, Lake Isabella office, 760/379-5646, www.fs.usda.gov/sequoia.

# 150 RIVERNOOK CAMPGROUND

🏊 ⛵ 🛶 🚣 🐕 ♿ 🚐 ⛺

**Scenic rating: 7**

on the North Fork of the Kern River

**Map 11.5, page 577**

This is a large, privately operated park near Isabella Lake a few miles from the head of the lake. Boat rentals are available at one of the nearby marinas. An optional side trip is to visit Keysville, the first town to become established on the Kern River during the gold rush days. The elevation is 2,665 feet.

**Campsites, facilities:** There are 30 pull-through sites with full hookups (30 and 50 amps) for RVs, 41 sites with partial hookups for RVs, and 59 sites for tents. Picnic tables, fire rings, and drinking water are provided. Restrooms with flush toilets and showers, three dump stations, and cable TV are available. Some facilities are wheelchair-accessible. Leashed pets are permitted.

**Reservations, fees:** Reservations are recommended. RV sites are $40-45 per night, tent sites are $35 per night, plus $5 per person per night for more than two people. Some credit cards are accepted. Open year-round.

**Directions:** From Bakersfield, drive east on Highway 178 for about 40 miles to the town of

Lake Isabella and Highway 155/Burlando Way. Turn left (north) and drive 10 miles to Kernville and the Kern River Highway/Sierra Way. Turn left on Sierra Way and drive 0.5 mile to the park entrance (14001 Sierra Way).

**Contact:** Rivernook Campground, 760/376-2705, www.rivernook.co.

# 151 LIVE OAK NORTH AND SOUTH

🏊 ⛵ 🛶 🐕 🚐 ⛺

**Scenic rating: 8**

on Isabella Lake

**Map 11.5, page 577**

This is an overflow campground in use only when other surrounding campgrounds are full. Live Oak is on the west side of the road, while Tillie Creek is on the eastern, lake side of the road. (Note that "North" and "South" are not displayed on the campground signs.)

**Campsites, facilities:** There are 59 sites for tents or RVs up to 30 feet (no hookups) at Live Oak North. There is one group site for up to 150 people at Live Oak. Picnic tables and fire grills are provided. Drinking water and restrooms with flush toilets are available. Supplies are available in nearby Wofford Heights. Leashed pets are permitted. No glass of any kind is allowed in the campground.

**Reservations, fees:** Reservations are not accepted. Sites are $24 per night, plus $7 per night for each additional vehicle, and it's $350 per night for the group site. Open May through September.

**Directions:** From Bakersfield, drive east on Highway 178 for about 40 miles to the town of Lake Isabella and Highway 155. Turn left (north) and drive six miles to the campground entrance road on the left (0.5 mile before reaching Wofford Heights).

**Contact:** Sequoia National Forest, Kern River Ranger District, Lake Isabella Office, 760/379-5646, www.fs.usda.gov/sequoia.

## 152 TILLIE CREEK

**Scenic rating: 9**

on Isabella Lake

**Map 11.5, page 577**

This is one of two camps (the other is Live Oak) near where Tillie Creek enters Isabella Lake, on the northwest shore of the lake near the town of Wofford Heights. Isabella Lake is a large lake, and with it comes a dynamic array of campgrounds, marinas, and facilities. It is set at 2,650 feet elevation in the foothills east of Bakersfield, fed by the Kern River, and dominated by water sports of all kinds.

**Campsites, facilities:** There are 155 sites for tents or RVs up to 45 feet and four group sites for tents or RVs up to 45 feet that can accommodate 80-150 people each (no hookups). Picnic tables and fire grills are provided. Drinking water and restrooms with showers and flush toilets are available. Dump station, playground, amphitheater, and a fish-cleaning station are nearby. Supplies are nearby in Wofford Heights. Some facilities are wheelchair-accessible. Leashed pets are permitted. No glass of any kind is allowed in the campground.

**Reservations, fees:** Reservations are accepted for individual sites and required for group sites at 877/444-6777 ($10 reservation fee) or www.recreation.gov ($9 reservation fee). Sites are $24 per night, plus $7 per night for each additional vehicle, and it's $210-525 per night for group sites. Open year-round.

**Directions:** From Bakersfield, drive east on Highway 178 for about 40 miles to the town of Lake Isabella and Highway 155. Turn left (north) and drive five miles to the campground (0.5 mile before reaching Wofford Heights).

**Contact:** Sequoia National Forest, Kern River Ranger District, Lake Isabella Office, 760/379-5646, www.fs.usda.gov/sequoia.

## 153 CAMP 9

**Scenic rating: 8**

on Isabella Lake

**Map 11.5, page 577**

This campground is primitive and sparsely covered, but it has several bonus features. It is along the northeast shore of Isabella Lake, known for good boating, waterskiing in the summer, and fishing in the spring. Other options include great rafting and kayaking waters along the North Fork of the Kern River (north of the lake), a good bird-watching area at the South Fork Wildlife Area (along the east side of the lake), and an off-highway-motorcycle park across the road from this campground. The elevation is 2,650 feet.

**Campsites, facilities:** There are 109 primitive sites for tents or RVs of any length (no hookups), and 11 group sites can accommodate 20-35 people each. Picnic tables and fire rings are provided. Drinking water, flush and vault toilets, dump station, boat launch, and fish-cleaning station are available. Supplies and a coin laundry are nearby in Kernville. Some facilities are wheelchair-accessible. Leashed pets are permitted. No glass of any kind is allowed in the campground.

**Reservations, fees:** Reservations are required for the group site at 877/444-6777 ($10 reservation fee) or www.recreation.gov ($9 reservation fee). Sites are $17 per night, plus $5 per night for each additional vehicle, and it's $90-160 per night for a group site. Open year-round.

**Directions:** From Bakersfield, drive east on Highway 178 for about 40 miles to the town of Lake Isabella and Highway 155. Turn right (south) and drive six miles to the campground entrance on the right (on the northeast shore of Isabella Lake). The campground entrance is just south of the small airport at Lake Isabella.

**Contact:** Sequoia National Forest, Kern River Ranger District, Lake Isabella Office, 760/379-5646, www.fs.usda.gov/sequoia.

# 154 HUNGRY GULCH

**Scenic rating: 9**

near Isabella Lake in Sequoia National Forest

**Map 11.5, page 577**

Hungry Gulch is on the western side of Isabella Lake but across the road from the shore. Nearby Boulder Gulch camp, directly across the road, is an alternative. There are no boat ramps in the immediate area. (For details about Isabella Lake, see the Pioneer Point listing in this chapter.)

**Campsites, facilities:** There are 74 sites for tents or RVs up to 30 feet (no hookups). Picnic tables and fire grills are provided. Drinking water, restrooms with flush toilets, and a fish-cleaning station are available. A playground is nearby. Supplies and a coin laundry are available in Lake Isabella. Leashed pets are permitted. No glass of any kind is allowed in the campground.

**Reservations, fees:** Reservations are accepted at 877/444-6777 ($10 reservation fee) or www.recreation.gov ($9 reservation fee). Sites are $24 per night, plus $7 per night for each additional vehicle. Open April through September.

**Directions:** From Bakersfield, drive east on Highway 178 for about 40 miles to the town of Lake Isabella and Highway 155. Turn left (north) and drive four miles on Highway 155 to the campground.

**Contact:** Sequoia National Forest, Kern River Ranger District, Lake Isabella Office, 760/379-5646, www.fs.usda.gov/sequoia.

# 155 BOULDER GULCH

**Scenic rating: 8**

on Isabella Lake

**Map 11.5, page 577**

Boulder Gulch lies fairly near the western shore of Isabella Lake, across the road from Hungry Gulch. Take your pick. Isabella is one of the biggest lakes in Southern California and a prime destination point for Bakersfield area residents. Fishing for trout and bass is best in the spring. The lake is stocked with trout in winter, and other species are bluegill, catfish, and crappie. By the dog days of summer, when people are bow-wowin' at the heat, water-skiers take over, along with folks just looking to cool off. Like a lot of lakes in the valley, Isabella is subject to drawdowns. The elevation is 2,650 feet. (For more information, see the Pioneer Point listing in this chapter.)

**Campsites, facilities:** There are 58 sites for tents or RVs up to 45 feet (no hookups). Picnic tables and fire grills are provided. Restrooms with flush toilets, drinking water, playground, marina, and fish-cleaning station are available. Supplies and a coin laundry are available in the town of Lake Isabella. Leashed pets are permitted. No glass of any kind is allowed in the campground.

**Reservations, fees:** Reservations are accepted at 877/444-6777 ($10 reservation fee) or www.recreation.gov ($9 reservation fee). Sites are $24 per night, plus $7 per night for each additional vehicle. Open April through September.

**Directions:** From Bakersfield, drive east on Highway 178 for about 40 miles to the town of Lake Isabella and Highway 155. Turn left (north) and drive four miles to the campground entrance.

**Contact:** Sequoia National Forest, Kern River Ranger District, Lake Isabella Office, 760/379-5646, www.fs.usda.gov/sequoia.

# 156 FRENCH GULCH GROUP CAMP

**Scenic rating: 9**

on Isabella Lake

**Map 11.5, page 577**

This is a large group camp on Isabella Lake at the southwest end of the lake about two miles north of Pioneer Point and the spillway. The elevation is 2,700 feet. (For recreation information, see the Pioneer Point listing in this chapter.)

**Campsites, facilities:** One large group site for tents or RVs of any length (no hookups) can accommodate up to 100 people. Picnic tables and fire grills are provided. Drinking water and restrooms with flush toilets are available. A store, coin laundry, and propane gas are nearby. Leashed pets are permitted. No glass of any kind is allowed in the campground.

**Reservations, fees:** Reservations are required at 877/444-6777 ($10 reservation fee) or www.recreation.gov ($9 reservation fee). The camp is $350 per night. Open year-round.

**Directions:** From Bakersfield, drive east on Highway 178 for about 40 miles to the town of Lake Isabella and Highway 155. Turn left (north) and drive three miles to the campground entrance on the right.

**Contact:** Sequoia National Forest, Kern River Ranger District, Lake Isabella Office, 760/379-5646, www.fs.usda.gov/sequoia.

## 157 PIONEER POINT

### Scenic rating: 9

on Isabella Lake in Sequoia National Forest

**Map 11.5, page 577**

Isabella Lake is one of the largest freshwater lakes in Southern California, and with it comes a dynamic array of campgrounds, marinas, and facilities. It is at 2,650 feet elevation in the foothills east of Bakersfield, fed by the Kern River and dominated by boating sports of all kinds. This camp is at the lake's southwest corner, between the spillway and the main dam, with a boat ramp available a mile east. Isabella is a first-class lake for waterskiing, but in the spring and early summer sailboarding is also excellent, best just east of the Auxiliary Dam. Boat rentals of all kinds are available at several marinas.

**Campsites, facilities:** There are 73 sites for tents or RVs up to 30 feet (no hookups). Picnic tables and fire grills are provided. Drinking water and restrooms with coin showers and flush toilets are available. A playground and fish-cleaning station are nearby. A boat ramp is three miles from camp. Supplies and a coin laundry are available in the town of Lake Isabella. Leashed pets are permitted. No glass of any kind is allowed in the campground.

**Reservations, fees:** Reservations are accepted at 877/444-6777 ($10 reservation fee) or www.recreation.gov ($9 reservation fee). Sites are $24 per night, plus $7 per night for each additional vehicle. Open year-round.

**Directions:** From Bakersfield, drive east on Highway 178 for about 40 miles to the town of Lake Isabella and Highway 155. Turn left (north) and drive 2.5 miles north on Highway 155 to the campground.

**Contact:** Sequoia National Forest, Kern River Ranger District, Lake Isabella Office, 760/379-5646, www.fs.usda.gov/sequoia.

## 158 KEYESVILLE SPECIAL MANAGEMENT AREA

### Scenic rating: 5

on the Kern River near Lake Isabella

**Map 11.5, page 577**

The Keyesville area originally was developed in the 1850s during the California gold rush; gold was first discovered in this area in 1851. Very few historical buildings remain, however, since much of the old town of Keyesville was composed of tents and small shacks along trails. Today, this camp is used primarily by OHV enthusiasts and miners and is an alternative to the more crowded and developed campgrounds around Lake Isabella. The Kern River runs through this 7,133-acre BLM area, and campsites are available near the river; dispersed camping is also allowed. The Sequoia National Forest borders this area to the north and west. Keyesville has multi-use trails and specific areas for recreational mining and OHV use. Hunting is allowed in season. Fishing for trout or bass is another option. Swimming is not recommended because of the swift water, undercurrents, and obstacles. A free permit is required for white-water rafting and is available at the forest service office in Lake Isabella (call 760/379-5646). Check for fire requirements before camping in this area.

**Campsites, facilities:** There is dispersed camping for tents or RVs up to 30 feet (no hookups). Picnic tables and fire rings are provided. Vault toilets are available. There is no drinking water. Garbage must be packed out. Leashed pets are permitted.

**Reservations, fees:** Reservations are not accepted. There is no fee for camping. A 14-day stay limit per year is enforced. Open year-round.

**Directions:** From Bakersfield, drive east on Highway 178 for approximately 40 miles to the town of Lake Isabella and Highway 155. Turn left (north) on Highway 155 and drive one mile to Keyesville Road. Turn left and drive 0.5 mile to the Special Management Area entrance.

**Contact:** Bureau of Land Management, Bakersfield Field Office, 661/391-6000, www.blm.gov/ca.

## 159 AUXILIARY DAM

### Scenic rating: 8

on Isabella Lake

**Map 11.5, page 577**

This primitive camp was designed to be an overflow area if other camps at Isabella Lake are packed. It's the only camp directly on the shore of the lake, and many people like it. In addition, a boat ramp is just a mile east for good lake access, and the sailboarding prospects adjacent to the campground are the best of the entire lake. The winds come up and sail right over the dam, creating a steady breeze in the afternoon that is not gusty. The elevation is 2,650 feet.

**Campsites, facilities:** There are primitive, undesignated sites for tents or RVs of any length (no hookups). Drinking water and restrooms

with flush toilets and showers are available. Supplies and a coin laundry are available in the town of Lake Isabella. Some facilities are wheelchair-accessible. Leashed pets are permitted. No glass of any kind is allowed in the campground.

**Reservations, fees:** Reservations are not accepted. Sites are $10 per night per vehicle or $50 for a season pass. Open year-round.

**Directions:** From Bakersfield, drive east on Highway 178 for about 40 miles to the town of Lake Isabella. Continue east on Highway 178 for one mile to the campground entrance.

**Contact:** Sequoia National Forest, Kern River Ranger District, Lake Isabella Office, 760/379-5646, www.fs.usda.gov/sequoia.

## 160 PARADISE COVE

### Scenic rating: 6

on Isabella Lake

**Map 11.5, page 577**

Paradise Cove is on the southeast shore of Isabella Lake at 2,600 feet elevation. A boat ramp is about two miles away to the west, near the South Fork Picnic Area. While the camp is not directly at the lakeshore, it does overlook the broadest expanse of the lake. This part of the lake is relatively undeveloped compared to the areas near Wofford Heights and the dam.

**Campsites, facilities:** There are 46 sites for tents and a primitive area for up to 80 RVs of any length (no hookups). Picnic tables and fire grills are provided in standard sites but not in the primitive area. Drinking water, restrooms with flush toilets and coin showers, dump station, and fish-cleaning station are available. A camp host is on-site. Some facilities are wheelchair-accessible. Supplies, a dump station, and a coin laundry are available in Mountain Mesa. Leashed pets are permitted. No glass of any kind is allowed in the campground.

**Reservations, fees:** Reservations are accepted at 877/444-6777 ($10 reservation fee) or www.recreation.gov ($9 reservation fee). Sites are $24 per night, plus $7 per night for each additional vehicle. Open year-round.

**Directions:** From Bakersfield, drive east on Highway 178 for about 40 miles to the town of Lake Isabella. Continue east on Highway 178 for six miles to the campground entrance.

**Contact:** Sequoia National Forest, Kern River Ranger District, Lake Isabella Office, 760/379-5646, www.fs.usda.gov/sequoia.

## 161 KOA LAKE ISABELLA/ KERN RIVER

### Scenic rating: 4

on Isabella Lake

**Map 11.5, page 577**

This KOA camp provides a good, clean option to the Forest Service camps on the southern end of Isabella Lake, Southern California's largest lake. It is set in South Fork Valley (elevation 2,600 feet), east of the lake off Highway 178. The nearest boat ramp is at South Fork Picnic Area (about a five-minute drive to the west), where there is a good view of the lake.

**Campsites, facilities:** There are 70 sites with full or partial hookups (30 amps) for tents or RVs up to 40 feet; some sites are pull-through. Picnic tables and fire rings are provided. Restrooms with flush toilets and showers, drinking water, playground, seasonal swimming pool, coin laundry, recreation room, pub, convenience store, dump station, firewood, and propane gas are available. Leashed pets are permitted with some restrictions.

**Reservations, fees:** Reservations are accepted at 800/562-2085. RV sites are $42-48 per night, tent sites are $29-37 per night, plus $5 per person per night for more than two people. Some credit cards are accepted. Open year-round.

**Directions:** From Bakersfield, drive east on Highway 178 for about 40 miles to the town of Lake Isabella. Continue east on Highway 178 for 10 miles to the campground entrance on the left (well signed).

**Contact:** KOA Lake Isabella/Kern River, 760/378-2001, www.koa.com.

## 162 SANDY FLAT

### Scenic rating: 6

on the Kern River in Sequoia National Forest

**Map 11.5, page 577**

This camp is opened as an overflow camp if Hobo is filled. It is about a mile from Hobo. It is a low-use campground, with less shade than Hobo; some sites are shaded—others, well, nope. It is used primarily as a boat launch area for kayakers and rafters. Fishing is fair for catfish, bass, and rainbow trout. The river is stocked with trout in the summer.

**Campsites, facilities:** There are 33 sites for tents or RVs up to 24 feet (no hookups), including six walk-in sites. Fire rings and picnic tables are provided. Vault toilets and drinking water are available. Some facilities are wheelchair-accessible. Leashed pets are permitted. No glass of any kind is allowed in the campground.

**Reservations, fees:** Reservations are accepted at 877/444-6777 ($10 reservation fee) or www.recreation.gov ($9 reservation fee). Sites are $23-25 per night, plus $7 per night for each additional vehicle. Open year-round.

**Directions:** From Bakersfield, drive east on Highway 178 for 35 miles to Borel Road (five miles from Lake Isabella). Turn right (south) at Borel Road and drive 0.3 mile to Old Kern Canyon Road. Turn right and drive one mile to the campground on your right.

**Contact:** Sequoia National Forest, Kern River Ranger District, Lake Isabella Office, 760/379-5646, www.fs.usda.gov/sequoia.

## 163 HOBO

**Scenic rating: 7**

on the Kern River in Sequoia National Forest

**Map 11.5, page 577**                    **BEST (**

The secret is out about Hobo: It is adjacent to a mineral hot springs, that is, an open-air springs, with room for about 10 people at once. The camp is also along the lower Kern River, about 10 miles downstream of the dam at Isabella Lake. Rafters sometimes use this camp as a put-in spot for an 18-mile run to the take-out at Democrat Picnic Area, a challenging Class IV run. The elevation is 2,300 feet.

**Campsites, facilities:** There are 24 sites for tents or RVs up to 22 feet (no hookups). Fire grills and picnic tables are provided. Drinking water and vault toilets are available. Some facilities are wheelchair-accessible. Leashed pets are permitted. No glass of any kind is allowed in the campground.

**Reservations, fees:** Reservations are not accepted. Sites are $23-25 per night, plus $7 per night for each additional vehicle. Open April through September.

**Directions:** From Bakersfield, drive east on Highway 178 for 35 miles to Borel Road (five miles from Lake Isabella). Turn right (south) at Borel Road and drive 0.3 mile to Old Kern Road. Turn right and drive two miles to the campground on your right.

**Contact:** Sequoia National Forest, Kern River Ranger District, Lake Isabella Office, 760/379-5646, www.fs.usda.gov/sequoia.

## 164 BRECKENRIDGE

**Scenic rating: 7**

in Sequoia National Forest

**Map 11.5, page 577**

This is a popular spot for people to visit with sport utility vehicles. It is a tiny, primitive camp set at 6,600 feet elevation near Breckenridge Mountain (there's a good lookout) in a little-traveled southwest sector of the Sequoia National Forest. From camp, it's a two-mile drive south up to the lookout, with sweeping views afforded in all directions. There are no other camps in the immediate area.

**Campsites, facilities:** There are eight tent sites. Picnic tables and fire grills are provided. Vault toilets are available. No drinking water is available. Garbage must be packed out. Leashed pets are permitted.

**Reservations, fees:** Reservations are not accepted. There is no fee for camping. Open May through September.

**Directions:** From Bakersfield, drive east on Highway 178 for about 40 miles to the town of Lake Isabella and Lake Isabella Boulevard. Turn right (south) on Lake Isabella Boulevard and drive two miles to a Y intersection with Kern River Canyon Road and Caliente Bodfish Road. Bear left on Caliente Bodfish Road and drive nine miles to the town of Havilah. Continue on Caliente Bodfish Road for two miles to Forest Road 28S06. Turn right and drive about 10 miles to the campground.

**Contact:** Sequoia National Forest, Kern River Ranger District, Lake Isabella Office, 760/379-5646, www.fs.usda.gov/sequoia.

## 165 KERN RIVER CAMPGROUND

**Scenic rating: 6**

at Lake Ming

**Map 11.5, page 577**

The campground is at Lake Ming, a small but exciting place. The lake covers just 205 surface acres, and with the weather so hot, the hot jet boats can make it a wild affair. It's become a popular spot for southern valley residents, only a 15-minute drive from Bakersfield. It is so popular for water sports that every year, beginning in March, the lake is closed to the public one weekend per month for private boat races and waterskiing competitions. The lake is restricted to sailing and sailboarding on the second weekend of every month and on Tuesday and Thursday afternoons. All other boating, including waterskiing, is permitted on the remaining days. All boats are required to have a permit; boaters may buy one at the park. Swimming is not allowed because there is a parasite in the water that has been known to cause swimmer's itch. Yikes. The lake is stocked with rainbow trout in the winter months, and they join a sprinkling of bluegill, catfish, crappie, and bass. The elevation is 450 feet. Maximum stay is 10 days.

**Campsites, facilities:** There are 50 sites for tents or RVs up to 28 feet. Picnic tables and fire rings are provided. Restrooms with flush toilets and coin showers, drinking water, dump station, playground, concession stand, picnic area, and boat ramp are available. Some facilities are wheelchair-accessible. A store is nearby. Leashed pets are permitted.

**Reservations, fees:** Reservations are not accepted. Sites are $12-24 per night, plus $7-11 per night for a second vehicle, $5 per night for a towed vehicle, and $4 per night per pet. Prices are discounted in winter. Open year-round.

**Directions:** From Bakersfield, drive east on Highway 178 for 11 miles to Alfred Harrell Highway. Turn left (north) on Alfred Harrell Highway and drive four miles to Lake Ming Road. Turn right on Lake Ming Road and follow the signs to the campground on the right, 0.25 mile west of the lake.

**Contact:** Kern County Parks and Recreation Department, 661/868-7000, www.co.kern.ca.us/parks.

# 166 TROY MEADOWS
🏞️🐕♿🚐⛺

### Scenic rating: 7
on Fish Creek in Sequoia National Forest

**Map 11.5, page 577**

Obscure? Yes, but what the heck, it gives you an idea of what is possible out in the boondocks. The camp is at 7,800 feet elevation right along Fish Creek. Black Rock Ranger Station is two miles northwest. You are advised to stop there before any backcountry trips. Note that off-highway vehicles (OHVs) are allowed in this area. Also note that Jackass National Recreation Trail is a short drive to the east; it runs north aside Jackass Creek to its headwaters just below Jackass Peak (9,245 feet).

**Campsites, facilities:** There are 70 sites for tents or RVs up to 20 feet (no hookups). Picnic tables and fire grills are provided. Drinking water and vault toilets are available. Garbage must be packed out. Some facilities are wheelchair-accessible. Leashed pets are permitted.

**Reservations, fees:** Reservations are not accepted. Sites are $17 per night, plus $7 per night per each additional vehicle. Open June through October, weather permitting.

**Directions:** Drive on U.S. 395 to Ninemile Canyon Road (four miles north of the town of Pearsonville, 48 miles south of Lone Pine). Turn west on Ninemile Canyon Road and drive 31 miles (the road becomes Sherman Pass Road) to the campground.

**Contact:** Sequoia National Forest, Kern River Ranger District, Kernville Office, 760/376-3781, www.fs.usda.gov/sequoia.

# 167 FISH CREEK
🏞️🐕🚐⛺

### Scenic rating: 8
in Sequoia National Forest

**Map 11.5, page 577**

This is a pretty spot at the confluence of Fish Creek and Jackass Creek. The elevation is 7,500 feet. The nearby trails are used by off-highway vehicles, which can make this a noisy campground during the day.

**Campsites, facilities:** There are 37 sites for tents or RVs up to 27 feet (no hookups). Picnic tables and fire grills are provided. Drinking water and vault toilets are available. Garbage must be packed out. Leashed pets are permitted.

**Reservations, fees:** Reservations are not accepted. Sites are $17 per night, plus $5 per night per each additional vehicle. Open June through October, weather permitting.

**Directions:** Take U.S. 395 to Ninemile Canyon Road (four miles north of the town of Pearsonville, 48 miles south of Lone Pine). Turn west on Ninemile Canyon Road and drive 28 miles (the road becomes Sherman Pass Road) to the campground.

**Contact:** Sequoia National Forest, Kern River Ranger District, Kernville Office, 760/376-3781, www.fs.usda.gov/sequoia.

## 168 KENNEDY MEADOWS

### Scenic rating: 8
on the South Fork of the Kern River in Sequoia National Forest

**Map 11.5, page 577**

This is a pretty Forest Service campground set amid piñon pine and sage country, with the Pacific Crest Trail running by the camp. That makes it a great trailhead camp, as well as a refreshing stopover for PCT through-hikers. A highlight is the nearby South Fork Kern River, which provides fishing for rainbow trout. The camp receives moderate use and is a lifesaver for PCT through-hikers.

**Campsites, facilities:** There are 37 sites for tents or RVs up to 30 feet (no hookups) and three sites for RVs of any length. Picnic tables and fire rings are provided. Drinking water (seasonal) and vault toilets are available. Garbage must be packed out. Leashed pets are permitted.

**Reservations, fees:** Reservations are not accepted. Sites are $17 per night, plus $5 per night per each additional vehicle. Open year-round, weather permitting.

**Directions:** Drive on U.S. 395 to Ninemile Canyon Road (four miles north of the town of Pearsonville, 48 miles south of Lone Pine). Turn west on Ninemile Canyon Road and drive

21 miles to a small store. Bear right at the store (still Ninemile Canyon Road) and continue for three miles to the campground.

**Contact:** Sequoia National Forest, Kern River Ranger District, Kernville Office, 760/376-3781, www.fs.usda.gov/sequoia.

## 169 LONG VALLEY

### Scenic rating: 5
near the Dome Land Wilderness

**Map 11.5, page 577**

This one is way out there. It's at road's end in Long Valley, a mile from the border of the Dome Land Wilderness to the east, and the camp is used primarily as a jumping-off spot for hikers. A trail from camp leads 2.5 miles west, climbing along a small stream and reaching the South Fork of the Kern River, in rugged and remote country. The elevation is 5,200 feet.

**Campsites, facilities:** There are 13 tent sites. Picnic tables and fire grills are provided. Vault toilets are available. No drinking water is available. Garbage must be packed out. Leashed pets are permitted.

**Reservations, fees:** Reservations are not accepted. There is no fee for camping, but donations are encouraged. Open year-round.

**Directions:** Drive on U.S. 395 to Ninemile Canyon Road (four miles north of the town of Pearsonville, 48 miles south of Lone Pine). Turn west on Ninemile Canyon Road and drive 11 miles to the BLM Work Station and Cane Brake Road. Turn left on Cane Brake Road (the dirt road opposite the BLM station) and drive six miles to Long Valley Road. Turn right and drive eight miles to the campground entrance road on the left. Turn left and drive one mile to the campground.

**Contact:** Bureau of Land Management, Bakersfield Field Office, 661/391-6000, www.blm.gov/ca.

## 170 CHIMNEY CREEK

### Scenic rating: 5

on the Pacific Crest Trail

**Map 11.5, page 577**

This BLM camp is at 5,900 feet elevation along the headwaters of Chimney Creek, on the southern flank of Chimney Peak (7,990 feet) two miles to the north. This is a trailhead camp for the Pacific Crest Trail, one of its relatively obscure sections. The PCT heads north from camp and in 10 miles skirts the eastern border of Dome Land Wilderness.

**Campsites, facilities:** There are 32 sites for tents or RVs up to 25 feet (no hookups). Picnic tables and fire grills are provided. Vault toilets are available. Drinking water is available seasonally at site 36 in the campground (at the very end of the campground road). Garbage must be packed out. Horses and leashed pets are permitted.

**Reservations, fees:** Reservations are not accepted; however, call to confirm access before planning a trip. There is no fee for camping, but donations are encouraged. Open year-round.

**Directions:** Drive on U.S. 395 to Ninemile Canyon Road (four miles north of the town of Pearsonville, 48 miles south of Lone Pine). Turn west on Ninemile Canyon Road and drive 11 miles to the BLM Work Station and Cane Brake Road. Turn left on Cane Brake Road (the dirt road opposite the BLM station) and drive three miles to the camp on the left.

**Contact:** Bureau of Land Management, Bakersfield Field Office, 661/391-6000, www.blm.gov/ca.

## 171 WALKER PASS WALK-IN

### Scenic rating: 6

on the Pacific Crest Trail southwest of Death Valley National Park

**Map 11.5, page 577**

Long-distance hikers on the Pacific Crest Trail treat this camp as if they were arriving at Valhalla. That's because it is right on the trail. The camp is at 5,200 feet elevation, southwest of Death Valley National Park. And if you guessed it was named for Joe Walker, the West's greatest trailblazer and one of my heroes, well, right you are. If you arrive by car instead of on the PCT, use this spot as a base camp. Because of its desert remoteness, very few hikers start trips from this location.

**Campsites, facilities:** There are two sites for tents or RVs up to 20 feet (no hookups), with limited parking, and 11 walk-in sites for tents only. Picnic tables and fire rings are provided. No drinking water is available at the campground, but a spring development is 0.1 mile west on Highway 178, in the bottom of the drainage by the 30-mph sign. Pit toilets are available. Hitching racks and corrals are available. Garbage must be packed out. Leashed pets are permitted.

**Reservations, fees:** Reservations are not accepted. There is no fee for camping, but donations are encouraged. A 14-day stay limit is enforced. Open year-round.

**Directions:** From Bakersfield, drive east on Highway 178 for about 40 miles to the town of Lake Isabella. Continue east on Highway 178 to Onyx and continue 14 miles to Walker Pass and the right side of the road (where a sign is posted for the Pacific Crest Trail). Park and walk 0.25 mile to the campground.

**Contact:** Bureau of Land Management, Bakersfield Field Office, 661/391-6000, www.blm.gov/ca.

# SANTA BARBARA AND VICINITY

The Santa Barbara region offers a unique mix of sun-swept beaches that stretch 200 miles and surprise inland coastal forests. Highlights include San Simeon, Hearst Castle, Cambria, Goleta, Cayucos, and the route through it all. Getting a campsite reservation at one of these stunning state beaches can feel like winning the lottery. These sites go fast and are filled every night of vacation season. Yet as popular as the coast is, just inland lie many remote, hidden campsites. Los Padres National Forest spans a matrix of canyons with small streams, mountaintop lookouts, and wilderness trailheads. Lake Nacimiento is one of the top family-friendly lakes for water sports, and it provides sensational fishing. San Antonio Reservoir is a great lake for bass. Cachuma Lake and Lake Casitas near Santa Barbara have produced some of the largest bass ever caught.

# SANTA BARBARA AND VICINITY

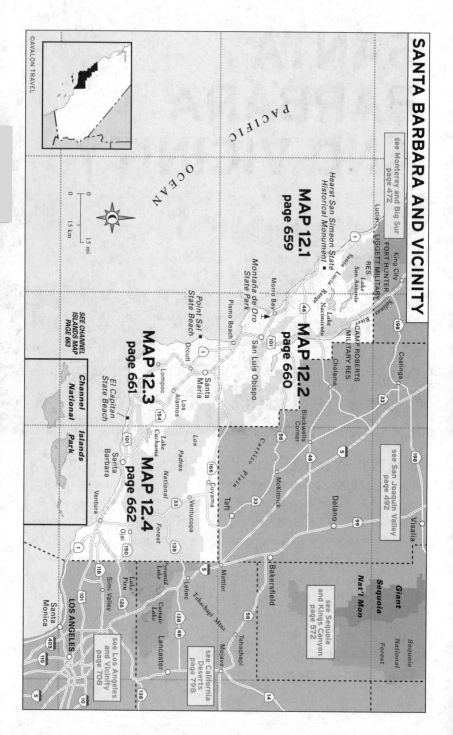

©AVALON TRAVEL

see Monterey and Big Sur
page 472

MAP 12.1
page 659

MAP 12.2
page 660

MAP 12.3
page 661

MAP 12.4
page 662

SEE CHANNEL
ISLANDS MAP
PAGE 663

see San Joaquin Valley
page 492

see Sequoia
and Kings Canyon
page 572

see California
Deserts
page 798

see Los Angeles
and Vicinity
page 708

Channel
Islands
National
Park

PACIFIC
OCEAN

Hearst San Simeon State
Historical Monument

Montaña de Oro
State Park

Point Sal
State Beach

El Capitan
State Beach

Giant
Sequoia
Nat'l Mon

Sequoia
National
Forest

Santa Lucia Range

Lake
San Antonio

Lake
Nacimiento

Salinas River

Carrizo Plain

Los
Padres
National
Forest

Tehachapi Mtns

Lucia

FORT HUNTER
LIGGETT MILITARY
RES

CAMP ROBERTS
MILITARY RES

King City

Coalinga

Visalia

Morro Bay

Pismo Beach

San Luis Obispo

Orcut

Santa
Maria

Lompoc

Los
Alamos

Lake
Cachuma

Santa
Barbara

Ventura

Ojai

Cholame

Blackwells
Corner

Cuyama

Ventucopa

Taft

McKittrick

Delano

Bakersfield

Lebec

Castaic
Lake

Lake
Piru

Pyramid
Lake

Simi Valley

Lancaster

Santa
Monica

LOS ANGELES

Mettler

Tehachapi

Mojave

15 mi

15 km

0

0

1

1

1

1

46

101

101

101

101

154

166

33

33

33

58

58

46

5

5

5

99

198

198

138

138

138

138

48

150

126

118

405

110

10

14

# Map 12.1

## Sites 1-3
## Page 664

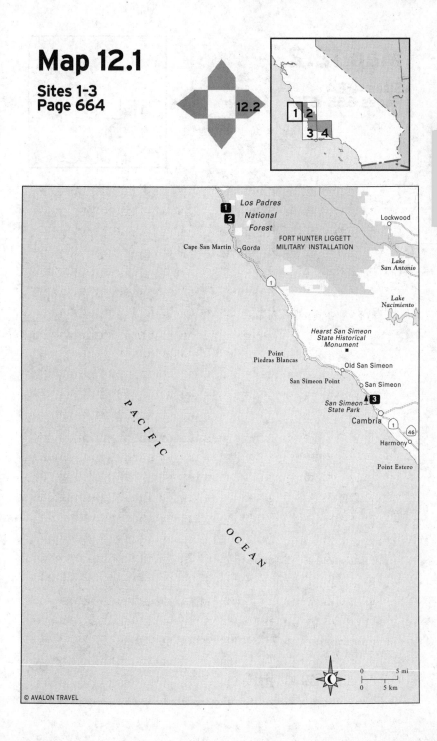

# Map 12.2

## Sites 4-24
## Pages 665-675

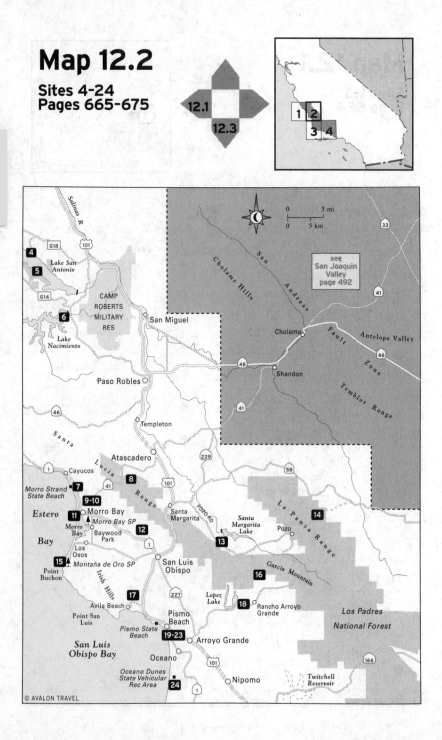

# Map 12.3

**Sites 25-35**
**Pages 676-681**

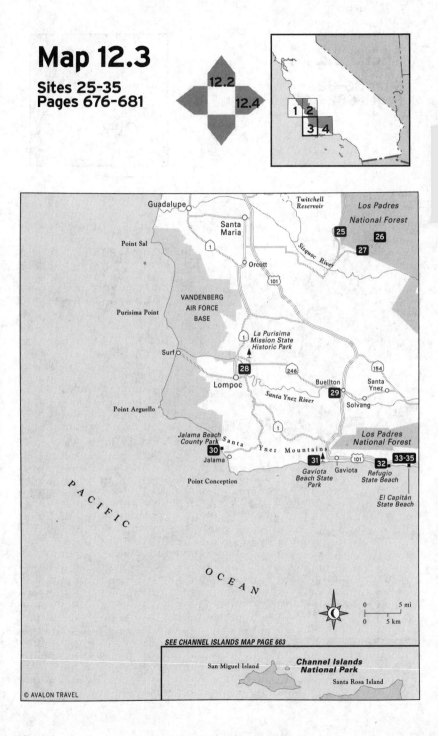

# Map 12.4

### Sites 36-82
### Pages 682-702

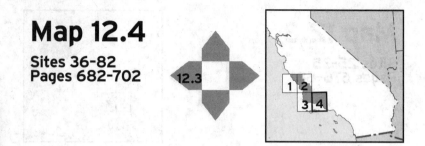

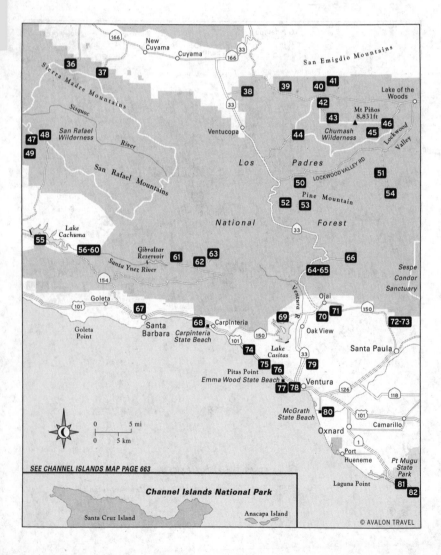

SEE CHANNEL ISLANDS MAP PAGE 663

*Channel Islands National Park*

© AVALON TRAVEL

# CHANNEL ISLANDS   Sites 83-87  Pages 703-705

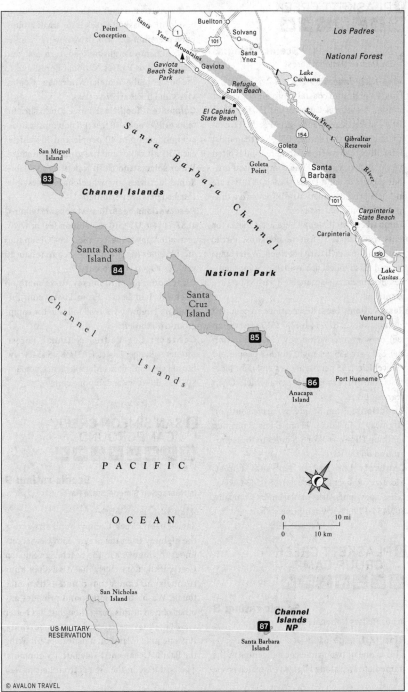

# 1 PLASKETT CREEK

### Scenic rating: 8

in Los Padres National Forest

**Map 12.1, page 659**

This is a premium coastal camp for Highway 1 cruisers, set at an elevation of just 100 feet along little Plaskett Creek above the Pacific Ocean. It is slightly farther south of Big Sur than most are willing to drive from Monterey and is often overlooked as a result. The campground provides access to Sand Dollar Beach. A little café in Lucia provides open-air dining with a dramatic lookout over the coast.

**Campsites, facilities:** There are 42 sites for tents or RVs up to 30 feet (no hookups). Picnic tables and fire grills are provided. Water spigots and flush toilets are available. Some facilities are wheelchair-accessible. Leashed pets are permitted.

**Reservations, fees:** Reservations are required for most sites at 877/444-6777 ($10 reservation fee) or www.recreation.gov ($9 reservation fee). Sites are $35 per night (for 6-8 people and two vehicles), $5 per night per person for bicyclists, and $10 per night per extra vehicle. Open year-round.

**Directions:** From Monterey, drive south on Highway 1 to Lucia. From Lucia, continue south on Highway 1 for 9.5 miles to the campground on the left.

**Contact:** Los Padres National Forest, Monterey Ranger District, 831/385-5434, www.fs.usda.gov/lpnf; Parks Management Company, 805/434-1996, www.campone.com.

# 2 PLASKETT CREEK GROUP CAMP

### Scenic rating: 8

in Los Padres National Forest

**Map 12.1, page 659**

This is one of two prime coastal camps in the immediate area along Highway 1, which is one of the prettiest drives in the West. The camp beside little Plaskett Creek is for small groups. For a premium day trip, drive north five miles to Nacimiento-Ferguson Road, turn east, and drive into Los Padres National Forest and to the border of the Ventana Wilderness. Coastal views and hikes are first class.

**Campsites, facilities:** Three group sites for tents or RVs up to 30 feet (no hookups) can accommodate up to 40 people and 10 vehicles each. Picnic tables and fire grills are provided. Water spigots and flush toilets are available. Some facilities are wheelchair-accessible. Leashed pets are permitted.

**Reservations, fees:** Reservations are required at 877/444-6777 ($10 reservation fee) or www.recreation.gov ($9 reservation fee). Group sites are $150 per night and can accommodate 10 vehicles. Open year-round.

**Directions:** From Monterey, drive south on Highway 1 to Lucia. From Lucia, continue south on Highway 1 for 9.5 miles to the campground on the left.

**Contact:** Los Padres National Forest, Monterey Ranger District, 831/385-5434, www.fs.usda.gov/lpnf; Parks Management Company, 805/434-1996, www.campone.com.

# 3 SAN SIMEON CREEK CAMPGROUND

### Scenic rating: 9

in Hearst San Simeon State Park

**Map 12.1, page 659**

San Simeon Creek Campground sits across the highway from the ocean, with easy access under the highway to the beach. San Simeon Creek, while not exactly the Mississippi, runs through the campground and adds a nice touch. Washburn campground provides another option at this park; though it has better views, the sites are exposed and can be windy. It is one mile inland on a plateau overlooking the Pacific Ocean and Santa Lucia Mountains. The best hike in the area is from Leffingwell

Landing to Moonstone Beach, featuring sweeping views of the coast from ocean bluffs and a good chance to see passing whales. There are three preserves in the park, including a wintering site for monarch butterfly populations, and it has an archaeological site dating from more than 5,800 years ago. In the summer, junior ranger programs and interpretive programs are offered. Hearst Castle is only five miles northeast, making this a natural overnight for visitors planning to take a tour.

**Campsites, facilities:** At San Simeon Creek camp, there are 134 sites for tents or RVs up to 35 feet (no hookups), 10 sites for tents only, and two hike-in/bike-in sites. Picnic tables and fire grills are provided. Drinking water, a dump station, and restrooms with flush toilets and coin showers are available. At Washburn camp, there are 70 sites for tents or RVs up to 31 feet (no hookups). Picnic tables and fire grills are provided. Drinking water, pit and flush toilets, and firewood are available. A grocery store, coin laundry, gas station, restaurants, and propane gas are two miles away in Cambria. Some facilities are wheelchair-accessible. Leashed pets are permitted in the campgrounds only.

**Reservations, fees:** Reservations are accepted at 800/444-7275 or www.reserveamerica.com ($8 reservation fee). Sites are $25 per night at San Simeon Creek, $20 per night at Washburn, plus $8 per night for each additional vehicle, plus $5 per person per night for hike-in/bike-in sites. Open year-round.

**Directions:** From Cambria, drive two miles north on Highway 1 to San Simeon Creek Road. Turn east and drive 0.2 mile to the park entrance on the right.

**Contact:** Hearst San Simeon State Park, 805/927-2035, www.parks.ca.gov; Hearst Castle tour reservations, 800/444-4445.

## 4 NORTH SHORE SAN ANTONIO

**Scenic rating: 7**

on Lake San Antonio

**Map 12.2, page 660**

At time of publication, Lake San Antonio is scheduled to open weekends only August-September 2017. The North Shore campground remains closed. Please call before planning a trip.

When full, Lake San Antonio makes a great year-round destination for adventure. It is a big, warm-water lake, long and narrow, at an elevation of 780 feet in the foothills north of Paso Robles. The camp features four miles of shoreline camping, with the bonus of primitive sites along Pleyto Points. The lake is 16 miles long, covers 5,500 surface acres, and has 60 miles of shoreline and average summer water temperatures in the 70s, making it an ideal place for fun in the sun. It is one of the top lakes in California for bass fishing, best in spring and early summer. It is also good for striped bass, catfish, crappie, sunfish, and bluegill. It provides the best wintering habitat in the region for bald eagles, and eagle-watching tours are available from the south shore of the lake. Of course, the size of the lake, along with hot temperatures all summer, makes waterskiing and water sports absolutely first-class. Note that boat rentals are not available here, but are at South Shore. Equestrian trails are also available.

**Campsites, facilities:** The campground has 200 sites for tents or RVs of any length (no hookups), 24 sites with full or partial hookups (30 amps) for tents or RVs of any length, and up to 1,800 primitive dispersed sites near the shoreline. The Los Robles HorseWorld is open to equestrian camping only. Mobile home rentals are also available. Fire grills and picnic tables are provided. Drinking water may not be available; bring your own to be sure. Restrooms, a dump station, boat ramp, hitching posts and corrals, general store, and volleyball are available. Some facilities are wheelchair-accessible. Leashed pets are permitted.

**Reservations, fees:** Reservations are accepted at 800/444-7275 or www.reserveamerica.com ($8 reservation fee). Sites are $32-45 per night, plus $15 per night for each additional vehicle and $2 per pet per night. Boat launch is $10 per day. Open year-round.

**Directions:** On U.S. 101, drive to the Jolon Road/G14 exit (just north of King City). Take that exit and turn south on Jolon Road and drive 27 miles to Pleyto Road (curvy road). Turn right and drive three miles to the North Shore entrance of the lake. Note: When arriving from the south or east on U.S. 101 near Paso Robles, it is faster to take the G18/Jolon Road exit.

**Contact:** Monterey County Parks, 805/472-2311, www.co.monterey.ca.us/parks.

## 5 SOUTH SHORE SAN ANTONIO
### 🚶 🚴 🏊 🛶 ⚓ 🏕 🦌 👥 🚐 ⛺

### Scenic rating: 7
on Lake San Antonio

**Map 12.2, page 660**

At time of publication, Lake San Antonio is scheduled to open weekends only August-September 2017. The campground remains closed. Please call before planning a trip.

Harris Creek, Redondo Vista, and Lynch are the three campgrounds near each other along the south shore of Lake San Antonio, a 16-mile reservoir that provides good bass fishing in the spring and waterskiing in the summer when full. There are also 26 miles of good biking and hiking trails in the park. A museum and a visitors center are available at the park's administration building. In the winter, the Monterey County Department of Parks offers a unique eagle-watching program, which includes boat tours. (See the North Shore San Antonio listing for more details about the lake.)

**Campsites, facilities:** Redondo Vista has 173 sites for tents or RVs (no hookups) and 86 sites with full hookups (30 amps) for tents or RVs; Lynch has 52 sites for tents and 54 sites with partial hookups for tents or RVs; Harris Creek has 88 sites for tents and 26 sites with partial hookups for tents or RVs. Group camping is available for groups reserving 10 or more sites. Mobile-home rentals are also available. Picnic tables and fire grills are provided. Flush toilets are available. Drinking water may not be available; bring your own to be sure. Restrooms with showers, dump station, marina, boat ramp, boat rentals, boat slips, bait and tackle, playground, recreation room, coin laundry, general store, and fishing licenses are available nearby. Leashed pets are permitted.

**Reservations, fees:** Reservations are accepted at 800/444-7275 or www.reserveamerica.com ($8 reservation fee). Tent sites are $32 per night, RV sites (hookups) are $38-45 per night, plus $15 per night for each additional vehicle and $2 per pet per night. Boat launch is $10 per day. Some credit cards are accepted. Off-season discounts are available. Open year-round.

**Directions:** From the north, on U.S. 101 (just north of King City), take the Jolon Road/G14 exit. Turn south on Jolon Road and drive 21 miles to Lockwood and Interlake Road (G14). Turn right and drive 18 miles to San Antonio Lake Road. Turn left and drive three miles to the South Shore entrance of the lake.

From the south, drive on U.S. 101 to Paso Robles and the 24th Street exit (G14 west). Take that exit and drive 14 miles to Lake Nacimiento Drive. Turn right and drive across Lake Nacimiento Dam to Interlake Road. Turn left and drive seven miles to Lake San Antonio Road. Turn right and drive three miles to the South Shore entrance.

**Contact:** South Shore, 805/472-2311, www.co.monterey.ca.us/parks.

# 6 LAKE NACIMIENTO RESORT

### Scenic rating: 8

at Lake Nacimiento

**Map 12.2, page 660**

This is the only game in town at Nacimiento, and the management plays it well. It's an outstanding operation, with headquarters for a great fishing or water-sports trip. When the lake is full, the fishing for white bass and largemouth bass can be incredible and the water play is also great. The lake has 165 miles of shoreline with many arms—ideal for bass fishing. The resort has a lake-view restaurant open during the summer, and the campsites provide limited tree cover with pines and oaks. Two camps are on the lake's shore, and the rest are set back about three-quarters of a mile from the lake. Lakeview lodging is also available.

**Campsites, facilities:** The campgrounds offer 297 sites with no hookups for tents or RVs of any length, 40 sites with full hookups for RVs up to 35 feet, and 12 group sites for 15-40 people each. Nineteen lodges, eight trailers, and two mobile homes are for rent. Picnic tables and fire grills are provided. Drinking water, restrooms with showers and flush toilets, dump station, boat ramp, boat docks, boat rentals, seasonal swimming pool, seasonal restaurant, coin laundry, general store, fishing licenses, swimming beaches, basketball and volleyball courts, and horseshoe pits are available. Some facilities are wheelchair-accessible. Leashed pets are permitted.

**Reservations, fees:** Reservations are accepted for tent sites and are required for RV sites with full hookups. Tent sites are $32 per night, RV sites (hookups) are $45 per night, plus $15 per extra vehicle and $2 per pet per night. Some credit cards are accepted. Open year-round.

**Directions:** From U.S. 101 north, drive to Paso Robles and the 46E exit; from U.S. 101 south, drive to Paso Robles and the 24th Street exit (same exit, different names depending on which direction you're coming from). Turn west on 24th Street (becomes Lake Nacimiento Drive/G14) and drive for nine miles. Bear right on Lake Nacimiento Drive and continue for seven miles to the resort entrance on the left. Note: If you cross the Lake Nacimiento dam, you've gone too far.

**Contact:** Lake Nacimiento Resort, 805/238-3256 or 800/323-3839, www.nacimientoresort.com.

# 7 MORRO STRAND STATE BEACH

### Scenic rating: 7

near Morro Bay

**Map 12.2, page 660**

A ton of Highway 1 cruisers plan to stay overnight at this state park. It is along the ocean near Morro Bay, right on the beach—a pretty spot year-round. The park features a three-mile stretch of beach that connects the southern and northern entrances to the state beach. Fishing, jogging, sailboarding, and kite flying are popular.

**Campsites, facilities:** There are 76 sites for tents or RVs up to 24 feet (no hookups). Picnic tables and fire grills are provided. Drinking water and flush toilets are available. Cold, outdoor showers are also available. Supplies and a coin laundry are in Morro Bay. Leashed pets are permitted, but not on the beach.

**Reservations, fees:** Reservations are accepted at 800/444-7275 ($10 reservation fee) or www.reserveamerica.com ($9 reservation fee). Sites may still be available on a first-come, first served basis. Sites are $35 per night, plus $8 per night for each additional vehicle. Open year-round.

**Directions:** On Highway 1, drive to Morro Bay. Take the Yerba Buena Street/Morro Strand State Beach exit. Turn west on Yerba Buena Street and drive one block to the campground.

**Contact:** Morro Strand State Beach, 805/772-8812; San Luis Obispo Coast District, 805/927-2065, www.parks.ca.gov.

## 8 CERRO ALTO

### Scenic rating: 7

near San Luis Obispo

**Map 12.2, page 660**

This camp is near Morro Creek, which runs most of the year but can disappear in late summer in dry years. Some sites are along the creek, nicely spaced, with sycamore and bay trees peppering the hillside. There are numerous hiking and mountain-biking trails. The best of these is Cerro Alto Trail, which is accessible from camp and then travels four miles up to Cuesta Ridge for sweeping views of Morro Bay.

**Campsites, facilities:** There are 22 sites for tents or RVs up to 30 feet (no hookups). Picnic tables and fire grills are provided. Drinking water and vault toilets are available. A camp host and pay phone are nearby. Some facilities are wheelchair-accessible. Leashed pets are permitted.

**Reservations, fees:** Reservations are accepted at 877/444-6777 ($10 reservation fee) or www.recreation.gov ($9 reservation fee). Sites are $25 per night, plus $10 per night per additional vehicle. Open year-round, weather permitting.

**Directions:** From U.S. 101 at Atascadero, take the Highway 41 west exit. Drive west on Highway 41 for eight miles to the campground on the left.

**Contact:** Los Padres National Forest, Santa Lucia Ranger District, 805/925-9538, www.fs.usda.gov/lpnf; Parks Management Co., 805/434-1996.

## 9 RANCHO COLINA RV PARK

### Scenic rating: 6

in Morro Bay

**Map 12.2, page 660**

This privately operated RV park is one of several camping options in the Morro Bay area. Folks who park here typically stroll the boardwalk, exploring the little shops. (For recreation, see the Morro Bay State Park listing in this chapter.) About 20 percent of the sites are long-term rentals.

**Campsites, facilities:** There are 57 sites with full hookups (30 and 50 amps) for RVs up to 40 feet. No tents. Picnic tables are provided. Restrooms with showers, laundry facilities, and a recreation room are available. Some facilities are wheelchair-accessible. Leashed pets are permitted.

**Reservations, fees:** Reservations are accepted. Sites are $45 per night. Monthly rates are available. Some credit cards are accepted. Open year-round.

**Directions:** From Morro Bay on Highway 1, drive one mile east on Atascadero Road/Highway 41 to the park at 1045 Atascadero Road.

**Contact:** Rancho Colina RV Park, 805/772-8420.

## 10 MORRO DUNES RV PARK

### Scenic rating: 6

in Morro Bay

**Map 12.2, page 660**

A wide array of side-trip possibilities and great natural beauty make Morro Bay an attractive destination. Most visitors will walk the boardwalk, try at least one of the coastal restaurants, and then head to Morro Bay State Park for hiking or sea kayaking. Other folks will head straight to the port for fishing, or just explore the area before heading north to San Simeon for the Hearst Castle tour. (See the Morro Bay State Park listing for more information.)

**Campsites, facilities:** There are 152 sites with full or partial hookups (30 and 50 amps) for RVs of any length and 16 sites for tents. Some sites are pull-through. Picnic tables and fire grills are provided. Restrooms with showers, drinking water, cable TV, Wi-Fi, coin laundry, general store, clubhouse, RV storage, RV supplies and repair, recreation hall, group facilities, horseshoes, firewood, ice, and dump station are available. Propane gas, a golf course, a playground, and boat rentals are nearby. Some facilities are wheelchair-accessible. Leashed pets are permitted.

**Reservations, fees:** Reservations are accepted. RV sites are $39-46 per night, tent sites are $30 per night, plus $2.20 per person per night for more than two people and $2.20 per pet per night. Weekly and monthly rates are available during the winter. Some credit cards are accepted. Open year-round.

**Directions:** Drive on Highway 1 to Morro Bay and the exit for Highway 41. Take that exit and turn west on Atascadero Road/Highway 41 and drive 0.5 mile to 1700 Embarcadero/Atascadero Road.

**Contact:** Morro Dunes RV Park, 805/772-2722, www.morrodunes.com.

## 11 MORRO BAY STATE PARK

### Scenic rating: 9

in Morro Bay

**Map 12.2, page 660**

Reservations are strongly advised at this popular campground. This is one of the premium stopover spots for folks cruising on Highway 1. The park offers a wide range of activities and exhibits covering the natural and cultural history of the area. The park features lagoon and natural bay habitat. The most prominent feature is Morro Rock. A "morro" is a small volcanic peak, and there are nine of them along the local coast. The top hike at the park climbs one of them, Black Hill, and rewards hikers with sensational coastal views. The park has a marina and golf course, with opportunities for sailing, fishing, and bird-watching. Activities include beach walks, kayaking in Morro Bay, ocean fishing on a party boat, and touring Hearst Castle.

**Campsites, facilities:** There are 94 sites for tents or RVs up to 35 feet (no hookups), 30 sites with partial hookups (15 and 30 amps) for RVs up to 35 feet, five hike-in/bike-in sites, and two group sites for 25-35 people. Picnic tables, food lockers, and fire rings are provided. Restrooms with flush toilets and coin showers, drinking water, dump station, Wi-Fi, museum exhibits, nature walks, and interpretive programs are available. A coin laundry, grocery store, propane gas, boat ramp, mooring, boat rentals, gas stations, and food service are available in Morro Bay. Some facilities are wheelchair-accessible. Leashed pets are permitted, but not on the beach.

**Reservations, fees:** Reservations are accepted at 800/444-7275 or www.reserveamerica.com ($8 reservation fee). Tent sites are $35 per night, RV sites (hookups) are $50 per night, plus $8 per night for each additional vehicle, plus $5 per person per night for hike-in/bike-in sites. Chorro Group Site is $165 per night, and Osos Group Camp is $100 per night. Open year-round.

**Directions:** On Highway 1, drive to Morro Bay and take the exit for Los Osos-Baywood Park/Morro Bay State Park. Turn south and drive one mile to State Park Road. Turn right and drive one mile to the park entrance on the right.

**Contact:** Morro Bay State Park, 805/772-7434; San Luis Obispo Coast District, 805/927-2065, www.parks.ca.gov.

## 12 EL CHORRO REGIONAL PARK

### Scenic rating: 6

near San Luis Obispo

**Map 12.2, page 660**

North of Morro Bay on the way to San Simeon and Hearst Castle, this can be a prime spot for RV travelers. Note that the campground isn't in the state park reservation system, which means there are times when coastal state parks can be jammed full and this regional park may still have space. Morro Bay, six miles away, provides many possible side trips. The park has full recreational facilities, including a golf course, volleyball, horseshoe pits, softball fields, hiking trails, and botanical gardens. Note that there's a men's prison about four miles away. For some people, this can be a real turnoff.

**Campsites, facilities:** There are 63 sites for tents or RVs up to 40 feet and some undesignated overflow sites; 45 sites have full hookups and the remaining sites have no hookups. Some primitive sites are pull-through. Fire grills and picnic tables are provided. Restrooms with flush toilets and showers, drinking water, playground, picnic area, off-leash dog area, and recreational facilities are available. Supplies and a coin laundry are nearby in San Luis Obispo. Leashed pets are permitted.

**Reservations, fees:** Reservations are accepted for groups only (minimum of three campsites, $9 reservation fee). Primitive tent sites are $25 per night, RV sites are $29 (partial hookups) and $37-40 (full hookups) per night, plus $13 per night for each additional vehicle and $3 per pet per night. Coastal Dunes camping is $49 per night. Group camping is $21 per unit for primitive camping or $80 for the backcountry group area. Campsites are discounted on weekdays and in the off-season. Maximum stay is two weeks. Some credit cards are accepted. Open year-round.

**Directions:** From San Luis Obispo, drive 4.5 miles north on Highway 1 to the park entrance on the right side of the highway.

**Contact:** El Chorro Regional Park, 805/781-5930, www.slocountyparks.org.

## 13 SANTA MARGARITA KOA

**Scenic rating: 6**

near Santa Margarita Lake

**Map 12.2, page 660**

Santa Margarita Lake should have a sign at its entrance that proclaims, "Fishing Only!" That's because the rules do not allow waterskiing or any water contact, including swimming, wading, using float tubes, or sailboarding. The excellent prospects for bass fishing, along with the prohibitive rules, make this lake a favorite

among anglers. Santa Margarita Lake covers nearly 800 acres, most of it long and narrow and set in a dammed-up valley in the foothill country at an elevation of 1,300 feet, just below the Santa Lucia Mountains. Horseback riding is available nearby.

**Campsites, facilities:** There are 65 sites for tents or RVs up to 40 feet; most have full or partial hookups (30 and 50 amps), and one site is pull-through. There are also 11 cabins, four lodges, and two yurts. Picnic tables and fire grills are provided. Restrooms with flush toilets and showers, drinking water, Wi-Fi, seasonal swimming pool, playground, coin laundry, convenience store, dump station, and propane gas are available. Some facilities are wheelchair-accessible. Leashed pets are permitted.

**Reservations, fees:** Reservations are accepted at 800/562-5619. RV sites are $40-50 per night, tent sites are $30-40 per night, plus $5 per person per night for more than two people over age six. Cabins are $65-95 per night, lodges are $115-195 per night, and yurts are $108 per night. Some credit cards are accepted. Open year-round.

**Directions:** From San Luis Obispo, drive north on U.S. 101 for eight miles to the Highway 58/Santa Margarita Lake exit. Take that exit and drive through the town of Santa Margarita to Estrada. Turn right on Estrada and drive eight miles (Estrada becomes Pozo Road) to Santa Margarita Lake Road. Turn left and drive 0.5 mile to the campground on the right.

**Contact:** Santa Margarita KOA, 805/438-5618, www.koa.com.

## 14 LA PANZA

**Scenic rating: 3**

in Los Padres National Forest

**Map 12.2, page 660**

This primitive spot sits at 2,200 feet elevation in the La Panza Range, an oak woodland area that is crisscrossed by numerous off-highway-vehicle and hiking trails and small streams. Some of the trails are not maintained. The Machesna Mountain Wilderness is to the south. Water is scarce.

**Campsites, facilities:** There are 12 sites for tents or RVs up to 16 feet (no hookups). Picnic tables and fire grills are provided. Vault toilets are available. There is no drinking water. Garbage must be packed out. Leashed pets are permitted.

**Reservations, fees:** Reservations are not accepted. Sites are $20 per night, plus $10 per each additional vehicle. Open year-round.

**Directions:** From San Luis Obispo, drive eight miles north on U.S. 101. Turn east on Highway 58 and drive four miles (two miles past Santa Margarita). Turn southeast on Pozo Road and drive for 16 miles to the town of Pozo and Pozo Grade Road. Turn right and drive five miles to Red Hill Road. Turn right and drive one mile to the camp on the left.

**Contact:** Los Padres National Forest, Santa Lucia Ranger District, 805/925-9538, www.fs.usda.gov/lpnf.

## 15 MONTAÑA DE ORO STATE PARK

🏃 🚴 🛶 🐕 🚐 ⛺

**Scenic rating: 9**

near Morro Bay

**Map 12.2, page 660**

This sprawling chunk of primitive land includes coastline, 8,500 acres of foothills, and 1,373-foot Valencia Peak. The name means "Mountain of Gold," and it's named for the golden wildflowers that bloom here in the spring. The camp is perched near a bluff, and while there are no sweeping views from campsites, they await nearby. Bluffs Trail is one of the best easy coastal walks anywhere, offering stunning views of the ocean and cliffs and, in the spring, tons of wildflowers over the course of just 1.5 miles. Another hiking option at the park is to climb Valencia Peak, a little butt-kicker of an ascent that tops out at 1,373 feet, providing more panoramic coastal views. These

are the two best hikes among 50 miles of trails for horses, mountain bikers, and hikers, with trails accessible right out of the campground.

**Campsites, facilities:** There are 48 sites for tents or RVs up to 27 feet (no hookups), four walk-in environmental sites (50- to 150-yard walk), four equestrian sites, and two group equestrian sites for up to 50 people and 25 horses. Picnic tables and fire grills are provided, but fires are not allowed at the environmental sites. Vault toilets are available. Drinking water is available only at the main campground; stock water is available at the equestrian campground. There is limited corral space and single-site equestrian camps have two stalls each. Garbage from equestrian and environmental sites must be packed out. Supplies and a coin laundry are available five miles away in the town of Los Osos. Leashed pets are permitted, except at the environmental sites and on trails.

**Reservations, fees:** Reservations are accepted at 800/444-7275 ($10 reservation fee) or www.reserveamerica.com ($9 reservation fee). Sites are $25 per night, plus $8 per night for each additional vehicle. The environmental sites are $20 per night, hike-in/bike-in sites are $5 per night, equestrian sites are $50, and group sites are $100-150 per night. Open year-round.

**Directions:** From Morro Bay, drive two miles south on Highway 1. Turn on South Bay Boulevard and drive four miles to Los Osos. Turn right on Los Osos Valley Road and drive five miles (it becomes Pecho Valley Road) to the park.

**Contact:** Montaña de Oro State Park, 805/528-0513; San Luis Obispo Coast District, 805/927-2065, www.parks.ca.gov.

## 16 HI MOUNTAIN

🏃 🐕 ⛺

**Scenic rating: 4**

in Los Padres National Forest

**Map 12.2, page 660**

At an elevation of 2,800 feet, this camp is on

the edge of the Santa Lucia Wilderness. You can reach the Hi Mountain Lookout if you continue hiking 1.5 miles past the campground. The Lookout has awesome 360-degree views from the 3,180-foot summit.

**Campsites, facilities:** There are 11 walk-in sites for tents only. Picnic tables and fire grills are provided. Vault toilets are available. There is no drinking water. Garbage must be packed out. Leashed pets are permitted.

**Reservations, fees:** Reservations are not accepted. There is no fee for camping, but an Adventure Pass ($30 annual fee or a $5 daily fee) per parked vehicle is required. Open year-round, weather permitting.

**Directions:** From San Luis Obispo, drive eight miles north on U.S. 101. Turn east on Highway 58 and drive four miles (four miles past Santa Margarita) to Pozo Road/Santa Margarita Lake. Turn right (southeast) and drive 16 miles to the town of Pozo and Hi Mountain Road. Turn right on Hi Mountain Road (next to the Pozo fire station) and prepare to hike or bike five miles to get to the campground. Four-wheel-drive vehicles are recommended.

Note: In winter and spring, multiple stream crossings are required, and a high-clearance vehicle may be necessary. Colson Canyon Road can become impassable. La Brea Canyon Road is washed out and closed.

**Contact:** Los Padres National Forest, Santa Lucia Ranger District, 805/925-9538, www.fs.usda.gov/lpnf.

# 17 AVILA HOT SPRINGS RESORT

**Scenic rating: 6**

on San Luis Obispo Bay

Map 12.2, page 660

The hot mineral pool is a featured attraction. This is a natural mineral hot springs with an artesian well that produces water directly into the spas at 104°F. A pizza kitchen and snack bar are available. Nearby recreation options include Avila State Beach and Pismo State Beach.

**Campsites, facilities:** There are 26 sites for tents only and 30 cabins (26 are rented monthly; two are rented nightly). Picnic tables and fire grills are provided. Restrooms with showers, heated swimming pool, hot mineral pool, spa, recreation room, arcade, playground, and a group barbecue pit is available. An 18-hole golf course is nearby. Pets are not permitted. Some facilities are wheelchair-accessible.

**Reservations, fees:** Reservations are accepted at 805/595-2359 ($10 nonrefundable reservation fee). Tent sites are $45 per night, plus $10 night for more than two people and $5 for extra vehicles. Cabins are $175-200 per night. Some credit cards are accepted. Open year-round.

**Directions:** From San Luis Obispo, drive south on U.S. 101 for nine miles to the Avila Beach Drive exit. Take that exit and drive a short distance to the park at 250 Avila Beach Drive.

**Contact:** Avila Hot Springs Resort, 805/595-2359, www.avilahotsprings.com.

# 18 LOPEZ LAKE RECREATION AREA

**Scenic rating: 7**

near Arroyo Grande

Map 12.2, page 660

Lopez Lake has become an example of how to do something right, with specially marked areas set aside exclusively for waterskiing, personal watercraft, and sailboarding, and the rest of the lake designated for fishing and low-speed boating. There are also full facilities for swimming, with a big swimming beach and two giant water slides, a children's wading pool, and a nice beach area. Another bonus is the scenic boat tours available on Saturdays, which get plenty of takers. A 25-mile trail system provides opportunities for biking, hiking, and horseback riding. That makes it perfect for just about everyone, and with good bass fishing, the lake has become very popular, especially on spring weekends when the bite is on. Other species include trout, bluegill, crappie, and catfish. Lopez Lake is set amid oak woodlands southeast of San Luis Obispo. The lake is shaped something like a horseshoe, has 940 surface acres with 22 miles of shoreline when full, and gets excellent weather most of the year. Features of the park in summer are ranger-led hikes and campfire shows. Many campsites overlook the lake or are nestled among oaks. Note: All boats must be certified mussel-free before launching.

**Campsites, facilities:** There are 143 sites with full hookups (20 and 30 amps) for tents or RVs, 211 sites for tents, and six group sites for 30-100 people each. An equestrian camp with 18 corrals will accommodate up to 10 vehicles. Picnic tables and fire rings are provided. Restrooms with showers, a playground, children's wading pool, coin laundry, convenience store, ice, snack bar, marina, boat ramp, mooring, boat fuel (dry land fueling only), tackle, boat rentals, and water slides are available. Some facilities are wheelchair-accessible. Leashed pets are permitted.

**Reservations, fees:** Reservations are required by phone or online ($9 reservation fee, $9 transaction fee per site). Tent sites are $25 per night, RV sites are $29 (water and electricity) and $40 (full hookups) per night, plus $13 per night for each additional vehicle and $3.50 per pet per night. Boat launching is $10 per day. Group sites are $21 per unit ($27 reservation fee), and coastal dunes camping is $49 per night. Site fees are discounted on weekdays and in the off-season. In summer there's a two-week maximum stay. Some credit cards are accepted. Open year-round.

**Directions:** From Arroyo Grande on U.S. 101, take the Grand Avenue exit. Turn east and drive through Arroyo Grande to Lopez Drive. Turn left (northeast) on Lopez Drive and drive 10 miles to the park.

**Contact:** Lopez Lake Recreation Area, 805/788-2381; Lopez Lake Marina, 805/489-1006, www.slocountyparks.org.

# 19 NORTH BEACH

**Scenic rating: 7**

in Pismo State Beach

Map 12.2, page 660

Pismo State Beach is nationally renowned for its beaches, dunes, and, in the good old days, clamming. The adjacent tree-lined dunes make for great walks or, for kids, great rolls. The beach is popular with bird-watchers, and the habitat supports the largest wintering colony of monarch butterflies in the United States. Plan on a reservation and having plenty of company in summer. This is an exceptionally popular state beach, either as an ultimate destination or as a stopover for folks cruising Highway 1. There are four restaurants and ATV rentals within two blocks. A trolley service provides a shuttle to the surrounding community. The clamming on minus low tides was legendary. Poaching has devastated the clamming here, with no legal clams taken for years.

**Campsites, facilities:** There are 103 sites for tents or RVs up to 36 feet. Fire grills and picnic tables are provided. Restrooms with showers and flush toilets, drinking water, Wi-Fi, and a dump station are available. Horseback-riding facilities, grocery store, ATV rentals, restaurants, coin laundry, and propane gas are nearby. Some facilities are wheelchair-accessible. Leashed pets are permitted at the campground and on the beach.

**Reservations, fees:** Reservations are accepted at 800/444-7275 or www.reserveamerica.com ($8 reservation fee). Sites are $35 per night, RV sites (hookups) are $50 per night, plus $8 per night for each additional vehicle. Sites discounted in off-season. Open year-round.

**Directions:** On Highway 1 in Pismo Beach, take the North Beach/State Campground exit (well signed) and drive to the park entrance.

**Contact:** Pismo State Beach, 805/473-7220, www.parks.ca.gov.

## OCEANO

**Scenic rating: 6**

in Pismo State Beach

**Map 12.2, page 660**

This is a prized state beach campground, with Pismo Beach and its sand dunes and coastal frontage a centerpiece for the state park system. Its beauty and recreational opportunities, as well as its location on the central coast on Highway 1, make it extremely popular. It fills to capacity most nights, and reservations are usually a necessity. (For more information on Pismo State Beach, see the North Beach listing in this chapter.)

**Campsites, facilities:** There are 40 sites for tents or RVs up to 31 feet (no hookups) and 42 sites with partial hookups for trailers and RVs up to 36 feet. Picnic tables and fire grills are provided. Drinking water and restrooms with flush toilets and coin showers are available. Horseback-riding facilities, grocery store, coin laundry, dump station, restaurants, and gas stations are nearby. Some facilities are wheelchair-accessible, including a fishing overlook at Oceano Lagoon. Leashed pets are permitted at the campground and beach.

**Reservations, fees:** Reservations are accepted at 800/444-7275 ($10 reservation fee) or www.reserveamerica.com ($9 reservation fee). Sites are $35 per night, RV sites (hookups) are $50 per night, plus $8 per night for each additional vehicle. Discounts are offered in the off-season. Open year-round.

**Directions:** From Pismo Beach, drive two miles south on Highway 1 to Pier Avenue. Turn right and drive 0.2 mile to the campground entrance.

**Contact:** Pismo State Beach, 805/473-7220, www.parks.ca.gov.

## 21 PISMO COAST VILLAGE RV RESORT

**Scenic rating: 7**

in Pismo Beach

**Map 12.2, page 660**

This big-time RV park gets a lot of use by Highway 1 cruisers. Its location near the ocean is a plus. Pismo Beach is well known for its sand dunes and beautiful coastal frontage.

**Campsites, facilities:** There are 400 sites with full hookups (30 and 50 amps) for RVs up to 40 feet. No tents are permitted. Picnic tables, fire rings, and satellite TV are provided. Restrooms with showers, free Wi-Fi, playgrounds, heated swimming pool, coin laundry, convenience store, firewood, ice, recreation room, propane gas, seasonal recreation programs, restaurant, RV supplies and repair, bicycle rentals, and a nine-hole miniature golf course are available. Some facilities are wheelchair-accessible. Leashed pets are permitted, with restrictions on certain breeds.

**Reservations, fees:** Reservations are accepted at 888/782-3224. Sites are $52-69 per night, plus $2 per night for each additional person. Group discounts are available in the off-season. There is a 29-day maximum stay. Some credit cards are accepted. Open year-round.

**Directions:** In Pismo Beach, drive on Highway 1/Pacific Coast Highway to the park at 165 South Dolliver Street/Highway 1.

**Contact:** Pismo Coast RV Resort, 805/773-1811, www.pismocoastvillage.com.

## 22 LE SAGE RIVIERA

**Scenic rating: 6**

near Pismo State Beach

**Map 12.2, page 660**

This year-round RV park can serve as headquarters for folks who are interested in visiting several nearby attractions, including neighboring Pismo State Beach and Lopez Lake, 10 miles to the east. The park is on the ocean side of Highway 1, 250 yards from the beach. Many sites are filled with seasonal renters.

**Campsites, facilities:** There are 60 sites with full hookups (30 and 50 amps) for self-contained RVs up to 55 feet; many are pull-through. No tents are permitted. Picnic tables are provided. Restrooms with showers, drinking water, and coin laundry are available. Stores, restaurants, and golf courses are nearby. Some facilities are wheelchair-accessible. Leashed pets are permitted, with certain restrictions.

**Reservations, fees:** Reservations are accepted at 866/489-5506. Sites are $45-55 per night, plus $3 per night for each additional person and $3 per night for each additional vehicle. Holiday rates are higher. Some credit cards are accepted. Open year-round.

**Directions:** In Pismo Beach on Highway 1, drive south on Highway 1 for 0.5 mile to the park on the right (west side) to 319 North Highway 1 (in Grover Beach).

**Contact:** Le Sage Riviera, 805/489-5506, www.lesageriviera.com.

## 23 OCEANO MEMORIAL PARK AND CAMPGROUND

Scenic rating: 7

in Oceano

Map 12.2, page 660

This San Luis Obispo county park is extremely busy during the summer and busy the rest of the year. The location is a bonus; it's within a quarter mile of the Pismo State Beach entrance, the site of great sand dunes and wide-open ocean frontage. Oceano has a fishing lagoon.

**Campsites, facilities:** There are 22 sites for tents or RVs up to 40 feet (full hookups) but no pull-through sites. Picnic tables and fire grills are provided. Drinking water, restrooms with coin showers and flush toilets, a basketball court, horseshoes, athletic field, and picnic area are available. A playground, coin laundry, grocery store, and propane gas are nearby. Leashed pets are permitted.

**Reservations, fees:** Reservations are required by phone or online ($9 reservation fee, $9 transaction fee per site). Tent sites are $25 per night, RV sites are $29 (water and electricity) and $40 (full hookups) per night, plus $13 per night for each additional vehicle and $3.50 per pet per night. Boat launching is $10 per day. Group sites are $21 per unit ($27 reservation fee), and coastal dunes camping is $49 per night. Site fees are discounted on weekdays and in the off-season. Summer stays are limited to four weeks maximum. Some credit cards are accepted. Open year-round.

**Directions:** From Pismo Beach, drive south on U.S. 101 to the Pismo Beach/Grand Avenue exit west to Highway 1. Take that exit and turn south on Highway 1 and drive 1.5 miles to Pier Avenue. Turn right on Pier Avenue and drive a short distance to Norswing. Turn left and drive to the end of the street and Mendel Avenue. Turn right and drive to Air Park Drive. Turn right and drive to the park on the right.

**Contact:** Oceano Memorial Park and Campground, 805/781-5930, www.slocountyparks.org.

## 24 OCEANO DUNES STATE VEHICULAR RECREATION AREA

Scenic rating: 6

south of Pismo Beach

Map 12.2, page 660

This is "national headquarters" for all-terrain vehicles (ATVs)—you know, those three- and four-wheeled motorcycles that turn otherwise normal people into lunatics. The camps are along 1-3 miles of beach and 1,500 acres of open sand dunes, and since not many make the walk to the campsites, four-wheel drives or ATVs are needed for access. The area covers 3,600 acres, including 5.5 miles of beach open for vehicles and 1,500 acres of sand dunes available for OHVs. They roam wild on the dunes here; that's the law, so don't go planning a quiet stroll. If you don't like 'em, you are strongly advised to go elsewhere. If this is your game, have fun and try to keep from killing yourself. Each fall, the National Sand Drags are held here. More than one million people visit each year. High tides can limit access. A beach towing service for RVs and trailers is available. Activities include swimming, surfing, surf fishing, horseback riding, and bird- and nutcase-watching.

**Campsites, facilities:** There are 1,000 sites for tents or RVs of any length (no hookups). Chemical and vault toilets are provided. There is no drinking water. Drinking water, horseback-riding facilities, grocery store, coin laundry, restaurants, gas stations, Wi-Fi, and dump station are nearby. Leashed pets are permitted at the campground and beach.

**Reservations, fees:** Reservations are accepted at 800/444-7275 ($10 reservation fee) or www.reserveamerica.com ($9 reservation fee). Sites are $10 per night per vehicle. Open year-round.

**Directions:** Drive on U.S. 101 to Arroyo Grande and take the Grand Avenue exit. Turn left (toward the beach) on Grand Avenue and drive four miles until the road ends at the North Entrance beach camping area. The South Entrance is one mile south. To get there from Highway 1, take Pier Avenue.

**Contact:** Oceano Dunes, 805/473-7220 or 805/773-7170, www.ohv.parks.ca.gov or www.parks.ca.gov.

## 25 COLSON CANYON

Scenic rating: 6

in Los Padres National Forest

**Map 12.3, page 661**

Colson is just a mile from the western border of Los Padres National Forest, making it far easier to reach than other Forest Service camps in this region. The camp is named after the canyon in which it sits, Colson Canyon. This area really has just two seasons when you should visit,

spring and fall. In the summer, it's hot and dry, with no water available, and is scarcely fit for habitation. The elevation is 2,100 feet.

**Campsites, facilities:** There are five sites for tents only. Picnic tables and fire grills are provided. There are no toilets or drinking water. Garbage must be packed out. Leashed pets are permitted.

**Reservations, fees:** Reservations are not accepted. There is no fee for camping. Open year-round.

**Directions:** From U.S. 101 in Santa Maria, take the Betteravia Road exit east and drive eight miles to a fork with Santa Maria Mesa Road. Bear left at the fork and drive southeast on Santa Maria Mesa Road to Tepusquet Road. Turn left on Tepusquet Road and drive 6.5 miles to Colson Canyon Road. Turn right on Colson Canyon Road/Forest Road 11N04 and drive four miles to the campground on the left. A high-clearance vehicle may be necessary. Colson Canyon Road can be impassable when wet, requiring a four-mile hike to reach the campground.

**Contact:** Los Padres National Forest, Santa Lucia Ranger District, 805/925-9538, www.fs.usda.gov/lpnf.

## 26 WAGON FLAT

Scenic rating: 6

on the North Fork of La Brea Creek in Los Padres National Forest

**Map 12.3, page 661**

Not many folks know about this obscure spot, and if it's a hot, late-summer day, they're probably better off for it. The camp is at an elevation of 1,400 feet, pretty in spring, but in summer often a hot, dry region of Los Padres National Forest. The bright spot is little La Brea Creek, which runs by the camp.

**Campsites, facilities:** There are three sites for tents only. Picnic tables and fire grills are provided. Pit toilets are available. Drinking water is not available. Garbage must be packed out. Leashed pets are permitted.

**Reservations, fees:** Reservations are not accepted. There is no fee for camping. An Adventure Pass ($30 annual fee or $5 daily pass) per parked vehicle is required. Open seasonally, road conditions permitting (call ahead during wet weather).

**Directions:** From U.S. 101 in Santa Maria, take the Betteravia Road exit east and drive eight miles to a fork with Santa Maria Mesa Road. Bear left at the fork and drive southeast on Santa Maria Mesa Road to Tepusquet Road. Turn left on Tepusquet Road and drive 6.5 miles to Colson Canyon Road. Turn right on Colson Canyon Road/Forest Road 11N04 and drive seven miles to La Brea Canyon Road.

Note: La Brea Canyon Road is washed out and closed. To continue, you will need to hike four miles to the campground. In the winter and spring, multiple stream crossings are required and a high-clearance vehicle may be necessary. Colson Canyon Road can become impassable.

**Contact:** Los Padres National Forest, Santa Lucia Ranger District, 805/925-9538, www. fs.usda.gov/lpnf.

## 27 BARREL SPRINGS

### Scenic rating: 7

in Los Padres National Forest

**Map 12.3, page 661**

This small, primitive camp sits at 1,000 feet elevation along La Brea Creek and is shaded by the oaks in La Brea Canyon. It is named after nearby Barrel Springs, which forms a small creek and feeds into La Brea Creek.

**Campsites, facilities:** There are six tent sites. Picnic tables and fire grills are provided. Vault toilets are available. There is no drinking water. Garbage must be packed out. Leashed pets are permitted.

**Reservations, fees:** Reservations are not accepted. There is no fee for camping. An

Adventure Pass ($30 annual fee or $5 daily pass) per parked vehicle is required. Open seasonally. Access roads may be closed in wet weather.

**Directions:** From U.S. 101 in Santa Maria, take the Betteravia Road exit east and drive eight miles to a fork with Santa Maria Mesa Road. Bear left at the fork and drive southeast on Santa Maria Mesa Road to Tepusquet Road. Turn left on Tepusquet Road and drive 6.5 miles to Colson Canyon Road. Turn right on Colson Canyon Road/Forest Road 11N04 and drive (or hike) eight miles to the campground.

Note: Colson Canyon Road can become impassable and La Brea Canyon Road is washed out and closed. To continue, you will need to hike eight miles to the campground. In the winter and spring, multiple stream crossings are required and a high-clearance vehicle may be necessary.

**Contact:** Los Padres National Forest, Santa Lucia Ranger District, 805/925-9538, www. fs.usda.gov/lpnf.

## 28 RIVER PARK

### Scenic rating: 4

in Lompoc

**Map 12.3, page 661**

River Park is next to the lower Santa Ynez River, which looks quite a bit different than it does up in Los Padres National Forest. A small fishing lake within the 45-acre park is stocked with trout and catfish. A camp host and resident ranger are on-site. Side-trip possibilities include the nearby La Purisima Mission State Historic Park and Jalama Beach. Before checking in you'd better get a lesson in how to pronounce Lompoc. It's "LOM-poke." If you arrive and say, "Hey, it's great to be in LOM-pock," they might just tell ya to get on back to the other cowpokes.

**Campsites, facilities:** There are 35 sites for RVs up to 40 feet (full hookups) and a group camping area for tents or RVs but no pull-through sites. Picnic tables and barbecues are provided. Restrooms with flush toilets and coin showers, drinking water, dump station, fishing pond, trail, sand volleyball, horseshoes, group facilities, and playground are available. Supplies and a coin laundry are nearby. Leashed pets are permitted with certain restrictions.

**Reservations, fees:** Reservations are not accepted for family sites but are required for groups at 805/875-8036. Sites are $5 per night plus $10 per vehicle, RV sites (full hookups) are $30 per night or $200 per week, hike-in/bike-in sites are $5 per night, and pets are free (maximum of two). Group fees are $15 per night per tent, $10 per night per RV, with a $25 minimum. Weekly rates are available. Some credit cards are accepted. Open year-round.

**Directions:** In Lompoc, drive to the junction of Highway 246 and Sweeney Road at the southwest edge of town and continue to the park at 401 East Highway 246.

**Contact:** Lompoc Parks and Recreation Department, 805/875-8100, www.cityoflompoc.com/parks_rec/river.

## 29 FLYING FLAGS RV RESORT AND CAMPGROUND

### Scenic rating: 3

near Solvang

**Map 12.3, page 661**

This is one of the few privately operated parks in the area that welcome tenters as well as RVers. Nearby side trips include the Santa Ynez Mission, just east of Solvang. The town of Solvang is of interest. It was originally a small Danish settlement that has expanded since the 1920s yet managed to keep its cultural heritage intact through the years. The town is exceptionally clean, an example of how to do something right. Wineries are nearby.

**Campsites, facilities:** There are 228 sites with full or partial hookups (30 and 50 amps) for RVs of any length and 125 sites for tents. Most sites are pull-through. Cabins and cottages are also available. Picnic tables are provided. Restrooms with showers, cable TV, playground, heated swimming pool, spa, coin laundry, convenience store, dump station, ice, recreation room, free Wi-Fi, Internet workstations, a dog park, arcade, five clubhouses, two splash zones, a fitness center, and propane gas are available. A nine-hole golf course, boat launch, and boat rentals are nearby. Some facilities are wheelchair-accessible. Leashed pets are permitted with certain restrictions.

**Reservations, fees:** Reservations are accepted. Sites are $26-98, plus $3 per person per night for more than two people, $5 per night for each additional vehicle, and $2 per pet per night for more than two dogs. Airstreams are $99-189 per night, cottages are $99-219 per night, and luxury tent villas are $99-199 per night. Holiday rates are higher. Weekly and monthly rates are available. Open year-round. Some credit cards are accepted.

**Directions:** From Santa Barbara, drive 45 miles north on U.S. 101 to Highway 246. Turn west (left) on Highway 246 and drive about 0.5 mile to Avenue of the Flags (a four-way stop). Turn left on Avenue of the Flags and drive about one block to the campground entrance on the left at 180 Avenue of the Flags.

**Contact:** Flying Flags RV Resort and Campground, 805/688-3716, www.flyingflags.com.

## 30 JALAMA BEACH COUNTY PARK

### Scenic rating: 8

near Lompoc

**Map 12.3, page 661**

This is a pretty spot where Jalama Creek empties into the ocean, about five miles north of Point Conception and just south of Vandenberg Air Force Base. The area is known for its sunsets and beachcombing. The camp is so popular that a waiting list is common in summer. Activities include surfing, sailboarding, and fishing for perch, cabezon, kelp bass, and halibut.

**Campsites, facilities:** There are 98 sites for tents or RVs up to 40 feet and two group sites for eight vehicles and 20-40 people each. Some sites have electrical (30 amps) hookups. Picnic tables and fire pits are provided. Restrooms with flush toilets and showers, drinking water, dump station, general store, snack bar, bait and tackle, picnic area, firewood, and ice are available. Note that the nearest gas station is 20 miles away. Some facilities are wheelchair-accessible. Leashed pets are permitted, but a vaccination certificate is required.

**Reservations, fees:** Reservations are not accepted for individual sites; a waiting list (first-come, first-served) is available when the camp fills. Group reservations are required at 805/934-6211 or online at www.reservations. sbparks.org ($25 reservation fee). Tent sites are $25 per night, RV sites (water and electricity) are $35 per night, plus $10 per night for each additional vehicle and $3 per pet per night. It's $200 per night for a group site. Weekly rates are available in the off-season. Some credit cards are accepted. Open year-round.

**Directions:** From Lompoc, drive about five miles south on Highway 1. Turn southwest on Jalama Road and drive 14 miles to the park.

**Contact:** Jalama Beach County Park, 805/736-6316 or 805/736-3504, www.countyofsb.org/parks.

# 31 GAVIOTA STATE PARK

## Scenic rating: 10

near Santa Barbara

Map 12.3, page 661

This is the granddaddy, the biggest of the three state beaches along U.S. 101 northwest of Santa Barbara. Spectacular and beautiful, the park covers 2,700 acres, providing trails for hiking and horseback riding, as well as a mile-long stretch of stunning beach frontage. Gaviota means "seagull" and was first named by the soldiers of the Portola Expedition in 1769, who learned why you always wear a hat (or a helmet) when they are passing overhead. The ambitious can hike the beach to get more seclusion. Trails to Gaviota Overlook (1.5 miles) and Gaviota Peak (3.2 miles one-way) provide lookouts with drop-dead gorgeous views of the coast and Channel Islands. Want more? There is also a 0.5-mile trail to the hot springs. This park is known for being windy and for shade being hard to find. Unfortunately, a railroad trestle crosses above the day-use parking lot. You know what that means? Of course you do. It means trains run through day and night, and with them comes noise. This is a popular beach for swimming and surf fishing, as well as boat launching and fishing.

**Campsites, facilities:** There are 41 sites for tents or RVs up to 30 feet (no hookups) and an area for hike-in/bike-in sites. Picnic tables and fire grills are provided. Restrooms with flush toilets and coin showers, drinking water, summer lifeguard service, and boat hoist (two-ton maximum weight) are available. A convenience store (summer only) is nearby. Some facilities are wheelchair-accessible. Leashed pets are permitted at campsites.

**Reservations, fees:** Reservations are accepted for about half the sites from Memorial Day weekend through Labor Day weekend at 800/444-7275 ($10 reservation fee) or www.reserveamerica.com ($9 reservation fee). Sites are $35-45 per night, plus $10 per night for each additional vehicle, $10 per person per night for hike-in/bike-in sites. Boat launching is $8 per day. Maximum stay is one week in summer and two weeks in winter. Open daily March through October; from November through February, the campground is open Friday through Sunday only.

**Directions:** From Santa Barbara, drive north on U.S. 101 for 30 miles to the Gaviota State Beach exit. Take that exit, turn west, and drive a short distance to the park entrance.

**Contact:** Gaviota State Park, Channel Coast

District, 805/968-1033 or 805/585-1850, www.parks.ca.gov.

## 32 REFUGIO STATE BEACH

🏃 🚴 🏊 🛶 ⚓ 🐕 ♿ 🚐 ⛺

### Scenic rating: 9

near Santa Barbara

**Map 12.3, page 661**

Refugio State Beach is the smallest of the three beautiful state beaches along U.S. 101 north of Santa Barbara. The others are Gaviota and El Capitán, which also have campgrounds. Palm trees planted close to Refugio Creek add a unique look to this beach and campground. This is a great spot for family campers with bikes, with a paved two-mile bike trail connecting Refugio campground with El Capitán. Fishing is often good in this area of the coast. Visitors can get a unique perspective of the coastline by taking the kayak tours offered by state park lifeguards from Memorial Day weekend through August. Campsite reservations are strongly advised and are often a necessity throughout the vacation season.

**Campsites, facilities:** There are 66 sites for tents or RVs up to 30 feet (no hookups), one hike-in/bike-in site, and three group sites for tents or RVs that can accommodate up to 80 people and 25 vehicles. Picnic tables and fire grills are provided. Restrooms with flush toilets and coin showers, drinking water, summer lifeguard service, summer convenience store, and food services are available. Some facilities are wheelchair-accessible; beach wheelchairs are available at no cost. Leashed pets are permitted at campsites.

**Reservations, fees:** Reservations are accepted at 800/444-7275 ($10 reservation fee) or www.reserveamerica.com ($9 reservation fee). Standard sites are $45 per night, premium sites are $55 per night, plus $10 per night for each additional vehicle; hike-in/bike-in sites are $10 per night, Anapamu and Yanonali group sites are $235 per night, and the Bouchard group site is $350 per night. Maximum stay is one week in summer and two weeks in winter. Open year-round, weather permitting.

**Directions:** From Santa Barbara, drive northwest on U.S. 101 for 23 miles to the Refugio State Beach exit. Take that exit and turn west (left) and drive a short distance to the campground entrance.

**Contact:** Refugio State Beach, Channel Coast District, 805/968-1033 or 805/585-1850, www.parks.ca.gov.

## 33 EL CAPITAN CANYON

🏃 🚴 🏊 🛶 ⚓ 🚐 ♿ ⛺

### Scenic rating: 8

near Goleta

**Map 12.3, page 661**    **BEST (**

El Capitan Canyon is a unique campground where you do not bring your own tent but rather rent permanent safari tents or cabins on-site. The tent cabins are situated on 12-by-14-foot wood platforms, and they come fully furnished with beds and linens. The safari tents are heated and have electricity. The park covers 65 acres in the coastal foothills north of Santa Barbara and offers visitors the best of both worlds: There are 2,200 acres of public land near the camp with backcountry hiking and mountain-biking trails, or for those who prefer the sand and surf, beach access is within walking distance and ocean kayaking and deep-sea fishing trips can be booked at the resort. In the summer live entertainment is available, including a concert series and the "Blues and Barbecue" event every Saturday night. Dogs are strictly prohibited in a mission to stop the spread of nonnative plants; this in turn has inspired a return of native habitat and the birds and wildlife that rely on it.

**Campsites, facilities:** There are 26 tent cabins, 108 cabins, and three yurts. Picnic tables and fire pits are provided. Restrooms with flush toilets and showers, drinking water, heated swimming pool, outdoor hot tub, yoga, a ropes course, children's playground, live music (Saturday nights May through October),

Wi-Fi, convenience store, massage service, free use of bicycles, and firewood are available. Horseback-riding facilities are nearby. Some facilities are wheelchair-accessible.

**Reservations, fees:** Reservations are recommended at 866/352-2729. Tent cabins are $145-170 per night, cabins are $195-795 per night, and yurts are $175-225. Discounts are available Monday through Thursday and in the off-season. Some credit cards are accepted. Open year-round.

**Directions:** From Santa Barbara, drive about 20 miles northwest on U.S. 101 to the El Capitán State Beach exit. Go straight on the frontage road paralleling the freeway for about 100 yards. Turn right at the sign for El Capitan Canyon on the mountain side of the freeway.

**Contact:** El Capitan Canyon, 805/685-3887, www.elcapitancanyon.com.

## 34 OCEAN MESA

**Scenic rating: 8**

near Goleta

**Map 12.3, page 661**

Ocean Mesa Campground sits on an inland bluff surrounded by Los Padres National Forest and overlooking the Pacific Ocean. Sites are paved and shaded, some with ocean views, while tenters can soak in the rolling hills. Plenty of amenities will keep you grounded, or it's just a 20-minute drive to downtown Santa Barbara for dining or tidepooling at El Capitán State Beach. On Saturday evenings there's live music at El Capitan Canyon.

**Campsites, facilities:** There are 20 sites for tents and 80 sites with full hookups for RVs up to 50 feet (some pull-through). Picnic tables and fire rings are provided. Drinking water, flush toilets, heated pool and spa, Wi-Fi, cable TV, convenience store and snack bar, yurt meeting space, and horseback-riding facilities are available. Leashed pets are permitted but not on the hiking trails.

**Reservations, fees:** Reservations are accepted

at 866/410-5783 or online at www.oceanmesa. com. Tent sites are $45-55 per night and RV sites are $75-95 per night. Open year-round; there's a two-night minimum stay on weekends.

**Directions:** From Santa Barbara, drive about 20 miles northwest on U.S. 101 to the El Capitán State Beach exit. Drive past the entrance to El Capitan Canyon to Calle Real. Turn right on Calle Real and drive to El Capitan Terrace Lane. Turn right on El Capitan Terrace Lane and drive to the office/store.

**Contact:** Ocean Mesa Campground, 866/410-5783, www.oceanmesa.com.

## 35 EL CAPITÁN STATE BEACH

**Scenic rating: 10**

near Santa Barbara

**Map 12.3, page 661**

This is one in a series of beautiful state beaches along the Santa Barbara coast. El Capitán has a sandy beach and rocky tidepools. The water is warm, the swimming good. A stairway descends from the bluffs to the beach, a beautiful setting, and sycamores and oaks line El Capitán Creek. A paved, two-mile bicycle trail is routed to Refugio State Beach, a great family trip. This is a perfect layover for Coast Highway vacationers, and reservations are usually required to ensure a spot. Refugio State Beach to the north is another option.

**Campsites, facilities:** There are 130 sites for tents or RVs up to 40 feet, one hike-in/bike-in site, two group sites for tents or RVs that can accommodate 50-125 people each, and five group sites for tents only that can accommodate 50-125 people each. There are no hookups. Picnic tables and fire grills are provided. Restrooms with flush toilets and coin showers, drinking water, summer lifeguard service, and a summer convenience store are available. Some facilities are wheelchair-accessible. Leashed pets are permitted in the campgrounds but not on the beach.

**Reservations, fees:** Reservations are accepted

at 800/444-7275 ($10 reservation fee) or www. reserveamerica.com ($9 reservation fee). Sites are $35 per night, plus $10 per night for each additional vehicle, and it's $10 per person per night for hike-in/bike-in sites. Group sites are $225, $235, $285, and $320 per night depending on size. Maximum stay is one week in summer and two weeks in winter. Open year-round, weather permitting.

**Directions:** From Santa Barbara, drive north on U.S. 101 for 20 miles to the Capitán State Beach exit. Turn west (left) and drive a short distance to the campground entrance.

**Contact:** El Capitán State Beach, Channel Coast District, 805/968-1033 or 805/585-1850, www.parks.ca.gov.

## 36 BATES CANYON

### Scenic rating: 7
in Los Padres National Forest

**Map 12.4, page 662**

This camp is on the northeast flank of the Sierra Madre, along a small stream in Bates Canyon, at 2,900 feet elevation. Note that the primitive access road out of camp to the south is often gated; it leads to the Sierra Madre Ridge, where a road contours right along the ridge on the border of the San Rafael Wilderness, passing from peak to peak.

**Campsites, facilities:** There are six tent sites. Picnic tables and fire grills are provided. Vault toilets are available. There is no drinking water. Garbage must be packed out. Some facilities are wheelchair-accessible. Leashed pets are permitted.

**Reservations, fees:** Reservations are not accepted. There is no fee for camping. An Adventure Pass ($30 annual fee or $5 daily pass) per parked vehicle is required. Open year-round. Note that access roads can be closed during and after heavy rains.

**Directions:** From Santa Maria, drive east on Highway 166 for 50 miles to Cottonwood Canyon Road. Turn right on Cottonwood Canyon Road and drive southwest for 7.5 miles to the campground.

**Contact:** Los Padres National Forest, Santa Lucia Ranger District, 805/925-9538, www. fs.usda.gov/lpnf.

## 37 ALISO PARK

### Scenic rating: 6
in Los Padres National Forest

**Map 12.4, page 662**

This primitive, quiet camp is at the foot of the Sierra Madre at 3,200 feet, directly below McPherson Peak (5,749 feet). It is just inside the northeast boundary of Los Padres National Forest, making it easily accessible from Highway 166.

**Campsites, facilities:** There are 10 sites for tents or RVs up to 28 feet (no hookups). Picnic tables and fire grills are provided. Pit toilets are available. Drinking water is not available. Garbage must be packed out. Some facilities are wheelchair-accessible. Leashed pets are permitted.

**Reservations, fees:** Reservations are not accepted. There is no fee for camping. An Adventure Pass ($30 annual fee or $5 daily pass) per parked vehicle is required. Open year-round.

**Directions:** From Santa Maria, drive east on Highway 166 for 59 miles to Aliso Canyon Road/Forest Road 10N04. Turn right on Aliso Canyon Road/Forest Road 10N04 and drive south about six miles to the campground at the end of the road.

**Contact:** Los Padres National Forest, Mount Piños Ranger District, 661/245-3731, www. fs.usda.gov/lpnf.

## 38 BALLINGER

### Scenic rating: 3

in Los Padres National Forest

**Map 12.4, page 662**

Ballinger Camp is right inside the boundary of Los Padres National Forest in the Mount Piños Ranger District, just six miles east of Highway 33. During the week, this camp receives very little use. On weekends, it gets moderate, even heavy use at times, from OHV owners. Note that the California "green sticker" or "red sticker" is required to ride OHVs here. The camp is at an elevation of 3,000 feet.

**Campsites, facilities:** There are 20 sites for tents or RVs up to 32 feet (no hookups). Picnic tables and fire grills are provided. Vault toilets are available. No drinking water is available. Garbage must be packed out. Leashed pets are permitted.

**Reservations, fees:** Reservations are not accepted. Sites are $20 per night, plus $10 per each additional vehicle. Open year-round.

**Directions:** From Maricopa, drive southwest on Highway 166 about 14 miles to Highway 33. Turn south on Highway 33 and drive about 3.5 miles to Ballinger Canyon Road/Forest Road 9N10. Turn left (east) and drive three miles to the campground.

**Contact:** Los Padres National Forest, Mount Piños Ranger District, 661/245-3731, www. fs.usda.gov/lpnf; Parks Management Company, 805/434-1996, www.campone.com.

## 39 VALLE VISTA

### Scenic rating: 8

in Los Padres National Forest

**Map 12.4, page 662**

The view of the southern San Joaquin Valley and the snowcapped Sierra is the highlight of this primitive camp. It is set at 4,800 feet elevation, near the boundary of Los Padres National Forest. Visitors have an opportunity to view condors, and you can usually spot a few buzzards, er, turkey vultures, circling around. If you don't bring your own water, they might just start circling you. Little-known fact: This camp sits exactly on the border of Kern County and Ventura County.

**Campsites, facilities:** There are seven sites for tents or RVs up to 22 feet (no hookups). Picnic tables and fire grills are provided. Pit toilets are available. No drinking water is available. Garbage must be packed out. Leashed pets are permitted.

**Reservations, fees:** Reservations are not accepted. There is no fee for camping. An Adventure Pass ($30 annual fee or $5 daily pass) per parked vehicle is required. Open year-round.

**Directions:** From Maricopa, drive south on Highway 166 about nine miles to Cerro Noroeste Road. Turn left and drive 12 miles to the campground on the left.

**Contact:** Los Padres National Forest, Mount Piños Ranger District, 661/245-3731, www. fs.usda.gov/lpnf.

## 40 CABALLO

### Scenic rating: 4

in Los Padres National Forest

**Map 12.4, page 662**

Caballo is at 5,850 feet elevation on a small creek that is the headwaters for Santiago Creek, on the northern flank of Mount Abel. The creek flows only about 10 days a year, usually before the opening of the campground, so do not count on it for water. This is one of several primitive camps in the immediate area—a take-your-pick offer. But it's an offer not many folks even know about.

**Campsites, facilities:** There are five sites for tents or RVs up to 16 feet (no hookups). Picnic tables and fire grills are provided. Pit toilets are available. No drinking water is available. Garbage must be packed out. Leashed pets are permitted.

**Reservations, fees:** Reservations are not accepted. There is no fee for camping. Open early May through October, weather permitting.

**Directions:** Drive on I-5 to just south of Lebec to the Frazier Park exit. Take that exit and drive west on Frazier Mountain Road to the town of Lake of the Woods and Cuddy Valley Road. Continue straight on Cuddy Valley Road for six miles to Mil Potrero Highway (signed "Pine Mountain Club"). Turn right and drive 10 miles to Forest Road 9N27. Turn right and drive a short distance to the campground. High-clearance vehicles are recommended for the dirt access road.

**Contact:** Los Padres National Forest, Mount Piños Ranger District, 661/245-3731, www.fs.usda.gov/lpnf.

## 41 MARIAN
🥾 🐎 🚙 ⛺

### Scenic rating: 4
in Los Padres National Forest

**Map 12.4, page 662**

Marian is extremely primitive, set on the outskirts of Los Padres National Forest at 6,600 feet elevation, between Brush Mountain to the immediate northwest and San Emigdio Mountain to the immediate southeast. The road in is rough, as is the route out of camp that leads three miles to the San Emigdio summit, at 7,495 feet. A network of Forest Service roads provides access to other camps in the area, as well as to Mount Abel (8,286 feet) and Mount Piños (8,831 feet). The access gate is usually locked in winter, when reaching this camp requires a two-mile hike. Nearby Toad Springs and Caballo are smaller but more easily accessible. Note that there is neither drinking water nor toilets.

**Campsites, facilities:** There are five sites for tents or RVs up to 16 feet (no hookups). Picnic tables and fire grills are provided. Drinking water and toilets are not available, so bring your own. Garbage must be packed out. Leashed pets are permitted.

**Reservations, fees:** Reservations are not accepted. There is no fee for camping. Open early May through October, weather permitting.

**Directions:** Drive on I-5 to just south of Lebec to the Frazier Park exit. Take that exit and drive west on Frazier Mountain Road to the town of Lake of the Woods and Cuddy Valley Road. Continue straight on Cuddy Valley Road for six miles to Mil Potrero Highway (signed "Pine Mountain Club"). Turn right and drive 10 miles to Forest Road 9N27. Turn right and drive one mile (passing Caballo campground) to the camp. Note: Four-wheel-drive or high-clearance vehicles are recommended.

**Contact:** Los Padres National Forest, Mount Piños Ranger District, 661/245-3731, www.fs.usda.gov/lpnf/lospadres.

## 42 TOAD SPRINGS
🐎 🚙 ⛺

### Scenic rating: 8
in Los Padres National Forest

**Map 12.4, page 662**

Toad Springs is at 5,700 feet elevation near Apache Saddle, on the northwest flank of Mount Abel (8,286 feet). It is at the head of Quatal Canyon with a spectacular badlands landscape. Water and toilets are not available, so forget this one for your honeymoon. Note that a landslide destroyed a primitive trail (about a mile out of camp) that once was led south out of camp for six miles to Mesa Springs and a trail camp. It is considered too dangerous for use.

**Campsites, facilities:** There are three sites for tents or RVs up to 16 feet (no hookups). Picnic tables and fire grills are provided. Toilets and drinking water not available. Garbage must be packed out. Leashed pets are permitted.

**Reservations, fees:** Reservations are not accepted. There is no fee for camping. Open early May through October, weather permitting.

**Directions:** Drive on I-5 to just south of Lebec to the Frazier Park exit. Take that exit and drive west on Frazier Mountain Road to the town of

Lake of the Woods and Cuddy Valley Road. Continue straight on Cuddy Valley Road for six miles to Mil Potrero Highway (signed "Pine Mountain Club"). Turn right and drive 10 miles to the campground on the left.

**Contact:** Los Padres National Forest, Mount Piños Ranger District, 661/245-3731, www. fs.usda.gov/lpnf.

## 43 CAMPO ALTO

### Scenic rating: 6

in Los Padres National Forest

**Map 12.4, page 662**

Campo Alto means "High Camp," and you'll find when you visit that the name fits. The camp is high (8,250 feet) on Cerro Noroeste/Mount Abel in Los Padres National Forest. Don't show up thirsty, as there's no drinking water. About half a mile from camp there is a trailhead on the southeast side of the road. From here, you can hike two miles to Grouse Mountain and, in another mile, reach remote, hike-in Sheep Camp.

**Campsites, facilities:** There are 15 sites for tents or RVs up to 30 feet (no hookups) and one group site. Picnic tables and fire grills are provided. Vault toilets are available. No drinking water is available. Garbage must be packed out. Leashed pets are permitted.

**Reservations, fees:** Reservations are not accepted. Sites are $20 per night, plus $10 for each additional vehicle; the group camp is $100 per night. Open May through October, weather permitting.

**Directions:** Drive on I-5 to just south of Lebec to the Frazier Park exit. Take that exit and drive west on Frazier Mountain Road to the town of Lake of the Woods and Cuddy Valley Road. Continue straight on Cuddy Valley Road and drive six miles to Mil Potrero Highway (signed "Pine Mountain Club"). Turn right and drive nine miles to Cerro Noroeste Road (Forest Road 9N07). Turn left and drive nine miles to the campground.

**Contact:** Los Padres National Forest, Mount Piños Ranger District, 661/245-3731, www. fs.usda.gov/lpnf; Parks Management Company, 805/434-1996, www.campone.com.

## 44 NETTLE SPRINGS

### Scenic rating: 4

in Los Padres National Forest

**Map 12.4, page 662**

This remote camp near the end of a Forest Service road in Apache Canyon borders the Chumash Wilderness. A mile east of camp, via the access road, is a primitive trailhead on the left side. This trail is routed four miles to Mesa Springs and a trail camp. The elevation is 4,400 feet.

**Campsites, facilities:** There are nine sites for tents or RVs up to 22 feet (no hookups). Picnic tables and fire grills are provided. Vault toilets are available, but there is no drinking water. Garbage must be packed out. Leashed pets are permitted.

**Reservations, fees:** Reservations are not accepted. There is no fee for camping. Open year-round.

**Directions:** From Maricopa, drive 14 miles south on Highway 166 to the Highway 33 exit. Turn south on Highway 33 and drive about 13 miles to Apache Canyon Road (Forest Road 8N06). Turn left and drive about 11 miles to the campground. Note: The last 10 miles are rough; high-clearance vehicles are advised.

**Contact:** Los Padres National Forest, Mount Piños Ranger District, 661/245-3731, www. fs.usda.gov/lpnf.

## 45 MOUNT PIÑOS

### Scenic rating: 7

in Los Padres National Forest

**Map 12.4, page 662**

This camp is set at 7,800 feet elevation, one

of three camps on the eastern flank of Mount Piños (8,831 feet). This is one of the few places on earth where it is possible to see flying California condors, the largest bird in North America. Note that a once-popular drive to the top of Mount Piños for beautiful and sweeping views is now closed after being recognized as a Chumash holy site. There's access to the Mount Piños summit trail 2.5 miles away on Mil Potrero Highway at the Chula Vista parking area. From there it's about two miles to the summit, which is a designated botanical area. July and August usually are the best months for wildflower displays. McGill (see listing in this chapter) provides a nearby camping alternative.

**Campsites, facilities:** There are 19 sites for tents or RVs up to 16 feet (no hookups). Picnic tables and fire rings are provided. Vault toilets are available, but there is no drinking water. Leashed pets are permitted.

**Reservations, fees:** Reservations are not accepted. Sites are $20 per night, plus $10 per night per each additional vehicle. Open late May through October, weather permitting.

**Directions:** Drive on I-5 to just south of Lebec to the Frazier Park exit. Take that exit and drive west on Frazier Mountain Road to the town of Lake of the Woods and Cuddy Valley Road. Continue straight on Cuddy Valley Road and drive about six miles to Mount Piños Highway. Bear left and drive five miles (the road name changes several times, but stay on the main road) to the campground.

**Contact:** Los Padres National Forest, Mount Piños Ranger District, 661/245-3731, www.fs.usda.gov/lpnf; Parks Management Company, 805/434-1996, www.campone.com.

## 46 MCGILL

### Scenic rating: 6

near Mount Piños in Los Padres National Forest

**Map 12.4, page 662**

The camp is set at 7,400 feet elevation, about four miles from the top of nearby Mount Piños. Although the road is closed to the top of Mount Piños, numerous hiking and biking trails in the area provide spectacular views. On clear days, there are vantage points to the high Sierra, the San Joaquin Valley, and Antelope Valley.

**Campsites, facilities:** There are 78 sites for tents or RVs up to 16 feet (no hookups) and two group sites for 60 and 80 people. Picnic tables and fire grills are provided. Pit toilets are available. There is no drinking water. Some facilities are wheelchair-accessible. Leashed pets are permitted.

**Reservations, fees:** Reservations are required for group sites at 877/444-6777 ($10 reservation fee) or www.recreation.gov ($9 reservation fee). Sites are $20 per night, the group site is $100-120 per night. Open late May through October.

**Directions:** Drive on I-5 to just south of Lebec to the Frazier Park exit. Take that exit and drive west on Frazier Mountain Road to the town of Lake of the Woods and Cuddy Valley Road. Continue straight on Cuddy Valley Road and drive about six miles to Mount Piños Highway. Bear left and drive about five miles to the campground on the right.

**Contact:** Los Padres National Forest, Mount Piños Ranger District, 661/245-3731, www.fs.usda.gov/lpnf; Parks Management Company, 805/434-1996, www.campone.com.

## 47 DAVY BROWN

### Scenic rating: 7

on Davy Brown Creek in Los Padres National Forest

**Map 12.4, page 662**

This pretty spot sits along little Davy Brown Creek at 2,100 feet elevation, deep in Los Padres National Forest. The border of the San Rafael Wilderness and an excellent trailhead are just two miles down the road (along Davy Brown Creek) to the northeast at Nira (see the Nira listing in this chapter for hiking options).

**Campsites, facilities:** There are 13 sites for

tents or RVs up to 25 feet (no hookups). Picnic tables and fire grills are provided. Vault toilets are available. No drinking water is available. Garbage must be packed out. Leashed pets are permitted.

**Reservations, fees:** Reservations are not accepted. Sites are $20 per night, plus $10 per each additional vehicle. Open year-round.

**Directions:** From U.S. 101 in Santa Barbara, take Highway 154 and drive northeast for 22 miles to Armour Ranch Road. Turn right on Armour Ranch Road and drive 1.5 miles to Happy Canyon Road. Turn right on Happy Canyon Road/County Route 3350 and drive 11 miles to Cachuma Saddle. Continue straight (north) on Sunset Valley/Cachuma Road/Forest Road 8N09 for four miles to the campground.

**Contact:** Los Padres National Forest, Santa Lucia Ranger District, 805/925-9538, www. fs.usda.gov/lpnf; Parks Management Company, 805/434-1996, www.campone.com.

## 48 NIRA

### Scenic rating: 8

on Manzana Creek in Los Padres National Forest

**Map 12.4, page 662**

Nira is a premium jumping-off spot for backpackers, set at 1,000 feet elevation along Manzana Creek, on the border of the San Rafael Wilderness. A primary wilderness trailhead is available, heading east into the San Rafael Wilderness through Lost Valley, along Fish Creek, and to Manzana Creek (and beyond), all in just six miles, with a series of hike-in camps available as the trail enters the wilderness interior. Today's history lesson? This camp was originally an NRA (National Recovery Act) camp during the Depression, hence the name Nira.

**Campsites, facilities:** There are 11 sites for tents or RVs up to 16 feet (no hookups). Picnic tables and fire grills are provided. Vault toilets, hitching posts, and horse trailer parking

are available. No drinking water is available. Garbage must be packed out. Some facilities are wheelchair-accessible. Leashed pets are permitted.

**Reservations, fees:** Reservations are not accepted. Sites are $20 per night, plus $10 per each additional vehicle. Open year-round, but access roads may be closed during and after heavy rains.

**Directions:** From U.S. 101 in Santa Barbara, take Highway 154 northeast and drive 22 miles to Armour Ranch Road. Turn right on Armour Ranch Road and drive 1.5 miles to Happy Canyon Road. Turn right on Happy Canyon Road and drive 11 miles to Cachuma Saddle. Continue straight (north) on Sunset Valley/ Cachuma Road/Forest Road 8N09 for six miles to the campground.

**Contact:** Los Padres National Forest, Santa Lucia Ranger District, 805/925-9538, www. fs.usda.gov/lpnf; Parks Management Company, 805/434-1996, www.campone.com.

## 49 FIGUEROA

### Scenic rating: 7

in Los Padres National Forest

**Map 12.4, page 662**

This is one of the more attractive camps in Los Padres National Forest. It is at 3,500 feet elevation beneath an unusual stand of oak and huge manzanita trees and offers a view of the Santa Ynez Valley. Nearby attractions include the Piño Alto Picnic Area, 2.5 miles away, offering a panoramic view of the adjacent wildlands with a 0.5-mile, wheelchair-accessible nature trail. An exceptional view is also available from the nearby Figueroa fire lookout. Though it requires a circuitous 10-mile ride around Figueroa Mountain to get there, Nira to the east provides the best trailhead in this area for the San Rafael Wilderness.

**Campsites, facilities:** There are 33 sites for tents or RVs up to 25 feet (no hookups). Picnic tables and fire grills are provided. Vault toilets are available. No drinking water is available. Garbage must be packed out. Leashed pets are permitted.

**Reservations, fees:** Reservations are not accepted. Sites are $20 per night, plus $10 per each additional vehicle. Open year-round.

**Directions:** Drive on Highway 154 to Los Olivos and Figueroa Mountain Road. Turn northeast on Figueroa Mountain Road and drive 12.5 miles to the campground. Note that the last 6.6 miles of Figueroa Mountain Road are not RV-friendly.

**Contact:** Los Padres National Forest, Santa Lucia Ranger District, 805/925-9538, www. fs.usda.gov/lpnf; Parks Management Company, 805/434-1996, www.campone.com.

## 50 REYES CREEK FAMILY AND EQUESTRIAN CAMP

### Scenic rating: 7

in Los Padres National Forest

**Map 12.4, page 662**

This developed Forest Service camp sits at the end of an old spur, Forest Road 7N11. The camp is at 3,960 feet elevation along Reyes Creek, which is stocked with trout in early summer. The Piedra Blanca/Gene Marshall Trail is routed out of camp to the south and climbs three miles to Upper Reyes backpack camp and beyond, up a ridge and down to Bear-Trap Creek and several trail camps along that creek. In all, the trail covers approximately 20 miles.

**Campsites, facilities:** There are 30 sites for tents or RVs up to 22 feet (no hookups). Picnic tables and fire grills are provided. Pit toilets and a corral are available, but there is no drinking water. Garbage must be packed out. A bar and café are nearby. Some facilities are wheelchair-accessible. Leashed pets are permitted.

**Reservations, fees:** Reservations are not accepted. Sites are $20 per night, plus $10 per each additional vehicle. Open year-round.

**Directions:** From Ojai, drive north on Highway 33 for 36 miles to Lockwood Valley

Road. Turn right on Lockwood Valley Road (Ozena Road) and drive about 3.5 miles to Forest Road 7N11. Turn right and drive about 1.5 miles to the village of Camp Scheideck and a T intersection. Bear left at the T intersection and drive 0.25 mile to the campground.

**Contact:** Los Padres National Forest, Ojai Ranger District, 805/646-4348, www.fs.usda. gov/lpnf; Parks Management Company, 805/434-1996, www.campone.com.

## 51 PINE SPRINGS

### Scenic rating: 6

near San Guillermo Mountain in Los Padres National Forest

**Map 12.4, page 662**

This primitive camp is at 5,800 feet elevation on a short spur road that dead-ends on the east flank of San Guillermo Mountain (6,569 feet). Pine Springs feeds the tiny headwaters of Guillermo Creek at this quiet spot. It gets little use, primarily from hunters in the fall.

**Campsites, facilities:** There are 12 sites for tents or RVs up to 22 feet (no hookups). Picnic tables and fire grills are provided. Vault toilets are available, but there is no drinking water. Garbage must be packed out. Leashed pets are permitted.

**Reservations, fees:** Reservations are not accepted. There is no fee for camping. An Adventure Pass ($30 annual fee or $5 daily pass) per parked vehicle is required. Open early May through October, weather permitting.

**Directions:** Drive on I-5 to just south of Lebec to the Frazier Park exit. Take that exit and drive west on Frazier Mountain Road to the town of Lake of the Woods and Lockwood Valley Road. Turn left on Lockwood Valley Road (take the left fork) and drive about 12 miles to Grade Valley Road (Forest Road 7N03). Turn left and drive 3.5 miles to Forest Road 7N03A. Turn right and drive one mile to the campground.

**Contact:** Los Padres National Forest, Mount

Piños Ranger District, 661/245-3731, www. fs.usda.gov/lpnf

# 52 PINE MOUNTAIN
🏃🐕⛺

### Scenic rating: 6
in Los Padres National Forest

**Map 12.4, page 662**

Pine Mountain, along with nearby Reyes Peak campground (a quarter mile to the east; see listing in this chapter), is a tiny, primitive campground in a pretty setting with a few trailheads close at hand. The two best nearby hikes lead to springs. A trail is routed out of camp and into Boulder Canyon for a mile down the mountain, where it meets another trail that turns left and heads a quarter mile to McGuire Spring Trail camp (piped spring water is available). It's advisable to obtain a Forest Service map. A popular launch area for hang gliders is 1.5 miles west of the campground. The elevation is 6,700 feet.

**Campsites, facilities:** There are six tent sites. Picnic tables and fire grills are provided. A pit toilet is available. There is no drinking water. Garbage must be packed out. Leashed pets are permitted.

**Reservations, fees:** Reservations are not accepted. Sites are $20 per night, plus $10 per each additional vehicle. Open April through early November, weather permitting.

**Directions:** From Ojai, drive north on Highway 33 for 33 miles to Reyes Peak Road. Turn right on Pine Mountain/Reyes Peak Road and drive five miles to the campground on the left.

**Contact:** Los Padres National Forest, Ojai Ranger District, 805/646-4348, www.fs.usda. gov/lpnf; Parks Management Company, 805/434-1996, www.campone.com.

# 53 REYES PEAK
🏃🐕⛺

### Scenic rating: 6
in Los Padres National Forest

**Map 12.4, page 662**

Reyes Peak is a primitive camp set at 6,800 feet elevation. Three short hikes in the immediate vicinity lead to trail camps. The closest is from a trailhead just to the west of camp, which provides an easy, half-mile hike north to Raspberry Spring (a backcountry camp is available there). A popular launch area for hang gliders is a half mile from camp. Nearby Pine Mountain campground (see listing in this chapter) provides an alternative for camping.

**Campsites, facilities:** There are six tent sites. Picnic tables and fire grills are provided. A pit toilet is available. There is no drinking water. Garbage must be packed out. Leashed pets are permitted.

**Reservations, fees:** Reservations are not accepted. Sites are $20 per night, plus $10 per each additional vehicle. Open April through early November, weather permitting.

**Directions:** From Ojai, drive north on Highway 33 for 33 miles to Reyes Peak Road. Turn right on Reyes Peak Road and drive 5.5 miles to the campground.

**Contact:** Los Padres National Forest, Ojai Ranger District, 805/646-4348, www.fs.usda. gov/lpnf; Parks Management Company, 805/434-1996, www.campone.com.

# 54 THORN MEADOWS FAMILY AND EQUESTRIAN CAMP
🏃🐕5%🚐⛺

### Scenic rating: 7
on Piru Creek in Los Padres National Forest

**Map 12.4, page 662**

The reward at Thorn Meadows is a small, quiet spot along Piru Creek at 5,000 feet elevation, deep in Los Padres National Forest. A trail out of camp leads three miles up to Thorn Point, a magnificent 6,935-foot lookout. It is by far the best view in the area, worth the 2,000-foot climb, and on a clear day you can see the Channel Islands.

**Campsites, facilities:** There are five sites for tents or RVs up to 16 feet (no hookups). Picnic tables and fire grills are provided. A toilet and a pipe corral are available. There is no drinking water. Garbage must be packed out. Leashed pets are permitted.

**Reservations, fees:** Reservations are not accepted. There is no fee for camping. An Adventure Pass ($30 annual fee or $5 daily pass) per parked vehicle is required. Open early May through October, weather permitting.

**Directions:** Drive on I-5 to just south of Lebec and the Frazier Park exit. Take that exit and drive west on Frazier Mountain Road to the town of Lake of the Woods and Lockwood Valley Road. Turn left on Lockwood Valley Road and drive about 12 miles to Mutau Flat Road (Forest Road 7N03/Grade Valley Road). Turn left and drive seven miles to Forest Road 7N03B. Turn right and drive one mile to the campground. A high-clearance vehicle is recommended.

**Contact:** Los Padres National Forest, Mount Piños Ranger District, 661/245-3731, www.fs.usda.gov/lpnf.

## 55 CACHUMA LAKE RECREATION AREA

### Scenic rating: 7

near Santa Barbara

**Map 12.4, page 662**

Cachuma is at 750 feet elevation in the foothills northwest of Santa Barbara, a once-big lake covering 3,200 acres. In low-rain years the drawdowns are so significant that you'd hardly recognize the place. After fishing, picnicking and camping come in a distant second and third in popularity, respectively.

Note: All boats must be certified mussel-free before launching. Watercraft under 10 feet and inflatables under 12 feet are prohibited on the lake.

**Campsites, facilities:** There are 420 sites for tents or RVs of any length and nine group areas for 8-30 vehicles (32-100 people). Some sites have full or partial hookups (30 amps) and/or are pull-through. Yurts and cabins are also available. Picnic tables and fire pits are provided. Drinking water, restrooms with flush toilets and coin showers, and coin laundry are available. Playground, general store, propane gas, seasonal swimming pool, full-service marina, fishing piers, bait and tackle, boat ramp, mooring, boat fuel, boat and water bike rentals, nature cruises, dump station, group facilities, RV storage, gas station, ice, and snack bar are nearby. Leashed pets are permitted, but they must be kept at least 50 feet from the lake.

**Reservations, fees:** Reservations are accepted online at www.sbparks.org (reservation fee $7 for tent sites, $20 for yurts and cabins). Tent sites are $25-30 per night, RV sites with partial and full hookups are $40-50 per night, $10 per night for each additional vehicle, $3 per pet per night. Yurts are $65-90 per night, cabins are $100-140 per night, and the group sites are $220-825 per night. Some credit cards are accepted. Open year-round.

**Directions:** From Santa Barbara, drive 18 miles north on Highway 154 to the campground entrance on the right.

**Contact:** Cachuma Lake Recreation Area, 805/686-5054, www.sbparks.org; Cachuma Marina and Boat Rentals, 805/688-4040; Cachuma Boat Tours, 805/686-5050 or 805/688-4515.

## 56 FREMONT

### Scenic rating: 7

near the Santa Ynez River in Los Padres National Forest

**Map 12.4, page 662**

As you travel west to east, Fremont is the first in a series of Forest Service campgrounds near the Santa Ynez River. This one is just inside the boundary of Los Padres National Forest at 900 feet elevation, nine miles east of Cachuma Lake to the west.

**Campsites, facilities:** There are 15 sites for tents or RVs up to 22 feet (no hookups). Picnic tables and fire grills are provided. Drinking water and flush toilets are available. Some facilities are wheelchair-accessible. Groceries are available within two miles and propane gas is available at Cachuma Lake nine miles away. Leashed pets are permitted.

**Reservations, fees:** Reservations are accepted at 877/444-6777 ($10 reservation fee) or www.recreation.gov ($9 reservation fee). Sites are $30 per night, plus $10 per night for each additional vehicle. Open early April through late October.

**Directions:** From Santa Barbara, drive northwest on Highway 154 for about 10 miles to Paradise Road/Forest Road 5N18. Turn right on Paradise Road/Forest Road 5N18 and drive 2.5 miles to the campground on the right.

**Contact:** Los Padres National Forest, Santa Barbara Ranger District, 805/967-3481, www.fs.usda.gov/lpnf; Parks Management Company, 805/434-1996, www.campone.com.

## 57 LOS PRIETOS
🏃 🛶 🚗 ⛺

### Scenic rating: 7
near the Santa Ynez River in Los Padres National Forest

**Map 12.4, page 662**

Los Prietos is across from the Santa Ynez River at an elevation of 1,000 feet, just upstream from nearby Fremont campground to the west. There are several nice hiking trails nearby; the best starts near the Los Prietos Ranger Station, heading south for two miles to Wellhouse Falls (get specific directions and a map at the ranger station). River access is available a quarter mile away at the White Rock day-use area.

**Campsites, facilities:** There are 38 sites for tents or RVs up to 22 feet (no hookups). Picnic tables and fire grills are provided. Drinking

water and flush toilets are available. Leashed pets are permitted.

**Reservations, fees:** Reservations are accepted at 877/444-6777 ($10 recreation fee) or www.recreation.gov ($9 reservation fee). Sites are $30 per night, plus $10 per night for each additional vehicle. Open early April through late October.

**Directions:** From Santa Barbara, take Highway 154 and drive 10 miles northeast to Paradise Road/Forest Road 5N18. Turn right on Paradise Road/Forest Road 5N18 and drive 3.8 miles to the campground.

**Contact:** Los Padres National Forest, Santa Barbara Ranger District, 805/967-3481, www.fs.usda.gov/lpnf; Parks Management Company, 805/434-1996, www.campone.com.

## 58 UPPER OSO FAMILY AND EQUESTRIAN CAMP
🏃 🛶 🐕 ♿ 🚗 ⛺

### Scenic rating: 7
near the Santa Ynez River in Los Padres National Forest

**Map 12.4, page 662**

This is one of the Forest Service campgrounds in the Santa Ynez Recreation Area. It is set in Oso Canyon at 1,100 feet elevation, one mile from the Santa Ynez River. This is a prime spot for equestrians, with horse corrals available at adjacent campsites. Note that at high water this campground can become inaccessible. A mile north of camp is the Santa Cruz Trailhead for a hike up Oso Canyon for a mile, then three miles up to Happy Hollow, and beyond that to a trail camp just west of Little Pine Mountain, elevation 4,508 feet. A trailhead into the San Rafael Wilderness is nearby, and once on the trail, you'll find many primitive sites in the backcountry.

**Campsites, facilities:** There are 23 sites for tents or RVs up to 22 feet (no hookups). Picnic tables and fire grills are provided. Drinking water, flush toilets, and garbage bins are available. Some facilities are wheelchair-accessible. Many sites have horse corrals and there is a horse-watering station. Leashed pets are permitted.

**Reservations, fees:** Reservations are accepted at 877/444-6777 ($10 reservation fee) or www.recreation.gov ($9 reservation fee). Sites are $30 per night, equestrian sites are $35 per night, and it's $10 per night for each additional vehicle. Open year-round, weather permitting.

**Directions:** From Santa Barbara, take Highway 154 and drive 10 miles northeast to Paradise Road/Forest Road 5N18. Turn right on Paradise Road/Forest Road 5N18 and drive six miles to Upper Oso Road. Turn left on Upper Oso Road and drive one mile to the campground at the end of the road.

**Contact:** Los Padres National Forest, Santa Barbara Ranger District, 805/967-3481, www.fs.usda.gov/lpnf; Parks Management Company, 805/434-1996, www.campone.com.

## 59 PARADISE

**Scenic rating: 7**

near the Santa Ynez River in Los Padres National Forest

**Map 12.4, page 662**

Here is yet another option among the camps along the Santa Ynez River. As you drive east it is the second camp you come to, just after Fremont. Trout are usually planted upriver of the campground during the spring. The best hiking trailheads nearby are at Upper Oso Camp and the Sage Hill Group Campground. Cachuma Lake is six miles west.

**Campsites, facilities:** There are 15 sites for tents or RVs up to 22 feet. Picnic tables and fire grills are provided. Drinking water and flush toilets are available. Groceries are available nearby. Some facilities are wheelchair-accessible. Leashed pets are permitted.

**Reservations, fees:** Reservations are accepted at 877/444-6777 ($10 reservation fee) or www.recreation.gov ($9 reservation fee). Single sites are $30 per night, double sites are $55 per night, plus $10 per night for each additional vehicle. Open year-round.

**Directions:** From Santa Barbara, take Highway 154 and drive 10 miles northeast to Paradise Road/Forest Road 5N18. Turn right on Paradise Road/Forest Road 5N18 and drive three miles to the campground on the right.

**Contact:** Los Padres National Forest, Santa Barbara Ranger District, 805/967-3481, www.fs.usda.gov/lpnf; Parks Management Company, 805/434-1996, www.campone.com.

## 60 SAGE HILL GROUP AND EQUESTRIAN CAMP

**Scenic rating: 7**

on the Santa Ynez River in Los Padres National Forest

**Map 12.4, page 662**

This is one in a series of camps along the Santa Ynez River in Los Padres National Forest. Sage Hill is at 2,000 feet elevation and was designed for large groups as well as equestrians, with horse corrals available next to one group site. A 3.5-mile loop trail starts at the back end of Sage Hill Group Camp. The first mile is a self-guided interpretive trail.

**Campsites, facilities:** Five group areas for tents or RVs up to 32 feet (no hookups) can accommodate 50-60 people each. Picnic tables and fire grills are provided. Drinking water and flush toilets are available. Horse corrals and hitching posts are in the Caballo group site. Some facilities are wheelchair-accessible. Leashed pets are permitted.

**Reservations, fees:** Reservations are required at 877/444-6777 ($10 reservation fee) or www.recreation.gov ($9 reservation fee). Sites are $125-150 per night. Open year-round, weather permitting.

**Directions:** From Santa Barbara, take Highway 154 and drive 10 miles northeast to Paradise Road/Forest Road 5N18. Turn right on Paradise Road/Forest Road 5N18 and drive five miles to the ranger station and the campground entrance road. Turn left and drive 0.5 mile to the campground.

**Contact:** Los Padres National Forest, Santa Barbara Ranger District, 805/967-3481, www. fs.usda.gov/lpnf; Parks Management Company, 805/434-1996, www.campone.com.

## 61 MONO HIKE-IN

### Scenic rating: 7
on Mono Creek in Los Padres National Forest

**Map 12.4, page 662**

Not many folks know about this spot. The camp is small and primitive, at 1,500 feet elevation on little Mono Creek. Also note that Little Caliente Hot Springs is one mile northeast of the campground. Mono Creek is a feeder to Gibraltar Reservoir, a long, narrow lake with no direct access.

**Campsites, facilities:** There are three tent sites. Picnic tables and fire grills are provided. Vault toilets are available. No drinking water is available. Garbage must be packed out. Leashed pets are permitted.

**Reservations, fees:** Reservations are not accepted. There is no fee for camping. An Adventure Pass ($30 annual fee or $5 daily pass) per parked vehicle is required. Open year-round, weather permitting.

**Directions:** From U.S. 101 in Santa Barbara, take Highway 154 and drive northeast for eight miles to East Camino Cielo/Forest Road 5N12. Turn right on East Camino Cielo/Forest Road 5N12 and drive 18 miles to the end of the paved road at Camuesa Road/Forest Road 5N15 (a dirt road). Continue on Camuesa Road for five miles to the old Juncal Campground (closed). Turn left (still on Forest Road 5N15) and drive seven miles to the parking area for Mono Hike-In. Park and hike approximately 100 yards to the campground.

**Contact:** Los Padres National Forest, Santa Barbara Ranger District, 805/967-3481, www. fs.usda.gov/lpnf.

## 62 P-BAR FLAT

### Scenic rating: 7
on the Santa Ynez River in Los Padres National Forest

**Map 12.4, page 662**

The best thing—or the worst thing, depending on how you look at it—about P-Bar Flat is a trailhead that is routed north into the remote wildlands of Los Padres National Forest. The camp is very small and primitive, set at 1,800 feet elevation along the Santa Ynez River. The trail starts by heading up Horse Canyon along a creek, but eventually it is routed 10 miles to Hildreth Peak, at 8,066 feet, a 6,000-foot butt-kicker of a climb. A lot of guys in prison get less punishment.

**Campsites, facilities:** There are four tent sites. Picnic tables and fire grills are provided. Vault toilets are available. No drinking water is available. Garbage must be packed out. Leashed pets are permitted.

**Reservations, fees:** Reservations are not accepted. There is no fee for camping. An Adventure Pass ($30 annual fee or $5 daily pass) per parked vehicle is required. Open year-round, weather permitting.

**Directions:** From U.S. 101 in Santa Barbara, take Highway 154 and drive northeast for eight miles to East Camino Cielo/Forest Road 5N12. Turn right on East Camino Cielo/Forest Road 5N12 and drive 18 miles to the end of the paved road at Camuesa Road/Forest Road 5N15 (a dirt road). Continue on Camuesa Road for five miles to the old Juncal Campground (closed). Turn left (still on Forest Road 5N15) and drive four miles to the campground.

**Contact:** Los Padres National Forest, Santa Barbara Ranger District, 805/967-3481, www. fs.usda.gov/lpnf.

## 63 MIDDLE SANTA YNEZ

**Scenic rating: 7**

on the Santa Ynez River in Los Padres National Forest

**Map 12.4, page 662**

Four camps border the Santa Ynez River between Gibraltar Reservoir to the west and little Jameson Lake to the east. Look them over and pick the one you like best. This one is at an elevation of 1,500 feet, about a half mile east of P-Bar Flat (see the P-Bar Flat listing in this chapter for information about a trailhead there).

**Campsites, facilities:** There are 13 tent sites. Picnic tables and fire grills are provided. Vault toilets are available. No drinking water is available. Garbage must be packed out. Leashed pets are permitted.

**Reservations, fees:** Reservations are not accepted. There is no fee for camping. An Adventure Pass ($30 annual fee or $5 daily pass) per parked vehicle is required. A senior discount is available. Open year-round, weather permitting.

**Directions:** From U.S. 101 in Santa Barbara, take Highway 154 and drive northeast for eight miles to East Camino Cielo/Forest Road 5N12. Turn right on East Camino Cielo/Forest Road 5N12 and drive 18 miles to the end of the paved road at Camuesa Road/Forest Road 5N15 (a dirt road). Continue on Camuesa Road for five miles to the old Juncal Campground (closed). Turn left (still on Forest Road 5N15) and drive three miles to the campground.

**Contact:** Los Padres National Forest, Santa Barbara Ranger District, 805/967-3481, www. fs.usda.gov/lpnf.

## 64 HOLIDAY GROUP CAMP

**Scenic rating: 7**

on Matilija Creek in Los Padres National Forest

**Map 12.4, page 662**

This group site, set at 2,000 feet elevation, is near the North Fork of the Matilija. It's only three miles uphill from Matilija Reservoir.

**Campsites, facilities:** One group site for tents or RVs up to 22 feet (no hookups) can accommodate up to 75 people. An adjacent parking lot has room for 10 vehicles. Picnic tables and fire grills are provided. Vault toilets are available, but there is no drinking water. Garbage must be packed out. Leashed pets are permitted.

**Reservations, fees:** Reservations are required at 877/444-6777 ($10 reservation fee) or www. recreation.gov ($9 reservation fee). The camp is $100-125 per night (includes up to 10 vehicles), plus $10 per night per each additional vehicle. Open year-round.

**Directions:** From Ojai, drive northwest on Highway 33 for nine miles to the campground entrance on the right.

**Contact:** Los Padres National Forest, Ojai Ranger District, 805/646-4348, www.fs.usda. gov/lpnf; Parks Management Company, 805/434-1996, www.campone.com.

## 65 WHEELER GORGE

**Scenic rating: 7**

on Matilija Creek in Los Padres National Forest

**Map 12.4, page 662**

This developed Forest Service camp at 2,000 feet elevation is one of the more popular spots in the area. The North Fork of the Matilija runs beside the camp and provides some fair trout fishing in the spring and good swimming holes in early summer. Interpretive programs are also available, a nice plus, and a nature trail is adjacent to the campground.

**Campsites, facilities:** There are 67 sites for tents or RVs up to 35 feet (no hookups), including six double sites. Picnic tables and fire grills are provided. Vault toilets are available, but there is no drinking water. Garbage must be packed out. Some facilities are wheelchair-accessible. Leashed pets are permitted.

**Reservations, fees:** Reservations are accepted at 877/444-6777 or www.recreation.gov ($9 reservation fee). Single sites are $25 per night, double sites are $50 per night, plus $10 per night for each additional vehicle. Winter rates are lower. Open year-round.

**Directions:** From Ojai, drive northwest on Highway 33 for 8.5 miles to the campground entrance on the left. Gates are locked at 10pm and no entry is allowed.

**Contact:** Los Padres National Forest, Ojai Ranger District, 805/646-4348, www.fs.usda. gov/lpnf; Parks Management Company, 805/434-1996, www.campone.com.

# 66 ROSE VALLEY

### Scenic rating: 8
in Los Padres National Forest

**Map 12.4, page 662**

The short walk to Rose Valley Falls, a 300-foot waterfall that provides a happy surprise, makes this camp a sure winner in late winter and spring. The walk to the waterfall is just a half-mile round-trip. Note that there are two views of it: a long-distance view of the entire waterfall, and at the base a view of just the lower tier (the limestone crumbles easily, so be careful near ledges). It is one of the scenic highlights in this section of Los Padres National Forest. The camp is at 3,400 feet elevation next to Rose Valley Creek, about two miles from Sespe Creek. If this campground is full, there is another campground, Middle Lion, two miles beyond Rose Valley camp.

**Campsites, facilities:** There are nine sites for tents or RVs up to 30 feet (no hookups). Picnic tables and fire grills are provided. Vault toilets are available. There is no drinking water. Horseback-riding facilities are nearby. Garbage

must be packed out. Some facilities are wheelchair-accessible. Leashed pets are permitted.

**Reservations, fees:** Reservations are not accepted. Sites are $20 per night, plus $10 per each additional vehicle. Open year-round, weather permitting.

**Directions:** From Ojai, drive north on Highway 33 for 15 miles to Sespe River Road/Rose Valley Road. Turn right on Sespe River Road/Rose Valley Road and drive 5.5 miles to the campground entrance.

**Contact:** Los Padres National Forest, Ojai Ranger District, 805/646-4348, www.fs.usda. gov/lpnf; Parks Management Company, 805/434-1996, www.campone.com.

# 67 SANTA BARBARA SUNRISE RV PARK

### Scenic rating: 3
in Santa Barbara

**Map 12.4, page 662**

This is the only RV park in Santa Barbara, and RV cruisers get a little of two worlds: The park is close to the beach, but the downtown shopping area isn't too far away, either. But it's also close to the highway, so noise can be a problem for RVs that are less than soundproof. In addition, access is difficult for RVs over 30 feet.

**Campsites, facilities:** There are 33 sites with full hookups (20, 30, and 50 amps) for RVs up to 45 feet, including four pull-through sites. Picnic tables, restrooms with free showers, cable TV, free Wi-Fi, and coin laundry are available. A grocery store, golf course, tennis courts, and propane gas are nearby. Leashed pets are permitted, with some breed restrictions.

**Reservations, fees:** Reservations are accepted. Sites start at $60 per night, plus $5 per person per night for more than two people. Some credit cards are accepted. Open year-round.

**Directions:** In Santa Barbara on U.S. 101 northbound, drive to the Salinas Street exit. Take that exit and drive to the park (well signed) at 516 South Salinas Street, near the highway exit.

In Santa Barbara on U.S. 101 southbound, drive to the Milpas Street exit. Take that exit and turn left on Milpas Street. Drive under the freeway to Carpinteria Street. Turn right and drive 0.5 mile to Salinas Street. Turn right and drive 0.5 mile to the park on the right.

**Contact:** Santa Barbara Sunrise RV Park, 805/966-9954 or 800/345-5018, www.santabararv.com.

## 68 CARPINTERIA STATE BEACH

🚶 🚴 🏊 ⛵ 🎣 🐕 ♿ 🚐 ⛺

**Scenic rating: 8**

near Santa Barbara

**Map 12.4, page 662**

First, plan on reservations, and then, plan on plenty of neighbors. This state beach is one pretty spot, and a lot of folks cruising up the coast like the idea of taking off their boots here for a while. This is an urban park; that is, it is within walking distance of downtown, restaurants, and shopping. You can love it or hate it, but this camp is almost always full. It features one mile of beach and 21 campgrounds, including seven group sites. Harbor seals can be seen December through May, along with an occasional passing gray whale. Protected tidepools contain starfish, sea anemones, crabs, snails, octopus, and sea urchins. In the summer, the visitors center features a living tidepool exhibit. Other state beaches to the nearby north are El Capitán State Beach and Refugio State Beach, both with campgrounds.

**Campsites, facilities:** There are 65 sites with no hookups for tents, 79 sites with full or partial hookups (30 amps) for RVs up to 30 feet, 29 sites with partial hookups for RVs up to 35 feet, 38 sites with no hookups for RVs up to 21 feet, one hike-in/bike-in site, and seven group sites that can accommodate 25-65 people each. Picnic tables and fire rings are provided. Drinking water, restrooms with flush toilets

and coin showers, and a picnic area are available. A convenience store, coin laundry, restaurants, and propane gas are nearby in the town of Carpinteria. Some facilities are wheelchair-accessible. Leashed pets are permitted, except on the beach.

**Reservations, fees:** Reservations are accepted at 800/444-7275 ($10 reservation fee) or www.reserveamerica.com ($9 reservation fee). Tent sites are $35-45 per night, premium tent sites are $50-60 per night; RV sites (hookups) are $50-80 per night, premium RV sites (hookups) are $60-80 per night; $10 per night for each additional vehicle. The hike-in/bike-in site is $10 per person per night, group sites are $180-430 per night. Open year-round.

**Directions:** From Santa Barbara, drive south on U.S. 101 for 12 miles to Carpinteria and the Casitas Pass Road exit. Take that exit and turn right on Casitas Pass Road and drive about a block to Carpinteria Avenue. Turn right and drive a short distance to Palm Avenue. Turn left and drive about six blocks to the campground at the end of Palm Avenue.

**Contact:** Carpinteria State Beach, 805/684-2811; Channel Coast District, 805/968-1033, www.parks.ca.gov.

## 69 LAKE CASITAS RECREATION AREA

🚴 ⛵ 🎣 🐕 🏇 ♿ 🚐 ⛺

**Scenic rating: 7**

north of Ventura

**Map 12.4, page 662**

Lake Casitas is known as one of Southern California's world-class fish factories. The lake is managed primarily for anglers, with more 10-pound bass produced here than anywhere, including the former state record, a bass that weighed 21 pounds, 3 ounces (other species include catfish, crappie, and sunfish). The ideal climate in the foothill country gives the fish a nine-month growing season and provides excellent weather for camping. Fishing at night is permitted on select weekends. Note: All boats must be certified mussel-free before launching (call 805/649-2233 for an appointment). Due to drought, please check current conditions for water levels, fishing restrictions, or camping requirements.

Casitas is north of Ventura at an elevation of 567 feet in the foothills bordering Los Padres National Forest. The lake has 32 miles of shoreline with a huge number of sheltered coves, covering 2,710 acres; waterskiing, personal watercraft, and swimming are not permitted. The park holds many special events, including the Ojai Wine Festival and the Ojai Renaissance Festival.

**Campsites, facilities:** There are 400 sites for tents or RVs of any length and three group sites for a maximum of 10 vehicles each; some sites have full or partial hookups (30 and 50 amps) and/or are pull-through. Picnic tables and fire rings are provided. Restrooms with flush toilets and showers, drinking water, two dump stations, playgrounds, general store, picnic areas, propane, ice, snack bar, water playground, and a full-service marina (including boat ramps, boat rentals, slips, fuel, tackle, and bait) are available. Some facilities are wheelchair-accessible. Leashed pets are permitted, except on the lake.

**Reservations, fees:** Reservations are accepted at 805/649-1122 ($9 reservation fee, $75 reservation fee for group sites) or online at www.casitaswater.org or www.lakecasitas.info. Tent sites are $26-30 per night, RV sites are $35-40 (water and electricity) and $55-60 (full hookups) per night, plus $12 per night for each additional vehicle and $3 per pet per night. The group sites are $250-350 per night with a two-night, 10-vehicle maximum. Some credit cards are accepted. Open year-round.

**Directions:** From Ventura, drive north on Highway 33 for 10.5 miles to Highway 150/Baldwin Road. Turn left (west) on Highway 150 and drive three miles to Santa Ana Road. Turn left and drive to the lake and campground entrance at 11311 Santa Ana Road.

**Contact:** Lake Casitas Recreation Area, 805/649-2233; Lake Casitas Marina, 805/649-2043; Nature Cruises, 805/640-6844, ext. 654, www.lakecasitas.info.

## 70 CAMP COMFORT PARK OJAI

**Scenic rating: 4**

on San Antonio Creek north of Ventura

Map 12.4, page 662

This Ventura County park gets missed by many. It's set in a residential area in the Ojai Valley foothill country at 1,000 feet elevation. San Antonio Creek runs through the park and there are shade trees. Lake Casitas Recreation Area is 10 miles away.

**Campsites, facilities:** There are 15 sites with full hookups (30 and 50 amps) for tents or RVs up to 34 feet. Picnic tables and fire pits are provided. Restrooms with flush toilets and showers, drinking water, coin laundry, cable TV, picnic areas, group facilities, clubhouse, and playground are available. Supplies are nearby. Leashed pets are permitted in the campground only.

**Reservations, fees:** Reservations are accepted in the off-season only ($10 nonrefundable reservation fee). Sites are $35-40 per night per vehicle, plus $1 per pet per night. Open year-round.

**Directions:** From Ventura, take Highway 33 north to North Creek Road. Turn right and drive 4.5 miles to the park at 11969 North Creek Road.

**Contact:** Camp Comfort Park Ojai, 805/654-3951, www.venturaparks.org.

## 71 DENNISON CAMPGROUND

**Scenic rating: 8**

in Ojai

Map 12.4, page 662

Dennison Campground is in the foothills of Ojai. This is a nice, calm place to relax, with shade trees and an outstanding view of the Ojai Valley. As a county park, it is often overlooked by out-of-towners. Lake Casitas, known for huge but hard-to-catch bass, is to the west.

**Campsite, facilities:** There are 46 sites for tents or RVs up to 35 feet (no hookups). Picnic tables and fire pits are provided. Drinking water, restrooms with flush toilets and coin showers, horseshoe pits, a playground, and a camp host are available.

**Reservations, fees:** Reservations are accepted online at www.venturaparks.org ($10 nonrefundable reservation fee). Sites are $21 per night (one RV, one tent maximum), plus $1 per pet per night. Call for group rates. Open year-round.

**Directions:** From Ventura, drive north on Highway 33 for 13 miles to East Ojai Avenue. Continue on East Ojai Avenue for 3.5 miles to a slight right on Ojai Santa Paula Road (Highway 150). Continue 1.5 miles to Dennison Park.

**Contact:** Ventura County Parks Department, 805/654-3951, www.venturaparks.org.

## 72 VENTURA RANCH KOA

### Scenic rating: 7

on Santa Paula Creek east of Ventura

**Map 12.4, page 662**

Ventura Ranch KOA is near little Santa Paula Creek in the foothill country adjacent to Steckel County Park. For those who want a well-developed park with a lot of amenities, the shoe fits. Note that at one time the two campgrounds, Ventura Ranch KOA and Steckel County Park, were linked. No more, and for good reason. Ventura Ranch KOA is a tight ship where the gates close at 10pm and quiet time ensures campers a good night's sleep. It is a good place to bring a family. Steckel County Park, on the other hand, has a problematic campground— loud noise, partying, and fights. So what do you do? Go next door to Ventura Ranch KOA, where the inmates aren't running the asylum, and the days are fun and nights are peaceful.

**Campsites, facilities:** There are 72 sites with full or partial hookups (20, 30, and 50 amps) for RVs up to 65 feet and a tent area for up to 400 people. Picnic tables and fire rings are provided. Restrooms with flush toilets and showers, drinking water, coin laundry, Wi-Fi for RVs, dump station, zipline, clubhouse, video room, RV storage, guided hikes, rock-climbing wall, and horseshoes are available. Supplies are nearby. Leashed pets are permitted.

**Reservations, fees:** Reservations are accepted for RV sites and are required for the tent area. RV sites are $39-69 per night, plus $10 per night for each additional vehicle. Tent sites are $38-47 per night. Group rates are available (minimum of eight RVs). Weekly and monthly rates are available. Some credit cards are accepted. Open year-round.

**Directions:** From Ventura, drive east on Highway 126 for 14 miles to Highway 150. Turn northwest on Highway 150 and drive five miles to the resort entrance on the right.

**Contact:** Ventura Ranch KOA, 805/933-3200 or 800/562-1899, www.venturaranchkoa.com.

## 73 RIVER VIEW CAMPGROUND

### Scenic rating: 7

in Steckel Park

**Map 12.4, page 662**

Santa Paula Creek flows through Steckel Park, a pretty county park that has put some work into their campground. It offers enough shade trees so that you don't feel jammed in, an aviary, fishing, and hiking. To the near north is the Sespe Wilderness, fronted by Santa Paula Ridge and the Topatopa Mountains. This area is also a refuge for the California condor.

**Campsites, facilities:** There are 48 sites for tents and RVs; 10 sites have full 20-, 30-, and 50-amp hookups. Picnic tables and fire pits are provided. Drinking water, restrooms with flush toilets and coin showers, horseshoe pits, a playground, a softball field, and a camp host are available. Leashed pets are permitted for a fee.

**Reservations, fees:** Reservations are accepted at www.venturaparks.org ($10 individual, $20 group reservation fee). Tent sites are $23 per night, RV sites are $36 per night (one RV, one tent maximum), pet fees are $1 per day (allowed only in campground). Winter rates are available. Open year-round.

**Directions:** From Ventura, drive east on Highway 126 for 14 miles to Highway 150. Turn left (northwest) on Highway 150 and drive five miles to the campground entrance on right.

**Contact:** Ventura County Parks Department, 805/654-3951, www.venturaparks.org.

## 74 HOBSON COUNTY PARK

### Scenic rating: 6

north of Ventura

**Map 12.4, page 662**

This county park is at the end of Rincon Parkway, kind of like a crowded cul-de-sac, with easy access to the beach and many side-trip possibilities. There is a great reef to explore at low tides. Emma Wood State Beach, San Buenaventura State Beach, and McGrath State Beach are all within 11 miles of the park.

**Campsites, facilities:** There are 31 sites for tents or RVs up to 34 feet; 15 sites have full hookups, including cable TV. Picnic tables and fire pits are provided. Restrooms with flush toilets and coin showers, drinking water, and a snack bar are available. Leashed pets are permitted in the campground, but not on the beach.

**Reservations, fees:** Reservations are accepted for RV sites with full hookups at www.venturaparks.org ($3 reservation fee). All other sites are first-come, first-served. Tent sites are $30-36 per night, RV sites are $43-48 per night (one RV, one tent maximum), pet fees are $1 per day. Winter rates are available. Open year-round.

**Directions:** From Ventura, drive northwest

on U.S. 101 for three miles to the State Beaches exit. Take that exit, turn north on West Pacific Highway, and drive five miles to the campground on the left.

**Contact:** Ventura County Parks Department, 805/654-3951, www.venturaparks.org.

## 75 FARIA COUNTY PARK

### Scenic rating: 7

north of Ventura

**Map 12.4, page 662**

This county park provides a possible base of operations for beach adventures, including surf fishing. It is along the ocean, with Emma Wood State Beach, San Buenaventura State Beach, and McGrath State Beach all within 10 miles.

**Campsites, facilities:** There are 42 sites for tents or RVs up to 34 feet; 10 sites have full hookups (30 amps), including cable TV. Picnic tables and fire pits are provided. Restrooms with flush toilets and coin showers, drinking water, a playground, and a snack bar are available. Leashed pets are permitted.

**Reservations, fees:** Reservations are not accepted. RV sites are $34-36 (no hookups and some without fire rings) and $48-53 (hookups) per night, plus $1 per pet per night. Open year-round.

**Directions:** From Ventura, drive north on U.S. 101 for three miles to the State Beaches exit. Take that exit, turn north on West Pacific Highway, and drive four miles to the campground.

**Contact:** Ventura County Parks Department, 805/654-3951, www.venturaparks.org.

## 76 RINCON PARKWAY

### Scenic rating: 5

north of Ventura

**Map 12.4, page 662**

This is basically an RV park near the ocean,

where the sites are created by parking end-to-end along old Highway 1. It is not quiet. Passing trains across the highway vie for noise honors with the surf. Emma Wood State Beach, San Buenaventura State Beach, and McGrath State Beach are all within 10 miles. Two activities are surf fishing and watching great sunsets.

**Campsites, facilities:** There are 127 sites for self-contained RVs up to 40 feet (no hookups). Supplies are available nearby. Leashed pets are allowed but not on the beach.

**Reservations, fees:** Reservations are not accepted. RV sites are $28 per night per vehicle, plus $1 per pet per night. Open year-round.

**Directions:** From Ventura, drive northwest on U.S. 101 for three miles to the State Beaches exit. Take that exit, turn north on West Pacific Highway, and drive 4.5 miles to the campground on the left.

**Contact:** Ventura County Parks Department, 805/654-3951, www.venturaparks.org.

## 77 EMMA WOOD STATE BEACH

### Scenic rating: 8

north of Ventura

**Map 12.4, page 662**

This is more of a parking lot than a campground with individual sites. And oh, what a place to camp: It is set along the ocean, a pretty spot with tidepools full of all kinds of little marine critters waiting to be discovered. It is also just a short drive from the town of Ventura and the Mission San Buenaventura. One downer, a big one for many, is noise from passing trains. Another downer: No toilets are available at night, so you must have a self-contained vehicle. The gate closes at 10pm and reopens at 6am.

**Campsites, facilities:** There are 86 sites for RVs up to 40 feet (no hookups). No tents are permitted. Chemical toilets are available for day use only. No drinking water is available. Supplies and a coin laundry are three miles

away. Leashed pets are permitted but not on the beach.

**Reservations, fees:** Reservations are required mid-May through Labor Day weekend at 800/444-7275 ($10 reservation fee) or www.reserveamerica.com ($9 reservation fee). Sites are $30-40 per night, plus $10 per night for each additional vehicle. Open year-round, weather and tides permitting.

**Directions:** From Ventura drive north on U.S. 101 for three miles to the State Beaches exit. Take that exit, drive under the freeway, and continue less than a mile to the park entrance on the left.

**Contact:** Emma Wood State Beach, Channel Coast District, 805/585-1850, www.parks.ca.gov.

## 78 VENTURA RIVER GROUP CAMP

### Scenic rating: 1

at Emma Wood State Beach near Ventura

**Map 12.4, page 662**

This is an extremely noisy area, and the campsites are also downright ugly. It is near the freeway and railroad tracks, and you get a lot of noise from both. It's not popular, either. What you have is mainly a dry riverbed. It is saved somewhat by a freshwater marsh at the southwest end of the beach that attracts red-tailed hawks, songbirds, and raccoons.

**Campsites, facilities:** There are four group tent sites for up to 30 people each, one group site for RVs of up to 45 feet that can accommodate up to 50 people, and 15 hike-in/bike-in sites. Picnic tables and fire rings are provided. Drinking water, chemical toilets, and cold showers are available. Leashed pets are permitted in the campground but not on the beach. Supplies are within one mile.

**Reservations, fees:** Reservations are required for the group sites at 800/444-7275 ($10 reservation fee) or www.reserveamerica.com ($9 reservation fee). The tent group camps are $130 per night, the RV group camp is $360 per night, and the hike-in/bike-in sites are $10 per person per night. Rates are lower October through April. Open year-round.

**Directions:** On U.S. 101 in Ventura, take the Main Street exit and turn west. Drive one mile on Main Street to the campground on the left.

**Contact:** Emma Wood State Beach, Channel Coast District, 805/585-1850, www.parks.ca.gov.

## 79 RESIDENCE CAMPGROUND

Scenic rating: 6

in Foster Park in Ventura

Map 12.4, page 662

The Ventura River meanders through this park and its campground. The park has shade trees, a small amphitheater, and an equestrian area and is close to the trailhead for the Ojai Valley trail. Fishing and hiking round out the recreation options. However, there have been complaints of traffic noise.

**Campsites, facilities:** There are 16 sites for tents and RVs; 10 sites have 20-, 30-, and 50-amp hookups. Picnic tables and fire pits are provided, and there is an area for group barbecues. Drinking water, restrooms with flush toilets, a playground, horseshoe pits, and a camp host are available. Leashed pets are permitted in the campground only.

**Reservations, fees:** Reservations are accepted in the off-season at www.venturaparks.org ($10 reservation fee). Tent sites are $20 per night; RV sites (hookups) are $34 per night (one RV and one tent maximum per site). Call for group reservation rates and fees. Pet fees are $1 per night. Winter rates are available. Open year-round.

**Directions:** From Ventura, drive north on Highway 33 for 4.5 miles to the North Ventura Avenue exit (immediately before the freeway ends). Turn right on North Ventura and then right again almost immediately onto Casitas

Vista. The park entrance is at 438 Casitas Vista Road.

**Contact:** Ventura County Parks Department, 805/654-3951, www.venturaparks.org.

## 80 MCGRATH STATE BEACH

Scenic rating: 9

south of Ventura

Map 12.4, page 662

McGrath State Beach has been closed since August 2014 due to flooding. Please contact the park directly before planning a trip.

This is a pretty spot just south of Ventura Harbor. Campsites are about 400 yards from the beach. This park features two miles of beach frontage, as well as lush riverbanks and sand dunes along the ocean shore. That gives rise to some of the best bird-watching in California. The north tip of the park borders the Santa Clara River Estuary Natural Preserve, where the McGrath State Beach Nature Trail provides an easy walk (wheelchair-accessible) along the Santa Clara River as it feeds into the estuary and then into the ocean. Rangers caution all considering swimming here to beware of strong currents and rip tides; they can be deadly. Beach access from the campground is limited due to flooding and nesting habitat protection. Campers must walk approximately half a mile or more to get around the inland lagoon.

**Campsites, facilities:** There are 174 sites for tents or RVs up to 30 feet (no hookups); 29 of the sites can be used as group sites. There is also a hike-in/bike-in site. Picnic tables and fire grills are provided. Restrooms with flush toilets and coin showers, drinking water, and a dump station are available. Supplies and a coin laundry are nearby. Some facilities are wheelchair-accessible. Leashed pets are permitted in campsites only.

**Reservations, fees:** Reservations are accepted online at 800/444-7275 ($10 reservation fee) or www.reserveamerica.com ($9 reservation fee). Sites are $35-45 per night, plus $10 per night for each additional vehicle, and the hike-in/bike-in site are $10 per person per night. For group prices and reservations, phone 805/648-3918. Open year-round, weather and river conditions permitting.

**Directions:** Drive on U.S. 101 to south of Ventura and the Seaward exit. Take that exit and drive to the stoplight and Harbor Boulevard. Turn west on Harbor Boulevard and drive four miles to the park (signed).

**Contact:** McGrath State Beach or Emma Wood State Beach, Channel Coast District, 805/585-1850, www.parks.ca.gov.

## 81 THORNHILL BROOME AND LA JOLLA GROUP

### Scenic rating: 7

in Point Mugu State Park

**Map 12.4, page 662**

Point Mugu State Park is known for its rocky bluffs, sandy beaches, rugged hills, and uplands. There are two major river canyons and wide grassy valleys sprinkled with sycamores, oaks, and a few native walnut trees. Of the campgrounds at Point Mugu, Thornhill Broome is more attractive than Sycamore Canyon (see listing in this chapter) for many visitors because it is on the ocean side of the highway (Sycamore Canyon is on the north side of the highway). It is a 2.5-mile walk to reach La Jolla Valley. While the beachfront is pretty and you can always just lie there in the sun and pretend you're a beached whale, the park's expanse on the east side of the highway in the Santa Monica Mountains provides more recreation. That includes two stellar hikes, the 9.5-mile Sycamore Canyon Loop and the seven-mile La Jolla Valley Loop. In all, the park covers 14,980 acres, far more than the obvious strip of beachfront. The park has more than 70 miles of hiking trails and five miles of ocean shoreline. Swimming, body surfing, and surf fishing are possible on the beach. Note: The front

gate for Thornhill Broome closes at 10pm and reopens at 8am.

**Campsites, facilities:** Thornhill Broome has 65 primitive sites for tents or RVs up to 31 feet (no hookups); La Jolla Group has a group camping area for tents only accommodating 9-50 people. There are also 10 environmental walk-in sites. Picnic tables and fire rings are provided at some sites; no open fires are allowed at the environmental walk-in sites. Drinking water and chemical toilets are available at Thornhill Broome; drinking water and flush toilets are available at La Jolla Group. Supplies can be obtained nearby. Note that nearby Sycamore Canyon has a dump station and nature center. Some facilities are wheelchair-accessible.

**Reservations, fees:** Reservations are accepted at 800/444-7275 ($10 reservation fee) or www.reserveamerica.com ($9 reservation fee). Environmental sites are first-come, first-served. Thornhill Broome sites are $35 per night, plus $12 per night for each additional vehicle; hike-in/bike-in sites are $10 per person per night; and La Jolla Group Camp is $225 per night. Open year-round but subject to closure during fire season.

**Directions:** From Oxnard, drive 15 miles south on Highway 1 to the camp entrance. Thornhill Broome is on the right, and La Jolla Group is on the left.

**Contact:** California State Parks, Angeles District, 818/880-0363 or 805/488-5223, www.parks.ca.gov.

## 82 SYCAMORE CANYON

### Scenic rating: 6

in Point Mugu State Park

**Map 12.4, page 662**

While this camp is across the highway from the ocean, it is also part of Point Mugu State Park, which covers 14,980 acres. That gives you plenty of options. One of the best is taking the Sycamore Canyon Loop, a long hiking route with great views that starts right at the camp.

In all, the 9.5-mile loop climbs to a ridge top and offers beautiful views of nearby canyons and long-distance vistas of the coast. Note: The front gate closes at 10pm and reopens at 8am.

**Campsites, facilities:** There are 55 sites for tents or RVs up to 31 feet (no hookups) and one hike-in/bike-in site. Picnic tables and fire grills are provided. Restrooms with flush toilets and showers (token required; bring $1 bills), drinking water, and a dump station are available. A weekend nature center is within walking distance. Supplies can be obtained nearby. Some facilities are wheelchair-accessible.

**Reservations, fees:** Reservations are accepted at 800/444-7275 ($10 reservation fee) or www.reserveamerica.com ($9 reservation fee). Sites are $45 per night, plus $12 per night for each additional vehicle, and it's $10 per person per night for the hike-in/bike-in site. Open year-round.

**Directions:** From Oxnard, drive south on Highway 1 for 16 miles to the camp entrance on the left.

**Contact:** California State Parks, Angeles District, 818/880-0363, www.parks.ca.gov.

## 83 SAN MIGUEL ISLAND
🚶🏊🎣 5% ⛺

**Scenic rating: 10**
in Channel Islands National Park

**Channel Islands map, page 663** BEST (

The trip to San Miguel starts with a three-hour boat ride. The island is distant, extremely rugged, and home to unique birds and much wildlife, including elephant seals and one of the largest seal and sea lion rookeries in the world (best on the south side of the island). Only rarely do people take advantage of this island paradise, limited to no more than 75 people at any one time on the entire island. To reach the campground, start from Cuyler Harbor, where you will be dropped off, and then hike up Nidever Canyon and take the left fork. Bring plenty of water and warm clothes, and be prepared for the chance of fog and wind; the boat

typically will not return to pick you up for several days. That's why camping here is like staking out your own personal island.

**Campsites, facilities:** There are nine primitive tent sites. Picnic tables and food lockers are provided. Pit toilets and windbreaks are available. No drinking water is available, and garbage must be packed out. No open fires are allowed; bring a camp stove for cooking. No pets are permitted.

**Reservations, fees:** Reserve transportation by calling Island Packers at 805/642-1393. After arranging transportation, you must obtain a camping reservation at 800/444-7275 ($10 reservation fee) or www.recreation.gov ($9 reservation fee). Sites are $15 per night. There is a fee for round-trip boat transportation. Open year-round, weather permitting.

**Directions:** To reach Island Packers in Ventura, take U.S. 101 south to Ventura and the Seaward exit. Take that exit, turn west on Seaward Avenue, and drive to Harbor Boulevard. Turn left on Harbor Boulevard and drive about two miles to Spinnaker Drive. Turn right and drive a short distance to the harbor. The boat ride is at least three hours each way.

**Contact:** Channel Islands National Park Visitor Center, 805/658-5730, www.nps.gov/chis.

## 84 SANTA ROSA ISLAND
🚶🏊🎣 5% ⛺

**Scenic rating: 10**
in Channel Islands National Park

**Channel Islands map, page 663** BEST (

Santa Rosa, the second-largest of the Channel Islands (the largest is Santa Cruz), is 10 miles wide and 15 miles long, and it holds many mysteries and adventures. A camping trip to Santa Rosa Island, available Friday through Sunday, will be an unforgettable experience even for those who think they've seen it all. The island is beautiful in the spring, when its grasslands turn emerald green and are sprinkled with wildflowers. There are many good hikes: The best is the Cherry Canyon Trail into the island's interior. Another great one is the five-mile Torrey Pines Trail. The Lobo Canyon Trail is a personal favorite. Because the boat ride to Santa Rosa is approximately 2.5 hours, longer than the trip to Santa Cruz, this island often receives fewer visitors than its nearby neighbor, which makes it even more special. Bring warm clothes because of the chance of fog and wind. The back beaches and sand dunes between Skunk Point and East Point are closed to hiking March through mid-September to protect nesting habitat for the snowy plover. The coastline around Sandy Point is closed year-round to protect seal rookeries.

**Campsites, facilities:** There are 15 primitive tent sites. Picnic tables and windbreaks are provided. Drinking water and pit toilets are available. No open fires are allowed; bring a camp stove for cooking. Garbage must be packed out.

**Reservations, fees:** Reservations are accepted at 800/444-7275 ($10 reservation fee) or www.recreation.gov ($9 reservation fee). Sites are $15 per night. Open year-round, weather permitting.

**Directions:** Reserve transportation via boat through Island Packers (805/642-1393) or by air through Channel Islands Aviation (805/987-1301).

To reach Island Packers in Ventura: Drive on U.S. 101 to Ventura and the Seaward exit. Take that exit and turn west on Seaward Avenue and drive to Harbor Boulevard. Turn left on Harbor Boulevard and drive about two miles to Spinnaker Drive. Turn right and drive a short distance to the harbor. The boat ride is at least 2.5 hours each way.

To reach Channel Islands Aviation in Camarillo: Drive on U.S. 101 to Camarillo to the exit for Los Posas West. Take that exit to Los Posas West and drive to Pleasant Valley. Turn right on Pleasant Valley and drive to Airport Way. Turn right on Airport Way and drive to Durley Avenue. Drive past the hangar and turn into the parking lot on the right. The office for Channel Islands Aviation is at 305 Durley Avenue, next to the Wave Point Café.

**Contact:** Channel Islands National Park Visitor Center, 805/658-5730, www.nps.gov/chis.

## 85 SANTA CRUZ ISLAND

🏃 🏊 🛶 🚣 5% ⛺

### Scenic rating: 10
in Channel Islands National Park

Channel Islands map, page 663 BEST (

Santa Cruz is the largest of the Channel Islands, perfect for camping and multiday visits. It covers 96 square miles, features a 2,450-foot mountain (Devil's Peak), and boasts an incredible array of flora and fauna, sheltered canyons, and sweeping ocean views. Kayaking through sea caves is outstanding, but it can be dangerous, so use caution. The Scorpion campground is set in a eucalyptus grove in a valley, with trailheads near camp that hikers can take to the surrounding ridgeline. A great three-mile hike from Prisoner's Harbor to Pelican Bay travels along the coast to a beautiful beach. The hike is on Nature Conservancy property and requires a guide from Island Packers; the hike can be arranged at the same time as the transportation.

**Campsites, facilities:** Scorpion campground has 40 hike-in sites. There are four primitive backcountry sites at Del Norte. Picnic tables are provided. Pit toilets are available. Drinking water is available at Scorpion but not at Del Norte. No open fires are allowed; bring a camp stove for cooking. Garbage must be packed out.

**Reservations, fees:** Reserve transportation by calling Island Packers at 805/642-1393. After arranging transportation, you must obtain a camping reservation at 800/444-7275 ($10 reservation fee) or www.reserveamerica.com ($9 reservation fee). Sites are $15 per night. There is a fee for round-trip boat transportation. Open year-round, weather permitting.

**Directions:** To reach Island Packers in Ventura, drive on U.S. 101 to Ventura and the Seaward exit. Take that exit and turn west on Seaward Avenue and drive to Harbor Boulevard. Turn left on Harbor Boulevard and drive about two miles to Spinnaker Drive. Turn right and drive a short distance to the harbor. The boat ride is at least one hour each way.

**Contact:** Channel Islands National Park Visitor Center, 805/658-5730, www.nps.gov/chis.

## 86 ANACAPA ISLAND
🏃 ⛰ 🏊 🚣 5% ⛺

### Scenic rating: 10
in Channel Islands National Park

**Channel Islands map, page 663** BEST

Little Anacapa, long and narrow, is known for its awesome caves, cliffs, and sea lion rookeries that range near huge kelp beds. After landing on the island, you face a 154-step staircase trail that leaves you perched on an ocean bluff. From there, it is a half-mile hike to the camp. Other trails venture past Inspiration Point and Cathedral Cove and provide vast views of the channel. The inshore waters are a marine preserve loaded with marine life and seabirds, and, with the remarkably clear water, this island makes a great destination for snorkeling and sea kayaking. At only 50 minutes, the boat ride here is the shortest one to the Channel Islands.

**Campsites, facilities:** There are seven primitive tent sites. Picnic tables are provided. Pit toilets are available. No drinking water is available. Garbage must be packed out. No open fires are allowed; bring a camp stove for cooking. Garbage must be packed out. No pets are permitted.

**Reservations, fees:** Reserve transportation by calling Island Packers at 805/642-1393. After arranging transportation, you must obtain a camping reservation at 800/444-7275 ($10 reservation fee) or www.recreation.gov ($9 reservation fee). Sites are $15 per night. There is a fee for round-trip boat transportation. Open year-round, weather permitting.

**Directions:** To reach Island Packers in Ventura, drive on U.S. 101 to Ventura and the Seaward exit. Take that exit and turn west on Seaward Avenue and drive to Harbor Boulevard. Turn

left on Harbor Boulevard and drive about two miles to Spinnaker Drive. Turn right and drive a short distance to the harbor. The boat ride is approximately one hour each way.

**Contact:** Channel Islands National Park Visitor Center, 805/658-5730, www.nps.gov/chis.

## 87 SANTA BARBARA ISLAND
🏃 ⛰ 🏊 5% ⛺

### Scenic rating: 10
in Channel Islands National Park

**Channel Islands map, page 663**

Note: At time of publication, Santa Barbara Island remained closed due to dock damage from Hurricane Marie. It is scheduled to reopen to the public in 2017. Please call before planning a trip.

This is a veritable dot of an island, well to the south of the four others that make up the Channel Islands. It is best known for its five miles of hiking trails, solitude, snorkeling, swimming, and excellent viewing of marine mammals. It is a breeding ground for elephant seals, with dolphins, sea lions, and whales (in the winter) all common in the area. The snorkeling can be wonderful, as you dive amid playful seals. The only negative is the long boat ride, three hours from the mainland. After landing, it is a steep hike to the campground (no stairs up the bluff), covering about half a mile. Most campers treat this as a wilderness backpacking experience with a long boat ride instead of a long hike.

**Campsites, facilities:** There are 10 primitive tent sites. Picnic tables are provided. Pit toilets are available. No drinking water is available. Garbage must be packed out. No open fires are allowed; bring a camp stove for cooking. No pets are permitted.

**Reservations, fees:** Reserve transportation by calling Island Packers at 805/642-1393. After arranging transportation, you must obtain a camping reservation 800/444-7275 ($10 reservation fee) or www.recreation.gov ($9 reservation fee). Sites are $15 per night. There is a fee for round-trip boat transportation. Open year-round, weather permitting.

**Directions:** To reach Island Packers in Ventura, drive on U.S. 101 to Ventura and the Seaward exit. Take that exit and turn west on Seaward Avenue and drive to Harbor Boulevard. Turn left on Harbor Boulevard and drive about two miles to Spinnaker Drive. Turn right and drive a short distance to the harbor. The boat ride is at least three hours each way.

**Contact:** Channel Islands National Park Visitor Center, 805/658-5730, www.nps.gov/chis.

# LOS ANGELES AND VICINITY

© DREAMSTIME.COM

It's stunning to realize that Los Angeles and its surrounding forests provide more campgrounds than even the Yosemite area. This region offers a tremendous range of national forests, canyons, mountains, lakes, coast, and islands. Angeles National Forest and San Bernardino National Forest hold more than one million acres, 1,000 miles of trails, and dozens of hidden campgrounds, including remote sites along the Pacific Crest Trail. The mountaintop views are best from Mount Baldy (10,064 feet), Mount San Jacinto (10,834 feet), and Mount San Gorgonio (11,490 feet). Great campgrounds nestle on the flanks of all three of these destinations. Big Bear is the region's top lake for fishing and boating. Though popular on weekends, there are relatively few people on weekdays. Other top lakes include Arrowhead, Castaic, and several smaller reservoirs.

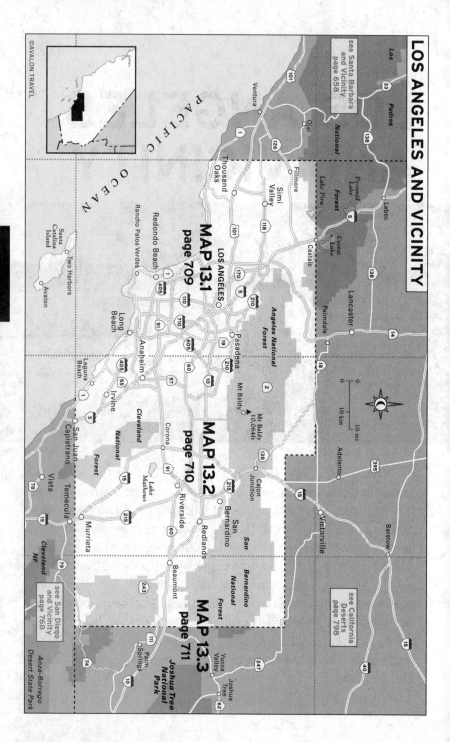

# LOS ANGELES AND VICINITY

see Santa Barbara
and Vicinity
page 658

©AVALON TRAVEL

PACIFIC

OCEAN

Santa Catalina Island

Two Harbors

Avalon

Redondo Beach

Rancho Palos Verdes

Long Beach

Laguna Beach

**LOS ANGELES
MAP 13.1
page 709**

**MAP 13.2
page 710**

**MAP 13.3
page 711**

see San Diego
and Vicinity
page 768

see California
Deserts
page 799

Los Padres

Ventura

Ojai

Thousand Oaks

Fillmore

Simi Valley

Castaic

Lake Piru

Pyramid Lake

Castaic Lake

Lebec

Lancaster

Palmdale

National Forest

Angeles National Forest

Pasadena

Mt Baldy

Mt Baldy 10,064ft

Anaheim

Irvine

San Juan Capistrano

Vista

Temecula

Murrieta

Cleveland National Forest

Corona

Lake Mathews

Riverside

Redlands

Beaumont

San Bernardino

San Bernardino National Forest

Cleveland NF

Anza-Borrego Desert State Park

Cajon Junction

Victorville

Adelanto

Barstow

Palm Springs

Yucca Valley

Joshua Tree

**Joshua Tree National Park**

101, 33, 138, 1, 126, 101, 5, 138, 14, 170, 210, 5, 110, 405, 91, 710, 605, 19, 210, 60, 57, 10, 2, 405, 55, 1, 5, 15, 215, 78, 15, 79, 243, 74, 10, 111, 247, 62, 40, 15, 395, 138, 215, 60

0 10 km
0 10 mi

# Map 13.1

**Sites 1-26**
**Pages 712-725**

**13.2**

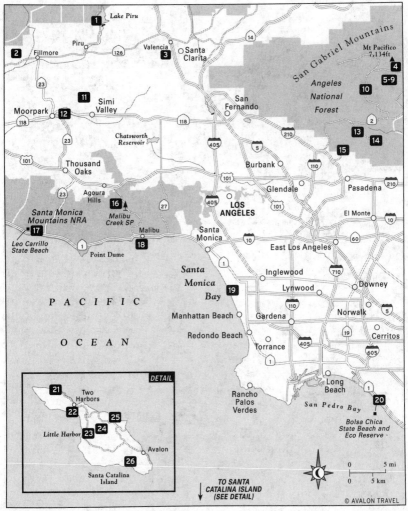

Lake Piru

**1**

Piru

Fillmore **2**

Valencia

Santa Clarita

**3**

126

14

San Gabriel Mountains

Mt Pacifico
7,134ft

**4**

**5-9**

Angeles National Forest

**10**

23

Simi Valley **11**

Moorpark

**12**

San Fernando

118

118

210

**2**

**13**

**14**

Chatsworth Reservoir

405

5

**15**

Thousand Oaks

101

23

101

Burbank

Glendale

Pasadena

210

23

Agoura Hills

Malibu Creek SP

**16**

27

405

**LOS ANGELES**

El Monte

101

10

Santa Monica Mountains NRA

**17**

Leo Carrillo State Beach

1

Point Dume

Malibu

**18**

Santa Monica

10

East Los Angeles

60

710

**P A C I F I C**

Santa Monica Bay

1

**19**

Inglewood

Lynwood

Downey

5

110

**O C E A N**

Manhattan Beach

Gardena

Norwalk

Redondo Beach

Torrance

1

405

**19**

Cerritos

605

**DETAIL**

**21**

Two Harbors

**22**

**25**

Little Harbor

**23** **24**

Avalon

**26**

Santa Catalina Island

Rancho Palos Verdes

Long Beach

1

San Pedro Bay

**20**

Bolsa Chica State Beach and Eco Reserve

0        5 mi
0      5 km

*TO SANTA CATALINA ISLAND (SEE DETAIL)*

© AVALON TRAVEL

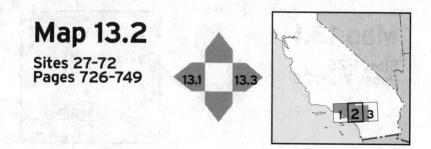

# Map 13.2

## Sites 27-72
## Pages 726-749

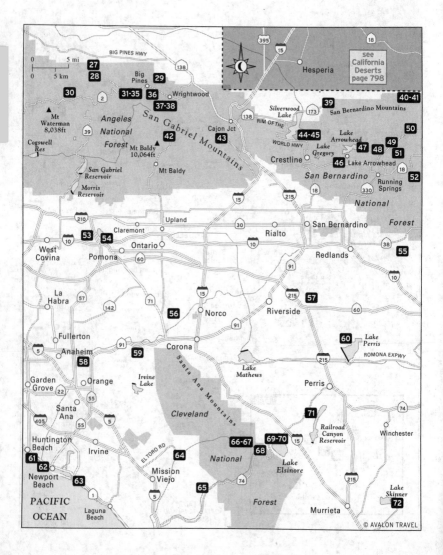

# Map 13.3

**Sites 73-107
Pages 749-766**

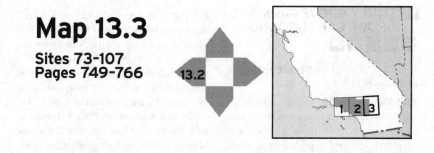

13.2

1 2 3

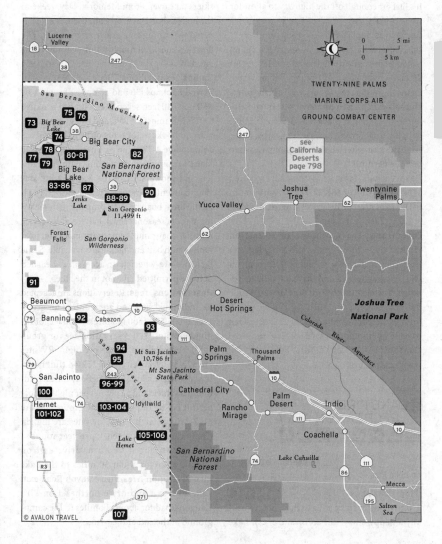

Lucerne Valley

18

38

247

San Bernardino Mountains

75 76

73 Big Bear Lake

74

38

Big Bear City

77

78

80-81

82

79

Big Bear Lake

San Bernardino National Forest

83-86

87

88-89

90

Jenks Lake

San Gorgonio 11,499 ft

Forest Falls

San Gorgonio Wilderness

91

Beaumont

10

79 Banning 92 Cabazon

93

111

94

Mt San Jacinto 10,786 ft

95

San Jacinto

Mt San Jacinto State Park

79

San Jacinto

243

96-99

100

74

103-104

Idyllwild

Hemet

101-102

San Jacinto Mtns

105-106

Lake Hemet

San Bernardino National Forest

R3

371

107

© AVALON TRAVEL

TWENTY-NINE PALMS

MARINE CORPS AIR

GROUND COMBAT CENTER

247

see California Deserts page 798

Joshua Tree

Twentynine Palms

62

Yucca Valley

62

**Joshua Tree National Park**

Colorado River Aqueduct

Desert Hot Springs

Palm Springs

Thousand Palms

10

Cathedral City

Palm Desert

Indio

Rancho Mirage

111

Coachella

74

Lake Cahuilla

111

86

10

Mecca

195

Salton Sea

0    5 mi
0    5 km

# 1 KENNEY GROVE PARK AND GROUP CAMPGROUND

🐕 🏕 ♿ 🚐 ⛺

### Scenic rating: 4

near Fillmore

**Map 13.1, page 709**

A lot of folks miss this spot, a park tucked away among orchards, coast live oaks, and eucalyptus groves, with several group campgrounds. It's just far enough off the highway to allow for some privacy.

**Campsites, facilities:** This group camp has 33 sites with partial hookups (30 amps) for RVs up to 40 feet (no pull-through sites) and 18 sites for tents. Picnic tables and fire pits are provided. Drinking water, restrooms with flush toilets and showers, an amphitheater, a softball field, horseshoes, and a playground are available. Supplies and a coin laundry are nearby. Some facilities are wheelchair-accessible. Leashed pets are permitted.

**Reservations, fees:** Reservations are required at 805/524-0750 or 888/327/2757. A minimum of five sites must be reserved. Group rates start at $315. Open year-round.

**Directions:** From Ventura, drive east on Highway 126 for 22 miles to Old Telegraph Road (before the town of Fillmore). Turn left on Old Telegraph Road and drive 0.6 mile to 7th Street. Turn left (northwest) and drive 0.3 mile to North Oak Avenue. Turn right and drive 0.5 mile to the park on the left at 823 North Oak Avenue in Fillmore.

**Contact:** County of Ventura, 805/524-0750, www.ventura.org.

# 2 LAKE PIRU RECREATION AREA

🏊 🚤 ♨ 🚣 ⛴ 🐕 ♿ 🚐 ⛺

### Scenic rating: 7

on Lake Piru

**Map 13.1, page 709**      **BEST (**

Things can get crazy at Lake Piru, but it's usually a happy crazy, not an insane crazy. Lake Piru (1,055 feet elevation) is shaped like a teardrop and covers 1,200 acres when full. This is a lake set up for waterskiing, with lots of fast boats. All others be forewarned: The rules prohibit boats under 12 feet or over 26 feet, as well as personal watercraft. Canoes and kayaks over eight feet are permitted in a special-use area. (All boats must be certified mussel-free before launching.) Bass and trout fishing can be quite good in the spring before the waterskiers take over. From Memorial Day weekend through Labor Day weekend, there is a designated swimming area safe from the boats. The tent sites consist of roughly 40-by-40-foot areas amid trees.

**Campsites, facilities:** There are 235 sites with partial hookups (30 and 50 amps) for tents or RVs up to 40 feet, seven sites with full hookups (30 and 50 amps) for RVs, and two group camps with no hookups for tents or RVs that can accommodate 4-12 vehicles. Fire pits and picnic tables are provided. Restrooms with flush toilets and showers, drinking water, dump station, convenience store, coin laundry, Wi-Fi, picnic area, boat storage, propane, fish-cleaning station, seasonal snack bar, ice, full-service marina, boat ramp, temporary mooring, boat rentals, and bait and tackle are available. Some facilities are wheelchair-accessible. Leashed pets are permitted, but not in the lake.

**Reservations, fees:** Reservations are accepted for individual sites and are required for group sites at 805/521-1500 ($8 reservation fee for individual sites; $20 reservation fee for group sites). Tent sites are $20-28 per night, RV sites are $22-32 (electricity) and $32-44 (full hookups) per night, plus $12-14 per day for each additional vehicle and $2 per pet per night. A boat permit is $10-13 per day. The group sites are $112-390 per night. Holiday rates are higher. Credit cards are accepted. Open year-round.

**Directions:** From Ventura, drive east on Highway 126 for about 30 miles to the Lake Piru Recreation Area/Piru Canyon Road exit. Take that exit and drive northeast on Piru Canyon Road for about six miles to the campground at the end of the road.

**Contact:** Lake Piru Recreation Area, 805/521-1500, www.camplakepiru.com.

## 3 VALENCIA TRAVEL VILLAGE

### Scenic rating: 5

in Valencia

Map 13.1, page 709

This huge RV park is in the scenic San Fernando foothills, just five minutes from Six Flags Magic Mountain. Lake Piru and Lake Castaic are only 15 minutes away. The camp was built on a 65-acre horse ranch. Note: There are roughly 300 long-term residents here, so temporary camping space may be limited.

**Campsites, facilities:** There are 381 sites, including about 300 with permanent residents, with full or partial hookups (30 and 50 amps) for RVs; most are pull-through. No tents are permitted. Picnic tables and fire pits (some sites) are provided. A market, two heated swimming pools, spa, lounge, video and games arcade, playground, shuffleboard, horseshoes, volleyball courts, table tennis, coin laundry, Wi-Fi, propane, and dump station are available. Some facilities are wheelchair-accessible. Leashed pets are permitted.

**Reservations, fees:** Reservations are recommended at 888/588-8678. RV sites (hookups) are $50-60 per night, plus $2 per person per night for more than two people (maximum of six people per site). Weekly and monthly rates are available, as well as some discounts. Some credit cards are accepted. Open year-round.

**Directions:** Drive on I-5 to Santa Clarita and Highway 126 west/Henry Mayo Road. Take that exit and drive west on Highway 126 for one mile to the camp on the left.

**Contact:** Valencia Travel Village, 661/257-3333, www.valenciatravelvillagellc.com.

## 4 MOUNT PACIFICO

### Scenic rating: 7

on the Pacific Crest Trail in Angeles National Forest

Map 13.1, page 709

This is one of the great primitive camps in Angeles National Forest. It is near the top of Mount Pacifico at an elevation of 7,134 feet, with the Pacific Crest Trail a half mile from camp. The views are outstanding, especially to the north of the sparse Antelope Valley and beyond. From here, the PCT passes through a series of ravines and draws and up short ridges, pleasant but not inspiring.

**Campsites, facilities:** There are eight tent sites. Picnic tables and fire grills are provided. Vault toilets are available. No drinking water is available. Garbage must be packed out. Leashed pets are permitted.

**Reservations, fees:** Reservations are not accepted. An Adventure Pass ($30 annual fee or $5 daily pass) per parked vehicle is required. Open mid-May through mid-November, weather permitting.

**Directions:** From Pasadena, drive north on I-210 for four miles to the exit for Highway 2/Angeles Crest Highway. Take that exit and drive north on Highway 2 for nine miles to Angeles Forest Highway/County Road N3. Turn left on Angeles Forest Highway and drive about 12 miles to the intersection with Santa Clara Divide Road/Forest Road 3N17 (look for the Mill Creek Summit sign). Turn right (east) and drive about six miles to Mount Pacifico Road. Turn left on the dirt road and drive four miles to the campground. High-clearance vehicles are recommended.

Note that at Mill Creek Summit, the gate is locked from November 15 to May 15 and it will be necessary to hike from the gate. When Santa Clara Divide Road is impassable because of weather conditions, it will be necessary to hike from Alder Saddle.

**Contact:** Angeles National Forest, Los Angeles

River Ranger District, 818/899-1900, www. fs.usda.gov/angeles.

## 5 HORSE FLATS

### Scenic rating: 7

near the San Gabriel Wilderness in Angeles National Forest

**Map 13.1, page 709**

This is one of several options in the immediate area: Chilao, Bandido Group Camp, and Coulter Group Camp are the other three. Horse Flats is at 5,700 feet elevation along a national recreation trail (Silver Moccasin Trail). Two trails into the San Gabriel Wilderness are nearby.

**Campsites, facilities:** There are 26 sites for tents or RVs up to 20 feet (no hookups). Picnic tables and fire pits are provided. Vault toilets, hitching rails, and horse corrals are available. No drinking water is available. Leashed pets are permitted.

**Reservations, fees:** Reservations are not accepted. Sites are $12 per night. Open April through mid-November, weather permitting.

**Directions:** From Pasadena, drive north on I-210 for four miles to the exit for Highway 2/Angeles Crest Highway. Take that exit and drive northeast on Highway 2 for 30 miles to Santa Clara Divide Road/Forest Road 3N17 at Three Points (signed). Turn left and drive three miles to Horse Flats Road. Turn left and drive one mile to the campground.

**Contact:** Angeles National Forest, Los Angeles River Ranger District, 818/899-1900, www. fs.usda.gov/angeles.

## 6 BANDIDO GROUP CAMP

### Scenic rating: 6

near the Pacific Crest Trail in Angeles National Forest

**Map 13.1, page 709**

This is an equestrian base camp for groups preparing to hike or ride into the surrounding wilderness. A trail out of the camp heads east and intersects with the Pacific Crest Trail a little over two miles away at Three Points, a significant PCT junction. Before heading out visitors must check in and register with the rangers at the Los Angeles River Ranger District office, two miles west of Three Points on Highway 2. The elevation is 5,840 feet.

**Campsites, facilities:** There are five group camps for tents or RVs up to 40 feet (no hookups) that accommodate 12-60 people each. The sites can be reserved individually or combined into a large group site for up to 150 people. Picnic tables and fire rings are provided. Pit toilets, corrals, and water troughs are available. There is no drinking water. Leashed pets are permitted.

**Reservations, fees:** Reservations are required at 877/444-6777 ($10 reservation fee) or www. recreation.gov ($9 reservation fee). The sites are $24-300 per night, depending on how many sites you reserve. Open April through mid-November, weather permitting.

**Directions:** From Pasadena, drive north on I-210 for four miles to the exit for Highway 2/Angeles Crest Highway. Take that exit and drive northeast on Highway 2 for 30 miles to Santa Clara Divide Road/Forest Road 3N17 at Three Points (signed). Turn left and drive two miles to the campground on the left.

**Contact:** Angeles National Forest, Los Angeles River Ranger District, 818/899-1900, www. fs.usda.gov/angeles.

# 7 CHILAO CAMPGROUND

### Scenic rating: 6

near the San Gabriel Wilderness in Angeles National Forest

**Map 13.1, page 709**

A national recreation trail runs right by here, so this popular trailhead camp gets a lot of use. Access to the Pacific Crest Trail is three miles north at Three Points (five miles if hiking the Silver Moccasin Trail), and parking is available there. An Adventure Pass is required to park at all trailheads. The elevation is 5,300 feet. Note: There is frequent bear activity, so use precautions.

**Campsites, facilities:** There are 83 sites for tents or RVs up to 40 feet (no hookups). Picnic tables and fire rings are provided. Drinking water and vault toilets are available. Some facilities are wheelchair-accessible. Leashed pets are permitted.

**Reservations, fees:** Reservations are not accepted. Sites are $12 per night. Open April through mid-November, weather permitting.

**Directions:** From Pasadena, drive north on I-210 for four miles to the exit for Highway 2/Angeles Crest Highway. Take that exit and drive northeast on Highway 2 for 27 miles to the campground entrance road (signed) on the left.

**Contact:** Angeles National Forest, Los Angeles River Ranger District, 818/899-1900, www.fs.usda.gov/angeles.

# 8 COULTER GROUP CAMP

### Scenic rating: 6

near the San Gabriel Wilderness in Angeles National Forest

**Map 13.1, page 709**

This is a popular group camp set near both a visitors center and a trailhead for the Pacific Crest Trail. Access to the PCT is 3.5 miles north at Three Points (5.5 miles if hiking the Silver Moccasin Trail), and parking is available. An Adventure Pass is required to park at the trailheads. The elevation is 5,300 feet. It is close to Chilao Campground.

**Campsites, facilities:** There is one group site for up to 50 people (no hookups) and RVs up to 40 feet. Four picnic tables, a barbecue pit, fire ring, vault toilet, and drinking water are available. Check posted signs for current water quality. Leashed pets are permitted.

**Reservations, fees:** Reservations are required at 877/444-6777 ($10 reservation fee) or www.recreation.gov ($9 reservation fee). The camp is $100 per night. Open April through mid-November, weather permitting.

**Directions:** From Pasadena, drive north on I-210 for four miles to the exit for Highway 2/Angeles Crest Highway. Take that exit and drive northeast on Highway 2 for 27 miles to the campground entrance road on the left (enter through the Little Pines Loop at Chilao Campground).

**Contact:** Angeles National Forest, Los Angeles River Ranger District, 818/899-1900, www.fs.usda.gov/angeles.

# 9 SULPHUR SPRINGS WALK-IN

### Scenic rating: 6

near the Pacific Crest Trail in Angeles National Forest

**Map 13.1, page 709**

This walk-in camp is on the South Fork of Little Rock Creek, a short distance from a trailhead for the Pacific Crest Trail. It is at 5,300 feet elevation amid pines and is a popular jumping-off point for hikes. It was formerly a drive-in camp, but the road washed out and the Forest Service has since made it a permanent walk-in site. Some familiar with this area may remember that campers with horses once used this site. No more—the equestrian facilities have been removed.

**Campsites, facilities:** There are six sites for

tents only. Picnic tables and stoves are provided. Pit toilets are available. There is no drinking water. Leashed pets are permitted.

**Reservations, fees:** Reservations are not accepted. There is no fee for camping. An Adventure Pass ($30 annual fee or $5 daily pass) per parked vehicle is required. Open April through mid-November, weather permitting.

**Directions:** From Pasadena, drive north on I-210 for four miles to the exit for Highway 2/Angeles Crest Highway. Take that exit and drive northeast on Highway 2 for 30 miles to Santa Clara Divide Road/Forest Road 3N17 at Three Points. Turn left on Santa Clara Divide Road/Forest Road 3N17 and drive 4.5 miles to Alder Saddle. Bear right (north), onto the pavement, and drive one mile to the Pacific Crest Trail (100 yards before the road closure gate). Park your vehicle and walk east (downhill) on the Pacific Crest Trail for 0.75 mile to the camp.

**Contact:** Angeles National Forest, Los Angeles River Ranger District, 818/899-1900, www.fs.usda.gov/angeles.

## 10 MONTE CRISTO
🚶 🐕 ♿ 🚐 ⛺

### Scenic rating: 7
on Mill Creek in Angeles National Forest

**Map 13.1, page 709**

This is a Forest Service camp on Mill Creek at 3,600 feet elevation, just west of Iron Mountain. The camp is situated under sycamore trees, which provide great color in the fall. In most years, Mill Creek flows six months out of the year.

**Campsites, facilities:** There are 22 sites for tents or RVs up to 30 feet (no hookups). Picnic tables and fire grills are provided. Drinking water and vault toilets are available. Some facilities are wheelchair-accessible. Leashed pets are permitted.

**Reservations, fees:** Reservations are not accepted. Sites are $12 per night. Open year-round.

**Directions:** From Pasadena, drive north on I-210 for four miles to the exit for Highway 2/Angeles Crest Highway. Take that exit and drive northeast on Highway 2 for nine miles to Angeles Forest Highway/County Road N3. Turn left on Angeles Forest Highway and drive about 10 miles to the campground on the right.

**Contact:** Angeles National Forest, Los Angeles River Ranger District, 818/899-1900, www.fs.usda.gov/angeles.

## 11 TAPO CANYON COUNTY PARK
🚐 ⛺

### Scenic rating: 7
off Tapo Canyon Road in Simi Valley

**Map 13.1, page 709**

The campground features a large undeveloped area for tents and slots with hookups for RVs. Highlights are a grassy picnic area and an arena for horseback riding; a camp host is a plus. This county park has quickly become a favorite site for youth groups.

**Campsites, facilities:** There are 16 sites with hookups (20, 30, and 50 amps) for RVs of any length. Picnic tables and fire rings are provided. Drinking water, restrooms with flush toilets, and coin showers are available. A dump station, equestrian arena, horse watering station, and hitching posts are also available. A camp host is on-site.

**Reservations, fees:** Reservations are accepted for the individual sites and are required for the group sites at 805/654-3951 or www.venturaparks.org ($10 reservation fee). Sites are $37 per night, $32 per night in winter, plus $1 per dog per night (limit two). Call for group rates.

**Directions:** From U.S. 101 north of Thousand Oaks, turn north on Highway 23 and drive eight miles to Highway 118. Merge onto Highway 118 east and drive 4.1 miles to Tapo Canyon Road, Exit 27. Take that exit and turn left onto Tapo Canyon Road. Drive three miles to the campground.

**Contact:** Tapo Canyon Park, Ventura, 805/654-3951, www.countyofventura.org.

## 12 OAK PARK

### Scenic rating: 3

in Simi Valley near Moorpark

**Map 13.1, page 709**

One of the frustrations at many state and national park campgrounds is that they are full from reservations, especially at the state beaches. The county parks often provide a safety valve, and Oak Park certainly applies—but not always. This oft-overlooked county park in the foothill country of Simi Valley has many trails offering good hiking possibilities. The camp is somewhat secluded, more so than many expect. The catch? Sometimes the entire campground is rented to a single group. Note: Gates close at dusk and reopen at 8am.

**Campsites, facilities:** There are 29 sites with partial hookups (20 and 30 amps) for RVs. Picnic tables and fire pits are provided. Drinking water, restrooms with flush toilets, and a dump station are available. Group facilities are available by reservation only. Horseshoe pits, a playground, and basketball and volleyball courts are nearby. Supplies and a coin laundry are within two miles. Leashed pets are permitted.

**Reservations, fees:** Reservations are accepted ($3 online registration fee, $10 phone registration fee). Sites are $31 per night (includes one RV, one vehicle, and one tent with no more than six people per site), hookups are $26, and dogs are permitted for $1 per night (limit two). Call for group sites. There is a 14-day stay limit. Off-season discounts are available. Open year-round, except Christmas Day.

**Directions:** From Ventura, drive south on U.S. 101 to Highway 23. Turn north on Highway 23 (which becomes Highway 123 east) and drive about three miles to the Collins Street exit. Continue straight through the intersection (it becomes Old Los Angeles Avenue) and drive 1.5 miles to the park entrance on the left.

**Contact:** Oak Park, 805/654-3951, www.countyofventura.org.

## 13 VALLEY FORGE TRAIL CAMP

### Scenic rating: 8

on the San Gabriel River in Angeles National Forest

**Map 13.1, page 709**

Valley Forge is a good camp for anglers or hikers who are looking for a short backpacking trip. A 2.5-mile hike is required to reach this campground. For hikers, a national recreation trail passes close to the camp. For anglers, there are small but feisty native trout. The elevation is 3,500 feet.

**Campsites, facilities:** There are six tent sites. Picnic tables and fire rings are provided. Pit toilets are available. No drinking water is available. Stream water can be used if it is boiled or pump-filtered. Garbage must be packed out. Leashed pets are permitted.

**Reservations, fees:** Reservations are not accepted. There is no fee for camping. An Adventure Pass ($30 annual fee or $5 daily pass) per parked vehicle is required. Open year-round, weather permitting.

**Directions:** From Pasadena, drive north on I-210 for four miles to the exit for Highway 2/Angeles Crest Highway. Take that exit and drive north on Highway 2 for 14 miles to Mount Wilson Road. Turn right on Mount Wilson Road, then immediately turn left into the parking lot. Access the Gabrielino National Recreation Trail, which is behind the restrooms, and hike 2.5 miles to the campground.

**Contact:** Angeles National Forest, Los Angeles River Ranger District, 818/899-1900, www.fs.usda.gov/angeles.

## 14 WEST FORK TRAIL CAMP

### Scenic rating: 8

on the West Fork of the San Gabriel River in Angeles National Forest

**Map 13.1, page 709**

It takes a circuitous drive and a four- to five-mile hike to reach this camp, but for backpackers it is worth it. The camp is on the West Fork of the San Gabriel River amid pine woodlands, with two national recreation trails intersecting at the campground. The canyon is deep and the river is beautiful. The elevation is 3,100 feet.

**Campsites, facilities:** There are seven tent sites. Picnic tables and fire rings are provided. Pit toilets are available. No drinking water is available. Stream water can be used if it is boiled or pump-filtered. Garbage must be packed out. Leashed pets are permitted.

**Reservations, fees:** Reservations are not accepted. There is no fee for camping. Open year-round.

**Directions:** From Pasadena, drive north on I-210 for four miles to the exit for Highway 2/Angeles Crest Highway. Take that exit and drive north on Highway 2 for 14 miles to Mount Wilson Road. Turn right on Mount Wilson Road, then immediately turn left into the parking lot. Access the Gabrielino National Recreation Trail, which is behind the restrooms, and hike five miles to the campground.

**Contact:** Angeles National Forest, Los Angeles River Ranger District, 818/899-1900, www.fs.usda.gov/angeles.

## 15 MILLARD TRAIL CAMP

### Scenic rating: 8

near Millard Falls in Angeles National Forest

**Map 13.1, page 709**

This tiny, pretty camp, set near a creek amid oak and alder woodlands, is best known as the launching point for some excellent hikes. The best is the half-mile hike to Millard Falls, where

you actually rock-hop your way upstream to the 60-foot waterfall, a drop-dead beautiful sight. On weekends, there can be lots of foot traffic through the campground with hikers on their way to the falls. Another trail out of camp leads to Inspiration Point and continues to San Gabriel Peak; it's a short walk to the campsites.

Note: Millard Trail Camp may close occasionally due to increased bear activity. Call 818/899-1900 for current conditions.

**Campsites, facilities:** There are six sites for tents only. Picnic tables and fire pits are provided. Vault toilets are available. No drinking water is available, but stream water may be boiled or filtered. Garbage must be packed out. Leashed pets are permitted.

**Reservations, fees:** Reservations are not accepted. There is no fee for camping. An Adventure Pass ($30 annual fee or $5 daily pass) per parked vehicle is required. Open year-round.

**Directions:** From Pasadena, drive north on I-10 to the exit for Lake Avenue. Take that exit north and drive 3.5 miles to Loma Alta Drive. Turn left (west) at Loma Alta Drive and drive one mile to Chaney Trail Road (at the flashing yellow light). Turn right at Chaney Trail and drive 1.5 miles (keep left at the fork) to the parking lot for the campground. It is a short walk on a fire road to the campground. Note: A gate is locked at Chaney Trail from 8pm to 6am, preventing drive-in access approximately 1.5 miles from the campground.

**Contact:** Angeles National Forest, Los Angeles River Ranger District, 818/899-1900, www.fs.usda.gov/angeles.

## 16 MALIBU CREEK STATE PARK

### Scenic rating: 9

near Malibu

**Map 13.1, page 709**

If you plan on staying here, be sure to get your reservation in early. This 6,600-acre state park is just a few miles out of Malibu between Highway 1 and U.S. 101, two major thoroughfares for vacationers. Despite its popularity, the park manages to retain a natural setting, with miles of trails for hiking, biking, and horseback riding, and inspiring scenic views. The park offers 15 miles of streamside trail through oak and sycamore woodlands and also some chaparral-covered slopes. It is an ideal spot for a break on a coastal road trip. This park was once used as a setting for the filming of some movies and TV shows, including *Planet of the Apes* and *M*A*S*H*.

**Campsites, facilities:** There are 57 sites for tents or RVs up to 30 feet (no hookups) and a group tent site for up to 60 people. Picnic tables are provided. No wood fires are permitted in the summer, but propane and charcoal barbecues are allowed. Drinking water, restrooms with flush toilets and coin showers, and a dump station are available. Some facilities are wheelchair-accessible. Leashed pets are permitted, but only in the campground area.

**Reservations, fees:** Reservations are accepted at 800/444-7275 or www.reserveamerica.com ($8 reservation fee). Sites are $45 per night, plus $8 per night for each additional vehicle, and $225 per night for the group site. Open year-round.

**Directions:** From U.S. 101: Drive on U.S. 101 to the exit for Las Virgenes Canyon Road (on the western border of Calabasas). Take that exit south and drive on Las Virgenes Canyon Road/County Road N1 for four miles to the park entrance on the right.

From Highway 1: Drive on Highway 1 to Malibu and Malibu Canyon Road. Turn north on Malibu Canyon Road and drive north for 5.5 miles (the road becomes Las Virgenes Canyon Road/County Road N1) to the park entrance on the left.

**Contact:** Malibu Creek State Park, 818/880-0367, www.parks.ca.gov.

# 17 LEO CARRILLO STATE PARK

### Scenic rating: 8

north of Malibu

**Map 13.1, page 709**

The camping area at this state park is in a canyon, and reservations are essential during the summer and on weekends the remainder of the year. Large sycamore trees shade the campsites. The Nicholas Flat Trail provides an excellent hike to the Willow Creek Overlook for beautiful views of the beach. In addition, a pedestrian tunnel leads to a wonderful coastal spot with sea caves, tunnels, tidepools, and patches of beach. This park features 1.5 miles of beach for swimming, surfing, and surf fishing. In the summer, lifeguards are posted at the beach. Many will remember a beach camp that was once popular here. Well, that sucker is gone, wiped out by a storm.

**Campsites, facilities:** There are 135 sites for tents or RVs up to 31 feet (no hookups), one hike-in/bike-in area for up to 24 people, and one group tent site for 9-50 people. Picnic tables and fire rings are provided. Restrooms with flush toilets and coin showers, drinking water, a dump station, a seasonal visitors center, Wi-Fi, summer programs, and a summer convenience store are available. Some facilities are wheelchair-accessible. Leashed pets are permitted. Front gates close at 10pm and reopen at 7am.

**Reservations, fees:** Reservations are recommended at 800/444-7275 or www.reserveamerica.com ($8 reservation fee). Sites are $45 per night, plus $10 per night for each additional vehicle, and $10 per person per night for the hike-in/bike-in site. The group tent site costs $225 per night. Open year-round.

**Directions:** From Santa Monica, drive north on Highway 1 for 28 miles to the park entrance (signed) on the right.

From Oxnard, drive south on Highway 1 for 20 miles to the park entrance (signed) on the left.

**Contact:** California State Parks, Angeles District, 310/457-8143, www.parks.ca.gov.

## 18 MALIBU BEACH RV PARK

### Scenic rating: 7

in Malibu

Map 13.1, page 709

This is one of the few privately developed RV parks in the region that provides some sites for tent campers as well. It's one of the nicer spots in the area, set on a bluff overlooking the Pacific Ocean, near both Malibu Pier (for fishing) and Paradise Cove. Each RV site and many of the tent sites have views of either the ocean or adjacent mountains. Sites with ocean views are charged a small premium. Whale-watching is best in March and April, and then again in October and November. Dolphin-watching is popular year-round.

**Campsites, facilities:** There are 35 sites for tents (four-person maximum per site) and 142 sites with full or partial hookups (30 and 50 amps) for RVs; some sites are pull-through. Picnic tables and barbecue grills are provided. Restrooms with showers, a spa, recreation room, playground, coin laundry, Wi-Fi, dog walk area, propane gas, ice, cable TV, dump station, and convenience store are available. Some facilities are wheelchair-accessible. Leashed pets are permitted, except in the tent area, and certain breeds are prohibited.

**Reservations, fees:** Reservations are recommended at 800/622-6052. Ocean-view RV sites (full hookups) are $145-210 per night, mountain-view RV sites (full hookups) are $110-155 per night, RV sites with partial hookups are $70-100 per night, tent sites are $50 per night, plus $10 per night for each additional vehicle, $5 per person per night for more than two people, and $3 per pet per night. Discounts are available weekdays and off-season. Credit cards are accepted. Open year-round.

**Directions:** Drive on Pacific Coast Highway/

Highway 1 to the Malibu area. The park is two miles north of the intersection of Highway 1 and Malibu Canyon Road on the east side of the road.

**Contact:** Malibu Beach RV Park, 310/456-6052, www.maliburv.com.

## 19 DOCKWEILER BEACH RV PARK

### Scenic rating: 8

near Manhattan Beach

Map 13.1, page 709

Dockweiler is L.A. County's only RV campground on the beach. This layover spot for coast cruisers is just a hop from the beach and the Pacific Ocean. There is access to a 26-mile-long coastal bike path.

**Campsites, facilities:** There are 118 sites with full hookups (20, 30, and 50 amps) for RVs up to 40 feet. No tents. Picnic tables and barbecue grills are provided. Restrooms with flush toilets and showers, dump station, and coin laundry are available. Some facilities are wheelchair-accessible. You can buy supplies nearby. Leashed pets are permitted, with a two-dog limit.

**Reservations, fees:** Reservations are accepted at 310/322-4951 or 800/950-7275 ($10 reservation fee). RV sites (full hookups) are $55-65 per night (depending on location and view), plus $3 per person per night for more than four people and $3 per pet per night. Holiday rates are an additional $4 per night. Open year-round, except in January. Some credit cards are accepted.

**Directions:** From Santa Monica, take I-405 south to I-105/Imperial Highway. Take I-105 and continue as it becomes Imperial Highway. When the road name changes to Imperial Highway, drive west for four miles to the park (signed) on the left.

**Contact:** Dockweiler Beach RV Park, Los Angeles County, 310/322-4951, www.reservations.lacounty.gov.

## 20 BOLSA CHICA STATE BEACH

🚶 🚲 🏊 ⛵ 🐾 ♿ 🚐

### Scenic rating: 7
near Huntington Beach

**Map 13.1, page 709**

This state beach extends three miles from Seal Beach to Huntington Beach City Pier. A bikeway connects it with Huntington State Beach, seven miles to the south. Across the road from Bolsa Chica is the 1,000-acre Bolsa Chica Ecological Preserve, managed by the Department of Fish and Game. The campground consists of basically a beachfront parking lot, but a popular one at that. A great little walk is available at the adjacent Bolsa Chica State Reserve, a 1.5-mile loop that provides an escape from the parking lot and entry into the 530-acre nature reserve, complete with egrets, pelicans, and many shorebirds. Lifeguard service is available during the summer. This camp has a seven-day maximum stay during the summer and a 14-day maximum stay during the winter. Surf fishing is popular for perch, cabezon, small sharks, and croaker. There are also occasional runs of grunion, a small fish that spawns in hordes on the sandy beaches of Southern California.

**Campsites, facilities:** There are 50 sites with full hookups (30 and 50 amps) available in a parking lot configuration for RVs up to 48 feet. Fire rings are provided. Restrooms with flush toilets and coin showers, drinking water, Wi-Fi, dump station, picnic areas, bicycle trail, volleyball, basketball, and food service (seasonal) are available. Some facilities are wheelchair-accessible, including a paved ramp for wheelchair access to the beach. Leashed pets are permitted at campsites.

**Reservations, fees:** Reservations are accepted at 800/444-7275 or www.reserveamerica.com ($8 reservation fee). Tent and RV sites (hookups) are $55 per night, premium beachfront sites are $65 per night, plus $10 per night for each additional vehicle. Open year-round.

**Directions:** Drive on Highway 1 to the park entrance (1.5 miles north of Huntington Beach).

**Contact:** Bolsa Chica State Beach, 714/846-3460, www.parks.ca.gov.

## 21 PARSONS LANDING HIKE-IN

🚶 🏊 ⛺ 5% 🏔

### Scenic rating: 10
on Catalina Island

**Map 13.1, page 709**          **BEST (**

This primitive campground is one of five on Catalina Island. It is on the island's northern end, seven miles from the island's isthmus and the village of Two Harbors. If you want to try to avoid the crowds, this is the area to visit; forget Avalon and head instead to Two Harbors.

Note: The ferry to Avalon is available from Long Beach, Dana Point, or San Pedro. The ferry to Two Harbors is available only from San Pedro. Once at Avalon, there is a Safari Bus (310/510-2800, $16-25 one-way) to Two Harbors that departs at noon.

**Campsites, facilities:** There are eight tent sites, each for up to six campers. Picnic tables, barbecue and fire rings, and a locker with firewood and 2.5 gallons of drinking water are provided. Chemical toilets are available. There are no sun shades, so bring your own. Firewood, charcoal, and propane are sold only at the ranger station (May through Labor Day). No radios are permitted.

Campers must first check in at Two Harbors Visitor Services to get a key for a lock box ($20) containing one bundle of wood and 2.5 gallons of water. A concessionaire rents a full array of camping equipment, including tents, sleeping bags, pads, stoves, and lanterns.

**Reservations, fees:** Reservations are required at 877/778-1487 or www.reserveamerica.com ($9.25 reservation fee); group reservations for 20 or more can be made at 310/510-2000, ext. 1246. Sites are $17-34 per adult, $8-14 per child (age 11 and under) per night. A fee is charged for the ferry ride to Avalon at Catalina Island from Dana Point, Long Beach, or San Pedro. Discounts are available weekdays and off-season. Open year-round, weather permitting, with a 10-day maximum stay.

**Directions:** Take the ferry boat to Avalon. From Avalon, take shuttle bus to Two Harbors. At Two Harbors, check in at the visitor information booth to validate your camping permit and obtain locker key for water and wood. From Two Harbors, hike seven miles to campsites. Note: A shuttle boat is sometimes available from Two Harbors to Emerald Bay; from Emerald Bay, it is a 1.5-mile hike to the campground.

**Contact:** For ferry information, camp reservations, or general information: Two Harbors Visitor Services, 310/510-4205; concessionaire, 877/778-1487 or 310/510-8368; www.visitcatalinaisland.com or www.visittwoharbors.com.

## 22 TWO HARBORS

### Scenic rating: 10

on Catalina Island

**Map 13.1, page 709**          **BEST (**

This campground is only a quarter-mile hike away from the village of Two Harbors. Nearby attractions include the Two Harbors Dive Station with snorkeling equipment, paddleboard rentals, and scuba tank fills to 3,000 psi. There are guided tours of the island and a scheduled bus service between Two Harbors and Avalon; a shuttle bus stops at all the interior campgrounds. An excellent hike is the nine-mile round-trip from Two Harbors to Emerald Bay, featuring a gorgeous coast and pretty valleys.

Note: The ferry to Avalon is available from Long Beach, Dana Point, or San Pedro. The ferry to Two Harbors is available only from San Pedro. Once at Avalon, there is a Safari Bus (310/510-2800, $16-25 one-way) to Two Harbors.

**Campsites, facilities:** There are 42 sites for tents, three group sites for 20-25 people each, and 13 tent cabins for up to six people each. Picnic tables and fire grills are provided. Drinking water, sun shades (at most sites), cold showers, and chemical toilets are available. Tent cabin sites also include cots, camp stove, and lantern. No radios are permitted. Firewood, charcoal, and propane are sold at the ranger station (May through Labor Day) and can also be ordered in advance. A general store, restaurant and saloon, snack bar, tennis courts, volleyball, coin laundry, and hot showers are available in the town of Two Harbors.

Campers must first check in at Two Harbors Visitor Services to get a key for a lock box ($20) containing one bundle of wood and 2.5 gallons of water. A concessionaire rents a full array of camping equipment, including tents, sleeping bags, pads, stoves, and lanterns.

**Reservations, fees:** Reservations are required at 877/778-1487 or www.reserveamerica.com ($9.25 reservation fee); group reservations for 20 or more can be made at 310/510-2000, ext. 1246. Sites are $24-27 per adult per night, $15-18 per child (age 11 and under) per night. A tent cabin is $60-80 per night. A fee is charged for the round-trip ferry ride to Avalon at Catalina Island from Dana Point, Long Beach, or San Pedro. Discounts are offered midweek and in winter. Open year-round, weather permitting, except for tent cabins (Apr.-Oct. only). Maximum stay is 10 days.

**Directions:** Take the ferry boat to Avalon. From Avalon, take the shuttle bus to Two Harbors. At Two Harbors, check in at the visitor information booth to validate your camping permit and obtain locker key for water and wood. From Two Harbors, hike 0.25 mile to campground.

**Contact:** For ferry information, camp reservations, or general information: Avalon, 877/778-8322; Two Harbors Visitor Services, 310/510-4205; concessionaire, 877/778-1487 or 310/510-8368; www.visitcatalinaisland.com or www.visittwoharbors.com.

## 23 LITTLE HARBOR HIKE-IN

### Scenic rating: 10

on Catalina Island

**Map 13.1, page 709**            **BEST (**

There is plenty to do here: You can swim, dive, fish, or go for day hikes. There are two sandy beaches near this camp. One is great for swimming and snorkeling, and the other has surf for boogie boarding. A Native American historical site is nearby. Two Harbors has several excellent hikes, including the nine-mile excursion to Emerald Bay. Of course, you could always take the shuttle bus. Many folks consider this to be the pick of the campgrounds on the island. It is a gorgeous place—small wonder that some big Hollywood flicks have been shot here.

Note: The ferry to Avalon is available from Long Beach, Dana Point, or San Pedro. The ferry to Two Harbors is available only from San Pedro. Once at Avalon, there is a Safari Bus (310/510-4205, $16-25 one-way) to Two Harbors.

**Campsites, facilities:** There are 21 tent sites, including eight group sites. Picnic tables and fire rings are provided. Drinking water, cold showers, sun shades (at most sites), pay telephone, shuttle bus service, and chemical toilets are available. No radios are permitted. Wood, charcoal, and propane are available from the ranger station (May-Labor Day), and it is recommended that you order in advance. Kayak and snorkel gear rentals are available in Two Harbors.

Campers must first check in at Two Harbors Visitor Services to get a key for a lock box ($20) containing one bundle of wood and 2.5 gallons of water. A concessionaire rents a full array of camping equipment, including tents, sleeping bags, pads, stoves, and lanterns.

**Reservations, fees:** Reservations are required 877/778-1487 or 310/510-8368 ($25 reservation fee) or online (no fee) at www.visitcatalinaisland.com; make group reservations for 20 or more at 310/510-8368, ext. 1414. Sites are $17-24 per adult per night, $8-14 per child age 11

and under per night. Tent cabins are $50-70 per night. A fee is charged for the round-trip ferry ride to Avalon at Catalina Island from Dana Point, Long Beach, or San Pedro. Discounts are offered midweek and in winter. Open year-round, weather permitting, with a maximum stay of 10 days.

**Directions:** Take the ferry boat to Avalon. From Avalon, take the shuttle/Safari bus (or hike or bike) to Little Harbor. Check in at the visitor information booth to validate your camping permit and obtain a locker key for water and wood. From Little Harbor, hike 6.8 miles to the campground. The campground is about 16 miles from Avalon.

**Contact:** For ferry information, camp reservations, or general information: Avalon, 877/778-8322; Two Harbors Visitor Services, 310/510-4205; concessionaire, 877/778-1487 or 310/510-8368; Wet Spot Rentals, 310/510-2229; www.visitcatalinaisland.com or www.visittwoharbors.com.

## 24 BLACK JACK HIKE-IN

### Scenic rating: 7

on Catalina Island

**Map 13.1, page 709**

This camp is named after Mount Black Jack (2,008 feet), the island's highest point, and it is a great place to hunker down for a spell. It's also the site of the old Black Jack Mine. This is the least popular campground on the island, viewed by most as a stopover site, not a base camp. From Black Jack Junction (accessible by shuttle bus), it is a 1.5-mile hike to the camp. Note that shuttle bus service is limited October through mid-June. The camp, at 1,500 feet elevation, is nine miles from Avalon and 11.8 miles from Two Harbors. If you stand in just the right spot, you can see the mainland, but Los Angeles will seem like a million miles away.

Note: The ferry to Avalon is available from Long Beach, Dana Point, or San Pedro. The ferry to Two Harbors is available only from

San Pedro. Once at Avalon, there is a Safari Bus (310/510-4205, $16-25 one-way) to Two Harbors.

**Campsites, facilities:** There are 11 tent sites with a maximum of six campers per site. Drinking water, picnic tables, fire rings, and cold showers are available. No radios are permitted. Chemical toilets are available. A pay phone is nearby. Firewood, charcoal, and propane are sold only at the ranger station (May through Labor Day). Kayak and snorkel gear at Two Harbors is available at West End Diver Center.

Campers must first check in at Two Harbors Visitor Services to get a key for a lock box ($20) containing one bundle of wood and 2.5 gallons of water. A concessionaire rents a full array of camping equipment, including tents, sleeping bags, pads, stoves, and lanterns.

**Reservations, fees:** Reservations are required at 877/778-1487 or www.reserveamerica.com ($9.25 reservation fee); group reservations for 20 or more can be made at 310/510-2000, ext. 1246. Sites are $17-34 per adult, $8-14 per child (age 11 and under) per night. A fee is charged for the round-trip ferry ride to Avalon at Catalina Island from Dana Point, Long Beach, or San Pedro. Discounts are offered midweek and in winter. Open year-round, weather permitting, with a maximum stay of 10 days.

**Directions:** Take ferry boat ride to Avalon. From Avalon, take the shuttle bus to Black Jack Junction. Check in at the visitor information booth to validate your camping permit and obtain a locker key for water and wood. From Black Jack Junction hike 1.3 miles to the campground.

**Contact:** For ferry information and reservations: Avalon, 877/778-8322; Two Harbors Visitor Services, 310/510-4205; concessionaire, 877/778-1487 or 310/510-8368; www.visitcatalinaisland.com or www.visittwoharbors.com.

## 25 CATALINA ISLAND BOAT-IN

**Scenic rating: 10**

on Catalina Island

**Map 13.1, page 709**   **BEST (**

Here is one of the most unusual and best camping experiences in California: the 17 boat-in sites at nine locations on Catalina Island. These primitive camps are on the north shore of the island, between Avalon and Two Harbors. You reach them by private boat or by paddling there (kayak rentals available). There are no overnight powerboat rentals on the island. A ranger checks each boat-in site daily and collects any fees. There are no moorings, so you must anchor your boat and use a dinghy to reach shore. Since these sites are primitive, they have no toilets, no drinking water, no fire rings, and no sun shade. That means you must plan your trip carefully.

Note: The ferry to Avalon is available from Long Beach, Dana Point, or San Pedro. The ferry to Two Harbors is available only from San Pedro. At Avalon, a Safari Bus (310/510-4205, $16-25 one-way) to Two Harbors runs once a day. Kayak rentals are available from Two Harbors Dive & Recreation Center.

**Campsites, facilities:** There are 17 primitive boat-in sites for tents (no moorings). Picnic tables are provided. Fishing is permitted with a license. There are no toilets; bring your own portable chemical toilet or buy waste-disposal bags from the ranger. There is no drinking water or shade. No campfires or beach fires are allowed. Charcoal and propane stoves are permitted; charcoal and propane are sold only at the ranger station (May through Labor Day). No radios are permitted. Garbage must be packed out. Leashed pets are permitted.

**Reservations, fees:** Reservations are required at 877/778-1487 or www.reserveamerica.com ($9.25 reservation fee). Sites are $20 per adult per night, $10 per child (age 2-11) per night. Open year-round, weather permitting, with a maximum stay of 10 days.

**Directions:** Reach the camp by private boat or take the ferry boat ride to Avalon. From Avalon or Two Harbors, rent a kayak and paddle to the campsite.

**Contact:** For ferry information, camp reservations, or general information: Avalon, 877/778-8322; Two Harbors Visitor Services, 310/510-4205; concessionaire, 877/778-1487 or 310/510-8368; www.visitcatalinaisland.com or www.campingcatalinaisland.com.

## 26 HERMIT GULCH
🚶 🚴 ⛰ 🏊 ⛵ 5% ⛺

### Scenic rating: 10
in Avalon on Catalina Island

**Map 13.1, page 709**

This is the closest campground to the town of Avalon, the gateway to Catalina. Reaching the camp requires a 1.5-mile hike up Avalon Canyon. If you're making a tourist trip, there are a ton of things to do: Visit Avalon's underwater city park, play the nine-hole golf course, rent a bicycle, or visit the famous casino. Scenic tours, glass-bottomed boat tours, and Wrigley Memorial and Botanical Gardens are available. Fishing can be excellent, including angling for white seabass, yellowtail, and, in the fall, even marlin. The best hiking experience in the Avalon area is found by taking the shuttle bus to the Airport in the Sky and from there hiking along Empire Landing Road. The route traces the island's curving, hilly northern shore, providing great views of secluded beaches, coves, and rock formations, and a chance to see wildlife, at times even buffalo. Note that free hiking permits are required. Also, if cycling outside of Avalon, a $50 permit is required! Taxi service is available in Avalon, but it is expensive.

Note: The ferry to Avalon is available from Long Beach, Dana Point, or San Pedro. The ferry to Two Harbors is available only from San Pedro. At Avalon, a Safari Bus (310/510-4205, $16-25 one-way) to Two Harbors runs once a day.

**Campsites, facilities:** There are 40 sites for tents, nine tent cabins, and one group site for up to 35 people. Picnic tables and barbecue pits are provided. Restrooms with flush toilets and coin showers, drinking water, ice, lockers, playground, coin microwave, vending machines, and pay phone are available. No radios are permitted. Fires are not allowed; any fires will result in a severe fine. Charcoal and propane are sold only at the ranger station (May through Labor Day). Some camping equipment is available for rent. Kayak and snorkel gear is available at West End Diver Center at Two Harbors.

Campers must first check in at Two Harbors Visitor Services to get a key for a lock box ($20) containing one bundle of wood and 2.5 gallons of water. A concessionaire rents a full array of camping equipment, including tents, sleeping bags, pads, stoves, and lanterns.

**Reservations, fees:** Reservations are required at 877/778-1487 or www.reserveamerica.com ($9.25 reservation fee); group reservations for 20 or more can be made at 310/510-2000, ext. 1246. Sites are $24-27 per adult per night, $15-18 per child per night (age 2-11). Tent cabins are $60-80 per night. A fee is charged for the round-trip ferry ride to Avalon at Catalina Island from Dana Point, Long Beach, or San Pedro. Discounts are offered midweek and in winter. Open year-round, weather permitting, with a maximum stay of 10 days.

**Directions:** Ride the ferry to Avalon. Check in at the visitor information booth to validate your camping permit and obtain a locker key for water and wood. In Avalon at Sumner Avenue, walk up Avalon Canyon (follow the "Avalon Canyon Road" sign) for 1.5 miles to the campground. The camp is across from the picnic area.

**Contact:** For ferry information, camp reservations, or general information: Avalon, 877/778-8322; Two Harbors Visitor Services, 310/510-4205; concessionaire, 877/778-1487 or 310/510-8368; www.visitcatalinaisland.com or www.visittwoharbors.com.

## 27 SYCAMORE FLATS

🐾 🚐 ⛺

**Scenic rating: 7**

on Big Rock Creek in Angeles National Forest

**Map 13.2, page 710**

Sycamore Flats is a developed camp just inside the northern boundary of Angeles National Forest, set at 4,200 feet on the southwest flank of Pinyon Ridge. While there are no trails leading out from this camp, a trailhead is at South Fork, which is two miles south.

**Campsites, facilities:** There are 12 sites for tents or RVs up to 18 feet (no hookups). Picnic tables and fire grills are provided. Drinking water and vault toilets are available seasonally; there is no drinking water in winter or in dry years. Garbage must be packed out. Leashed pets are permitted.

**Reservations, fees:** Reservations are not accepted. There is no fee for camping. An Adventure Pass ($30 annual fee or $5 daily pass) per parked vehicle is required. Open year-round, weather permitting.

**Directions:** From Palmdale (at the junction of Highway 14 and Highway 138), take Highway 138 southeast and drive about 10 miles to Pearblossom and Longview Road. Turn south (right) and drive a short distance to Avenue W/Valyermo Road. Turn left on Avenue W/Valyermo Road and drive about 20 miles into the national forest (past the ranger station) to Big Rock Road. Turn right on Big Rock Road and drive about two miles to the campground entrance.

**Contact:** Angeles National Forest, Santa Clara/Mojave Rivers Ranger District, 661/269-2808, www.fs.usda.gov/angeles.

## 28 SOUTH FORK

🚶 🚐 🐾 🚗 ⛺

**Scenic rating: 7**

on Big Rock Creek in Angeles National Forest

**Map 13.2, page 710**

This excellent trailhead camp sits at 4,500 feet elevation along South Fork Creek. One trail climbs 2.2 miles to the west to Devils Punchbowl County Park, topping out at Devils Chair (the trail includes a steep descent and climb). There are two other options: One meanders south along Big Rock Creek, and the other heads east on High Desert National Recreation Trail (also called Manzanita Trail).

**Campsites, facilities:** There are 21 sites for tents or RVs up to 16 feet (no hookups). Picnic tables and fire rings are provided. Vault toilets are available. No drinking water is available. Garbage must be packed out. Leashed pets are permitted.

**Reservations, fees:** Reservations are not accepted. There is no fee for camping. An Adventure Pass ($30 annual fee or $5 daily pass) per parked vehicle is required. Open year-round, weather permitting.

**Directions:** From Palmdale (at the junction of Highway 14 and Highway 138), take Highway 138 southeast and drive about 10 miles to Pearblossom and Longview Road. Turn south (right) and drive a short distance to Avenue W/Valyermo Road. Turn left on Avenue W/Valyermo Road and drive about 20 miles into the national forest (past the ranger station) to Big Rock Road. Turn right on Big Rock Road and drive about two miles up the canyon (past the Sycamore Flat campground entrance) to the South Fork campground entrance.

**Contact:** Angeles National Forest, Santa Clara/Mojave Rivers Ranger District, 661/269-2808, www.fs.usda.gov/angeles.

## 29 TABLE MOUNTAIN

🐾 ♿ 🚐 ⛺

**Scenic rating: 6**

in Angeles National Forest

**Map 13.2, page 710**

This family campground accommodates both tents and RVs. The road leading in is a paved two-lane county road, easily accessible by any vehicle. The nearby Big Pines Visitor Information Center, one mile south, can provide maps and information on road conditions. The camp elevation is 7,200 feet. A rough road for four-wheel-drive rigs leads out of camp north along the Table Mountain Ridge.

**Campsites, facilities:** There are 111 single sites and two double sites for tents or RVs up to 32 feet (no hookups) and a group site for up to 32 people. Picnic tables and fire pits are provided. Drinking water, vault toilets, and an amphitheater (available for groups by reservation) are available. Some facilities are wheelchair-accessible. Leashed pets are permitted.

**Reservations, fees:** Reservations are accepted at 877/444-6777 ($10 reservation fee) or www.recreation.gov ($9 reservation fee). Single sites are $20 per night, double sites are $40 per night, plus $5 per night extra vehicle fee, and the group site is $80 per night. Open May to November, weather permitting.

**Directions:** Drive on I-15 to Cajon Junction (north of San Bernardino) and the exit for Highway 138 west. Take that exit and drive west on Highway 138 to Angeles Crest Highway/Highway 2. Turn west on Angeles Crest Highway and drive five miles to Wrightwood, then continue for three miles to Big Pines and Table Mountain Road. Turn right on Table Mountain Road and drive one mile to the campground.

**Contact:** Angeles National Forest, Santa Clara/Mojave Rivers Ranger District, 661/269-2808, www.fs.usda.gov/angeles; Big Pines Information Station, 760/249-3504, www.americanll.com.

## 30 BUCKHORN
🏞️ 🐕 ♿ 🚐 ⛺

### Scenic rating: 9
near Snowcrest Ridge in Angeles National Forest

| Map 13.2, page 710 | BEST ( |
|---|---|

This is a prime jumping-off spot for backpackers in Angeles National Forest. The camp, at 6,300 feet elevation, nestles among huge pine and cedar trees along a small creek near Mount Waterman (8,038 feet). A great day hike begins here, a tromp down to Cooper Canyon and the PCT; hikers will be rewarded by beautiful Cooper Falls on this three-hour round-trip. Want a weekend trip? You got it: The Burkhart National Recreational Trail descends into Caruthers Canyon, where hikers can access the High Desert National Recreational Trail and head east to Devil's Punchbowl County Park to Vincent's Gap and the Pacific Crest Trail.

**Campsites, facilities:** There are 38 sites for tents or RVs up to 18 feet (no hookups). Picnic tables and fire pits are provided. Drinking water and vault toilets are available. Some facilities are wheelchair-accessible. Leashed pets are permitted.

**Reservations, fees:** Reservations are not accepted. Sites are $12 per night. Open April through mid-November, weather permitting.

**Directions:** From Pasadena, drive north on I-210 for four miles to the exit for Highway 2/Angeles Crest Highway. Take that exit and drive northeast on Highway 2 for 35 miles to the signed campground entrance.

**Contact:** Angeles National Forest, Los Angeles River Ranger District, 818/899-1900, www.fs.usda.gov/angeles.

## 31 JACKSON FLAT GROUP CAMP WALK-IN
🏞️ 🐕 ⛺

### Scenic rating: 4
near the Pacific Crest Trail in Angeles National Forest

| Map 13.2, page 710 |
|---|

This is a good spot for a group to overnight, assess themselves, and get information before heading out into the surrounding wildlands. The camp is in the Angeles National Forest high country at 7,500 feet elevation, near the end of a short spur road. It takes a 200-yard walk to reach this campground from the parking area. There are two nature trails and an observation deck on-site. The Pacific Crest Trail passes just north of camp and can be reached by a short connecting link trail.

**Campsites, facilities:** There are three tent-only group sites: one for 40 people and two for 30 people each. Picnic tables, bear boxes (mandatory), and fire pits are provided. Drinking water and flush toilets are available. Leashed pets are permitted.

**Reservations, fees:** Reservations are required at 877/444-6777 ($10 reservation fee) or www.recreation.gov ($9 reservation fee); search for Jackson Flats (with an "s") online. Sites are $130-150 per night. Open early May through October, weather permitting.

**Directions:** Drive on I-15 to Cajon Junction (north of San Bernardino) and the exit for Highway 138 west. Take that exit and drive west on Highway 138 to Angeles Crest Highway/Highway 2. Turn west on Angeles Crest Highway and drive five miles to Wrightwood, then continue for three miles to Big Pines. Bear left (still on Angeles Crest Highway) and drive two miles to a Forest Service road (opposite the sign for Grassy Hollow Campground). Turn right and drive one mile to the campground parking lot. Walk 200 yards to the campground. Gates close at 10pm.

**Contact:** Angeles National Forest, Santa Clara/Mojave Rivers Ranger District, 661/269-2808 or 760/249-3526 for information, www.fs.usda.gov/angeles or www.americanll.com.

## 32 APPLETREE

### Scenic rating: 6

near Jackson Lake in Angeles National Forest

**Map 13.2, page 710**

This is one of four camps on Big Pines "Highway" near Jackson Lake. This "lake" is more of a pond and is about a half mile to the west, just up the road. Lake and Peavine Camps are between Appletree and Jackson Lake, while Mountain Oak is just beyond the lake. Any questions? Rangers can answer them at the

nearby Big Pines Information Station and ski complex. The elevation is 6,200 feet.

**Campsites, facilities:** There are eight tent sites. Picnic tables and fire rings are provided. Vault toilets are available. There is no drinking water. Garbage must be packed out. Some facilities are wheelchair-accessible. Leashed pets are permitted.

**Reservations, fees:** Reservations are not accepted. There is no fee for camping. An Adventure Pass ($30 annual fee or $5 daily pass) is required. Open year-round, weather permitting.

**Directions:** Drive on I-15 to Cajon Junction (north of San Bernardino) and the exit for Highway 138 west. Take that exit and drive west on Highway 138 to Angeles Crest Highway/Highway 2. Turn west on Angeles Crest Highway and drive five miles to Wrightwood, and then continue for three miles to Big Pines and Big Pines Highway/County Road N4. Bear right on Big Pines Highway and drive two miles to the campground.

**Contact:** Angeles National Forest, Santa Clara/Mojave Rivers Ranger District, 661/269-2808, www.fs.usda.gov/angeles.

## 33 MOUNTAIN OAK

### Scenic rating: 4

near Jackson Lake in Angeles National Forest

**Map 13.2, page 710**

This is one of four camps within a mile of little Jackson Lake on Big Pines Highway. The others are Lake, Peavine, and Appletree. This camp is about a quarter mile northwest of the lake. The elevation is 6,200 feet.

**Campsites, facilities:** There are 17 sites for tents or RVs up to 18 feet (no hookups). Picnic tables and fire pits are provided. Drinking water and flush toilets are available. Groceries and propane gas are nearby. Leashed pets are permitted.

**Reservations, fees:** Reservations are accepted at 877/444-6777 ($10 reservation fee) or www.recreation.gov ($9 reservation fee). Sites are $20-40 per night. Open May through November, weather permitting.

**Directions:** Drive on I-15 to Cajon Junction (north of San Bernardino) and the exit for Highway 138 west. Take that exit and drive west on Highway 138 to Angeles Crest Highway/ Highway 2. Turn west on Angeles Crest Highway and drive five miles to Wrightwood, and then continue for three miles to Big Pines and Big Pines Highway/County Road N4. Bear right on Big Pines Highway and drive three miles to the campground.

**Contact:** Angeles National Forest, Santa Clara/ Mojave Rivers Ranger District, 661/269-2808, www.fs.usda.gov/angeles or www.americanll. com.

## 34 LAKE CAMPGROUND

### Scenic rating: 8
on Jackson Lake in Angeles National Forest

Map 13.2, page 710

This is a pretty setting on the southeast shore of little Jackson Lake. Of the four camps within a mile, this is the only one right beside the lake. The elevation is 6,100 feet.

**Campsites, facilities:** There are eight sites for tents or RVs up to 18 feet (no hookups). Picnic tables, food lockers, and fire pits are provided. Drinking water and vault toilets are available. Leashed pets are permitted.

**Reservations, fees:** Reservations are accepted at 877/444-6777 ($10 reservation fee) or www. recreation.gov ($9 reservation fee). Sites are $20 per night. Open May through November, weather permitting.

**Directions:** Drive on I-15 to Cajon Junction (north of San Bernardino) and the exit for Highway 138 west. Take that exit and drive west on Highway 138 to Angeles Crest Highway/ Highway 2. Turn west on Angeles Crest Highway and drive five miles to Wrightwood,

and then continue for three miles to Big Pines and Big Pines Highway/County Road N4. Bear right on Big Pines Highway and drive 2.5 miles to the campground.

**Contact:** Angeles National Forest, Santa Clara/ Mojave Rivers Ranger District, 661/269-2808, www.fs.usda.gov/angeles or www.americanll. com.

## 35 PEAVINE

### Scenic rating: 4
near Jackson Lake in Angeles National Forest

Map 13.2, page 710

This tiny camp is one of four in the immediate area, just half a mile east of little eight-acre Jackson Lake. This area is popular for snow play in the winter. The elevation is 6,100 feet.

**Campsites, facilities:** There are four tent sites. Picnic tables and fire pits are provided. Vault toilets are available. There is no drinking water. Garbage must be packed out. A store and propane gas are nearby. Some facilities are wheelchair-accessible. Leashed pets are permitted.

**Reservations, fees:** Reservations are not accepted. There is no fee for camping. An Adventure Pass ($30 annual fee or $5 daily pass) per parked vehicle is required.

**Directions:** Drive on I-15 to Cajon Junction (north of San Bernardino) and the exit for Highway 138 west. Take that exit and drive west on Highway 138 to Angeles Crest Highway/ Highway 2. Turn west on Angeles Crest Highway and drive five miles to Wrightwood, and then continue for three miles to Big Pines and Big Pines Highway/County Road N4. Bear right on Big Pines Highway and drive and drive 2.7 miles to the campground.

**Contact:** Angeles National Forest, Santa Clara/ Mojave Rivers Ranger District, 661/269-2808, www.fs.usda.gov/angeles.

## 36 BLUE RIDGE

### Scenic rating: 8

on the Pacific Crest Trail in Angeles National Forest

**Map 13.2, page 710**

Blue Ridge, high in Angeles National Forest at 8,000 feet elevation, makes a good jumping-off spot for a multiday backpacking trip. The Pacific Crest Trail runs right alongside the camp. Guffy, also beside the PCT, provides an option two miles to the southeast. Note that some of the surrounding area is closed to vehicles to protect the yellow-legged frog.

**Campsites, facilities:** There are eight sites for tents or RVs up to 20 feet. Picnic tables and fire rings are provided. Vault toilets are available. No drinking water is available. Garbage must be packed out. Leashed pets are permitted.

**Reservations, fees:** Reservations are not accepted. There is no fee for camping. An Adventure Pass ($30 annual fee or $5 daily pass) per parked vehicle is required. Open May through November, weather permitting.

**Directions:** Drive on I-15 to Cajon Junction (north of San Bernardino) and the exit for Highway 138 west. Take that exit and drive west on Highway 138 to Angeles Crest Highway/Highway 2. Turn west on Angeles Crest Highway and drive five miles to Wrightwood, and then continue for three miles to Big Pines. Bear left (still on Angeles Crest Highway) and drive 1.5 miles to Blue Ridge Road (adjacent to Inspiration Point). Turn left on Blue Ridge Road and drive three miles to the campground.

**Contact:** Angeles National Forest, Santa Clara/Mojave Rivers Ranger District, 661/269-2808 or 661/269-2808 for information, www.fs.usda.gov/angeles.

## 37 LUPINE WALK-IN

### Scenic rating: 7

on Prairie Fork Creek in Angeles National Forest

**Map 13.2, page 710**

This little-known, hard-to-reach camp, set at 6,500 feet elevation along Prairie Fork Creek, is now a walk-in camp. It is closed to vehicles in order to protect the yellow-legged frog. A challenging butt-kicker hike on a primitive trail starts here. The trail leads from the camp over Pine Mountain Ridge, down into a canyon, and then winds to the east up Dawson Peak—long, difficult, and completed by few.

**Campsites, facilities:** There are 11 sites for tents only. Picnic tables and fire pits are provided. Vault toilets are available. No drinking water is available. Garbage must be packed out. Leashed pets are permitted.

**Reservations, fees:** Reservations are not accepted. There is no fee for camping. An Adventure Pass ($30 annual fee or a $5 daily pass) is required. Open May through November, weather permitting.

**Directions:** Drive on I-15 to Cajon Junction (north of San Bernardino) and the exit for Highway 138 west. Take that exit and drive west on Highway 138 to Angeles Crest Highway/Highway 2. Turn west on Angeles Crest Highway and drive five miles to Wrightwood, and then continue for three miles to Big Pines. Bear left (still on Angeles Crest Highway) and drive 1.5 miles to Blue Ridge Road (adjacent to Inspiration Point). Turn left on Blue Ridge Road and drive five miles to the locked gate. From here, you can hike, bike, or ride a horse for three miles to the campground.

**Contact:** Angeles National Forest, Santa Clara/Mojave Rivers Ranger District, 661/269-2808, www.fs.usda.gov/angeles.

## 38 GUFFY HIKE-IN

### Scenic rating: 7

on the Pacific Crest Trail in Angeles National Forest

**Map 13.2, page 710**

A short trail right out of this camp connects with the Pacific Crest Trail, making Guffy a backpacker's special. The camp and access road are closed to vehicles in order to protect the yellow-legged frog. The elevation is 8,300 feet.

**Campsites, facilities:** There are six tent sites. Picnic tables and fire rings are provided. Vault toilets are available. No drinking water is available. Garbage must be packed out. Leashed pets are permitted.

**Reservations, fees:** Reservations are not accepted. There is no fee for camping, but an Adventure Pass ($30 annual fee or a $5 daily pass) is required. Open May through November, weather permitting.

**Directions:** From I-15 near Cajon, take Highway 138 west. Turn west on Angeles Crest Highway/Highway 2 and drive five miles to Wrightwood. Continue for three miles to Big Pines. Bear left and continue on Angeles Crest Highway for 1.5 miles to Blue Ridge Road. Turn left (opposite Inspiration Point) on Blue Ridge Road and park. From here, you can hike, bike, or ride a horse six miles to the campground.

**Contact:** Angeles National Forest, Santa Clara/ Mojave Rivers Ranger District, 661/269-2808, www.fs.usda.gov/angeles.

## 39 MOJAVE RIVER FORKS REGIONAL PARK

### Scenic rating: 7

near Silverwood Lake

**Map 13.2, page 710**

You can usually find a spot here—it's quiet and enjoyable. Full hookups are a bonus for RV drivers, as is the park's proximity to Silverwood Lake—which is only nine miles away but does not have any sites with hookups. The sites are well spaced, but the nearby "river" is usually dry. The elevation at this 840-acre park is 3,200 feet.

**Campsites, facilities:** There are 25 sites with full hookups (20 and 30 amps) for RVs up to 40 feet, 25 sites with no hookups for RVs, 25 walk-in tent sites, and group sites for 200-300 people each. Several sites are pull-through. Picnic tables and fire grills are provided. Restrooms with showers and flush toilets, drinking water, and a dump station are available. Leashed pets are permitted.

**Reservations, fees:** Reservations are accepted online at www.sbcountyparks.com ($5 reservation fee) and are required for group sites. Sites with hookups are $40 per night, sites without hookups are $30 per night, walk-in tent sites are $20 per night, plus $5 per night for more than four people (six people max) and $1 per pet per night. Call for group rates. Some credit cards are accepted. Campers must show proof of current vehicle registration and insurance. Open year-round.

**Directions:** From I-15, drive to Cajon Junction (north of San Bernardino) and the exit for Highway 138/Silverwood. Take that exit east and drive nine miles to a fork with Highway 173. Bear left at the fork on Highway 173 and drive six miles to the park on the right.

**Contact:** Mojave River Forks Regional Park, 760/389-2322, www.sbcountyparks.com.

## 40 BIG PINE FLATS

### Scenic rating: 6

in San Bernardino National Forest

**Map 13.2, page 710**

This is a favorite staging area for off-highway vehicle (OHV) users, with many OHV trails nearby. It is a pretty spot set at 6,800 feet elevation in San Bernardino National Forest and provides a little of both worlds: You are surrounded by wildlands near Redondo Ridge, yet you're not a long drive (about 45 minutes) from

Big Bear Lake to the south. Any questions? The firefighters at Big Pine Flats Fire Station, just across the road, can answer them.

**Campsites, facilities:** There are 19 sites for tents or RVs up to 30 feet (no hookups). Picnic tables and fire grills are provided. Drinking water is available but limited; owners of trailers and RVs should fill up their water tanks prior. Vault toilets are available. Some facilities are wheelchair-accessible. Leashed pets are permitted.

**Reservations, fees:** Reservations are not accepted. Sites are $22-24 per night, plus $5 per night per extra vehicle. Open mid-May through mid-October.

**Directions:** Drive on Highway 30 to the junction with Highway 330 (east of San Bernardino near Highland). Take Highway 330 north (signed "Mountain Resorts") and drive 35 miles to the dam on Big Bear Lake and a fork with Highway 38. Continue straight on Highway 38 and drive about four miles to the town of Fawnskin and Rim of the World Highway. Turn left and drive seven miles (after 0.5 mile it becomes Forest Road 3N14, a dirt road) to Big Pine Flats Fire Station and the campground on the right.

**Contact:** San Bernardino National Forest, Mountaintop Ranger District, Big Bear Ranger Station/Discovery Center, 909/382-2790, www. fs.usda.gov/sbnf.

## 41 BIG PINE GROUP AND EQUESTRIAN
🚶🐴♿🚙⛺

### Scenic rating: 3
in San Bernardino National Forest

**Map 13.2, page 710**

This camp is adjacent to the Big Pine Flats Fire Station and is used by equestrians and OHV riders. A trailhead for the Pacific Crest Trail is about two miles to the southeast of the camp via Forest Road 3N14. The elevation is 6,700 feet.

**Campsites, facilities:** One group camp for tents or RVs up to 32 feet (no hookups) can accommodate up to 25 people. Picnic tables and fire grills are provided. Vault toilets and drinking water are available. Horse facilities include corrals, hitching racks, a staging area, and water troughs. Some facilities are wheelchair-accessible. Leashed pets are permitted.

**Reservations, fees:** Reservations are required at 877/444-6777 ($10 reservation fee) or www. recreation.gov ($9 reservation fee). The camp is $100-110 per night. Open mid-May through mid-November.

**Directions:** Drive on Highway 30 to the junction with Highway 330 (east of San Bernardino near Highland). Take Highway 330 north (signed "Mountain Resorts") and drive 35 miles to the dam on Big Bear Lake and a fork with Highway 38. Continue straight on Highway 38 and drive about four miles to the town of Fawnskin and Rim of the World Highway. Turn left and drive seven miles (after 0.5 mile it becomes Forest Road 3N14, a dirt road) to Forest Road 3N16. Turn left and drive 0.25 mile to the campground on the right.

**Contact:** San Bernardino National Forest, Mountaintop Ranger District, Big Bear Ranger Station/Discovery Center, 909/382-2790, www. fs.usda.gov/sbnf.

## 42 MANKER FLATS
🚶🐴🚙⛺

### Scenic rating: 7
near Mount Baldy in Angeles National Forest

**Map 13.2, page 710**　　　　BEST (

This camp is best known for its proximity to Mount Baldy and the nearby trailhead to reach San Antonio Falls. The trail to San Antonio Falls starts at an elevation of 6,160 feet, a third of a mile up the road on the left. Then it's a 1.5-mile saunter on a ski park maintenance road to the waterfall, a pretty 80-footer. The wild and ambitious can continue six more miles and climb to the top of Mount Baldy (10,064 feet) for breathtaking 360-degree views. Making this all-day butt-kicker is like a baptism for Southern California hikers.

**Campsites, facilities:** There are 21 sites for tents or RVs up to 16 feet (no hookups). Picnic tables and fire grills are provided. Drinking water and flush toilets are available. Leashed pets are permitted. There is no drinking water in dry years.

**Reservations, fees:** Reservations are not accepted. Sites are $14 per night ($10 with Adventure Pass), $5 per night for each additional vehicle ($3 with Adventure Pass). Open May through September.

**Directions:** Drive on I-10 to Ontario and the exit for Highway 83. Take that exit and drive north on Highway 83 to Mount Baldy Road. Continue north on Mount Baldy Road for nine miles to the campground.

**Contact:** Angeles National Forest, San Gabriel River Ranger District, 626/335-1251 or 909/982-2829, www.fs.usda.gov/angeles.

## 43 APPLEWHITE

### Scenic rating: 5

near Lytle Creek in San Bernardino National Forest

**Map 13.2, page 710**

Note: This camp sustained damage from the 2016 Blue Cut fire and remained closed at time of publication. Contact the ranger station for updates before planning a trip.

Nothing like a little insiders' know-how, especially at this camp, set at 3,300 feet elevation near Lytle Creek. You can reach the Middle Fork of Lytle Creek by driving north from Fontana via Serra Avenue to the Lytle Creek area. To get to the stretch of water that is stocked with trout by the Department of Fish and Game, turn west on Middle Fork Road, which is 1.5 miles before the campground at Apple White. The first mile upstream is stocked every other week in spring and early summer.

**Campsites, facilities:** There are 44 sites for tents or RVs up to 30 feet (no hookups). Picnic

tables and fire grills are provided. Restrooms with flush toilets and drinking water are available. A store is nearby. Some facilities are wheelchair-accessible. Leashed pets are permitted.

**Reservations, fees:** Reservations are not accepted. Single sites are $10 per night, double sites are $15 per night, plus $5 per night for each additional vehicle. Open Friday through Tuesday year-round.

**Directions:** Drive to Ontario and the junction of I-10 and I-15. Take I-15 north and drive 11 miles to the Sierra Avenue exit. Take that exit and turn left, go under the freeway, and continue north (into the national forest) for about nine miles to the campground on the right.

**Contact:** San Bernardino National Forest, Front Country Ranger District, Lytle Creek Ranger Station, 909/382-2851, www.fs.usda.gov/sbnf.

## 44 MESA–SILVERWOOD LAKE

### Scenic rating: 8

on Silverwood Lake in Silverwood Lake State Recreation Area

**Map 13.2, page 710**

This state park campground is on the west side of Silverwood Lake at 3,355 feet elevation, bordered by San Bernardino National Forest to the south and high desert to the north. The hot weather and proximity to San Bernardino make it a winner with boaters, who have 1,000 surface acres of water and 13 miles of shoreline to explore. All water sports are allowed. It's a great lake for waterskiing (35-mph speed limit), water sports (5-mph speed limit in major coves), and sailboarding, with afternoon winds usually strong in the spring and early summer. Note that the quota on boats is enforced, with a maximum of 166 boats per day, and that boat-launch reservations are required on summer weekends and holidays. There are also designated areas for boating, waterskiing, and fishing to reduce conflicts. Fishing varies dramatically according to season, with trout planted in the cool months and largemouth bass, bluegill, striped bass, catfish, and crappie caught the rest of the year. (Note: All boats must be certified mussel-free before launching.) A large sandy swimming beach is on the lake's southeast side at the Sawpit Recreation Area. The park also has a modest trail system with both nature and bike trails. Miller Canyon is off-limits during bald eagle nesting season.

**Campsites, facilities:** There are 134 sites for tents or RVs up to 32 feet (no hookups), with a few for RVs of any length, and four hike-in/bike-in sites. Some sites are pull-through. Picnic tables and fire rings (fire restriction may be in effect) are provided. Restrooms with flush toilets and coin showers, drinking water, Wi-Fi, dump station, boat ramp, marina, boat rentals, and small store are available. Some facilities are wheelchair-accessible. Leashed pets are permitted.

**Reservations, fees:** Reservations are accepted at 800/444-7275 or www.reserveamerica.com ($8 reservation fee). Sites are $45-50 per night, plus $8 per night for each additional vehicle, and $5 per night per person for hike-in/bike-in sites. Open year-round.

**Directions:** Drive on I-15 to Cajon Junction (north of San Bernardino) and the exit for Highway 138 east. Take that exit and drive east on Highway 138 for 12 miles to the park entrance on the right.

**Contact:** Silverwood Lake State Recreation Area, 760/389-2303 or 760/389-2281; Silverwood Lake Marina, 760/389-2299, www.parks.ca.gov.

## 45 WEST FORK GROUP CAMPS

**Scenic rating: 4**

at Silverwood Lake in Silverwood Lake State Recreation Area

Map 13.2, page 710

This is a large camping complex for groups at Silverwood Lake. For more information on Silverwood Lake, see the Mesa—Silverwood Lake listing in this chapter.

**Campsites, facilities:** There are six group camps for tents or RVs of any length (no hookups): three group camps for up to 40 people and three group camps for up to 100 people. Picnic tables and fire rings (fire restriction may be in effect) are provided. Restrooms with flush toilets and coin showers and drinking water are available. Some facilities are wheelchair-accessible. Shaded picnic areas, fishing, hiking, swimming, boating, food service, and a store are available nearby. A dump station is available at Mesa campground. Leashed pets are permitted.

**Reservations, fees:** Reservations are required at 800/444-7275 or www.reserveamerica.com ($8 reservation fee). Sites are $325 per night. Open April through October.

**Directions:** Take I-15 to Cajon Junction (north of San Bernardino) and the exit for Highway 138 east. Take that exit and drive east on Highway 138 for 12 miles to the park entrance on the right.

**Contact:** Silverwood Lake State Recreation Area, 760/389-2303 or 760/389-2281, www.parks.ca.gov.

## 46 DOGWOOD

**Scenic rating: 6**

near Lake Arrowhead in San Bernardino National Forest

Map 13.2, page 710

So close, yet so far—that's the paradox between

Lake Arrowhead and Dogwood. The lake is just a mile away, but there is no public access. The lake is ringed by gated trophy homes. The elevation is 5,600 feet. Any questions? The rangers at the Arrowhead Ranger Station, about 1.5 miles down the road to the east, can answer them.

**Campsites, facilities:** There are 57 sites for tents or RVs up to 40 feet, 19 sites for tents or RV sites with partial hookups (30 amps), and 11 sites for tents only. Picnic tables and fire grills are provided. Drinking water, restrooms with flush toilets and coin showers, and a dump station are available. An amphitheater and campfire programs are available. A store is nearby. Some facilities are wheelchair-accessible. Leashed pets are permitted.

**Reservations, fees:** Reservations are accepted at 877/444-6777 ($10 reservation fee) or www.recreation.gov ($9 reservation fee). Single sites are $30-32 per night, and it's $5 per night for each additional vehicle. Open mid-May through October.

**Directions:** Drive on Highway 30 to San Bernardino and Highway 18 (two miles east of the junction of Highway 30 and I-215). Turn north on Highway 18 and drive 15 miles to Rim of the World Highway. Continue on Highway 18 for 0.3 mile to the road immediately after Daley Canyon Road. Turn left and make an immediate right on the Daley Canyon access road. Drive a short distance to the campground entrance on the left.

**Contact:** San Bernardino National Forest, Mountaintop Ranger District, Arrowhead Ranger Station, 909/382-2782, www.fs.usda.gov/sbnf.

# 47 NORTH SHORE

### Scenic rating: 8
on Lake Arrowhead in San Bernardino National Forest

**Map 13.2, page 710**

Of the two camps at Lake Arrowhead, this one is preferable. It is at 5,300 feet elevation near the northeastern shore of the lake, which provides decent trout fishing in the spring and early summer from a boat. Note that this is a private lake, and there is no shore access. To the nearby north, Deep Creek in San Bernardino National Forest is well worth exploring; a hike along the stream to fish for small trout (catch-and-release only) or see a unique set of small waterfalls is highly recommended.

**Campsites, facilities:** There are 28 single sites and a few double sites for tents or RVs up to 22 feet (no hookups). Picnic tables and fire rings are provided. Drinking water and flush toilets are available. A store is nearby. Some facilities are wheelchair-accessible. Leashed pets are permitted.

**Reservations, fees:** Reservations are accepted at 877/444-6777 ($10 reservation fee) or www.recreation.gov ($9 reservation fee). Single sites are $22-44 per night, plus $5 per night for each additional vehicle. Open May through September.

**Directions:** Drive on Highway 30 to San Bernardino and the Waterman exit. Take that exit and drive north on Waterman Avenue until it becomes Highway 18. Continue on Highway 18/Rim of the World Highway and drive 17 miles to Highway 173. Turn left on Highway 173 and drive north for 1.6 miles to the stop sign. Turn right (still on Highway 173) and drive 2.9 miles to Hospital Road. Turn right and continue 0.1 mile to the top of the small hill. Turn left just past the hospital entrance and continue a short distance to the campground.

**Contact:** San Bernardino National Forest, Mountaintop Ranger District, Big Bear Ranger Station/Discovery Center, 909/382-2790, www.fs.usda.gov/sbnf.

## 48 TENT PEG GROUP

**Scenic rating: 5**

near the Pacific Crest Trail in San Bernardino National Forest

**Map 13.2, page 710**

This camp would be a lot easier to reach with a helicopter than a vehicle. But that's why Tent Peg is a well-loved camp for the few who book it: It's a primitive camp for groups at 5,400 feet elevation, complete with trailhead. A rough jeep road heads out of camp to the west and down into Deep Creek. In addition, there is a trailhead for a three-mile hike down the canyon to the south to Fisherman's Hike-In campground, set along Deep Creek. The trout are small but willing (catch-and-release only).

**Campsites, facilities:** There is one group camp that can accommodate 10-30 people and five vehicles. Picnic tables and fire grills are provided. Vault toilets are available. No drinking water is available. A store is approximately five miles away. Some facilities are wheelchair-accessible. Leashed pets are permitted.

**Reservations, fees:** Reservations are required at 877/444-6777 ($10 reservation fee) or www.recreation.gov ($9 reservation fee). The camp is $120-130 per night. Open mid-May through October.

**Directions:** From San Bernardino, drive east on Highway 30 to the junction with Highway 330 (east of San Bernardino near Highland). Take Highway 330 north (signed "Mountain Resorts") and drive to Running Springs and the junction with Highway 18. Turn east on Highway 18 and drive to Green Valley Road. Turn left on Green Valley Road and drive three miles to Forest Road 3N16 (a dirt road). Turn left and drive four miles (you will cross two creeks that vary in depth depending on season; high clearance is recommended but is typically not necessary) to the campground (one mile past the town of Green Valley Lake) to an intersection with Forest Road 3N34. Bear left on Forest Road 3N34 and drive one mile to the campground on the left.

**Contact:** San Bernardino National Forest, Mountaintop Ranger District, Arrowhead Ranger Station, 909/382-2782, www.fs.usda.gov/sbnf.

## 49 CRAB FLATS

**Scenic rating: 4**

near Crab Creek in San Bernardino National Forest

**Map 13.2, page 710**

Four-wheel-drive cowboys and dirt-bike enthusiasts often make this a base camp, known as a staging area for off-highway vehicles (green sticker required). It is a developed Forest Service camp set at a fork in the road at 6,200 feet elevation. A challenging jeep road and motorcycle trail heads west into Deep Creek Canyon. Note that Tent Peg Group camp (see listing in this chapter) is just a half mile to the west on Forest Road 3N34 (hiking trails are available there).

**Campsites, facilities:** There are 27 sites for tents or RVs up to 28 feet (no hookups). Picnic tables and fire rings are provided. Drinking water and vault toilets are available. Leashed pets are permitted.

**Reservations, fees:** Reservations are accepted at 877/444-6777 ($10 reservation fee) or www.recreation.gov ($9 reservation fee). Sites are $20-22 per night. Open mid-May through October.

**Directions:** From San Bernardino, drive east on Highway 30 to the junction with Highway 330 (east of San Bernardino near Highland). Take Highway 330 north (signed "Mountain Resorts") and drive to Running Springs and the junction with Highway 18. Turn east on Highway 18 and drive to Green Valley Road. Turn left on Green Valley Road and drive three miles to Forest Road 3N16 (a dirt road). Turn left and drive four miles (you will cross two creeks that vary in depth depending on season; high clearance is recommended but is typically not necessary) to an intersection. Bear left at the intersection and drive a very short distance to the campground entrance on the right.

**Contact:** San Bernardino National Forest, Mountaintop Ranger District, Arrowhead Ranger Station, 909/382-2782, www.fs.usda. gov/sbnf.

## 50 FISHERMAN'S HIKE-IN

### Scenic rating: 8

on Deep Creek in San Bernardino National Forest

#### Map 13.2, page 710

Get here and you join the 5 Percent Club. Fisherman's Hike-In is a secluded, wooded campground deep in San Bernardino National Forest at 5,400 feet elevation. Deep Creek, a designated Wild and Scenic River, runs alongside, providing stream trout fishing and a beautiful setting. It's worth the significant effort required to get here. Anglers tromp along the stream via a primitive route along the creek (which looks more like a deer trail than a hiking trail). The trout are small but well colored, and the first cast into the head of a pool often results in a strike. Remember, it is catch-and-release fishing only in this area.

**Campsites, facilities:** There are four tent sites for groups of up to eight people per site. Picnic tables and fire grills are provided. Vault toilets are available. No drinking water is available. Garbage must be packed out. Horses and leashed pets are permitted, but corrals and water troughs are not available.

**Reservations, fees:** Reservations are required at 877/444-6777 ($10 reservation fee) or www.recreation.gov ($9 reservation fee). Sites are $10 per night. Open year-round, weather permitting.

**Directions:** From San Bernardino, drive east on Highway 30 to the junction with Highway 330 (east of San Bernardino near Highland). Take Highway 330 north (signed "Mountain Resorts") and drive to Running Springs and the junction with Highway 18. Turn east on

Highway 18 and drive to Green Valley Road. Turn left on Green Valley Road and drive three miles to Forest Road 3N16 (a dirt road). Turn left and drive four miles (you will cross two creeks that vary in depth depending on season; high clearance is recommended but is typically not necessary) to the campground (one mile past the town of Green Valley Lake) to an intersection with Forest Road 3N34. Bear left on Forest Road 3N34 and drive west for 1.3 miles to Forest Service Trail 2W07 on your left. Park and take this hiking trail for 2.5 miles southwest to Deep Creek. The campground is on the other side of the creek.

**Contact:** San Bernardino National Forest, Mountaintop Ranger District, Arrowhead Ranger Station, 909/382-2782, www.fs.usda. gov/sbnf. For fire information, call Big Bear Discovery Center, 909/866-3437; Arrowhead Ranger Station, 909/382-2782.

## 51 GREEN VALLEY

### Scenic rating: 4

near Green Valley Lake in San Bernardino National Forest

#### Map 13.2, page 710

This camp sits along Green Valley Creek at an elevation of 7,000 feet. Little Green Valley Lake is a mile to the west; it is privately owned, but public access is allowed. It's quiet and intimate at this lake, and kayaks and rowboats can be rented. The lake is stocked with trout by the Department of Fish and Game and it is also a good spot to take a flying leap and belly flop when water levels are high enough.

**Campsites, facilities:** There are 37 sites for tents or RVs up to 22 feet (no hookups). Picnic tables and fire grills are provided. Drinking water and flush toilets are available. A store and coin laundry are nearby. Leashed pets are permitted.

**Reservations, fees:** Reservations are accepted at 877/444-6777 ($10 reservation fee) or www. recreation.gov ($9 reservation fee). Single sites are $22-24 per night, double sites are $44 per night, plus $5 per night for each additional vehicle. Open May through October.

**Directions:** From San Bernardino, take Highway 30 east to the junction with Highway 330 (east of San Bernardino near Highland). Take Highway 330 north (signed "Mountain Resorts") and drive to Running Springs and the junction with Highway 18. Turn east on Highway 18 and drive to Green Valley Lake Road. Turn left on Green Valley Lake Road and drive five miles to the campground (one mile past the town of Green Valley Lake).

**Contact:** San Bernardino National Forest, Mountaintop Ranger District, Arrowhead Ranger Station, 909/382-2782, www.fs.usda. gov/sbnf.

## 52 SHADY COVE GROUP AND WALK-IN

**Scenic rating: 7**

near the Children's Forest in San Bernardino National Forest

**Map 13.2, page 710**

The highlight here is the adjacent short looped trail through the Children's Forest. The camp is excellent for Boy Scout and Girl Scout troops. The walk to the camp is about 100 yards. The elevation is 7,500 feet.

**Campsites, facilities:** There are three group sites for up to 30 people each. Picnic tables and fire grills are provided. Drinking water and vault toilets are available. Some facilities are wheelchair-accessible. Leashed pets are permitted.

**Reservations, fees:** Reservations are required at 877/444-6777 ($10 reservation fee) or www. recreation.gov ($9 reservation fee). The group sites are $90-100 per night. Note: The camp is gated for safety; groups are given a combination. Open May through mid-October, weather permitting.

**Directions:** From San Bernardino and Highway 330, drive north on Highway 330 to

the town of Running Springs. Continue just past Running Springs to Keller Peak Road (just past Deer Lick Fire Station). Turn right (south) on Keller Peak Road and drive four miles to the Children's Forest. Bear left to the parking area. The walk-in sites are 100 yards from the parking area.

**Contact:** San Bernardino National Forest, Mountaintop Ranger District, Arrowhead Ranger Station, 909/382-2782, www.fs.usda. gov/sbnf.

## 53 LOS ANGELES/POMONA/ FAIRPLEX KOA

**Scenic rating: 4**

in Pomona

**Map 13.2, page 710**

This is what you might call an urban RV park. Then again, the L.A. County Fairgrounds are right across the street, and there's something going on there every weekend. Frank G. Bonnelli Regional Park, which includes Puddingstone Lake, is only 15 minutes away. Note that about 100 of the sites are occupied by permanent residents.

**Campsites, facilities:** There are 188 pull-through sites with full hookups (50 amps) for RVs and 11 tent sites. Two cabins are also available. Restrooms with showers, pool and spa, convenience store, dump station, dog walk, and coin laundry are available. Some facilities are wheelchair-accessible. Leashed pets are permitted, with certain restrictions.

**Reservations, fees:** Reservations are accepted. RV sites (full hookups) are $60.89-70.18 per night, tent sites are $39.27-41.53 per night, plus $10 per night for each additional vehicle and $6 per person per night for more than two people. Camping cabins are $64.72-75.90 per night. Some credit cards are accepted. Open year-round.

**Directions:** Drive on I-10 to the exit for Fairplex Drive (five miles west of Pomona). Take that exit north (toward the mountain)

and drive two miles to McKinley Avenue. Turn right on McKinley Avenue and drive one mile to White Avenue. Turn left and drive about 0.5 mile (0.2 mile south of Arrow Street) to the park on the right (2200 North White Avenue).
**Contact:** Los Angeles/Pomona/Fairplex KOA, 909/593-8915, www.koa.com.

## 54 EAST SHORE RV PARK

**Scenic rating: 7**

at Puddingstone Lake

Map 13.2, page 710

Considering how close Puddingstone Lake is to so many people, the quality of fishing and waterskiing might be a surprise to newcomers. The lake covers 250 acres and is an excellent recreation facility. For the most part, rules permit waterskiing and personal watercraft between 10am and sunset, making it an excellent lake for fishing for bass and trout (in season) during the morning and evening. All water sports are allowed, with specific days and hours for power-boating and personal watercraft. A ski beach is on the north shore, and there is a large, sandy swimming beach on the southwest shore about a mile away. The lake is just south of Raging Waters in San Dimas and is bordered to the south by Bonnelli Regional Park; a golf course and equestrian facilities are adjacent. The park has roughly 50 monthly residents. Insider's tip: One nice tent site on a hilltop with trees provides more privacy.
**Campsites, facilities:** There are 518 sites with full hookups (20, 30, and 50 amps) for RVs of any length, 25 walk-in sites for tents, and three group tent sites. Some sites are pull-through. Restrooms with showers, cable TV, Wi-Fi, recreation room, swimming pools, general store, playground, basketball, volleyball, horseshoes, propane gas delivery, 24-hour ranger service, and coin laundry are available. A hot-tub facility is nearby. Some facilities are wheelchair-accessible. Leashed pets are permitted at RV sites but not at tent sites.

**Reservations, fees:** Reservations are accepted at 800/809-3778. RV sites are $43-58 per night for up to two people, tent sites are $30 per night for up to three people, plus $3 per night for each additional person and $3 per pet per night. Group, monthly, and seasonal rates are available. Some credit cards are accepted. Open year-round.
**Directions:** Drive on I-10 to the exit for Fairplex Drive (five miles west of Pomona). Take that exit north to Via Verde (the first traffic light). Turn left on Via Verde and drive to the first stop sign at Campers View. Turn right on Campers View and drive into the park.
**Contact:** East Shore RV Park, 909/599-8355 or 800/809-3778, www.eastshorervpark.com.

## 55 YUCAIPA REGIONAL PARK

**Scenic rating: 7**

near Redlands

Map 13.2, page 710

This is a great family-oriented county park, complete with water slides and paddleboats for the kids and fishing access and hiking trails for adults. Three lakes are stocked weekly with catfish in the summer and trout in the winter, the closest thing around to an insurance policy for anglers. Spectacular scenic views of the Yucaipa Valley, the San Bernardino Mountains, and Mount San Gorgonio are possible from the park. The park covers 885 acres in the foothills of the San Bernardino Mountains. A one-acre swimming lagoon and two water slides make this a favorite for youngsters. The Yucaipa Adobe and Mousley Museum of Natural History is nearby.
**Campsites, facilities:** There are 42 sites for RVs of any length and nine sites for tents. All RV sites have full hookups (20, 30, and 50 amps) and/or are pull-through. Picnic tables and fire rings are provided at most sites. Drinking water and restrooms with flush toilets and showers are available, and shade ramadas are available

at tent sites. A seasonal swimming lagoon and water slides, fishing ponds, seasonal paddle-boat and aquacycle rentals, Wi-Fi (in office), ATM, DVD rentals, pay phone, seasonal snack bar, picnic shelters, playground, volleyball (bring net), horseshoes, group facilities, bait shop, and dump station are nearby. The water slide is open Memorial Day weekend through Labor Day weekend. Some facilities are wheelchair-accessible. Leashed pets are permitted.

**Reservations, fees:** Reservations are accepted at www.sbcountyparks.com ($10 reservation fee). Tent sites are $25 per tent per night, RV sites (full hookups) are $40 per night, plus $1 per pet per night. Weekly, senior, and youth group rates are available. Some credit cards are accepted. Additional charges apply for fishing, swimming, and use of the water slide. Proof of vehicle registration is required for campers. Maximum stay in any 30-day period is 14 days. Open year-round.

**Directions:** Drive on I-10 to Redlands and the exit for Yucaipa Boulevard. Take that exit and drive east on Yucaipa Boulevard to Oak Glen Road. Turn left and continue two miles to the park on the left.

**Contact:** Yucaipa Regional Park, 909/790-3127, www.sbcountyparks.com.

## 56 PRADO REGIONAL PARK

### Scenic rating: 6

on Prado Park Lake near Corona

**Map 13.2, page 710**

Prado Park Lake is the centerpiece of a 2,280-acre recreation-oriented park that features hiking trails, an equestrian center, athletic fields, shooting range, dog-training facility, and 36-hole golf course. The lake is small and used primarily for paddling small boats and fishing, which is best in the winter and early spring when trout are planted, and then in early summer for catfish and bass. Gas motors, inflatables, sailboarding, swimming, and water/body contact are not permitted. The shooting facility, the site of the 1984 Olympic shooting venue, is outstanding.

**Campsites, facilities:** There are 75 sites with full hookups (30 and 50 amps) for RVs of any length, 15 tent sites, and nine group sites. Most sites are pull-through. Picnic tables and fire rings are provided. Restrooms with showers, coin laundry, pay phone, snack bar, picnic area, playground, group facilities, boat ramp, and bait shop are available. A playing field with softball, soccer, and horseshoes is on-site. Some facilities are wheelchair-accessible. Leashed pets are permitted.

**Reservations, fees:** Reservations accepted at 909/597-4260 or 877/387-2757 at www.sbcountyparks.com ($7 reservation fee). Sites are $40 per night, good for four people and two vehicles, plus $1 per pet per night. Group sites are $5 per person per night with a 20-person minimum. Weekly rates are available. A fee is charged for fishing. Campers must show proof of vehicle registration and insurance. Some credit cards are accepted. Open year-round, with a maximum 14-day stay in a 30-day period.

**Directions:** Drive on Highway 91 to Highway 71 (west of Norco and Riverside). Take Highway 71 north and drive four miles to Highway 83/Euclid Avenue. Turn right on Euclid Avenue and drive one mile to the park entrance on the right.

**Contact:** Prado Regional Park, 909/597-4260 or 877/387-2757, www.sbcountyparks.com.

## 57 RANCHO JURUPA PARK

### Scenic rating: 4

near Riverside

**Map 13.2, page 710**

Lord, it gets hot in the summertime, but there is shade and grass at this 200-acre park. The setting is along the Santa Ana River, amid cottonwood trees and meadows. This Riverside County park stocks trout and catfish in a three-acre fishing lake. Hiking, cycling, and equestrian trails are also available in the park. Shaded picnic sites are a plus. Summer visitors will find that the nearest lake for swimming and water sports is Lake Perris, about a 20-minute drive away. The elevation is 780 feet.

**Campsites, facilities:** There are 67 sites: 12 sites with full hookups and 55 sites with partial hookups (30 and 50 amps) for tents or RVs of any length. Picnic tables and fire grills are provided. Drinking water, flush toilets with showers, and a dump station are available. Some facilities are wheelchair-accessible. Leashed pets are permitted.

**Reservations, fees:** Reservations are accepted for the individual sites and required for the group camp at 800/234-7275 ($8 reservation fee, $15 for group camp). Tent sites are $25 per night, RV sites (partial hookups) are $35 per night, plus $1 per pet per night and $1 per horse per night. Group sites are $150 per night for primitive tent camping or $225 per night for a developed site; youth group camping is available. A fishing fee is charged. Some credit cards are accepted. Open year-round, with a maximum 14-day stay in a 28-day period.

**Directions:** Drive on I-215 to Riverside and Highway 60. Take Highway 60 east and drive seven miles to Rubidoux Boulevard. Turn left on Rubidoux Boulevard and drive 0.5 mile to Mission Boulevard. Turn left on Mission Boulevard and drive about one mile to Crestmore Road. Turn right and drive 1.5 miles to the park gate on the left (4800 Crestmore Road).

**Contact:** Rancho Jurupa Park, 800/234-7275 or 951/684-7032, www.rivcoparks.org.

## 58 ORANGELAND RV PARK

### Scenic rating: 1

near Disneyland

**Map 13.2, page 710**

This park is about three miles east of Disneyland. If the other RV parks near Disneyland are filled, this is a useful alternative.

Note that about half of the sites are filled with long-term renters.

**Campsites, facilities:** There are 195 sites for RVs of any length (full hookups); some sites are pull-through. Picnic tables are provided. Restrooms with showers, two fire grills, a playground, heated swimming pool, spa, exercise room, coin laundry, convenience store, Wi-Fi, car wash, shuffleboard court, billiards, dump station, ice, and recreation room are available. Some facilities are wheelchair-accessible. Leashed pets are permitted, with certain restrictions.

**Reservations, fees:** Reservations are recommended. Deluxe RV sites (full hookups) are $85 per night, preferred sites are $80 per night, premium sites are $75 per night, and regular sites are $70, plus $2 per person for more than eight and $1 per pet per night. Weekly and monthly rates are available. Some credit cards are accepted. Open year-round.

**Directions:** Drive on I-5 to Anaheim and the exit for Katella Avenue. Take that exit east for Katella Avenue and drive two miles (passing Anaheim Stadium and the Santa Ana River) to Struck Avenue. Turn right and drive 200 yards to the park on the right (1600 West Struck Avenue).

**Contact:** Orangeland RV Park, 714/633-0414, www.orangeland.com.

## 59 CANYON RV PARK GROUP CAMPGROUND

### Scenic rating: 6

near Yorba Linda

**Map 13.2, page 710**

The group campground is in a mature grove of cottonwood and sycamore trees, with natural riparian wildland areas and open spaces nearby. It is near the Santa Ana River (swimming or wading at the lake or creek is prohibited). The Santa Ana River Bicycle Trail runs through this park, which runs from Orange in Riverside County to Huntington Beach and the Pacific Ocean. Side-trip possibilities include Chino Hills State Park to the north, Cleveland National Forest to the south, and Lake Matthews to the southeast. The park is also close to Disneyland and Knott's Berry Farm. Canyon RV Park is a private group campground operating under a long-term lease from Orange County. It is at Featherly Regional Park.

**Campsites, facilities:** There are 140 sites with full hookups (30 and 50 amps) for RVs up to 45 feet and 10 cabins. Picnic tables and fire pits are provided. Restrooms with flush toilets and showers, two dump stations, a seasonal swimming pool, horseshoes, firewood, ice, and two playgrounds are available. A visitors center and two amphitheaters are on-site. A convenience store, coin laundry, and propane are also available. Restaurants are nearby. Some facilities are wheelchair-accessible. Leashed pets are permitted, with some restrictions.

**Reservations, fees:** Reservations are accepted by phone or website. RV sites (full hookups, 50 amp) are $75 per night, plus $10 per night for tents within RV sites, $5 per night for each additional vehicle, $2 per person per night for more than two people, and $1 per dog per night. Cabins are $75 per night. Weekly rates are available. Call for youth-group rates. Some credit cards are accepted. Open year-round.

**Directions:** Drive on I-5 to Highway 91 in Anaheim. Take Highway 91 east and drive 13 miles to the exit for Gypsum Canyon Road. Take that exit to Gypsum Canyon Road. Turn left, drive under the freeway, and drive about one block to the park entrance on the left.

**Contact:** Canyon RV Park, 714/637-0210, www.canyonrvpark.com.

## 60 LAKE PERRIS STATE RECREATION AREA

**Scenic rating: 7**

on Lake Perris

**Map 13.2, page 710**   BEST (

Lake Perris is a great recreation lake with first-class fishing for spotted bass, and many fishing records have been set here. In the summer, it's an excellent destination for boating and water sports. It is at 1,500 feet elevation in Moreno Valley, just southwest of the Badlands foot-hills. The lake has a roundish shape, covering 2,200 acres, with an island that provides a unique boat-in picnic site. There are large ski beaches on the northeast and southeast shores and a designated sailing cove on the northwest side, an ideal spot for various water sports; inflatables are not permitted. Swimming is also excellent, but it's allowed only at the developed beaches a short distance from the campground. The recreation area covers 8,300 acres and includes 10 miles of paved bike trails (including a great route that circles the lake), 15 miles of equestrian trails, and five miles of hiking trails. Summer campfire and junior ranger programs are offered. There is also a special area for scuba diving, and a rock-climbing area is just south of the dam. Note: All boats must be certified mussel-free before launching.

**Campsites, facilities:** There are 177 sites for tents only, 254 sites with partial hookups (30 amps) for tents or RVs up to 31 feet, seven primitive horse camps with corrals and water troughs, and six group sites with no hookups for 25-100 people each. Picnic tables and fire grills are available. Restrooms with flush toilets and coin showers, drinking water, Wi-Fi, dump station, playground, convenience store, two swimming beaches, boat launch, and fishing boat rentals are available. Some facilities are wheelchair-accessible. Leashed pets are permitted, with certain restrictions, except at the beach or in the water.

**Reservations, fees:** Reservations are accepted for individual sites at 800/444-7275 or www.

reserveamerica.com ($8 reservation fee). Tent sites are $30 per night, RV sites are $45 per night, hike-in/bike-in sites are $4 per person per night (no vehicles), equestrian sites are $21 per night, plus $10 per night for each additional vehicle. Group sites are $275 per night plus $8 per vehicle. Reserve group and equestrian sites at 951/940-5603. Open year-round.

**Directions:** From Riverside, drive southeast on I-215/Highway 60 for about five miles to the I-215/Highway 60 split. Bear south on 215 at the split and drive six miles to Ramona Expressway. Turn left (east) and drive 3.5 miles to Lake Perris Drive. Turn left and drive 0.75 mile to the park entrance.

**Contact:** Lake Perris State Recreation Area, 951/940-5600; Lake Perris Marina, 951/657-2179, www.parks.ca.gov.

## 61 SUNSET VISTA RV PARK

**Scenic rating: 7**

in Huntington Beach

**Map 13.2, page 710**

This RV park is operated by the city of Huntington Beach and is a helpful layover for Highway 1 cruisers. Bolsa Chica State Beach provides an alternative spot to park an RV. The best nearby adventure is the short loop walk at Bolsa Chica State Reserve (see the Bolsa Chica State Beach listing in this chapter for more information).

**Campsites, facilities:** There are 46 sites with partial hookups (30 and 50 amps) for RVs up to 45 feet. Fire rings are provided. Drinking water, outdoor cold showers, flush toilets, and a dump station are available. Supplies are available within a mile. Some facilities are wheelchair-accessible. Leashed pets are permitted.

**Reservations, fees:** Reservations are accepted online or by mail (print out the online reservation form and mail it). Sites are $70 per night, with a one-time processing fee of $10. Discounts are available for seniors and people with disabilities. Open October through May.

**Directions:** Drive on I-405 to Huntington Beach and the exit for Beach Boulevard. Take that exit west and drive on Beach Boulevard to Highway 1/Pacific Coast Highway. Turn right (north) and drive approximately one mile to 1st Street. Turn left and drive a short distance to the park entrance at 103 Pacific Coast Highway in Huntington Beach.

**Contact:** Huntington Beach, Parks Department, 714/536-5280, www.sunsetvista-camping.huntingtonbeachca.gov.

## 62 NEWPORT DUNES WATERFRONT RESORT

**Scenic rating: 9**

in Newport Beach

**Map 13.2, page 710**

This five-star resort in a pretty spot on the bay has a beach, boat ramp, and storage area as bonuses. The resort received the "Mega Park of the Year Award 2003" from the California Travel Parks Association. It is situated on 100 acres of Newport Bay beach, beautiful and private, without public access. It features one mile of beach and a swimming lagoon, beachfront sites, and 24-hour security. A one-mile promenade circles the resort and is popular for cycling and inline skating. Nearby to the west is Corona del Mar State Beach, and to the south is Crystal Cove State Park. The park is five minutes' walking distance from Balboa Island and is next to the largest estuary in California, the Upper Newport Bay Ecological Reserve.

**Campsites, facilities:** There are 382 sites with full hookups (30 and 50 amps) for tents or RVs up to 50 feet and 24 cottages. Picnic tables are provided. Restrooms with showers, heated swimming pool and spa, waveless saltwater lagoon, 440-slip marina, satellite TV, Wi-Fi, organized activities, beach volleyball, coin laundry, market, waterfront restaurant, café, fitness center, game room/video arcade, group facilities, dog run, playground, RV and boat storage, RV and boat wash, and marina with boat launch ramp are available. Boat, kayak, sailboard, golf cart, and bicycle rentals are available, along with lessons for various water sports. Some facilities are wheelchair-accessible. Leashed pets are permitted, with some restrictions, including a maximum of two leashed pets; no pit bulls or Rottweilers, and no pets in the cottages. No smoking in cottages.

**Reservations, fees:** Reservations are accepted up to two years in advance (up to one year in advance for the week of July 4) at 800/765-7661. Rates for RV sites (full hookups) vary widely: Standard RV sites are $79-189 per night; select, partial-view RV sites are $64-150 per night; beachfront RV sites are $99-479 per night; cottages are $90-345 per night; plus $20 per night for each additional vehicle and $2 per pet per night. Nightly rates are roughly half in winter. Monthly, weekly, and group rates are available. Note that long-term stays are limited to 5.5 months. Some credit cards are accepted. Open year-round.

**Directions:** Drive on I-405 to the exit for Highway 55. Take that exit south and drive on Highway 55 to Highway 73. Turn south on Highway 73 and drive three miles to the Jamboree Road exit. Take that exit, turn right, and drive south on Jamboree Road for five miles to Back Bay Drive. Turn right and drive a short distance to the resort on the left.

**Contact:** Newport Dunes Waterfront Resort, 949/729-3863, www.newportdunes.com.

# 63 MORO CAMPGROUND

### Scenic rating: 9

in Crystal Cove State Park

**Map 13.2, page 710**

First, let's get this straight: This park does not provide beach camping. That aside, this place is still very special. Crystal Cove is a gorgeous park that covers 2,791 acres and features 3.5 miles of coast. A 1,140-acre underwater park is popular with scuba divers and snorkelers, the inland acreage is popular with mountain bikers and hikers, and the beach is popular with swimmers and surfers. The on-site Crystal Cove Historic District contains quaint coastal cottages (some available for rent), a restaurant, and visitor services. Most of the park's backcountry is grass hills and woodlands, and the backcountry camps here are rarely full. Guided nature hikes are offered in the day-use area.

**Campsites, facilities:** The Moro Campground has 28 RV sites with partial hookups and 30 tent sites. Picnic tables are provided. Showers and flush toilets are available. Some facilities are wheelchair-accessible. Leashed pets are permitted, but are not allowed on the beach or in the backcountry.

There are also 32 backcountry hike-in sites at three environmental campgrounds: Lower Moro, Upper Moro, and Deer Canyon. These campsites require a hike of 3.5-4.5 miles. A permit is required and is available online or at the Moro Campground kiosk. Picnic tables are provided. Pit toilets are available. No drinking water is available. No fires are permitted; bring a backpacking stove for cooking. Garbage must be packed-out.

**Reservations, fees:** Reservations are for tent and RV sites are accepted at 800/444-7275 or www.reserveamerica.com ($8 reservation fee). Reservations for cottages can be made online at www.crystalcovebeachcottages.org. Tent sites are $55 per night (four-person limit), RV sites are $75 per night, plus $15 per night for each additional vehicle. Environmental sites are $25 per night. Cottage rentals run $35-69 per night. Registration at the visitors center is required. Open year-round.

**Directions:** Drive on Highway 1 to the park entrance (three miles south of Corona del Mar) on the east side of the highway. Register at the visitors center. The Moro camps require a 3.5- to 4-mile walk. The Deer Canyon camp requires a 4.5-mile walk.

**Contact:** Crystal Cove State Park, 949/494-3539; Orange Coast District, Central Sector, 949/492-0802, www.crystalcovestatepark.com or www.parks.ca.gov.

## 64 O'NEILL REGIONAL PARK AND EQUESTRIAN CAMP

🏃 🚴 🐎 🛶 ♿ 🚐 ⛺

### Scenic rating: 6

near Cleveland National Forest

**Map 13.2, page 710**

This Orange County park is just far enough off the main drag to get missed by most of the RV cruisers on I-5. It is near Trabuco Canyon, adjacent to Cleveland National Forest to the east. About 70 percent of the campsites are under a canopy of sycamore and oak, and, in general, the park is heavily wooded. The park covers 3,800 acres and features 18 miles of trails, including those accessible by equestrians. Several roads near this park lead to trailheads into Cleveland National Forest. Rangers occasionally post mountain lion warnings at this park. The elevation is 1,000 feet.

**Campsites, facilities:** There are 79 sites for tents and RVs of any length (no hookups), five equestrian sites for up to six horses per site, and two group camping areas for 20-80 people each. A few sites are pull-through. Picnic tables and fire rings are provided. Restrooms with flush toilets and showers, drinking water, playground, picnic area, amphitheater, horseshoes, firewood, and a dump station are available. Horse corral, water faucets, small corrals, and an arena are available at equestrian sites. An interpretive center is open on weekends. A store is nearby. Some facilities are wheelchair-accessible. Leashed pets are permitted but not in wilderness areas.

**Reservations, fees:** Reservations are recommended for individual sites and are required for group sites at 800/600-1600 or www.reserveamerica.com ($8 reservation fee). Sites are $20 per night, plus $3 per horse per night and $5 per each additional vehicle. Call for group rates. Some credit cards are accepted. Open year-round.

**Directions:** From I-5 in Laguna Hills, take the County Road S18/El Toro Road exit and drive east (past El Toro) for 7.5 miles. Turn right onto Live Oak Canyon Road/County Road S19 and drive about three miles to the park on the right. **Contact:** O'Neill Regional Park, 949/923-2260 or 949/923-2256, www.ocparks.com.

## 65 CASPERS WILDERNESS PARK

🏃 🚴 🚣 ♿ 🚐 ⛺

### Scenic rating: 6

on San Juan Creek

**Map 13.2, page 710**

This 8,500-acre protected wilderness preserve is best-known for coastal stands of live oak and magnificent stands of California sycamore. It is a popular spot for picnics, day hikes (30 miles of trails), horseback riding, and cycling. Seasonal wildflower displays and running streams add to the rich beauty, and abundant wildlife can be seen from the park's numerous trails. Much of the pristine and protected land is bordered to the south by the San Juan Creek and to the east by the Cleveland National Forest and the San Mateo Canyon Wilderness. Highway 74 provides access.

**Campsites, facilities:** There are 42 sites with no hookups and 13 sites with electrical hookups only for tents or RVs of any length, 22 equestrian sites, and five sites for groups of up to 60 people. Picnic tables, fire pits, and barbecues are provided. Drinking water, restrooms with flush toilets and showers, a dump station, corrals, amphitheater, museum with interpretive programs, and a playground are available. Some facilities are wheelchair-accessible. Pets are not allowed.

**Reservations, fees:** Reservations are required at 800/600-1600 or online at www.reserveamerica.com; group reservations are required at 949/923-2210. Single sites are $20-26 per night, plus $5 per night per additional vehicle and $3 per horse per night. Group sites are $240-360 per night. Youth group discounts are available. Some credit cards are accepted. Open year-round.

**Directions:** Drive on I-5 to San Juan

Capistrano and Highway 74/Ortega Highway. Turn east on Ortega Highway and drive 7.5 miles northeast to the signed park entrance on the left.

**Contact:** Caspers Wilderness Park, Orange County, 949/923-2210, www.ocparks.com.

## 66 FALCON GROUP CAMPS

### Scenic rating: 4

in the Santa Ana Mountains in Cleveland National Forest

**Map 13.2, page 710**

At an elevation of 3,300 feet, Falcon is near the trailheads for the San Juan and Chiquito Trails, which both lead into the backcountry and the Santa Ana Mountains. There are three group campgrounds, with limited parking at Lupine and Yarrow Campgrounds.

**Campsites, facilities:** There are three group sites for tents or RVs (no hookups). Sage Camp accommodates 30 people and six RVs up to 40 feet; Lupine Camp accommodates 40 people and eight RVs up to 20 feet; and Yarrow Camp accommodates 70 people and 10 RVs up to 30 feet. Picnic tables and fire rings are provided. Drinking water and vault toilets are available. A store is within five miles. Leashed pets are permitted.

**Reservations, fees:** Reservations are required at 877/444-6777 ($10 reservation fee) or www.recreation.gov ($9 reservation fee). Sites are $60-120 per night. Open year-round, weather permitting.

**Directions:** Drive on I-15 to Lake Elsinore and the Central exit to Highway 74 west. Take that exit and drive west on Highway 74 for 12 miles (the road becomes Grand Avenue for a couple of miles in Lake Elsinore, then bears right) to Forest Road 6S05 (Long Canyon Road). Turn right and drive approximately 4.5 miles to the campground entrance on the left.

**Contact:** Cleveland National Forest, Trabuco Ranger District, 951/736-1811, www.fs.usda.gov/cleveland.

## 67 BLUE JAY

### Scenic rating: 4

in the Santa Ana Mountains in Cleveland National Forest

**Map 13.2, page 710**

The few hikers who know of this spot like it and keep coming back, provided they time their hikes when temperatures are cool. The trailheads to San Juan Trail and Chiquito Trail (which is accessed from the San Juan Trail), both of which lead into the backcountry and the Santa Ana Mountains, are adjacent to the camp. A Forest Service map is strongly advised. The elevation is 3,400 feet.

**Campsites, facilities:** There are 50 sites for tents or RVs up to 20 feet (no hookups). Picnic tables and fire rings are provided. Drinking water and vault toilets are available. A store is within five miles. Leashed pets are permitted.

**Reservations, fees:** Reservations are not accepted. Sites are $20 per night, plus $5 per night per additional vehicle. Open year-round, weather permitting.

**Directions:** From Lake Elsinore, take Route 74 south for 5.7 miles to the sign for Blue Jay campground. Turn right and proceed 5.1 miles to the campground on the right.

**Contact:** Cleveland National Forest, Trabuco Ranger District, 951/736-1811, www.fs.usda.gov/cleveland.

## 68 EL CARISO CAMPGROUND

### Scenic rating: 5

near Lake Elsinore in Cleveland National Forest

**Map 13.2, page 710**

This pretty, shaded spot at 2,600 feet elevation is just inside the border of Cleveland National Forest, with Lake Elsinore to the east. On the drive in there are great views to the east, looking down at Lake Elsinore and across the desert country.

**Campsites, facilities:** There are 25 sites for tents or RVs up to 22 feet (no hookups). Picnic tables and fire rings are provided. Drinking water and vault toilets are available. Leashed pets are permitted.

**Reservations, fees:** Reservations are not accepted. Sites are $15 per night. Open year-round, weather permitting.

**Directions:** Drive on I-15 to Lake Elsinore and the Central exit to Highway 74 west. Take that exit and drive west on Highway 74 for 12 miles (the road becomes Grand Avenue for a couple of miles in Lake Elsinore, then bears right) to the campground on the right.

Drive on I-5 to San Juan Capistrano and Highway 74/Ortega Highway. Turn east on the Ortega Highway and drive 24 miles northeast (into national forest) to the campground.

**Contact:** Cleveland National Forest, Trabuco Ranger District, 951/736-1811, www.fs.usda.gov/cleveland.

## 69 LAKE ELSINORE WEST MARINA AND RV RESORT

**Scenic rating: 7**

on Lake Elsinore

Map 13.2, page 710

This privately operated RV park has 1,000 feet of lake frontage, and boat rentals are nearby. Note that about a third of the sites are occupied by long-term renters. (For information about Lake Elsinore, see the La Laguna Resort listing in this chapter.)

**Campsites, facilities:** There are 184 sites with full hookups (50 amps) for RVs up to 40 feet and 60 lakeshore tent sites. Picnic tables and cable TV are provided. Restrooms with showers, dump station, horseshoe pit, clubhouse, Wi-Fi, convenience store, group facilities, propane, and boat ramp are available. Some facilities are wheelchair-accessible. Leashed pets are permitted, with some restrictions.

**Reservations, fees:** Reservations are accepted at 800/328-6844 or at www.lakeelsinoremarina.

com. RV sites (full hookups) are $38 per night, tent sites are $28 per night, plus $3 per person per night for more than five people and $1 per pet per night. Monthly and weekly rates are available. Some credit cards are accepted. Open year-round.

**Directions:** Drive to the junction of I-15 and Highway 74. At that junction, take Highway 74 west/Central Avenue and drive west for four miles to the entrance to the park on the left (32700 Riverside Drive).

**Contact:** Lake Elsinore West Marina, 951/678-1300 or 800/328-6844, www.lakeelsinoremarina.com.

## 70 LA LAGUNA RESORT

**Scenic rating: 7**

on Lake Elsinore

Map 13.2, page 710        BEST (

The weather is hot and dry enough in this region to make the water in Lake Elsinore more valuable than gold. Elsinore is a huge, wide lake—the largest natural freshwater lake in Southern California—where water-skiers, personal-watercraft riders, and sailboarders can find a slice of heaven. This camp is along the north shore, where there are also several trails for hiking, biking, and horseback riding. There is a designated area near the campground for swimming and water play; a gently sloping lake bottom is a big plus. Fishing has improved greatly in recent years and the lake is stocked with trout and striped bass. Other fish species include channel catfish, crappie, and bluegill. Night fishing is available. Anglers have a chance to fish for Whiskers, a very special catfish. It is a hybrid channel catfish that was stocked in 2000. It is a genetic cross between a blue and channel catfish, meaning that Whiskers could grow to more than 100 pounds. If you like thrill sports, hang gliding and parachuting are also available at the lake and, as you scan across the water, you can often look up and see these daredevils soaring overhead.

The recreation area covers 3,300 acres and has 15 miles of shoreline. The elevation is 1,239 feet. While the lake is huge when full, in low-rain years Elsinore's water level can be subject to extreme and erratic fluctuations. Boaters planning to visit this lake should call first to get the latest on water levels and quality. Those familiar with this area will remember it was once named Lake Elsinore Campground and Recreation Area.

**Campsites, facilities:** There are 120 sites with partial hookups for tents or RVs up to 40 feet, 10 sites for RVs only with full hookups (30 amps), 51 tent sites, and 10 group sites for groups of 30-150 people. Picnic tables and fire pits are provided at some sites. Restrooms with flush toilets and showers, drinking water, picnic area, and dump station are available. Supplies and coin laundry are nearby. Some facilities are wheelchair-accessible. Leashed pets are permitted.

**Reservations, fees:** Reservations are accepted at 800/416-6992 ($8 reservation fee). Tent sites are $25-30 per night, RV sites (electricity, sewer, and water) are $38 per night, plus $3 per night per additional person (more than five people), $5 per night per additional vehicle, and $1 per pet per night. Some credit cards are accepted. Open year-round.

**Directions:** Drive to the junction of I-15 and Highway 74. At that junction, take Highway 74 west/Central Avenue. Drive a short distance on Central Avenue to Collier. Turn right on Collier and drive 0.25 mile to Riverside Drive. Turn left and drive approximately 1.5 miles to the campground on the left.

**Contact:** La Laguna Resort, 800/328-6844 or 951/471-1212, www.lakeelsinoremarina.com or www.rockymountainrec.com; City of Lake Elsinore, 951/674-3124, ext. 265.

# 71 PALM VIEW RV PARK

### Scenic rating: 5

near Lake Elsinore

**Map 13.2, page 710**

This privately operated RV park is in a quiet valley at 700 feet elevation and has a duck pond. The sites are fairly rustic, with some shade trees. The park's recreation area offers basketball, volleyball, horseshoes, tetherball, and a playground. For you wonderful goofballs, bungee jumping and parachuting are available in the town of Perris. Note that 50 percent of the sites are occupied by long-term renters.

**Campsites, facilities:** There are 41 sites with full hookups (30 amps) for RVs, nine tent sites, and a group tent area that can accommodate up to 200 people. Some sites are pull-through. Picnic tables and fire rings are provided. Restrooms, dump station, recreation area, seasonal swimming pool, coin laundry, playground, convenience store, ice, and firewood are available. Some facilities are wheelchair-accessible. Leashed pets are permitted.

**Reservations, fees:** Reservations are not accepted. RV sites (full hookups) are $32 per night, tent sites are $25 per night, plus $3 per person per night for more than four people. Monthly and weekly rates are available. Open year-round.

**Directions:** Drive to the junction of I-15 and Highway 74. At that junction, take Highway 74/Central Avenue and drive east on Highway 74 for 4.5 miles to River Road. Turn right (south) and drive one mile to the park on the left (22200 River Road).

**Contact:** Palm View RV Park, 951/657-7791.

## 72 LAKE SKINNER RECREATION AREA

🚶 🏊 🚣 🎣 🐾 🏕 ⛵ 🛶

**Scenic rating: 7**

on Lake Skinner

Map 13.2, page 710

Lake Skinner is set within a Riverside County park at an elevation of 1,470 feet in sparse foothill country, where the water can sparkle. The lake covers 1,200 surface acres and there is a speed limit of 10 mph (only four-stroke engines are allowed). No water-contact sports are permitted—no waterskiing, swimming, or sailboarding—however, a half-acre swimming pool is available in summer. An amphitheater lies alongside a splash pad (April through October) for those hot days when the family just needs to cool off. Bird-watching is a prized activity, and visitors can regularly spot a wide variety of birds, such as herons, owls, and hawks. Fishing can be good, including trophy-sized bass and trout, along with catfish and bluegill. The fishing records here include a 39.5-pound striped bass, 33-pound catfish, and 14-pound, 8-ounce largemouth bass. The recreation area also provides hiking trails.

**Campsites, facilities:** There are 241 sites for tents or RVs of any length, an overflow area, and two group camping areas; 184 sites have full hookups, 16 sites have electricity (50 amps) and water, and 41 sites have water only. Many sites are pull-through. Picnic tables and fire grills are provided. Restrooms with flush toilets and coin showers, drinking water, playground, convenience store, picnic area, group facilities, ice, bait, dump station, swimming pool (in the summer), boat ramp, marina, mooring, boat rentals, and propane gas are available. Some facilities are wheelchair-accessible. Leashed pets are permitted.

**Reservations, fees:** Reservations are accepted at 800/234-7275 or www.reserveamerica.com ($8 reservation fee). Tent sites are $20-25 per night; RV sites are $35 (full hookups), $30 (water and electricity), or $23 (no hookups) per night; the overflow area is $13 per night; plus $5 per night per additional vehicle and $1 per pet per night. It's $150-320 per night for group sites (with special rates for youth groups). Weekly and monthly rates are available. Some credit cards are accepted. Open year-round.

**Directions:** Drive on I-15 to Temecula and the exit for Rancho California. Take that exit and drive northeast 9.5 miles to the park entrance on the right.

**Contact:** Lake Skinner Recreation Area, 951/926-1541 or 800/234-7275, www.rivco-parks.org.

## 73 HANNA FLAT

🚶 🐾 🚻 🚙 🏕

**Scenic rating: 8**

near Big Bear Lake in San Bernardino National Forest

Map 13.3, page 711

Over the years, Hanna Flat has been one of the largest, best maintained, and most popular of the Forest Service camps in the Big Bear Lake District (Serrano Campground is the most popular). The camp is at 7,000 feet elevation on the slopes on the north side of Big Bear Lake, just under three miles from the lake. Big Bear is a beautiful mountain lake covering more than 3,000 acres, with 22 miles of shoreline and often excellent trout fishing and waterskiing. A trailhead for the Pacific Crest Trail is a mile by road north of the camp.

**Campsites, facilities:** There are 85 sites for tents or RVs up to 35 feet (no hookups). Picnic tables and fire grills are provided. Drinking water and vault toilets are available. Some facilities are wheelchair-accessible. Leashed pets are permitted.

**Reservations, fees:** Reservations are accepted at 877/444-6777 ($10 reservation fee) or www.recreation.gov ($9 reservation fee). Single sites are $26-28 per night, double sites are $52-56 per night, plus $5 per night for each additional vehicle. Open May through September.

**Directions:** Drive on Highway 30 to the junction with Highway 330 (east of San Bernardino near Highland). Take Highway 330 north (signed "Mountain Resorts") and drive 28 miles (Highway 330 becomes Highway 18/Rim of the World Highway) to the Big Bear Lake Dam and a fork with Highway 38 and Highway 18. Continue straight on Highway 38 and drive approximately four miles to the town of Fawnskin and Rim of the World Highway. Turn left and drive three miles (after 0.5 mile, it becomes Forest Road 3N14, a dirt road) to the campground on the left.

**Contact:** San Bernardino National Forest, Mountaintop Ranger District, Big Bear Ranger Station/Discovery Center, 909/382-2790, www. fs.usda.gov/sbnf.

## 74 SERRANO

### Scenic rating: 8

on Big Bear Lake in San Bernardino National Forest

**Map 13.3, page 711**   **BEST (**

This campground opened in the 1990s and became the first National Forest campground to offer state-of-the-art restrooms and hot showers. That is why it costs more to camp here. Regardless, it has since become the most popular campground in the region. Location is also a big plus, as this is one of the few camps at Big Bear within walking distance of the lakeshore. It covers 60 acres, another big plus. Another bonus is a paved trail that is wheelchair-accessible. Want more? Big Bear is the jewel of Southern California lakes, the Lake Tahoe of the South, with outstanding trout fishing and waterskiing. All water sports are allowed. The lake is stocked with trout and catfish, and it also has large- and smallmouth bass, crappie, bluegill, and sunfish. Swimming is excellent at this lake, with large, sandy beaches around the shoreline. However, the water is cold. A trailhead for the Pacific Crest Trail is nearby, and Canada is only 2,200 miles away. The elevation is 6,800 feet.

**Campsites, facilities:** There are 111 sites for tents or RVs up to 55 feet; some sites have full hookups (30 amps). Picnic tables and fire rings are provided. Restrooms with flush toilets and coin showers, drinking water, a camp host, interpretive trails and programs, and a dump station are available. A store is nearby. Some facilities are wheelchair-accessible. Leashed pets are permitted.

**Reservations, fees:** Reservations are accepted at 877/444-6777 ($10 reservation fee) or www. recreation.gov ($9 reservation fee). Single sites are $30-32 per night, double sites are $60-64 per night, plus $5 per night per each additional vehicle. Open April through November.

**Directions:** Drive on Highway 30 to the junction with Highway 330 (east of San Bernardino near Highland). Take Highway 330 north (signed "Mountain Resorts") and drive 28 miles (Highway 330 becomes Highway 18/Rim of the World Highway) to the Big Bear Lake Dam and a fork with Highway 38 and Highway 18. Continue straight on Highway 38 and drive about 2.5 miles to Fawnskin and North Shore Lane (signed "Serrano Campground"). Turn right on North Shore Lane and drive to the campground entrance.

**Contact:** San Bernardino National Forest, Mountaintop Ranger District, Big Bear Ranger Station/Discovery Center, 909/382-2790, www.fs.usda.gov/sbnf; Serrano Campground, 909/866-8021.

## 75 HOLCOMB VALLEY

### Scenic rating: 7

near the Pacific Crest Trail in San Bernardino National Forest

**Map 13.3, page 711**

This camp is near the Holcomb Valley Historic Area, at 7,400 feet elevation in the mountains about four miles north of Big Bear Lake. On the way in on Van Dusen Canyon Road you will pass a trailhead for the Pacific Crest Trail (two miles southeast of the camp). From here you can make the two-mile climb southwest to Bertha Peak, at 8,198 feet, overlooking Big Bear to the south.

**Campsites, facilities:** There are 19 sites for tents or RVs up to 25 feet (no hookups). Picnic tables and fire grills are provided. Vault toilets are available. No drinking water is available. Leashed pets are permitted.

**Reservations, fees:** Reservations are not accepted. Sites are $20-22 per night. Open year-round, but access is based on road conditions.

**Directions:** Drive on Highway 30 to the junction with Highway 330 (east of San Bernardino near Highland). Take Highway 330 north (signed "Mountain Resorts") and drive 28 miles (Highway 330 becomes Highway 18/Rim of the World Highway) to the Big Bear Lake Dam and a fork with Highway 38 and Highway 18. Continue straight on Highway 38 and drive about 10 miles to Van Dusen Canyon Road/Forest Road 3N09. Turn left and drive three miles (a dirt road) to Forest Road 3N16. Turn left and drive to the campground on the right.

**Contact:** San Bernardino National Forest, Mountaintop Ranger District, Big Bear Ranger Station/Discovery Center, 909/382-2790, www. fs.usda.gov/sbnf.

are available. No drinking water is available. Leashed pets are permitted.

**Reservations, fees:** Reservations are required at 877/444-6777 ($10 reservation fee) or www. recreation.gov ($9 reservation fee). The camp is $120-130 per night. Open mid-May through September.

**Directions:** Drive on Highway 30 to the junction with Highway 330 (east of San Bernardino near Highland). Take Highway 330 north (signed "Mountain Resorts") and drive 28 miles (Highway 330 becomes Highway 18/ Rim of the World Highway) to the Big Bear Lake Dam and a fork with Highway 38 and Highway 18. Continue straight on Highway 38 and drive about 10 miles to Van Dusen Canyon Road/Forest Road 3N09. Turn left (dirt road) and drive four miles to Forest Road 3N16. Turn right and drive 1.7 miles to Forest Road 3N79. Turn right and drive 0.5 mile to the campground. Trailers are not recommended.

**Contact:** San Bernardino National Forest, Mountaintop Ranger District, Big Bear Ranger Station/Discovery Center, 909/382-2790, www. fs.usda.gov/sbnf.

## 76 TANGLEWOOD GROUP CAMP

**Scenic rating: 4**

on the Pacific Crest Trail in San Bernardino National Forest

**Map 13.3, page 711**

This primitive group camp is off an old spur road with the trailhead for the Pacific Crest Trail—the primary highlight. It is set at 7,400 feet elevation in a flat but wooded area northeast of Big Bear Lake. It is about a 10- to 15-minute drive from Big Bear City.

**Campsites, facilities:** One group campsite for tents or RVs up to 32 feet (no hookups) can accommodate up to 40 people. Picnic tables and fire grills are provided. Vault toilets

## 77 BLUFF MESA GROUP CAMP

**Scenic rating: 7**

near Big Bear Lake in San Bernardino National Forest

**Map 13.3, page 711**

Bluff Mesa Group Camp is one of several camps south of Big Bear Lake. A highlight is the trailhead (signed on the access road on the way in) for the half-mile walk to the Champion Lodgepole Pine, the largest lodgepole pine in the world: 400 years old, 112 feet tall, with a circumference of 20 feet. Many Forest Service roads are available nearby for self-planned side trips. The elevation is 7,600 feet.

**Campsites, facilities:** There is one group campsite for tents or RVs up to 20 feet (no hookups) that can accommodate up to 40 people.

Picnic tables and fire grills are provided. Vault toilets are available. No drinking water is available. Garbage must be packed out. Some facilities are wheelchair-accessible. Leashed pets are permitted.

**Reservations, fees:** Reservations are required at 877/444-6777 ($10 reservation fee) or www.recreation.gov ($9 reservation fee). The camp is $120-130 per night. Open mid-May through mid-October.

**Directions:** Drive on Highway 30 to the junction with Highway 330 (east of San Bernardino near Highland). Take Highway 330 north (signed "Mountain Resorts") and drive 28 miles (Highway 330 becomes Highway 18/Rim of the World Highway) to the Big Bear Lake Dam and a fork with Highway 38 and Highway 18. Turn right at Highway 18 and drive about four miles to Mill Creek Road. Turn right on Mill Creek Road and drive about 1.5 miles to the sign at the top of the hill and Forest Road 2N10. Turn right on Forest Road 2N10 and drive three miles (dirt road) to Forest Road 2N86. Turn right on Forest Road 2N86 and drive 0.25 mile to the campground.

**Contact:** San Bernardino National Forest, Mountaintop Ranger District, Big Bear Ranger Station/Discovery Center, 909/382-2790, www.fs.usda.gov/sbnf; fire regulations: Discovery Center, 909/866-3437.

## 78 HOLLOWAY'S MARINA AND RV PARK

⛱ 🚤 🚐 🛖 🚶 ♿ 🚍

### Scenic rating: 6

on Big Bear Lake

**Map 13.3, page 711**

This privately operated RV park is a good choice at Big Bear Lake, with boat rentals, ramp, and full marina available. Big Bear is the jewel of Southern California's lakes, covering more than 3,000 surface acres with 22 miles of shoreline. Its cool waters make for excellent trout fishing, and yet, by summer, it has heated up enough to make for superb waterskiing. A bonus in the summer is that a breeze off the lake keeps the temperature in the mid-80s. Note that about one-third of the sites are occupied by long-term renters. (For details about the lake, see the Serrano listing in this chapter.)

**Campsites, facilities:** There are 116 sites with full hookups (30 and 50 amps) for RVs up to 40 feet. Limited group camping is available. Picnic tables and fire grills are provided. Restrooms with flush toilets and showers, drinking water, dump station, cable TV, convenience store, ice, propane gas, coin laundry, playground, basketball court, horseshoe pits, and full marina with boat rentals are on the premises. A pirate ship tour is available. Leashed pets are permitted, including on rental boats.

**Reservations, fees:** Reservations are accepted at 800/448-5335. RV sites (full hookups) are $50-60 per night, plus $10 per night for each additional vehicle. Monthly rates are available. Some credit cards are accepted. Open year-round, weather permitting.

**Directions:** Drive on Highway 30 to the junction with Highway 330 (east of San Bernardino near Highland). Take Highway 330 north (signed "Mountain Resorts") and drive 28 miles (Highway 330 becomes Highway 18/Rim of the World Highway) to the Big Bear Lake Dam and a fork with Highway 38 and Highway 18. Turn left on Highway 18 and drive three miles to Edgemoor Road. Turn left at Edgemoor Road and drive 0.25 mile to the park entrance on the left.

**Contact:** Holloway's Marina and RV Park, 909/866-5706 or 800/448-5335, www.hollowaysmarina.com.

## 79 BOULDER GROUP CAMP

🛖 🚐 ⛺

### Scenic rating: 6

near Big Bear Lake in San Bernardino National Forest

**Map 13.3, page 711**

This is a primitive camp at 7,500 feet elevation, just far enough away from some prime attractions to make you wish you could move the camp to a slightly different spot. The headwaters of Metcalf Creek are hidden in the forest on the other side of the road, tiny Cedar Lake is about a half-mile drive north, and Big Bear Lake is about two miles north. You get the idea.

**Campsites, facilities:** There is one group campsite for tents and RVs up to 20 feet (no hookups) that can accommodate up to 40 people. Picnic tables and fire grills are provided. Vault toilets are available. No drinking water is available. Garbage must be packed out. A store and coin laundry are nearby. Leashed pets are permitted.

**Reservations, fees:** Reservations are required at 877/444-6777 ($10 reservation fee) or www.recreation.gov ($9 reservation fee). The camp is $120-130 per night. Open mid-May through mid-October.

**Directions:** Drive on Highway 30 to the junction with Highway 330 (east of San Bernardino near Highland). Take Highway 330 north (signed "Mountain Resorts") and drive 28 miles (Highway 330 becomes Highway 18/Rim of the World Highway) to the Big Bear Lake Dam and a fork with Highway 38 and Highway 18. Turn right at Highway 18 and drive about four miles to Mill Creek Road. Turn right on Mill Creek Road and drive about 1.5 miles to the sign at the top of the hill and Forest Road 2N10. Turn right on Forest Road 2N10 and drive about two miles to the campground entrance road (Forest Road 2M10B). Turn right and drive to the camp.

**Contact:** San Bernardino National Forest, Mountaintop Ranger District, Big Bear Ranger Station/Discovery Center, 909/382-2790, www.fs.usda.gov/sbnf; fire regulations: Discovery Center, 909/866-3437.

# 80 PINEKNOT

**Scenic rating: 6**

near Big Bear Lake in San Bernardino National Forest

**Map 13.3, page 711**

This popular, developed Forest Service camp is just east of Big Bear Lake Village (on the southern shore of the lake) about two miles from the lake. It is a popular spot for mountain biking, with several ideal routes available. Of the camps at Big Bear, this is the closest to supplies. The elevation is 7,000 feet. (For details about the lake, see the Serrano listing in this chapter.)

**Campsites, facilities:** There are 47 sites for tents or RVs up to 35 feet (no hookups). Picnic tables and fire grills are provided. Drinking water and flush toilets are available. A store and coin laundry are nearby. Leashed pets are permitted.

**Reservations, fees:** Reservations are accepted at 877/444-6777 ($10 reservation fee) or www.recreation.gov ($9 reservation fee). Sites are $26-28 per night, plus $5 per night per each additional vehicle. Open May through mid-October.

**Directions:** Drive on Highway 30 to the junction with Highway 330 (east of San Bernardino near Highland). Take Highway 330 north (signed "Mountain Resorts") and drive 28 miles (Highway 330 becomes Highway 18/Rim of the World Highway) to the Big Bear Lake Dam and a fork with Highway 38 and Highway 18. Turn right at Highway 18 and drive about six miles to Summit Boulevard. Turn right and drive through the parking area to the road on the left (just before the gate to the ski area). Turn left and drive 0.25 mile to the campground on the right.

**Contact:** San Bernardino National Forest, Mountaintop Ranger District, Big Bear Ranger Station/Discovery Center, 909/382-2790, www.fs.usda.gov/sbnf.

## 81 BUTTERCUP GROUP CAMP

**Scenic rating: 5**

near the town of Big Bear Lake in San
Bernardino National Forest

**Map 13.3, page 711**

This is a forested camp designed for large
groups looking for a developed site near Big
Bear Lake. It is about four miles from the
southeast side of the lake, just outside the Snow
Summit Ski Area. The elevation is 7,000 feet.

**Campsites, facilities:** One group campsite
for tents or RVs up to 25 feet (no hookups) can
accommodate up to 40 people. Picnic tables
and fire rings are provided. Drinking water
and vault toilets are available. A store and coin
laundry are nearby. Garbage must be packed
out. Some facilities are wheelchair-accessible.
Leashed pets are permitted.

**Reservations, fees:** Reservations are required
at 877/444-6777 ($10 reservation fee) or www.
recreation.gov ($9 reservation fee). The camp
is $120-130 per night. Open mid-May through
mid-October.

**Directions:** Drive on Highway 30 to the junction with Highway 330 (east of San Bernardino
near Highland). Take Highway 330 north
(signed "Mountain Resorts") and drive 28 miles
(Highway 330 becomes Highway 18/Rim of the
World Highway) to the Big Bear Lake Dam and
a fork with Highway 38 and Highway 18. Turn
right at Highway 18 and drive about six miles
to Summit Boulevard. Turn right and drive
through the parking area to the road on the
left (just before the gate to the ski area). Turn
left and drive 0.5 mile (past Pineknot Camp) to
the campground on the right.

**Contact:** San Bernardino National Forest,
Mountaintop Ranger District, Big Bear Ranger
Station/Discovery Center, 909/382-2790, www.
fs.usda.gov/sbnf; fire regulations: Discovery
Center, 909/866-3437.

## 82 JUNIPER SPRING GROUP CAMP

**Scenic rating: 3**

in San Bernardino National Forest

**Map 13.3, page 711**

This is a little-known group camp, set at 7,700
feet elevation in a desertlike area about 10 miles
east of Big Bear Lake. It is little known because
there are not a lot of reasons to camp here. You
need to be creative. Got a Scrabble game? Want
to watch the junipers grow? Or maybe watch
the features of the land change colors as the day
passes? You get the idea.

**Campsites, facilities:** One group camp
for tents and RVs up to 20 feet (no hookups)
can accommodate up to 40 people. Picnic tables and fire grills are provided. Vault toilets
are available. No drinking water is available.
Garbage must be packed out. Leashed pets are
permitted.

**Reservations, fees:** Reservations are required
at 877/444-6777 ($10 reservation fee) or www.
recreation.gov ($9 reservation fee). The camp is
$120-130 per night. Open year-round.

**Directions:** Drive on I-10 to Redlands and
Highway 38. Take Highway 38 northeast and
drive about 40 miles (1.5 miles past Onyx
Summit) to Forest Road 2N01 on the right.
Turn right (dirt road) and drive three miles to
a Forest Service road (opposite the sign on the
left posted Forest Road 2N04). Turn right and
drive into the campground.

**Contact:** San Bernardino National Forest,
Mountaintop Ranger District, Big Bear Ranger
Station/Discovery Center, 909/382-2790, www.
fs.usda.gov/sbnf; fire regulations: Discovery
Center, 909/866-3437.

## 83 COUNCIL GROUP CAMP

### Scenic rating: 5

near Jenks Lake and the San Gorgonio Wilderness in San Bernardino National Forest

**Map 13.3, page 711**

This is a group camp in a pretty wooded area a half mile from little Jenks Lake (there is a nice, easy walk around the lake) and a few miles north of the northern border of the San Gorgonio Wilderness. There are several other camps in the area.

**Campsites, facilities:** One group campsite for tents or RVs up to 22 feet (no hookups) can accommodate up to 50 people. Picnic tables and fire rings are provided. Drinking water and vault toilets are available. Some facilities are wheelchair-accessible. Leashed pets are permitted.

**Reservations, fees:** Reservations are required at 877/444-6777 ($10 reservation fee) or www. recreation.gov ($9 reservation fee). The camp is $200-210 per night. Open May through mid-November.

**Directions:** Drive on I-10 to Redlands and Highway 38. Take Highway 38 northeast and drive 26 miles to the campground on the left, just past the Barton Flats Visitor Center.

**Contact:** San Bernardino National Forest, Mountaintop Ranger District, Big Bear Ranger Station/Discovery Center, 909/382-2790, www. fs.usda.gov/sbnf; fire regulations: Discovery Center, 909/866-3437.

## 84 BARTON FLATS

### Scenic rating: 7

near Jenks Lake in San Bernardino National Forest

**Map 13.3, page 711**

This is one of the more developed Forest Service camps in San Bernardino National Forest. The camp, at 6,500 feet elevation, is about two miles from Jenks Lake, a small, pretty lake with good

hiking and a picnic area. Barton Creek, a small stream, runs nearby, although it may be waterless in late summer. The San Gorgonio Wilderness, one mile to the south, is accessible via Forest Service roads to the wilderness area trailhead. Permits are required for overnight camping within the wilderness boundaries and are available at Forest Service ranger stations. Those driving in on Highway 38 should stop at the Mill Creek Ranger Station in Redlands.

**Campsites, facilities:** There are 52 sites for tents or RVs of any length (no hookups). Picnic tables and fire grills are provided. Drinking water, a dump station, and restrooms with coin showers and flush toilets are available. Some facilities are wheelchair-accessible. Leashed pets are permitted.

**Reservations, fees:** Reservations are accepted at 877/444-6777 ($10 reservation fee) or www. recreation.gov ($9 reservation fee). Sites are $28-30 per night, multifamily sites are $60 per night, plus $5 per night for each additional vehicle. Open May through mid-November.

**Directions:** Drive on I-10 to Redlands and Highway 38. Take Highway 38 northeast and drive 27.5 miles to the campground on the left.

**Contact:** San Bernardino National Forest, Mountaintop Ranger District, Big Bear Ranger Station/Discovery Center, 909/382-2790, www. fs.usda.gov/sbnf; campground, 909/389-4517.

## 85 SAN GORGONIO

### Scenic rating: 7

near the San Gorgonio Wilderness in San Bernardino National Forest

**Map 13.3, page 711**

San Gorgonio is one in a series of Forest Service camps along Highway 38 and about 2.5 miles from Jenks Lake. (See the Barton Flats listing in this chapter for details.) The elevation is 6,500 feet.

**Campsites, facilities:** There are 51 single sites and three group sites (for up to 15 people) for tents or RVs of any length (no hookups). Picnic tables and fire grills are provided. Drinking water and restrooms with flush toilets and coin showers are available. Some facilities are wheelchair-accessible. Leashed pets are permitted.

**Reservations, fees:** Reservations are accepted at 877/444-6777 ($10 reservation fee) or www.recreation.gov ($9 reservation fee). Sites are $26-28 per night group sites are $56 per night, plus $5 per night for each additional vehicle. Open mid-May through mid-October.

**Directions:** Drive on I-10 to Redlands and Highway 38. Take Highway 38 northeast and drive 28 miles to the campground.

**Contact:** San Bernardino National Forest, Mountaintop Ranger District, Big Bear Ranger Station/Discovery Center, 909/382-2790, www.fs.usda.gov/sbnf.

## 86 OSO AND LOBO GROUP

**Scenic rating: 6**

near the San Gorgonio Wilderness in San Bernardino National Forest

**Map 13.3, page 711**

Oso and Lobo Group Camps are directly adjacent to each other at 6,600 feet elevation. The camps are about three-quarters of a mile from the Santa Ana River. Little Jenks Lake is two miles away to the west, and the northern border of the San Gorgonio Wilderness is just a few miles to the south.

**Campsites, facilities:** There are two group sites for tents or RVs of any length (no hookups): Oso can accommodate 100 people and Lobo can accommodate 75 people. Picnic tables and fire grills are provided. Drinking water and vault toilets are available. Leashed pets are permitted.

**Reservations, fees:** Reservations are required at 877/444-6777 ($10 reservation fee) or www.recreation.gov ($9 reservation fee). Sites are $300-410 per night. Open May through mid-October, weather permitting.

**Directions:** From I-10 in Redlands, drive 29 miles east on Highway 38 to the campground entrance road on the left.

**Contact:** San Bernardino National Forest, Mountaintop Ranger District, Big Bear Ranger Station/Discovery Center, 909/382-2790, www.fs.usda.gov/sbnf; fire regulations: Discovery Center, 909/866-3437.

## 87 SOUTH FORK

**Scenic rating: 7**

near the Santa Ana River in San Bernardino National Forest

**Map 13.3, page 711**

This is an easy-access Forest Service camp just off Highway 38, set at 6,400 feet elevation near the headwaters of two rivers, the South Fork River and the Santa Ana River. It is part of the series of camps in the immediate area, just north of the San Gorgonio Wilderness. This one is a four-mile drive from little Jenks Lake. (See the Barton Flats listing in this chapter for more details.)

**Campsites, facilities:** There are 24 sites for tents or RVs up to 30 feet (no hookups). Picnic tables and fire rings are provided. Drinking water and vault toilets are available. Leashed pets are permitted.

**Reservations, fees:** Reservations are not accepted. Sites are $22-24 per night, plus $5 per night for each additional vehicle. Open mid-May through September.

**Directions:** Drive on I-10 to Redlands and Highway 38. Take Highway 38 northeast and drive 29.5 miles to the campground entrance road.

**Contact:** San Bernardino National Forest, Mountaintop Ranger District, Big Bear Ranger Station/Discovery Center, 909/382-2790, www.fs.usda.gov/sbnf.

## 88 HEART BAR FAMILY AND SKYLINE GROUP CAMPS

### Scenic rating: 4

in San Bernardino National Forest

**Map 13.3, page 711**

It's a good thing there is drinking water at this camp. Why? Because Heart Bar Creek often isn't much more than a trickle and can't be relied on for water. The camp is at 6,900 feet elevation near Big Meadows and Aspen Grove. A challenging butt-kicker of a hike has a trailhead about a half mile away to the north off a spur road, midway between the camp and the fire station. The trail travels along Wildhorse Creek to Sugarloaf Mountain (9,952 feet, about 8-9 miles one-way to the top). Insider's note: Just past the midway point on the trail to Sugarloaf Mountain is a trail camp on Wildhorse Creek.

**Campsites, facilities:** There are 89 sites for tents or RVs up to 40 feet (no hookups) and one group tent site for up to 25 people. Picnic tables and fire grills are provided. Drinking water and vault toilets are available. Some facilities are wheelchair-accessible. Leashed pets are permitted.

**Reservations, fees:** Reservations are accepted for individual sites and required for the group site at 877/444-6677 ($10 reservation fee) or www.recreation.gov ($9 reservation fee). Sites are $23-50 per night and the group site is $100-110 per night, plus $5 per night for each additional vehicle. Open mid-May through early October.

**Directions:** Drive on I-10 to Redlands and Highway 38. Take Highway 38 northeast and drive 33.5 miles to Forest Road 1N02. Turn right and drive one mile to the campground.

**Contact:** San Bernardino National Forest, Mountaintop Ranger District, Big Bear Ranger Station/Discovery Center, 909/382-2790, www.fs.usda.gov/sbnf; fire regulations: Discovery Center, 909/866-3437.

## 89 HEART BAR EQUESTRIAN AND WILD HORSE EQUESTRIAN

### Scenic rating: 5

in San Bernardino National Forest

**Map 13.3, page 711**

You might not meet Mr. Ed here, but bring an apple anyway. Heart Bar is a horse camp on Heart Bar Creek, less than a mile east of Heart Bar Family Camp. Wild Horse is just a tenth of a mile before Heart Bar Family Camp. A good trail leading into the San Gorgonio Wilderness starts four miles down the road at Fish Creek Meadows. It heads west for three miles to Fish Creek and then up Grinnell Mountain to the north peak of the Ten Thousand Foot Ridge. A wilderness permit is required. The elevation is 7,000 feet.

**Campsites, facilities:** Heart Bar has 46 corrals, 11 stables, and one group site for tents or RVs up to 22 feet (no hookups) that can accommodate up to 65 people. Campers without horses are not permitted. Wild Horse has 11 equestrian sites, including three double sites, and 24 corrals. Picnic tables and fire grills are provided. Drinking water, coin showers, and flush toilets are available. Water is available for horses. Some facilities are wheelchair-accessible. Leashed pets are permitted.

**Reservations, fees:** Reservations are required at 877/444-6677 ($10 reservation fee) or www.recreation.gov ($9 reservation fee). Wild Horse sites are $28-30 per night, the group camp at Heart Bar is $260-270 per night, and it's $5 per night for each additional vehicle. Open May through early October.

**Directions:** From San Bernardino, take I-10 east to Redlands and Highway 38. Take Highway 38 northeast and drive 33.5 miles to Forest Road 1N02. Turn right and drive a mile to the Heart Bar Group Campground on the right. Continue for 0.1 mile to the Wild Horse camp on the left. To reach Heart Bar Group Equestrian Campground, continue another 0.1 mile.

**Contact:** San Bernardino National Forest, Mountaintop Ranger District, Big Bear Ranger Station/Discovery Center, 909/382-2790, www. fs.usda.gov/sbnf; fire regulations: Discovery Center, 909/866-3437.

## 90 COON CREEK CABIN GROUP CAMP

### Scenic rating: 4

on the Pacific Crest Trail in San Bernardino National Forest

**Map 13.3, page 711**

Backpackers call this the "Coon Creek jump-off" because it is on the Pacific Crest Trail at 8,200 feet elevation and provides a "jump-off" for a trek on the Pacific Crest Trail. The camp is on Coon Creek, but the creek often runs dry by summer. Note that in the off-season the access road, Forest Road 1N02, can be gated; campers must hike or cross-country ski to the camp.

**Campsites, facilities:** There is one group camp for tents only for up to 25 people and 10 vehicles (no trailers or RVs). Picnic tables and fire grills are provided. Vault toilets are available. No drinking water is available. Leashed pets are permitted.

**Reservations, fees:** Reservations are required at 877/444-6777 ($10 reservation fee) or www. recreation.gov ($9 reservation fee). The camp is $100-110 per night. Open year-round.

**Directions:** From San Bernardino, take I-10 east to Redlands and Highway 38. Take Highway 38 northeast and drive 33.5 miles to Forest Road 1N02. Turn right and drive five miles to the campground entrance (dirt road).

**Contact:** San Bernardino National Forest, Mountaintop Ranger District, Big Bear Ranger Station/Discovery Center, 909/382-2790, www. fs.usda.gov/sbnf; fire regulations: Discovery Center, 909/866-3437.

## 91 BOGART PARK

### Scenic rating: 4

in Cherry Valley

**Map 13.3, page 711**

This county park is overlooked by many vacationers on I-10, and it is as pretty as it gets for this area. There are two miles of horse trails and some hiking trails for a recreation option during the cooler months. It covers 414 acres of Riverside County foothills at the north end of Cherry Valley. The elevation is 2,800 feet. Bears frequent this area, so store your food properly and avoid scented products. The park is closed to camping Monday, Tuesday, and Wednesday nights.

**Campsites, facilities:** There are 26 sites for tents or RVs up to 40 feet (no hookups), a group campground for tents that can accommodate up to 100 people, and a group equestrian campground. Fire grills and picnic tables are provided. Drinking water and flush toilets are available. The equestrian camp has 11 corrals, stalls, and water troughs. Supplies are available in Beaumont. Some facilities are wheelchair-accessible. Leashed pets are permitted.

**Reservations, fees:** Reservations are accepted for individual sites and are required for the group camp at 800/234-7275 ($7 reservation fee). Developed sites are $12 per night, and primitive sites are $10 per night. The group site is $144 per night, the group equestrian camp is $120 per night, plus $1 per night per pet or horse. Youth group rates are available. Open year-round but closed on Tuesday and Wednesday.

**Directions:** From San Bernardino, take I-10 east to Beaumont and the exit for Beaumont Avenue. Take that exit north and drive four miles to Brookside. Turn right and drive 0.5 mile to Cherry Avenue. Turn left at Cherry Avenue and drive to the park on the right (9600 Cherry Avenue).

**Contact:** Bogart Park, 951/845-3818; Riverside County Parks, 800/234-7275, www.rivcoparks. org.

## 92 BANNING STAGECOACH KOA

### Scenic rating: 2

in Banning

**Map 13.3, page 711**

Banning Stagecoach KOA (formerly Pine Ranch RV Park) is considered the gateway to mile-high Idyllwild. Banning may not seem like a hotbed of civilization at first glance, but this clean, comfortable park is a decent spot to make camp while exploring some of the area's hidden attractions, including Agua Caliente Indian Canyons and the Lincoln Shrine. It is set at 2,400 feet elevation, 22 miles from Palm Springs. A good side trip is to head south on curving "Highway" 240 up to Vista Point in the San Bernardino National Forest.

**Campsites, facilities:** There are 94 RV sites with full hookups (30 and 50 amps); many sites are pull-through. There are also five tent sites and three park models. Picnic tables and fire grills are provided. Restrooms with showers, cable TV, playground, swimming pool, clubhouse, coin laundry, Wi-Fi, dump station, ice, horseshoes, and propane gas are available. Leashed pets are permitted, with certain restrictions.

**Reservations, fees:** Reservations are recommended at 800/562-4110. RV sites are $40-45 per night, tent sites are $25 per night, and park models are $80 per night, plus $2 per additional person per night over 6 people and $1 per night for each additional vehicle. Some credit cards are accepted. Open year-round.

**Directions:** From San Bernardino, take I-10 east to Banning and the exit for Highway 243. Take that exit south and take 8th Street south for one block to Lincoln. Turn left on Lincoln and drive two blocks to San Gorgonio. Turn right and drive one mile to the park.

**Contact:** Banning Stagecoach KOA, 951/849-7513, www.koa.com.

## 93 WILDERNESS WALK-IN CAMPS

### Scenic rating: 10

in Mount San Jacinto State Park

**Map 13.3, page 711**     **BEST (**

This is one of the most spectacular getaways in the western United States. It includes a tram ride that will take you from 2,643 feet to 8,516 feet elevation, with stunning views across the desert and especially heart-breaking sunsets. On clear days, you can see the Salton Sea 50 miles to the south. From the tram, you then hike up to 2.75 miles to the camps, set at 9,100 feet, an ideal launch point for the hike to the Mount San Jacinto summit, at 10,834 feet the second-highest peak in Southern California. From Round Valley Camp, it is a 7.5-mile round-trip (just add another mile round-trip from Tamarack Valley Camp). On clear days from the summit, you can see 100 miles, including the Channel Islands, Mexico, and Nevada. On summer weekends, these campgrounds are often filled for dates more than a month in advance. Insider's tip: Be prepared for all types of weather conditions; weather can turn cold/rainy/snowy/windy quickly here. Snow camping is allowed.

**Campsites, facilities:** There are 25 tent sites at Round Valley, 12 tent sites at Tamarack Valley, and six sites at Little Round Valley. Groups are limited to 15 people. Pit toilets are available. No drinking water is available. Stream water (seasonal) must be boiled or pump-filtered before use. No campfires are permitted. Bring a camp stove (propane or gas) for cooking. Smoking is not allowed. Garbage must be packed out. No firearms or wheels are permitted. Horses are allowed, but bring weed-free feed and water for the horses. Cell phone reception is virtually nonexistent.

**Reservations, fees:** Reservations are accepted online and are highly recommended for Friday and Saturday nights in peak season. Sites are $25 per person. A camping permit is required and can be obtained at the park office or by mail to Mount San Jacinto State Park (P.O. Box 308, Idyllwild, CA 92549; include a stamped, self-addressed envelope); or apply online up to eight weeks in advance. A fee is charged for the tram ride. Open year-round, except when the tram is closed for maintenance.

**Directions:** From Banning, drive east on I-10 for 12 miles to the Highway 111/Palm Springs exit. Take that exit to Highway 111 and drive south nine miles to Tramway Road. Turn right and drive three miles to the parking area for Palm Springs Aerial Tramway. Ride the tram to Mountain Station. Hike 2.25 miles to Round Valley Camp, or continue from Round Valley Camp for another 0.5 mile to Tamarack Valley Camp.

**Contact:** Mount San Jacinto State Park, 951/659-2607, www.parks.ca.gov; Palm Springs Aerial Tramway, 888/515-8726, www.pstramway.com.

## 94 BLACK MOUNTAIN GROUP CAMP

### Scenic rating: 6

near Mount San Jacinto in San Bernardino National Forest

**Map 13.3, page 711**

This is a beautiful scenic area, particularly to the north on the edge of the San Jacinto Wilderness and to the east of Mount San Jacinto State Park. The camp, at 7,500 feet elevation, is within a mile of a trailhead for the Pacific Crest Trail. You can turn southeast and hike along Fuller Ridge for another mile to the border of Mount San Jacinto State Park. Note that Black Mountain Lookout is just a two-mile drive, close to Boulder Basin Camp.

**Campsites, facilities:** One group camp for tents and RVs up to 25 feet (no hookups) can accommodate up to 100 people and up to 25 vehicles. Picnic tables and fire rings are provided. Vault toilets are available. Drinking water is available at Cinca Posa Spring, about two miles away. Leashed pets are permitted.

**Reservations, fees:** Reservations are required at 877/444-6777 ($10 reservation fee) or www.recreation.gov ($9 reservation fee). The camp is $60-120 per night. Open May through mid-October.

**Directions:** Drive on I-10 to Banning and Highway 243/Pines to Palms Scenic Highway. Turn south on Pines to Palms Scenic Highway and drive about 15 miles to Forest Road 4S01. Turn left on Forest Road 4S01 and drive eight miles (a narrow dirt road) to the campground on the right. Trailers are not advised.

**Contact:** San Bernardino National Forest, San Jacinto Ranger District, 909/382-2922, www.fs.usda.gov/sbnf.

## 95 BOULDER BASIN

### Scenic rating: 8

near the San Jacinto Wilderness in San Bernardino National Forest

**Map 13.3, page 711**

This camp is on the top of the world for these parts: 7,300 feet elevation, adjacent to the Black Mountain Fire Lookout with great views in all directions and highlighted by Tahquitz Peak (8,828 feet) 10 miles to the southeast. Boulder Basin is also near the San Jacinto Wilderness (to the northeast) and makes a good trailhead camp for hikers. A trail starting at Black Mountain Lookout leads west, dropping steeply into a canyon and also into a designated scenic area.

**Campsites, facilities:** There are 34 sites for tents or RVs up to 15 feet (no hookups). Note that trailers and RVs are not recommended. Picnic tables and fire rings are provided. Vault toilets are available, but there is no drinking water. Leashed pets are permitted.

**Reservations, fees:** Reservations are accepted at 877/444-6777 ($10 reservation fee) or www.recreation.gov ($9 reservation fee). Sites are $10 per night, plus $5 per night per additional vehicle. Open May through mid-October.

**Directions:** Drive on I-10 to Banning and

Highway 243/Pines to Palms Scenic Highway. Turn south on Pines to Palms Scenic Highway and drive about 15 miles to Forest Road 4S01/ Black Mountain Road. Turn left and drive six miles (a narrow dirt road) to the campground on the right. RVs are not advised.

**Contact:** San Bernardino National Forest, San Jacinto Ranger District, 909/382-2922, www. fs.usda.gov/sbnf.

## 96 DARK CANYON

### Scenic rating: 7

in the San Jacinto Mountains in San Bernardino National Forest

**Map 13.3, page 711**

This pretty setting is on the slopes of the San Jacinto Mountains at 5,800 feet elevation. Hikers can drive to the Seven Pines Trailhead less than a mile north of camp at the end of Forest Road 4S02. The trail leads east for three miles into Mount San Jacinto State Park to Deer Springs, where there is a trail camp and a junction with the Pacific Crest Trail. A wilderness permit is required. While the North Fork of the San Jacinto River runs near the campground, access is closed to protect the mountain yellow-legged frog.

**Campsites, facilities:** There are 15 sites for tents or RVs up to 17 feet (no hookups). Picnic tables and fire grills are provided. Drinking water and vault toilets are available. Leashed pets are permitted.

**Reservations, fees:** Reservations are not accepted. Sites are $12 per night, plus $5 per night per additional vehicle. Open mid-May through mid-September.

**Directions:** Drive on I-10 to Banning and Highway 243/Pines to Palms Scenic Highway. Turn south on Pines to Palms Scenic Highway

and drive about 13 miles to Forest Road 4S02. Turn left on Forest Road 4S02 and drive three miles (narrow paved road) to the campground.

**Contact:** San Bernardino National Forest, San Jacinto Ranger District, 909/382-2922, www. fs.usda.gov/sbnf.

## 97 MARION MOUNTAIN

### Scenic rating: 7

in San Bernardino National Forest

**Map 13.3, page 711**

You get good lookouts and a developed campground at this spot. Nearby Black Mountain is a good side trip that includes a drive-to scenic lookout point. In addition, there are several trailheads in the area. The best one starts near this camp and heads up the slopes to Marion Mountain and east into adjacent Mount San Jacinto State Park. The elevation is 6,400 feet.

**Campsites, facilities:** There are 24 sites for tents or RVs up to 15 feet (no hookups). Picnic tables and fire grills are provided. Drinking water and vault toilets are available. Leashed pets are permitted.

**Reservations, fees:** Reservations are accepted at 877/444-6777 ($10 reservation fee) or www. recreation.gov ($9 reservation fee). Sites are $10 per night, $5 per night per additional vehicle. Open mid-May through mid-October.

**Directions:** Drive on I-10 to Banning and Highway 243/Pines to Palms Scenic Highway. Turn south on Pines to Palms Scenic Highway and drive about 13 miles south to Forest Road 4S02. Turn left on Forest Road 4S02 and drive two miles (narrow paved road) to the campground.

**Contact:** San Bernardino National Forest, San Jacinto Ranger District, 909/382-2922, www. fs.usda.gov/sbnf.

## 98 FERN BASIN

🚶 🐕 🚙 ⛺

**Scenic rating: 7**

near Mount San Jacinto State Park in San
Bernardino National Forest

**Map 13.3, page 711**

This is a nearby alternative to Stone Creek
(you'll pass it on the way in) and Dark Canyon
(another three miles in). Marion Mountain
Trailhead is accessible within half a mile of the
campground by driving east on Forest Road
4S02.

**Campsites, facilities:** There are 22 sites for
tents or RVs up to 15 feet (no hookups). Picnic
tables and fire rings are provided. Drinking
water and vault toilets are available. Leashed
pets are permitted.

**Reservations, fees:** Reservations are accepted
at 877/444-6777 ($10 reservation fee) or www.
recreation.gov ($9 reservation fee). Sites are $10
per night, plus $5 per night per additional ve-
hicle. Open mid-May through mid-October.

**Directions:** Drive on I-10 to Banning and
Highway 243/Pines to Palms Scenic Highway.
Turn south on Pines to Palms Scenic Highway
and drive about 13 miles south to Forest Road
4S02. Turn left on Forest Road 4S02 and drive
one mile (narrow paved road) to the campground on the left.

**Contact:** San Bernardino National Forest, San
Jacinto Ranger District, 909/382-2922, www.
fs.usda.gov/sbnf.

## 99 STONE CREEK

🚶 🐕 ♿ 🚙 ⛺

**Scenic rating: 7**

in Mount San Jacinto State Park

**Map 13.3, page 711**

This is a wooded camp in Mount San Jacinto
State Park. The elevation is 5,900 feet, and it's
a quarter mile off the main road along Stone
Creek, just outside the national forest boundary. It is less than a mile from Fern Basin and
less than three miles from Dark Canyon. The

best trailhead in the immediate area is Seven
Pines Trail out of Marion Mountain Camp, a
half mile from this camp.

**Campsites, facilities:** There are 50 sites for
tents or RVs up to 24 feet (no hookups). Picnic
tables and fire rings are provided. Drinking
water and vault toilets are usually available.
However, camp alerts may be in effect depending upon weather: sites may be walk-in
or self-pay with no water and no firewood or
charcoal fires. Supplies and a coin laundry are
three miles away in Pine Cove. Some facilities
are wheelchair-accessible. Leashed pets are
permitted.

**Reservations, fees:** Reservations are accepted
at 800/444-7275 ($10 reservation fee) or www.
reserveamerica.com ($9 reservation fee). Sites
are $20 per night, plus $8 per night for each additional vehicle. Discounts are offered in winter. Open year-round.

**Directions:** Drive on I-10 to Banning and
Highway 243/Idyllwild Panoramic Highway.
Turn south on Idyllwild Panoramic Highway
and drive about 13 miles south to the park entrance on the left.

**Contact:** Mount San Jacinto State Park,
951/659-2607; Inland Empire District, 951/443-
2423, www.parks.ca.gov.

## 100 GOLDEN VILLAGE PALMS RV RESORT

🏊 🐕 ♿ 🚐

**Scenic rating: 5**

in Hemet

**Map 13.3, page 711**

This RV resort is for those age 55 and over. It
is the biggest RV park in Southern California.
The grounds are lush, with gravel pads for RVs.
It is near Diamond Valley Lake, about 10 miles
south, a new lake that is the largest reservoir in
Southern California. A golf course is nearby,
Lake Hemet is 20 miles east, and winery tours
are available in Temecula, a 30-minute drive.
About 250 of the 1,019 sites are rented on a
year-round basis.

**Campsites, facilities:** There are 1,019 sites with full hookups (20, 30, and 50 amps) for RVs up to 45 feet; some sites are pull-through. There are no tent sites. Restrooms with flush toilets and showers, drinking water, cable TV, Wi-Fi, business services, three heated swimming pools, three spas, a recreation room, fitness center, billiard room, coin laundry, large clubhouse, banquet and meeting rooms, organized activities, pavilion, church services, concerts, library, ballroom, shuffleboard, nine-hole putting green, volleyball courts, and horseshoe pits are available. A day-use area with propane barbecues is also available. Some facilities are wheelchair-accessible. Leashed pets are permitted (pet run available).

**Reservations, fees:** Reservations are accepted at 866/477-6154. RV sites (hookups) start at $183 per night, plus $10 per person per night for more than two people and $2 per pet per day. Group rates are available. Weekly, monthly, and annual rates are available. Open year-round.

**Directions:** Drive to the junction of I-215 and Highway 74 (near Perris). At that junction, take Highway 74 east and drive 14 miles to Hemet (the highway becomes Florida Avenue in Hemet) and continue to the resort on the left.

**Contact:** Golden Village Palms RV Resort, 951/925-2518, www.goldenvillagepalms.com.

## 101 CASA DEL SOL RV PARK RESORT

### Scenic rating: 3

in Hemet

**Map 13.3, page 711**

Hemet is a retirement town, so if you want excitement, the four lakes in the area are the best places to look for it: Lake Perris to the northwest, Diamond Valley Lake and Lake Skinner to the south, and Lake Hemet to the east. The elevation at this 20-acre resort is 1,575 feet. Note that many of the sites are taken by year-round or long-term rentals.

**Campsites, facilities:** There are 358 sites with full hookups (30 and 50 amps) for RVs up to 45 feet. Restrooms with flush toilets and showers, drinking water, cable TV, Wi-Fi, ice, library, heated swimming pool, spa, recreation room, exercise room, billiard room, shuffleboard courts, golf driving cage, dog runs, and coin laundry are available. Some facilities are wheelchair-accessible. Leashed pets are permitted.

**Reservations, fees:** Reservations are accepted at 888/925-2516. RV sites (hookups) are $55 per night, plus $10 per person per night for more than two people. Weekly and monthly rates are available; discounts are available. Some credit cards are accepted. Open year-round.

**Directions:** Drive to the junction of I-215 and Highway 74 (near Perris). At that junction, take Highway 74 east and drive 15 miles to Hemet (the highway becomes Florida Avenue in Hemet) and to Kirby Avenue. Turn right (south) on Kirby Avenue and drive a half block to the resort at 2750 West Acacia Avenue.

**Contact:** Casa del Sol RV Park Resort, 951/925-2515, www.casadelsolrvpark.com.

## 102 MOUNTAIN VALLEY RV RESORT

### Scenic rating: 3

in Hemet

**Map 13.3, page 711**

This is one of three RV parks in the Hemet area. Four lakes in the area provide side-trip possibilities: Lake Perris to the northwest, Lake Skinner and Diamond Valley Lake to the south, and Lake Hemet to the east. Golf courses are nearby.

**Campsites, facilities:** There are 170 sites with full hookups (30 and 50 amps) for RVs up to 40 feet. Restrooms with flush toilets and showers, cable TV, drinking water, a fireside room, heated swimming pool, enclosed spa, fitness center, golf driving cage, card-access laundry, billiards room, meeting room, group facilities, Wi-Fi, and telephone hookups are available. A store and propane gas are nearby.

Some facilities are wheelchair-accessible. Leashed pets are permitted, with some breeds prohibited.

**Reservations, fees:** Reservations are accepted at 800/926-5593. RV sites (hookups) are $35-60 per night, plus $5 per person per night for more than two people and $2 per pet per night. Weekly, monthly, and annual rates are available. Some credit cards are accepted. Open year-round.

**Directions:** Drive to the junction of I-215 and Highway 74 (near Perris). At that junction, take Highway 74 east and drive 15 miles to Hemet (the highway becomes Florida Avenue in Hemet) and continue to South Lyon Avenue. Turn right on South Lyon Avenue and drive to the park at the corner of Lyon and South Acacia (235 South Lyon).

**Contact:** Mountain Valley RV Resort, 951/925-5812, www.mountainvalleyrv.com.

## 103 IDYLLWILD COUNTY PARK

**Scenic rating: 6**

near San Bernardino National Forest

**Map 13.3, page 711**

This Riverside County park covers 202 acres, set at 5,300 feet elevation and surrounded by Mount San Jacinto State Park, San Jacinto Wilderness, and the San Bernardino National Forest lands. That provides plenty of options for visitors. The park has equestrian trails and an interpretive trail. The top hike in the region is the ambitious climb up the western slopes to the top of Mount San Jacinto (10,804 feet), a terrible challenge of a butt-kicker that provides one of the most astounding views in all the land. (The best route, however, is out of Palm Springs, taking the aerial tramway, which will get you to 8,516 feet elevation before you hike out the rest.)

**Campsites, facilities:** There are 88 sites for tents or RVs up to 40 feet (no hookups). Fire grills and picnic tables are provided. Drinking

water and restrooms with flush toilets and coin showers are available. A store, coin laundry, and propane gas are nearby. There is no drinking water in dry years. Some facilities are wheelchair-accessible. Leashed pets are permitted.

**Reservations, fees:** Reservations are accepted at 800/234-7275 ($8 reservation fee). Sites are $25 per night, plus $2 per pet per night. Some credit cards are accepted. Open year-round.

**Directions:** Drive on I-10 to Banning and Highway 243/Idyllwild Panoramic Highway. Turn south on Idyllwild Panoramic Highway and drive to Idyllwild and Riverside County Playground Road. Turn west on Riverside County Playground Road and drive 0.5 mile (follow the signs) to the park entrance on the right.

**Contact:** Idyllwild County Park, 951/659-2656, www.rivcoparks.org.

## 104 IDYLLWILD

**Scenic rating: 8**

in Mount San Jacinto State Park

**Map 13.3, page 711**

This is a prime spot for hikers and one of the better jumping-off points for trekking in the area. Elevation is 5,400 feet. There are no trails from this campground. But a half mile north is Deer Spring Trail, which is connected with the Pacific Crest Trail and then climbs on to Mount San Jacinto (10,834 feet) and its astounding lookout.

**Campsites, facilities:** There are 24 sites for tents only, nine sites for tents or RVs up to 24 feet (three with full hookups, six with partial), and one hike-in/bike-in site. Fire grills and picnic tables are provided. Drinking water, restrooms with flush toilets and coin showers, and Wi-Fi are available. Supplies and coin laundry (100 yards) are nearby. Some facilities are wheelchair-accessible. Leashed pets are permitted.

**Reservations, fees:** Reservations are accepted

at 800/444-7275 or www.reserveamerica.com ($8 reservation fee). Sites are $25 per night, plus $8 per night for each additional vehicle, and $3 per person per night for the hike-in/bike-in site. Open year-round.

**Directions:** In Idyllwild, drive to the north end of town on Highway 243 to the park entrance on the left (next to the fire station).

From I-10 in Banning, take the A Street exit onto Highway 243. Drive south on Highway 243 for 23.8 miles to the campground on the right, just before the town of Idyllwild.

**Contact:** Mount San Jacinto State Park, 951/659-2607; Inland Empire District, 951/443-2423, www.parks.ca.gov.

## 105 LAKE HEMET

### Scenic rating: 7

near Hemet

**Map 13.3, page 711**

Lake Hemet covers 420 acres, is set at 4,340 feet elevation, and sits near San Bernardino National Forest just west of Garner Valley. Many campsites have lake views. It provides a good camping/fishing destination, with large stocks of trout each year, and yep, catch rates are good. The lake also has bass, bluegill, and catfish. Boating rules prohibit boats under 10 feet, canoes, sailboats, inflatables, and swimming—no swimming or wading at Lake Hemet. The boat speed limit is 10 mph.

**Campsites, facilities:** There are 275 sites for RVs up to 40 feet, 250 dry sites for tents, and four group sites for a minimum of 25 people, including equestrian groups. Park-model cabins are also available. All sites have full hook-ups (20 amps). Picnic tables and fire rings are provided. Restrooms with flush toilets and coin showers, drinking water, dump station, playground, basketball and volleyball courts, horseshoes, boat ramp, boat rentals, convenience store, coin laundry, and propane gas are available. No generators are permitted at

campsites. Some facilities are wheelchair-accessible. Leashed pets are permitted.

**Reservations, fees:** Reservations are accepted and are required for the group sites at 951/659-2680 ($9 reservation fee). Tent sites are $30 per night, double and triple sites are $35-40 per night, RV sites are $35-40 per night, plus $5 per person per night for more than two people, $15 per night for additional vehicle, and $3 per pet per night. Some credit cards are accepted. Open year-round.

**Directions:** From Palm Desert, drive southwest on Highway 74 for 33 miles (near Lake Hemet) to the campground entrance on the left. For directions if arriving from the west (several options), phone 951/659-2680, ext. 2.

**Contact:** Lake Hemet, 951/659-2680, www.lakehemet.org.

## 106 HURKEY CREEK PARK

### Scenic rating: 5

near Lake Hemet

**Map 13.3, page 711**

This large Riverside County park is just east (across the road) of Lake Hemet, beside Hurkey Creek (which runs in winter and spring). The highlight, of course, is the nearby lake, known for good fishing in the spring. No swimming is permitted. The camp elevation is 4,800 feet. The park covers 59 acres.

**Campsites, facilities:** There are 130 sites and five group sites for tents or RVs up to 40 feet (no hookups) that can accommodate up to 100 people each. Fire grills and picnic tables are provided. Drinking water, restrooms with flush toilets and coin showers, a playground, and picnic areas are available. Some facilities are wheelchair-accessible. A small general store is nearby and a dump station is at Lake Hemet. Leashed pets are permitted.

**Reservations, fees:** Reservations are accepted for individual sites and required for the group sites at 800/234-7275 ($8 reservation fee). Sites are $25 per night, plus $2 per pet per night.

Group sites are $6 per person with a minimum of 40 people. Some credit cards are accepted. Open year-round.

**Directions:** From Palm Desert, drive southwest on Highway 74 for 32 miles (near Lake Hemet) to the campground entrance on the right.

**Contact:** Hurkey Creek Park, 951/659-2050, www.rivcoparks.org.

## 107 ANZA RV RESORT

### Scenic rating: 4

near Anza

**Map 13.3, page 711**

This is a year-round RV park at 4,100 feet elevation, with many nearby recreation options. Lake Hemet is 16 miles away, with hiking, motorbiking, and jeep trails nearby in San Bernardino National Forest. Pacific Crest Trail hikers are welcome to clean up and to arrange for food and mail pickup. Note that most sites are filled with long-term renters.

**Campsites, facilities:** There are 116 sites for tents and RVs; many have full hookups (30 and 50 amps) and some sites are pull-through. Picnic tables are provided. Restrooms with showers, catch-and-release fishing pond, horseshoe pits, coin laundry, convenience store, dump station, ice, recreation room, and propane gas are available. Leashed pets are permitted, with certain restrictions.

**Reservations, fees:** Reservations are accepted at 888/763-4819. RV sites (hookups) are $21 per night, tent sites are $13-15 per night, plus $1 per person per night for more than two people. Discounts are offered on weekdays. Credit cards are accepted online only. Open year-round.

**Directions:** From Palm Desert, drive west on Highway 74 for 24 miles to Highway 371. Turn left on Highway 371 and drive west to the town of Anza and Kirby Road. Turn left on Kirby Road and drive 3.5 miles to the campground on the left at Terwilliger Road (look for the covered wagon out front).

**Contact:** Anza RV Resort, 951/763-4819 or 888/763-4819, www.anzarvresort.com.

# SAN DIEGO AND VICINITY

The weather, ocean and beaches, lakes and fishing, state forests and parks, mountains, hiking, biking, and water sports make San Diego one of the best regions to live in California. Everywhere are campgrounds and parks, from primitive to deluxe. Cleveland National Forest provides remote mountains with canyons, hidden streams, small campgrounds, and a terrain of forests. Some of the more remote sections of Cleveland National Forest, as well as Cuyamaca Rancho State Park, provide access to wildlands and primitive campsites. Several campgrounds are at Palomar State Park and in the nearby national forest. And there are developed RV parks in the San Diego area that cost as much as fine hotel rooms in other parts of the state—and they're worth it.

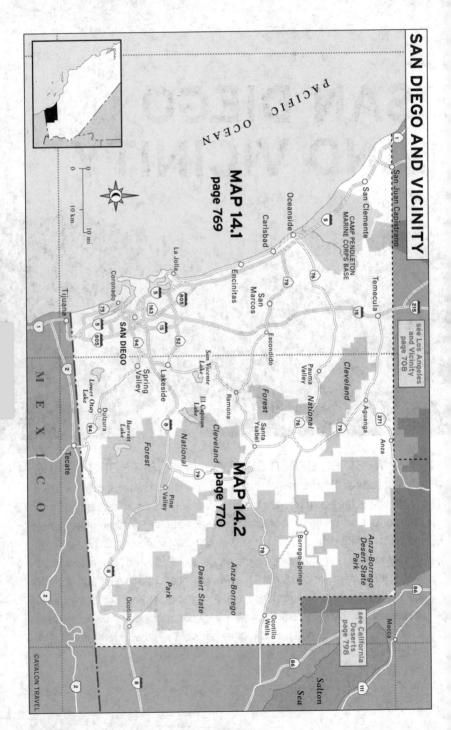

SAN DIEGO AND VICINITY

MAP 14.1
page 769

MAP 14.2
page 770

PACIFIC OCEAN

see Los Angeles and Vicinity page 708

see California Deserts page 798

©AVALON TRAVEL

# Map 14.1

**Sites 1-15
Pages 771-778**

14.2

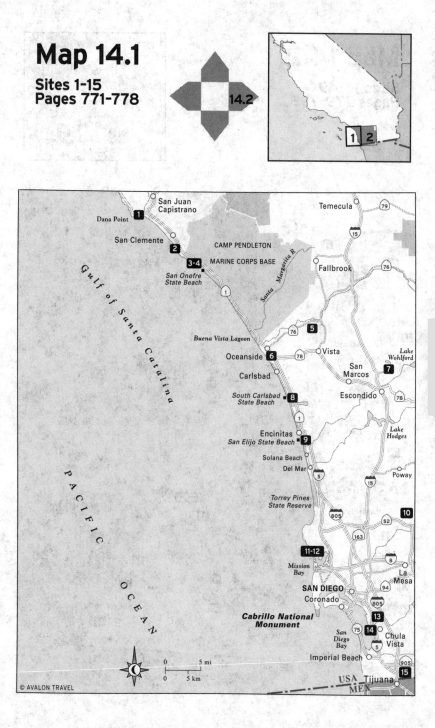

# Map 14.2

**Sites 16-49
Pages 779-795**

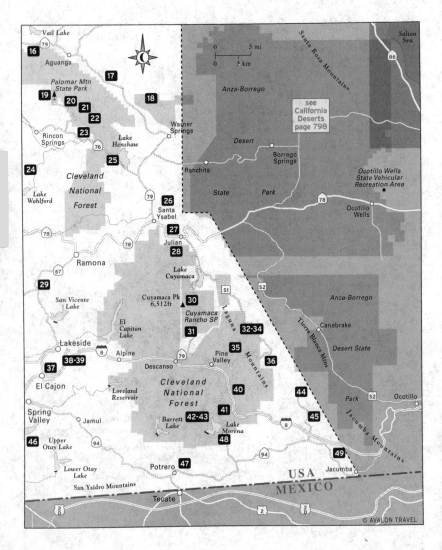

# 1 DOHENY STATE BEACH

🚶 🚴 ⛵ 🏊 🎣 🐕 ♿ 🚐 ⛺

### Scenic rating: 10

on Dana Point Harbor

**Map 14.1, page 769**    **BEST (**

Doheny is a gorgeous park with a campground that requires working the reservation system the first morning campsites become available. Some campsites are within steps of the beach, yet this state beach is right in town, at the entrance to Dana Point Harbor. It is a pretty spot with easy access off the highway. A lifeguard service is available in the summer, and campfire and junior ranger programs are also offered. A day-use area has a lawn with picnic area and volleyball courts. Bonfire rings are set up on the beach. Surfing is popular, but note that it is permitted at the north end of the beach only. San Juan Capistrano provides a nearby side trip, just three miles away.

**Campsites, facilities:** There are 113 sites for tents or RVs up to 35 feet (no hookups), one hike-in/bike-in site, and a group site for up to 40 people. Picnic tables and fire grills are provided. Drinking water, restrooms with flush toilets and coin showers, dump station, Wi-Fi, aquarium, and seasonal snack bar are available. Propane gas and gasoline are nearby. Some facilities are wheelchair-accessible. Leashed pets are permitted in the campground only, not on the beach.

**Reservations, fees:** Reservations are accepted at www.reserveamerica.com ($8 reservation fee). Inland sites are $40 per night, premium beachfront sites are $60 per night, plus $15 per night for each additional vehicle and $5 per person per night for the hike-in/bike-in site (photo ID required). The group site is $300 per night. Open year-round.

**Directions:** Drive on I-5 to the exit for Pacific Coast Highway/Camino de las Ramblas (three miles south of San Juan Capistrano). Take that exit and drive to Dana Point/Harbor Drive (second light). Turn left and drive one block to the park entrance. Doheny State Beach is about one mile from I-5.

**Contact:** Doheny State Beach, 949/496-6172; Orange Coast District, San Clemente Sector, 949/492-0802, www.parks.ca.gov.

# 2 SAN CLEMENTE STATE BEACH

🚶 🚴 ⛵ 🏊 🎣 🐕 ♿ 🚐 ⛺

### Scenic rating: 8

near San Clemente

**Map 14.1, page 769**

The campground at San Clemente State Beach is set on a bluff, not on a beach. A few campsites have ocean views. Surfing is popular on the north end of a one-mile beach. The beach is popular for swimming, body surfing, and skin diving. Of the three local state beaches that provide easy access and beachfront camping, this one offers full hookups. The others are Doheny State Beach to the north and San Onofre State Beach to the south. A feature at this park is a two-mile long interpretive trail, along with hike-in/bike-in campsites. Surfing camp is held here during the summer.

**Campsites, facilities:** There are 160 sites, and 72 sites have full hookups (30 amps) for tents or RVs up to 40 feet. There is one hike-in/bike-in site. Two group sites (one with hookups) for tents or RVs hold up to 50 people and 20 vehicles. Picnic tables and fire grills are provided. Restrooms with flush toilets and coin showers, a dump station, Wi-Fi, summer lifeguard service, and summer programs are available. A store, coin laundry, and propane gas are nearby. Some facilities are wheelchair-accessible. Leashed pets are permitted in the campground only.

**Reservations, fees:** Reservations are accepted at 800/444-7275 ($10 reservation fee) or www.reserveamerica.com ($9 reservation fee). Tent sites are $35-40 per night, RV sites (with hookups) are $45-65 per night, plus $15 per night for each additional vehicle; the group sites are $250-300 per night, and it's $5 per person per night for the hike-in/bike-in site. Open year-round.

**Directions:** From I-5 in San Clemente, take the Avenida Calafia exit. Drive west for a short distance to the park entrance on the left.

**Contact:** San Clemente State Beach, 949/492-3156; Orange Coast District, 949/492-0802, www.parks.ca.gov.

## 3 BLUFF AREA

### Scenic rating: 7

in San Onofre State Beach near San Clemente

Map 14.1, page 769

This camp may appear perfect at first glance, but nope, it is very noisy. Both the highway and train tracks are very close. You can practically feel the ground rumble, and that's not all: With Camp Pendleton just on the other side of the freeway, there is considerable noise from helicopters and other operations. Too bad. This is one of three parks along the beach near San Clemente, just off the busy Coast Highway. The campground is on top of a 90-foot bluff. This state beach covers more than 3,000 acres, featuring 3.5 miles of sandy beaches and access trails on the neighboring bluffs. This area is one of the most popular in California for surfing and is also good for swimming. The San Onofre Nuclear Power Plant is nearby. Other state beaches in the area are San Clemente State Beach and Doheny State Beach, both to the north.

**Campsites, facilities:** There are 175 sites for tents or RVs up to 38 feet (no hookups) and one group site for up to 50 people. Picnic tables and fire rings are provided. Drinking water, flush toilets, cold outdoor showers, and a dump station are available. A store, coin laundry, and propane gas are within about five miles. Some facilities are wheelchair-accessible. Leashed pets are permitted at the campground and beach but must stay on designated trails to access the beach.

**Reservations, fees:** Reservations are accepted at 800/444-7275 ($10 reservation fee) or www.reserveamerica.com ($9 reservation fee).

Sites are $40 per night, plus $15 per night for each additional vehicle, and it's $250 per night for the group site. Open mid-May through October, weather permitting.

**Directions:** From San Clemente, drive south on I-5 for three miles to the Basilone Road exit. Take that exit and drive south on Basilone Road for two miles to the park.

**Contact:** San Onofre State Beach, 949/492-4872; Orange Coast District Office, 949/492-0802 or 949/366-8500, www.parks.ca.gov.

## 4 SAN MATEO

### Scenic rating: 9

in San Onofre State Beach near San Clemente

Map 14.1, page 769

This state beach is considered one of the best surf breaks in the United States—it's well known as the outstanding Trestles Surfing Area. The camp is set inland and includes a nature trail, featuring a marshy area where San Mateo Creek meets the shoreline. Although this is a state beach, the camp is relatively far from the ocean; it is a 1.5-mile walk to the beach. But it sure is a lot quieter than the nearby option, Bluff Area campground.

**Campsites, facilities:** There are 157 sites for tents or RVs up to 35 feet; 67 sites have partial hookups (30 amps). Picnic tables and fire grills are provided. A dump station and restrooms with coin showers and flush toilets are available. A store, propane gas, and coin laundry are nearby. Some facilities are wheelchair-accessible. Leashed pets are permitted.

**Reservations, fees:** Reservations are accepted at 800/444-7275 ($10 reservation fee) or www.reserveamerica.com ($9 reservation fee). Sites are $40 per night, plus $15 per night for each additional vehicle, and RV sites (hookups) are $45-65 per night. The group site is $200 per night. Off-season discounts are available. Open year-round.

**Directions:** Drive on I-5 to the southern end of San Clemente and the Cristianitos Road exit.

Take that exit and drive east on Cristianitos Road for 1.5 miles to the park entrance on the right.

**Contact:** San Onofre State Beach, 949/492-4872; Orange Coast District Office, 949/492-0802 or 949/366-8500, www.parks.ca.gov.

## 5 GUAJOME COUNTY PARK

**Scenic rating: 5**

in Oceanside

**Map 14.1, page 769**

*Guajome* means "home of the frog" and, yep, so it is with little Guajome Lake and the adjacent marsh, both of which can be explored on a delightful two-mile hike. The lake provides a bit of fishing for warm-water species, mainly sunfish and catfish. Swimming is prohibited. Because of the wetlands, a huge variety of birds stop here on their migratory journeys, making this a favorite area for bird-watching. A historical adobe house in the park is a must-see. The park covers 557 acres and features several miles of trails for hiking and horseback riding, as well as a nearby museum with antique gas and steam engines and farm engines.

**Campsites, facilities:** There are 33 sites with full hookups (30 amps) for tents or RVs up to 45 feet; a few sites are pull-through. Group camping (at least 10 sites) is available by reservation. A camping cabin is also available. Picnic tables and fire grills are provided. Drinking water, restrooms with flush toilets and showers, dump station, basketball court, and playgrounds are available. An enclosed pavilion and gazebo can be reserved for groups. A store and propane gas are nearby. Leashed pets are permitted.

**Reservations, fees:** Reservations are accepted at 858/565-3600 or 877/565-3600 or online at www.sdparks.org ($5 reservation fee). Sites are $34 per night, the cabin is $155 per night, plus $4 per night per each additional vehicle and $1 per pet per night. Some credit cards are accepted. Open year-round.

**Directions:** From Oceanside, drive east on

Highway 76/Mission Avenue for seven miles to Guajome Lakes Road. Turn right (south) on Guajome Lakes Road and drive to the entrance.

**Contact:** San Diego County Parks Department, Guajome County Park, 760/724-4489, www.sdparks.org.

## 6 PARADISE BY THE SEA RV RESORT

**Scenic rating: 7**

in Oceanside

**Map 14.1, page 769**

This is a classic oceanfront RV resort, but no tenters need apply. It's an easy walk to the beach. The main coastal rail line runs adjacent to the resort, so expect some noise. For boaters, Oceanside Marina to the immediate north is the place to go. Oceanside is an excellent headquarters for deep-sea fishing, with charter trips available; contact Helgren's Sportfishing (760/722-2133) to arrange charters. Legoland is six miles from the resort, and the Wave Waterpark and Mission San Luis Rey are seven miles away. Camp Pendleton, a huge Marine Corps training complex, is to the north.

**Campsites, facilities:** There are 102 sites with full hookups (30 amps) for RVs up to 40 feet; a few sites are pull-through. Picnic tables are provided. Showers, flush toilets, cable TV, Wi-Fi, heated swimming pool, spa, clubhouse, banquet room, coin laundry, RV supplies, and convenience store are available. Boat rentals are nearby. Leashed pets are permitted, with certain breeds prohibited.

**Reservations, fees:** Reservations are accepted online at www.rvatparadise.com ($8 reservation fee). In summer, sites are $90-200, plus $5 per person per night for more than five people, $15 per night for each additional vehicle, and $3 per pet per night. Off-season, sites are $65-90, plus $3 per person per night for more than four people, $5 per night for each additional vehicle, and $3 per pet per night. There is a 90-day limit per stay. Weekly and monthly rates are available. RV rentals are available. Credit cards are accepted. Open year-round.

**Directions:** Drive on I-5 to Oceanside and the Oceanside Boulevard exit. Take that exit and drive west on Oceanside Boulevard for 0.5 mile to South Coast Highway. Turn left on South Coast Highway and drive to the park on the right (1537 South Coast Highway).

**Contact:** Paradise by the Sea RV Resort, 760/439-1376, www.rvatparadise.com.

## ❼ DIXON LAKE RECREATION AREA

**Scenic rating: 7**

near Escondido

### Map 14.1, page 769

Little Dixon Lake is the centerpiece of a regional park in the Escondido foothills. The camp is at an elevation of 1,405 feet, about 400 feet above the lake's shoreline. No private boats or swimming are permitted, and a 5-mph speed limit for rental boats keeps things quiet. When the lake is full, the water is clear, with fair bass fishing (a few huge lunkers). The best success for bass is in the spring, with trout fishing best in the winter and early spring. Catfish are stocked in the summer, trout in winter and spring. In the summer, the lake is open at night for fishing for catfish. A pretty, easy hike is Jack Creek Nature Trail, a one-mile walk to a seasonal 20-foot waterfall. No wood fires are permitted, but charcoal and gas are allowed.

**Campsites, facilities:** There are 45 sites for tents or RVs up to 35 feet; 11 sites have full hookups (30 amps). A cabin is also available. Picnic tables, fire grills, and food lockers are provided. Drinking water, restrooms with flush toilets and showers, picnic shelters, boat rentals, bait, ice, snack bar, and playground are available. Some facilities are wheelchair-accessible. No pets are allowed in the recreation area.

**Reservations, fees:** Reservations are accepted at 760/741-3328 ($5 reservation fee). Standard sites are $18-28 per night, and deluxe sites (with full hookups) are $28-35 per night. Groups can be accommodated. Some credit cards are accepted. Discounts are offered off-season. Open year-round.

**Directions:** Drive on I-15 to the exit for El Norte Parkway (four miles north of Escondido). Take that exit northeast and drive four miles to La Honda Drive. Turn left and drive about one mile to Dixon Lake.

**Contact:** Dixon Lake Recreation Area, City of Escondido, 760/839-4680, www.lakedixon. com.

## ❽ SOUTH CARLSBAD STATE BEACH

**Scenic rating: 9**

near Carlsbad

### Map 14.1, page 769

No reservation? Then likely you can forget about staying here. This is a beautiful state beach, and, as big as it is, the sites go fast to the coastal cruisers who reserved a spot. The campground is on a bluff, with half the sites overlooking the ocean. The nearby beach is accessible by stairs. This is a phenomenal place for scuba diving and snorkeling, thanks to a nearby reef. This is also a popular spot for surfing and body surfing. Legoland is one mile away.

**Campsites, facilities:** There are 220 sites for tents or RVs up to 35 feet; some sites have full or partial hookups. Picnic tables and fire rings are provided. Drinking water, restrooms with flush toilets and showers, Wi-Fi, and a dump station are available. Lifeguard service is not provided. Garbage must be packed out. Supplies and a coin laundry are available in Carlsbad. Some facilities are wheelchair-accessible. Leashed pets are permitted, but not on the beach.

**Reservations, fees:** Reservations are accepted at 800/444-7275 ($10 reservation fee) or www.reserveamerica.com ($9 reservation fee). Developed sites are $35 per night, premium sites are $50 per night, plus $15 per night for each additional vehicle. Open year-round, with limited facilities in the winter.

**Directions:** Drive on I-5 to Carlsbad and the exit for Palomar Airport Road. Take that exit and drive west for 0.3 mile to Carlsbad Boulevard South. Turn south on Carlsbad Boulevard South and drive three miles to Poinsettia Avenue and the park entrance on the right.

**Contact:** South Carlsbad State Beach, 760/438-3143; San Diego Coast District, 619/688-3260, www.parks.ca.gov.

## 9 SAN ELIJO STATE BEACH

### Scenic rating: 9

in Cardiff by the Sea

**Map 14.1, page 769**

These are bluff-top campgrounds and about half the sites overlook the ocean. Swimming and surfing are good, with a reef nearby for snorkeling and diving. What more could you ask for? Well, for one thing, how about not so many trains? Yep, train tracks run nearby and the trains roll by several times a day. So much for tranquility. Regardless, it is a beautiful beach just north of the small town of Cardiff by the Sea. Nearby San Elijo Lagoon at Solana Beach is an ecological preserve. Though this is near a developed area, there are numerous white egrets, as well as occasional herons and other marine birds. Reservations are usually required to get a spot between Memorial Day weekend and Labor Day weekend.

**Campsites, facilities:** There are 144 sites for tents or RVs up to 22 feet (no hookups) and 28 sites for tents or RVs up to 35 feet (full hookups). A hike-in/bike-in site is available (4pm-9am, first-come, first-served, one night maximum stay). Picnic tables and fire rings are provided. Drinking water, restrooms with flush toilets and coin showers, Wi-Fi, coin laundry, dump station, and a small store are available. Lifeguard service is not provided. Garbage must be packed out. Some facilities are wheelchair-accessible. Leashed pets are permitted, but not on the beach.

**Reservations, fees:** Reservations are accepted at 800/444-7275 ($10 reservation fee) or www.reserveamerica.com ($9 reservation fee). Inland sites are $35 per night, inland RV sites (hookups) are $60 per night, ocean sites are $50 per night, and ocean RV sites (hookups) are $75 per night, plus $15 per night for each additional vehicle. Call for the hike-in/bike-in fee. Open year-round.

**Directions:** Drive on I-5 to Encinitas and the Encinitas Boulevard exit. Take that exit and drive west on Encinitas Boulevard for one mile to U.S. 101 (South Coast Highway). Turn south (left) on U.S. 101 and drive two miles to the park on the right.

**Contact:** San Elijo State Beach, 760/753-5091; San Diego Coast District, 619/688-3260 or 760/720-7001, www.parks.ca.gov.

## 10 SANTEE LAKES RECREATION PRESERVE

### Scenic rating: 8

near Santee

**Map 14.1, page 769**

This is a 190-acre park built around a complex of seven lakes. The park is best known for fishing; lakes are stocked with large numbers of trout and catfish, with fantastic lake records including a 39-pound catfish, 13-pound rainbow trout, 13.9-pound largemouth bass, and 2.5-pound bluegill. Rowboats, pedal boats, kayaks, and canoes are available for rent. So how many lakes can you boat on? Answer: Only one, Lake 5. Fishing is allowed on all lakes, and float tubing is permitted for campers only on four lakes. No swimming or water/body contact is allowed and no private motorized boats are permitted.

This small regional park lies 20 miles east of San Diego at a 400-foot elevation and receives more than 100,000 visitors per year. The

Carlton Oaks Country Club is half a mile away and is open to the public.

**Campsites, facilities:** There are 300 sites with full hookups (50 amps) for RVs of any length and nine tent sites. Some sites are pull-through and some campsites are lakefront. Ten cabins are also available. Picnic tables are provided and some sites have barbecue grills. Restrooms with flush toilets and showers, drinking water, dump station, boat rentals, seven playgrounds, seasonal swimming pool, general store, picnic area, amphitheater, RV storage, recreation center, Wi-Fi, pay phone, propane, and coin laundry are available. Some facilities are wheelchair-accessible. Leashed pets are permitted in the campground.

**Reservations, fees:** Reservations are accepted at 619/596-3141 and www.santeelakes. com. RV sites are $45-60 per night and include pull-through, deluxe (pull-through and back-in), lakefront sites, and back-in sites. Lakefront cabins and floating cabins range $125-150 per night, a camping club site is $37 per night, plus $2 per night for each additional vehicle and $1 per pet per night. Discounts are offered Sunday through Thursday. Weekly and monthly rates are available. Some credit cards are accepted. Open year-round.

**Directions:** Drive on I-8 to El Cajon and Highway 67. Take the Highway 67 exit north (toward Santee) and drive one mile to Bradley Avenue. Take that exit and drive a short distance to Bradley Avenue. Turn left and drive one mile to Cuyamaca Street. Turn right and drive 1.6 miles to Mission Gorge Road. Turn left (west) and drive 0.3 mile to Fanita Parkway. Turn right and drive a short distance to the campground entrance on the left at 9310 Fanita Parkway.

**Contact:** Santee Lakes Recreation Preserve, Padre Dam Municipal Water District, 619/596-3141, www.santeelakes.com.

## 11 CAMPLAND ON THE BAY

### Scenic rating: 8

on Mission Bay

**Map 14.1, page 769**     **BEST (**

This is one of the biggest campgrounds this side of the galaxy. The place has a prime location overlooking Kendall Frost Wildlife Preserve and is set on Mission Bay, a beautiful spot that's a boater's paradise with a private beach. Waterskiing, sailboarding, and ocean access for deep-sea fishing are preeminent. SeaWorld, just north of San Diego, offers a premium side trip. This campground is consistently rated one of San Diego's best.

**Campsites, facilities:** There are more than 558 sites, most with full or partial hookups (30 and 50 amps) for tents or RVs up to 45 feet. Picnic tables and fire pits are provided. Restrooms with flush toilets and showers, drinking water, cable TV, phone, Wi-Fi, swimming pools, spa, recreation hall, arcade, playground, café, dump station, coin laundry, grocery store, amphitheater, RV and boat storage, RV supplies, propane gas, boat ramp, marina, boat docks, water toy rentals, boat and bike rentals, and organized activities and events are available. Leashed pets are permitted, with certain restrictions.

**Reservations, fees:** Reservations are accepted at 800/422-9386 ($25 site-guarantee fee), online (www.campland.com), or by fax to 858/581-4206. RV sites are $50-417 per night, tent sites are $55-65 per night, plus $10-15 per night for each additional vehicle or boats and trailers, $10 per person per night for more than four people, and $3 per night per pet. Winter rates are discounted. Weekly rates are available during the winter. Some credit cards are accepted. Open year-round.

**Directions:** Drive on I-5 south to San Diego and the Balboa-Garnet exit. Take that exit to Mission Bay Drive and drive to Grand Avenue. Turn right and drive one mile to Olney Street. Turn left on Olney Street and drive to Pacific

Beach Drive. Turn left and drive a short distance to the campground entrance.

From northbound I-5 in San Diego, take the Grand-Garnet exit. Stay in the left lane to Grand Avenue. Turn left on Grand Avenue and drive to Olney Street. Turn left on Olney Street and continue as above.

**Contact:** Campland on the Bay, 800/422-9386, administration office 858/581-4200, fax 858/581-4206, www.campland.com.

## 12 SANTA FE PARK RV RESORT

🏊 🐕 🏃 ♿ 🚐

### Scenic rating: 5

in San Diego

Map 14.1, page 769

This resort is a short drive from a variety of side trips, including the San Diego Zoo, SeaWorld, the historic San Diego Mission and Presidio Park, golf courses, beaches, sportfishing, and Tijuana.

**Campsites, facilities:** There are 129 sites with full hookups (20, 30, and 50 amps) for RVs up to 40 feet (at three pull-through sites). RVs must not be older than 15 years. Picnic tables and barbecues are provided. Restrooms with flush toilets and showers, drinking water, playground, heated swimming pool, spa, dump station, satellite TV, Wi-Fi, recreation room, mini theater, fitness center, and coin laundry are available. Some facilities are wheelchair-accessible. Leashed pets under 25 pounds are permitted, with some restrictions.

**Reservations, fees:** Reservations are accepted online or at 800/959-3787. RV sites (hookups) and pull-through RV sites (hookups) are $74-105 per night, plus $4 per person per night for more than three people and $3.50 per pet per night. Discounts are offered on weekdays and in the off-season. Weekly and monthly rates are available. Some credit cards are accepted. Open year-round.

**Directions:** Drive on I-5 south to San Diego and Exit 23 for Balboa-Garnet. Take that exit,

get in the left lane, and drive a short distance to the second stoplight and Damon Street. Turn left and drive 0.25 mile to Santa Fe Street. Turn left and drive 1.4 miles to the resort on the right (5707 Santa Fe Street).

On northbound I-5, drive to Exit 23 for Grand-Garnet. Take that exit and continue as it feeds to East Mission Bay Drive. Continue through four traffic signals to Damon Street. Turn right and drive 0.25 mile to Santa Fe Street. Turn left and drive 1.4 miles to the resort on the right (5707 Santa Fe Street). Note: On Santa Fe Street, disregard the sign for "Not a through street."

**Contact:** Santa Fe Park RV Resort, 858/272-4051 or 800/959-3787, www.santafepark.com.

## 13 SAN DIEGO METROPOLITAN KOA

🚲 🏊 🏕 🐕 🏃 ♿ 🚐 ⛺

### Scenic rating: 6

in Chula Vista

Map 14.1, page 769

This is one in a series of parks set up primarily for RVs cruising I-5. Chula Vista is between Mexico and San Diego, allowing visitors to make side trips east to Lower Otay Lake, north to the San Diego attractions, south to Tijuana, or "around the corner" on Highway 75 to Silver Strand State Beach. Nearby San Diego Bay is beautiful, with excellent waterskiing (in designated areas), sailboarding, and a great swimming beach.

**Campsites, facilities:** There are 200 sites for RVs of any length (full hookups), 63 sites for tents, 27 cabins, and eight lodges. Many sites are pull-through. Picnic tables and barbecue grills are provided. Restrooms with flush toilets and showers, drinking water, Wi-Fi, playground, dump station, coin laundry, heated swimming pool, spa, bike rentals, propane gas, seasonal organized activities, and convenience store are available. Some facilities are wheelchair-accessible. Leashed pets are permitted.

**Reservations, fees:** Reservations are accepted

at 800/562-9877. RV sites (hookups) are $50-80 per night, tent sites are $45-60 per night, plus $5 per night for each additional vehicle. Camping cabins are $75-110 per night, and lodges are $125-210 per night. Off-season discounts are offered. Some credit cards are accepted. Open year-round.

**Directions:** From I-5 in Chula Vista, take the exit for E Street and drive east on E Street for three miles to 2nd Avenue. Turn left (north) on 2nd Avenue and drive 0.75 mile to the park on the right (111 North 2nd Avenue).

**Contact:** San Diego Metropolitan KOA, 619/427-3601, www.sandiegokoa.com.

## 14 CHULA VISTA RV RESORT

🚲 🏊 ⛵ 🛶 🎣 🐕 🛝 ♿ 🚐 🏪

### Scenic rating: 8

in Chula Vista

**Map 14.1, page 769**

This RV park is about 50 yards from San Diego Bay, a beautiful, calm piece of water where waterskiing is permitted in designated areas. Each site is landscaped to provide some privacy. The park has its own marina with 552 slips. An excellent swimming beach is available, and conditions in the afternoon for sailboarding are also excellent. Bike paths are nearby.

**Campsites, facilities:** There are 237 sites with full hookups (30 and 50 amps) for RVs. Some sites are pull-through. No tents are permitted. Picnic tables and cable TV are provided. Restrooms with flush toilets and showers, drinking water, Wi-Fi, fitness center, playgrounds, heated swimming pool and spa, game room, two waterfront restaurants, marina, fishing pier, free boat launch, coin laundry, propane gas, bicycle rentals, car rentals, picnic area, meeting rooms, and general store are available. Some facilities are wheelchair-accessible. Leashed pets up to 20 pounds are permitted, with certain restrictions.

**Reservations, fees:** Reservations are accepted at 800/770-2878 or www.chulavistarv.com (deposit required). RV sites are $75-99, plus $3 per night per additional person for more than four people, $3 per night for each additional vehicle, and $3 per pet per night. Boat slips are $1-2 per foot per night. Weekly and monthly rates are available. Off-season discounts are offered. Some credit cards are accepted. Open year-round.

**Directions:** Drive on I-5 to Chula Vista and the exit for J Street/Marina Parkway. Take that exit, turn left, and drive 0.5 mile west to Sandpiper Way. Turn left and drive a short distance to the park on the left (460 Sandpiper Way).

**Contact:** Chula Vista RV Resort, 619/422-0111, www.chulavistarv.com.

## 15 LA PACIFICA RV RESORT

🏊 🐕 ♿ 🚐 🏪

### Scenic rating: 6

in San Ysidro

**Map 14.1, page 769**

This RV park is less than two miles from the Mexican border. Note that many sites are filled with long-term renters, but some sites are available for overnight use.

**Campsites, facilities:** There are 179 sites with full hookups (30 and 50 amps) for RVs up to 40 feet. Many sites are pull-through. Picnic tables are provided at most sites. Restrooms with flush toilets and showers, heated swimming pool, whirlpool, clubhouse, video and book library, cable TV, Wi-Fi, recreation room, dump station, coin laundry, and propane gas are available. All facilities are wheelchair-accessible. Leashed pets are permitted with restrictions.

**Reservations, fees:** Reservations are accepted at 888/786-6997 or online; group reservations must be made by phone. RV sites are $39-49 per night, plus $5 per person for more than four people. Weekly and monthly rates are available. Credit cards are accepted. Open year-round.

**Directions:** From the San Diego area, drive south on I-5 to San Ysidro and the exit for Dairymart Road. Take that exit east to Dairymart Road and drive a short distance to

San Ysidro Boulevard. Turn left and drive to the park on the left.

**Contact:** La Pacifica RV Resort, 1010 San Ysidro Boulevard, 619/428-4411, www.lapacificarvresortpark.com.

## 16 DRIPPING SPRINGS

### Scenic rating: 7

near the Agua Tibia Wilderness in Cleveland National Forest

**Map 14.2, page 770**

This is one of the premium Forest Service camps available, set just inside the national forest border near Vail Lake and adjacent to the Agua Tibia Wilderness. Dripping Springs Trail is routed south out of camp, starting at 1,600 feet elevation and climbing near the peak of Agua Tibia Mountain, at 4,779 feet.

**Campsites, facilities:** There are 33 sites for tents or RVs up to 22 feet (no hookups), including several double sites and five equestrian sites. Picnic tables and fire rings are provided. Drinking water and vault toilets are available. Supplies are nearby in Temecula. Leashed pets are permitted.

**Reservations, fees:** Reservations are accepted at 877/444-6777 ($10 reservation fee) or www.recreation.gov ($9 reservation fee). Sites are $15-30 per night, plus $5 per night per additional vehicle. Open June through February (closed March through May for protection of an endangered species, the arroyo southwestern toad).

**Directions:** From I-15 in Temecula, drive 11 miles southeast on Highway 79 to the campground.

**Contact:** Cleveland National Forest, Palomar Ranger District, 760/788-0250, www.fs.usda.gov/cleveland.

## 17 OAK GROVE

### Scenic rating: 4

near Temecula Creek in Cleveland National Forest

**Map 14.2, page 770**

Oak Grove campground is on the northeastern fringe of Cleveland National Forest at 2,800 feet elevation. Easy access from Highway 79 makes this a popular camp. The Palomar Observatory is five miles up the mountain to the west, but there is no direct way to reach it from the campground and it cannot be viewed from camp. Lake Henshaw is about a half-hour drive to the south. A boat ramp and boat rentals are available there.

**Campsites, facilities:** There are 81 sites for tents, including 12 double sites, or RVs up to 32 feet (no hookups). Picnic tables and fire grills are provided. Drinking water and flush toilets are available. Propane gas and groceries are nearby. Leashed pets are permitted.

**Reservations, fees:** Reservations are accepted at 877/444-6777 ($10 reservation fee) or www.recreation.gov ($9 reservation fee). Sites are $15-30 per night, plus $5 per night per additional vehicle. Open year-round.

**Directions:** Drive on I-15 to the Highway 79 exit. Take that exit and drive south on Highway 79 to Aguanga. Continue southeast on Highway 79 for 6.5 miles to the camp entrance.

**Contact:** Cleveland National Forest, Palomar Ranger District, 760/788-0250, www.fs.usda.gov/cleveland.

## 18 INDIAN FLATS

### Scenic rating: 5

near the Pacific Crest Trail in Cleveland National Forest

**Map 14.2, page 770**

Indian Flats is a remote campground at 3,600 feet elevation just north of Pine Mountain. The Pacific Crest Trail passes only two miles down the road to the south. A two-mile hike south on the PCT will take you down into a canyon and the home of Agua Caliente Creek.

**Campsites, facilities:** There are 17 sites for tents or RVs up to 15 feet and a group site for 20-50 people. Picnic tables and fire grills are provided. Vault toilets are available. There is no drinking water. Leashed pets are permitted.

**Reservations, fees:** Reservations are not accepted. Sites are $12 per night, plus $5 per night per additional vehicle. Open June through February (closed March through May for protection of an endangered species, the arroyo southwestern toad).

**Directions:** From El Cajon, drive east on I-8 to Highway 79 (near Descanso Junction). Turn north on Highway 79 and drive to the town of Warner Springs. Continue two miles on Highway 79 to Forest Road 9S05. Turn right on Forest Road 9S05 and drive six miles to the campground.

**Contact:** Cleveland National Forest, Palomar Ranger District, 760/788-0250, www.fs.usda.gov/cleveland.

## 19 PALOMAR MOUNTAIN STATE PARK
🚶 🚴 ⛵ 🏕 ♿ 🚐 ⛺

**Scenic rating: 5**

near the Palomar Observatory

**Map 14.2, page 770**

The long-distance views from Palomar Mountain State Park are spectacular. The park features 14 miles of trails, including several loop trails. This camp offers some fishing in Doane Pond (state fishing laws are in effect here—great for youngsters learning to fish). There are numerous hikes, including Boucher Trail (four miles) and Lower Doane Valley Trail (three miles). The view from Boucher Lookout is stunning, at 5,438 feet elevation looking out over the valley below. This developed state park is a short drive from the Palomar Observatory (not part of the park). There are four other campgrounds in the immediate area. At the Palomar Observatory you'll find the 200-inch Hale Telescope, America's largest telescope. This is a private, working telescope, run by the California Institute of Technology. Observatory tours are available, and the telescope can be viewed (but not used) by the public. The campground elevation is 4,700 feet.

**Campsites, facilities:** There are 32 sites for tents or RVs up to 27 feet (no hookups) and trailers up to 24 feet, three group sites for 15-25 people, and one hike-in/bike-in site. Picnic tables, fire grills, and food lockers are provided. Drinking water and restrooms with flush toilets and coin showers are available. Some facilities are wheelchair-accessible. Leashed pets are permitted in the campground but not on trails.

**Reservations, fees:** Reservations are accepted at 800/444-7275 ($10 reservation fee) or www.reserveamerica.com ($9 reservation fee) and are recommended for Cedar Grove Group (April through November) and for Doane Valley (April through October). Sites are $30 per night, plus $8 per night for each additional vehicle. It's $5 per night for the hike-in site and $90-145 per night for group sites. A fishing license is required for fishing pond; buy one before arrival. Open year-round.

**Directions:** Drive on I-15 to the Highway 76 exit (east of Oceanside). Take that exit and drive east on Highway 76 for approximately 25 miles to County Road S6 (which brings you to the top of Palomar Mountain). At the top of the mountain, turn left and drive about 50 feet to State Park Road/County Road S7. Turn left on State Park Road/County Road S7 and drive about 3.5 miles to the park entrance.

**Contact:** Palomar Mountain State Park, 760/742-3462, Colorado Desert District, 760/767-4087; Palomar Observatory, 760/742-2119, www.parks.ca.gov; Friends of Palomar Mountain State Park, www.friendsofpalomarsp.org.

## 20 FRY CREEK

### Scenic rating: 6

near the Palomar Observatory in Cleveland National Forest

**Map 14.2, page 770**

A small, seasonal stream, Fry Creek, runs near this camp at 5,200 feet elevation. On a clear night, you can see forever from Palomar Mountain. Literally. That's because the Palomar Observatory, just a short distance from this forested camp, houses America's largest telescope. With the 200-inch Hale Telescope, it is possible for scientists to see 100 billion galaxies. It is open to public touring (check for current hours), but you cannot touch the telescope.

**Campsites, facilities:** There are 20 sites for tents or RVs up to 15 feet. No trailers are allowed. Picnic tables and fire rings are provided. Drinking water and vault toilets are available. A store and coin showers are nearby. Leashed pets are permitted.

**Reservations, fees:** Reservations are accepted at 877/444-6777 ($10 reservation fee) or www.recreation.gov ($9 reservation fee). Sites are $15 per night, plus $5 per night per additional vehicle. Open April through November, weather permitting.

**Directions:** Drive on I-15 to the Highway 76 exit (east of Oceanside). Take that exit and drive east on Highway 76 for 25 miles to County Road S6 (which brings you to the top of Palomar Mountain). Turn left on County Road S6 and drive about nine miles to the campground entrance on the left. The road is not recommended for trailers.

**Contact:** Cleveland National Forest, Palomar Ranger District, 760/788-0250, www.fs.usda.gov/cleveland.

## 21 OBSERVATORY

### Scenic rating: 6

near the Palomar Observatory in Cleveland National Forest

**Map 14.2, page 770**

This Forest Service camp is a popular spot for campers visiting the nearby Palomar Observatory, which houses the largest telescope in America. The elevation is 4,800 feet. There are four other camps in the immediate area. The trailhead for Observatory Trail starts at this camp: a two-hour hike to the observatory with one short, steep climb, highlighted by a vista deck with a sweeping view of Mendenhall Valley, and then onward to the top and to the viewing area to catch a glimpse of the telescope. Tours are available, but the telescope itself is not open to the public. Part of the campground has been converted into an "astronomy-friendly" environment: Bright lights (lanterns and white lights) are not permitted after 9pm in the north end of the campground. The campground hosts monthly star parties, where you can camp and spend the night viewing the cosmos and learning about the stars.

**Campsites, facilities:** There are 37 sites for tents or RVs up to 27 feet (no hookups). Picnic tables and fire grills are provided. Drinking water and restrooms with flush toilets and coin showers (high season only) are available. Some facilities are wheelchair-accessible. Leashed pets are permitted.

**Reservations, fees:** Reservations are accepted at 877/444-6777 or www.recreation.gov ($9 reservation fee). Single sites are $15 per night; double sites are $30 per night. Open May through November.

**Directions:** Drive on I-15 to the Highway 76 exit (east of Oceanside). Take that exit and drive east on Highway 76 for 25 miles to County Road S6 (which brings you to the top of Palomar Mountain). Turn left on County Road S6 and drive about 8.5 miles to the campground entrance on the right. The road is not recommended for large trailers.

**Contact:** Cleveland National Forest, Palomar Ranger District, 760/788-0250, www.fs.usda.gov/cleveland.

## 22 CRESTLINE GROUP CAMP

### Scenic rating: 6

near the Palomar Observatory in Cleveland National Forest

**Map 14.2, page 770**

This Forest Service camp is designed expressly for large groups. (For adventure information, see the Palomar Mountain State Park listing in this chapter.) The elevation is 4,800 feet.

**Campsites, facilities:** One group site for tents or RVs up to 27 feet accommodates up to 50 people. Picnic tables and fire grills are provided. Drinking water and vault toilets are available. Some facilities are wheelchair-accessible. A store is nearby. Leashed pets are permitted.

**Reservations, fees:** Reservations are required at 877/444-6777 ($10 reservation fee) or www.recreation.gov ($9 reservation fee). The site is $75 per night. Open May through November.

**Directions:** Drive on I-15 to the Highway 76 exit (east of Oceanside). Take that exit and drive east on Highway 76 for 25 miles to County Road S6 (which brings you to the top of Palomar Mountain). Turn left on County Road S6 and drive about 6.5 miles to the campground at the junction of County Roads S6 and S7. The road is not recommended for trailers.

**Contact:** Cleveland National Forest, Palomar Ranger District, 760/788-0250, www.fs.usda.gov/cleveland.

## 23 OAK KNOLL

### Scenic rating: 6

near the Palomar Observatory

**Map 14.2, page 770**

Oak Knoll campground is at 3,000 feet

elevation in San Diego County foothill country among giant old California oaks. It is at the western base of Palomar Mountain, and to visit the Palomar Observatory and its awesome 200-inch telescope requires a remarkably twisty 10-mile drive up the mountain (the telescope is not open to the public, but the observatory is open). The campground management suggests you bring your telescope or borrow one of theirs for nighttime stargazing. A good side trip is the Boucher Lookout in Palomar Mountain State Park. Trailheads for hikes on Palomar Mountain include Observatory Trail (starting at Observatory) and Doane Valley Loop (starting in Palomar Mountain State Park).

**Campsites, facilities:** There are 46 sites for tents or RVs up to 35 feet; many sites have full or partial hookups (30 amps). Picnic tables and fire barrels (some with built-in grills) are provided. Drinking water, restrooms with flush toilets and coin showers, library, video arcade, Wi-Fi, recreation hall, pavilion, seasonal activities, playground, swimming pool, baseball diamond, horseshoes, basketball court, coin laundry, propane gas, and camp store are available. Leashed pets are permitted, with certain restrictions.

**Reservations, fees:** Reservations are accepted. Sites are $25-45 per night, plus $5 per person per night for more than two people, $5 per night for each additional vehicle, and $3 per pet per night. Cabins are $119-139 per night. Monthly rates are available. Open year-round.

**Directions:** Drive on I-15 to the Highway 76 exit (east of Oceanside). Take that exit and drive east on Highway 76 for 21 miles to South Grade Road/County Road S6. Turn left and drive a short distance to the campground on the left.

**Contact:** Oak Knoll Campground, 760/742-3437, www.oakknoll.net.

## 24 WOODS VALLEY KAMPGROUND

**Scenic rating: 5**

near Lake Wohlford

Map 14.2, page 770

This privately operated 20-acre park is popular with families. Lake Wohlford is about 10 miles to the south and has a lake speed limit of 5 mph. When full, the lake is stocked with rainbow trout, brown trout, steelhead, channel catfish, and blue catfish. Insider's tip: A bald eagle winters at Lake Wohlford.

**Campsites, facilities:** There are 59 sites for RVs of any length and 30 sites for tents. Three group sites accommodate 10-18 people each. Many of the RV sites have partial hookups, and some have full hookups (30 amps). Picnic tables and fire barrels are provided. Drinking water, restrooms with flush toilets and showers, dump station, coin laundry, swimming pool, catch-and-release fishing pond, small animal farm, playground, volleyball, horseshoes, recreation hall, group facilities, and supplies are available. Leashed pets are permitted, with some dogs prohibited.

**Reservations, fees:** Reservations are accepted. Sites are $31-45 per night, plus $3 for each additional person, $3 per night for each additional vehicle, and $3 per pet per night. The group sites are $290-522 per night. Weekly and monthly rates are available. Open year-round.

**Directions:** From San Diego, drive north on I-15 to the Escondido area, take the Via Rancho Parkway exit, and continue to Via Rancho Parkway. Turn right (name changes to Bear Valley Parkway) and drive approximately nine miles to a T intersection and Valley Parkway. Turn right on Valley Parkway and drive approximately six miles (name changes to Valley Center Road) to Woods Valley Road. Turn right and drive 2.2 miles to the park on the left.

**Contact:** Woods Valley Kampground, 760/749-2905, www.woodsvalley.com.

## 25 LAKE HENSHAW RESORT

**Scenic rating: 7**

near Santa Ysabel

Map 14.2, page 770

Lake Henshaw has only one camp, but it's a good one (with cabin rentals a big plus). The camp is on the southern corner of the lake, at 2,727 feet elevation near Cleveland National Forest. Like many reservoirs, Lake Henshaw is often plagued by low water levels, and drought only makes it worse. When it's full, swimming, water-body contact, canoes, and rafts are not permitted and a 10-mph speed limit is in effect. The fishing is best for catfish, especially in the summer, and at times decent for bass, with the lake-record bass weighing 14 pounds, 4 ounces. Other fish species are trout, bluegill, and crappie. A mobile home park is also on the premises.

**Campsites, facilities:** There are four acres of open sites for tents or RVs of any length (no hookups) and 16 sites with full hookups (20 amps) for tents or RVs up to 28 feet. Cabins are also available. Picnic tables and fire pits are provided. Restrooms with flush toilets and showers, cabins, swimming pool, spa, picnic area, clubhouse, playground, dump station, coin laundry, propane gas, boat and motor rentals, boat launch, bait and tackle, café, and convenience store are available. Some facilities are wheelchair-accessible. A golf course is 10 miles away. Leashed pets are permitted.

**Reservations, fees:** Reservations are not accepted. RV sites are $25 per night, tent sites are $20 per night, plus $1 per additional person per night, $2 per pet per night, and $7.50 per person per day for lake use. Weekly rates are available. Boat launching is $5 per day. Cabins are $65-87 per night. Some credit cards are accepted. Open year-round.

**Directions:** From Santa Ysabel, drive seven miles north on Highway 79 to Highway 76. Turn east on Highway 76 and drive four miles to the campground on the left.

**Contact:** Lake Henshaw Resort, 760/782-3501, www.lakehenshawresort.com.

## 26 STAGECOACH TRAILS

🧍🏊🎠♿🚐🏕️

### Scenic rating: 6

near Julian

**Map 14.2, page 770**

You want space? You've got space. That includes 600,000 acres of public lands bordering this RV campground, making Stagecoach Trails Resort ideal for those who love horseback riding and hiking. Forty corrals and two round pens at the campground let you know right away that this camp is very horse-friendly. It is more than a horse camp, however, with amenities for various types of campers. The resort provides the perfect jumping-off place for trips into neighboring Anza-Borrego Desert State Park and onto the Pacific Crest Trail, which is 2.5 miles away. The resort's name comes from its proximity to the old Wells Fargo Butterfield Stage Route. While the scenic rating merits a 6, if the rating were based purely on cleanliness, professionalism, and friendliness, this resort would rate a 10.

**Campsites, facilities:** There are 250 sites with full hookups (30 amps) for RVs of any length, along with a large dispersed camping area for tents. Most RV sites are pull-through. Other choices include wagon cabins and camp cabins. Picnic tables and fire rings are provided. Drinking water, restrooms with flush toilets and showers, a heated pool, 40 horse corrals, a roping area, guided horseback riding, convenience store, ATM, coin laundry, Wi-Fi, group facilities, horseshoe pits, shuffleboard, 24-hour security, and propane gas are available. Some facilities are wheelchair-accessible. Leashed pets are permitted.

**Reservations, fees:** Reservations are accepted. RV sites are $37 per night (fee for electricity), tent sites are $27 per night, plus $3 per person per night for more than four people (six people maximum) and $10 per night per horse.

Cabins are $35-145 per night. Some credit cards are accepted. Open year-round.

**Directions:** From Santa Ysabel, turn north on Highway 79 and drive 14 miles to County Road S2/San Felipe Road. Turn right and drive 17 miles to Highway 78. Turn right (west, toward Julian) and drive 0.3 mile to County Road S2 (Great Southern Overland Stage Route). Turn left and drive four miles to the resort on the right (at mile marker 21 on Road S2). Note: There are various ways to get here. Since equestrian campers towing horse trailers and other campers may need alternative directions, and those not towing rigs might want shortcut directions, call the resort for driving details.

**Contact:** Stagecoach Trails Park, 760/765-3765, www.stagecoachtrails.com.

## 27 PINEZANITA RV PARK AND CAMPGROUNDS

🎣🐕🚐🏕️

### Scenic rating: 6

near Julian

**Map 14.2, page 770**

Set at an elevation of 4,680 feet in dense pine and oak, this camp has had the same owners, the Stanley family, for more than 30 years. The fishing pond is a great attraction for kids (no license is required); no swimming allowed. The pond is stocked with bluegill and catfish, some of which are 12 inches or longer. Two possible side trips include Lake Cuyamaca, five miles to the south, and William Heise County Park, about 10 miles to the north as the crow flies.

**Campsites, facilities:** There are 210 sites with full or partial hookups (30 and 50 amps) for RVs, 32 sites for tents, and three cottages. Picnic tables and fire rings are provided. Restrooms with flush toilets and showers, drinking water, a general store, ice, propane, bait and tackle, fishing pond, and dump station are available. Leashed pets are permitted, but not in the cottages.

**Reservations, fees:** Reservations are accepted by phone only. Sites are $25 per night per vehicle, plus $5 per night for electricity, $2 for sewer hookup, $3 per night per person for more than two people, and $3 per night per pet, with a maximum of three pets. Cottages are $145-165 per night with a $50 deposit. Some credit cards are accepted. Open year-round.

**Directions:** From El Cajon, drive east on I-8 to Highway 79 (near Descanso Junction). Turn north on Highway 79 and drive 20 miles to Julian and the campground on the left.

**Contact:** Pinezanita RV Park and Campgrounds, 760/765-0429, www.pinezanita.com.

## 28 WILLIAM HEISE COUNTY PARK

### Scenic rating: 6

near Julian

**Map 14.2, page 770**

This beautiful county park at 4,200 feet elevation offers hiking trails and a playground, all amid woodlands with a mix of oak and pine. Cabins provide a bonus opportunity for those who do not want to tent camp. A great hike starts right at camp (at the tent camping area), signed "Nature Trail." It joins Canyon Oak Trail and, after little more than a mile, links with Desert View Trail. You will reach an overlook with a view of the Anza-Borrego Desert and the Salton Sea. The park features more than 900 acres of mountain forests of oak, pine, and cedar. A popular equestrian trail is Kelly Ditch Trail, which is linked to Cuyamaca Rancho State Park and Lake Cuyamaca. The vast Anza-Borrego Desert State Park lies to the east, and the historical mining town of Julian is five miles away. Julian is known for its Apple Day Festival each fall.

**Campsites, facilities:** There are 21 sites with partial hookups (30 amps) for tents or RVs up to 40 feet, 40 sites for tents or RVs up to 40 feet (no hookups), 41 sites for tents only, two youth group sites for up to 30 people each, and six cabins. Group camping (at least 10 sites) is available by reservation. Picnic tables and fire grills are provided. Restrooms with flush toilets and showers, drinking water, coin laundry, dump station, picnic areas, and a playground are available. Supplies are available five miles away in Julian. Leashed pets are permitted.

**Reservations, fees:** Reservations are accepted and are required for group sites at 877/565-3600 ($5 reservation fee). RV sites (partial hookups) are $34 per night, tent and RV sites (without hookups) are $27 per night, the youth and group sites are $55-100 per night, and cabins are $67 per night, plus $1 per pet per night. Discounts for seniors and travelers with disabilities are available. Some credit cards are accepted. Open year-round.

**Directions:** From El Cajon, drive east on I-8 to Highway 79 (near Descanso Junction). Turn north on Highway 79 and drive to Julian and Highway 78. Turn west (left) on Highway 78 and drive to Pine Hills Road. Turn left (south) on Pine Hills Road and drive two miles to Frisius Drive. Turn left (south) on Frisius Drive and drive two miles to the park.

**Contact:** San Diego County Parks and Recreation Department, 760/765-0650, www.sdparks.org.

## 29 DOS PICOS COUNTY PARK

### Scenic rating: 5

near Ramona

**Map 14.2, page 770**

*Dos picos* means "two peaks," and this park is the highlight of a landscape featuring old groves of oaks and steep, boulder-strewn mountain slopes. Some of the oaks are 300 years old. The park covers 78 acres and has a nature trail. As a county park, this camp is often missed. The park is quite picturesque, with plenty of shade trees and a small pond. Fishing is allowed in the pond, but swimming is prohibited. Several nearby recreation options are in the area, including Lake Poway and Lake Sutherland. The elevation is 1,500 feet.

**Campsites, facilities:** There are 57 sites (partial hookups) for RVs to 40 feet, 11 sites for tents or RVs up to 40 feet (no hookups), one youth group area for up to 25 people, and two cabins. Group camping (at least 10 sites) is available by reservation. Picnic tables and fire grills are provided. Restrooms with flush toilets and showers, drinking water, dump station, playground, horseshoes, and soccer field are available. Supplies and a coin laundry are one mile away in Ramona. Leashed pets are permitted.

**Reservations, fees:** Reservations are accepted and are required for group sites at 877/565-3600 ($5 reservation fee). RV sites with partial hookups are $34 per night, tent sites and RV sites (without hookups) are $27 per night, the youth and group sites are $55-100 per night, and cabins are $67 per night, plus $1 per pet per night. Discounts for seniors and campers with disabilities are available. Some credit cards are accepted. Open year-round.

**Directions:** From I-8 in El Cajon, take the exit for Highway 67 and drive north for 22 miles to Mussey Grade Road. Turn right (a sharp turn) on Mussey Grade Road and drive two miles to the park.

**Contact:** San Diego County Parks Department, Dos Picos County Park, 760/789-2220, www.sdparks.org.

## 30 PASO PICACHO

🏃 🚵 🏊 🐕 🚐 ⛺

### Scenic rating: 6

in Cuyamaca Rancho State Park

**Map 14.2, page 770**

This camp is at 5,000 feet elevation in Cuyamaca Rancho State Park, best known for Cuyamaca Peak, at 6,512 feet. Stonewall Peak Trail is accessible from across the street. This five-mile (sun-exposed) round-trip features a climb to the summit at 5,700 feet. Long-distance views are highlighted by the Salton Sea and the Anza-Borrego State Desert. It's the most popular hike in the park, a fair to moderate grade, and is completed by a lot of families.

Another, more ambitious, hike is the trail up to Cuyamaca Peak, starting at the southern end of the campground, a 6.5-mile round-trip tromp (alas, on a paved road—at least it's closed to traffic) with a climb of 1,600 feet in the process. The view from the top is breathtaking, with the Pacific Ocean and Mexico visible to the west and south, respectively. *Cuyamaca* means "the rain beyond."

**Campsites, facilities:** There are 85 sites for tents or RVs up to 30 feet long and 10 feet tall (no hookups), five cabins, a nature den cabin, and four wood cabins. Fire grills and picnic tables are provided. Restrooms with flush toilets and coin showers, drinking water, Wi-Fi, and dump station are available. Supplies are nearby in Cuyamaca. Leashed pets are permitted.

**Reservations, fees:** Site reservations for April through November are accepted at 800/444-7275 ($10 reservation fee) or www.reserveamerica.com ($9 reservation fee). December through March, sites are first-come, first-served. Sites are $30 per night. Equestrian sites are $35 per night, plus $8 per night for each additional vehicle. Group sites are $355 per night. Open year-round.

**Directions:** From El Cajon, drive east on I-8 to Highway 79 (near Descanso Junction). Turn north (left) and drive 13.5 miles to the park entrance on the left.

**Contact:** Cuyamaca Rancho State Park, 760/765-3020, www.parks.ca.gov or www.crspia.org.

## 31 GREEN VALLEY

🏃 🚵 🏊 🐕 ♿ 🚐 ⛺

### Scenic rating: 6

in Cuyamaca Rancho State Park

**Map 14.2, page 770**

Cuyamaca Peak (6,512 feet) looms overhead to the northwest of this camp. A trailhead is available (look for the picnic area) at the camp (elevation 4,000 feet) for an easy five-minute walk to Green Valley Falls, and it can be continued out to the Sweetwater River in a 1.5-mile round-trip. The park covers 25,000 acres with trails for hiking, mountain biking, and horseback riding. Green Valley is the southernmost camp in Cuyamaca Rancho State Park.

**Campsites, facilities:** There are 81 sites for tents or RVs up to 30 feet long and 10 feet tall (no hookups), 15 equestrian sites, four cabins, and one hike-in/bike-in site. Picnic tables and fire grills are provided. Restrooms with flush toilets and coin showers, drinking water, Wi-Fi, and a dump station are available. A store and propane gas are nearby. Some facilities are wheelchair-accessible. Leashed pets are permitted.

**Reservations, fees:** Reservations are accepted at 800/444-7275 ($10 reservation fee) or www.reserveamerica.com ($9 reservation fee). Sites are $30 per night, equestrian sites are $35 per night, plus $8 per night for each additional vehicle, and $5 per person per night for the hike-in/bike-in site. Open April through November.

**Directions:** From El Cajon, drive east on I-8 to Highway 79 (near Descanso Junction). Turn north (left) on Highway 79 and drive seven miles to the campground entrance on the left (near mile marker 4).

**Contact:** Cuyamaca Rancho State Park, 760/765-3020, www.parks.ca.gov or www.crspia.org.

## 32 LAGUNA

**Scenic rating: 6**

near Little Laguna Lake in Cleveland National Forest

**Map 14.2, page 770**

Laguna is set on Little Laguna Lake, one of the few lakes in America where "Little" is part of its official name. That's because for years everybody always referred to it as "Little Laguna Lake," and it became official. Yep, it's a "little" lake all right, a relative speck, and the lake can occasionally dry up. The camp is on its eastern side at an elevation of 5,550 feet. A trailhead for the Pacific Crest Trail is a mile north on

the Sunrise Highway. Big Laguna Lake, which is actually a pretty small lake, is one mile to the west.

**Campsites, facilities:** There are 104 sites for tents or RVs up to 40 feet (no hookups). Eight sites are limited to two people each to protect the endangered Laguna Skipper butterfly. Picnic tables and fire grills are provided. Drinking water and restrooms with flush and pit toilets and coin showers are available. A store and propane gas are nearby. Some facilities are wheelchair-accessible. Leashed pets are permitted.

**Reservations, fees:** Reservations are accepted at 877/444-6777 ($10 reservation fee) or www.recreation.gov ($9 reservation fee). Sites are $23 per night, plus $6 per night per additional vehicle and $2 per pet (for more than one). Open year-round.

**Directions:** From San Diego, drive east on I-8 about 50 miles to the Laguna Junction exit for the Sunrise Highway. Turn north on the Sunrise Highway and drive 11 miles to the town of Mount Laguna. Continue north on Sunrise Highway for 2.5 miles to the campground entrance road on the left.

**Contact:** Cleveland National Forest, Descanso Ranger District, 619/445-6235, www.fs.usda.gov/cleveland; Laguna Mountain Visitor Center, 619/473-8547.

## 33 EL PRADO GROUP CAMP

**Scenic rating: 3**

in Cleveland National Forest

**Map 14.2, page 770**

El Prado Group Camp is directly adjacent to Laguna and is an alternative to nearby Horse Heaven Group Camp. Five separate group sites are available. Certain areas are fenced off to protect habitat for the endangered Laguna Skipper butterfly. The elevation is 5,500 feet.

**Campsites, facilities:** There is one group site for tents or RVs up to 40 feet (no hookups) and four group sites for tents only that can accommodate 30-50 people each. Picnic tables and fire grills are provided. Drinking water and vault toilets are available. At Yerba Santa campground, flush toilets are available and some facilities are wheelchair-accessible. Supplies are available in Mount Laguna. Leashed pets are permitted.

**Reservations, fees:** Reservations are required at 877/444-6777 ($10 reservation fee) or www. recreation.gov ($9 reservation fee). Sites are $45-75 per night. Open Memorial Day weekend through mid-October, weather permitting.

**Directions:** From San Diego, drive east on I-8 about 50 miles to the Laguna Junction exit for the Sunrise Highway. Turn north on the Sunrise Highway and drive 11 miles to the town of Mount Laguna. Continue north on Sunrise Highway for 2.5 miles to the campground entrance road on the left.

**Contact:** Cleveland National Forest, Descanso Ranger District, 619/445-6235, www.fs.usda. gov/cleveland.

## 34 HORSE HEAVEN GROUP CAMP

🚶 🐕 � 🏕

### Scenic rating: 3

near the Pacific Crest Trail in Cleveland National Forest

**Map 14.2, page 770**

Horse Heaven is on the northeastern border of Cleveland National Forest at 5,500 feet elevation, near Mount Laguna in the Laguna Recreation Area. The Pacific Crest Trail passes near the camp. Laguna and El Prado Group Camp provide nearby options. Side-trip possibilities include visiting Little Laguna Lake to the immediate west and Desert View Picnic Area to the south at Mount Laguna. Despite its name, the campground has no equestrian sites.

**Campsites, facilities:** There are three group sites for tents or RVs up to 27 feet (no hookups) that can accommodate 40, 70, and 100 people respectively. Picnic tables and fire grills are provided. Drinking water and vault toilets

are available. You can buy supplies in Mount Laguna. Leashed pets are permitted.

**Reservations, fees:** Reservations are required at 877/444-6777 ($10 reservation fee) or www. recreation.gov ($8 reservation fee). Sites are $60-150 per night. Open Memorial Day weekend through Labor Day weekend.

**Directions:** From San Diego, drive east on I-8 about 50 miles to the Laguna Junction exit for the Sunrise Highway. Turn north on the Sunrise Highway and drive 11 miles to the town of Mount Laguna. Continue north on Sunrise Highway for two miles to the campground entrance road on the left.

**Contact:** Cleveland National Forest, Descanso Ranger District, 619/445-6235, www.fs.usda. gov/cleveland.

## 35 WOODED HILL GROUP

🚶 🐕 � 🏕

### Scenic rating: 5

near the Pacific Crest Trail in Cleveland National Forest

**Map 14.2, page 770**

This camp is on the southern flank of Mount Laguna. The Pacific Crest Trail is within one mile of Burnt Rancheria Campground, a mile up the road to the northwest. The elevation is 6,000 feet.

**Campsites, facilities:** One group site for tents or RVs up to 40 feet (no hookups) can accommodate up to 110 people. Picnic tables and fire grills are provided. Drinking water and vault toilets are available. A store is nearby. Leashed pets are permitted.

**Reservations, fees:** Reservations are required at 877/444-6777 ($10 reservation fee) or www. recreation.gov ($9 reservation fee). Sites are $110-165 per night. Open Memorial Day weekend through Labor Day weekend.

**Directions:** From San Diego, drive east on I-8 about 50 miles to the Laguna Junction exit for the Sunrise Highway. Turn north on the Sunrise Highway and drive about eight miles to the campground entrance road on the left.

**Contact:** Cleveland National Forest, Descanso Ranger District, 619/445-6235, www.fs.usda. gov/cleveland.

## 36 BURNT RANCHERIA

### Scenic rating: 6

near the Pacific Crest Trail in Cleveland National Forest

**Map 14.2, page 770**

Burnt Rancheria is high on the slopes of Mount Laguna in Cleveland National Forest, at an elevation of 6,000 feet. It is quiet and private with large, roomy sites. The Pacific Crest Trail is approximately one mile from camp. Desert View Picnic Area, a mile north, provides a good side trip. Wooded Hill Group campground is one mile away.

**Campsites, facilities:** There are 109 sites for tents or RVs up to 40 feet (no hookups). Picnic tables and fire grills are provided. Drinking water, vault toilets, and coin showers are available. Supplies are nearby in Mount Laguna. Some facilities are wheelchair-accessible. Leashed pets are permitted.

**Reservations, fees:** Reservations are accepted at 877/444-6777 ($10 reservation fee) or www. recreation.gov ($9 reservation fee). Sites are $23 per night, plus $8 per night per additional vehicle and $2 per pet (for more than one). Open mid-April through October, weather permitting.

**Directions:** From San Diego, drive east on I-8 about 50 miles to the Laguna Junction exit for the Sunrise Highway. Turn north on the Sunrise Highway and drive about 10 miles north to the campground entrance road on the right.

**Contact:** Cleveland National Forest, Descanso Ranger District, 619/445-6235, www.fs.usda. gov/cleveland.

## 37 VACATIONER RV RESORT

### Scenic rating: 3

near El Cajon

**Map 14.2, page 770**

This well-maintained resort is 25 minutes from San Diego and 40 minutes from Mexico. Discount tickets to area attractions such as the San Diego Zoo, SeaWorld, and the Wild Animal Park are available. There is the very real chance of getting highway noise if you have a site at the back of the park. The RV sites are on asphalt and gravel, and there are many shade trees. The elevation is 260 feet.

**Campsites, facilities:** There are 147 sites with full hookups (30 and 50 amps) for RVs up to 40 feet, including 13 pull-through sites. A group campground is available. Restrooms with flush toilets and showers, drinking water, coin laundry, recreation room, horseshoe pits, phone access, Wi-Fi, heated swimming pool, spa, cable TV, free video library, RV storage, and picnic area with barbecues are available. A store is nearby. Some facilities are wheelchair-accessible. Leashed pets up to 20 pounds are permitted, with certain restrictions.

**Reservations, fees:** Reservations are accepted at 877/626-4409. Standard RV sites are $50 per night; premium RV sites are $60 per night; deluxe, luxury, and elite RV sites are $65-80 per night; add $2 per person per night for more than two people, $2 per night for each additional vehicle, and $2 per pet per night. Some credit cards are accepted. Open year-round.

**Directions:** From El Cajon, drive east on I-8 for three miles to the Greenfield Drive exit. Take that exit, turn north, and drive 100 feet to East Main Street. Turn left (west) and drive 0.5 mile to the park on the left.

**Contact:** Vacationer RV Resort, 619/442-0904 or 877/626-4409, www.vacationerrv.com.

## 38 RANCHO LOS COCHES RV PARK

🏊 🐾 🚐 ⛰

### Scenic rating: 5

near Lake Jennings

**Map 14.2, page 770**

This is not your typical RV park. This place has plenty of charm and a private setting. There is an abundance of history here, too. The park land was once the smallest Mexican land grant of the 19th century. The former ranch was also once a station for the Jackass Mail and Butterfield Stage routes. Windmill House, built in 1925, is featured prominently on the property and is a local historical landmark. Nearby Lake Jennings provides an option for boaters and anglers and also has a less developed camp on its northeast shore. Vista Point on the southeastern side of the lake provides a side trip. (For more information, see the Lake Jennings County Park listing in this chapter.) Casinos are nearby.

**Campsites, facilities:** There are 142 sites with full hookups (30 and 50 amps) for RVs up to 50 feet and four tent areas. Restrooms with flush toilets and showers, drinking water, free digital cable TV, dump station, heated swimming pool, spa, recreation hall, fitness room, Frisbee golf, horseshoes, table tennis, Wi-Fi, and coin laundry are available. A store and gas station are one mile away. Leashed pets are permitted, with certain restrictions.

**Reservations, fees:** Reservations are accepted online or at 800/630-0448. RV sites (full hookups) are $45-55 per night (depending on size), tent sites are $25-30 per night, plus $3 per person per night for more than two people. Weekly and monthly rates are available. RV rentals are available. Open year-round.

**Directions:** From El Cajon, drive east on I-8 to the Los Coches Road exit. Take that exit and drive under the freeway to Highway 8 Business Route. Turn right on Highway 8 Business Route and drive 0.25 mile to the park entrance on the left (13468 Highway 8 Business).

**Contact:** Rancho Los Coches RV Park, 619/443-2025, www.rancholoscochesrv.com.

## 39 LAKE JENNINGS COUNTY PARK

🚶 🏊 🚐 🐾 ♿ 🚐 ⛰

### Scenic rating: 6

on Lake Jennings

**Map 14.2, page 770**

Lake Jennings, at 108 acres, is a nice little backyard fishing hole and recreation area set at 700 feet elevation, with easy access from I-8. Most people come here for the fishing; the lake is stocked with trout and catfish. It has quality prospects for giant catfish, as well as largemouth bass, bluegill, and, in cool months, rainbow trout. The lake-record blue catfish is 60 pounds. Note that while shore fishing is available on a daily basis, boats are permitted on the lake Friday through Sunday November through August. Night fishing is allowed on weekends during the summer. A fishing permit is required. The highlights here are evening picnics, summer catfishing, and a boat ramp and rentals. Swimming and water/body contact are prohibited. Miles of hiking trails are routed through chaparral-covered hills. Only one camp is available right at the lake, and this is it.

**Campsites, facilities:** There are 35 sites with full hookups (30 amps) for RVs up to 35 feet, 37 sites with partial hookups (20 amps) for RVs up to 25 feet, 26 tent sites, five tipis, and a youth group area for up to 35 people. Some sites are pull-through. Picnic tables and fire grills are provided. Restrooms with flush toilets and showers, drinking water, nature trail, clubhouse, Wi-Fi, pavilion, horseshoes, and dump station are available. A store is nearby. Some facilities are wheelchair-accessible. Leashed pets are permitted.

**Reservations, fees:** Reservations are accepted online at www.lakejennings.org ($8 reservation fee). Tent sites are $28-30 per night; RV sites are $33-38 (partial hookups) and $40-42 (full hookups) per night, plus $1 per pet per night.

The youth group area is $75 per night, the adult and family group area is $100 per night, and tipis are $65-75 per night (no pets), plus $2 per night for each additional person, $2 per night per additional vehicle, and $1 per night per pet. Per person fees are charged for fishing. Open year-round.

**Directions:** From San Diego, drive east on I-8 for 21 miles to Lake Jennings Park Road. Turn north (left) on Lake Jennings Park Road and drive one mile to the park entrance.

**Contact:** Helix Water District, campground information 619/390-1623, www.lakejennings.org.

## 40 CIBBETS FLATS

### Scenic rating: 5

on Troy Canyon Creek in Cleveland National Forest

**Map 14.2, page 770**

Cibbets Flat is at the southern flank of the Laguna Mountains near Troy Canyon Creek, and Kitchen Creek runs adjacent to the camp. It is an obscure, fairly remote camp and staging area for the Pacific Crest Trail. A trailhead for the PCT is a mile southeast of camp, used mostly by hikers heading north across the Laguna Mountains. The elevation is 4,200 feet.

**Campsites, facilities:** There are 24 sites for tents or RVs up to 27 feet (no hookups), including a few double sites. Picnic tables and fire grills are provided. Drinking water and vault toilets are available. Leashed pets are permitted.

**Reservations, fees:** Reservations are not accepted. Sites are $14-28 per night. Open year-round.

**Directions:** From El Cajon, drive east on I-8 for about 50 miles to Boulder Oaks, then continue a short distance to the exit for Kitchen Creek/Cameron Station. Turn north on Kitchen Creek Road and drive 4.5 miles to the campground entrance on the right.

**Contact:** Cleveland National Forest, Descanso Ranger District, 619/445-6235, www.fs.usda.gov/cleveland.

## 41 BOULDER OAKS EQUESTRIAN

### Scenic rating: 4

near Lake Morena in Cleveland National Forest

**Map 14.2, page 770**

Boulder Oaks is easy to reach, just off I-8, yet it is a very small camp with an important trailhead for the Pacific Crest Trail running right by it. This camp also is designed as a trailhead camp for equestrians. The elevation is 3,300 feet, set in the southern end of Cleveland National Forest and the Laguna Mountains. This campground is closed March through May to protect the breeding activity of the arroyo southwestern toad, an endangered species.

**Campsites, facilities:** There are 32 sites, including six double sites for tents or RVs up to 27 feet (no hookups) and 17 equestrian sites. Picnic tables and fire grills are provided. Vault toilets are available. Drinking water is limited and is only available in summer months; bring your own. No wood or charcoal fires are allowed when water is not available. Leashed pets are permitted.

**Reservations, fees:** Reservations are not accepted for individual sites but are required for equestrian sites at 877/444-6777 ($10 reservation fee) or www.recreation.gov ($9 reservation fee). Sites are $12-24 per night, plus $5 per night for additional vehicle. Open mid-June through February.

**Directions:** From El Cajon, drive east on I-8 to Pine Valley, then continue east for four miles to Buckman Springs Road. Take the Buckman Springs off-ramp, turn right (south) on Buckman Springs Road, and drive a short distance to a four-way stop sign at Old Highway 80. Turn left and drive 2.5 miles to the campground.

**Contact:** Cleveland National Forest, Descanso

Ranger District, 619/445-6235, www.fs.usda.gov/cleveland.

## 42 BOBCAT MEADOW

### Scenic rating: 6

in Cleveland National Forest

**Map 14.2, page 770**

This camp, along with nearby Corral Canyon, caters primarily to OHV users. The camp is shaded with live oaks and is a 10-minute drive from Corral Canyon camp. This camp is similar, but it has no water. The more spacious sites and privacy can make up for that. Off-highway vehicles are allowed. The elevation is 3,800 feet.

**Campsites, facilities:** There are 20 sites for tents or RVs up to 27 feet (no hookups). Fire pits are provided. Vault toilets are available. No drinking water is available. Garbage must be packed out. Leashed pets are permitted.

**Reservations, fees:** Reservations are not accepted. There is no fee for camping. An Adventure Pass ($30 annual fee or $5 daily fee per parked vehicle) is required. A DMV green sticker is required for OHVs. Open year-round.

**Directions:** From El Cajon, drive east on I-8 to Pine Valley, then continue east for four miles to Buckman Springs Road. Take the Buckman Springs off-ramp, turn right (south) on Buckman Springs Road, and drive 3.6 miles to Corral Canyon Road, signed "Camp Morena." Turn right and drive 6.2 miles (the road becomes Forest Service Road 17S04) to Four Corners Trailhead. Bear left (Forest Service Road 17S04) and drive a mile to the campground on the left.

**Contact:** Cleveland National Forest, Descanso Ranger District, 619/445-6235, www.fs.usda.gov/cleveland.

## 43 CORRAL CANYON

### Scenic rating: 6

in Cleveland National Forest

**Map 14.2, page 770**

This is a primitive camp adjacent to a network of OHV trails leading 24 miles into the Corral Canyon area, hence the name. Most of the routes lead into a chaparral landscape. The camp is at 3,500 feet elevation and is used primarily by the OHV crowd.

**Campsites, facilities:** There are 20 sites for tents or RVs up to 27 feet (no hookups). Fire rings are provided. Drinking water may be available but may not be potable. Vault toilets are available. Garbage must be packed out. Leashed pets are permitted.

**Reservations, fees:** Reservations are not accepted. There is no fee for camping. An Adventure Pass ($30 annual fee or $5 daily fee per parked vehicle) is required. DMV green sticker is required for OHVs. Open year-round.

**Directions:** From El Cajon, drive east on I-8 to Pine Valley, then continue east for four miles to Buckman Springs Road. Take the Buckman Springs off-ramp, turn right (south) on Buckman Springs Road, and drive 3.6 miles to Corral Canyon Road, signed "Camp Morena." Turn right and drive 6.2 miles (the road becomes Forest Service Road 17S04) to the Four Corners Trailhead. Continue straight on Corral Canyon Road for one mile to the campground on the right.

**Contact:** Cleveland National Forest, Descanso Ranger District, 619/445-6235, www.fs.usda.gov/cleveland.

## 44 COTTONWOOD

### Scenic rating: 4

in the McCain Valley Recreation Area

**Map 14.2, page 770**

This camp is on the western edge of the McCain Valley Recreation Area. Like most

Bureau of Land Management camps, it is little known and little used, but is occasionally frequented by backcountry horseback riders. Off-highway vehicles are not allowed. The elevation is 4,000 feet.

**Campsites, facilities:** There are 25 sites for tents or RVs up to 35 feet (no hookups). Picnic tables and fire grills are provided. Drinking water and vault toilets are available. Two group horse corrals are also available. Leashed pets are permitted.

**Reservations, fees:** Reservations are not accepted. Sites are $6 per night. Open year-round.

**Directions:** From El Cajon, drive east on I-8 for 70 miles to the Boulevard/Campo exit. Take that exit right, then at the frontage road, turn left immediately and drive east (just south of the interstate) for two miles to McCain Valley Road. Turn left on McCain Valley Road and drive about 13 miles to the campground.

**Contact:** Bureau of Land Management, El Centro Field Office, 760/337-4400, www.blm. gov/ca.

## 45 LARK CANYON OHV

🏃 🚷 🐾 🚐 ⛺

### Scenic rating: 5

in the McCain Valley Recreation Area

**Map 14.2, page 770**

Few know of this small camp at 4,000 feet elevation in the McCain Valley National Cooperative and Recreation Area. It is near a popular off-highway-vehicle area. Many dirt bikers use it as their base camp.

**Campsites, facilities:** There are 15 sites for tents or RVs up to 35 feet (no hookups) and group campsites are available. Picnic tables, fire rings, and trash service are provided. Vault toilets are available, but there is no drinking water. Firewood is scarce so bring it with you. Leashed pets are permitted.

**Reservations, fees:** Reservations are not accepted. Sites are $6 per night. Open year-round.

**Directions:** From El Cajon, drive east on I-8 for 70 miles to the Boulevard/Campo exit. Take that exit right, then at the frontage road, turn left immediately and drive east (just south of the interstate) for two miles to McCain Valley Road. Turn left at McCain Valley Road and drive three miles to the campground.

**Contact:** Bureau of Land Management, El Centro Field Office, 760/337-4400, www.blm. gov/ca.

## 46 SWEETWATER SUMMIT REGIONAL PARK

🏃 🚴 🏄 🚐 🐎 👫 👨‍🦽 🚐 ⛺

### Scenic rating: 7

near Sweetwater Reservoir in Bonita

**Map 14.2, page 770**

This regional park overlooks the Sweetwater Reservoir in Bonita. The campground is set right on the summit, overlooking the Sweetwater Valley. This camp has equestrian sites with corrals for the horses. There are 15 miles of trails in the park for hiking, mountain biking, and horseback riding. There are several golf courses nearby and it is 15 minutes from Tijuana. The Chula Vista Nature Center is nearby on the shore of south San Diego Bay.

**Campsites, facilities:** There are 113 sites: 56 sites (full hookups) for RVs to 45 feet, 46 sites (partial hookups, 20 amps) for tents or RVs up to 45 feet, and 11 equestrian sites with corrals. Picnic tables and fire grills are provided. Restrooms with flush toilets and showers, drinking water, covered pavilion, exercise course, playground, and dump station are available. Some facilities are wheelchair-accessible. Leashed pets are permitted.

**Reservations, fees:** Reservations are accepted at 858/565-3600 or 877/565-3600 ($5 reservation fee). Sites are $29-33 per night, plus $2 per horse per night and $1 per pet per night. Open year-round.

**Directions:** From San Diego, drive south on I-805 for 10 miles to Bonita Road. Turn east on Bonita Road and drive to San Miguel Road. Bear right on San Miguel Road and drive two miles to the park entrance on the left.

**Contact:** San Diego County Parks Department, Sweetwater Summit Regional Park, 619/472-7572, www.sdparks.org.

## 47 POTRERO COUNTY PARK

**Scenic rating: 4**

near the Mexican border

**Map 14.2, page 770**

If you are looking for a spot to hole up for the night before getting through customs, this is the place. This park covers 115 acres, set at an elevation of 2,300 feet. It is a broad valley peppered with coastal live oaks amid grassy meadows and rocky foothills. The average summer high temperature is in the 90°F range, and the average winter low is 34°F. There is occasional light snowfall in the winter. *Potrero* means "pasturing place." Some of the summer grazers are rattlesnakes, occasionally spotted here. Side trips include the railroad museum and century-old historical stone store in Campo, as well as the Mexican community of Tecate. In fact, it is just a heartbeat away from the customs inspection station in Tecate. A good side trip is to the nearby Tecate Mission Chapel, where you can pray that the guards do not rip your vehicle up in the search for contraband. Insider's tip: In the spring you may hear the evening call of the Pacific tree frog.

**Campsites, facilities:** There are 39 sites with partial hookups (20, 30, and 50 amps) for RVs up to 45 feet, seven tent sites, and a youth group site for up to 45 people. Group camping (at least 10 sites) is available by reservation. Picnic tables and fire grills are provided. Restrooms with flush toilets and showers, drinking water, playground, ball fields, and dump station are available. Picnic areas, ball fields, and a dance pavilion are available. You can buy supplies in Potrero. Leashed pets are permitted.

**Reservations, fees:** Reservations are accepted at 858/565-3600 or 877/565-3600 or online at www.sdparks.org ($5 reservation fee). Tent sites are $22 per night, RV sites (partial hookups) are $27 per night, plus $1 per pet per night. Group sites are $100 per night, and the youth group site is $50 per night. Open year-round.

**Directions:** From El Cajon, drive east on Highway 94 for 42 miles (near the junction of Highway 188) to Potrero Valley Road. Turn north on Potrero Valley Road and drive one mile to Potrero Park Road. Turn right (east) on Potrero Park Road and drive one mile to the park entrance.

**Contact:** San Diego County Parks Department, 619/478-5212, www.sdparks.org.

## 48 LAKE MORENA RV PARK

**Scenic rating: 6**

in Lake Morena County Park near Campo

**Map 14.2, page 770**

This camp is near the southern side of Lake Morena, a great lake for fishing and off-season vacations. It is one of three camps near the lake and the best for RVs. Lake Morena, at 3,200 feet elevation, is a large reservoir in the San Diego County foothills and is known for big bass. It is also known for fluctuating water levels. Swimming is prohibited at this lake.

**Campsites, facilities:** There are 41 sites with full or partial hookups (30 and 50 amps) for RVs up to 40 feet. Some picnic tables are provided. Fires are not allowed. Restrooms with flush toilets and showers, a dump station, propane gas, and coin laundry are available. Some facilities are wheelchair-accessible. Leashed pets are permitted, with certain restrictions.

**Reservations, fees:** Reservations are recommended. RV sites are $33 per night. Some credit cards are accepted. Open year-round.

**Directions:** From El Cajon, drive east on I-8 to Buckman Springs Road. Take the Buckman Springs off-ramp, turn right (south) on Buckman Springs Road, and drive 5.5 miles to Oak Drive. Turn right on Oak Drive and drive 1.5 miles to Lake Morena Drive. Turn left on Lake Morena Drive and drive a short distance to the park on the right (2330 Lake Morena Drive).

**Contact:** Lake Morena RV Park, 619/478-5677, www.sdparks.org.

# 49 THE OAKS AT SACRED ROCKS

🏃 🏊 🐎 ♿ 🚐 ⛺

**Scenic rating: 5**

in Boulevard

**Map 14.2, page 770**

The Oaks at Sacred Rocks sits on 163 acres and has hiking trails. The elevation is 3,800 feet. The town of Boulevard is centrally situated for a wide variety of recreation possibilities. About 10 miles to the north is Mount Laguna, with hiking trails available. About 30 minutes to the south is the nearest point of entry to Mexico at Tecate. Fishing at Lake Morena or Lake Cuyamaca is also a possibility, as is soaking in nearby hot springs. A casino is four miles away. A train museum is available in Campo, about 16 miles away.

**Campsites, facilities:** There are 151 RV sites with full hookups (20, 30, and 50 amps) for RVs up to 45 feet, a primitive tent camping area, and a group camping area for up to 1,000 people. Picnic tables and fire rings are provided at some sites. A clubhouse, restrooms with showers, horseshoes, volleyball court, coin laundry, gift shop, general store, Wi-Fi, group campfire area, and organized activities and classes are available. A swimming pool and hot tub are available (May through October). Golf carts are allowed. Some facilities are wheelchair-accessible. Leashed pets are permitted, with some breeds prohibited.

**Reservations, fees:** Reservations are accepted at http://theoaksatsacredrocks.com. RV sites are $30-55 per night, cabins are $60 per night, and tent camping is $20 per night (plus $10 each additional person). Horse camping is also available. Weekly, monthly, and group rates are available. Credit cards are accepted. Open year-round.

**Directions:** From El Cajon, drive east on I-8 for approximately 50 miles (past Alpine) to the Crestwood/Live Oak Springs Road exit. Take that exit and turn east and drive 0.5 mile to Church Street. Turn right and drive 4.2 miles to Highway 94. Turn left (east) and drive 1.1 miles to the resort on the right, at 1331 Shasta Way.

**Contact:** The Oaks at Sacred Rocks RV Park and Campground, 619/766-4480, http://theoaksatsacredrocks.com.

# CALIFORNIA DESERTS

The broad expanse of the California deserts includes Mojave National Preserve, Joshua Tree National Park, Death Valley, and Anza-Borrego Desert State Park. Remote and with relatively few visitors, Mojave National Preserve is where three major landscapes join: the Sonoran Desert, the Colorado Desert, and the Mojave Desert. Highlights include the Kelso Dunes, a series of volcanic cliffs. Joshua Tree National Park, edged in by mountains and peppered with the peculiar Joshua trees, is where the high desert (Mojave) meets the low desert (Colorado) and where rock piles lure climbers. Death Valley is the largest national park in the lower 48, yet there are only nine campgrounds. Highlights include Badwater, the lowest point in the United States. Anza-Borrego Desert State Park covers 600,000 acres, the largest state park in California. Canyons, badlands, and barren ridges are home to endangered desert bighorn.

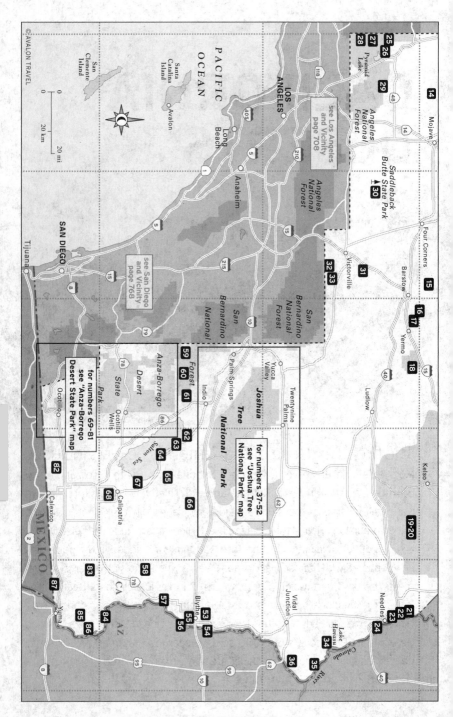

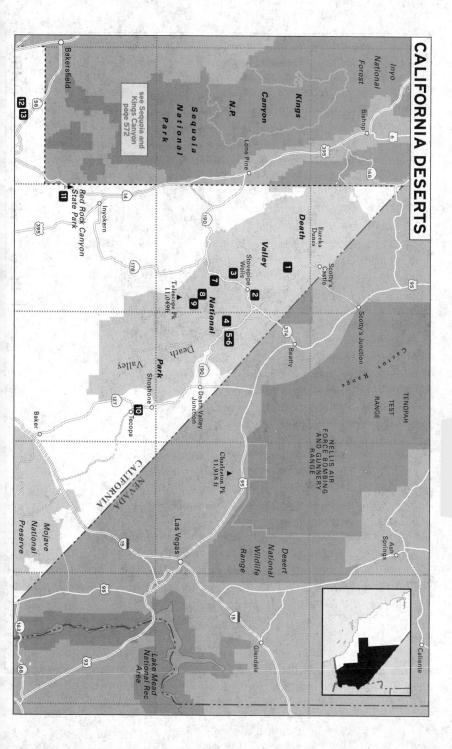

CALIFORNIA DESERTS

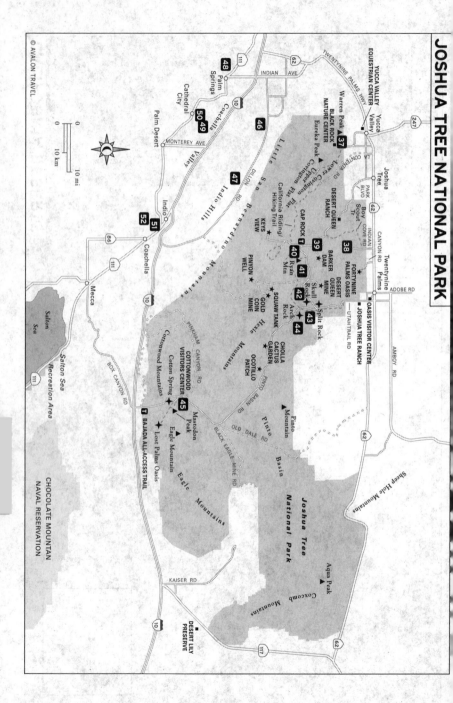

JOSHUA TREE NATIONAL PARK

© AVALON TRAVEL

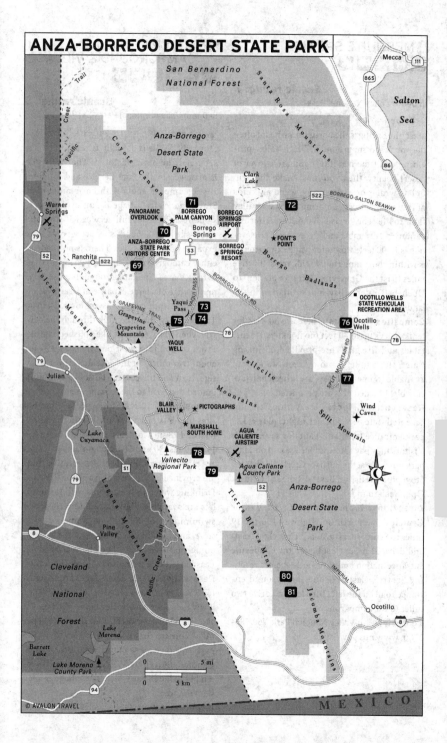

# ANZA-BORREGO DESERT STATE PARK

# 1 MESQUITE SPRING

**Scenic rating: 7**

in Death Valley National Park

**Map page 799**

Mesquite Spring is the northernmost and often the prettiest campground in Death Valley, providing you time it right. If you are a lover of desert beauty, then you must make this trip in late winter or early spring, when all kinds of tiny wildflowers can bring the stark valley floor to life. The key is soil moisture, courtesy of rains in November and December. The elevation is 1,800 feet. Mesquite Spring campground is within short range of two side trips. It is five miles (past the Grapevine Entrance Station) to Ubehebe Crater, a pay-off destination in the landscape.

**Campsites, facilities:** There are 30 sites for tents or RVs up to 30 feet (no hookups). Picnic tables and fire grills are provided. Drinking water, flush toilets, and a dump station are available. Some facilities are wheelchair-accessible. Leashed pets are permitted.

**Reservations, fees:** Reservations are not accepted. Sites are $14 per night, plus a $25 park entrance fee that is valid for seven days. Visitors may pay the entrance fee and obtain a park brochure at the Furnace Creek, Grapevine, Stovepipe Wells, or Beatty Ranger Stations. Open year-round.

**Directions:** From Furnace Creek Visitor Center, drive north on Highway 190 for 19 miles to Scotty's Castle Road. Turn right (east) and drive 33 miles (just before the Grapevine entrance station and three miles before reaching Scotty's Castle) to the campground entrance road on the left. Turn left and drive two miles to the campground.

**Contact:** Death Valley National Park, 760/786-3200, www.nps.gov/deva.

# 2 STOVEPIPE WELLS CAMPGROUND & VILLAGE

**Scenic rating: 4**

in Death Valley National Park

**Map page 799**

Stovepipe Wells is actually two adjoined but separately managed facilities. The Wells side is managed by the Park Service and provides rustic camping spots with basic amenities. Stovepipe Wells Village is run by a concessionaire and has 14 full-service RV sites and an on-site hotel. The RV sites are set on a large expanse of desert gravel. There is no shade in either campground except for two lonely trees in the RV area. The campgrounds lie at sea level on the edge of a large expanse of Death Valley.

A worthwhile side trip is to Mosaic Canyon Trail, an easy one-mile walk through the canyon where the walls look like polished marble. From camp, head west on Highway 190 for about two miles. At the Mosaic Canyon Trail sign, turn and travel a short distance on a well-graded dirt road to the parking area.

**Campsites, facilities:** Stovepipe Wells has 190 sites for tents or RVs of any length (no hookups) and 28 sites for tents only. The Village has 14 RV sites (30 and 50 amp hookups); all sites are pull-through. Picnic tables and fire rings are provided and there is also a group fire ring. Drinking water and restrooms with flush toilets are available. Showers, a dump station, a swimming pool ($4 for tent campers), camp store, and gasoline are available at the Village. Some facilities are wheelchair-accessible. Leashed pets are permitted at campsites only.

**Reservations, fees:** Reservations are accepted for RV sites at the Village at 760/786-2387 or www.escapetodeathvalley.com. Village RV sites are $33.30 per night. Tent sites are $14 per night and are first-come, first-served. A $25 park entrance fee is required for both campgrounds. Stovepipe Wells is open mid-September through early May; the Village is open year-round.

**Directions:** From Los Angeles and I-5, take

Exit 162 to State Route 14 N/Antelope Valley Freeway and drive 0.6 mile toward Palmdale/Lancaster. Merge onto CA-14N/State Route 14 N and continue for 68.9 miles. Turn right onto CA-14 N/Aerospace Hwy/Midland Trail and drive 48.8 miles. Continue onto US-395 N for 41.5 miles, then turn right onto CA-190 E and drive for 14.6 miles. Turn right to stay on CA-190 East. Continue for 61.1 miles to Stovepipe Wells Village.

**Contact:** Stovepipe Wells Village, 760/786-2387, www.escapetodeathvalley.com; Death Valley National Park, 760/786-3244, www.nps.gov/deva.

## 3 EMIGRANT
👣 🐕 ⛺

### Scenic rating: 4
in Death Valley National Park

Map page 799

The key here is the elevation, and Emigrant, at 2,100 feet, is out of the forbidding subzero elevations of Death Valley. That makes it one of the more habitable camps. From the camp, a good side trip is to drive south 21 miles on Emigrant Canyon Road, then turn east on Upper Wildrose Canyon Road for seven miles, the last two miles a rough dirt road. That done, you come to the trailhead for Wildrose Peak, on the left side of the road at the parking area for the Charcoal Kilns. A trail climbs 4.2 miles to the peak, with awesome views in the last two miles; the last mile is a butt-kicker.

**Campsites, facilities:** There are 10 sites for tents only. Picnic tables are provided. Drinking water and flush toilets are available. Campfires are not permitted during the summer. Leashed pets are permitted at campsites only.

**Reservations, fees:** Reservations are not accepted. There is no fee for camping. There is a $25 park entrance fee per vehicle that is valid for seven days. Open year-round.

**Directions:** In Stovepipe Wells Village, drive eight miles southwest on Highway 190 to the campground on the right.

**Contact:** Death Valley National Park, 760/786-3200, www.nps.gov/deva.

## 4 FURNACE CREEK
👣 🏕 🐕 ♿ 🚐 ⛺

### Scenic rating: 5
in Death Valley National Park

Map page 799

This is a well-developed national park site that provides a good base camp for exploring Death Valley, especially for newcomers. The nearby visitors center includes Death Valley Museum and offers maps and suggestions for hikes and drives in this unique wildland. This camp offers some shady sites, a rarity in Death Valley, but these are packed close together with noisy neighbors, and RV generators are a factor when the campground is full. It's open all year, but keep in mind that the daytime summer temperatures commonly exceed 120°F, making this area virtually uninhabitable in the summer. The elevation is 190 feet below sea level.

**Campsites, facilities:** There are 136 sites for tents or RVs up to 35 feet (full hookups) and two group sites for up to 10 vehicles and 40 people each. Picnic tables and fire rings are provided. Drinking water, flush toilets, a dump station, and evening ranger programs are available. Campfires are not permitted during summer. Some facilities are wheelchair-accessible. Leashed pets are permitted at campsites only.

**Reservations, fees:** Reservations are accepted mid-October through mid-April at 877/444-6777 or www.recreation.gov ($9 reservation fee). Sites are first-come, first-served the rest of the year. Standard sites are $22 per night, RV sites with hookups are $36 per night, plus a $25 park entrance fee per vehicle that is valid for seven days. Group sites are $60 per night. Open year-round.

**Directions:** From Stovepipe Wells, drive east on Highway 190, turning right at the intersection with Scotty's Castle Road. Furnace Creek Campground will be on the left shortly before Furnace Creek Ranch and the visitors center.

**Contact:** Death Valley National Park, 760/786-3200, www.nps.gov/deva.

## 5 TEXAS SPRING

### Scenic rating: 2

in Death Valley National Park

Map page 799

Although this camp is slightly more protected than Sunset camp, there's limited shade and no shelter. The lower half of the campground is for tents only. It is open only in winter. The upper end of the camp has trails that provide access to the historic springs and a viewing area. The nearby visitors center, which features the Death Valley Museum, offers maps and suggestions for hikes and drives. The lowest point in the United States, Badwater, set 282 feet below sea level, is to the southwest. This camp has one truly unique feature: bathrooms that are listed on the National Historic Register.

**Campsites, facilities:** There are 92 sites for tents or RVs of any length (no hookups). Picnic tables and fire rings are provided. Drinking water, flush toilets, and a dump station are available. Campfires are not permitted in the summer. Some facilities are wheelchair-accessible. Leashed pets are permitted.

**Reservations, fees:** Reservations are not accepted. Sites are $16 per night, plus a $25 park entrance fee per vehicle that is valid for seven days. Open mid-October through mid-April.

**Directions:** From Furnace Creek Ranch, drive south on Highway 190 for 0.25 mile to the signed campground entrance on the left.

**Contact:** Death Valley National Park, 760/786-3200, www.nps.gov/deva.

## 6 SUNSET

### Scenic rating: 4

in Death Valley National Park

Map page 799

This camp is another enormous section of asphalt where the campsites consist of white lines for borders. Sunset is one of several options for campers in the Furnace Creek area of Death Valley, with an elevation of 190 feet below sea level. It is advisable to make your first stop at the nearby visitors center for maps and suggested hikes (according to your level of fitness) and drives.

**Campsites, facilities:** There are 270 sites for RVs of any length (no hookups). Drinking water, flush toilets, and a dump station are available. Campfires are not permitted in the summer. Some facilities are wheelchair-accessible. Leashed pets are permitted at campsites.

**Reservations, fees:** Reservations are not accepted. Sites are $14 per night, plus a $25 park entrance fee per vehicle that is valid for seven days. Open mid-October through mid-April.

**Directions:** From Furnace Creek Ranch, turn south on Highway 190 and drive 0.25 mile to the signed campground entrance and turn left into the campground.

**Contact:** Death Valley National Park, 760/786-3200, www.nps.gov/deva.

## 7 WILDROSE

### Scenic rating: 4

in Death Valley National Park

Map page 799

Wildrose is on the road that heads out to the primitive country of the awesome Panamint Range, eventually coming within range of Telescope Peak, the highest point in Death Valley National Park (11,049 feet). The elevation at the camp is 4,100 feet.

**Campsites, facilities:** There are 23 sites for tents or RVs up to 25 feet (no hookups). Picnic

tables and fire rings are provided. Drinking water (April through November only) and pit toilets are available. Campfires are not permitted during the summer. Leashed pets are permitted at campsites only.

**Reservations, fees:** Reservations are not accepted. There is no fee for camping; there is a $25 park entrance fee per vehicle that is valid for seven days. Open year-round.

**Directions:** From Stovepipe Wells Village, drive south on Highway 190 for eight miles to Emigrant Canyon Road (just past the Emigrant rest area). Turn left (east) on Emigrant Canyon Road and drive 22 miles to the campground entrance on the left.

**Contact:** Death Valley National Park, 760/786-3200, www.nps.gov/deva.

## 8 THORNDIKE
🚶 🐕 ⛺

### Scenic rating: 4
in Death Valley National Park

**Map page 799**

This is one of Death Valley National Park's little-known camps. It is in the high country at 7,400 feet elevation. It's free, of course. Otherwise the park service would have to actually send somebody out to tend to the place. Nearby are century-old charcoal kilns that were built by Chinese laborers and tended by Shoshone workers. The trailhead that serves Telescope Peak (11,049 feet), the highest point in Death Valley, can be found in nearby Mahogany Flat.

**Campsites, facilities:** This backcountry campground is accessible only by foot or high-clearance vehicle; it has six sites for tents. Picnic tables and fire rings are provided. Pit toilets are available. No drinking water is available. Campfires are not permitted in the summer. Garbage must be packed out. Leashed pets are permitted at campsites only.

**Reservations, fees:** Reservations are not accepted. There is no fee for camping. There is a $25 park entrance fee per vehicle that is

valid for seven days. Open March through November.

**Directions:** In Death Valley at Stovepipe Wells Village, drive south on Highway 190 for eight miles to Emigrant Canyon Road (just past the Emigrant rest area). Turn left (east) on Emigrant Canyon Road and drive 21 miles to Wildrose Canyon Road. Turn left and drive nine miles to the camp. (The road becomes extremely rough; a high-clearance vehicle is required.)

**Contact:** Death Valley National Park, 760/786-3200, Death Valley National Park, 760/786-3200, www.nps.gov/deva.

## 9 MAHOGANY FLAT
🚶 🐕 ⛺

### Scenic rating: 5
in Death Valley National Park

**Map page 799**

This is one of two primitive, hard-to-reach camps (the other is Thorndike) in the Panamint Range high country. It is one of the few shaded camps, offering beautiful piñon pines and junipers. What makes it popular, however, is the trail to Telescope Peak leading out from camp. Only the ambitious and well conditioned should attempt the climb, a seven-mile trip one-way with breathtaking (literally) views of both Panamint Valley and Death Valley. The elevation at the campground is 8,200 feet, and Telescope Peak tops out at 11,049 feet, which translates to a climb of 2,849 feet.

**Campsites, facilities:** There are 10 sites for tents only. Picnic tables and fire rings are provided. Pit toilets are available. No drinking water is available. Campfires are not permitted during the summer. Garbage must be packed out. The campground is accessible only by foot or high-clearance four-wheel-drive vehicle. Leashed pets are permitted at campsites only.

**Reservations, fees:** Reservations are not accepted. There is no fee for camping. There is a $25 park entrance fee per vehicle that is valid for seven days. Open March through November, weather permitting.

**Directions:** From Stovepipe Wells Village, drive south on Highway 190 for eight miles to Emigrant Canyon Road (just past the Emigrant rest area). Turn left (east) on Emigrant Canyon Road and drive 21 miles to Wildrose Canyon Road. Turn left and drive nine miles (passing Thorndike campground) to the end of the road and the camp.

**Contact:** Death Valley National Park, 760/786-3200, www.nps.gov/deva.

## 10 TECOPA HOT SPRINGS CAMPGROUND

### Scenic rating: 3

north of Tecopa

**Map page 799**

Nobody gets here by accident. This Inyo County campground is out there in no-man's land, and if it weren't for the hot springs and the good rockhounding, all you'd see around here would be a few skeletons. Regardless, it's quite an attraction in the winter, when the warm climate is a plus and the nearby mineral baths are worth taking a dunk in. Rockhounds will enjoy looking for amethysts, opals, and petrified wood in the nearby areas. The elevation is 1,325 feet.

**Campsites, facilities:** There are 250 sites for tents or RVs of any length (with partial hookups of 30 amps). Some sites are pull-through. Picnic tables and fire grills are provided. Restrooms with flush toilets and showers, a dump station, mineral pools, play equipment, and Wi-Fi are available. There is no drinking water. Groceries and propane gas are available within 10 miles. Leashed pets are permitted.

**Reservations, fees:** Reservations are accepted. Sites for tents or self-contained RVs are $16 per night, RV sites (with hookups) are $20-22 per night ($3 per night for electricity), plus $5 per person per night for more than two people and $5 per night for each additional

vehicle. A bath pass is $7; bath passes are included with campsites. Weekly and monthly rates are available. Open year-round.

**Directions:** From Baker, drive north on Highway 127 for 58 miles to a county road signed "Tecopa Hot Springs" (south of the junction of Highway 178 and Highway 127). Turn right (east) and drive five miles to the park and campground entrance.

**Contact:** Tecopa Hot Springs Campground, Inyo County Parks and Recreation, 760/852-4377, www.inyocountycamping.com.

## 11 RED ROCK CANYON STATE PARK

### Scenic rating: 8

near Mojave

**Map page 799**

This unique state park is one of the prettiest spots in the region year-round. A gorgeous series of geologic formations, most of them tinted red, makes it a worthwhile visit in any season. The park also has paleontology sites, as well as remnants of some 1890s-era mining operations. A great, easy hike is the two-mile walk to Red Cliffs Natural Preserve, where there are awesome 300-foot cliffs and columns, painted red by the iron in the soil. Part of this area is closed February through June to protect nesting raptors. For those who don't hike, a must is driving up Jawbone Canyon Road to see Jawbone and Last Chance Canyons. Hikers have it better. The park also has excellent wildflower blooms March through May. A primitive off-highway vehicle (OHV) trail is also available; check regulations. The elevation is 2,600 feet.

**Campsites, facilities:** There are 50 sites for tents or RVs up to 30 feet (no hookups). Picnic tables and fire grills are provided. Drinking water, pit toilets, dump station, picnic area, and seasonal visitors center and campfire programs are available. In spring and fall, volunteers lead nature walks. Some facilities are wheelchair-accessible. Leashed pets are permitted in the campground only.

**Reservations, fees:** Reservations are not accepted. Sites are $25 per night, and it's $6 for each additional vehicle. Open year-round.

**Directions:** Drive on Highway 14 to the town of Mojave (50 miles east of the Los Angeles Basin area). Continue northeast on Highway 14 for 25 miles to the park entrance on the left.

**Contact:** Red Rock Canyon State Park, 661/946-6092, www.parks.ca.gov.

## 12 BRITE VALLEY AQUATIC RECREATION AREA

### Scenic rating: 7

at Brite Lake

**Map page 799**

Brite Valley Lake is a speck of a water hole (90 acres) on the northern flank of the Tehachapi Mountains in Kern County, at an elevation of 4,000 feet. No gas motors are permitted on the lake, so it's perfect for canoes, kayaks, or inflatables. No swimming is permitted. Use is moderate, primarily by picnickers and anglers. The lake is stocked with trout in the spring; other species include catfish and bluegill. A golf course is nearby.

**Campsites, facilities:** There are six sites with full hookups and 12 sites with partial hookups (20 amps) for RVs of any length, as well as a tent camping area. Group camping is also available. Picnic tables and fire grills are provided. Drinking water, restrooms with flush toilets and showers, a dump station, a playground, picnic pavilions (available by reservation), and a fish-cleaning station are available. Supplies are available about eight miles away in Tehachapi. Leashed pets are permitted.

**Reservations, fees:** Reservations are not accepted for individuals, but large RV clubs may reserve sites at 661/822-3228, ext. 10. Tent sites are $15 per night; RV sites are $20 (partial hookups) and $30 (full hookups) per night. Fishing fees are $5 per person, and each angler

over age 16 must have a California fishing license. Open year-round.

**Directions:** From Bakersfield, drive east on Highway 58 for 40 miles toward the town of Tehachapi. Take the Highway 202 exit and drive three miles west to Banducci Road. Turn left and drive for about one mile to the park on the right.

**Contact:** Tehachapi Valley Recreation and Parks District, 661/221-3228, www.tvrpd.org; Brite Lake Campground, 661/221-2832.

## 13 INDIAN HILL RANCH AND RV PARK

### Scenic rating: 7

near Tehachapi

**Map page 799**

This is a unique park with two seasonal ponds stocked with largemouth bass and catfish. Crappie and bluegill are other fish species. The campground is open year-round and offers spacious, private sites with oak trees and a view of Brite Valley. Some sites have lake views, while others have hill views. A bonus is the hiking trails in the park. The elevation is 5,000 feet. Although this area is known for being windy, this campground is somewhat sheltered from the wind.

**Campsites, facilities:** There are 37 sites with full or partial hookups for RVs; nearly half of the sites are pull-through. A group site accommodates up to 40 people. Picnic tables and fire pits are provided. Restroom with flush toilets and showers (seasonal), a dump station, coin laundry, Wi-Fi, horseshoes, firewood, propane, and two stocked fishing ponds are available. Small leashed pets are permitted, with certain restrictions.

**Reservations, fees:** Reservations are accepted. Lakeside sites (partial and full hookups) are $30-40 per night, lake-view sites (water and 30-amp) are $25 per night, and A section sites (full hookups) are $20 per night, plus $6 per night per extra person (four-person occupancy). The group site is $400 per night. Monthly rates are available. No credit cards are accepted. Open year-round, with some seasonal lakeside sites closed November through mid-May.

**Directions:** Drive on Highway 58 to Tehachapi and Exit 148 for Tehachapi/Highway 202. Take that exit to Tucker Road. Turn right and drive south one mile to Highway 202/Valley Boulevard. Turn right (west) and drive four miles to Banducci Road. Turn left and drive 0.75 mile to Arosa Road. Turn left and drive 1.7 miles to the park.

**Contact:** Indian Hill Ranch and RV Park, 18061 Arosa Road, 661/822-6613, www.indianhillranch.com.

## 14 TEHACHAPI MOUNTAIN PARK

### Scenic rating: 7

southwest of Tehachapi

**Map page 798**

This county park is overlooked by most out-of-towners. It is a pretty spot covering 5,000 acres, set on the slopes of the Tehachapi Mountains, with elevations in the park ranging from 5,500 to 7,000 feet. The roads to the campgrounds are steep, but the sites are flat. Trails for hikers and equestrians are available, but no horses are allowed at the campground. An interpretive trail, Nuooah Nature Trail, is available. This park is popular not only in spring but in winter, when the elevation is high enough to get snow (chains often required for access). The park lies eight miles southwest of the town of Tehachapi on the southern side of Highway 58 between Mojave and Bakersfield. Woody's Peak, at almost 8,000 feet, overlooks the park from its dominion in the Tehachapi Mountains, the dividing line between the San Joaquin Valley and the Los Angeles Basin.

**Campsites, facilities:** There are 61 sites for tents or RVs of any length (no hookups), a group campsite for up to 40 people, a group campsite for up to 150 people, and group lodging with 10 cabins for a minimum of 40 people. Picnic tables and fire grills are provided. Open fires may be banned; check for updates. Drinking water (natural spring) and pit toilets are available. Some facilities are wheelchair-accessible. Leashed pets are permitted.

**Reservations, fees:** Reservations are not accepted for individual sites but are required for the group sites and group cabins at 661/868-7000. Sites are $18 per night per vehicle, rates for seniors and travelers with mobility issues are $12 per night, plus $4 per pet per night. Sierra Flats Group Site is $75 per night, and Tehachapi Mountain Group Site (includes 10 cabins) is $300 per night. Open year-round, weather permitting.

**Directions:** In Tehachapi, take Tehachapi Boulevard to the Curry Street exit. Take that exit south and drive about three miles to Highline Road. Turn right on Highline Road and drive two miles to Water Canyon Road. Turn left on Water Canyon Road and drive three miles to the park.

**Contact:** Kern County Parks Department info line, 661/868-7000, www.co.kern.ca.us/parks/tehachapi.asp.

## 15 OWL CANYON

### Scenic rating: 3

near Barstow

**Map page 798**

The primary attraction of Owl Canyon camp is that the surrounding desert is sprinkled with exposed fossils of ancient animals. Guess they couldn't find any water. Well, if people try hiking without a full canteen, there may soon be some human skeletons out here, too. Actually, rangers say that the general public is unlikely to spot fossils because it takes some basic scientific knowledge to identify them. The sparse BLM land out here is kind of like an ugly dog you learn to love: After a while, when you look closely, you learn it has a heart of gold. This region is best visited in the spring and fall, of course, when hiking allows a fresh, new look at what may appear to some as a wasteland. The beauty is in the detail of it—tiny critters and tiny flowers seen against the unfenced vastness, with occasional fossils yet to be discovered. The elevation is 2,600 feet.

**Campsites, facilities:** There are 30 sites for tents or RVs of any length (no hookups). Two horse corrals are available at a separate group site. Picnic tables, shade ramadas, and fire grills are provided. Limited potable water (hand pump) and vault toilets are available. A campground host is on-site fall through spring. Some trash service may be offered, but prepare to pack out all garbage. Some facilities are wheelchair-accessible. Leashed pets are permitted.

**Reservations, fees:** Reservations are not accepted. Sites are $6 per night. Open year-round.

**Directions:** Drive on I-15 to Barstow to the exit for 1st Street. Take that exit and drive north on 1st Street (crossing the Mojave River Bridge) for 0.75 mile to Irwin Road. Turn left and drive eight miles to Fossil Bed Road. Turn left and drive two miles to the campground on the right.

**Contact:** Bureau of Land Management, Barstow Field Office, 760/252-6000, www.blm.gov/ca.

## 16 CALICO GHOST TOWN REGIONAL PARK

**Scenic rating: 4**

near Barstow

**Map page 798**

Let me tell you about this ghost town: There are probably more people here now than there have ever been. In the 1880s and 1890s it was a booming silver mine town, and there are still remnants of that. Alas, it now has lots of restaurants and shops. Recreation options include riding on a narrow-gauge railroad, touring what was once the largest silver mine in California, and watching an old-style melodrama with villains and heroes. This is a 480-acre park with self-guided tours, hiking trails, gold panning, summer entertainment, and a museum, with festivals held throughout the year. Whatever you do, don't take any artifacts you may come across, such as an old nail, a jar, or anything; you will be doomed with years of bad luck. No foolin'. A park representative told the story of a man from the East Coast who nabbed a beautiful rock on his visit. He then was plagued with years of bad luck, including broken bones, disappointment in his love life, and several family deaths. In desperation, he flew back to California and returned the rock to its rightful place.

**Campsites, facilities:** There are 265 sites for tents and RVs up to 45 feet; 104 sites have full or partial hookups (20, 30, and 50 amps), and some sites are pull-through. There are also three group camping areas, six cabins, and a bunkhouse. Fire pits are provided. Restrooms with flush toilets and showers, drinking water, and three dump stations are available. Pay phone, restaurants, and shops are on-site. Groceries, propane gas, and laundry facilities are 10 miles away. Some facilities are wheelchair-accessible. Leashed pets are permitted.

**Reservations, fees:** Reservations are accepted at 800/892-2542 ($7 reservation fee) and www.sbcountyparks.com. Tent sites are $30 per night, RV sites are $35 (partial hookups) and $40 (full hookups) per night, and it's $1 per pet per night. Cabins are $50 per night, and the bunkhouse is $160 (up to 20 people, two-night minimum). Some credit cards are accepted. Open year-round.

**Directions:** From Barstow, drive northeast on I-15 for seven miles to the exit for Ghost Town Road. Take that exit and drive north on Ghost Town Road for three miles to the park on the left.

**Contact:** Calico Ghost Town Regional Park, San Bernardino County, 760/254-2122, www.sbcountyparks.com or www.calicotown.com.

## 17 BARSTOW CALICO KOA

🏕️ 🏊 🏕️ 🐕 🏇 ♿ 🚐 ⛺

### Scenic rating: 3

near Barstow

**Map page 798**

Don't blame me if you end up way out here. Actually, for vacationers making the long-distance grind of a drive on I-15, this KOA can seem like the promised land. It has received awards for its cleanliness, and a nightly quiet time ensures that you have a chance to get rested. Vegetation screening between sites enhances privacy. But hey, as long as you're here, you might as well take a side trip to Calico Ghost Town, about three miles to the northeast at the foot of the Calico Mountains. A unique side trip is the Calico Early Man Site, about five miles to the north; tours are available. Primitive stone tools are believed to have been discovered here in 1942. Rockhounding, hiking, and an outlet mall are other nearby options. The elevation is 1,900 feet.

**Campsites, facilities:** There are 15 tent sites and 66 sites with full or partial hookups (30 and 50 amps) for RVs of any length; many sites are pull-through. Cabins are also available. Picnic tables and fire grills are provided. Drinking water, restrooms with flush toilets and showers, a dump station, playground with climbing wall, swimming pool (seasonal), recreation room, Wi-Fi, archery range, convenience store, propane gas, ice, and coin laundry are available. Some facilities are wheelchair-accessible. Leashed pets are permitted.

**Reservations, fees:** Reservations are accepted at 800/562-0059. RV sites are $50-60 per night, tent sites are $35-50 per night, plus $4-5 per person per night for more than two people. Cabins are $133 per night; the safari tent is $79-83 per night (up to eight people). Credit cards are accepted. Open year-round.

**Directions:** From Barstow, drive northeast on I-15 for seven miles to the exit for Ghost Town Road. Take that exit and drive left under the freeway to a frontage road at the Shell gas station. Turn left at the frontage road and drive 0.25 mile to the campground on the right.

**Contact:** Barstow Calico KOA, 760/254-2311, www.koa.com/campgrounds/barstow.

## 18 AFTON CANYON

🏕️ 🐕 🚐 ⛺

### Scenic rating: 6

near Barstow in the East Mojave National Scenic Area

**Map page 798**

This camp is at 1,400 feet elevation in a desert riparian habitat along the Mojave River. This is one of several Bureau of Land Management tracts near the Mojave National Preserve. Side-trip options include the Rainbow Basin Natural Area (about an hour's drive), Soda Springs, and the Calico Early Man Site. Remember, rivers in the desert are not like rivers in cooler climates. There are no fish worth eating.

**Campsites, facilities:** There are 22 sites for tents or RVs up to 30 feet (no hookups). Picnic tables, shade ramadas, and fire rings are provided. Vault toilets are available. Drinking water is available intermittently, so bring your own water. Some trash service is offered but be prepared to pack out all garbage. Leashed pets are permitted.

**Reservations, fees:** Reservations are not accepted. Sites are $6 per night. Open year-round.

**Directions:** From Barstow, drive east on I-15 for 37 miles to Afton Road. Turn right (south) and drive three miles to the campground. Note: Four-wheel-drive or high-clearance vehicles are recommended since the access road can be rough and have washouts.

**Contact:** Bureau of Land Management, Barstow Field Office, 760/252-6000, www.blm.gov/ca.

# 19 MID HILLS

🚶 🏕 🚙 ⛺

## Scenic rating: 4

in the Mojave National Preserve

**Map page 798**

This is a primitive campground among the junipers and piñon trees in a mountainous area at 5,600 feet elevation. It is one of two little-known camps in the vast desert that is managed by the National Park Service. About half of the campsites were burned in the 2005 Hackberry Fire; most of the piñon and juniper trees burned as well. An eight-mile one-way trail starts across from the entrance to Mid Hills and meanders down to the Hole-in-the-Wall Campground. It's a pleasant walk in spring and fall.

**Campsites, facilities:** There are 26 sites for tents or RVs up to 22 feet (no hookups). Picnic tables and fire grills are provided. Drinking water, trash service, and pit toilets are available. Leashed pets are permitted.

**Reservations, fees:** Reservations are not accepted. Sites are $12 per night. Open year-round.

**Directions:** Drive on I-40 to Essex Road (near Essex, 116 miles east of Barstow). Take that exit and drive north on Essex Road for 10 miles to Black Canyon Road. Turn north and drive nine miles (at Hole-in-the-Wall campground, the road becomes dirt) and continue seven miles to Wild Horse Canyon Road. Turn left and drive two miles (rough, dirt road) to the campground on the right. Watch for storm damage on all roads.

Note: Storms have caused flash flooding and damage to roads. Reduce speed and use caution when traveling through the park. Call 760/252-6100 or 760/252-6108 for updates.

**Contact:** Mojave National Preserve, 760/252-6100, www.nps.gov/moja.

# 20 HOLE-IN-THE-WALL AND BLACK CANYON

🚶 🏕 🚙 ⛺

## Scenic rating: 6

in the Mojave National Preserve

**Map page 798**

This is the largest and best-known of the camps in the vast Mojave National Preserve. There are three camps in this area: Hole-in-the-Wall, Black Canyon Group, and Black Canyon Equestrian. All are set at 4,400 feet elevation. An interesting side trip is to the Mitchell Caverns in the nearby Providence Mountains State Recreation Area.

**Campsites, facilities:** There are 35 sites for tents or RVs of any length (no hookups), two walk-in sites, one group site for up to 50 people, and an equestrian camp for up to 30 people. Picnic tables and fire grills are provided. Drinking water, pit and vault toilets, trash service, and a dump station are available. The group site has a picnic shelter and corrals are provided at the equestrian site. Leashed pets are permitted.

**Reservations, fees:** Reservations are not accepted at Hole-in-the-Wall, but they are required at Black Canyon for groups of at least 15 people, seven vehicles, or seven horses (call 760/928-2572 or 760/252-6104). Sites at Hole-in-the-Wall are $12 per night. Sites at Black Canyon are $25 per night. Open year-round.

**Directions:** From I-40, take Essex Road (near Essex, 116 miles east of Barstow) north for 10 miles to Black Canyon Road. Turn north and drive nine miles to the campgrounds.

Note: Storms have caused flash flooding and damage to roads. Reduce speed and use caution when traveling through the park. Call 760/252-6100 or 760/252-6108 for updates.

**Contact:** Mojave National Preserve, 760/252-6100, www.nps.gov/moja.

## 21 RAINBO BEACH RESORT

### Scenic rating: 6

on the Colorado River

**Map page 798**  **BEST (**

The big bonus here is the full marina, making this resort on the Colorado River the headquarters for boaters and water-skiers. And headquarters it is, with tons of happy folks who are extremely well lubed, both inside and out. This resort boasts 800 feet of river frontage. A 60-site mobile home park is adjacent to the RV park. (For boating details, see the Needles Marina Park listing in this chapter.)

**Campsites, facilities:** There are 60 sites with full hookups (30 and 50 amps) for RVs. Some sites are pull-through. Picnic tables are provided. Restrooms with showers, coin laundry, swimming pool, heated spa, recreation room, launch ramp, and a restaurant and full-service bar are available. A boat dock is nearby. Leashed pets are permitted.

**Reservations, fees:** Reservations are accepted. Sites are $35 per night. Seasonal rates are available. Some credit cards are accepted. Open year-round.

**Directions:** Take I-40 to Needles and River Road. Turn north on River Road and drive 1.5 miles to the resort on the right.

**Contact:** Rainbo Beach Resort, 3520 Needles Highway, 760/326-3101, www.rainbobeach.com.

## 22 NEEDLES MARINA PARK

### Scenic rating: 6

on the Colorado River

**Map page 798**

Bring your suntan lotion and a beach towel. This section of the Colorado River is a big tourist spot where the body oil and beer can flow faster than the river. There are a ton of hot bodies and hot boats, and waterskiing dominates the adjacent calm-water section of the Colorado River. However, note that upstream of the Needles-area put-in is the prime area for waterskiing. Downstream is the chance for canoeing or kayaking. Meanwhile, there's also an 18-hole golf course adjacent to the camp, but most folks head for the river. Compared to the surrounding desert, this park is almost a golden paradise. A mobile home park is adjacent to the RV park.

**Campsites, facilities:** There are 158 sites with full hookups (30 and 50 amps) for tents or RVs, along with six cabins. Some sites are pull-through. Picnic tables are provided. Restrooms with flush toilets and showers, drinking water, heated pool, spa, recreation room, Wi-Fi, picnic area, boat ramp, boat slips, store, gas, and laundry facilities are available. Some facilities are wheelchair-accessible. Leashed pets are permitted.

**Reservations, fees:** Reservations are accepted ($2 reservation fee). Waterfront sites are $48 per night, non-waterfront sites are $50 per night, plus $5 per night for air conditioning, $10 per night per person for more than four people, and $5 per pet per night. Cabins are $100 per night ($100 deposit, two-night minimum). Reduced snowbird fees are offered October through March. Some credit cards are accepted. Open year-round.

**Directions:** Take I-40 to Needles and the exit for J Street. Take that exit and drive to Broadway. Turn left on Broadway and drive 0.75 mile to Needles Highway. Turn right (north) on Needles Highway and drive 0.5 mile to the park on the left.

**Contact:** Needles Marina Park, 760/326-2197, www.needlesmarinapark.com.

## 23 NEEDLES KOA

### Scenic rating: 2

near the Colorado River

**Map page 798**

At least you've got the Needles KOA out here—winner of the 2012 KOA President's Award. The swimming pool will help you get a new start, while side trips include venturing to the nearby Colorado River or heading north to Lake Mead. Of course, you could always go to Las Vegas. Nah.

**Campsites, facilities:** There are 93 pull-through sites with full hookups (30 and 50 amps) and 18 pull-through sites with partial hookups (30 and 50 amps) for tents or RVs of any length. Five cabins are also available. Restrooms with flush toilets and showers, drinking water, recreation room, swimming pool, playground, Wi-Fi, store, propane gas, and coin laundry are available. Some facilities are wheelchair-accessible. Leashed pets are permitted.

**Reservations, fees:** Reservations are accepted at 800/562-3407 or www.koa.com. RV sites are $35-40 per night, tent sites are $30 per night, plus $2 per person per night for more than two people. Cabins are $50-70 per night. Credit cards are accepted. Discounts are available. Open year-round.

**Directions:** Take I-40 to Needles and the exit for West Broadway. Take that exit to Needles Highway. Turn northwest on Needles Highway and drive 0.75 mile to National Old Trails Highway. Turn left and drive one mile to the park on the right.

**Contact:** Needles KOA, 5400 National Old Trails Highway, 760/326-4207, www.koa.com.

## 24 PIRATE COVE RESORT

### Scenic rating: 7

on the Colorado River

**Map page 798**

Campsites are situated in the main area of the park along 2.5 miles of shoreline peninsula. The park features 24 group areas. The adjacent Colorado River provides the main attraction, the only thing liquid around these parts that isn't contained in a can or bottle. The natural response when you see it is to jump in the water, and everybody does so, with or without

a boat. You'll see lots of wild and crazy types having the time of their lives on the water. The boating season is a long one here, courtesy of that desert climate. Fishing is good for catfish, smallmouth bass, bluegill, striped bass, and sometimes crappie. There are 3,800 miles of off-road trail in the immediate area.

**Campsites, facilities:** There is a large grassy area for tents and more than 600 sites for RVs or tents; 157 sites have full or partial hookups (20, 30, and 50 amps) and a few are pull-through. There are also 24 group camping areas. Picnic tables and fire grills are provided at most sites. Restrooms with flush toilets and showers, coin laundry, store, ice, two dump stations, covered picnic area, marina, bait, and boat ramp are available. Volleyball, basketball, horseshoes, and putting green are also available. An 18-hole golf course is nearby. Some facilities are wheelchair-accessible. Leashed pets are permitted, with restrictions.

**Reservations, fees:** Reservations are accepted at 866/301-3000 or 760/326-9000 or online at http://reservations.piratecoveresort.com ($10 reservation fee). Tent sites are $20 per night, RV sites are $40 (partial hookups) and $50 (full hookups) per night; peninsula sites have full hookups and are $50 per night with an eight person maximum per site. Pet fee is $2 per pet per night. Long-term rates are available in the winter, with a limit of five months. Some credit cards are accepted. Open year-round.

**Directions:** From Needles, drive east on I-40 for 11 miles to Park Moabi Road. Turn left on Park Moabi Road and continue 0.5 mile to the park entrance at the end of the road.

**Contact:** Pirate Cove Resort, 760/326-9000, www.piratecoveresort.com.

## 25 KINGS

### Scenic rating: 5

near Piru Creek in Los Padres National Forest

**Map page 798**

The Hungry Valley State Vehicular Recreation

Area is just five miles to the east. Figure it out: This is a primitive but well-placed camp for four-wheel-drive and off-highway vehicles. The camp is near Piru Creek, off a short spur road, so it feels remote yet is close to one of California's top off-road areas.

**Campsites, facilities:** There are seven sites for tents or RVs up to 16 feet (no hookups). Picnic tables and fire grills are provided. Vault toilets are available. No drinking water is available. Garbage must be packed out. Leashed pets are permitted.

**Reservations, fees:** Reservations are not accepted. There is no fee for camping, but an Adventure Pass ($30 annual fee or a $5 daily fee) per parked vehicle is required. Open year-round.

**Directions:** Drive on I-5 to south of Gorman and the Gorman-Hungry Valley Road exit (the northern exit for the Hungry Valley Recreation Area). Take that exit and turn south on Hungry Valley Road (Forest Road 8N01) and drive six miles to Gold Hill Road (Forest Road 8N01). Turn right and drive six miles to Forest Road 18N01A. Turn left and drive 0.75 mile to the campground.

**Contact:** Los Padres National Forest, Mount Piños Ranger District, 661/245-3731, www.fs.usda.gov/lpnf.

## 26 LOS ALAMOS

### Scenic rating: 4

near Pyramid Lake in Angeles National Forest

**Map page 798**      **BEST (**

Los Alamos is at an elevation of 2,600 feet near the southern border of the Hungry Valley State Vehicular Recreation Area, about 2.5 miles north of Pyramid Lake. Pyramid Lake is a big lake, covering 1,300 acres with 20 miles of shoreline, and is extremely popular for water-skiing and fast boating (35 mph speed limit), as well as for sailboarding (best at the northern launch point), fishing (best in the spring and early summer and in the fall for striped

bass), and swimming. A lifeguard is on duty at the boat launch area during the summer. Note: All boats must be certified mussel-free before launching.

**Campsites, facilities:** There are 93 sites and three group sites for tents or RVs up to 26 feet (no hookups) that can accommodate up to 40 people each. Picnic tables and fire pits are provided. Drinking water, flush toilets, dump station, volleyball courts, fish-cleaning stations, and a camp store are available. Boat rentals are nearby and a boat ramp is at the Emigrant Landing Picnic Area. Some facilities are wheelchair-accessible. Leashed pets are permitted.

**Reservations, fees:** Reservations are accepted and are required for the group site at 877/444-6777 ($10 reservation fee) or www.recreation.gov ($9 reservation fee). Sites are $20-25 per night, plus $10 per night per each additional vehicle and $5 per night for additional person (more than six people). Group sites are $85-125 per night. Open year-round.

**Directions:** Drive on I-5 to eight miles south of Gorman and the Smokey Bear Road exit. Take the Smokey Bear Road exit and drive west about 0.75 mile and follow the signs to the campground.

**Contact:** Parks Management Company, 805/434-1996; Angeles National Forest, Santa Clara/Mojave Rivers Ranger District, 661/269-2808, www.fs.usda.gov/angeles.

## 27 DUTCHMAN

### Scenic rating: 6

on Alamo Mountain in Los Padres National Forest

**Map page 798**

These spots at Dutchman are best known by four-wheel-drive enthusiasts rumbling around the area. The big attraction is access to Miller Jeep Trail, a gnarly black-diamond route that can bend metal and alter minds. This camp also provides an alternative to the Hungry Valley State Vehicular Recreation Area to the nearby northeast. (Note: The place is called Dutchman Flat, but the camp itself is just Dutchman.) The elevation is 6,800 feet.

**Campsites, facilities:** There are eight primitive sites. Picnic tables and fire grills are provided. Pit toilets are available. No drinking water is available. Garbage must be packed out. Leashed pets are permitted.

**Reservations, fees:** Reservations are not accepted. There is no fee for camping, but an Adventure Pass ($30 annual fee or a $5 daily fee) per parked vehicle is required. Open early May through October, weather permitting.

**Directions:** Drive on I-5 to south of Gorman and the Gorman-Hungry Valley Road exit (the northern exit for the Hungry Valley Recreation Area). Take that exit and turn south on Hungry Valley Road (Forest Road 8N01) and drive six miles to Gold Hill Road (Forest Road 8N01). Turn right and drive 13 miles to Twin Pines campground. To reach Dutchman, at Twin Pines campground, turn right at Forest Road 7N01 and drive three miles to the campground.

**Contact:** Los Padres National Forest, Mount Piños Ranger District, 661/245-3731, www.fs.usda.gov/lpnf.

## 28 HALF MOON
👣 🐕 🚐 ⛺

### Scenic rating: 7
near Piru Creek in Los Padres National Forest

**Map page 798**

Half Moon is a primitive camp set along Piru Creek at 4,700 feet elevation. Adjacent to camp, Forest Road 7N13 follows the creek for a few miles, then dead-ends at a trailhead that continues along more remote stretches of this little stream. Hikers should also consider the trail to nearby Thorn Point for a beautiful lookout. Piru Creek OHV Trail 128 also starts here.

**Campsites, facilities:** There are 10 sites for tents or RVs up to 22 feet (no hookups). Picnic tables and fire grills are provided. Vault toilets are available. No drinking water is available.

Garbage must be packed out. Leashed pets are permitted.

**Reservations, fees:** Reservations are not accepted. There is no fee for camping, but an Adventure Pass ($30 annual fee or a $5 daily fee) per parked vehicle is required. Open mid-May to mid-November, weather permitting.

**Directions:** Drive on I-5 to just south of Lebec and the Frazier Park exit. Take that exit and drive west on Frazier Mountain Road to the town of Lake of the Woods and Lockwood Valley Road. Turn left on Lockwood Valley Road and drive about 12 miles to Grade Valley Road (Forest Road 7N03). Turn left and drive 11 miles to the campground on the left. High-clearance or four-wheel-drive vehicles are recommended; access requires crossing a creek in which the current can be fairly fast and high, especially in the spring.

**Contact:** Los Padres National Forest, Mount Piños Ranger District, 661/245-3731, www.fs.usda.gov/lpnf.

## 29 SAWMILL
👣 🐕 🚐 ⛺

### Scenic rating: 7
on the Pacific Crest Trail in Angeles National Forest

**Map page 798**

This is a classic hikers' trailhead camp. It is at 5,200 feet elevation, right on the Pacific Crest Trail and just one mile from the junction with Burnt Peak Canyon Trail. For a good day hike, head southeast on the Pacific Crest Trail for one mile to Burnt Peak Canyon Trail, turn right (southwest), and hike just over a mile to Burnt Peak, at 5,788 feet elevation. Note that this camp is inaccessible after the first snow.

**Campsites, facilities:** There are eight sites for tents or RVs up to 16 feet (no hookups). Note that RVs are not recommended. Picnic tables and fire pits are provided. Vault toilets are available. No drinking water is available. Garbage must be packed out. Leashed pets are permitted.

**Reservations, fees:** Reservations are not accepted. There is no fee for camping. An Adventure Pass ($30 annual fee or $5 daily pass) per parked vehicle is required. Open year-round, weather permitting.

**Directions:** Drive on I-5 to the Tehachapi Mountains near the small town of Castaic and Lake Hughes Road. Turn northeast on Lake Hughes Road and drive 27 miles to the town of Lake Hughes and Pine Canyon Road/County Road N2. Turn left on Pine Canyon Road and drive 10 miles to Bushnell Summit Road. Turn left and drive two miles to the campground on the left.

**Contact:** Angeles National Forest, Santa Clara/Mojave Rivers Ranger District, 661-269-2808, www.fs.usda.gov/angeles.

## 30 SADDLEBACK BUTTE STATE PARK
🏃 🐕 ♿ 🚐 ⛺

**Scenic rating: 8**

near Lancaster

**Map page 798**

This 3,000-acre park was originally established to preserve ancient Joshua trees. In fact, it used to be called Joshua Tree State Park, but folks kept getting it confused with Joshua Tree National Park, so it was renamed. The terrain is sparsely vegetated and desertlike, with excellent hiking trails up the nearby buttes. The best hike is Saddleback Loop, a five-mile trip that features a 1,000-foot climb to Saddleback Summit at 3,651 feet. On rare clear days, there are fantastic views in all directions, including the Antelope Valley California Poppy Preserve, the surrounding mountains, and the Mojave Desert. On the typical hazy day, the poppy preserve might as well be on the moon; you can't even come close to seeing it. The elevation is 2,700 feet.

**Campsites, facilities:** There are 40 sites for tents or RVs up to 30 feet (no hookups). A group camp is available for up to 30 people and 12 vehicles. Picnic tables, shade ramadas, and fire grills are provided. Drinking water, flush toilets, and dump station are available. A visitors center is nearby. Some facilities are wheelchair-accessible. Leashed pets are permitted in the campground only.

**Reservations, fees:** Reservations are not accepted; call 661-946-6092 for group camping. Sites are $20 per night, plus $5 per night for each additional vehicle, and it's $100 per night for the group site. Open year-round.

**Directions:** Take Highway 14 north to Lancaster and the exit for Avenue J. Take that exit and drive east on Avenue J for 17 miles to the park entrance on the right. Or drive south on Highway 14 to Lancaster to the exit for 20th Street west. Take that exit, turn left, and drive to Avenue J. Turn east on Avenue J and drive 17 miles to the park entrance on the right.

**Contact:** Saddleback Butte State Park, Mojave Desert Information Center, 661-942-0662, www.parks.ca.gov.

## 31 SHADY OASIS VICTORVILLE
🏊 🐕 🏍 ♿ 🚐 ⛺

**Scenic rating: 3**

near Victorville

**Map page 798**

Most long-distance trips on I-15 are grueling endurance tests, with drivers making the mistake of trying to get a decent night's sleep at a roadside rest stop. Why endure the torture, especially with Shady Oasis way out here, in Victorville of all places? Where the heck is Victorville? If you are exhausted and lucky enough to find the place, you won't be making any jokes about it. Note: There are some permanent residents at this former KOA.

**Campsites, facilities:** There are 136 sites for tents or RVs up to 53 feet, many with full or partial hookups (50 amps) and some pull-through. There are also eight cabins. Picnic tables and fire grills are provided. Drinking water, restrooms with flush toilets and showers, recreation room, seasonal heated swimming pool, playground, Wi-Fi, convenience store, propane gas, and coin laundry are available. Some facilities are wheelchair-accessible. Leashed pets are permitted.

**Reservations, fees:** Reservations are accepted at 760/245-6867. Tent sites are $20-25 per night, RV sites are $40 for partial hookups (water and electricity) and $45 for full hookups per night. Camping cabins are $45 per night. Some credit cards are accepted. Open year-round.

**Directions:** Drive on I-15 to Victorville and Stoddard Wells Road (north of Victorville). Turn south on Stoddard Wells Road and drive a short distance to the campground.

**Contact:** Shady Oasis Victorville, 16530 Stoddard Wells Road, 760/245-6867, http://shadyoasis.tripod.com.

## 32 HESPERIA LAKE CAMPGROUND

### Scenic rating: 5

in Hesperia

**Map page 798**

This is a slightly more rustic alternative than the usual Hesperia campgrounds. There is a small lake/pond for recreational fishing along with a small fishing fee, but no fishing license is required. Boating and swimming are not allowed, but youngsters usually get a kick out of feeding the ducks and geese that live at the pond. A lake-record 268-pound sturgeon was caught and released back into the lake.

**Campsites, facilities:** There are 52 sites, some with partial hookups (30 and 50 amps), for tents or RVs up to 40 feet. Picnic tables and fire pits are provided. Drinking water, restrooms with flush toilets and showers, a playground, and a fishing pond are available. Some facilities are wheelchair-accessible. Leashed pets are permitted.

**Reservations, fees:** Reservations are accepted at 800/521-6332. Sites are $35 per night (reservations require a two-night minimum), plus $2 per night per pet and $18 to fish at the pond. Some credit cards are accepted. Open year-round.

**Directions:** Drive on I-15 to Hesperia and the exit for Main Street. Take that exit and drive east on Main Street for 9.5 miles (the road curves and becomes Arrowhead Lake Road) to the park on the left.

**Contact:** Hesperia Lake Campground, 760/244-5951 or 800/521-6332, www.hesperiaparks.com.

## 33 MOJAVE NARROWS REGIONAL PARK

### Scenic rating: 7

on the Mojave River

**Map page 798**

Almost no one except the locals knows about this little county park. It is like an oasis in the Mojave Desert. There are two small lakes: the larger Horseshoe Lake and Pelican Lake. No private boats are allowed, and rental rowboats and pedal boats are available on weekends. Swimming and water/body contact are prohibited. It is at 2,000 feet elevation and provides a few recreation options, including a pond stocked in season with trout and catfish, horseback-riding facilities, and equestrian trails. Hiking includes a wheelchair-accessible trail. The Mojave River level fluctuates here, almost disappearing in some years in summer and early fall. One of the big events of the year, the Huck Finn Jubilee, is on Father's Day in June. Note: The gate closes each evening.

**Campsites, facilities:** There are 68 sites for tents or RVs of any length, including seven pull-through sites and 38 sites with full hookups (15 and 30 amps). Nine group areas for up to 150 people are also available. Picnic tables and barbecue grills are provided. Drinking water, restrooms with flush toilets and showers, dump station, playground, picnic shelters, bait, horse rentals, and horseback-riding facilities are available. A store is three miles from the campground. Some facilities are wheelchair-accessible. Leashed pets are permitted.

**Reservations, fees:** Reservations are accepted for RV and group sites ($7 reservation fee for RV sites, $20 for groups). Tent sites are $30 per night, RV sites (hookups) are $40 per night, group areas are $20 per unit per night, plus $5 per night per additional person (over six people), $1 per night per pet, and an $8 per day fishing fee. Rates increase on holidays and during special events. Weekly rates are available. Discounts are offered for seniors. Some credit cards are accepted. Open year-round.

**Directions:** Take I-15 to Victorville and the exit for Bear Valley Road. Take that exit and drive east on Bear Valley Road for six miles to Ridgecrest. Turn left on Ridgecrest, drive three miles, and make a left into the park.

**Contact:** Mojave Narrows Regional Park, 760/245-2226, www.cms.sbcounty.gov/parks.

## 34 HAVASU LANDING RESORT AND CASINO

### Scenic rating: 7

on the western shore of Lake Havasu

**Map page 798**                    **BEST (**

Situated on the western shore of Lake Havasu, this full-service resort is run by the Chemehuevi Indian Tribe. It even includes a casino with slot machines and a card room. The resort is situated in a desert landscape in the Chemehuevi Valley. A boat shuttle operates from the resort to the London Bridge and Havasu City, Arizona. A mobile-home park is within the resort and an airstrip is nearby. Some RV sites are waterfront and some are rented for the entire winter. Permits are required for off-road vehicles and can be obtained at the resort. This is one of the most popular boating areas in the southwestern United States. The lake is 45 miles long, covers 19,300 acres, and is at the low elevation of 482 feet. Havasu was created when the Parker Dam was built across the Colorado River.

**Campsites, facilities:** There are 180 sites with full hookups (30 and 50 amps) for RVs up to 40 feet, three large tent camping areas, and mobile home rentals. Picnic tables, restrooms with flush toilets and showers, a dump station, coin laundry, picnic areas, restaurant and lounge, casino, 24-hour security, 24-hour marina with gas dock, bait and tackle, general store and deli, boat launches, boat slips, fish-cleaning room, dry storage, boat shuttle, and boat launch and retrieval service are available. Activities include movie nights and potluck socials. An ATM is on-site. An airport is nearby. Some facilities are wheelchair-accessible. Leashed pets are permitted.

**Reservations, fees:** Reservations are accepted at 760/858-4592 or online at www.havasulanding.com. Sites for tents and self-contained RVs are $20 per night, RV sites are $27-32 per night, plus $2 per person per night for more than two people and $10 per night for each additional vehicle. Holiday rates are higher. Weekly and monthly rates are available. A boat-launch fee is charged. Some credit cards are accepted. Open year-round.

**Directions:** From Needles, drive south on Highway 95 for 19 miles to Havasu Lake Road. Turn left and drive 17.5 miles to the resort on the right.

From Blythe, drive north on Highway 95 for 79 miles to Havasu Lake Road. Turn right and drive 17.5 miles to the resort on the right.

**Contact:** Havasu Landing Resort and Casino, 760/858-4592, www.havasulanding.com; Lake Havasu Tourism Bureau, 928/453-3444 or 800/242-8278, www.golakehavasu.com; Lake Havasu Area Chamber of Commerce, 928/855-4115, www.havasuchamber.com.

## 35 BLACK MEADOW LANDING

### Scenic rating: 7
south of Lake Havasu on the Colorado River

**Map page 798**

This area of the Colorado River attracts a lot of people, so reservations are highly recommended. Hot weather, warm water, and proximity to Las Vegas make this one of the top camping and boating hot spots in the West. Vacationers are here year-round, although fewer people use it in the late winter. Black Meadow Landing is a large resort with hundreds of RV sites, lodging, and a long list of amenities. Some sites—A Row—have water views. Once you arrive, everything you need for a stay should be available within the resort.

**Campsites, facilities:** There are 350 sites with full hookups (30 amps) for RVs up to 53 feet, and tent camping is available. Park-model cabins, kitchen cabins, and a motel are also options. Restrooms with flush toilets and showers, drinking water, picnic tables, picnic areas, horseshoe pit, restaurant, convenience store, recreation room (winter only), bait and tackle, propane, full-service marina, boat launch, boat slips, boat and RV storage, a swimming lagoon, and a five-hole golf course are available. Leashed pets are permitted.

**Reservations, fees:** Reservations are accepted at 877/642-8278. Waterfront RV sites (A and Z Rows, full hookups) are $55-60 per night, B Row sites are $55-60 per night, D and E Rows (water only) are $35 per night. RV park sites (1-168) are $35-40 per night, golf course RV sites (169-209) are $35-40 per night, plus $6 per person per night for more than two people and $6 per night for each additional vehicle. Weekly and monthly rates are available. Some credit cards are accepted. Open year-round.

**Directions:** From Southern California: Take I-10 east to Blythe and turn north on U.S. 95. Continue to Vidal Junction at the intersection of U.S. 95 and Highway 62. Turn east on Highway 62 and drive to Earp and Parker Dam Road. Continue straight on Parker Dam Road and drive to a Y intersection and Black Meadow Landing Road (near Parker Dam). Bear left on Black Meadow Landing Road and drive approximately nine miles to the resort at the end of the road.

From Northern California: From Barstow, take I-40 east and drive to Needles. Continue east on I-40 to Arizona Highway 95. Drive south on Arizona Highway 95 to Lake Havasu City. Continue south to the Parker Dam turn-off. Turn west and drive across the dam to a Y intersection and Black Meadow Landing Road. Bear right on Black Meadow Landing Road and drive approximately nine miles to the resort at the end of the road. Note: Towed vehicles are not allowed to cross the dam.

**Contact:** Black Meadow Landing, 760/663-4901, www.blackmeadowlanding.com; Lake Havasu Tourism Bureau, 928/453-3444 or 877/242-8278, www.golakehavasu.com; Lake Havasu Area Chamber of Commerce, 928/855-4115, www.havasuchamber.com.

## 36 RIVERLAND RV PARK

### Scenic rating: 6
on the Colorado River near Parker Dam

**Map page 798**

This resort is in the middle of a very popular boating area, particularly for waterskiing. Check out the park's live webcam for an on-the-spot feel for the place and the weather. Summer is the busiest time because of the sunshine and warm water. In the winter, although temperatures can get pretty cold, around 40°F at night, the campground fills with retirees from the snow and rain country. Even though the resort is way out there on the Colorado River, there are plenty of services, including a convenience store, swimming beach, and full-service marina. Insider's tip: One of the best spots for catfish is a few miles down the road below Parker Dam.

**Campsites, facilities:** There are 85 sites with

full hookups (50 amps) for RVs up to 42 feet. There are also six bungalows and eight RV rentals. Picnic tables are provided. Restrooms with flush toilets and showers, drinking water, cable television, Wi-Fi, convenience store, coin laundry, full-service marina with gas dock, boat launch, boat slips, boat and RV storage, swimming beach, fishing pier, bait, recreation room (winter only), volleyball court, and horseshoe pits are available. An ATM is on-site and an 18-hole golf course is about 20 minutes away in Arizona. Some facilities are wheelchair-accessible. Leashed pets are permitted, with restrictions.

**Reservations, fees:** Reservations are accepted at 760/663-3733. Sites are $58-79 per night, bungalows are $156-172 per night, and RV rentals are $184-210 per night. Weekly rates are available; monthly rates are available November through May. Some credit cards are accepted. Open year-round.

**Directions:** From Southern California, take I-10 east to Blythe and turn north on U.S. 95. Continue to Vidal Junction at the intersection of U.S. 95 and Highway 62. Turn east on Highway 62 and drive to Earp and Parker Dam Road. Continue straight on Parker Dam Road and drive five miles to the resort on the right.

**Contact:** Riverland RV Park, 760/663-3733, www.riverlandresort.net.

## 37 BLACK ROCK CAMP AND HORSE CAMP

🧍 🐕 ♿ 🚐 ⛺

### Scenic rating: 4

in Joshua Tree National Park

**Joshua Tree map, page 800**

This is the fanciest darn public campground this side of the desert. Why, it actually has drinking water. The camp is at the mouth of Black Rock Canyon, at 4,000 feet elevation, which provides good winter hiking possibilities amid unique (in other words, weird) rock formations, about a half-hour drive from the campground. Show up in summer and you'll

trade your gold for a sip of water. The camp is near the excellent Black Rock Canyon Visitor Center and a trailhead for a four-mile round-trip hike to a rock wash. If you scramble onward, the route continues all the way to the top of Eureka Peak, at 5,518 feet, an 11-mile round-trip. But hey, why not just drive there?

**Campsites, facilities:** There are 100 sites for tents or RVs up to 35 feet (no hookups) and 15 equestrian sites for up to six people and four horses per site. Picnic tables and fire grills are provided. Drinking water, flush toilets, and a dump station are available. The horse camp has hitching posts and a water faucet. Some facilities are wheelchair-accessible. Leashed pets are permitted, but not on trails.

**Reservations, fees:** Reservations are accepted October through May at 877/444-6777 ($10 reservation fee) or www.recreation.gov ($9 reservation fee). Sites are $15 per night, plus a $25 per vehicle park entrance fee. Open year-round, weather permitting.

**Directions:** From the junction of I-10 and Highway 62 near Palm Springs, drive northeast on Highway 62 for 22.5 miles to Yucca Valley and Joshua Lane. Turn right (south) on Joshua Lane and drive about five miles to the campground.

**Contact:** Joshua Tree National Park, 760/367-5500 or 760/362-4367, www.nps.gov/jotr; Visitors Center, 760/367-5522; Black Rock Nature Center, 760/365-6204.

## 38 INDIAN COVE CAMPGROUND

🧍 🐕 🚐 ⛺

### Scenic rating: 4

in Joshua Tree National Park

**Joshua Tree map, page 800**

This is one of the campgrounds near the northern border of Joshua Tree National Park. The vast desert park, covering 1,238 square miles, is best known for its unique granite formations and scraggly-looking trees. If you had to withstand the summer heat here, you'd look scraggly too. Drinking water is available at the Indian Cove Ranger Station, two miles from the campground.

**Campsites, facilities:** There are 101 sites for tents or RVs up to 35 feet (no hookups) and 13 group sites for tents only for up to 60 people. Picnic tables and fire grills are provided. Drinking water and vault toilets are available. Gas, groceries, and laundry services are available in Twentynine Palms (seven miles) or Joshua Tree (12 miles). Leashed pets are permitted, but not on trails.

**Reservations, fees:** Reservations are accepted October through May at 877/444-6777 ($10 reservation fee) or www.recreation.gov ($9 reservation fee). Sites are $15 per night, group sites are $25-40 per night, plus a $25 per vehicle park entrance fee. Open year-round.

**Directions:** From the junction of I-10 and Highway 62 near Palm Springs, drive northeast on Highway 62 for 22 miles to Yucca Valley, continue to the small town of Joshua Tree, and then continue nine miles to Indian Cove Road. Turn right and drive three miles to the campground.

**Contact:** Joshua Tree National Park, 760/367-5500 or 760/362-4367, www.nps.gov/jotr.

## 39 HIDDEN VALLEY

### Scenic rating: 7

in Joshua Tree National Park

**Joshua Tree map, page 800**

This is one of California's top campgrounds for rock-climbers. Set at 4,200 feet elevation in the high desert country, this is one of several camping options in the area. A trailhead is available two miles from camp at Barker Dam, an easy one-mile loop that features the Wonderland of Rocks. The hike takes you next to a small lake with magical reflections of rock formations off its surface. The RV sites here are snatched up quickly and this campground fills almost daily with rock-climbers.

**Campsites, facilities:** There are 44 sites for tents or RVs up to 25 feet (no hookups). Picnic tables and fire grills are provided. Vault toilets are available. There is no drinking water. Leashed pets are permitted.

**Reservations, fees:** Reservations are not accepted. Sites are $10 per night, and there's a $25 park entrance fee per vehicle. Open year-round.

**Directions:** From the junction of I-10 and Highway 62 near Palm Springs, drive northeast on Highway 62 for 22 miles to Yucca Valley, then continue to the small town of Joshua Tree and Park Boulevard. Turn south on Park Boulevard and drive 14 miles to the campground on the left.

**Contact:** Joshua Tree National Park, 760/367-5500 or 760/362-4367, www.nps.gov/jotr.

## 40 RYAN

### Scenic rating: 4

in Joshua Tree National Park

**Joshua Tree map, page 800**

This is one of the high desert camps in the immediate area (see also the Jumbo Rocks listing in this chapter). Joshua Tree National Park is a forbidding paradise: huge, hot, and waterless (most of the time). The unique rock formations look as if some great artist made them with a chisel. The elevation is 4,300 feet. The best hike in the park starts here—a three-mile round-trip to Ryan Mountain is a 1,000-foot climb to the top at 5,470 feet elevation. The view is simply drop-dead gorgeous, not only of San Jacinto, Tahquitz, and San Gorgonio peaks, but of several beautiful rock-studded valleys as well as the Wonderland of Rocks.

**Campsites, facilities:** There are 31 sites for tents or RVs up to 25 feet (no hookups). Picnic tables and fire grills are provided. Vault toilets are available. There is no drinking water. Leashed pets are permitted.

**Reservations, fees:** Sites are $10 per night, and there is a $25 park entrance fee per vehicle. Open year-round.

**Directions:** From the junction of I-10 and

Highway 62 near Palm Springs, drive northeast on Highway 62 to Twentynine Palms and Utah Trail. Turn right (south) on Utah Trail and drive about 20 miles to the campground entrance on the left.

**Contact:** Joshua Tree National Park, 760/367-5500 or 760/362-4367, www.nps.gov/jotr.

## 41 SHEEP PASS GROUP CAMP

### Scenic rating: 4

in Joshua Tree National Park

**Joshua Tree map, page 800**

Several campgrounds are in this stretch of high desert. Ryan campground (see listing in this chapter), just a couple of miles down the road, has an excellent trailhead for a trek to Ryan Mountain, the best hike in the park. Temperatures are routinely over 100°F here in the summer. (For details on this area, see the White Tank listing in this chapter.)

**Campsites, facilities:** There are six group camps for tents or RVs up to 25 feet (no hookups) that can accommodate 20-50 people. Picnic tables and fire grills are provided. Vault toilets are available. There is no drinking water. Leashed pets are permitted.

**Reservations, fees:** Reservations are accepted at 877/444-6777 or at www.recreation.gov ($9 reservation fee). Sites are $25-40 per night, plus a $25 park entrance fee per vehicle. Open year-round.

**Directions:** From the junction of I-10 and Highway 62 near Palm Springs, drive northeast on Highway 62 to Twentynine Palms and Utah Trail. Turn right (south) on Utah Trail and drive about 16 miles to the campground on the left.

**Contact:** Joshua Tree National Park, 760/367-5500 or 760/362-4367, www.nps.gov/jotr.

## 42 JUMBO ROCKS

### Scenic rating: 4

in Joshua Tree National Park

**Joshua Tree map, page 800**

Joshua Tree National Park covers more than 1,238 square miles. It is striking high-desert country with unique granite formations that seem to change color at different times of the day. At 4,400 feet, this camp is one of the higher ones in the park, with adjacent boulders and rock formations that look as if they have been strewn about by an angry giant. It is a popular site for rock-climbing.

**Campsites, facilities:** There are 124 sites for tents and a limited number of RVs up to 35 feet (no hookups). Picnic tables and fire grills are provided. Vault toilets are available. There is no drinking water. Leashed pets are permitted.

**Reservations, fees:** Reservations are not accepted. Sites are $10, and there is a $25 park entrance fee per vehicle. Open year-round.

**Directions:** From the junction of I-10 and Highway 62 near Palm Springs, drive northeast on Highway 62 to Twentynine Palms and Utah Trail. Turn right (south) on Utah Trail and drive about nine miles to the campground on the left side of the road.

**Contact:** Joshua Tree National Park, 760/367-5500 or 760/362-4367, www.nps.gov/jotr.

## 43 BELLE

### Scenic rating: 4

in Joshua Tree National Park

**Joshua Tree map, page 800**

This camp is at 3,800 feet elevation in rocky high country. It is one of six camps in the immediate area. (For more details, see the White Tank listing in this chapter.)

**Campsites, facilities:** There are 18 sites for tents or RVs up to 25 feet (no hookups). Picnic tables and fire grills are provided. Vault toilets are available. There is no drinking water. Leashed pets are permitted.

**Reservations, fees:** Reservations are not accepted. Sites are $10 per night, and there is a $25 park entrance fee per vehicle. Open year-round.

**Directions:** From the junction of I-10 and Highway 62 near Palm Springs, drive northeast on Highway 62 to Twentynine Palms and Utah Trail. Turn right (south) on Utah Trail and drive eight miles to Pinto Basin Road. Turn left (heading toward I-10) and drive about 1.5 miles to the campground on the left.

**Contact:** Joshua Tree National Park, 760/367-5500 or 760/362-4367, www.nps.gov/jotr.

## 44 WHITE TANK

### Scenic rating: 4
in Joshua Tree National Park

**Joshua Tree map, page 800**

Joshua Tree National Park is a unique area where the high and low desert meet. Winter is a good time to explore the beautiful boulder piles and rock formations amid scraggly Joshua trees. There are several trails in the area, with the best near Black Rock Campground, Hidden Valley, and Cottonwood. The elevation is 3,800 feet.

**Campsites, facilities:** There are 15 sites for tents and a limited number of RVs up to 25 feet (no hookups). Picnic tables and fire grills are provided. Vault toilets are available. There is no drinking water. Leashed pets are permitted.

**Reservations, fees:** Reservations are not accepted. Sites are $10 per night, and there is a $25 park entrance fee per vehicle. Open year-round.

**Directions:** From the junction of I-10 and Highway 62 near Palm Springs, drive northeast on Highway 62 to Twentynine Palms and Utah Trail. Turn right (south) on Utah Trail and drive eight miles to Pinto Basin Road. Turn left (heading toward I-10) and drive three miles to the campground on the left.

**Contact:** Joshua Tree National Park, 760/367-5500 or 760/362-4367, www.nps.gov/jotr.

## 45 COTTONWOOD

### Scenic rating: 4
in Joshua Tree National Park

**Joshua Tree map, page 800**

If you enter Joshua Tree National Park at its southern access point, this is the first camp you will reach. The park visitors center, where maps are available, is a mandatory stop. This park is vast, high-desert country, highlighted by unique rock formations, occasional scraggly trees, and vegetation that manages to survive the bleak, roasting summers. This camp is set at 3,000 feet elevation. A trailhead departs for an easy one-mile nature trail, where small signs have been posted to identify different types of vegetation. You'll notice, however, that they all look like cacti (the plants, not the signs, heh, heh).

**Campsites, facilities:** There are 62 sites for tents or RVs up to 35 feet (no hookups) and three tent-only group sites for 15-25 people. Picnic tables and fire grills are provided. Drinking water, flush toilets, and a dump station are available. Some facilities are wheelchair-accessible. Leashed pets are permitted.

**Reservations, fees:** Reservations are accepted for group sites only at 877/444-6777 ($10 reservation fee) or www.recreation.gov ($9 reservation fee). Sites are $15 per night, group sites are $30 per night, and park entrance is $25 per vehicle. Open year-round.

**Directions:** From Indio, drive east on I-10 for 35 miles to the exit for Pinto Basin Road/Twentynine Palms (near Chiriaco Summit). Take that exit and drive north for seven miles (entering the park) to the campground on the right.

**Contact:** Joshua Tree National Park, 760/367-5500 or 760/362-4367, www.nps.gov/jotr.

## 46 SAM'S FAMILY SPA

**Scenic rating: 5**

near Palm Springs

**Joshua Tree map, page 800**

Hot mineral pools attract swarms of winter vacationers to the Palm Springs area. This 50-acre park, set 13 miles outside of Palm Springs, provides an alternative to the more crowded spots nearby and is one of the few parks to allow tent campers. The therapeutic pools here are partially enclosed. The elevation is 1,000 feet. (For information on the tramway ride to Desert View west of Palm Springs, or the hike to Mount San Jacinto, see the Sky Valley Resort listing in this chapter.)

**Campsites, facilities:** There are 170 sites for tents and RVs up to 42 feet (with full hookups of 30 and 50 amps). Six mobile-home rentals and a motel are also available. Picnic tables are provided. There is a separate area with barbecues. Restrooms with showers, a playground, heated swimming pool, heated wading pool, four hot mineral pools, dry sauna and steam rooms, Wi-Fi, coin laundry, and convenience store are available. Some facilities are wheelchair-accessible. Leashed pets are permitted in the campground only.

**Reservations, fees:** Reservations are accepted online only, not by telephone. Sites are $55 per night, plus $10 per night per person for more than four people. An electricity deposit ($50) is required at time of registration. Weekly and monthly rates are available. Some credit cards are accepted. Open year-round.

**Directions:** From I-10 and Palm Springs, take the Palm Drive exit (to Desert Hot Springs). Drive north on Palm Drive for about two miles to Dillon Road. Turn right (east) on Dillon Road and drive 4.5 miles to the park on the right, at 70-875 Dillon Road.

**Contact:** Sam's Family Spa, 760/329-6457, www.samsfamilyspa.com.

## 47 SKY VALLEY RESORT

**Scenic rating: 5**

near Palm Springs

**Joshua Tree map, page 800**

This 140-acre park is much like a small town, complete with RV homes, an RV park, and park-model rentals and seasonal restaurants. But it's the nine hot spring pools that bring people in. One of the best adventures in California is just west of Palm Springs, taking the aerial tram up from Chino Canyon to Desert View, a ride/climb of 2,600 feet for remarkable views to the east across the desert below. An option from there is hiking the flank of Mount San Jacinto, including making the ascent to the summit (10,804 feet), a round-trip butt-kicker of nearly 12 miles. Golf courses are nearby. Note that there are 260 permanent residents.

**Campsites, facilities:** There are 618 sites with full hookups (30 and 50 amps) for RVs up to 42 feet. Restrooms with showers, cable TV, four swimming pools, nine natural hot mineral whirlpools, two laundry rooms, two large recreation rooms, fitness centers, children's playroom, seasonal grocery store, chapel program, seasonal tennis and golf lessons, pickleball court, Wi-Fi, activities director, shuffleboard, tennis, horseshoes, crafts room, and walking paths are available. Propane gas is nearby. Some facilities are wheelchair-accessible. Leashed pets are permitted.

**Reservations, fees:** Reservations are recommended (especially in winter) at 888/894-7727, 760/329-8400, or online. Sites are $55-64 per night, plus $5 per person per night for more than two people. The weekly rate is $330 for up to two people. Discounts are offered off-season. Monthly rates are available. Some credit cards are accepted. Open year-round.

**Directions:** From I-10 and Palm Springs, take the Palm Drive exit (to Desert Hot Springs). Drive north on Palm Drive for three miles to Dillon Road. Turn right on Dillon Road and drive 8.5 miles to the park on the right.

**Contact:** Sky Valley Resort, 74-711 Dillon Road, 760/329-2909, www.skyvalleyresort.com.

## 48 HAPPY TRAVELER RV PARK

### Scenic rating: 1

in Palm Springs

Joshua Tree map, page 800

Are we having fun yet? They are at Happy Traveler, which is within walking distance of Palm Springs shopping areas and restaurants. The nearby Palm Springs Air Museum has a collection of World War II aircraft. A casino is one mile away.

**Campsites, facilities:** There are 130 sites with full hookups (30 and 50 amps) for RVs up to 40 feet. No tents or tent trailers are permitted. Picnic tables are provided. Restrooms with showers, cable TV, Wi-Fi, swimming pool, spa, clubhouse, shuffleboard, propane, seasonal activities, and coin laundry are available. Leashed pets are permitted with restrictions, including a maximum of two pets.

**Reservations, fees:** Reservations are accepted. Sites are $55 per night. Weekly and monthly rates are available. Credit cards are not accepted. Open year-round.

**Directions:** From I-10 and Palm Springs, take the exit for Highway 111/Palm Canyon Drive. Drive 12 miles south on Palm Canyon Drive to Mesquite Avenue. Turn right on Mesquite Avenue and drive to the park on the left.

**Contact:** Happy Traveler RV Park, 211 West Mesquite, 760/325-8518, www.happytravel-errv.com.

## 49 OUTDOOR RESORT OF PALM SPRINGS

### Scenic rating: 6

near Cathedral City

Joshua Tree map, page 800

This is considered a five-star resort, beautifully landscaped, huge, and offering many activities: swimming pools galore, a 27-hole golf course, tons of tennis courts, spas, and on and on. The 137-acre park is four miles from Palm Springs. Note that this is a lot-ownership park with lots for sale. About a quarter of the sites are available for rent to vacationers. One of the best adventures in California is just west of Palm Springs: taking the aerial tram up from Chino Canyon to Desert View, a ride/climb of 2,600 feet for remarkable views to the east across the desert below.

**Campsites, facilities:** There are 1,213 sites with full hookups (30 and 50 amps) for RVs up to 45 feet. RV rentals are also available. Restrooms with showers, eight swimming pools, spas, 14 lighted tennis courts, 27-hole golf course, two clubhouses, snack bar, café, beauty salon, coin laundry, Wi-Fi, convenience store, fitness center, and planned activities are available. Some facilities are wheelchair-accessible. Leashed pets are permitted.

**Reservations, fees:** Reservations are accepted at 800/843-3131 (California only). Sites start at $70-80 per night, plus $1 per pet per night with a two-pet maximum. RV rentals are $32-75 per night. Guest registration fee is $10. Monthly rates are available. Some credit cards are accepted. Open year-round.

**Directions:** From I-10 and Palm Springs, continue on I-10 Cathedral City and the exit for Date Palm Drive. Take that exit and drive south on Date Palm Drive for two miles to Ramon Road. Turn left and drive to the resort on the right.

**Contact:** Outdoor Resort, 69-411 Ramon Road, 760/347-6777, www.outdoorresort.com.

## 50 PALM SPRINGS OASIS RV PARK

### Scenic rating: 2

in Cathedral City

**Joshua Tree map, page 800**

This popular wintering spot is for RV cruisers looking to hole up in the Palm Springs area for a while. Palm Springs is only six miles away. This is a seniors-only park: Children are not allowed, and one person must be at least 55 years of age to check in; anyone else must be at least 40.

**Campsites, facilities:** There are 140 sites with full hookups (30 and 50 amps) for RVs up to 45 feet. Restrooms with showers, cable TV, Wi-Fi, two swimming pools, spa, tennis and shuffleboard courts, coin laundry, dump station, dog run, game room, and propane gas are available. An 18-hole golf course is adjacent to the park. Some facilities are wheelchair-accessible. Leashed pets are permitted, with a two-pet maximum.

**Reservations, fees:** Reservations are accepted. Sites are $49-61 per night, plus $2 per person per night for more than two people and a $3 per night resort fee. Weekly, monthly, and off-season rates are available. Some credit cards are accepted. Open year-round.

**Directions:** From I-10 and Palm Springs, continue on I-10 to Cathedral City and the exit for Date Palm Drive. Take that exit and drive south on Date Palm Drive for four miles to Gerald Ford Drive and the park on the left corner.

**Contact:** Palm Springs Oasis RV Park, 36-100 Date Palm Drive, 760/328-4813 or 800/680-0144.

## 51 INDIAN WELLS CAREFREE RV RESORT

### Scenic rating: 2

in Indio

**Joshua Tree map, page 800**

Indio is a good-sized town midway between the Salton Sea to the south and Palm Springs to the north, which is about 20 miles away. In the summer, it is one of the hottest places in America. In the winter, it is a favorite for "snowbirds"; that is, RV and trailer owners from the snow country who migrate south for the winter. About half of the sites are filled with long-term renters.

**Campsites, facilities:** There are 305 sites with full hookups (50 amps) for RVs up to 45 feet; some are pull-through. No tents are permitted. Restrooms with showers, cable TV, Wi-Fi, three swimming pools, two therapy pools, horseshoes, basketball, water volleyball, shuffleboard courts, driving net and putting green, recreation room, planned activities, ice, mini dog run, picnic area, RV storage, and coin laundry are available. Some facilities are wheelchair-accessible. Leashed pets are permitted.

**Reservations, fees:** Reservations are accepted at 800/789-0895 and online. Sites are $47-69 per night. Weekly and monthly rates are available. Some credit cards are accepted. Open year-round.

**Directions:** From I-10 in Indio, take the exit for Jefferson Street. Stay in the right lane and drive to the stoplight at Jefferson. Turn right at Jefferson and drive south for three miles to the park on the left.

**Contact:** Indian Wells RV Resort, 47-340 Jefferson Street, 760/347-0895, www.carefreervresorts.com.

## 52 OUTDOOR RESORTS INDIO

### Scenic rating: 7

in Indio

**Joshua Tree map, page 800**

For owners of tour buses, motor coaches, and lavish RVs, it doesn't get any better than this in Southern California. Only RVers in Class A motor homes are allowed here. This resort bills itself as the "ultimate RV resort" and has been featured on the Travel Channel and in the *Wall Street Journal*. About 25 percent of the sites are available for rent; all sites are owned by RVers. This park is close to golf, shopping, and restaurants. Jeep tours of the surrounding desert canyons and organized recreation events are offered.

**Campsites, facilities:** There are 419 sites with full hookups (50 amps) for Class A motor homes with a minimum length of 34 feet; no trailers or pickup-truck campers are permitted. Restrooms with showers, cable TV, Wi-Fi, swimming pools, pickleball courts, tennis courts, sauna, spas, café, fitness center, clubhouse, coin laundry, and an 18-hole golf course are available. Some facilities are wheelchair-accessible. Leashed pets are permitted, with a two-pet maximum.

**Reservations, fees:** Reservations are accepted. Sites are $75-145 per night, plus $5 per night per additional person more than four (six people maximum). Rates include greens fees, tennis, and pickleball. Discounts are offered in summer. Some credit cards are accepted. Open year-round with a minimum stay of four nights.

**Directions:** From I-10 in Indio, take the exit for Indio Boulevard/Jefferson Street. Stay in the right lane and drive to the stoplight at Jefferson. Turn right at Jefferson and drive south for three miles to Avenue 48. Turn left and drive 0.25 mile to the park on the left side of the road.

**Contact:** Outdoor Resorts Indio, 80-394 Avenue 48, 760/775-7255 or 800/892-2992, www.orindio.com.

## 53 MIDLAND LONG TERM VISITOR AREA

### Scenic rating: 4

west of Blythe

**Map page 798**

Like its neighbor to the south (Mule Mountain), this camp is attractive to snowbirds, rockhounds (geodes and agates can be collected), and stargazers. The campground is on the southwest slope of the Big Maria Mountains, a designated wilderness, set at an elevation of 250 feet. The campsites are on flattened desert pavements consisting of alluvium. The desert landscape is extremely stark.

**Campsites, facilities:** There are numerous dispersed sites for tents or RVs of any length (no hookups). Barbecue stands and fire rings are provided. Drinking water and toilets are not available. A dump station and trash service are provided.

**Reservations, fees:** Reservations are not accepted. Sites are $40 for up to 14 nights, or $180 per season. Fees are charged mid-September through mid-April. Summer camping is free, with a 14-day limit. Open year-round.

**Directions:** From Blythe, drive east on I-10 a short distance to Lovekin Boulevard. Turn left and drive about eight miles to the campground on the right.

**Contact:** Bureau of Land Management, Palm Springs Field Office, 760/833-7100, www.blm.gov/ca.

## 54 MAYFLOWER COUNTY PARK

### Scenic rating: 6

on the Colorado River

**Map page 798**

The Colorado River is the fountain of life around these parts and, for campers, the main attraction of this county park. It is a popular spot for waterskiing. There is river access in the

Blythe area. Fishing is good for channel and flathead catfish, striped bass, large- and smallmouth bass, bluegill, and crappie. This span of water is flanked by agricultural lands, although there are several developed recreation areas on the California side of the river south of Blythe near Palo Verde.

**Campsites, facilities:** There are 27 tent sites and 152 sites for RVs of any length (with partial hookups of 30 and 50 amps). Youth group camping (20-person minimum) is available. Picnic tables and fire grills are provided. Drinking water, restrooms with flush toilets and free showers, dump station, shuffleboard, lawn bowling, horseshoes, and boat ramp are available. Some facilities are wheelchair-accessible. Leashed pets are permitted.

**Reservations, fees:** Reservations are not accepted. Tent sites are $20 per night, RV sites are $32 (partial hookups) and $37 (full hookups) per night, plus a $6 boat launch fee and $1 per pet per night. Weekly and monthly rates are available. Some credit cards are accepted. Open year-round.

**Directions:** Drive on I-10 to Blythe and Highway 95. Take Highway 95 north (it becomes Intake Boulevard) and drive 3.5 miles to 6th Avenue. Turn right at 6th Avenue and drive 2.5 miles to Colorado River Road. Bear left and drive 0.5 mile to the park entrance.

**Contact:** Mayflower County Park, 760/922-4665, www.rivcoparks.org.

## 55 RIVIERA RV RESORT

**Scenic rating: 6**

near Blythe

**Map page 798**

This RV park is set up for camper-boaters who want to hunker down for a while along the Colorado River and cool off. Access to the park is easy off I-10, and a marina is available, both big pluses for those showing up with trailered boats. Swimming lagoons are another bonus. A

golf course is within 10 miles. Note that about half of the sites are rented year-round.

**Campsites, facilities:** There are 287 sites for RVs of any length (with full hookups of 30 and 50 amps); some sites are pull-through. Tents are allowed, and seven park-model cabins are available. Picnic tables are provided. Restrooms with showers, heated swimming pool, spa, cable TV, Wi-Fi, coin laundry, convenience store, card room, 24-hour security, RV and boat storage, arcade, recreation center, boat ramps, boat fuel, bike and boat rentals, and propane gas are available. Some facilities are wheelchair-accessible. Leashed pets are permitted, with certain restrictions.

**Reservations, fees:** Reservations are accepted at 760/922-5350 or 855/922-5350. RV sites are $44.11-59.49 per night, tent sites are $25-29.11 per night, plus $3 per person for more than four adults and $10 per night for each additional vehicle; cabins are $127.37 per night with a two-night minimum. Holiday rates are higher. Monthly rates are available. Credit cards are accepted. Open year-round.

**Directions:** Drive on I-10 to Blythe and continue east for two miles to the exit for Riviera Drive. Take that exit east and drive two miles to the park on the right.

**Contact:** Riviera RV Resort, Blythe, 500 Riviera Drive, 760/922-5350 or 855/922-5350, www.rivierarvresort.com.

## 56 DESTINY MCINTYRE RV RESORT

**Scenic rating: 3**

on the Colorado River

**Map page 798**

This RV park sits on the outskirts of Blythe on the Colorado River, with this stretch of river providing good conditions for boating, waterskiing, and other water sports. A swimming lagoon is a big plus, along with riverfront beach access. Fishing is an option, with a variety of fish, including striped bass, largemouth bass, and catfish, providing fair results.

**Campsites, facilities:** There are 40 tent sites and 30 RV sites with full hookups (30 and 50 amps), including 11 pull-through sites. Picnic tables and fire rings are provided. Drinking water, restrooms with flush toilets and showers, dump station, propane gas, store, bait, ice, and boat ramp and boat fuel are available. Some facilities are wheelchair-accessible. Leashed pets are permitted.

**Reservations, fees:** Reservations are accepted at 760/922-8205 or http://destinyrv.com. Premium sites are $20-37 per night, deluxe and standard sites are $35 per night, dry tent sites are $10 per night, plus $4 per person (over age 9) per night for more than two people and $10 per night for each additional vehicle. Monthly rates are available. Some credit cards are accepted. Open year-round.

**Directions:** Drive on I-10 to Blythe to the exit for Intake Boulevard south. Take that exit and drive south on Intake Boulevard for 6.5 miles to the junction with 26th Avenue (it takes off to the right) and the park entrance on the left. Turn left and enter the park.

**Contact:** Destiny McIntyre RV Resort, 760/922-8205, www.destinyrv.com.

## 57 PALO VERDE COUNTY PARK

🥾 🏊 🛶 🚤 🎣 ♿ 🚐 ⛺

### Scenic rating: 5

near the Colorado River

**Map page 798**

This is the only game in town, with no other camp around for many miles. It is near a bend in the Colorado River, not far from the Cibola National Wildlife Refuge. A boat ramp is available at the park, making it a launch point for adventure. This stretch of river is a good one for powerboating and waterskiing. The best facilities for visitors are available here and on the west side of the river between Palo Verde and

Blythe, with nothing available on the east side of the river.

**Campsites, facilities:** There are 20 sites for tents or RVs of any length (no hookups). Picnic tables, fire rings, restrooms with flush toilets, and shade ramadas are available. No drinking water is available. A boat ramp is available. A store, coin laundry, and propane gas are in Palo Verde. Some facilities are wheelchair-accessible. Leashed pets are permitted.

**Reservations, fees:** Reservations are not accepted. Sites are $15 per night with a seven-day limit. Open year-round.

**Directions:** Drive on I-10 to Highway 78 (two miles west of Blythe). Take Highway 78 south and drive about 20 miles (three miles past Palo Verde) to the park entrance road on the east side.

**Contact:** Palo Verde County Park, Imperial County, 760/482-4236, www.icpds.com.

## 58 MULE MOUNTAIN LONG TERM VISITOR AREA

🥾 🏕 ♿ 🚐 ⛺

### Scenic rating: 4

west of Blythe

**Map page 798**

Mule Mountain is out in the middle of nowhere, but rockhounds and stargazers have found it anyway; it's ideal for both activities. There are two campgrounds, Coon Hollow and Wiley's Well, along with dispersed camping. Rockhounding, in particular, can be outstanding, with several geode and agate beds nearby. Hobby rock-collecting is permitted. Commercial rock-poaching is not. The site, ideal for winter camping, attracts snowbirds and is set in a desert landscape at an elevation of 150 feet. Bradshaw Trail runs east to west through the visitors area.

**Campsites, facilities:** There are 29 sites at Coon Hollow and 14 sites at Wiley's Well for tents or RVs up to 35 feet (no hookups). Picnic tables, shade ramadas, and fire grills are provided. Vault toilets and trash service are available. There is no drinking water. A dump station is nearby, halfway between the two campgrounds, and is available mid-September through mid-April. Some facilities are wheelchair-accessible. Leashed pets are permitted.

**Reservations, fees:** Reservations are not accepted. Sites are $40 for up to 14 nights or $180 per season, with a 14-day stay limit every 28 days. Open year-round.

**Directions:** From Blythe, drive west on I-10 about 15 miles to Wiley's Well Road. Turn left (south) and drive about nine miles (the road turns to dirt) to Wiley's Well. Continue another three miles to reach Coon Hollow. Dispersed camping is allowed once you pass the sign that indicates you're in the visitors center.

**Contact:** Bureau of Land Management, Palm Springs Field Office, 760/833-7100, www.blm.gov/ca.

## 59 TOOL BOX SPRINGS
🏃 🐕 ⛺

**Scenic rating: 5**

in San Bernardino National Forest

**Map page 798**

This is a lightly used campground well off the beaten track. More like off the beaten universe. That makes it perfect for people who want to be by themselves when they go camping. Ramona Trail begins at the campground, heads north, and provides a 3.5-mile one-way hike, with a 1,500-foot loss and then gain in elevation. In the winter, call for road conditions to determine accessibility. The elevation is 6,500 feet.

**Campsites, facilities:** There are six tent sites as well as dispersed camping. Picnic tables and fire grills are provided. Vault toilets are available, but there is no drinking water. Garbage must be packed out. Leashed pets are permitted.

**Reservations, fees:** Reservations are not accepted. There is no fee for camping. An Adventure Pass ($30 annual fee or $5 daily pass) per parked vehicle is required. Open year-round, but subject to closure during fire season.

**Directions:** From Hemet, drive east on Highway 74 into San Bernardino National Forest and continue just past Lake Hemet to Forest Road 6S13. Turn right on Forest Road 6S13 (paved, then dirt) and drive four miles to a fork. Bear left at the fork and continue on Forest Road 6S13 for 4.5 miles to the camp on the left.

**Contact:** San Bernardino National Forest, San Jacinto Ranger District, 909/382-2921, www.fs.usda.gov/sbnf.

## 60 PINYON FLAT
🏃 🐕 ♿ 🚐 ⛺

**Scenic rating: 6**

near Cahuilla Tewanet Vista Point in San Bernardino National Forest

**Map page 798**

The Cahuilla Tewanet Vista Point is just two miles east of the camp and provides a good, easy side trip, along with a sweeping view of the desert to the east on clear days. A primitive trail is two miles to the southeast via Forest Road 7S01 off a short spur road (look for it on the left side of the road). This hike crosses a mix of sparse forest and high-desert terrain for 10 miles, passing Cactus Spring five miles in. Desert bighorn sheep are sometimes spotted in this area. The elevation is 4,000 feet.

**Campsites, facilities:** There are 18 sites for tents or RVs up to 15 feet (no hookups). Picnic tables and fire rings are provided. Drinking water and vault toilets are available. Some facilities are wheelchair-accessible. Leashed pets are permitted.

**Reservations, fees:** Reservations are not accepted. Sites are $8 per night. Open year-round.

**Directions:** Drive on I-10 to Palm Springs and Highway 111. Turn south on Highway 111 and drive to Rancho Mirage and Highway 74. Turn right (south) on Highway 74 and drive 14 miles (a slow, twisty road) to the campground on the right.

**Contact:** San Bernardino National Forest, San

Jacinto Ranger District, 909/382-2921, www.
fs.usda.gov/sbnf.

## 61 LAKE CAHUILLA COUNTY PARK

**Scenic rating: 7**

near Indio

Map page 798

Lake Cahuilla covers just 135 acres, but those
are the most-loved 135 acres for miles in all directions. After all, water out here is as scarce
as polar bears. This 710-acre Riverside County
park provides large palm trees and a 10-acre
beach and water-play area (no swimming or
boating is allowed). The lake is stocked with
trout in the winter and in the summer with
catfish; other species include largemouth and
striped bass, crappie, and carp up to 30 pounds.
An equestrian camp is also available, complete
with corrals, and equestrian and hiking trails
are on nearby public land. Morrow Trail is popular, and the trailhead is near the park's ranger
station. A warning: The wind can really howl
through here, and temperatures well over 100°F
are typical in the summer.

**Campsites, facilities:** There are 55 RV sites
with partial hookups (30 and 50 amps), 10 RV
sites (water only), a primitive camping area
with 30 sites for tents or RVs (no hookups), a
large group area, and an equestrian area with
20 sites (partial hookups) and horse corrals.
Maximum RV length is 45 feet, except in the
equestrian area where any length can be accommodated. Fire grills and picnic tables are
provided. Restrooms with showers, a dump station, and a seasonal swimming pool are available. Some facilities are wheelchair-accessible.
Leashed pets are permitted.

**Reservations, fees:** Reservations are accepted at 800/234-7275 ($7 reservation fee).
Tent sites are $15 per night, RV sites are $22-
35 per night, group camping is $150-210, and
it's $1 per pet per night. Weekly rates are avail-
able during the winter. Maximum stay is two

weeks. Some credit cards are accepted. Open
year-round; closed Tuesday through Thursday
May through October.

**Directions:** Drive on I-10 to Indio and the exit
for Monroe Street. Take that exit and drive
south on Monroe Street to Avenue 58. Turn
right (west) and drive two miles to the park at
the end of the road.

**Contact:** Lake Cahuilla County Park, 760/564-
4712, www.rivcoparks.org.

## 62 HEADQUARTERS

**Scenic rating: 5**

in the Salton Sea State Recreation Area

Map page 798

The giant Salton Sea is a vast, shallow, and
unique lake—the center of a 360-square-mile
basin and one of the world's inland seas. Salton
Sea was created in 1905 when a dike broke and,
in turn, the basin was flooded with saltwater.
The lake is 35 miles long, but it has an average depth of just 15 feet. This is the northernmost campground, set at the recreation area
headquarters just south of the town of Desert
Beach at an elevation of 227 feet below sea level.
Fishing for tilapia is popular, and this is also
one of Southern California's most popular
boating areas. Because of the low altitude, at-
mospheric pressure allows high performance
for many ski boats. If winds are hazardous, a
red beacon on the northeast shore of the lake
will flash. If you see it, get to the nearest shore.
Camp use is moderate year-round but is lowest
in the summer thanks to temperatures that can
hover in the 110°F range for days.

**Campsites, facilities:** There are 15 sites with
full hookups (30 amps) for RVs up to 40 feet,
30-40 sites for tents or RVs with no hookups,
and several hike-in/bike-in sites. Picnic tables,
fire grills, and shade ramadas are provided.
Drinking water, restrooms with flush toilets
and coin showers, dump station, fish-cleaning
station, and visitors center with Wi-Fi access
are available. A store is within two miles. Some

facilities are wheelchair-accessible. Leashed pets are permitted in the campgrounds and on roadways only.

**Reservations, fees:** Reservations are accepted October through May at 800/444-7275 or www. reserveamerica.com ($8 reservation fee). Sites (no hookups) are $15-20 per night, RV sites (full hookups) are $30 per night, and hike-in/bike-in sites are $10 per person per night. Boat launching is $3 per day. Open year-round.

**Directions:** From Los Angeles, take I-10 east to Indio and the exit for the Highway 86 Expressway. Take that exit and drive south for 12 miles to 66th Avenue. Turn left and drive less than one mile to Mecca and Highway 111. Turn right (south) on Highway 111 and drive 12 miles to the entrance on the right.

**Contact:** Salton Sea State Recreation Area, 760/331-9944 or 760/393-3059, www.parks. ca.gov.

# 63 MECCA BEACH

🚶 🚲 🏊 🎣 🚐 🐴 ♿ 🚙 ⛺

**Scenic rating: 4**

in the Salton Sea State Recreation Area

**Map page 798**

This is one of the camps in the Salton Sea State Recreation Area on the northeastern shore of the lake. The big attractions are the waterfront sites, which are not available at nearby Headquarters campground (see listing in this chapter).

**Campsites, facilities:** There are 50 sites (no hookups) for tents or RVs of any length, four sites with full hookups (30 amps), and several hike-in/bike-in sites. Picnic tables and fire grills are provided. Drinking water, restrooms with flush toilets and showers, an amphitheater, and a fish-cleaning station are available. A dump station is one mile north of Headquarters campground and a store is within 3.5 miles. Some facilities are wheelchair-accessible. Leashed pets are permitted in the campgrounds and on roadways only.

**Reservations, fees:** Reservations are not

accepted. Sites are $15-20 per night, RV sites (hookups) are $30 per night, and it's $10 per person per night for hike-in/bike-in sites. Boat launching is $3 per day. Open October through May.

**Directions:** From the Los Angeles area, take I-10 east to Indio and the exit for the Highway 86 Expressway. Take that exit and drive south for 12 miles to 66th Avenue. Turn left and drive less than one mile to Mecca and Highway 111. Turn right (south) on Highway 111 and drive 12.5 miles to the entrance on the right.

**Contact:** Salton Sea State Recreation Area, 760/393-3052 or 760/393-3059, www.parks. ca.gov.

# 64 SALT CREEK PRIMITIVE AREA

🚶 🚲 🏊 🎣 🚣 🐴 ♿ 🚙 ⛺

**Scenic rating: 4**

in the Salton Sea State Recreation Area

**Map page 798**

Waterfront campsites are a bonus at this campground, even though the campground consists of just an open area on hard-packed dirt. Birding hikes are available during winter months. Several trails leave from camp, or nearby the camp, and head 1-2 miles to the Bat Cave Buttes, which are in the Durmid Hills on Bureau of Land Management property. There are bats in the numerous caves to explore, although the nearby OHV traffic has reduced their numbers. From the buttes, which are up to 100 feet above sea level, hikers can see both the north and south ends of the Salton Sea simultaneously. This is the only easily accessible place to view both shores of the Salton Sea. Many people believe the buttes are the southernmost point of the San Andreas Fault; the fault does not exist above ground south of here. (For details on the Salton Sea State Recreation Area, see the Headquarters listing in this chapter.)

**Campsites, facilities:** There are 200 primitive sites for tents or RVs of any length (no hookups) and several hike-in/bike-in sites. Drinking water and vault toilets are available. Fires are permitted in metal containers only. Leashed pets are permitted in the campgrounds and on roadways only.

**Reservations, fees:** Reservations are not accepted. Sites are $15 per night or $10 per person per night for hike-in/bike-in sites. Open October through May.

**Directions:** From Los Angeles, take I-10 east to Indio and the exit for the Highway 86 Expressway. Take that exit and drive south for 12 miles to 66th Avenue. Turn left and drive less than one mile to Mecca and Highway 111. Turn right (south) on Highway 111 and drive 17.5 miles to the entrance on the right.

**Contact:** Salton Sea State Recreation Area, 760/393-3052 or 760/393-3059, www.parks.ca.gov.

## 65 FOUNTAIN OF YOUTH SPA

### Scenic rating: 4

near the Salton Sea

**Map page 798**

Natural artesian steam rooms are the highlight here, but close inspection reveals that nobody seems to be getting any younger. This is a vast private park on 90 acres, set near the Salton Sea. Though this park has 1,000 sites for RVs, almost half of the them have seasonal renters. This park is popular with snowbird campers, and about 2,000 people live here during the winter. (See the Red Hill Marina County Park listing in this chapter for side-trip options.)

**Campsites, facilities:** There are 835 sites with full hookups (30 and 50 amps) and 165 "dry camp" sites with no hookups for tents or RVs. Park home rentals are available. Restrooms with flush toilets and showers, cable TV, natural artesian steam rooms, swimming pools, artesian mineral water spa, three freshwater spas, recreation halls, dump stations, fitness room, library, picnic areas, nine-hole desert-style golf course, horseshoes, organized activities, craft and sewing room, Wi-Fi, coin laundry, beauty parlor, masseur, church services, propane gas, and groceries are available. Some facilities are wheelchair-accessible. Leashed pets are permitted.

**Reservations, fees:** Reservations are not accepted. RV sites are $45-57 per night, dry camp sites are $22 per night, plus $2 per person per night for more than two people. Park home rentals are $595-695 per week. Discounts are offered off-season. Weekly and monthly rates are available. Some credit cards are accepted. Open year-round.

**Directions:** From Los Angeles: Take I-10 east to Indio and the exit for the Highway 86 Expressway. Take that exit and drive south for 12 miles to Avenue 62. Turn right and drive less than one mile to Highway 111. Turn left (south) on Highway 111 and drive 44 miles to Hot Mineral Spa Road. Turn left (north) on Hot Mineral Spa Road and drive approximately four miles to Spa Road. Turn right and drive approximately 1.5 miles to the park on the left.

From Calipatria: Take Highway 111 north to Niland, then continue north for 15 miles to Hot Mineral Spa Road. Turn right (north) on Hot Mineral Spa Road and drive approximately four miles to Spa Road. Turn right and drive about 1.5 miles to the park on the left.

**Contact:** Fountain of Youth Spa, 888/800-0772 or 760/354-1340, www.foyspa.com.

## 66 CORN SPRINGS

### Scenic rating: 4

in BLM desert

**Map page 798**

Just think: If you spend a night here, you can say to darn near anybody, "I've camped someplace you haven't." I don't know whether to offer my condolences or congratulations, but Corn Springs offers a primitive spot in the middle of nowhere in desert country. A 0.5-mile interpretive trail can easily be walked in athletic shoes. It is divided into 11 stops with different vegetation, wildlife habitat, and cultural notes at each stop. The side trip to Joshua Tree National Park to the north (40-minute drive to closest entrance) is also well worth the adventure. So is the aerial tram ride west of Palm Springs (one-hour drive) for an incredible view of the desert. On the other hand, if it's a summer afternoon, tell me, just how do you spend the day here when it's 115°F?

**Campsites, facilities:** There are eight sites for tents or RVs up to 22 feet (no hookups) and one group site for tents or RVs (one or two only) up to 22 feet that can accommodate up to 25 people. Picnic tables, fire grills, and shade ramadas are provided. Drinking water and vault toilets are available. Some facilities are wheelchair-accessible. Leashed pets are permitted.

**Reservations, fees:** Reservations are not accepted. Sites are $6 per night. Open year-round.

**Directions:** From Indio, drive east on I-10 for 60 miles to the Corn Springs Road exit. Take that exit to Old Chuckwalla Valley Road. Turn right (south) onto Old Chuckwalla Valley Road and drive 0.5 mile to Corn Springs Road. Turn right and drive 10 miles on a dirt road to the campground on the left.

**Contact:** Bureau of Land Management, Palm Springs Field Office, 760/833-7100, www.blm.gov/ca.

## 67 RED HILL MARINA COUNTY PARK

### Scenic rating: 3

near the Salton Sea

**Map page 798**

It's called Red Hill Marina, but the marina washed away in the mid-1970s. This county park is near the south end of the Salton Sea, one of the weirdest places on earth. At 228 feet below sea level, this vast body of water covers 360 square miles and is 35 miles long, but with an average depth of just 15 feet. Hundreds of species of birds stop by this area as they travel along the Pacific Flyway. Several wildlife refuges are in the immediate area, including two separate chunks of the Imperial Wildfowl Management Area, to the west and south, and the huge Wister Waterfowl Management Area, northwest of Niland. Fishing is often good for corvina in spring and early summer.

**Campsites, facilities:** There are 37 seasonal sites for RVs or tents. There are also nine overnight spaces, some with full or partial hookups, plus eight "dry camping" spaces. Picnic tables, cabanas, and barbecue pits are provided. Drinking water and restrooms with flush toilets and showers are available. There is no dump station. Leashed pets are permitted.

**Reservations, fees:** Reservations are not accepted, but filling out an online check-in form is recommended. Dry camp tent sites are $5 per day with a seven-day maximum stay; dry camp RV sites are $15 per night. RV sites are $25 (partial hookups) and $35 (full hookups) per night, plus $2 per night for each additional vehicle. Monthly rates are available. Open year-round.

**Directions:** From Mecca, drive south on Highway 111 to Niland and continue to Sinclair Road. Turn right and drive 3.5 miles to Garst Road. Turn right and drive 1.5 miles to the end of Garst Road at Red Hill Road. Turn left on Red Hill Road and drive to the park at the end of the road.

From El Centro, drive north on Highway 111 to Brawley and Highway 78/Main Street. Turn west (left) on Highway 78/Main Street and drive a short distance to Highway 111. Turn right (north) and drive to Calipatria. Continue north on Highway 111 just outside of Calipatria to Sinclair Road. Turn left on Sinclair Road and drive to Garst Road. Turn right and drive 1.5 miles to where it ends at Red Hill Road. Turn left at Red Hill Road and drive to the end of the road and the marina and campground.

**Contact:** Red Hill Marina, 7581 Garst Rd., Calipatria, 760/482-4236, www.icpds.com.

## 68 WIEST LAKE COUNTY PARK

### Scenic rating: 4
on Wiest Lake

**Map page 798**

This is a developed county park along the southern shore of Wiest Lake, which adjoins the Imperial Wildfowl Management Area to the north. Wiest Lake is just 50 acres, set 110 feet below sea level, and a prized area with such desolate country in the surrounding region. Waterskiing and sailboarding can be excellent, although few take advantage of the latter. Swimming is allowed when lifeguards are on duty. The lake is most popular for fishing, with trout planted in winter and catfish in summer. The lake also has bass and bluegill. The Salton Sea, about a 20-minute drive to the northwest, is a worthy side trip.

**Campsites, facilities:** There are 30 sites with full hookups (50 amps) for RVs up to 45 feet and 10 tent sites. Picnic tables, shade ramadas, and fire grills are provided. Drinking water and restrooms with flush toilets and showers, a boat ramp, and a dump station are available. A store, coin laundry, and propane gas are available within five miles. Some facilities are wheelchair-accessible. Leashed pets are permitted.

**Reservations, fees:** Reservations are not accepted. RV sites with full hookups are $35 per night, RV sites with partial hookups are $25 per night, dry RV sites are $15 per night, and tent sites are $5 per night, plus $2 per night for each additional vehicle. Monthly rates are available. Open year-round.

**Directions:** From El Centro, drive north on Highway 111 to Brawley and Highway 78/Main Street. Turn west (left) on Highway 78/Main Street and drive a short distance to Highway 111. Turn right (north) on Highway 111 and drive four miles to Rutherford Road (well signed). Turn right (east) and drive two miles to the park entrance on the right.

**Contact:** Wiest Lake County Park, 760/482-4236, www.icpds.com.

## 69 CULP VALLEY PRIMITIVE CAMP AREA

### Scenic rating: 4
near Peña Springs in Anza-Borrego Desert State Park

**Anza-Borrego map, page 801**

Culp Valley is near Peña Springs, which is more of a mudhole than a spring. A 600-yard hike takes you to an overlook of Hellhole Canyon and an eastern view of the Borrego Valley. Campground elevation is 3,400 feet.

**Campsites, facilities:** This is a primitive, open camping area for tents or RVs of any length (no hookups). Vault toilets are available. No drinking water is available. Fires are permitted in metal containers only. Garbage and ashes must be packed out. Leashed pets are permitted in the campground, but not on trails.

**Reservations, fees:** Reservations are not accepted. There is no fee for camping. Open year-round.

**Directions:** From Julian, at the junction of Highway 78 and Highway 79, drive east on Highway 78 (steep and curvy) for 10 miles to Highway S2. Turn left (north) and drive 16 miles to Highway S22/Borrego Salton Seaway. Turn right (east) and drive 10 miles to the campground entrance road on the left.

**Contact:** Anza-Borrego Desert State Park, Visitor Center, 760/767-4205; Colorado Desert District, 760/767-5311, www.parks.ca.gov.

## 70 BORREGO PALM CANYON

### Scenic rating: 6
in Anza-Borrego Desert State Park

**Anza-Borrego map, page 801**

This is one of the best camps in Anza-Borrego Desert State Park, with two excellent hikes available. The short hike into Borrego Palm Canyon is like being transported to another world, from the desert to the tropics, complete with a small waterfall, a rare sight in these parts. Panorama Overlook Trail also starts here. An excellent visitors center is available, offering an array of exhibits and a slide show. The elevation is 775 feet. Anza-Borrego Desert State Park is one of the largest state parks in the continental United States, covering more than 600,000 acres and with 500 miles of dirt roads. The park is appropriately named for the desert bighorn sheep (*borrego* in Spanish) that live in the mountains.

**Campsites, facilities:** There are 65 sites for tents or RVs up to 25 feet (no hookups), 52 sites with full hookups (30 amps) for RVs up to 35 feet, and five group tent sites for 9-25 people each. Picnic tables, shade ramadas, and fire grills are provided. Drinking water, restrooms with flush toilets and showers, and a dump station are available. A store, coin laundry, and propane gas are nearby. Some facilities are wheelchair-accessible. Leashed pets are permitted.

**Reservations, fees:** Reservations are accepted seasonally at 800/444-7275 or www.reserveamerica.com ($8 reservation fee). Sites are $25 per night, RV sites (full hookups) are $35 per night, additional vehicles cost $8 per night, and group sites are $80 per night. Senior discounts are available. Open year-round, with sites first-come, first-served May through October.

**Directions:** From Julian, at the junction of Highway 78 and Highway 79, drive east on Highway 78 (steep and curvy) for 19.5 miles to Yaqui Pass Road/County Road S3. Turn left (north) and drive eight miles to Borrego Springs and Palm Canyon Drive. Turn left (west) and drive 4.5 miles to the campground entrance road on the right.

**Contact:** Anza-Borrego Desert State Park, Visitor Center, 760/767-4205; Colorado Desert District, 760/767-5311, www.parks.ca.gov.

## 71 VERN WHITAKER HORSE CAMP

👫 🐕 ♿ 🚐 ⛺

### Scenic rating: 5

in Anza-Borrego Desert State Park

**Anza-Borrego map, page 801**

This camp is popular during spring and fall, with lighter use during the winter. The 30 miles of horse trails attract equestrian campers. Campers are expected to clean up after their horses, and garbage bins are available for manure.

**Campsites, facilities:** There are 10 equestrian sites for tents or RVs up to 24 feet (no hookups). Picnic tables and fire grills are provided. Restrooms with flush toilets and coin showers, drinking water, picnic areas, group gathering area, horse-washing station, and horse corrals are available. Some facilities are wheelchair-accessible. Leashed pets are permitted in the campground but not on trails or in wilderness.

**Reservations, fees:** Reservations are accepted at 800/444-7275 or www.reserveamerica.com ($8 reservation fee). Sites are $25 per night, which includes two horses; it's $2 per additional horse per night. Open October through April.

**Directions:** From Julian, at the junction of Highway 78 and Highway 79, drive east on Highway 78 (steep and curvy) for 19.5 miles to Yaqui Pass Road/County Road S3. Turn left (north) and drive eight miles to Palm Canyon Drive. Turn left and drive to Borrego Springs and bear right (at the traffic circle) onto northbound Borrego Springs Road. Drive four miles on Borrego Springs Road to Henderson Canyon Road. Bear right and drive a short distance to the campground entrance road (look for the metal sign). Turn left and continue four miles to the camp. Note: Part of the last four miles is on a private road; please respect the property owner's rights.

**Contact:** Anza-Borrego Desert State Park, Visitor Center, 760/767-4205; Colorado Desert District, 760/767-5311, www.parks.ca.gov.

## 72 ARROYO SALADO PRIMITIVE CAMP AREA

### Scenic rating: 5
in Anza-Borrego Desert State Park

**Anza-Borrego map, page 801**

This camp is a primitive spot set along (and named after) an ephemeral stream, the Arroyo Salado. About eight miles to the west is the trailhead for Thimble Trail, which heads south into a wash in the Borrego Badlands. The elevation is 880 feet.

**Campsites, facilities:** This is a primitive, open camping area for tents or self-contained RVs (no hookups). Vault toilets are available. No drinking water is available. Fires are allowed in metal containers only; open fires are not allowed. Garbage and ashes must be packed out. Leashed pets are permitted in the campground but not on trails or in wilderness.

**Reservations, fees:** Reservations are not accepted. There is no fee for camping. Open year-round.

**Directions:** From Julian, at the junction of Highway 78 (steep and curvy) and Highway 79, drive east on Highway 78 for 19.5 miles to Yaqui Pass Road/County Road S3. Turn left (north) and drive eight miles to Borrego Springs and Palm Canyon Drive. Turn right on Palm Canyon Drive (becomes Highway 522) and drive 20 miles (past Fonts Point) to the campground entrance on the right.

**Contact:** Anza-Borrego Desert State Park, Visitor Center, 760/767-4205; Colorado Desert District, 760/767-5311, www.parks.ca.gov.

## 73 YAQUI PASS PRIMITIVE CAMP AREA

### Scenic rating: 1
in Anza-Borrego Desert State Park

**Anza-Borrego map, page 801**

This extremely primitive area is beside rough Yaqui Pass Road at an elevation of 1,730 feet.

The camping area is a large, open, sloping area of asphalt, where it is darn near impossible to get an RV level. The trailhead for Kenyon Loop Trail is to the immediate south. This spot is often overlooked because the Tamarisk Grove camp nearby provides shade, drinking water, and a feature trail.

**Campsites, facilities:** This is a primitive, open camping area for tents or self-contained RVs of any length (no hookups). Drinking water and toilets are not available. No open fires are allowed. Garbage must be packed out. Leashed pets are permitted, but not on trails or in wilderness.

**Reservations, fees:** Reservations are not accepted. There is no fee for camping. Open year-round.

**Directions:** From Julian, at the junction of Highway 78 and Highway 79, drive east on Highway 78 (steep and curvy) for 19.5 miles to Yaqui Pass Road/County Road S3. Turn left (north) and drive 2.5 miles to the campground entrance on the right. The access road is rough and the camping area has few level areas for large RVs, so only small RVs are recommended.

**Contact:** Anza-Borrego Desert State Park, Visitor Center, 760/767-4205; Colorado Desert District, 760/767-5311, www.parks.ca.gov.

## 74 YAQUI WELL PRIMITIVE CAMP AREA

### Scenic rating: 2
in Anza-Borrego Desert State Park

**Anza-Borrego map, page 801**

This camp is used primarily as an overflow area if the more developed Tamarisk Grove camp is full. Cactus Loop Trail, a 2.5-mile loop hike that passes seven varieties of cacti, starts at Tamarisk Grove. The elevation is 1,400 feet.

**Campsites, facilities:** This is a primitive, open camping area for tents or self-contained RVs (no hookups). Vault toilets are available. No drinking water is available. Fires are permitted in metal containers only. Garbage and ashes must be packed out. Open fires are not permitted. Leashed pets are permitted, but not on trails or in wilderness.

**Reservations, fees:** Reservations are not accepted. There is no fee for camping. Open year-round.

**Directions:** From Julian, at the junction of Highway 78 and Highway 79, drive east on Highway 78 (steep and curvy) for 19.5 miles to Yaqui Pass Road/County Road S3. Turn left (north) and drive a short distance to the campground entrance road on the left. The access road is rough and the camping area has few level areas for large RVs, so only small RVs are recommended.

**Contact:** Anza-Borrego Desert State Park, Visitor Center, 760/767-4205; Colorado Desert District, 760/767-5311, www.parks.ca.gov.

## 75 TAMARISK GROVE

🚶 🐕 ♿ 🚐 ⛺

### Scenic rating: 7

in Anza-Borrego Desert State Park

**Anza-Borrego map, page 801**

Tamarisk is one of three camps in the immediate area, so if this camp is full, primitive Yaqui Well to the immediate west and Yaqui Pass to the north on Yaqui Pass Road provide alternatives. Cactus Loop Trail, with the trailhead just north of camp, provides a hiking option. This 1.5-mile loop passes seven varieties of cacti, some as tall as people. Side trips to Julian and Borrego Springs are just 30-45 minutes away. The elevation is 1,400 feet at this campground.

**Campsites, facilities:** There are 27 sites for tents or RVs up to 21 feet (no hookups) and 11 cabins. Picnic tables, shade ramadas, and fire grills are provided. Restrooms with coin showers and vault toilets are available. There is no drinking water. Some facilities are wheelchair-accessible. Leashed pets are permitted in the campground but not on trails or in wilderness.

**Reservations, fees:** Reservations are accepted at 800/444-7275 or www.reserveamerica.com ($8 reservation fee). Sites are $25 per

night, cabins are $25-60 per night, plus $8 per night for each additional vehicle. Open October through April.

**Directions:** From Julian, at the junction of Highway 78 and Highway 79, drive east on Highway 78 (steep and curvy) for 19.5 miles to Yaqui Pass Road/County Road S3. Turn left (north) and drive 0.5 mile to the campground on the right.

**Contact:** Anza-Borrego Desert State Park, Visitor Center, 760/767-4205; Colorado Desert District, 760/767-5311, www.parks.ca.gov.

## 76 OCOTILLO WELLS SVRA

🚶 🚲 🐕 🚙 ⛺

### Scenic rating: 4

in Ocotillo Wells near Anza-Borrego Desert State Park

**Anza-Borrego map, page 801**

This can be a wild place, a giant OHV camp where the population of Ocotillo Wells can go from 10 to 5,000 overnight, no kidding. Yet if you arrive when there is no off-road event, it can also be a lonely, extremely remote destination. Some locals call the OHV crowd "escapees" and watch stunned as they arrive every February for two or three weeks. OHV events are held here occasionally. Mountain bikers also use these trails. One great side note is that annually there is "Desert Cleanup Day," when OHV users will clean up the place; the date changes every year. The non-OHV crowd can still use this camp but most come in the winter on weekdays, when activity is lower. The landscape is barren desert, dry as an iguana's back. A few shade ramadas are provided. The area covers 72,000 acres, ranging from below sea level to an elevation of 400 feet. It is adjacent to Anza-Borrego Desert State Park, another 600,000 acres of wildlands. The wash-and-ridge terrain includes a butte with dunes, a sand bowl, a blow sand dune, and springs. After wet winters, the blooms of wildflowers can be excellent. While this area is well known as a wild play area for the OHV crowd, it is also a place where on most days you can literally disappear and see no one. All drivers should watch for soft ground. Many vehicles get stuck here and have to be towed out. Also, dispersed camping is allowed in most of these state park lands.

**Campsites, facilities:** There are more than 100 dispersed primitive sites for tents or RVs of any length (no hookups). Camping is not allowed in the Shell, Reef, Devils Slide, and Blow Sand areas. Picnic tables and fire rings are provided. Vault toilets and shade ramadas are available in the Pumpkin Patch, Quarry, Cove, Main Street, Holly Road, and Hidden Valley areas. There is no drinking water. A coin-shower building is near the ranger station, and another is 3.5 miles east at Holmes Camp. A visitors center across from the ranger station offers telescope viewing and an amphitheater with interpretive programs from October through April. A store, restaurants, propane, and auto supplies are available four miles away in Ocotillo Wells. A gas station is at the corner of S-22 and Highway 86-S in Salton City. Leashed pets are permitted.

**Reservations, fees:** Reservations are not accepted. There is no fee for camping. There is a 30-day maximum stay per year. Open year-round.

**Directions:** From Julian, at the junction of Highway 78 and Highway 79, drive east on Highway 78 for 31.5 miles to Ranger Station Road. Turn left and drive 0.25 mile to the ranger station. Note that this road is curvy with some tight turns. Longer RVs may prefer to take San Felipe Road (S2) east from Highway 79 instead.

**Contact:** Ocotillo Wells SVRA, 760/767-5391, www.parks.ca.gov or www.ohv.parks.ca.gov.

## 77 FISH CREEK

**Scenic rating: 3**

in Anza-Borrego Desert State Park

**Anza-Borrego map, page 801**

This primitive camp is just inside the eastern border of Anza-Borrego Desert State Park at the foot of the Vallecito Mountains to the west. This is the closest camp to the Ocotillo Wells State Vehicular Recreation Area, which is 12 miles to the north. RVs are not recommended because of the steep access road. Note that the Elephant Tree Discovery Trail is a few miles north of camp.

**Campsites, facilities:** There are six sites for tents. Vault toilets are available and some sites have fire rings. No drinking water is available. Garbage must be packed out. Leashed pets are permitted.

**Reservations, fees:** Reservations are not accepted. There is no fee for camping. Open year-round.

**Directions:** From Julian, at the junction of Highway 78 and Highway 79, drive east on Highway 78 (steep and curvy) for 34 miles to Ocotillo Wells and Split Mountain Road. Turn right (south) and drive seven miles to the campground access road. Drive two miles to the campground entrance on the left.

**Contact:** Anza-Borrego Desert State Park, Visitor Center, 760/767-4205; Colorado Desert District, 760/767-5311, www.parks.ca.gov.

## 78 VALLECITO COUNTY PARK

**Scenic rating: 3**

near Anza-Borrego Desert State Park

**Anza-Borrego map, page 801**

This county park in the desert gets little attention in the face of the other nearby attractions. This is a 71-acre park built around a sod reconstruction of the historic Vallecito Stage Station. It was part of the Butterfield Overland Stage from 1858 to 1861. The route carried mail and passengers from Missouri to San Francisco in 25 days, covering 2,800 miles. *Vallecito* means "little valley." It provides a quiet alternative to some of the busier campgrounds in the desert. One bonus is that it is usually 10 degrees cooler here than at Agua Caliente. A covered picnic area is a big plus. Other nearby destinations include Agua Caliente Hot Springs, Anza-Borrego Desert State Park to the east, and Lake Cuyamaca and Cuyamaca Rancho State Park about 35 miles away. The elevation is 1,500 feet.

**Campsites, facilities:** There are 44 sites for tents or RVs up to 40 feet (no hookups), one group area for up to 15 RVs, one equestrian area with eight sites and two corrals, and one youth camping area for up to 50 people. Picnic tables and fire rings are provided. Drinking water, flush toilets, a large covered picnic area, and a playground are available. Some facilities are wheelchair-accessible. Leashed pets are permitted.

**Reservations, fees:** Reservations are accepted at 858/565-3600 or 877/565-3600 ($5 reservation fee) and online at www.reservations.sdparks.org. Sites are $22 per night, the youth group area is $50-75 per night, plus $1 per pet per night, $2 per horse per night, and $4 per night per additional vehicle. Some credit cards are accepted. Open Labor Day weekend through Memorial Day weekend; closed June, July, and August.

**Directions:** From El Cajon, drive east on I-8 for about 75 miles to the town of Ocotillo (the first town after crossing from San Diego County to Imperial County) and County Road S2/Imperial Highway. Turn north (left) on County Road S2/Imperial Highway and drive 30 miles to the park entrance.

**Contact:** San Diego County Parks Department, 858/694-3049, www.sdparks.org; campground, 760/765-1188.

# 79 AGUA CALIENTE REGIONAL PARK

### Scenic rating: 3

near Anza-Borrego Desert State Park

**Anza-Borrego map, page 801**

This is a popular park in winter. It has two naturally fed pools: A large outdoor thermal pool is kept at its natural 90°F, and an indoor pool is heated to 102°F and outfitted with jets. Everything is hot here. The weather is hot, the coffee is hot, and the water is hot. And hey, that's what *"agua caliente"* means—hot water, named after the nearby hot springs. Anza-Borrego Desert State Park is also nearby. If you would like to see some cold water, Lake Cuyamaca and Cuyamaca Rancho State Park are about 35 miles away. The elevation is 1,350 feet. The park covers 910 acres with several miles of hiking trails.

**Campsites, facilities:** There are 106 sites with full or partial hookups (30 amps) for RVs up to 40 feet, 35 sites with no hookups for tents or RVs, and a group area for up to 100 people. Seven camping cabins are also available. Picnic tables and fire grills are provided. Restrooms with flush toilets and showers, drinking water, outdoor and indoor pools, picnic area, and a playground with horseshoes and shuffleboard are available. Groceries and propane gas are nearby. Some facilities are wheelchair-accessible. Leashed pets are permitted, but not on trails.

**Reservations, fees:** Reservations are accepted at 858/565-3600 or 877/565-3600 ($5 reservation fee) and online at www.reservations.sdparks.org. Tent sites are $24 per night, RV sites are $33 (full hookups) and $29 (partial hookups) per night, and the group area is $100 per night. Some credit cards are accepted. Open Labor Day weekend through Memorial Day weekend; closed June, July, and August.

**Directions:** From El Cajon, drive east on I-8 about 75 miles to the town of Ocotillo (the first town after crossing from San Diego County to Imperial County) and County Road S2/

Imperial Highway. Turn north (left) on County Road S2/Imperial Highway and drive 25 miles to the park entrance.

From Julian, take Highway 78 east and drive 12 miles to County Road S2/San Felipe Road. Turn right on County Road S2/San Felipe Road and drive 21 miles south to the park entrance.

**Contact:** San Diego County Parks Department, 858/694-3049, www.sdparks.org, campground, 760/765-1188.

## 80 MOUNTAIN PALM SPRINGS PRIMITIVE CAMP AREA

🖐 🐕 🚐 ⛰

### Scenic rating: 4
in Anza-Borrego Desert State Park

**Anza-Borrego map, page 801**

A plus for this camping area is easy access from County Road S2, but no water is a giant minus. Regardless of pros and cons, only hikers will get the full benefit of the area. A trail leads south to Bow Willow Creek (and Bow Willow) and onward into Bow Willow Canyon. The Carrizo Badlands Overlook is on the southeast side of Sweeney Pass, about a 10-minute drive south on County Road S2. The elevation is 760 feet.

**Campsites, facilities:** This is a primitive, open camping area for tents or RVs of any length (no hookups). Vault toilets are available. No drinking water is available. Fires are permitted in metal containers only. Garbage and ashes must be packed out. Leashed pets are permitted, but not on trails or in wilderness.

**Reservations, fees:** Reservations are not accepted. There is no fee for camping. Open year-round.

**Directions:** From El Cajon, drive east on I-8 for about 75 miles to the town of Ocotillo (the first town after crossing from San Diego County to Imperial County) and County Road S2/Imperial Highway. Turn north (left) on

County Road S2/Imperial Highway and drive 27.5 miles to the campground entrance road on the left (about 0.5 mile past the Bow Willow campground turnoff). Turn left and continue 0.75 mile to the camp.

**Contact:** Anza-Borrego Desert State Park, Visitor Center, 760/767-4205; Colorado Desert District, 760/767-5311, www.parks.ca.gov.

## 81 BOW WILLOW

🖐 🐕 🚐 ⛰

### Scenic rating: 4
near Bow Willow Canyon in Anza-Borrego Desert State Park

**Anza-Borrego map, page 801**

Rugged Bow Willow Canyon can be explored by hiking the trail that starts at this camp. A short distance east of the camp, the trail forks to the south to Rockhouse Canyon. For a good side trip, drive back to County Road S2 and head south over Sweeney Pass for the view at the Carrizo Badlands Overlook.

**Campsites, facilities:** There are 16 sites for tents or RVs up to 24 feet (no hookups). Picnic tables, fire rings, and shade ramadas are provided. Vault toilets are available. There is no drinking water. Leashed pets are permitted in the campground but not on trails.

**Reservations, fees:** Reservations are not accepted. Sites are $15 per night, plus $5 per night per additional vehicle. Open year-round.

**Directions:** From El Cajon, drive east on I-8 about 75 miles to the town of Ocotillo (the first town after crossing from San Diego County to Imperial County) and County Road S2/Imperial Highway. Turn north (left) on County Road S2/Imperial Highway and drive 27 miles to the gravel campground entrance road on the left.

**Contact:** Anza-Borrego Desert State Park, Visitor Center, 760/767-4205; Colorado Desert District, 760/767-5311, www.parks.ca.gov.

## 82 RIO BEND RV AND GOLF RESORT

### Scenic rating: 5

near El Centro

**Map page 798**

This resort is 50 feet below sea level near Mount Signal, about a 20-minute drive south of the Salton Sea. For some, this region is a godforsaken wasteland, but hey, that makes arriving at this park all the more like coming to a mirage in the desert. This resort is a combination RV park and year-round community with park models for sale. Management does what it can to offer visitors recreational options, including a nine-hole golf course. It's hot and sizzling most of the year, but dry and cool in the winter, which is the best time to visit.

**Campsites, facilities:** There are 500 sites for RVs to 40 feet, including 460 sites with full hookups (30 and 50 amps). Group sites have partial hookups. Picnic tables are provided. Cable TV and restrooms with showers are available. Two small, stocked lakes for catch-and-release fishing, a café, heated swimming pool, spa, shuffleboard, pickleball, volleyball, horseshoes, bocce ball, pet park, nine-hole golf course and pro shop, library, pool table, club room, organized activities, coin laundry, and Wi-Fi are available on a seasonal basis. Some facilities are wheelchair-accessible. A small store is nearby. Leashed pets are permitted.

**Reservations, fees:** Reservations are accepted. Sites are $50 per night, pull-through sites (full hookups) are $70 per night, plus $3 per person for more than two people. Discounts are offered off-season. Weekly, monthly, and annual rates are available. Some credit cards are accepted. Open year-round.

**Directions:** From El Centro, drive west on I-8 for seven miles to the Drew Road exit. Take that exit and drive south on Drew Road for 0.25 mile to the park on the right.

**Contact:** Rio Bend RV and Golf Resort, 1589 Drew Road, 760/352-7061 or 800/545-6481, www.riobendrvgolfresort.com.

## 83 IMPERIAL SAND DUNES RECREATION AREA

### Scenic rating: 1

east of Brawley

**Map page 798**

There are many camping options at Imperial Sand Dunes Recreation Area. There isn't a tree within sight, but the people who wind up here all have the same thing in common: They're ready to ride across the dunes in their dune buggies or off-highway vehicles (weather permitting). Note that several areas are off-limits to motorized vehicles and camping because of plant and habitat protection; hiking in these areas is allowed. Other recreation options include watching the sky and waiting for a cloud to show up.

**Campsites, facilities:** There are 19 dispersed campgrounds for tents or RVs of any length (no hookups) in the North Dunes area and 6 dispersed campground for tents or RVs of any length (no hookups) in the South Dune campground area. A few sites have camping pads. Vault toilets and garbage bins are available at some sites. There is no drinking water. Leashed pets are permitted.

**Reservations, fees:** Reservations are not accepted, but season permits are required October through mid-April and are available at 800/832-7664 or online at www.isdpermits.com. With an advance permit, sites are $35 per week or $150 per season. Permits purchased on-site are $50 per week or $150 per season with a 14-day stay limit every 28 days. Open year-round.

**Directions:** From Brawley, drive east on Highway 78 for 27 miles to Gecko Road. Turn south on Gecko Road and drive three miles to the campground entrance on the left. To reach Roadrunner Camp in the North Dunes campground, continue for two miles to the campground at the end of the road.

**Contact:** Bureau of Land Management, El Centro Field Office, 760/337-4400, www.blm.gov/ca. For information on closed areas, contact the Imperial Sand Dunes ranger station (760/337-4400).

## 84 PICACHO STATE RECREATION AREA

🏃 🏊 🛶 ⛴ 🐕 ♿ 🚐 ⛺

### Scenic rating: 6

near Taylor Lake on the Colorado River

**Map page 798**

To get here, you really have to want it. Picacho State Recreation Area is way out there, requiring a long drive north out of Winterhaven on a spindly little road. The camp is on the southern side of Taylor Lake on the Colorado River. The park is the best deal around for many miles, though, with boat ramps, waterskiing, good bass fishing, and, occasionally, crazy folks having the time of their lives. The sun and water make a good combination. This recreation area includes eight miles of the lower Colorado River. Park wildlife includes wild burros and bighorn sheep, with thousands of migratory waterfowl on the Pacific Flyway occasionally taking up residence. More than 100 years ago, Picacho was a gold-mining town with a population of 2,500 people. Visitors should always carry extra water and essential supplies.

**Campsites, facilities:** There are 54 sites for tents or RVs up to 35 feet (no hookups), two group sites for up to 50 people each, two group boat-in campsites for groups of up to 100 people, and five up-river sites (no hookups). Picnic tables and fire grills are provided. Drinking water, vault and chemical toilets, dump station, solar showers, and two boat launches are available. Some facilities are wheelchair-accessible. Leashed pets are permitted.

**Reservations, fees:** Reservations are accepted for boat-in sites and group sites ($20 non-refundable reservation fee) at 760/996-2963. Individual sites are $20-25 per night, group sites are $75 per night for up to 12 vehicles, group boat-in sites are $75 per night for a minimum of 15 people, plus $5 per person per night for additional people. Open year-round.

**Directions:** From El Centro, drive east on I-8 to Winterhaven and the exit for Winterhaven/4th Avenue. Take that exit to Winterhaven Drive. Turn left on Winterhaven Drive and drive 0.5 mile to County Road S24/Picacho Road. Turn right and drive 24 miles (crossing rail tracks, driving under a railroad bridge and over the American Canal; the road becoming dirt for the last 18 miles) to the campground. The road is not suitable for large RVs. The drive takes 1-2 hours from Winterhaven. In summer, thunderstorms can cause flash flooding, making short sections of the road impassable.

**Contact:** Picacho State Recreation Area, Salton Sea State Recreation Area, 760/996-2963, www.parks.ca.gov.

## 85 SENATOR WASH RECREATION AREA

🏊 🛶 ⛴ 🐕 🚐 ⛺

### Scenic rating: 6

near Senator Wash Reservoir in Arizona

**Map page 798**

Senator Wash Reservoir Recreation Area features two campgrounds, named (surprise) Senator Wash South Shore and Senator Wash North Shore. This recreation area is approximately 60 acres, with many trees of various types and several secluded camping areas. At Senator Wash North Shore (where there are fewer facilities than at South Shore), campsites are both on the water as well as farther inland. Gravel beaches provide access to the reservoir. Boat ramps are nearby. This spot provides boating, fishing, OHV riding, wildlife-viewing, and opportunities for solitude and sightseeing.

**Campsites, facilities:** There are numerous dispersed sites for tents or RVs of any length (no hookups). South Shore has restrooms with flush toilets, outdoor showers, trash cans, a dump station, and drinking water. North Shore has two vault toilets and no drinking water; a boat ramp is approximately a quarter mile away (there is no camping at the boat ramp). A buoyed swimming area and boat ramp are available, providing boat-in access to campsites. Leashed pets are permitted.

**Reservations, fees:** Reservations are not accepted. Sites are $15 per night. The day-use fee is $10 per vehicle, $15 per vehicle for overnight, or $75 annually per vehicle (up to five people per vehicle). A $1 per person fee is charged for each person over the five-person limit. There is a maximum 14-day stay limit per 28 days. Open year-round.

**Directions:** Take I-8 to Yuma, Arizona, and the exit for 4th Avenue. Take that exit and drive to Imperial Highway/County Road S24. Turn north and drive 22 miles to Senator Wash Road. Turn left and drive about three miles south to Mesa Campground. Turn left and drive 200 yards to the South Shore Campground access road on the right. Turn right and drive to the reservoir and campground.

**Contact:** Bureau of Land Management, Yuma Field Office, 928/317-3200, www.blm.gov/az.

## 86 SQUAW LAKE

### Scenic rating: 6

near the Colorado River

**Map page 798**

Take your pick. There are two camps near the Colorado River in this area (the other is Senator Wash). This one is near Squaw Lake, created by the nearby Imperial Dam on the Colorado River. These sites provide opportunities for swimming, fishing, boating, and hiking, featuring direct boat access to the Colorado River. Wildlife includes numerous waterfowl, as well as quail, coyotes, and reptiles. A speed limit of 5 mph is enforced on the lake; no wakes are permitted. The no-wake zone ends at the Colorado River.

**Campsites, facilities:** There are 125 sites for RVs of any length (no hookups) and dispersed sites for tents. Picnic tables and barbecue grills are provided. Four restrooms with flush toilets

and coin showers (fee) are available. Drinking water is available at a central location. Trash and gray-water disposal are available. Two boat ramps and a dump station are nearby. Two buoyed swimming areas are available. Some facilities are wheelchair-accessible. Leashed pets are permitted.

**Reservations, fees:** Reservations are not accepted. Sites are $15 per night. The day-use fee is $10 per vehicle, and it's $15 per vehicle for overnight or $75 annually per vehicle (up to five people per vehicle). A $1 per person fee is charged for each person over the five-person limit. There is a year-round 14-day stay limit for every 28 days. Open year-round.

**Directions:** Drive on I-8 to Yuma, Arizona, and the exit for 4th Avenue. Take that exit and drive to Imperial Highway/County Road S24. Turn north and drive 22 miles to Senator Wash Road. Turn left and drive about four miles (well signed) to the lake and campground on the right.

**Contact:** Bureau of Land Management, Yuma Field Office, 928/317-3200, www.blm.gov/az.

## 87 MIDWAY

### Scenic rating: 6

in the Imperial Sand Dunes Recreation Area

**Map page 798**

This is OHV headquarters, a place where people bring their three-wheelers, four-wheelers, and motorcycles. That's because a large area has been set aside just for this type of recreation. The good news is that this area has become more family-oriented because of increased enforcement, eliminating much of the lawlessness and lunatic behavior of the past. As you drive in, you enter the Buttercup Recreation Area, part of the Imperial Sand Dunes Recreation Area. You can camp almost anywhere you like, and nobody beefs. Note that several areas are off-limits to motorized vehicles and camping because of plant and habitat protection; hiking in these areas is allowed. (See the Imperial Sand

Dunes Recreation Area listing in this chapter for more options.)

**Campsites, facilities:** There are several primitive sites for tents or RVs of any length (no hookups). Vault toilets are available. No drinking water is available. Leashed pets are permitted.

**Reservations, fees:** Reservations are not accepted, but camping permits are required and are available online at www.isdpermits.com. Permits are $35 per week (in advance), $50 per week (on-site), or $150 per season with a 14-day stay limit every 28 days. Open year-round, weather permitting.

**Directions:** From El Centro, drive east on I-8 for about 40 miles to Gray's Wells Road (signed "Sand Dunes"). Take that exit and drive (it bears to the right) to a stop sign. Continue straight on Gray's Wells Road and drive three miles to another stop sign. To reach Buttercup Recreation Area, turn left and drive a short distance. To reach Midway, continue straight on Gray's Wells Road for 1.5 miles (the road turns from pavement to dirt and then dead-ends); camping is permitted anywhere in this region.

**Contact:** Bureau of Land Management, El Centro Field Office, 760/337-4400, www.blm.gov/ca. For more information on closed areas, contact the Buttercup Ranger Station (760/344-7657).

# RESOURCES

© LYNN BENDICKSON/123RF.COM

# NATIONAL FORESTS

The Forest Service (www.fs.fed.us) provides many secluded campgrounds and allows camping except where it is specifically prohibited. Forest Service campgrounds may be remote with no drinking water or facilities, but they are often low cost or free. Some campgrounds are first-come, first-served while others can be reserved at Recreation.gov (877/444-677 or www.recreation.gov).

When popular campsites are full on summer weekends, lesser-known Forest Service sites can often save your trip. Most of these camps are subject to winter closure because of snow or mud.

Dogs are permitted in national forests (no fee), but leashes may be required. Always carry documentation of current vaccinations.

## Adventure Pass

In Southern California's Angeles, Cleveland, Los Padres, and San Bernardino National Forests, an Adventure Pass (909/382-2622, $5 per day, $30 annual pass) is required for each vehicle parked in any of the 25 recreation areas. Note that the pass is required for parking only (e.g., at the trailhead, day-use area, near a fishing stream, etc.) but may also be required when camping at a fee-free Forest Service campsite. Passes are available at national forest offices in Southern California and at retail outlets and online vendors. Major credit cards are accepted at most retail and online outlets and at some Forest Service offices. When purchasing the annual pass, you may also buy an annual second-vehicle Adventure Pass ($5).

For more information, visit the Forest Service website (www.fs.fed.us).

## Interagency Pass

An Interagency Pass (http://store.usgs.gov, $80 annually) is available in lieu of an Adventure Pass. The Interagency Pass is honored nationwide at all Forest Service, National Park Service, Bureau of Land Management, Bureau of Reclamation, and U.S. Fish and Wildlife Service sites charging entrance fees. It is valid for 12 months from the month of purchase and is available at most national forest or grassland offices or online.

## Senior Pass

The Senior Pass ($10) is a lifetime pass available for U.S. residents who are age 62 and older. It is accepted at more than 2,000 federal recreation sites, including national parks, U.S. Fish and Wildlife refuges, and many U.S. national forests. In Southern California, the Senior Pass supplants the Adventure Pass. The Senior Pass can also provide discounts for national forest campgrounds and boat ramps.

## National Forest Reservations

Some of the more popular camps (and most group camps) are on a reservation system. Reservations can be made up to 240 days in advance and up to 360 days in advance for groups. To reserve a site, contact Recreation. gov (877/444-6777, www.recreation.gov). The reservation fee is $9 online and $10 by phone; major credit cards are accepted. Holders of the Interagency Pass, Golden Age, or Golden Access Passes will receive a 50 percent discount for campground fees (except group sites). The Recreation.gov website is used for the trailhead lotteries for Half Dome in Yosemite National Park.

## National Forest Maps

National Forest maps (406/329-3024, www. nationalforeststore.com) are among the best you can get for the price, detailing backcountry streams, lakes, hiking trails, and logging roads for access. Maps are available online or at forest service offices. Major credit cards are accepted when ordering by phone. Most maps of national forests cost $10; wilderness maps cost $8-12; forest atlases cost $12-36.

## Forest Service Information

In California, most camping trips are on Friday and Saturday nights when few sites are available. Sunday through Thursday you can often have your pick of sites, especially in the more distant areas away from national parks. Forest Service personnel can be helpful for obtaining camping or hiking trail information. If you do not have a reservation at a popular destination, call the Forest Service in advance to determine availability.

For specific information on a national forest, contact the following offices:

**USDA Forest Service**
Pacific Southwest Region
1323 Club Drive
Vallejo, CA 94592
707/562-8737
www.fs.usda.gov

**Angeles National Forest**
701 North Santa Anita Avenue
Arcadia, CA 91006
626/574-1613
www.fs.usda.gov/angeles

**Cleveland National Forest**
10845 Rancho Bernardo Road, No. 200
San Diego, CA 92127-2107
858/673-6180
www.fs.usda.gov/cleveland

**Eldorado National Forest**
100 Forni Road
Placerville, CA 95667
530/622-5061
www.fs.usda.gov/eldorado

**Humboldt-Toiyabe National Forest**
1200 Franklin Way
Sparks, NV 89431
775/331-6444
www.fs.usda.gov/htnf

**Inyo National Forest**
351 Pacu Lane, Suite 200
Bishop, CA 93514
760/873-2400
www.fs.usda.gov/inyo

**Klamath National Forest**
1312 Fairlane Road
Yreka, CA 96097-9549
530/842-6131
www.fs.usda.gov/klamath

**Lake Tahoe Basin Management Unit**
35 College Drive
South Lake Tahoe, CA 96150
530/543-2600
www.fs.usda.gov/ltbmu

**Lassen National Forest**
2550 Riverside Drive
Susanville, CA 96130
530/257-2151
www.fs.usda.gov/lassen

**Los Padres National Forest**
6755 Hollister Avenue, Suite 150
Goleta, CA 93117
805/968-6640
www.fs.usda.gov/lospadres

**Mendocino National Forest**
825 North Humboldt Avenue
Willows, CA 95988
530/934-3316
www.fs.usda.gov/mendocino

**Modoc National Forest**
800 West 12th Street
Alturas, CA 96101
530/233-5811
www.fs.usda.gov/modoc

**Plumas National Forest**
P.O. Box 11500
159 Lawrence Street
Quincy, CA 95971
530/283-2050
www.fs.usda.gov/plumas

**San Bernardino National Forest**
602 South Tippecanoe Avenue
San Bernardino, CA 92408-2607
909/382-2600
www.fs.usda.gov/sanbernardino

**Sequoia National Forest**
Giant Sequoia National Monument
1839 South Newcomb Street
Porterville, CA 93257
559/784-1500
www.fs.usda.gov/sequoia

**Shasta-Trinity National Forest**
3644 Avtech Parkway
Redding, CA 96002
530/226-2500
www.fs.usda.gov/shastatrinity

**Sierra National Forest**
1600 Tollhouse Road
Clovis, CA 93611
559/297-0706
www.fs.usda.gov/sierra

**Six Rivers National Forest**
1330 Bayshore Way
Eureka, CA 95501
707/442-1721
www.fs.usda.gov/sixrivers

**Stanislaus National Forest**
19777 Greenley Road
Sonora, CA 95370
209/532-3671
www.fs.usda.gov/stanislaus

**Tahoe National Forest**
631 Coyote Street
Nevada City, CA 95959
530/265-4531
www.fs.usda.gov/tahoe

# STATE PARKS

The California State Parks system provides many popular campgrounds in spectacular settings. These campgrounds include drive-in numbered sites, tent spaces, and picnic tables, with showers and bathrooms provided nearby. Reservations are often necessary during the summer.

Most camping trips are on Friday and Saturday nights in summer, when few sites are available at marquee destinations. Popular areas that book quickly include Steep Ravine Environmental Cabins on the Marin coast, Doheny State Beach near Dana Point, and the beachfront campgrounds at Monterey Bay. Many campgrounds along the California coast are popular in summer and require planning and advance reservations in order to secure a campsite.

Although many parks are well known, there are still some little-known gems in the state parks system where campers can enjoy seclusion, even in summer. Consider a spot in the Redwood Empire, Sacramento, the San Joaquin Valley, and the northern Sierra Nevada where sites rarely sell out. Or try to plan a trip Sunday through Thursday, when you can have your pick of sites. In addition, there is a sprinkling of first-come, first-served sites, including walk-in sites, where you can often score a surprise find.

Camping fees have risen from $12 per night to $35 per night at most parks. The beautiful settings and security of nearby park rangers keep them desirable, and many find them ideal for self-contained RVs.

## State Park Reservations

Most of the state park campgrounds are on a reservation system; campsites can be booked up to seven months in advance. Reservations can be made at ReserveAmerica.com (800/444-7275, www.reserveamerica.com, $10 reservation fee); major credit cards are accepted online. There is a rush on reservations on the first Monday of the month in December, January, February, and March. There are also hike-in/bike-in sites at many of the parks available on a first-come, first-served basis.

In 2017, the State Park reservation system may shift to a new concessionaire. However, the reservation phone number will remain the same for a seamless transition.

Camping discounts of 50 percent are available for holders of the Disabled Discount Pass ($3.50). Free camping is allowed for holders of the Distinguished Veteran Pass.

For general information about California State Parks, contact:

### California Department of Parks and Recreation
Public Information Office
P.O. Box 942896
1416 9th Street
Sacramento, CA 94296
800/777-0369
www.parks.ca.gov

# NATIONAL PARKS

California's national parks are America's greatest natural wonders. The landscape varies from the spectacular yet crowded Yosemite Valley, the showpiece of the world, to little-seen Lava Beds National Monument and its caves in the remote north of the state.

Reservations for campsites are available five months in advance for many of the national parks in California. Reservations can be made at Recreation.gov (877/444-6777, www.recreation.gov). The reservation fee is $9 online ($10 by phone); major credit cards are accepted. There is a rush on reservations on the first Monday of the month for Point Reyes National Seashore and on the 15th of the month for Yosemite National Park. In addition to campground fees, expect to pay a park entrance fee of $20-30 per vehicle (good for seven days).

The Annual Pass (http://store.usgs.gov, $80) provides free entry at all national parks. The Forest Service Interagency Pass (http://store.usgs.gov, $80 annually) can be added to the National Parks Pass, which eliminates entrance fees at sites managed by the U.S. Fish and Wildlife Service, the U.S. Forest Service, and the Bureau of Land Management. The Senior Pass ($10) provides free entry for life at national parks and other federal sites.

### National Park Service
Pacific West Region
One Jackson Center
1111 Jackson Street, Suite 700

Oakland, CA 94607
510/817-1304
www.nps.gov

### Cabrillo National Monument
1800 Cabrillo Memorial Drive
San Diego, CA 92106-3601
619/557-5450
www.nps.gov/cabr

### Channel Islands National Park
1901 Spinnaker Drive
Ventura, CA 93001
805/658-5730
www.nps.gov/chis

### Death Valley National Park
P.O. Box 579
Death Valley, CA 92328-0579
760/786-3200
www.nps.gov/deva

### Devils Postpile National Monument
P.O. Box 3999
Mammoth Lakes, CA 93546
760/934-2289 (summer only)
www.nps.gov/depo

### Golden Gate National Recreation Area
Fort Mason, Building 201
San Francisco, CA 94123-0022
415/561-4700
www.nps.gov/goga

### Joshua Tree National Park
74485 National Park Drive
Twentynine Palms, CA 92277-3597
760/367-5500
www.nps.gov/jotr

### Lassen Volcanic National Park
P.O. Box 100
Mineral, CA 96063-0100
530/595-4444
www.nps.gov/lavo

### Lava Beds National Monument
1 Indian Well Headquarters
Tulelake, CA 96134
530/667-2282
www.nps.gov/labe

### Mojave National Preserve
2701 Barstow Road
Barstow, CA 92311
760/252-6100
www.nps.gov/moja

### Pinnacles National Park
5000 Highway 146
Paicines, CA 95043
831/389-4485
www.nps.gov/pinn

### Point Reyes National Seashore
Point Reyes Station, CA 94956-9799
415/464-5100
www.nps.gov/pore

### Redwood National and State Parks
1111 2nd Street
Crescent City, CA 95531
707/465-7335
www.nps.gov/redw

### Santa Monica Mountains National Recreation Area
401 West Hillcrest Drive
Thousand Oaks, CA 91360
805/370-2301
www.nps.gov/samo

### Sequoia and Kings Canyon National Parks
47050 Generals Highway
Three Rivers, CA 93271-9700
559/565-3341
www.nps.gov/seki

### Smith River National Recreation Area
P.O. Box 228
Gasquet, CA 95543
707/457-3131
www.fs.usda.gov/srnf

### Whiskeytown National Recreation Area
P.O. Box 188
Whiskeytown, CA 96095
530/246-1225 or 530/242-3400
www.nps.gov/whis

### Yosemite National Park
P.O. Box 577
Yosemite National Park, CA 95389
209/372-0200
www.nps.gov/yose

# U.S. ARMY CORPS OF ENGINEERS

Some of the family camps and most of the group camps operated by the U.S. Army Corps of Engineers (www.spn.usace.army.mil) are on a reservation system. Reservations can be made up to 240 days in advance and up to 360 days in advance for groups. To reserve a site, call 877/444-6777 or visit the website www.recreation.gov. The reservation fee is usually $10; major credit cards are accepted. Holders of Golden Age or Golden Access passports receive a 50 percent discount for campground fees (except group sites).

### South Pacific Division
333 Market Street
San Francisco, CA 94105
415/977-8272

### Sacramento District
1325 J Street
Sacramento, CA 95814
916/557-5100

### Los Angeles District
915 Wilshire Boulevard, Suite 980
Los Angeles, CA 90017-3401
213/452-3908

# BUREAU OF LAND MANAGEMENT

Most of the Bureau of Land Management (BLM) campgrounds are in remote areas, such as the deserts of Southern California (outside designated parklands), the Lost Coast and the King Range on the Northern California coast. Many of these sites are primitive; there is often no fee for camping. Holders of Golden Age or Golden Access passports receive a 50 percent discount (except group camps).

**Bureau of Land Management**
California State Office
2800 Cottage Way, Suite W-1834
Sacramento, CA 95825-1886
916/978-4400
www.blm.gov/ca

**California Desert District Office**
22835 Calle San Juan de los Lagos
Moreno Valley, CA 92553
951/697-5200
www.blm.gov/ca/cdd

**Alturas Field Office**
708 West 12th Street
Alturas, CA 96101
530/233-4666
www.blm.gov/ca/alturas

**Arcata Field Office**
1695 Heindon Road
Arcata, CA 95521-4573
707/825-2300
www.blm.gov/ca/arcata

**Bakersfield Field Office**
3801 Pegasus Drive
Bakersfield, CA 93308
661/391-6000
www.blm.gov/ca/bakersfield

**Barstow Field Office**
2601 Barstow Road
Barstow, CA 92311
760/252-6000
www.blm.gov/ca/barstow

**Bishop Field Office**
351 Pacu Lane, Suite 100
Bishop, CA 93514
760/872-5000
www.blm.gov/ca/bishop

**Eagle Lake Field Office**
2950 Riverside Drive
Susanville, CA 96130
530/257-0456
www.blm.gov/ca/eaglelake

**El Centro Field Office**
1661 South 4th Street
El Centro, CA 92243
760/337-4400
www.blm.gov/ca/elcentro

**Folsom Field Office**
63 Natoma Street
Folsom, CA 95630
916/985-4474
www.blm.gov/ca/folsom

**Hollister Field Office**
20 Hamilton Court
Hollister, CA 95023
831/630-5000
www.blm.gov/ca/hollister

**Palm Springs/South Coast Field Office**
P.O. Box 581260
North Palm Springs, CA 92258-1260
760/251-4800
www.blm.gov/ca/palmsprings

**Redding Field Office**
355 Hemsted Drive
Redding, CA 96002
530/224-2100
www.blm.gov/ca/redding

**Ridgecrest Field Office**
300 South Richmond Road

Ridgecrest, CA 93555
760/384-5400
www.blm.gov/ca/ridgecrest

### Ukiah Field Office
2550 North State Street
Ukiah, CA 95482
707/468-4000
www.blm.gov/ca/ukiah

# OTHER VALUABLE RESOURCES
## State Forests
### Jackson Demonstration State Forest
802 North Main Street
Fort Bragg, CA 95437
707/964-5674
http://calfire.ca.gov

### Mountain Home Demonstration State Forest
P.O. Box 517
Springville, CA 93265
559/539-2321 (summer)
559/539-2855 (winter)
http://calfire.ca.gov

## County/Regional Park Departments
### Del Norte County Parks
840 9th Street, Suite 11
Crescent City, CA 95531
707/464-7230
www.co.del-norte.ca.us

### East Bay Regional Park District
P.O. Box 5381
Oakland, CA 94605-0381
888/327-2757
www.ebparks.org

### Humboldt County Parks
1106 2nd Street
Eureka, CA 95501
707/445-7651
www.co.humboldt.ca.us

### Marin Municipal Water District
220 Nellen Avenue
Corte Madera, CA 94925
415/945-1455
www.marinwater.org

### Midpeninsula Regional Open Space District
330 Distel Circle
Los Altos, CA 94022-1404
650/691-1200
www.openspace.org

### Pacific Gas and Electric Company
Corporate Real Estate/Recreation
5555 Florin-Perkins Road, Room 100
Sacramento, CA 95826
916/386-5164
www.pge.com

### Sacramento County Regional Parks
3711 Branch Center Road
Sacramento, CA 95827
916/875-6961
www.regionalparks.saccounty.net

### San Diego County Parks and Recreation Department
2454 Heritage Park Row
San Diego, CA 92110
858/694-3049
www.sandiegocounty.gov/parks

### San Luis Obispo County Parks Department
1087 Santa Rosa Street
San Luis Obispo, CA 93408
805/781-5930
www.slocountyparks.org

### San Mateo County Parks and Recreation Department
455 County Center, 4th floor
Redwood City, CA 94063-1646
650/363-4020
http://parks.smcgov.org

**Santa Barbara County Parks
and Recreation Department**
610 Mission Canyon Road
Santa Barbara, CA 93105
805/568-2461
http://cosb.countyofsb.org/parks

**Santa Clara County Parks Department**
298 Garden Hill Drive
Los Gatos, CA 95032-7669
408/355-2200
www.sccgov.org

**Sonoma County Regional Parks**
2300 County Center Drive, Suite 120-A
Santa Rosa, CA 95403
707/565-2041
www.sonomacounty.com

# State and Federal Offices
**U.S. Fish and Wildlife Service**
1849 C Street NW
Washington, DC 20240
800/344-9453
www.fws.gov

**U.S. Geological Survey**
Branch of Information Services
P.O. Box 25286, Bldg. 810
MS 306, Federal Center
Denver, CO 80225
888/275-8747 or 303/202-4700
www.usgs.gov

**California Department of Fish and Wildlife**
1416 9th Street, 12th floor
Sacramento, CA 95814
916/445-0411
www.wildlife.ca.gov

# Information Services
**Lake County Visitor Information Center**
P.O. Box 1025
6110 East Highway 20

Lucerne, CA 95458
707/274-5652 or 800/525-3743
http://lakecounty.com

**Mammoth Lakes Visitors Bureau**
P.O. Box 48
2520 Main Street
Mammoth Lakes, CA 93546
888/466-2666 or 760/934-2712
www.visitmammoth.com

**Mount Shasta Visitors Bureau**
300 Pine Street
Mount Shasta, CA 96067
530/926-4865 or 800/926-4865
http://mtshastachamber.com

**The Nature Conservancy of California**
201 Mission Street, 4th floor
San Francisco, CA 94105-1832
415/777-0487
www.nature.org

**Plumas County Visitors Bureau**
550 Crescent Street
P.O. Box 4120
Quincy, CA 95971
530/283-6345 or 800/326-2247
http://plumascounty.org

**Shasta Cascade Wonderland Association**
1699 Highway 273
Anderson, CA 96007
530/365-7500 or 800/474-2782
www.shastacascade.com

# Map Companies
**Map Link**
30 South La Patera Lane, Unit 5
Goleta, CA 93117
805/692-6777
or 800/962-1394
www.maplink.com

**Olmsted and Bros. Map Company**
P.O. Box 5351
Berkeley, CA 94705
510/658-6534

**Tom Harrison Maps**
2 Falmouth Cove
San Rafael, CA 94901-4465
415/456-7940
www.tomharrisonmaps.com

**U.S. Forest Service**
National Forest Store
Attn: Map Sales
P.O. Box 8268
Missoula, MT 59807
406/329-3024
www.nationalforestmapstore.com

**U.S. Geological Survey**
345 Middlefield Road
Menlo Park, CA 94025
650/329-4390
www.usgs.gov

# Index